Frommer's®

W9-BIT-874

Southeast Asia

5th Edition

by Jason Armbrecht, Brian Calvert, Jennifer Eveland & Jen Lin-Liu

Wiley Publishing, Inc.

Published by:

Wiley Publishing, Inc.

111 River St.
Hoboken, NJ 07030-5774

ISBN: 978-0-470-12009-5

Editor: Leslie Shen
Production Editor: Eric T. Schroeder
Cartographer: Andrew Murphy
Photo Editor: Richard Fox
Anniversary Logo Design: Richard Pacifico
Production by Wiley Indianapolis Composition Services

Front cover photo: Thailand, Bangkok, Damnoen Saduak Floating Market: Group of four women traders in boats laden with flowers
Back cover photo: Cambodia, Angkor Wat: Buddhist monks standing by columns of library of temple, rear view

For information on our other products and services or to obtain technical support, please contact our Customer Care Department within the U.S. at 800/762-2974, outside the U.S. at 317/572-3993 or fax 317/572-4002.

Wiley also publishes its books in a variety of electronic formats. Some content that appears in print may not be available in electronic formats.

Manufactured in the United States of America

5   4   3   2   1

Contents

4   Thailand   73

by Jason Armbrecht

5   Laos   226

by Jason Armbrecht

6 Vietnam

280

by Brian Calvert

7 Cambodia

405

by Brian Calvert

List of Maps

About the Authors

Jason Armbrecht (Thailand and Laos) first spent time in Southeast Asia during an around-the-world trip in 2002. His fascination with the region's cultures and people combined with a lack of viable TV options after college basketball season brought him back in 2005. He currently lives in Bangkok with his girlfriend, Yasirin, and teaches English to kindergarteners with varying degrees of success. This is his first assignment for Frommer's.

Brian Calvert (Vietnam and Cambodia) has worked as a journalist in Asia for 5 years, including 4 years at a newspaper in Phnom Penh, the *Cambodia Daily*, reporting new stories from across the country as well as training Cambodian journalists. He has traveled extensively in Vietnam, and in 2002 interviewed Phan Van Khai, the prime minister at that time. He now works in Washington, D.C.

Jennifer Eveland (Singapore and Malaysia) spent part of her childhood in Singapore, has studied in Hong Kong, lived for a spell in Bangkok, and has traveled extensively throughout East and Southeast Asia. She is the author of *Frommer's Singapore & Malaysia* and has authored previous editions of *Frommer's Thailand*. She writes regularly for the *International Herald Tribune* and contributes travel and lifestyle stories to numerous local and international magazines. She lives in Toa Payoh, one of Singapore's older New Towns, with her husband, a Singaporean musician and producer, their baby son, and their four cats.

Jen Lin-Liu (Bali) is a freelance writer based in Beijing. She is currently working on a book about learning how to cook in China that will be published in 2008 by Harcourt. She was born in Chicago, raised in Southern California, and went to college and graduate school at Columbia University in New York. She has traveled and reported from a dozen Asian countries and enjoys going to Southeast Asia as frequently as possible to escape Beijing's cold winters. She would like to thank her boyfriend, Craig Simons, for "roughing it" with her in Bali.

An Invitation to the Reader

In researching this book, we discovered many wonderful places—hotels, restaurants, shops, and more. We're sure you'll find others. Please tell us about them, so we can share the information with your fellow travelers in upcoming editions. If you were disappointed with a recommendation, we'd love to know that, too. Please write to:

Frommer's Southeast Asia, 5th Edition
Wiley Publishing, Inc. • 111 River St. • Hoboken, NJ 07030-5774

An Additional Note

Please be advised that travel information is subject to change at any time—and this is especially true of prices. We therefore suggest that you write or call ahead for confirmation when making your travel plans. The authors, editors, and publisher cannot be held responsible for the experiences of readers while traveling. Your safety is important to us, however, so we encourage you to stay alert and be aware of your surroundings. Keep a close eye on cameras, purses, and wallets, all favorite targets of thieves and pickpockets.

Other Great Guides for Your Trip:

Frommer's Singapore & Malaysia
Frommer's Thailand
Frommer's Vietnam
Frommer's Hong Kong

Frommer's Star Ratings, Icons & Abbreviations

Every hotel, restaurant, and attraction listing in this guide has been ranked for quality, value, service, amenities, and special features using a **star-rating system.** In country, state, and regional guides, we also rate towns and regions to help you narrow down your choices and budget your time accordingly. Hotels and restaurants are rated on a scale of zero (recommended) to three stars (exceptional). Attractions, shopping, nightlife, towns, and regions are rated according to the following scale: zero stars (recommended), one star (highly recommended), two stars (very highly recommended), and three stars (must-see).

In addition to the star-rating system, we also use **eight feature icons** that point you to the great deals, in-the-know advice, and unique experiences that separate travelers from tourists. Throughout the book, look for:

Finds	Special finds—those places only insiders know about
Fun Fact	Fun facts—details that make travelers more informed and their trips more fun
Kids	Best bets for kids and advice for the whole family
Moments	Special moments—those experiences that memories are made of
Overrated	Places or experiences not worth your time or money
Tips	Insider tips—great ways to save time and money
Value	Great values—where to get the best deals
Warning	Warning—traveler's advisories are usually in effect

The following **abbreviations** are used for credit cards:

AE	American Express	DISC	Discover	V	Visa
DC	Diners Club	MC	MasterCard		

Frommers.com

Visit our website at **www.frommers.com** for additional travel information on more than 3,500 destinations. We update the site regularly, to give you instant access to the most current trip-planning information available. At Frommers.com, you'll find scoops on the best airfares, lodging rates, and car rental bargains. You can even book your travel online through our reliable travel booking partners. Other popular features include:

- Online updates of our most popular guidebooks
- Vacation sweepstakes and contest giveaways
- Newsletters highlighting the hottest travel trends
- Online travel message boards with featured travel discussions

What's New in Southeast Asia

Much of what is so fascinating to travelers in Southeast Asia is the ephemeral: that friendly shopkeeper who invites you to sample something new, a hole-in-the-wall antiques store, a local specialty served at street side, seemingly impromptu festivals, and the kindness of strangers. These serendipitous moments—some call them "trail magic"—are what make exploring this part of the world so memorable and yet so maddening for the publisher of a guidebook to chronicle. Those quaint little corners are as fickle as shooting stars and can often be found only by searching, only to disappear or change if sought after again. Our advice: Search away! Follow a passion—an interest in local cuisine, history, or architecture—and ask around. Go where the locals go. Accept invites where appropriate and take your time—things unfold slowly in this part of the world. Visitors come away with their own unique experiences and impressions in even the shortest visit to this diverse region.

Below we list a few of the major changes in this updated edition. Travelers to Southeast Asia need to be hip to fluctuations in the international airline scene in today's cautious climate. While some Asian airlines have eliminated North American routes, many North American carriers have begun offering rock-bottom rates for premium flights, and there are even some new international connections. Check with ticket consolidators or carriers that sell regional multi-stop tickets: See Cathay Pacific (www.cathay.com), for example, or look into special travel passes arranged by ASEAN (www.asean-tourism.com).

Safety is on the mind of every traveler these days, and despite the public-relations disaster of the SARS crisis, avian influenza, and some political hot spots in the region, the well-informed traveler in Southeast Asia can be sure of a trouble-free trip and manageable adventures.

THAILAND

Tourists in Thailand woke up on the morning of September 20, 2006, to discover that this once idyllic Southeast Asian paradise, renowned worldwide as the "Land of Smiles," was now under the rule of a military junta, and they fled by the thousands.

Well, maybe that's a bit of an exaggeration. For visitors here during the coup, the only inconvenience was that tourist spots in Bangkok were shut down for a day. Unless they saw an English-language newspaper or got a call from a nervous friend or loved one, chances are travelers outside of Bangkok were not immediately aware that anything in the capital was amiss.

True, the country is currently ruled by the military, but by the time you read this, new elections will hopefully have been held (although this seems increasingly unlikely) and civilian government restored. The worry is that the junta will drag its feet setting up new elections, causing unrest amongst a population already wary of its motives. But for now, we'll cross our fingers and think happy thoughts.

Although the coup was not violent, it should be noted that the far south of the country *is* violent, as Muslim extremists terrorize the Buddhist population, police, and military. Attacks blamed on Muslim groups have moved north from the immediate border areas of Pattani, Narathiwat, and Yala provinces to Hat Yai in Songkhla Province, a major transit point in the south. Although these attacks were isolated incidents, they did target tourist areas and at least two foreign nationals were killed. Travel to the far south is generally discouraged, although train service to Butterworth in Malaysia is generally considered safe, as it stays west of the most troublesome provinces.

In more positive travel news, the shiny **Suvarnabhumi International Airport,** plagued by construction delays and cost overruns, finally opened in September 2006. (*Warning:* At press time, it was still undergoing repairs to some cracks in its runways and water leakage in its terminal building. For the time being, the old airport will temporarily reopen to handle some domestic, nonconnecting flights—so make sure you know which airport you're flying in and out of.) The new airport is roughly 30km (8 miles) east of central Bangkok and in the future will be connected to the city's skytrain system by a high-speed rail link. If history is any guide, this link will most likely be completed some time *after* its scheduled completion date of October 2008. When this line is complete, the airport will only be a 15-minute ride from downtown, but for now, the options are bus, taxi, limo, rental car, or a layover in the **Novotel Suvarnabhumi Airport Hotel** (✆ 02131-1111), the only hotel serving the airport.

As for shiny new things in **Bangkok,** the **JW Marriott** (✆ 02656-7700), located in the heart of the busy Sukhumvit shopping area, is leading the way in in-room, high-tech convenience

and is a new addition to this guide. Just across the street is the **Majestic Grande** (✆ 02262-2999), a classy midrange choice and one of the best values in the city. On the Chao Phraya, the **Millennium Hilton** (✆ 02442-2000) adds another name to the already prestigious list of luxury riverfront spots. Back in the city center, the massive **Siam Paragon** adds additional acres of shopping space to already crowded Siam Square, housing as well the world-class **Siam Ocean World.**

Pattaya expects to see even more business with the new airport just over an hour's drive away, and the **Amari Orchid Resort & Tower** (✆ 02255-3767) is hoping to cash in. By mid-2007, it will have added a five-star luxury wing to the current four-star property. Already completed is the hotel's posh new **Mantra** (✆ 03842-9591), one of the best new restaurants in the country. On the south end of the beach, the **Sheraton Pattaya** (✆ 03825-9888) is a new secluded getaway.

Further east, the islands of **Koh Samet** and **Koh Chang,** once solely the domain of backpackers, have new luxury resorts: the exclusive, all-villa **Paradee** (✆ 03864-4283) on Samet; and the **Amari Emerald Cove** (✆ 03955-2000), one of the chain's best, on Chang.

The most popular island destinations continue to be **Koh Samui** and **Phuket,** back to full speed after the 2004 tsunami. Both islands are slowly sinking from the weight of the resorts that have been built in recent years. Of these, a special nod goes to **Sala Samui** (✆ 07724-5888), a new honeymoon spot/love nest on Samui.

The beachfronts of **Krabi,** a nice alternative to busy Phuket, have also seen their fair share of construction, as both the **Sofitel Phokeethara** (✆ 07562-7800) and the **Central Krabi Bay Resort** (✆ 07563-7789) were opening their doors at the time of this writing (too close to press time to be reviewed in this edition).

Koh Phi Phi, thoroughly destroyed by the 2004 tsunami, is back to its old tricks and has added a truly unique boutique resort, **Zeavola** (© **07562-7024**), that hearkens back to rural Thailand of the 1950s.

In **Chiang Mai, The Chedi** (© **05325-3333**) is the new standard bearer for luxury in the northern capital. Also new to this edition is the trendsetting **D2 Hotel** (© **05399-9999**), a surprisingly hip "lifestyle hotel" from the usually traditional Dusit hotel chain. A real find is the **Baan Orapin** (© **05324-3677**), a family-run bed-and-breakfast that is a must for those looking for a break from large, impersonal hotels. It's highly recommended—and not just because the owner and I attended the same college (Go Heels!).

In the far north near the once mysterious **Golden Triangle,** those with the means should look into the **Four Seasons Tented Camp** (© **05391-0200**), a super-luxe, super-exclusive resort. Getting to the camp requires a Kurtzian ride up the Mekong; once there, you will be pampered and wined and dined between *mahout* (elephant riding) classes.

LAOS

French military men in the early 19th century bemoaned the posting of disciplined officers to Laos, telling of how the languid pace and earthly delights spoiled the man and made mush out of good soldiers. Things haven't changed much; in fact, after a visit to Laos, it's hard to get back into the rat race.

Security for travelers is not an issue, but some reports over the last decade give pause (see "Staying Safe," p. 45). The main north–south highway, Route 13, has been free of insurgent activity for some time now, but public bus company employees still carry machine guns just in case, which can be seen as either reassuring or terrifying. The national carrier, once called Lao Aviation, has renamed itself **Lao Airlines** (www.laoairlines.com); it has acquired a number of new planes and flies new routes, offering better service and a stronger commitment to safety (though it still has yet to pass international safety standards).

Much of the recent foreign investment in Laos has gone towards improving the roads. Not long ago, roads outside of the major towns were unpaved and many were impassable during the rainy season. The highways are much improved now, but rural roads are still reserved for the hardy. One good way to get around in style is to book with **Luang Say Cruises** (© **071/252-553;** www.asian-oasis.com), either for its northern trip from the Thai border to Luang Prabang—with an overnight at its luxurious eco-lodge—or on the luxury **Vat Phou** flagship in the far south. **Diethelm Travel** (© **021/213-833;** www.diethelmtravel.com) is still the country's leader for deluxe classic tours.

Sadly, **Vientiane,** the capital, has its first official eyesore. The 14-story **Don Chan Palace** (© **021/244-288**) opened in 2005 and has been successfully courting the Asian business community. The terrific new **Green Park Boutique Hotel** (© **021/263-063**) also opened its doors in 2005, joining the Settha Palace as the most luxurious digs in the capital. For those in search of value for your money, look no further than the **Vayakorn Guesthouse** (© **021/241-911**), a guesthouse in name (and price) only. In foodie news, **Le Central** (© **021/243-703**) is another on the growing list of Vientiane's fine French restaurants, serving some of the best desserts in town.

Luang Prabang, a UNESCO World Heritage city of quaint French colonial buildings and stunning original temples along the Mekong, is the country's premier attraction. Many of the old colonials have been converted into stylish boutique hotels, with all renovations sticking to strict guidelines from UNESCO in hopes of retaining the town's history and charm. The **Villa Santi Hotel** (✆ 071/212-267) continues to set the standard, but newcomer **Apsara** (✆ 071/254-670), with loftlike open-plan rooms, and the newly expanded **Les 3 Nagas** (✆ 071/252-079), are both luxurious alternatives. The more affordable but no less stylish **Sala Prabang** (✆ 071/252-460) has also expanded, adding seven additional naturally styled rooms to its already prominent riverside presence. The **Maison Souvannaphoum** (✆ 071/254-609), once the residence of the former prime minister Prince Souvannaphouma, has recently reopened its doors as a Coulours of Angsana property and has quickly established itself as a top downtown choice.

Eco-tourism is still what brings many travelers to rural Laos, and the folks at **Green Discovery** (✆ 021/223-022; www.greendiscoverylaos.com) lead adventurous trips out into the back of beyond.

VIETNAM

In the past few years, Vietnam has fashioned itself into a tourism powerhouse. Luxury and service have become the hallmarks of a country that was once on the map only for intrepid backpackers. The economy is thundering along, and in the service sector, this means choices upon choices. And while the very shape of Vietnam lends itself to linear travel, it won't be long before the country becomes a region-specific locale that visitors will want to visit time and again. Vietnam is now a member of the WTO, and in 2006 hosted a massive meeting of Asia-Pacific partners, with U.S. President George W. Bush in attendance. A certain pride is welling into the people along the old tourist trail, and Vietnam's war years are well behind it. Meanwhile, international investment continues to pour in, bringing with it international standards, styles, and sensibilities, and, while it was always evident in Saigon, the entire country has a bustling feeling that is infectious and a joy for today's traveler.

Despite its newfound place in Southeast Asia's tourism arena, Vietnam remains relatively cheap. Prices are rising in lodging from small guesthouses to luxury resorts, and in most restaurants. The increase is marginal, however, and service and quality remain high priorities. Leave the well-trod path, though, and you'll still find a seductive, sleepy Vietnam, where poised fruit sellers push bicycles through clattering streets, where old Chinese inscriptions line the walls, and where crowded public markets offer all the sights and sounds visitors have come to love and seek out in Vietnam. Plenty of discoveries await travelers, but, at the end of a day or a week of adventuring, comfort and good prices remain, right where you want them to be.

For evidence of real change, visit **Hanoi.** It's beginning to resemble Saigon, albeit less glitzy and glassy. But more and more cars are replacing motorcycles, and more motorcycles are replacing bicycles. An urgency has taken hold here in recent years, and Hanoi is emerging as a hip little capital, with a growing number of locals and expats involved in interesting affairs, from art to music and other entertainment. A good bet is the up-and-running **Sheraton Hanoi** (✆ 04/719-9000), whose appearance on a small lake away from the city center has sprouted a small street of boutiques and good eats, called **Xuan Dieu Street** (pronounced Shuan Zee-oh). New to the restaurant section of this edition is **Vine** (✆ 04/719-8001), where fine dining in a wonderfully conceived atmosphere is on offer.

Halong Bay seems to have enough natural beauty to absorb any influx thrown at it, and the mountains that jut from the crystal sea are as beckoning as ever. Now, though, it's even easier to get at some real adventure here, as many budget hotels offer excursions that include kayaking or nights spent on old junks. For luxury, go aboard *Jewel of the Bay* (© 04/828-0702; www.buffalo tours.com) or the old French steamer *Emeraude* (© 04/934-0888; www.emeraude-cruises.com).

While you're in the north, don't miss a visit to **Sapa,** a once quiet, now bustling hive of activity for some of Vietnam's many hill tribes. As expected, all the development that's come to Sapa has taken away some of its quiet charm, but that only means you can get farther into neighboring areas with tours to other villages, valleys, and markets. Trek in the shadow of **Fansipan,** the region's highest mountain, and enjoy the cool air, or just wander Sapa, a gathering spot for the hill-tribe men and women, who are starting to combine traditional swaddling with the trappings of a globalized world—hot-pink hats or knock-off sneakers, for example. Getting here by train and bus has become increasingly easy, and new to this edition is the **Topas Eco-Lodge** (© 020/872-404), possibly the most mesmerizing, peaceful locale in the country.

Colonial **Hue** offers visitors many chances to travel through Vietnam's varied past, from its time under Chinese rule to the American war. The hotel scene is not what it could be—and is bound to get better—but for now, there's the **Hotel Saigon Morin** (© 054/823-526) and the new, inspiring **La Résidence Hôtel & Spa** (© 054/837-475).

One of the best singular cities in Vietnam remains **Hoi An,** an ancient old town protected as a UNESCO World Heritage Site. It can make for days of entertaining wanderings, but equally tempting are the southern tip of China Beach and its breaking waves. Between the old town and the sea lies a real look at modern Vietnam, from *pho* shops to river fishing boats; travel between the two by rented bicycle. In the old town, the **Hoi**

An Cargo Club & Patisserie (© 0510/910-489) manages to retain the classic feel of a European street cafe—it's an excellent place to sip coffee and contemplate the historic setting around you—while at the **Wan Lu** noodle shop (© 0510/861-212), you'll feel like you've stepped back in time.

Nha Trang, once known as a party town on the backpackers' Southeast Asian circuit, has grown up into a bona fide beach destination; new to this edition is the **Evason Hideaway at Ana Mandara** (© 058/522-222), an ultra-luxurious resort accessible only by boat, set among lush forests on a secluded beach at the edge of a mountain range.

To beat the heat, do what French colonialists did, and travel to the high plateau of **Dalat,** where you can stay in renovated villas from a time long gone at **Evason Ana Mandara Villas & Spa** (© 063/560-719; www.evasonhideaways.com), new to this edition. It's reasonably priced for the experience it offers. Or choose a traditional stay in the hotel that started it all, the **Sofitel Dalat Palace** (© 063/825-444), where a vintage Citroën tour of the town's old architecture is not to be missed.

Ho Chi Minh City (Saigon) remains the country's business nexus and is busy as ever. Food, entertainment, shopping—all things remain unrivaled in old Saigon, but some of the classic stays in the city have been re-done so many times they've lost their charm. Enter the newest downtown hotel, **Park Hyatt Saigon** (© 08/824-1234), which has managed to recapture what was lost, through brilliant design and attitude. That said, there's still nothing like a drink at the rooftop bar of the **Rex Hotel** (© 08/829-2185). Finally, an old favorite among Vietnamese, and new to this edition, is the **Song Ngu** (© 08/832-55017), where fabulous seafood with good prices can be found.

CAMBODIA

Cambodia remains a land of rugged mystery, a shadowy, war-ravaged country that has yet to turn the corner and is still developing. The ruling party in a coalition government, the CPP, has consolidated its grip on power, while a fractured royalist party is looking for its identity. Legislation remains shockingly slow, and exploitation of natural resources is still endemic. Corruption remains king, and the country has remained unable to come to grips with its past. A tribunal is underway for former leaders of the infamous Khmer Rouge, but the process has been bogged down in red tape and foot dragging. The country has yet to rise to its potential, and people living in rural areas are as poor as ever, but Cambodia isn't an uninteresting destination.

The good news, though, is that **Siem Reap,** the gateway city to the famed temples of **Angkor,** is outpacing the rest of the nation. Once a dusty, crumbling town travelers had to put up with in order to view the awe-inspiring temples, Siem Reap has blossomed into a place worthy of a visit. Great investments have been put into airports and roads, police seem on their best behavior, and an entire bar and restaurant area has matured around the Old Market, where you can still have cheap, wholesome food at a place like the **Khmer Kitchen Restaurant** (© 012/763-468), but where you can also eat ice-cream sundaes in an air-conditioned, nonsmoking cafe, the **Blue Pumpkin** (© 063/963-574), which makes excellent sandwiches to pack to the temples. On the hotel scene, the combination of whip-smart service, a community-minded philosophy, and attention to out-of-the-way temples makes the **Amansara** (© 063/760-333) an unrivaled host in Cambodia, and beyond. For a great stay at a moderate hotel, with a quiet environment and quaint pool, seek out the **Auberge Mont Royal d'Angkor** (© 063/964-044).

In the next few years, the temple to see will be **Ta Prohm,** which was left much how the French found it: being swallowed by the jungle. Giant trees wrap their limbs around manmade stone, putting humanity in a perspective different from that of other temples. Development is underway, though, to reclaim this temple, to pull it back from the edge of the forest, and this will mean the loss of some of its magic. The time to go is now.

Phnom Penh, meanwhile, remains a fascinating capital in Southeast Asia. Not as dust-blown as it once was, Phnom Penh's growth is accelerating, and the word "sleepy" no longer applies here. More and more cars are choking the streets, and where once a visitor got around on the back of a motorcycle, he or she can now find a more placid ride in the chaos via **tuk-tuk,** a cushioned, shaded cart pulled behind a motorcycle. Rent one for a day and drive around the city, or see the important genocide sites, **Tuol Sleng** or **Choeung Ek,** which are grim reminders of Cambodia's past but really put the place into perspective. A less grisly attraction in Phnom Penh is the riverfront, along Sisowath Boulevard, which has sprouted numerous boutiquette hotels and fine restaurants in recent years. It's still a bit toutish, but solace can be found on a **Mekong cruise,** which costs as little as US$10 (£5.50) an hour. Stay in a hotel overlooking the river and you'll be blessed every morning with a spectacular sunrise.

New to this edition is a brief introduction to the small beach town of **Kep,** one of the country's best-kept secrets. In the past, a rough road and hard ride to the "Cambodian Riviera" kept many away, but the road is better now and a bus service brings passengers to Kep's doorstep. The beach is placid, if a little rustic, but numerous activities are available—from day trips to tropical islands to motorcycle rides through jungly mountains. These, combined with several quality places to stay—like the **Knai Bang Chatt** (☏ **012/ 879-486**) and the **Veranda Natural Resort** (☏ **012/888-619**)—make Kep an imperative destination for anyone interested in seeing Cambodia beyond its ancient temples or shadowy capital.

SINGAPORE

After 2006, Singapore's tourism industry will never be the same again. The government's approval for two **casinos** marks the end of an era for the squeaky-clean city-state.

The first casino will be built by **Las Vegas Sands,** which is investing S$5 billion (US$3.16 billion/£1.6 billion) to create a casino in Singapore's downtown area, just across the marina from the financial district and downtown convention center. With an eye on the meetings, incentives, convention, and exhibits (MICE) travel segment, the huge complex will also feature 110,000 sq. m (1,184,040 sq. ft.) of meeting space, two 2,000-seat theaters, three hotel towers, an **ArtScience Museum,** luxury retail outlets, dining venues in floating pavilions on the bay, plus innovative public spaces that include a rooftop park with a 360-degree city view, an ice-skating rink, and indoor canals.

The second casino is being developed by **Genting International** and **Star Cruises,** which will invest S$5.2 billion (US$3.3 billion/£1.65 billion) to build an enormous facility on **Sentosa Island.** Geared towards family and leisure activities, the casino will be supported by spa-resort accommodations, restaurants and bars, plus retail and entertainment outlets. Perhaps the most exciting part of the package will be the addition of **Universal Studios Singapore,** promised to be Asia's largest, with 22 attractions in themed "worlds," including "Journey to Madagascar," and a DreamWorks Digital Animation Studio. Also in the works is the **Quest Marine Life Park,** with the largest single marine tank in the world and an interactive dolphin habitat. The **Equarius Water Park** will feature water rides and a maritime museum. Three amphitheaters will host international entertainment, including a resident show from the creators of **Cirque du Soleil.**

While the estimated completion date for these projects is 2010, super-efficient Singapore may have everything up and running much sooner than that.

In the future, also look to **Singapore Airlines** to be the first airline to use the massive Airbus 380 for commercial passenger flights. These double-decker jets have 49% more floor space than Boeing's 747, but incorporate only 35% more seats, allowing room for fun extras like bars, gyms, and duty-free shops. The mammoth plane will be rolled out in 2007 for the "kangaroo route" between Sydney, Singapore, and London.

MALAYSIA

In 2007, Malaysia celebrates **50 years of independence,** and the tourism board has a host of activities for travelers—from music festivals to international sporting events and big nationwide sales—that will showcase the country to the world. August will be the most exciting month, with a week-long international fireworks competition and a lion dance exhibition leading up to Malaysia's Independence Day celebrations on August 31, with parades, outdoor fairs, concerts, and fireworks. Also in 2007, the **Eye on Malaysia,** a 60m (197-ft.) Ferris wheel with views over Kuala Lumpur, will open in its Lake Gardens location.

Malaysia's budget carrier **AirAsia,** which offers some of the cheapest airfares around the country and the region, is teaming up with **Virgin Atlantic** and

EasyJet to introduce the world's first low-cost long-haul flights. Starting in July 2007, the airline is planning to offer trips between KL and London for as low as half the price you'd pay on a normal carrier. The deal will also give AirAsia's partners access to **Kuala Lumpur International Airport,** creating a nice Asian hub for their operations as well. AirAsia also plans to offer RM100 (US$28/£14) flights to China. The move will pave the way for Malaysia's KLIA to become a coveted gateway for budget flights from around the world into Southeast Asia and within the Asia Pacific region.

BALI

Tourism is once again on the rebound after terrorists struck Bali for the second time, in October 2005. Sadly, the more remote areas of Bali—the safest places to visit—have felt the greatest impact due to the drop in tourism. Security has tightened, with the addition of bomb-sniffing dogs at many resorts and in downtown areas, and hotels have slashed prices—you can get a private villa with a plunge pool for less than $200 per night these days. Bali's outstanding service, beautiful landscape, and deluxe hotels at reasonable prices still make it a very appealing place to visit.

A top area full of world-class restaurants and deluxe hotels near— but not in—the action in downtown **Kuta** is Seminyak. New to this edition is the **Sofitel Seminyak Bali** (© 361/730730), formerly the Royal Seminyak. The outstanding two-story private villas have undergone renovations and are now some of the best beachside villas in Seminyak; bargain hard. Staying in this area also puts you near the clubbing scene; check out the most happening nightclub, **Hu'u Bar** (© 361/736443), located on the beach just south of Seminyak.

In the island's south is picturesque **Jimbaran Bay.** You'll find great amenities here at the **Ritz-Carlton Bali** (© 361/702222), which boasts one of the best pools on the island—an infinity pool built in a cliffside just above a beautiful beach with crashing waves. The outstanding spa recently added an Aquatonic therapy pool, a huge Jacuzzi with currents and jets that give you a workout and a massage. Try the Ritz's new **Dava** restaurant, which features pan-Asian delights.

Also in southern Bali, the resort area of **Nusa Dua** is home to several outstanding properties, including the very private **Balé** (© 361/775111) and **Kayumanis** (© 361/770777), both of which have a strict no-child policy for extra peace and quiet. Conversely, if you are bringing the kids, check out **Ayodya Resort Bali** (© 361/771102). A great value in the south is **Rumah Bali** (© 361/771256), a bed-and-breakfast resort that features the island's best cooking school, **Bumbu Bali** (© 361/774502). The school also serves tasty food, or you can check out **Tao** (© 361/772902), a new fusion restaurant with a beachside pool nearby.

In the rice paddies of **Ubud** is possibly the best new resort in all of Bali: the **Chedi Club at Tanah Gajah** (© 361/975685), with private butler service, a private plunge pool, a huge outdoor tub, and plenty of complimentary bonuses like a free minibar, afternoon tea, and breakfast in bed. Also check out **Ubud Hanging Garden** (© 361/982700), a resort built on the side of a steep gorge.

In Bali's north, the village of **Pemuteran** is a great base for diving and snorkeling trips to the nearby island of Menjangan. Try **Reef Seen Aquatics** (© 362/92339; www.reefseen.com) for snorkeling, diving, and basic but nicely appointed rooms for around US$40 (£22). The best of Pemuteran's resorts is the **Matahari Beach Resort & Spa** (© 362/92312).

1

The Best of Southeast Asia

To the Western visitor, Southeast Asia is an assault on the senses, an immersion into a way of life utterly unlike that to which we're accustomed. From bustling cities like Bangkok, Singapore, and Kuala Lumpur to tiny fishing villages and thatched rural hamlets, from the jungles of Malaysian Borneo to the deluxe resorts of Bali, from the temples of Luang Prabang in Laos to the bacchanal of Patpong in Thailand, Southeast Asia offers a glimpse of the extraordinary, an explosion of colors, sounds, smells, textures, and life that will send you home with a wider vision of the human experience. In this chapter, we share our picks of the region's unrivaled highlights.

1 The Most Unforgettable Travel Experiences

- **Making Merit** (Thailand & Laos): For centuries, the *sangha,* or monkhood, has lived off the donations of food and money from the community. The tradition continues to this day: Every morning, monks walk the streets around their temple not just to receive their daily food, but also to allow the giver to make merit. By giving food in this lifetime, Buddhists believe that they will not go hungry in the next lifetime. If you are interested in making merit this way, talk to your hotel's concierge. You might be able to join kitchen staff as they head to a nearby monastery in the early morning or wait on the right byway to greet and feed a column of monks. In Luang Prabang, this tradition has become a tourist attraction of sorts and is a must-see. See chapters 4 and 5.

- **Staying in a Hill-Tribe Village near the China Border** (Laos): They still ask visitors, "Why do you come here, anyway?" in villages along the Nam Ha River in northern Laos. Thanks to the folks who run the Nam Ha Ecotourism Project, these vast tracts of pristine jungle won't be overrun by tourists anytime soon, and the many ethnic minority groups who've lived here in isolation won't be turned into human zoo exhibits. It is heartening to know that the money you spend on a trek goes to support a model of sustainable eco-tour development in a fragile region. And it is good, hearty jungle trekking or river kayaking that takes you through lush jungle terrain where you're likely to see monkeys and exotic birds. You'll arrive in villages where kayaks are still an oddity, and spend fun evenings around the fire communicating by charades or stick figures in a notebook. It's not about the villages being "pristine"; it's about the fact that your visit is part of a cultural exchange. You can have a positive effect on people with your heart *and* your tourist dollars. See chapter 5.

- **Participating in a Baci Ceremony** (Laos): The Baci is a touching Lao ceremony used to say welcome or farewell and to honor achievements.

Southeast Asia

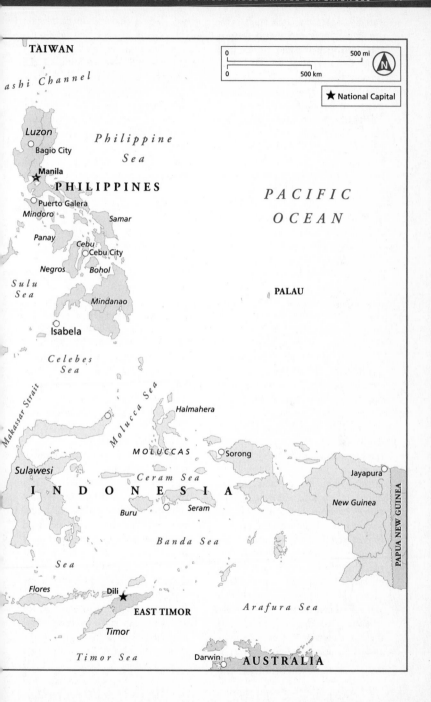

Participants sit in a circle and receive group blessings, after which there is traditional dancing and *lao lao,* rice wine. It's a chance for the ultra-friendly Lao people to express their hospitality to you, their honored guest. See chapter 5.

- **Sailing the South China Sea** (Vietnam): With the sky above us a deep, red afterglow, we rounded a buoy marking the shipping lane off coastal Nha Trang and, with the wind now at our backs, settled the Hobie Cat into a perfect fan-tail, the mainsail and jib billowing on opposite sides as the rudders gave a low moan and the boat gained speed. Riding low swells, we sped toward a coast where twinkling lights might have belonged to a child's train set, and the sky continued its show, now in orange. Heavenly. Opportunities for watersports and sailing are many as you travel along Vietnam's coast. Most resorts have boats for rent, and Nha Trang is a good bet, as is the area off Mui Ne Beach near Phan Thiet, which is becoming a very popular wind- and kitesurfing spot. See chapter 6.

- **Waiting for the Magic Hour at Angkor Wat** (Cambodia): You'll want to plan your day around it, and temple aficionados all have their favorite spots; but whether from a hillside overlooking a glowing temple facade or from the heights of the main temple itself, with the horizon framed by the famed ancient towers, be sure to see an Angkor sunset. Sunrise is equally worth the early-morning ride. At the more popular viewing spots, like Bakeng Hill, you'll ooh and aah in concert with lots of other travelers. Nobody likes crowds, but there is a certain cool oneness here, and the odd didgeridoo player or cross-legged character in meditation is a nice throwback to the old hippie-trail days in the region. See chapter 7.

- **Sipping a Singapore Sling in the Long Bar at the Raffles Hotel** (Singapore): Ah, the Long Bar, home of the Singapore Sling. Come in the afternoon, before the tourist rush. Sheltered by long timber shutters that close out the tropical sun, the air cooled by lazy punkahs (small fans that wave gently back and forth above), you can sit back in an old rattan chair and have a saronged waitress serve you sticky alcoholic creations while you toss back a few dainty crab cakes. Life can be so decadent. Okay, so the punkahs are electric and, come to think of it, the place is air-conditioned (not to mention that it costs a small fortune), but it's fun to imagine the days when Somerset Maugham, Rudyard Kipling, or Charlie Chaplin would be sitting at the bar sipping Slings and spinning exotic tales of their world travels. Drink up, my friend; it's a lovely high. See chapter 8.

- **Walking the Streets of Georgetown** (Penang, Malaysia): Evidence of former British colonization and early Chinese, Indian, and Arab immigration is apparent in many major cities in Malaysia, but Penang has a special charm. In some ways, the city still operates the way it did half a century ago. The shophouses are filled with small businesses—bicycle-repair shops, hardware stores, Chinese medicine halls, and coffee shops. From upstairs windows, you can still see laundry hanging on bamboo poles. Life hums in these streets, and for anyone who has witnessed the homogenization of Singapore or the modernization of Kuala Lumpur,

Penang is a charming reminder of what life might have been like in these old outposts. See chapter 9.

- **Observing Open-Air Public Cremations** (Bali): Hindus believe that cremation is the only way a soul can be freed of its earthly body and travel to its next incarnation (or to enlightenment), so cremations are joyous occasions, full of floats and fanfare that can resemble a Mardi Gras parade. Complicated towers hold the body, carried aloft by cheering men. At the burning ground, the body is placed in a receptacle resembling a winged lion, a bull, or some other fabulous creature, and is set on fire. It's beautiful and awesome, a marvelous show of pageantry and faith, and yet a natural part of everyday life. Western visitors are welcomed. See chapter 10.

2 The Best Towns & Villages

- **Chiang Saen** (Thailand): Crumbling 11th-century temples take you back to the birthplace of the Lanna Kingdom, one of Thailand's wealthiest and most influential. The nearby **Golden Triangle,** a notorious trade point for the international opium industry, has a new museum and riverside views of Laos, Thailand, and Myanmar. See chapter 4.

- **Luang Prabang** (Laos): This town, proclaimed a World Heritage Site by UNESCO for its glorious Buddhist temples, is also a charming retreat. Shady lanes are lined with French-style country homes that have been restored and converted to house cafes, galleries, shops, and some quaint guesthouses. The sunset over the lazy Mekong is the perfect end to a day spent in Luang Prabang. See chapter 5.

- **Hoi An** (Vietnam): The small size of Hoi An belies its importance to Vietnam; it was once a major trading port, with canals leading right up to merchants' quarters for easy delivery of goods. The canals are now peaceful streets, but little else has changed. Almost every building in central Hoi An is a historic Vietnamese-, Japanese-, and Chinese-influenced residence or meeting hall. See chapter 6.

- **Phnom Penh** (Cambodia): Few countries' capitals could be called quaint or fall under the category of a "town," and that's the very charm of this riverside burg. They say you either love it or hate it, that it's a place for expats and not tourists, but in a short stroll through the town center, you'll come across a unique mix. First you'll encounter a row of tourist cafes, the streets buzzing with motorbikes and choked with dust, but turn the corner and you'll find a quiet alley, a row of colonials, a lone kid kicking a soccer ball, and a grim-looking grandmother breaking into a smile as you walk by. There's something special here. See chapter 7.

- **Ubud** (Bali): This is the cultural heart of Bali, bursting with art and greenery and some of the best food on the island. Even though it's dependent on tourism and is far from a typical Balinese village, you still get a sense of a real town, with real life going on around you. Ubud is the richest region in Bali for art production and, because of its central location, the town is the perfect base for exploring the rest of the island. See chapter 10.

3 The Best Beaches

- **Chaweng Beach** (Koh Samui, Thailand): Chaweng is real fun in the sun. The beach itself is gorgeous, with bungalows nestled in the trees just beyond the sand. Behind the beach lies a small town full of life, from wonderful Thai and seafood eateries to shopping and wild nightlife options. See chapter 4.

- **Mai Khao Beach** (Phuket, Thailand): Look to your right—nobody. Look to your left—nobody. Just 17km (11 miles) of deserted beachfront, the longest beach on Phuket, with only one resort (which also happens to be one of the island's best) dotting its shores. Not a place to come if you want to party, though, since the only excitement occurs during the Songkran festival in April, when hundreds of baby sea turtles are released into the ocean. See chapter 4.

- **Mui Ne Beach** (Phan Thiet, Vietnam): Just a few hours from Ho Chi Minh City (Saigon), Phan Thiet is the latest getaway in Vietnam. Oceanside development is in full swing here, and there are some great boutique resorts along the stunning white sands of Mui Ne Beach. Golfers will enjoy the Nick Faldo–designed course, the seafood here is good, and the town of Phan Thiet itself is an interesting little fishing port worth a wander. There are some great day trips to enormous remote dunes and smaller fishing villages. See chapter 6.

- **Tanjung Rhu** (Langkawi, Malaysia): This huge, secluded cove has one of the longest stretches of private beach ever. Wide with soft sand, the beach has cooling shady spots provided by palm trees overhead and beautiful deep-blue waters for good swimming. Best of all, there's only one resort here (and the beach is kept picture perfect), so you won't have to elbow for space or suffer jet skis. See chapter 9.

- **Lombok** (off coast of Bali, Indonesia): The pure white-sand beaches of Lombok, with clear aqua-blue water lapping against them, are sometimes so private that you can have one all to yourself. And Lombok is just a short hop from neighboring Bali. See chapter 10.

4 The Best Outdoor Adventures

- **Exploring Phang Nga Bay** (Thailand): From the island of Phuket, sea-canoe operators guide visitors through the caves hidden deep inside the craggy island-rocks of Phang-Nga Bay. Outside, the islands thrust up to the sky, their jagged edges laced with scattered trees. Lie flat in your canoe to slip through the small cave openings, inside which you'll find magnificent chambers believed to have once hidden pirate operations. See chapter 4.

- **Caving & Kayaking in Vang Vieng** (Laos): Countless caves and caverns are hidden in the magnificent mountains surrounding Vang Vieng, a small village along the Nam Song River. Some of them are well known and some are barely on the map. Kayak tours on the Nam Song include some fun caves that you'll swim into; you can test your mettle on natural mud slides. Spend your days exploring and evenings talking about it over drinks in this laid-back little backpacker town. See chapter 5.

- **Sea Kayaking in Halong Bay** (Vietnam): The more than 3,000 arresting limestone karst formations rising out of Halong Bay's peaceful blue-green waters provide a natural obstacle course for paddling. Moving among them, you'll pass in and among intriguing grottoes and caverns. Nights are spent camping out in natural parks or on the deck of a mother ship. See chapter 6.

- **Trekking to Hill-Tribe Villages in Sapa** (Vietnam): Dressed in elaborate costumes of leggings, tunics, and headdresses, Hmong and Yao people (among other groups) gather to sell their weavings, fine dyed clothing, or crude but intricate metalwork in the central market. In fact, the town of Sapa is famed for an ephemeral "love market," where people from surrounding villages converge to find that special someone. A trip to Sapa means that the hill tribes come to you, but don't limit your trip to the town; be sure to get off into the countryside and trek in the shadow of Fansipan, the highest mountain in the region. Among lush terraced rice fields, you can visit many villages on even the shortest trek and experience different hill-tribe traditions and cultures. See chapter 6.

- **Jungle Trekking in Taman Negara** (Malaysia): With suitable options for all budgets, levels of comfort, and desired adventure, Malaysia's largest national park opens the wonders of primary rainforest and the creatures who dwell in it to everyone. From the canopy, walk high atop the forest on night watches for nocturnal life. This adventure is as stunning as it is informative. See chapter 9.

- **Hiking Gunung Agung** (Bali): Bali's highest mountain/volcano, Gunung Agung (3,014m/9,886 ft.), is sacred to the Balinese, whose traditions call it "the center of the world." Climbing the steaming peak is a serious trek that calls for a guide and proper supplies. Most hotels can arrange for it, but you will have to start out in the middle of the night or very early in the morning to make the top by sunrise. Nearby **Gunung Batur** is a less strenuous and no less rewarding half-day climb. See chapter 10.

5 The Most Intriguing Temples, Shrines, Palaces & Archaeological Sites

- **Grand Palace & Wat Phra Kaeo** (Bangkok, Thailand): These two places are number one on every travel itinerary to Bangkok, and rightly so. The palace is indeed grand, with mixtures of traditional Thai and European Victorian architecture. Wat Phra Kaeo, the royal temple that houses Thailand's revered and mysterious Emerald Buddha, is a small city in itself, with a dozen or more picturesque outer buildings and monuments that devour rolls of film. See chapter 4.

- **Ayutthaya** (north of Bangkok, Thailand): Before Bangkok, there was Ayutthaya. This was the thriving capital of Siam that the first Europeans saw when they visited amazing Thailand. Ruling a rich and powerful kingdom of over a million inhabitants, the monarchy supported the arts, especially literature. As the city grew, international trade was encouraged. Today, all that remains are brick remnants of a grand palace and many temples that were sacked during the Burmese invasion. It's best to hire a guide who can walk you through and point out the significance of each site. See chapter 4.

- **Sukhothai** (central Thailand): Founded in the 13th century, Sukhothai ("Dawn of Happiness") was the capital of the first unified state in what is today Thailand. Its borders grew to include parts of Burma to the west and extended as far as Luang Prabang to the east. Now a UNESCO World Heritage Site, the Sukhothai Historical Park encompasses the ruins of the former royal palace as well as over 20 temples. Best enjoyed from the seat of a bicycle and in combination with a trip to nearby Sri Satchanalai. See chapter 4.

- **Wat Xieng Thong** (Luang Prabang, Laos): The glittering Xieng Thong, built in 1560, sits grandly on a peninsula jutting into the Mekong River. The facades of two of its buildings are covered by glittering glass mosaics; another building contains an ornate chariot with the heads of seven dragons and the remains of a king. About a dozen English-speaking monks roam the premises; all are excellent conversationalists. See chapter 5.

- **Plain of Jars** (Xieng Khouang, Laos): How did hundreds of huge stone urns, some measuring 2.7m tall (9 ft.), come to be placed on a few meadows in northern Laos? No one really knows, and that's what's fun here. The most prevalent explanation is that the urns were made by prehistoric folks in the area about 2,000 years ago to be used as sarcophagi, but there's lots of room for conjecture. See chapter 5.

- **Tomb of Khai Dinh** (Hue, Vietnam): Khai Dinh was an egotistical, eccentric emperor who was bad for the people of Vietnam but great for the tomb he left behind. A gaudy mix of Gothic, baroque, and classical Chinese architecture, the exterior is remarkable. The stunning interior is completely covered with intricate glass and ceramic mosaic work. See chapter 6.

- **Cao Dai Holy See Temple** (Tay Ninh, north of Ho Chi Minh City, Vietnam): This is the spiritual home base of the Cao Dai religion, a faith characterized by philosophical inclusion and influence gathered from all beliefs, including the world's great scientists and humanitarians. Its headquarters is like a fantasyland of colored mosaic and elaborate painting. Followers are dressed in colorful robes during the picturesque daily procession. It's quite unique. See chapter 6.

- **Angkor Wat** (Cambodia): One of the world's man-made wonders, Angkor Wat is the Disneyland of temples in Asia. This ancient city was known to the Western world only in myth until it was rediscovered and hacked free of jungle overgrowth in the late 1800s. The magnificent temples are arrayed over a 97-sq.-km (37-sq.-mile) compound that dates from the rise and fall of the mighty Angkor civilization (A.D. 802–1295). A visit here is unforgettable. See chapter 7.

- **Thian Hock Keng Temple** (Singapore): One of Singapore's oldest Chinese temples, it is a fascinating testimony to Chinese Buddhism combined with traditional Confucian beliefs and natural Taoist principles. Equally fascinating is the modern world that carries on just outside the old temple's doors. See chapter 8.

- **Jame Mosque** (Kuala Lumpur, Malaysia): Built at the central point of the city, this is one of the oldest mosques in Kuala Lumpur. It is the heart of Malay Islam, as evidenced by the Muslim shops, eateries, and daily activities carried on in the streets surrounding it. See chapter 9.

- **Jalan Tokong** (Malacca, Malaysia): This street, in the historic heart of the city, has a Malay mosque, a Chinese temple, and a Hindu temple living peacefully side by side—the perfect example of how the many foreign religions that came to Southeast Asia shaped its communities and learned to coexist in harmony. See chapter 9.

- **Uluwatu** (Bali): This dramatic cliff-side temple overlooks the crashing waves of Bali's southern beaches. Watch the Balinese pray and perform dances. The frolicking monkeys provide comedic relief from all the romance at sunset. See chapter 10.

- **Basakih Temple** (Bali): Built in homage of Gunung Agung, the island's feisty, smoke-belching creator, the Basakih Temple does justice to the awe and grandeur of the Balinese creation myths surrounding the volcano. The spires of individual family shrines and temples are something like Chinese pagodas, and the place is always abuzz with local worshippers. You're likely to get pulled into a ceremony here. See chapter 10.

6 The Best Museums

- **National Museum** (Bangkok, Thailand): From prehistory to recent events, this museum—the former palace of the brother of King Rama I—answers many questions about Thai history and culture through the ages. Inside buildings that are themselves works of fine Thai design, you'll find Buddha images, ancient artifacts, royal paraphernalia, and fine arts. Rama's sister also lived here, and her house is decorated in the same style as it was in the late 1700s. See chapter 4.

- **Vietnam National Museum of Fine Arts** (Hanoi, Vietnam): Proper art museums are few and far between in the region, and this large colonial house has a nice collection of newer works and historic pieces. You'll find nothing too controversial or groundbreaking, but some good examples of lacquer and silk painting, woodblock, and folk and expressive work in oil. If you see anything you like, you're sure to find good copies in any of the city's many galleries. See chapter 6.

- **Cham Museum** (Danang, Vietnam): This open-air colonial structure houses the largest collection of Cham sculpture in the world. Not only are relics of this ancient Hindu-inspired culture rare, but the religious artwork itself—more than 300 pieces of sandstone—is also voluptuous, captivating, and intense. See chapter 6.

- **National Museum** (Phnom Penh, Cambodia): Don't miss this repository for the statues and relief sculpture that have been recovered from the Angkor temples and other ancient sites throughout Cambodia. Organized in a convenient chronology, it's a short course in Khmer art history. Later pieces are particularly expressive. See chapter 7.

- **Tuol Sleng, Museum of Genocide** (Phnom Penh, Cambodia): Be warned that a visit here is quite intense—too much for some. The museum is simply the shell of Cambodia's largest prison from 1975 to 1979, when the entire country was turned into a concentration camp. Originally a high school, Tuol Sleng was the site of horrible atrocities and, though there are some photo exhibits, the main experience of the museum is in wandering the small cells and learning the tragic tale from experienced local guides. See chapter 7.

- **Images of Singapore** (Sentosa Island, Singapore): No one has done a better job than this museum in chronicling for the public the horrors of the Pacific theater and Japanese occupation in Southeast Asia. Video and audio displays take you on a chronological journey through Singapore's World War II experience. The grand finale is the Surrender Chambers, life-size wax dioramas of the fateful events. Other dioramas depict traditional cultural festivals and historical figures throughout Singapore's early development. See chapter 8.

7 The Best Festivals & Celebrations

- **Songkran** (Thailand): Every year from April 13 to 15, Thais welcome the New Year (according to their calendar). Because Songkran falls in the middle of the hottest season in an already hot country, how do you think people celebrate? Every Thai heads out into the streets with water guns and buckets of ice water—sometimes laced with talcum powder, just to add to the mess—and spends the next 3 days soaking one another—and *you*. Foreigners are especially favorite targets. Don't get mad: Arm thyself! Water bazookas are on sale everywhere. Have a ball! See chapter 4.

- **Dragon Boat Races** (Laos): Celebrating the end of Buddhist Lent, dragon boat races are held in every riverside town in Laos (and that's most towns, really). The races are exciting, the betting is frenzied, and there's always a small carnival with handmade rides and the standard rigged games of skill. See chapter 5.

- **That Luang Festival** (Vientiane, Laos): In early November, thousands of Buddhist followers from all over the country, and even a few neighboring countries, converge on the spectacular That Luang temple in Vientiane. There are alms-giving ceremonies and flower processions, and then the whole affair dissolves into a carnival that stretches over several days. See chapter 5.

- **Chinese New Year** (Singapore): If you're in Southeast Asia around the end of January or the beginning of February, hop up to Hong Kong or down to Singapore for the festivities. It's a 3-day party, with parades (complete with dragons and stilt walkers) and fireworks. See chapter 8.

- **Thaipusam** (Singapore & Malaysia): Around the end of January and the beginning of February, Hindus celebrate Thaipusam. Men give thanks for prayers answered by carrying *kavadis,* huge steel racks attached to their bodies with skewers piercing the skin. Cheeks are pierced, and fruits are hung from the skin using sharp hooks. A parade of devotees carry these things in a deep trance—and the next day they wake up virtually unharmed. See chapters 8 and 9.

8 The Best Resorts & Luxury Hotels

- **The Oriental, Bangkok** (Bangkok, Thailand): The original address in Thailand, the Oriental has seen modernization detract from its charms of yesterday, but there's still ambience all around. See p. 98.

- **JW Marriott Phuket Resort & Spa** (Phuket, Thailand): One of the most relaxing resorts in Thailand, the JW Marriott is set on a secluded 17km (11-mile) stretch of white-sand beach far from the debaucherous din of Patong. An ideal getaway. See p. 183.

- **Four Seasons Resort Chiang Mai** (Chiang Mai, Thailand): Set in the hills of the Mae Rim Valley north of Chiang Mai, luxurious Lanna-style pavilions overlook working terraced rice paddies. Each suite has its own *sala* from which to admire the grounds and surrounding hills. See p. 210.

- **La Résidence Phou Vao** (Luang Prabang, Laos): Lording it over the town in boutique luxury, the gardens and large suites of the Phou Vao (formerly the Pansea) are comfort, and the atmosphere is done to a T. This is typical of other Orient Express properties in the region. See p. 263.

- **Settha Palace Hotel** (Vientiane, Laos): Once the address of note for visitors to the French colony, the Settha Palace only recently returned from obscurity and is now one of the finest hotels in the region. It's a nice marriage of colonial elegance and modern comfort. See p. 248.

- **Sofitel Metropole Hanoi** (Hanoi, Vietnam): The history of the Metropole, one of the country's premier grande dames, tells the history of the last tumultuous century in Vietnam. If the walls could only talk. Though everything is luxurious and comfortable and you're in a prime downtown location, you'll certainly feel like you've walked into old Indochina. See p. 305.

- **Evason Hideaway at Ana Mandara** (Nha Trang, Vietnam): Earth-toned private villas are secreted away in a secluded cove near Nha Trang that can only be reached by boat. Set into the forested beach or rocky coast, and each with a private pool, the Hideaway's villas portend good things for Vietnam's luxury getaways. Nothing else in the country comes close. Yet. See p. 360.

- **Sofitel Dalat Palace** (Dalat, Vietnam): It's real old-world opulence in the king's former castle in Vietnam's central highlands. Private spaces are decorated in a cool colonial baroque style, while service is, in short, kingly. See p. 369.

- **Amansara** (Siem Reap, Cambodia): If there's one place to splurge on a jaunt through Southeast Asia, this is the one. Built around former King Sihanouk's private guesthouse, the Amansara is flawless in detail and service, making it a perfect base of operations for exploring the temples of Angkor. See p. 436.

- **Raffles Hotel** (Singapore): For old-world opulence, Raffles is second to none. This is a pure fantasy of the days when tigers still lurked around the perimeters. See p. 469.

- **Shangri-La Hotel, Singapore** (Singapore): What sets this hotel apart from other city properties is its sprawling grounds. The Shang is a meticulously landscaped tropical oasis, with lush garden views from every angle. Three individual wings give you a choice of accommodations styles: urban contemporary, natural resort, and Asian opulence. See p. 476.

- **Hilton Kuala Lumpur** (Kuala Lumpur, Malaysia): The coolest of the cool stay at the new Hilton. The rooms feel like suites, decorated in slickety slick contempo style with the latest entertainment and IT built in—even in the bathrooms. See p. 558.

- **Four Seasons Resort Langkawi** (Langkawi, Malaysia): Raising the bar, this resort is an exotic Moorish paradise on the most gorgeous beach in Malaysia. Rooms and public areas drip with the ambience of the *Arabian Nights*. Three words: To. Die. For. See p. 587.

- **Four Seasons Resort at Jimbaran Bay** (Jimbaran, Bali): With its individual bungalows and plunge pools overlooking the blue sea and its famous Four Seasons pampering, this is one of the great hotels in the world. See p. 624.

- **Amandari** (Ubud, Bali): The Amandari offers another sybaritic Bali experience, with individual bunga-lows overlooking a deep-green gorge. If you can afford it (or the Four Seasons Resort at Jimbaran Bay), do it. Even if you can't, do it. See p. 630.

- **Chedi Club at Tanah Gajah** (Ubud, Bali): The private villas offer plunge pools, indoor and outdoor Bose speaker systems, huge outdoor bath-tubs, butlers that cater to your every demand, and plenty of complimentary services that make other hotels seem stingy. See p. 630.

9 The Best Hotel Bargains

- **Majestic Grande** (Bangkok, Thailand): The Majestic could rightly be called either a small-scale luxury hotel or a bloated boutique hotel. Regardless of the label, it's in a prime spot off bustling Sukhumvit, with rooms going for half the price of the large chains. See p. 107.

- **Tamarind Village** (Chiang Mai, Thailand): If you're going to travel on a budget, do it with style—and style is what Tamarind Village has wrapped up in its quiet courtyard in the middle of Old Town. Rooms are new and rather spartan in concrete and rattan, but everything is tip-top. See p. 208.

- **Day Inn Hotel** (Vientiane, Laos): So it's just a few notches above your average guesthouse, but there's a comfortable, laid-back feel here, and this many long-stay visitors can't be wrong. You'll find rooms for US$32 (£18). See p. 249.

- **Spring Hotel** (Ho Chi Minh City, Vietnam): Not especially luxurious, but rooms in this privately owned downtown property (one of few non-governmental places in Saigon) start at US$36 (£20). It's light on amenities but very comfortable, convenient, and friendly. See p. 393.

- **Goldiana** (Phnom Penh, Cambodia): It's no-frills, but friendly and cheap, set in a quiet neighborhood south of the town center. The hotel is popular with long-staying visitors and NGO workers. See p. 424.

- **SHA Villa** (Singapore): This boutique hotel is packed with Southeast Asian charm. It has an attentive staff and an ideal location, close to Orchard Road. See p. 481.

- **Swiss-Inn** (Kuala Lumpur, Malaysia): Location, location, location! Right in the center of Kuala Lumpur's bustling Chinatown, the Swiss-Inn is the perennial favorite for travelers here. A comfortable choice, plus it's so close to everything. See p. 560.

- **Heeren House** (Malacca, Malaysia): Bargain or no bargain, this boutique hotel in the heart of the old city is the place to stay in Malacca if you want to really get a feel for the local atmosphere. See p. 570.

- **Telang Usan Hotel** (Kuching, Malaysia): An informal place, Telang Usan is homey and quaint, and within walking distance of many major attractions in Kuching. See p. 592.

- **The *Losmen* (Homestays) of Bali.** These small-time accommodations will give you a large, comfortable (though no-frills) room or bungalow with a big, often fancy breakfast for about US$5 a night for two. See chapter 10.

- **Ritz-Carlton Bali** (Jimbaran, Bali): Okay, it's certainly not cheap, but the resort—with spectacular amenities and massive grounds made for strolling—offers great value for money. See p. 625.

10 The Best Local Dining Experiences

- **Street Food** (Bangkok, Thailand): On every street, down every alley, you'll find someone setting up a cart with an umbrella. Noodles, salads, and satay are favorites, and some hawkers set up tables and stools on the sidewalk for you to take a load off. This is Thai cafe life! See chapter 4.

- **Kua Lao** (Vientiane, Laos): Kua Lao serves traditional Lao cuisine in a restored colonial—it's the premier Lao restaurant in the country. The extensive menu goes on for pages. There is an entire page of vegetarian entrees and another entire page of something you don't see often: traditional Lao desserts. See p. 251.

- **Pho** (Vietnam): Don't leave the country without sampling one, if not many, bowls of this delicate noodle soup, made with vermicelli (thin rice noodles), chicken *(ga)* or beef *(bo)*, and several fresh accompaniments, according to the chef's whim or local flavor: basil, mint, chile peppers, and bean sprouts. See chapter 6.

- **Ngon Restaurant** (Ho Chi Minh City, Vietnam): It may be a restaurant, but it's really like the classroom for Vietnam Cuisine 101. It's loud and busy, but diners have their choice of food from the many authentic street stalls that line the central courtyard. Locals eat here; and though there is an English menu, go with a Vietnamese friend or ask for a recommendation from the friendly (but always busy) staff. See p. 396.

- **Hawker Centers** (Singapore): Think of them as shopping malls for food—great food! For local cuisine, who needs a menu with pictures when you can walk around and select anything you want as it's prepared right before your eyes? See chapter 8.

- **Gurney Drive Food Stalls** (Penang, Malaysia): Penang is king for offering a variety of Asian cuisines, from Chinese to Malay, Indian, and everything else in between. Visiting this large hawker center by the sea is like taking "Intro to Penang 101." See p. 581.

- **Warungs** (Bali): Like a local cafe, the Balinese equivalent of the greasy-spoon diner in America, *warungs* can be found on every street corner. If you're not put off by a bit of grime, you'll discover the food can be authentic, delicious, and cheap. See chapter 10.

11 The Best Markets

- **Chatuchak Weekend Market** (Bangkok, Thailand): One word describes it: huge. You can easily get lost and certainly spend hours wandering this labyrinth. Don't buy anything until you spend at least a half day wandering down the endless aisles eyeballing the multitude of merchandise available. See chapter 4.

- **Night Bazaar** (Chiang Mai, Thailand): Most of those gorgeous handicrafts you find all over Thailand are made in the north, and at Chiang Mai's sprawling Night Bazaar, you'll find the widest selection, best quality, and best prices. See chapter 4.

- **Morning Market** (Vientiane, Laos): Laos's famous market is three huge buildings with traditional tiered roofs. Silver handicrafts, fabrics, jewelry, electronics, books, and much, much more occupy each building's several floors. The aisles are wide and made for wandering and poking through the wares, and the proprietors are friendly, gentle bargainers. See chapter 5.

Tips Everything Has a Price: Haggling

Prices are never marked in the small shops and at street vendors in Southeast Asia. You must bargain. The most important thing to remember when bargaining is to keep a friendly, good-natured banter between you and the seller. Before you start out, it's good to have some idea of how much your purchase is worth, to give you a base point for negotiation. A simple "How much?" is the place to start, to which the vendor will reply with the top price. Check at a few vendors before negotiating, and never accept the first price! Try a smile and ask, "Is that your best price?" Vendors will laughingly ask for your counteroffer. Knock the price down about 50%—they'll look shocked, but it's a starting point for bidding. Just remember to smile and be friendly, and remain willing to walk away (or fake it). *Caveat:* If it's a larger, more expensive item, don't get into major bargaining unless you're serious about buying. If the shopkeeper agrees on what you say you're willing to pay, it's considered rude not to make the purchase. See the individual country chapters for more on shopping.

- **Central Market** (Hoi An, Vietnam): On the banks of the busy Perfume River lies this entire city block of narrow, roofed aisles. Products of every description are for sale inside: handicrafts, household items, and services such as facials and massages. On the outskirts, an entire warehouse is devoted to silk and silk tailoring. See chapter 6.

- **Central Market** (Phnom Penh, Cambodia): This is where it all happens in Phnom Penh. The main building is a massive Art Deco rotunda with wings extending in all directions. It's an anthill of activity on any given day, and you can get some interesting bargains and unique finds. See chapter 7.

- **Arab Street** (Singapore): Sure, Singapore is a shopper's paradise, but it needs more places like Arab Street, where small shops lining the street sell everything from textiles to handicrafts. Bargaining is welcome. See chapter 8.

- **Central Market** (Kuala Lumpur, Malaysia): This is one-stop shopping for all the rich arts and handicrafts Malaysia produces—and it's air-conditioned, too. See chapter 9.

12 The Best Shopping Bargains

- **Antiques** (Thailand): Before you head out on vacation, visit some Asian galleries in your home country and take a look at the prices of the items you like. Once you're here, you'll be amazed at how little these things really cost. Most places will be glad to pack and ship purchases for you, and you'll still come out ahead. See chapter 4.

- **Tailored Silk Suits** (Thailand; also Hanoi, Hoi An, and Ho Chi Minh City, Vietnam): For a fraction of what you'd pay at home, you can have a lined silk (or wool) suit tailored in a day or less, including a fitting or two.

Bring pictures of your favorite designer outfits for a clever copy, plus an empty suitcase or two for the trip home. See chapters 4 and 6.

- **Hand-Woven Textiles** (Laos): The Laos hand-weave textured fabrics piece by piece on primitive wooden looms. Such painstaking work costs more than a few dollars, but, ranging from sophisticated silk to gaily colored ethnic prints, the designs are pure art and uniquely Laotian. See chapter 5.
- **Silver or Lacquer Handicrafts** (Vietnam): The workmanship is tops and the prices low throughout Vietnam, particularly for lacquerware. Bargain hard and make sure that the silver is genuine. See chapter 6.

- **Silver Filigree Jewelry** (Malaysia): Silver is worked into detailed filigree jewelry designs to make brooches, necklaces, bracelets, and other fine jewelry. See chapter 9.
- **Pewter** (Malaysia): Malaysia is the home of Selangor Pewter, one of the largest pewter manufacturers in the world. Its many showrooms have all sorts of items to choose from. See chapter 9.
- **Fabric & Woodcarvings** (Bali): Even with the "rich man's tax" for tourists in Bali, just about anything you buy on the island is a bargain compared with the same stuff back home. Commissioned fabric and woodcarvings are a particularly good deal. See chapter 10.

13 The Hottest Nightlife

- **Patpong** (Bangkok, Thailand): Yes, *that* Patpong. If go-go bars and sex shows aren't your style, you'll still find plenty to do. After you're finished shopping in the huge night market, you'll see plenty of restaurants, pubs, and discos that cater to folks who prefer more traditional nightlife. See chapter 4.
- **Disco Lives!** (Laos): Go to a disco . . . any disco. It's like a bad junior-high dance and just as innocent. In the basement of Vientiane's Lao Plaza Hotel is a reasonable big-city facsimile, but ask around in any small town for what's going on. The music is Asian pop, but it's refreshing to watch young gentlemen ask the ladies to the floor with a bit of pomp and circumstance, and then it's cheek-to-cheek or stilted boogie until the big cheer when the music stops. It hearkens back to an America of the 1950s. See chapter 5.
- **Ho Chi Minh City** (Vietnam): From the tawdry to the socialite scene,

you'll find it in Ho Chi Minh City (Saigon). With rooftop garden bars like Saigon Saigon and cool spots like Q Bar, the city has a rollicking scene. Most evenings begin with an elegant (but very reasonable) French or Vietnamese dinner; then it's bar-hopping time in the compact downtown, mingling with trendy locals and fun-loving expats. See chapter 6.
- **Singapore:** Nightlife is becoming increasingly sophisticated in Singapore, where locals have more money for recreation and fun. Take the time to choose the place that suits your personality. Jazz club? Techno? Cocktail lounge? Wine bar? Good old pub? It has it all. See chapter 8.
- **Bangsar** (near Kuala Lumpur, Malaysia): Folks in Kuala Lumpur know to go to Bangsar for nighttime excitement. A couple blocks of concentrated restaurants, cafes, discos, pubs, and wine bars will tickle any fancy. There's good people-watching, too. See chapter 9.

2

Introducing Southeast Asia

While the rest of the world's continents fit into nice, tidy compartments, the nations that make up Southeast Asia—Cambodia, Indonesia, Laos, Malaysia, Singapore, Thailand, and Vietnam—often have more differences than similarities. Diverse geographical features, histories, religious and cultural heritages, economies, and politics across the region mean that the shortest journey offers cross-cultural comparison and new perspective.

Safety is a primary concern for travelers these days, and while it is important to stay updated on internal issues in any given country and to steer clear of any hot spots, the adventurous tourist paths through this vibrant region are ripe for exploration and replete with mystery, beauty, and ancient culture and wisdom.

1 The Region Today

The region's many differences mean an array of choices for vacationers. With so many options, how can you decide which is the perfect beach or the most intriguing cultural or adventure locale? In this chapter, we provide an overall view of the region and explain some of the special features and unique attractions of each destination to help you decide. And in the chapters that follow, we'll help you plan your trip from soup to nuts.

Geographically, Southeast Asia is diverse and stunning. The lush tropical rainforests of peninsular Malaysia and Borneo are some of the oldest in the world. Beautiful islands and beaches are many, including large resort areas like Thailand's Phuket or Indonesia's Bali, plus countless other gorgeous isles, atolls, and sandy strips that are relatively unexploited. Divers and snorkelers flock from around the world for stunning coral reefs bursting with colorful life in Thailand, Malaysia, and Indonesia. You can find adventures in the wild while jungle

trekking, sea and river kayaking, or visiting ethnic villages and sacred peaks.

Southeast Asia is also a cultural melting pot, a crossroads of influences from China, south Asia, and Tibet. Consider the Sri Lankans, who transplanted Theravada Buddhism, with its serene and orthodox ways, from Myanmar to Thailand and Laos. Or the Indian traders, who brought ancient Hinduism to Cambodia, influencing the architecture of the magical city of Angkor. Or the Hindus who settled on Bali, mixing their dogma with local animism to create a completely unique sect. Meanwhile, seafaring Arab merchants imported Islam to coastal areas of Malaysia and Indonesia, adding another interesting facet to the region. In Vietnam, the only Southeast Asian nation to fall directly under the control of past Chinese empires, China's cultural influences are still strong. And, on top of that, Europeans from the late 1400s onward imported Western culture to cities such as Hong Kong, Singapore, Penang, and

Malacca; the European colonial imprint is still visible in the architecture and cuisine of most countries in the region. Crossing an international border in Southeast Asia is stepping into another world.

Economic and political developments have changed the face of tourism in the region. While cosmopolitan stops like Singapore, Kuala Lumpur, and Bangkok guarantee the best luxury hotels, finest dining, and most refined cultural attractions, up-and-coming cities such as Hanoi, Ho Chi Minh City (Saigon), and Chiang Mai promise cultural curiosities around every street corner as they struggle to justify traditional customs with modern development. Thailand's 3 decades of tourism development have created very familiar facilities for travelers, for example, but those looking for a more down-and-dirty experience can head off to nearby Cambodia or Laos, countries still off the beaten path of most tourist agendas. For every luxurious Bali, there's a laid-back Tioman Island (Malaysia). For every busy Bangkok, there's a charming Luang Prabang (Laos).

It is important, of course, to talk about those Southeast Asian nations that have political or safety concerns, and the sections that follow discuss political turmoil in more detail. Steer clear of any sectarian or political tension, and know that the relative stability of many countries in Southeast Asia is rather short-lived; flash political upheavals are not uncommon. Refer to your country's overseas travel bureau or to the U.S. State Department (click "Travel Warnings" at www.travel.state.gov) to learn about current travel warnings in the area.

THAILAND

Each year, Thailand sees more international travelers than any of its neighbors, enticing everyone from luxury vacationers to young shoestring backpackers, Japanese junkets, and European group tours. You'll meet young professionals on

hiatus, naive tourists prowling for that "One Night in Bangkok," and soul-searchers hanging around for the Buddhist Dharma and Asian hospitality. Many trips to Southeast Asia either start here or end up here, and it is a good orientation.

Travelers usually arrive in **Bangkok,** staying for a few days to take in the city's bizarre mix of royal palaces and skyscrapers, pious monks amid rush-hour commuters, and sidewalk noodle vendors serving bankers in suits. That's not to mention the city's nightlife, with that seedy element that made the city infamous. Heading south, find the legendary beaches and resorts of **Phuket** island; **Koh Samui,** in the Gulf of Thailand, is a comparable alternative. Another attraction, the northern hills around **Chiang Mai,** presents a world of adventure trekking and tribal culture along well-worn—but well-worth-it—travel paths. Throughout the country, you'll have opportunities for **outdoor adventure** and **extreme sports,** organized by very professional firms that you can count on for safety and reliability.

And at the end of the day, there's that unbeatable taste of **Thai cuisine**—tangy soups, hearty coconut curries, and the freshest seafood.

LAOS

Travelers who complain that Thailand has become too touristy can look to Laos. Here is a country where foreigners are still greeted as gracious guests rather than cash cows. Rarely will you find tacky souvenir stalls or tourist kitsch—just quiet towns with laid-back markets, townsfolk carrying on their trades, and farmers tending to their chores. Life is set to the pace of Buddhism, tranquillity and compassion the hallmarks, and Lao people are very kind and welcoming.

Some people fear that Laos will follow Thailand's accelerated development model, that the ethnic villages in the north will be turned into safari parks and the country's beautiful temples transformed into theme attractions. But the infrastructure of this developing nation won't yet support that, and Lao people are in no rush to cash in on the nation's peacefulness.

For a capital city, **Vientiane** is startlingly parochial. With every other building dedicated to an international development agency, it's an eye-opening reminder that Laos is one of the 10 poorest countries in the world. Next stop is **Luang Prabang,** UNESCO World Heritage Site, a paradise of gorgeous Buddhist temples—dozens of them amid shady streets that lead to the Mekong River. If you have time, **Xieng Khouang,** east of Vientiane, is the home of Southeast Asia's Stonehenge, the **Plain of Jars,** huge mysterious stone monoliths that have somehow survived bombs and guerilla insurgents. **Eco-tourism** is growing rapidly, and some new and interesting avenues into the Lao jungle and rivers connect remote ethnic villages (especially in the north).

VIETNAM

If the thought of Vietnam stirs flashbacks of televised war coverage or scenes from dark movies, guess again. One of the fastest-growing destinations in the region also happens to be one of the most beautiful, most friendly, and most convenient places to travel.

Vietnam's major destinations fall in a line, and most visitors choose to travel from north to south, starting in Hanoi and ending in Ho Chi Minh City (Saigon), or vice versa. Convenient tourist buses connect the main coastal stops, and there are increasing options for individual travelers as well.

In the south, **Ho Chi Minh City,** or **Saigon,** is the gateway to the beautiful **Mekong Delta** region. Heading north, you'll pass through **Dalat,** a hill station in the cool mountains, and then on to **Nha**

Trang, an emerging seaside getaway. Farther north, **Hoi An** is one of the region's most charming villages and a picturesque labyrinth of cobblestone streets, historic buildings, and lots of shopping. Still farther, the former capital city at **Hue** is filled with many architectural gems of Chinese and European influence. The cultural amalgam is best defined in **Hanoi,** where Vietnamese, French, and Chinese cultures collide. From here, head east to see gorgeous **Halong Bay,** with hundreds of craggy rock formations jutting straight up from the sea; or travel to the far north to **Sapa,** where you visit Vietnam's hill-tribe people in the mountains that divide northern Vietnam from China.

CAMBODIA

It wasn't long ago that Cambodia was off the map, a land plagued by general lawlessness and banditry as the result of years of strife. In recent times, visitors have braved the remnants of the country's chaos and, by hook or by crook, made their way to Siem Reap and Southeast Asia's premier cultural attraction, **Angkor Wat,** the magnificent temple ruins of the mighty Angkor civilization of A.D. 800 to 1200.

The good news is that, though it will take years to catch up economically with its growing neighbors, Cambodia is on the mend. It will take at least a few generations to heal after the tragic events of the mid-1970s, when the entire country was turned into a concentration camp under Pol Pot, but Cambodia is now looking to the future. Bolstered by international humanitarian aid organizations, the country is enjoying a protracted period of peace not seen in many years. **Phnom Penh,** the capital, and **Siem Reap,** the access village for the Angkor temples, are safe, and the countryside is open to more adventurous travelers ready to brave the rough roads and basic amenities and accommodations. Many still limit their trip in Cambodia to the temples of

Angkor, however. Convenient direct flights from the larger cities throughout the region simplify the process.

It's important to remember that the country is still littered with UXO, unexploded ordnance, including dormant bombs and land mines. In the rural areas, it's important to stay on well-worn trails and, farther afield, to go with a knowledgeable guide. After a peaceful election in 2003, the situation in Phnom Penh is stable, but visitors should stay informed before going, as the country has a history of flash political upheaval.

SINGAPORE

All of Southeast Asia's cultures seem to converge on Singapore, making it perhaps one of the best places to begin your exploration of the region. Excellent **museums** explore Asian civilizations, Southeast Asian art, and even World War II history. The city's hundreds of restaurants provide a wealth of choices in terms of **cuisine,** offering a glimpse of many regional specialties in one stop. And some of the best regional **fine arts, crafts,** and **antiques** end up in Singapore showrooms.

To be honest with you, Singapore gets trashed regularly by complaints that it is too Western, too modern, too sanitary—too Disneyland. Walk the streets of **Chinatown, Little India,** and the Malay Muslim area at **Kampong Glam,** and you can see where the buildings have been renovated and many former inhabitants have retired from traditional crafts. But some of these places have a few secrets left that are very rewarding if you are observant. For the past 200 years, Singapore has invented itself from many contributing cultures. If you consider the country today, you'll realize it is still keeping up that tradition.

MALAYSIA

Possibly one of the most overlooked countries in Southeast Asia, Malaysia is one of my favorites for one very special reason:

It's not Thailand! After so much time spent traveling around Thailand listening to every hawker yell "Hello! Special for you!" and every backpacker bragging about US$5 roach-infested guesthouses, I look forward to Malaysia just to escape the tourism industry. Beaches on the islands of **Langkawi** and **Sabah** are just as beautiful as Thailand's, and resorts here are equally as fine. The quaint British colonial influences at **Penang, Malacca,** and **Kuching** (Sarawak) add to the beauty, as do the mysterious Arab-Islamic influences all over the country. That's not to mention an endless number of **outdoor adventures,** from mountain climbing to jungle trekking to scuba diving—in fact, the rainforest here is far superior.

Why is Malaysia so underestimated? To be honest, after experiencing the relative "freedom" and tolerance of Thai culture, many travelers find Malaysian culture too strict and prohibitive. Personally, I think it's a fair trade—in Thailand, when I talk to Thai people, I'm often treated like a tourist with a fat wallet. In Malaysia, when I meet local people, I end up having interesting conversations and cherished personal experiences. And I don't have to suffer through blatant prostitution and drug abuse—the sad, sleazy side of the Thai tourism industry.

One word of caution regarding travel in Malaysia: On April 23, 2000, a group of tourists was kidnapped from the diving resort at Sipadan Island, off the east coast of Sabah (Malaysian Borneo). Abu Sayyaf, the Filipino Muslim separatists who were responsible for the incident, still remain at large in the southern islands of the Philippines close to Borneo. Exercise caution when traveling to this area.

BALI (INDONESIA)

Memories of the 2002 and 2005 bombings in southern Bali are written large on our collective image of the island, and no

Myanmar (Burma): To Go or Not to Go?

In preparing this guide, we were confronted with problematic political realities in Myanmar—realities that made us question the advisability of sending readers there. The brutality and unfairness of the military government of Myanmar have been met with sanctions and embargoes from the international community. Political leaders like the resilient Aung San Suu Kyi are being punished, and any dissent is met with house arrest and prison.

Since the early 1990s, the junta has encouraged tourism, and a visit to Myanmar is in fact a unique glimpse into rich Buddhist tradition, ancient culture, and stunning natural beauty. But while some encourage tourism and believe that Western visitors give voice to the troubles of Burma, other voices shout for a moratorium on tourism to this troubled land, saying that visitors' dollars subsidize and support tyranny.

Because of the precarious political climate in Myanmar, we've decided to exclude the country from this edition. Those not so easily dissuaded, however, can find more information on the subject at the **Burma Project at the Open Society Institute** (www.soros.org/burma) or at www.burmadebate.org. If you do decide to go to Myanmar, we suggest sticking with a reputable international tour operator. Good regional providers include **Diethelm Travel** (1 Inya Rd., Kamayut Township; ✆ 951/527-110 or 951/527-117; fax 951/527-135; www.diethelm-travel.com) and **Exotissimo Travel** (#0303 Sakura Tower, 339 Bogyoke Aung San St., Kyauktada Township, Yangon; ✆ 951/255-427 or 951/255-388; fax 951/255-428; myanmar@exotissimo.com).

doubt the whole world is familiar with Indonesia's history of civil unrest: ethnic and religious conflict, the struggle for independence in East Timor and now Aceh, and anti-Western bombings and riots in Jakarta. Yet tourism is on the upswing in Bali, and those who visit are taking advantage of great hotel deals on an island well known for spectacular beaches, lush rice paddies, and welcoming people

Until the bombings, Bali was the one safe haven, an enclave of upscale resorts separate from troubles on the larger islands of Indonesia. Now, in the wake of the bombings, Bali struggles to regain its international allure. The **beaches** remain the stuff of legend, supporting dreamy resorts that cater to anyone from families to escapist honeymooners and well-heeled paradise seekers. **Watersports** enthusiasts flock to Bali for surfing, snorkeling, scuba diving, and swimming as well as wind- and kitesurfing. Those who can pull themselves away from the seaside can venture into villages lively with local smiles and markets packed with eye-boggling handicrafts and treasures, or take off into the jungle or up among high volcanic peaks for rigorous trekking. The town of **Ubud** is set among delightful Hindu temples and gorgeous mountain scenery—famed for its terraced rice fields—and supports a unique community of local and expat artists. Bali still has much to offer, and the friendly Balinese islanders are eager to see a return of the Western visitors who've brought so much to this magical isle.

2 A Southeast Asian Cultural Primer

The diverse ethnic groups in the region, from socialite city dwellers to remote enclaves of subsistence farmers, each have a unique history, cultural practices, and religions. The region is a veritable cornucopia of cultures that have intertwined and adopted various elements, beliefs, and practices from one another.

THE CULTURAL MAKEUP OF SOUTHEAST ASIA
THAILAND

Over centuries, migrating cultures have blended to create what is known as "Thai" today. Early waves of southern Chinese migrants combined with Mon peoples from Burma, Khmers from Cambodia, Malays, and Lao people—it is said that Thailand's King Rama I could trace ancestry to all these—plus European, Indian, Han Chinese, and Arab families. Of the 75% of the population that calls itself Thai, a great number of people in northeastern Isaan are of Lao ancestry. In the past century, Thailand has also become home to many migrating hill tribes in the north—tribes who've come from Vietnam, Laos, Myanmar, and southern China, many as refugees. As you travel south toward the Malaysian border, you find Thai people who share cultural and religious affinity with their southern Malay neighbors. Also in the past 50 years, Thailand has seen a boom in Chinese immigrants.

The Thais are a warm and peaceable people, with a culture that springs from Indian and Sri Lankan origins. Early Thais adopted many Brahman practices, evident in royal ceremony and social hierarchy— Thailand is a very class-oriented culture. Even their cherished national story, the *Ramakien,* the subject of almost all Thai classical dances and temple murals, finds its origin in the Indian Hindu epic the *Ramayana.* Thai Buddhism follows the Theravada sect, imported from Sri Lanka along with the classic bell-shape stupa seen in many temple grounds.

Perhaps the two main influences in Thai life today are spirituality and the royal family. In nearly every household throughout the country, you'll find a spirit house to appease the property's former inhabitants, a portrait of the king in a prominent spot and perhaps pictures of a few previous kings, a dais for Buddha images and religious objects, and portraits of each son as he enters the monkhood, as almost all sons do.

LAOS, VIETNAM & CAMBODIA

Together, the countries of Laos, Vietnam, and Cambodia make up one of the most ethnically diverse regions of Southeast Asia. Outside the cities, little English is spoken in any of these countries except by tour guides and others who have frequent contact with Western visitors. Much of the architecture and art in Cambodia and Laos is influenced by Buddhism and includes some of the world's most renowned temples, along with exquisitely sculpted Buddha images. The temple complexes of Angkor Wat in Cambodia are among the architectural wonders of the ancient world, while the finest temples in Laos are found in the ancient capital of Luang Prabang.

Note: The ethnic minorities, or hill tribes, of northern Vietnam, Laos, and Thailand all share a common heritage with one another, originating from either Himalayan tribes or southern Chinese clans. You'll find startling similarities in the customs and languages of all these people.

LAOS In Laos, approximately half the population is ethnic Lao descended from centuries of migration, mostly from southern China. A landlocked country with few natural resources, Laos has had

Buddha & Buddhism in Southeast Asia

Born **Siddhartha Gautama Buddha** in the year 563 B.C., the historical Buddha was an Indian prince. A passing sage predicted the child's future as a great holy man and, to spare him the tortuous life of the saint, Siddhartha was kept sheltered behind palace walls. As a child, he knew nothing of sickness and death. He married, had children, and lived a carefree life, though one plagued by a certain soul sickness and discontent. His journey began when he first spied a sick man and a corpse. Renouncing his princely cloaks, he concluded that life is suffering. Resolving to search for relief from earthly pain, he went into the forest and lived there for many years as a solitary ascetic, ultimately following his moderate "middle way" and achieving enlightenment and **nirvana** (escape from the cycle of reincarnation) while in meditation under the Bodhi tree.

Buddha's peripatetic teaching is the basis of all Buddhism. Upon his death, two schools arose and spread throughout Asia. The oldest and probably closest to the original practice is **Theravada** (Doctrine of the Elders), sometimes referred to as **Hinayana** (the Small Vehicle), which prevails in Sri Lanka, Laos, Thailand, and Cambodia and posits the enlightenment of individuals in this life, one at a time. The other school is **Mahayana** (the Large Vehicle), practiced in eastern Asia and Vietnam, which speaks of group enlightenment (we all go at once).

Buddhism has one aim only: to abolish suffering. To do so, according to Buddhism, one must transcend the ego, the "self," and attachment to the fleeting pleasures in an ever-changing material world, in order to see things clearly—with wisdom—and find peace.

There is no god in Buddhism; the Buddha is but an example. Buddhist practices, particularly Theravada, center on meditation and require that individuals, according to Buddha himself, look within and come to understand

little luck entering the global trade scene and remains dependent on the international donor community. If you think the Thais are laid-back, you'll have to check the Laos for a pulse. In fact, Lao culture is most often compared with that of the Thais because the two share common roots of language and culture, although the Thais will never admit it because they often look down upon their northern neighbors. Large communities of ethnic minorities live in agrarian and subsistence communities, particularly in the north, and carry on rich traditional crafts and practices.

VIETNAM   In Vietnam, the ethnic Vietnamese are a fusion of Viet, Tai (a southern Chinese group), Indonesian, and Chinese who first settled here between 200 B.C. and A.D. 200. Although Vietnam has no official religion, several religions have significantly impacted Vietnamese culture, including Buddhism, Confucianism, Taoism, and Animism. Animism, which is the oldest religious practice in Vietnam and many other Southeast Asian countries, is centered on belief in a spirit world.

Ancient cultural traditions lean toward borrowings from the mandarins of old the **Four Noble Truths:** the existence of suffering; its arising; the path to eliminating suffering; and, its ultimate passing by practice of the Eightfold Path, a road map to right living and good conduct.

Buddhist philosophy pervades every aspect of life, morality, and thought in the countries of Thailand, Laos, and Cambodia. The monastic community, called the **sangha,** is supported by local people and serves as the cultural touchstone and often an important avenue of education. Monks live in the "supramundane," free from the usual human concerns of finding food, clothing, and shelter. Instead, they focus on the rigorous practice of meditation, study, and austerities prescribed by the Theravada tradition. Mahayana traditions from China hold important sway over life in parts of the Malay Peninsula, Thailand, and Vietnam.

Lay practitioners adopt the law of **karma,** in which every action has effects and the energy of past action, good or evil, continues forever and is "reborn." Merit is gained by entering the monkhood (which most males do for a few days or months), helping in the construction of a monastery or a stupa, contributing to education, giving alms, or performing any act of kindness, no matter how small. When monks go with their alms bowls from house to house, they are not begging, but offering laypersons an opportunity to **"make merit"** by supporting them.

Buddha images are honored and revered in the Eastern tradition and are said to radiate the essence of Buddha, ideals that we should revere and struggle to achieve; but the images themselves are not holy or spiritually charged, per se. Buddhism does not seek converts, and, as long as they follow some simple rules of conduct, tourists are welcome guests at most Buddhist fetes and festivals.

Chinese dynasties that claimed sovereignty over Vietnam. In the 1900s, the French added a new flavor to the mix. Modern Vietnam is defined by its pell-mell rush to capitalism.

CAMBODIA The population of Cambodia is made up primarily of ethnic Khmers who have lived here since around the 2nd century A.D. and whose religion and culture have been influenced by interaction with Indians, Javanese, Thais, Vietnamese, and Chinese. The achievements of the ancient Angkor empire were a long time ago, and modern Khmer culture still struggles in the aftermath of many years of war and terror. Relative political stability is new here, and Cambodia has far to go to catch up economically and with the infrastructure of the other countries in the region. Basic medical necessities are still lacking; land mines still cover the countryside and kill an estimated four people each day. Time and effort by civil authorities and NGOs (nongovernmental organizations) will only tell. Life in Cambodia is marked by devout Buddhist ritual, much like its neighbors, which fosters a pervasive gentleness among the Khmer.

SINGAPORE

Seventy-eight percent of Singaporeans trace their heritage to migrating waves from China's southern provinces, particularly from the Hokkien, Teowchew, Hakka, Cantonese, and Hainanese dialect groups. Back then, the Chinese community was driven by rags-to-riches stories—the poor worker hawking vegetables who opened a grocery store and then started a chain of stores and now drives a Mercedes. This story still motivates them today.

But it's not just Chinese who have dominated the scene. The island started off with a handful of Malay inhabitants; then came the British colonials with Indian administrators, followed by Muslim Indian moneylenders, Chinese merchants, Chinese coolie laborers, and Indian convict labor, plus European settlers and immigrants from all over Southeast Asia. Over 2 centuries of modern history, each group made its contribution to "Singaporean culture."

Today, as your average Singaporean struggles to balance traditional values with modern demands of globalization, his country gets raked over the coals for being sterile and overly Westernized. Older folks are becoming frustrated by younger generations who discard their traditions in their pursuit of "The 5 Cs"—career, condo, car, credit card, and cash. Temples and ethnic neighborhoods are finding more revenue from tourists than from the communities they once served. Although many lament the loss of the good old days, most are willing to sacrifice a little tradition to be Southeast Asia's most stable and wealthiest country.

MALAYSIA

Malaysia's population consists primarily of ethnic Malays, labeled Bumiputeras, a political classification that also encompasses tribal people who live in peninsular Malaysia and Borneo. Almost all Malays are Muslim, and conservative values are the norm. The ruling government party supports an Islam that is open and tolerant to other cultures, but a growing minority favors strict Islamic law and government, further marginalizing the country's large Chinese and Indian population. These foreign cultures migrated to Malaysia during the British colonial period as trading merchants, laborers, and administrators. Today, Malaysia recognizes ethnic Chinese and Indian citizens as equals under national law. However, government development and education policies always seem to favor Bumiputeras.

Among the favorite Malaysian recreational pastimes are kite flying, using ornately decorated paper kites, and top spinning. Some still practice silat, a Malaysian form of martial arts.

BALI (INDONESIA)

No country in Southeast Asia has a more ethnically diverse population than Indonesia, with more than 350 ethnic groups with their own languages and cultures scattered among the 6,000 inhabited islands of this vast archipelago of more than 14,000 islands.

Of all the islands, Bali stands out for its especially rich cultural life, which is inextricably linked with its Hindu beliefs. Life here is marked by a unique flow of ritual; whether painting, carving, dancing, or playing music, it seems that all Balinese are involved in the arts or practice devout daily rituals of beauty. Flower offerings to the gods are a common sight, and the Balinese are forever paying homage to Hindu deities at more than 20,000 temples and during the 60 annual festivals on the island.

The majority of the island's population is native Balinese; there are quite a few people from other parts of Indonesia who are here for work opportunities. English is widely spoken in the tourist parts of Bali, which means that just about everywhere you go someone will speak enough to help you out.

ETIQUETTE

"Different countries, different customs," as Sean Connery said to Michael Caine in *The Man Who Would Be King*. And although each destination covered in this book proves that rule by having its own twists on etiquette, some general pointers will allow you to go though your days of traveling without inadvertently offending your hosts. (For etiquette tips in individual countries, see the relevant chapters.)

GREETINGS, GESTURES & SOCIAL INTERACTION In these modern times, the common **Western handshake** has become extremely prevalent throughout Southeast Asia, but it is by no means universal. There are a plethora of traditional greetings, so when greeting someone—especially an older man and even more especially a woman of any age—it's safest to wait for a gesture or observe those around you and then follow suit. In Muslim culture, for instance, it is not acceptable for men and women not related by blood or marriage to touch.

In interpersonal relations in strongly Buddhist areas (Laos, Vietnam, and Thailand), it helps to **take a gentle approach** to human relationships. A person showing anger or ill temper would be regarded with surprise and disapproval. A gentle approach will take you much further.

Here's an important, delicate matter: In countries with significant Muslim and Hindu cultures (Malaysia, Singapore, and Bali), **use only your right hand in social interaction.** Traditionally, the left hand is used only for personal hygiene. Not only should you eat with your right hand and give and receive all gifts with your right hand, but you should also make sure that you make all gestures, especially **pointing** (and, even more especially, pointing in temples and mosques), with your right hand. In all the countries discussed in this book, it's also considered more polite to point with your knuckle (with your hand facing palm down) than with your finger.

In all destinations covered in this guide, ladies seated on the floor should never sit with their legs crossed in front of them—instead, tuck your legs to the side. Men may sit with legs crossed. Both men and women should also **avoid showing the bottoms of the feet,** which are considered the lowliest, most unclean part of the body. If you cross your legs while on the floor or in a chair, don't point your soles toward other people. Also be careful not to use your foot to point or gesture. **Remove your shoes** when entering a temple or private home. And don't ever step over someone's body or legs.

On a similar note, in Buddhist and Hindu cultures, the head is considered the most sacred part of the body; therefore, **do not casually touch another person's head**—and this includes patting children on the head.

DRESSING FOR CULTURAL SUCCESS The basic rule is simple: **Dress modestly.** Except perhaps on the grounds of resorts and in heavily touristed areas such as Bali's Kuta and Thailand's beaches, foreigners displaying navels, chests, or shoulders, or wearing short shorts or short skirts, will attract stares. Although shorts and bathing suits are accepted on the beach, you should avoid parading around in them elsewhere, no matter how hot it is.

TEMPLE & MOSQUE ETIQUETTE Many of Southeast Asia's greatest and most remarkable sights are its places of worship, usually Buddhist *wats,* Hindu temples, and Islamic mosques *(masjids).* When visiting these places, more so than at any other time, it's important to observe certain rules of decorum.

When visiting the **mosques,** be sure to dress appropriately. Neither men nor women will be admitted wearing shorts. Ladies should not wear short skirts or sleeveless, backless, or low-cut tops. Both men and women are required to leave

Tips   The Biggest Cultural No-Nos

- **Showing too much skin.** Except perhaps in Singapore, Bangkok, and other heavily touristed areas—where modest Southeast Asians are more accepting of beachwear at the beach and sexier attire at discos—dress with respect for the locals and their traditions. And don't wear shorts or short skirts to a temple or mosque—it'll get you tossed out.
- **Photographing a member of a hill tribe without permission.** There's nothing a visitor wants more than to take away indelible images of the colorful, rustic lifestyles of the Southeast Asian ethnic minorities. However, many rural people are superstitious about photographs or might resent the intrusion of privacy. Ask first.
- **Losing your temper in Laos, Thailand, or Vietnam.** Many people follow Buddhist traditions in their daily life, approaching even unfortunate events with calm cheerfulness. They would be shocked and dismayed at anger or ill temper, and raising your voice won't achieve any purpose whatsoever. No matter how frustrated you become, keep it under wraps, or the people around you will see to it that you never get what you need.
- **Using offensive body language.** Muslims, Hindus, and Buddhists all reserve the left hand for "unclean" toilet duties, never for pointing at anyone or anything, handing objects to others, eating, or touching other people. Similarly, in Buddhist and Hindu cultures, the head is revered as the most sacred part of the body, while the feet are the lowest. Never touch another person's head or shoulders, and never point or gesture with your feet.
- **Looking (or being) poor in Singapore.** You probably won't run into too many cultural faux pas in cosmopolitan Singapore, but poverty is the pits in this city. Bring your smartest clothes if you want to impress people here.
- **Not belching after a meal in Bali.** Releasing a good burp after a meal is considered a compliment to the chef.

their shoes outside. Also, never enter the mosque's main prayer hall; this area is reserved for Muslims only. No cameras or video cameras are allowed, and remember to turn off cellphones and pagers. You should not plan to go to the mosques between 11am and 2pm on Friday, the Sabbath day.

Visitors are welcome to walk around and explore most **temples** and **wats.** As in the mosques, remember to dress appropriately—some temples might refuse to admit you if you're showing too much skin—and to leave your shoes outside.

Photography is permitted in most temples, although some, such as Wat Phra Kaeo in Thailand, prohibit it. Never climb on a Buddha image, and if you sit down, never point your feet in the direction of the Buddha. Do not cross in front of a person who is in prayer. Also, women should never touch a monk, try to shake his hand, or even give something to one directly (the monk will provide a cloth for you to lay the item upon, and then he will collect it). Monks are not permitted to touch women or to speak directly to them anywhere but inside a temple or wat.

3

Planning Your Trip to Southeast Asia

The later chapters in this guide provide specific information on traveling to and getting around Southeast Asia's individual countries, but in this chapter we give you some region-wide tips and information that will help you plan your trip.

1 Visitor Information

Destination Southeast Asia: Pre-Departure Checklist

- Are there any special requirements for your destination? Vaccinations? Visas, passports, or IDs? Bug repellents? Appropriate attire?
- Are you carrying a current, government-issued passport?
- Did you check to see if any travel advisories have been issued by the U.S. State Department (www.travel.state.gov) regarding your destination?
- Do you have the address and phone number of your country's embassy or consulate with you?
- Did you find out your daily ATM withdrawal limit?
- Do you have your credit card PINs? Is there a daily withdrawal limit on credit card cash advances?
- If you purchased traveler's checks, have you recorded the check numbers and stored the documentation separately from the checks?
- Do you have photocopies of the appropriate pages of your passport stored separately from the passport itself?
- Did you bring your ID cards that could entitle you to discounts, such as AARP cards and student IDs?
- Did you leave a copy of your itinerary with someone at home?
- Did you stop the newspaper and mail delivery, and leave a set of keys with someone reliable?
- Did you pack your camera, an extra set of batteries, and enough film? If you packed film in checked baggage, did you invest in protective pouches to shield film from airport X-rays? If going digital, do you have a strategy for saving files? Enough memory?
- Do you have a safe, accessible place to store money, like a money belt?
- Did you bring emergency drug prescriptions and extra glasses or contact lenses?
- To check in at an airline kiosk with an e-ticket, do you have the credit card you bought your ticket with or a frequent-flier card?
- Do you have the measurements for people you plan to buy clothes for on your trip?

2 Entry Requirements & Customs

ENTRY REQUIREMENTS

Many countries covered in this guide require only a **valid passport** for citizens of the U.S., U.K., Canada, Australia, and New Zealand. For information on how to get a passport, go to "Passports" in the "Fast Facts" section of this chapter—the websites listed provide downloadable passport applications as well as the current fees. For an up-to-date listing of passport requirements around the world, go to the "Foreign Entry Requirement" page of the U.S. State Department at **www.travel.state.gov**.

Note that Vietnam, Laos, and Cambodia require all visitors to have entry **visas.** Though most international airports offer visas upon arrival, and there are more overland points where you can apply with passport photos and money when you arrive, if you plan to enter Vietnam, Laos, or Cambodia from rural overland points, you often need to obtain a visa beforehand (you may even need to specify which entry point). See individual country chapters for specific information.

BALI (INDONESIA) Visitors from the U.S., Canada, most of Europe, Australia, and New Zealand are given a visa upon arrival for a fee of US$30. The only official gateways to Bali are Ngurah Rai Airport or the seaports of Padang Bai and Benoa. If you want to stay longer than 30 days, you must get a tourist or business visa before coming to Indonesia. Tourist visas cannot be extended, while business visas can be extended for 6 months at Indonesian immigration offices.

CAMBODIA All visitors are required to carry a passport and visa. A 1-month visa can be obtained upon entry at the Phnom Penh or Siem Reap international airports for US$20. Bring two passport photos for your application, or be fined. Visa on arrival is now available at the land crossing from Poi Pet (Thailand) and the boat-crossing point from Chau Doc in Vietnam for just US$22.

LAOS Visitors need a valid passport and visa to visit Laos. There are a number of entry sites where visas are granted upon arrival: by air to Vientiane or Luang Prabang, or when crossing from Thailand over the Friendship Bridge between Vientiane and Nong Khai, or between Chiang Khong and Houay Xai in the far north, and Mukdahan and Savannakhet or Chong Mek and Vung Tao (near Pakse) in the far south. A 30-day visa at these arrival points costs US$30. You will also need a passport-sized photo. When coming from Vietnam, be sure to have a pre-arranged visa. At an embassy outside of Laos, the going rate for a 30-day visa is US$35; you'll have to wait up to 5 days for processing (less in Bangkok). For a fee, travel agents in Thailand and other countries in the region can help you jump over the bureaucratic hurdles and get a visa in 1 day.

MALAYSIA To enter Malaysia, you must have a valid passport. Citizens of the U.S. do not need visas for tourism and business visits. Citizens of Canada, Australia, New Zealand, and the U.K. do not require a visa for tourism or business visits not exceeding 1 month.

SINGAPORE To enter Singapore, you'll need a valid passport. Visas are not necessary for citizens of the U.S., Canada, the U.K., Australia, and New Zealand. Upon entry, visitors from these countries will be issued a 30-day pass for a social visit only, except for Americans, who get a 90-day pass.

THAILAND All visitors to Thailand must carry a valid passport with proof of onward passage (either a return or through ticket). Visas are not required for stays of up to 30 days for citizens of the

Tips **Passport Savvy**

Allow plenty of time before your trip to apply for or renew a passport; processing normally takes 3 weeks but can take longer during busy periods (especially spring). And keep in mind that if you need a passport in a hurry, you'll pay a higher processing fee. When traveling, safeguard your passport in an inconspicuous, inaccessible place like a money belt and keep a copy of the critical pages with your passport number in a separate place. If you lose your passport, visit the nearest consulate or embassy of your native country as soon as possible for a replacement.

U.S., Australia, Canada, New Zealand, or the U.K., but 3-month tourist visas can be arranged before arrival.

VIETNAM Residents of the U.S., Canada, Australia, New Zealand, and the U.K. need both a passport and a valid visa to enter Vietnam. A tourist visa usually lasts 30 days and costs US$60. You need to specify your date of entry and exit. Though there's no official policy, tourist visas can commonly be extended with little hassle. Multiple-entry business visas are available that are valid for up to 3 months; however, you must have a sponsoring agency in Vietnam, and it can take much longer to process. For short business trips, it's less complicated simply to enter as a tourist.

CUSTOMS
WHAT YOU CAN BRING INTO SOUTHEAST ASIA
Allowable amounts of tobacco, alcohol, and currency are comparable in all countries: usually 2 cartons of cigarettes, up to 2 bottles of liquor, and between US$3,000 and US$10,000. Check individual chapters for exact amounts. Plant material and animals fall under restrictions across the board.

WHAT YOU CAN TAKE HOME FROM SOUTHEAST ASIA
Restrictions on what you can take out of the various nations of Southeast Asia are loose, at best. Expect a red flag if you have any kind of plant materials or animals, but the most notable restriction has to do with antiques. To prevent the kind of wholesale looting of the region's treasures in the recent colonial past, you might be stopped if you are carrying any Buddhist statuary or authentic antiques or religious artifacts. This does not apply to tourist trinkets, however aged and interesting. In fact, despite any salesman's claim of authenticity, you'll be hard-pressed to find authentic antiques.

U.S. CITIZENS For specifics on what you can bring back and the corresponding fees, download the invaluable free pamphlet *Know Before You Go* online at **www.cbp.gov**. (Click on "Travel" and then "Know Before You Go! Online Brochure.") Or contact **U.S. Customs & Border Protection (CBP),** 1300 Pennsylvania Ave. NW, Washington, DC 20229 (© **877/287-8667**), and request the pamphlet.

CANADIAN CITIZENS For a clear summary of Canadian rules, write for the booklet *I Declare,* issued by the **Canada Border Services Agency (© 800/461-9999** in Canada, or 204/983-3500; www.cbsa-asfc.gc.ca).

U.K. CITIZENS For information, contact **HM Customs & Excise (© 0845/010-9000,** or 020/8929-0152 from outside the U.K.; www.hmce.gov.uk).

AUSTRALIAN CITIZENS   A helpful brochure available from Australian consulates or Customs offices is *Know Before You Go.* For more information, contact the **Australian Customs Service** (© 1300/363-263; www.customs.gov.au).

NEW ZEALAND CITIZENS   Most questions are answered in a free pamphlet available at New Zealand consulates and Customs offices: *New Zealand Customs Guide for Travellers, Notice no. 4.* For more information, contact **New Zealand Customs,** The Customhouse, 17–21 Whitmore St., Box 2218, Wellington (© **04/473-6099** or 0800/428-786; www.customs.govt.nz).

3 Money

The East Asian financial crisis is now a distant memory, and the countries of Southeast Asia are generally gaining economic clout in the world; but the rate of exchange, not to mention the price of most goods and services, means that travel in the region is very budget-friendly. In places like Laos or Cambodia, you'll find that you can live quite well on very little, and the region's resort destinations and luxury accommodations in general come at a fraction of what you might pay in your home country. **ATM** service is good in the larger cities but can be scant, at best, in some of the region's backwaters, with no service whatsoever in places like Laos. **Traveler's checks,** an anachronism elsewhere in the world, are still not a bad idea, especially in the developing countries of the region. Note that the **U.S. dollar** is the de facto currency for many Southeast Asian countries, particularly in Laos, Vietnam, and Cambodia. Hotels, in particular, prefer doing business in U.S. dollars to dealing in local currency, a practice that helps them stay afloat amid fluctuating currency values. In some parts, everybody down to the smallest shop vendor quotes prices in U.S. dollars, and particularly the big-ticket items are best handled with green-backs instead of large stacks of local currency.

While dealing in U.S. dollars can make things less complicated, always keep in mind local currency values so you know if you're being charged the correct amount.

In this book, we've listed **hotel, restaurant, and attraction rates** in whatever form the establishments quoted them—in U.S. dollars where those were quoted, and in local currencies (with U.S. dollar and British pound equivalents) where those were used.

Note that, with the exception of the Singapore dollar, Malaysian ringgit, and Hong Kong dollar (which have remained stable), all other Southeast Asian national currencies are still in a state of flux. Before you budget your trip based on rates we give in this book, be sure to check the currency's current status. You can find a comprehensive currency converter at **www.oanda.com/convert/classic**.

CURRENCY

You will have to rely on local currency when traveling in many rural areas where neither traveler's checks nor credit cards are accepted. The U.S. dollar is the most readily accepted foreign currency throughout Southeast Asia, and it's a good idea to carry some greenbacks as backup.

It's not a bad idea to try and exchange at least some money—just enough to cover airport incidentals and transportation to your hotel—before you leave home (though don't expect the exchange rate to be ideal), so you can avoid lines at airport ATMs; most international arrival points in the region, however, have 24-hour exchange counters. You can exchange money at your bank or local American Express or Thomas Cook office. If you're far away from a bank with currency-exchange services, American Express offers traveler's checks and foreign currency, though with a $15 order fee and additional shipping costs, through www.americanexpress.com or © **800/807-6233.**

Listed below are the currencies of all destinations in this guide.

BALI (INDONESIA)   Indonesia's main currency is the **rupiah (Rp),** with bills of Rp100, 500, 1,000, 5,000, 10,000, 20,000, 50,000, and 100,000. Coins come in denominations of Rp25, 50, 100, and 500. After wild fluctuations in the 1990s, the rupiah has stabilized in recent years to **Rp9,000 = US$1.**

CAMBODIA   The monetary unit is the **riel,** which is available in 100, 200, 500, 1,000, 5,000, 10,000, 20,000, 50,000, and 100,000 riel notes. Cambodia's volatile exchange rate typically fluctuates, but is currently at **4,000 riel = US$1.** It's a good idea to bring a supply of U.S. dollars, as the dollar is considered Cambodia's second currency and is accepted—even preferred—by many hotels, guesthouses, and restaurants. If paying in dollars, you'll get the small change in riel.

LAOS   The primary unit of currency is the **kip** (pronounced *keep*), which comes in denominations of 500, 1,000, 2,000, 5,000, 10,000, and 20,000 notes. The exchange rate is approximately **10,000 kip = US$1.** As in Cambodia, many tourist establishments prefer payment in U.S. dollars. In many areas of Laos, both U.S. dollars and Thai baht are preferred over the local currency.

MALAYSIA   The **ringgit (RM),** which is also referred to as the Malaysian dollar, is the unit of currency. One ringgit equals 100 sen, and notes come in RM1, 2, 5, 10, 20, 50, 100, 500, and 1,000. Coins come in denominations of 1, 2, 5, 10, and 50 sen, as well as RM1. The exchange rate is approximately **RM3.57 = US$1.**

SINGAPORE   The **Singapore dollar (S$),** commonly referred to as the Sing dollar, is the local unit of currency, with notes issued in denominations of S$2, $5, $10, $50, $100, $500, and $1,000; coins come in denominations of 1, 5, 10, 20, and 50 cents and the gold-colored S$1. The exchange rate is approximately **S$1.60 = US$1.**

THAILAND   The Thai **baht (B)** is made up of 100 satang. It comes in colored notes of 20 (green), 50 (blue), 100 (red), 500 (purple), and 1,000 (khaki) baht. Coins come in denominations of 1, 2, 5, and 10 baht, as well as 25 and 50 satang. The exchange rate is approximately **40B = US$1.**

VIETNAM   The main unit of Vietnamese currency is the **dong (VND),** which comes in denominations of 500,000, 200,000, 100,000, 50,000, 10,000, 5,000, 1,000, 500, and 200 notes. There are no coins. Most tourist venues accept dollars, and even in small towns you will at least be able to exchange greenbacks, if not use dollars directly. The exchange rate is approximately **16,000VND = US$1.**

ATMs

The easiest and best way to get cash away from home is from an ATM. The **Cirrus**

⌜Tips Small Change

When you change money, ask for some small bills or loose change. Petty cash will come in handy for tipping and public transportation. Consider keeping the change separate from your larger bills, so that it's readily accessible and you'll be less of a target for theft.

((*©* 800/424-7787; www.mastercard.com) and PLUS ((*©* 800/843-7587; www. visa.com) networks span the globe; look at the back of your bank card to see which network you're on, then call or check online for ATM locations at your destination. Be sure you know your personal identification number (PIN) and daily withdrawal limit before you depart. *Note:* Many banks impose a fee every time you use a card at another bank's ATM, and that fee can be higher for international transactions (up to $5 or more) than for domestic ones (where they're rarely more than $2). In addition, the bank from which you withdraw cash may charge its own fee. For international withdrawal fees, ask your bank.

CREDIT CARDS

Credit cards are another safe way to carry money. They provide a convenient record of all your expenses, and they generally offer relatively good exchange rates. You can get cash advances from your credit cards at banks or ATMs, provided you know your PIN. Keep in mind that you'll pay interest from the moment of your withdrawal, even if you pay your monthly bills on time. Also, note that many banks now assess a 1% to 3% "transaction fee" on *all* charges you incur abroad (whether you're using the local currency or your native currency). Before you leave home,

call your credit card company to find out if there's a daily limit on cash advances.

For tips and telephone numbers to call if your wallet is stolen or lost, go to "Lost & Found" in the "Fast Facts" section of this chapter.

TRAVELER'S CHECKS

In most parts of the world, traveler's checks are an anachronism from the days before ATMs made cash accessible at any time. But be forewarned that the developing countries in Southeast Asia have scant ATM service, especially in rural areas. Traveler's checks are a sound alternative to traveling with dangerously large amounts of cash, and they can be replaced if lost or stolen.

You can buy traveler's checks at most banks. They are offered in denominations of $20, $50, $100, $500, and sometimes $1,000. Generally, you'll pay a service charge ranging from 1% to 4%.

The most popular traveler's checks are offered by **American Express** ((*©* 800/807-6233, or 800/221-7282 for card holders—this number accepts collect calls, offers service in several foreign languages, and exempts Amex gold and platinum cardholders from the 1% fee); **Visa** ((*©* 800/732-1322, or AAA members can call (*©* 866/339-3378 to get checks up to $1,500 for a $9.95 fee); and **MasterCard** ((*©* 800/223-9920).

Tips Dear Visa: I'm Off to Bangkok!

Some credit card companies recommend that you notify them of any impending trip abroad so that they don't become suspicious when the card is used numerous times in a foreign destination (and block your charges). Even if you don't call your credit card company in advance, you can always call the card's toll-free emergency number (see "Lost & Found" under "Fast Facts," p. 70) if a charge is refused—a good reason to bring the phone number with you. But perhaps the most important lesson here is to carry more than one card with you on your trip; a given card might not work for any number of reasons, so having a backup is the smart way to go.

American Express, Thomas Cook, Visa, and MasterCard all offer **foreign-currency traveler's checks,** which are useful if you're traveling to one country; they're accepted at locations where dollar checks may not be.

If you carry traveler's checks, keep a record of their serial numbers separate from your checks in the event that they are stolen or lost. You'll get a refund faster if you know the numbers.

4 When to Go

With a few exceptions, wherever and whenever you travel in Southeast Asia, you are likely to encounter hot and humid weather. All of Southeast Asia lies within the tropics, and the countries closest to the equator—Singapore, Malaysia, Indonesia, and southern Thailand—have the hottest annual temperatures. Vietnam, Laos, Cambodia, and the rest of Thailand located 10 to 20 degrees above the equator also have high humidity but slightly cooler temperatures. The mountainous northern regions of Thailand, Laos, and Vietnam get pretty chilly during the winter months between November and March, so bring a pullover.

Monsoon winds make weather patterns confusing to keep track of. The basic rule of thumb is this: Between the months of October and February, winds from the northeast create heavy rainfall and rough seas along the eastern coasts of Vietnam, Cambodia, Thailand (including Koh Samui), Malaysia, and Singapore; however, western coasts along Thailand (including Phuket) and Malaysia are peaceful and calm. In May, the winds shift, bringing rains and swelling seas from the northwest down upon the western coast of Thailand and Malaysia until October. Nearly every place has a dry and hot spell in March

and April—Bangkok swelters! The cooler months of October through March are also the most pleasant times to visit Hong Kong, while the most rain usually falls between July and September during typhoon season.

Singapore and Malaysia are hot and humid year-round, with annual average maximum and minimum daily temperatures of 90°F and 72°F (32°C and 22°C) and year-round humidity above 90%. Most major cities are located at or near sea level, where average daytime temperatures are in the range of 80° to 90°F (27°–32°C) year-round. The best way to escape the heat and humidity is to head for the hills and mountains in the higher-altitude regions of Thailand, Malaysia, Vietnam, and Laos.

HOLIDAYS & FESTIVALS Some of the holidays celebrated in Southeast Asia might affect your vacation plans, either positively or negatively. Wherever you are, you won't want to miss Chinese New Year or the many lunar festivals and myriad events like dragon-boat races and small Buddhist fetes, but some holidays simply mean that businesses and attractions are closed. See the individual destination chapters for listings of the major holidays celebrated in each country.

5 Travel Insurance

Check your existing insurance policies and credit card coverage before you buy travel insurance. You may already be covered for lost luggage, canceled tickets, or medical expenses.

The cost of travel insurance varies widely, depending on the cost and length of your trip, your age and health, and the type of trip you're taking, but expect to

Travel in the Age of Bankruptcy

Airlines go bankrupt, so protect yourself by **buying your tickets with a credit card.** The Fair Credit Billing Act guarantees that you can get your money back from the credit card company if a travel supplier goes under (and if you request the refund within 60 days of the bankruptcy). **Travel insurance** can also help, but make sure it covers against "carrier default" for your specific travel provider. And be aware that if a U.S. airline goes bust mid-trip, a 2001 federal law requires other carriers to take you to your destination (albeit on a space-available basis) for a fee of no more than $25, provided you rebook within 60 days of the cancellation.

pay between 5% to 8% of the vacation itself. You can get estimates from various providers through **InsureMyTrip.com**.

TRIP-CANCELLATION INSURANCE Trip-cancellation insurance will help you retrieve your money if you have to back out of a trip or depart early, or if your travel supplier goes bankrupt. Permissible reasons for trip cancellation can range from sickness to natural disasters to the State Department declaring a destination unsafe for travel.

For more information, contact one of the following recommended insurers: **Access America** (© 866/807-3982; www.accessamerica.com), **Travelex Insurance Services** (© 888/457-4602; www.travelex-insurance.com), **Travel Guard International** (© 800/826-4919; www.travelguard.com), **Travel Insured International** (© 800/243-3174; www.travelinsured.com).

MEDICAL INSURANCE For travel overseas, most U.S. health plans (including Medicare and Medicaid) do not provide coverage, and the ones that do often require you to pay for services upfront and reimburse you only after you return home. As a safety net, you may want to buy travel medical insurance, particularly if you're heading to a remote or high-risk area where emergency evacuation might be necessary.

If you require additional medical insurance, try **MEDEX Assistance** (© 410/453-6300; www.medexassist.com) or **Travel Assistance International** (© 800/821-2828; www.travelassistance.com; for general information on services, call the company's Worldwide Assistance Services, Inc., at © 800/777-8710).

LOST-LUGGAGE INSURANCE On flights within the U.S., checked baggage is covered up to $2,500 per ticketed passenger. On international flights (including U.S. portions of international trips), baggage coverage is limited to approximately $9.07 per pound, up to approximately $635 per checked bag. If you plan to check items more valuable than what's covered by the standard liability, see if your homeowner's policy covers your valuables, get baggage insurance as part of your comprehensive travel-insurance package, or buy Travel Guard's "BagTrak" product.

If your luggage is lost, immediately file a lost-luggage claim at the airport, detailing the luggage contents. Most airlines require that you report delayed, damaged, or lost baggage within 4 hours of arrival. The airlines are required to deliver luggage, once found, directly to your house or destination free of charge.

6 Health & Safety

STAYING HEALTHY

Health concerns should comprise much of your preparation for a trip to Southeast Asia, and staying healthy on the road takes vigilance. Tropical heat and mosquitoes are the biggest dangers. Travelers should also exercise caution over dietary change and cleanliness. Just a few pre-trip precautions and general prudence, though, is all that you need for a safe and healthy trip.

GENERAL AVAILABILITY OF HEALTH CARE

The best hospitals and health-care facilities are located in the large cities of countries that have the greatest number of Western visitors—Singapore, Hong Kong, Kuala Lumpur (Malaysia), and Bangkok (Thailand). In rural areas of these countries and throughout the lesser-developed countries of Vietnam, Cambodia, and Laos, there are limited health-care facilities: Hospitals are few and far between and are generally of poor quality. Even in heavily touristed Bali, you're better off evacuating to one of the more developed countries if faced with a serious medical situation. Over-the-counter medications are available anywhere, but it's a good idea to bring antidiarrheal medication and rehydration salts, among others.

Contact the **International Association for Medical Assistance to Travelers (IAMAT)** (© 716/754-4883, or 416/652-0137 in Canada; www.iamat.org) for tips on health concerns and lists of local, English-speaking doctors in the countries you're visiting. The U.S. **Centers for Disease Control and Prevention** (© 800/311-3435; www.cdc.gov) provides up-to-date information on health hazards by region or country and offers tips on food safety. You can find listings of reliable clinics overseas at the **International Society of Travel Medicine** (www.istm.org). The

website **www.tripprep.com**, sponsored by a consortium of travel medicine practitioners, may also offer helpful advice on traveling abroad.

COMMON AILMENTS

TROPICAL ILLNESSES Among Southeast Asia's tropical diseases carried by mosquitoes are **malaria, dengue fever,** and **Japanese encephalitis.** Reports about malaria prophylactics vary. While most local health agencies tell you not to waste your time with antimalarial drugs, the CDC still advises people to take tablets, most of which cause uncomfortable side effects. In truth, your only sure way to avoid mosquito-borne diseases is to avoid being bitten. Repellents that contain **DEET** are the most effective, but more gentle alternatives (see baby-care products in any pharmacy) provide DEET-free mosquito protection without the chemicals. Also be aware that malaria mosquitoes bite between the hours of 5 and 7 in the morning and the evening, so it's important to exercise caution at those times (wearing long sleeves and long trousers is a good idea, as is burning mosquito coils). Dengue-fever mosquitoes bite during the day.

Hepatitis A can be contracted from water or food, and **cholera** epidemics sometimes occur in remote areas. **Bilharzia, schistosomiasis,** and **giardia** are parasitic diseases that can be contracted from swimming in or drinking from stagnant or untreated water in lakes or streams.

Anyone contemplating sexual activity should be aware that **HIV** is rampant in many Southeast Asian countries, along with other STDs such as gonorrhea, syphilis, herpes, and hepatitis B.

DIETARY RED FLAGS Unless you intend to confine your travels to the big cities and dine only at restaurants that serve Western-style food, you will likely be sampling some new cuisine. This could lead initially to upset stomach or diarrhea, which usually lasts just a few days as your body adapts to the change in your diet.

Except for Singapore, where tap water is safe to drink, **always drink bottled water** and **never use tap water for drinking or even brushing teeth.** Peel all fruits and vegetables and avoid raw shellfish and seafood. Also beware of ice unless it is made from purified water. (Any suspicious water can be purified by boiling for 10 min. or treating with purifying tablets.)

If you're a vegetarian, you will find that Southeast Asia is a great place to travel; vegetarian dishes abound throughout the region. In terms of hygiene, restaurants are generally better options than street stalls, but don't forgo good local cuisine just because it's served from a cart. Be sure to carry diarrhea medication as well as any prescription medications you might need. It's acceptable to wipe down utensils in restaurants, and in some places locals even ask for a glass of hot water for just that purpose (some travelers even carry their own plastic chopsticks or cutlery). Bringing antiseptic hand-washing gel is also not a bad idea for when you're out in the sticks.

So, how can you tell if something will upset your stomach before you eat it? Trust your instincts. Avoid buffet-style places, especially on the street, and be sure all food is cooked thoroughly and made to order. If your gut tells you not to eat that gelatinous chicken foot, don't eat it. If your hosts insist but you're still afraid, explain about your "foreign stomach" with a regretful smile and accept a cup of tea instead. Be careful of raw ingredients, common in most Asian cuisines, but realize that questions like, "Are these vegetables washed in clean water?" are inappropriate anywhere. Use your best judgment or simply decline.

BUGS, BITES & OTHER WILDLIFE CONCERNS There are all kinds of creepy critters to be aware of in any tropical climate. In rural accommodations, mosquito nets are often required and, if so, are always provided by hoteliers. Check your shoes in the morning (or wear sandals) just in case some ugly little thing is taking a nap in your Nikes. Keep an eye out for snakes and poisonous spiders when in jungle terrain or when doing any trekking. Having a guide doesn't preclude exercising caution. **Rabies** is rampant, especially in rural areas of the less-developed nations, and extreme care should be taken when walking, particularly at night. In places like Thailand, dogs are simply fed and left to roam free, and you are likely to run into some ornery mutts. A walking stick or umbrella is a suitable deterrent when out in the countryside. It's also important to know that all dogs have been hit with hurled stones sometime in their life, and, a nod to Pavlov here, the very act of reaching to the ground for a handful of stones is often enough to send an angry dog on the run, for fear of being pelted. If you are bitten, wash the wound immediately and, even if you suffer just the slightest puncture or scrape, seek medical attention and a series of rabies shots (now quite a simple affair of injections in the arm in a few installments over several weeks).

RESPIRATORY ILLNESSES SARS hit the region hard in the winter and spring of 2003. Singapore reported some cases and essentially closed to tourism, and though most other countries in the region reported no cases of the disease, places like Thailand suffered the fallout of the regionwide scare. There have been no reported cases of SARS since 2004. **Tuberculosis** is a concern in more remote areas where testing is still uncommon.

The **avian influenza,** also called the **bird flu,** is another public-relations nightmare in Southeast Asia. A number of cases have been reported in Thailand and Vietnam, and millions of chickens suspected of carrying the illness have been slaughtered. The victims of the bird flu have been few in number (statistically insignificant, really) and are mostly isolated to people working in the poultry industry. The countries affected have been unusually forthright about reporting new cases, and the disease is yet limited in scope. It is important to note that you cannot contract bird flu from consuming cooked chicken.

Air quality is not good in the larger cities like Bangkok or Ho Chi Minh City; with no emissions standards, buses, trucks, and cars belch some toxic stuff, so visitors with respiratory concerns or sensitivity should take caution.

SUN/ELEMENTS/EXTREME WEATHER EXPOSURE Sun and heatstroke are a major concern anywhere in Southeast Asia. Limit your exposure to the sun, especially during the first few days of your trip and, thereafter, from 11am to 2pm. Use a sunscreen with a high protection factor, and apply it liberally. Asians are still big fans of parasols, so don't be shy about using an umbrella to shade yourself (all the Buddhist monks do). Remember that children need more protection than adults.

Always be sure to drink plenty of bottled water, which is the best defense against heat exhaustion and the more serious, life-threatening heatstroke. Also remember that coffee, tea, soft drinks, and alcoholic beverages should not be substituted for water because they are diuretics that dehydrate the body. In extremely hot and humid weather, try to stay out of the midday heat, and confine most of your daytime traveling to early morning and late afternoon. If you ever feel weak, fatigued, dizzy, or disoriented, get out of the sun immediately and go to a shady, cool place. To prevent sunburn, always wear a hat and apply sunscreen to all exposed areas of skin.

Be aware of major weather patterns; many island destinations are prone to typhoons or severe storms.

WHAT TO DO IF YOU GET SICK AWAY FROM HOME

Hospitals and **emergency numbers** are listed under "Fast Facts" in each destination chapter. Any foreign embassy or consulate can provide a list of area doctors who speak English. If you get sick, consider asking your hotel concierge to recommend a local doctor—even his or her own. You can also try the emergency room at a local hospital. Many hospitals also have walk-in clinics for cases that are not life-threatening; you may not get immediate attention, but you won't pay the high price of an emergency-room visit. In the larger cities of Southeast Asia, health care at hospitals and private clinics is of an international caliber and quite affordable.

You will need to pay in advance for any medical treatment and be reimbursed later. See "Medical Insurance," under "Travel Insurance," above, for details.

If you suffer from a chronic illness, consult your doctor before your departure. Pack **prescription medications** in your carry-on luggage, and keep them in their original containers, with pharmacy labels—otherwise they won't make it through airport security. Also bring the generic name of prescription medicines, in case a local pharmacist is unfamiliar with the brand name. Prescription medication is readily available, often over the counter.

STAYING SAFE

The good news is that anonymous, violent crime is not an issue in most countries in the region, but petty theft, pick-pocketing, and purse snatching are common. It is a good idea to carry a hidden travel wallet with your passport and documents, and keep an eye on valuables in public.

Avoiding "Economy-Class Syndrome"

Deep vein thrombosis, or as it's known in the world of flying, "economy-class syndrome," is a blood clot that develops in a deep vein. It's a potentially deadly condition that can be caused by sitting in cramped conditions—such as an airplane cabin—for too long. During a flight (especially a long-haul flight), get up, walk around, and stretch your legs every 60 to 90 minutes to keep your blood flowing. Other preventative measures include frequent flexing of the legs while sitting, drinking lots of water, and avoiding alcohol and sleeping pills. If you have a history of deep vein thrombosis, heart disease, or other conditions that puts you at high risk, some experts recommend wearing compression stockings or taking anticoagulants when you fly; always ask your physician about the best course for you. Symptoms of deep vein thrombosis include leg pain or swelling, or even shortness of breath.

Road conditions vary throughout the region, but most large cities, from Bangkok to Ho Chi Minh, are busy and chaotic. Even for intrepid travelers who push their limits out in the wilds, crossing big-city streets, even at prescribed crossings, can be the greatest risk on your trip; move slowly and exercise caution. Rural roads in places like Laos and Cambodia are often no more than dirt tracks. And even where the roads are good, Western visitors are often shocked at the seeming lack of rules and the fact that, on most roads, might is right: The biggest, fastest, and most aggressive vehicle takes precedence, and belligerent horn blowing is the rule. It is best to rent a car with a hired driver instead of trying to drive yourself. On some bus rides, you might want to just keep your eyes on the scenery and not the road ahead.

In places like the beach towns of Thailand, motorbike accidents are all too common and you're sure to meet one or two road-rashed victims. Exercise extreme caution on rented bikes, especially if you're inexperienced, and always wear a helmet.

Dicey political situations arise and pass with frequency; it's important to check travel warnings with the U.S. State Department (www.travel.state.gov) or the most up-to-date sources on the region. Places like Laos, Cambodia, Indonesia, and southern Thailand are known to flare with separatist movements and terrorism, while the September 2006 military coup in Thailand showed that even supposedly stable countries are susceptible to political turmoil. Stay abreast of any and all news before traveling.

Nancy Reagan's advice about drugs couldn't be more apt for a trip to Southeast Asia: "Just say no." Grown, produced, and shipped throughout the region, drugs like heroin, opium, and marijuana are readily available. There are island spots and mountain retreats where it might seem like the thing to do, but in all cases here, national laws are strict. Many visitors find themselves in an intensive language school of another variety (in other words, jail) in short order if they can't bribe their way out of it. It's certainly not worth it anywhere.

7 Specialized Travel Resources

TRAVELERS WITH DISABILITIES

Most disabilities shouldn't stop anyone from traveling. There are more options and resources out there than ever before. Larger hotels in the major cities of the region have adequate facilities for visitors with disabilities, though in rural destinations, specialized amenities are scant at best.

Many travel agencies offer customized tours and itineraries for those with disabilities. Among them are **Flying Wheels Travel** (℃ **507/451-5005;** www.flying wheelstravel.com), **Access-Able Travel Source** (℃ **303/232-2979;** www. access-able.com), and **Accessible Journeys** (℃ **800/846-4537** or 610/521-0339; www.disabilitytravel.com). **Avis Rent a Car** has an "Avis Access" program that offers such services as a dedicated 24-hour toll-free number (℃ **888/879-4273**) for customers with special travel needs; special car features such as swivel seats, spinner knobs, and hand controls; and accessible bus service.

Organizations that offer assistance to disabled travelers include **MossRehab** (www.mossresourcenet.org), the **American Foundation for the Blind (AFB)** (℃ **800/232-5463;** www.afb.org), and **SATH (Society for Accessible Travel & Hospitality)** (℃ **212/447-7284;** www. sath.org). **AirAmbulanceCard.com** is now partnered with SATH and allows you to preselect top-notch hospitals in case of an emergency.

For more information specifically targeted to travelers with disabilities, the online magazine **Gimp on the Go** (www.gimponthego.com) has destination reviews, travel tips, bulletin boards, and links to other sites. Also check out the magazines *Emerging Horizons* (www. emerginghorizons.com), published quarterly, and *Open World,* published by SATH.

GAY & LESBIAN TRAVELERS

Acceptance of alternative lifestyles in Southeast Asia, like anywhere, runs the gamut. One thing to remember is that many of the societies and cultures of the region are, by tradition, very modest, and public displays of affection of any kind

are not acceptable. Gay nightlife choices are many and varied in larger cities like Bangkok, Singapore, and Hong Kong, but in rural areas, provincial attitudes vary and intolerance is not uncommon.

The **International Gay and Lesbian Travel Association (IGLTA)** (℃ **800/448-8550** or 954/776-2626; www.iglta. org) is the trade association for the gay and lesbian travel industry. It offers an online directory of gay- and lesbian-friendly travel businesses; go to its website and click on "Members."

Many agencies offer tours and travel itineraries specifically for gay and lesbian travelers. Among them are **Above and Beyond Tours** (℃ **800/397-2681;** www. abovebeyondtours.com), **Now, Voyager** (℃ **800/255-6951;** www.nowvoyager. com), and **Olivia Cruises & Resorts** (℃ **800/631-6277;** www.olivia.com).

Gay.com Travel (℃ **800/929-2268** or 415/644-8044; www.gay.com/travel or www.outandabout.com) is an excellent online successor to the popular *Out & About* print magazine. It provides updated information about gay-owned, gay-oriented, and gay-friendly lodging, dining, sightseeing, nightlife, and shopping establishments in destinations worldwide.

The following travel guides are available at many bookstores, or you can order them from any online bookseller: *Spartacus International Gay Guide* (Bruno Gmünder Verlag; www.spartacusworld. com/gayguide), *Odysseus: The International Gay Travel Planner* (Odysseus Enterprises Ltd.), and the *Damron* guides (www.damron.com), with separate, annual books for gay men and lesbians.

SENIOR TRAVEL

Seniors traveling in the region can bask in the glow of filial piety and the region's notorious Confucian respect for elders, but they are less likely to enjoy the major discounts found in the West. Mention the fact that you're a senior when you make your travel reservations, though. In some cases, people over 60 qualify for reduced admission to theaters, museums, and other attractions, as well as discounted fares on public transportation.

Members of **AARP** (formerly known as the American Association of Retired Persons), 601 E St. NW, Washington, DC 20049 (© **888/687-2277;** www.aarp.org), often get discounts on hotels, airfares, and car rentals. AARP offers members a wide range of benefits, including *AARP: The Magazine* and a monthly newsletter. Anyone over 50 can join.

Many reliable agencies and organizations target the 50-plus market. **Elderhostel** (© **877/426-8056;** www.elderhostel.org) arranges study programs for those 55 and over. **ElderTreks** (© **800/741-7956;** www.eldertreks.com) offers small-group tours to off-the-beaten-path or adventure-travel locations, restricted to travelers 50 and older. **INTRAV** (© **800/456-8100;** www.intrav.com) is a high-end tour operator that caters to the mature, discerning traveler (not specifically seniors), with trips around the world that include guided safaris, polar expeditions, private-jet adventures, and small-boat cruises down jungle rivers.

Recommended publications offering travel resources and discounts for seniors include: the quarterly magazine *Travel 50 & Beyond* (www.travel50andbeyond.com); *Travel Unlimited: Uncommon Adventures for the Mature Traveler* (Avalon); *101 Tips for Mature Travelers,* available from Grand Circle Travel (© **800/221-2610** or 617/350-7500; www.gct.com); and *Unbelievably Good Deals and Great Adventures That You Absolutely Can't Get Unless You're Over 50* (McGraw-Hill), by Joann Rattner Heilman.

More and more seniors are considering Southeast Asia as a retirement destination.

If you fall into this category, take a look at *Retire to Asia* (www.retiretoasia.com), an e-book by Ken Silver, or **www.retire-asia.com**, a highly informative website by a British expat living in Vientiane. Although it is geared towards those considering a move to the region, it also has some of the most up-to-date nuts-and-bolts travel information available online.

FAMILY TRAVEL

If you have enough trouble getting your kids out of the house in the morning, dragging them thousands of miles away might seem like an insurmountable challenge. The rough roads of Southeast Asia can be a bit much, and concerns about communicable disease in rural areas should certainly be weighed. However, more accessible destinations and larger cities offer a glimpse into ancient civilizations and varied cultures that delights the kid in all of us. Most hotels can arrange extra beds at little additional cost, and connecting-room capability is common. To locate those accommodations, restaurants, and attractions that are particularly kid-friendly, refer to the "Kids" icon throughout this guide.

Familyhostel (© **800/733-9753;** www.learn.unh.edu/familyhostel) takes the whole family, including kids 8 to 15, on moderately priced U.S. and international learning vacations. Lectures, field trips, and sightseeing are guided by a team of academics.

Recommended family-travel websites include **Family Travel Forum** (www.familytravelforum.com), **Family Travel Network** (www.familytravelnetwork.com), **Traveling Internationally with Your Kids** (www.travelwithyourkids.com), and **Family Travel Files** (www.thefamilytravelfiles.com).

WOMEN TRAVELERS

Women traveling together or alone will find exploring this region particularly pleasant and easy. The Buddhist and

Islamic codes of conduct and ethics followed by many mean that you will be treated with respect and courtesy.

Although you will almost never find local women dining or touring alone, as a visitor, your behavior will be accepted. You will rarely, if ever, be approached or hassled by strangers. At the same time, you can feel free to start a conversation with a stranger without fear of misinterpretation. *Note:* If you are traveling with a man, public displays of affection are not welcome, and it's you, the female, who will be scorned. Also, you will have to take even more care than your male counterpart to dress modestly, meaning no cleavage- or midriff-baring tops, miniskirts, or short shorts. Otherwise, you risk offending people on the grounds of either religious or local moral standards. Though wearing revealing clothing or sunbathing topless might appear to be tolerated, that's only because your hosts wish to avoid confrontation. Deep inside, it is very embarrassing.

It's still not advisable to take risks that you wouldn't normally take at home. Don't hitchhike, accept rides, or walk around late at night, particularly in dimly lit areas or in unfamiliar places. Be acutely aware of purse or jewelry snatchers in large cities. When meeting strangers in nightclubs, for example, buy your own drinks and keep an eye on them. In Cambodia, where a system of impunity prevails, precautions are highly recommended—and that includes within the temple complex of Angkor.

Check out the award-winning website **Journeywoman** (www.journeywoman.com), a "real-life" women's travel network where you can sign up for a free e-mail newsletter and get advice on everything from etiquette and dress to safety; or the travel guide *Safety and Security for Women Who Travel,* by Sheila Swan and Peter Laufer (Travelers' Tales, Inc.), offering common-sense tips on safe travel.

AFRICAN-AMERICAN TRAVELERS

Black Travel Online (www.blacktravel online.com) posts news on upcoming events and includes links to articles and travel-booking sites.

Agencies and organizations that provide resources for black travelers include **Rodgers Travel** (© 800/825-1775; www.rodgerstravel.com) and **Henderson Travel & Tours** (© 800/327-2309 or 301/650-5700; www.hendersontravel.com), which has specialized in trips to Africa since 1957.

For more information, check out the following collections and guides: *Go Girl: The Black Woman's Guide to Travel & Adventure* (Eighth Mountain Press), a compilation of travel essays by writers including Jill Nelson and Audre Lorde; *Travel and Enjoy Magazine* (© 866/266-6211; www.traveland enjoy.com); and *Pathfinders Magazine* (© 877/977-PATH; www.pathfinders travel.com), which includes articles on everything from Rio de Janeiro to Ghana as well as information on upcoming ski, diving, golf, and tennis trips

STUDENT TRAVEL

This region has become a hot destination for budget-minded students, who often hit the shores in Southeast Asia and travel for extended periods of time. From bases like Bangkok's Khao San Road, backpackers roam the rugged highways and byways, paving the way for high-end tourism. Places like southern Thailand are attracting a young, spring-break crowd.

Any discounts to be found in Southeast Asia come from hard bargaining or tolerance for the most basic accommodations, but it's not a bad idea to have an **International Student Identity Card (ISIC),** which offers substantial savings on plane tickets and some entrance fees. It also provides you with basic health and life insurance and a 24-hour help line. The card is available from **STA Travel** (📞 **800/781-4040** in North America; www.statravel.com, or www.statravel.co.uk in the U.K.), the biggest student travel agency in the world. If you're no longer a student but are still under 26, you can get an **International Youth Travel Card (IYTC)** from the same people, which entitles you to some discounts (but not on museum admissions). **Travel CUTS** (📞 **800/667-2887** or 416/614-2887; www.travelcuts.com) offers similar services for both Canadians and U.S. residents. Irish students may prefer to turn to **USIT** (📞 **01/602-1600;** www.usitnow.ie), an Ireland-based specialist in student, youth, and independent travel.

SINGLE TRAVELERS

By and large, travelers in Southeast Asia are seekers of some kind, so many prefer to go it alone. For independent travelers, solo journeys are opportunities to make friends and meet locals. There is also a certain camaraderie that develops on long bus rides or in the uncertainty and wonder shared with fellow travelers. A trip that starts out solo often ends in friendships that last a lifetime.

For advice about hopping off the track and finding your own path, check out **Vagabonding** (www.vagabonding.net), which has information both practical and spiritual about the ways of the wanderer. Another inspiration is *The Art of Travel,* by Alain de Botton (Penguin Press). For more practical information, check out Eleanor Berman's latest edition of *Traveling Solo: Advice and Ideas for More Than 250 Great Vacations* (Globe Pequot), which has advice on traveling alone, either solo or as part of a group tour.

If going by tour, it is important to know that single travelers are often hit with a "single supplement" to the base price. To avoid it, you can agree to room with other single travelers or find a compatible roommate before you go, from one of the many roommate-locator agencies.

Travel Buddies Singles Travel Club (📞 **800/998-9099;** www.travelbuddiesworldwide.com), based in Canada, runs small, intimate, single-friendly group trips and will match you with a roommate free of charge. **TravelChums** (📞 **212/787-2621;** www.travelchums.com) is an Internet-only travel-companion matching service with elements of a personals-type site, hosted by the respected New York–based Shaw Guides travel service.

Many reputable tour companies offer singles-only trips. **Singles Travel International** (📞 **877/765-6874;** www.singlestravelintl.com) offers singles-only trips to places like London, Fiji, and the Greek Islands. **Backroads** (📞 **800/462-2848;** www.backroads.com) offers more than 160 active-travel trips to 30 destinations worldwide, including Bali, Morocco, and Costa Rica.

8 Planning Your Trip Online

SURFING FOR AIRFARES

The most popular online travel agencies are **Travelocity** (www.travelocity.com or www.travelocity.co.uk), **Expedia** (www.expedia.com www.expedia.co.uk, or www.expedia.ca), and **Orbitz** (www.orbitz.com).

In addition, most airlines now offer online-only fares that even their phone agents know nothing about. For the airlines that fly to and from your destination, go to "Getting There," p. 53.

Other helpful websites for booking airline tickets online include:

- www.biddingfortravel.com
- www.cheapflights.com
- www.hotwire.com

Frommers.com: The Complete Travel Resource

For an excellent travel-planning resource, we highly recommend **Frommers.com** (www.frommers.com), voted Best Travel Site by *PC Magazine*. We're a little biased, of course, but we guarantee that you'll find the travel tips, reviews, monthly vacation giveaways, bookstore, and online-booking capabilities to be thoroughly indispensable. Special features include our popular **Destinations** section, where you can access expert travel tips, hotel and dining recommendations, and advice on the sights to see in more than 3,500 destinations around the globe; the **Frommers.com Newsletter,** with the latest deals, travel trends, and money-saving secrets; and our **Travel Talk** area featuring **Message Boards,** where Frommer's readers post queries and share advice, and where our authors sometimes show up to answer questions. Once you finish your research, the **Book a Trip** area can lead you to Frommer's preferred online partners' websites, where you can book your vacation at affordable prices.

- www.kayak.com
- www.lastminutetravel.com
- www.opodo.co.uk
- www.priceline.com
- www.sidestep.com
- www.site59.com
- www.smartertravel.com

SURFING FOR HOTELS

In addition to **Travelocity, Expedia, Orbitz, Priceline,** and **Hotwire** (see above), the following websites will help you with booking hotel rooms online:

- www.hotels.com
- www.quickbook.com
- www.travelaxe.net

- www.travelweb.com
- www.tripadvisor.com

It's a good idea to **get a confirmation number** and **make a printout** of any online booking transaction.

SURFING FOR RENTAL CARS

For booking rental cars online, the best deals are usually found at rental-car company websites, although all the major online travel agencies also offer rental-car reservations services. Priceline and Hotwire work well for rental cars, too; the only "mystery" is which major rental company you get, and for most travelers the difference between Hertz, Avis, and Budget is negligible.

9 The 21st-Century Traveler

INTERNET ACCESS AWAY FROM HOME

Internet cafes in Southeast Asia are many and affordable, preferable to expensive hotel business centers (you'll also meet lots of fellow travelers at Internet cafes). Of course, using your own laptop or PDA (personal digital assistant) gives you the most flexibility, but connections in

hotels are expensive and wireless hotspots are, as yet, few.

WITHOUT YOUR OWN COMPUTER

In most parts of Southeast Asia, you'll find **Internet cafes** on every street corner, everything from informed, efficient services—even help managing digital photo files and burning CDs—to basic storefront spots or a place that's just terminals under a thatch roof by the beach. Be warned that rural destinations in places like Laos have little or no service. Backpacker ghettos are always a good bet for finding cheap and reliable service. Avoid **hotel business centers** unless you're willing to pay exorbitant rates.

Most major airports now have **Internet kiosks** scattered throughout their gates. These give you basic Web access for a per-minute fee that's usually higher than cybercafe prices.

To retrieve your e-mail, ask your **Internet Service Provider (ISP)** if it has a Web-based interface tied to your existing e-mail account. If your ISP doesn't have such an interface, you can use the free **mail2web** service (www.mail2web.com) to view and reply to your home e-mail. For more flexibility, you may want to open a free, Web-based e-mail account with **Yahoo! Mail** (http://mail.yahoo.com) or **Google's Gmail** (http://google.gmail. com). Your home ISP may be able to forward your e-mail to the Web-based account automatically.

WITH YOUR OWN COMPUTER

More and more hotels, cafes, and retailers are signing on as Wi-Fi (wireless fidelity) "hotspots." Some places provide **free wireless networks.** With your own wireless-capable computer, connection is a snap.

If Wi-Fi is not available, most business-class hotels offer dataports for laptop modems, some using an Ethernet network cable. You can bring your own cables, but most hotels offer them as well. In addition, major Internet Service Providers (ISP) have **local access numbers** around the world, allowing you to go online by placing a local call. Check your ISP's website or call its toll-free number and ask how you can use your current account away from home, and how much it will cost.

Wherever you go, bring a **connection kit** of the right power and phone adapters, a spare phone cord, and a spare Ethernet network cable—or find out whether your hotel supplies them to guests.

Most Southeast Asian countries run on **220-volt electrical currents.** Some hotels have 110-volt service. Plugs are two-pronged, with either round or flat prongs. If you're coming from the U.S. and you must bring electrical appliances, bring your own converter and adapter (a surge protector is a good idea for a laptop, too). Check the "Fast Facts" section of individual country chapters for more details.

CELLPHONE USE

The three letters that define much of the world's wireless capabilities are **GSM** (Global System for Mobiles), a big, seamless network that makes for easy cross-border cellphone use throughout Europe and dozens of other countries worldwide. In the U.S., T-Mobile, AT&T Wireless, and Cingular use this quasi-universal system; in Canada, Microcell and some Rogers customers are GSM, and all Europeans and most Australians use GSM.

If your cellphone is on a GSM system, and you have a world-capable multiband phone such as many Sony Ericsson, Motorola, or Samsung models, you can make and receive calls across civilized areas around much of the globe. Just call your wireless operator and ask for "international roaming" to be activated on your account. Unfortunately, per-minute charges can be high—usually $1 to $1.50 in Western Europe and up to $5 in places like Russia and Indonesia.

For many, **renting a phone** is a good idea. (Even world-phone owners will have to rent new phones if they're traveling to non-GSM regions, such as Japan or Korea.) While you can rent a phone from any number of overseas sites, including kiosks at airports and at car-rental agencies, we suggest renting the phone before you leave home. North Americans can rent

Online Traveler's Toolbox

Veteran travelers usually carry some essential items to make their trips easier. Following is a selection of handy online tools to bookmark and use.

- **Airplane Food** (www.airlinemeals.net)
- **Airplane Seating** (www.seatguru.com; www.airlinequality.com)
- **C.I.A. World Factbook** (www.cia.gov), for annotated statistics and information about countries worldwide
- **Elephant Guide** (www.elephantguide.com), for current information on each country in the region, with articles from international press and stories from individual travelers
- **Foreign Languages for Travelers** (www.travlang.com)
- **MasterCard ATM Locator** (www.mastercard.com), **Visa ATM Locator** (www.visa.com)
- **Mekong Express** (www.visit-mekong.com), a cross-referenced site for all of the countries in Indochina
- **Time & Date** (www.timeanddate.com)
- **Travel Warnings** (www.travel.state.gov, www.fco.gov.uk/travel, www.voyage.gc.ca, or www.dfat.gov.au/consular/advice). Generally, U.S. warnings are the most paranoid; Australian warnings are the most relaxed.
- **Universal Currency Converter** (www.oanda.com/convert/classic)
- **Weather** (www.intellicast.com; www.weather.com)

one before leaving home from **InTouch USA** (© **800/872-7626;** www.intouchglobal.com) or **RoadPost** (© **888/290-1606** or 905/272-5665; www.roadpost.com). InTouch will also, for free, advise you on whether your existing phone will work overseas; simply call © **703/222-7161** between 9am and 4pm EST, or go to http://intouchglobal.com/travel.htm.

For trips of more than a few weeks spent in one country, **buying a phone** can be economically attractive, as many nations have cheap prepaid phone systems. Once you arrive at your destination, stop by a local cellphone shop and get the cheapest package; you'll probably pay less than $50 for a phone and a starter calling card. Local calls may be as low as 10¢ per minute, and in many countries incoming calls are free.

True wilderness adventurers, or those heading to less-developed countries, should consider renting a **satellite phone ("satphone").** It's different from a cellphone in that it connects to satellites and works where there's no cellular signal or ground-based tower. Satphones are much more expensive to buy or rent than cellphones, however, and this cost, combined with the improved cellphone coverage throughout Southeast Asia, makes cellphones the much more sensible option.

10 Getting There

BY PLANE

If you're flying to Southeast Asia, you will more than likely arrive via one of the region's three main hubs: Bangkok, Singapore, or Hong Kong, from where you can pick up flights to any other destination in Southeast Asia. Your home country's national carriers will almost certainly connect with all three of these airports. In addition, check with Southeast Asian–based airlines for fare deals: Cathay Pacific, Thai Airways, Malaysian Airlines, and Singapore Airlines. United also has new direct flights between the U.S. West Coast and Vietnam.

TO BANGKOK

The following international airlines provide service to Bangkok's Suvarnabhumi International Airport.

FROM THE U.S. Service is provided by the national carrier, Thai Airways, as well as United Airlines, Northwest Airlines, Cathay Pacific Airways, All Nippon Airways, Asiana Airlines, Japan Air Lines, China Airlines, Eva Airways, Korean Air, Malaysia Airlines, and Singapore Airlines.

FROM CANADA Air Canada flies to Bangkok from Vancouver via Hong Kong and Tokyo.

FROM THE U.K. Airlines with flights from the U.K. to Bangkok include Thai Airways, British Airways, and Singapore Airlines.

FROM AUSTRALIA Service is provided by Qantas Airways, Thai Airways, Singapore Airlines, Jetstar Airlines, Tiger Airways, and British Airways.

FROM NEW ZEALAND Airlines with flights from New Zealand to Bangkok include Qantas Airways, Cathay Pacific, Singapore Airlines, Thai Airways, Malaysia Airlines, Air New Zealand, and Jetstar Airways.

TO SINGAPORE

The following carriers fly to Singapore's Changi International Airport.

FROM THE U.S. Singapore Airlines has the most weekly flights from the U.S. to Changi Airport. United Airlines and Northwest Airlines are the only U.S. airlines offering flights to Singapore.

FROM CANADA Singapore Airlines provides service from Canada.

Tips **Getting Through the Airport**

- Arrive at the airport 1 hour before a domestic flight and 2 hours before an international flight; if you show up late, tell an airline employee and he or she will probably whisk you to the front of the line.
- Beat the ticket-counter lines by using airport electronic kiosks or even online check-in from your home computer, from where you can print out boarding passes in advance. Curbside check-in is also a good way to avoid lines.
- Bring a current, government-issued photo ID such as a driver's license or passport. Children under 18 do not need government-issued photo IDs for flights within the U.S., but they do for international flights to most countries.
- Speed up security by removing your jacket and shoes before you're screened. In addition, remove metal objects such as big belt buckles. If you've got metallic body parts, a note from your doctor can prevent a long chat with the security screeners.
- Use a TSA-approved lock for your checked luggage. Look for Travel Sentry certified locks at luggage or travel shops and Brookstone stores (or online at www.brookstone.com).

FROM THE U.K. You can fly to Singapore via Singapore Airlines, British Airways, and Qantas Airways.

FROM AUSTRALIA Singapore Airlines, Qantas Airways, Ansett Australian Airlines, British Airways, and KLM Royal Dutch Airlines all provide service to Singapore.

FROM NEW ZEALAND Singapore Airlines and Air New Zealand offer New Zealand–Singapore flights.

FLYING FOR LESS: TIPS FOR GETTING THE BEST AIRFARE

- Passengers who can book their ticket **long in advance,** who can **stay over Saturday night,** or who **fly midweek** or **at less-trafficked hours** may pay a fraction of the full fare. If your schedule is flexible, say so, and ask if you can secure a cheaper fare by changing your flight plans.

- Search **the Internet** for cheap fares (see "Planning Your Trip Online").

- Keep an eye on local newspapers for **promotional specials** or **fare wars,** when airlines lower prices on their most popular routes. You rarely see fare wars offered for peak travel times, but if you can travel in the off-months, you may snag a bargain

- Try to book a ticket **in its country of origin.** For instance, if you're planning a one-way flight from Johannesburg to Bombay, a South Africa–based travel agent will probably have the lowest fares. For multi-leg trips, book in the country of the first leg; for example, book New York–London–Amsterdam–Rome–New York in the U.S.

- **Consolidators,** also known as bucket shops, are great sources for international tickets, although they usually can't beat Internet fares within North America. Start by looking in Sunday newspaper travel sections; U.S. travelers should focus on the *New York Times, Los Angeles Times,* and *Miami*

Herald. U.K. travelers should search in the *Independent,* the *Guardian,* or the *Observer.* For less-developed destinations, small travel agents who cater to immigrant communities in large cities often have the best deals. *Beware:* Bucket-shop tickets are usually nonrefundable or rigged with stiff cancellation penalties, often as high as 50% to 75% of the ticket price, and some put you on charter airlines, which may leave at inconvenient times and experience delays. One reliable agency specializing in Southeast Asia–bound flights is **Join-Us Travel** (✆ 800/324-5359; www.joinustravel.com). Several reliable consolidators are worldwide and available online. **STA Travel** (✆ 800/781-4040; www.statravel.com) has been the world's lead consolidator for students since purchasing Council Travel, but its fares are competitive for travelers of all ages. **ELTExpress (Flights.com)** (✆ 800/TRAV-800; www.eltexpress.com) has excellent fares worldwide, particularly to Europe. It also has "local" websites in 12 countries. **FlyCheap** (✆ 800/FLY-CHEAP; www.1800flycheap.com), owned by package-holiday megalith MyTravel, has especially good fares to sunny destinations. **Air Tickets Direct** (✆ 800/778-3447; www.airticketsdirect.com) is based in Montreal and leverages the currently weak Canadian dollar for low fares; it also books trips to places that U.S. travel agents won't touch, such as Cuba.

- Join **frequent-flier clubs.** Frequent-flier membership doesn't cost a cent, but it does entitle you to better seats, faster response to phone inquiries, and prompter service if your luggage is stolen or your flight is canceled or delayed. And you don't have to fly to earn points; **frequent-flier credit**

Tips   Coping with Jet Lag

Jetlag is a pitfall of traveling across time zones. If you're flying north–south and you feel sluggish when you touch down, your symptoms will be the result of dehydration and the general stress of air travel. When you travel east–west or vice versa, however, your body becomes thoroughly confused about what time it is, and everything from your digestive system to your brain is knocked for a loop. Traveling east, say from Chicago to Paris, is more difficult on your internal clock than traveling west, say from London to Hawaii, because most peoples' bodies are more inclined to stay up late than fall asleep early.

Here are some tips for combating jet lag:

- **Reset your watch** to your destination time before you board the plane.
- **Drink lots of water** before, during, and after your flight. Avoid alcohol.
- **Exercise** and **sleep well** for a few days before your trip.
- If you have trouble sleeping on planes, **fly eastward on morning flights.**
- **Daylight** is the key to resetting your body clock. At the website for **Outside In** (www.bodyclock.com), you can get a customized plan of when to seek and avoid light.

cards can earn you thousands of miles for doing your everyday shopping. With more than 70 mileage awards programs on the market, consumers have never had more options. Consider which airlines have hubs in the airport nearest you, and, of those carriers, which have the most advantageous alliances, given your most common routes. To play the frequent-flier game to your best advantage, consult Randy Petersen's **Inside Flyer** (www.insideflyer.com). Petersen and friends review all the programs in detail and post regular updates on changes in policies and trends.

LONG-HAUL FLIGHTS: HOW TO STAY COMFORTABLE

- Your choice of airline and airplane will definitely affect your legroom. Find details about U.S. airlines at **www.seatguru.com**. For international airlines, the research firm Skytrax has posted a list of average seat pitches at **www.airlinequality.com**.
- Emergency-exit seats and bulkhead seats typically have the most legroom.

Emergency-exit seats are usually left unassigned until the day of a flight (to ensure that the seat is filled by someone able-bodied); it's worth getting to the ticket counter early to snag one of these spots for a long flight. Many passengers find that bulkhead seating (the row facing the wall at the front of the cabin) offers more legroom, but keep in mind that bulkheads are where airlines often put baby bassinets, so you may be sitting next to an infant.

- To have two seats for yourself in a three-seat row, try for an aisle seat in a center section toward the back of coach. If you're traveling with a companion, book an aisle and a window seat. Middle seats are usually booked last, so chances are good you'll end up with three seats to yourselves.
- Ask about entertainment options. Many airlines offer seatback video systems where you get to choose your movies or play video games—but only on some of their planes. (Boeing 777s are your best bet.)

- To sleep, avoid the last row of any section or the row in front of an emergency exit, as these seats are the least likely to recline. Avoid seats near high-traffic toilet areas. Avoid seats in the back of many jets—these can be narrower than those in the rest of coach. You may also want to reserve a window seat so you can rest your head and avoid being bumped in the aisle.
- Get up, walk around, and stretch every 60 to 90 minutes to keep your blood flowing. See "Avoiding 'Economy-Class Syndrome,'" under "Health & Safety," p. 46.
- Drink water before, during, and after your flight to combat the lack of humidity in airplane cabins. Avoid alcohol, which will dehydrate you.
- If you're flying with kids, don't forget to carry on toys, books, pacifiers, and chewing gum to help them relieve ear pressure buildup during ascent and descent.

11 Packages for the Independent Traveler

Package tours are simply a way to buy the airfare, accommodations, and other elements of your trip (such as car rentals, airport transfers, and sometimes even activities) at the same time and often at discounted prices.

One good source of package deals is the airlines themselves. Most major airlines offer air/land packages, including **American Airlines Vacations** (© 800/321-2121; www.aavacations.com), **Delta Vacations** (© 800/221-6666; www.deltavacations.com), **Continental Airlines Vacations** (© 800/301-3800; www.covacations.com), and **United Vacations** (© 888/854-3899; www.unitedvacations.com). Several big **online travel agencies**—Expedia, Travelocity, Orbitz, Site59, and Lastminute.com—also do a brisk business in packages.

Travel packages are also listed in the travel section of your local Sunday newspaper. Or check ads in the national travel magazines such as *Arthur Frommer's Budget Travel Magazine, Travel & Leisure, National Geographic Traveler,* and *Condé Nast Traveler.*

⸢Tips⸥ Ask Before You Go

Before you invest in a package deal or an escorted tour:

- Always ask about the **cancellation policy.** Can you get your money back? Is a deposit required?
- Ask about the **accommodations choices** and **prices** for each. Then look up the hotels' reviews in a Frommer's guide and check their rates online for your specific dates of travel. Also find out what types of rooms are offered.
- Request a complete **schedule.**
- Ask about the **size** and **demographics** of the group.
- Discuss what is included in the **price** (transportation, meals, tips, airport transfers, and so on).
- Finally, look for **hidden expenses.** Ask whether airport departure fees and taxes, for example, are included in the total cost—they rarely are.

12 Escorted General-Interest Tours

Escorted tours are structured group tours, with a group leader. The price usually includes everything from airfare to hotels, meals, tours, admission costs, and local transportation.

Whether you want to ride an elephant through the jungle, trek among indigenous people, shake hands with an orangutan, swim beneath a waterfall, snorkel in a clear-blue lagoon, lounge on a white-sand beach, or wander through exotic markets, there's a Southeast Asia tour packager for you, offering a wide range of options using the finest and most reliable travel services available in the region.

Among the most experienced and knowledgeable tour operators specializing in Southeast Asia are **Absolute Asia** and **Asia Transpacific Journeys.** In-country tour providers **Diethelm** and **Exotissimo** can do anything from arranging deluxe tours to just helping out with small details or bookings. Most companies allow clients to design their own trip or deviate from exact schedules (often at a small cost). Companies like **Intrepid,** among others, offer unique itineraries for solo travelers. See individual destination chapters for other in-country tour operators.

Here are the top outfitters:

- **Abercrombie & Kent** (1520 Kensington Rd., Suite 212, Oakbrook, IL 60523; ⓒ **800/554-7016;** fax 630/954-3324; www.abercrombieandkent.com), offers Southeast Asia programs with numerous comprehensive itineraries. This well-known luxury-tour operator can take you to Thailand (on spa tours, too), Cambodia, Vietnam, Indonesia, and Laos, with stays at the finest hotels in Southeast Asia, such as the Oriental in Bangkok and the Sofitel Metropole in Hanoi.
- **Absolute Asia** (180 Varick St., 16th floor, New York, NY 10014; ⓒ **800/736-8187;** fax 212/627-4090; www.absoluteasia.com), founded in 1989, offers an array of innovative itineraries, specializing in individual or small-group tours customized to your interests, with experienced local guides and excellent accommodations. Talk to these folks about tours that feature art, cuisine, religion, antiques, photography, wildlife study, archaeology, and soft adventure—they can plan a specialized trip to see just about anything you can dream up for any length of time. They can also book you on excellent coach programs in Indochina.
- **Asia Transpacific Journeys** (2995 Center Green Court, Boulder, CO 80301; ⓒ **800/642-2742** or 303/443-6789; fax 303/443-7078; www.asiatranspacific.com) coordinates tours to every corner of South and Southeast Asia and the Pacific. It deals with small groups and custom programs that include luxury accommodations. The flagship package, the 23-day "Passage to Indochina" tour, takes you through the major attractions of Laos, Vietnam, and Cambodia with a well-planned itinerary, and it is but one of many fun tours that promote cultural understanding. It's a model of sustainable tourism and a highly recommended choice.
- **Backroads** (801 Cedar St., Berkeley, CA 94710; ⓒ **800/462-2848** or 510/527-1555; fax 510/527-1444; www.backroads.com), the cycling and hiking specialist, has an 11-day bike tour of Vietnam and Angkor Wat, an 8-day Thailand Golden Triangle tour, and others. Check out the website; Backroads is always coming up with innovative itineraries in the region.

- **Diethelm Travel** (Kian Gwan Building II, 140/1 Wireless Rd., Bangkok 10330, Thailand; ✆ **662/255-9150;** fax 662/256-0248; www.diethelm travel.com), a Swiss-based tour company, has offices throughout the region (it's a popular choice for European tour groups). The folks here are friendly and helpful; they also operate as de facto tourist information centers in places like Laos. Diethelm has full tour programs and, like Exotissimo (below), can help with any details for travelers in-country, arrange car rental or vans for small groups, and offer discount options to all locations.

- **Exotissimo Travel** (40 bis, Rue du fg Poissonniére, 75010 Paris, France, ✆ **149/490-360,** fax 149/490-369; or Saigon Trade Center, 37 Ton Duc Thang, District 1, Ho Chi Minh City, Vietnam, ✆ **08/825-1723,** fax 08/829-5800; www.exotissimo.com), a French outfit and outbound (in-country) agency with offices in every major city in the region, has excellent guides on-site. Agents not only can arrange all-inclusive tours, but also are helpful with all travel details, from ticketing to visas. See the office locations in each chapter.

- **Imaginative Traveller** (1 Betts Ave., Martlesham Heath, Suffolk IP5 7RH, U.K.; ✆ **0800/316-2717;** fax 0280/742-3045; www.imaginative-traveller.com), a U.K.–based firm, gets rave reviews for organizing all sorts of bicycling, trekking, and motorcycling adventures throughout Southeast Asia, particularly Indochina.

- **Intrepid Travel** (11 Spring St., Fitzroy, Victoria, 3065 Australia; ✆ **613/9473-2626;** fax 613/9419-4426; or ✆ **877/488-1616** in the U.S.; www.intrepidtravel.com), a popular Australian operator, is probably the best choice for an off-the-beaten-track tour of Asia. Intrepid caters trips for the culturally discerning, those with humanitarian goals, those in search of comfort and adventure, those on a budget, or those looking for a looser structure and lots of options. Its name is its motto, and with some of the best guides in Asia, these folks will take you to the back of beyond safely, in style, and with lots of laughs.

Despite the fact that escorted tours require big deposits and predetermine hotels, restaurants, and itineraries, many people derive security and peace of mind from the structure they offer. Escorted tours—whether they're navigated by bus, motor coach, train, or boat—let travelers sit back and enjoy the trip without having to drive or worry about details. They take you to the maximum number of sights in the minimum amount of time with the least amount of hassle. They're particularly convenient for people with limited mobility and they can be a great way to make new friends.

On the downside, you'll have little opportunity for serendipitous interactions with locals. The tours can be jam-packed with activities, leaving little room for individual sightseeing, whim, or adventure—plus they often focus on the heavily touristed sights, so you miss out on many a lesser-known gem.

13 Special-Interest Trips

For cultural tours and museum tours, contact any of the smaller local travel agents listed in each chapter. For the amateur ethnographer, contact any of the eco-tour outfitters below or those listed in specific sections (particularly in the north of Thailand, Laos, Vietnam, or western Cambodia).

OUTDOOR AVENTURES & ECO-TOURS If you live life like a Mountain Dew commercial or just like to get out into the sticks, you can find any number of small outfitters to suit you in many parts of Southeast Asia. Consider first what kind of terrain you'd like to explore—the choices are anything from jungle to dry plains, coastal estuaries to inland rivers. The best areas to get out and get your boots wet are in the furthest reaches of Thailand, Laos, and Vietnam.

In the north of Thailand, go with **Contact Travel** (73/7 Charoen Prathet Rd., Chiang Mai; © 05327-7178; fax 05327-9505; www.activethailand.com) for cycling, off-road, and other eco-adventures. In the far south of Thailand, **Paddle Asia** (9/71 Thanon Rasdanusorn, Phuket; © 07624-0952; fax 07621-6145; www.paddleasia.com) has some of the best nature kayaking trips—you're guaranteed to see some exciting wildlife.

In Laos, **Green Discovery** (54 Setthathirat Rd., Nam Phu Fountain Circle, Vientiane; © 021/223-022; www.greendiscoverylaos.com) runs great rafting and kayaking adventures anywhere in the country and has some unique village and cultural tours as well.

In the north of Vietnam, the folks at **Handspan** (80 Ma May St., Hanoi; © 04/962-0446; fax 04/926-0445; www.handspan.com) as well as **Buffalo Tours** (13 Hang Muoi, Hanoi; © 04/828-0702; www.buffalotours.com) put together exciting kayaking adventures in Halong Bay, hiking trips to Sapa, and jeep trips up to Dien Bien Phu. In central Vietnam, the old French colonial hill station of Dalat plays host to a great outfitter, **Phat Tire Ventures** (73 Truong Cong Dinh, Dalat; © 063/823-104; fax 063/829-422; www.phattireventures.com), that can help you rock climb, mountain bike, or trek with the most professional guides and experienced technicians.

In Bali, **Sobek Tours** (© 361/287059) and **Bali Adventure Tours** (© 361/721480; www.baliadventuretours.com) can both arrange fun day and overnight itineraries to volcanoes, the jungle, and rural villages.

The folks at **Exotissimo Travel** have offices throughout Southeast Asia and are the best for arranging all kinds of rural adventures. See individual chapters for office locations.

DIVING TRIPS There are more dive outfits in Southeast Asia than we could possibly list. Be sure to choose a PADI-accredited dive company and ask lots of questions before any trip: What is the ratio of diver to instructor? Does the company have its own boat?

For details, check specific chapters of this book. In Thailand, look under **Phuket** or **Koh Tao**; in Vietnam, try **Nha Trang**; in Cambodia, **Sihanoukville**; in Malaysia, **Langkawi.**

COOKING SCHOOLS The varied cuisine of the countries of Southeast Asia is a veritable banquet for the gourmet or the fearless eater, and there's no better way to learn about and participate in a culture than to take a cooking class. Opportunities abound.

In Thailand, a favorite option is the upscale **Blue Elephant Restaurant and Cooking School** (233 S. Sathorn Rd., Bangkok; © 02673-9353; www.blueelephant.com), set in an old mansion in the heart of the city. The restaurant is a popular luxury chain from Europe that has returned to its roots and set up shop in the Thai capital. It's not to be missed. In the north of Thailand, try the **Chiang Mai Cookery School** (1–3 Moonmuang Rd., Chiang Mai; © 05320-6388; www.thaicookeryschool.com). In the far south, there are lots of small resorts with cooking schools attached.

In northern Laos, enjoy a fun and informative day at **Tamnak Lao Restaurant and Cooking School** (Sakhalin Rd.,

Ban Wat Sene, Luang Prabang; © **071/ 252-525**), where you'll not only get the dish on Lao specialties and some unique derivations, but also learn a good bit about local culture, history, and language.

In central Vietnam, Ms. Vy, who runs the **Mermaid (Nhu Y) Restaurant** (02 Tran Phu St., Hoi An; © **0510/861-527;** www.hoianhospitality.com) and several other establishments in town, offers great cooking programs of varying length.

14 Getting Around Southeast Asia

Regional flights in Southeast Asia are affordable and convenient—a great way to get around if your time is short. That said, half the fun of traveling is getting there—many walk away from land travel in this part of the world saying, "I'll never do it again, but what a trip!" When the massive Soviet 4×4 nearly lays on its side in the deep ruts of a washed-out road in Laos, or that rattle-trap motorbike you rented in hill-tribe country in the north of Vietnam catches a flat and leaves you stranded, you might curse yourself or the very road you're on, but you'll have lots of stories to tell when you get back.

BY PLANE

Myriad routes into the region are served by international carriers, including Silk Air (the regional arm of Singapore Airlines), Malaysia Airlines, Thai Airways, Cathay Pacific, Vietnam Airlines, and Garuda Indonesia. Domestic carriers include Pelangi Air, Air Asia, and Berjaya Air in Malaysia; Lao Airlines in Laos; and Bangkok Airways and P.B. Air in Thailand and Cambodia.

Bear in mind that international airports are not restricted to capital cities. In addition to Bangkok, Thailand has international access via Chiang Mai and Chiang Rai (to China and Laos), U-Tapao and Phuket (to Cambodia), and Phuket and Koh Samui (to Singapore and Kuala Lumpur). You can fly into Malaysia at Penang, Langkawi, and Tioman Island, and to Borneo destinations direct from Singapore. Laos has international access at both Luang Prabang and Pakse, in addition to the capital, Vientiane. Vietnam

has international flights to both Ho Chi Minh City (Saigon) and Hanoi. And in Cambodia, you can fly directly to Siem Reap, the access city to Angkor Wat, from Bangkok, U-Tapao (near Pattaya), Phuket, Vientiane, Vietnam, and Singapore.

Check out the UNESCO World Heritage routes, a new schedule of flights offered by Bangkok Airways. Originating in Bangkok, this tour connects Sukhothai (Thailand) with Luang Prabang (Laos), Hue (Vietnam), and Angkor Wat (Cambodia).

Ask any travel agent for information, and be sure to research all flight options for the most direct routes and best fares. Each chapter gives specific details for booking.

BY TRAIN

With a few exceptions, trains that operate throughout Southeast Asia are poorly maintained, overcrowded, and slow. While trains used to be a good option for long distances, the recent increase in budget airlines offering rock-bottom prices has made train travel a less appealing option. The most popular rail route—and the only one with interconnecting service among countries in all of Southeast Asia—runs from Singapore to Bangkok (and vice versa) through the heart of the Malaysian peninsula, with stops along the way at the cities of Johor Bahru, Malacca, Kuala Lumpur, and Butterworth (for Penang). It takes 6 hours from Singapore to Kuala Lumpur, and another 35 hours from Kuala Lumpur to Bangkok. You can board the train at the Singapore Railway Station in Tanjong

Pagar, at the Kuala Lumpur Central Railway Station on Jalan Hishamuddin, and in Bangkok at the Hua Lamphong Railway Station on Rama IV Road.

Upscale travelers with unlimited budgets can book passage on one of the world's foremost luxury trains, the *Eastern & Oriental Express,* which covers the distance between Singapore and Bangkok in 42 hours. Find more details in the Thailand chapter.

Reliable rail service also runs north to south along coastal Vietnam, with interesting new luxury cars that connect Hanoi, the capital, with the northern hill country and make a further connection to the vast rail networks of China.

BY BUS

Buses are good on the budget and often the best way into the back of beyond. Bus trips in the region range from VIP tours with air-conditioning and video monitors to rattle-trap, overcrowded, break-down mobiles. Thai and Malay buses are quite reliable and a good option, connecting the far north of Thailand with the far southern tip of Malaysia and on to Singapore. In Laos and Cambodia, local buses, with the exception of a few interior routes, are rough. Check specific "Getting There" sections in individual chapters before embarking on long hauls. Also, check each country's individual visa requirements, as you often need to pre-arrange visas for land crossings.

BY BOAT

There are lots of unique boat adventures in the region. More and more travelers are heading down the Mekong, starting from the town of Chiang Khong in northern Thailand and ending in Luang Prabang in Laos. Luxury riverboats run the same trip, as well as trips in the far south of Laos between Pakse and Si Phan Don (look for LuangSay Cruises under the relevant sections). Boat trips in Vietnam's Halong Bay, just east of Hanoi, are very popular; outfitters like Handspan and Buffalo Tours run great excursions. Don't miss the new boat connections along the Mekong tributaries between Vietnam's Mekong Delta and Phnom Penh, Cambodia's capital. Boats also connect Cambodia's capital, Phnom Penh, with Siem Reap, the town that supports Angkor Wat, along the Mekong as it flows through Tonle Sap Lake.

BY CAR

Car rental is affordable in Southeast Asia. In the developing countries—Vietnam, Laos, Cambodia—it is a good idea (and costs not much more) to hire a car with driver. Insurance is often unavailable. Road rules vary, and in some places seem nonexistent—though there is always a method to the madness—so it's not a bad idea to spring for a driver where affordable. Be sure to research details and invest in good maps before heading out.

15 Tips on Accommodations

Affordable luxury is the name of the game in the countries of Southeast Asia. For what you might pay for a cracker-box room in big cities in the U.S. and Europe, you can go in style in Indochina and the countries on the Malay Peninsula. Pay over $100 and you'll live like royalty. Budget travelers and young backpackers flock to the region, and a big part of the charm is spending $2 to $5 per night; it makes the budget go on and on. If your trip is short, live it up! Go for a luxury room and take advantage of affordable spa treatments (at a fraction of what you'd pay elsewhere). Midrange boutique hotels and rustic eco-friendly rural resorts are also a new trend as developers discover that *refurbished* is cool, and that location—whether overlooking the Mekong or set in a tropical rainforest—is everything.

You'll find many of the major chains represented in the region. **Sheraton** has hotels throughout Thailand and in the major stops in Vietnam. **Inter-Continental** has high-end business properties in Bangkok, Phnom Penh, and Singapore. **Hilton** has fine properties in Hanoi (Vietnam), Bangkok and Phuket (Thailand), throughout Malaysia and Singapore, and on Bali. The French hoteliers at **Accor** host a number of **Sofitel** and **Novotel** hotels in the region; many of the big-city properties are aimed at the business market, but in Vietnam Sofitel takes the cake with some of the most unique refurbished hotels going, and in Cambodia it has a top resort as well. **Four Seasons** has fine properties in Bangkok and outside of Chiang Mai. **JW Marriott** has a hotel in Bangkok and a luxury resort on Phuket. **Le Meridien** boasts top resorts and golf in Thailand and Bali (Indonesia).

There are also a few good local chains. The **Amari** group is a Swiss-managed hotel chain with semiluxurious properties in all of the major stops in Thailand; service is conscientious and there is a good consistency among its many hotels (and good rates). In Vietnam, and now Cambodia, the **Victoria** hotels are a charming blend of atmosphere and connection to place, without sacrificing all of the comforts of home—quite unique. **Pansea** hotels, now individually branded under the management of the luxury **Orient Express** group, host some of the most unique and luxurious sanctuaries that take you away from it all, but remind you of local culture—find them in Laos, Thailand, and Cambodia. **Aman Resorts** are in a class all their own, with their sprawling villa properties in Indonesia, and now in Cambodia, all at rock-star prices.

Villa rental is a popular choice in island destinations. Balinese villas are a particular steal, best over a longer period of time and with hired staff. In places like Thailand's Phuket, you'll find timeshares and long-term rates for private, serviced, beachside places that are quite enticing (beware the hard sell, though).

Each of the countries in Southeast Asia sets its own star standards for hotels, usually one through five. Note that a five-star might only be rated so because of the quantity, not quality, of services offered.

SAVING ON YOUR HOTEL ROOM

The **rack rate** is the maximum rate that a hotel charges for a room. Hardly anybody pays this price, however, except in high season or on holidays. To lower the cost of your room:

- **Ask about special rates or other discounts.** You may qualify for corporate, student, military, senior, frequent-flier, trade-union, or other discounts. Find out the hotel policy on children—do kids stay free in the room or is there a special rate?
- **Dial direct.** When booking a room in a chain hotel, you'll often get a better deal by calling the individual hotel's reservations desk rather than the chain's main number.
- **Book online.** Many hotels offer Internet-only discounts, or supply rooms to Priceline, Hotwire, or Expedia at rates much lower than the ones you can get through the hotel itself. There are lots of regional websites offering very low rates, but many are unreliable fly-by-night operations. Shop around.
- **Remember the law of supply and demand.** Resort hotels are most crowded and therefore most expensive on weekends, so discounts are usually available for midweek stays. Business hotels in downtown locations are busiest during the week, so you can expect big discounts over the weekend. Many hotels have high-season and low-season prices, and

booking even one day after high season ends can mean big discounts.

- **Look into group or long-stay discounts.** If you come as part of a large group, you should be able to negotiate a bargain rate. Likewise, if you're planning a long stay (at least 5 days), you might qualify for a discount. As a general rule, expect 1 night free after a 7-night stay.
- **Avoid excess charges and hidden costs.** When you book a room, ask whether the hotel charges for parking. Use your own cellphone, pay phones, or prepaid phone cards instead of dialing direct from hotel phones, which usually have exorbitant rates. If possible, opt for Internet cafes over in-room access or the hotel business center. These services are dramatically overpriced at most hotels and resorts. And don't be tempted by the room's minibar offerings. Finally, ask about local taxes and service charges, which can increase the cost of a room by 15% or more.
- **Book an efficiency.** A room with a kitchenette allows you to shop for groceries and cook your own meals. This is a big money saver, especially for families on long stays.

LANDING THE BEST ROOM

Somebody has to get the best room in the house. It might as well be you. You can start by joining the hotel's frequent-guest program, which may make you eligible for upgrades. A hotel-branded credit card usually gives it owner "silver" or "gold" status in frequent-guest programs for free. Always ask about a corner room. They're often larger and quieter, with more windows and light, and they often cost the same as standard rooms. When you make your reservation, ask if the hotel is renovating; if it is, request a room away from the construction. Ask about nonsmoking rooms, rooms with views, rooms with twin, queen-, or king-size beds. If you're a light sleeper, request a quiet room away from vending machines, elevators, restaurants, bars, and discos. Ask for a room that has been most recently renovated or redecorated.

If you aren't happy with your room when you arrive, ask for another one. Most lodgings will be willing to accommodate you.

In resort areas, ask the following questions before you book a room:

- What's the view like? Cost-conscious travelers may be willing to pay less for a back room facing the parking lot, especially if you don't plan to spend much time in your room.
- Does the room have air-conditioning or ceiling fans? Do the windows open? If they do, and the nighttime entertainment takes place alfresco, you may want to find out when show time is over.
- What's included in the price? Your room may be moderately priced, but if you're charged for beach chairs, towels, sports equipment, and other amenities, you could end up spending more than you bargained for.
- How far is the room from the beach and other amenities? If it's far, is there transportation to and from the beach, and is it free?

16 Tips on Dining

Southeast Asia is a real playground for adventurous foodies; from high-class hotel restaurants and power-lunch points to street-side stalls with local specialties, you'll find it all. The cuisine of each country is unique, and crossing borders often means a new course in manners, food, and culture. In this guide, we list the safest of options by and large, making sure to designate any dining that could be deemed "adventurous"—but the adventurous in fact have lots of opportunities to try new foods, from oddities like freshly killed snake to fried crickets and grubs. It's not all that funky, though, and much of the best local cuisine is not found in restaurants but in markets and in street-side stalls, something that puts some people off. Our advice: Get adventurous! When eating in open-air joints, just be careful that things are cooked fresh and aren't sitting out, and be careful of raw ingredients like vegetables or some fish pastes. If you find yourself playing charades to get your food, laughing, smiling, and squatting on a tiny plastic stool, talking to locals and eating a meal that costs pennies to the approving nods of your new friends, then you're in the right place. Wherever possible, ask locals what's good and you'll be in store for a cool, cultural adventure.

Try *pho* and the many regional specials throughout Vietnam; enjoy cover-the-table spreads in Thailand and Malaysia, where spices are fiery and a meal is always an event; and don't miss crispy duck or *babi guling*—suckling pig—in Bali. The choices are endless. The usual varieties of international fare can be found throughout the region—in fact, every big city has its Chinese, Italian, sushi, and French. In parts of Indochina, Laos and Vietnam in particular, chefs carry on long traditions from colonial times, and the French cuisine is as good as you'll get anywhere. Chinese communities abound and, of course, so does good Chinese in its myriad forms—from dim sum to Peking duck.

All but the fanciest restaurants are open early until late. Tipping is not expected but always appreciated, and just rounding up the bill to the next dollar amount is often more than enough.

For drinkers, there are few restrictive laws or cultural taboos—in fact, drinking is a big part of most cultures in Southeast Asia. Local rice wines and whiskeys abound and foreign guests are always invited. Sometimes the stuff is pretty potent—toxic, even—so be warned. European visitors left their mark on the region with brewing and distilling technologies, and each country produces its own local beers to go along with the many imports. Fresh fruit is falling off the trees in the tropical climes of Southeast Asia, so good fresh juices are available everywhere. Coffee is grown throughout the region, and though local roasting processes are a bit different, local brews are delicious. Tap water is not potable in most regions, but bottled water is available everywhere; and perhaps the best advice for travel in the region is to stay hydrated. If you're thirsty, then it's too late. Drink lots.

17 Suggested Itineraries

Routes through the region are as varied as the rag-tag bunch that travels them. With the many convenient air connections, you can choose your destinations and connect them as you like, but here are a few suggestions to get you started.

TOURING INDOCHINA Clockwise or counterclockwise routes starting in Bangkok and including northern Thailand, Laos, Vietnam, and Cambodia are popular and avoid boring backtracking.

Connecting northern Thailand with Laos by boat is appealing, and flying from Vientiane, the Lao capital, to Hanoi or Ho Chi Minh City is a better choice than the rough overland route (which also leaves you in the middle of the north–south route, whereas a flight will get you to a terminus). After a sweep down the coast of Vietnam, connect with Cambodia overland (or by boat from the Mekong Delta) and continue on to

Angkor Wat by bus, boat, or plane. There is frequent air service between Angkor Wat and Bangkok.

This itinerary can take anywhere from a few weeks to 6 months, depending on your inclinations. Highlights include the historic temple towns of Thailand, hill-tribe treks throughout the region, sleepy Luang Prabang, busy Hanoi and Ho Chi Minh City (Saigon), all of the stops along coastal Vietnam (historical and recreational), and, of course, Angkor Wat. After a trip like this, you'll have earned your time on the beaches of Thailand, Malaysia, or Bali.

HEADING DOWN THE MALAY PENINSULA Starting in Bangkok and heading south, you can connect the major resort destinations of southern Thailand with a tour down the length of Malaysia to Singapore and end up in Bali.

You can do this trip in a fly-by-night week or stretch it out over a few months.

Highlights include pristine beaches (maybe even *The Beach*) in Thailand; great food, affordable cosmopolitan comforts, and unique cultural stops in Malaysia; "shop-till-you-drop" spending in Singapore; and the tranquil beaches of Bali.

BASING YOURSELF IN A HUB From Bangkok, Singapore, or other major urban centers, travelers can make short forays into the countryside or to the resort of their choice from a comfortable, familiar base in a big city with all the comforts of home. Many visitors aim for the cultural and historic sights recommended by UNESCO—places like Luang Prabang (Laos); Hoi An, Hue, and Halong Bay (Vietnam); Sukhothai and Ayuthaya (Thailand); and the temples of Angkor Wat (Cambodia)—all reachable via larger cities. Or start in a comfy hub and connect with local outfitters for short adventure trips before coming back to hot showers and room service.

18 Recommended Books & Films

BALI (INDONESIA) *Bali Sekala and Nishkala: Essays on Religion, Ritual and Art,* by Fred B. Eiseman, Jr., is the seminal text on the labyrinth of beliefs and practices on the island.

CAMBODIA Henry Kamm's *Cambodia: Report from a Stricken Land* is a good start to finding some context to the country's late troubles. *Brother Number One: A Political Biography,* by David P. Chandler, provides insight into the insanity of the Khmer Rouge.

There are many personal accounts by survivors of the years of violence and chaos in Cambodia. *Stay Alive, My Son,* by Pin Yathay, and *First They Killed My Father,* by Loung Ung, are both heart-wrenching stories of life under genocide in the mid-1970s.

With the reopening of Cambodia's borders to international aid came another era of chaos, this one marked by a general

lawlessness and unrestrained vice. *The Quality of Mercy*, by William Shawcross, examines the international response to Cambodia's post–Khmer Rouge refugee crisis, while *Off the Rails in Phnom Penh: Into the Dark Heart of Guns, Girls, and Ganja,* by Amit Gilboa, is a portrait of that time.

On film, the best depiction of Cambodia is *The Killing Fields,* a 1984 movie about the rise of the Khmer Rouge and the last days of freedom in Phnom Penh. *City of Ghosts*, a moody film by Matt Dillon, captures a certain feel of the country's underbelly, and *Tomb Raider* is a fanciful romp that was filmed at Angkor in 2000.

LAOS *Stalking the Elephant Kings,* by C. Kremmer, is a personal account of travel in Laos and one man's obsession to find the truth about the last dynasty—it's a good primer to Lao history and culture.

Another Quiet American, by Brett Dakin, a witty account of recent travels in the country, paints the state of the nation through the eyes of a young American working as a consultant for the National Tourism Authority in Vientiane.

The Ravens: Pilots of the Secret War of Laos and *Air America: The Story of the CIA's Secret Airline,* both by C. Robbins, tell the heretofore untold tale of the undeclared war in Laos. And *Tragedy in Paradise: A Country Doctor at War in Laos* is a memoir by Dr. Charles Weldon, recalling his experiences from 1963 to 1974 working hand-in-hand with Air America as chief of public health for USAID Laos.

SINGAPORE If you're having trouble finding books about Singapore in bookstores where you live, wait until you arrive and then browse local shelves, where you'll find tons of books about the country and its history, culture, arts, food, and local fiction. For interesting and informative reads that you can find (or order) through your neighborhood bookstore, here's a good place to start:

From Third World to First: The Singapore Story: 1965–2000, by Lee Kuan Yew, details the history and policies behind Singapore's remarkable economic success written by the man who was at the helm.

The Singapore Story: Memoirs of Lee Kuan Yew, by Lee Kuan Yew, offers an intimate account of Minister Mentor Lee's personal journey, and will unravel some of the mysteries behind one of the world's most talked-about leaders.

Crossroads: A Popular History of Malaysia & Singapore, by Jim Baker, is a readable history of Singapore and Malaysia from a longtime resident and expert.

The Singapore Grip, by J. G. Farrell, is a highly enjoyable work of historical fiction written by a Booker Prize winner that takes you back to Singapore on the brink of World War II to examine the last days of the British Empire.

Few knew that Louis L'Amour was a Merchant Marine in Southeast Asia. In *West from Singapore,* the famous author creates his brand of fascinating American West storytelling, only this tale takes place in the waters around pre–World War II Singapore.

THAILAND *Anna and the King,* the original late-19th-century work of Anna Leowens, governess for the children of the progressive King Rama IV, tells of the kingdom's opening to the West. Don't miss the film of the same name starring Jodie Foster (though due to gross historical inaccuracies, the film was banned from public release in Thailand).

Also banned in Thailand is *The Revolutionary King,* by William Stevenson, a biography of the revered King Bhumibol Adulyadej. Given unprecedented access to the king and royal family, Stevenson shows a side of the monarchy that few have seen. The book treats His Majesty as a real person (referring to him by his nickname, "Lek," meaning small) and delves into taboo subjects, such as the murder of the king's older brother Ananda, making it quite controversial.

The Beach, by Alex Garland, and the popular film of the same name featuring Leonardo DiCaprio, tells the tale of the impossibility of modern Utopia, the very thing that so many Asia adventurers seek. Though not about Thailand exclusively, Tiziano Terzani's *A Fortune-Teller Told Me* is a well-crafted portrait of the interlocking cultures of Asia and of the Westerner's search for personal destiny.

Carol Hollinger's *Mai Pen Rai Means Nevermind* is a personal history of time spent in the kingdom some 30 years ago, but the cultural insights are quite current. *Patpong Sisters,* by Cleo Odzer, and *Sex Slaves,* by Louise Brown, are both interesting exposés of the Thai sex industry.

Books on Thai Buddhism are many. Try Phra Peter Parrapadipo's *Phra Farang,* literally "The Foreign Monk," which tells the story of an Englishman turned Thai Buddhist monk. The writings of Jack Kornfield, particularly *A Path With Heart,* are a good introduction.

VIETNAM   *The Quiet American,* by Graham Greene, which was made into a Hollywood film starring Michael Caine in 2002, is a classic tale of espionage in the old colony. In fact, much of what is written—or popular—about Vietnam chronicles the country's recent strife, particularly the American War years. The list is long; below are but a few.

In Retrospect: The Tragedy and Lessons of Vietnam, by former American Secretary of Defense Robert S. McNamara and Brian DeMark, is quite popular in Vietnam (a copy stands in a glass case at the War Museum in Ho Chi Minh City), as it tells the tale of American deceit and misinformation from the perspective of one of its more remorseful arbiters. *A Bright Shining Lie,* by Neil Sheehan, is a similar explication. Pulitzer Prize–winning *Fire in the Lake,* by Francis Fitzgerald, is a sociological exploration of the war years and aftermath.

Personal accounts like *Dear America: Letters Home from Vietnam,* by Bernhard Edelman, or the Vietnamese classic *The Sorrow of War,* by Bao Ninh, tell of the experiences of soldiers and civilians caught in the fray. *The Girl in the Picture: The Story of Kim Phuc and the Photograph That Changed the Course of the Vietnam War,* by Denise Chong, is self-explanatory.

Robert Olen Butler won a Pulitzer Prize for *A Good Scent from a Strange Mountain,* a collection of short stories recounting the legacy of war through disparate voices. This book is one of the best you can read while traveling in the country. *Catfish and Mandala,* by Andrew X. Pham, is a Vietnamese American's travel odyssey and coming to terms with the past.

The Vietnam War was fertile terrain for Hollywood in the 1980s, with award-winning classics like Francis Ford Coppola's *Apocalypse Now, The Deer Hunter* with Robert DeNiro, and Oliver Stone's *Platoon* and *Born on the Fourth of July,* a true story about returnee Ron Kovic. *The Fog of War* is a uniquely candid hindsight look by Robert McNamara, the secretary of defense during the war. Films like Tran Anh Hung's *The Scent of Green Papaya* and *Cyclo* are more tranquil, studied views of Vietnamese culture. And *Indochine,* starring Catherine Deneuve, is a historic portrait of the tumultuous end of colonialism in Vietnam.

FAST FACTS: Southeast Asia

ATM Networks   Note that Laos has no international ATMs; however, international ATMs abound in the major cities of most countries in Southeast Asia. See "Money" (p. 38), earlier in this chapter, or in each individual country chapter.

Camera & Film   Film is easy to get in all of these countries and is usually much cheaper than in the West (the exceptions being Singapore and Hong Kong, where it costs about the same). Digital camera supplies are readily accessible.

Car Rentals   See the "Getting Around" section in each country's chapter. In most places, it's best to hire a driver when renting a car because road conditions and traffic rules (or the seeming lack thereof) can make driving yourself a bit harrowing; if this sounds like a luxury, know that hiring a driver for a day is affordable, for the most part, and drivers are often great sources of local information.

Currency See "Money," p. 38.

Drugstores You'll find over-the-counter medications readily available in each country. It's best to bring enough of any medication that you require regularly, and know the generic name of the medicines you carry, in case you lose one or run out.

Electricity Most countries run on 220 volts, with two-pronged (flat or round) plugs. Use a converter for U.S. appliances (some hotels actually run on 110 volts), and use a surge protector for a laptop.

Embassies & Consulates See the "Fast Facts" sections in each country's chapter.

Emergencies See the "Fast Facts" sections in each country's chapter.

Etiquette & Customs Customs vary, but in the mostly Buddhist and Muslim countries of Southeast Asia, modesty in dress and conduct is the general rule. Be sure to read the "Etiquette" section in chapter 2 (p. 33), as well as in the specific country chapters.

Appropriate Attire: Though the cultures and religions of the many nations of Southeast Asia are often more different than alike, they all agree on respect for one another and staying covered in public. Ratty or revealing clothes are out of place here, as anywhere.

Business Etiquette: Be on time, shake hands when greeting, and look people in the eye: The basics are all the same here, but it gets tricky when different cultural modes of thought and communication come into play (volumes are written on the subject). You might have to change your definition of "Yes" and "No," for example. See "Etiquette" in the individual country chapters for more details.

Gestures: Throughout Southeast Asia, a scooping form of the wave that Westerners use to say "hello" means "come here." Be aware of issues in most countries over eating with only the right hand (the left is considered dirty) or of how to offer things to people (commonly with both hands). See "Etiquette" in the individual country chapters, as there are some varied specifics here.

Photography: Be aware that there are some superstitions about photography among hill tribes. In general, it's a good idea to ask before shooting portraits or taking photos in houses of worship. Be careful not to photograph police or military installations or activity.

Holidays See "Holidays & Events" under "When to Go," earlier in this chapter, and check the "When to Go" sections in each individual country chapter.

Internet Access The Internet is accessible just about anywhere and everywhere you'll travel. The farther you are from urban centers, the slower the dial-up connections (at slightly inflated prices), but the region's boom in young backpackers and local online gamers means that you'll find a cybercafe in nearly any location. Avoid hotel business centers, when possible, as they charge exorbitant rates.

Language English is spoken just about everywhere in the countries of Southeast Asia, and wherever you go, you'll be sure to find helpful folks eager to practice a few phrases on you (certainly touts and people who want your tourist dollars will know a few words). Don't let this distract you from picking up some of the local lingo; a little goes a long way.

Laundromats Laundromats are few and far between, but affordable laundry service is available everywhere. Though often prohibitively expensive in large hotels, a short walk usually brings you to a local launderer where you'll pay by the kilo (extra for delicate items that require special care or ironing). Do not expect same-day service, as most places rely on air drying.

Liquor Laws Drinking ages vary (in most countries, it's either 18 or 20), but you won't find too many constraints placed on the purchase or consumption of alcohol in the region. Bars in the major cities are open late and, in some rural areas or at beachside, are mandated only by the whims of the owner. Beer, wine, and liquor—both familiar imports and local rice-based varieties—are sold anywhere and everywhere.

Lost & Found Be sure to tell all of your credit card companies the minute you discover that your wallet has been lost or stolen, and file a report at the nearest police precinct. Your credit card company or insurer might require a police report number or record of the loss. Most credit card companies have an emergency toll-free number to call (collect) if your card is lost or stolen; they might be able to wire you a cash advance immediately or deliver an emergency credit card in a day or two.

Visa cardholders should call (C) **800/847-2911** in the U.S. or 410/581-9994 collect. **MasterCard** holders should call (C) **800/307-7309** in the U.S. or 636/722-7111 collect. **American Express** cardholders and traveler's-check holders should call (C) **800/221-7282** in the U.S. or go to the nearest Amex representative. To see if there are local emergency credit card numbers in your destination, check the "Money" section in the individual country chapters.

If you need emergency cash over the weekend when all banks and American Express offices are closed, you can have money wired to you via **Western Union** ((C) **800/325-6000;** www.westernunion.com).

Mail Postage rates are comparable to those in Western countries, though service Is often less reliable and very slow, especially from the developing countries of Laos and Cambodia. Express services such as DHL and FedEx are growing in number and abundant in large cities. Many souvenir or antiques dealers can arrange shipping on items large and small.

Newspapers & Magazines In the major urban centers like Singapore and Bangkok, foreign-press material is available everywhere. There are also good local English-language papers, like the *Bangkok Post* or the *Nation,* Singapore's *Straits Times,* and the *Wall Street Journal Asia,* that will keep you connected. Don't pass up small-press editions or *Time Out* guides to local happenings and attractions; expat newspapers are also a good glimpse into daily life in each country.

Passports Allow plenty of time before your trip to apply for a passport; processing normally takes 3 weeks but can take longer during busy periods (especially spring). And keep in mind that if you need a passport in a hurry, you'll pay a higher processing fee.

For Residents of Australia: You can pick up an application from your local post office or any branch of Passports Australia, but you must schedule an interview at the passport office to present your application materials. Call the

Australian Passport Information Service at ☎ **131-232**, or visit the government website at www.passports.gov.au.

For Residents of Canada: Passport applications are available at travel agencies throughout Canada or from the central Passport Office, Department of Foreign Affairs and International Trade, Ottawa, ON K1A 0G3 (☎ **800/567-6868**; www.ppt.gc.ca).

For Residents of Ireland: You can apply for a 10-year passport at the Passport Office, Setanta Centre, Molesworth Street, Dublin 2 (☎ **01/671-1633**; www.irl gov.ie/iveagh). Those under 18 and over 65 must apply for a 3-year passport. You can also apply at 1A South Mall, Cork (☎ **021/272-525**), or at most main post offices.

For Residents of New Zealand: You can pick up a passport application at any New Zealand Passports Office or download it from the website. Contact the Passports Office at ☎ **0800/225-050** in New Zealand or 04/474-8100, or log on to www.passports.govt.nz.

For Residents of the United Kingdom: To pick up an application for a standard 10-year passport (5-yr. passport for children under 16), visit your nearest passport office, major post office, or travel agency or contact the United Kingdom Passport Service (☎ **0870/521-0410**; www.ukpa.gov.uk).

For Residents of the United States: Whether you're applying in person or by mail, you can download passport applications from the U.S. State Department website at http://travel.state.gov. To find your regional passport office, either check the State Department website or call the National Passport Information Center at ☎ **877/487-2778.**

Police See the "Fast Facts" sections in individual country chapters.

Restrooms Public restrooms can be a bit of a shocker for first-time visitors. Especially in rural areas, toilets often flush manually, with a few scoops of water from a larger cistern, and paper is to be deposited not in the toilet, but in a separate wastebasket. Standards of cleanliness vary, but many public toilets would make a run-down roadside gas station in the U.S. seem like a temple. Squat toilets are common, but most major hotels have amenities familiar to the Western visitor.

Safety See "Health & Safety," p. 43.

Smoking The region is more or less a smoker's paradise, and there are few restraints on the habit in most destinations. In fact, in rural areas of the developing countries, smoking is even allowed on buses (a bit much, really). New laws in Bangkok ban smoking in restaurants, and similar rules are in place in the larger cities. If you're a smoker, be sure to read the rules before heading to Singapore (see "Fast Facts: Singapore," p. 464).

Taxes Each country has its version of a VAT tax added to restaurant and hotel bills. It can go as high as 20%, so be sure to inquire beforehand.

Telephones See the "Fast Facts" sections in individual country chapters.

Time Zone The countries of Southeast Asia are between 7 and 8 hours ahead of Greenwich Mean Time. That means 12 or 13 hours ahead of New York, and 3 or 4 hours behind Sydney.

Tipping Though not as common as in the U.S., a small gratuity for taxi drivers, bellhops, and restaurant staff is appreciated.

Useful Phone Numbers U.S. Dept. of State Travel Advisory ℂ 202/647-5225 (manned 24 hr.); U.S. Passport Agency ℂ 202/647-0518; U.S. Centers for Disease Control International Traveler's Hot Line ℂ 404/332-4559.

Water Apart from in urban Singapore, *don't drink the water.* Buy inexpensive bottled drinking water, available everywhere. Some restaurants serve safe, treated ice and water.

4

Thailand

by Jason Armbrecht

Traffic and tranquillity, beaches and bargains, ancient palaces and stunning temples: Thailand has much to offer the millions who visit every year. The world caught on to Thailand's magic years ago, and foreign investors, with the encouragement of the Thai government, have seized on this fascination. Luxury resorts are popping up in virtually every town and island, turning once remote and unspoiled beaches and towns into bustling package-tour destinations, some virtually unrecognizable to those just a couple years removed from their last visit.

The opening of Bangkok's space-age airport, Suvarnabhumi, with the capacity to handle 45 million travelers a year and eventually 100 million with planned expansion, will only make Thailand a more convenient destination, recent political turmoil notwithstanding.

That's not to say Thailand has lost its charm; far from it. The authentic Thai way of life with its vibrant Buddhist culture is just outside the comfortable bubble of five-star resorts and luxury tour buses: All you have to do is wander the streets and soak it in.

In bustling Bangkok, find canal and riverside communities, a sprawling Chinatown, an ultramodern cityscape, and giant outdoor markets that are a heady mix of sights, sounds, and smells.

Beyond urban Thailand are flat plains carpeted with rice paddies and dotted with tiny villages, mountains of luxuriant teak forests where elephants once roamed wild, long stretches of white-sand beach, acres of coconut palms and rubber plantations, and clear-blue waters against towering rock cliffs. Rural life is languid and hospitable, and behind every warm Thai smile there is true kindness.

Outdoor-adventure opportunities abound: sail, paddle, dive, and snorkel in the sea; trek to villages; ride the rivers; or go on four-wheel-drive adventures in the rugged upcountry. Rural Thailand is ripe for exploration by bus, train, car, motorbike, and boat, and visitors are limited only by their tolerance for adventure.

Gorgeous tropical island beaches play host to laid-back bungalow guesthouses and posh, Thai-style five-star resorts. The cuisine is captivating, a unique blend of sweet, sour, and salty tastes tempered with fiery spice. And whether shopping the sprawling bazaars or visiting Thailand's notorious nightlife, you're sure to have some *sanuk,* or fun, Thai style.

1 Getting to Know Thailand

THE LAY OF THE LAND

Thailand is in the center of Southeast Asia, roughly equidistant from China and India, and shares cultural affinities with both. It borders Myanmar (Burma) to the north and west, Laos to the northeast, Cambodia (Kampuchea) to the east, and Malaysia to the south. Thailand's southwestern coast stretches along the Andaman

Sea, and its southern and southeastern coastlines border the Gulf of Thailand (still often called the Gulf of Siam).

Thailand covers approximately 289,668 sq. km (112,970 sq. miles)—about the size of France. The country is divided into six major geographic zones, within which there are 73 provinces.

THE REGIONS IN BRIEF

NORTHERN THAILAND Northern Thailand (the forehead of the elephant) is a relatively cool, mountainous region at the foothills of the Himalayas. Like most of Thailand, the cool hills in the north are well suited for farming, particularly for strawberries, asparagus, peaches, litchis, and other fruits. At higher elevations, many hilltribe farmers cultivate opium poppies, a crop that is rarely profitable (and ruinous to farmers who become addicted), though the agricultural program advanced by the king is introducing more productive crops. The cities in the north that are covered in this chapter are Chiang Mai and Chiang Rai.

THE CENTRAL PLAIN The Central Plain is an extremely fertile region, providing the country and the world with much of its abundant rice crop. The main city of the area is Phitsanulok, northeast of which are the impressive remains of Sukhothai, Thailand's first capital. To the south is Lopburi, an ancient Mon-Khmer settlement.

THE SOUTHEAST COAST The southeast coast is lined with seaside resorts, such as Pattaya and the islands Ko Samet and Ko Chang. Farther east, in the mountains, is Thailand's greatest concentration of sapphire and ruby mines.

WESTERN THAILAND On the opposite side of the country, west of Bangkok, are mountains and valleys carved by the Kwai River, made infamous during World War II by the "Death Railway," built by Allied prisoners of war who worked and lived under horrifying conditions, and a bridge (made famous by the film *Bridge on the River Kwai*) over the river near Kanchanaburi. Just to the north of Bangkok (which is in every way the center of the country, along the Chao Phraya River banks) is Ayutthaya, Thailand's second capital after Sukhothai.

THE SOUTHERN PENINSULA The long, narrow Southern Peninsula (the elephant's trunk) extends south to the Malaysian border. It was on the west coast of the peninsula, in the Andaman Sea, that the "Christmas Tsunami" struck on December 26, 2004. The result of a 9.0 earthquake in Aceh Indonesia, the waves claimed 5,000 victims in Thailand alone. Coastal Phuket was buffeted by the waves, but reconstruction was quick, while areas in Phang Nga Province, particularly Khao Lak, as well as the popular resort island of Ko Phi Phi near Krabi, were flattened. International aid continues to flow in. The eastern coastline along the Gulf of Thailand, unaffected by the disaster, extends more than 1,802km (1,117 miles); the western shoreline runs 716km (444 miles) along the Andaman Sea. This region is the most tropical in the country, with heavy rainfall during monsoon seasons. The northeast monsoon, roughly from November to April, brings clear weather and calm seas to the west coast; the southwest monsoon, March to October, brings similar conditions to the east coast. There are glamorous beach resorts here (people visit them even during the rainy season, as it doesn't rain all day), such as the western islands of Phuket and nearby Ko Phi Phi. The east-coast islands of Koh Samui and Ko Phangan are comparable.

ISAN Finally, Isan, the broad and relatively infertile northeast plateau (the ear of the elephant), is the least developed region in Thailand, bordered by the Mekong River

Thailand

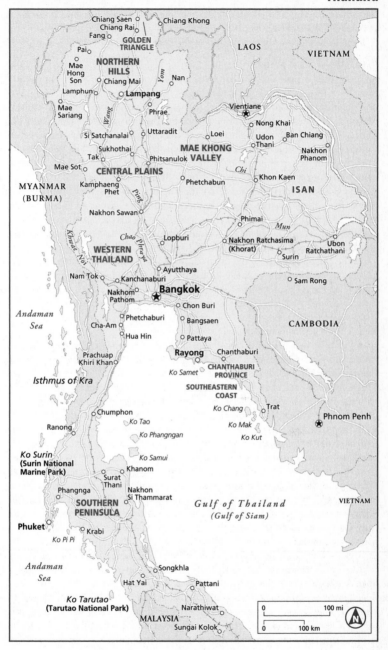

(Mae Nam Khong in Thai). Isan is dusty in the cool winter and muddy during the summer monsoon. Fewer tourists make their way to Isan than any other part of the country, so we've opted not to cover it in this chapter.

A LOOK AT THE PAST

Archaeologists believe that Thailand was a major thoroughfare for *Homo erectus* en route from Africa to China and other parts of Asia. Modern civilization did not arrive in Thailand until about a thousand years ago, when waves of people migrated from central and southern China, settling primarily in what is now Vietnam, Laos, Thailand, and Myanmar (Burma). These people, who are called *Tai,* became dispersed over a vast area of space, sharing a cultural and linguistic commonality. The **early Tais** lived in nuclear families with household collectives, called *muang,* or village, establishing loosely structured feudal states.

From the 6th century, Southeast Asia underwent a gradual period of **Indianization.** Merchants and missionaries from India introduced Brahmanism and Buddhism to the region, as well as Indian political and social values and art and architectural preferences. At the same time the **Mon,** migrants from Burma, were responsible for establishing Sri Lankan Buddhism in central Thailand.

By the early 9th century, the expansionist **Khmer** empire had risen to power in Cambodia, engulfing the region. Magnificent Khmer temples, originally built for the worship of Hindu deities before conversion to Buddhism and distinguished by their corncob-shaped *prang,* or towers, were constructed in outposts increasingly farther afield until the Khmer's eventual collapse in the 13th century. You can still find many Khmer ruins in Thailand, especially in Isan.

In 1259, several powerful centers of Tai power in northern Thailand, southern China, and Laos were united by **King Mengrai,** who established the first capital of the **Lanna Kingdom** at Chiang Rai in 1263, and later at Chiang Mai in 1296. The Lanna Kingdom saw the rise of a scholarly Buddhism, with strict adherence to orthodox ways. Citizens enjoyed the benefits of infrastructure projects for transportation and irrigation, developed medicine and law, and created artistic expression through religious sculpture, sacred texts, and poetry. But the Mongols, under the fierce expansionist leadership of **Kublai Khan,** forced their way into the region. Mengrai, forming strategic alliances with neighboring kingdoms, succeeded in keeping the Mongols at bay.

In the vacuum left by the departing Khmers, a tiny kingdom based in **Sukhothai** rose to fame after its crown prince, Rama, single-handedly defeated an invasion from neighboring Mae Sot at the Burmese border. Upon his coronation in 1279, **Ramkhamhaeng,** or "Rama the Bold," set the scene for what is recognized as the first truly Siamese civilization, mixing all the people of the central plains—Tai, Mon, Khmer, and indigenous populations, with threads of India and China interwoven in their cultural tapestry. In response to the Khmer's hierarchical rule, Ramkhamhaeng established himself as an accessible king. He was a devout Buddhist, adopting the orthodox and scholarly Theravada Buddhism. A patron of the arts, the king commissioned many great Buddha images, initiated splendid architectural projects, and developed the modern Thai written language. After his death in 1298, his successors failed to rule wisely and Sukhothai's brilliant spark faded almost as quickly at it had ignited.

Next came the kingdom of **Ayutthaya,** which swallowed what was left of Khmer outposts and the Sukhothai Kingdom. Incorporating the strengths of its population—Tai military manpower and labor, Khmer bureaucratic sensibilities, and Chinese commercial talents—the empire grew wealthy and strong. Following Khmer models, the king rose above his subjects atop a huge pyramid-shape administration. A fortified city was built, with temples that glittered as much as any in Sukhothai. This was the Kingdom of Siam that the first Europeans, the Portuguese, encountered in 1511.

Burmese invasion forces took Chiang Mai's Lanna Kingdom in 1558 and finally Ayutthaya in 1569. However, during the occupation, **Prince Naresuan,** descended from Sukhothai kings, in a historic battle scene atop an elephant, challenged the Burmese crown prince and defeated him with a single blow. Ayutthaya continued through the following 2 centuries in grand style, and while its Southeast Asian neighbors were falling under colonial rule, the court of Siam retained its own sovereignty. Thailand has the distinction of being the only Southeast Asian nation never to have been colonized, a point of great pride for Thais today. Unfortunately, the final demise of Ayutthaya was two more Burmese invasions in the 1760s.

The Siamese did not hesitate to build another kingdom. **Taksin,** a provincial governor, rose to power on the merits of his military excellence, charisma, and a firm belief that he was divinely appointed to rule. Rebuilding the capital at Thonburi, on the western bank of the Chao Phraya River (opposite present-day Bangkok), within 3 years he reunited the lands under the previous kingdom. But Taksin suffered from paranoia—he had monks killed, along with eventually his own wife and children. Regional powers were quick to get rid of him—he was swiftly kidnapped, covered in a velvet sack, and beaten to death with a sandalwood club.

These same regional powers turned to **Chaophraya Chakri** in 1782 to lead the land. Crowned **King Ramathibodi,** he was the first king of Thailand's present dynasty, the **Chakri Dynasty.** He moved the capital across the river to Bangkok, where he built the **Grand Palace** and great temples. The city grew around a network of canals, with the river as the central channel for trade and commerce. Rama I reinstated Theravada Buddhist doctrine, reestablished the state ceremonies of Ayutthaya, and revised all laws. He also wrote the ***Ramakien,*** based upon the Indian *Ramayana,* a legend that has become the subject for many Thai classical arts.

King Mongkut (1851–68) with his son, **King Chulalongkorn** (1868–1910), led Siam into the 20th century as an independent nation, establishing an effective civil service, formalizing global relations, and introducing industrialization-based economics. It was King Mongkut who hired Anna Leonowens (of *The King and I*) as an English tutor for his children. Thai people want everyone to know that Mongkut was not the overbearing, pushover fop described in her account. Historians side with the Thais, for she is barely mentioned in court accounts—the story had its origins more in her imagination than in realty.

During the reign of **King Prajadhipok,** Rama VII (1925–35), the growing urban middle class became increasingly discontent. Economic failings and bureaucratic bickering weakened the position of the monarchy, which was delivered its final blow by the Great Depression. In 1932, a group of midlevel officials staged a coup d'etat, and Prajadhipok abdicated in 1935.

Democracy had a shaky hold on Siam. Over the following decades, government leadership changed hands fast and frequently, many times the result of hostile takeover with the military at the helm. In 1939, the nation adopted the name Thailand—"Land of the Free."

During **World War II,** democracy was stalled in the face of the Japanese invasion in 1941. Thailand chose to side with the Japanese, but at the war's end, no punitive measures were taken against Thailand; the Thai ambassador in Washington had failed to deliver his country's declaration of war against the Allies.

Thailand managed to stay out of direct involvement in the **Vietnam War;** however, it continues to suffer repercussions from the burden of refugees. The U.S. pumped billions into the Thai economy, bringing riches to some and relative affluence to many, but further impoverishing the poor. Communism became an increasingly attractive political philosophy, and a full-scale insurrection seemed imminent. In June 1973, thousands of Thai students demonstrated in the streets, demanding a new constitution and the return to democratic principals. Tensions grew until October, when armed forces attacked a demonstration at Thammasat University in Bangkok, killing 69 students and wounding 800, paralyzing the capital with terror and revulsion.

The constitution was restored, a new government was elected, and democracy once again wobbled on. Many students, however, were not yet satisfied and continued to complain that the financial elite were still in control and still resisting change. In 1976, student protests again broke out, and there was a replay of the grisly scene of 3 years before at Thammasat University. The army seized control to impose and maintain order, conveniently spiriting away some bodies and prisoners, and another brief experiment with democracy was at an end. **Thanin Kraivichien** was installed as prime minister of a new right-wing government, which suspended freedom of speech and the press, further polarizing Thai society.

In 1980, **Prem Tinsulanonda** was named prime minister, and during the following 8 years, he managed to bring remarkable political and economic stability to Thailand. The Thai economy continued to grow steadily through the 1980s, fueled by Japanese investment and Chinese capital in flight from Hong Kong. Leadership since then has seen quite a few changes, including a military coup in 1991 and another student crackdown in 1992. It was under **Gen. Chavalit Yongjaiyudh**'s administration that the economic crisis hit Thailand in July 1997. While his government sat on its hands in indecision over how to proceed, connections between public officials and bad financial institutions became more apparent, and international investors lost confidence in Thailand. While in August 1997 Thailand accepted $17 billion in bailouts from the International Monetary Fund, political in-fighting stalled the government's action until November of the same year, when **Chuan Leekpai,** a previous prime minister, was elected into office again to try to straighten things out.

Economic stability was restored under the leadership of "the CEO Prime Minister" **Thaksin Shinawatra,** elected in 2000. From the outside, Thaksin's government appeared to be stable, and he was able to successfully court a great deal of foreign investment. Internally, however, discontent in the south and amongst the middle class in Bangkok was steadily growing over what was seen as the Thaksin regime's inherent corruption, subversion of democratic institutions, and inability to curb the increasing violence by Muslim separatists in the far south. This growing wave of discontent overtook the government in the form of an Army-led coup on September 19, 2006, leaving the country under a military junta calling itself the Council for Democratic Reform, now renamed the **Council for National Security (CNS).** The CNS, composed of the major coup leaders and headed by **Gen. Sonthi Boonyaratglin** (with Prime Minister Surayad Chulanont as the junta's public face), dissolved Parliament, suspended the constitution, and placed restrictions on political gatherings.

THAILAND TODAY

Today, under a pyramid of king, nation, and religion, Thais enjoy far more freedom than any of their neighbors. King Bhumibol Adulyadej holds a position outside of government, but is recognized as the defender of all Thai people. On a few occasions, he has put his foot down when government monkey business has not been beneficial to his people.

Recently the monkeys have been working overtime, however, and Thailand's political situation is in flux since the September 2006 coup. The CNS military government now rules the country, and elections once scheduled for within a year's time of the coup have now been pushed back to sometime in 2008.

Understandably, this has caused increased grumbling among the populace, both those who supported and those who disapproved of the coup. For the coup to be beneficial for the country, everyone agrees that the junta should release the reins of government, allowing a legitimately elected government to be put in place as soon as possible—but recent Thai history suggests that the country could be in for a bumpy ride.

THAILAND'S PEOPLE & CULTURE

Thailand is a true melting pot of people and cultures. Thais descended from people of southern China, who for centuries absorbed Mon, Khmer, Lao, Persian, Indian, and Malay people and influences. The hill-tribe peoples of the north descended from Tibeto-Burman people who migrated from the Himalayas.

RELIGION Thai culture cannot be fully appreciated without some understanding of Buddhism, which is followed by 90% of the population. Although Buddhism first came to Thailand in the 3rd century B.C., when missionaries were sent from India, it was not until the 14th century that the *sangha* (monastic order) was established. Even Thai kings humbly don the monk's robes at age 13.

Other faiths in Thailand include Islam, Christianity, Hinduism, and Sikhism. Sunni Islam is followed by more than two million Thais, mostly in the south.

CUISINE Thai cuisine is the best of Chinese food ingredients and preparation combined with the sophistication of Indian spicing and topped off with red and green chilis. Basic ingredients include a cornucopia of shellfish, fresh fruits, and vegetables—asparagus, tamarind, bean sprouts, carrots, mushrooms of all kinds, various kinds of spinach, and bamboo shoots, combined with pungent spices such as basil, lemongrass, mint, chili, garlic, and coriander. Thai cooking employs coconut milk, curry paste, peanuts, and a variety of noodles and rice.

Among the dishes you'll find throughout the country are: *tom yum goong,* a Thai hot-and-sour shrimp soup; *satay,* charcoal-broiled chicken, beef, or pork strips skewered on a bamboo stick and dipped in a peanut-coconut-curry sauce; spring rolls; *larb,* a spicy chicken or ground-beef concoction with mint and lime flavoring; salads, most with a dressing of onion, chili pepper, lime juice, and fish sauce; *pad thai* (Thai noodles), rice noodles usually served with shrimp, eggs, peanuts, fresh bean sprouts, lime, and a delicious sauce; *khao soi,* a northern curried soup served at small food stalls; a wide range of curries; spicy *tod man pla,* one of many fish dishes; sticky rice, served in the north and made from glutinous rice, prepared with vegetables and wrapped in a banana leaf; and Thai fried rice, a simple rice dish made with whatever the kitchen has on hand. "American fried rice" usually means fried rice topped with one egg, over easy, and meat. For dessert, the local fruit, from pineapple to papaya, is delicious. Also try local favorites like rambutan (similar to litchi), jackfruit, and pungent durian.

*A **word of caution:*** Thais enjoy incredibly spicy food, normally much more fiery than is tolerated in even the most piquant Western cuisines. Protect your own palate by saying *"Mai phet, farang,"* meaning "Not spicy, foreigner."

ETIQUETTE

Disrespect for the royal family and religious figures, sites, and objects will cause great offense. While photography is generally permitted in temples, never stand above a Buddha image or point your feet in the direction of the Buddha. Women should never touch a monk; when handing a monk an offering, he will provide a cloth for you to lay the item upon, and he will collect it.

In Thailand, the head is the most sacred part of the body, and the feet are the lowliest; therefore, do not touch another person's head or even tousle the hair of a child. Shoes should be removed when entering a temple or private home. Don't ever step over someone's body or legs, and avoid pointing your feet at people or Buddhist images. Pointing with the finger is also rude; Thais use a palms-up hand gesture when signifying direction or indicating a person or thing. Beckoning looks like a wave goodbye.

In public, it is important to avoid confrontation or shows of anger or frustration. While banging your fist on the counter might get you better service back home, in Thailand you'll be promptly ignored. Most Thais are Buddhist, and a person showing ill temper is regarded with surprise and disapproval. A gentle approach will take you farther, and patient persistence is more effective in any situation. Note, too, that "Thai Time" dictates that appointments are loosely kept, and offense at someone's tardiness is met with confusion.

The traditional Thai greeting is called the *wai:* Place your palms together in prayer, raise the tips of your fingers to your chin, and make a subtle bow from the waist while bending your knees slightly. It's also used to say thank you and good-bye. The person of lower social status initiates a wai. In general, you should not wai to children or to someone providing a service to you. Also, don't expect a monk to return a wai; they're exempt from the custom. In a business setting, a handshake is more appropriate.

Address a Thai person by his or her first name preceded by "Khun." Don't be surprised if you are solely addressed by your first name—such as Mr. John or Ms. Mary. Close friends will use nicknames, which are much easier to remember.

You wouldn't know it by the current fashion trends in urban Bangkok, where tiny miniskirts and bare midriffs are common, but Thai people are quite modest. Conservative dress—longer shorts, trousers, and shirts that cover the shoulder—are the standard. Though a tropical climate, it is offensive to wear bathing suits around town or go topless on the beach. It is particularly inappropriate for men or women to wear shorts, halter tops, or miniskirts in temples. Cover thyself in the presence of the Buddha.

LANGUAGE

Thai is derived from Mon, Khmer, Chinese, Pali, Sanskrit, and, increasingly, English. It is a tonal language, with distinctions based on inflection—low, mid, high, rising, or falling tone—rather than stress, and it can elude most speakers of Western languages. Central Thai is the official language, but there are regional dialects.

One interesting aspect of the language that can be confusing to first-time visitors is that the polite words roughly corresponding to our *sir* and *ma'am* are determined not by the gender of the person addressed, but by the gender of the speaker; females say *ka* and males say *khap* (the formal pronunciation is *khrap*, but the *r* is rarely heard in everyday usage). Unfortunately, there is no universal transliteration system, so you will see the usual **Thai greeting** written in Roman letters as *sawatdee, sawaddi, sawasdee, sawusdi,* and so forth.

USEFUL THAI PHRASES

Note: **All phrases end in *khap* for men and *ka* for women.**

Hello	**Sa-wa-dee-khap (male); sa-wa-dee-ka (female)**
Thank you	**Kahp-koon-khap/ka**
How are you?	**Sa-bai-dee-mai-khap/ka**
I am fine	**Sa-bai-dee-khap/ka**
Excuse me	**Kor-toht-khap/ka**
I understand	**Kao-jai-khap/ka**
I don't understand	**Mai-kao-jai-khap/ka**
Do you speak English?	**Khun-poot-pa-sa-angrit-dai-mai-khap/ka?**
Where is the toilet?	**Hawng-nam-yoo-tee-nai-khap/ka?**
Do you have . . . ?	**Mee . . . mai-khap/ka?**
drinking water	**nam-deum**
coffee/tea w/milk/sugar	**cafe/cha sai/nohm/wan**
How much?	**Tao-rai?**
That's expensive/very expensive	**Paeng/paeng maak**
Can I get a discount?	**Loht-dai-mai-khap/ka?**
Bus station	**Satani-rot-meh.**
Train station	**Satani-rot-fai.**
Stop here	**Yoot-tee-nee-khap/ka**
Not spicy, please	**Mai-pet-khap/ka**

2 The Best of Thailand in 2 Weeks

Thailand is known worldwide for its Buddhist temples and beautiful beaches. Fortunately for visitors, the recent growth of no-frills airlines providing service throughout the country means that all the top spots are no more than an inexpensive hour-long flight from Bangkok. The following 2-week plan starts you off in Bangkok (temples) and then takes you south to Phuket, Koh Phi Phi, and Krabi (beaches), all now fully recovered from the 2004 tsunami. The last stop is Chiang Mai in the north (more temples), before returning to Bangkok or heading to your next destination.

Days ❶–❸: Bangkok ★★★

Not to be missed, the capital is Thailand's most happening and vibrant city. It is also extremely congested, so you'll want to stay at a hotel with easy access to the BTS skytrain. On your first day, take the skytrain to Saphan Taksin pier on the Chao Phraya River and hop a tourist boat heading north. Stop off at **Wat Po** to see the giant **Reclining Buddha,** followed by the **Grand Palace** and **Wat Phra Kaeo,** which houses the **Emerald Buddha.** On your second day, start shopping! If it's the weekend, head to **Chatuchak Market,** a full day in itself. If it's a weekday, then **Sukhumvit Road** beckons—hit the malls during the day before strolling through infamous **Patpong** and its **Night Market.** On your third day, take a cruise upriver to the old capital of **Ayutthaya,** home to an array of temples in varying states of decay.

Days ❹–❺: Phuket 🐨🐨🐨

Fly directly to Phuket, one of Thailand's most beautiful islands. Relax by getting a massage or enjoying the beach (or both) during the day; then head to **Patong** for some adventurous nightlife. If you're up for it after a night on the town, a little daylight adventure can be had by kayaking in **Phang Nga Bay.**

Days ❻–❼: Koh Phi Phi 🐨🐨🐨

Hop a morning ferry to Phi Phi and you'll be settled in at your resort by lunch. **Snorkeling** and **scuba diving** are the activities *du jour.* Leonardo DiCaprio fans should choose a day tour that stops at *The Beach.*

Days ❽–❾: Railay Beach 🐨🐨

A longtail boat from your resort drops you off at a ferry for the short hop back to the mainland and Railay Beach in Krabi Province. Spend the afternoon at one of the beach's **climbing schools,** battling gravity on sheer karst peaks. The next day, give your body a rest on the white sands of **Phra Nang Beach.** Wade out to **Happy Island** at low tide.

Day ❿: Transit to Chiang Mai

There are no direct flights from Krabi to Chiang Mai, which means you'll have a stopover in Bangkok, a full day of travel, and a necessary break from the sun.

Days ⓫–⓭: Chiang Mai 🐨🐨🐨

Rent a bicycle or hire a tuk-tuk and visit some of Chiang Mai's 300 temples. Don't miss **Wat Chedi Luang** and **Wat Phra Singh.** When you're templed out, browse the locally made handicrafts at the famous **Night Bazaar.** The next morning, hire a *songtao* for the drive to the top of **Doi Suthep** mountain and get blessed by a monk at **Wat Phra That.** If you've fallen in love with Thai food, take a half-day **cooking class;** if you're not shopped out, hop on a white songtao to **Sankamphaeng Road,** a retail paradise. To cap off your northern adventure (especially if you have an extra day or two), take a **jungle trek** and visit the local hill tribes.

Day ⓮: Bangkok or Beyond

Fly back to Bangkok to tie up any loose ends—for instance, sometimes it's easier to mail your souvenirs home than lugging them on the plane—or head to the next port of call on your Southeast Asian adventure.

3 Planning Your Trip to Thailand

VISITOR INFORMATION

The **Tourism Authority of Thailand (TAT)** publishes pamphlets and maps as well as current schedules for festivals and holidays. Visit its useful website at **www.tat.org**. Once in the country, you'll also find many free tourist maps and resources.

ENTRY REQUIREMENTS

All visitors to Thailand must carry a valid passport with proof of onward passage (either a return or through ticket). Visa applications are not required if you are staying up to 30 days and are a national of one of 41 designated countries, including Australia, Canada, Ireland, New Zealand, the U.K., and the U.S. New Zealanders may stay up to 3 months. The **Immigration Division of the Royal Thai Police Department** is at 507 Soi Suan Phu (off Sathorn Tai Rd., south of Silom area and Sala Daeng BTS station; ✆ **02287-3101**). A visa extension costs a whopping 1,900B (US$48/£27). It is best to always have a proper visa and exit the country by the date stamped in your passport (or make the proverbial "visa run" over border points with Myanmar, Laos, Cambodia, or Malaysia). Visitors who overstay their visa will be fined 500B (US$13/£7) for each extra day, payable in cash upon exiting the country. For exhaustive visa particulars, try the unofficial but informative site www.thaivisa.com.

CUSTOMS REGULATIONS
Tourists are allowed to enter the country with 1 liter of alcohol and 200 cigarettes (or 250g of cigars or smoking tobacco) per adult, duty free. There are no restrictions on the import of foreign currencies or traveler's checks, but you cannot export foreign currency in excess of 10,000B (US$250/£140) unless declared to Customs upon arrival.

MONEY
The Thai unit of currency, the **baht,** is written on price tags and elsewhere as the letter B crossed with a vertical slash (written "B" in this chapter, as in "100B"). One baht is divided into 100 satang, though you'll rarely see a satang coin. Yellow coins represent 25 and 50 satang; silver coins come in 1, 2, 5, and 10B. Bank notes come in denominations of 20 (green), 50 (blue), 100 (red), 500 (purple), and 1,000 (khaki). While the exchange rate is still experiencing some flux following the 1997 Asian economic crisis, it's relatively stable. This edition uses the rate of **40 baht = US$1.**

ATMs   Most major banks throughout the country now have ATMs, which are also increasingly common in major tourist spots.

CURRENCY EXCHANGE   The largest banks in Thailand—try **Bangkok Bank, Thai Farmers Bank, Siam Commercial Bank,** or **Bank of Ayudhya**—all perform debit and cash advance services through the MasterCard/Cirrus or Visa/PLUS networks. *Note:* Time changes between here and home can affect your ability to withdraw cash on two consecutive business days.

TRAVELER'S CHECKS   Traveler's checks can be cashed in most banks or big hotels.

CREDIT CARDS   Nearly all international hotels and larger businesses accept credit cards, though it's cash-only in rural parts. Despite protests from credit card companies, many establishments add a 3% to 5% surcharge for payment. Use discretion in using your card—all major credit card companies list Thailand as a high-risk area for fraud. Don't let your card out of your sight, even for a moment, and be sure to keep all receipts. To report a lost or stolen credit card, call the emergency service numbers listed under "Lost & Found" in "Fast Facts: Thailand" (p. 89).

WHEN TO GO
CLIMATE   Thailand has two distinct climate zones: tropical in the south and tropical savanna in the north. The northern and central areas of the country (including Bangkok) experience three distinct seasons. The hot season lasts from March to May, with temperatures averaging in the upper 90s Fahrenheit (mid-30s Celsius); April is the hottest month. This period sees very little rain, if any at all. The rainy season begins in June and lasts until October; the average temperature is 84°F (29°C), with 90% humidity. While the rainy season brings frequent showers, it's rare for them to last for a whole day or for days on end. Daily showers come in torrents, usually in the late afternoon or evening. The cool season, from November through February, has temperatures from the high 70s to low 80s Fahrenheit (mid- to upper 20s Celsius), with moderate and infrequent rain showers. In the north during the cool season

(which is also the peak season for tourism), day temperatures can be as low as 60°F (16°C) in Chiang Mai and 41°F (5°C) in the hills.

The southern Malay Peninsula has intermittent showers year-round and daily ones during the rainy season (temperatures average in the low 80sF/high 20sC). If you're traveling to Phuket or Koh Samui, it will be helpful to note that the two islands alternate peak seasons. Optimal weather on Phuket occurs between November and April, when the island welcomes the highest numbers of travelers. Alternately, Koh Samui's good weather lasts from about February to October.

PUBLIC HOLIDAYS & EVENTS   Many holidays are based on the Thai lunar calendar, with numerous regional Buddhist fetes. The national holidays are **New Year's Day,** on January 1; **Makha Puja,** which falls in February; **Chakri Day,** on April 6; **Songkran,** the **Thai New Year,** celebrated from April 13 to 15; **Coronation Day,** on May 5; **Visakha Puja,** which falls in May; **Asalha Puja,** which falls in July; **Her Majesty the Queen's Birthday,** on August 12; **Chulalongkorn Day,** on October 23; **His Majesty the King's Birthday,** on December 5; **Constitution Day,** on December 10; and **New Year's Eve,** on December 31.

HEALTH & SAFETY

HEALTH CONCERNS   See chapter 3's "Health & Safety" section (p. 43) for information on the major health issues that affect travelers to Southeast Asia and recommended precautions for avoiding the most common diseases. It's also a good idea to check the most recent information at the **Centers for Disease Control** (click "Travelers' Health" at **www.cdc.gov**).

Don't drink the tap water in Thailand, even in the major hotels. Most hotels provide bottled water in or near the minibar or in the bathroom; use it for brushing your teeth as well as for drinking. Most restaurants serve bottled or boiled water and ice made from boiled water, but always ask to be sure. You may also want to exercise caution when eating from roadside and market stalls or in smaller local restaurants.

Air quality is not good in Bangkok, which has no emissions standards. Buses, trucks, and cars belch some toxic stuff, so visitors with respiratory concerns or sensitivity should take caution.

Thailand suffered fallout from the regionwide **SARS** scare in the winter and spring of 2003, but there have been no reported cases in the region since 2004. A number of cases of **avian influenza,** also called the **bird flu,** have been reported in Thailand, but the disease has been mostly isolated to people working in the poultry industry. Note that you cannot contract bird flu from consuming cooked chicken.

SAFETY CONCERNS   Visitors to Thailand should refer to their home country's overseas travel bureau or with the **U.S. State Department** (click "Travel Warnings" at **www.travel.state.gov**) to learn more about the present situation in the area. The far south of Thailand has seen attacks by Muslim extremists on the Buddhist population, police, and military. Attacks blamed on Muslim groups have moved north from the immediate border areas of Pattani, Narathiwat, and Yala provinces to Hat Yai in Songkhla Province, a major transit point in the south. Although these attacks were isolated incidents, they did target tourist areas; at least two foreign nationals were killed. Travel to the far south is generally discouraged.

The early-evening hours of New Year's Eve 2006 and the early-morning hours of New Year's Day 2007 saw eight bombs detonated in and around Bangkok, killing three and wounding over 30, including three foreigners. Widely believed to be an effort to discredit the government and instill a sense of fear in the public by those disgruntled with the new regime (although the Muslim insurgency in the south cannot be ruled out), no individual or group has claimed responsibility or been charged. The political situation in Thailand is still very volatile, thus tourists should always be aware of their surroundings (especially in crowded areas), avoid political gatherings of any size, and keep abreast of the current political situation before and during their trip. In addition to the U.S. State Department website (above), local newspaper websites include **www.bangkokpost.com** and **www.nationmultimedia.com**.

Anonymous violent crime in Thailand is rare; however, petty crimes such as purse snatching and pickpocketing are common. Overland travelers should take care on overnight buses and trains, popular targets for small-time thieves.

Road conditions vary throughout the country, but Bangkok is busy and chaotic. Crossing the streets can be the greatest risk on your trip; move slowly and exercise caution. In the beach towns, motorbike accidents are all too common—always wear a helmet if you decide to rent a vehicle.

GETTING THERE

BY PLANE   On September 28, 2006, aging Don Muang International Airport shut its doors after 92 years of service. The ultramodern **Suvarnabhumi International Airport** (say Su-va-na-*poom*) took its place and now handles all domestic and international flights into and out of Bangkok. **Thai Airways** (✆ **800/426-5204** in the U.S.; head office at 485 Silom Rd., Bangkok, ✆ **02280-0060;** www.thaiair.com) covers virtually all Southeast Asian nations on its routes. If you leave Thailand by air, you're required to pay a 700B (US$18/£9.80) international departure tax.

From North America, **Thai Airways** has daily flights from Los Angeles; **United Airlines** and **Northwest Airlines** connect many airports in North America to Bangkok; and **Air Canada** flies to Bangkok from Vancouver via Hong Kong and Tokyo.

From the U.K., **British Airways** has two or three daily nonstop flights from London to Bangkok.

From Australia, **Thai Airways** serves Bangkok from Sydney daily and from Brisbane, Melbourne, and Perth three times a week. **Qantas** has two daily flights from Sydney and one from Melbourne, both direct; it can also connect Adelaide, Brisbane, and Canberra daily. **British Airways** flies twice daily from Sydney.

Note that while most international flights arrive in Bangkok, you can also fly direct to Phuket, Koh Samui, Hat Yai, and Chiang Mai from regional destinations like Hong Kong, Singapore, Kuala Lumpur in Malaysia, Vientiane and Luang Prabang in Laos, and Phnom Penh and Siem Reap in Cambodia.

Tips Airport Update

At press time, the new Suvarnabhumi International Airport was undergoing repairs to cracks in its runways and water leakage in its terminal building. For the time being, the old airport will temporarily reopen to handle domestic, nonconnecting flights—including some of those on Thai Airways and a few of the budget airlines. The timetable for repairs is uncertain at this writing, so for all domestic flights, it's best to check in advance which airport you'll be flying in and out of.

BY TRAIN Thailand is accessible via train from Singapore and peninsular Malaysia. Malaysia's **Keretapi Tanah Melayu Berhad (KTM)** rail service begins in Singapore (*C* **65/222-5165**), stopping in Kuala Lumpur (*C* **603/273-8000**) and Butterworth (Penang) (*C* **604/323-7962**), before heading for Thailand, where it joins service with the State Railway of Thailand. Bangkok's **Hua Lampong Railway Station** is centrally located on Krung Kassem Road (*C* **02223-7010**).

The *Eastern & Oriental Express* (*C* **800/524-2420** in the U.S., or 65/392-3500 in Singapore; www.orient-express.com) operates a 2-night/3-day journey between Singapore and Bangkok that makes getting there almost better than being there. The romance of 1930s colonial travel is joined with modern luxury on this luxurious train. Departures are limited; current fares start at US$1,780 (£979) per person one-way during high season. There are also onward connections to Chiang Mai with a stop in Ayutthaya.

BY BUS From every major city in peninsular Malaysia (and even Singapore), you can pick up a bus to Thailand. VIP buses cost more but have reclining seats and more legroom; traveling overland along the length of the southern peninsula is best by train, however. Buses connect with Laos over the Lao-Thai Friendship Bridge to Vientiane and at other southern border crossings, and with Cambodia via Poipet.

GETTING AROUND

Transportation within Thailand is accessible, efficient, and inexpensive. If your time is short, fly. But if you have the time to take in the countryside and you care to see a bit of provincial living, travel by bus, train, or private car.

BY PLANE Most convenient are domestic flights on **Thai Airways** (6 Larn Luang Rd., Bangkok; *C* **02535-2084**), which connects Bangkok and 27 domestic cities, including Chiang Mai, Chiang Rai, Mae Hong Son, Phitsanulok, Loei, Surat Thani, and Phuket. **Bangkok Airways** (99/4 Moo 14 Vibhavadirangsit Rd., Chatuchak; *C* **02265-5678**) connects Bangkok with Koh Samui, Phuket, Ranong, U Tapao (near Pattaya), Sukhothai, and Chiang Mai, and has international flights from Singapore and Phnom Penh. Budget airline **Air Asia** (*C* **02515-9999** in Bangkok; www.airasia. com) flies between Bangkok and Chiang Mai, Chiang Rai, Phuket, Krabi, Hat Yai, and Surat Thani for super-cheap (book ahead).

BY TRAIN Bangkok's **Hua Lampong Railway Station** (*C* **02223-7010**, or 1690 for information hot line), now easily reached by subway, is a convenient, user-friendly facility. Clear signs point the way to public toilets, coin phones, and a food court. A post office, information counter, police box, ATMs and money-changing facilities, convenience shops, baggage check, and restaurants surround a large open area.

From this hub, the State Railway of Thailand provides regular service to destinations north as far as Chiang Mai, northeast to Udon Thani, east to Pattaya, and south to Thailand's southern border with continuing service to Malaysia. Complete schedules and fare information can be obtained at any railway station or by calling Hua Lampong Railway Station directly at the numbers listed above.

The various fare classes of trains are based on speed and comfort. The fastest is the Special Express, which is the best choice for long-haul, overnight travel. These trains cut travel time by as much as 60% and have sleeper cars, which are a must for the really long trips. Rapid trains are the next best option. Prices vary by class, from air-conditioned sleeper cars in first class down to the straight-backed, hard seats in third class.

> **Tips · Telephone Dialing at a Glance**
>
> - **To place a call from your home country to Thailand:** Dial the international access code (011 in the U.S. and Canada, 0011 in Australia, 0170 in New Zealand, 00 in the U.K.), plus Thailand's country code (**66**), and then the phone number (for example, a Bangkok number would be 011 66 2000-0000). *Important note:* When making international calls to Thailand, be sure to omit the **0** that appears before all phone numbers in this guide (thus you will only dial eight digits after the 66 country code).
> - **To call a cellphone number in Thailand:** Dial an **8** before the number, whether you're calling domestically or internationally (for example, 011 66 82000-0000).
> - **To place a direct international call from Thailand:** Dial the international access code (**00**), plus the country code, the area or city code, and the number (for example, to call the U.S., you'd dial 00 1 000/000-0000).
> - **International country codes are as follows:** Australia, 61; Cambodia, 855; Canada, 1; Hong Kong, 852; Indonesia, 62; Laos, 856; Malaysia, 60; Myanmar, 95; New Zealand, 64; the Philippines, 63; Singapore, 65; U.K., 44; U.S., 1; Vietnam, 84.

BY BUS Thailand has a very efficient and inexpensive bus system, highly recommended for budget travelers and short-haul trips. Options abound, but the major choices are government or private, air-conditioned or non-air-conditioned. Most travelers use the private, air-conditioned buses. Buses are best for short excursions; long-haul buses are an excellent value, but they can be slow and uncomfortable.

Bangkok has three major bus stations, each serving a different part of the country. All air-conditioned public buses to the west and the southern peninsula arrive and depart from the **Southern Bus Terminal** (© 02434-7192), on Nakhon Chaisi and Phra Pinklao Road (near Bangkok Noi Station), west of the river over the Phra Pinklao Bridge from the Democracy Monument. Service to the east coast (including Pattaya) arrives and departs from the **Eastern Bus Terminal,** also known as **Ekamai** (© 02391-8097), on Sukhumvit Road opposite Soi 63 (Ekamai BTS skytrain station). Buses to the north arrive and leave from the **Northern Bus Terminal,** aka **Mo Chit** (© 02576-5599), Kampaengphet 2 Road, Mo Chit, near the Chatuchak Weekend Market, and a short taxi or bus ride from the Mo Chit skytrain station. VIP buses leave from locations in town.

BY CAR Renting a car is a snap in Thailand, although self-driving in Bangkok traffic is discouraged. Outside the city, it's a good option, though Thai drivers are quite reckless and American drivers must reorient themselves to driving on the left. Among the many car-rental agencies, both **Avis** (© 02255-5300) and **Budget** (© 02566-5067) have convenient offices around the country.

You can rent a car with or without a driver. All drivers are required to have an international driver's license. At press time, self-drive rates started at 1,500B (US$38/£21) per day for a small Honda sedan.

Local tour operators in larger destinations like Chiang Mai, Phuket, and Koh Samui will rent cars for considerably cheaper than the larger, more well-known agencies. Sometimes the savings are up to 50%. These companies rarely require international driver's licenses. Always ask if you will still be covered by their insurance policy.

TIPS ON ACCOMMODATIONS
Thailand accommodations run the gamut, but you can expect a high standard of comfort and service at affordable rates. In places like Phuket and Koh Samui, rainy season brings discounts of 30% and 50%. You can negotiate with hotel reservations agents—there are always special discounts, packages, or free add-ons for extra value, and it never hurts to ask.

TIPS ON DINING
Larger Thai cities and towns play host to many Western restaurants, but go for authentic Thai wherever possible. One-dish meals like noodle soup, fried rice, or noodles are popular for solo travelers, but Thai meals are best when shared family style. There are many regional variations, but the most notable are the barbecue, sticky rice, and spicy papaya salads in Isan (the northeast) and the fiery coconut curries of the south; always ask about regional specials. Most family meals consist of a meat or fish dish (often a whole fish), fried or steamed vegetables, a curry, stir-fried dishes of meat and vegetables, and a soup, such as fiery *tom yum*. Meals are lengthy and boisterous affairs, and food is picked at slowly (often accompanied by local beer, rice wine, or strong whiskey). Table manners are casual and practical.

Be cautious with street eats: Check out the stall to see that it's clean and the ingredients are fresh. Most places temper spices for foreigners, but always ask.

You're not expected to tip at a Thai restaurant, but rounding up the bill or leaving 20B (US50¢/£0.30) on top of most checks is acceptable.

TIPS ON SHOPPING
Shopping is a full contact sport in Thailand. In markets and smaller shops, bargaining is the name of the game. If your suggested price is accepted, it is rude to walk away without finishing the sale. Keep in mind that in high-traffic tourist areas, prices are always inflated. In shopping malls and boutiques, prices are fixed. Some shops charge a 3% charge on credit card purchases.

FAST FACTS: Thailand

American Express There is no specific agent that handles American Express services in Thailand anymore, but there is an **American Express** office at 388 Pahonyothin Rd., in Bangkok. You can reach the office at ℂ **02273-5296** during business hours (Mon–Fri 8:30am–5pm) or call the customer service hot line (ℂ **02273-5544**) with any problems or questions.

Business Hours Government offices (including branch post offices) are open Monday through Friday from 8:30am to 4:30pm, with a lunch break between noon and 1pm. Businesses are generally open from 8am to 5pm. Shops often stay open from 8am until 7pm or later, 7 days a week. Department stores are generally open from 10am to 7pm.

Drugstores Pharmacies carry brand-name medications; pharmacists often speak some English and are very helpful.

Electricity All outlets are 220 volts AC (50 cycles), with two flat- or round-pronged holes. If you use a 110-volt hair dryer, electric shaver, or battery charger, bring a transformer and adapter. If you're bringing a laptop, don't forget a surge protector.

Embassies & Consulates Most countries have embassies in Bangkok; the U.S., Australia, Canada, and the U.K. also have consulates in Chiang Mai. Most embassies have 24-hour emergency services for their citizens. See "Fast Facts" in the Bangkok and Chiang Mai sections for contact information.

Emergencies Call ℂ **1699** or 1155 for the tourist police. Don't expect many English speakers at normal police posts outside the major tourist areas. It is a good idea to contact your embassy in case of emergencies, both medical and legal.

Internet Access You'll find Internet cafes everywhere in Thailand. See the "Fast Facts" sections in specific destination sections for details.

Language Central (often called Bangkok) Thai is the official language. English is spoken in the major cities at most hotels, restaurants, and shops, and is the second language of the professional class. See "Language," p. 80, for more information.

Liquor Laws The official drinking age in Thailand is 18, but laws are loosely followed—you can buy alcohol in most areas any time of day or night, with exceptions for certain Buddhist holidays and election days. All restaurants, bars, and nightclubs sell booze, and you can pick up take-away-size packages from just about anywhere. Nightspots close between midnight and 2am.

Lost & Found Your home embassy in Thailand is the place to contact if you've lost your travel documents and need them replaced. For more information, see "Embassies & Consulates," above.

If you have lost anything or had your valuables stolen, call the national police hot line at ℂ **1155**. Believe it or not, there have been several reports of lost items being returned to the appropriate consulate by taxi drivers and bus attendants.

To report a lost or stolen credit card in Thailand, call: **American Express** (ℂ **02273-5544**), **Diners Club** (ℂ **02238-3660**), **MasterCard** (ℂ **02670-4088**), or **Visa** (ℂ **02256-7326**).

If you need emergency cash over the weekend, when all banks and American Express offices are closed, you can have money wired to you via **Western Union** (ℂ **02/254-7000** in Bangkok), which has branches in Bangkok and in many provincial capitals. *One word of warning:* Western Union's exchange rate is not favorable, so use this service only in an emergency.

Mail Airmail postcards to the U.S. cost 12B to 15B (US30¢–US40¢/£0.15–£0.20), depending on the size of the card; first-class letters cost 19B (US50¢/£0.25) per 10 grams. Rates to Europe are about the same. Airmail delivery usually takes 7 days.

Air parcel post costs 950B (US$24/£13) per kilogram. Surface or sea parcel post costs 550B (US$14/£7.70) for 1 kilogram (and takes 3 or 4 months for delivery). International Express Mail (EMS) costs 600B (US$15/£8.40) for a document and 800B (US$20/£11) for a parcel from 1 to 250 grams, with delivery guaranteed in 3 to 5 days. See individual destination sections for local post offices and their hours.

Shipping by air freight is expensive. Major international delivery services have their main dispatching offices in Bangkok, though they deliver throughout the country; these include **DHL Thailand,** Sathorn Road (© **02345-5000**); **FedEx,** Rama IV Road (© **02229-8800**); and **UPS Parcel Delivery Service,** 16/1 Soi 44/1 Sukhumvit Rd. (© **02712-3300**). Many businesses will also pack and mail merchandise for you at a reasonable price.

Newspapers & Magazines The major domestic English-language dailies are the *Bangkok Post* and the *Nation,* distributed in the morning in the capital and later in the day around the country. They cover the domestic political scene, as well as international news from AP, UPI, and Reuters wire services.

Police In an emergency, call the tourist police at © **1699** or 1155 to connect with English speakers 24 hours a day.

Safety Petty crimes, such as purse snatching or pickpocketing, are common in Thailand. Overland travelers should take care on overnight buses and trains, popular targets for small-time thieves. Beware of bringing strangers to your hotel room—there are many incidents of drugging and robbery (especially by prostitutes).

Watch out for credit card scams: Carry a minimum of cards, don't allow them out of your sight, and keep all receipts. Don't carry unnecessary valuables, and keep those you do have in your hotel safe.

A special warning: Be wary of strangers who offer to guide you (particularly in Bangkok), take you to any shop (especially jewelry shops), or buy you food or drink. This most frequently occurs near tourist attractions. Without exception, this is a scam of some kind. These folks invariably want to sell you fake gems or waste your time and earn a commission. Just walk away.

See "Health & Safety," p. 84, for more tips on keeping yourself safe.

Taxes Hotels charge a 7% government value-added tax (VAT) and typically add a 10% service charge; hotel restaurants add 8.25% government tax. Smaller hotels quote the price inclusive of these charges.

Telephones The international country code for Thailand is **66.** Major hotels in Thailand offer international direct dialing (IDD), long-distance service, and in-house fax transmission. However, hotels levy a surcharge on local and long-distance calls, which can add up to 50% in some cases. Credit card or collect calls are a much better value, but most hotels add a hefty service charge for these, too.

Major post offices have special offices or booths for overseas calls, as well as fax and telex service, usually open from 7am to 11pm. Guesthouses and travel agents in tourist areas offer long-distance calling or call-back service on their private line or use very affordable net-to-phone connections of varying quality. Local calls can be made from any red or blue public pay phone. Card phones are your best bet; buy a Telephone Organization of Thailand (TOT) card, for use in yellow phones, anywhere.

For directory assistance, dial © **1133**. See "Telephone Dialing at a Glance," p. 87, for details on how to make calls to and from Thailand.

Time Zone Thailand is 7 hours ahead of Greenwich Mean Time. During winter months, Bangkok is 7 hours ahead of London, 12 hours ahead of New York, and 15 hours ahead of Los Angeles.

Tipping If no service charge is added to your check in a fine-dining establishment, a 10% to 15% tip is appropriate. In local shops, a small tip of 10B (US25¢/£0.15) or so is common. Airport or hotel porters expect tips, but just 20B to 50B (US50¢–US$1.25/£0.30–£0.70) is acceptable. Feel free to reward good service wherever you find it. Tipping taxi drivers is not expected, but accepted. Carry small bills, as many drivers either don't have change or won't admit having any.

Toilets The better restaurants and hotels will have Western toilets. Shops and budget hotels will have the Asian-style "squatty potty" toilet, a hole in the floor with foot pads on either side. Near the toilet is a water bucket or sink with a small ladle. The water is for flushing and cleaning the toilet. Don't count on these places having toilet paper. Some shopping malls have dispensers outside the restroom that charge 2B (US5¢/£0.03) for toilet paper. Dispose of it in the wastebasket provided, not down the drain.

Water Don't drink the tap water, even in the major hotels. Most hotels provide bottled water in or near the minibar or in the bathroom; use it for brushing your teeth as well as drinking. Most restaurants serve bottled or boiled water and ice made from boiled water, but always ask to be sure.

4 Bangkok ★★★

With an estimated population of 10 million in a country of only 64 million, Thailand's capital is the urban and cultural heart of the land: where all trends originate, where all roads meet, an exaggeration of every aspect of life in the kingdom. Choked with traffic, polluted, and corrupt, the city is also the financial capital of one of the fastest-growing economies in the world. Central Bangkok is all columns of glass and steel, hulking shopping complexes, and hotels linked at the city center by an elevated monorail, the BTS skytrain, and a slick new subway.

Bangkok was founded when King Rama I moved the city across the river from Thonburi in 1782. Today, the capital's stunning temples share space with skyscrapers and Starbucks; luxury condominiums stand stridently just a stone's throw from labyrinthine slums along dirty canals; glittering shopping malls cast their shadows over dusty open-air street bazaars. The city is less "Asian" than what many visitors often expect, but there are still gems to find in and among the new construction and suburban sprawl, and exploring Bangkok is certainly a highlight.

GETTING THERE

Bangkok has a massive new airport, three bus terminals, and a centrally located train station. Affordable taxis and tuk-tuks (three-wheeled, motorized trishaws/pedicabs) cruise the broad avenues. The BTS skytrain, the city's elevated rail line, and the new

Bangkok subway mean direct connection between the domestic train station and the northern bus terminal.

BY PLANE Bangkok is a major hub for air travel in Southeast Asia, with around 100 airlines providing service. In September 2006, Don Muang International Airport was replaced by the ultramodern **Suvarnabhumi International Airport** (say Su-va-na-*poom*). Claiming the second-largest terminal building in the world behind Hong Kong, Suvarnabhumi is a city unto itself, located about 30km (19 miles) east of Bangkok.

Passengers will find the following services available upon arrival: luggage storage for 100B (US$2.50/£1.40) per day; currency-exchange banks with the same rates as those in town; ATMs; phone-rental booths; **Airport Information** (© 02132-9328) and **Tourism Authority of Thailand (TAT)** booths; Association of Thai Travel Agents desks; Thai Hotel Association desks; Thai and international restaurants; massage services; convenience stores; and the **Novotel Suvarnabhumi Airport Hotel** (© 02131-1111).

Note: Be warned that the new airport's arrivals area is very small, poorly marked, and usually packed with touts offering rides to your hotel. Read the following information carefully to determine the best way to get to your destination. You can also go to **www.bangkokairportonline.com** for reliable, up-to-date airport information.

To get from the airport to the town center, it is anywhere from a 45- to 90-minute ride. Most of the larger hotels offer pickup service for a fee, or you can easily arrange for an air-conditioned minibus, taxi, or limousine to your hotel.

Taxi stands are on the ground level of the terminal building, as well as at the transport center, easily accessible by free airport shuttle buses that stop outside of the arrivals hall (second floor). Charges will be according to the meter, plus a 50B (US$1.25/£0.70) surcharge for airport service.

Private limousine services have air-conditioned sedans for hire from booths in the arrivals hall. Trips to town start at 900B (US$23/£13). Advance booking is not necessary.

The **Airport Express** is a convenient and inexpensive alternative, with regular departures from 5am to midnight. The four routes currently offered are from Suvarnabhumi to Silom Road; to Khao San Road; to Sukhumvit Road; and to Hualamphong Railway Station (via Siam Center). Stops include many major hotels. Tickets cost just 150B (US$3.75/£2.10).

The **transport center,** a short shuttle ride from the airport terminal, handles all city bus service to and from Bangkok, buses to outlying provinces (including Nong Khai on the border with Laos), and all car-rental companies. Take a free airport shuttle from outside of the arrivals hall (second floor).

City buses leave regularly and have clearly marked routes (the no. 552 bus is the most convenient, stopping at the On Nut BTS station). **Interprovincial buses** with service to Pattaya (130B/US$3.25/£1.80), Trat/Ko Chang (311B/US$7.75/£4.35), and Nong Khai/Vientiane, Laos (454B/US$11/£6.35) leave less frequently throughout the day.

Car-rental companies at Suvarnabhumi include **Avis** (© 084/700-8157), **National** (© 089/133-6126), **Budget** (© 089/841-3004), and **Hertz** (© 086/779-5456). Daily rentals start at 1,200B (US$30/£17) for a Toyota pickup or 2,000B (US$50/£28) for a Honda Civic sedan. Pickup and drop-off is at the transport center.

BY TRAIN The Thai rail network is extremely well organized, connecting Bangkok with major cities throughout the country. (You can also travel by train to Bangkok from Singapore, via Kuala Lumpur and Butterworth, Malaysia.)

All trains to and from the capital stop at **Hua Lampong Railway Station (② 1690** or 02223-7010), east of Chinatown at the intersection of Rama IV and Krung Kasem roads. The station has many services, including baggage check and a small food court. The information counter is helpful. From the station, connect to your destination by subway, metered taxi, or tuk-tuk.

BY BUS   Bangkok has three major bus stations, each serving a different part of the country. Buses to the west and the southern peninsula arrive and depart from the **Southern Bus Terminal (② 02434-7192)**, on Nakhon Chaisi, west of the river over the Phra Pinklao Bridge from the Democracy Monument. Service to the east coast arrives and departs from the **Eastern Bus Terminal,** also known as **Ekamai (② 02391-8097)**, on Sukhumvit Road opposite Soi 63 (Ekamai BTS skytrain station). Buses to the north arrive and leave from the **Northern Bus Terminal,** aka **Mo Chit (② 02936-2841)**, Kampaengphet 2 Road, Mo Chit, near the Chatuchak Weekend Market (easily reached by the BTS skytrain or the MRT subway). VIP buses leave from locations in town.

CITY LAYOUT

Vintage 19th-century photographs of Bangkok show the Chao Phraya River bustling with humble longtail boats and elaborate royal barges. Built along the banks of the broad, S-shaped river, the city spread inland through a network of *klongs* (canals) that rivaled the intricacy—though never the elegance—of Venice.

The **Historic District,** along the Chao Phraya River, contains most of the city's historical sights, such as the Grand Palace, and most of the city's original *wats* (temples with resident monks). Following the river south, you'll run into the narrow lanes of Bangkok's **Chinatown** and, farther down, a row of the city's finest riverside hotels, including the Oriental and the Peninsula. Inland from the river, Bangkok's central **business district** is situated on Sathorn, Silom, and Surawongse roads, beginning at Charoen Krung (or "New") Road. Bangkok's main shopping thoroughfare, on **Rama I Road,** between Payathai and Ratchadamri roads, sports huge modern shopping complexes like the World Trade Center and Siam Square. East of Rama I, **Sukhumvit Road** has acres of expat condos, restaurants, shopping, and nightlife.

Get to know the Thai word *soi,* meaning "lane." Larger thoroughfares in the city have names, and *sois* are the many numbered side streets along their length, odd and even numbers on alternate sides. For example, Sukhumvit Soi 5 is the home of the Amari Boulevard Hotel, while Sukhumvit Soi 8, a few minutes' walk east and across the street, is where you'll find Le Banyan restaurant. Note that closely numbered *sois* are not necessarily near each other.

STREET MAPS   Nancy Chandler's *Map of Bangkok* (160B/US$4/£2.25) is a detailed, colorful source for finding specific hotels, restaurants, and shopping. The free *Thaiways Map of Bangkok* and *Metropolitan Map* (available in most hotels) are both chock-full of adverts and detailed city maps with specific insets. Bus maps are many and helpful if you go that route.

GETTING AROUND

It can take more than 2 hours by taxi to get from one side of town to the other during rush hour, so it's best to avail yourself of the many new options below. Taxis are affordable, but at the wrong time of day can be a real nightmare.

BY SKYTRAIN   The **Bangkok Mass Transit System (BTS skytrain)** is an elevated railway system high above the maddening traffic. Trains access Bangkok's central areas and now connect with the **MRTA subway.** Single-journey tickets cost from 15B to 40B (US40¢–US$1/£0.20–£0.55). Buy ticket cards at platform vending machines: Choose your numbered destination from a map, press the corresponding button on the map, and pay in a slot (get small change at the info counter as needed). Ticket cards let you through the turnstile and are required for exit, so be sure to hang on to them during the ride. Also available are 1- and 3-day passes and stored-value cards. The skytrain operates daily between 6am and midnight.

BY SUBWAY   Bangkok's new subway line makes a reverse "C" though town, conveniently linking Hua Lampong Railway Station with the Chatuchak Weekend Market and bus-terminal area, with connections to the BTS skytrain at Silom Road and on Sukhumvit at Asok. Hours of operation are 6am to midnight. Subway tokens cost between 15B and 39B (US40¢–US$1/£0.20–£0.55), depending on distance traveled. Tap the token on the turnstile screen to enter, and put the token in the turnstile slot when exiting at your destination.

BY RIVERBOAT   Efficient and scenic, the public riverboats on the Chao Phraya are a great way to get around the sights in the city center and are a remarkable window on local life. Boats operated by the **Chao Phraya Express Company** (© 02222-5330) trace the river's length, with stops at many piers (*tha* in Thai) on both the Thonburi side (west) and in central Bangkok (east). Good maps are posted at each stop. Most sightseers will board near Saphan Taksin BTS station, the last stop on the Silom Line as it meets the river. The major stops going into town from Saphan Taksin are: Tha Ratchawong (in Chinatown off Ratchawong Rd.), Tha Thien (near Wat Po), Tha Chang (near the Temple of the Emerald Buddha), and Tha Maharaj (near Wat Mahathat). There is a range of boats available.

   Tourist express boats are the fastest and most convenient, with guides talking over a microphone about the sights you'll pass at riverside. Short trips start at 19B (US50¢/£0.70); an all-day pass, good for all riverboats, is 75B (US$1.90/£1.05).

   Express boats are long, white boats with pointed bow, bench seats, and open sides. Mention your destination when you board, and the attendant will tell you if it's the right boat (avoid the long-haul boats with colored flags on top). Trips start at 9B to 15B (US20¢–US40¢/£0.15–£0.20).

   Cross-river ferries are another category; these are useful for getting to places like Wat Arun or other sights in Thonburi.

   Private boats are also for hire for tours. See "Bangkok's Waterways," under "What to See & Do" (p. 115), for details.

BY BUS   Bangkok buses are cheap and frequent, if a little bit confusing (and ticket takers are not always so helpful). Air-conditioned buses cost from 11B to 21B (US25¢–US50¢/£0.15–£0.30) and save you from inhaling lots of pollution. Buy a map, bring small change, and be careful of pickpockets.

BY TAXI   Taxis are everywhere. The meter starts at 35B (US90¢/£0.50) for the first 3km (2 miles); thereafter, it's about 5B (US15¢/£0.05) per kilometer. It is a good idea to have your hotel concierge or a Thai friend write out any destination in Thai. Avoid drivers who want to barter a flat fare. Tipping is appreciated.

BY CAR   You'd have to be a bit mad to drive yourself around Bangkok, what with the crazy traffic, left-side driving (if you're not used to it), and aggressive tactics of cabs

Bangkok Metro Lines

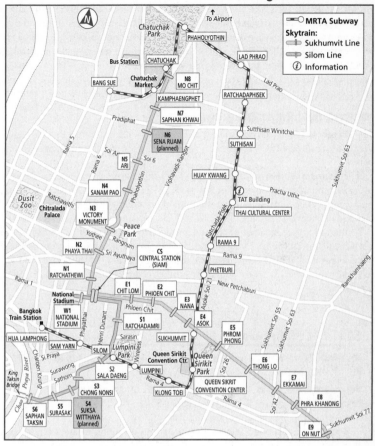

and trucks. It is best to hire a car with a driver. Contact **Diethelm Travel** (© 02255-9150; www.diethelmtravel.com), a leader in the region, for assistance.

BY TUK-TUK As much a national symbol as the elephant, the tuk-tuk, a small, three-wheeled, open-sided vehicle powered by a motorcycle engine, is noisy (named for the put-put sound it makes), smoky, and good fun. Drivers whip around city traffic like kamikazes. They are not good for long hauls or during rush hour, but for short trips or off-peak hours, they're convenient and a real kick, especially for first-time visitors to Thailand.

All tuk-tuk fares are negotiated, usually beginning at 40B (US$1/£0.55) for short trips. Bargain hard, but remember you'll always end up paying more than locals. *Warning:* Tuk-tuk drivers are notorious for talking travelers into shopping trips (and collecting commissions). Drivers will offer a very low fare, but will waste your time by stranding you at small, out-of-the-way gem and silk emporiums, all places that scam you and where the driver gets a cut. Insist on being taken where you want to go directly: Say, "No shopping!"

BY MOTORCYCLE TAXI   On every street corner, packs of drivers in colored vests play checkers, motorcycles standing by, waiting to shuttle passengers around the city. They are fast and can weave through traffic, but they are not so safe. Motorbike taxis are popular for short hops to the end of longer *sois,* or side streets, and cost from 10B (US25¢/£0.15) for short trips. Keep your knees tucked in.

ON FOOT   It is safe to walk around any part of town, but Bangkok is so spread out and the pollution so heavy that you'll want to stick to small areas.

VISITOR INFORMATION & TOURS

The **Bangkok Tourist Division** has offices at major tourist destinations throughout the city. Call ℂ **02225-7612** with any questions, or check out www.bangkoktourist. com.

The **Tourism Authority of Thailand (TAT)** offers general information about the provinces and operates a useful hot line at ℂ **1672.** It has two counters in Suvarnabhumi International Airport, open from 8am to midnight. The branch office at Ratchadamnoen Nok Avenue (ℂ **02282-9773**), near the Grand Palace, is helpful.

Numerous travel agencies offer local tours. **Diethelm Travel** (ℂ **02255-9150;** www.diethelmtravel.com), a leader in the region, can arrange excursions of any length. **World Travel** (ℂ **02233-5900**) and **Sea Tours** (ℂ **02216-5783**) also have good services, with branches in some hotels. Any hotel concierge can make the necessary arrangements.

FAST FACTS: Bangkok

American Express There is an office with limited services at 388 Pahonyothin Rd. (ℂ **02273-5544**).

Bookstores **Asia Books** carries a wide selection of regional works at its main branch, 221 Sukhumvit Rd., between Soi 15 and 17 (ℂ **02252-7277**), and its many outlets in town and throughout the country.

Bookazine has a good selection at its various locations, in Patpong on the first floor at CP Tower, 313 Silom Rd. (ℂ **02231-0016**); in Ploenchit on the third floor at Amarin Plaza, 498–502 Ploenchit Rd. (ℂ **02256-9304**); and at 286 Siam Square, opposite Siam Center (ℂ **02619-1015**).

Books Kinokuniya has shops in Pathumwan at the Isetan department store, 6th floor, World Trade Center, Ratchadamri Road (ℂ **02255-9834**); at the Emporium shopping complex, 3rd floor, 622 Sukhumvit Rd., Soi 24 (ℂ **02664-8554**); and a huge outlet in the Siam Paragon mall (ℂ **02610-9500**).

Numerous used bookstores willing to buy and trade can be found along Khao San Road and Soi Rambuttri in Banglampoo, Bangkok's main backpacker haunt.

Currency Exchange Most banks will exchange foreign currency Monday through Friday from 8:30am to 3:30pm. Exchange booths affiliated with the major banks are found in all tourist areas, open daily from as early as 7am to as late as 9pm.

The largest banks in Thailand—such as **Bangkok Bank, Thai Farmers Bank, Siam Commercial Bank,** and **Bank of Ayudhya**—all perform debit and cash advance services through the MasterCard/Cirrus or Visa/PLUS networks.

Many international banks also maintain offices in Bangkok, including **Bank of America,** 87/2 CRC Tower, Wireless Rd. (② 02305-2800); **Chase Manhattan,** Bubhajit Building, Sathorn Nua Road (② 02234-5992); **Citibank,** 82 Sathorn Nua Rd. (② 02232-2000); **National Australia Bank,** 90 Sathorn Nua Rd. (② 02236-6016); and **Standard Chartered Bank,** 90 Sathorn North, Silom (② 02636-1000). However, even if your bank has a branch in Thailand, your home account is considered foreign here—conducting personal banking will require special arrangements before leaving home.

Drugstores Bangkok has a great many pharmacies, though the drugs dispensed differ widely in quality, and generic knockoffs are common. Pack any prescription medications you require and go to a hospital for refills.

Embassies **U.S.:** 120–22 Wireless Rd. (② 02205-4000; http://thailand.usembassy. gov). **Canada:** 15th floor, Abdulrahim Place, 990 Rama IV Rd. (② 02636-0540; www.bangkok.gc.ca). **Australia:** 37 S. Sathorn Rd. (② 02344-6300; www. thailand.embassy.gov.au). **New Zealand:** 93 Wireless Rd. (② 02254-2530; www. nzembassy.com/thailand). **U.K.:** 14 Wireless Rd. (② 02305-8333; www.british embassy.gov.uk/thailand).

Emergencies In any emergency, first call Bangkok's **tourist police** at its direct-dial four-digit number (② 1155) or at ② 02678-6800. Someone at both numbers will speak English. Ambulance service is handled by private hospitals; see "Hospitals," below, or contact your hotel's front desk. For operator-assisted overseas calls, dial ② 100.

Hospitals The best facility going is luxurious **Bumrungrad Hospital,** 33 Soi 3, Sukhumvit Rd. (② 02667-1000). The **BNH Hospital** (Bangkok Nursing Home) is at 9 Convent Rd., between Silom and Sathorn roads, south of Rama IV Road (② 02632-0052). Bring your passport and be ready to put up a deposit as high as 20,000B (US$500/£280) before admittance. Bills must be settled before checking out.

Internet Access Most shopping malls and even the smallest hotels these days have at least a few Internet terminals, and you can't take a step without hitting one in places like Khao San Road, the backpacker area, or along busy Silom Road near Patpong. Prices usually range from 30B to 50B (US75¢–US1.25/ £0.40–£0.70) per hour. Big hotels charge exorbitant rates and are not worth it.

Luggage Storage Suvarnabhumi International Airport offers luggage storage for 100B (US$2.50/£1.40) per day per bag, 24 hours a day. Most hotels will allow you to store luggage while away on trips in the countryside.

Mail If you're shipping a parcel from Bangkok, take advantage of the packing service offered by the **General Post Office (GPO) Post & Telegraph Office,** Charoen Krung Road (② 02233-1050), open 24 hours. Small cardboard packing cartons start at just 10B (US25¢/£0.15); packing service is available during normal office hours. Telegraph and telephone service are available in the north end of the building. Ask at your hotel for branch offices located closer to you.

Newspapers & Magazines Bangkok Post and the *Nation,* English-language dailies, both cover local, national, and international news, plus happenings around town, TV listings, and other useful information (25B/US60¢/£0.35).

Metro Magazine (100B/US$2.50/£1.40), found at most bookstores, is a good source of current information on what's happening in Bangkok, especially the entertainment and social scene. *Falang* spins tales of backpacker debauchery and daring-do; like *Metro*, it has a listing section in the back with advice on travel in Thailand (100B/US$2.50/£1.40). *Where, Look East,* and *Thailand Magazine* are slick monthly English-language magazines distributed free and emphasizing events in and features on Bangkok, with lesser coverage of other Thai cities and provinces.

Police Call the **tourist police** at ℂ **1155** or 02678-6800, 24 hours, for assistance. English is spoken.

Safety Bangkok is a safe city, but be careful of pickpockets as you would any-where. Don't seek out trouble—avoid public disagreements or hostility (espe-cially with locals), and steer clear of gambling activities. The city is safe, even alone at night in most parts, but rely on your gut instinct—if you get a bad feel-ing about a place or situation, remove yourself from the scene to avoid getting caught in someone else's drama.

Telephones Beware of hotel surcharges on international calls, usually 25% to 40% (check with the hotel operator). Your best bet is the yellow, blue, or gray phones found in front of most convenience stores and in public places; these accept prepaid cards or coins. For information within the Bangkok metropoli-tan area, dial ℂ **1133**. See "Fast Facts: Thailand," earlier in this chapter, for additional information.

WHERE TO STAY

Bangkok supports a rich variety of hotels in all price categories—and luxury at a frac-tion of what you would pay elsewhere. Many hotels quote rates in U.S. dollars. Remember that prices listed here are the "rack rates" and should be considered only a guideline—be sure to search for discounts. Rates do not include the additional 7% value-added tax (VAT) and frequent service charge of 10%.

ALONG THE RIVER
Very Expensive

The Oriental, Bangkok 𝒜𝒜 A high-ranking member in the pantheon of the world's finest hotels, the Oriental makes for perhaps the most memorable stay in Bangkok. Its history dates from the 1860s, when the original hotel, no longer stand-ing, was established by two Danish sea captains soon after King Mongkut (Rama IV) reopened Siam to world trade. The hotel has withstood occupation by Japanese and American troops and played host to a long roster of Thai and international dignitaries and celebrities, including adventurous authors Joseph Conrad, Somerset Maugham, Noël Coward, Graham Greene, John Le Carré, and James Michener. Rooms in the older wing, built in 1876, pack the most colonial richness and charm. Those in the newer buildings (ca. 1958 and 1976) are certainly more spacious, some with better views of the river, but they sacrifice some of that Oriental hotel romance. It's the level and range of service, however, that distinguishes the Oriental from other riverfront hotels, and everyone from honeymooners and corporate execs to well-heeled tourists is treated like a diplomat. Even if you don't stay, stop by for high tea in the oldest building, now called the Authors' Wing and housing luxury suites. The area was recently renovated and is one of the best-preserved pieces of old Bangkok.

48 Oriental Ave., Bangkok 10500 (on the riverfront off Charoen Krung Rd./New Rd.). © **800/526-6566** or 02236-0400. Fax 02236-1937. www.mandarin-oriental.com. 393 units. US$370 (£204) superior; US$440 (£242) deluxe; from US$510 (£281) suite. AE, DC, MC, V. 5-min. walk to Saphan Taksin BTS station. **Amenities:** 4 restaurants; lounge w/world-class live jazz performances; 2 outdoor pools; 2 lighted outdoor tennis courts; state-of-the-art fitness center; luxurious spa w/sauna, steam, massage, and traditional Thai beauty treatments; concierge; tour desk; car rental; limo service; helicopter transfer service; tour boats for river excursions; business center; upmarket shopping arcade; salon; 24-hr. room service; babysitting; laundry service; dry cleaning; nonsmoking rooms; executive-level rooms; cooking school. *In room:* A/C, satellite TV, dataport, minibar, fridge, hair dryer, safe, IDD phone.

The Peninsula Bangkok ✸✸✸   Whether you land on the helicopter pad and promenade into the exclusive top-floor lounge, roll in from the airport in one of the hotel's Rolls-Royce limousines, or step lightly off the wood-decked, custom barges that ply the Chao Phraya, you'll feel like you've "arrived" however you get to the Peninsula, one of Bangkok's most deluxe accommodations. Every possible amenity is available here, from elegant dining to great activities and top-of-the-line business services. The rooms, some of the largest in town, all have river views and are done in a refined Thai and Western theme—a good marriage of Thai tradition and high-tech luxury, with wooden paneling, silk wallpaper, and attractive carpets. The technical features may make you feel like you've walked into a James Bond movie: Bedside control panels operate everything from the three phones and voice mail to the TV and even the mechanized curtains. The large marble bathrooms have separate vanity counters and a large tub with a hands-free phone and built-in TV monitor. "Ask and it will be done" seems to be the rule about service, and the multilingual staff is friendly and very accommodating.

333 Charoennakorn Rd., Klongsan, Bangkok 10600 (just across the Chao Praya River from Saphan Taksin station). © **866/382-8388** in the U.S.; 02861-2888 in Bangkok. www.peninsula.com. 370 units. US$240 (£132) standard; US$300 (£165) deluxe; US$500–US$3,000 (£275–£1,650) suite. AE, DC, MC, V. **Amenities:** 3 restaurants; 2 bars; 60m (197-ft.) 3-tiered pool; tennis court; state-of-the-art fitness center; full spa w/sauna, steam, massage, and aromatherapy; concierge; tour desk; car rental; fleet of Rolls-Royce limos; rooftop helicopter pad; tour boats and complimentary ferry service; business center; fine shopping; extensive salon; 24-hr. room service; babysitting; laundry service; dry cleaning; nonsmoking rooms; rooms for those w/limited mobility; executive-level rooms. *In room:* A/C, satellite TV, free Wi-Fi, minibar, hair dryer, safe, CD player, IDD phone.

Expensive

Bangkok Marriott Resort & Spa ✸✸ *Kids*   On the banks of the Chao Phraya, across the river and a few miles downstream from the heart of Bangkok, this resort is somewhat removed from the action and best reached via longtail boat. It's a short trip downriver, but you feel the crazy city release you from its grip. Once at the property, the big city seems a distant memory. The three wings of the hotel surround a large landscaped pool area with lily ponds and fountains, and there is a wonderful spa for a uniquely calming Bangkok experience. Boats go to and from the River City shopping mall every half-hour until evening. Stay here if you want to explore Bangkok yet at the same time escape.

257/1–3 Charoen Nakhorn Rd., at the Krungthep Bridge, Bangkok 10600 (on the Thonburi/east side of the Chao Phraya River, 15 min. by boat from River City). © **800/228-9290** or 02476-0022. Fax 02476-1120. www.marriott hotels.com. 413 units. US$245–US$275 (£135–£151) double; from US$345 (£190) suite. AE, DC, MC, V. **Amenities:** 6 restaurants; 3 bars; bakery, landscaped pool w/Jacuzzi; 2 outdoor lighted tennis courts; fitness center w/sauna; spa w/massage and beauty treatments; children's programs; concierge; tour desk; limo service; dinner cruises; business center; adjoining shopping arcade; salon; 24-hr. room service; babysitting; laundry service; dry cleaning; nonsmoking rooms. *In room:* A/C, satellite TV, dataport, minibar, fridge, safe, IDD phone.

Where to Stay & Dine in Bangkok

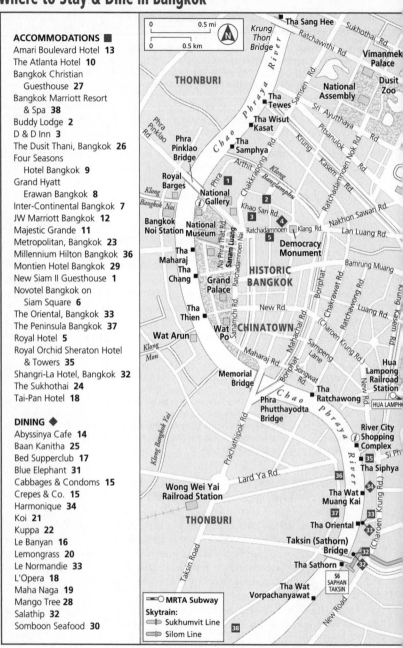

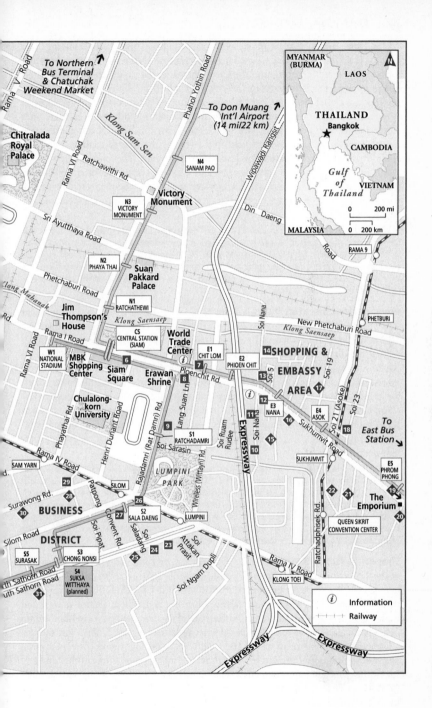

Millennium Hilton Bangkok ☆ Originally built by Sofitel, the building now housing the Millennium was vacant for 10 years before Hilton took over and opened for business in 2005. Jutting into the Chao Phraya on the Thonburi side, the Hilton boasts some of the best views in the city, highlighted by the appropriately named rooftop jazz club ThreeSixty and the vertigo-inducing glass elevator that accesses it. All rooms and facilities are sleek, modern, and oriented towards the river. Like other Thai Hiltons, the guest rooms lack almost any Thai touches, but are comfortable nonetheless: carpeting to comfort your feet, large bay windows to comfort your eyes, and mirror-laden marble bathrooms to comfort your vanity. The fourth-floor pool has a unique 1-foot-deep shelf with loungers and tables placed in the water, so you can sun, soak your feet, enjoy a cocktail, and watch the boats cruise the river. There's regular ferry service to the main pier in the event that you tire of being a spectator and decide to join the game.

123 Charoennakorn Rd., Klongsan, Bangkok 10600 (on the Thonburi side of the Chao Phraya River, a 10-min. boat ride from Saphan Taksin pier). ℂ 02442-2000. Fax 02442-2020. www.bangkok.hilton.com. 543 units. US$170–S$210 (£94–£116) double; from US$230 (£127) suite. AE, DC, MC, V. **Amenities:** 3 restaurants; bar and lounge; bakery; pool overlooking river; spa w/ sauna, steam, massage; concierge; tour desk; car rental; complimentary ferry service; business center; salon; 24-hr. room service; babysitting. *In room:* A/C, satellite TV, Internet access, minibar, coffeemaker, hair dryer, safe, IDD phone.

Royal Orchid Sheraton Hotel & Towers ☆ The Royal Orchid has magnificent views of the Chao Phraya and makes an excellent base for shopping or sightseeing. The rooms are spacious, pastel hued, and trimmed with warm teakwood, lending a refined and distinctly Thai ambience. The Sheraton Towers, a hotel within a hotel on the 26th through 28th floors (with its own check-in desk and express elevator), offers more ornate decor and a higher level of service for a premium; Sheraton Tower suites, for example, come with 24-hour butlers and personal fax machines. Recent renovations added the luxurious Mandara spa and state-of-the-art fitness center. The large pool area makes it easy to forget the big, crowded city. Try the hotel's many fine-dining options like "Etc . . . . " A walkway leads to the popular River City shopping complex next door.

2 Captain Bush Lane, Siphya Rd., Bangkok 10500 (next to River City mall). ℂ 800/325-3535 or 02266-0123. Fax 02236-8320. www.royalorchidsheraton.com. 740 units. US$200–US$270 (£110–£149) double; from US$300 (£165) suite. AE, DC, MC, V. 15-min. walk to Saphan Taksin BTS station. **Amenities:** 4 restaurants; lounge; 2 outdoor pools open 24 hr.; outdoor lighted tennis court; 24-hr. fitness center w/sauna; luxurious spa w/private plunge pools, steam, massage, and beauty treatments; concierge; tour desk; car rental; limo service; 24-hr. business center; small shopping arcade; 24-hr. room service; babysitting; laundry service; dry cleaning; executive-level rooms. *In room:* A/C, satellite TV w/pay movies, Internet access, minibar, fridge, hair dryer, safe, IDD phone.

Shangri-La Hotel, Bangkok ☆☆ The modern, opulent Shangri-La, on the banks of the Chao Phraya, boasts acres of polished marble and two towers with breathtaking views of the river. All units are outfitted with lush carpeting, teak furniture, and marble bathrooms. The views are terrific from the higher-floor deluxe rooms, and most have either a balcony or a small sitting room, making them closer to junior suites and a particularly good value for on-the-river upscale accommodations. For such an enormous place, the level of service and facilities is surprisingly good. The moody Chi Spa, whose design was inspired by Tibetan temple architecture, is one of the top hotel spas in town—highly recommended. The luxurious Krung Thep Wing adds another 17-story tower to the grounds, as well as a riverside swimming pool, restaurant, and breakfast lounge. Guests here register in their spacious rooms, surrounded by colorful Thai paintings and glistening Thai silk.

89 Soi Wat Suan Plu, Charoen Krung Rd. (New Rd.), Bangkok 10500 (adjacent to Sathorn Bridge, w/access off Chaoren Krung Rd. at south end of Silom Rd.). ✆ **800/942-5050** or 02236-7777. Fax 02236-8579. www.shangri-la. com. 799 units. 8,600B–12,300B (US$215–US$308/£120–£172) double; from 13,500B (US$338/£189) suite. AE, DC, MC, V. Next to Saphan Taksin BTS station. **Amenities:** 10 restaurants; lounge and bar; spa; 2 outdoor pools w/outdoor Jacuzzi; 2 outdoor lighted tennis courts; 2 squash courts; fitness center w/Jacuzzi, sauna, steam, massage, and aerobics classes; spa; concierge; tour desk; car rental; limo service; helicopter transfer; city shuttle service; dinner cruises; business center; small shopping arcade; salon; 24-hr. room service; laundry service; dry cleaning; nonsmoking rooms; executive-level rooms. *In room:* A/C, satellite TV, dataport, minibar, fridge, coffeemaker, hair dryer, safe, IDD phone.

BANGLAMPHU & KHAO SAN ROAD

Most of the major tourist sights are here, making sightseeing on foot more feasible, though it's quite a long ride from commercial Bangkok. For budget travelers, the widest range of low-price accommodations is found in this area around Khao San Road. There are a number of good values, but the best of the lot is the **New Siam II Guesthouse** (50 Trok Rong Mhai, Phra Ahtit Rd.; ✆ **02282-2795**), with a pool and spotless fan and air-conditioned rooms going for 720B (US$18/£10) and 840B (US$22/£12), respectively. On Khao San Road, the **Buddy Lodge** (265 Khao Sa Rd.; ✆ **02629-4477**) is your best choice, with tidy air-conditioned rooms from 2,200B (US$55/£31). The **D & D Inn** (68-70 Khao San Rd.; ✆ **02629-5252**) has clean but basic doubles starting at only 750B (US$19/£11).

Moderate

Royal Hotel ⍟ Near Thammasat University along the big, busy boulevard of Ratchadamnoen, the cozy Royal Hotel is just a 5-minute walk from the Royal Palace. It's good for budget-minded sightseers who don't want to stay on crazy Khao San, but short of being near some of the major sights, the Royal isn't particularly convenient for getting around Bangkok. The glitzy lobby, with polished marble floors, chandeliers, and massive Corinthian columns, was built in the 1950s and is a fun architectural pastiche from the Art Deco era. The hotel gained fame as the major field hospital during the May 1991 democracy demonstrations. Clean, kitschy rooms have lots of overly florid filigree and pink, ruffled dusters, but are spacious and have high ceilings. With a small pool and all the basic amenities, you're just a short walk from the useful tour services on Khao San, but it's quiet and a bit more grown-up here.

Ratchadamnoen Ave., Bangkok 10200 (2 blocks east of National Museum). ✆ **02222-9111.** Fax 02224-2083. 300 units. 1,700B (US$43/£24) double; from 4,000B (US$100/£56) suite. AE, MC, V. **Amenities:** 2 restaurants; lobby bar; outdoor pool; tour desk; car rental; courtesy car or limo; salon; 24-hr. room service; laundry service; dry cleaning. *In room:* A/C, satellite TV w/in-house movies, minibar.

THE BUSINESS DISTRICT

Don't be put off by the "business district" name, which is merely to distinguish this area from the others. This part of town is connected by skytrain and subway and is home of Silom Road, the center of Bangkok nightlife.

Very Expensive

Metropolitan, Bangkok ⍟ The Metropolitan is fashioned after the famed property in London and is one of Bangkok's hippest houses of style, home to those who took Corey Hart's '80s hit "I Wear My Sunglasses at Night" literally. The chic, modular lobby and crisply dressed staff could easily be mistaken for the velvet-rope crowd at an upscale urban club. Rooms are elegantly angular and quite stark at first glance. It takes a little getting used to, but there are lots of warm touches, like earth-toned fabrics and overstuffed pillows, to offset the crisp, contemporary lines. Bathrooms are large, with big sunken tubs. This is a stylish little getaway with some cool dining choices and a slick bar for you and your sunglasses-bedecked brethren to check out.

27 S. Sathorn Rd., Tungmahamek, Sathorn, Bangkok 10120. (C) **02625-3320.** Fax 02625-3320. www.metropolitan. como.bz. 171 units. US$240–US$300 (£132–£165) double; from US$1,499 (£824) suite. AE, MC, V. Short cab ride from Sala Daeng BTS station, soon just a short walk to the Lumpini subway stop. **Amenities:** 2 restaurants; bar; outdoor pool; great fitness center; spa w/massage, Jacuzzi, sauna, and steam; airport transfer; business center w/Internet access; shopping arcade; 24-hr. room service; laundry service; dry cleaning. *In room:* A/C, satellite TV w/DVD and CD players, wireless Internet access, minibar, fridge, safe, IDD phone.

The Sukhothai 𝒞𝒞𝒞 Find a welcome, if studied, serenity in this hotel's maze of low pavilions, contemporary lines, and earthy textures and tones. Broad, colonnaded public spaces surround peaceful lotus pools. Symmetry and simplicity form the back-drop for brick *chedis* (stupas or mounds), terra-cotta friezes, and celadon ceramics evoking the ancient kingdom of Sukhothai. Large guest rooms are done in fine Thai silk, mellow teak, and celadon tile. Gigantic luxurious bathrooms feature oversize tubs, separate shower and toilet stalls, and two full-size wardrobes. The Sukhothai is second to none in service and privacy, and now offers an indulgent spa experience as well.

13/3 S. Sathorn Rd., Bangkok 10120 (south of Lumphini Park, near intersection of Rama IV and Wireless roads, next to the YWCA). (C) **02287-0222.** Fax 02287-4980. www.sukhothai.com. 220 units. 11,900B (US$298/£167) double; from 15,600 (US$390/£218) suite. AE, DC, MC, V. **Amenities:** 4 restaurants; bar and lobby lounge; 25m (82-ft.) out-door pool; outdoor lighted tennis court; air-conditioned racquetball court; state-of-the-art fitness center w/Jacuzzi, sauna, steam, massage, and aerobics classes; concierge; limo service; 24-hr. business center w/cutting-edge technol-ogy; salon; 24-hr. room service; babysitting; executive-level rooms. *In room:* A/C, satellite TV w/in-house movies, fax, dataport w/direct Internet access, hair dryer, safe, IDD phone.

Expensive

The Dusit Thani, Bangkok 𝒞 "The Dusit" was once the city's grandest address, but Bangkok has built up around the old girl, and now the Dusit lies in the shadow of the skytrain and a hulking highway flyover. Still, the location is one of the best, just at the edge of the busiest part of Silom Road and a short walk from the skytrain, sub-way, and Lumpini Park. The lobby has splashing fountains, and the large outdoor pool is surrounded by thick foliage—a great escape after a day of sightseeing. Renovated rooms have brought the Dusit into the 21st century: They eschew the traditional Thai motif of years past for a more up-to-date business look, with club rooms adding high-speed Internet access and flatscreen TVs. The common areas are now the sole reposi-tories of Thai decor, but even these are being modernized. The Devarana spa is world class, and there are numerous quality in-house dining choices as well.

Rama IV Rd., Bangkok 10500 (at corner of Silom and Rama IV rds., opposite Lumpini Park). (C) **02236-0450.** Fax 02236-6400. http://bangkok.dusit.com. 532 units. US$220–US$280 (£121–£154) double; from 10,660B (US$267/£149) suite. AE, DC, MC, V. Near Sala Daeng BTS station. **Amenities:** 8 restaurants; lounge; bar; library w/high tea; small landscaped pool; driving range and chipping green; fitness center; spa w/massage, sauna, steam, and cafe; concierge; limo service; business center; shopping arcade; salon; 24-hr. room service; babysitting; laundry service; dry cleaning; executive-level rooms. *In room:* A/C, satellite TV w/VCR, Internet access, minibar, fridge, hair dryer, safe, IDD phone.

Montien Hotel Bangkok 𝒞 The Montien is a slick and comfortable business hotel in the very heart of Silom, right at the terminus of the two busy Patpong *sois.* Set up in two large wings, each with dark teak hallways and bright, pleasant rooms, the Montien has seen some good upgrades in recent years and offers lots of services and upmarket amenities at a price that would put you in a dull cell in other parts of the world. Unique here, too, are the resident psychics at the mezzanine level's Astrologers' Terrace, open daily from 10:30am to 7pm.

54 Surawong Rd., Bangkok 10500 (near Patpong). ℂ **02233-7060**. Fax 02236-5218. www.montien.com. 475 units. 6,000B–8,000B (US$150–US$200/£84–£112) double; from 9,000B (US$225/£126) suite. AE, DC, MC, V. 10-min. walk to Sala Daeng BTS station. **Amenities:** 3 restaurants; bar; lounge and karaoke; outdoor pool; fitness center w/sauna; tour desk; limo service; business center; 24-hr. room service; babysitting; laundry service; dry cleaning; executive-level rooms. *In room:* A/C, satellite TV, Internet access, minibar, fridge, hair dryer, safe, IDD phone.

Inexpensive

Bangkok Christian Guesthouse A wholesome yin to the debaucherous yang of the nearby red-light district, the Bangkok Christian Guesthouse is on a small *soi* just one street back from Sala Daeng BTS station and is a convenient, quiet, and comfortable choice (just a short walk from sin to salvation, or vice versa). This tranquil two-story guesthouse, originally a Presbyterian missionary residence, was converted into a lodge in the late 1960s, and is now operated by the Church of Christ in Thailand. The recently refurbished rooms are large and simple. The best ones are on the second floor overlooking the large lawn, with its sitting area, goldfish pond, and teak pavilion. Amenities include a cozy lounge and library, an affordable canteen restaurant, and a friendly and helpful staff.

123 Saladaeng, Soi 2, Convent Rd., Bangkok 10500 (1 block south of Silom Rd. off the corner of Convent Rd.). ℂ **02233-6303**. Fax 02237-1742. www.bcgh.org. 30 units. 1,540B (US$39/£22) double; 1,980B (US$50/£28) triple. No credit cards. 10-min. walk to Sala Daeng BTS station. **Amenities:** Restaurant; laundry service. *In room:* A/C, no phone.

SUKHUMVIT ROAD: THE SHOPPING/EMBASSY AREA

Accessed along its entire length by the convenient skytrain, Sukhumvit Road is the heart of upscale, commercial Bangkok. Here you'll find many of the town's finest large shopping complexes, good restaurants, and thronging street life.

Very Expensive

Four Seasons Hotel Bangkok ★★★ The Four Seasons is a modern palace. The entry is grand, with a sweeping staircase, giant Thai murals, and gold sunbursts on the vaulted ceiling. The impeccable service begins at the threshold, and an air of luxury pervades any stay in this modern city resort. Rooms are some of the most spacious in town, with Thai murals, plush carpeted dressing areas, and large bathrooms. Unique cabana rooms face the pool and terrace area, which is filled with palms, lotus pools, and all sorts of tropical greenery. If you can ignore the new condominium blocks overlooking the area, this is a real hideaway. The Four Seasons Spa is one of the best in Bangkok, and the in-house dining is excellent. The executive upgrade for just US$35 (£19) is more than worth it

155 Ratchadamri Rd., Bangkok 10330 (just south of Rama I Rd.). ℂ **02254-1000** or 02251-6127. Fax 02253-9195. www.fourseasons.com. 353 units. US$280–US$320 (£154–£176) double; US$420–US$490 (£231–£270) cabana room/suite; from US$540 (£297) suite. AE, DC, MC, V. Adjacent to Ratchadamri BTS station. **Amenities:** 7 restaurants; lobby lounge w/high tea and live jazz; landscaped outdoor pool; state-of-the-art fitness center; spa w/massage, sauna, and steam; limo service; concierge; 24-hr. business center; shopping arcade (w/Jim Thompson Silk); salon; 24-hr. room service; babysitting; laundry service; dry cleaning; nonsmoking rooms; executive-level rooms. *In room:* A/C, satellite TV, dataport, minibar, hair dryer, safe, IDD phone, iPod.

Grand Hyatt Erawan Bangkok ★★★ Bangkok's old grande dame, the Grand Hyatt is tops in comfort, convenience, and style. Don't miss the hotel shrine, a monument to prosperity and good luck dating from the 1956 construction of the hotel. Public spaces are grand, with giant columns, balustrade staircases, and rich indoor landscaping. The works of dozens of contemporary Thai artists grace hallways and spacious guest rooms, where earth-toned silks, celadon accessories, antique-finish furnishings, parquet floors, Oriental rugs, large bathrooms, and city views abound. Accommodations have just been given a technological upgrade and now feature individual reading lights, Internet access, and compact control panels. In addition to the facilities one expects from a five-star hotel, there is a delightful fifth-floor pool terrace here, where a waterfall tumbles down a rocky wall into a full-size hot tub. The in-house dining is some of the best in the city.

494 Ratchadamri Rd., Bangkok 10330 (corner of Rama I Rd.). ℂ **800/233-1234** or 02254-1234. Fax 02254-6308. www.bangkok.grand.hyatt.com. 387 units. US$290–US$305 (£160–£168) double; US$545 (£300) suite. AE, DC, MC, V. 5-min. walk to Chit Lom BTS station. **Amenities:** 8 restaurants; lounge; disco; wine bar; rooftop pool and garden; outdoor grass tennis court; 2 squash courts; fitness center w/Jacuzzi, sauna, steam, and massage; spa; concierge; tour desk; limo and helicopter service; 24-hr. business center; shopping arcade; salon; 24-hr. room service; babysitting; laundry service; dry cleaning; nonsmoking rooms; executive-level rooms. *In room:* A/C, satellite TV, dataport, minibar, hair dryer, safe, IDD phone.

Inter-Continental Bangkok ⟨★★⟩

Formerly Le Meridien, the Inter-Continental has a great location near Chit Lom BTS station and downtown shopping. Rooms are immaculate, done in a bland but familiar business-hotel style and set in a glass-and-steel tower block with unobstructed views of the city. High-end suites are without rival, and service is ultraprofessional and attentive. You pay a premium here, but you get perks like wireless Internet access, excellent amenities, and fine dining; don't miss its branch of the popular Shin Daikoku Japanese restaurant.

973 Ploenchit Rd., Lumphini, Pathumwan, Bangkok 10330 (near intersection of Rama I and Ratchadamri rds). ℂ **800/225-5843** or 02656-0444. Fax 02656-0555. www.intercontinental.com. 381 units. US$300–US$350 (£165–£193) double; from US$360 (£198) suite. AE, DC, MC, V. Adjacent to Chit Lom BTS station. **Amenities:** 3 restaurants; tower lounge w/live music; karaoke; rooftop pool; health club; spa w/Jacuzzi, sauna, steam, massage, and beauty treatments; concierge; tour desk; car rental; limo service; business center; shopping arcade; salon; 24-hr. room service; babysitting; laundry service; dry cleaning; nonsmoking rooms; executive-level rooms. *In room:* A/C, satellite TV, dataport, minibar, fridge, coffeemaker, hair dryer, safe, IDD phone.

JW Marriott Bangkok ⟨★★⟩

If you're looking for luxury but also need to stay wired for business back home (or you just have a bunch of high-tech gadgets), look no further than the JW Marriott. All rooms and common areas have wireless Internet access, and executive-level guests enjoy a plush lounge of their own. The JW has recently added a new class of rooms with the Disneyesque moniker "Rooms of the Future." Less grand than the name implies, these rooms are decorated in a pleasing contemporary style with the plush bedding common to all Marriott properties and large marble-laden bathrooms. What makes them unique are the power strips that allow you to hook up your electronic devices to the room's flatscreen TV. The technology is by no means "futuristic," but it is extremely convenient: You can hook up your camera and iPod and reminisce about your Asian adventures, with your favorite tunes as a soundtrack. For those looking for less sedentary perks, the hotel has an extensive health club with an attached juice bar. In-house dining is some of the best in the city, and the skytrain is but a short walk away.

4 Sukhumvit Rd., Soi 2, Bangkok 10110. ℂ **02656-7700**. Fax 02656-7711. www.marriott.com. 441 units. 6,800B (US$170/£95) superior; 8,800 B (US$220/£123) executive; from 11,400B (US$285/£160) suite. AE, DC, MC, V. Ploenchit BTS station. **Amenities:** 5 restaurants; 3 bars; outdoor pool; fitness center; spa w/sauna, steam, and attached juice bar; concierge; car rental; limo service; salon; 24-hr room service; babysitting; laundry service; dry cleaning. *In room:* A/C, satellite TV, dataport, minibar, coffeemaker, hair dryer, safe, IDD phone.

Expensive

Amari Boulevard Hotel ⟨★⟩

In the heart of the busy Nana shopping area of Sukhumvit Road (near the BTS Nana station), the Amari Boulevard is a good value.

The Krung Thep Wing has spacious rooms with terrific city views, while the original has less expensive rooms, some with balcony. Also see its popular business address, the nearby **Amari Watergate** (✆ 02653-9000).

2 Soi 5, Sukhumvit Rd., Bangkok 10110 (north of Sukhumvit Rd., on Soi 5). ✆ **02255-2930.** Fax 02255-2950. www.amari.com. 315 units. US$205–US$265 (£113–£146) double; US$375 (£206) suite. AE, DC, MC, V. 5-min. walk to Nana BTS station. **Amenities:** Restaurant; rooftop pool; fitness center; concierge; tour desk; limo service; business center; 24-hr. room service; massage; babysitting; laundry service; dry cleaning. *In room:* A/C, satellite TV, minibar, fridge, safe, IDD phone.

Novotel Bangkok on Siam Square ★★ This elegant and opulent high-rise hotel in the Siam Square shopping area is one of this French chain's best. The marble-and-glass entrance leads to an expansive gray-stone interior, complemented by soft leather sofas and chairs. Renovated guest rooms are sharp: business chic dominated by purples and dark blues, minus superfluous Thai touches. Bathrooms have the TV's sound wired in, which is wholly unnecessary yet strangely satisfying. Novotel is perfect for business or shopping trips and close to the skytrain. Don't miss the popular disco.

Siam Sq. Soi 6, Bangkok 10330 (in Siam Sq. off Rama I Rd.). ✆ **02255-6888.** Fax 02254-1328. www.novotel.com or www.novotelbkk.com. 465 units. 6,120B–7,650B (US$153–US$191/£86–£107) double; from 7,200B (US$180/£101) suite. AE, DC, MC, V. Siam BTS station. **Amenities:** 4 restaurants; huge popular disco; outdoor pool; fitness center w/massage; concierge; tour desk; limo service; business center w/Internet access; shopping arcade; salon; 24-hr. room service; babysitting; laundry service; dry cleaning; nonsmoking rooms; executive-level rooms. *In room:* A/C, satellite TV, minibar, fridge, safe, IDD phone.

Moderate

Majestic Grande ★★ *Value* For location and price, you can't beat the Majestic Grande. Just off busy Sukhumvit Road and a short walk or shorter complimentary tuk-tuk ride to the skytrain, the Majestic is perfect for shoppers, sightseers, and partyers alike. Rooms are smaller than those in the more expensive hotels in the area, but they are modern and super-clean. Wood flooring around the beds is flanked by smooth marble leading to tidy bathrooms, some with separate tubs and showers. Facilities are also on the small side, but are all present and accounted for: pool, fitness center, business center, and two restaurants. A highly professional staff round out the plaudits, making the Majestic the top mid-range choice on Sukhumvit.

12 Sukhumvit Soi 2, Bangkok 10110 (just south of Sukhumvit Rd.). ✆ **02262-2999.** Fax 02262-2900. www.majesticgrande.com. 251 units. 3,200B–4,200B (US$80–US$105/£45–£59) double; 4,400B–5,400B (US$110–US$135/£62–£76) executive double; from 6,700B (US$168/£94) suite. AE, DC, MC, V. 5-min. walk from Ploenchit BTS station. **Amenities:** 2 restaurants; lobby lounge; small outdoor pool; fitness center w/sauna, steam, Jacuzzi, and massage; concierge; tour desk; car rental; business center; 24-hr. room service; babysitting; laundry service; dry cleaning. *In room:* A/C, satellite TV, wireless and broadband Internet access, minibar, safe, coffeemaker, hair dryer, IDD phone.

Tai-Pan Hotel This modern white tower rises above a quiet *soi* off Sukhumvit (which means the city is your oyster). Rooms have comfortable sitting areas, city views, and all the facilities you'd expect from a more expensive hotel. Recent renovations have added new beds and fresh carpeting, as well as a small day spa. The excellent coffee shop has bargain buffet breakfasts and lunches. The staff is attentive and helpful.

25 Sukhumvit Soi 23, Bangkok 10110 (1 block north of Sukhumvit Rd.). ✆ **02260-9888.** Fax 02259-7908. www.taipanhotel.com. 150 units. 4,400B (US$110/£62) double; 6,000B (US$150/£84) deluxe; from 8,000B (US$200/£112) suite. AE, DC, MC, V. 10-min. walk to Asok BTS station. **Amenities:** Coffee shop; small pool; small fitness center; spa; business center w/Internet access; 24-hr. room service; laundry service; dry cleaning. *In room:* A/C, satellite TV, minibar, fridge, IDD phone.

Inexpensive
The Atlanta Hotel *(Finds)*   This is the first hotel I stayed at in Bangkok and is still one of my favorites. A great budget choice, the Atlanta is a real slice of history. The oldest "original" hotel in the city (without renovation), the Atlanta was built in 1952 by Dr. Max Henne, a Renaissance man and early expat; it's now managed by his son. For years the Atlanta was *the* foreign visitor's address of note. The lobby is original Art Deco and quite unique. Enjoy fine Thai food in the canteen (guests only), grab a book from the small library, or take in a film—a good youth-hostel vibe pervades. Rooms are concrete basic, and only a few suites have hot water. Service is quirky (a sign explains: NO COMPLAINTS AT THESE PRICES), and the "no drugs and no sex tourism" policy tends to the holier-than-thou. It seems that the staff considers all Asian women prostitutes, so even if you're married, mixed-race couples tend to get a less than welcome reception. The works of journalists and photographers in residence line the walls. The hotel is often full, so it's best to book ahead by fax.

78 Soi 2, Sukhumvit Rd., Bangkok 10110 (at the very end of Soi 2, a 5- to 10-min. walk or a 10B/US25¢/£0.15 motorbike taxi ride). ℭ **02252-6069.** Fax 02656-8123. www.theatlantahotel.bizland.com. 49 units. 450B–600B (US$11–US$15/£6.30–£8.40) fan room; 550B–700B (US$14–US$18/£7.70–£9.80) A/C double. No credit cards. **Amenities:** Restaurant; small outdoor pool; small gym area; good tour desk; laundry service; Internet access; library (w/light table for photographers). *In room:* A/C, safe (bring your own lock).

THE AIRPORT AREA
Until the new airport's skytrain link begins service (scheduled for 2008), Suvarnabhumi's sole access to Bangkok is by road. It will take anywhere from 45 to 90 minutes to get to destinations in the city center, depending on traffic.

Novotel Suvarnabhumi Airport Hotel *(★)*   The Novotel is the only show in town at Suvarnabhumi. Once the BTS train begins operation, the hotel will be connected to the airport terminal by way of underground walkway, but until then frequent shuttle buses leave from outside the arrivals area and will return you to the airport any time of day or night. The Novotel is as much a business hotel as a layover spot, sporting extensive convention and business facilities. Rooms are comfortable affairs, with soothing carpeting and large marble bathrooms. The spa has treatments catering to the weary traveler. Day rates are also available, allowing visitors access to all hotel facilities.

999 Suvarnabhumi Airport Hotel, Moo 1 Nongprue Bang Phli, Bangkok 10541. ℭ **02131-1111.** Fax 02131-1188. www.novotel.com. 612 units. 5,000B (US$125/£70) deluxe; 6,200 (US$155/£87) executive deluxe; 8,500B (US$213/£119) suite. Day rates from 4,500B (US$113/£63). **Amenities:** 4 restaurants; lobby lounge; coffee shop; outdoor pool; fitness center; spa w/massage and beauty treatments; concierge; tour desk; car rental; business center; salon; 24-hr. room service; children's programs; babysitting; laundry service; dry cleaning. *In room:* A/C, satellite TV, wireless and broadband Internet access, minibar, hair dryer, safe, IDD phone.

WHERE TO DINE
If you like your local Thai restaurant back home, you'll love the many choices in Bangkok, from simple noodle stands to sophisticated, upmarket joints. The city also offers a spectacular array of excellent European, Chinese, and other Asian cuisine that is expensive by local standards but a bargain in the West. Check local papers for any big "foodie" events, and get brave and try street food.

ALONG THE RIVER
Very Expensive
Le Normandie *(★★★)* FRENCH   The ultra-elegant Normandie, atop the renowned Oriental hotel, with its panoramic views, is the apex in formal dining in Thailand. The

room glistens in gold and silver, from place settings to chandeliers. Some of the highest-rated master chefs from France have made guest appearances here, adding their own unique touches to the menu. Choose from a limited selection of daily specials. The beef filet main course, in a red-wine sauce, is divine. The set menu includes a cheese course, coffee, and a sinful dessert. Order any wine you can imagine from the extensive list.

At the Oriental, 48 Oriental Ave. (off Charoen Krung/New Rd., overlooking the river). © 02236-0400. Reservations required at least 1 day in advance. Jacket/tie required for men. Main courses 850B–3,500B (US$21–US$88/£12–£49); set menu w/wine selections 5,200B (US$130/£73). AE, DC, MC, V. Daily noon–2:30pm and 7–10pm (closed Sun lunch). 10-min. walk from Saphan Taksin BTS station.

Expensive

Blue Elephant ⚔ THAI   The Blue Elephant franchises have been serving their brand of royal Thai cuisine throughout Europe and the Middle East since 1980. It was only in 2002 that the company opened a branch in Bangkok. Set in a 100-year-old colonial building that served as the Imperial Japanese Command Center during World War II, the restaurant is an oasis of refinement on busy South Sathorn Road. The dining rooms are decorated with traditional Thai-style statues and carvings, but they retain their colonial charm. The menu is a mix of classic Thai recipes and the chefs' original creations. If you have any questions about a particular dish, a member of the very professional waitstaff is always eager to assist.

The Blue Elephant has an excellent cooking school on the third floor of the building (see "Cultural Pursuits," p. 121). Also look for the Blue Elephant Cafe on the fourth floor of Siam Paragon mall.

233 S. Sathorn Rd. © 02673-9353. Reservations recommended. Main courses 190B–680B (US$4.75–US$17/£2.65–£9.50); set menus 980B–1300B (US$25–US$33/£14–£18). AE, DC, MC, V. Daily 11:30am–2:30pm and 6:30–10:30pm. Surasak BTS station.

Salathip ⚔⚔ THAI   Salathip, on the river terrace of the Shangri-La Hotel, is arguably Bangkok's most romantic Thai restaurant. Classical music and traditional

---

Moments   Dinner & Lunch Cruises on the Chao Phraya

While there are a number of tour operators that offer dinner cruises along the Chao Phraya, if you want to eat the finest food, I have only one solid recommendation. The **_Manohra_** ⚔⚔, a converted antique rice barge, cruises the river nightly, serving a six-course Thai dinner that's delicious (and not overly spicy). The quality is excellent, especially considering that most other dinner cruises serve lukewarm, indescribable food. The set menu runs 1,500B (US$38/£21) per person, and _Manohra_ sets sail at 7:30pm (but you can pick it up at the Oriental pier, where it stops at about 7:40pm). Call the **Bangkok Marriott Resort & Spa** (© 02476-0022) for details, and be sure to book in advance to make sure the boat isn't rented out for a private party.

The _Horizon II_ makes daily trips to Ayutthaya and back as well as evening cruises in town for a romantic candlelit meal. Cruises start at just 1,800B (US$45/£25). They leave every Monday, Wednesday, Friday, and Saturday at 8am for all-day trips or 7:30pm for dinner cruises (2,200B/US$55/£31). Contact the **Shangri-La Hotel** (© 02236-7777) for more information.

Tips **Bangkok Street Eats**

Ask any Bangkokian to take you to their favorite restaurant and you'll most likely be eating at street side or in a small, open-air eatery. In fact, the many night bazaars and hawker stalls are where you'll find the best eats throughout Thailand. Eating at street side will challenge your senses with the pungent aromas of garlic, chili, and barbecued meats, as well as the cacophony of music, lights, and voices. For the best open-air dining, try **Thong Lo,** a collection of busy stalls just adjacent to the Thong Lo BTS stop. **Suan Lum Night Bazaar,** next to Lumpini Park, is another good choice.

cuisine are superbly presented in aging, carved-teak pavilions perched over a lotus pond and overlooking the river (there are also air-conditioned dining rooms). Set menus introduce you to a range of courses. Here's an example: Thai spring rolls, pomelo salad with chicken, spicy seafood soup, snapper with chili sauce, and your choice of Thai curries. There is live music nightly as well as Thai dancing and a culture show.

At the Shangri-La Hotel, 89 Soi Wat Suan Plu (overlooking Chao Phraya River, near Taksin Bridge). ✆ 02236-7777. Reservations recommended. Main courses 280B–1,200B (US$8–US$30/£3.90–£17). AE, DC, MC, V. Daily 6:30–10:30pm. Saphan Taksin BTS station.

Moderate
Harmonique 🌟🌟 THAI   Hard to find, Harmonique is set in the courtyard of a century-old mansion and just oozes character—a great stop if you're touring the riverfront or visiting the antiques stores of nearby River City. Enter through the crook of a dangling banyan tree to find courtyard seating and an open-air dining area with Thai antiques. The cuisine is Thai tailored to Western tastes, but it's still very good—the *tom yum* with fish is delicious, served only as spicy as you like and with enormous chunks of fish. The sizzling grilled seafood platter is nice and garlicky (chilis on the side). Harmonique also has good Western desserts like brownies, great with a cool tea on a hot day. It's an atmospheric spot to relax.

22 Chaoren Krung Rd. (New Rd.), Soi 34. ✆ 02630-6270. Main courses 70B–200B (US$1.75–US$5/£1–£2.80). AE, MC, V. Mon–Sat 11am–10pm. 15-min. walk from Saphan Taksin BTS station.

BANGLAMPHU & KHAO SAN ROAD
Khao San Road is Bangkok's busy backpacker ghetto and where you'll find every manner of food, from Israeli and halal cuisine to Italian fare to tasty Thai served at street side. Have a seat somewhere along the busy road, order up a fruit shake, and watch the nightly parade of young travelers. **Cafe Primavera** (56 Phra Sumen Rd.; **02281-4718**), across from Phra Sumen Fort, serves excellent pizzas and pastas. Just down the street is **Baan Pla Sod** (114 Phra Ahtit Rd.; ✆ **02629-3339**). The name means "house of fresh fish," and other than a couple tofu dishes, that's all they serve. At this popular dinner spot for locals, no English is spoken, but menus have translations.

Inexpensive
May Kaidee 🌟 *Finds* VEGETARIAN/THAI   Don't come for atmosphere—it's more or less just tables in a little alleyway—but bring your appetite for healthy and delicious Thai vegetarian dishes. Ms. May (pronounced *My*) has developed a real following, as much for her wry smile and kindness as for the great curries and soups

she serves. The best *massaman* (potato and peanut) curry in Thailand and an array of dishes—from sweet green curry to good stir-fries—come with your choice of white or a unique short-grained brown rice. For dessert, don't pass up the black sticky rice with mango. May has a good cookbook for sale and also offers cooking classes. Look for her second location at 33Samsen Rd.

At the eastern terminus of Khao San Rd., in a small alley behind the first row of buildings (behind Burger King; ask around—everyone knows this place). ✆ **089137-3173.** Main course 60B–120B (US$1.50–US$3/£0.85–£1.70). No credit cards. Daily 9am–11pm.

THE BUSINESS DISTRICT

Silom Road is where you'll find Patpong, the busy red-light district, a tourist night market, and a host of good dining choices.

Moderate

Baan Khanitha ✫✫ THAI   While the new location on busy Sathorn Road lacks some of the charm of its previous incarnation, Baan Khanitha still offers authentic Thai in a comfortable, classy atmosphere. You'll start off with a free tray of finger foods, the dried condiments for making your own little spicy spring rolls called *mienkham,* and then you'll graduate to shared dishes of curry, from spicy red to mellow yellow and green; light salads; and good seafood as you like it. The pomelo salad is a find. Follow up with good Thai desserts. Thais actually come here, a rarity for upscale Thai eateries, and the place is always packed: both good signs. Be sure to call ahead. There's another location at 36/1 Sukhumvit Soi 23 (✆ **02258-4128**).

69 S. Sathorn Rd. ✆ **02675-4200.** Reservations highly recommended. Main courses 140B–480B (US$3.50–US$12/£1.95–£6.70). AE, MC, V. Daily 11am–2pm and 6–11pm. 5-min. walk from Ploen Chit BTS station.

Mango Tree ✫ THAI   In a lovely 80-year-old Siamese restaurant house with its own tropical garden, the Mango Tree offers a quiet retreat from the hectic Patpong area. Live traditional music and classical Thai decorative touches fill the house with charm, and the attentive staff serves well-prepared dishes from all regions of the country. The mild green chicken curry and the crispy spring rolls are both excellent—but the menu is extensive, so feel free to experiment. Only trouble is, the food isn't exactly authentic—though it's still quite good.

37 Soi Tantawan, Bangrak (off west end of Surawong Rd., across from Tawana Ramada Hotel). ✆ **02236-2820.** Reservations recommended. Main courses 150B–360B (US$3.75–US$9/£2.10–£5.05). AE, DC, MC, V. Daily 11:30am–midnight. 10-min. walk from Sala Daeng BTS station.

Somboon Seafood ✫✫ SEAFOOD   This one's for those who would sacrifice atmosphere for excellent food. Though it's packed nightly, you'll still be able to find a table, as the place is huge. The staff is extremely friendly—between them and the picture menu, you'll be able to order the best dishes and get the finest recommendations. Peruse the large aquariums outside to see all the live seafood options, such as prawn, fishes, lobsters, and crabs (guaranteed freshness). The house specialty, chili crab curry, is especially good, as is the *tom yang goong* soup (spiced to individual taste).

169/7–11 Surawongse Rd. (just across from the Peugeot building). ✆ **02233-3104.** Reservations not necessary. Seafood at market prices (about 800B/US$20/£11 for 2 people). No credit cards. Daily 4–11pm.

SUKHUMVIT ROAD: THE SHOPPING/EMBASSY AREA

Expensive

Bed Supperclub ✫✫ INTERNATIONAL   This is the coolest place in Bangkok, hands down. Come for a drink in the bar, at least, and stick around for when the place busts open into a full-on club. It serves meals at one seating only (8:30pm); the best part is that, as the name suggests, you eat in long shared beds. You walk up a concrete gang-plank to enter the giant cylinder-shaped building via large airplane airlocks. One side of the room is the bar, while the other is the dining area, where you'll be assigned your slot on one of the two big beds that line the walls. The two-story, glowing white-and-neon interior alone is unique. Four-course meals are ordered from a limited menu. Dessert is pure decadence of rich chocolate specials and cakes. The waitstaff wears tight spacesuits and angel wings, the music is funky trance spun by a DJ, and the food is fantastic.

26 Sukhumvit Soi 11, Klongtoey-Nua (at the end of Soi 11). © 02651-3537. www.bedsupperclub.com. Reservations required. Men should wear trousers, not shorts. Set menu 1,350B (US$34/£19) Tues–Thurs; 1,750B (US$44/£25) Fri–Sat. AE, MC, V. Tues–Thurs 7:30pm–midnight; Fri–Sat 7:30pm–2am. Dinner served promptly at 8:30pm (best to be early). Nana BTS station.

Koi 🐟🐟 JAPANESE   Modern modular Japanese pavilions set in a quiet, fountain-laden garden. Slick black and blood-red interior, moody candle lighting, beautiful people doing beautiful-people things at the bar. A case of style over substance, maybe? Not at all. One of the hippest new restaurants in the city, Koi serves outstanding Japanese food with subtle California twists and some of the best sushi in town. One of the house specialty rolls is braised shrimp over a California roll. Someone less mature than me would describe it thusly—a circular sushi fort guarding helpless teriyaki shrimp, mushrooms, and asparagus—but I won't. Both this less mature indi-vidual and I would, however, describe it as delicious—as we would anything on the menu containing the words "sushi" or "chocolate cake." The service is decidedly unpretentious for a restaurant of such style, but if you see a waiter wearing anything besides solid black, I'll buy you a shot of sake.

26 Sukhumvit Soi 20, Klongtoey (a 5-min. walk down Soi 20). © 02258-1590. www.koirestaurantbkk.com. Reser-vations recommended. Main courses 320B–2,300B (US$4–US$58/£4.50–£32). AE, MC, V. Tues–Sat 6pm–midnight. Asok BTS station.

Le Banyan 🐟🐟 FRENCH   A spreading banyan tree on the edge of the gardenlike grounds inspires the name. The upscale dining area is warm in tone, furnished with sisal matting and white-clapboard walls adorned with Thai carvings, old photos, and prints of early Bangkok. The house special is a dish for two: pressed duck with goose liver, shallots, wine, and Armagnac to make the sauce. Other fine choices include a rack of lamb a la Provençal and salmon with lemongrass. There are daily specials and a list of fine wines as well. If you come on foot, you'll run the gauntlet of all the girly bars at the entrance of the *soi,* but find this little upscale gem and enjoy an evening of fine dining and effusive service.

59 Sukhumvit Soi 8 (1 block south of Sukhumvit Rd.). © 02253-5556. www.le-banyan.com. Reservations recom-mended. Main courses 400B–1,300B (US$10–US$33/£5.60–£18). AE, DC, MC, V. Mon–Sat 6–10pm. 10-min. walk from Nana BTS station.

Tips **Dinner & Dance**

For an evening of Thai culture and cuisine, try the **Sala Rim Nam,** at the Orien-tal (© 02236-0400), which stages Thai dance performances. An opulent evening night out here costs 1,850B (US$46/£26) per person. An affordable cultural evening can be found at the **Supatra River House** (© 02411-0305) on Friday and Saturday nights; call ahead for details

---

Tips **Cricket, anyone?**

Grasshoppers, beetles that look like cockroaches, scorpions, ants, and grubs are a favorite snack for folks from Isan, in the northeast, where bugs are in fact cultivated for the dining table and are an important source of protein. Don't miss the snack stands selling these on Sukhumvit or Khao San. How do they taste? Crickets are like popcorn, and the beetles are something like—hate to say it— crispy chicken. A great photo op.

Maha Naga 👁️👁️ THAI/WESTERN FUSION   Classy Maha Naga is an oasis of luxury Thai dining in the heart of the Sukhumvit area. The restaurant design features a fountain courtyard surrounded by high-peaked, lavishly decorated, and air-conditioned Thai pavilions—it makes for a quiet, romantic evening or a fun night for private groups. The food is delicious, a bold marriage of Thai and Western traditions in unique dishes like pork chops with spicy Thai *som tam* (papaya salad) flavor, whole lobster done in a chili sauce, or imported New Zealand grilled filet with Thai spice and mint. Elsewhere, fusion dishes come out rather bland, but the unique fare at Maha Naga breaks new ground.

2 Sukhumvit Soi 29, Klongtoey. ℂ **02662-3060**. Reservations recommended. Main courses 350B–950B (US$8.75–US$24/£4.90–£13). AE, DC, MC, V. Daily 11:30am–2:30pm and 6–11pm. 10-min. walk south from Phrom Pong BTS station.

Moderate

Kuppa 👁️ INTERNATIONAL   This cafe restaurant in a quiet neighborhood is worth a visit if only to see the unique space, a former warehouse (and reputedly a C.I.A. hangout). Now its chic, modern interior houses the offices of owner and interior designer Robin Lourvanij, who shares her time and heart between Bangkok and Australia. Come for the coffee and don't miss the hulking roaster machine, a centerpiece of the dining area where Kuppa roasts its own blend weekly. The food is delicious: a healthy sampling of unique Thai and Western fare and good stuff to fill the homesick tummies of expats and visitors. Grilled items are great, there are lots of weekly specials, and guest chefs from Australia make periodic visits. Dessert is something sinful with good coffee. A second location can be found in the Playground! shopping center at 818 Soi Sukhumvit 55 (ℂ **02714-9517**).

39 Sukhumvit Soi 16, Klongtoey (a 10 min. walk down Soi 16). ℂ **02663-0495**. Main courses 165B–695B (US$4.15–US$17/£2.30–£9.75). AE, MC, V. Tues–Sun 10:30am–10:30pm. Asok BTS station.

Lemongrass 👁️👁️ THAI   Nouvelle Thai cuisine tailored to Western tastes is the specialty of this pleasant restaurant. Just a short walk from the skytrain (near Phrom Pong) and right across from the hulking Emporium shopping center, Lemongrass is set in a small Thai mansion handsomely converted and furnished with antiques. A visit here makes it easy to forget busy Bangkok outside. Try house favorites pomelo salad or chicken satay. Also excellent are the *tom yang kung* (a spicy sweet-and-sour prawn soup with ginger shoots) and the tender, juicy lemongrass chicken.

5/1 Sukhumvit Soi 24 (south of Sukhumvit Rd. on Soi 24). ℂ 02258-8637. Reservations highly recommended. Main courses 150B–455B (US$3.75–US$11/£2.10–£6.40). AE, DC, MC, V. Daily 11am–2pm and 6–11pm. Phrom Pong BTS station.

L'Opera 👁️ ITALIAN   With its sister restaurant in Vientiane, Laos, L'Opera Bangkok has been hosting visitors and expats since it first opened in the 1970s—back when Soi 39 was but a dusty little alley with cows grazing out front. Now it's a sophis-ticated enclave and it's got the formula just right: dim lights in a glassed-in pavilion, cool jazz in the air, and good, affordable Italian. Come with friends and fill the table. Start with a decadent seafood salad. For a main course, go for the fresh fish done as you like or any of the grilled items or fine pastas.

53 Sukhumvit Soi 39, Klongtoey. ⓒ **02258-5606**. Main courses 200B–900B (US$5–US$23/£2.80–£13). AE, MC, V. Daily 6–11pm. 15-min. walk or 30B tuk-tuk ride from Phrom Pong BTS station.

Inexpensive

Abyssinya Cafe 𝒦 *Finds* ETHIOPIAN Confession: Before eating at Abyssinya, I had never eaten Ethiopian food—or even thought about Ethiopian food for that mat-ter. All dishes here are served on a homemade flatbread called *injera* and prepared with spices imported from Addis Abbaba. No utensils, only hands. The restaurant was opened by Tigist Fekade, an Ethiopian native, because she couldn't find coffee in Bangkok that compared with the stuff back home. (Fun fact: Coffee is named after the Kaffa region of Ethiopia.) True enough, the coffee is amazing, and every Saturday and Sunday the cafe holds a coffee ceremony where coffee freshly roasted and brewed over a charcoal fire is served to a diverse mix of people from around the world. Like the cafe itself, the ceremony is a unique experience and a crash course in Ethiopian culture.

16/11 Sukhumvit Soi 3 (a 5-min. walk down Soi 3, just past the Grace Hotel). ⓒ **02655-3436**. Main courses 200B–250B (US$5–US$6/£2.80–£3.50). AE, MC, V. Daily 11am–10pm.

Cabbages & Condoms 𝒦𝒦 THAI Here's a theme restaurant with a purpose. Opened by local hero Mechai Viravaidya, founder of the Population & Community Development Association, the restaurant helps fund population control, AIDS awareness, and a host of rural development programs. Set in a large compound, the two-story restaurant has air-conditioned indoor dining—but if you sit on the garden terrace, you'll be in a fairyland of twinkling lights: quite romantic. Share a whole fish done as you like or, for something on the sweet side, try the *gaang kua goong sapparot* (a sweet curry with shrimp and pineapple). There's also a large selection of vegetable and bean-curd entrees. Before you leave, be sure to check out the gift shop's whimsi-cal condom-related merchandise. The restaurant hands out condoms instead of din-ner mints.

10 Sukhumvit Soi 12. ⓒ **02229-4610**. Reservations recommended. 100B–450B (US$2.50–US$11/£1.40–£6.30). AE, DC, MC, V. Daily 11am–10pm. 15-min. walk from Asok BTS station.

Crepes & Co. 𝒦𝒦 *Kids* EUROPEAN Popular among Bangkok foreign residents (and their kids), this is the place to satisfy that sweet tooth. Crepes & Co. serves them up light and fluffy and filled with any of dozens of combinations, both savory and sweet—all of them delicious. It also has good Mediterranean main courses, great cof-fee, and a nice selection of tea. Everything is excellent.

18/1 Sukhumvit Soi 12. ⓒ **02653-3990**. Reservations recommended. Main courses 110B–495B (US$3–US$13/£1.55–£6.95). AE, DC, MC, V. Mon–Sat 9am–midnight; Sun 8am–midnight. 15-min. walk from Asok BTS station.

WHAT TO SEE & DO

When Rama I established Bangkok as the new capital city in the 1780s, he built a new palace and royal temple on the banks of the Chao Phraya River. The city sprang up around the palace and spread outward from this point as population and wealth grew. Today, this area contains most of Bangkok's major historic sights, including a great number of *wats,* or Buddhist temples, that were built during the last 200 years. If

Confident, O Merciful Fat

ing to you. I beg you to gra

sion, the special favour I no

make known by miracles th

Heaven, so that she may be

Church on earth, through C

you're short on time, the most interesting and easily accessible wats to catch are Wat Phra Kaeo, the royal wat that houses the Emerald Buddha at the Grand Palace, and Wat Po, home of the reclining Buddha.

BANGKOK'S WATERWAYS

The history of Bangkok was written on its waterways, and Bangkok was once known as the "Venice of the East." Most of these *klongs* have been paved over, but the magnificent Chao Phraya River (River of Kings) cuts through the heart of the city. On the Thonburi side (opposite Bangkok), the labyrinthine canals offer an intimate glimpse of traditional Thai life. You'll see people using the river to bathe and wash their clothes; floating kitchens in sampans serve rice and noodles to customers in other boats. Hire a private boat to see the busy riverside area in style and to tour the narrow canals of neighboring Thonburi. Boat charter is available anywhere, really, and the touts will find you, especially at the main sites. It is best to arrange hourly trips at the riverfront kiosk near the **River City** shopping mall, at the **Grand Palace** (℡ **02225-6179**), or at the skytrain exit at the **Saphan Taksin BTS station.** Trips cost 900B (US$23/£13) per hour, per boat. Be specific about destinations and times.

HISTORIC TREASURES

Grand Palace 💥💥💥   Rama I built the oldest buildings in the square-mile complex when he moved the capital from Thonburi to Bangkok in the 1780s. It was the official residence and housed the offices of the kings until 1946, when the royal family moved to Chitralada Palace. These days, the palace is used only for royal ceremonies. The focal point of the compound is the Chakri Maha Prasad, an intriguing mixture of Victorian architecture topped with a Thai temple-style roof that today houses the ashes of royal family members. The Amarinda Vinichai Hall is the venue for the highest royal ceremonies, including coronations. The Dusit Hall is a perfect example of Thai architecture in the highest order.

Near the river on Na Phra Lan Rd., near Sanam Luang. ℡ **02222-0094**. Admission 250B (US$6.25/£3.50). Price includes Wat Phra Kaeo and the Coin Pavilion inside the Grand Palace grounds, as well as admission to the Vimanmek Palace (near the National Assembly). Daily 8:30am–3:30pm; most individual buildings are closed to the public except on special days proclaimed by the king. Take the Chao Phraya Express Boat to the Tha Chang Pier, then walk east and south.

Jim Thompson's House 💥   Jim Thompson was a New York architect who served in the O.S.S. (Office of Strategic Services, now the C.I.A.) in Thailand during World War II and afterward settled in Bangkok. He almost single-handedly revived Thailand's silk industry, employing Thai Muslims as skilled silk weavers and building up a thriving industry. After expanding his sales to international markets, Thompson mysteriously disappeared in 1967 while vacationing in the Cameron Highlands in Malaysia. Despite extensive investigation, his disappearance has never been resolved.

His Thai house is composed of six linked teakwood houses from central Thailand that were rebuilt according to Thai architectural principles, but with Western additions (such as a staircase and window screens). In some rooms, the floor is made of Italian marble, but the wall panels are pegged teak. Volunteers guide you through rooms filled with Thompson's splendid collection of Khmer sculpture, Chinese porcelain, Burmese carving (especially a 17th-century teak Buddha), and antique Thai scroll paintings.

Soi Kasemsan 2 (on a small soi off Rama I Rd., opposite the National Stadium). ℡ **02216-7368**. Admission 100B (US$2.50/£1.40). Daily 9am–5:30pm.

Exploring Bangkok

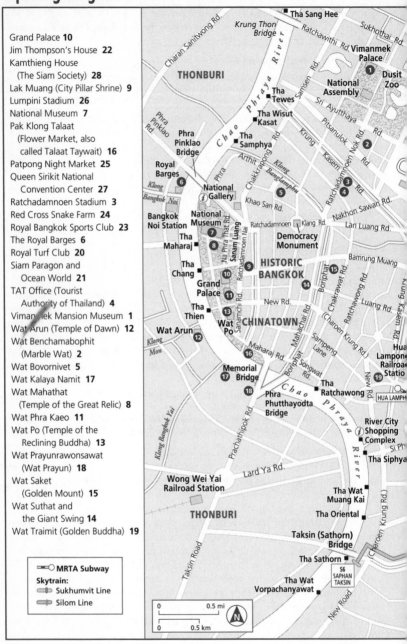

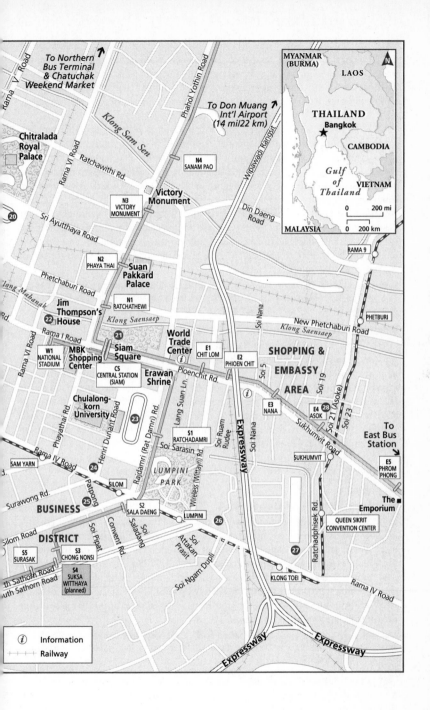

To Northern Bus Terminal & Chatuchak Weekend Market

To Don Muang Int'l Airport (14 mi/22 km)

Chitralada Royal Palace

Klong Sam Sen

Rama V Road
Rama VI Road
Ratchawithi Rd.
Phahol Yothin Road
Wipawadi Rangsit

N4 SANAM PAO

MYANMAR (BURMA) — **LAOS**

THAILAND — Bangkok

CAMBODIA

Gulf of Thailand — **VIETNAM**

MALAYSIA

| 0 | 200 mi |
| 0 | 200 km |

N3 VICTORY MONUMENT

Victory Monument

Sri Ayutthaya Road

Din Daeng Road

20

RAMA 9

N2 PHAYA THAI

Suan Pakkard Palace

Phetchaburi Road

Klang Mahanak

N1 RATCHATHEWI

Jim Thompson's House

22

Rama VI Road

Rama I Road

Klong Saensaep

New Phetchaburi Road

Klong Saensaep

PHETBURI

21

MBK Shopping Center

Siam Square

World Trade Center

E1 CHIT LOM

E2 PHLOEN CHIT

SHOPPING & EMBASSY AREA

Soi Nana

Soi Nana

Soi 5

W1 NATIONAL STADIUM

CS CENTRAL STATION (SIAM)

Erawan Shrine

Ploenchit Rd.

Phayathai Rd.

Chulalong-korn University

Henri Dunant Road

23

Lang Suan Ln.

E3 NANA

Sukhumvit Road

E4 ASOK

28

Soi 19

Soi 21 (Asoke)

Soi 23

To East Bus Station

S1 RATCHADAMRI

Rama IV Road

SAM YARN

24

Rajdamri (Rat Damri) Rd.

Soi Sarasin

LUMPINI PARK

Soi Ruam Rudee

Wireless (Wittayu) Rd.

SUKHUMVIT

E5 PHROM PHONG

The Emporium

Surawong Rd.

25

Patpong

SILOM

BUSINESS

Silom Road

S5 SURASAK

DISTRICT

Soi Pipat

S3 CHONG NONSI

Convent Rd.

Soi Saladang

S2 SALA DAENG

LUMPINI

26

Soi Attakan Prasit

Ratchadphisek Rd.

QUEEN SIKRIT CONVENTION CENTER

27

th Sathorn Road

South Sathorn Road

S4 SUKSA WITTHAYA (planned)

Soi Ngam Dupli

KLONG TOEI

Rama IV Road

Expressway

Expressway

Expressway

ⓘ Information

┼┼┼┼ Railway

National Museum ★★ The National Museum, a short (15-min.) walk north of the Grand Palace and the Temple of the Emerald Buddha, is the country's central treasury of art and archaeology. It was originally the palace that the brother of Rama I built as part of the Grand Palace complex in 1782. Rama V converted the palace into a museum in 1884. Today, it is the largest museum in Southeast Asia and takes quite a lot of time to see.

One important stop is the Red House, a traditional 18th-century Thai building that was originally the living quarters of Princess Sri Sudarak. Another essential stop is the Phuttaisawan (Buddhaisawan) Chapel, built in 1787 to house the Phra Phut Sihing, one of Thailand's most revered Buddha images, brought here from its original home in Chiang Mai. The main building of the royal palace contains gold jewelry, some from the royal collections, and Thai ceramics, including many pieces in the five-color *bencharong* style. The Old Transportation Room has ivory carvings, elephant chairs, and royal palanquins. There are also rooms of royal emblems and insignia, stone carvings, woodcarvings, costumes, textiles, musical instruments, and Buddhist religious artifacts. Fine art and sculpture are found in the newer galleries at the rear of the museum compound.

Na Phra That Rd. (about ½ mile north of the Grand Palace). ✆ 02224-1333. Admission 40B (US$1/£0.55). Wed–Sun 9am–4pm. Free English-language tours: Buddhism/culture Wed 9:30am; art/culture/religion Thurs 9:30am; call the museum or check a newspaper for more details and current schedule.

Vimanmek Mansion Museum ★ Built in 1901 by King Chulalongkorn the Great (Rama V) as the Celestial Residence, this beautiful golden-teakwood mansion was restored in 1982 for Bangkok's bicentennial and was reopened by Queen Sirikit as a private museum with a collection of the royal family's memorabilia. An intriguing and informative 1-hour tour takes you through a series of apartments and rooms (81 in all) in what is said to be the largest teak building in the world—the thought of all that gorgeous teakwood is staggering. The original **Abhisek Dusit Throne Hall** houses a display of Thai handicrafts, and nine other buildings north of the mansion display photographs, clocks, fabrics, royal carriages, and other regalia.

193/2 Ratchavitee Rd., Dusit Palace grounds (opposite the Dusit Zoo, north of the National Assembly Building). ✆ 02281-8166. Admission 100B (US$2.50/£1.40); included in Grand Palace fee. Daily 9am–4pm.

THE WATS

Wat Arun (Temple of Dawn) ★★★ The 86m-high (282-ft.) Khmer-inspired tower rises majestically from the banks of the Chao Phraya, across from Wat Po. This religious complex served as the royal chapel during King Taksin's reign (1809–24), when Thonburi was the capital of Thailand. The original tower was only 16m (52 ft.) high, but it was expanded during the rule of Rama III (1824–51) to its current height. The exterior is decorated with floral and decorative motifs made of colorful ceramic shards, which were donated to the monastery by local people at the request of Rama III. Wat Arun is a sight to behold shimmering in the sunrise, but truly the best time to visit is in late afternoon for sunset.

West bank of the Chao Phraya, opposite Tha Thien Pier. ✆ 02465-5640. Admission 20B (US50¢/£0.30). Daily 8am–5:30pm. Take a water taxi from Tha Thien Pier (near Wat Po) or cross the Phra Pinklao Bridge and follow the river south on Arun Amarin Rd.

Wat Benchamabophit (Marble Wat) Wat Benchamabophit, simplified for tourists as the Marble Wat because of the white Carrara marble from which it's constructed, is an early-20th-century temple designed by Prince Narai, the half brother of

THE TRAVELOCITY GUARANTEE

...THAT SAYS EVERYTHING YOU BOOK WILL BE RIGHT, OR WE'LL WORK WITH OUR TRAVEL PARTNERS TO MAKE IT RIGHT, RIGHT AWAY.

*To drive home the point,
we're going to use the word "right" in every single sentence.*

Let's get right to it. Right to the meat! Only Travelocity guarantees everything about your booking will be right, or we'll work with our travel partners to make it right, right away. Right on!

Here's a picture taken smack dab right in the middle of Antigua, where the Guarantee also covers you.

The Guarantee covers all but one of the items pictured to the right.

For example, what if the ocean view you booked actually looks out at a downright ugly parking lot? You'd be right to call – we're there for you. And no one in their right mind would be pleased to learn the rental car place has closed and left them stranded. Call Travelocity and we'll help get you back on the right track.

Now, you may be thinking, "Yeah, right, I'm so sure." That's OK; you have the right to remain skeptical. That is until we mention help is always right around the corner. Call us right off the bat, knowing our customer service reps are there for you 24/7. Righting wrongs. Left and right.

Now if you're guessing there are some things we can't control, like the weather, well you're right. But we can help you with most things – to get all the details in righting,* visit travelocity.com/guarantee.

*Sorry, spelling things right is one of the few things not covered under the Guarantee.

I'd give my right arm for a guarantee like this, although I'm glad I don't have to.

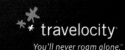

You'll never roam alone.

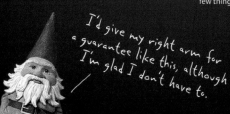

©2006 Travelocity.com LP. CST # 2056372-50.

Rama V. It's the most modern and one of the most beautiful of Bangkok's royal wats. Unlike the older complexes, there's no truly monumental *wihaan* or *chedi* dominating the grounds. Many smaller buildings reflect a melding of European materials and designs with traditional Thai religious architecture. Even the courtyards are paved with polished white marble. Walk inside the compound, beyond the main *bot*, to view the many Buddha images that represent various regional styles. In the early mornings, monks chant in the main chapel, sometimes so intensely that it seems as if the temple is going to lift off.

Si Ayutthaya Rd. (south of the Assembly Building near Chitralada Palace). ✆ **02281-2501.** Admission 20B (US50¢/£0.30). Daily 8am–5pm.

Wat Mahathat (Temple of the Great Relic) ✿

Built to house a relic of the Buddha, Wat Mahathat is one of Bangkok's oldest shrines and the headquarters for Thailand's largest monastic order. Also the home of the Mahachulalongkorn Buddhist University, the most important center for the study of Buddhism and meditation, Wat Mahathat offers some programs in English.

Adjacent to it, between Maharat Road and the river, is the city's biggest **amulet market,** where a fantastic array of religious amulets, charms, talismans, and traditional medicine is sold. Each Sunday, hundreds of worshippers squat on the ground studying tiny images of the Buddha with magnifying glasses, hoping to find one that will bring good fortune or ward off evil.

Na Phra That Rd. (near Sanam Luang Park, between the Grand Palace and the National Museum). ✆ **02222-6011.** Suggested donation 20B (US50¢/£0.30). Daily 9am–5pm.

Wat Phra Kaeo ✿✿✿

When Rama I built the Grand Palace, he included this temple, the royal temple most revered by the Thai people. The famed **Emerald Buddha,** a 0.6m-tall (2-ft.) northern Thai–style image made from green jasper, sits atop a towering gold altar. The statue dons a different costume for each of the three seasons in Thailand, changed by the king himself, who climbs up to the image because it can be lowered for no one.

Historians believe that artists created the statue in the 14th century. The Emerald Buddha hid inside a plaster Buddha image until 1434, when movers accidentally dropped it, setting it free. The king at Chiang Mai demanded that it be brought to his city, but three attempts failed. Each time, the elephant transporting the image stopped at the same spot in Lampang, so the king gave in to the will of the spirits and built a *chedi* (sacred monument) for it there. Thirty-two years later, King Tiloka of Chiang Mai brought the image to Chiang Mai. The Emerald Buddha stayed in the Wat Chedi Luang until 1552, when a later king from Luang Prabang carted it off to Laos. When the king moved the capital of Laos to Vientiane, the image followed him. Rama I finally recaptured the statue in a successful invasion of Laos and placed it in Wat Phra Kaeo, where it remains today.

The wat compound is a small city in itself, including a library with stunning Ayutthaya-style mother-of-pearl inlay doors; a reliquary like a golden bell-shaped Sri Lankan–style chedi; a *wihaan* (hall) bejeweled with chipped porcelain mosaics; and a miniature model of Angkor Wat, the sprawling temple complex at the ancient Khmer capital, with its corn-shape chedis. Murals on the surrounding walls tell the story of the *Ramayana* (one of the two great epics of India).

In the Grand Palace complex. ✆ **02222-0094.** Admission 250B (US$6.25/£3.50); included in Grand Palace fee. Daily 8:30am–3:30pm. Take the Chao Phraya Express Boat to Tha Chang Pier, then walk east and south.

Wat Po (Temple of the Reclining Buddha) ✦✦✦ Wat Po (Wat Phra Chetuphon) was built by Rama I in the 16th century and is the oldest and largest Buddhist temple in Bangkok. Considered Thailand's first public university, the temple's many monuments and artworks explain principles of religion, science, and literature.

Most people go straight to the enormous Reclining Buddha in the northern section. It's more than 46m (151 ft.) long and 16m (53 ft.) high, and was built during the mid-19th-century reign of Rama III. The statue is brick, covered with layers of plaster and always-flaking gold leaf; the feet are inlaid with mother-of-pearl illustrations of 108 auspicious *laksanas* (characteristics) of the Buddha. Behind the Buddha, a line of 108 bronze bowls, each also representing one of the laksanas, awaits visitors to drop coins (acquired nearby for a 20B/US50¢/£0.30 donation for luck).

Outside, the grounds contain 91 *chedis* (stupas or sacred mounds), four *wihaans,* and a *bot* (the central shrine in a Buddhist temple). The Traditional Medical Practitioners Association Center teaches traditional Thai massage and medicine. Stop in for a massage (360B/US$9/£5 per hr.) or ask about the 7- to 10-day massage courses.

Maharat Rd., near the river (about ½ mile south of the Grand Palace). ℂ 02222-0933. Admission 50B (US$1.25/ £0.70). Daily 8am–5pm; massages offered until 6pm.

Wat Saket (Golden Mount) ✦ Wat Saket is easily recognized by its golden chedi atop a fortresslike hill near the pier for Bangkok's east–west *klong* ferry. The wat was restored by King Rama I, and 30,000 bodies were brought here during a plague in the reign of Rama II. The hill, which is almost 80m (262 ft.) high, is an artificial construction begun during the reign of Rama III. Rama IV brought in 1,000 teak logs to shore it up because it was sinking into the swampy ground. Rama V built the golden chedi to house a relic of Buddha, said to be from India or Nepal, given to him by the British. The concrete walls were added during World War II to keep the structure from collapsing.

The Golden Mount, a short but breathtaking climb that's best made in the morning, is most interesting for its vista of old Rattanakosin Island and the rooftops of Bangkok. Every late October to mid-November (for 9 days around the full moon), Wat Sakhet hosts Bangkok's most important temple fair, when the Golden Mount is wrapped with red cloth and a carnival erupts around it, with food and trinket stalls, theatrical performances, freak shows, animal circuses, and other monkey business.

Ratchadamnoen Klang and Boriphat rds. Free admission to wat; suggested donation 5B (US15¢/£0.05) for the chedi. Daily 9am–5pm.

Wat Suthat and the Giant Swing The temple is among the oldest and largest in Bangkok, and Somerset Maugham declared its roofline the most beautiful. It was begun by Rama I and finished by Rama III; Rama II carved the panels for the wihaan's doors. It houses a beautiful 14th-century Phra Buddha Shakyamuni that was brought from Sukhothai, and the ashes of King Rama VIII, Ananda Mahidol, brother of the current king, are contained in its base. The wall paintings for which it is known were done during Rama III's reign.

The huge teak arch in front—also carved by Rama II—is all that remains of an original giant swing, which was used until 1932 to celebrate and thank Shiva for a bountiful rice harvest and to ask for the god's blessing on the next. The minister of rice, accompanied by hundreds of Brahman court astrologers, would lead a parade around the city walls to the temple precinct. Teams of men would ride the swing on arcs as high as 25m (82 ft.) in the air, trying to grab a bag of silver coins with their teeth. Due to injuries and deaths, the dangerous swing ceremony has been discontinued.

Sao Chingcha Sq. (near the intersection of Bamrung Muang and Ti Thong rds.). ℂ 02222-0280. Suggested donation 20B (US50¢/£0.30). Daily 9am–9pm.

Wat Traimit (Golden Buddha)   Thirteenth-century Wat Traimit is notable only for its central statue, a nearly 3m-high (10 ft.), 5-ton Buddha in gold. The statue was discovered by accident in 1957 when an old stucco image was being moved from a storeroom by a crane, which dropped it and shattered the plaster shell, revealing the shining gold beneath. The graceful seated statue was cast during the Sukhothai period and later covered with plaster to hide it from the Burmese.

Traimit Rd. (west of Hua Lampong Railway Station, just west of the intersection of Krung Kasem and Rama IV rds.). Suggested donation 20B (US50¢/£0.30). Daily 9am–5pm. Walk southwest on Traimit Rd. and look for a school on the right with a playground; the wat is up a flight of stairs overlooking the school.

CULTURAL PURSUITS

Thai culture is not something to observe but to participate in, and festivals, classes, and cultural activities abound. Check with the **TAT** (ℂ 02250-5500) or the **Bangkok Tourist Division** (ℂ 02225-7612, or visit the information offices around the city) and keep an eye on magazines like *Metro* or local newspapers like the *Nation* and the *Bangkok Post* for major events during your stay.

THAI COOKING   Fancy a chance to learn cooking techniques from the pros? Thai cooking is fun and easy, and there are a few good hands-on courses in Bangkok. Learn about Thai herbs, spices, and unique local veggies (you'll never look at a produce market the same way again). Lectures on Thai regional cuisine, cooking techniques, and menu planning complement classroom exercises to prepare all your favorite dishes. The best part is afterwards, when you get to eat them. The **Blue Elephant** (ℂ 02673-9353; www.blueelephant.com) is the best in town, with classes starting at 2,800B (US$70/£39).

THAI MASSAGE ✦✦✦   A traditional Thai massage is a must-do for visitors and is quite unique. You don't just lie back and passively receive a Thai massage; instead, you are an active participant as masseuses manipulate your limbs to stretch each muscle, then apply acupressure techniques to loosen up tense muscles and get energy flowing. It's been described as having yoga "done" to you—your body will be twisted, pulled, and sometimes pounded in the process.

The home of Thai massage, **Wat Po,** is school to almost every masseuse in Bangkok, and has cheap massages in an open-air pavilion within the temple complex—a very interesting, but not necessarily relaxing, experience (see "The Wats," above; ℂ 0222-0933; 360B (US$9/£5) per hr.).

Bangkok supports some fine spas, most in the larger hotels. **Le Banyan Tree Spa** (ℂ 02679-1054; www.banyantree.com) and the **Shangri-La Hotel's Chi Spa** (ℂ 02236-7777; www.shangri-la.com) are among the finest places going, but they're just two of the many fine spas in town (in hotels and out).

There are countless massage places around Bangkok, many offering fine services at very reasonable rates (as low as 200B/US$5/£2.80 per hr.). Many places have NO SEX or other blatant signs indicating the place is hanky-panky free (and if you're looking for hanky-panky, those signs are just as blatant).

THAI BOXING ✦✦   *Muaythai,* or Thai boxing, is Thailand's national sport. A visit to the two venues in Bangkok, or to the many fight-nights in towns all over Thailand (as much festival as sport), is a fun window into Thai culture. The pageant of the fighters' elegant pre-bout rituals, live musical performances, and frenetic gambling activity are a real spectacle. In Bangkok, catch up to 15 bouts nightly at either of two stadiums. The air-conditioned **Ratchadamnoen Stadium** (Ratchadamnoen Nok Ave.; ℂ **04024-3065**) hosts fights on Monday, Wednesday, Thursday, and Sunday, while the muggier **Lumphini Stadium** (Rama IV Rd.; ℂ **02251-4303**) has bouts on Tuesday, Friday, and Saturday. Tickets are 2,000B (US$50/£28) for ringside seats, 1,500B (US$38/£21) for second-class seats, and 1,000B (US$25/£14) for nosebleed seats. Go for second-class seats. Not for the squeamish.

MEDITATION   **Wat Mahathat,** or the Temple of the Great Relic (see "The Wats," above), serves as one of Thailand's largest Buddhist universities and has become a popular center for meditation lessons and practice, with English-speaking monks overseeing students of Vipassana, or Insight Meditation. Three-hour sessions begin daily at 7am, 1pm, and 6pm (ℂ **02222-6011**). Donations are requested.

OUTDOOR ACTIVITIES

Most hotels, certainly the finest five-star properties, support quality fitness centers complete with personal trainers and top equipment. **California,** just along Silom Road near Patpong at Liberty Square (ℂ **02631-1122**), is a large, convenient facility open to day visitors.

GOLF   Golf enthusiasts will be happy to know that you don't have to go far to enjoy some of Thailand's best courses; there are a number of courses, some of championship quality, in or near the city center.

- **Pinehurst Golf & Country Club,** 73 Phaholythin Rd., Klong Luang, Pathum Thani (ℂ **02516-8679;** www.pinehurst.co.th), sports three 9-hole courses at par 27 each. This prestigious club served as the venue for the 1992 Johnnie Walker Classic (greens fees: 1,700B/US$43/£24 weekdays, 2,300B/US$58/£32 weekends).
- **Rose Garden Golf Club,** 53/1 Moo 4, Petchkasem Highway, Sam Phran, Nakhon Pathom (ℂ **03432-2770;** www.rose-garden.com), an esteemed par-72 course, offers a pretty game, with scenery enhanced by wooded surrounds (greens fees: 900B/US$23/£13 weekdays, 1,500B/US$38/£21 weekends).
- **Royal Thai Army Golf Club,** 459 Ram Indra Rd., Bang Kaen, Bangkok (ℂ **02521-5211**), has both an old course and a new course to choose from. This well-maintained course was host to the Thai Open (greens fees: 1,400B/US$35/£20).

SHOPPING

You're bound to shop in Bangkok. With the abundance of Thai silk, good tailors, artwork, hill-tribe crafts, silver, gems, and porcelain, shopping is inevitable, but prices are low and the whole process is good fun—bargain hard! At the city's many **street bazaars,** you can find cheap batik clothing, knockoff watches, jeans, designer wear, and all sorts of souvenirs. Buy a bag to tote it all back home.

The best hotel shopping arcades are those at the **Oriental,** the **Four Seasons,** and the **Peninsula** hotels; prices are high. For Thai silk, try the **Jim Thompson Thai Silk Company,** the town's most famous (main store: 9 Surawong Rd., near Silom; ℂ **02632-8100;** www.jimthompson.com).

Pick up a copy of Nancy Chandler's *The Market Map* (160B/US$4/£2.25) with detailed insets of specific shopping areas. If you encounter problems with merchants, call the tourist police (ℂ **1155**).

> **Warning   Jewelry Scams**
>
> For every reputable gem dealer in Bangkok, there are at least 100 crooks wait-
> ing to catch you in the latest scam. To avoid being ripped off, follow this sim-
> ple rule: Refuse offers from touts for free city shopping junkets.

SHOPPING AREAS

ALONG THE RIVER   One of the finest collections of art and antiques dealers anywhere in the kingdom is at **River City,** a large convention hall at riverside near
Bangkok's finest hotels. Sticker shock is the rule, but you get what you pay for—and
quality is what you get here. Nearby **Charoen Krung Road** hosts lots of high-end
shopping venues for everything from jewelry to antiques, carpets to fine tailoring. All
shops can arrange shipping.

SUKHUMVIT ROAD   This area is lined with shops from one end to the other, as
well as some of Bangkok's biggest shopping malls (see "Department Stores & Shopping Malls," below). For antiques, stop in **L'Arcadia** (12/2 Sukhumvit Soi 23;
© 02259-1517), where you'll find fine Burmese and Thai furniture and carvings. For
gems, try **Uthai's Gems** (28/7 Soi Ruam Rudee; © 02253-8582), down Ruam
Rudee, a busy shortcut *soi* parallel to Wireless just south of Ploen Chit.

SILOM ROAD   This area is packed with outdoor shopping (see the **Patpong Night
Market,** discussed below). There are any number of fine jewelry shops, silk retailers,
and tailors here.

MARKETS

Visiting Bangkok's many markets is as much cultural as consumer experience: The
markets are where the Thai economy happens. Bargaining is fast and furious. The
Weekend Market (Chatuchak), near the Mo Chit BTS stop, is the city's most
famous, covering a vast area and overcrowded on any given Saturday or Sunday. The
riverside **Chinatown** area is a labyrinth of shopping. **Khao San Road,** the popular
backpacker area, is a great place to pick up anything from travel trinkets to cool
T-shirts. The city's two night markets, **Patpong Night Market** (Patpong Soi 1, off
Silom) and **Suan Lum Night Market** (east of Lumpini Park on Rama IV Road), are
great stops for souvenirs and more.

DEPARTMENT STORES & SHOPPING MALLS

The size and opulence of Bangkok's many malls and shopping plazas are a shock to first-
time visitors in search of the exotic. Highlights include the cavernous **Siam Paragon**
(99/1 Rama I Rd., opposite the Siam BTS stop; © 02610-9000; www.siamparagon.
co.th), one of the largest malls in Asia, with designer outlets, a gourmet market and food
court offering everything from fast food to fine dining, an IMAX theater, a bowling
alley, and even an opera theater. Paragon's **Siam Ocean World** ✯✯ (© 02687-2000)
deserves special mention—it's a world-class aquarium with a large shark tank that you can
walk through via glass tunnel. Great for both kids and adults. Open daily from 9am to
10pm; admission is 450B (US$11/£6.30) for adults, 280B (US$7/£3.95) for children.

Next door is **Siam Discovery Center** (Rama I Rd.; © 02658-1000; www.siam
discoverycenter.co.th) and adjoining **Siam Center,** both offering additional acres of
high-end shopping.

Also near Siam, the **MBK Center** (at Rama I and Phayathai rds.; National Stadium BTS station; ℂ **02620-9000;** www.mbk-center.co.th) and its **Tokyu Department Store** are a real trip to teenybopper Thailand. This mall supports lots of more affordable local shops—a crowded exercise in how Bangkok shops.

Finally, the **Emporium** (622 Sukhumvit Soi 24; ℂ **02269-1000;** www.emporium thailand.com) has all of the designer outlets you could imagine, plus a great food court and a cinema.

BANGKOK AFTER DARK

One night in Bangkok, right? Despite recent legislation restricting bar hours, the action is still fierce and furious in Thailand's hedonistic capital and a rollicking good time can always be found. If the Bangkok debauch isn't your scene, know that the town is not all red-light district by any means: There are all kinds of events, clubs, and bars. Check *Metro Magazine, BK Magazine,* the *Bangkok Post,* or the *Nation* for current happenings.

THE PERFORMING ARTS

There are a number of Thai dance and dinner theaters for tourists (see "Dinner & Dance," p. 112, for specific recommendations).

There are two major theaters for Thai and international performances: the **National Theater** (1 Na Phra That Rd.; ℂ 02222-1092) and the **Thailand Cultural Center** (Thiem Ruammit Rd. off Ratchadaphisek Rd., Huai Khwang; ℂ **02247-0028**), both with a regular schedule of performances. Contact them directly or check local papers.

The **Joe Louis Theater** (in the Suan Lum Night Market adjacent to Lumpini Park; ℂ 02252-9683) holds nightly **puppet theater** performances of stories from the *Ramakien* as well as comic vignettes of rural Thai life. Shows are nightly at 7:30 and 8:45pm. Tickets start at 900B (US$23/£13).

THE BAR & CLUB SCENE

There are nighttime adventures to be found down any soi in town. If you'd just like to unwind with an evening cocktail, check out what's happening at your hotel's lobby bar; many set up jazzy live music to entertain folks. Stop by the **Bamboo Bar,** at the Oriental (Oriental Lane off Charoen Krung Rd.; ℂ 02236-0400), or the **Living Room,** at the Sheraton Grande Sukhumvit (250 Sukhumvit Rd.; ℂ 02649-8888). Both present some of the best jazz in the city; the Living Room also hosts a weekly Sunday Jazzy Brunch Buffet from 11:30am to 3pm.

SILOM ROAD & PATPONG Most visitors won't leave Bangkok without a stroll around Patpong, the famous sex strip and night market with myriad vendors and blocks of bars and clubs. The Patpong scene centers around Soi Patpong 1 and Soi Patpong 2 between Surawong and Silom roads. It's the home of Bangkok's raunchier sex shows, but most visitors come to wander the market area (lots of pirated goods).

Despite its rep as a go-go center, there are lots of good bars in Patpong. **O'Reilly's Irish Pub** (62 Silom Rd., at corner of Soi Thaniya just east of Patpong; ℂ 02632-7515) is a lively bar full of locals and travelers and features nightly drink specials. The **Barbican** (9/4–5 Soi Thaniya off Silom Rd.; ℂ 02234-3590) is a stylish hangout with great food and live music. The **Irish Exchange,** across from Patpong on Convent Road (next to Silom Complex at 1/5–6 Sivadon Building; ℂ 02266-7160), caters to expats with live music after office working hours. If it's margaritas you crave, **Coyote on Convent** (1/2 Convent Rd.; 02631-2325) has 75 varieties to choose from.

Head to Silom Soi 4 (between Patpong 2 and Soi Thaniya off Silom Rd.), where you'll find small home-grown clubs spinning great music as well as the city's prominent gay clubs: **Telephone Bar** (114/11–13 Silom Soi 4; ✆ 02234-3279) and the **Balcony** (86–8 Silom Soi 4; ✆ 02235-5891).

SIAM SQUARE   Siam Square, on Rama I Road between Henri Dunant and Phayathai roads, is where you'll find Bangkok's **Hard Rock Cafe** (424/3–6 Siam Sq. Soi 11; ✆ 02254-0830), featuring good live bands.

A great disco, **Concept CM²**, has nightly live or DJ music—a very popular place in the basement of the Novotel Bangkok on Siam Square (Siam Sq. Soi 6; ✆ 02209-8888). **Spasso,** in the Grand Hyatt Erawan Bangkok (494 Ratchadamri Rd.; ✆ 02254-1234), is a great Italian restaurant that turns into an upscale club with live music acts nightly.

A little bit north of this area (a short taxi ride away), near the Victory Monument BTS station (a cab ride up Phayathai Rd.), check out live jazz and blues at **Saxophone Pub and Restaurant** (✆ 02246-5472).

KHAO SAN ROAD   The backpackers on Khao San Road still party on despite more and more restrictions. Start at **Gulliver's,** on the corner of Khao San and Chakrabongse roads, and then explore the back lanes off Khao San for small dance clubs (some the size of broom closets) and hangouts. You'll find lots of travelers in their 20s and a perpetually laid-back atmosphere—anything goes. In the middle of Khao San, don't miss **Lava** (249 Khao San Rd.; ✆ 02281-6565), a popular basement

The Bangkok Sex Scene

Since the 1960s—and particularly since the Vietnam War—Bangkok has been the sin capital of Asia, with sex clubs, bars, massage parlors, and prostitutes concentrated in the **Patpong, Nana Plaza,** and **Soi Cowboy** districts. Sex is for sale in many quarters of Bangkok, and surprise at seeing the many older Western gentlemen strutting about town with lovely young Thai ladies is a common impression for first-time visitors.

Despite recent efforts and restrictions by the Taksin government, Bangkok's skin trades are thriving. Go-go bars and clubs are really little more than fronts for prostitution, and very thinly veiled fronts at that. The men and women in the clubs are all available to take out of the bar for a "bar fine." "Modern" or "physical" massage parlors are where patrons choose ladies by number from behind glass for an oil massage and more, with negotiations. If this is your scene, take great care: Apart from the condom thing (use one), prostitutes are known to slip you drugs (which happens), rob your hotel room while you're sleeping (which happens), or get you mixed up with illegal activities (which also happens). Child prostitution, slavery, and violence against sex workers are still common. If you encounter any problem, report it to the tourist police (✆ 1155).

Note that a startling increase in HIV-positive cases in the last 20 years brought on mandated as well as grass-roots efforts to educate about use of condoms, but AIDS is still a major concern among sex workers.

dance club. For a mellower evening, head west of Khao San to riverside **Phra Athit Road,** where there are any number of small cafes with live music.

SUKHUMVIT ROAD One of the most happening areas of Bangkok, the small sois along busy Sukhumvit host Bangkok's top clubs and good bars. **Q Bar** ⟨✿✿⟩ (34 Sukhumvit Soi 11; ⓒ 02252-3274) is *the* place for the slick urban hip of Bangkok; its only rival is the similarly ab-fab **Bed Supperclub** ⟨✿✿✿⟩ (p. 111; 26 Sukhumvit Soi 11; ⓒ 02651-3537). Both are ultramodern, have great expat DJs, and boom-boom-boom late into the night 7 days a week.

The **Conrad Hotel** (87 Wireless Rd., across from the U.S. Embassy; ⓒ 02690-9999) is home of two of Bangkok's newest and best spots: **87** is an ultrachic, ultraexclusive club, while the **Diplomat Bar** ⟨✿⟩ fills with, well, diplomats from the U.S. Embassy as well as Bangkok's hobnobbers.

For bars along Sukhumvit, try the **Bull's Head** (Sukhumvit Soi 33/1; ⓒ 02259-4444), a fun local pub that draws crowds with frequent theme parties and a clubhouse attitude. **Bruahaus Bangkok** (President Park, at the end of Sukhumvit Soi 24; ⓒ 02661-1111) is a popular brewpub, as is **Taurus Brew House** (Sukhumvit Soi 26; ⓒ 02661-2207), which packs 'em in—especially on weekends—for home brews and live pop music.

If you're in the mood for dancing, **Royal City Avenue (RCA)** is a 2km stretch of bars, restaurants, and clubs between Rama IX and New Phetchaburi roads. Mostly frequented by young, well-heeled Thais, RCA has clubs spinning everything from trance to American pop. It's always happening on the weekends and decidedly un-sex-touristy.

On the other hand, if you're looking for something similar to the Patpong sex-show scene, Sukhumvit has a couple of popular go-go areas: **Soi Cowboy** (between Soi Asoke and Sukhumvit Soi 21), the oldest go-go scene dating from Vietnam War days; and **Nana Plaza,** just on Sukhumvit Soi 4.

SIDE TRIPS FROM BANGKOK
EASY DAY TRIPS
See "Visitor Information & Tours" (p. 96) for recommended agencies that can make all the arrangements for the following excursions.

The **Muang Boran** (ⓒ 02323-9253) ⟨✿✿⟩, or **Ancient City,** is roughly 45 minutes east of Bangkok in Samut Prakan. Best reached by group tour, Muang Boran is a collection of scaled-down replicas of over 100 of Thailand's most famous and architecturally significant structures. The grounds housing the models cover 320 acres in the shape of Thailand, with each structure generally set in its correct location. Open daily 8am from 5pm. Admission is 300B (US$8/£4.20) for adults, 200B (US$5/£2.80) for children.

The **Floating Market at Damnoen Saduak** ⟨✿⟩, Ratchaburi, is about 40 minutes south of Nakhon Pathom. Some tours combine the Floating Market with a visit to the Rose Garden or with the River Kwai sights (see below for more on each). At a real floating market, food vendors sell their goods from small boats to local folk in other boats or in *klong*-side homes. Damnoen is as precise a duplicate as you could imagine and great for photographers.

Besides its rose garden, the attractive if somewhat touristy **Rose Garden Country Resort** (ⓒ 02295-3261; www.rose-garden.com) is known for its all-in-one show of Thai culture, which includes Thai classical and folk dancing, Thai boxing, sword fighting, and cock fighting—a convenient way for visitors with limited time to digest some canned Thai culture. It's 32km (20 miles) west of Bangkok on the way to Nakhon Pathom on Highway 4. Admission is 40B (US$1/£0.55) for the grounds,

430B (US$11/£6) for the show. It's open daily from 8am to 5pm; the cultural show is at 3:45pm. Call for details.

KANCHANABURI

120km (74 miles) NW of Bangkok

Really more than a day trip (best as an overnight), Kanchanaburi is home of the famed **Bridge over the River Kwai** and the notorious internment camps for Allied troops forced into servitude (and death) by the Japanese during World War II in an effort to link Burma and Thailand by rail. Made legendary by the film of the same name, the Bridge over the River Kwai lives on in name only; the existing bridge is just a little rattle-trap trestle that crosses not the River Kwai but a tributary (but that doesn't stop souvenir hawkers and the tourist infrastructure that has grown up around the bridge). There are, however, lots of good excursions in the area, many caves and waterfalls in the surrounding hills, and a few good hotels and riverside guesthouses; it's a popular escape from the heat, traffic, and pollution of Bangkok.

You can connect by train from Bangkok's **Hua Lampong Railway Station** (✆ **1690** or 02223-7010) on regular weekend junkets starting in the early morning, or go by daily ordinary trains from **Bangkok Noi Station** (✆ **02411-3102**), with slow, twice-daily connections to **Kanchanaburi Station** (✆ **03456-1052**) for 300B (US$8/£4.20) round-trip. The rail trips here are quite scenic and a great experience, though a long, hot ride. There are also frequent regular buses from the **Southern Bus Terminal** (✆ **02434-5557**), but if you're going by road, it's perhaps best to opt for a rented car (see "Getting Around," p. 86).

For overnight lodging, consider the **Felix River Kwai Resort** (9/1 Moo 3 Tambon, Kanchanaburi; ✆ **03455-1000**). The Felix has rooms starting at 2,200B (US$55/£31) and is the best for comfort, but places like the **Jungle Raft Resort** (Lam Khao Ngu; ✆ **02377-5556**)—which is just as it says, a bunch of jungle rafts—are certainly far more atmospheric and adventurous. Budget guesthouses are chockablock at riverside near the bridge.

AYUTTHAYA ★★

76km (47 miles) N of Bangkok

From 1350 until its fall to the Burmese in 1767, Ayutthaya was Thailand's capital and home to 33 kings and numerous dynasties. At its zenith and until the mid–18th century, Ayutthaya was a majestic city with three palaces and 400 splendid temples on an island threaded by canals—a site that impressed European visitors.

The architecture of Ayutthaya is a fascinating mix of Khmer (ancient Cambodian) and early Sukhothai style, with large cactus-shaped obelisks called *prangs* the hallmark. The town is encircled by water, and the central island area of Ayutthaya is itself the site; modern buildings and busy canalside streets are in and among the ruins of this once-great city. It is flat, so going by rented bicycle is a good choice. Highlights are **Wat Mahathat,** a crumbling but stunning example of the Ayutthaya style (don't miss the Buddha head in the tree trunk), and **Wihaan Phra Mongkol Bopit,** which houses a massive Buddha. The **Ayutthaya Historical Study Center** and nearby **Chao Sam Phraya National Museum** offer useful background information. The TAT office at the museum offers a detailed map.

Train and bus connections are frequent from Bangkok's **Hua Lampong Railway Station** (✆ **1690** or 02223-7010) and **Northern Bus Terminal** (✆ **02936-2841**), respectively.

All-day river cruises are a popular option to and from Ayutthaya. Contact **River Sun Cruises** (✆ **02266-9316**) directly or book through any riverside hotel; departure points are the **Oriental** (✆ **02236-0400**), the **Shangri-La Hotel** (✆ **02236-7777**), and the River City pier daily at approximately 7:30am (and include a stop at Bang Pa-In). The *Manorha* ✺✺ (✆ **02476-0022**), a 60-year-old teak rice barge converted to a luxury liner, leaves every Monday and Thursday for a 3-day/2-night cruise to Ayutthaya; the cost is US$1,150 (£633) for two.

If you're stuck overnight, the **Krungsri River Hotel** (7/2 Rojana Rd.; ✆ **03524-4333**), near the train station, is a good choice. Convenient but basic is the **Ayothaya Hotel** (12 Moo Tessabarn Soi 2; ✆ **03523-2855**), with rooms from 1,200B (US$30/£17).

5 An Introduction to the Eastern Seaboard

Tracing the coastline directly east of Bangkok, there are a few resort spots that are attractive as much for their proximity to Bangkok as anything. Closest is **Pattaya,** one of Thailand's earliest holiday developments and famous (or infamous) for its wild nightlife. The town is always hopping late into the night—guys come from all over the world to live it up. Continuing east from Pattaya, **Ko Samet,** in Rayong Province, is a small island with loads of affordable, makeshift bungalow resorts and a few high-end choices. It is a low-luxe, laid-back little retreat reached by a short ferry ride from the mainland at the town of Ban Phe (via Rayong). And **Ko Chang,** the last stop before Cambodia to the east, has earned a hushed following among young budget travelers because its remote location has kept development to a minimum. The cement trucks are rolling, though, and the island, Thailand's third largest, has sprouted a few high-end resorts. Ko Chang is reached via the nondescript town of Trat.

6 Pattaya

147km (91 miles) E of Bangkok

The current incarnation of **Pattaya** claims its founders' day as June 29, 1959, when a few truckloads of American troops stationed in nearby Isan arrived in overflowing trucks, rented houses along the beach, and had such a hoot that they told their friends. Word spread and, over time, the town became the R & R capital for war-weary American troops over the next many years. The legacy of those early visitors is today's adult playground: hundreds of go-go clubs, beer bars, and massage parlors at beachside.

Tourism boomed in the 1980s, and because unchecked resort development was not accompanied by infrastructure upgrades, beaches became veritable toilets of raw sewage. Despite cleanup projects, the beach is not at all pleasant.

In 2005, over 5 million of Thailand's 11 million foreign tourists visited Pattaya. This number will only increase now that Suvarnabhumi International Airport is up and running. Just an hour's drive away, Pattaya is as convenient a first stop when you step off the plane as Bangkok.

Pattaya supports a host of international resorts, retreats set in sprawling, manicured seaside gardens. It would like to be a family destination, and, along with fine accommodations, there are some family activities here, but the mammoth sex-tourism industry kind of puts the kibosh on any wholesome family fun. Neighboring **Jomtien** and **Dongtan** beaches are popular alternatives with less seedy activities and cleaner beaches, but mostly just condominiums—good for day visits.

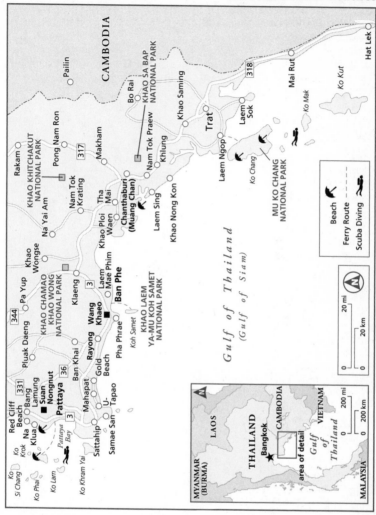

Pattaya Beach Road is the heart of the town, a long strip of hotels, bars, restaurants, and shops overlooking Pattaya Bay. Pattaya 2nd and Pattaya 3rd roads run parallel to Beach Road and form a busy central grid of small, crowded sois bound by North Pattaya Road and South Pattaya Road and bisected by Central Pattaya Road. At both the far northern and southern ends of the strip are two bluffs. Due south is condo-lined Jomtien Beach, a 15-minute ride from Pattaya.

GETTING THERE

BY TRAIN Weekday train service leaves from Bangkok's **Hua Lampong Railway Station** at 6:55am and returns from Pattaya at 2:20pm. The 5-hour trip through the countryside is pleasant and costs only 31B (US80¢/£0.45). There's no service on the

Pattaya

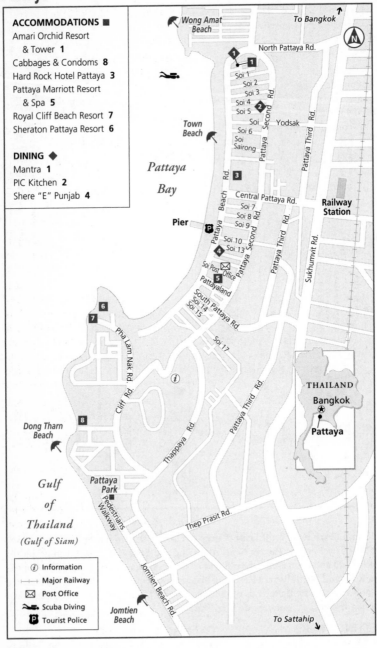

ACCOMMODATIONS ■

Amari Orchid Resort
& Tower **1**
Cabbages & Condoms **8**
Hard Rock Hotel Pattaya **3**
Pattaya Marriott Resort
& Spa **5**
Royal Cliff Beach Resort **7**
Sheraton Pattaya Resort **6**

DINING ◆

Mantra **1**
PIC Kitchen **2**
Shere "E" Punjab **4**

Wong Amat Beach

To Bangkok

North Pattaya Rd.

Soi 1
Soi 2
Soi 3
Soi 4
Soi 5

Yodsak

Town Beach

Soi 6
Soi Sairong

Pattaya Bay

Central Pattaya Rd.
Soi 7
Soi 8
Soi 9

Pattaya Beach Rd.

Pattaya Second Rd.

Pattaya Third Rd.

Railway Station

Pier

Soi 10
Soi 13

Soi Post Office
Pattayaland

Sukhumvit Rd.

South Pattaya Rd.
Soi 14
Soi 15

Soi 17

Pha Lam Nak Rd.

Cliff Rd.

i

THAILAND

Bangkok

Pattaya

Dong Tharn Beach

Gulf

of

Thailand

(Gulf of Siam)

Pattaya Park

Pedestrians Walkway

Thappaya Rd.

Pattaya Third Rd.

Thep Prasit Rd.

Jomtien Beach Rd.

Jomtien Beach

To Sattahip

i Information
—|— Major Railway
⊠ Post Office
🤿 Scuba Diving
🅿 Tourist Police

130

weekends. Call Hua Lampong in Bangkok (© **1690** or 02223-7010) or in Pattaya (© **03842-9285**) for information. A shared *songtao* (covered pickup truck) to town from the Pattaya train station is just 20B (US50¢/£0.30).

BY BUS Buses depart from Bangkok's **Eastern Bus Terminal** (Sukhumvit Rd., opposite Soi 63, at Ekamai BTS station; © **02391-8097**) every half-hour from 5am to 10pm daily. For air-conditioned coach service, the fare is 124B (US$3/£1.75). There's also regular bus service from Bangkok's **Northern Bus Terminal (Mor Chit)** (© **02936-2841**).

Air-conditioned buses to and from Bangkok use the bus station in Pattaya on North Pattaya Road (© **03842-9877**). A songtao to town is 20B (US50¢/£0.30).

BY TAXI Cabs from Suvarnabhumi International Airport's taxi counter go for 1,050B (US$26/£15). Any hotel concierge can negotiate a fare of about 1,500B (US$38/£21) with a metered taxi driver to take you to or from Pattaya resort, door to door.

GETTING AROUND

BY MINIBUS/SONGTAO Songtao (called **baht buses** here) follow regular routes up and down the main streets. Fares in Pattaya start at 20B (US50¢/£0.30). It's about 30B (US75¢/£0.40) to get to Jomtien (bargain hard!). Some hotels operate minibuses as well.

BY CAR **Avis** has an office at the Dusit Resort (© **03836-1628**), with self-drive rates from about 2,480B (US$62/£35) per day for a Toyota Vigo four-wheel-drive sport vehicle. **Budget** has an office at Liabchayhard Beach Road (© **03871-0717**) and offers comparable rates. **VIA Rent-a-Car** (215/15–18 Pattaya 2nd Rd., opposite Royal Garden Plaza; © **03872-3123**) has a good reputation and, like the many firms along Pattaya Beach Road, offers better rates (from 900B/US$23/£13). Read contracts closely.

BY MOTORCYCLE Let's be honest, Pattaya's busy roads are full of drunk and reckless foreign drivers on motorbikes, but the brave (or foolish) can rent 150cc motorcycles for 200B (US$5/£2.80) a day (no insurance). Big choppers and Japanese speed bikes (500cc) will go for from 500B to 900B (US$13–US$23/£7–£13) per day. Demand a helmet and, as always, "Renter beware."

FAST FACTS: PATTAYA

There are many independent **money-changing booths,** 24-hour **bank** exchange desks (with better rates), and **ATMs** at every turn in town. **Bangkok Pattaya Hospital** (© **03842-7751**) has full services and English-speaking staff. In Pattaya, the number for the **tourist police** is © **1699** or 03842-9371. **Internet access** costs 40B to 60B per hour (US$1–US$1.50/£0.55–£0.85) at a number of cafes along the water (try Soi Yamato). The **post office** is on Soi Post Office near the Royal Garden Plaza (© **03842-9341**).

WHERE TO STAY

Pattaya accommodations range from seedy to stylish. The town supports a few more isolated, peaceful getaways as well. Reserve ahead in high season.

EXPENSIVE

Amari Orchid Resort & Tower ⭐ On the northern end of busy Pattaya, just out of the fray but close enough to walk there, the Amari has tidy rooms, good amenities, and a helpful staff. The open-air lobby is inviting and guest rooms are large, trimmed in dark wood with parquet floors and pleasing, contemporary lines. There's a playground and lots of space in the grassy central area. Amari also has good in-house dining (see "Mantra," under "Where to Dine," below). At press time, a new luxury wing with some 300 rooms was under construction and due to open in 2007. One to watch.

Pattaya Beach, Pattaya 20150 (on the very northernmost end of the beachfront rd.). ✆ **02255-3767**. Fax 02255-3718. www.amari.com. 236 units. US$177–US$253 (£97–£139) double; from US$377 (£207) suite. **Amenities:** 3 restaurants; 3 bars; outdoor pool; 9-hole miniature golf; 2 tennis courts; fitness center; Jacuzzi; playground and kids' club; tour desk; business center w/Internet access; salon; 24-hr. room service; babysitting; laundry service; dry cleaning; nonsmoking rooms. *In room:* A/C, satellite TV, minibar, fridge, safe, IDD phone.

Hard Rock Hotel Pattaya ⭐⭐ *(Kids)* The ultramodern Hard Rock Hotel is a rollicking, good-time oasis in the heart of sordid Pattaya. This is one place in town you might feel okay bringing the kids, and they're sure to have a ball in the sandy-edged pool, game area, and Internet cafe. Rooms are compact and purposely sparse, done in immaculate whites set against bright blue or orange. Each room features larger-than-life murals of your favorite rock-'n'-roll idols, from Elvis to John Lennon. Large family suites are a good option and now come with Xbox for the kids. The lobby and adjoining Hard Rock Cafe feature the chain's typical minimuseum of musical memorabilia; the Lil' Rock kids' club is one of the best going; the spa is tops; and the pool area is compact but has lots of shady areas and massage *salas*—a kind of low, Thai-style pavilion that is a better alternative than the beach.

Beach Rd., P.O. Box 99, Pattaya 20260 (next to Montien Hotel). ✆ **03842-8755**. Fax 03842-1673. www.hardrock hotels.net. 320 units. US$137–US$211 (£75–£116) double; US$337 (£185) suite. AE, MC, V. **Amenities:** 3 restaurants; Hard Rock Cafe w/live rock music; huge outdoor lagoon-style pool; fitness center; spa w/massage, Jacuzzi, sauna, and steam; watersports equipment; children's club; game room; tour desk; limo service; shopping arcade; salon; 24-hr. room service; babysitting; laundry service; dry cleaning; nonsmoking rooms; executive-level rooms; "e-bar" Internet lounge. *In room:* A/C, satellite TV, minibar, fridge, coffeemaker, hair dryer, safe, IDD phone, CD player.

Pattaya Marriott Resort & Spa ⭐⭐ *(Kids)* Right in the center of Pattaya Beach and adjoining the Royal Garden Plaza shopping complex, the Marriott has a quiet courtyard garden and landscaped pool area (with the largest pool in Pattaya)—so you can almost forget Pattaya city just beyond the walls. Spacious balconied rooms have views of the gardens or the sea and are done in a tidy, upscale style common to all Thai Marriotts, with lots of nice little Thai touches and plush bedding. This resort makes for a great retreat full of all the requisite creature comforts. The adjoining Royal Garden Plaza means access to fine dining and entertainment.

218 Beach Rd., Pattaya 20150. ✆ **03841-2120**. Fax 03842-9926. www.marriott.com. 300 units. US$220–US$290 (£121–£160) double; from US$490 (£270) suite. AE, DC, MC, V. **Amenities:** 3 restaurants; lounge; pool w/swim-up bar; 2 lighted grass tennis courts; large fitness center; spa w/Jacuzzi, sauna, and steam; Thai herbal spa; watersports equipment; children's programs; game room; tour desk; limo service; adjacent shopping mall w/more than 50 shops; salon; 24-hr. room service; babysitting; laundry service; dry cleaning; nonsmoking rooms; executive-level rooms; Ripley's Believe It or Not! museum; Motion Master Theater. *In room:* A/C, satellite TV w/in-house movies, dataport, minibar, fridge, coffeemaker, safe, IDD phone.

Royal Cliff Beach Resort ⭐⭐⭐ Comprising the Royal Cliff Grand & Spa, the Royal Wing & Spa, the Royal Cliff Beach Hotel, and the Royal Cliff Terrace, this luxurious compound provides a range of accommodations and is tops in Pattaya. Each property has its own charm. High-end **Royal Cliff Grand** and all-suite **Royal Wing** are the best choices, catering to the well-heeled business traveler. Everything is luxe, from the columned public spaces, chandeliers, and fountains to the large and opulent guest rooms. The Grand's spacious rooms are set in a contemporary, scallop-shaped tower and have marble bathrooms with separate shower stalls and twin sinks. The **Royal Cliff Beach Hotel,** the most affordable choice, is Pattaya's top family resort. Rooms here are also spacious, with bleached wood and pastel decor and large terraces, most with bay views. Two-bedroom suites are perfect for families. The beachfront **Royal Cliff Terrace** was the resort's first property and is the most secluded. Recently renovated rooms now boast contemporary decor as well as nice ocean views. The property is far from town and very quiet.

353 Phra Tamnak Rd., Pattaya 20150 (on cliff, south end of Pattaya Bay). ℂ 03825-0421. Fax 03825-0514. www.royalcliff.com. 1,072 units. 5,800B–8,200B (US$145–US$205/£81–£115) deluxe double; from 11,500B (US$288/£161) suite. AE, DC, MC, V. **Amenities:** All Royal Cliff Beach Resort properties share all facilities, including: 10 restaurants; 5 bars (many w/live music); 5 outdoor landscaped pools; golf course; 4-hole putting green; 6 outdoor lighted tennis courts; fully equipped fitness center w/spa, sauna, steam, and massage; Jacuzzi; watersports equipment; concierge; tour desk; limo service; business center; salon; 24-hr. room service; babysitting; laundry service; dry cleaning; nonsmoking rooms. *In room:* A/C, satellite TV, minibar, fridge, hair dryer, safe, IDD phone.

Sheraton Pattaya Resort 🎯🎯   Perched in the hills south of Pattaya's main beach, the Sheraton is the top choice for a quiet and luxurious getaway. The guest rooms and pavilions descend the hillside, flanking a maze of gardens, waterfalls, and freeform swimming pools. Decorated in pleasing pastel peaches and sea greens, the guest quarters are spacious and contain oversize king or queen beds. There's an attractive man-made white-sand beach by the water. While the rocky waterfront isn't the most inviting place for a dip, the adventurous will find the water much cleaner than that of Pattaya's main beach.

437 Phra Tamnak Rd., Pattaya 20150 (on cliff, south end of Pattaya Bay). ℂ 03825-9888. Fax 03825-9899. www.sheraton.com/pattaya. 156 units. US$220–US$360 (£121–£198) double; from US$1,500 (£825) villa. AE, DC, MC, V. **Amenities:** 3 restaurants; bar; 3 outdoor pools; fitness center; spa; tour desk; limo service; boutique; salon; 24-hr. room service; babysitting; laundry service. *In room:* A/C, satellite TV w/DVD player, dataport, wireless and broadband Internet access, minibar, coffeemaker, hair dryer, safe, IDD phone.

MODERATE

Cabbages & Condoms   This lush, comfortable resort was built by Khun Meechai and the same folks who support sustainable rural development and health education throughout Thailand (see their restaurants in both Bangkok and Chiang Rai, on p. 114 and p. 222, respectively). Rooms are cozy here, and the property is a luxurious oasis in the far south of Pattaya. An atmospheric, affordable escape.

366/11 Moo 12 Phra Tam Nak 4 Rd., Nongprue, Banglamung (south of town on the hilltop, not far from the Royal Cliff). ℂ 03825-0556. Fax 03825-0034. www.cabbagesandcondoms.co.th. 53 units. 3,500B–4,500B (US$88–US$112/ £49–£63) deluxe; from 4,500B (US$112/£63) suite. AE, MC, V. **Amenities:** Restaurant; large outdoor pool; spa w/massage; tour desk; limited room service; laundry service. *In room:* A/C, satellite TV, minibar, fridge.

WHERE TO DINE

Busy Pattaya is chockablock with small storefront bars and eateries. You'll find the big fast-food chains well represented (including two Starbucks along the beachfront road). The **Royal Garden** shopping complex (south of town) and the large **Big C Festival Center** (on Pattaya 2nd Rd., north end of town) support a number of very familiar restaurants.

EXPENSIVE

Mantra ✹✹✹   Part of Amari's expanding empire on the far north of the main beach, Mantra would be right at home 90 miles west in Bangkok or even 8,000 miles east in New York City. By far the most stylish restaurant in Pattaya, newly opened Mantra also serves by far the best food in town. The menu is eclectic: Australian beef, Indian curries, Peking duck, pizza, sushi, and dim sum are among the many choices prepared in open-air stations on the restaurant's main floor. The Sunday brunch is something special and worth the trip from Bangkok even if you're not staying in Pattaya. It's partially a buffet, as the salads, sandwiches, sushi, and desserts are all laid out, but you can also have main dishes cooked to order. We had a four-cheese pizza, pork tenderloin with béarnaise sauce, Peking duck, chicken tikka, Chinese fried vegetables, barbecued shrimp, sushi . . . another pizza, I think (I lost track after a while). Without question the most enjoyable meal I've had in Thailand. Mantra's stylish bar is a happening place on the weekends, too.

At the Amari, 240 Moo 5, Pattaya Beach Rd. (north end of Pattaya). ℂ 03842-9591. www.mantra-pattaya.com. Main courses 120B–2,400B (US$3–US$60/£1.70–£34); Sun brunch 950B (US$24/£13). AE, DC, MC, V. Mon–Sat 6pm–1am; Sun 11am–3pm and 6pm–1am.

MODERATE

PIC Kitchen ✹ THAI   Named for the Pattaya International Clinic (PIC) Hospital next door (don't worry, they're unrelated), PIC has a nice atmosphere of small teak pavilions, both air-conditioned and open-air, and both Thai-style floor seating and romantic tables. Delicious and affordable Thai cuisine is served a la carte or as lunch and dinner set menus. The spring rolls and deep-fried crab claws are mouthwatering. Other dishes come pan-fried, steamed, or charcoal-grilled, with spice added to taste. At night, groove to a live jazz band from 7pm to 1am.

Soi 5 Pattaya 2nd Rd. ℂ 03842-8374. Main courses 100B–550B (US$2.50–US$14/£1.40–£7.70). AE, DC, MC, V. Daily 8am–midnight.

Shere "E" Punjab NORTHERN INDIAN   An inviting little storefront right along the main beach road at town center, Shere "E" Punjab has candlelit tables in air-conditioned comfort. It offers a range of northern Indian cuisine and tandoori-grilled dishes. Everything is cooked to order with fresh ingredients and everything is authentic, a far better choice than the faux-Western eateries in town.

216 Soi 11 Beach Rd. ℂ 03842-0158. Main courses 120B–360B (US$3–US$9/£1.70–£5.05). AE, MC, V. Daily noon–1am.

WHAT TO SEE & DO

Wat Khao Prayai is a small temple complex high above Pattaya to the south, with a 10m (33-ft.) gold Buddha surveying town. The **Pattaya Elephant Village** (info at the Tropicana Hotel, Beach Rd.; ℂ 03842-8158) stages elephant shows daily at 2:30pm and offers jungle treks as well. **Ngong Nooch** (ℂ 03842-2958) is a botanical garden with a culture show on the outskirts of town.

For something completely unusual, **Ripley's Believe It or Not!** (Royal Garden Plaza, 218 Beach Rd., 3rd floor; ℂ 03871-0294) is hilarious, with unusual exhibits and oddities. It's open from 11am to midnight daily; admission is 380B (US$9.50/£5.30). Equally strange, yet very impressive, is the **Sanctuary of Truth** ✹ (206/5 Moo 5, Naklua; ℂ 03836-7229), a 100m-tall (328 ft.) wood structure of intricately carved Thai, Khmer, Chinese, and Lao gods and goddesses. Construction is ongoing; carpenters have worked on the structure since 1981 and expect to finish around 2025.

OUTDOOR ACTIVITIES

GOLF   The hills around Pattaya are known as the "Golf Paradise of the East," with many international-class courses within a short 40km (25-mile) radius of the city.

- **Bangphra International Golf Club,** 45 Moo 6, Tambon Bang Phra, Sri Racha (✆ **03834-1149**), is the finest course in Pattaya, although it's a long drive (greens fees: 980B/US$25/£14 weekdays, 1,800B/US$45/£25 weekends).
- **Laem Chabang International Country Club,** 106/8 Moo 4 Tambon Bung, Sri Ratcha (✆ **03837-2273**), is a 9-hole course designed by Jack Nicklaus with very dramatic scenery (greens fees: 2,500B/US$63/£35 weekdays, 3,000B/US$75/£42 weekends).
- **Siam Country Club,** 50 Tambol Poeng, Banglamung (✆ **03824-9381;** fax 03824-9387; www.siamcountryclub.com), is a short hop from Pattaya and believed to be one of the country's most challenging courses. Closed for renovation at the time of writing, but scheduled to reopen in mid-2007.

WATERSPORTS   Efforts at cleanup are ongoing, but the bay in Pattaya is still quite polluted. Sad that development ruined the one thing that drew travelers here in the first place. Beach sand is coarse; swimming, if you dare, is best either at the very north of Pattaya Beach or a 15-minute drive south, over the mountain, to Jomtien Beach.

   The bay is full of boats ready to take you to outlying islands like **Ko Khrok, Ko Lan,** and **Ko Sok** for a day of private beach lounging or snorkeling starting at 500B (US$13/£7) per head on a full boat (more for a private charter). It'll cost you a bit more to access far-flung **Bamboo Island** or **Ko Man Wichai**—some 2,000B (US$50/£28). Contact **Adventure Divers,** 219/56 Soi Yamato (✆ **03836-4453**), for scuba trips.

   Paragliding around the bay behind a motorboat is a popular beachfront activity; a 5-minute flight costs from 500B (US$13/£7). Jomtien Beach hosts **windsurfing** and **sea-kayaking;** boards and boats are rented along the beach for rates starting at 200B (US$5/£2.80) per hour.

PATTAYA AFTER DARK

Pattaya is all flashing neon and blaring music down even the smallest soi, an assault on the senses. Places like the south Pattaya pedestrian area, "Walking Street," are lined with open-air watering holes with bar girls luring passersby: The nightlife finds you in this town with an imploring, "You, mister, where you go?" Go-go bars are everywhere and red-light "Bar Beer" joints are springing up as fast as local officials can close them down. The city is a larger version of Bangkok's Patpong, complete with "Boyz Town," a row of gay clubs in south Pattaya. The same debauch that brings so many to Pattaya is pretty sad in the light of day, though, when bleary-eyed revelers stumble around streets once glowing with neon, now bleak and strewn with garbage.

   There are a few spots without the sleaze. **Hopf Brewery** (219 Beach Rd.; ✆ 03871-0650) makes its own fine brand of suds, and the in-house Hopf Band plays everything from old Herb Alpert tunes to newer jazzy sounds. **Shenanigan's** (✆ 03871-0641) is a fun Irish bar at the Royal Garden complex (near the Marriott), with the front entrance on Pattaya 2nd Road. **Henry J. Bean's** (on the beach near the Amari Hotel; ✆ 03842-8161) has a live band and a light, friendly atmosphere.

The town's campy cabaret shows are touristy good fun. Pattaya's most beautiful *katoeys* (transsexuals) don sequined gowns and feather boas to strut their stuff for packed houses nightly. Both **Tiffany's** (464 Moo 9, 2nd Rd.; ✆ **03842-9642**) and **Alcazar** (78/14 Pattaya 2nd Rd., opposite Soi 5; ✆ **03803841-0224**) have hilarious shows much like those in other tourist towns in Thailand. Tickets start at 500B (US$13/£7). The biggest disco, **Palladium** (78/33–35 Pattaya 2nd Rd.; ✆ **03836-1376**), is a cavernous dance hall with pulsing music, karaoke, and snooker.

7 Ban Phe & Ko Samet ✶

220km (136 miles) E of Bangkok on Hwy. 3 via Pattaya (or 185km/115 miles via Pattaya bypass)

Tiny **Ko Samet** first became popular with Thais from the poetry of Sunthon Phu, a venerated 19th-century author and Rayong native who set his best-known epic on this "tropical island paradise." Just 1km (a half-mile) wide, Ko Samet is split by a rocky ridge. The east coast is lined with budget bungalows. Ko Samet is a national park (you'll pay 400B/US$10/£5.60 to enter Diamond Beach), but it's unclear what's being protected here. It's best to arrive on a weekday for ease in finding a room, but stick around for the weekend to join in with the big groups from Bangkok. The island is accessed from the town of **Ban Phe,** 35km (22 miles) east of Rayong city.

GETTING THERE

BY BUS   Buses leave Bangkok every hour between 5am and 7pm for the 3½-hour journey, departing from the city's **Eastern Bus Terminal (Ekamai),** on Sukhumvit Road opposite Soi 63 (✆ **02391-8097**). The one-way trip to the ferry landing at Ban Phe costs 167B (US$4.10/£2.35). If you're coming from Pattaya, you'll have to wait on the highway and flag down anything heading east.

BY MINIBUS   **Samet Island Tour** (109/22 Moo 10 Pratumnak Rd., Pattaya; ✆ **03871-0676**) runs regular routes from Pattaya (trip time: 1 hr.; 460B/US$13/ £6.45 round-trip). Private cars can also be arranged.

BY CAR   Take Highway 3 east from Bangkok along the longer, more scenic coastal route (trip time: 3½–4 hr.), or the quicker route via Highway 3 east to Pattaya, then Highway 36 to Rayong, then the coastal Highway 3 to Ban Phe (trip time: about 3 hr.).

GETTING TO & AROUND THE ISLAND

Connect by bus from central Rayong to the ferry pier at Ban Phe (✆ **03865-1508**). From there, ferries leave for Ko Samet's northern ferry terminal at Na Dan every half-hour (trip time: 40 min.; 50B (US$1.25/£0.70) or when full. The first boat departs at 8am and the last at 6pm. Several agents at the pier in Ban Phe sell passage directly to Vong Deuan beach for as little as 60B (US$1.50/£0.85).

After arriving at the ferry terminal on the northern tip of Ko Samet, you can catch a **songtao** (covered pickup truck) to other beaches for between 20B and 50B (US50¢–US$1.25/£0.30–£0.70). Or you can rent **scooters** with good suspension for about 400B (US$10/£5.60) per day. There is one road on Samet connecting the main town, Samet village, halfway down the eastern shore of the island to Vong Deuan.

FAST FACTS: KO SAMET

Ko Samet has no banks or ATMs, but any resort can change money. The **post office** is at the Naga Bar, along the main road south of Diamond Beach.

WHERE TO STAY & DINE

With few exceptions, accommodations are basic, but rates are higher than at other "undeveloped" island resorts because food and water must be imported from the mainland. Hotel and transport touts pounce at the pier.

All of the bungalows offer some sort of dining experience, mostly bland local food and beer, with some Western breakfast offerings. In the evenings on Vong Deuan beach, tables are set up under twinkling lights alongside big seafood barbecues brimming with the day's catch. It's very pretty. Try **Sea Horse.**

AO KIEW

Paradee ⊛   This well may be the first of many superluxe resorts on Ko Samet, but for now it's the only option and an attractive one at that. Best reached by boat, the Paradee occupies a sliver of land at the southern tip of Samet that offers ocean access on both the east and west coasts (something for both sunrise and sunset enthusiasts). Most of the resort's thatch-roofed villas come with a private pool and Jacuzzi, and all are spacious with imposing four-poster beds, sizable bathrooms, and furnished wood patios. Numerous high-tech amenities include flatscreen TVs, DVD players, and free broadband Internet access. Here's a unique touch: Give the chef a day's notice and he'll do his best to prepare any meal you desire. When the resort works all the kinks out, it has the potential to be truly special.

76 Moo 4, Tumbol Phe, Rayong, Ko Samet 21160 (on southern tip of island, best reached by direct boat). ⓒ 03864-4283. Fax 03864-4290. www.paradeeresort.com. 40 units. 13,500B (US$338/£189) garden villa; 18,000B (US$450/£252) garden villa w/pool; 22,500B–27,500B (US$563–US$688/£315–£385) beachfront villa w/pool. AE, MC, V. **Amenities:** Restaurant; 2 bars; fitness center; spa; watersports equipment; tour desk; 24-hr. room service; babysitting; Internet cafe; DVD library. *In room:* A/C, satellite TV w/DVD player, free Internet access, minibar, safe, IDD phone.

AO PRAO

This is the only beach on the west coast, reached either by pickup or motorbike from the ferry or else directly by ferry. **Le Vimarn** (ⓒ **03864-4104**), a hillside collection of bungalows and villas, offers the highest standard on Ao Prao. Bungalows start at 7,800B (US$195/£109). Next door is the more affordable **Ao Prao Resort** (ⓒ **03861-6881**), Le Vimarn's sister property, with bungalows from 4,800B (US$120/£67). Contact either of these resorts for direct ferry service.

VONG DEUAN

This area is the most happening beach in Samet. Busy, with lots of bungalows and open-air eateries, Vong Deuan has a good vibe in the evening and it's a fun party spot on the weekend. The beach is about halfway down the island and can be reached by ferry directly from Ban Phe for just 60B (US$1.50/£0.85) one-way.

Malibu Garden Resort (ⓒ **03864-4020**) has clean, spartan rooms starting at just 1,150B (US$27/£16) at its central motel-style campus. It has an in-house tour operator and provides direct boat connection. **Vongdeuan Resort** (ⓒ **03864-4171;** www.vongdeuan.com) is a similar budget standard just next door.

8 Trat & Ko Chang ⊛

400km (248 miles) E of Bangkok

Trat's dramatic, wooded landscape crests at the Khao Bantat Range, which separates Thailand's easternmost province from neighboring Cambodia. The local economy relies on rubber and chili plantations, fish farming, and fishing. Memories of territorial conflicts with nearby Cambodia are fresh, but the situation is calm. Trat Province is the gateway to the tranquil, unspoiled acres of **Mu Ko Chang National Park,** 52 heavily wooded islands, most accessible by ferry from the cape at Laem Ngop. **Ko Chang** is scenically beautiful and very, very quiet.

GETTING THERE

BY BUS   There are numerous daily departures from Bangkok's **Eastern Bus Terminal (Ekamai)** to Trat (✆ **02391-8097;** trip time: 5–6 hr.; 257B/US$6/£3.60). Less frequent buses leave from Bangkok's **Northern Bus Terminal** (✆ **02936-2852;** 266B/US$6.65/£3.70). From Pattaya, you'll have to flag down westbound buses along Sukhumvit Road; it's a 3½-hour trip. Pattaya tour companies can also arrange direct minivans.

BY CAR   Take Highway 3 east from Bangkok to Chonburi, then Highway 344 southeast to Klaeng (bypassing Pattaya and Rayong), then the coastal Highway 3 east through Chanthaburi and south to Trat (trip time: about 5–6 hr.).

GETTING TO & AROUND THE ISLAND

From Trat, you'll hop a shared songtao to the pier at Ao Thammachat or Center Point for just 30B (US75¢/£0.40). Seven ferries depart **Ao Thammachat** daily from 7am to 7pm (trip time: 30 min.; 30B/US75¢/£0.40) and land on Ko Chang at the **Ao Sapparos** ferry terminal. Ferries from **Center Point** leave every hour from 6am to 6pm (trip time: 40 min; 50B/US$1.25/£0.70), landing at **Dan Kao Cabana Pier.** Less frequent boats leave from the **Laem Ngop** pier (50B/US$1.25/£0.70), a similar 30B ride from Trat.

Once on the island, you can hop a **songtao** to your destination, starting at 50B (US$1.25/£0.70) for a 15-minute ride to White Sand Beach (touts from the many bungalows will offer free rides if you stay at their place).

VISITOR INFORMATION

The **TAT** has an office in Trat (Moo 1 Trat-Laem Ngop Rd.; ✆ **03959-7259**) and provides information about the nearby islands.

WHERE TO STAY & DINE

If you're arriving in the late evening and get stranded in Trat, the **Muang Trad Hotel,** 4 Sukhumvit Rd. (✆ **03951-1091**), 1 block south of the bus terminal, has rooms from 650B (US$16/£9.10) with air-conditioning.

EXPENSIVE

Amari Emerald Cove Resort & Spa 🏖🏖   The Amari has an easy and effective formula for success in Thailand: well-maintained, professionally staffed resorts with comfortable rooms and excellent dining. Well, maybe it's not that easy, but they sure make it look easy—and the Emerald Cove is a case in point. Some of the most attractive rooms in the Amari chain, with beautiful rosewood floors and comfortable modern furnishings, line an immaculately kept courtyard, the crown jewel being the beachfront 50m (164 ft.) lap pool. During the day, the ever-vigilant staff will assist you with your every need. At night, you have the choice of excellent Thai or Italian cuisine.

88/8 Moo 4, Ko Chang 23170. ✆ **03955-2000.** Fax 03955-2001. www.amari.com. 165 units. US$190 (£105) superior; US$222 (£122) deluxe; US$385 (£212) suite. AE, MC, V. **Amenities:** 3 restaurants; 2 bars; large outdoor pool; children's pool; fitness center; spa; Jacuzzi; sauna; tour desk; car rental; 24-hr. room service; massage; babysitting; laundry service. *In room:* A/C, satellite TV, Wi-Fi, minibar, coffeemaker, hair dryer, safe, IDD phone.

> **Tips Malaria?**
>
> Malaria is endemic to the heavily forested islands of Mu Ko Chang National
> Park and the jungle-covered foothills of Trat Province, but no cases have been
> reported in a number of years. It's all the buzz on the boat ride over, but don't
> believe the hype. Still, it is a good idea, as anywhere in Thailand, to avoid get-
> ting bitten. Bring insect repellent (with DEET if possible), and keep skin covered
> up at dusk and dawn.

Panviman ✶ Before the Amari (above) opened, the Panviman was the most luxurious choice on the island. The spacious grounds are meticulously manicured, and the
pool is a beautiful little meander flanked on one side by a casual bar, on the other by
the resort's fine dining—everything oriented to great views of the sea (with the accompanying great sunsets). Check out the little garden gnomes all about. Rooms are set in
high-peaked, Thai-style buildings with arching *naga* roofs. They're done in tile and
teak, each with canopy bed, large sitting area, balcony, and huge stylish bathroom. It's
not a private beach, but the resort is far south of central White Sand Beach, so even
in high season you might have a vast stretch of sand to yourself.

8/15 Klong Prao Beach, Ko Chang 23120 (a short ride south of White Sand Beach on the west coast of the island).
ⓒ 03955-1290, or 02910-8660 in Bangkok. Fax 03955-1283. www.panviman.com. 50 units. 7,500B (US$188/£103)
double. MC, V. **Amenities:** Restaurant; bar; outdoor pool; fitness center; Jacuzzi; watersports equipment; tour desk;
car rental; transfer services; limited room service; massage; laundry service; Internet access. *In room:* A/C, satellite TV,
minibar, fridge, coffeemaker, safe, IDD phone.

MODERATE
Banpu (9/11 Moo 4, White Sand Beach; ⓒ 03955-1234) is typical of the atmospheric bungalows along White Sand Beach. Rooms start at 2,500B (US$63/£35).

WHAT TO SEE & DO
Ko Chang, Thailand's second-largest island after Phuket, is the anchor of the 52-
island **Mu Ko Chang National Park.** Thickly forested hills rise from its many rocky
bays, forming a swaying hump reminiscent of a sleeping elephant (*chang* means elephant). Although they are not indigenous to the island, there are opportunities for elephant treks. The best choice by far is the **Ban Kwan Chang Elephant Camp.**
Supported by the Asian Elephant Foundation, the camp offers half-day tours that
include feeding, bathing, and riding (the elephants). Contact Jungle Way Bungalows
at ⓒ 089-223-4795 for information.

Cambodia is visible from the eastern shore of Ko Chang. **Hat Sai Khao (White
Sand Beach),** on the island's west coast, is the most popular beach. Twenty minutes
by boat farther south is **Hat Khlong Phrao,** with clusters of bungalows, an inland
canal, and a fishing settlement. There is good snorkeling off Ko Chang's south coast;
contact tour operators for details and to arrange passage by boat.

---

9 An Introduction to the Southern Peninsula: East Coast & Islands

Thailand's slim Malay Peninsula extends 1,250km (775 miles) south from Bangkok
to the Malaysia border. The towns of **Cha-Am** and royal **Hua Hin** are just a short hop

The Southern Peninsula: East Coast

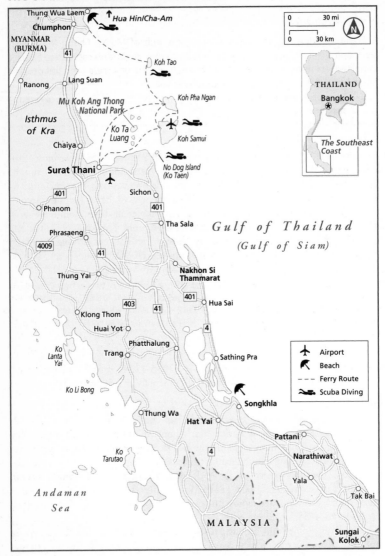

south of Bangkok, and the ancient temples of **Phetchaburi,** the last outpost of the Khmer empire, are a good day trip from there.

Passing through coastal towns like Prachuap Kiri Khan and Chumphon, heading further south you come to **Surat Thani,** a popular jumping-off point for islands in the east: Koh Samui, Koh Pha Ngan, and Koh Tao. If the beach resorts of Phuket dominate the tourist landscape on the west coast, so too, **Koh Samui,** a developed but laid-back resort island in the Gulf of Siam, dominates the east. Nearby **Koh Pha**

Ngan, famed for its wild full-moon parties, is gaining prominence as a rustic resort destination, as is **Koh Tao** for its access to some of Thailand's best dive sites.

10 Hua Hin & Cha-Am

Hua Hin: 265km (164 miles) S of Bangkok, 223km (138 miles) N of Chumphon; Cha-Am: 240km (149 miles) S of Bangkok, 248km (154 miles) N of Chumphon

Hua Hin and **Cha-Am,** neighboring towns on the Gulf of Thailand, are together the country's oldest resort area. Developed in the 1920s as a relaxing getaway for Bangkok's elite, the beautiful seaside of "Thailand's Riviera" was a mere 3- to 4-hour journey from the capital by train, thanks to the southern railway's completion in 1916. The royal family was the first to embrace these two small fishing villages as the perfect location for both summer vacations and health retreats. In 1924, King Vajiravudh (Rama VI) built the royal Mareukatayawan Palace amid the tall evergreens that lined these stretches of golden sand. At the same time, the Royal Hua Hin Golf Course opened as the first course in Thailand. As Bangkok's upper classes began building summer bungalows along the shore, the State Railway opened the Hua Hin Railway Hotel for tourists, which stands today as the Sofitel Central Hua Hin Resort, and until his recent health problems, the King of Thailand spent much of his time at his regal residence just north of town. Today, the area's clean sea and beaches support some unique resorts, and nearby **Phetchaburi** (see "Side Trips from Hua Hin & Cha-Am," later in this section) is a fascinating and easy day trip to experience a bit of Thai history and culture.

Plan your trip for the months between November and May to get the most sunshine and least rain, but note that from about mid-December to mid-January, Hua Hin and Cha-Am reach peak levels and bookings should be made well in advance (at higher rates). This is also increasingly true for weekends year-round, as more and more weekenders from Bangkok are making Hua Hin their destination of choice.

GETTING THERE

BY PLANE There is an airport here, but no domestic connections.

BY TRAIN Both Hua Hin and Cha-Am are reached via the train station in Hua Hin. Ten trains make the daily trek from Bangkok's **Hua Lampong Railway Station** (© **1690** or 02223-7010). The trip is just over 4 hours.

The **Hua Hin Railway Station** (© **03251-1073**) is at the tip of Damnoenkasem Road, which slices through the center of town straight to the beach. Pickup-truck taxis *(songtao)* or tuk-tuks to town start at 50B (US$1.25/£0.70).

BY BUS The bus is the most efficient choice for travel from Bangkok. Buses depart from Bangkok's **Southern Bus Terminal** (© **02434-7192**) every 20 minutes from 5am to 10pm (151B/US$3.75/£2.10). There are also five daily buses to Cha-Am between 5am and 2pm (130B/US$3.25/£1.80).

Buses from Bangkok arrive in Hua Hin at the air-conditioned bus station on Srasong Road, 1 block north of Damnoenkasem Road (© **03251-1230**). From here it's easy to find a songtao or tuk-tuk to take you to your destination. The Cha-Am bus station is on the main beach road (© **03242-5307**).

Minibuses can be arranged at any hotel or travel agent in either Bangkok or Hua Hin. Regular minivan departures leave from the west side of the traffic circle at Bangkok's busy Victory Monument (a stop on the BTS skytrain) between 5:30am and 6pm and cost 180B (US$4.50/£2.50).

BY CAR   From Bangkok, take Route 35, the Thonburi–Paktho Highway, southwest and allow 2 to 4 hours, depending on traffic.

GETTING AROUND

Despite all the tourist traffic, **Hua Hin** is easy to navigate. The main artery, Petchkasem Road, runs parallel to the waterfront about 4 blocks inland. Wide Damnoenkasem Road cuts through Petchkasem and runs straight to the beach. On the north side of Damnoenkasem toward the waterfront, you'll find a cluster of guesthouses, restaurants, shopping, and nightspots lining the narrow lanes.

Smaller **Cha-Am** is a 25-minute drive north of Hua Hin along Petchkasem Road. Ruamchit Road, also known as Beach Road, hugs the shore and is lined with shops, restaurants, hotels, and motels. Cha-Am's resorts line the 8km (5-mile) stretch of beach that runs south from the village toward Hua Hin.

BY SONGTAO   Pickup-truck taxis follow regular routes in Hua Hin, passing the railway station and bus terminals at regular intervals. Flag one down that's going in your direction. Fares range from 10B to 20B (US25¢–US50¢/£0.15–£0.30) within town, while stops at outlying resorts will cost up to 50B (US$1.25/£0.70). Trips between Hua Hin and Cha-Am are between 100B and 200B (US$2.50–US$5/£1.40–£2.80).

BY TUK-TUK   Tuk-tuks rides are negotiable, as always, but expect to pay as little as 40B (US$1/£0.55) for a ride within town.

BY MOTORCYCLE TAXI   Within each town, motorcycle-taxi fares begin at 20B (US50¢/£0.30). The taxi drivers, identifiable by colorful numbered vests, are a good way to get to your resort if you're in Cha-Am after hours (about 100B/US$2.50/£1.40).

BY TRISHAW   Trishaws, or *samlors,* can be hired for short distances in town (from 20B/US50¢/£0.30). You can also negotiate an hourly rate.

BY CAR/MOTORCYCLE   **Avis** has a desk at both the Sofitel Central Hua Hin Resort (℃ 03251-2021) and the Dusit Resort & Polo Club in Cha-Am (℃ 03252-0008). **Budget** has an office at the Grand Hotel (℃ 03251-4220). Self-drive rates start at 1,210B (US$30/£17). Cheaper alternatives can be rented from stands near the beach on Damnoenkasem Road. A 100cc motorcycle goes for 200B (US$5/£2.80) per day.

VISITOR INFORMATION

The **Hua Hin Tourist Information Center** (℃ 03251-1047 or 03253-2433) is in the center of town, tucked behind the city shrine at the corner of Damnoenkasem and Petchkasem roads. Open daily from 8:30am to 8pm. In Cha-Am, the **TAT office** (℃ 03247-1005 or 03247-1006) is inconveniently located on the corner of Petchkasem Road and Narathip Road.

FAST FACTS: HUA HIN & CHA-AM

IN HUA HIN   All major **banks** are along Petchkasem Road to the north of Damnoenkasem; there are also many money changers throughout the town. The main **post office** (℃ 03251-1350) is on Damnoenkasem Road near the Petchkasem intersection. Hua Hin has **Internet cafes** along the more-traveled shopping streets. The **Hua Hin Hospital** (℃ 03252-0371) is in the north of town along Petchkasem Road. Call the **tourist police** at ℃ 03251-5995.

IN CHA-AM **Banks** and the **Muangphet Thonburi Hospital** (☏ 03241-5190) are centered along Petchkasem Road, while the **post office** is on Beach Road. **Internet access** is available along the beach road. Call the **tourist police** at ☏ 03251-5995.

WHERE TO STAY IN HUA HIN
VERY EXPENSIVE
Chiva-Som International Health Resort ✸✸✸ Chiva-Som is a new beginning for many. One of the finest high-end health resorts in the region, this peaceful campus is a sublime collection of handsome pavilions, bungalows, and central buildings dressed in fine teak and sea-colored tiles nestled in landscaped grounds just beyond a pristine beach. But what brings so many to Chiva-Som are its spa programs: From Chi Gong to chin-ups, muscle straining to massage, a stay at Chiva-Som is a chance to escape the workaday world and focus on development of body and mind. Leave the kids at home, turn off the cellphone, and change the suit for loose-fitting cotton because, whether just to relax or to start a new chapter in life, a visit to Chiva-Som is proactive. Upon check-in, you'll fill out an extensive survey, have a brief medical check-up, and meet with a counselor who can tailor a program to fit your needs, goals, and budget or package you have booked (there is a wide range). Guests might focus on early-morning yoga, stretching, and tough workouts, or go for gentle massages, aromatherapy, even isolation chambers and past-life regression workshops. The choices are many, and the personal trainers, staff, and facilities are unmatched in the region. The resort's spa cuisine is not all granola and oats, but rather simple, healthy fare, and there is a nice bond that develops between guests and staff in weekly barbecues and frequent "mocktail" parties. The spa treatments are fantastic: Don't pass up the signature Chiva-Som massage. Day-spa visitors are welcome.

73/4 Petchkasem Rd., Hua Hin 77110 (5-min. drive south of Hua Hin). ☏ 03253-6536. Fax 03251-1615. www. chivasom.com. 57 units. All rates are quoted per person: US$380 (£209) oceanview double; US$485 (£267) pavilion; from US$655 (£195) suite. Nightly rate includes 3 spa-cuisine meals per day, health and beauty consultations, daily massage, and participation in fitness and leisure activities. Contact the resort about other packages. AE, DC, MC, V. **Amenities:** 2 restaurants; ozonated indoor swimming pool and outdoor swimming pool; golf course nearby; amazing fitness center w/personal trainers and exercise classes; his-and-hers spas w/steam and hydrotherapy treatments, massage, beauty treatments, floatation, and medical advisement; watersports equipment; bike rental; concierge; tour desk; limo service; salon; 24-hr. room service; laundry service; dry cleaning; nonsmoking rooms; library. *In room:* A/C, satellite TV, minibar, fridge, safe, IDD phone.

EXPENSIVE
Anantara Resort Hua Hin ✸✸ The Anantara is a collection of teak pavilions surrounded by lily ponds, and from the hotel's most luxurious rooms and their wide balconies, you can hear chirping frogs and watch buzzing dragonflies. More affordable rooms cluster around a manicured courtyard. All accommodations are furnished in Thai style with teak-and-rattan furniture. Deluxe units have either garden or sea view, with terrace rooms offering large patios perfect for private barbecues. Suites have enormous aggregate bathtubs that open to guest rooms via a sliding door. Both suites and lagoon rooms offer exclusive use of the lagoon pool (adults only), as well as other fine perks. Fine-dining options are many and the resort's spa is large and luxurious.

43/1 Petchkasem Beach Rd., Hua Hin 77110. ☏ 03252-0250. Fax 03252-0259. www.anantara.com. 197 units. US$300–US$360 (£165–£198) deluxe; US$390 (£215) superior lagoon; from US$570 (£314) suite. AE, DC, MC, V. **Amenities:** 4 restaurants; lounge; 2 outdoor pools; children's pool; outdoor lighted tennis courts; fitness center; spa w/sauna, steam, massage; Jacuzzi; watersports equipment and instruction; bike and motorcycle rental; children's playground; concierge; tour desk; car rental; limo service; shopping arcade; salon; 24-hr. room service; babysitting; laundry service; dry cleaning; nonsmoking rooms. *In room:* A/C, satellite TV, minibar, fridge, coffeemaker, hair dryer, safe, IDD phone.

Hilton Hua Hin Resort & Spa 🌟🌟

Right in the heart of downtown Hua Hin, this massive tower overlooks the main beach. It's a Hilton, which means a fine room standard and courteous staff. Accommodations are spacious and well appointed, with balconies overlooking the sea. New spa suites are particularly classy, with sleek contemporary Thai decor. The marble lobby with quiet reflection pools is welcoming, the beachside pool is luxurious, and there are extensive indoor facilities and activities for rainy days. The Hua Hin Resort is a top international standard and the best location for strolling the main beach area, in-town shopping, and nightlife.

33 Narsdamri Rd., Hua Hin 77110 (on the main beach and in the heart of downtown shopping). © 03251-2888. Fax 02250-0999. www.huahin.hilton.com. 296 units. US$190–US$263 (£105–£145) double; US$280 (£154) suite. AE, DC, MC, V. **Amenities:** 3 restaurants; 2 bars; outdoor pool; 2 tennis courts; 2 squash courts; large fitness center; spa w/massage, Jacuzzi, sauna, and steam; concierge; tour desk; car rental; shopping arcade; salon; 24-hr. room service; babysitting; laundry service; dry cleaning. *In room:* A/C, satellite TV w/in-house movies, wireless and broadband Internet access, minibar, fridge, coffeemaker, hair dryer, safe, IDD phone.

Hua Hin Marriott Resort & Spa 🌟 (Kids)

From the giant swinging couches in the main lobby to the large central pavilions, the Marriott is done in a grand, if exaggerated, Thai style. It attracts large groups, but is a good choice for families. Ponds, pools, boats, golf, tennis, and other sports venues dot the junglelike grounds leading to the open beach area. There is a good children's club, and the staff throughout the hotel seems to really enjoy kids, not just tolerate them. The hotel is relatively far from the busy town center, but provides shuttle service. Deluxe rooms are the best choice—large, amenity-filled, and facing the sea. Terrace rooms at beachside are worth the bump up. The spa is luxurious, too.

107/1 Petchkasem Beach Rd., Hua Hin 77110. © 800/228-9290 in the U.S., or 03251-1881. Fax 03251-2422. 216 units. US$180–US$200 (£99–£110) double; US$250–US$260 (£138–£143) beachfront; from US$440 (£242) suite. AE, DC, MC, V. **Amenities:** 3 restaurants; lounge; outdoor pool; golf course nearby; outdoor lighted tennis courts; fitness center; spa; watersports equipment; bike rental; children's playground and zoo; concierge; tour desk; car rental; limo service; shopping arcade; salon; 24-hr. room service; massage; babysitting; laundry service; dry cleaning; nonsmoking rooms. *In room:* A/C, satellite TV, minibar, coffeemaker, safe, IDD phone.

Sofitel Central Hua Hin Resort 🌟🌟🌟

The original Hua Hin Railway Hotel opened in the 1920s and is the classiest, most luxurious hotel going. There's a cool, calm colonial effect to the whitewashed buildings, shaded verandas and walkways, fine wooden details, red-tile roofs, and immaculate gardens with topiaries. A small museum contains photography and memorabilia, and the original 14 bedrooms are preserved for posterity. Subsequent additions and renovations over the years have expanded the place into a large and modern full-facility property without sacrificing a bit of its former charm. The original rooms have their unique appeal, but the newer rooms are larger, brighter, and more comfortable. With furnishings that reflect the hotel's old beach-resort feel, they are still modern and cozy. Sofitel's three magnificent outdoor pools are finely landscaped and have sun decks under shady trees. The spa, in its own beachside bungalow, provides full-service health and beauty treatments, and the fitness center is extensive.

1 Damnoenkasem Rd., Hua Hin 77110 (in the center of town by the beach). © 800/221-4542 in the U.S., or 03251-2021. Fax 03251-1014. www.sofitel.com. 214 units. 10,970B–12,382B (US$274–US$310/£154–£173) double; from 15,207B (US$380/£213) suite. DC, MC, V. **Amenities:** 5 restaurants; lounge and bar; 3 outdoor pools; putting green and miniature golf; golf course nearby; outdoor lighted tennis courts; fitness center; spa w/massage; watersports

equipment; bike rental; kids' club; concierge; tour desk; car rental; limo service; business center; shopping arcade; salon; 24-hr. room service; babysitting; laundry service; dry cleaning; nonsmoking rooms; executive-level rooms; daily crafts and language lessons; nature tours; billiards room. *In room:* A/C, satellite TV, minibar, fridge, hair dryer, safe, IDD phone.

MODERATE

For affordable, in-town accommodations, try **PP Villa** (11 Damnoenkasem Rd.; ✆ 03253-3785), with tidy rooms from 950B (US$24/£13); or the **Fresh Inn Hotel** (132 Naretdamri Rd., across from the Hilton; ✆ 03251-1389), with clean doubles starting at 1,700B (US$43/£24).

WHERE TO STAY IN CHA-AM
MODERATE
Regent Cha-Am Beach Resort & Spa ✿   No relation to the Regent chain, the Regent Cha-Am is a sprawling property, the combination of three resorts for a total of some 708 rooms (at the Regent Resort and more luxury Regency Wing and Regent Chalet). There are lots of services, large pools, watersports, squash, and a small fitness area. The main resort is a massive courtyard, while the Chalet is a separate, quieter bungalow facility (the best choice). Standard rooms are comfortable and affordable, done up like the average chain hotel but very clean and cozy. The resort is on the road between Hua Hin and Cha-Am—it's a long ride to either. Come with your own wheels or else be stuck here. The Regent is busy year-round, mostly on the weekends.

849/21 Petchkasem Rd., Cha-Am 76120. ✆ 03245-1240. Fax 03245-1277. www.regent-chaam.com. 708 units. 4,718B–6,120B (US$118–US$153/£66–£86) double; from 6,591B (US$165/£92) suite. AE, MC, V. **Amenities:** 3 restaurants; lounge; 3 pools; outdoor lighted tennis courts; squash courts; fitness center; Jacuzzi; watersports equipment; bike and motorcycle rental; game room; tour desk; limo service; business center; salon; 24-hr. room service; massage; babysitting; laundry service; dry cleaning. *In room:* A/C, satellite TV, minibar, fridge, IDD phone.

WHERE TO DINE
The resorts have more restaurants than there is room to list; no matter where you stay, you'll have great in-house dining options. The main piers in both Hua Hin and Cha-Am are busy every morning, when fishing boats return with their loads. Nearby open-air restaurants serve fresh seafood at a fraction of what you'd pay in Bangkok. In town, there are lots of small storefront eateries, tourist cafes, and seafood places along the beach. The **Night Market,** on Dechanuchit Road west of Petchkasem Road in the north end of Hua Hin, is a great spot for authentic local eats for very little.

Itsara ✿ THAI   In a two-story seaside home built in the 1920s, this restaurant has a real laid-back charm, from the noisy open kitchen to the terrace seating and views of the beach—quite atmospheric. It's a good place to get together with friends, cover the table with dishes, and enjoy the good life. Specialties include a sizzling hot plate of glass noodles with prawn, squid, pork, and vegetables. Fresh seafood and meats are prepared steamed or deep-fried, and can be served with either salt, chili, or red-curry paste.

7 Napkehard St., Hua Hin (seaside, a 50B/$1.25/£0.70 trishaw ride north from the town center). ✆ 03253-0574. Reservations recommended for Sat dinner. Main courses 60B–380B (US$1.50–US$9.50/£0.85–£5.30). AE, MC, V. Daily 11am–10pm.

WHAT TO SEE & DO
The stunning Khmer-style temples of **Phetchaburi** (described at the end of this section) are the most significant cultural sights near Hua Hin and Cha-Am, but most folks are here simply to escape Bangkok and to enjoy the beaches.

The **Sofitel Central Hua Hin Resort** (see "Where to Stay in Hua Hin," above), originally built in the 1920s for Thai royals and their guests, is itself an attraction. Visitors are welcome to tour the grounds or enjoy **high tea** in a quaint garden area (daily 3:30–6pm; 420B/US$11/£5.90).

Shoppers will enjoy Hua Hin's 2-block-long **Night Market** (on Dechanuchit Rd. west of Petchkasem Rd., in the north end of town), which is busy from dusk until late with small food stalls and vendors selling tasty treats and fun trinkets. On Damnoenkasem Road near the beach, you can also browse local handicrafts and batik clothing.

For nightlife, your best bet is Hua Hin. A 15-minute stroll through the labyrinth of sois between Damnoenkasem, Poolsuk, and Dechanuchit roads near the beach reveals all sorts of small places to stop for a cool cocktail and some fun.

OUTDOOR ACTIVITIES

GOLF   Hua Hin is a golf getaway for Bangkokians. It's best to make reservations. The larger hotels run shuttles to all courses.

- **Royal Hua Hin Golf Course,** Damnoenkasem Road near the Hua Hin Railway Station (© **03251-2475**), was Thailand's first championship golf course, opened in 1924. Don't miss the many topiary figures along its fairways (greens fees: 1,200B/US$30/£17 weekdays, 1,500B/US$38/£21 weekends).
- **Springfield Royal Country Club,** 193 Huay-Sai Nua, Petchkasem Road, Cha-Am (© **03270-9222**), designed by Jack Nicklaus in 1993, is in a beautiful valley setting—the best by far (greens fees: 3,500B/US$88/£49).

WATERSPORTS   Most resorts forbid noisy jet skis, but the beaches are lined with young entrepreneurs renting them out for 1,000B (US$25/£14) per half-hour. Windsurfers and Hobie Cats are available at most resorts or through small outfits along the beach, starting at 400B (US$10/£5.60) and 1,100B (US$27/£15) per hour, respectively. Call **Western Tours** (11 Damnoenkasem Rd.; © **03253-3303**) to ask about snorkeling trips to outer islands for about 1,800B (US$45/£25) per person.

SIDE TRIPS FROM HUA HIN & CHA-AM

PHETCHABURI

Phetchaburi dates from the same period as Ayutthaya and Kanchanaburi, and later served as an important military city. Phetchaburi's palace and historically significant temples are the highlights of an excellent day trip—it's just an hour from Hua Hin. The main attraction is **Phra Nakhorn Khiri,** a 19th-century summer palace of King Mongkut (Rama IV) in the hills overlooking the city, reachable by cable car. You'll also find a collection of important royal temples and the summer palaces of other kings. **Western Tours** (11 Damnoenkasem Rd.; © **03253-3303**) has a day excursion every Thursday that costs 1,300B (US$33/£18).

KHAO SAM ROI YOT NATIONAL PARK

Just 40 minutes' drive south of Hua Hin, Khao Sam Roi Yot, or the "Mountain of Three Hundred Peaks," offers great short hikes to panoramic views of the sea. Of the park's two caves, Kaew Cave is the most interesting, housing a *sala* pavilion that was built in 1890 for King Chulalongkorn.

11 Surat Thani

644 km (399 miles) S of Bangkok

Surat Thani is believed to have been an important center of the Sumatra-based Srivi-jaya Empire in the 9th and 10th centuries. Today, it's known to foreigners as the gate-way to beautiful Koh Samui and to Thais as a rich agricultural province. Surat is the main jumping-off point for the eastern islands **Koh Samui, Koh Pha Ngan,** and **Koh Tao** (each described in the following sections of this chapter), as well as the navigable jungles of **Khao Sok National Park.**

GETTING THERE & GETTING AROUND

Surat Thani is built up along the south shore of the Tapi River. **Talad Mai Road,** 2 blocks south of the river, is the city's main street, with the TAT office at its west end, and the bus station and central market at its east end. Frequent **songtao** run along Talad Mai; prices are based on distance, but rarely exceed 20B (US50¢/£0.30).

BY PLANE   **Thai Airways** (© 02535-2084 in Bangkok), **Air Asia** (© 02515-9999 in Bangkok), and **One-Two-Go** (© 01141-1126) all have daily flights from Bangkok to Surat Thani (trip time: 70 min.). You can grab a shared minivan to town for 80B (US$2/£1.10). The local Thai Airways office is at 3/27–28 Karoonrat Rd. (© 07727-2610), just south of town.

BY TRAIN   Ten trains to Surat Thani leave daily from Bangkok's **Hua Lampong Railway Station** (© 1690 or 02223-7010; trip time: 13 hr.). A second-class sleeper is 788B (US$20/£11); a second-class seat is 438B (US$11/£6.15). The Surat Thani train station is very inconvenient, but minitrucks meet trains to transport folks to town for 20B (US50¢/£0.30) shared ride, or if you roll in on the morning train, you can just hop on one of the travel-agent buses to the ferry.

BY BUS   Two VIP 24-seater buses leave daily from Bangkok's **Southern Bus Termi-nal** (© 02434-7192; trip time: 10 hr.; 755B/US$19/£11). Air-conditioned buses leave daily from Phuket's bus terminal off Phang-nga Road opposite the Royal Phuket City Hotel (© 07621-1977; trip time: 5 hr.; 200B/US$5/£2.80). Also from Phuket, minivans travel to Surat Thani daily (trip time: 4 hr.; 300B/US$7.50/£4.20)—you can find them across from the Montri Hotel on Suthat Road. The Surat Thani bus terminal is on Kaset II Road, a block east of the main road.

BY MINIVAN   The best way to travel between southern cities is by privately operated air-conditioned minivans. They are affordable and run on regular schedules between Surat Thani and Chumphon, Ranong, Nakhon Si Thammarat, Hat Yai, and beyond. The best way to arrange these trips is by consulting your hotel's front desk. You can go door-to-door to the hotel of your choice, usually for around 200B (US$5/£2.80).

BY CAR   Take Highway 4 south from Bangkok to Chumphon, then Highway 41 south direct to Surat Thani.

VISITOR INFORMATION

For information about Surat Thani, Koh Samui, and Koh Pha Ngan, contact the **TAT** office at 5 Talad Mai Rd., Surat Thani (© 07728-8818), near the Wang Tai Hotel.

FAST FACTS: SURAT THANI

Major **banks** along Talad Mai Road have ATMs and will perform currency exchanges. The **Post Office** and **Overseas Call Office** are together on Na Muang and Chonkasean roads near the center of town. The **Taksin Hospital** (✆ **07727-3239**) is at the north end of Talad Mai Road. The **tourist police** (✆ **07720-0475**) are with the TAT on Talad Mai Road.

WHERE TO STAY

For most, Surat Thani is just a stopping-off point for trips to the islands. If you have a layover, the best choice in town is the **Wang Tai Hotel** (1 Talad Mai Rd.; ✆ **07728-3020**), just south of the town center, with large, clean rooms from 950B (US$24/£13). More convenient to the market and town transport is the **BJ Hotel** (17/1 Donnok Rd.; ✆ **07721-7410**), with bare-bones rooms from 500B (US$13/£7). The **Siam Thara** (1/144 Donnock Rd.; ✆ **07727-3740**) is a similar standard but showing some age.

WHAT TO SEE & DO

Surat is a typical small Thai city and, for most foreign visitors, little more than a transportation hub to the islands of Koh Samui and Koh Pha Ngan. Most people will want to press on. If it is your only stop in Thailand (on the way to Koh Samui, for example), give the town a wander and see what Thai life is all about (take the small streets and find a wat). Outside of town, popular day trips include the **Monkey Training College** (24 Moo 4, Tambon Thungkong; ✆ **07722-7351**), where monkeys are trained to get coconuts.

SIDE TRIPS FROM SURAT THANI

KHAO SOK NATIONAL PARK ⛺

Khao Sok, known for its stunning scenery and exotic wildlife, is convenient to both Surat Thani and Phuket. The park is some 646 sq. km (252 sq. miles) in area, traced by jungle waterways and steep trails among craggy, limestone cliffs—imagine the jutting formations of Phang Nga Bay or Krabi, only inland. Rising some 1,000m (3,280 ft.), and laced with shaggy patches of forest, the dense jungle habitat of the park is literally crawling with life. Among the underbrush and thick vines hanging from the high canopy, tigers, leopards, golden cats, and even elephants still wander freely, and visitors commonly spot Malaysian sun bear, gibbons, mangur, macaques, civets, flying lemur, and squirrels. Keep your eyes peeled for the more than 200 species of birds, like hornbills, woodpeckers, and kingfishers. As for the flora, there is every variety—the Raffelesia, the largest flower in the world and a parasite, finds vines from which to draw its nourishment (the largest are up to 1m/3¼ ft. wide).

One of the best ways to get up close with the varied fauna of the park is by kayak along the nether reaches of the large reservoir. Jungle animals are skittish, so your chances of seeing something rare by noisily tromping through the bush are slim at best. Contact the folks at **Paddle Asia** (9/71 Thanon Rasdanusorn, in Phuket; ✆ **07624-0952;** fax 07621-6145; www.paddleasia.com) for details.

12 Koh Samui

84km (52 miles) E of Surat Thani

Koh Samui lies 84km (52 miles) off the east coast in the Gulf of Thailand, near the mainland commercial town of Surat Thani. The island is hilly, densely forested, and rimmed with coconut-palm plantations. Since the 1850s, Chinese merchants sailed from as far as Hainan Island in the South China Sea to trade coconuts and cotton, the island's two most profitable products.

Koh Samui

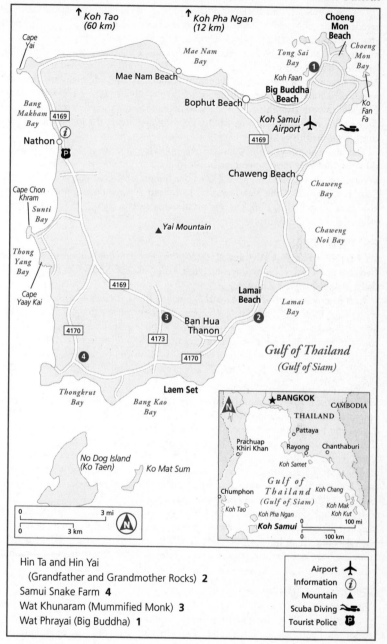

Hin Ta and Hin Yai
   (Grandfather and Grandmother Rocks) **2**
Samui Snake Farm **4**
Wat Khunaram (Mummified Monk) **3**
Wat Phrayai (Big Buddha) **1**

Airport ✈
Information ⓘ
Mountain ▲
Scuba Diving ≈
Tourist Police 🅿

Once a popular hippie haven of pristine beaches, idyllic bungalows, and thatched eateries along dirt roads, Samui is now an international resort area with all of the attendant comforts and crowding. If you came here as a backpacker in the past, you may not want to come back to see McDonald's and a Wal-Mart–style shopping outlet where hammocks once hung. An international airport was opened in 1988 and now greets up to 20 packed daily flights. After the 2004 tsunami, many travelers who were worried about another disaster, or felt uneasy about visiting the west coast of Thailand so soon after the tragedy, decided to make Samui their beach destination of choice. Fine hotels and large resorts are popping up all over the island, making any comparisons with Phuket apt.

The high season on Koh Samui is from mid-December to mid-January. January through April have the best weather, before its gets hot. October through mid-December are the wettest months, with November bringing extreme rain and winds that make the east side of the island rough for swimming. August sees a brief increase in visitors, a mini–high season, but the island's west side is often buffeted by summer monsoons from the mainland.

GETTING THERE

BY PLANE   **Bangkok Airways** (② 02265-5555 in Bangkok) connects Samui with Bangkok and Phuket. From Singapore, **Silk Air** (② 02236-5301-3 in Bangkok) flies daily, as does Bangkok Airways.

Koh Samui Airport (② 07742-5012) is a little slice of heaven—open-air pavilions with thatch roofs surrounded by gardens and palms. If you're staying at a larger resort, airport shuttles can be arranged when you book your room. There's also a convenient minivan service: Book your ticket at the transportation counter upon arrival and you'll get door-to-door service for 100B (US$2.50/£1.40). If you depart Koh Samui via the airport, an additional 300B (US$8/£4.20) airport tax is usually added to your ticket charge.

BY FERRY   If you're traveling overland, **Songserm** (② 07728-7124 in Surat Thani) runs a convenient ferry loop from Surat Thani with stops in Koh Samui, Koh Pha Ngan, and Koh Tao, finishing at Chumphon (and back again). The total trip is about 4 hours, while the Surat–Samui leg is 2 hours. Rates are as follows: Surat–Samui, 200B (US$5/£2.80); Samui–Pha Ngan, 150B (US$3.75/£2.10); Pha Ngan–Koh Tao, 250B (US$6.25/£3.50); Koh Tao–Chumphon, 400B (US$10/£5.60). The morning boat leaves at 8am. There are a number of smaller companies that make boat connection, as well as speedboats, but Songserm is the best.

If you book ahead at a resort, most will arrange transport from the Koh Samui ferry pier at Nathon to your hotel; otherwise, **songtao** make the trip to most beaches on the east coast for as little as 30B (US75¢/£0.40) if they can get a packed truckload from the boat landing (and it can be very packed). If you haven't booked a room in advance, drivers will make stops along the way to help you find a place.

GETTING AROUND

With a total area of 233 sq. km (91 sq. miles), you can trace Samui's entire coastline by car in about 2½ hours. The Koh Samui Airport is in the northeast corner of the island. The hydrofoils, car ferry, and express boats arrive on the west coast, in or near (depending on the boat) **Nathon,** just a tiny town with a few banks, the TAT office, and the main post office (few visitors spend much time here). The main road (Hwy. 4169, also called the "ring road") circles the island. The long east-coast stretch between **Chaweng** and **Lamai** beaches is the most popular destination for visitors and, consequently, where you'll find the greatest concentration of hotels and bungalows. The south coast has a few little hideaways, too.

BY SONGTAO   Songtao are the easiest and most efficient way to get around the island. They advertise their destinations—to such beaches as Lamai, Chaweng, and Mai Nam—with colorfully painted signs and all follow Route 4169, the ring road, around the island. For many trips, you have to change trucks between north and south routes. You can hail one anywhere along the highway or along beach roads. To visit a site off the beaten track (or one other than that painted on a truck's sign), ask the driver to make a detour. Most stop running regular routes after sundown, after which some will hang around outside the discos in Chaweng to take night owls home to other beaches. The cost is 50B (US$1.25/£0.70) one-way, with steep fares (up to 300B/US$7.50/£4.20) after hours.

BY TAXI   Unmetered taxis loiter outside most resorts and on virtually every street corner in Chaweng. If you're used to Bangkok's metered taxis, the prices here will come as a shock. A ride between beaches will set you back 200B (US$5/£2.75) with some bargaining; rides to and from the airport usually run 400B to 500B (US$10–US$13/£5.60–£7). Taxis can be a good option if you need to get somewhere quickly; otherwise, stick to songtaos.

BY CAR   Koh Samui's roads are narrow, winding, and poorly maintained, with few lights at night to guide you. Road accidents are many, but renting a car is a far better idea than going by motorcycle. Your defensive driving skills will be required to navigate around slow-moving trucks and motorcycles at the side of the road, not to mention the occasional wandering dog.

   Budget Car Rental has an office at the Samui Airport (© **07742-7188**). It rents a host of vehicles, starting with Suzuki Caribians at just 1,450B (US$36/£20) a day. **Avis,** at the Santiburi Dusit Resort (© **07742-5031**), offers similar services and does pickup and delivery as well. Beachside rental companies and travel agents rent for as low as 700B (US$18/£9.80) per day, but don't expect solid insurance coverage.

BY MOTORCYCLE   Road accidents injure or kill an inordinate number of tourists and locals each year on Samui, mostly motorcycle riders. Still, two wheels and a motor is still the most popular way to get around the island. The roads on Samui are busy, so stay left and close to the shoulder of the road to make way for passing cars and trucks. And go easy: Hot-shotting around the island lands many in the hospital, or worse. The fine for not wearing a helmet is 500B (US$13/£7), but it's enforced irregularly. Travel agencies and small operators rent motorcycles in popular beach areas. Honda scooters go for as little as 150B (US$3.75/£2.10) per day.

VISITOR INFORMATION

The **TAT** information center is on Thawiratchaphakdi Road, just north of the main ferry terminal in Nathon (© **07742-0504**). You'll also find a host of free small-press magazines and maps at retailers throughout Samui.

FAST FACTS: KOH SAMUI

All the major **banks** are in Nathon along waterfront Thawiratchaphakdi Road. In Chaweng, you'll find numerous money changers and ATMs; try Krung Thai Bank, opposite Starbucks. Hotels and guesthouses also accept traveler's checks. If you need medical attention, **Bandon International Hospital** (✆ 07742-5382) is a fine facility north of Chaweng with English-speaking physicians who make house calls.

For **Internet access,** there are a number of places in Chaweng—one option is the kind folks at **Multi Travel & Tour** (164/3 Moo 2 Chaweng; ✆ **07741-3969**). For the **tourist police,** dial ✆ **07742-1281.** The main **post office** (✆ **07742-1013**) is on Chonwithee Road in Nathon, but you probably won't hike all the way back to the main pier for posting. Any hotel or guesthouse will handle it for you, and stamps can be purchased in small provision shops in beach areas.

WHERE TO STAY

Twenty years ago, there were but a few makeshift beachside bungalow compounds along the nearly deserted coast of Samui. Today, luxury resorts stand shoulder-to-shoulder with homey guesthouses, chic modern facilities next to motel cellblocks, all vying for supremacy over the choicest beachside real estate. Even if your budget is tight, you can still enjoy the same sand as those in the more exclusive joints.

MAE NAM BAY

Mae Nam Bay is 12km (7½ miles) from the ferry pier, at the midpoint of Samui's north shore, facing nearby Koh Pha Ngan. The beach is narrow and long, with coarse sand and shaded by trees. The water is deep enough for swimming.

Very Expensive

Santiburi Dusit Resort ★★★   The sprawling Santiburi Dusit is the ultimate in relaxed luxury on the island. The resort design is influenced by late Thai royal architecture, with spacious and airy interiors—a simplicity accented with luxurious Jim Thompson Thai silks and tidy floral arrangements. The gardens and beachfront are picturesque and quiet, and the staff is motivated to please, making this not only the best resort on the island, but also comparable to any of the fine properties in the kingdom. The top villas front the beach, while the others are set among lush greenery around a central pool and spa. Each bungalow is a luxe suite, with living and sleeping areas divided by glass and flowers. The bathroom is masterfully outfitted in wood and black tiles, the centerpiece a large, round sunken tub. Standard features such as a video player and stereo system make each villa as convenient as your own home. Guests can take advantage of windsurfing and sailing on the house, while duffers can enjoy the only 18 holes on the island at the nearby Santiburi Country Club. The resort also has its own gorgeous Chinese junk, anchored in the bay for dinner cruises or for hiring out to tour surrounding islands. For a more affordable but equally indulgent stay, try Santiburi's sister property, **Bophut Resort & Spa,** just a short hop down the beach.

12/12 Moo 1, Tambol Mae Nam, Koh Samui 84330. ✆ 07742-5031. Fax 07742-5040. www.santiburi.com. 71 units. 19,000B–24,000B (US$475–US$600/£266–£336) suite; 24,000B–47,520B (US$600–US$1,188/£336–£665) villa. AE, DC, MC, V. **Amenities:** 2 restaurants; 2 bars; lounge; outdoor pool; outdoor lighted tennis courts; fitness center; spa; Jacuzzi; sauna; watersports equipment; concierge; car rental; limo service; salon; 24-hr. room service; massage; babysitting; laundry service; dry cleaning; Internet access. *In room:* A/C, satellite TV w/DVD player (and DVD library), stereo, Wi-Fi, minibar, fridge, hair dryer, safe, IDD phone.

Moderate/Inexpensive

Coco Palm Resort A good budget choice, Coco Palm's bungalows are basic and comfortable. The place attracts lots of families on a budget, but is still quite peaceful. Deluxe bungalows are worth a bump-up; though still with just shower-in-room bathrooms, they are airy and have vaulted cathay ceilings. Seaside bungalows are worth the additional jump in price for their location.

26/4 Moo 4, Mae Nam Beach, Koh Samui 84330. © **07724-7288.** Fax 07742-5321. www.cocopalmsamui.com. 86 units. 1,200B (US$30/£17) cottage; 1,800B–3,200B (US$45–US$80/£25–£45) deluxe; 5,500B–9,000B (US$138–US$225/£77–£126) villa. MC, V. **Amenities:** Restaurant; small outdoor pool; tour desk; jeep and motorcycle rental; transfer service; laundry service. *In room:* A/C, TV, minibar, no phone.

Mae Nam Resort   These 36 bungalows form a secluded little village in overgrown jungle gardens with tall lush greenery. Each has teak paneling and floors, rattan furnishings, a small bathroom with polished stone walls, and a small deck. Beachfront bungalows will have you stepping off your balcony right into the silky, palm-shaded sand for very little, considering the neighboring Santiburi Dusit Resort's beachfront villas run about 32,800B (US$820/£459). Okay, so Mae Nam Resort can't compare to five-star luxury, but it's still the same sand and view.

Mae Nam Beach, Koh Samui 84330 (next to the Santiburi Dusit Resort). © **07724-7287.** Fax 07742-5116. www.maenamresort.com. 41 units. 1,200B (US$30/£17) double w/fan; 1,400B–2,000B (US$35–US$50/£20–£28) double w/A/C; 2,700B (US$68/£38) A/C bungalow. AE, MC, V. **Amenities:** Restaurant; jeep and motorcycle rental; transfer service; limited room service; laundry service. *In room:* No phone.

BOPHUT BEACH

Bophut Beach is on the north coast just east of Mae Nam. The beach is thin and the sand is coarse, but the little commercial strip is fun and convenient.

Moderate

Peace Resort   Closed at press time due to bungalow renovation and construction of a new lobby, the Peace Resort promises an even higher standard of understated luxury after its scheduled reopening in 2007. Once just a few family-owned bungalows, that same relaxed spirit pervades the Peace Resort, but these new free-standing bungalows are really more like small luxury suites. All have vaulted ceilings with design schemes that are either finely crafted wood or cooler, almost Mediterranean numbers in pastel tiles with designer flat-stone masonry and smooth stucco. Spring for a larger seaside room. The central pool is not particularly large, but it's cozy and near the beach. There's a small, open-air restaurant where you can enjoy a cool drink, the company of good friends, and the calm of this tranquil bay with the big Buddha winking from the next beach. Peace indeed.

Bophut Beach, Koh Samui 94320 (central Bophut). © **07742-5357.** Fax 07742-5343. www.peaceresort.com. 102 units. 5,300B–10,000B (US$132–US$250/£74–£140) garden bungalow; 12,000B (US$300/£168) beachview villa. MC, V. **Amenities:** Restaurant; bar; outdoor pool; spa (across the road); kids' club and playground; tour desk; car and motorbike rental; limited room service (6am–11:30pm); babysitting; laundry service; Internet access. *In room:* A/C, satellite TV, minibar, fridge, safe, no phone.

TONGSAI BAY

Tongsai Bay is a scenic cove dominated by the hillside Tongsai Bay resort. The beach itself is rather uninspiring with very rough sand, but it is quite private.

Very Expensive

The Tongsai Bay 🏵🏵   The luxe Tongsai Bay resort dominates this stunning, rocky section of coast. Built theatrically down a hillside, the white-stucco, red-tile-roofed bungalows and buildings are reminiscent of the Mediterranean, though the palm trees are pure Thai. Between the half-moon cove's rocky bookends, the coarse-sand beach invites you to idle away the days. The all-suite resort has some very unique touches that set it apart—each unit has plenty of outdoor terrace space, with sea views or a private walled courtyard. Terrace suites have outdoor tubs, while the Tongsai Grand Villas have not only tubs but also gazebos; the Tongsai Pool Villas manage to add on a private pool to boot. The villas are designed in unique harmony with nature, some even with small stands of trees growing though the middle of them. You'll find plenty of spots to hide out with a hammock under a shade tree. Service is tip-top: From the landscapers to management, there is no friendlier staff on the island.

84 Moo 5, Ban Plailaem, Bophut, Koh Samui 84320 (northeast tip of island). © **07742-5015.** Fax 07742-5462. Bangkok reservations office: © 02254-0056; fax 02254-0054. www.tongsaibay.co.th. 83 units. 12,500B (US$312/£175) beachfront suite; 15,300B (US$383/£214) cottage suite; 25,900B (US$648/£363) Tongsai Grand Villa; 29,400B (US$735/£412) Tongsai Pool Villa. AE, DC, MC, V. **Amenities:** 3 restaurants; 2 bars; outdoor pool; outdoor lighted tennis court; fitness center; spa w/massage and beauty treatments; watersports equipment; tour desk; car rental; limo service; limited room service; laundry service; dry cleaning; snooker room; Internet cafe; small DVD library. *In room:* A/C, satellite TV w/DVD player, minibar, fridge, coffeemaker, hair dryer, safe, IDD phone.

CHOENG MON

Choeng Mon is a gracefully shaped crescent about 1km (½ mile) long. Palm trees shading sunbathers reach right to the water's edge; swimming is excellent, with few rocks near the central shore. Choeng Mon is isolated, but there are many good local services and transport.

Very Expensive

Sala Samui ★★ If you're on your honeymoon, anniversary, or are just in love and want to get away from it all, look no further that the Sala Samui. Pool villas offer the most privacy, with daybeds, outdoor bathrooms (use the mosquito nets in the evenings), and small pools set in a secluded courtyard. Bedrooms are minimally decorated, with whitewashed walls offset by wood trimming and furnishings. If you do decide to leave your luxury lair, the resort offers two common swimming pools and access to a lovely part of the beach. Honeymooners are a large part of the clientele here and the staff goes out of its way to make each couple feel welcome.

10/9 Moo 5, Bophut, Koh Samui 84320. © **07724-5888.** Fax 07724-5889. www.salasamui.com. 69 units. US$240 (£132) deluxe; US$320–US$600 (£176–£330) villa; US$750 (£413) presidential villa. AE, MC, V. **Amenities:** Restaurant; bar; wine cellar; 2 outdoor pools; fitness center; spa w/massage; watersports equipment; tour desk; car rental; limited room service; laundry service. *In room:* A/C, TV, minibar, coffeemaker, hair dryer, safe, IDD phone.

Samui Peninsula Spa & Resort ★★ If you can, do stay at the Peninsula; you'll be treated like royalty in a fine private suite, your own luxury pool villa, or a new deluxe pavilion set around a three-tier pool at the highest point of this expanding hillside resort. Rooms are sanctuaries done in dark wood and silk, brimming with classic Thai style and featuring incredible panoramic views of the surrounding bay. It's a long walk to the beach proper, but you may not want to leave this ultra-comfy compound. The water in the central infinity-edge pool appears to drop off into the placid bay below, and the resort dining and services are tops.

24/73 Moo 5, Bophut Beach, Koh Samui 84320 (on the rocky point between Mae Nam and Bophut). © **07742-8100.** Fax 07742-8122. www.samuipeninsula.com. 132 units. 11,000B–15,000B (US$275–US$375/£154–£210) deluxe; from 12,000B (US$300/£168) suite; from 27,000B (US$675/£378) villa. AE, MC, V. **Amenities:** 2 restaurants; bar; 2 outdoor pools; watersports equipment; tour desk; car rental; limo service; 24-hr. room service; massage; laundry service; dry cleaning; Internet access. *In room:* A/C, satellite TV w/in-house movies, minibar, fridge, safe, IDD phone.

Expensive

Imperial Boat House Hotel ★ You've got a pretty unique concept here—34 authentic teak rice barges have been dry-docked and converted into charming freestanding suites. The less expensive rooms in the three-story buildings are fine but not nearly as atmospheric. Hotel facilities are extensive, the beach is one of the nicest on the island, and if you can't get a boat suite, at least you can swim in the boat-shaped swimming pool.

83 Moo 5, Tambon Bophut, Koh Samui 84320 (southern part of beach). ⓒ **07742-5041**. Fax 07742-5460. www. imperialhotels.com. 210 units. US$140–US$190 (£77–£105) double; US$220 (£121) honeymoon suite; US$270 (£149) boat suite. AE, DC, MC, V. **Amenities:** 2 restaurants; bar; 2 outdoor pools; fitness center; spa; Jacuzzi; sauna; watersports equipment; concierge; tour desk; car rental; limo service; business center; 24-hr. room service; massage; babysitting; laundry service; dry cleaning. *In room:* A/C, satellite TV, minibar, fridge, hair dryer, safe, IDD phone.

White House Beach Resort & Spa ★★
This resort in the graceful Ayutthaya style, built around a central garden with a lotus pond and swimming pool, is by far the top choice in Choeng Mon for comfort at reasonable cost. The lobby is impeccably decorated with original Thai artwork. The spacious and elegant rooms flank a central walkway that's lined with orchids. Each house accommodates four spacious rooms, which have separate sitting areas, huge beds, fine furnishings, and large bathrooms. By the beach, there's a pool with a bar and an especially graceful teak *sala*. The resort's quality Swiss management team is very efficient and assures a pleasant stay. This is top comfort spilling onto a beautiful stretch of white-sand beach.

59/3 Moo 5, Choeng Mon Beach, Koh Samui 84320. ⓒ **07724-7921**. Fax 07724-5318. www.hotelthewhitehouse. com. 40 units. 5,000B–5,600B (US$125–US$140/£70–£78) double; 6,200B–6,600B (US$155–US$165/£87–£92) suite. AE, MC, V. **Amenities:** 2 restaurants; bar; outdoor pool; Jacuzzi; tour desk; jeep and motorcycle rental; transfer service; massage; laundry service. *In room:* A/C, satellite TV, minibar, fridge, coffeemaker, safe.

CHAWENG & CHAWENG NOI BAYS
The beaches at Chaweng are the most popular and the most overdeveloped on Samui. If you came to get away from it all, go elsewhere. Still, most of the resorts here are private, cozy, affordable, and convenient to the busy strip. North Chaweng beaches are rocky; the south is better for swimming.

Expensive
Amari Palm Reef Resort & Spa ★★
This is the finest of Amari's many hotels in Thailand by virtue of the luxury suites at beachside and the comfortable design of the oceanside pool and dining. Accommodations in the main block and new blocks across the road are not particularly luxurious, though they're very clean with parquet floors. Suites face the sea and are designed in a seamless marriage of contemporary and traditional Thai, with large decks giving way to huge glass sliders, lovely sunken seating areas, massive plush beds, and designer bathrooms with separate shower, tub, and his-and-her sinks. The rocks and coral along the beach mean you'll have to take a bit of a walk for swimming, but the scenery is lovely and you can expect the same high standard of service as at all Amari hotels. The resort is far enough from the Chaweng strip to be quiet and comfortable (but close enough to party). Great for families.

Chaweng Beach, Koh Samui 84320 (north end of the main strip). ⓒ **07742-2015**. Fax 07742-2394. www.amari. com. 187 units. US$230 (£127) superior; US$280 (£154) deluxe; US$395 (£217) suite. AE, MC, V. **Amenities:** 3 restaurants; 2 outdoor pools; squash court; spa w/massage, Jacuzzi, sauna, and steam; bike rental; kids' club; tour desk; car rental; babysitting; laundry service; dry cleaning; nonsmoking rooms. *In room:* A/C, satellite TV, minibar, fridge, coffeemaker, hair dryer, safe, IDD phone.

Coral Bay Resort ★
Far from the boom-boom bass of Chaweng but close enough to commute, the Coral Bay—a collection of large, upscale thatch bungalows—crests a picturesque hill on the northern end of Chaweng. Rooms are in rows along the hillside (a bit of trudging to get to some); each has a large balcony, some shared with adjoining rooms. The decor is lavish, with bamboo and coconut-inlaid cabinets,

intricate thatch, and fine hangings; some rooms feature unique graphic mosaics as well: There's nothing like it on Samui. Spring for a deluxe unit with canopy bed. Bathrooms are small garden landscapes with waterfall showers and designer flat-stone masonry. The central pool area is high above the rock-and-coral beach below (not good for swimming), and large thatch pavilions house the open lobby and fine dining. Coral Bay offers a high standard of comfort and service throughout; it also provides good information on self-touring (or can make arrangements).

9 Moo 2, Bophut, Chaweng Beach, Koh Samui 84320 (north end of Chaweng as the road crests the 1st big hill). ℂ 07742-2223. Fax 07742-2392. www.coralbay.net. 53 units. 6,000B–7,500B (US$150–US$188/£84–£105) deluxe bungalow; from 8,500BB (US$213/£119) family bungalow; all rooms add beachfront surcharge. AE, MC, V. **Amenities:** 2 restaurants; bar; pool; spa; Jacuzzi; sauna; kids' club; tour desk; car rental; massage; babysitting; laundry service; nonsmoking rooms; Internet access; library and video lounge. *In room:* A/C, minibar, fridge, safe, IDD phone.

Imperial Samui Hotel 🏵🏵   A member of the Thai-owned Imperial group, the hotel is set in a large hill-top grove of coconut palms a short drive south of busy Chaweng. You can't walk it, but it does have frequent shuttle service to town—and unlike most resorts on or near Chaweng, this one's quiet. The saltwater pool has an organic design with large boulders, a central island, and a vanishing edge overlooking the bay below: charming. Spacious rooms have balconies with sea views, lots of floral prints and rattan, large bathrooms with potted plants, and easy access (via steps) to the beach. The sprawling hillside location means a bit of hill hiking to some of the furthest rooms, but for seclusion and comfort, this is a great choice.

86 Moo 3, Ban Chaweng Noi, Koh Samui 84320 (middle of Chaweng Noi Beach). ℂ 07742-2020. Fax 07742-2396. www.imperialhotels.com. 155 units. US$210 (£116) premier sea-facing unit; from US$230 (£127) suite. AE, DC, MC, V. **Amenities:** 2 restaurants; lounge; 2 outdoor pools (freshwater and seawater); outdoor lighted tennis courts; spa; Jacuzzi; watersports equipment and dive center; bike rental; concierge; tour desk; car rental; limo service; 24-hr. room service; massage; babysitting; laundry service; dry cleaning; snooker and badminton. *In room:* A/C, satellite TV w/free in-house movies, minibar, fridge, coffeemaker, hair dryer, safe, IDD phone.

Poppies Samui 🏵🏵   The famed Balinese resort runs this popular annex in Samui. On the south end of busy Chaweng, Poppies is indeed an oasis. Luxury cottages, all the same, have thatch roofs and Thai–Balinese appointments. Renovations at the time of writing promise new floors, remodeled bathrooms, and flatscreen TVs. Although rooms are set close together, they're well situated for optimum privacy. This is a popular honeymoon choice, and the service and standards throughout are tops. The central pool is small but cozy and the hotel dining is some of the best going (see "Where to Dine," below).

P.O. Box 1, Chaweng, Koh Samui 84320 (on the south end of the Chaweng strip). ℂ 07742-2419. Fax 07742-2420. www.poppiessamui.com. 24 units. 11,500B (US$288/£161) double; rates vary depending on season. AE, MC, V. **Amenities:** Restaurant; pool; tour desk; limited room service; massage; laundry service. *In room:* A/C, satellite TV, minibar, fridge, coffeemaker, safe, IDD phone.

Moderate

Baan Chaweng 🏵   This is a very good mid-range choice. You're right in the heart of Chaweng here, but far enough removed from the thumping bass to get a peaceful night's sleep. Quiet paths lead past rooms and bungalows, through the lovely gardens and palms of the main courtyard, to a cozy beachfront pool and restaurant. Guest rooms are comfortable and sparsely decorated, though not displeasingly so. Superior units are in modern two-story blocks furthest removed from the beach, while free-standing deluxe bungalows and villas take the prime spots and are not a bad upgrade. The hotel's restaurant, Leelawadee, has terrace seating right on the beach and serves very good seafood.

Chaweng Beach, Koh Samui 84320 (middle of Chaweng Beach). ⓒ **07742-2403**. Fax 07742-2404. www.baan chaweng.com. 60 units. 3,300B (US$83/£46) superior; 3,800B–5,000B (US$95– US$125/£53–£70) villa; 3,500B–6,500B (US$88–US$163/£49–£91) bungalow. AE, MC, V. **Amenities:** Restaurant; pool; tour desk; limo service; massage; laundry service; Internet access. In room: A/C, satellite TV, minibar, hair dryer, safe, IDD phone.

Chaweng Resort   Like a small-time Florida development, the Chaweng Resort consists of two columns of free-standing bungalows leading to the sea. Cottages are basic but spacious, with lots of overdone filigree. Bathrooms are plain but spotless. The larger suites are a good value for families. The grounds are nicely landscaped, the central pool is small but cozy, and there are lots of fun Thai touches and statues throughout. Current cosmetic renovations will mean a carved concrete lobby not unlike a Hindu temple (or a wedding cake). The Thai/Continental restaurant overlooks the beach. The place is not luxurious, but it's a good family choice bustling with activity.

Chaweng Beach, Koh Samui 84320 (middle of Chaweng Beach). ⓒ **07742-2230**, or 02651-0016 in Bangkok. Fax 07751-0018. www.chawengresort.com. 70 units. 2,400B–3,400B (US$60–US$85/£34–£48) double; 3,900B (US$98/£55) beachfront double; 5,000B–5,500B (US$125–US$138/£70–£77) suite. AE, DC, MC, V. **Amenities:** Restaurant; pool; tour desk; massage; laundry service; Internet access. In room: A/C, satellite TV, minibar, fridge.

LAMAI BAY

The long sand beach on Lamai Bay is comparable to Chaweng's, but caters more to the young backpacker set. There are a few comfy new resorts in and among the budget bungalows, however, and the wide range of services, cafes, and nightlife make Lamai the best budget choice and a popular spot.

Very Expensive

Renaissance Koh Samui Resort & Spa   Recently rebranded as a Marriott resort, the Renaissance is tucked away on rocky hills that rise from a quiet cove just north of Lamai's main beach. The elegant open-air lobby surrounds a flower-laden reflecting pool guarded by two imposing *chao fa* (ornamental hooks common to Thai temple roofs). At night, the staff hosts lessons on folding towels into the intricate animal figures you'll find in every room. Deluxe units, in blocks set on the highest part of the compound, are very chic with large puffy beds and tile showers leading to a raised bathtub on the balcony (with bamboo blinds for privacy). Free-standing villas descend towards the beach and boast private terraces with pools, towering vaulted ceilings, and classical Thai decor done on a grand scale. The lovely beachfront infinity pool surrounds a budding leelawadee tree; the poolside bar is a great perch for watching the dazzling sunsets.

208/1 Moo 4, T. Maret, Lamai, Koh Samui 84310 (on the northeast end of Lamai on the hilltop). ⓒ **07742-9300**. Fax 07742-9333. www.marriott.com. 78 units. US$350 (£193) deluxe; from US$415 (£228) suite; from US$450 (£252) villa. AE, DC, MC, V. **Amenities:** 4 restaurants; poolside bar; 2 outdoor pools; health club; spa w/Jacuzzi, sauna, and steam; watersports equipment (including free sea kayaks); tour desk; car rental; business center; shopping; limited room service; babysitting; laundry service; dry cleaning. In room: A/C, satellite TV w/DVD and CD players, Internet access, minibar, fridge, coffeemaker, safe, IDD phone.

Expensive

Pavilion Samui Boutique Resort   The newly renovated Pavilion is more the rococo of a small-time mafia don's private sanctuary than "boutique," but it *is* a tidy hotel with good service. Public spaces are surrounded by lots of greenery. Suites and spa rooms have huge luxury bathrooms, some even a courtyard area where you can enjoy a Jacuzzi and shower under the stars. Off-season guests will be sure to encounter renovations, as the owner likes to present a new look each year for return customers. There's a fine spa, the small pool and dining pavilion are right on the surf, and the proximity to Lamai's nightlife is a plus for most guests.

124/24 Moo 3, Lamai Beach, Koh Samui 84310 (north end of Lamai Beach). © 07742-4030. Fax 07742-4029. www.pavilionsamui.com. 62 units. 10,000B (US$250/£140) superior spa; from 12,000B (US$300/£168) suite. AE, DC, MC, V. **Amenities:** Restaurant; bar; outdoor pool; spa; Jacuzzi; steam bath; tour desk; car rental; transfer service; limited room service; laundry service. *In room:* A/C, TV, minibar, safe.

Moderate

Spa Samui Resorts ★ (Value)   For long-term stays or just a daytime spa visit, the Spa Samui Resorts is a unique choice offering a "healthy good time." The popular cleansing-and-fasting series rejuvenates your system with prepared detox drinks and tablets plus twice-daily colonic enemas. Some balk at the thought of paying $300 per week, on top of room rates, to "not eat," but it is a good, professional program. The laid-back spa resort on the sea just north of Lamai has been around for years and is still in full swing, a rustic grouping of old bungalows and open-air dining and massage pavilions, but it now has a more comfortable property in the south of Lamai, high in the hills above town, as well as new two-bedroom villas with private pools. Rooms at the new resort range from simple, affordable bungalows to large private suites with balconies. All rooms are fitted with a colonic board for daily enemas. The spa has a cozy pool, herbal steam bath in a stone grotto, massage, body wraps, and facial treatments. Classes and workshops on yoga, meditation, and massage techniques can fill your day—or you can just put your feet up, colon all sparkling clean, and have a go at that novel you've been lugging around (or writing). All of the spa services are available for day visitors as well. The vegetarian Spa Restaurant serves excellent dishes with particular care to cleansing the body (see "Where to Dine," below).

Lamai Beach, Koh Samui 84320 (just south, in the hills over Lamai Beach). © 07723-0855. Fax 07742-4126. www.spasamui.com. 73 units. 500B–2,500B (US$12–US$63/£7–£35) double; 3,500B (US$88/£49) suite; 7,200B–7,700B (US$180–US$193/£101–£108) villa. MC, V. **Amenities:** Restaurant; juice bar; pool; spa; sauna; massage; laundry service. *In room:* A/C, minibar, fridge, safe.

LAEM SET BAY

Laem Set Bay is a small rocky cape on Samui's southeast coast, with dramatic scenery that has prompted the construction of a few well-known hotels.

Moderate/Inexpensive

Laem Set Inn ★★   Distinctive in a landscape of cookie-cutter high-end resorts, the Laem Set Inn sets its own standard of style, traditional luxury, and fine service in this isolated corner of paradise. This cozy hideaway on the far southern end of the island is a collection of uniquely designed Thai suites ranging from rustic thatch bungalows to private pool villas. Some suites were constructed from rural teak homes from outlying islands that were saved from the wrecking ball (or desertion), moved here, and carefully rebuilt. Family suites have bunk beds, private bathrooms for kids, and small dining nooks. The most exclusive accommodations are the private two-bedroom suites decorated with hand-hewn furniture and a certain regional grace. Large porches bookend all villas and provide a perch for drinking in views beyond the pounding surf to nearby No Dog Island. Kayaks, mountain bikes, and snorkel gear are available to explore this location's stunning scenery. Wireless Internet comes standard in all areas, free of charge. The elevated pool seamlessly blends with the gulf, reflecting sea and sky, and the pavilion restaurant serves gourmet fare and delicious Thai seafood. This boutique inn is true rustic luxury, far from the crowds—an ideal getaway.

110 Moo 2, Hua Thanon, Laem Set, Koh Samui 84310. © 07742-4393. Fax 07742-4394. www.laemset.com. 30 units. 1,200B (US$30/£17) seaview bungalow w/fan; 2,750B (US$69/£39) seafront bungalow w/fan; 4,350B–8,000B (US$109–US$200/£61–£112) standard double; from 8,150B (US$204/£114) suite. MC, V. **Amenities:** 2 restaurants;

bar; outdoor pool; fitness center; Jacuzzi; sauna; watersports equipment; bike and motorcycle rental; children's programs; concierge; tour desk; car rental; limo service; business center; limited room service; massage; babysitting; laundry service. *In room:* A/C, wireless Internet access, minibar, fridge, coffeemaker, hair dryer, safe, IDD phone.

WEST COAST
Very Expensive
Le Royal Meridien Baan Taling Ngam ★★★   A true five-star, Le Royal Meridien is peaceful and isolated on the western side of the island some 40 minutes' drive from the Samui Airport. Built on the side of a hill, the resort's accommodations include deluxe rooms and suites, along with one- to three-bedroom beach and cliff villas. The hilltop lobby and restaurant, as well as the guest rooms, have fantastic views of the sea and resort gardens, and the main pool appears to spill over its edges into the coconut-palm grove below. Guest rooms combine Thai furniture, fine textiles, and louvered wood paneling, including the sliding doors to the huge tanning terrace. Bathrooms feature oversize tubs and sophisticated black slate and wood. The two-bedroom villas afford the most value and convenience for families. The resort's only drawback is that the beach is small, and while some may seek out the privacy this place promises, the cost is isolation from the "action" on the other parts of the island—at least a 30-minute drive away. Le Royal Meridien has kayaks, catamarans, snorkeling gear, and windsurfers for rent, as well as tennis, mountain bikes, a fine spa, PADI dive school, and no fewer than seven outdoor pools so no one gets bored. Dining at the hilltop Lom Talay is as gorgeous as the Thai and Asian cuisine served, while the Promenade serves locally caught fresh seafood by the beach.

295 Moo 3, Taling Ngam Beach, Koh Samui 84140. © 800/225-5843 in the U.S., or 07742-3019. www.lemeridien. com. 72 units. US$265–US$295 (£146–£162) double; US$475 (£261) suite; US$375–US$615 (£206–£338) villa. AE, DC, MC, V. **Amenities:** 3 restaurants; lounge; 7 pools; outdoor lighted tennis courts; fitness center; spa w/massage; Jacuzzi; sauna; watersports equipment and dive center; bike rental; concierge; tour desk; car rental; limo service; salon; 24-hr. room service; babysitting; laundry service; dry cleaning. *In room:* A/C, satellite TV, minibar, fridge, IDD phone.

WHERE TO DINE
BOPHUT BEACH
For fine baked goods, try **Angela's Harbourside Cafe** (© 07742-7212).

Mangrove ★★ INTERNATIONAL   For romantic, elegant dining, the Mangrove is the best on Samui. It's on a quiet stretch of rural road (near the airport), and though removed from the bustling tourist areas like Chaweng, that is in fact the very appeal here. It's still just a short drive from Chaweng. The casual open-air dining area overlooks a grove of mangroves, of course, and echoes with the sounds of forest and jungle. The menu changes monthly to cater to the oft-returning expat clientele. For a starter, try the crab salad and ask about any daily specials. I had a delicious lamb chop marinated in herbs de Provence. The place is run by a friendly young (but very experienced) French/Belgian couple who go to great lengths. Don't scrimp on dessert; try the rich chocolate mouse and follow it up with a Rum Ginger, the Mangrove's signature after-dinner drink.

32/6 Moo 4, Bophut (on the airport rd. between Bophut and Big Buddha beaches). © 07742-7584. Main courses 430B–520B (US$11–US$13/£6–£7.30). Daily 5:30pm–last order (closed on the last 3 days of each month).

TONGSAI BAY
Chef Chom's ★ THAI   Even if you're not fortunate enough to stay at the Tongsai Bay resort, Chef Chom's makes a trip to this corner of the island worthwhile. Chom descends from a long line of cooks, some of whom worked in the palace kitchen of

Princess Vibhavadee Rangsit in Bangkok. The menu is a mix of southern Thai (spicy) and royal Thai (sweet) cuisines and utilizes only the freshest ingredients. For a nice selection of tastes, try the Tongsai Platter, which offers six distinct dishes, including the excellent *gai hom toey* (chicken in pandan leaves). The cool ocean breezes, candle-light, and soft Thai classical music in the background all make for a romantic evening.

At the Tongsai Bay resort, Moo 5, Ban Plailaem, Bophut (northeast tip of island). © 07724-5480. Reservations recommended in peak season. Main courses 120B–480B (US$3–US$12/£1.70–£6.70). AE, MC, V. Daily 7:30–10pm.

CHAWENG BEACH
Chaweng is where you'll find the most variety, from McDonald's to fine dining.

Betelnut 𝕱 INTERNATIONAL   California cuisine, anyone? Down a quiet soi off the south end of Chaweng, you'll be greeted at the door by Jeffrey Lord, owner, pro-prietor, and rollicking raconteur who delivers fine wit and witticisms along with good victuals. The menu is divided into "Eats Big" and "Eats Small," not necessarily apps and main courses (but could be), and runs the gamut from "Buddha Jumped Over the Wall" (an ostrich steak) to clam chowder with green curry. I had a delicious sesame-encrusted salmon katsu, indicative of the international fare here. The blackened tuna with salsa and the soft-shell crabs with green papaya and mango salad are also good choices. Come with friends, order a spread of tapas, and pick from among the fine wine selections for a great evening.

46/27 Chaweng Blvd. (south of Tradewinds Hotel and the town center, down a small soi). © 07741-3370. Main courses 300B–725B (US$7.50–US$18/£4.20–£10). MC, V. Daily 6–10pm.

Poppies 𝕱 THAI/INTERNATIONAL   Known for its Balinese flair, Poppies is equally famous for fresh seafood by the beach. The romantic atmosphere under the large thatch pavilion is enhanced by soft lighting and live international jazz music. Though it specializes in fresh seafood, the kitchen also offers international and Thai classics as well as a sizable vegetarian menu. Thai dishes are tempered to the Western palate, but say *Ow pet* ("I want it spicy") and chef Wantanee will crank up the heat for you.

South Chaweng Beach. © 07742-2419. Reservations recommended during peak season. Main courses 195B–995B (US$5–US$25/£2.75–£14). AE, MC, V. Daily 7am–10pm.

Vechia Napoli 𝕱 ITALIAN   Listen to the dulcet tones of quiet Italian folk music and watch lazy fans languidly churn cool air as you lean back in a rattan chair; you might think you've been transported to a small town in rural Napoli, and the simple authentic cuisine of this restaurant completes the picture. Tomato and mozzarella with a splash of pesto, a glass of red, and good conversation; you won't believe you're just a stone's throw from busy Chaweng (down a little alley with seedy massage places and bars, but that somehow lends to the atmosphere). You'll find it all here: great pastas, grilled specials, pizzas, and the house special—shellfish soup with king prawns, fresh crab, mussels, and clams done in a special Neapolitan broth. Follow it up with a real gelato or tiramisu and espresso.

166/31 Moo 2, in central Chaweng. © 07723-1229. Main courses 180B–550B (US$3–US$11/£2.50–£7.70). MC, V. Daily 11am–11pm.

LAMAI BEACH
Spa Restaurant VEGETARIAN   This place is not just about veggies (you'll find a few seafood and chicken dishes as well); it's for anyone who'd like to enjoy a health-ful, tasty dish. Go for the delicious curries, or try one of the excellent local dishes. But leave plenty of time for an herbal steam and massage at the health center, too.

Rte. 4169, between Chaweng and Lamai beaches. © 07723-0855. Reservations recommended in peak season. Main courses 40B–350B (US$1–US$8.75/£0.55–£4.90). MC, V. Daily 6:30am–10pm.

WHAT TO SEE & DO

Busy Samui supports all kinds of activities, from scuba diving to bungee jumping, jungle trekking to cooking schools. Most folks come here for beach fun and frolic, and you'll find all kinds of such activities—sailing, jet skis, and parasailing—right at beachside.

The gold-tiled **Wat Phrayai (Big Buddha),** more than 24m (79 ft.) tall, sits atop Koh Faan (Barking Deer Island), a small islet connected to the shore by a dirt causeway almost 305m (1,000 ft.) long. Though of little historic value, it's an imposing presence on the northeast coast and is one of Samui's primary landmarks. It's open all day; a 20B (US50¢/£0.30) contribution is recommended. It's easy to reach: Just hop on any songtao going to Big Buddha Beach. You can't miss it.

Koh Samui's famed **Wonderful Rocks**—the most important of which are the unique **Hin Ta** and **Hin Yai,** or Grandfather and Grandmother Stones, shaped like the male and female anatomy—are at the far southern end of Lamai Beach. To get there, flag down any songtao to Lamai Beach.

The **Mummified Monk** at Wat Khunaram is certainly worth a visit if you're bent on seeing roadside oddities. He died in the meditation mudra, legs folded lotus style, and was embalmed that way; you can see him behind glass in a small pavilion at the right as you enter **Wat Khunaram,** itself a worthy example of a typical Thai town temple. At the entrance to the monks' pavilion, a few coins are the cost of the resident monk's blessing with water. Take off your shoes, smile, and kneel, and he will put water on your head and say a few good words, for whatever it's worth. The wat is along the main road, Route 4169, as it shoots inland far south of Lamai.

The **Samui Monkey Theater** (© 07724-5140) is just south of Bophut village on 4169 Road. A vaudeville-style act demonstrates how monkeys collect coconuts—more fun for kids than for adults. Showtimes are 10:30am, 2pm, and 4pm daily; the cost is 150B (US$3.75/£2.10) for adults, 50B (US$1.25/£0.70) for children.

Samui's **snake farm** is at the far southwest corner of the island on 4170 Road (© 07742-3247), with daily shows at 11am and 2pm; tickets cost 250B (US$6.25/£3.50).

For daily Thai cooking and fruit-carving lessons, the **Samui Institute of Thai Culinary Arts (SITCA)** (© 07741-3172; www.sitca.net) is a professional operation and a great way to have fun—especially if your beach plans get rained out. Lunch and dinner courses cost 1,600B (US$40/£22) each.

OUTDOOR ACTIVITIES

KAYAKING **Blue Stars Sea Kayaking,** at the Gallery Lafayette next to the Green Mango in Chaweng (© 07723-0497), and easy to contact through most booking agents, takes people to the Mu Koh Ang Thong National Marine Park for kayaking and snorkeling. The rubber canoes are perfect for exploring the caverns beneath limestone cliffs. The 4-hour trip costs 2,000B (US$50/£28) per person.

SCUBA DIVING & SNORKELING Local aquanauts agree that the best scuba diving is off **Koh Tao,** a small island north of Koh Pha Ngan and Koh Samui, and many of the operations on Samui coordinate with larger on-site dive centers there while also offering good day trips from Samui. Conditions vary with the seasons (Oct–Mar are the best months). The cluster of tiny islands south of Samui, **Mu Koh**

Ang Thong National Marine Park, is often a more reliable destination. Follow the advice of a local dive shop on where to go, as many have schools on Samui and offer trips ranging further afield. You can try **Samui International Diving School** (© 07742-2386 in Chaweng; www.planet-scuba.net), with eight locations around the island; **Easy Divers** (© 07741-3373); or **Big Blue** (© 07745-6179).

THE SPA SCENE

Traditional massage is available in any number of storefronts in Chaweng and everywhere along the beach. Expect to pay between 200B and 400B (US$5–US$10/£2.80–£5.60) per hour for services.

Ban Sabai, at Big Buddha Beach (© 07724-5175; www.ban-sabai.com), is a great choice for a relaxing seaside massage. It offers all treatments, from aromatherapy to body waxing, in its lush, Thai-style compound. Personal attention is this spa's hallmark, and the well-informed staff can tailor a program to your every need. Treatments start at just 750B (US$19/£11) for a 1-hour massage.

The **Spa Resort,** in Lamai (© 07723-0855; www.spasamui.com), has been a leader on the island for years and continues to provide good, affordable day programs, as well as its signature fasting retreat and all-inclusive packages. **Tamarind Retreat** (© 07723-0571; www.tamarindretreat.com) is a more exclusive (and expensive) choice set apart in a jungle area just off the beach at Lamai.

KOH SAMUI AFTER DARK

Any given evening along the Chaweng strip is certain to be disrupted at least a few times by roaming pickup trucks with crackling PA systems blaring out advertisements in Thai and English for local **Thai boxing** bouts. Grab one of their flyers for times and locations, which vary.

For bars and discos, Chaweng is the place to be. A mainstream kind of fun seems to always be happening at the **Reggae Pub** (indicated on just about every island map—back from the main road around the central beach area). In this huge thatch mansion, the stage thumps with funky international acts, the dance floor jumps (even during low season, it does a booming business), and the upstairs pool tables are good for sporting around. Just outside is a collection of open-air bars, also found along Chaweng's beach road. The **Green Mango** has its own street, just off the beachfront road in the northern end of Chaweng, and boom-boom-booms late every night as the town's number-one dance location. A good place to meet that special someone or two.

Most beachside bars consist of a younger backpacker crowd lounging on cushions in the sand. Of these, the **Ark Bar** (© 07742-2047), across from the Center Point shopping center, is the most happening. The Irish-owned **Tropical Murphy's** (© 07741-3614), across from McDonald's in south Chaweng, is indeed a slice of

---

Warning   **Just say "Mai!"**

"Mai" means "no," and Nancy Reagan's ardent, much-parodied plea couldn't be more apt. Thai authorities hope to put the kibosh on Haad Rin's monthly Full Moon Parties (and other "Half-Moon" and "No-Moon" excuses to rage). This means undercover drug busts by the very guy who just sold you that bag of oregano and bribing your way out of police custody.

Ireland along the Chaweng strip. It's always full and open late; it's the best place to have a friendly pint and be assured you won't have to scream over the thumping bass of house music. Good Irish bands visit from time to time.

Zico's (© 07723-1560), a unique Brazilian restaurant, has a slick, big-city kind of bar that will be a comfort to any Hollywood-style players who miss their playground. Zico's modern facade looks over the busy main drag in the south of Chaweng near the Central Resort compound. **Coco Blues Company** (© 07741-4354), on the north end of Chaweng's main drag, hosts nightly live music, either the house band or international acts, and also serves decent Cajun food.

Over at Lamai Beach, there are some open-air bars geared to budget backpackers, but many are the sleazier bar-beer variety. On Bophut Beach, be sure to stop by friendly and laid-back **Frog & Gecko Bar** (in Fisherman's Village; © 07742-5248), especially for its popular pub quiz on Wednesday evenings.

Sunday afternoons, be sure to truck on over to the **Secret Garden Pub** ☆☆, on Big Buddha Beach (© 07724-5253), for live music and a barbecue on the beach. Many a famous performer (Gerry played here, man!) has jumped up on stage, and there have been times when the pub has hosted thousands. It's not exactly "secret," but still highly recommended. Festivities usually kick off around 5pm.

SIDE TRIPS FROM KOH SAMUI
MU KOH ANG THONG NATIONAL MARINE PARK ☆

Forty islands northwest of Koh Samui have been designated a national park. Mu Koh Ang Thong National Marine Park is known for its scenic beauty and rare coral reefs. Many of these islands are limestone rock towers (similar to Phang Nga Bay off Phuket), once used by pirates marauding in the South China Sea.

You can book a private boat from Nathon Pier, or you can take a day trip via sea kayak, paddling through the scenery for better views. The latter runs about 2,000B (US$50/£28) with **Blue Stars Sea Kayaking** (see "Outdoor Activities," above).

13 Koh Pha Ngan

75km (47 miles) E of Surat Thani

Visible from Koh Samui and about two-thirds its size, with similar terrain and flora, Koh Pha Ngan has some beautiful beaches and, along the further reaches of the island—the rugged north and west coasts, accessible only by bumpy road or special boat—a few cozy resorts and a measure of rustic tranquillity.

The southeastern peninsula of **Haad Rin** is the locus of the monthly **Full Moon Party,** a multiday beachside rave with all the Day-Glo, strobe lights, and debauchery you can handle; attendance at the raves, especially in high season, numbers in the thousands of partyers moving to the mix of a European DJ, gobbling tabs of Ecstasy and magic mushrooms, and letting loose, very loose: something like Ibiza meets a Phish show at the beach. The aftermath of the party is a beautiful white-sand beach strewn with party garbage and buzzing with flies.

If you're interested in attending, boats from Koh Samui leave at regular intervals all day and night (stopping at around 1am) and many revelers just make a night of it, crash on the beach, and come back to Samui in the morning. *A word of warning:* Beware of theft at Full Moon Parties—do yourself a favor and lock all your valuables in a hotel safe.

GETTING THERE

BY BOAT   Frequent boats link Surat Thani, Koh Samui, Koh Pha Ngan, Koh Tao, and Chumphon. From Samui's Nathon Pier, the trip to Koh Pha Ngan takes just over an hour and costs 150B (US$3.75/£2.10). Contact **Songserm,** in Koh Samui (© 07742-0157). Special boats from Samui's Big Buddha Beach and Bophut Beach also make regular trips for 100B (US$2.50/£1.40), more during Full Moon Parties at inflated rates. *Note:* Unfortunately, the muster point in Pha Ngan is not well organized, just a bare pier and one gruff attendant. Come armed with the patience of Buddha, especially any time near the full moon.

GETTING AROUND

Jeep and **motorbike** rentals on Koh Pha Ngan are available anywhere in Haad Rin or near the ferry pier at Thong Sala, on the southwest coast. Caribeener jeeps start at 900B (US$23/£13); regular motorbikes go for 150B (US$3.75/£2.10) and up. The island roads are steep and treacherous, especially the popular southern reaches east of Thong Sala near Haad Rin. Many interior roads, including the trek to the secluded Thong Nai Pan area in the north, are hilly, muddy tracks. **Songtaos** follow regular routes between Thong Sala ferry pier and Haad Rin, as well as up the west coast; rides start at 350B (US$8.75/£4.80), more at night or during party time.

FAST FACTS: KOH PHA NGAN

There are branches of **Siam City Bank,** with exchange and ATM services, along both the main street of Thong Sala and in Haad Rin. **Internet access** is chockablock around the island; prices are 2B (US5¢/£0.05) per minute. The **tourist police** operates a small information kiosk on the north end of the ferry offices at Thong Sala pier; call © 07742-1281 for info or © 1155 in an emergency.

WHERE TO STAY & DINE

Cheap eats abound in busy Haad Rin, but your best bet for a good meal outside of your chosen resort is limited to mostly budget storefronts blaring DVD movies at high decibels. One bright spot is **Om Ganesh** (© 07737-5123), near the main ferry pier. It has great curries and set menus (all-you-can-eat Indian *thali* meals) for little: authentic, delicious, and very popular.

BAAN TAI BEACH

Just east of the ferry landing at Thong Sala, Ban Tai Beach is a quiet stretch of sand on the island's southwest coast. The water is shallow and not great for swimming, but the beaches are lovely, and there are a few convenient little resorts far from the hubbub of Haad Rin but close enough to visit. Try **First Villa** (145/1 Moo 1, Bantai Beach; © 07737-7225), with basic bungalows from 1,020B (US$26/£14), or nearby **Mac Bay Resort** (Baan Tai Beach, Koh; © 07723-8443), with a similar plain standard and rates.

HAAD RIN

Haad Rin is a narrow peninsula on the island's southeast tip, with a large number of bungalows on both the west and east sides and busy shopping streets and footpaths leading between them. There are lots of small bungalow resorts, all quite basic. On the busier west side, try **Phangan Buri Resort & Health Spa** (120/1 Haad Rin Nai Beach, Haad Rin; © 07737-5481), with standard rooms from 2,900B (US$73/£41). Or check out hilltop **Sea Breeze Bungalow** (94/11 Moo 6, Haad Rin; © 07737-5162), a quiet, lofty perch high enough above town for a bit of quiet but close enough to walk down and join the festivities. Rooms start at 400B (US$10/£5.60) for fan only (double at Full Moon times).

The **Sanctuary** (P.O. Box 3, Koh Pha Ngan 84280; www.thesanctuarythailand. com) bills itself as an alternative boutique resort. It offers all kinds of healthy activities like yoga, massage, and fasting programs. Accommodations range from 80B (US$2/£1.10) dorms to family houses for 1,200B (US$30/£17). You'll need to arrange a taxi boat from Haad Rin to Haad Tien (50B/US$1.25/£0.70).

NORTHEAST COAST

Secluded on its own stretch of beach 17km (11 miles) from the ferry pier and north of busy Haad Rin, this area features great beaches with a few budget stops as well as the island's best resort. Thong Nai Pan is a scenic choice, easily reached by boat (contact Panviman below) or, less easily, by bumpy dirt road. **Panviman** ℱ (22/1 Moo 5, Thong Nai Pan Noi Bay; ℭ/fax **07744-5101;** www.panviman.com) is the best standard on Pha Ngan and has picturesque rooms overlooking the bay, lots of services, and a unique tiered pool area. Open but still under construction at press time, the **Santhiya Resort & Spa** (ℭ 07723-**8333;** www.santhiya.com), once finished, might take the mantle of "best on the beach." Deluxe rooms start at 12,000B (US$300/£168).

NORTHWEST COAST

The northwest coast has good beaches and is far from the monthly "do" at Haad Rin, a relief for many. Resorts here are quiet and affordable and growing in number and quality of amenities. **Green Papaya** (Haad Salad, on the far northwest of the island; ℭ/fax **07737-4230**) is a mellow little courtyard hotel with rooms from 3,400B (US$85/£48). The next-door **Salad Beach Resort** (ℭ **07734-9274**) is same-same.

WHAT TO SEE & DO

The rugged roads of Pha Ngan beg to be explored, and interior roads connect small towns worth seeing as a window into a way of laid-back island living that is slowly disappearing.

Wat Kow Tahm ℱ is a well-known international meditation center and temple compound just north of the road near Thong Sala pier. Since 1988, Steve and Rosemary Weissmann (from the U.S. and Australia, respectively) have been offering courses in Insight Meditation, or Vipassana. The emphasis is on the development of compassionate understanding through the practice of formal walking and sitting meditation. There are frequent Dharma talks and 10- and 20-day retreats for meditators of all experience levels; prices start at 34,000B (US$850/£468) for 10 days. The temple is also open to day visitors and has an overlook with one of the best views on the island. Check the informative website at www.watkowtahm.org or address inquiries to: RETREATS, Wat Kow Tahm, P.O. Box 18, Koh Pah Ngan, Surat Thani 84280.

14 Koh Tao

Tiny Koh Tao developed differently from its neighbors—it skipped the slow-growth years of thatch shacks and candlelit meals and went straight to corrugated tin roofs and video-playing bars. There are still lots of rustic choices on the island, but the current trend is small, all-inclusive resorts owned and operated by dive companies with head offices in Samui and elsewhere. Visitors spend their days out on the water on **scuba tours** to the fine coral sites around the island, then return to the comfort of private bungalows where they can relax and debrief after the day's exploration (many of these places even have air-conditioned classrooms for studying diving specifics). Avoid Koh Tao in the stormy November-to-December season, when the monsoon whips up and winds cloud the normally transparent seas.

Songserm (☎ **07742-0157** on Koh Samui, ☎ **07750-6205** in Chumphon, ☎ **07745-6274** on Koh Tao) connects from nearby islands. From Chumphon, the fare is a steep 450B (US$11/£6.30); from Koh Samui, 300B (US$7.50/£4.20); and from Koh Pha Ngan, 170B (US$4.25/£2.40). Once you get to the main town, you'll find scuba operators and accommodations booking offices.

For advance booking with a dive service, contact a dive office such as **Big Blue Diving Koh Tao** (in Mae Haad; ☎ **07745-6050;** www.bigbluediving.com) or **Easy Divers** (in Mae Haad at the catamaran jetty; ☎ **07745-6010;** www.thaidive.com).

15 The Far South & on to Malaysia

From Surat Thani going south, Thailand slowly gives way to Malay culture; Buddhism, predominant elsewhere in the kingdom, is replaced by rich Islamic influence, a gradual process without any precise border. **Nakhon Si Thammarat** is an ancient Buddhist city of note with many temples worth visiting. The far southern **Hat Yai** is a major transport hub and a destination more popular with Malay and Singaporean tourists, mostly a stopover for onward travel to (or connecting from) Malaysia.

Warning: Two recent bomb attacks targeted tourist areas in Hat Yai: In April 2005, a bomb was set off in Hat Yai International Airport, killing two, and in September 2006, six separate bombs killing four people, including a Canadian, were detonated in downtown Hat Yai. While these were isolated events, and most of the violence occurs further south in the border areas with Malaysia, caution is advised if you plan on using Hat Yai as a transit point.

NAKHON SI THAMMARAT

Nakhon Si Thammarat, one of the oldest cities in southern Thailand, has long been a religious capital. **Wat Mahatat** houses a hair of the Buddha and is the town's central attraction and important pilgrimage point for Thai Buddhists. This region is the locus for traditional Thai puppet play, and **Ban Nang Thalung Suchart Subsin** (Mr. Subsin's House of Shadow Plays), at 110/18 Si Thammasok Soi 3 (☎ **07534-6394**), makes for an interesting visit.

Thai Airways and **PB Air** each connect Nakhon with Bangkok. All north–south **trains** make a stop here, and affordable **minivans** can be arranged from any hotel (the best way to get around the south).

Thai Hotel (1375 Ratchadamnoen Rd; ☎ **07534-1509**) is a basic and convenient standard lodging, with rooms starting at 390B (US$9.75/£5.45).

HAT YAI

It's a town full of tourists behaving badly, mostly men from nearby Malaysia and Singapore attracted by this rowdy, slightly sleazy, inexpensive, consumer playground. For Westerners, Hat Yai is mostly a gateway to Malaysia by train or bus, or a stepping-off point for rugged Tarutao National Park. Hat Yai's busy **Night Market** is certainly worth a wander, and the beaches at nearby **Songkhla** are not a bad day trip.

Hat Yai International Airport welcomes frequent flights from Malaysia and Singapore via Silk Air, Malaysia Airlines, and Thai Airways, and there are connections available to Bangkok and Phuket.

Five trains depart daily from Bangkok's **Hua Lampong Railway Station** (© **1690** or 02223-7010) to Hat Yai, which is a major rail hub, and there are daily connections with Malaysia. Minibuses connect from other parts of the region, and long-distance buses connect from Bangkok's **Southern Bus Terminal** (© **02435-1199**).

A number of fine hotels cater to Malay tourists. Try the **Regency Hotel** (23 Prachathipat Rd.; © **07423-4400**), with rooms from 900B (US$23/£13), or the popular backpacker haunt, **Cathay Guest House** (93/1 Niphat Uthit 2 Rd.; © **07424-3815**), with dorms from 100B (US$2.50/£1.40) and reasonable singles from 160B (US$4/£2.25).

Hat Yai is also the gateway to **Tarutao National Park,** a chain of 51 islands originally settled by sea gypsies and later used as prison colonies. The jumping-off point for Tarutao is Ban Pak Bara, a port city reached by bus from Hat Yai.

16 An Introduction to the Southern Peninsula: West Coast & Islands

This stunning length of coast, dotted by some of the finest resorts in the region, is now well known for the tragic events of December 2004, when a massive tsunami struck the shores here, leaving a path of destruction. Many lives were lost and this long, heavily populated coast was left in ruins. Today, there are few signs left of the destruction, as resorts were quick to rebuild and remodel post-tsunami. In the unlikely event of another tsunami, the government has installed an early warning system, and evacuation routes to high ground are well marked.

The island of **Phuket** was one of the earliest tourist developments in the kingdom and from humble origins has grown into a top international resort area: the best choice for comfort and services on the west coast. Phuket may be the largest and best known, though it is but one of many in the brilliant blue Andaman Sea; rocky islets, atolls, and leafy jungle coastline play host to a roster of island resorts and getaways. It is a great area to island-hop via bus and ferry connections, and there are opportunities for snorkeling, trekking, and laid-back luxury in every quarter.

The province of **Krabi** encompasses all the land east of Phuket, including Koh Phi Phi and Koh Lanta, but "Krabi" typically refers to the small port town and nearby beaches of the Krabi Resort area and Ao Nang Beach. In places like Railay Beach, you'll find dynamic stone-tower landscapes (famous for rock climbing), great beaches, and a range of resorts. It's a popular alternative to busy Phuket.

Officially part of Krabi Province but often visited from Phuket, the island of **Koh Phi Phi** followed Phuket's development model, though on a smaller scale. Phi Phi was hit hard by the tsunami, but has quickly been rebuilt.

Koh Lanta is a large island southeast of Krabi Town. Once just budget resorts and bungalows, it now hosts a number of luxury resorts with many more under construction.

The high season on the west coast is from November to April—bookings must be made in advance, especially on Phuket, and discounted rates are hard to come by. Still, western winter months are the time for water activities, when the Andaman is calm and the skies clear (and when the snow falls thick in many parts of the world). In superpeak season, from the Christmas holiday to about January 10, most places tack on steep surcharges.

The Southern Peninsula: West Coast

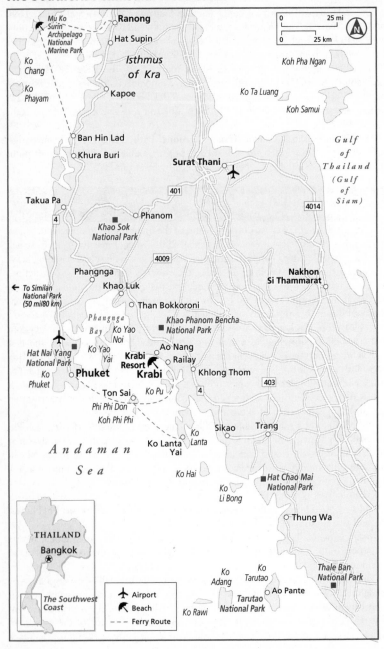

17 Phuket ✭✭✭

At its best, this island in the Andaman Sea is idyllic: It has long sandy beaches (some with dunes), warm water, excellent snorkeling and scuba diving off Koh Similan, ideal windsurfing conditions, mountains, fine resorts, and some of the best seafood in all of Thailand. At its worst, it is overdeveloped and overrun with tour groups; its raucous nightlife and areas like busy Patong's pulsing commercial strip are a bit too much for those in search of beachside tranquillity.

Over the years, the Thai government has granted economic incentives to encourage developers to shape the island into an international first-class resort. The 2004 tsunami was merely a speed bump, development wise, as today construction continues to spread to previously remote beaches, and tourism numbers are almost back to pre-tsunami days. As groups pour in from Singapore, Hong Kong, and Europe, the backpackers head off to nearby Koh Phi Phi and Krabi, or to islands on the eastern gulf like Samui and Pha Ngan.

But many of the resorts are attractive and elegant and designed to give you the illusion of tropical solitude in busier areas. It's nearly impossible to find a totally secluded beach, but there are a number of very attractive and comfortable facilities with a high level of service—not a bad trade-off for those in search of all the luxuries. If on a family holiday, Phuket is a good choice.

GETTING THERE

BY PLANE   **Thai Airways** (✆ 02525-2084 in Bangkok for domestic reservations) flies at least 10 times daily from Bangkok, from 7am to 9:30pm (trip time: 1 hr., 20 min.), and has a daily flight from Chiang Mai (trip time: 2 hr.). It also connects Phuket with international flights to and from Frankfurt, Hong Kong, Perth, Singapore, and Tokyo. The local Thai Airways office in Phuket is at 78 Ranong Rd. (✆ 07621-1195 for domestic, 07621-2499 for international).

Silk Air (✆ 02236-5301-3 in Bangkok) has daily connections with Singapore.

Bangkok Airways (✆ 02229-3434 in Bangkok, 07724-5601 on Koh Samui) connects Phuket with both Koh Samui and Bangkok at least three times daily. The Bangkok Airways office in Phuket is at 158/2–3 Yaowarat Rd., Phuket Town (✆ 07622-5033, or 07632-7114 at Phuket Airport).

Phuket Airlines (✆ 02535-6382), **Air Asia** (✆ 02515-9999; www.airasia.com), **Nok Air** (✆ 02900-9955), and **One-Two-Go** (✆ 01141-1126) all connect Phuket with Bangkok daily.

The attractive, modern **Phuket International Airport** (✆ 07732-7230) is in the north of the island, about a 40-minute drive from town or from Patong Beach. It has banks, money-changing facilities, car-rental agents (see "Getting Around," below), and a post office. The Phuket Tourist Business Association booth can help you make hotel arrangements if you haven't booked a room in advance.

Many resorts will pick you up at the airport upon request for a fee, usually steep, though some include this with your rate. The airport limousine counter, operated by **Tour Royale** (✆ 07634-1214), offers many options for getting to your hotel from the airport. The cheapest way is the **minibus,** which operates every hour on the hour from 9am to 11pm daily. Stopping between Patong, Kata, Karon, and Phuket Town, prices run from 80B to 180B (US$2–US$4.50/£1.10–£2.50), depending on how far you're going (180B gets you as far south as Kata Beach). **Taxi** service from the airport, also arranged at the limousine counter, will cost between 400B (US$10/£5.60) to Phuket

Phuket

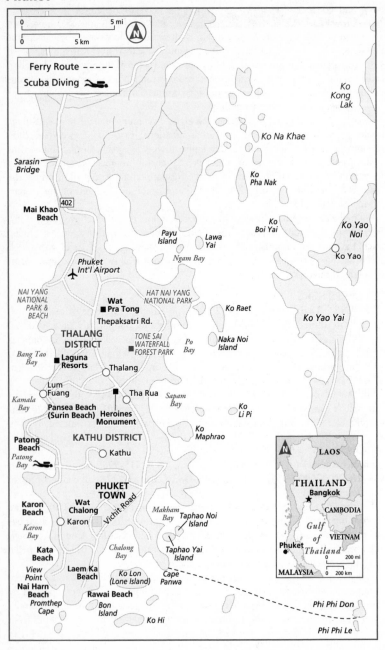

0 5 mi
0 5 km

Ferry Route - - - - -
Scuba Diving

Ko Kong Lak

Ko Na Khae

Sarasin Bridge

Ko Pha Nak

Mai Khao Beach

402

Payu Island   *Lawa Yai*

Ko Boi Yai

Ko Yao Noi

Phuket Int'l Airport

Ngam Bay

Ko Yao

NAI YANG NATIONAL PARK & BEACH

HAT NAI YANG NATIONAL PARK

Wat Pra Tong
Thepaksatri Rd.

Ko Raet

Ko Yao Yai

THALANG DISTRICT

TONE SAI WATERFALL FOREST PARK

Po Bay

Naka Noi Island

Bang Tao Bay

Laguna Resorts

Thalang

Lum Fuang

Kamala Bay

Pansea Beach (Surin Beach)

Tha Rua

Sapam Bay

Heroines Monument

Ko Li Pi

KATHU DISTRICT

Patong Beach

Kathu

Ko Maphrao

Patong Bay

PHUKET TOWN

Karon Beach

Wat Chalong

Makham Bay   Taphao Noi Island

Karon Bay

Karon

Vichit Road

Kata Beach

Chalong Bay

Taphao Yai Island

View Point

Laem Ka Beach

Ko Lon (Lone Island)

Cape Panwa

Nai Harn Beach

Rawai Beach

Promthep Cape

Bon Island

Ko Hi

LAOS

THAILAND
Bangkok ★

CAMBODIA

Gulf
of

VIETNAM

Phuket ●

Thailand

0 200 mi
0 200 km

MALAYSIA

Phi Phi Don

Phi Phi Le

Town and 650B (US$16/£9.10) to Kata Beach. The **airport bus** connects with Phuket Town and costs 52B (US$1.25/£0.75). Buses depart roughly every hour from 6:30am to 9:30pm.

BY BUS   Three air-conditioned 24-seat VIP buses leave daily from Bangkok's **Southern Bus Terminal** (✆ 02434-7192), best as an overnight, and cost from 1,045B (US$26/£15). Regular air-conditioned buses cost 541B (US$13/£7.60). Standard buses make frequent connections to Surat Thani and nearby towns on the mainland (trip time from Surat: 6 hr.; 200B/US$5/£2.80).

The intercity bus terminal is at the **City Park Complex** (Phangnga Rd.; ✆ 07621-1480), east of Phuket Town just opposite the Royal Phuket City Hotel. For information on how to get from here to the beaches, see "Getting Around," below.

BY MINIVAN   Minivans to and from Surat Thani, Krabi, Nakhon Si Thammarat, Ranong, and other southern cities leave on regular schedules throughout the day. In each city, minivan operators work with the hotels and arrange free pickup, so it's best to book through your hotel front desk or a travel agent (especially since the operators who man the phones at minivan companies rarely speak English). Tickets from destinations in the south, such as Surat Thani and Hat Yai, go for between 200B and 350B (US$5–US$8.75/£2.80–£4.90).

GETTING AROUND

Public transportation is a problem on Phuket that never seems to get solved. If you've spent any time in other parts of the country, you'll know that the covered pickup trucks that cruise the streets picking up and dropping off passengers are called *songtao,* while the noisy motorized three-wheel demons are known as tuk-tuks. Not so on Phuket! Here, the people call the minitrucks **tuk-tuks,** while **songtao** are the giant colorful buses that ply the main roads (a few people also call them **baht buses**). Tuk-tuk drivers, in an attempt to generate more business, have lobbied successfully for exclusive rights to transport people *between* beaches, the lone exception being between Kata and Karon. This means the songtao buses are only permitted to travel from each beach to Phuket Town—you can't hop from beach to beach on them. For these trips, you have to negotiate with the tuk-tuk drivers (see below for tips).

BY SONGTAO   The local bus terminal is in front of the Central Market on Ranong Road in Phuket Town. Fares to the most popular beaches range from 20B to 30B (US50¢–US75¢/£0.30–£0.40). Songtao buses leave when full, usually every 30 minutes, from 7am to 6pm between Phuket Town and the main beaches on the west coast. Other than the route through Karon and Kata beaches, they do not operate routes between beaches.

BY TUK-TUK & DAIHATSU MINI   Within Phuket Town, tuk-tuk trucks cost about 20B to 40B (US50¢–US$1/£0.30–£0.55) for in-town trips: a good way to get to the bus station or to Phuket Town's restaurants. In the west-coast beaches, tuk-tuks and small Daihatsu minitrucks roll around town honking at any tourist on foot, especially in Patong, and charge more, about 200B (US$5/£2.80) from Patong Beach to Karon Beach, with higher prices late at night

BY MOTORCYCLE TAXI   Drivers, identifiable by colored vests, make short trips in Phuket Town or along Patong Beach for 20B to 40B (US50¢–US$1/£0.30–£0.55).

BY CAR   Self-driving is popular on Phuket, but extreme caution applies. Roads between the main beaches in the west and connecting with Phuket Town across the

---

Tips **Special Event**

If you are on Phuket in October, don't miss the **Vegetarian Festival,** a colorful tradition passed down from early Thai-Chinese settlers. For 9 days, not only do devotees refrain from meat consumption, but many also submit to physical self-mutilation through walking over coals and practicing extreme body-piercing with long skewers or swords, all acts of merit making and penance to the spirits who helped early inhabitants ward off malaria. Early-morning processions follow through the streets of Phuket Town, with onlookers clad in white for the occasion.

---

center of the island are dangerously steep and winding, with more than a few hairpin turns, lots of traffic, and motorbikes zipping around unpredictably. As in other parts of the kingdom, drivers pass aggressively, even on blind curves, and drivers will want to be very defensive and alert at all times.

Avis has a counter at Phuket Airport (© **07653-1243**). Plan on spending around 1,500B to 1,800B (US$38–US$45/£21–£25) per day for a Suzuki Caribian four-wheel-drive sport vehicle. **Budget** (© **07620-5396**) is a bit cheaper; it has an airport location as well as counters at a number of hotels (JW Marriott, Evason Resort, and Club Andaman Beach Resort in Patong). Both companies offer sedans, and both also have sound insurance coverage available, which is highly recommended.

BY MOTORCYCLE   Also along the Patong strip, the same car-rental guys will provide you with a bike for cheap. A 100cc Honda scooter goes for 200B (US$5/£2.80) per day, while a 400cc Honda CBR or a 600cc Honda Shadow chopper will set you back at least 600B (US$15/£8.40) per day. Significant discounts can be negotiated if you plan to rent for a longer time. Wear your helmet (there are sometimes-enforced fines of 500B/US$13/£7 for going without), keep to the left, and let cars pass. Exercise caution: You're sure to meet up with a few road-rashed travelers in any beach area, and there is no quicker way to end a vacation than on slippery, treacherous roads, especially for inexperienced riders.

ISLAND LAYOUT

Phuket Town, the island's commercial center, is in the southeast. Picturesque stretches of sand dot the western coast from Nai Harn, on the southern tip, to Bang Tao, about 30km (19 miles) north. Beginning in the south, you'll find Kata Noi, Kata, Karon, Patong, Surin, and a number of smaller beaches all along this corridor. A busy coastal road links the popular tour towns in the south, but destinations north of Patong require short detours from the main highway. Inland Phuket, with its winding mountain roads, buzzes with traffic, and many visitors rent vehicles to tour the island's smaller byways or make the trip to jungle parks like Khao Phra Thaeo National Park in the northeast, famed for diverse flora and fauna.

THE BEACHES   There's a beach for everyone in Phuket, from exclusive hideaways with luxury hotels to backpacker towns and even campgrounds. Each beach is distinct—selecting the appropriate area makes all the difference.

Nai Harn Beach, in the far south of the busy west coast of Phuket, is an isolated area with a few fine resorts. Going north from here, you'll find **Kata Beach, Kata Noi**

Beach, and **Karon Beach.** Developed but not overwhelmingly so (far from over-the-top Patong), these beaches are home to resorts large and small. In general, this is the least expensive area on Phuket, with still a few holdout budget places that haven't been bulldozed and made high-end yet. Sandy beaches are long and picturesque; the water is deep, with some nice wave breaks. This beach area has more restaurants than the remote bays, and some shopping, nightlife, and travel-agent options as well. But you won't find rowdy crowds here—and even with all the development, the area manages to maintain a laid-back character.

North of Kata and Karon bays, you'll pass through **Relax Bay,** a small cove with a few resorts, before rolling down the mountain to **Patong Beach,** the most famous (perhaps infamous) strip on the island. Patong's draw is its raucous nightlife, busy shops and restaurants, and brash neon-radiating pulse: Can you hear the bass? Accommodations run the gamut here.

Still north of Patong, **Kamala Bay, Surin Beach,** and **Pansea Beach** have more secluded resorts on lovely beaches for those who still want the convenience of nearby Patong, but cherish the serenity of a quiet resort. Just north is **Bang Tao Beach,** home to the Laguna Resort Complex of luxury hideaways. Beautiful **Hat Nai Yang National Park** is a remote area with good diving, just north of Laguna, and, in the far north are **Mai Khao Beach** and the JW Marriott.

VISITOR INFORMATION

The **TAT** office in Phuket Town is at 73–75 Phuket Rd. (© **07621-2213**), but there is far better information through any hotel concierge or tour desk. You'll find lots of free maps on offer (all filled with advertisements). For driving around the island, pick up the very detailed *Periplus Editions Map of Phuket* at any bookstore. Restaurants and hotel lobbies are good places to pick up a number of free local publications: *Phuket Food-Shopping-Entertainment* is packed with dining suggestions and ads for many of the island's activities; *What's on South* has some useful information on Phuket, Koh Phi Phi, and Krabi; and there's a few fun ultraglossy local magazines for sale.

FAST FACTS: Phuket

Currency Exchange Banks are in Phuket Town, with many larger branches on Ranong and Rasada roads. There are bank offices at the airport, as well as branches of major Thai banks at Kata, Karon, and Patong beaches. See each destination section for more information. Money changers are in major shopping areas on each beach and at most resorts, but banks offer the best rates.

Hospitals The **Bangkok Phuket Hospital** (2/1 Hongyok-Uthit Rd., off Yaowarat Rd. in Phuket Town; © **07625-4421**) has English-speaking staff and high-quality facilities, and accepts international medical insurance.

Internet Access Internet service is fairly easy to find on the island. There are cafes aplenty in Patong; the best are further away from the beach.

Mail The general post office in Phuket Town (© **07621-1020**) is at the corner of Thalang and Montri roads.

Police The emergency number for the **tourist police** is the fast-dial four-digit © **1155**. For **marine police,** call © **07621-4368.**

WHERE TO STAY

The island's accommodations and restaurants below are divided by beach area, to help you simplify your choices. Hotel listings provide high-season rack rates, an almost fictitious fee but a good point of departure for gauging price. Expect to pay from 30% to as much as 50% below the listed rates, especially in low season.

PHUKET TOWN

Most just pass through the island's commercial hub, but there are some high-class facilities if you're stuck, plus a few restaurants worth the trip, especially if Phuket island is your only destination (see "Where to Dine," later in this section).

If you're in a pinch and looking for a budget spot, the **Tavorn Hotel** (74 Rasada Rd., Amphur Muang; ✆ **07621-1333**) is an old standby at the town center with rooms starting at 550B (US$14/£7.70). The hotel has seen better days, though; in fact, it has seen much better days—a little museum in the beat-up old lobby testifies to the fact. A careful renovation could bring the old gal back to her former glory days, when she was the choice of kings, but for now it's pretty rough. **Phuket Island Pavillion** (133 Satoon Rd.; ✆ **07621-0444**) has better rooms starting at just 1,500B (US$38/£21).

Expensive

Royal Phuket City Hotel ✦   For a small town like Phuket, this hotel is surprisingly cosmopolitan. A true city hotel, Royal Phuket's facilities include one of the finest fitness centers going, a full-service spa with massage, a large outdoor swimming pool, and a very professional business center. Above the cavernous marble lobby, guest rooms are smart—in contemporary hues and style, but dull with views of the busy little town below that pale in comparison to the beachfront just a short ride away. Pickles Restaurant serves international cuisine; the Chinatown Restaurant is one of the most posh in town. Few indeed stay in Phuket Town, but if you're stuck here, go for style.

154 Phang-Nga Rd., Amphur Muang, Phuket 83000 (to the east of Phuket Town, across from the intercity bus terminal). ✆ 07623-3333. Fax 07623-3335. www.royalphuketcity.com. 251 units. 4,155B–4,986B (US$105–US$125/£58–£70) double; from 7,122B (US$178/£100) suite. AE, DC, MC, V. **Amenities:** 2 restaurants; lobby lounge; outdoor pool; golf course nearby; fitness center w/sauna, steam, massage, and spa; tour desk; limo service; business center; 24-hr. room service; babysitting; laundry service; dry cleaning; nonsmoking rooms; executive-level rooms. *In room:* A/C, satellite TV, dataport, minibar, fridge, hair dryer, safe, IDD phone.

NAI HARN BEACH
Very Expensive

Le Royal Meridien Phuket Yacht Club ✦✦   Perched above the northern edge of Nai Harn Beach, overlooking the public beach and yachts beyond, the Yacht Club is one of the earliest luxury accommodations in Phuket, yet it still rivals nearly anything on the island for setting and comfort. Staff members in pith helmets greet with heel-clicking salutes and, as you enter, the pagoda-style foyer gives way to the terraced gardens overflowing with pink and white bougainvillea. Common areas are terra-cotta tile and open-air with views. All rooms have large balconies for viewing the beach, the Andaman Sea, and Promthep Cape from every angle. Interiors are spacious and decorated with cheerful fabrics and wicker furniture; bathrooms are huge, many with sunken tubs, and come with luxury amenities. The resort is more sedate and romantic than the many noisy family establishments on the island, exemplified by the Yacht Club's sister property, Le Meridien Phuket Beach Resort (p. 178).

23/3 Viset Rd., Nai Harn Beach, Phuket 83130 (above Nai Harn Beach, 18km/11 miles south of Phuket Town). *℡* **0800/225-5843** or 07638-1156. Fax 07638-1164. www.lemeridien.com. 110 units. 13,200B US$330/£182) double; from 17,200B (US$430/£241) suite. AE, DC, MC, V. **Amenities:** 3 restaurants; patio lounge; outdoor pool; 2 outdoor lighted tennis courts; small fitness center; spa w/Jacuzzi, steam, massage, and face and body treatments; extensive watersports equipment; tour desk; car rental; limo service; business center; small boutique; salon; 24-hr. room service; babysitting; laundry service; dry cleaning; nonsmoking rooms. *In room:* A/C, satellite TV w/pay movies, Internet access, minibar, fridge, coffeemaker, hair dryer, safe, IDD phone.

KATA BEACH

Arguably one of the nicest beaches in Phuket, Kata is a wide strip of soft sand and rolling surf. Rent an umbrella for 100B (US$2.50/£1.40) per day, get a massage, or grab a kayak or surfboard and hit the waves (okay, the small waves, mostly). Unfortunately, the most choice real estate near the beach is taken up by the sprawling **Club Med Phuket** (*℡* **07633-0455;** www.clubmed.com), a branch of the famous chain.

Expensive

Kata Beach Resort *⊛* With its soaring granite-and-marble lobby and fine rooms, the Kata is the best choice on Kata Beach proper and attracts not only individual tourists looking for comfort, but also a burgeoning international conference market. Go for a deluxe beachview room in the central building—the slightly higher-priced choice, but the view really is lovely. All units have balconies and are attractively decorated. *Hint:* For the best views of the bay and Crab Island beyond, ask for a room on the third floor, not the fourth (palm fronds obstruct the view).

5/2 Patak Rd., Kata Beach, Phuket 83100 (on the Kata Beach strip). *℡* **07633-0530**, or 02939-4062 in Bangkok. Fax 07633-0128. www.katagroup.com. 200 units. 5,700B (US$143/£80) superior double; 6,200B (US$155/£87) deluxe seaview double; from 12,000B (US$300/£165) suite. AE, DC, MC, V. **Amenities:** 2 restaurants; outdoor pool; fitness center w/sauna and massage; watersports equipment; children's center; concierge; tour desk; limo service; business center; shopping arcade; salon; limited room service; babysitting; laundry service; dry cleaning. *In room:* A/C, satellite TV, minibar, fridge, hair dryer, safe, IDD phone.

Katathani Phuket Beach Resort *⊛ (Kids)* Occupying a nearly kilometer-long stretch of lovely Kata Noi Beach, the Kata Thani is a haven of understated luxury. Divided into two wings, each with its own lobby, rooms and suites have been recently renovated to a very high standard. The beachfront Thani wing is all suites, notable for their fine ocean views. The Bhuri wing, across the street, is where the more affordable superior rooms can be found. Attractive new wood floors, remodeled marble bathrooms, and comfortable beds make these a decent value. Wide, well-groomed lawns surround sizable pools and lead to the graceful curve of the pristine cove. If at any time you feel like you're walking on a putting green, you probably are—putters and balls are available at the oceanside bar. Kata Noi is a bit out of the fray, just over the hill from the main Kata beach and far from the raucous strip at Patong, but the hotel is fully self-contained and can arrange transport for any excursion. *Note:* The Katathani is usually quite crowded and very popular with families. This is not the resort for a quiet, romantic getaway.

3/24 Patak Rd., Kata Noi Beach, Phuket 83100 (north end of Kata Noi Beach). *℡* **07633-0124.** Fax 07633-0426. www.katathani.com. 479 units. US$250–US$280 (£138–£154) superior; from US$310 (£171) suite. AE, DC, MC, V. **Amenities:** 6 restaurants; 2 lounges; 5 outdoor pools; golf course nearby; 2 outdoor lighted tennis courts; fitness center; aromatherapy spa; Jacuzzi; sauna; watersports equipment/scuba diving; game room; tour desk; car rental; limo service; salon; 24-hr. room service; massage; babysitting; laundry service; dry cleaning; library. *In room:* A/C, satellite TV, minibar, coffeemaker, hair dryer, safe, IDD phone.

Mom Tri's Boathouse and Villa Royale *⊛⊛* At the quieter south end of Kata Beach, the **Boathouse** is a longtime favorite with many return visitors. More inn than resort, there's a real home-style feeling here. Comfortable, attractive rooms all face the sea, each with a terrace overlooking courtyard pool and beach beyond, but not particularly luxurious (though clean and adequate). Nothing about the hotel calls attention to itself; instead, it's the friendly, attentive staff that makes it special. The Boathouse restaurant is an old favorite for the visiting connoisseur (see "Where to Dine"). It offers good cooking classes, too.

For a very special stay, stop in at Mom Tri's latest venture, **Villa Royale,** a collection of superluxe suites. An artist and architect, Mom Tri built these hillside villas perched over a steep cliff with stunning views of the sea. Each is sumptuously decorated in a unique mix of local materials: dark teaks, mosaics of bamboo and coconut, black tile with stone inlay, and elegant weavings. No two units are the same—the Toey Talay even has its own wine cellar. Walk through the grounds and you'll discover museum-worthy pieces of art from Mom Tri's personal collection, including an antique hand-carved gate from Chiang Mai. Mom Tri's Kitchen, the hotel's companion restaurant, offers some of the best dining on the island (see "Where to Dine").

Kata Beach, Phuket 83100. ⓒ **07633-0015.** Fax 07633-0561. www.boathousephuket.com or www.villaroyal ephuket.com. 36 units at the Boathouse; 27 units at Villa Royale. 7,500B (US$188/£105) Boathouse double; from 14,000B (US$350/£196) Boathouse suite; from 11,500B (US$288/£161) Villa suite. AE, DC, MC, V. **Amenities:** 3 restaurants; lounge; outdoor pool; golf course nearby; fitness center; Jacuzzi; limo service; limited room service (7am–10:30pm); massage; babysitting; laundry service; dry cleaning; library. *In room:* A/C, satellite TV, minibar, fridge, coffeemaker, hair dryer, safe, IDD phone.

Moderate

Kata Palm Resort & Spa ★ (Value) (Kids)   For the price and facilities, you can't beat the Kata Palm. It's stuck behind the oceanfront Club Med, making it a bit of a hike to get to the beach, but the pool more than makes up for the lack of beach access. A wandering affair, the pool wraps around a central lounge area and is beautifully landscaped with palm trees, orchids, and leelawadee flowers. Rooms are in three-story blocks, some with direct access to the pool from attached patios. Deluxe units in the newer block furthest from the lobby are your best bet. Four-poster daybeds, tasteful Thai decor, and bathrooms with separate shower and faux-antique tub make these a good upgrade. The Kata Palm is popular with families and offers one of the best values on Phuket.

60 Kata Rd., Kata Beach, Phuket 83100. ⓒ **07628-4334.** Fax 07628-4324. www.katapalmresort.com. 180 units. 4,300B (US$108/£60) superior; 5,300B–6,100B (US$128–US$158/£74–£85) deluxe; 9,150B (US$229/£128) suite. AE, DC, MC, V. **Amenities:** 3 restaurants; 2 pool bars; 2 outdoor pools; children's pool; fitness center; spa w/massage; kid's club; tour desk; salon; limited room service; babysitting; laundry service; Internet access; shuttles to Patong. In room: A/C, satellite TV, minibar, fridge, coffeemaker, IDD phone.

Marina Phuket Resort ★   These simple cottages, tucked in the jungle above a scenic promontory between Kata and Karon beaches, are quite comfortable and the best choice of the many mid-range places nearby. Rates vary according to the view, but all have a jungle bungalow charm, connected by hilly walkways and boardwalks past the lush hillside greenery (keep your eyes peeled for wildlife). Guest rooms are decorated in Thai style but are not particularly luxurious: Standard rooms have plain tile floors and basic built-in furniture; superior rooms are just a bit larger, with more flourishes like fine Thai fabrics, higher ceilings, and good views. It is a hike down to the rocky shore and the swimming isn't great, but there is a good seaside restaurant. The in-house **Marina Divers** (ⓒ **07638-1625**) is a PADI dive center that conducts classes, rents equipment, and leads good multi-day expeditions.

47 Karon Rd., Karon Beach, Phuket 83100 (on bluff at south end of Karon Beach Rd.). ℭ **07633-0625.** Fax 07633-0516. www.marinaphuket.com. 104 units. US$120–US$260 (£66–£143) double; US$500 (£275) villa. MC, V. **Amenities:** Restaurant; pool; limited room service; laundry service; dive center. *In room:* A/C, satellite TV, minibar, no phone.

Inexpensive

Katanoi Bay Inn   Here's a no-muss-no-fuss pick for Phuket. This budget accommodation provides you with a comfortable, very clean room without making you pay out the nose for resort facilities you might not even use. Rooms have balconies and good firm beds. There is little else in the way of facilities, but quiet Kata Noi Beach is just across the road (near the Katathani hotel).

4/16 Moo 2 Patak Rd., Kata Noi Beach, Phuket 83100 (Kata Noi is south of Kata Beach). ℭ/fax **07633-3308.** www.phuket.com/katanoibayinn. 28 units. 700B–1,700B (US$18–US$43/£9.80–£24) double. MC, V. **Amenities:** Restaurant; tour desk; car rental; laundry service; dry cleaning; Internet terminal. *In room:* Fridge, no phone.

KARON BEACH

Karon Beach is a long, straight stretch of beach lined with upper- and mid-range hotels and resorts. You'll find heaps of tailors, gift shops, small restaurants, Internet service, and minimarts on the north end of the beach.

Expensive

Andaman Seaview Hotel   Here's one that is highly recommended if you can book it (the word is out and it is often full). Bright and airy public spaces—done in Mediterranean hues of light blue and white, a Sino-Portuguese theme—are flanked by ponds and give way to a large central courtyard, garden, and meandering pool. Rooms overlook the pool area and are large and nicely appointed, better than most in this category. Deluxe units are massive, featuring marble bar areas and his-and-hers sinks. Bright primary colors dominate and everything sparkles. There is a charm throughout that is less about luxury than about the warm welcome, tidy appearance of the place, and friendly crowd. The restaurant is a de rigueur hotel coffee shop, but you'll want to dine at poolside: In fact, do everything at poolside. You're just across the street from Karon Beach here.

Karon Rd., Phuket 83100 (along the main strip at Karon Beach). ℭ **07639-8111.** Fax 07639-8177. www.andaman phuket.com. 161 units. 5,900B (US$148/£83) superior double; 8,800B (US$220/£123) deluxe double. AE, MC, V. **Amenities:** Restaurant; poolside bar; 2 outdoor pools; small fitness center; small spa; Jacuzzi; gift shop; 24-hr. room service; massage; laundry service; dry cleaning; Internet access; tailor. *In room:* A/C, satellite TV, minibar, fridge, coffeemaker, safe, IDD phone.

Hilton Phuket Arcadia Resort & Spa   Recently rebranded as a Hilton hotel, this modern, full-facility resort is a massive presence on Karon Beach, and after some upgrades is beginning to meet Hilton's high standards. Accommodations are spread amongst three separate wings, with the 12-story Lotus wings providing the most panoramic views. Rooms are attractive but bland, with standard bathroom facilities, and most with full or partial sea views. The newest addition to this sprawling campus is the luxury spa, a miniature Thai village with 15 villas connected by raised teakwood walkways. There are numerous facilities here, but chances are you won't be the only one using them at any given time—you don't stay at a Hilton for the solitude. If the pools get too crowded, Karon Beach is just a short hop across the street.

78/2 Patak Rd., Karon Beach, Phuket 83100 (middle of Karon Beach Rd.). ℭ **07639-6433.** Fax 07639-6136. www.phuketarcadia.com. 658 units. 5,200B–6,800B (US$130–US$170/£73–£95) double; from 14,400B (US$360/£202) suite. AE, DC, MC, V. **Amenities:** 8 restaurants; lounge and karaoke; 3 large outdoor pools; golf course nearby; putting green; 3 outdoor lighted tennis courts; 2 squash courts; fitness center w/Jacuzzi, sauna, steam, and massage;

spa; game room; tour desk; limo service; salon; 24-hr. room service; babysitting; laundry service; dry cleaning. *In room:* A/C, satellite TV, Internet access, minibar, coffeemaker, safe.

Moderate

Karon Beach Resort This is the only Karon Beach property with direct beach access (from all others, you'll have to walk across the road). Newly renovated, it is quite often full. Rooms are midsize, with dark wooden entries, clean tile floors, and some Thai touches, but are most noteworthy for their orientation to the sea: Balconies are stacked in receding, semicircular tiers and all look out on the pool below (1st-floor units with direct pool access) or to the beach and sea beyond. You'll find good watersports rentals nearby. This is a cozy beachside choice and an affordable option for young couples.

51 Karon Rd., Tambon Karon, Phuket 83100 (south end of Karon Beach, just as the road bends up to cross to Kata). © 07633-0006. Fax 07633-0217. www.katagroup.com. 81 units. 6,500B (US$163/£91) double; from 18,000B (US$450/£252) suite. AE, MC, V. **Amenities:** 2 restaurants; 2 outdoor pools; tour desk; car rental; courtesy car and airport transfer; massage; laundry service; Internet access. *In room:* A/C, satellite TV, minibar, fridge, safe (50B/ US$1.25/£0.70 fee), IDD phone.

Inexpensive

Golden Sand Inn One of only a few acceptable budget accommodations on this part of the island (they're either getting converted into swanky digs or falling into disrepair as in Patong), the Golden Sand is clean, reasonably quiet, and well maintained. The location isn't bad, on the northernmost end of Karon and not far from all the town services and the beach. Rooms are large and like those in a beat-up roadside motel. It does have a nice coffee shop, though, and a small pool. Off-season rates are cheap-cheap.

Karon Beach, Phuket 83100 (across hwy. from north end of beach above traffic circle). © 07639-6493. Fax 07639-6117. 125 units. 1,500B–2,500B (US$38–US$63/£21–£35) double. AE, DC, MC, V. **Amenities:** Restaurant; pool; laundry service. *In room:* A/C, TV, minibar, fridge, safe.

RELAX BAY

Le Meridien Phuket Beach Resort ★ *Kids* Le Meridien Phuket is tucked away on secluded Relax Bay, with a lovely 549m (1,800-ft.) beach and 16 hectares (40 acres) of tropical greenery. This is one of the largest resorts on the island, and throughout the year it's packed with Asian and European vacationers. The advantages of a larger resort are its numerous facilities—two big pools, watersports, four tennis courts, a putting green and practice range, and a fine fitness center. The disadvantage is the crowds. The staff is helpful but harried, and can often be found "dug in" behind the front desk like soldiers in a trench readying for the onslaught of the many big groups here. The resort caters to families, though, and there are lots of activities and a good day-care center that kids just seem to love. The large complex combines Western and traditional Thai architecture, and one of the advantages to its U-shaped layout is that it ensures that 80% of the rooms face the ocean. Each cheerful room has modern furnishings of rattan and teak, as well as a balcony with wooden deck chairs. No fewer than 10 restaurants give you all kinds of dining options.

8/5 Tambol, Karon Noi, P.O. Box 277, Relax Bay, Phuket 83000. © 0800/225-5843 or 07634-0480. Fax 07634-0479. www.lemeridien.com. 470 units. US$310–US$370 (£171–£204) double; from US$395 (£217) suite. AE, DC, MC, V. **Amenities:** 10 restaurants; 4 pubs w/games and live shows; 2 large outdoor pools; golf driving range and on-site pro; miniature golf; outdoor lighted tennis courts; squash courts; fitness center; watersports equipment and dive center; bike rental; excellent children's center; game room; concierge; tour desk; car rental; limo service; business center; shopping arcade; salon; 24-hr. room service; massage; babysitting; laundry service; dry cleaning; nonsmoking rooms. *In room:* A/C, satellite TV, minibar, fridge, coffeemaker, hair dryer, safe, IDD phone.

PATONG BEACH

Patong's got it all, but it's all stacked in a heap and glowing with neon. The area pulses with shopping, dining, and nightlife activity, late into the evening. In the downtown area, it's all touts catcalling and the beeping horns of passing tuk-tuks wanting to take you for a ride (quite literally); but Patong does have tons of services and some good accommodations (the best find creative ways to make you feel like you're not in Patong).

Expensive

Amari Coral Beach Resort & Spa ★★   The Coral Beach gets the nod for its wonderful location atop the rocks high above Patong, at the southern tip well away from the din of Patong's congested strip, but close enough for access to the mayhem. The beachfront below is rocky, but it's a good place to search for sea creatures at low tide. The whole resort, from the very grand terraced lobby to the guest rooms and fine pool, is situated toward incredible views of the huge bay below. The rooms have seafoam tones, cozy balconies, and all the comforts of home. The hotel's Italian restaurant, La Gritta (see "Where to Dine"), is special, and there's also live music nightly.

2 Meun-ngern Rd., Phuket 83150 (south of and uphill from Patong Beach). ☏ **07634-0106**. Fax 07634-0115. www.amari.com. 200 units. 6,800B–7,950B (US$170–US$199/£95–£111) double; from 10,300B (US$258/£144) suite. AE, DC, MC, V. **Amenities:** 3 restaurants; lounge; 2 outdoor pools; outdoor lighted tennis court; fitness center; brand-new spa; game room; tour desk; car rental; limo service; salon; 24-hr. room service; massage; babysitting; laundry service; dry cleaning; dive center. *In room:* A/C, satellite TV, minibar, safe.

Holiday Inn Resort Phuket ★★ *Kids*   The older buildings at this Holiday Inn are modern, concrete blocks and not particularly luxurious, but the newly renovated Busakorn Wing features more stylish rooms with Thai decor, teak appointments, carvings, and pottery. If on a honeymoon, go for a newer room; if with the kids, the old block will do the trick (and save some money). In fact, what distinguishes the Holiday Inn is its excellent offerings for traveling families. The central pool areas have elaborate fountains and a fun meander suited to kids of all ages, and the hotel has active kids' programs, family activities and excursions, and a children's center, not to mention babysitting for when mom and dad need a night out. There are even family suites, with separate "kid's rooms" that have jungle or pirate theme decor, TVs with video and PlayStation, toys, and bunk beds. The hotel also has self-service launderettes so you don't have to pay hotel laundry prices for the biomass of play clothes your kids will rip through: quite unique. Also unique is the hotel's minibar scheme, whereby rooms have just a bare fridge and guests visit a small convenience store in the lobby to choose what they would like; it's all delivered to your room at a cost of only a small bump-up from the retail price.

52 Thaweewong Rd., Patong Beach, Phuket 83150 (Patong Beach strip). ☏ **0800/HOLIDAY** or 07634-0608. Fax 07634-0435. www.phuket.holiday-inn.com. 369 units. 5,800B (US$145/£81) standard double; 7,000B (US$175/£98) Busakorn studio; 8,500B (US$213/£119) family suite. AE, DC, MC, V. **Amenities:** 3 restaurants; lounge; 4 outdoor pools; fitness center; spa w/massage, sauna, and steam; tip-top children's center and programs; tour desk; car rental; limo service; business center; 24-hr. room service; massage; babysitting; laundry service; self-service laundry; dry cleaning. *In room:* A/C, satellite TV, minibar, fridge, coffeemaker, hair dryer, safe, IDD phone.

Impiana Phuket Cabana Resort & Spa ★★   The Impiana is the only high-end property in Patong with direct beachfront access. It was heavily damaged by the 2004 tsunami, shutting its doors for almost a year. Renovations are almost complete (at press time, the finishing touches were being put on the new spa) and she's now better than ever. Cabanas have been refitted with polished stone floors, vaulted ceilings, and recessed lighting. Each is fashioned in a pleasingly minimal contemporary boutique style. The beach is only steps away, a major selling point, but there is also a beachfront infinity-edge pool if the strip gets too crowded. The location means that you are right in the thick of things, but the rooms are far enough removed from the main drag for privacy.

41 Thaweewongse Rd., Patong Beach, Phuket 83150 (middle of Beach Rd.). ℂ 07634-0138. Fax 07634-0178. www. impiana.com. 70 units. 8,800B–10,500B (US$220–US$263/£123–£147) double; 10,500B–15,000B (US$263–US$375/ £147–£210) suite. AE, DC, MC, V. **Amenities:** 2 restaurants; 2 bars; pool; spa; watersports equipment; concierge; tour desk; car rental; limo service; limited room service; babysitting; laundry service; dry cleaning; Internet access. *In room:* A/C, satellite TV, minibar, fridge, hair dryer, safe, IDD phone.

Novotel Coralia Phuket ✦
Set high in the hills on the north end of Patong, the Novotel is a lovely hideaway. It is typical of Accor hotels anywhere: good services and comfortable rooms done in a local style. What sets this apart is the three-tiered pool at the center of the property and its dynamic view of the beach and sea from this towering point. The lobby is under an enormous steep Thai roof, and from its luxury massage pavilions to the many fine-dining choices, guests are constantly wrapped in comfort and reminded of Thai culture.

Kalim Beach Rd., Patong Beach, Phuket 83150 (on the hill north of town, just as the road heads uphill). ℂ 07634-2777. Fax 07634-2168. www.novotelphuket.com or www.accorhotels.com. 215 units. 9,000B–11,000B (US$225–US$275/£126–£154) double; from 13,000B (US$325/£182) suite. AE, MC, V. **Amenities:** 3 restaurants; 3 bars; pool w/multiple tiers; 2 tennis courts; fitness center; sauna; kids' club; tour desk; car rental; business center w/Internet access; shopping; 24-hr. room service; massage; babysitting; laundry service; dry cleaning. *In room:* A/C, satellite TV, minibar, fridge, safe, IDD phone.

Moderate
Budget accommodations are best along Kata and Karon beaches in the southern end of the island. In Patong, the budget hotels are generally run-down, even seedy, owing to the hostess-bar and go-go scene. A notable exception is the deluxe rooms at the **Baumanburi** (239/1 Rat-U-Thit Pi Rd.; ℂ 07634-5951). While the standard units are depressing cells, the deluxe rooms are in a separate block overlooking the attractive pool and garden area—a steal at only 4,000B (US$100/£56) a night. Another 1,000B (US$25/£14) gets you direct access to the pool from your private patio. If you must have direct access to the beach, the **Patong Beach Bungalows** (39 Thaweewong Rd.; ℂ 07634-0117) joins the Impiana Phuket Cabana Resort as the only shows in town. Basic but clean bungalows start at 3,000B (US$75/£42), with a 40% discount in low season.

NORTHWEST COAST: PANSEA BEACH (SURIN BEACH)
Also known as Surin Beach, the Pansea area has coconut plantations, steep slopes leading down to the beach, and small, private coves dominated by two of the most secluded and divine hotels on the island.

Very Expensive
Amanpuri ✦✦✦ The discreet and sublime Amanpuri is the Phuket address for international celebrities. It is the most elegant and secluded resort in Thailand and quite possibly all of Southeast Asia. The lobby is an open-air pavilion with a standing Buddha near a lovely swimming pool and stairs leading to the beach. Free-standing pavilion suites dot the dense coconut-palm grounds; each is masterfully designed in traditional Thai style, with teak-and-tile floors, sliding teak doors, exquisite built-ins, and well-chosen accents, including antiques. Private *salas* (covered patios) are perfect for romantic dining or secluded sunbathing.

Pansea Beach, Phuket 83110 (north end of cove). (C) **07632-4333**. Fax 07632-4100. 53 units. US$700–US$800 (£385–£440) gardenview pavilion; US$950–US$1650 (£523–£908) seaview pavilion; from US$2400 (£1,320) villa. AE, DC, MC, V. **Amenities:** 2 restaurants; pool; golf course nearby; outdoor lighted tennis courts; squash courts; fitness center; spa; sauna; watersports equipment and instruction; private yacht fleet; concierge; limo service; limited room service; babysitting; laundry service; dry cleaning; library. In room: A/C, minibar, fridge, stereo, IDD phone.

The Chedi, Phuket &&& Like its august neighbor Amanpuri (above), the Chedi commands an excellent view of the bay below and has its own private stretch of sand. From the exotic lobby—with columns and lily pond—to the sleek private bungalows, it is one of the most handsome properties on the island. It's quality with a big price tag, but this romantic getaway has it down to the details. Each room is a thatched minisuite with a lovely private deck and top amenities. The black-tile swimming pool is large and luxurious. The snappy staff can arrange any watersports, sightseeing tours, or activities. The fine service here caters to the likes of honeymooners and celebrities, and everyone is a VIP. While it may not be as outwardly impressive as its extraordinary neighbor, the Chedi is quiet, comfortably informal, and very relaxing. There's a top-notch cooking school as well.

118 Moo 3, Choeng Talay, Pansea Beach, Phuket 83110 (next to the Amanpuri). (C) **07632-4017**. Fax 07632-4252. www.ghmhotels.com. 108 units. 16,200B–25,200B (US$405–US$630/£227–£353) 1-bedroom cottage; 21,100B–32,800B (US$528–US$820/£295–£459) 2-bedroom cottage; 29,700B–38,600B (US$743–US$965/£416–£540) suite. AE, DC, MC, V. **Amenities:** 3 restaurants; bar; outdoor pool; 2 outdoor lighted tennis courts; spa; watersports equipment; children's center; game room; concierge; tour desk; car rental; limo service; 24-hr. room service; massage; babysitting; laundry service; dry cleaning; volleyball and badminton. In room: A/C, satellite TV, minibar, coffeemaker, safe, IDD phone.

BANG TAO BAY (LAGUNA RESORT COMPLEX)

Twenty minutes south of the airport and just as far north of Patong Beach on the western shore of Phuket, this isolated area is Phuket's "integrated resort" of five high-end properties that share the island's most top-rated facilities. Among them you'll find world-class spas, countless restaurants, and the island's best golf course. The grounds are impressively landscaped, and the hotel properties are scattered among the winding lagoons, all navigable by boat. The best thing about staying here is that you can dine at any of the fine hotel restaurants, connecting by boat or free shuttle, and be charged on one simple bill at whatever resort you're staying at.

Very Expensive

Banyan Tree Phuket &&& Banyan Tree is a famous hideaway for honeymooners and high society (paparazzi-free for your protection). There is nothing like it for people of means who need an escape. Private villas with walled courtyards (many with private pool or Jacuzzi) are spacious and grand, lushly styled in teakwood. The style throughout is low Thai pavilions, with good Thai touches like platform beds and murals depicting the *Ramakien*, an ancient Thai saga. The resort can arrange private barbecues at your villa, as well as private massages in your room or in outdoor pavilions. The reception area is a large open *sala* with lovely lotus pools. A small village in itself, the spa provides a wide range of beauty and health treatments in luxurious rooms. The Tamarind Restaurant serves delicious, light, and authentic spa cuisine. The main pool is truly impressive—a freeform lagoon, landscaped with greenery and rock formations—with a flowing water canal. There's a top-notch golf course on site, a private tour office, and the beach just a short walk away. Understandably, many guests never leave their villa, much less the resort.

33 Moo 4, Srisoonthorn Rd., Cherngtalay District, Amphur Talang, Phuket 83110 (north end of beach). ℂ **0800/525-4800** or 07632-4374. Fax 07632-4375. www.banyantree.com. 121 units. US$700–US$800 (£385–£440) villa; US$1,000 (£550) pool villa; US$1,650 (£908) spa pool villa; from US$1,550 (£853) 2-bedroom villa. AE, DC, MC, V. **Amenities:** 6 restaurants; lounge; outdoor lagoon-style pool; golf course; 3 outdoor lighted tennis courts; fitness center; award-winning spa w/spa pool, sauna, steam, and massage; watersports equipment; tour desk; car rental; limo service; 24-hr. room service; babysitting; laundry service; dry cleaning. *In room:* A/C, satellite TV w/pay movies, minibar, fridge, coffeemaker, safe, IDD phone.

Dusit Laguna Resort, Phuket ⭐ *(Kids)*   The Dusit hotel group has some fine properties in Thailand, and the Dusit Laguna is no exception. Older rooms are midsize and done with pastel tiles, faux columns, and bathrooms that open to the living area via wide, wooden doors. There are lots of Thai touches throughout—some tacky, others (like some of the large, traditional hangings) quite pleasing. New club rooms are part of the Dusit's effort to shed its traditional image and appeal to a younger, hipper crowd. Sleek and modern, decked out in royal blues and golds, these units all have ocean views and are a complete departure, style wise, from the other rooms. Of the hotel's fine-dining options, particularly of note is the quaint Italian restaurant, La Trattoria, serving authentic Italian in a chic but laid-back gardenside pavilion decorated in cool whites and blues. The well-landscaped gardens at seaside have an especially delightful waterfall and an excellent pool, and the grounds open onto a long, wide, white-sand beach flanked by two lagoons. Facilities for kids are great: a kids' corner, babysitting, playground, and computer games.

390 Srisoontorn Rd., Cherngtalay District, Phuket 83110 (south end of beach). ℂ **07632-4320.** Fax 07632-4174. http://phuket.dusit.com. 226 units. US$385–US$445 (£212–£245) double; US$500 (£275) club double; from US$700 (£385) suite. AE, DC, MC, V. **Amenities:** 4 restaurants; lounge; freeform outdoor pool; golf course nearby; pitch and putt on premises; outdoor lighted tennis courts; fitness center; spa w/Jacuzzi, sauna, steam, and massage; watersports equipment; bike rental; tour desk; car rental; limo service; business center; shopping arcade; salon; 24-hr. room service; babysitting; laundry service; dry cleaning; nonsmoking rooms. *In room:* A/C, satellite TV, minibar, fridge, coffeemaker, safe, IDD phone.

Sheraton Grande Laguna Phuket ⭐⭐   The granddaddy of the lagoon in terms of size, the Sheraton is a sprawling luxury campus of two- and three-story hotel-style pavilions. Rooms are quite large, with tile floors, cozy sitting areas, balconies, and newly refurbished bathrooms. Those looking for more privacy should consider the Grande Villas: These one- to four-bedroom suites provide nice perks like exclusive access to facilities such as the villa pool (no kids allowed). The main pool is a long, winding meander. There are good amenities for kids of all ages, from a children's club to beach games and sailboat rental at the private, sandy put-in at the lagoon. And don't miss the Sheraton's two pet elephants, Ning Nong and Yum Yum, who can assist you in all of your pachyderm-related needs. With both fine dining and more casual eateries and cafes (including a good bakery), plus a very professional staff, the Sheraton is a fine, reliable, familiar choice.

10 Moo 4, Bang Tao Bay, Phuket 83110. ℂ **07632-4101.** Fax 07632-4108. www.starwoodhotels.com. 335 units. US$325–US$380 (£179–£209) double; from US$550 (£303) villa. AE, DC, MC, V. **Amenities:** 6 restaurants; bar and lounge; 2 outdoor pools; golf course nearby; 2 outdoor lighted tennis courts; fitness center; spa; watersports equipment; bike rental; kids' club; tour desk; car rental; limo service; business center w/Internet access; shopping; 24-hr. room service; babysitting; laundry service; dry cleaning; nonsmoking rooms. *In room:* A/C, satellite TV, minibar, fridge, coffeemaker, hair dryer, safe, IDD phone.

NAI YANG BEACH

Hat Nai Yang National Park is a long stretch of shoreline peeking out from underneath a dense forest of palms, casuarina, and other indigenous flora. It's become an area known for the yearly release of baby turtles into the wild. This area is good if you want to leave the crowds behind, but be warned that it is isolated and quite rustic. For accommodations, the best standard by far is the secluded **Arahmas Resort & Spa** (© **07631-6000;** www.arahmas.com), with luxury rooms from 6,300B (US$158/ £88). The **Indigo Pearl** (tel] **07632-7006;** www.indigo-pearl.com), formerly the Pearl Village, had completed renovations and was just opening at press time, with rooms starting at US$212 (£117).

MAI KHAO BEACH
Mai Khao is a marvelous beach on the northwestern shore near the airport. It's where sea turtles lay their eggs during December and January; efforts are ongoing to protect the breeding grounds, since turtle eggs are a local delicacy.

Very Expensive
JW Marriott Phuket Resort & Spa ★★★ Relaxation. If ever a resort fully embodied this ethos, it is the Marriott. From the moment you set foot in this beach-side paradise, you are encouraged to let the troubles of the outside world slip away. Set on a desolate and windswept stretch of Mai Khao Beach, the relaxing sounds of birds and flowing water follow you wherever you step. Comfortable spots to curl up and read are around every corner, from daybeds on stairwell landings to reading nooks in each beautifully appointed room. Arrivals at night will be awed by the opulence of oversized torches lining the circular drive; the wide, low pavilions of the lobby surround an enormous black reflecting pool that sparkles with torchlight. There are no services outside of the hotel, and it is a 30-minute drive to the nearest tourist area—there are regular shuttles—but the resort facilities are so complete that guests needn't leave. Rooms are private getaways with open-plan bathrooms and the aforementioned reading corner, with Thai cushions and lovely balconies that give way to sumptuous gardens: a hidden Eden. Enjoy the very professional service, fine spa treatments, sports, activities, and dining. The hotel can arrange transport anywhere on the island, and there are a host of excursions to choose from at the helpful tour desk.

231 Moo 3, Mai Khao, Talang, Phuket 83110. © **07633-8000.** Fax 07634-8360. www.marriott.com. 265 units. US$630–US$680 (£347–£374) deluxe double; from US$1,500 (£825) suite. AE, DC, MC, V. **Amenities:** 5 restaurants; 3 bars; 2 outdoor pools; 2 tennis courts; top-notch fitness center w/lots of activities; extensive spa; Jacuzzi; sauna; watersports equipment (Hobie Cat and runabouts); complimentary bikes; children's center and kids' club; teen activity center w/computers; concierge; tour desk; car rental; limo service; business center; shopping arcade; convenience store; salon; 24-hr. room service; massage; babysitting; laundry service; dry cleaning; nonsmoking rooms; executive-level rooms. *In room:* A/C, satellite TV w/in-house movies, dataport, minibar, fridge, coffeemaker, hair dryer, safe, IDD phone.

WHERE TO DINE
From tip to tip, north to south, it's over a 1-hour drive on Phuket, but hired tuk-tuks, hotel transport, or even self-drive vehicles mean that for dining and nightlife, you can choose from any establishments on the island. The beach areas in the west are chock-ablock with small, storefront eateries, while Patong features everything from the obligatory McDonald's and Starbucks to designer sushi chains.

PHUKET TOWN
Though it's a long ride from the west-coast beach areas, a night out in Phuket Town is worth it for some fine meals and a taste of local culture.

Salvatore ★ ITALIAN *"Va bene!"* It's the real thing here: pasta, grilled dishes, huge salads, pizza, and a great wine list in a large, air-conditioned dining room at the town center. Salvatore himself comes to your table and will make you something special. There are lots of Italian restaurants in all of the resort areas of Thailand, but this one is the best, with an unpretentious atmosphere and good food that draws many regular customers. Fine pasta, lasagna, steaks, cacciatore dishes, and a range of daily specials are all made with fresh ingredients. All the extras—like the important spices, garnishes, even prosciutto, and, of course, the wine—are imported. Don't miss the dessert of Limoncello Truffle, a liqueur meringue that goes great with the strong coffee.

15 Rasada Rd., Tambol Taladyai, in central Phuket Town. (C) 07622-5958. Main courses 200B–750B (US$5–US$19/ £2.80–£11). AE, MC, V. Daily 11:30am–2:30pm and 6–11pm.

KATA & KARON BEACHES

The busy road between Kata and Karon (as well as the many side streets) is chock-ablock with small cafes and restaurants serving affordable Thai and Western food. Stop by **Euro Deli** (58/60 Karon Rd.; (C) 07628-6265) for a good sandwich; it's open from 8am to 1am.

Expensive

The Boathouse 𝓰𝓰𝓰 THAI/INTERNATIONAL   So legendary is the Thai and Western cuisine at the Boathouse, the inn where it resides (see "Where to Stay," earlier in this section) offers popular holiday packages for visitors who wish to come and take lessons from its chef. A large bar and separate dining area sport nautical touches, and through huge picture windows diners can watch the sun set over the watery horizon. The cuisine combines the best of East and West and utilizes only the finest ingredients. If you're in the mood for the works, the Phuket lobster is one of the most expensive dishes on the menu, but is worth every baht. The Boathouse also has an excellent selection of international wines—over 500 labels. And if that doesn't tickle your taste buds, **Mom Tri's Kitchen,** another upscale venture from the folks at the Boathouse, is just up the hill and serves similar fine cuisine from its luxury perch. Bon appétit.

At the Boathouse Inn, 114 Patak Rd., Kata Beach. (C) 07633-0557. www.boathousephuket.com. Reservations recommended during peak season. Main courses 280B–850B (US$7–US$21/£3.90–£12); seafood at market prices. AE, DC, MC, V. Daily 7am–10:30pm.

Moderate

Mom Tri's Gung THAI/JAPANESE   A less formal affair than Mom Tri's other culinary offerings (see above), Gung serves fine Thai and Japanese fare. The menu is short, but what is offered is of the highest quality. For starters, I had the tapas plate, a nice selection of grilled and fried seafood, followed by the grilled teriyaki sea bass—very light and with just the right amount of sauce. With outdoor terrace seating right on the beach, Gung is the perfect place to kick back and enjoy beach life.

2/2 Moo 2 Patak Rd. (next to the Boathouse), Kata Beach. (C) 07633-0015. Reservations recommended for dinner during peak season. Main courses 160B–480B (US$4–US$12/£2.25–£6.75). AE, DC, MC, V. Daily 11:30am–11pm.

On the Rock   Part of the Marina Phuket Resort (see "Where to Stay," earlier in this section), this unassuming little restaurant serves tip-top Thai meals from a scenic deck high above the south end of Karon Beach. Newly renovated but still laid-back and charmingly rustic, it offers some of the best views of the beach below. Try the seafood basket, a medley of grilled and fried ocean critters. There are steaks and French entrees like chicken *cordon bleu,* but stick with the better Thai dishes for a great meal in a great atmosphere.

47 Karon Rd., Karon Beach (on bluff at south end of Karon Beach Rd.). (C) 07633-0625. Fax 07633-0516. www. marinaphuket.com. Main courses 200B–750B (US$2–US$19/£2.80–£11). AE, MC, V. Daily 8am–11pm.

PATONG BEACH

Some of the best seafood dining in busy Patong doesn't come from any upscale restaurant, but from the small **Seafood Night Market,** in the north end of Patong along busy Rat-U-Thit Road. It's really just a collection of outdoor restaurants sharing a large open-air dining area. Visitors who approach or show any interest will be attacked with menus and implored to choose from among the restaurants. It can be a bit off-putting, but just pick a menu or a kind face (the others will disperse) and order from a wide selection of fresh seafood, prepared as you like it. It's good food at a fraction of restaurant prices.

Baan Rim Pa THAI   In a beautiful Thai-style teak house, Baan Rim Pa offers dining in a romantic indoor setting or from outdoor terraces with gorgeous views of the bay. Among high-end travelers, the restaurant has long been one of the most popular stops on the island, so be sure to reserve your table early. The Thai cuisine features seafood, plus a variety of other meat and vegetable dishes, including a rich duck curry and a sweet honey chicken dish. The seafood basket is a fantastic assortment of prawns, mussels, squid, and crab. The owner has opened up a few other restaurants on the cliffside next to Baan Rim Pa: **Da Maurizio** (© 07634-4079) and the Japanese restaurant **Otowa** (© 07634-4235).

223 Kalim Beach Rd., on the cliffs just north of Patong Beach. © 07634-0789. Reservations necessary. Main courses 350B–1,200B (US$8.75–US$30/£4.90–£17). AE, DC, MC, V. Daily noon–10pm.

La Gritta ☆ ITALIAN   Similar to the Amari chain's other fine Italian restaurants of the same name, this one is notable for its views of Patong Beach below—the best in town, really. It's classic northern Italian cuisine: antipasti, salads, soups, grilled entrees, and pastas accompanied by an extensive wine list. The cooks use all fresh ingredients and serve a colorful antipasti plate that makes a great shared appetizer. *Note:* For a romantic evening, La Gritta is best visited after 8pm, unless your idea of romantic is listening to the lobby band rip through Ricky Martin's oeuvre.

At the Amari Coral Beach Resort, 2 Meun-ngern Rd., south of and uphill from Patong Beach. © 07634-0106. Main courses 210B–540B (US$5.25–US$14/£2.95–£7.55). AE, MC, V. Daily 11am–11:30pm.

Patong Seafood Restaurant SEAFOOD   Take an evening stroll along the lively Patong Beach strip and you'll find quite a few open-air seafood restaurants displaying their catch of the day on chipped-ice buffet tables out front. The best of them all is the casual Patong Seafood, for the freshest selection of seafood that includes several types of local fish, lobster, squid (very tender), prawn, and crab. The menu has a fantastic assortment of preparation styles, with photos of popular Thai noodles and Chinese stir-fry dishes. Service is good, and it's popular enough that it doesn't employ a carnival barker like most along the strip; it just attracts with the food rather than promoting with ploys.

Patong Beach Rd., Patong Beach. © 07634-0247. Reservations not accepted. Main courses 80B–250B (US$2–US$6.25/£1.10–£3.50); seafood at market prices. AE, DC, MC, V. Daily 7am–11pm.

Sala Bua ☆ THAI   Heavily damaged by the 2004 tsunami, Sala Bua is back to its stylish beachside ways. The lunch menu features light Thai dishes, plus Western sandwiches and burgers. More pricey evening fare includes southern-Thai-style seafood favorites—local Phuket lobster, huge juicy tiger prawns, and fresh fish steaks in a variety of local preparations—expensive, but a good value. The imported New Zealand tenderloin is award-winning. For dessert, try the unique sticky-rice sushi rolls with sweet coconut milk and mango. Sala Bua is a far more intimate option than the crowded seafood joints across the street.

At the Impiana Phuket Cabana Resort, 94 Thaweewong Rd., Patong Beach (at the north end of the beach). (C) 07634-2100. Reservations recommended on weekends. Main courses 320B–1,360B (US$8–US$34/£4.50–£19). AE, DC, MC, V. Daily 6:30pm–midnight.

BANG TAO BAY (LAGUNA RESORT COMPLEX)

The many hotel restaurants of the five-star properties in the Laguna Resort Complex could fill a small guidebook on their own. You can't go too wrong in any of the hotels, really, and here, more than anywhere, it's a question of getting what you pay for; from superluxurious fine dining to laid-back grills or snack corners, everything's covered. One restaurant just outside the complex is worth mentioning, however—it's where all the hotel managers eat when they get out of work.

Tatanka 🐾🐾 INTERNATIONAL Billed as "globe-trotter cuisine," dining at Tatanka is indeed a foray into the realm of a culinary nomad. Harold Schwarz, the young owner and well-traveled chef, puts to use his many years in hotel restaurants around the world (his resume is written on the bathroom wall, each tile featuring another of Harold's many stops). "Fusion" is a battered and broken term in restaurant parlance, but dishes here are a creative melding of Mediterranean, pan-American, and Asian influence. The emphasis is on variety: Selections from the tapas menu include vegetable quesadillas, California crab cakes, stuffed calamari cups, wonton wafers, and rolls. The menu is updated frequently and depends on what is fresh that day, but may feature anything from Peking duck to pizza, gazpacho to Thai *tom yum* (hot-and-sour soup with shrimp). Ask what's good and enjoy.

382/19 Moo 1, Srisoontorn Rd., Cherngtalay (at the entrance of the Laguna Resort Complex in Bangtao Bay). (C) 07632-4349. Main courses 150B–420B (US$3.75–US$11/£2.10–£5.90). MC, V. Daily 6pm–last order.

WHAT TO SEE & DO

There's lots to do on Phuket. Beach and outdoor activities top the list, and you'll find the beachfront areas full of tour operators, each vying for your business and offering similar trips (or copycat tours). Opportunities abound to visit the island's rustic bays, explore the many beaches, and take day trips to the jungle interior or to scenic Phang Nga Bay to the north.

If Phuket is your only destination in Thailand, you'll certainly want to get to some of the small rural temples and to **Phuket Town,** but the island's sights pale in comparison to culturally rich areas like Bangkok or Chiang Mai. Still, there are a few Buddhist temples that are quite notable. The most famous one among Thai visitors is **Wat Chalong,** on the Bypass Road, about 8km (5 miles) south of Phuket Town. Chalong was the first resort on Phuket, back when the Thais first started coming to the island for vacations. Nowadays, the discovery of better beaches on the west coast has driven most tourists away from this area, but the temple still remains the center of Buddhist worship. While the temple compound itself is pretty standard in terms of modern temples, the place comes to life during Buddhist holy days. Also worth visiting is **Wat Pra Tong,** along Highway 402 in Thalang, just south of the airport—it's the most unique temple on the island.

Sea gypsies, the indigenous people of the southern islands, are fast disappearing from Phuket as commercial-fishing interests and shoreline development continue to threaten their livelihood of subsistence fishing. Gypsy villages are simple, floating shacks and longtail boats. Visits to some of the larger settlements in Phang Nga Bay are included in many island day trips.

For a unique view of gorgeous **Phang Nga Bay,** book a trip aboard the *June Bahtra,* a restored Chinese sailing junk, to cruise the islands. Full-day trips include lunch and hotel transfers. Adults pay 2,300B (US$58/£32), not including alcoholic beverages, and children up to 12 pay 1,500B (US$38/£21). Contact **East West Siam,** 128/3 Chalermprakiat Rd., Patong (© **07637-6192**), to book. For a different perspective of Phang Nga Bay, see "Sea Kayaking" under "Outdoor Activities," below.

Hat Nai Yang National Park, 90 sq. km (35 sq. miles) of protected land in the northwest corner of the island, offers a peaceful retreat from the rest of Phuket's tourism madness. There are two fantastic reasons to make the journey out to the park. The first is for Phuket's largest coral reef in shallow water, only 1,400m (460 ft.) from the shore. The second is for the giant leatherback turtles that come to nest every year between November and February. Park headquarters is a very short hop from Phuket Airport off Highway 402.

The **Gibbon Rehabilitation Project** 😊😊 (© **07626-0492**; www.gibbonproject. org), off Highway 4027 at the Bang Pae waterfall in the northeastern corner of the island, cares for mistreated gibbons, placing them in more caring and natural surroundings (among other gibbons). Volunteer guides offer tours. Open daily from 10am to 4pm; admission is free, but donations are accepted and appreciated.

At **Butterfly Garden & Insect World** (71/6 Moo 5, Yaowarat Rd.; © **07621-0861;** www.phuketbutterfly.com), you get a crash course in the history and life cycles of insects followed by a walk through an enclosed garden housing thousands of butterflies bred on the premises. Don't forget your camera. Open daily from 9am to 5pm. Admission is 300B (US$7.50/£4.20) for adults and 150B (US$3.75/£2.10) for children 4 to 10.

OUTDOOR ACTIVITIES

Most of the noisier watersports activities are concentrated along Patong Beach—so swimmers can enjoy the other beaches without the buzz of a jet ski or power boat. **Jet skis** are technically illegal, but can still be rented for 30 minutes at 700B (US$18/£9.80). A 10-minute **parasailing** ride is 6,700B (US$18/£94), and you can rent outboard runabouts by the hour or the day. **Hobie Cats** go for 600B (US$15/£8.40) per hour; **windsurfing** boards for 200B (US$5/£2.80) per hour. There are no specific offices to organize these activities, just small operators with hand-painted signs at the beaches.

BUNGEE JUMPING   The **Jungle Bungy Jump** awaits! If you have the nerve to jump out 50m (164 ft.) over the water, call the "bungee hot line" at © **07632-1351.** It's in Kathu, near Patong. The charge is 1,600B (US$40/£22) per jump. It has a 100% safety record—knock wood.

GOLF   There are some fine courses on Phuket; golf junkets bring vacationing expats and international tourists alike.

- **Banyan Tree Club & Laguna,** 34 Moo 4, Srisoonthorn Road, at the Laguna Resort Complex on Bang Tao Bay (© **07627-0991;** fax 07632-4351; www.banyan tree.com), is the best option, a par-71 resort course (greens fees: 3,250B/US$81/ £46, plus caddie fee; guests of the Laguna Resort Complex receive a discount).
- **Blue Canyon Country Club,** 165 Moo 1, Thepkasattri Road, near the airport (© **07632-8088;** fax 07632-8086; www.bluecanyonclub.com), has two world-class tracks, the Lakes and Canyon courses—the latter host to the Johnnie Walker Classic in 1994 and 1998, won by Tiger Woods (greens fees: 3,600B/US$90/£50 Lakes course, 5,300B/US$133/£74 Canyon course).

- **Phuket Country Club,** 80/1 Vichitsongkram Rd., west of Phuket Town (© **07632-1038;** fax 07632-1721; www.phuketcountryclub.com), an older course that dates back to 1989, has beautiful greens and fairways, plus a giant lake (greens fees: 3,000B/US$75/£42).

HORSEBACK RIDING   A romantic and charming way to see Phuket's jungles and beaches is on horseback. **Phuket Riding Club,** 95 Viset Rd., Chaweng Bay (© **07628-8213**), and **Phuket Laguna Riding Club,** 394 Moo 1, Bangthao Beach (© **07632-4199;** www.phuket-bangtao-horseriding.com), welcome riders of all ages and experience levels and can provide instruction for beginners and children. Prices start at 300B (US$7.50/£4.20) per hour.

SCUBA DIVING   With access to the nearby **Similan Islands,** Phuket is a popular scuba destination, one of the most affordable (and safe) places to get certified. There are three decompression chambers on the island and a strong dive community. The problem is, there are something like 40 companies, and all can arrange day trips to the nearby coral wall and wrecks as well as overnight or long-term excursions to the Similan Islands (as well as PADI courses, dive-master courses, and 1-day introductory lessons and open-water certification). Open-water courses can cost as little as 10,000B (US$250/£140).

Many storefront operations are just consolidators for other companies, so ask if they have their own boats and whether they're PADI certified. Also check on the ratio of divers to instructor or Divemaster; anything more than five to one is not acceptable, and should be more like two to one for beginner courses. Below are a few choices:

- **Scuba Cat** (94 Thaweewong Rd., Patong Beach; © **07629-3120;** www.scubacat. com) has got the best thing going on Phuket. With over 10 years of experience, a large expat staff, and its own fleet of boats, it's a very professional outfit offering the full range of day trips and luxury live-aboards for anyone from beginner to expert (and at competitive prices). You can't miss the small practice pool in front of its beachside Patong office (in fact, you have to cross a small bridge to get in the place). The staff is very helpful and welcoming.
- **Fantasea Divers** (main office: 219 Rat-U-Thit Rd., Patong Beach; © **07628-1388;** fax 07628-1389; www.fantasea.net) is another reputable firm on Phuket. The dive packages include live-aboard trips to the Burmese coast and 4-day PADI certification courses, in addition to full-day dives around Phuket.
- **Sea Bees Diving** (1/3 Moo 9, Viset Rd., Chalong Bay; © **07638-1765;** fax 07628-0467; www.sea-bees.com) is another good outfit offering day trips from US$80 (£44).

SEA KAYAKING   **Phang Nga Bay National Park** 🐸🐸, a 1½-hour drive north of Phuket (3 hr. by boat), hosts great day trips by sea kayak. The scenery is stunning, with limestone karst towers jutting precariously from the water's surface, creating more than 120 small islands. These craggy rock formations (the backdrop for the James Bond classic *The Man with the Golden Gun*) look straight out of a Chinese scroll painting. Sea kayaks are perfect for inching your way into the many breathtaking caves and chambers that hide beneath the jagged cliffs. All tours include the hour-plus rides to and from Phang Nga, the cruise to the island area, paddle guide, kayak, and lunch. The company that pioneered the cave trips is **Sea Canoe** (367/4 Yaowarat Rd.; © **07621-2172;** fax 07621-2252; www.seacanoe.net). It's much imitated, but still the best choice for day trips through island caves to central lagoons (called *hongs*). The standard day trip runs 2,950B (US$74/£41) per person. It's touristy, you'll be sitting two to an inflated boat, and you'll be paddled by a guide going in and out of the caves (frustrating if you like to actually paddle yourself)—but the scenery is great and the caves are stunning (and there's free time for paddling on your own later). It also offers multi-day and more adventurous "self-guided" tours.

The folks at **Paddle Asia** (9/71 Thanon Rasdanusorn; 🕾 **07624-0952;** fax 07621-6145; www.paddleasia.com) make Phuket their home and do trips throughout the region, with a focus more on custom adventure travel, not day junkets. It has great options for anyone from beginner to expert. On any trip, you'll get to paddle real decked kayaks, not inflatables. A highlight is its trip to Khao Sok National Park (p. 148), a 3-day adventure in which you're sure to see some amazing jungle wildlife. In Phuket, it can arrange either offshore paddling to outlying islands or custom adventures.

TREKKING   To experience the wild side of Phuket's interior, try a rainforest trek through **Khao Phra Thaeo National Park,** in the north part of the island. **Phuket Nature Tour** (🕾 07625-5522) takes small groups through 3.5km (2.25 miles) of jungle paths past waterfalls and swimming holes. A typical half-day excursion includes hotel transfers, English-speaking jungle guides, and drinks.

Then there's **elephant trekking,** a perennial favorite for children, and a great time for adults, too. Elephants are not indigenous to Phuket, so what you get here is more or less a pony ride, but arguments over captive elephant-tour programs aside, the kids dig it (and the elephants do better here than when paraded around city streets for owners to collect coins). **Siam Safari Nature Tours** (45 Chaofa Rd., Chalong; 🕾 07628-0116; www.siamsafari.com) coordinates daily treks on elephants, Land Rovers, river rafts, and traditional wooden junks. The four-in-one half-day eco-adventure includes 6 hours of elephant trekking through jungles to rubber estates, jeep touring to see local wildlife, watching trained monkeys pick coconuts, and a relaxing cruise on a wooden junk to Chalong Bay. A full-day tour includes canoeing and elephant trekking in Khao Sok National Park, with a Thai lunch.

YACHTING   The crystal-blue waters of the Andaman Sea near Phuket are an old salt's dream. Every December, Phuket hosts the increasingly popular **King's Cup Regatta,** in which nearly 100 international racing yachts compete. For more information, check out www.kingscup.com.

There are more and more options for chartering yachts in Phuket. For details, contact **Asia Marine** (c/o Phuket Boat Lagoon, 20/7-8 Thepkasatri Rd., Tambon Koh Kaew, Phuket 83200; 🕾 07623-9111; www.thaimarine.com).

THE SPA SCENE 🕸🕸🕸

If you've come to Phuket to escape and relax, there's no better way to accomplish your goal than to visit one of the island's spas. Even the smallest resort now offers full spa services (of varying quality), and you can find good, affordable massage along any beach and in storefronts in the main tourist areas.

For luxury treatments, the most famous and exclusive facility here is the **Spa at the Banyan Tree Phuket** (p. 181; 🕾 07632-4374 for reservations; www.lagunaphuket.com/spa). In secluded garden pavilions, you'll be treated regally and can choose from many types of massage, body and facial treatments, or health and beauty programs. Expect to pay for the luxury—figure at least 2,000B (US$50/£28) per individual treatment.

> *Moments*   **The Best Sunset**
>
> From the cliffs atop Promthep Cape on the southern tip of the island, the view of the sky as it changes colors—from deep reds to almost neon yellows—can't compete with the best fireworks. The place isn't exactly a secret, so get here early (around 6pm or so) on weekends.

In Phuket Town, the **Cheraim Spa Village** (16 Wichitsongkram Rd.; ℂ 07624-9670; www.cheraimspavillage.com) offers a wide variety of treatments ranging from massage to seaweed wraps, all in a relaxing garden setting. Highly recommended.

Let's Relax (Rat-U-Thit Rd., Patong; ℂ 07634-0913) is a more affordable little day spa in and among many similar services—some a bit dodgy, but this one is okay—just off Patong Beach. One-hour Thai massage begins at 350B (US$8.75/£4.90).

SHOPPING

Patong Beach is the center of handicrafts and souvenir shopping on Phuket; the main streets and small sois are chockablock with storefront tailors, leather shops, jewelers, and ready-to-wear clothing boutiques. Vendors line the sidewalks, selling everything from batik clothing, T-shirts, and pirated CDs to local arts, northern-hill-tribe handicrafts, silver, and souvenir trinkets. Everywhere in Patong, they have the rotten habit of hassling passersby. Prices are a bit inflated, but a bit of haggling gets you the same cool goods that you'd otherwise find only in the far north or in Bangkok.

PHUKET AFTER DARK

From the huge billboards and glossy brochures, **Phuket FantaSea** ✮✮ (ℂ 07638-5111 for reservations; www.phuket-fantasea.com), the island's premier theme attraction, seems like it could be touristy and ridiculous. Surprise—it is! But it's fun in the same way Atlantic City can be fun. This big theme park has a festival village lined with glitzy shops, games, entertainment, and snacks. A wander here will keep you busy until the show starts. There's a huge buffet in the palatial Golden Kinaree Restaurant; afterwards, visitors proceed to the Palace of the Elephants for the show. The in-your-face advertising for the place alone is enough to put you off (witness the trucks driving around town with loudspeakers and posters plastered on anything flat), but it's worth a trip. Many places include transport in the price of the ticket. The show is at Kamala Beach, north of Patong, on the coastal road. The stage is dark on Thursdays. The park opens at 5:30pm, the buffet begins at 6:30pm, and the show is at 9pm. Tickets for the show are 1,000B (US$25/£14) for adults and 750B (US$19/£11) for children, while dinner and transfer fees usually add 500B (US$13/£7) for adults and 300B (US$7.50/£4.20) for children. Ask about the rates at any hotel concierge, as they often have deals.

Dino Park Mini Golf (ℂ 07633-0625; www.dinopark.com) is for kids young and old. There's golf for the kids, and a restaurant and bar for mom and dad. It's located on the south of Karon Beach, next to the Marina Phuket Resort.

Phuket's resident cabaret troupe can be found at **Simon Cabaret,** 100/6–8 Moo 4, Patong Karon Road (ℂ 07634-2011). There are shows at 7:30 and 9:30pm nightly for 600B (US$15/£8.40) adults, 400B (US$10/£5.60) kids; it's on the south end of Patong. It's a featured spot on every planned tour agenda, so it draws busloads. The glitzy transsexual show caters mostly to Asian tourists—the lip-sync numbers of popular Asian pop songs keep the audience roaring. It can be a lot of fun. In between the comedy are dance numbers with pretty impressive sets and costumes; performers are available for photos after the show.

You can catch Thai boxing at **Vegas Thai Boxing** (at Patong Simon Shopping Arcade, Soi Bangla, Patong). Bouts start every night at 7pm and last until 3am. Fight-night info is all over town and admission is free.

Patong nightlife is wild. Lit up like a little Las Vegas, the beach town hops and it's Saturday every night of the week. Shops and restaurants stay open late, and tourists choose from an array of bars, nightclubs, karaoke lounges, snooker halls, massage parlors, go-go bars, and dance shows a la Bangkok's Patpong or the streets of Pattaya. Bangla Road, perpendicular to the beach road on the north end of Patong, is the little red-light district in town, where the hostess girls line up and reel in passersby (it goes something like: "Hey, handsome man, where you go?"). It's pretty seedy, but it's a funny scene. A few bars about halfway down the road are always packed for views of the informal tabletop dancing. The curvaceous, costumed dancers are mostly transsexuals (*Important:* No photos!).

Molly Malone's (© 07629-2771) and **Scruffy Murphy's** (© 07629-2590), both along the main strip in Patong, are the obligatory beachside Irish pubs. Good atmosphere, good service, good pints. Both are fine places to start the night, end the night, or spend the whole night (they'll wake you up at closing time). There are also a few discos in town; just ask around to find out what's going on.

18 Krabi (Ao Nang, Railay ★★ & Khlong Mouang Beaches)

814km (505 miles) S of Bangkok, 211km (131 miles) SW of Surat Thani, 165km (102 miles) E of Phuket, 42km (26 miles) E of Koh Phi Phi

Krabi is a popular alternative to busy Phuket. Ferries and minivans connect the town of Krabi (few stay here) to the nearby beach and tourist strip at **Ao Nang** and to the farther-flung beaches: **Railay Beach,** the famed "climbers' beach" with its stunning karst towers, is accessed by boat, while **Khlong Mouang Beach,** only recently developed, is north of Ao Nang.

GETTING THERE

There are boat and bus connections between Krabi and Phuket, as well as connections via Surat Thani with the east-coast islands of Koh Samui and Koh Pha Ngan.

BY PLANE   **Thai Airways** (© 02535-2084) flies four times daily from Bangkok. Budget carriers **Air Asia** (© 02515-9999), **Nok Air** (© 02900-9955), and **One-Two-Go** (© 01141-1126) have daily connections. From the airport, you can catch a minivan to town for 60B (US$1.50/£0.85), with higher prices for further beaches. Taxis start at 350B (US$8.75/£4.90).

BY BUS   Two air-conditioned VIP 24-seater buses leave daily from Bangkok's **Southern Bus Terminal** (© 02435-1199; trip time: 12 hr.; 710B/US$18/£9.95) to Krabi Town. Frequently scheduled air-conditioned minibuses leave daily from Surat Thani to Krabi (trip time: 2¾ hr.; 200B/US$5/£2.80). Three air-conditioned minibuses leave daily from Phuket Town to Krabi (trip time: 3½ hr.; 300B/US$8/£4.20).

BY BOAT   Twice-daily trips leave from Koh Phi Phi to Krabi (trip time: 2 hr.; 250B/US$6.25/£3.50). There are two daily boats from Koh Lanta to Krabi in high season (trip time: 2½ hr.; 200B/US$5/£2.80).

GETTING AROUND

Krabi Town is the commercial hub in the area, but few stay. There is frequent **song-tao** service between Krabi Town and Ao Nang Beach; just flag down a white pickup (trip time: 30 min.; 20B/US50¢/£0.30). **Railay Beach** is not an island, but is cut off by its high cliffs from the mainland and reachable only by boat from the pier in Krabi Town (45 min.) or from the beach at Ao Nang, at the small pavilion across from the Prah Nang Inn (20 min.). **Khlong Mouang Beach** is some 25km (16 miles) from Krabi Town.

VISITOR INFORMATION

There's a small branch of the **TAT** (© **07561-2740**) on Utarakit Road in Krabi Town, on the north end of the esplanade along the river. Free maps and info are available at hotels.

FAST FACTS: KRABI

Most services in Krabi Town are on Utarakit Road, paralleling the waterfront (to the right as you board the ferry). Here you'll find a number of **banks** with ATM service. The **post office** and **police station** (© **07563-7208**) are south on Utarakit Road, to the left as you leave the pier. There are also a few banks in Ao Nang, near the Phra Nang Inn.

WHERE TO STAY & DINE

Outside of the resorts, your dining options are just small storefront eateries and tourist cafes. In Ao Nang, try **Ao Nang Cuisine** for good Thai fare, or stop in any of the small beachside eateries. In Railay, there are lots of little beachside bars and restaurants as well.

RAILAY BEACH
Very Expensive

Rayavadee 🟊🟊🟊 Rayavadee is one of the finest resorts in Thailand. Handsome two-story rounded pavilions are large and luxurious, offering every modern conven-ience and utmost privacy; the first-floor sitting areas have a central hanging lounger with cushions, while second-story bedrooms are all silk and teak. Private bathrooms come complete with Jacuzzi tubs and luxury products. The resort grounds lie at the base of towering cliffs on the island's most choice piece of property, a triangle of land in which each point accesses the beach. It all comes with an over-the-top price tag, though—and the sun sets the same for the bungalow dwellers next door. Still, every-thing at Rayavadee *is* tip-top, and from your airport pickup to private boat transfer to great dining and professional service, you'll get the regal treatment.

214 Moo 2, Tambol Ao Nang, Amphur Muang, Krabi 81000 (30 min. northwest of Krabi Town by longtail boat or 70 min. from Phuket via the resort's own launch). © **07562-0740.** Fax 07562-0630. www.rayavadee.com. 77 units. 22,300B (US$558/£312) deluxe pavilion; 28,300B (US$708/£396) hydropool pavilion; 35,000B (US$875/£490) family pavilion; from 72,000B (US$1,800/£1,008) specialty villa. AE, DC, MC, V. **Amenities:** 2 restaurants; lounge and library; outdoor pool w/children's pool; outdoor lighted tennis courts; air-conditioned squash court; fitness center; spa; Jacuzzi; sauna; watersports equipment and scuba center; concierge; 24-hr. room service; massage; laundry serv-ice. *In room:* A/C, satellite TV, minibar, fridge, safe, IDD phone.

Moderate/Inexpensive

Sand Sea Resort (© **07562-2170;** www.krabisandsea.com), just next to Rayavadee, is typical of the good mid-range bungalows here, with clean air-conditioned rooms from 900B (US$23/£13). **Diamond Cave Resort** (© **07562-2589**), at the north end of Railay Beach, has small private bungalows with fan from 500B (US$13/£7). If you're looking for hotel-style accommodations, the **Railay Princess Resort & Spa** (© **07562-2998**) has tidy rooms overlooking the pool for 3,200B (US$80/£45) in high season and 1,350B (US$34/£19) in low season.

AO NANG BEACH
Moderate
Krabi Resort   The Krabi Resort is the only property in Ao Nang with direct beach access. It's a compound of two hotel blocks and an array of free-standing beachside bungalows. Tidy grounds surround a fine swimming pool, but other resort amenities are unused and aging. More private seaview bungalows are the best choice; they're large and clean with parquet floors, high ceilings, rattan furnishings, and lots of little Thai touches. The place is just north of the main shopping and restaurant area at Ao Nang, but a lovely beach walk. Ask about overnight trips to rustic bungalows on nearby Poda Island.

53–57 Patthana Rd., Ao Nang Beach, Krabi 81000 (overlooking beach at Ao Nang). © 07563-7051. 75 units. 3,200B–6,260B (US$80–US$157/£45–£88) bungalow; from 6,560 (US$164/£92) suite. MC, V. **Amenities:** Restaurant; lounge; pool; outdoor lighted tennis courts; fitness center; watersports equipment; bike rental; tour desk; limited room service; massage; laundry service. *In room:* A/C, satellite TV, minibar, fridge, safe, IDD phone.

KHLONG MOUANG BEACH
Very Expensive
Sheraton Krabi Beach Resort   This expansive resort is set in a U-shaped configuration, the buildings connected by boardwalks suspended over tidal mangrove flats. Moderate-size rooms are immaculate and done in fine tile and dark-wood furnishings. The beachside pool is large and luxurious; the fine health and fitness area has good programs, ranging from kickboxing to meditation. The spa, too, is a real treat. Service is excellent all around.

155 Moo 2, Baan Khlong Mouang Beach, Nong Talay, Krabi 81000 (15km/9 miles north of Ao Nang, 26km/16miles from Krabi Town). © 07562-8000. Fax 07562-8028. www.sheraton.com. 246 units. US$295–US$315 (£162–£173) double; US$500 (£275) suite. AE, DC, MC, V. **Amenities:** 3 restaurants; 3 bars; outdoor pool; tennis court (w/shoe and racket rental); fitness center; spa w/massage; Jacuzzi; sauna; sailboat and kayak rental; mountain-bike rental; kids' club; library area w/games, videos, and Internet access; tour desk; car rental; shopping arcade; 24-hr. room service; babysitting; laundry service; nonsmoking rooms. *In room:* A/C, satellite TV, dataport, minibar, fridge, coffeemaker, hair dryer, safe, IDD phone.

WHAT TO SEE & DO
Most head straight for the beaches to relax and play. Popular activities are day boat trips, snorkeling, and rock climbing at Railay.

Just a short tuk-tuk ride northeast of Krabi Town, however, you'll find **Wat Tham Sua (Tiger Temple),** a stunning hilltop pilgrimage point and meditation center. The beaches and stunning cliffs of **Railay Beach** are certainly worth a day trip even if you don't stay there (see "Where to Stay & Dine," above). In the daytime, longtail boats wait just offshore at Ao Nang and boat drivers consolidate passengers at a small pavilion just across from the Phra Nang Inn for the 20-minute, 60B (US$1.50/£0.85) ride. From the docks in Krabi Town, it's a 40-minute, 100B (US$2.50/£1.40) ride.

The craggy karst cliffs of Railay make it one of the best-known **rock-climbing** spots in the region (if not the world). It's "sport climbing" done on mapped routes, with safety bolts already drilled into the rock; a number of companies offer full- and half-day courses. There are many routes suitable for beginners, too. Start with a lesson at

King Climbers (① 07563-7125; www.railay.com) or **Cliffs Man** (① 07562-1768; www.cliffsman.com). Half-day courses begin at about 800B (US$20/£11), while full-day courses are from 1,500B (US$38/£21).

If you visit Railay, don't miss secluded **Phra Nang Beach** , one of the most scenic beaches in Thailand. Access from Railay is by a footpath that wraps around the Rayavadee resort. Monkeys hop around the beachfront trees here; at low tide, you can walk across a sandbar to nearby **Happy Island,** which also has a number of sport-climbing routes.

Full-day **boat trips** and **snorkeling** can be arranged at any beachfront tour agent or hotel near Krabi. You'll be taken to a few small coral sites and any number of secluded coves, starting at 800B (US$20/£11) for a half-day. Day kayak tours to out-lying islands or the mangroves near **Ao Luk** are also becoming popular for visitors to Ao Nang. Contact **Sea, Land & Trek Co.** (① 07563-7364) or **Sea Kayak Krabi** (① 07563-0270) for details.

19 Koh Phi Phi ★★★

42km (26 miles) W of Krabi, 160km (99 miles) SW of Phuket

The December 26, 2004, tsunami devastated Phi Phi; most of the central isthmus of this tiny island was wiped out and the loss of life was considerable. Soon after the tsunami, there was talk that development would be curbed and the island would only be open to day trips. The talk was short lived, however, and nowadays Phi Phi is back and better (or worse) than ever.

Phi Phi is two islands: **Phi Phi Don** is the main barbell-shaped island whose central isthmus (the barbell handle) is packed with amenities; all visitors arrive at the busy ferry port in Phi Phi Don's Loh Dalam Bay. The sandy beaches at Ton Sai Bay, just opposite, are good for swimming. Smaller **Phi Phi Lei** is south of the main island and famed for its coveted swallow nests and the courageous pole-climbing dare-devils who go get them (the nests fetch a hefty price for the making of a gourmet soup). The smaller island is protected as a natural park, but is visited as part of most day trips.

Phi Phi is where the filmmakers of *The Beach* chose to stage their Hollywood version of tropical Utopia, and some tours will take you to Makan, the site of the filming. Small beachfront outfits rent snorkel gear and conduct longtail boat tours to quiet coves for as little as 500B (US$13/£7).

GETTING THERE

Ferries make regular connections from Phuket, Krabi, and Koh Lanta. Boats from the pier in central Krabi Town run three times daily (at 10:30am, 2:30pm, and 4pm) for 250B (US$6.25/£3.50). Boats from Ao Nang/Railay depart at 8:30am and charge 300B (US$7.50/£4.20). From Phuket, ferries leave from the pier near Phuket Town at 8:30am and 1:30pm, with rates as low as 250B (US$6.25/£3.50), including free transfer from your hotel. And from Koh Lanta, one boat a day leaves at 8:30am and costs 250B (US$6.25/£3.50).

FAST FACTS: KOH PHI PHI

Services on Koh Phi Phi are in Ton Sai Bay, on the central isthmus of Phi Phi Don. **Siam Commercial Bank** has an ATM; there are a number of currency-exchange booths as well. **Internet cafes** are ubiquitous and average 2B per minute (US$3/£1.65

per hr.). A small **post office** can be found towards the middle of the village. The **tourist police** booth is next to the main pier.

WHERE TO STAY & DINE

Ton Sai Bay is the commercial center of Phi Phi and has been overrun with budget accommodations, turning it into a virtual backpacker ghetto. The best of the budget set are the **Phi Phi Hotel** and its sister property, the **Phi Phi Banyan Villa** (*©* **07561-1233**), with comfortable rooms starting at 1,800B (US$45/£25) and 2,500B (US$63/£35), respectively. The best resorts are on the isolated beaches in the northeast corner of the island and can be reached by longtail boat from Ton Sai pier. Some ferries from Krabi or Phuket will drop you off directly at your resort.

While the nicer resorts usually have the best food on the island, it's always nice to mix things up. Ton Sai Bay is developing a wide variety of dining choices. Most are simple beachside cafes, but **Le Grand Bleu,** by the main pier, stands out as the best of the bunch, serving fine French fare with a good selection of wines. For all of your bread needs, **PP Bakery** is an old standby.

VERY EXPENSIVE

Zeavola 👁👁   The only true luxury resort on the island, Zeavola is referred to in reverential tones by the locals, and not just for its hefty price tag. Many Thais long for a return to their rural village roots, a time when life was simple. That is what Zeavola is trying to create—a return to traditional 1950s Thai living. Sand walkways cut through palm trees, and scaavola plants lead to free-standing thatch-roofed teak suites. Each is luxuriously appointed with polished teakwood floors, oversize daybeds, and both indoor and outdoor rain showers. The living areas extend past glass doors to covered teakwood patios, where privacy is supplied by electronically controlled bamboo blinds. What makes the suites truly unique, however, are the rustic flourishes: old-fashioned copper piping, wooden taps, pottery sink basins, and *mon ing* cushions (the traditional triangular Thai pillows) for the patios. This rustic theme extends to the fine hillside spa but not, for obvious reasons, to the resort's first-class PADI dive center and private dive boat. A luxurious trip to the past. *Hint:* The beachfront suite trades privacy for the sea view; some garden suites have partial ocean views without the loss of privacy.

Laem Tong Beach, Koh Phi Phi, Krabi 81000. Phuket office: 111 Hongyok Utid Rd., Taladyai, Phuket 83000. *©* **07562-7024.** Fax 07562-7025. www.zeavola.com. 33 units. 16,000B (US$400/£224) village suite; 18,000B (US$450/£252) garden suite; 29,000B (US$725/£406) beachfront suite. AE, MC, V. **Amenities:** 2 restaurants (Thai, Italian); saltwater pool; spa; watersports equipment; tour desk; airport transfer; laundry service; wireless and broadband Internet access; PADI dive center. *In room:* A/C, TV w/DVD/CD player, minibar, coffeemaker, hair dryer, safe, IDD phone.

EXPENSIVE

Holiday Inn Resort Phi Phi Island   The Holiday Inn has a lot of things going for it—a great location on beautiful Laem Tong beach, lovely manicured lawns, hammocks gently swaying under beachfront palm trees. Unfortunately, the bungalows are rather basic and uninspired, with guesthouse-quality bathrooms. The restaurants offer decent fare, though. Bottom line: unparalleled location, but lodgings are a little lacking. Try Phi Phi Island Village (below) first.

Laem Tong Beach, Koh Phi Phi, Krabi 81000. Phuket office: 100/435 Moo 5 Chalermprakiet Rama 9 Rd., T. Rassada, Phuket 83000. *©* **07626-1860.** Fax 07626-1866. www.holiday-inn.com. 77 units. 8,200B–9,400B (US$205–US$235/£115–£132) bungalow. AE, MC, V. **Amenities:** 2 restaurants; bar; outdoor pool; fitness center; tour desk; room service; massage; laundry service. *In room:* A/C, minibar, IDD phone.

Phi Phi Island Village Beach Resort & Spa   Set on quiet Loh Ba Kao Bay just south of Laem Tong Beach, Phi Phi Island Village offers a variety of elevated wood-and-cement huts spread amongst the palms. The bungalows are large and comfortable with all of the creature comforts (it's the only resort on this part of the island with satellite TV), but they're starting to show their age—just normal wear and tear—which is understandable since this was the first resort on the island. Beachfront studios were the only rooms damaged by the 2004 tsunami and have been renovated to a very high standard. Of all of the island's resorts, this one offers the most facilities, making it thoroughly self-sufficient and the best option for an extended stay on Phi Phi.

Loh Ba Kao Bay (20. min by longtail boat from main pier), Koh Phi Phi, Krabi 81000. Phuket office: 89 Satoon Rd. Phuket 83000. (© 07621-5014. Fax 07621-4918. www.ppisland.com. 100 units. 6,100B–7,700B (US$153–US$193/ £85–£108) bungalow; 10,500B (US$263/£147) beachfront studio; 25,000B (US$603/£350) pool villa. AE, MC, V. **Amenities:** 3 restaurants; 3 bars; 2 outdoor pools; spa; Jacuzzi; sauna; tour desk; babysitting; laundry service; Internet cafe; longtail boats to main pier; PADI dive center. *In room:* A/C, satellite TV, minibar.

OUTDOOR ACTIVITIES

Next to lounging on the beach, **snorkeling** and **scuba diving** are the most popular activities in and around Phi Phi. Most resorts offer free snorkeling equipment, or you can rent from one of the storefronts on Ton Sai Bay. **Moskito Diving** (© 07560-1154) caters to all experience levels and offers a variety of day trips as well as live-aboards on its state-of-the-art 85-foot dive boat. Other PADI-certified outfits include **Aquanauts Scuba** (© 07421-2640; www.aquanauts-scuba.com) and **Visa Diving** (© 07561-8106).

20 Koh Lanta

70km (43 miles) SE of Krabi

Small Muslim fishing villages dot the east coast of Lanta Yai (Big Lanta), a less-developed region of the south. You'll have to cross Lanta Noi (Small Lanta) to get to the main beach areas of Lanta Yai. Business is booming, and where there were once only backpacker haunts, luxury and midrange bungalows are slowly taking over. Much of the development is taking place in the protected Moo Koh Lanta National Marine Park, meaning that the new construction must meet environmental impact standards. Local laws also govern the height and size of new resorts as the locals try to keep the island looking as natural as possible. We'll see.

GETTING THERE

Minivans from Krabi Town and Trang make connections to Lanta; the cost is from 250B (US$6.25/£3.50) for bus/boat/bus door-to-door service. After two short ferry crossings, most transport stops in **Saladan,** near the ferry pier on the northern tip of Lanta Yai. In the high season, daily ferries connect Koh Lanta with Koh Phi Phi (250B/US$6.25/£3.50). You can also connect with Phuket via Phi Phi. In the low season, a chartered boat is your only option.

WHERE TO STAY
VERY EXPENSIVE

On developing Phra Ae Beach (Long Beach), **Layana Resort & Spa** (272 Moo 3 Saladan; © 07560-7100; www.layanaresort.com) offers first-class accommodations and is the best on the beach. Luxury pavilions and suites start at 10,000B (US$250/£1,400).

Pimalai Resort & Spa   From Krabi Town or the airport, you can ride in style: first by luxury van, then by picturesque private boat ride directly to the resort in high season (a short four-wheel-drive ride to another pier in low season). Getting here is an adventure in itself that pays dividends when you check in to your own luxury suite. A fine marriage of comfort and proximity to nature, the large, free-standing villas are partly walled compounds with rooms done in hardwoods and luxurious bathrooms with outdoor showers. Each unit has a large veranda, some overlooking the sea or at least in earshot of the crashing surf of the picturesque beach below (a good swimming beach). The high-end suites are spectacular. The resort is thoroughly self-contained, with services like a library, a beautiful spa, and good day trips.

99 Moo 5, Ba Kan Tiang Beach, Lanta Yai Island, Krabi 81150 (on the far southeast coast of Lanta Yai). ⓒ 07560-7999. Fax 07560-7998. www.pimalai.com. 86 units. 11,000B–15,500B (US$275–US$388/£154–£217) double; 23,500B–34,500B (US$588–US$863/£329–£4683) pavilion suite; from 24,000B (US$600/£336) villa. AE, DC, MC, V. **Amenities:** 3 restaurants; bar; pool; fitness center; spa w/massage; Jacuzzi; watersports equipment; mountain-bike rental; tour desk; car rental; limo transfer; business center w/Internet access; 24-hr. room service; laundry service; library w/good book selection; dive center. *In room:* A/C, satellite TV (some w/DVD players), minibar, fridge, safe, IDD phone.

MODERATE/INEXPENSIVE

Budget accommodations along the west coast of Lanta are basic bungalows starting as low as 300B (US$7.50/£4.20); keep an eye out for new hotels springing up. **Moonlight Bay Resort** (69 Moo 8, Klongtob; ⓒ 07568-4401) is typical of the good bungalow resorts and offers cozy accommodations and basic services starting at 1,000B (US$25/£14).

21 An Introduction to Central Thailand

Going north from Bangkok, travelers tracing the route of the Chao Phraya River travel back in time as they push upstream and beyond. Starting with the ruins of **Ayutthaya** (see "Side Trips from Bangkok," p. 126), the towns as you go north are the successive historical capitals of old Siam, and the vast Central Plain and the nation's greatest architectural wonder, **Sukhothai,** are the very founding point of the Thai kingdom in 1238. Even further north is the land of Lanna and the distinct ancient kingdom once centered around Chiang Mai (covered in section 23, below).

Phitsanulok, 377km (234 miles) north of Bangkok, is the commercial hub of the region, but despite a visit to the town's noted **Wat Yai,** an important Thai pilgrimage temple, most travelers just pass through on their way to Sukhothai. The **Phitsanulok Station** (ⓒ 05525-8005) is served by regular rail connection from Bangkok's **Hua Lampong Railway Station** (ⓒ 1690 or 02223-7010). If you're stuck for the night, try **Topland Hotel** (68/33 Akathodsarod St.; ⓒ 05524-7800; www.toplandhotel. com), with rooms going for 2,000BB (US$50/£28).

22 Sukhothai ✶✶✶ & Si Satchanalai ✶

Sukhothai: 427km (265 miles) N of Bangkok, 58km (36 miles) E of Phitsanulok; Si Satchanalai: 56km (35 miles) N of Sukhothai

The emergence of Sukhothai (which means "Dawn of Happiness" in Pali) in 1238 as an independent political state signified the birth of the first unified kingdom known as Thailand. Today, Sukhothai is a world-renowned historical site; it is to Thailand what Angkor Wat is to Cambodia.

New Sukhothai, built along the banks of the Yom River, is the access point for the main attraction, **Sukhothai Historical Park** (or Muang Kao, which means Old City), situated some 12km (7½ miles) west of the town center.

Si Satchanalai Historical Park, also along the Yom River, is 56km (35 miles) north of New Sukhothai. Another legacy of the Sukhothai Kingdom, the ancient city is crumbling—but that's part of its charm, and it's certainly worth the 1-day detour. If you're traveling from Phitsanulok, the drive takes you across wide plains of rice paddies, cotton fields, and mango and lemon groves—a glimpse into another era.

GETTING THERE

BY PLANE   Bangkok Airways has a private airport near Sukhothai, with at least one daily flight connecting Bangkok, Sukhothai, and Chiang Mai. For information, call ℂ **02229-3456** in Bangkok, ℂ **05328-1519** in Chiang Mai, or ℂ **05564-7224** at the Sukhothai airport.

BY TRAIN   The nearest railroad station is at Phitsanulok (see above). From Phitsanulok's intercity bus terminal on Highway 12, buses leave hourly for the 1-hour trip to New Sukhothai (30B/US75¢/£0.40).

BY BUS   Three daily air-conditioned buses leave from Bangkok's **Northern Bus Terminal** (ℂ **02936-2841**) for the 7-hour trip (256B/US$6.40/£3.60). Four daily air-conditioned buses leave from Chiang Mai's **Arcade Bus Terminal** (ℂ **05324-2664**) for the 5½-hour trip (153B–373B/US$3.80–US$9.30/£2.15–£5.20).

The Sukhothai bus station is about 3km (2 miles) west of New Sukhothai. Public songtaos charge 20B (US50¢/£0.30) for the ride to New Sukhothai. Drivers will try to bargain, but you should just hop in a songtao with the locals.

BY CAR   Take Singhawat Road east from Phitsanulok, then Highway 12.

WHERE TO STAY & DINE

Pailyn Sukhothai Hotel (10/2 Moo 1, Jarodvithithong; ℂ **05561-3310**), a roadside motel about 4km (2½ miles) east of the old city, offers the highest standard, with doubles running 1,200B (US$30/£17). It's nothing special, but fine for short stays. In New Sukhothai, the **Lotus Village** (170 Ratchathanee St.; ℂ **05562-1484**) has fan and air-conditioned rooms from 600B (US$15/£8.40) and 900B (US$23/£13), respectively. You can also contact the guesthouse for drivers and certified park guides.

In the super-inexpensive category, **Ban Thai Guesthouse** (38 Pravet Nakhon Rd.; west side of Yom River; ℂ **05561-0163**) is a collection of A-frame teak bungalows starting from just 200B (US$5/£2.80). It's quite basic, but a good place to get useful local info.

Like most small cities and towns in Thailand, you can find good eats at the central market from early 'til late. **Dream Cafe** (86/1 Singhawat Rd.; ℂ **05561-2081**) is a great choice, with fine, funky Thai atmosphere and great eats.

EXPLORING SUKHOTHAI ★★★

Named a UNESCO World Heritage Site in 1978, a 1988 preservation project kept the monuments upright and added the museum and park facilities.

You can reach the historic park of Sukhothai by public bus, by three-wheeled motorcycle taxi *(samlor),* or by private car. The samlors that cruise around New Sukhothai can be hired to trek you out to the monuments and take you for a 3-hour tour around the park, at a cost of about 300B (US$7.50/£4.20).

The historical park is open daily from 6am to 6pm. Purchase a combination ticket with admission to the National Museum, Historic Park (all areas), and Si Satchanali National Park for 150B (US$3.75/£2.10)—a good value. A basic map is available at the museum, but better maps are to be found at the bike-rental shops near the entrance. Since the site is too spread out for walking, it's best to either go by guided tour in a car, by samlor, or by rented bicycle (available at the entrance). There are also tram tours.

A network of walls and moats defines the perfect rectangle that is the central city. The **Ramkamhaeng National Museum,** with its detailed models and artifacts from the site, is a good place to start. **Wat Mahatat,** composed of several small towers and chedis, is an imposing monument and the site's most important. Don't miss the fine relief work on the southeast corner. The remains of the **Royal Palace** and **Wat Sri Sawai** are also highlights. Don't miss the temples, pottery kilns, and small pilgrimage mounds outside the city walls. A visit to **Sri Satchanalai,** some 56km (35 miles) north, makes for a good day trip.

23 An Introduction to Northern Thailand

If lazy beach days aren't your thing, the historic cities of **Chiang Mai, Chiang Rai,** and the small but interesting **Golden Triangle** (Chiang Saen), a former cowboy town for the opium trade, are a welcome change for visitors who want to experience Thailand's rugged rural beauty.

The majority of northern Thais trace their heritage to the Tai people who migrated from southern China in waves between the 1st and 8th centuries. King Mengrai, a brilliant leader who united the Tai tribes, established the first capital of the Lanna Kingdom at Chiang Rai in 1262. It was about this time that Kublai Khan invaded Burma. For added protection, King Mengrai forged ties with the Sukhothai Kingdom to the south, and in 1296 he moved his capital to Chiang Mai. For the next century, the Lanna Kingdom absorbed most of the northern provinces and, in alliance with the Sukhothai, held off invasion from the Mons and Khmers. After taking control of Sukhothai, Ayutthaya tried to conquer Chiang Mai and failed each time. The Lanna Kingdom enjoyed wealth and power until 1556, when the Burmese captured the capital. It remained in their hands until 1775, when King Taskin (of Ayutthaya) took it for Siam.

North of Chiang Mai and its satellite cities, travelers enter a mountainous region that promises lots of adventure. Rugged hills, proximity to Myanmar (Burma) and Laos, and the diverse ethnic hill-tribe groups living here distinguish northern Thailand from the rest of the country. The mighty Mekong River flows southeast from the

Tips **Special Event**

Loi Krathong is a visually delightful 3-day festival held nationwide on the full moon of the 12th lunar month—usually in October or November—in honor of the water spirits. Crowds gather at ponds, klongs, rivers, and temple fountains to float small banana-leaf boats bearing candles, incense, a flower, and a coin in offering to wash away the past year's sins. Since this festival dates from the Sukhothai era, celebrations are especially widespread throughout the province.

Northern Thailand

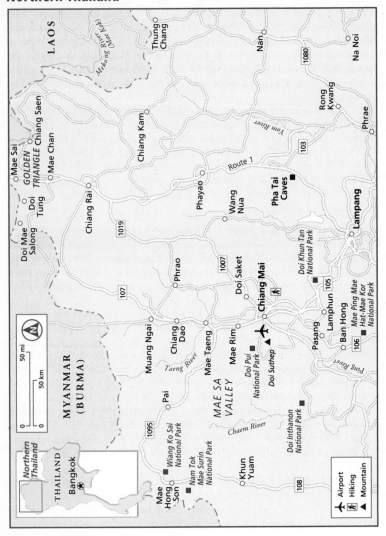

Golden Triangle, the opium-producing region straddling Myanmar and Laos, and the river traces a path along dense jungles and teak forests. This is the land of the elephants, of the ancient Lanna culture, of backwater border towns and adventure around every turn.

Northern Thailand is home to the majority of Thailand's more than half a million **ethnic hill tribes,** which are classified in six primary groups: the Karen, Akha, Lahu, Lisu, Hmong (Meo), and Mien (Yao), each with subgroups that are linked by history, lineage, language, costume, social organization, and religion. With close ethnic, cultural, and linguistic ties to the cultures of their Lao, Chinese, Burmese, and Tibetan ancestors and neighbors, each group retains, to this day, traditional costume, religion, art, and daily practices.

Keep in mind that November through May are the best months for trekking, with February, March, and April (when southern Thailand gets extremely hot) usually being the least crowded months. *Trekkers beware:* During the rainy season, June through October, paths become mudslides due to frequent showers.

24 Chiang Mai ★★★

Chiang Mai (New City) was founded in 1296 by King Mengrai as the capital of the first independent Thai state, Lanna Thai (Kingdom of One Million Rice Fields). It became the cultural and religious center of the northern Tai, those people who had migrated from southern China to dwell in Thailand, and remained through the turbulent period of recurring Burmese attacks. The Burmese were occupiers; in fact, Burmese influence on culture is still strong. Ongoing Thai–Burmese conflicts led to alliances with Siam and, in 1939, the city became Thai.

These days, Chiang Mai is a booming town of some 200,000 people (in a province of some 1.6 million). Most residents are native born, but there are an increasing number of transplants from Bangkok drawn to the slower pace and friendly locals. Chiang Mai's heart is the Old City, an area surrounded by vestiges of walls and moats originally constructed for defense; yet Chiang Mai is also a modern city with a growing infrastructure of modern shopping malls and condominiums. The contrast is part of the town's charm.

GETTING THERE

BY PLANE Lao Airlines (✆ 05340-4033) connects Chiang Mai to Vientiane and Luang Prabang five times each week, while **Air Mandalay** (✆ 05327-6884) has limited flights to Yangon, Myanmar (Burma). **Silk Air** (✆ 05327-6459), the regional arm of Singapore Airlines, connects with Singapore.

Within Thailand, **Thai Airways** (240 Propokklao Rd.; ✆ 05321-0431), **Bangkok Airways** (✆ 05328-1519, or 02229-3434 in Bangkok), and budget carriers **Air Asia** (✆ 02515-9999 in Bangkok; www.airasia.com), **Nok Air** (✆ 02900-9955), and **One-Two-Go** (✆ 01141-1126) fly from Bangkok to Chiang Mai daily (trip time: 1 hr., 10 min.) and make regional connections.

The **Chiang Mai International Airport** has several banks for changing money, a post and overseas call office, and an information booth. Taxis from the airport charge a flat 100B (US$2.50/£1.30) to town. Buy a ticket from the taxi booth in the arrivals hall, then proceed to the taxi queue.

BY TRAIN Of the seven daily trains from Bangkok to Chiang Mai, the 8:30am Sprinter (trip time: 11 hr.) is the quickest, but you sacrifice a whole day to travel and spend the entire trip in a seat. A second-class air-conditioned seat will run 511B (US$13/£7.15). Other trains take between 13 and 15 hours. For overnight trips, second-class sleeper berths are a good choice, costing 881B (US$22/£12) for an upper berth with air-conditioning, 691B (US$17/£6.70) for a lower berth with air-conditioning. In Bangkok, contact **Hua Lampong Railway Station** (✆ 1690 or 02223-7010) up to 90 days in advance. For local train information in Chiang Mai, call ✆ 05324-5363; for advance booking, call ✆ 05324-2094. Reservations cannot be made over the phone, but you can check availability.

BY BUS Buses from Bangkok to Chiang Mai are many and varied—from rattle-trap, open-air numbers to fully reclining VIP vehicles. The trip takes about 10 hours. From Bangkok's **Northern Bus Terminal** (© **02936-2841**), there are numerous departures (about 900B/US$23/£13 for VIP bus). There's also frequent service between Chiang Mai and Mae Hong Son, Phitsanulok, and Chiang Rai.

Chiang Mai's **Arcade Bus Terminal** (© **05324-2664**) is on Kaeo Nawarat Road, 3km (2 miles) northeast of Tha Pae Gate; some buses arrive at **Chang Puak Station** (© **05321-1586**), north of Chang Puak Gate on Chotana Road.

GETTING AROUND

The heart of Chiang Mai is the **Old City,** completely surrounded by a moat and a few remains of the massive wall, laid out in a square aligned with the cardinal directions. Several of the original gates have been restored and serve as handy reference points, particularly **Tha Pae Gate** to the east. All major streets radiate from the Old City.

The main business and shopping area is the 1km (half-mile) stretch between the east side of the Old City and the **Ping River.** Here you will find the Night Bazaar, many shops, trekking agents, hotels, and restaurants. To the west of town and visible from anywhere in the city is the imposing wall of **Doi Suthep** mountain, where, at its crest, you'll find the most regal of all Chiang Mai Buddhist compounds, **Wat Phra That Doi Suthep.**

BY SONGTAO Songtaos (covered pickups) cover all routes. These red pickup trucks fitted with two long bench seats are also known locally as *seelor* (four wheels). Hail one going in your general direction and tell the driver your destination. (*Tip:* Have your hotel or guesthouse concierge write your destination in Thai before you head out.) Ask the price and bargain hard.

BY TUK-TUK The ubiquitous tuk-tuk (motorized three-wheeler) is the next best option to the songtao. Fares are negotiable—you will have to bargain hard to get a good rate—but expect to pay at least 40B (US$1/£0.55) for any ride.

BY CAR **Avis** (© **05320-1574**) has an office conveniently located at the airport, while **Budget** (© **05320-2871**) will deliver; prices start at 1,500B (US$38/£21). **North Wheels** (127/2 Moonmuang Rd.; © **05321-6189**) is a good choice and typical of the more budget services in town.

BY MOTORCYCLE Many guesthouses along the Ping River and shops around Chaiyapoom Road (north of Tha Pae Gate in the Old City) rent 100cc to 150cc motorcycles for about 200B (US$5/£2.80) per day (with discounts for longer periods); 250cc Hondas (and larger) are also available. Wear a helmet.

BY BICYCLE Cycling in the city is fun and practical, especially for getting around to the temples within the Old City. Bikes are available at any of the many guesthouses in or around the Old City; they go for about 50B (US$1.25/£ 0.70) per day.

VISITOR INFORMATION

The **TAT** office is at 105/1 Chiang Mai-Lamphun Rd. (© **05324-8604**), 400m (1,312 ft.) south of the Nawarat Bridge on the east side of the Ping River. Around town, you can find lots of free local magazines with maps and lists of events.

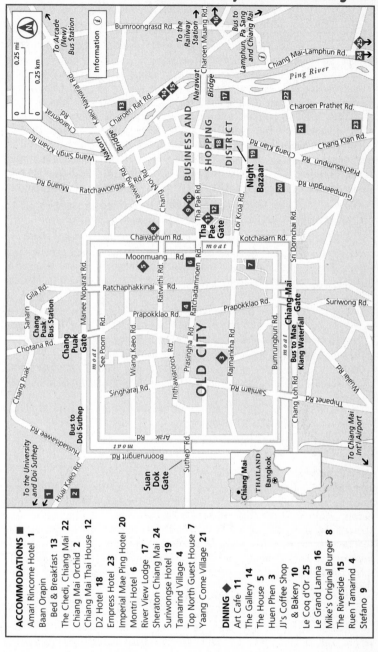

Where to Stay & Dine in Chiang Mai

N

0.25 mi
0.25 km

Information (i)

To Arcade (New) Bus Station

Bumroongrasd Rd.

To the Railway Station

Bus to Lamphun, Pa Sang and Chiang Rai

Chiang Mai-Lamphun Rd.

Ping River

Charoen Muang Rd.

Charoen Prathet Rd.

Charoen Rat Rd.

Narawat Bridge

Chang Klan Rd.

Kaeo Nawarat Rd.

Charoenrat Rd.

BUSINESS AND

SHOPPING

DISTRICT

Chang Klan Rd.

Prachasumpun Rd.

Wang Singh Kham Rd.

Ratchawongse Rd.

Muang Rd.

Taiwang Rd.

Moon Rd.

Chang Moi Rd.

Tha Pae Rd.

Night Bazaar

Gumpaengdin Rd.

Chaiyaphum Rd.

Tha Pae Gate

Loi Kroa Rd.

Kotchasarn Rd.

Sri Dornchai Rd.

Moonmuang Rd.

moat

Manee Noparat Rd.

Ratchaphakkinai Rd.

Ratwithi Rd.

Ratchadamnoen Rd.

Gila Rd.

Sanam

Chang Puak Bus Station

Chang Puak Gate

Prapokklao Rd.

Prapokklao Rd.

Chiang Mai Gate

Suriwong Rd.

Chotana Rd.

Manee Noparat Rd.

See Poom Rd.

Wiang Kaeo Rd.

Prasingha Rd.

Rajmankha Rd.

Bumrungburi Rd.

Bus to Mae Klang Waterfall Gate

OLD CITY

Chang Puak

Bus to Doi Suthep

Hussadisawee Rd.

Huai Kaeo Rd.

Singharaj Rd.

Inthawarorot Rd.

Samlarn Rd.

Chang Loh Rd.

Thipanet Rd.

Wualai Rd.

To Chiang Mai Int'l Airport

Arak Rd.

Suthep Rd.

Boonruangrit Rd.

moat

Suan Dok Gate

To the University and Doi Suthep

Chiang Mai

THAILAND

Bangkok

ACCOMMODATIONS ■

Amari Rincome Hotel **1**
Baan Orapin
Bed & Breakfast **13**
The Chedi, Chiang Mai **22**
Chiang Mai Orchid **2**
Chiang Mai Thai House **12**
D2 Hotel **18**
Empress Hotel **23**
Imperial Mae Ping Hotel **20**
Montri Hotel **6**
River View Lodge **17**
Sheraton Chiang Mai **24**
Suriwongse Hotel **19**
Tamarind Village **4**
Top North Guest House **7**
Yaang Come Village **21**

DINING ◆

Art Cafe **11**
The Gallery **14**
The House **5**
Huen Phen **3**
JJ's Coffee Shop & Bakery **10**
Le Coq d'Or **25**
Le Grand Lanna **16**
Mike's Original Burger **8**
The Riverside **15**
Ruen Tamarind **4**
Stefano **9**

FAST FACTS: Chiang Mai

Bookstores **Backstreet Books** (✆ 05387-4143) and **Gecko Books** (✆ 05387-4066) are neighbors on Chang Moi Kao, a side street north of eastern Tha Pae Road just before it meets the city wall. Both have a good selection of new and used books and do exchanges at the usual rate: two for one, depending on the condition. **Bookazine** (Chiang Inn Plaza, 100/1 Chang Klan Rd., ground floor; ✆ 05381-8995) is cramped, but has a comprehensive selection. Also try **Suriwong Book Centre** (54/1–5 Sri Dornchai; ✆ 05328-1052) and the appropriately named **Thapae Gate Books** (2 Chaiyapoom Rd.; ✆ 05387-4066).

Consulates **U.S.:** 387 Wichayanond Rd. (✆ 05325-2629). **Canada:** 151 Chiang Mai–Lampang Superhighway, T. Tahsala (✆ 05385-0147). **Australia:** 165 Sirimangklachan Rd. (✆ 05322-1083). **U.K.:** 198 Bumrungraj Rd. (✆ 05320-3405).

Currency Exchange For convenient bank ATMs and money changers, go to Chang Klan Road and Charoen Prathet Road, around the Night Bazaar.

Emergencies In case of emergency, dial ✆ **1699** to reach the tourist police.

Hospitals Chiang Mai hospitals offer excellent emergency and general care, with English-speaking nurses and physicians. The best private hospital is **McCormick**, on Kaeo Nawarat Road (✆ 05392-1777), out toward the Arcade Bus Terminal.

Internet Access In the Old City, there are numerous small, inexpensive cafes with service sometimes costing only 15B (US40¢/£0.20) per hour. Try **NET Generation**, 404/4 Tha Pae Rd. (✆ 01568-7470), or **Buddy Internet**, near the Kad Suan Kaew (Central) shopping complex (✆ 05340-4550).

Mail The most convenient branch is at 186/1 Chang Klan Rd. (✆ 05327-3657). The general post office is on Charoen Muang (✆ 05324-1070), near the train station.

WHERE TO STAY
NEAR THE PING RIVER
Very Expensive

The Chedi, Chiang Mai ✰✰   Upon arrival, The Chedi resembles a fortress with towering white walls providing protection from the onslaught of tuk-tuks and noise beyond. However, the interior reveals a sleek modern hideaway with little to remind you that you are in fact still in Chiang Mai. Reflecting pools and manicured gardens line an inner courtyard dominated by an 80-year-old whitewashed colonial building. Formerly the British consulate, it now houses the hotel's bar and restaurant and provides a welcome charm to the otherwise stark exterior architecture. Airy rooms are decorated in a chic contemporary Asian style that is more focused on "contemporary" than "Asian." Stunning black-marble bathrooms open up to the bedroom by way of folding teak doors, and balconies overlook a riverfront swimming pool surrounded by lotus ponds (try for a fourth-floor room for the best view). Added perks like butler service, complimentary minibar, and free laundry service make the very spacious suites worth the steep price tag.

123 Charoen Prathet Rd., Chiang Mai 50100 (on the river 5 blocks south of Tha Pae Rd.). ℂ **05325-3333**. Fax 05325-3352. www.ghmhotels.com. 84 units. 10,400B (US$260/£146) deluxe; 15,600B (US$390/£218) suite. AE, DC, MC, V. **Amenities:** Restaurant; 2 bars; lounge; outdoor pool; fitness center; spa; tour desk; car rental; limo service; business center; boutique; 24-hr. room service; babysitting; laundry service; dry cleaning. *In room:* A/C, satellite TV, wireless and broadband Internet access, minibar, coffeemaker, hair dryer, safe, IDD phone.

Expensive

D2 Hotel ☀☀ The Dusit hotel chain is trying to appeal to a younger, hipper crowd by updating its image; this "lifestyle hotel" is one of its first efforts at capturing the demographic. From the lobby to the restaurants to the guest rooms, every corner of the hotel is bathed in a postmodern minimalist cool. Oranges and browns are the dominant colors, and the furniture and decor seamlessly blend sharp lines with rounded edges—everything flows. More important, the style of the furnishings does not translate into a lack of comfort. Rooms are very livable and have all the finer creature comforts: daybeds, flatscreen TVs with DVD players, and well-stocked bathrooms. An upgrade to the club deluxe level allows access to the chic club lounge, with free cocktails and Internet service. Dusit's famous Devarana Spa is the one part of the hotel that the young'uns were not allowed to get their hands on—it retains its traditional Thai elegance. The hotel's staff exudes a laid-back cool, but is very attentive and helpful. An enjoyable and unique choice.

100 Chang Klan Rd., Chiang Mai 50100 (2 blocks south of Tha Pae Rd., 2 blocks west of river, just north of Night Bazaar). ℂ **05399-9999**. Fax 05399-9900. www.d2hotels.com. 131 units. US$154 (£85) deluxe; US$179 (£98) club deluxe; from $256 (£141) suite. AE, DC, MC, V. **Amenities:** Restaurant; bar; outdoor pool; fitness center; spa; concierge; car rental; business center; 24-hr. room service; babysitting. *In room:* A/C, satellite TV w/DVD player, Internet access, minibar, coffeemaker, hair dryer, safe, IDD phone.

Imperial Mae Ping Hotel ☀ This imposing, crescent-shaped tower hotel is one of the city's most popular choices for its style and good location—just a short stroll from the Night Bazaar, yet far enough away to get a good night's sleep. The unusual two-story lobby interprets Thai architectural elements in bold white-and-gold accents; the decor throughout is a nice mix of modern and traditional. Large, bright guest rooms feature traditional blond-teak furnishings and contemporary Thai elements like sculpted lamp bases, reproductions of temple murals, and Thai weavings. Deluxe rooms have better-than-average amenities for just a small jump in price. Be sure to ask for a room with a mountain view.

153 Sri Dornchai Rd., Chiang Mai 50100 (corner of Kampaengdin Rd., 2 blocks southwest of Night Bazaar). ℂ **05327-0160**. Fax 05327-0181. www.imperialmaeping.com. 371 units. 4,500B–5,500B (US$113–US$138/£63–£77) double; from 10,000B (US$250/£140) suite. AE, DC, MC, V. **Amenities:** 3 restaurants; lounge and beer garden (p. 218); outdoor pool; fitness center; tour desk; limo service; business center; salon; 24-hr. room service; massage; babysitting; laundry service; dry cleaning; nonsmoking rooms, executive-level rooms. *In room:* A/C, satellite TV, minibar, fridge.

Sheraton Chiang Mai ☀☀ Chiang Mai's best high-rise hotel is just a short ride south of town. This is "the" place if you're coming to town for business. From the enormous pillars, chandeliers, frescoes, and filigree of the grand lobby to its international standard of guest rooms and service, everything is tip-top. What the Sheraton lacks in local touches, it more than makes up for with comfortable familiarity. Complimentary shuttles to the Night Bazaar and the airport help offset the out-of-the-way locale.

318/1 Chiangmai-Lamphun Rd., Chiang Mai 50007 (south of city center, across Mengrai Bridge on east bank of river). ℂ **05327-5300**. Fax 05327-5299. www.sheraton-chiangmai.com or www.starwoodhotels.com. 526 units. 7,200B–8,400B (US$180–US$210/£101–£118) double; 11,000B (US$275/£154) executive deluxe; from 17,000B

(US$425/£238) suite. AE, DC, MC, V. **Amenities:** 3 restaurants; lounge; outdoor pool; golf course nearby; fitness center; sauna; concierge; tour desk; car rental; limo service; business center; 24-hr. room service; massage; babysitting; laundry service; dry cleaning; nonsmoking rooms; executive-level rooms. *In room:* A/C, satellite TV, minibar, fridge, hair dryer, IDD phone.

Yaang Come Village ⋆   Named after the massive 40-year-old yaang tree that provides shade for the reception area, the Yaang Come is a small oasis in developing Chiang Mai. The idea behind the resort is to re-create the feel of a traditional Thai Lue village (the Thai Lue migrated from Yunnan Province to northern Thailand a couple centuries ago). While I wouldn't say that they've fully realized this goal—I'm not sure how prevalent Jacuzzis and wireless Internet access were in Thai Lue villages—the resort does have a laid-back charm. The lavishly decorated open-air reception leads to an inner courtyard dominated by a swimming pool and Jacuzzi. Flanking the pool area are the guest rooms, which are housed in brick buildings with Lanna-style roofs. All are well appointed with red-tile floors, balconies, glossy tile bathrooms, and unique wall murals painted by artisans from nearby Nan province. The hotel is outside of the bustle on a quiet street south of the Night Bazaar, yet still within striking distance of the action.

90/3 Sri Dornchai Rd., Chiang Mai 50100 (between Chang Klan and Charoen Prathet rds., midway between Old City and river). ℭ 05323-7222. Fax 05323-7230. www.yaangcome.com. 42 units. 6,000B–7,000B (US$150–US$175/£84–£98) double; 9,000B (US$225/£126) family room; 15,000 (US$375/£210) suite. AE, MC, V. **Amenities:** Restaurant; bar; outdoor pool and Jacuzzi; tour desk; car rental; limo service; massage; laundry service; wireless Internet access. *In room:* A/C, satellite TV w/DVD player, Internet access, minibar, coffeemaker, hair dryer, IDD phone.

Moderate
Baan Orapin Bed & Breakfast ⋆⋆ *(Finds*   For those looking for a more intimate and personal stay in Chiang Mai, the Baan Orapin is a real gem. Owned and operated by Khun Opas Chao, who spent over a decade studying and working in the U.S. and U.K., the hotel is set on land that has been in his family for over 100 years. Two-story Lanna-style buildings surround the 90-year-old mansion and attached gardens. While the rooms and suites are rustic in comparison with the larger resorts and hotels, they are stylish and extremely clean, with sturdy teakwood furniture, mosquito netting for the beds, and handicrafts to add some local flavor. Large bathrooms are outfitted in beautifully polished, locally made green-and-blue tiling. Khun Opas is a wealth of information about the town and its history; he and his staff will bend over backwards to attend to your every need. A truly unique experience.

150 Charoenraj Rd., Chiang Mai 50100 (east side of river, north of Narawatt Bridge). ℭ 05324-3677. Fax 05324-7142. www.baanorapin.com. 12 units. 1,900B (US$48/£27) double; 2,400B–3,000B (US$60–US$75/£34–£42) suite; 4,000B (US$100/£56) family villa. AE, MC, V. **Amenities:** Restaurant; tour desk; Internet access. *In room:* A/C, satellite TV, fridge.

Empress Hotel ⋆   This 17-story tower, opened in 1990, is south of the main business and tourist area, which makes it especially quiet. The hotel has all the amenities and—even when swarming with tourist groups—doesn't seem overrun. The impressive public spaces are decorated with elaborate gem-encrusted stupas and golden elephant statues. Large guest rooms with picture windows are done in a tasteful, modern interpretation of Asian decor in rose and peach tones. Bathrooms are small, but decked out in marble and stocked with good complimentary amenities. Newly renovated deluxe rooms are done in beiges and dark reds with polished wood floors and understated Lanna artwork. Very classy. Ask to be on the mountain side—there are nice views from upper floors.

199/42 Chang Klan Rd., Chiang Mai 50100 (15-min. walk south of Night Bazaar, 2 blocks from river). © 05327-0240. Fax 05327-2467. www.empresshotels.com. 375 units. 3,500B–4,000B (US$88–US$100/£49–£56) double; 4,700B (US$118/£66) deluxe; from 10,000B (US$250/£140) suite. AE, DC, MC, V. **Amenities:** 3 restaurants; lobby lounge and disco (p. 218); pool; fitness center w/sauna; concierge; tour desk; business center; shopping arcade; salon; 24-hr. room service; massage; babysitting; laundry service; dry cleaning; executive-level rooms; Internet. *In room:* A/C, satellite TV, minibar, fridge, hair dryer.

River View Lodge ★★   River View has a great location and is the kind of place that people return to again and again (well-known guide-map maker Nancy Chandler, for instance, makes this her home when she is researching). The hotel's riverside locale makes for a peaceful retreat, and yet it's only a short hop to the city's main business and shopping district. What with the quaint, shady garden, small but cozy riverside pool, open-air cafe, and quiet sitting areas scattered about, there's a good laid-back vibe here. The staff is friendly enough, and informed if a bit "eccentric," to give it a word. Large guest rooms have fresh terra-cotta tile floors with simple wood furnishings and no-fuss decor set against one wall of red-brick facing. Some units have balconies as well. Bathrooms have shower stalls only.

25 Charoen Prathet Rd., Soi 2, Chiang Mai 50100 (on river 2 blocks south of Tha Pae Rd.). © 05327-1109. Fax 05327-9019. www.riverviewlodgch.com. 36 units. US$41–US$51 (£23–£28) double. MC, V. **Amenities:** Restaurant; small pool; laundry service. *In room:* A/C.

Suriwongse Hotel ★   For the shopper or party animal looking to be close to the Night Bazaar area, this hotel is tops. The unique hardwood paneling in the lobby lends warmth to the place. Spacious, teak-trimmed rooms have clean carpet, firm beds, and are done in cool off-white and pastels (if you can ignore the red bordello drapes). Higher-priced rooms have similar amenities but offer a balcony and better views. The town's McDonald's and Starbucks franchises are both within a stone's throw (if throwing stones is your thing).

110 Chang Klan Rd., Chiang Mai 50100 (corner of Loi Kroa Rd., just southwest of Night Bazaar, halfway between Old City and river). © 05327-0051. Fax 05327-0063. www.suriwongsehotels.com. 180 units. 2,400B–3,500B (US$60–US$88/£33–£48) double; from 4,800B (US$120/£66) suite. Seasonal rates available. AE, DC, MC, V. **Amenities:** 2 restaurants; lounge; pool; tour desk; business center; shopping; limited room service; massage; babysitting; laundry service; dry cleaning; nonsmoking rooms. *In room:* A/C, satellite TV, minibar, fridge, IDD phone.

Inexpensive

Chiang Mai Thai House ★★ (Value)   Set on a quiet soi 2 blocks from Tha Pae Gate and a 10-minute walk to the Night Bazaar, the Thai House in basketball parlance would be considered a "tweener"—somewhere between a guesthouse and a hotel. Opened in 2005, the rooms and bathrooms (the all-in-one shower variety) are spotless, and a quick perusal of the house rules shows management is dead set on keeping them that way. Spacious air-conditioned rooms have wood floors and small fridges, with first-floor air-con units sporting an attached small garden sitting area. Fan rooms are just as spacious and a good choice during the cooler months. Hallway balconies overlook the relaxing pool area. The tour desk can help book excursions ranging from rafting and cycling to all-day cooking classes. The restaurant serves decent Thai fare. Overall, this is a great value.

5/1 Tha Pae Rd., Soi 5, Chiang Mai 50100 (2 blocks east of Tha Pae Gate). © 05390-4110. Fax 05390-4737. www.chiangmaithaihouse.com. 37 units. 500B (US$13/£7) double w/fan; 900B (US$23/£13) double w/A/C. AE, MC, V. **Amenities:** Restaurant; outdoor pool; tour desk; laundry service; computer room. *In room:* TV, Internet access, IDD phone.

IN THE OLD CITY
Moderate
Tamarind Village ★★   Passing down a long, shaded lane lined with new-growth bamboo, follow meandering walkways among the whitewashed buildings of this stylish little hideaway in the heart of the Old City. It's hard to believe that you're in Chiang Mai. Rooms at the Tamarind are marvels of concrete flatwork burnished to an almost shining glow. Complemented by straw mats and chic contemporary Thai furnishings, they make for a pleasing, minimalist feel (if you're a minimalist, that is). Bathrooms are spacious, with double doors connecting to the vaulted-ceilinged guest rooms. There's an almost Mediterranean feel to the whole complex, what with all of the arched, covered terra-cotta walks joining buildings in a village-style layout. At press time, five new rooms were being added, as well as a full-service spa promising Jacuzzi and sauna facilities. Add that to the already excellent poolside restaurant (see "Where to Dine," below) and you have the makings of a unique city resort.

50/1 Rathcadamnoen Rd., Sriphom, Chiang Mai 50200 (a short walk toward the center of the Old City from Tha Pae Gate). ℂ 05341-8896. Fax 05341-8900. www.tamarindvillage.com. 40 units. 4,200B (US$105/£59) double; 5,600B (US$140/£78) deluxe; 9,800B (US$245/£137) suite. MC, V. **Amenities:** Restaurant; bar; outdoor pool; tour desk; laundry service; dry cleaning. *In room:* A/C, satellite TV, minibar, fridge, hair dryer, IDD phone.

Inexpensive
Montri Hotel ★ *Value*   The earliest address of note for foreigners in Chiang Mai, the Montri is still a convenient, inexpensive gem located just inside the Old City and across from Tha Pae Gate. Newly renovated rooms with built-in cabinets, valances, and new furniture are attractive, comfortable, and a very good value; the rest are pretty basic cells, though comfy and clean. Dark parquet floors are standard throughout and bathrooms are of the shower-in-room style. Ask for a back-facing room; you'll get more peace, and from higher floors can see Doi Suthep. If you're arriving by plane, make sure you request a free airport transfer when you make your booking.

2–6 Ratchadamnoen Rd., Chiang Mai 50100 (just northwest across from Tha Pae Gate). ℂ 05321-1069. Fax 05321-7416. 75 units. 750B (US$19/£11) double. MC, V. **Amenities:** Restaurant; tour desk; small business center; laundry service. *In room:* A/C, satellite TV, minibar, fridge.

Top North Guest House   South of Tha Pae and down one of the Old City's narrow lanes, laid-back Top North is comfortable and affordable. The small central pool is unique in this category and is a popular hangout for backpackers going upscale. There are many room standards, all with high ceilings. Top-category units (600B/$15/£8) are large and clean, with tile floors and bathrooms with tubs. Time is not kind to budget hotels, however, and indeed some of the furnishings look like they've gone a few rounds with an angry, caged ape. Rooms on the lower echelon vary in price and amenities (with or without A/C or TV), but all at least have hot-water showers. Top North's extras include a good tour operation, an Internet cafe, and a bar that shows DVDs in the evenings. Its sister property, **Top North Hotel** (ℂ 05327-9623-5), is an old standby just south of the Tha Pae Gate within the Old City; it offers a slightly higher class of rooms but seems to attract a rougher lot (it's good in a pinch, though).

15 Moon Muang Rd., Soi 2, Chiang Mai 50100. ℂ 05329-8900. Fax 05327-8485. www.topnorthgroup.com. 90 units. 400B (US$10/£5.60) double w/fan; 500B–600B (US$13–US$15/£7–£8.40) double w/A/C. MC, V. **Amenities:** Restaurant; outdoor pool; bike and motorcycle rental; tour desk; laundry service; Internet cafe. *In room:* A/C, TV.

WEST SIDE/UNIVERSITY AREA
Expensive/Moderate
Amari Rincome Hotel ✸   This tranquil hotel complex is a favorite because of its elegant, yet traditional, Thai atmosphere. The public spaces are decorated with local handicrafts, and the professional staff wears intricately embroidered costumes. Superior rooms are elaborately adorned with Burmese tapestries and carved-wood accents in local style, but are looking a little worn. Recently renovated deluxe rooms are more in keeping with Amari's high standards: business beiges with plush carpeting and modern Lanna decorations. There is a gorgeous garden and pool area, the dining at La Gritta is great, and the hotel is near some of the better upscale shops and galleries in town. The staff is as professional as they come, will know your name from the moment you cross the threshold, and can help with any eventuality (tours, transport, and so on). A very comfortable choice.

1 Nimmanhaeminda Rd., off Huay Kaeo Rd., Chiang Mai 50200 (near superhighway northwest of Old City). 𝄆 05322-1130. Fax 05322-1915. www.amari.com. 158 units. US$167 (£92) superior; US$197 (£108) double; US$409 (£225) suite. AE, DC, MC, V. **Amenities:** 3 restaurants; lounge; 2 outdoor pools; outdoor lighted tennis court; concierge; tour desk; limo service; business center; shopping arcade; salon; 24-hr. room service; massage; babysitting; laundry service; dry cleaning; nonsmoking rooms; executive-level rooms. *In room:* A/C, satellite TV, minibar, fridge, hair dryer, IDD phone.

Chiang Mai Orchid ✸   The Orchid has attractive facilities and friendly service and is just next to the town's most popular hangout, the Kad Suan Kaew (Central) shopping complex. Spacious, quiet rooms are pleasantly decorated with local woodcarvings. The lobby and other public spaces are furnished with clusters of chic, low-slung rattan couches and decorated with flowers. The Orchid covers all the bases in terms of amenities, from dining to car rental and a knowledgeable tour desk.

100–102 Huai Kaeo Rd., Chiang Mai 50200 (northwest of Old City, next door to Kad San Kaew/Central shopping complex). 𝄆 05322-2099. Fax 05322-1625. www.chiangmaiorchid.com. 267 units. 1,550B–2,550B (US$39–US$69/£22–£36) double; from 7,850B (US$196/£110) suite. AE, DC, MC, V. **Amenities:** 3 restaurants; lounge and pub; outdoor pool; fitness center; sauna; children's playground; tour desk; car rental; limited room service; massage; babysitting; laundry service. *In room:* A/C, satellite TV, dataport, minibar, fridge.

SANKAMPAENG ROAD
Very Expensive
Mandarin Oriental Dhara Dhevi, Chiang Mai   The same folks who set the standard for riverside luxury in their historic property in Bangkok now bring a new ultra-luxe resort to Chiang Mai. Lying east of town along the busy stretch of Sankampaeng Road, the resort is intended to be a living museum, re-creating a traditional Lanna palace and its attendant village. Upon arrival, a horse-drawn cart whisks you across a moat into the miniature city, dropping you off at the lavishly decorated lobby. A reproduction of a Burmese palace, it is quite impressive and—like the nearby spa, a teakwood extravagance modeled after the Mandalay Palace—wholly unique in a resort setting. Accommodations are of the suite-only variety, roughly divided between the older villas and pavilions and the just completed colonial suites. Arranged like miniature Lanna villages, the villa and pavilion suites surround verdant compounds of rice terraces and gardens that are worked daily by a family of buffalo. Villa suites are grand two-story teakwood rice barns, while pavilion suites are impressive takes on traditional Thai houses, each incorporating different ethnic influences on Lanna architecture. All have attached Thai-style *salas* and are appointed as if for royalty, in rich teak, silk, and all the finest fittings. The newest suites borrow heavily from 19th-century English and

Burmese colonial style. Pastel tones, chandeliers dangling from towering ceilings, and stunning open-plan marble bathrooms give these rooms a sense of refinement unmatched in Chiang Mai. To take a simple stroll through the grounds is to be bombarded with the history of Lanna architecture and culture. If your head starts to spin, a cultural expert is available to give guided tours.

51/4 Chiang Mai–Sankampaeng Rd., Moo 1 T Tasala, Chiang Mai 50000. (C) 05388-8929. Fax 05399-9928. www. mandarinoriental.com. 142 units. US$450–US$2,000 (£248–£1,100) colonial suite; US$600–US$1,600 (£330–£880) villa; US$1,300–US$2,650 (£715–£1,458) residence; US$6,000 (£3,300) royal villa. AE, MC, V. **Amenities:** 3 restaurants; 2 bars; outdoor pool; tennis court; health club; extensive spa; children's center; concierge; tour desk; car rental; limo service; business center; shopping village; 24-hr. room service; massage; babysitting; laundry service; dry cleaning; cooking school; library. *In room:* A/C, satellite TV, minibar, fridge, coffeemaker, hair dryer, safe, IDD phone.

OUTSIDE CHIANG MAI
Very Expensive
Four Seasons Resort Chiang Mai   Northern Thailand's finest resort is isolated from the bustle of the city on 8 hectares (20 acres) of landscaped grounds in the Mae Rim Valley. The beautiful central area features terraced rice paddies and even a resident family of water buffalo used to work the fields. Two-story Lanna-style pavilions overlook the tranquil scenery. Spacious suites are understatedly elegant with polished teak floors and vaulted ceilings, decorated with traditional Thai fabrics and art, each with an adjoining private *sala*. Bathrooms are particularly large and luxurious. The pool is a spectacle with a vanishing edge overlooking fields and mountains. At night, torches are lit in those fields, lending a mysterious air to the views from the resort's restaurants. The location gives full access to the picturesque Mae Rim Valley, which guests can explore by borrowing a complimentary mountain bike. If you're worried about being far from Chiang Mai, there are regular shuttles to and from the main business and shopping district. There's even a fine cooking school. The *pièce de résistance* is the luxurious Lanna Spa, which offers a standard of luxury and service without rival in the region.

Mae Rim–Samoeng Old Rd., Mae Rim, Chiang Mai 50180 (20 min. north of city off Chiang Mai–Mae Rim Rd.). (C) 800/545-4000 in the U.S., or 05329-8181. Fax 05329-8190. www.fourseasons.com. 80 units. US$425–US$525 (£234–£289) pavilion suite; from US$1,050 (£578) residence suite. AE, DC, MC, V. **Amenities:** 3 restaurants; bar; 2 pools; 2 outdoor lighted grass tennis courts; fitness center w/sauna and steam; spa w/steam, massage, and salon; complimentary mountain bikes; children's activities; concierge; car rental; shuttle to town; business center; 24-hr. room service; babysitting; laundry service; dry cleaning; library. *In room:* A/C, satellite TV w/in-house movies, minibar, fridge, hair dryer, safe, IDD phone.

WHERE TO DINE
Northern-style cuisine, called Lanna, is influenced by the Burmese and other ethnic minorities who live in the area. Among the most distinctive northern Thai dishes are *khao miao* (glutinous or sticky rice), often served in a knotted banana leaf; *sai ua* (Chiang Mai sausage); *khao soi* (a spicy, curried broth with vegetables and glass noodles); as well as many other slightly sweet meat and fish curries. The formal northern meal is called *khan toke*, referring to the custom of sharing a variety of main courses (eaten with the hands) with guests seated around *khan toke* (low, lacquered teak tables).

NEAR THE PING RIVER
Expensive
Le Coq d'Or 🌂🌂 FRENCH   In a romantic English country house setting, Le Coq d'Or is second to none in Chiang Mai for excellent atmosphere, food, presentation, and service. Professional waiters serve from a list of imported beef, lamb, and fish

prepared in French and Continental styles. Presentation is done on fine white linen and real china. Try the chateaubriand, rare, with a delicate gravy and béarnaise on the side. The poached Norwegian salmon is a fine light choice. For starters, try the foie gras or a unique salmon tartar wrapped in smoked filet and served with toast, a sour-cream-and-horseradish sauce, and capers. A nice wine list complements the meal. Don't wait for a special occasion.

68/1 Koh Klang Rd. (5-min. drive south of the Westin, following the river). ✆ **05328-2024**. Reservations recommended for weekend dinners. Main courses 650B–3,600B (US$16–US$90/£9.10–£50). AE, DC, MC, V. Daily noon–2pm and 6:30–10:30pm.

Moderate

The Gallery ✿ THAI
Built in 1892 and one of the oldest original wooden structures in Chiang Mai, the Gallery is the most tranquil and romantic of the choice riverside restaurants on the eastern bank of the Ping River. This was the auspicious spot where, during her visit to Chiang Mai in 1996, Hillary Clinton chose to set sail her float at the Loi Kratong Festival. The menu offers a nice mix of northern Thai specialties and more traditional Thai dishes. Candlelight, soft Thai music, and a great view of the river and the city's twinkling lights beyond top off a lovely evening of dining. If you're in the mood for after-dinner jazz, stop by the attached Tha Chang Jazz Club, with nightly live performances.

25–29 Charoenrat Rd. (east side of river, north of Narawatt Bridge). ✆ **05324-8601-1**. Main courses 60B–450B (US$1.50–US$11/£0.80–£6.30). AE, MC, V. Daily noon–1am.

The House ✿✿ PACIFIC RIM/FUSION
This cozy bistro is set in an old colonial-style edifice decorated in placid pale tones, with seating in rattan chairs around linen-draped tables. The menu is a constantly evolving roster of regionally influenced classical dishes, grilled items, imported steaks, lamb, and seafood when available fresh. A good stop for a light lunch when touring or an evening of fine dining.

199 Moonmuang Rd. (just north of Tha Pae Gate on the inside edge of the city moat). ✆ **05341-9011**. Main courses 290B–950B (US$7.25–US$24/£4.05–£13). AE, DC, MC, V. Daily 11am–2:30pm and 6–10:30pm.

Le Grand Lanna ✿✿ THAI
Chiang Mai's most opulent Thai restaurant is indeed grand. In the shopping area of Sankampaeng Road, Le Grand Lanna is set on a large parcel of lush terrain. Diners choose from the deluxe Lanna Thai pavilions, various open deck areas, pondside courtyards among banyan trees, and unique theme rooms. Evening meals are all candlelight, outdoor torches, and the dulcet tones of traditional music. The fine Thai cuisine is very affordable. Try the whitefish with lemon-coleslaw marinade, one of the delicious and varied curries, or the *gaeng hang lan mop,* a dry, fiery red curry that will knock your socks off (best mollified by a sweet mango chutney). Follow up with great homemade ice cream in local litchi or taro flavors.

51/4 Chiang Mai–Sankampaeng Rd., Moo 1 T. Tasala (4km/2½ miles east on Charoen Muang near the end of shoppers' row; follow signs and turn right/south down a small lane). ✆ **05311-3300**. Main courses 100B–250B (US$2.50–US$6.25/£1.40–£3.50). AE, MC, V. Daily 11am–10pm.

The Riverside ✿✿ THAI/INTERNATIONAL
Casual and cool is what the Riverside is all about. It's a tavern with riverside terrace views—make sure you get here before the dinner rush so you have your pick of tables. There's live music, from blues to soft rock, plus great Thai and Western food (including burgers) and a full bar. Even if you just stop by for a beer, it's a convivial place that always has a jolly crowd of travelers, locals, and expats. Riverside also operates a dining cruise at 8pm (board at

7:15pm) for just 70B (US$1.75/£1) per person; drinks and dining are a la carte. Call ahead to reserve.

9–11 Charoenrat Rd. (east side of river, north of Narawatt Bridge). ℂ **05324-3239.** Main courses 160B–255B (US$4–US$6.25/£2.25–£3.60). AE, MC, V. Daily 10am–2am.

Ruen Tamarind ⍟ THAI/INTERNATIONAL   Part of the expanding Tamarind Village (see "Where to Stay," above), Ruen Tamarind offers a fine selection of northern Thai cuisine with a couple of international favorites thrown in for the less adventurous. A must-try is the *tort mun pla,* or fried fish cakes, a common dish with a unique twist: The cakes are marinated with small chunks of banana and are served with peanut sauce. Delicious. In the evenings, the restaurant's candlelit tables spread onto the hotel's lovely pool deck. Live jazz is performed every night; Fridays feature traditional Thai dance performances.

At the Tamarind Village, 50/1 Rathcadamnoen Rd., Sriphom (a short walk toward the center of the Old City from Tha Pae Gate). ℂ **05341-8896.** Main courses 130B–220B (US$4.25–US$5.50/£1.80–£3.10). MC, V. Daily 11am–5pm and 7–11pm.

Stefano ⍟ ITALIAN   Stefano is in a busy alley off Tha Pae Road, a lively and popular place with an extensive catalog of northern Italian cuisine, from steaks to excellent pizzas and pastas. Portions are big, the wine list is deep, and there are good daily set menus and specials. Meet lots of young backpackers splashing out after long, rugged journeys in the north.

2/102 Chang Mai Kao Rd. (just to the east of Tha Pae Gate). ℂ **05387-4189.** Main courses 120B–360B (US$3–US$8/£1.70–£5.05). AE, MC, V. Daily 11am–10:30pm.

AROUND THE OLD CITY
Inexpensive
Huen Phen THAI   Huen Phen, near Wat Phra Sing, is an authentic local choice. There's an English menu, but just peek in the open kitchen and see what looks good. The restaurant serves good *kao soi,* Chiang Mai's famed noodle stew, but try the specialty: *khanom jeen namngeua,* a beef stew in a hearty broth. It'll keep you warm when those storms come blowing in off Doi Suthep.

112 Rachamangla Rd. ℂ **05381-4548.** Main courses 15B–50B (US40¢–US$1.25/£0.20–£0.70). No credit cards. Daily 8:30am–4pm.

Mike's Original Burger ⍟⍟ AMERICAN   I've been to nearly 30 countries, but until Mike's came into my life, I had yet to find a cheeseburger that could compare to even an average American burger (McDonald's does not count, by the way). If your kids or husband start whining about eating Thai food every day, this should pacify them for a while. Just a simple street-side counter, Mike's serves hot dogs and excellent teriyaki chicken wraps as well as the aforementioned burgers. This is a place for those who like to eat food that had parents, so if you're a vegetarian, well, you can munch on some condiments. The perfect stop before exploring the wats or after exploring a couple bottles of Beer Singh.

Chaiyaphum Rd. (at corner of Changmoi Rd., just north of Tha Pae Gate). ℂ **086/269-9145.** Main courses 110B–165B (US$2.75–US$4/£1.55–£2.30). Daily 9am–3am.

SNACKS & CAFES
Kalare Food & Shopping Center (89/2 Chang Klan Rd., at Soi 6, behind the Night Bazaar; ℂ **05327-2067**) is where you'll find a small food court next to the nightly Thai culture show; call for hours. **JJ's Coffee Shop & Bakery** (388 Tha Pae Rd.;

℃ 05323-4007) is a popular breakfast spot that also has an extensive menu of sandwiches, burgers, and salads. Right across from the Tha Pae Gate, the **Art Cafe** (291 Tha Pae Rd.; ℃ **05320-6365**) serves everything from pizza to enchiladas and is a good spot for people-watching.

WHAT TO SEE & DO
THE WATS

Chiang Mai has more than 700 temples, the largest concentration outside of Bangkok, and unique little sights are around every corner. In one very full day, you can hit the highlights in Old Chiang Mai if you go by tuk-tuk.

Wat Chedi Luang ⟨⟨⟨ Because this temple is near the Tha Pae Gate, most visitors begin their sightseeing here, where there are two wats of interest. This complex, which briefly housed the Emerald Buddha now at Bangkok's Wat Phra Kaeo, dates from 1411 when the original *chedi* (mound) was built by King Saen Muang Ma. The already-massive edifice was expanded to 84m (276 ft.) in height in the mid-1400s, only to be ruined by a severe earthquake in 1545, just 11 years before Chiang Mai fell to the Burmese. (It was never rebuilt.) A Buddha still graces its exterior, and it's not unusual to spot a saffron-robed monk bowing to it as he circles the chedi.

　　Wat Phan Tao, also on the grounds, has a wooden *wihaan* (spirit house) and *bot* (central shrine in a Buddhist temple), reclining Buddha, and fine carving on the eaves and door. After leaving the temple, walk around to the monks' quarters on the side, taking in the traditional teak northern architecture and delightful landscaping.

Prapokklao Rd., south of Ratchadamnoen Rd. Suggested donation 20B (US50¢/£0.30). Daily 6am–5pm.

Wat Chet Yot (Seven Spires)　　Also called Wat Maha Photharam, Wat Chet Yot is one of the central city's most elegant sites. The chedi was built during the reign of King Tilokkarat in the late 15th century (his remains are in one of the smaller chedis), and in 1477, the World Sangkayana convened here to revise the doctrines of the Buddha. The unusual design of the main rectangular chedi with seven peaks was copied from the Maha Bodhi Temple in Bodh Gaya, India, where the Buddha first achieved enlightenment. The temple also has architectural elements of Burmese, Chinese Yuan, and Ming influence. The extraordinary proportions; the angelic, levitating *devata* (Buddhist spirits) figures carved into the base of the chedi; and the juxtaposition of the other buildings make Wat Chet Yot a masterpiece. The Lanna-style Buddha hidden in the center was sculpted in the mid–15th century; a door inside the niche containing the Buddha leads to the roof on which rests the **Phra Kaen Chan (Sandalwood Buddha).** There is a nice vista from up top, but only men are allowed to ascend the stairs.

On the superhighway near the Chiang Mai National Museum (north of the intersection of Nimanhemin and Huai Kaeo rds., about 1km/half-mile on the left). Suggested donation 20B (US50¢/£0.30). Daily 6am–5pm.

Wat Chiang Man　　Thought to be Chiang Mai's oldest wat, it was built during the 14th century by King Mengrai, the founder of Chiang Mai, on the spot where he first camped. Like many of the wats in Chiang Mai, this complex reflects varied architectural styles. Some of the structures are pure Lanna. Others show influences from as far away as Sri Lanka; notice the typical row of elephant supports. Wat Chiang Man is most famous for its two Buddhas: **Phra Sritang Khamani** (a miniature crystal image also known as the **White Emerald Buddha**) and the marble **Phra Sri-la Buddha.** Unfortunately, the *wihaan* that safeguards these religious sculptures is almost always closed.

North of the intersection of Nimanhemin and Huai Kaeo rds., about 1km (half-mile) on the left.

Wat Phra Singh   This compound was built during the zenith of Chiang Mai's power, and is one of the more venerated shrines in the city. It's still the site of many important religious ceremonies, particularly during the Songkran Festival. More than 700 monks study here, and you will probably find them especially friendly and curious. King Phayu, of Mengrai lineage, built the chedi in 1345, principally to house the cremated remains of King Kamfu, his father. As you enter the grounds, head to the right toward the 14th-century library. Notice the graceful carving and the characteristic roofline with four separate elevations. The sculptural devata figures, in both dancing and meditative poses, are thought to have been made during King Muang Kaeo's reign in the early 16th century. They decorate a stone base designed to keep the fragile *sa* (mulberry bark) manuscripts elevated from flooding and vermin.

On the other side of the temple complex is the 200-year-old Lai Kham (Gilded Hall) Wihaan, housing the venerated image of the **Phra Singh,** or **Sighing Buddha,** brought to the site by King Muang Ma in 1400. The original Buddha's head was stolen in 1922, but the reproduction in its place doesn't diminish the homage paid to this figure during Songkran. Inside are frescoes illustrating the stories of Sang Thong (the Golden Prince of the Conch Shell) and Suwannahong. These images convey a great deal about the religious, civil, and military life of 19th-century Chiang Mai during King Mahotraprathet's reign.

Samlarn and Ratchadamnoen rds. Suggested donation 20B (US50¢/£0.30). Daily 6am–5pm.

Wat Suan Dok   This complex is special less for its architecture (the buildings, though monumental, are undistinguished) than for its contemplative spirit and pleasant surroundings. The temple was built amid the pleasure gardens of the 14th-century Lanna Thai monarch, King Ku Na. Unlike most of Chiang Mai's other wats (more tourist sights than working temples and schools), Wat Suan Dok houses quite a few monks who seem to have isolated themselves from the distractions of the outside world. Among the main attractions in the complex are the bot, with a very impressive **Chiang Saen Buddha** (one of the largest bronzes in the north), dating from 1504, and some garish murals; the chedi, built to hold a relic of the Buddha; and a royal cemetery with some splendid shrines. There is also an informal "monk chat," where monks and lay visitors can share views, every Monday, Wednesday, and Friday from 5 to 7pm. Unique.

Suthep Rd. (from the Old City, take the Suan Dok Gate and continue 1.6km/1 mile west). Suggested donation 20B (US50¢/£0.30). Daily 6am–5pm.

MUSEUMS

Chiang Mai City Arts and Cultural Center   In the building adjacent to the Three Kings Monument in the heart of the Old City, this new museum houses a permanent exhibit that walks visitors through a tour of prehistory to the present. Another section houses short-term local exhibits of all types.

Propokklao Rd. ℂ 05321-7793. Admission 90B (US$2.25/£1.25). Tues–Sun 8:30am–5pm.

Chiang Mai National Museum   While its collection of historic treasures is not nearly as extensive as that of Bangkok's National Museum, this quick stop does provide something of an overview of the region, the city, and its history. The Lanna Kingdom, Tai people, and hill tribes are highlighted in simple displays with English explanations.

Just off the superhighway northwest of the Old City near Wat Chet Yot. ℂ 05322-1308. Admission 30B (US75¢/£0.40). Daily 9am–4pm.

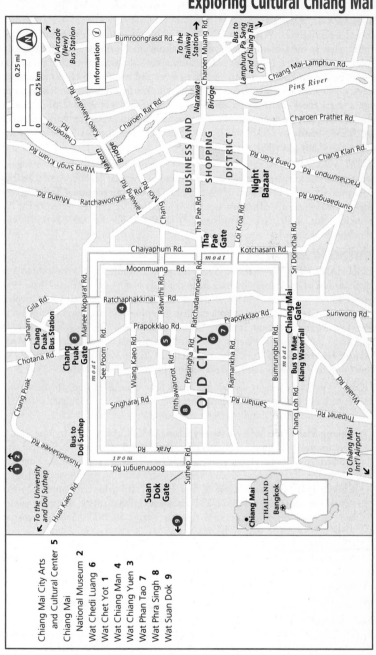

Chiang Mai City Arts
  and Cultural Center **5**
Chiang Mai
  National Museum **2**
Wat Chedi Luang **6**
Wat Chet Yot **1**
Wat Chiang Man **4**
Wat Chiang Yuen **3**
Wat Phan Tao **7**
Wat Phra Singh **8**
Wat Suan Dok **9**

CULTURAL PURSUITS

THAI COOKING   If you love Thai food and want to learn how to make it, look into a class at the **Chiang Mai Cookery School** ☆, the oldest establishment of its kind in Chiang Mai. It has five 1-day courses, each designed to teach Thai cooking basics but with a different menu—of up to seven dishes—so you can attend as many days as you want and still gain quite a bit of skill. You'll have hands-on training and a lot of fun. Classes start at 10am and last until 4pm; they cost 990B (US$25/£14) for the day. Contact the main office at 1–3 Moonmuang Rd., opposite the Tha Pae Gate (© 05320-6388; fax 05320-6387; www.thaicookeryschool.com). Look for the RECOMMENDED BY FROMMER'S sign in the window.

THAI MASSAGE   Northern-style Thai massage is something closer to yoga, in which your muscles are stretched and elongated to enhance flexibility and relaxation. There are a number of schools in Chiang Mai. Try the **International Training Massage (ITM),** where a 5-day course is 3,500B (US$85/£49). Contact the school at 17/7 Morakot Rd., Hah Yaek Santitham (© **05321-8632;** fax 05322-4197; www.itmthaimassage.com).

OUTDOOR ACTIVITIES

ELEPHANT RIDING   One of Thailand's greatest treasures, the domesticated Asian elephant has worked alongside men since the early history of Siam, and these gentle giants are an important symbol of the kingdom. There are a total of 14 elephant camps near Chiang Mai, some with animals in rather dire condition. Far above the rest is the **Young Elephant Training Center,** in Lampang (see "Side Trips from Chiang Mai," below), where visitors work with the animals. Of the others, try **Maetamann Elephant Camp** (535 Rimtai, Maerim, Chiang Mai; © 05329-7060). Day tours include a few hours of hill trekking in a basket on elephant-back.

GOLF   Golf is the activity du jour in Chiang Mai, especially among the many Western retirees and vacationing Thais. All courses below are open to the public and offer equipment rental. Call ahead to reserve a tee time.

- **Chiang Mai Green Valley Country Club,** 183/2 Chotana Rd., in Mae Rim, 20 minutes north of town on Route 107 (© **05329-8249;** fax 05329-7426), is in excellent condition with flat greens and fairways that slope toward the Ping River (greens fees: 1,700B/US$30/£24 weekdays, 2,700B/US$50/£38 weekends).
- **Chiang Mai Highlands Golf & Spa Resort,** 167 Moo 2, Tambol On-Nuar (© **081961-0028;** fax 01951-5233), is a new hillside course about 20 minutes east of town off Highway 1317 (greens fees: 1,400B/US$35/£20 weekdays, 2,500B/US$63/£35 weekends).
- **Chiang Mai–Lamphun Country Club,** Baan Thi Road, 10km (6¼ miles) east of Sankamphaeng (© **05324-8397;** fax 05324-8937), in a valley to the east, is a fine 18-hole course (greens fees: 1,400B/US$35/£20 weekdays, 1,800B/US$45/£25 weekends).

TREKKING   For jungle trekking, a number of outfitters arrange trips from Chiang Mai. **Contact Travel** (73/7 Charoen Prathet Rd., Chiang Mai; © **05327-7178;** fax 05327-9505; www.activethailand.com) is in a category all its own—it can combine treks and village stays with multi-sport adventures by jeep, bicycle, and kayak.

Small operators that cater to the backpacker market offer tours and treks for as little as 500B (US$13/£7) per day. This can mean you'll be in a large group, with care and feeding at a lower standard, but that's budget trekking for you. **Top North Tours**

(41 Moonmuang Rd., Chiang Mai; © 05320-8788) and **Queen Bee Travel Service** (5 Moonmuang Rd. Chiang Mai; © 05327-5525) are both good.

THE SPA SCENE

Most hotels offer massage and beauty treatments, and there are lots of street-side massage places of varying quality and reputation. The **Four Seasons Resort** (Mae Rim–Samoeng Old Rd.; © 05329-8181) has some of the finest spa facilities in Thailand and, though it comes with a high price tag, the quality and service are over the top. **Oasis Spa** (© 05381-500; www.chiangmaioasis.com), with three convenient locations in and around the Old City, is more affordable, has a variety of treatments, and comes highly recommended by the general manager of the Amari Rincome (it was the only spa he visited that didn't offer a "special massage"). **Let's Relax,** in Chiang Mai Pavilion (145/27 Changklan Rd., on the 2nd floor above McDonald's; © 05381-8498), has good rates and makes for a relaxing break from shopping.

SHOPPING

If you plan to shop in Thailand, save your money for Chiang Mai. Quality craft pieces and handmade traditional items still sell for very little, and large outlets for fine antiques and high-end goods abound in and around the city. Many shoppers pick up an affordable new piece of luggage to tote their finds home. If you find that huge standing Buddha or oversize Thai divan you've been searching for, don't worry: All stores can arrange shipping.

The **Night Bazaar** , on Chang Klan Road between the Old Town and the river, is the city's premier attraction. Shopping starts around 6pm each night and slows down at about 11pm. The actual Night Bazaar is a modern, antiseptic, three-story building, but the indoor and outdoor market extends south to Sri Dornchai Road and far beyond. Many shops and stalls remain open throughout the day and evening, too, especially along Chang Klan Road. Some stalls have grandiose names, like Harrods (with the familiar logo), and most carry Bangkok-produced counterfeits of international name-brand clothing, watches, and luggage. There are thousands of pirated audiotapes and videodiscs, acres of burnished brown "bone" objects, masks, woodcarvings, opium pipes, opium weights, you name it.

AROUND THE OLD CITY   Small shops and boutiques line the areas around the Night Bazaar and Old City. Try **Ginger** (39/1 Loi Kroh; © 05320-6842) for fine designer clothing and jewelry. Sleek designs steal the show at **Living Space** (276–278 Tha Pae Rd.; © 05387-4299), with its collection of home furnishings, celadon, and lacquerware. **Nova Collection** (201 Tha Pae Rd.; © 05327-3058) carries a unique line of decorative jewelry in contemporary styles with Asian influences and also has 1- to 5-day courses in jewelry making. **Princess Jewelry** (41 Changklan Rd., near Chiang Inn Plaza; © 05327-3648) offers customized and ready-made jewelry and personalized service. For silk, try **City Silk** (336 Tha Pae Rd., 1 block east of the gate; © 05323-4388).

WEST SIDE   Across from the Amari Rincome Hotel, **Nantawan Arcade** (95 Nimanhemin Rd.) has many notable antiques, crafts, and curio shops that make for fun browsing. **Gong Dee Gallery** (© 05321-5768) has a fine collection of gifts and original artwork, the best of the many here.

SANKAMPHAENG ROAD   Shopaholics will be thrilled by the many outlets along the Chiang Mai–Sankamphaeng Road (Rte. 1006). Rent your own wheels or hop on the white songtaos that follow this busy road due east of town. After several kilometers, you'll reach the many shops, showrooms, and factories extending along a 9km (5½-mile) strip. These feature anything from lacquerware to ready-made clothes, silver to celadon pottery.

For pottery, try **Baan Celadon** (7 Moo 3, Chiang Mai–Sankamphaeng Rd.; ⓒ 05333-8288) and **Siam Celadon** (38 Moo 13, Chiang Mai–Sankamphaeng Rd.; ⓒ 05333-1526). For silver pieces, **Louis Silverware** (99/1 Chiang Mai–Sankamphaeng Rd.; ⓒ 05333-8494) has traditional silversmiths on the premises so you can see the various stages of the jewelry-making process. And the **Thai Silk Village** (120/11 Moo 3, Chiang Mai–Sankamphaeng Rd.; ⓒ 05333-8357) takes you from silkworm to loom to scarf.

CHIANG MAI AFTER DARK

The Night Bazaar area is the center of nighttime activity—there are lots of small bars, clubs, and go-go joints here. If you get tired and hungry along the way, you'll want to stop at **Kalare Food & Shopping Center** (89/2 Chang Klan Rd., at Soi 6, behind the Night Bazaar; ⓒ 05327-2067), which has free cultural dance shows nightly.

For a more studied cultural performance, the **Old Chiang Mai Cultural Center,** 185/3 Wulai Rd. (ⓒ 05327-4093), stages a good show at 7pm every night for 270B (US$6.75/£3.80), which includes dinner. Enjoy a *khan toke* meal accompanied by live music and dance. Yup, it's touristy, but a rollicking good time.

The following are just a few bars and clubs among the many to choose from. **Good View** (13 Charoenrat Rd.; ⓒ 05324-1866) and the **Riverside** (9/11 Charoenrat Rd.; ⓒ 05324-3239) are both popular riverfront restaurants that feature live music.

Directly east of the Night Bazaar and in the large compound of the old Diamond Hotel, **River Bar** (33/11 Jarenprathat Rd.; ⓒ 05320-6169) has live music nightly, as does the equally raucous outdoor **Imperial Mae Ping Beer Garden** (p. 205; 153 Sridonchai Rd.; ⓒ 5328-3900). The **Bubble Disco,** at Pornping Tower Hotel (46 Charoen Prathit Rd.; ⓒ 05327-0099), and the **Crystal Cave Disco,** at the Empress Hotel (p. 206; Chang Klan Rd.; ⓒ 05327-0240), are two popular haunts but seem to take turns getting shut down.

Outside of town in Doi Suthep–Pui National Park, the controversial **Chiang Mai Night Safari** ([tel **05399-9000;** www.chiangmainightsafari.com) offers a chance to ride around in open-air trams and hopefully glimpse some of the 60 species of animals on show, including giraffes, Asian elephants, impalas, perhaps even a cheetah. Rumors of animal deaths due to mishandling and the ill-conceived plan to serve rare species at the park's restaurant have caused public outcries and protests. The park is open Monday through Friday from 1pm to midnight, Saturday and Sunday from 2pm to midnight. Admission is 500B (US$13/£7) for adults and 250B (US$9/£3.50) for children.

SIDE TRIPS FROM CHIANG MAI

If you have time for only a day trip, Wat Phra That Doi Suthep, Chiang Mai's famed mountain and temple, is the best choice.

WAT PHRA THAT DOI SUTHEP ✦✦✦

The jewel of Chiang Mai, Wat Phra That glistens in the sun on the slopes of Doi Suthep mountain. At 1,000m (3,280 ft.), the temple occupies an extraordinary site with a cool refreshing climate, expansive views over the city, and the mountain's idyllic forests, waterfalls, and flowers.

The Mae Hong Son Loop

Seasoned travelers, given the option, never backtrack, and the "loop" through the rugged hills north and west of Chiang Mai is gaining popularity for that very reason. Connecting the towns of Pai and Mae Hong Son, the circuit continues to out-of-the-way Mae Sariang before returning to Chiang Mai. For all but the adventurous, going by tour or by hired car with driver is recommended, though a self-drive means freedom to take side trips and explore at one's own pace. The road, especially in the northernmost points, is serpentine and precipitous, and calls for good driving skills (watch for anything from smoke-belching buses to buffalo). Give yourself 4 days to do it, staying at least a night in each town.

Your first stop is **Pai,** 135km (84 miles) northwest of Chiang Mai. It's a quiet town, with mountains on all sides and a laid-back vibe (lots of travelers get "stuck" here). Overnight rafting trips on the Pai River with **Thai Adventure Rafting** (Rangsiyanon Rd.; ℂ **05369-9111**) are popular July through January.

Guesthouses abound in Pai. Try **Rim Pai Cottages,** in the town center (ℂ **05369-9133**). The one high-end choice is **Belle Villa Resort** (113 Moo 6, Tumol Viengtai; ℂ **05369-8226-7**; www.bellevillaresort.com), just outside of town, with cozy stilted villas starting from 2,707B (US$68/£38).

Between Pai and Mae Hong Son, you'll find the **Lod,** or **Spirit Cave,** some 8km (5 miles) north of the highway. This large, awe-inspiring cave is filled with colorful stalagmites and stalactites; the small caverns will keep you exploring for hours. Hire a guide with a lantern at the entrance; you'll pay 100B (US$2.50/£1.40), plus 200B (US$5/£2.80) for ferry crossings.

Mae Hong Son, the next stop on the loop, sits on the very edge of Myanmar and is the largest town amid the scenic woodlands, waterways, and unique hill-tribe villages of the area. The town is famed for cool weather, an eerie morning mist, and bursts of fall foliage. It's a good base for trekking. Contact **Rose Garden Tours** (86/4 Khunlumprapas Rd.; ℂ/fax **05361-1577**; www.rosegarden-tours.com), which arranges treks and visits to nearby **Padung Villages,** peopled by the famed **"long-necked Karen."**

The best place to stay in town is the luxury **Imperial Tara Mae Hong Son Hotel** (149 Moo 8, Tampon Pang Moo; ℂ **05361-1021**; www.imperial hotels.com), with rooms from US$70 (£39). A good in-town budget choice is **Bai Yoke Chalet** (90 Khunlumprapas, Chong Kham; ℂ **05361-1536**), where you'll pay 950B (US$24/£13) and up.

Mae Sariang is just a cozy river town and the best halfway stopover on the long southern link between Mae Hong Son and Chiang Mai. Driving in the area, along Route 108, takes you past pastoral villages, scenic rolling hills, and a few enticing side trips to small local temples and waterfalls. Mae Sariang offers only basic accommodations; try **Riverhouse Hotel** (77 Langpanich Rd.; ℂ **05362-1201**).

In the 14th century, during the installation of a relic of the Buddha in Wat Suan Dok (in the Old City), the holy object split in two, with one part equaling the original size. A new wat was needed to honor the miracle. King Ku Na placed the new relic on a sacred white elephant and let it wander freely through the hills. The elephant climbed to the top of Doi Suthep, trumpeted three times, made three counterclockwise circles, and knelt down, choosing the site for Wat Phra That.

The site is highly revered, and Thai visitors come to make an offering—usually flowers, candles, incense, and small squares of gold leaf that are applied to a favored Buddha or to the exterior of a chedi—and to be blessed.

The site is open from 7am to 5pm. The suggested donation is 20B (US50¢/£0.30). To get here, take the 35B (US90¢/£0.50) minibus from Chiang Mai's Chang Puak Gate or hire a songtao for 400B (US$10/£5.60) round-trip. It's best to wear long trousers; visitors in shorts are offered a sarong for decency. Also bring a sweater or jacket, as it gets cold up here.

LAMPANG

The sprawling town of Lampang (originally called Khelang Nakhon) was once famous for its exclusive reliance on the horse and carriage for transportation long after the car was introduced. In fact, old-style horse buggies can still be rented near the center of town next to the City Hall. Sprawling Lampang has some of the finest Burmese temples in Thailand, and short tours by horse and carriage, the town's traditional mode of transport, are popular.

About 54km (33 miles) east of town, don't miss the **Young Elephant Training Center** (© **05422-9042**). The center is not a tourist attraction per se—and nothing like the pony-ride atmosphere of most elephant camps. Instead, the focus at the Young Elephant Training Center is on the animals, their care, and their interaction with humans. It has unique programs in which homestay visitors learn how to be elephant mahouts.

DOI INTHANON NATIONAL PARK

Thailand's tallest mountain, **Doi Inthanon**—at 2,563m (8,406 ft.)—is 47km (29 miles) south of Chiang Mai. It crowns a 932-sq.-km (363-sq.-mile) national park filled with impressive waterfalls and wild orchids. There is a road to the summit, and along the way is the 30m-high (98-ft.) **Mae Klang Falls,** a popular picnic spot with food stands. Admission is 200B (US$5/£2.80).

25 Chiang Rai

180km (112 miles) NE of Chiang Mai, 780km (484 miles) NE of Bangkok

Chiang Rai is Thailand's northernmost province. The Mekong River makes its borders with Laos to the east and Myanmar (Burma) to the west. The smaller yet scenic Mae Kok River, which supports many hill-tribe villages along its banks, flows right through the provincial capital of the same name.

Chiang Rai lies some 565m (1,853 ft.) above sea level in a wide fertile valley, and its cool, refreshing climate, tree-lined riverbanks, and popular Night Market lure travelers weary of traffic congestion and pollution in Chiang Mai. Although Chiang Rai has some passable hotels and restaurants and a few small attractions, most just use this as a base for trips to Chiang Saen and the Golden Triangle.

GETTING THERE

BY PLANE **Thai Airways** (© 05321-0431 in Chiang Mai) has four daily flights from Bangkok to Chiang Rai (trip time: 85 min.). **Air Asia** (© 02515-9999) has three daily flights; **Bangkok Airways** (© 05327-6176 in Chiang Mai) has between three and five connections daily. The **Chiang Rai International Airport** (© 05379-3048) is 10km (6¼ miles) north of town. Taxis to town are 200B (US$5/£2.80).

BY BUS Three air-conditioned VIP 24-seat buses leave daily from Bangkok's **Northern Bus Terminal** (© 02936-2852) to Chiang Rai (trip time: 11 hr.; 900B/US$23/£13). Buses leave from Chiang Mai's **Arcade Bus Terminal** (© 05324-2664) roughly every hour between 6am and 5:30pm (trip time: 3½ hr.; 77B/US$1.95/£1 non-A/C; 108B/US$2.70/£1.50 A/C; 194B/US$4.85/£2.70 VIP). Chiang Rai's **Khon Song Bus Terminal** (© 05371-1369) is near the Night Market in the center of town. Tuk-tuks and *samlors* (motorized pedicabs) connect to hotels for 30B to 60B (US75¢–US$1.50/£0.40–£0.85).

BY CAR The fast, not particularly scenic route from Bangkok is Highway 1 north, direct to Chiang Rai. A slow, scenic approach on blacktop mountain roads is Route 107 north from Chiang Mai to Fang, then Route 109 east to Highway 1.

GETTING AROUND

Chiang Rai is a small city, with most services grouped around the main north–south street, Phaholythin Road. The Mae Kok River forms the north edge of town. The bus station is near the central Night Market just off Phaholythin Road. The town is compact enough to explore on foot; however, there are **samlors** and **tuk-tuks,** which charge 30B to 60B (US75¢–US$1.50/£0.40–£0.85) in town.

BY MOTORCYCLE A good choice to get out of town. **Soon Motorcycle,** 197/2 Trirath Rd. (© 05371-4068), charges 150B (US$4/£2.10) for a 100cc motorbike.

BY CAR **Budget** has a branch at the Golden Triangle Inn (see "Where to Stay & Dine," below; 590 Phaholythin Rd.; © 05371-1339), with standard rates beginning at 1,550B (US$38/£22) for a Honda Jazz.

VISITOR INFORMATION

The **TAT** (© 05374-4674) is at 448/16 Singhakai Rd., near Wat Phra Singh on the north side of town. Good free maps and info are available anywhere.

FAST FACTS: CHIANG RAI

To exchange currency, look for the several **banks** on Phaholythin Road in the center of town, open daily from 8:30am to 10pm. The **Overbrook Hospital** (© 05371-1366) is on the north side of town at Singhakai and Trairat roads, west of the TAT. There are a few **Internet cafes** along the main drag, Phaholythin Road, with average service going for 30B (US75¢/£0.40) per hour. The **tourist police** (© 05371-7796) is next to the TAT on Singhakai Road. The **post office** is 2 blocks north of the clock tower on Uttarakit Road.

WHERE TO STAY & DINE

With the exception of the expensive resort across the river, most Chiang Rai hotels are within walking distance of the sights and shopping. As for dining options, after 7pm the **Night Market** is the best for budget eats, but beyond that there are a few good restaurants to choose from.

Look for a branch of Bangkok's **Cabbages & Condoms** (620/25 Thanalai Rd.; ℂ **05371-9167**), a good Thai restaurant that promotes its unique humanitarian work. The **Golden Triangle Cafe** ☆, at the Golden Triangle Inn (see below), serves great regional treats from a menu that is a short course in Thai cuisine. **BaanChivit-Mai Bakery** (ℂ **05371-2357**), conveniently located across from the bus station, offers an all-day breakfast menu, breads and pastries, and Internet service.

Tip: Be sure to sample the town's delicacies, like the huge *ching kong* catfish, caught in April and May; litchis, which ripen in June and July; and the sweet *nanglai* pineapple wine.

EXPENSIVE

Dusit Island Resort, Chiang Rai ☆☆   Chiang Rai's best resort hotel occupies a large delta island in the Mae Kok River and offers comfort at the expense of atmosphere. The lobby is grand, with panoramic views of the water. Rooms are luxuriously appointed with pastel cottons and teak trim. The resort has manicured grounds, a pool, and numerous facilities that make the place quite self-contained. Tenth-floor dining at the Peak offers sweeping views, while the Chinatown restaurant serves good Cantonese. Stop by the Music Room bar in the evening.

1129 Kraisorasit Rd., Amphur Muang, Chiang Rai 57000 (over bridge at northwest corner of town). ℂ 05371-5777. Fax 05371-5801. http://chiangrai.dusit.com. 271 units. 4,000B–6,000B (US$100–US$150/£56–£84) superior/deluxe double; from 8,400B (US$220/£118) suite. AE, DC, MC, V. **Amenities:** 3 restaurants; lounge and pub; outdoor pool; lighted tennis courts; fitness center w/Jacuzzi, sauna, steam, and massage; game room; concierge; tour desk; car rental; limo service; 24-hr. room service; babysitting; laundry service; dry cleaning; nonsmoking rooms; executive-level rooms. *In room:* A/C, satellite TV, minibar, fridge, safe, IDD phone.

MODERATE

Wiang Inn Hotel ☆   The best of the downtown choices, its rooms are clean and spacious with all of the de rigueur Lanna decorations (in case you'd forgotten where you were). It's just a short stroll to the bus station and Night Market, making it a popular stop for tour groups and often full—book ahead.

893 Phaholyothin Rd., Chiang Rai 57000 (just south of the bus station). ℂ 05371-1533. Fax 05371-1877. www.wianginn.com. 260 units. 2,200B–2,800B (US$55–US70/£31–£39) double; from 5,000B (US$125/£70) suite. AE, DC, MC, V. **Amenities:** 2 restaurants; karaoke bar and lobby lounge; outdoor pool; tour desk; limited room service; massage; babysitting; laundry service; dry cleaning. *In room:* A/C, satellite TV, minibar, IDD phone.

INEXPENSIVE

Golden Triangle Inn ☆☆   The Golden Triangle is set in its own quiet little garden patch. Large rooms have terra-cotta floors and traditional-style furniture and decor. The staff is helpful, the Thai restaurant is excellent, and the in-house travel agency, Golden Triangle Tours, is the best choice in town for arranging travel in the area.

590 Phaholyothin Rd., Amphur Muang, Chiang Rai 57000 (2 blocks north of bus station). ℂ 05371-1339. Fax 05371-3963. www.goldenchiangrai.com. 30 units. 800B (US$20/£11) double. MC, V. **Amenities:** Restaurant; tour desk; car rental; laundry service. *In room:* A/C, no phone.

WHAT TO SEE & DO

There are a number of fine wats in town: **Wat Phra Kaeo,** on Trairat Road in the northwest quadrant, is the best known of the northern wats because it once housed the Emerald Buddha now at Bangkok's royal Wat Phra Kaeo. **Wat Phra Singh,** a restored 15th-century temple, is 2 blocks east of Wat Phra Kaeo. The Burmese-style **Wat Doi Tong** (Phra That Chomtong) sits atop a hill above the northwest side of town, up a steep staircase off Kaisornrasit Road, and offers an overview of Chiang Rai and a panorama of the Mae Kok Valley. It's said that King Mengrai himself chose the site for his new Lanna capital from this very hill.

The **Mae Kok River** is one of the most scenic attractions in the area. You can hire a longtail boat for day trips to outlying villages. Most of the **hill-tribe villages** within close range of Chiang Rai have long ago been set up for routine visits by group tours (not recommended), but there are a few good outfitters. The best operation is **Golden Triangle Tours,** at the Golden Triangle Inn, 590 Phaholythin Rd. (© **05371-1339;** www.goldenchiangrai.com). It offers everything from 1-day hill-tribe treks to week-long adventures.

26 Chiang Saen ⊀ & the Golden Triangle

239km (148 miles) NE of Chiang Mai, 935km (580 miles) NE of Bangkok

The small village of **Chiang Saen** has a sleepy, rural charm, as if the waters of the Mekong carried a palpable calm from nearby Myanmar (Burma) and Laos. Chiang Saen was abandoned for the new Lanna Thai capitals of Chiang Rai and then Chiang Mai, in the 13th century, and today the decaying regal wats, crumbling fort walls, and overgrown moat contribute greatly to its appeal. After visiting the museum and local sights, most travelers head west along the Mekong to the **Golden Triangle,** the north's prime attraction. It is actually less mysterious than its reputation and more like a row of souvenir stalls leading to a giant riverside golden Buddha statue, but if you stand at the crook of the river, you can see Laos on the right and Myanmar (Burma) on the left.

GETTING THERE

BY BUS   Buses from Chiang Rai's **Kohn Song Bus Terminal** (© 05371-1224) leave every 15 minutes from 6am to 6pm (trip time: 1½ hr.; 29B/US75¢/£0.40). The bus drops you on Chiang Saen's main street; the museum and temples are within walking distance. Public **songtaos,** or pickups, make frequent trips between Chiang Saen and the Golden Triangle for about 20B (US50¢/£0.30).

BY CAR   Take the superhighway Route 110 north from Chiang Rai to Mae Chan, then Route 1016 northeast to Chiang Saen.

GETTING AROUND

Route 1016 is the village's main street, also called Phaholythin Road, which terminates at the Mekong River. Along the river road there are a few guesthouses, eateries, and souvenir, clothing, and food stalls.

BY BICYCLE/MOTORCYCLE   It's a great 45-minute bike ride from Chiang Saen to the prime nearby attraction, the Golden Triangle. The roads are well paved and pretty flat. You'll see a few rental outlets along the river that charge 40B (US$1/£0.55) per day.

BY SAMLOR   Motorized pedicabs hover by the bus stop in town to take you to the Golden Triangle for 60B (US$1.50/£0.85) one-way.

BY SONGTAO   These pickup-truck taxis can be found on the main street across from the market; rides to the Golden Triangle cost only 20B (US50¢/£0.30).

BY LONGTAIL BOAT   Longtail-boat captains wait down by the river and offer Golden Triangle tours to visitors. One popular option is a trip to the Golden Triangle with a short stop at a Lao village on the way, costing 800B (US$20/£11) for 2 hours.

The village is just a couple of market stalls, but you can find interesting cheap Chinese goods, Lao silks, or the "I bought this in Laos" souvenir. Others enjoy the half-hour cruise upriver, take a walk around the village of Sob Ruak after they've seen the Golden Triangle, and then continue on by bus.

VISITOR INFORMATION

The nearest **TAT** office is in Chiang Rai. You can pick up a useful map at the Chiang Saen National Museum (see below).

FAST FACTS: CHIANG SAEN

There's a **Siam Commercial Bank** in the center of the main street, Phaholythin Road (Rte. 1016), close to the bus stop and **post office.** You'll also see a currency-exchange booth at the Golden Triangle.

WHERE TO STAY
VERY EXPENSIVE

For a truly unique experience, consider a stay at the **Four Seasons Tented Camp Golden Triangle** (© 05391-0200; www.fourseasons.com/goldentriangle), a super-luxe, super-exclusive resort. Getting to the camp requires a Kurtzian ride up the Mekong; once there, you will be pampered and wined and dined between *mahout* (elephant riding) classes.

Anantara Resort Golden Triangle ⋆⋆   The Anantara is a triumph of upscale local design. Every detail will remind you that you're in the scenic hill-tribe region: The resort features fine local weavings, carved teak panels, and expansive views of the juncture of the Ruak and Mekong Rivers. The balconied guest rooms have splendid views and are so spacious and private, you'll feel like you're in your own bungalow. Tiled foyers lead to large bathrooms; the bedrooms are furnished in teak and traditional fabrics.

229 Moo 1, Chiang Saen 57150 (above river, 12km/7½ miles northwest of Chiang Saen). © **800/225-5843** in the U.S., or 05378-4084. Fax 05378-4090. www.anantara.com. 90 units. US$299 (£164) double; US$449 (£247) suite. AE, DC, MC, V. **Amenities:** 3 restaurants; lounge and bar; outdoor pool; outdoor lighted tennis courts; fitness center; Mandara Spa; Jacuzzi; sauna; bike rental; concierge; tour desk; car rental; limo service; business center; shopping arcade; salon; limited room service; massage; babysitting; laundry service. *In room:* A/C, satellite TV w/in-house movies, minibar, fridge, coffee/tea-making facilities, hair dryer, safe, IDD phone.

MODERATE/INEXPENSIVE

The next step down from the luxurious Anantara Resort is the **Imperial Golden Triangle Resort** (222 Golden Triangle, Sob Ruak; © **05378-4001;** www.imperial hotels.com), about 11km (7 miles) northwest of Chiang Saen. It's a clean but uninspired hotel, with rooms starting at 2,000B (US$50/£28). There are great views of the river from the top floor. In tiny Chiang Saen, the **Chiang Saen River Hill Hotel** (714 Moo 3 Tambol Viang; © **05365-0826**) has clean, basic air-conditioned rooms from 1,100B (US$28/£15). It's a 5-minute samlor ride from the bus stop.

WHAT TO SEE & DO

Allow a half-day to see all of Chiang Saen's historic sights before exploring the Golden Triangle. The **Chiang Saen National Museum** (702 Phaholythin Rd.; © **05377-7102;** closed Mon–Tues) is a good first stop, with an overview of artifacts from 15th- to 17th-century Lanna Thai. Admission is 30B (US75¢/£0.40).

The temples of Chiang Saen are all within walking distance. **Wat Pa Sak** is the best preserved; the oldest is **Wat Phra Chedi Luang.** All are fine samples of Lanna temples.

Tips **Onward to Laos**

Many make Chiang Rai or Chiang Saen their last port of call in the land of Thai and then head overland to rugged but inviting Laos. It is possible to travel downriver 70km (43 miles) to Chiang Khong, a small border town from which you can catch a boat or bus into the "Land of a Thousand Elephants," Laos. Buses and local songtao also make the connection from either Chiang Rai or Chiang Saen. For more information, see chapter 5, "Laos."

The infamous **Golden Triangle,** 12km (7½ miles) northwest of Chiang Saen, is the point where Thailand, Myanmar (Burma), and Laos meet at the confluence of the broad, slow, and silted Mekong and Mae Ruak rivers. Once a no-man's-land of the international drug trade, the area is a unique vantage point for life in the north.

The **Hall of Opium** ★★ (*©* **05365-2151;** www.goldentrianglepark.org) located 10km (6¼ miles) northwest of Chiang Saen, is a sprawling museum overlooking the Mekong. A visit here provides a walk through the curious cultivation of poppies and the history of the opium trade. There is also information about the Thai war on drugs.

5

Laos

by Jason Armbrecht

Laos is a forgotten land. Most conversations about traveling to Southeast Asia focus on exploring Bangkok, finding the perfectly deserted white-sand beach, or visiting the temples at Angkor Wat. Talk rarely drifts to Laos. Many people may not know it's a viable travel option, much less what there is to see and do here. Part of this ignorance is a result of the shroud of Laos's communist government, which became politically and economically isolated after taking power in 1975. An air of mystery then drifted over the country.

In recent years, more light has shined on Laos, and the world is slowly discovering what the country and its people have to offer. Following in the footsteps of its more prosperous neighbors, Laos is making a concerted effort to build its fledgling tourism industry. One of the poorest countries in the world, Laos's designation by the United Nations as a "least-developed country" ensures an influx of money from both foreign governments and nongovernmental organizations (NGOs) alike.

Although some of this aid money goes to sustain the donor (case in point: the ubiquitous shiny white Range Rovers seen throughout the country), much of it's spent on developing the country's infrastructure. While improving, the roads are still primitive by Western standards—which means getting from point A to point B is, more often than not, an adventure. But for the stout of heart (and iron of stomach), these adventures are part of Laos's allure—they'll take you to

places that are well worth some minor discomfort.

Vientiane, a perennial candidate for the "sleepiest capital in the world" crown, may be shocking to some. But a few days spent wandering the streets and watching the sun set over the Mekong makes a good introduction to "Lao time." A couple hours north of Vientiane, you'll find **Vang Vieng,** a backpacker town set on the Nam Song River. Surrounded by gorgeous karst peaks, Vang Vieng is a great base for kayaking, trekking, and caving. Further north lies **Luang Prabang,** ancient capital and UNESCO National Heritage Site. With its almost three dozen temples, French colonial architecture, and rich history, Luang Prabang is a magical town and not to be missed. In the far north, the **Nam Ha Biodiversity Conservation Area,** in Luang Namtha, offers off-the-beaten-path adventures. The pre-Angkorian temple **Wat Phou** sits in the southern province of Champasak. Finally, remnants of an even older civilization are in evidence at the mysterious **Plain of Jars,** in the heart of Xieng Khouang province.

Sixty percent of Lao people are practicing Buddhists, and that fact colors every facet of life. Temples and stupas dominate the architecture of even the smallest village, and you're sure to spot groups of monks in colorful robes on their early-morning *pintabat,* or alms rounds, especially in Luang Prabang. Buddhist acceptance and compassion play an important part in Lao culture; arguments are the exception, and the *sangha,* or monastic community, fosters a strict moral code. Even the shortest visit to Laos offers unique insight into Buddhist culture.

With recent infrastructure development and rising tourism, many fear for the natural and cultural resources of this peaceful land-locked nation. If Laos follows neighboring Thailand's model, as it does in many areas, its forests and waterways may be further exploited and, by packaging tourism for mass consumption, ethnic villages may become human zoos. Working with United Nations agencies, the Lao government is taking steps to see that rural development proceeds slowly in order to protect these vital resources.

Laos is a place to tread lightly, but foreign travelers are made quite welcome and encouraged to do their part to preserve and participate in cultural practices. The beauty of Laos exists not only along the Mekong at sunset, but also in smiles at the market or impromptu Lao lessons on the street corner, things that are easily missed if you're in a hurry. It's an enchanting land that demands you slow your pace to match its own, and even the shortest visit might add tranquillity to your travels.

1 Getting to Know Laos

THE LAY OF THE LAND

Comprising 147,201 sq. km (57,408 sq. miles), roughly the size of Great Britain or the state of Utah, Laos shares borders with China and Myanmar in the north and the northwest, Cambodia in the south, Thailand in the west, and Vietnam in the east. The country is divided into 16 provinces. Seventy percent of its land is mountain ranges and plateaus, and with an estimated population of nearly 5.7 million, Laos is one of the most sparsely populated countries in Asia. Natural landmarks include the Annamite Mountains along the border with Vietnam, as well as the Mekong River, which flows from China and along Laos's border with Thailand. About 55% of the landscape is pristine tropical forest, sheltering such rare and wild animals as elephants, leopards, the Java mongoose, panthers, gibbons, and black bears.

A LOOK AT THE PAST

Laos can trace its history as a unified state to the Kingdom of Lane Xang Hon Khao ("one million elephants under a white parasol"). Formed in 1353 by an exiled prince named Fa Ngum, its capital was Muang Xiang Thong, later renamed Luang Prabang, or "Great Prabang," in honor of a gold Buddha image *(prabang)* given to the kingdom by the court at Angkor. For 300 years, Lane Xang was an important and powerful trading center, occupying present-day Laos as well as parts of northern Thailand, Vietnam, and Cambodia.

In 1707, a secession crisis caused the kingdom to split into three smaller principalities: Vientiane, Luang Prabang, and Champassak. Over the next 100 years, Siam gradually established domination over these mini-kingdoms, sacking Vientiane in 1828 after a rebellion by their handpicked king.

Toward the end of the 19th century, Siamese hegemony was replaced by French rule. By 1907, through treaty as well as force, Siam was obliged to cede all lands east of the Mekong to the French, who in turn united this territory and named it Laos.

World War II saw the occupation of French Indochina by the Japanese, who forced King Sisavangvong to declare Laos's independence in 1945. Japan's surrender later that year created a power vacuum, which the French and the recently organized Lao Issara

("Free Laos") movement, headed by former prime minister Prince Phetsarath, hoped to fill. Early the next year, the French defeated the combined forces of the Laos Issara and Vietminh, and Prince Phetsarath, along with his half-brothers Prince Souvanna Phouma and Prince Souphannavong, set up a government-in-exile in Thailand.

Over the next 7 years, the French gradually granted sovereignty to Laos, culminating in full independence in 1953. During this period, Souvanna Phouma returned to Laos to negotiate with the French, while Souphannavong (the "Red Prince") set up the Lao Patriotic Front (widely known as the Pathet Lao) in northwestern Vietnam. Accompanying invading Vietminh forces, the Pathet Lao soon established a stronghold in the northeastern town of Sam Neua.

The late 1950s and early 1960s saw numerous attempts at coalition building between the neutralists, rightists, and communists mediated by Prince Phetsarath, but these governments all collapsed. The Second Geneva Convention held in 1961 and 1962 re-established Laos's neutrality and formed another coalition government under Souvanna Phouma. This one failed as well and the country descended into civil war. The Pathet Lao, with help from North Vietnamese troops still in Laos in violation of the Geneva Conventions, took control over most of eastern and northeastern Laos.

As the civil war and the wider Indochina conflict intensified, the U.S. began its secret bombing campaign over eastern Laos, targeting communist bases and the Ho Chi Minh Trail. From 1964 to 1973, the U.S. dropped more tonnage of bombs on Xieng Khouang, Huaphan, and Phongsali provinces than were dropped on the whole of Europe during World War II. It is estimated that an average of one bombing run was flown every 8 minutes for 9 years.

With the U.S. trying to end its involvement in the region, a ceasefire was reached in 1973, and by 1975, with the U.S. fully withdrawn, the whole of Laos fell to the Pathet Lao. The Lao People's Democratic Republic (LPDR) was formed with Kaysone Phomvihane, a longtime behind-the-scenes communist organizer, installed as prime minister and Prince Souphannavong as president. Draconion political and economic policies followed, including the relocation of many members of the previous government, including the royal family, into "re-education camps" (the king died within 4 years). An additional 10% of the population fled the country, with an estimated 250,000 eventually settling in the U.S.

During the 1980s and 1990s, progressively more liberalized economic policies were introduced to stir the stagnant economy, producing a more capitalist system. Tourism was also embraced, as the government could not ignore the tourist boom occurring throughout Southeast Asia, especially in neighboring Thailand. Concerted governmental efforts, as well as improved relations with Thailand and the resultant Thai–Lao Friendship Bridge connecting Nong Khai and Vientiane, have helped Laos court the tourist dollar. While only an estimated 33,000 travelers visited Laos in 1991, over one million arrived in 2005, bringing in almost US$150 million and making tourism one of the leading sources of foreign exchange.

Unfortunately, the relaxation of economic policies has not gone hand in hand with the easing of political controls. Although they have been inept at implementing strict socialist doctrine, the communist People's Revolutionary Party retains a stranglehold on power to this day.

THE LAO PEOPLE & CULTURE

In a recent study, a group of Russian ethnologists estimated that there are more than 100 distinct ethnic groups in Laos, but it is commonly believed that Laotians fall into

Laos

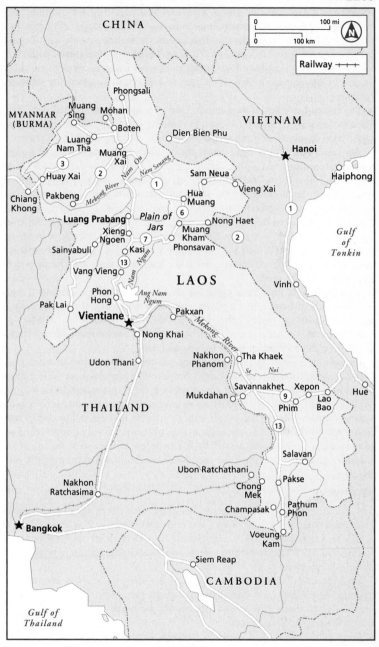

68 different groups. Only 47 groups have been fully researched and identified; sadly, many are disappearing by attrition or intermarriage. All Lao ethnicities fit into one of three categories. The lowlanders are **Lao Loum,** the majority group, who live along the lower Mekong and in Vientiane. The **Lao Theung,** low mountain dwellers, live on mountain slopes, and the **Lao Soung** are the hill tribes, or *montagnards.* Eighty percent of the population lives in villages or small hamlets, practicing subsistence farming.

The earliest Lao religions were animist, and most hill tribes still practice this belief, often in combination with Buddhism. In minority villages, you'll see elaborate spirit gates, small structures of bamboo and wood often depicting weapons to protect the village (tread lightly if you come across one of these markers, as they are of great significance; touching or even photographing them is a major faux pas). Buddhism predominates, though, and 60% to 80% of all Laotians are practicing Theravada Buddhists. In the morning, monks walk the streets collecting food or alms, eagerly given by the Laotians, who believe it will aid them in the next life. Laotians worship regularly and can often be seen making temple visits. Most young males spend at least 3 months in a *wat,* or monastery, usually around the time of puberty or before they marry. Impressive religious art and architecture are created in a singular Lao style, particularly the "standing" or "praying for rain" Buddha, upright with hands pointing straight down at the earth.

Music and dance are integral to the Lao character, and you'll get a taste of it during your stay. Folk or *khaen* music is played with a reed mouth organ, often accompanied by a boxed string instrument. The *lamvong* is the national folk dance, in which participants dance in concentric circles. Don't miss a **Baci ceremony,** in which a circle of celebrants chant and sing to honor or bless an event.

Laotians are friendly and easygoing, but you might find it hard to make a close friend. Language will usually be a barrier. Solo travelers probably have the best chance of making entry into society, and any effort with the Lao language goes a long way. While Laos suffered brutally throughout its colonial history and most horrifically during the Vietnam War, the Lao people want to move on to peace and prosperity rather than dwell on the past. It's very unlikely that an American will be approached with recrimination, but memories are still fresh. Lao people still deal with war fallout literally and figuratively, a result of the unexploded bombs (UXO) that litter 50% of the country.

ETIQUETTE

The Lao are generally tolerant people, but there are a few things to keep in mind. First, upon entering a temple or *wat,* you must always remove your shoes. There will usually be a sign, but a good rule of thumb is to take them off before mounting the last flight of stairs. You should also take off your shoes before entering a private home, unless told otherwise.

Dress modestly. It's unusual to see bare Lao skin above the elbow or even above the midcalf. Longer shorts and even sleeveless tops are permissible for foreigners of both sexes, but short shorts or skirts and bare bosoms and navels will cause stares and possibly offense, especially in a *wat.*

Avoid public displays of affection between men and women. Remember that monks are not permitted to touch women or even to speak directly to them anywhere but inside a temple; therefore, women should never try to shake hands with or even hand something directly to a monk. On buses, you'll find that Lao people will change seats so that monks sit only near men.

The traditional greeting (also a gesture of thanks and farewell) is called the *nop* or *wai,* a slight bow performed with hands in a prayer position. There are many subtleties to the gesture, but best to just return the greeting if you're given one.

The head is considered the most sacred part of the body, while the feet are the lowliest. Therefore, do not casually touch another person's head or even nonchalantly tussle the hair of a child. Don't sit with your legs crossed or otherwise point your feet at something or someone, especially Buddha images. As in most cultures, pointing with the finger is also considered rude; Laotians often use a palms-up hand gesture when signifying direction or indicating a person or thing. If you are seated on the floor, men may sit with the legs crossed, but women should tuck them to one side.

Lao people take a gentle approach to human relationships. A person showing violence or ill temper is regarded with surprise and disapproval. A calm approach will take you further. Patient persistence and a smile always win out, especially when haggling. It is important to haggle, of course, but just one or two go-rounds are usually enough, and "no" means no.

LANGUAGE

The Lao language resembles Thai, with familiar tones and sounds found in each. While some vocabulary words might cross over, the two tongues—spoken and written—are quite distinct. However, many Lao understand Thai (learned from school texts and TV), so if you've picked up some words and phrases in Thailand, they'll still be useful here; people will understand and correct you with the appropriate Lao phrase.

Thankfully, many people in Vientiane and Luang Prabang speak English, and older citizens will usually be able to speak French. Russian is not uncommon, and Chinese is growing in accord with the rising Chinese population (mostly in the north).

Like Thai, Lao has no officially recognized method of Roman alphabet transliteration. As a result, even town and street names have copious spelling irregularities, so for the vocabulary below, only phonetic pronunciations are listed. Most Lao will understand you, even without proper tones, and will appreciate your efforts to speak their language.

When trying to figure out the correct pronunciation of certain names, it's helpful to remember that the original transliteration of Lao was done by francophones, so consider the French pronunciation when faced with a new word. For example, in Vientiane (pronounced wee-en-*chan*), the wide central avenue spelled Lane Xang is pronounced *Lahn Sahng.* Also in Vientiane, Mixay sounds like *Mee*-sigh. Phonexay is *Pawn*-sigh. It takes a while, but it's easy to pick up.

USEFUL LAO PHRASES

Hello	**Sa bai dee**
Good-bye	**Laa gawn**
Thank you	**Khawp jai**
Thank you very much	**Khawp jai lai lai/khawp jai deuh**
You're welcome/it's nothing	**Baw pen nyahng**
No problem	**Baw mi banhaa**

How are you?	**Sa bai dee baw?**
I'm fine/I'm not fine	**Sabai dee/baw sabai**
Yes	**Chow**
No	**Baw/baw men**
Excuse me	**Khaw toht**
I don't understand	**Baw kao jai**
Do you speak English/French?	**Passah Angit/Falang dai baw?**
How do you say that in Lao?	**Ani passah Lao ee-yahng?**
Where is the toilet?	**Hawng nam yoo sai?**
May I wear shoes here?	**Sai gup pen nyanhg baw?**
Where are you going?	**Pai sai?**
I'm going traveling/to the market/to eat	**Pai tiao/pai talat/pai gin kao**
I want to go to . . .	**Koi yak pai . . .**
Do you have . . . ?	**Mii . . . baw?**
drinking water	**nam-deum**
a room	**hawng**
I would like . . .	**Kaaw . . .**
coffee (black)/with cream	**café dahm/café sai nom**
tea	**nam saa**
How much kip/baht/dollar?	**Tao dai keep/baht/dollah?**
Expensive/too expensive	**Paeng/paeng poht**
Can you make it cheaper?	**Loht dai baw?**
Help!	**Soi neh!**
Call the police!	**Toh–ha tam louat!**

2 The Best of Laos in 1 Week

Tourism in Laos is still a relatively new phenomenon and as such, the number of tourist "spots" is still very limited. The only stop that must be included on any Laos itinerary is the ancient capital of Luang Prabang. While some visitors get stuck for weeks or even months in Luang Prabang, the suggested plan below calls for only a couple of days there out of 1 week in the country. This gives you enough time to hit the two most important and interesting cities, Vientiane and Luang Prabang, as well as mix in some outdoor adventure along the caves and rivers in and around Vang Vieng.

Days ❶–❷: Vientiane 🐸🐸

If you're arriving from Bangkok, the capital will most likely be the site of your introduction to Laos time. Stay at the **Settha Palace,** the most luxurious downtown hotel. Get used to the pace of the sleepiest capital in the world by walking the tree-lined streets. Head over to the **Morning Market,** home of the best bargain handmade silks and handicrafts in Laos, and bargain hard (and politely). Afterwards, sip a Beer Lao at one of the makeshift bars and restaurants lining the Mekong River and watch the sun set over neighboring Thailand. Head back to your hotel and cap off the night with the fine French cuisine at **La Belle Epoque.** The next morning, hire a jumbo and visit the odd but fascinating statues at the **Buddha Park,** followed by stops at **Wat Si Saket,** home to over 10,000 Buddha statues, and the golden **Phra That Luang.** Spend the rest of the afternoon ducking into the many silk and clothing stores lining the streets near the riverfront. For dinner, experience the best of Lao cuisine at **Kua Lao.** After your meal, hear the latest travel news and gossip at **Khop Chai Deu.**

Days ❸–❹: Vang Vieng ⋆

Take the early bus to Vang Vieng, a 4-hour journey. Once settled, get a local map from your hotel, rent a bicycle, and trek out to **Phu Kham Cave,** stopping at some of the smaller caves along the way. Spend your evening by the river watching the sun dip behind the distant karst peaks. For your second day, set up a **kayaking** tour on the Nam Song River with Green Discovery.

Days ❺–❼: Luang Prabang ⋆⋆⋆

An early morning minibus on winding roads through beautiful mountain scenery (keep your camera within reach) drops you off in Luang Prabang before dinner. The long journey will leave you a little worse for the wear, so splurge and have a mind-erasing spa treatment at **La Résidence Phou Vao.** Wake up at dawn and **make merit** by giving rice to the monks receiving their daily alms. Stroll the streets of the temple district and admire the glass mosaics at **Wat Xieng Thong.** Duck into any of the numerous smaller temples and chat with one of the novice monks in residence. After lunch, get a break from the heat at the **Royal Palace Museum.** Then cross the street and hike to the top of **Mount Phousi** to enjoy the panoramic view. Spend the evening dining at **L'Elephant,** followed by a stroll through the **Night Market.** The next morning, take a longtail boat up the Mekong to the **Pak Ou Caves.** Spend the afternoon back in the temple district, soaking up the atmosphere at a street-side cafe and, at dusk, listening to the monks chant their evening prayers.

Day ❽: Try to Leave

As hard as it might be to accept, the real world beckons. Say goodbye to Lao time. Fly to Bangkok and connect with your return flight home.

3 Planning Your Trip to Laos

VISITOR INFORMATION

The Lao Tourism Authority serves as more of an administrative arm of the government than an information service for visitors. It provides some basic brochures if contacted at the **National Tourism Authority of Lao P.D.R.,** 08/02 Lane Xang Ave., P.O. Box 2511, Vientiane, Lao P.D.R. (✆ **021/212-248** or 021/212-251; fax 021/212-769; www.tourismlaos.gov.la). The information office in Vientiane has a few good English speakers and is not a bad place to start.

   Sayo Magazine (www.sayolaos.com) is available at hotels and bookstores for US$2.50/£1.40 and features articles on local dining, fashion, and happenings.

   The official Visit Laos website, **www.visit-laos.com,** is sponsored by both the Lao government and private organizations. This site is detailed and accurate, and provides links to other sources of information in the region. For current domestic and international news and government affairs, log on to **www.laoembassy.com,** sponsored and maintained by the Lao Embassy in Washington, D.C. Below are Lao embassy and consulate locations overseas.

- **In the U.S.:** 2222 S St. NW, Washington, DC 20008 (© **202/332-6416;** fax 202/332-4923; www.laoembassy.com); or 317 E. 51st St., New York, NY 10022 (© **212/832-2734;** fax 212/750-0039; www.laoembassy.com/laomission/index.html).
- **In Australia:** 1 Dalmain Crescent, O'Malley, Canberra, ACT 2606 (© **02/6286-4595;** fax 02/6290-1910).
- **In Thailand:** 520/502/1–3 Soi Sahakarnpramoon, Wangthonglang, Bangkok 10310, Pracha Uthit Road (end of Soi Ramkhamhaeng 39; © **539-6667-8** or 539-7341; fax 539-3827 or 539-6678; www.bkklaoembassy.com).

ORGANIZED TOURS & TRAVEL AGENTS

In chapter 3, we've outlined major tour operators that organize trips throughout the region (see p. 58). Getting around underdeveloped Laos can be difficult, making organized travel the simplest option here.

Independent travel is quite feasible, though, and the same companies that organize group tours can help with hotel and travel arrangements and even create independent tour itineraries.

The most established and widely represented agencies provide basic, mainstream tours to most provinces for either short trips or extended visits. Destinations include in and around Vientiane, Luang Prabang, Xieng Khouang (Plain of Jars), and Champasak, plus visits to Laos's hill tribes, adventure trips, and ecotourism excursions. When arranging travel with even the larger tour operators, be absolutely clear about the specifics (meals included, driver's expenses, taxes, and so forth). Many tour companies offer the world and come up short. Below are recommended tour operators that offer Laos itineraries.

- **Diethelm Travel,** Namphu Square, Setthathirat Road, P.O. Box 2657, Vientiane (© **021/213-833;** fax 021/217-151 or 021/216-204; www.diethelmtravel.com), is open Monday through Friday from 8am to noon and 1:30 to 5pm, Saturday from 8am to noon, and operates almost like a de facto tourist information and help center. The folks here are the most professional in the country and can arrange deluxe, personalized trips that cover all the necessities. Offices are in all major towns (locations are listed in the sections on each town in this chapter).
- **Exotissimo Travel,** Pangkham Street, Vientiane (© **021/241-861** or 021/215-920; fax 021/262-001; www.exotissimo.com), is a slick and helpful French-owned company. It offers fine upscale group, individual, classic, and ecotourism itineraries.
- **Inter-Lao Tourism,** 07/073 Luang Prabang Rd., P.O. Box 2912, Vientiane (© **021/214-832** or 021/219-249; fax 021/216-306; www.interlao.laopdr.com), is helpful and has convenient offices in Luang Prabang and Xieng Khouang.
- **Green Discovery,** 54 Setthathirat Rd., Nam Phu Fountain Circle, Vientiane (© **021/223-022;** www.greendiscoverylaos.com), offers exciting rafting, kayaking, climbing, cycling, and trekking excursions ranging from 1-day trips to 1-month expeditions. The helpful international staff caters to both budget travelers and well-heeled adventurers.

ENTRY REQUIREMENTS

Visitors need a valid passport and visa to visit Laos. There are a number of entry sites where visas are granted upon arrival: by air to Vientiane or Luang Prabang, or when crossing from Thailand over the Friendship Bridge between Vientiane and Nong

> ⌒ *Tips* **Booking Air Travel in Laos**
>
> Making your own air arrangements from Vientiane or Luang Prabang is simple, and most travel offices can help for a small fee.
>
> **Lao Airlines** has offices in Vientiane at 2 Pangkham Rd. (✆ **021/212-057,** or 021/214-427 for reservations; www.laoairlines.com), the best place to book domestic flights. Smaller booking offices, like **Lao Air Booking Co.** (44/3 Setthathirat Rd., just south of Namphu in Vientiane; ✆ **021/216-761**) or **Blue Bird** (2 Pangkham Rd., across from the Lao Airlines office; bluebird@laotel.com), are good choices for purchasing regional connections on international carriers.

Khai, or between Chiang Khong and Houayxai in the far north, and Mukdaharn and Savannakhet or Chong Mek and Vung Tao (near Pakse) in the far south. When coming from Vietnam, be sure to have a prearranged visa. A 30-day visa costs US$30 (£17). At an embassy outside of Laos, the going rate for a 30-day visa is US$35 (£19), and you'll have to wait up to 5 days for processing (less in Bangkok). For a fee, travel agents in Thailand and other countries in the region can help you jump over the bureaucratic hurdles and get a visa in 1 day. Check the Lao Embassy site at **www.laoembassy.com** for details.

Once in Laos, you can extend your visa up to 30 days at US$2 (£1.10) per day. It's best to do this through a travel agent. Many hotels, guesthouses, and tour operators offer the service as well; **Diethelm Travel,** described above, has a counter devoted solely to visa affairs. **Lao Tourism** (08/02 Lane Xang Ave., adjacent to the National Tourism Authority; ✆ **021/216-671**) is a government agency and a good choice.

Visa overstay costs US$5 (£2.75) per day, levied when you exit the country.

CUSTOMS REGULATIONS

You may bring 500 cigarettes, 100 cigars, or 500g of tobacco; 1 liter of alcohol; two bottles of wine; and unlimited amounts of money, all for personal use, into Laos without taxation or penalty—not that the Customs officials do much, if any, searching. However, if you purchase silver or copper items during your stay, you might be required to pay duty upon exiting Laos, according to their weight. Antiques, especially Buddha images or parts thereof, are not permitted to leave the country.

MONEY

The **kip** (pronounced *keep*), the official Lao unit of currency, comes in denominations of 500, 1,000, 2,000, 5,000, and, only recently issued by the Lao government, 10,000 and 20,000 notes. The new notes are an improvement, but with the current exchange rate (at press time, **10,000 kip = US$1**), that still means that the largest unit of currency is just US$2/£1.10. For your larger purchases, you'll want to use **U.S. dollars,** accepted widely, or **Thai baht,** commonly accepted but more popular near the border. Be prepared to handle bricks of Lao cash when you exchange foreign currency.

Laos is still very much a cash country, especially outside Vientiane. Virtually all hotel and guesthouse rates, upmarket restaurant prices, transportation charges, and expensive items' price tags are quoted in U.S. dollars. Use kip for smaller purchases, local transportation, and pocket money. Remember to exchange your kip into dollars or baht before leaving Laos. Kip cannot be exchanged outside of the country.

CURRENCY EXCHANGE   You can exchange currency at Wattay International Airport, hotels, banks, and on the black market, with the rate of exchange worst at hotels and best on the black market (though the difference is negligible). Because the U.S. dollar is so widely accepted, it's not a bad idea to change traveler's checks to dollars at a major bank (usually for a 2% fee) before going for any extended time out of the larger towns.

TRAVELER'S CHECKS   Traveler's checks in U.S. dollars and other major currencies are accepted in all banks in Vientiane and Luang Prabang, and some in Xieng Khouang and Pakse, but rarely by vendors.

CREDIT CARDS   Credit cards are gaining wider acceptance at hotels and restaurants, but the majority are still cash-only. Lao Airlines accepts American Express, MasterCard, and Visa. You can get cash advances on your Visa card at **La Banque Pour Le Commerce Extérieur Lao (BCEL)** and at **Lane Xang Bank** branches in larger towns throughout the country. Both banks have local ATM service but have yet to make the international link.

To report a lost or stolen American Express card, contact **Diethelm Travel,** Setthathirat Road, Namphu Square, Vientiane (© **021/213-833** or 021/215-920; www.diethelmtravel.com). For other cards, call the hot lines in Bangkok (p. 96).

WHEN TO GO

High season for tourism is November through March and the month of August, when weather conditions are favorable, plus the Lao New Year in the middle of April. Accommodations run at full capacity and transportation can be overbooked at these times.

CLIMATE   Laos's tropical climate ushers in a wet monsoon season lasting from early May through October, followed by a dry season from November through April. In Vientiane, average temperatures range from 71°F (22°C) in January to 84°F (29°C) in April. The northern regions, which include Xieng Khouang, get chilly from November to February and can approach freezing temperatures at night in mountainous areas. Beginning in mid-February, temperatures gradually climb, and April can see temperatures over 100°F (38°C). In order to avoid the rain and heat, the best time to visit the south is probably November through February. In the mountains of the north, May through July means still-comfortable temperatures.

PUBLIC HOLIDAYS & EVENTS   Businesses and government offices close for these holidays, but restaurants remain open. Ask about local festivals; on the full moon of each month, called a *boun,* there's always a festival somewhere—not to be missed.

- **International New Year's Day:** January 1, nationwide. Your standard countdown and party, sans Dick Clark.
- **Lao New Year (Pimai Lao):** Full moon in mid-April, nationwide. The Luang Prabang festivities include a procession, a fair, a sand-castle competition on the Mekong, a Miss New Year pageant, folk performances, and cultural shows. Make sure you're booked and confirmed in hotels before you go.
- **Buddhist Lent (Boun Khao Phansaa):** At local temples, worshippers in brightly colored silks greet the dawn on Buddhist Lent by offering gifts to the monks and pouring water into the ground as a gesture of offering to their ancestors. Lent begins in July and lasts 3 months. Monks are meant to stay at their temple throughout this time, for more rigorous practice. Lent ends in the joyous **Boun**

Ok Phansa holiday in September, usually commemorated with boat races (below), carnivals, and the release of hundreds of candle-bearing paper and bamboo floats on the country's rivers.

- **Dragon Boat Races (Bun Song Hua):** Held at different times in late summer and early fall in every riverside town, these races celebrate the end of Buddhist Lent. Teams of 50 paddle longboats in a long sprint, and winners parade through town. The **Vientiane Boat Race Festival** (Vientiane and Savannakhet) is held the second weekend in October. The **Luang Prabang Boat Races** are held in early September along the Nam Kan, with a major market day preceding the races and festivities throughout the night on race day.
- **That Luang Festival:** Full moon in early November, Vientiane. This major Buddhist fete draws the faithful countrywide and from nearby Thailand. Before dawn, thousands join in a ceremonial offering and group prayer, followed by a procession. For days afterward, a combined trade fair and carnival offers handicrafts, flowers, games, concerts, and dance shows.
- **Hmong New Year:** End of November/beginning of December, in the north. Although this is not a national holiday, it's celebrated among this northern hill tribe.
- **National Day:** December 2, nationwide. The entire country celebrates a public holiday, while in Vientiane, you'll find parades and dancing at That Luang temple.

HEALTH & SAFETY

HEALTH CONCERNS   See chapter 3's "Health & Safety" section (p. 43) for information on the major health issues that affect travelers to Southeast Asia and recommended precautions for avoiding the most common diseases. It's also a good idea to check the most recent information at the **Centers for Disease Control** (click "Travelers' Health" at **www.cdc.gov**).

No water in Laos is considered potable, so stick with bottled water. Also, Lao cuisine uses many fresh ingredients and garnishes, and condiments made from dried fish that might have been stored under unsanitary conditions. Exercise caution when eating from roadside and market stalls and smaller local restaurants.

In Laos, medical facilities are scarce and rudimentary. Emergency medical facilities exist in Vientiane, but outside the capital you'll require medical evacuation. Contact information is provided under "Fast Facts: Laos," below.

SAFETY CONCERNS   Visitors to Laos should refer to their home country's overseas travel bureau or with the **U.S. State Department** (click "Travel Warnings" at **www.travel.state.gov**) to learn more about the present situation in the area. Laos is not a dangerous destination, but it's important to remember that the current climate of calm and openness to visitors is historically quite new. Visitors should keep an ear to the ground when in country.

Travelers in the countryside should also remember that bus and boat breakdowns are frequent. Additionally, road conditions and poor infrastructure make rural travel unpredictable. Hospital facilities, even in the capital, are rudimentary at best, and any serious medical conditions require evacuation. UXO, unexploded ordnance left from years of conflict, is still a major concern, especially in Xieng Khouang near the Plain of Jars. It should also be mentioned that Lao Airlines has yet to pass any international standards for safety.

Warning: Although the period between 2000 and 2005 saw sporadic attacks by Hmong rebels on buses traveling via Route 13, just north of Vang Vieng, things have quieted down since then and hundreds of the rebels have surrendered to government forces. Still, the threat lingers, and local buses that ply the route have an employee on board with a concealed automatic weapon just in case.

GETTING THERE

Official land borders are with China, Vietnam, and Thailand *only*, and not all border points are open to Western nationals. For example, to China, the crossing point is at Boten, and though it looks encouraging on a map, you cannot cross north of Muang Sing. Similarly, the Laos–Vietnam borders in the north at Dien Bien Phu and Sam Neua are not open; only in the south at Lao Bao can you cross to and from Vietnam.

BY PLANE   Bangkok is Laos's main link with global air routes. In addition, regular flights from neighboring Vietnam and Cambodia make it easy to hop a direct flight from anywhere in Southeast Asia to Vientiane's **Wattay International Airport.** See the individual country chapters for carriers to the destinations mentioned above.

Lao Airlines (formerly Lao Aviation) runs both domestic and international routes. The main office in Vientiane is at 2 Pangkham Rd. (© 021/212-057, or 021/214-427 for reservations; www.laoairlines.com). Lao Airlines connects Vientiane with Bangkok, Chiang Mai, Kunming, Hanoi, Ho Chi Minh City, Phnom Penh, and Siem Reap. It's also possible to fly from Bangkok, Chiang Mai, Hanoi, or Siam Reap directly to Luang Prabang. Other convenient routes link Cambodia (Phnom Penh and Siem Reap) and Pakse. **Thai Airways, Bangkok Airways,** and **Vietnam Airlines** also provide service to Laos. Check www.bangkokair.com for information about new Bangkok Airways routes between the UNESCO World Heritage Sites of Bangkok, Sukhothai, Luang Prabang, and Hue.

Note: There is an international departure tax of US$10/£5.50, payable in any currency (dollars/euros/baht/kip).

BY TRAIN   The State Railway of Thailand's northeastern line originates at Bangkok's Hua Lampong Railway Station (© 02223-7010 or 1690). Running north, it connects many major provincial capitals in Isaan, Thailand's northeastern region, before terminating at Nong Khai, opposite Vientiane.

Once in Nong Khai, hire a tuk-tuk from the train station to the immigration checkpoint at the Thai–Lao Friendship Bridge (about 40B/US$1/£0.55 per person for the trip; open daily 8:30am–5pm). Once across to Laos, you can take a taxi, tuk-tuk, or minibus to Vientiane. Prices are set at 300B/US$7.50/£4.15 for a taxi, 250B/US$6.25/£3.45 for a tuk-tuk, and 350B/US$8.75/£4.80 per person for a minibus. There is also frequent bus service to the Morning Market in Vientiane for just 3,000 kip (US30¢/£0.15). Walk to the bus stop on the far side of the gravel parking lot and wait for the no. 14 bus. Another choice is to hire a tuk-tuk to the Nong Khai bus station and take the Nong Khai/Vientiane bus for 55B/US$1.40/£0.80 (six departures daily).

Connecting with Pakse in the south of Laos is also possible by train from Bangkok via the Thai terminus at Ubon Ratchathani. From Ubon to the Lao border and on to Pakse means two long bus rides (the best you'll get from the Lao border to Pakse is an overcrowded *songthaew,* or pickup truck).

BY BUS   Tourist buses—the VIP, reclining-seat, air-conditioned variety—connect Bangkok and Vientiane via the Friendship Bridge. The overnight trip can be booked through most tour services for about 700B (US$18/£9.60) and will leave you at the Thai side of the border. Buses also run regularly from both Nong Khai and Udonthani, for 55B (US$1.40/£0.80) and 80B (US$2/£1.10) respectively, via the Friendship Bridge.

BY BOAT   The Mekong border crossing between Thailand's Chiang Khong (near Chiang Mai) and Laos's Houayxay is popular. From the border, it's a lazy 2-day boat ride on the Mekong to Luang Prabang (see "Getting Around," below). At the time of this writing, a 15-day visa was available on arrival.

Additional ferry crossing points along the Mekong are between Mukhdahan (Thailand) and Thakhek (Laos), and between Mukhdahan (near Ubon in Thailand) and Chong Mek (Laos).

GETTING AROUND
Navigating on foot through Laos's small cities is easy. You can use taxis and tuk-tuks (covered carts behind motorbikes) in Vientiane, Luang Prabang, and Pakse, or you can rent bicycles and motorbikes in Vientiane, Luang Prabang, and Vang Vieng.

Getting around the country, however, is a different story. Laos's underdeveloped infrastructure begs caution. See "Health & Safety," above, and note the poor road conditions, especially during the rainy season and in the north. Often-overcrowded public transport relegates road and river travel to only the hearty.

That said, these very obstacles are what attract many to traveling in Laos; there's nothing like the feel of pulling into a northern town covered in dust or hopping from a boat to a muddy riverbank in a rural village to be greeted by a friendly delegation of kids. For many, though, the difficulties outweigh (or overshadow) any reward. Arm yourself with the most up-to-date information if you're traveling far out of Vientiane and Luang Prabang, and consider carefully the travel options below.

Tips **Telephone Dialing at a Glance**

- **To place a call from your home country to Laos:** Dial the international access code (011 in the U.S. and Canada, 0011 in Australia, 0170 in New Zealand, 00 in the U.K.), plus Laos's country code (**856**), the city or local area code (**21** for Vientiane, **71** for Luang Prabang), and the phone number (for example, 011 856 21 000-000). *Important note:* Omit the initial "0" in all Laos phone numbers when calling from abroad.

- **To place a call within Laos:** Dial the city or area code preceded by a 0 (the way numbers are listed in this book), and then the local number (for example, 021 000-000).

- **To place a direct international call from Laos:** Dial the international access code (**00**), plus the country code, the area or city code, and the number (for example, to call the U.S., you'd dial 00 1 000/000-0000).

- **International country codes are as follows:** Australia, 61; Cambodia, 855; Canada, 1; Hong Kong, 852; Indonesia, 62; Malaysia, 60; Myanmar, 95; New Zealand, 64; the Philippines, 63; Singapore, 65; Thailand, 66; U.K., 44; U.S., 1; Vietnam, 84.

BY PLANE   Contact **Lao Airlines** (© 021/212-057; www.laoairlines.com) for details on domestic routes. Ticket prices are about US$35/£19 from Luang Prabang to Oudomsay, US$136/£75 from Luang Prabang to Pakse. Lao Airlines accepts payment in U.S. dollars, traveler's checks, Lao kip, and most major credit cards.

   Lao Westcoast Helicopter Company (© 021/512-023) will charter a whirlybird to take you where you need to go, at your convenience. Similarly, **Lao Flying Service** (© 021/222-687; laofly@laotel.com) offers chartered fixed-wing options (strictly small planes) and sells blocks of time and package deals for charter, air taxi, and aerial survey throughout the country.

BY BUS   Korean-made public buses and minibuses connect most towns; however, many areas (especially in the north) are still served only by *songthaew*, four-valve pickup trucks fitted with open-sided covers and bench seats. Private companies handle long-haul routes from Vientiane north to Luang Prabang and south to Savannakhet. Regular buses are often overcrowded, which can mean sitting on a plastic chair in the center aisle with a bag of chickens or pigs wriggling at your feet. These buses stop frequently for new passengers and rest stops at rural roadsides. It's good grist for travel journals, but harrowing. VIP buses, when available, are a good choice. They boast more legroom, they don't overbook, and they keep unscheduled stops to a minimum.

BY CAR   One alternative is to hire a private car with a driver (self-drive vehicles are virtually impossible to find). Contacts for car hires are listed in each corresponding section to follow.

BY BOAT   **Tour boats** operated by **Luang Say Cruises** (© 021/215-958 in Vientiane, or 071/252-553 in Luang Prabang; www.asian-oasis.com) are a luxury option along the Mekong both in the north between Thailand and Luang Prabang and in the south from Pakse. See the appropriate sections for details.

   Riverboats ply the length of the Mekong in Laos, and smaller boats of the longtail variety navigate lesser waterways throughout the country (particularly in the north). On some routes, departures are so infrequent that travelers need to charter boats for themselves, a true exercise in patience. The 2-day **slow boat** from the Thai border town of Houayxay (with an overnight in Pak Beng) is popular.

   Another option is a **speedboat** hire, which gets you there much faster but via a bone-jarring ride that, though brief, is more uncomfortable and much more dangerous than riding the barge (ear plugs are recommended; many opt for the helmets offered, too). Local boats from Pakse to Champasak and farther south are a possibility but are similarly uncomfortable and loosely scheduled.

TIPS ON ACCOMMODATIONS

Book your hotel early during peak season (Aug and Nov–Mar), using travel agents and tour operators as necessary. Also be aware that most hotels in Luang Prabang are full during the Lao New Year, when thousands of tourists, both foreign and Lao, pour into the city for the festivities. Both standards and prices are generally good.

TIPS ON DINING

Lao cuisine is varied and interesting, with sticky rice (or glutinous rice) a staple that, over a longer visit, sometimes loses its appeal through redundancy. Lao fare mixes Thai and Chinese traditions, with a bit of French thrown in for good measure (and a few unique regional favorites). Try it at real restaurants whenever possible—the street stands aren't up to those in neighboring countries. French colonial influence is clear in the many excellent Continental options in Vientiane and Luang Prabang.

TIPS ON SHOPPING

You'll undoubtedly leave with a few pieces of hand-woven Lao textiles, handcrafted silver, and other lovely objects. Many things are one of a kind, so if you see something you like, get it. Remember that the Lao do, of course, haggle. For foreigners, the starting price might be high, but bargaining here is not as relentless as it is in Laos's neighboring countries.

FAST FACTS: Laos

American Express The country's one Amex representative is **Diethelm Travel,** Namphu Square, Setthathirat Road, Vientiane (© **021/213-833** or 021/215-920; www.diethelmtravel.com).

Business Hours With a few exceptions, hours are 8:30am to noon and 1:30 to 5pm Monday through Friday, 8am to noon on Saturday. Restaurants are open from about 11am to 2pm and 6 to 10pm daily; many are closed for lunch on Sunday.

Drug Laws Opium is openly grown in northeast Laos and is easily available, as is marijuana. Neither is legal, and although you might see many travelers indulging, it is highly recommended that you don't. You could face high fines or jail if you're caught.

Electricity Laos runs on 220-volt electrical currents. Plugs are two-pronged, with either round or flat prongs. If you're coming from the U.S. and you must bring electrical appliances, bring your own converter and adapter. Outside of Vientiane and Luang Prabang, electricity is sketchy, and sometimes available for only a few hours a day. A surge protector is a must for laptops.

Embassies **U.S.:** Thatdam Bartholonie Road, Vientiane (© **021/267-000;** fax 021/212-584; http://vientiane.usembassy.gov). **Australia:** Nehru Road, Bane Phonsay, Vientiane (© **021/413-600;** www.laos.embassy.gov.au). The Australian embassy also assists nationals of Canada, New Zealand, and the U.K.

Emergencies In Vientiane, dial © **191** for police, © **190** for fire, and © **195** for an ambulance. For medical evacuation, call **Lao Westcoast Helicopter Company** (© **021/512-023**), in Vientiane.

Hospitals Medical care in Laos is primitive by Western standards. For major problems, most foreigners choose to hop the border to Thailand for the **Nong Khai Wattana General Hospital** (just over the Friendship Bridge). In an emergency, call © **66-42/465-201.** Vientiane has one 24-hour **International Medical Clinic,** Mahosot Hospital, on Fa Ngum Road at the Mekong riverbank (© **021/ 214-022**). For emergency evacuation, call **Lao Westcoast Helicopter Company** (© **021/512-023**), in Vientiane.

Internet Access You can find Internet cafes in the main tourist towns. The cheapest service is found in Vientiane and Luang Prabang, where connections are generally fast. Wireless access is now available in both cities, but connections are slow.

Language The national language of Laos is *Lao,* which is similar to Thai. Many people understand Thai, and in Vientiane and Luang Prabang, many speak

English. A rare few also speak Russian and French, and Mandarin Chinese is growing concurrently with the Chinese population (mostly in the north). See "Language," p. 231, for more information.

Liquor Laws There are no real liquor laws in Laos, but most bars refuse to admit patrons under the age of 18. Bars usually close around midnight.

Mail A letter or postcard should take about 10 days to reach the U.S. Overseas postage runs about 33,000 kip (US$3.30/£1.80) for 100g, and up to 107,000 kip (US$11/£5.90) for 500g. Postcards are 4,000 kip (US40¢/£0.20). The mail service is unreliable, however, so if you're sending something important, use an express-mail service. **FedEx** (✆ 021/223-278) and **DHL** (✆ 021/216-830) have offices in the major cities.

Safety Buddhist Laos is an extremely safe country by any standard. Violent or even petty crime is not a big risk for tourists. There have been rare instances of robbery or rape in remote areas, however. Thus, solo travelers should take care when off the beaten path, even on a day hike. Some of the country's highways, like Route 13 near Kasi and Route 7 in the northeast, have seen rebel and bandit attacks in the past. Although attacks usually target locals, not foreigners, ask around before going too far afield. Of course, petty crime does exist. Watch your belongings, and don't leave valuables in your hotel rooms. When trekking in the north near the Plain of Jars or in the south around the Ho Chi Minh Trail, beware of unexploded bombs. Don't stray into remote areas, and don't touch anything on the ground. See "Health & Safety," p. 237, for more information.

Telephones The international country code for Laos is **856**. International calls are charged at a flat 2,000 kip (US20¢/£0.10) rate. There are just 300 phone booths in the whole country, and only a few can make international calls. Most newer hotels have international direct dialing at surcharges of about 10%. Collect calls are impossible, and the long-distance companies haven't made it to Laos yet. Internet cafes often have Internet phone service at 2,000 kip (US20¢/£0.10) per minute and charge 2,000 kip (US20¢/£0.10) for callback service. See "Telephone Dialing at a Glance," p. 239, for details.

Phone booths in Laos accept only prepaid phone cards, even for local calls. You can buy phone cards at the post office, telephone office, and minimarts. Laos has no coins.

Mobile phones have come to Laos. If you have a GSM phone with a replaceable SIM card, you can arrange prepaid service in any telecom outlet in the country. Coverage is surprisingly extensive. **Lao Telecom** (www.laotel.com) and **Tango** (✆ 021/253-001; www.tangolao.com) are the best and offer a flat international rate of 2,000 kip (US20¢/£0.10) per minute.

Time Zone Laos is 7 hours ahead of Greenwich Mean Time, in the same zone as Bangkok. That makes it 12 hours ahead of the U.S. Eastern Standard Time during the winter months, and 3 hours behind Sydney.

Tipping Tipping has arrived in Laos, particularly in Vientiane. Feel free to tip bellhops, chauffeurs, and tour guides, and to leave 5% to 10% or round up your bill in upscale restaurants. Foreign currency, especially U.S. dollars, is appreciated.

Toilets You'll find Western toilets (sit-down style) in most hotels for foreigners. Out in the boonies, it's mostly the Asian-style "squatty-potty" toilets. Bring your own toilet paper; sanitary hand wipes or lotions are a good idea, too. You'll notice a bowl and a pail of water nearby for flushing (put two or three buckets in). On rural roads, buses just pull to the side for bathroom breaks. In villages, find a convenient tree.

Water Drink only boiled or bottled water, available everywhere for 1,000 kip (US10¢/£0.06). Be wary of ice in any but the finest restaurants. Some people even use boiled or bottled water for tooth brushing.

4 Vientiane ★★

Vientiane (wee-en-*chan*) is one of the few world capitals that lack the look and feel of what most Westerners would consider a "city," much less a capital. Quiet, provincial, sleepy: These are terms that come to mind on seeing Vientiane for the first time. And if you drive into town, you might not even realize when you're actually in the city proper, as "metropolitan" Vientiane blends seamlessly with the countryside. Just a short ride in any direction from Lane Xang, the main north–south avenue, will quickly carry you into the beginnings of rural Laos.

But for better or worse, the slow march to modernity seems inevitable, as the massive influx of foreign aid and manpower from both foreign governments and NGOs is bound to reshape the city and dramatically affect those who inhabit it. While recent infrastructure and telecommunications improvements portend greater future transformation, change has still come slowly in Vientiane. Traffic is only a trickle on the city center's beautiful tree-lined boulevard, the people are always armed with their easy and ready smiles, and the city is asleep by 11pm every night.

The city was ransacked by the Siamese in 1828, so it lacks some of the ancient history you find in the former capital of Luang Prabang, but many of Vientiane's temples have been beautifully reconstructed. **That Luang** is the preeminent Buddhist temple in the country and the scene of a huge festival every November. The **Patuxay Victory Monument** is a peculiarly Lao version of the Arc de Triomphe. The **Morning Market** comprises a full city block of goods to explore. And the **Mekong**, lined with picturesque colonials and cozy thatched bars, rolls through the very heart of the city and glows pink at sunset—not to be missed. It's worth a stay of several days to take it all in and enjoy Vientiane's laid-back atmosphere—while it lasts.

GETTING THERE

For more information on arriving by plane or by train, see p. 238.

BY PLANE Vientiane is Laos's major international hub for air travel. If you're arriving via **Wattay International Airport** in Vientiane, a taxi to town will cost 50,000 kip (US$5/£2.75).

BY BUS The **Northern Bus Station** (©021/260-555) connects Vientiane with all destinations in Laos. The bus station at the **Morning Market** (© 021/216-507), which is called **Talat Sao** in Lao, is the hub for local buses as well as those linking Vientiane with Nong Khai and Udonthani in Thailand via the Friendship Bridge.

Vientiane

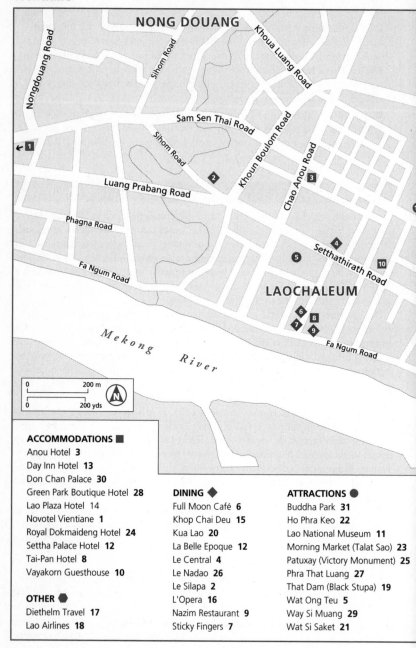

NONG DOUANG

Nongdouang Road
Sihom Road
Khoua Luang Road
Sam Sen Thai Road
Sihom Road
Luang Prabang Road
Khoun Boulom Road
Chao Anou Road
Phagna Road
Fa Ngum Road

LAOCHALEUM

Setthathirath Road
Fa Ngum Road

Mekong River

0   200 m
0   200 yds

ACCOMMODATIONS ■
Anou Hotel **3**
Day Inn Hotel **13**
Don Chan Palace **30**
Green Park Boutique Hotel **28**
Lao Plaza Hotel **14**
Novotel Vientiane **1**
Royal Dokmaideng Hotel **24**
Settha Palace Hotel **12**
Tai-Pan Hotel **8**
Vayakorn Guesthouse **10**

OTHER ⬣
Diethelm Travel **17**
Lao Airlines **18**

DINING ◆
Full Moon Café **6**
Khop Chai Deu **15**
Kua Lao **20**
La Belle Epoque **12**
Le Central **4**
Le Nadao **26**
Le Silapa **2**
L'Opera **16**
Nazim Restaurant **9**
Sticky Fingers **7**

ATTRACTIONS ●
Buddha Park **31**
Ho Phra Keo **22**
Lao National Museum **11**
Morning Market (Talat Sao) **23**
Patuxay (Victory Monument) **25**
Phra That Luang **27**
That Dam (Black Stupa) **19**
Wat Ong Teu **5**
Way Si Muang **29**
Wat Si Saket **21**

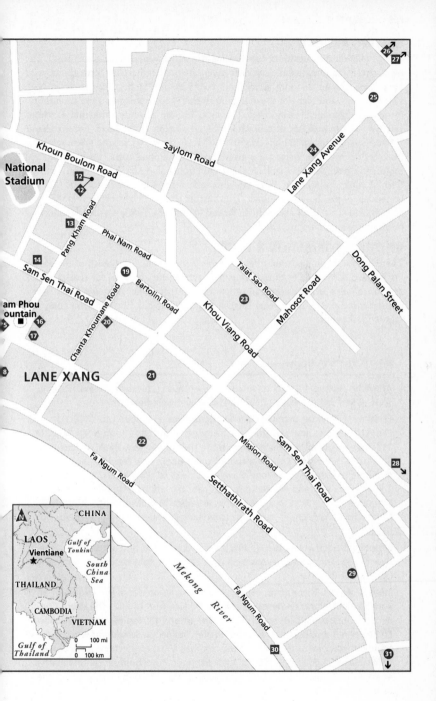

GETTING AROUND

The city lies on the east side of the Mekong River (the western bank is Thailand). The main streets, running parallel to each other, are Samsenthai and Setthathirat, with Lane Xang, the north–south artery, intersecting them. The heart of the city is Nam Phu Fountain, and many of the directions in this chapter are given in relation to it.

Central Vientiane is easily covered on foot. You can also hire a **tuk-tuk,** a covered cart behind a motorbike, or a **jumbo,** a bigger version of the same. Drivers charge about 5,000 kip to 10,000 kip (US50¢–US$1/£0.28–£0.55) around town; settle the price before you ride. Bikes are a great way to get around town. Both bicycle and motorcycle rentals are available at many storefronts along Fa Ngum Road near the river or along Samsenthai. You can also rent a car with driver for 600,000 kip (US$60/£33) per day around town. Trips further afield will cost between US$80 and US$90 (£44–£50). Call **Asia Vehicle Rental** (② 021/217-493; www.avr.laopdr.com) or inquire at any hotel front desk.

VISITOR INFORMATION & TOURS

There is a tourist information office on Lane Xang Avenue, just north of the Morning Market. Also see "Organized Tours & Travel Agents" (p. 234) for tour providers in Laos, all of which have helpful offices in Vientiane. The *Vientiane Times* (www. vientianetimes.org.la) is the local English-language paper, a fun read with good listings of local events.

FAST FACTS: Vientiane

American Express Vientiane's Amex representative is **Diethelm Travel,** Namphu Square, Setthathirat Road (② 021/213-833; www.diethelmtravel.com).

Currency Exchange **Banque Pour Le Commerce Extérieur Lao (BCEL)** is on Pangkham Street down by the river, just west of the Lane Xang Hotel (② 021/ 213-200), or just a short distance from the river at **Lao May Bank,** 39 Pankham St. (② 021/330-001). At these and most other banks, you can exchange money in all major currencies, change traveler's checks to U.S. dollars, and get cash advances on Visa and MasterCard. You can also exchange money at **Banque Setthathirat,** near Wat Mixay. All banks are open Monday through Friday from 8:30am to 3:30pm. Other banks line Lane Xang Avenue; exchange counters dot the city.

Emergencies For police, dial ② 991; for fire, dial ② 190; and for an ambulance, dial ② 195. For medical evacuation, call **Lao Westcoast Helicopter Company** (② 021/512-023).

Internet Access There are numerous Internet cafes on riverside Fa Ngum or on parallel Setthathirat or Samsenthai (each 1 block further from the river). Connections are generally good. Expect to pay around 100 kip per minute (US60¢/ £0.35 per hr.) at most Internet cafes. **Planet Online,** on Settathirat west of the fountain, was one of the first in town and has a fast connection. **Joma Bakery Café** charges 25,000 kip (US$2.50/£1.40) per hour. Hotel business centers charge at least three times this rate. Wireless service has arrived in Vientiane, but the connections are slow and finicky.

Mail The general post office is at the corner of Khou Vieng Road and Lane Xang Avenue, opposite the Morning Market. Hours are Monday through Friday from 8am to noon and 1 to 5pm, Saturday and Sunday from 8am to noon. EMS and FedEx services are just next door.

Telephones The city code for Vientiane is **21**. The central telephone office, where you can place local and international direct dial (IDD) calls, is located on Setthathirat Road just east of Nam Phu Circle (Nam Phu Fountain). It's open from 8am to 10pm daily. You can also send faxes.

WHERE TO STAY

Vientiane has some good options that range from luxury rooms to backpacker dives. Book ahead, especially in late November and early December, and ask for a discount if you come during the rainy season (some places post their low-season rates). Hotels accept U.S. dollars, Lao kip, or Thai baht. Be warned that the prices listed below do not always include a government tax of 10% or any additional service charges (sometimes applicable in high season).

EXPENSIVE

Don Chan Palace ⚅ "It's on the river. You can't miss it." That's all you need to know to find the Don Chan Palace. While Vientiane has a law banning buildings taller than the seven-story Victory Monument, the 14-story Don Chan brushed aside this inconvenience by being built on an island in the Mekong. Set just south of the city business center (a 15-min. walk or short shuttle-bus ride) and resembling a life-sized dollhouse, it really is an awful eyesore. That said, the views of the Mekong and surrounding areas, especially from the rooftop restaurant, are spectacular. With its vast convention hall and extensive business facilities, the Don Chan was clearly designed to cater to the Asian business traveler. Rooms are business-hotel standard, with muted colors and few traditional Lao touches, but they're comfortable nonetheless. The real draw here is the unparalleled views, so ask for a room on the Mekong/sunset side, where you can enjoy the scenery from your own small balcony.

Unit 6 Piawat Village, Sistanak District, Vientiane. ⓒ **021/244-288.** Fax 021/244-111. www.donchanpalacelaopdr. com. 230 units. US$150–US$180 (£83–£99) double; US$300–US$500 (£165–£275) suite. AE, MC, V. **Amenities:** 3 restaurants; bar and disco; bakery; coffee shop; pool; outdoor gym; spa; sauna; steam room; concierge; travel agency; shuttle-bus service (to city center and airport); business center; laundry service. *In room:* A/C, satellite TV, Internet access, minibar, coffeemaker, hair dryer, safe, IDD phone.

Green Park Boutique Hotel ⚅⚅ Combining the traditional and contemporary into a seamless whole can be difficult, but the Green Park has succeeded in doing just that. Raised tile pathways set amongst jar fountains lead from the elegant reception area to the central courtyard, where contemporary Lao-style pavilions surround a lovely swimming pool and adjacent reflecting pool. Stylish guest rooms boast rich wood floors, beautiful Lao silks draped over chic teakwood furniture, and all the modern conveniences, including free wireless Internet access. Cozy balconies have views of the pools and the newly planted frangipani trees that dot the surrounding garden areas. Set next to the undeveloped Nong Chanh Park, Vientiane's largest, and a 15-minute walk to the Morning Market, the Green Park is far enough away to feel secluded but not too far to feel isolated from the city. Add to this tranquil setting an eager-to-please staff that caters to guests' every whim and you get a hotel that has set the bar extremely high for future boutique properties in Vientiane.

248 Khouvieng Rd., P.O. Box 9698, Vientiane. ℂ 021/263-063. Fax 021/263-064. www.greenparkvientiane.com. 34 units. US$115 (£63) classic; US$125 (£69) deluxe; US$250–US$380 (£138–£209) suite. MC, V. **Amenities:** Restaurant; lounge; outdoor pool; spa; Jacuzzi; shuttle service to town; business center; laundry service. *In room:* A/C, satellite TV, wireless Internet access, minibar, coffeemaker, hair dryer, safe, IDD phone.

Lao Plaza Hotel ℛ   Popular with business travelers, the Lao Plaza is the most familiar international hotel in Laos. It's in a convenient central location, and the accommodations are bland but comfortable. Sizable rooms are either beige or blue, with solid wood furniture, thick rugs, firm beds, and small marble-tiled bathrooms with terry-cloth robes. The pool is big and inviting. The May Yuan restaurant has admirable Chinese food, while a cheery cafe has buffet meals and a deli/bakery. The Plaza is sufficiently self-contained and convenient to any destination in town, and one of only a few accommodations in Laos where you might forget that you're in Laos.

63 Samsenthai Rd., P.O. Box 6708, Vientiane. ℂ 021/218-800. Fax 021/218-808. www.laoplazahotel.com. 142 units. US$100–US$120 (£55–£66) superior single/twin; US$130–US$140 (£72–£77) executive single/twin; US$250–US$450 (£138–£248) suite. AE, MC, V. **Amenities:** 2 restaurants; bar; popular nightclub; beer garden; bakery; nice pool; gym; Jacuzzi; sauna; travel agency; car service; business center w/Internet access; bookstore and gift shop; massage; laundry service; conference rooms; nonsmoking rooms. *In room:* A/C, satellite TV, Internet access, minibar, coffeemaker, hair dryer, safe, IDD phone.

Novotel Vientiane ℛ   Just a short ride west of the town center, the Novotel Vientiane is a pleasant oasis from the dusty streets and downtown tuk-tuk clamor. The lobby is decorated in a classic Art Deco theme, with stylish woodwork and a domed ceiling painted in a muted pastel yellow—an attractive invitation to Novotel's fine rooms and services. Renovated deluxe rooms have fine wood furniture and marble bathrooms. Standard rooms are done in pastels with cane furnishings and plain tile bathrooms. Everything is ultratidy. All units feature hangings and artwork that keep your mind in Indochina. Adjoining the lobby is a well-appointed Continental restaurant with indoor and outdoor by-the-pool seating. The staff is friendly and helpful, and the hotel offers a wealth of facilities and services, including use of its smart business center and chic executive lounge. It's a bit far from town but has very convenient amenities and good transportation. The busy disco, Dtec, is always a happening spot.

Unit 9, Samsenthai Rd., P.O. Box 585, Vientiane. ℂ 800/221-4542 or 021/213-570. Fax 021/213-572. www.novotel. com. 201 units. US$90 (£50) superior; US$107 (£59) deluxe; US$450 (£248) suite. AE, MC, V. **Amenities:** Restaurant; 3 bars; nice outdoor pool; tennis; health club; sauna; steam bath; free and frequent transport to the town center; business center w/Internet access; gift shop; 24-hr. room service; massage; babysitting; dry cleaning. *In room:* A/C, satellite TV, Wi-Fi, minibar, coffeemaker, hair dryer, safe, IDD phone.

Settha Palace Hotel ℛℛ   Once the distinguished address for visitors from the adjacent colonies of Indochina, this masterfully restored, early-20th-century French colonial mansion traced a long history of decline before its multimillion-dollar face-lift and 1999 reopening. A small circular drive leads to the columned marble entry, where light coming through the large windows lends a softness to the lobby that is not unlike stepping into a sepia photograph of a distant time. Rooms are cozy, with antique details, dark-wood reproduction furnishings, and stalwart four-poster beds. Bathrooms are small but elegant. If a stay at the Palace is a trip to the past, modern amenities like in-room Internet access and satellite TV will keep you connected in the present. The hotel's elegant restaurant, La Belle Epoque (p. 250), serves excellent Continental cuisine. With service unmatched in town, the Palace offers quality far exceeding its price tag.

6 Pangkham (P.O. Box 161), Vientiane. ℂ **021/217-581.** Fax 021/217-583. www.setthapalace.com. 29 units. US$180 (£99) deluxe; US$280 (£154) junior suite; US$380 (£209) suite. AE, MC, V. **Amenities:** Restaurant; bar; outdoor pool (nonguests welcome for US$4/£2.20); Jacuzzi; car service; business center w/Internet access; room service; laundry service; dry cleaning. *In room:* A/C, satellite TV, Wi-Fi, minibar, safe, IDD phone.

MODERATE

Royal Dokmaideng Hotel ⚿   The Royal is owned and managed by a Taiwanese group and often fills with big groups and conventioneers. The hotel has large rooms that are devoid of character; many are a bit musty or use too much aerosol to cover it up (ask to see the room first). But the spacious suites are good for families, and the Chinese restaurant is bright and inviting, as is the small courtyard pool. With a central location on Lane Xang Avenue, just north of the Morning Market, the Royal Dokmaideng is a favorite for business travelers. Be sure to ask for a nonsmoking room. There's a popular karaoke area on the second floor.

Lane Xang Ave., P.O. Box 3925, Vientiane. ℂ **021/214-455.** Fax 021/214-454. 80 units. US$37–US$47 (£20–£26) double; US$70 (£39) suite. MC, V. **Amenities:** Restaurant; bar; small courtyard pool; basic gym; sauna; laundry service; conference room; nonsmoking rooms. *In room:* A/C, TV, minibar, IDD phone.

Tai-Pan Hotel ⚿ Ⓥ𝑎𝑙𝑢𝑒   This very attractive midsize hotel is convenient to downtown, on a quiet street just off the Mekong, and offers the amenities and service of its larger, high-end competition. Standard rooms are compact, with double beds only, while the deluxe rooms are spacious. All are cheerful, with dark parquet floors and painted wood furniture set against bright yellow walls and floral bedspreads. Sizable bathrooms are done in blinding white, with clean tile and tubs. Ask for a third-floor room with a balcony and river view. With a sister property in Bangkok, the Tai-Pan is popular for business travelers and the long-staying humanitarian workers. The lobby restaurant is tops, the location can't be beat, and the hotel has a new pool and tidy fitness center.

22/3 François Nginn Rd., Ban Mixay, Muong Chanthabury, Vientiane. ℂ **021/216-906.** Fax 021/216-223. www.travelao.com. 44 units. US$74 (£41) double; US$80 (£44) deluxe; US$90 (£50) junior suite; US$102–US$167 (£56–£92) suite. AE, MC, V. **Amenities:** Restaurant; bar; small pool; health club; Jacuzzi; sauna; airport transfer; conference rooms; computer rental; Internet access. *In room:* A/C, satellite TV, minibar, IDD phone.

INEXPENSIVE

Anou Hotel Ⓥ𝑎𝑙𝑢𝑒   Here's a bargain for you: The Anou has clean, bright, good-size rooms, some with tidy beige carpeting and others with hardwood floors. The beds are comfortable and the bathrooms are livable, with tile floors and spiffy marble counters. Some are the shower-in-room variety, without tubs, so let the hotel know if that matters to you. The suites are simply huge, all with wood floors, but they're just oversize versions of the standard rooms (with a larger fridge). The restaurant is inviting, and the hotel has a good location in downtown Chinatown. Surrounded by shops and restaurants, the area is abuzz with activity into the evening and can get pretty noisy.

01–03 Heng Boun St., Vientiane. ℂ **021/213-630.** Fax 021/213-632. www.anouhotel.laopdr.com/anou_services.htm. 40 units. US$20–US$22 (£11–£12) double; US$30 (£17) suite. AE, MC, V. **Amenities:** Restaurant; bar; laundry service. *In room:* A/C, TV, minibar, IDD phone.

Day Inn Hotel ⚿ Ⓕ𝑖𝑛𝑑𝑠   This charming little inn in the shadow of the Lao Plaza was once the Indian embassy, and it retains some of that urban, colonial dignity in its large, airy rooms, with their high ceilings and tall French doors. Though it's all a bit simple, and the bright sea-green color scheme is a little overpowering, you're in an ideal downtown location. Rooms are furnished in basic but tidy wicker, with hard

beds and clean bathrooms (some with a tub). The Day Inn is like an upscale guest-house, really, but it has the standard in-room amenities of a proper hotel. Ask for a room in the front, where doors and windows open to small private balconies. The staff is extremely cheerful and very helpful, making this an all-around pleasant stay.

059/3 Pangkham Rd., P.O. Box 4083, Vientiane. ℂ **021/223-848**. Fax 021/222-984. dayinn@laopdr.com. 25 units. US$27 (£15) single; US$32 (£18) double; US$47 (£26) suite. No credit cards. **Amenities:** Restaurant; laundry service; Internet access in lobby. *In room:* A/C, satellite TV, minibar, safe, IDD phone.

Vayakorn Guesthouse ⭐⭐ *Value*   This is one of the best deals in town. Centrally located and offering nicer digs than many of the more expensive hotels in town, "guesthouse" is a misnomer. Clean, comfortable rooms come with wood floors, soft beds, and spotless shower-only bathrooms. Amenities, as well as views, are almost nonexistent, but you can't complain at these prices. A deal like this is difficult to keep hush-hush and the word has been out for a while, so be sure to book ahead.

091 Nokeo Koummane St., Ban Mixay, Vientiane. ℂ **021/241-911**. vayakone@laotel.com. 22 units. US$15 (£8.25) twin; US$18 (£9.90) double. MC, V. **Amenities:** Restaurant (breakfast only); laundry service. *In room:* A/C, satellite TV.

WHERE TO DINE

French is very big in the Lao capital, and good international restaurants of this ilk actually outnumber those serving Lao fare. You'll find some great, affordable fine dining. A few local specialties to watch out for are *khao poun,* rice vermicelli with vegetables, meat, or chiles, in coconut milk; *laap,* minced meat, chicken, or fish tossed with fresh mint leaves; or a tasty Lao-style pâté. Try sticky rice, eaten with the hands, as an accompaniment to most Lao dishes (it's a thrice-a-day staple for Laotians).

EXPENSIVE

La Belle Epoque ⭐⭐ FRENCH/CONTINENTAL   In the atmospheric Settha Palace Hotel (p. 248), you can't beat the atmosphere of La Belle Epoque—colonial elegance mixed with Vientiane's laid-back charm. The service is efficient, and the menu covers a wide range of Continental specialties, with meat, game, and seafood prepared to order. Imported Australian steaks and salmon top a fine list of specialties, like grilled lamb with ratatouille or terrine of duck liver marinated in wine. Try one of the creative appetizers, like the goat-cheese pastry. Don't pass up the crème brûlée. You would pay an arm and a leg for such a meal anywhere but here.

Settha Palace Hotel, 6 Pangkham St. ℂ **021/217-581**. Reservations recommended. Main courses US$4.50–US$21 (£2.50–£12). AE, MC, V. Daily 7am–10:30pm.

Le Nadao ⭐⭐ FRENCH   Once a hush-hush eatery of just a few tables, where ordering a souffle meant a long, languid wait, Le Nadao's Lao-born and French-trained chef and owner, Mr. Sayavouth, is reaching a wider market at his larger location adjacent to the Patuxay Monument, Vientiane's Arc de Triomphe. Le Nadao means "Stars in the Ricefield," and indeed this little star now plays host to Vientiane's best and brightest business folks and dignitaries. The dining room is a converted teak house, very rustic and soothing, with a corrugated metal ceiling showing through rough slats, warm indirect lighting, and live local music. The menu is classic French: no fusion, no foolin'. You might start with calamari pan-fried in cream Catalonian style, followed by roast partridge in a rich gravy with potatoes and a lightly fried Mekong filet with lemon, capers, and local organic brown rice. Dessert is chocolate mousse—so rich you'll melt—or a unique "tulip" of pastry with local fruit and ice cream. Bring someone special and make a long evening of it.

Patouxay (on the west side of the Victory Monument roundabout). ✆ **020/550-4884**. Main courses US$4–US$30 (£2.20–£17). No credit cards. Daily noon–1:30pm and 7–10:30pm.

L'Opera ✮✮ ITALIAN For over 10 years, L'Opera has been serving up "real Italian" cuisine and garnering nothing but praise. It features homemade egg-noodle pasta, fine grilled and broiled entrees, daily specials, and fantastic desserts and espresso. There is also a large selection of pizza Lao, which is a surprisingly good combination of tomatoes, cheese, chiles, Lao sausage, and pineapple. The ambience is a rather formal Italy-meets-Lao, with linen tablecloths, brick walls, and wood-beam ceilings in a large, open setting. Lao staff in fine restaurants often act as if their foreign patrons are armed and dangerous, but here the service is confident and professional. Groups of four or more can try the Opera Menu of nine different special appetizers, pastas, and main courses for US$25 (£14) per person.

On the Fountain Circle. ✆ **021/215-099**. Main courses US$6–US$18 (£3.30–£9.90). AE, MC, V. Daily 11:30am–2pm and 6–10pm.

MODERATE

Full Moon Café ✮ INTERNATIONAL Boasting Lao, Thai, Chinese, Vietnamese, and Indian daily specials, this is the place to go if you're not sure which Asian country's cuisine you want to sample. Other places stretch themselves thin through too much variety, but the Full Moon covers all the culinary bases pretty well. The main menu is a mix of tasty Western and Thai staples, while the tapas menu offers up a few interesting selections, most notably the "Water Buffalo Wings" and "Pig Between the Sheets." Of course, if I see "Pig Between the Sheets" on a menu, I'm going to order it. And of course, this being Laos, it wasn't quite what I expected (it was a little like French toast), but it was good nonetheless. If you're simply looking for a place to beat the heat, order a frappe/cappu/mocha-ccino, sink into one of the oversize cushions lining the dining area, and relax.

020 François Nginn Rd. (across from the Tai-Pan Hotel). ✆ **021/243-373**. Main courses US$2–US$4.50 (£1.10–£2.50). MC, V. Mon–Sat 9am–midnight.

Khop Chai Deu ✮ LAO/INTERNATIONAL The name means "Thank you very much." No matter how short your stay in Vientiane, you can't miss this place even if you want to. Just south and west of the Nam Phu Fountain and set in a large colonial building, Khop Chai Deu is the crossroads for expats, backpackers, and tourists. Folks come to get connected with the local scene as much as anything. The menu is extensive, with some tasty barbecue and good Lao selections. Consider the Lao Discovery set, which walks you through various short courses of typical Lao dishes. The old standbys of fried rice, noodles, and spring rolls are featured on the menu's "backpackers page," while the "expatriate relief page" has pizza, spaghetti, and other microwavable favorites from home. Sit on one of the many balconies of this multitiered building, pull up a chair in the courtyard or at the bar, get into some NGO shop-talk, or share notes with English teachers and backpackers. Khop Chai Deu is abuzz late into the evening, and the 5,000 kip (US50¢/£0.30) draft beer flows freely.

54 Setthathirat Rd., southwest of Nam Phu Fountain. ✆ **021/212-106**. Main courses US$2–US$5 (£1.10–£2.75); set menu US$5.70 £3.15). MC, V. Daily 7am–10:30pm (bar open later).

Kua Lao ✮✮ LAO Kua Lao serves excellent Lao fare in a traditional atmosphere that makes for a unique dining experience. Set in a restored colonial mansion, there's music and Lao dancing each evening. It's a bit of tourist kitsch, but the staff is very kind and their desire to infuse your dining experience with Lao culture is quite genuine. Nowhere else will you find such an extensive menu of Lao food with English descriptions (and pictures), and many will appreciate the numerous options for vegetarians, not to mention a whole page of tempting Lao desserts. Try the *laap* (or *larp*), a mince of fish, chicken, or beef mixed with spices and mint; it's excellent when accompanied by a basket of sticky rice and eaten by hand. The set menus are a bargain at US$10 (£5.50), especially for smaller groups hoping to sample a larger selection. If you're going upcountry or heading out to the back of beyond, this is a good place for a primer on Lao cuisine.

111 Samsenthai Rd. (at the intersection with Chanta Khoumane). ⓒ 021/214-813. Main courses US$2–US$6 (£1.10–£3.30); set menu US$10 (bp)5.50). No credit cards. Daily 11am–2pm and 5–11:30pm.

Le Central ⭐⭐ FRENCH/CONTINENTAL   This is an elegant yet casual addition to the growing stable of French fine-dining options in Vientiane. Le Central scored a coup by stealing one of the chefs from La Belle Epoque. His new twists on Asian favorites (deep-fried spring roll filled with goat cheese and cashew nuts, anyone?) and a nice selection of French and Chilean wines complement the Continental main menu. The aforementioned spring rolls are excellent; the braised lamb shank is melt-in-your-mouth tender. However, the highlight of the meal will undoubtedly be the Chef's Specialty: mid-cooked chocolate cake with custard and gingerbread ice cream. Outstanding. Even if you eat dinner somewhere else, the freshly baked cakes and pies are worth a look for dessert.

077/8 Setthatirath Rd. ⓒ 021/243-703. Main courses US$3.50–US$10 (£1.95–£5.50). MC, V. Daily 11:30am–2pm and 6:30–10:30pm.

Le Silapa ⭐⭐ (Finds) FRENCH/CONTINENTAL   For cozy atmosphere and authentic French cuisine, this is a find in Vientiane (if you can find it). The effusive French proprietor will make you feel welcome. There's a great wine list to go with tasty meals like whitefish subtly garnished with capers, lemon, and parsley. The food is a lot more sophisticated than you might expect from such an unassuming storefront.

17/1 Sihom Rd., Ban Haysok. ⓒ 021/219-689. Main courses US$4.75–US$13 (£2.60–£7.15); set lunch US$5.50 (£3). MC, V. Mon–Sat 11:30am–2pm and 6–10pm.

Sticky Fingers ⭐⭐ INTERNATIONAL   Started by Australians who came to Laos with the U.N. and are involved in NGO work, Sticky Fingers serves up soups, salads, sandwiches, and snacks in a relaxed atmosphere. It's got the corner on the casual business lunch and the after-work crowd. Try a burger, sandwich, or steak, and be sure to choose from the impressive list of homemade dips and sauces (available for carryout). This is the place to grab a falafel or get your hummus fix and a respite from the afternoon heat.

10/3 François Nginn Rd., across from the Tai-Pan Hotel. ⓒ 021/215-972. Main courses US$2.80–US$7.50 (£1.55–£4.10). No credit cards. Tues–Sun 10am–11:30pm.

INEXPENSIVE

Nazim Restaurant ⭐ INDIAN   For great Indian cuisine at affordable prices, Nazim has cornered the market in Laos and now has branch locations in Vang Vieng and Luang Prabang. Serving up anything from biryani to tandoori to any kind of curry you can imagine, Nazim offers a survey of Indian cuisine (and the beer to wash it down) in a no-frills storefront along the Mekong. The staff can sometimes act as if

---

Finds **Vientiane's Street Fare**

The busy area of **Ban Haysok** on the western edge of the town center is Vientiane's small **Chinatown** and an excellent place for an evening stroll and some great snacks. One-dish meals of rice or noodles, Lao/Chinese desserts, and super-sweet banana pancakes are sold by street vendors. It's an area that stays up late for sleepy Vientiane, and its charm is in the clamorous chaos. Don't miss it.

The many storefronts along riverside **Fa Ngum Road** are popular gathering spots for travelers, and across the street, on the riverside, are a row of thatched-roof eateries serving all the basics. This is a great spot for viewing the Mekong and neighboring Thailand at sunset.

---

taking your order is an unspeakable bother, but the food is tasty and the prices are reasonable, making this a popular backpacker spot and an expat standby.

Fa Ngum Rd. (© 021/223-480. www.nazim.laopdr.com. Main courses US$1–US$2.50 (£0.55–£1.40). No credit cards. Daily 10:30am–10:30pm.

SNACKS & CAFES

Joma Bakery Café, across from the fountain on Setthathirat Road (© 021/215-265), is renovated and spruced up, with fine breads and good coffee, as well as wireless Internet access. Next door is the newly opened **Dao-Fa,** offering the same fine crepes and pastas as its sister branch in Luang Prabang. The **Scandinavian Bakery,** off Nam Phu Fountain Circle, has good fresh bread and is always packed with travelers. It's a good place to pick up a foreign newspaper and people-watch on the terrace. **Xayoh Café,** just across from the Lao National Culture Hall (© 020/612-051), serves pub grub of all sorts and is a good place to relax and have a beer or a coffee anytime. For excellent desserts, including a chocolate and wine sampler, try **Le Central** (see above).

WHAT TO SEE & DO

Most sights are within the city limits, which means you'll be able to cover them by bicycle or even on foot, getting to know the city intimately—and getting to know the city intimately might be the real attraction in this little burg.

Buddha Park ★★ **Finds Kids**   It's said that if a fool persists in his folly, he will become wise. Buddha Park is a fanciful sculpture garden full of Hindu and Buddhist statues, and it is a concrete testament to the obsession of Luang Pu, a shamanist priest who conceived and started building the park in the 1950s. The statues are captivating, whether they are snarling, reposing, or saving maidens in distress (or carrying them to their doom—it's hard to tell). The huge reclining Buddha is outstanding; you can climb on its arm for a photo. There is also a large pumpkin-esque dome to climb, itself filled with sculptures. The dusty and bumpy bus ride here provides clear views of Thailand across the Mekong.

About 24km (15 miles) southeast of town (take bus no. 14 from the Morning Market). Admission 5,000 kip (US50¢/£0.30), plus an additional 2,000 kip (US20¢/£0.10) for jumbo parking and 2,000 kip (US20¢/£0.10) to use a camera. Daily 7:30am–5:30pm.

Ho Phra Keo ★★   Built by King Setthathirat in 1565, Phra Keo was constructed to house an emerald Buddha that the king took from Thailand (which the Thais took back in 1779). Today there are no monks in residence, and the *wat* is actually a museum of religious art, including a Khmer stone Buddha and a wooden copy of the famous Luang Prabang Buddha. In the garden, there's a transplanted jar from the Plain of Jars (p. 277).

On Setthathirat Rd., opposite Wat Si Saket. Admission 5,000 kip (US50¢/£0.30). Daily 8am–noon and 1–4pm.

Lao National Museum Housed in an interesting old colonial structure that was once used for government offices, the Museum of the Revolution has photos, artifacts, and re-creations of the Lao struggle for independence against the French and Americans. The exhibits (firearms, chairs used by national heroes, and the like) are rather scanty, barely scratching the surface of such a complicated subject, but most are in English at least. Archaeological finds and maps presented on the first floor (probably because there is no other museum to house them at present) help make a visit here worthwhile. One of the most interesting exhibits is in the last room before you exit, sort of a Laos trade and commodities exhibit of produce, handiwork, and manufactured goods. Though dated, it will give you some idea of Laos's geography and commerce.

Samsenthai Rd., near the Lao Plaza Hotel. Admission 5,000 kip (US50¢/£0.30). Daily 8am–noon and 1–4pm.

Morning Market (Talat Sao) ★★ Full of surprises around every corner, the Morning Market is the hub of local commerce and really where the action is. Here you can find anything from the Thai version of a Britney Spears CD to a Buddhist keepsake from one of the tourist shops or trinket salesmen. Great deals can be found on Lao silks if you bargain hard. This is the Laos version of mall culture, and sometimes the everyday tool department or stationery area gives a special glimpse into daily life. Enjoy a good wander and hassle-free shopping. There are few touts, but, as always in crowded places, mind your valuables.

On Talat Sao Rd., off Lane Xang Ave. Daily 7am–5pm.

Patuxay (Victory Monument) ★ This monument was completed in 1968 and dedicated to those who fought in the war of independence against the French. Ironically, the monument is an arch modeled on the Parisian Arc de Triomphe. Its detailing is typically Lao, however, with many *kinnari* figures—half woman, half bird. It's an imposing sight, and you can climb up for a good city view. Once on top, numerous signs forbid the use of cameras (government paranoia, perhaps), but no one seems to take heed. This is the town's main teenage strutting ground and is crowded on weekends.

At the end of Lane Xang Ave. Admission 3,000 kip (US30¢/£0.15). Daily 8am–4pm.

Phra That Luang ★★ This is the preeminent stupa in Lao, a national symbol that's an imposing 44m (144 ft.) high. It is not the original; the first, built in 1566 by King Setthathirat over the ruins of a 12th-century Khmer temple, was destroyed when the Siamese sacked Vientiane in 1828. It was rebuilt by the French in 1900, but the Lao people criticized it as not being true to the original. It was torn down in 1930 and remodeled to become what you see today. As you approach, the statue in front depicts Setthathirat. After you enter the first courtyard, look to the left to see a sacred Bodhi tree, the same variety Buddha sat under to achieve enlightenment. It has a tall, slim trunk, and the shape of its foliage is almost perfectly round. According to the Laotians, Bodhi trees appear only in sacred places; legend has it that the site originally housed a stupa containing a piece of the Buddha's breastbone. The stupa is built in stages. On the second level, there are 30 small stupas, representing the 30 Buddhist perfections, or stages to enlightenment. That Luang is the site of one of Laos's most important temple festivals, which takes place in early November.

At the end of That Luang Rd. Admission 5,000 kip (US50¢/ £0.30). Daily 8am–noon and 1–4pm.

That Dam (Black Stupa)   This ancient stupa was probably constructed in the 15th century or even earlier, though it has never been dated. It is rumored to be the resting place of a mighty seven-headed *naga,* or dragon, that protected the local residents during the Thai invasion in the early 1800s. (*Note:* The name is pronounced *tat dahm,* not with the mildly invective intonation.)

In the center of the traffic circle at the intersection of Chanta Khumman and Bartholomie Rd.

Wat Ong Teu ★   Wat Ong Teu is in a particularly auspicious location, surrounded by four temples: Wat Inpeng to the north, Wat Mixay to the south, Wat Haysok to the east, and Wat Chan to the west. Its name comes from its most famous inhabitant, a huge (*ongteu*) bronze Buddha. The temple, famous for its beautifully carved wooden facade, was built in the early 16th century and rebuilt in the 19th and 20th centuries. Home to the Patriarch of Lao Buddhism, the temple also serves as a national center for Buddhist studies.

Intersection of Setthathirat and Chau Anou rds. Daily 8am–5pm.

Wat Si Muang   Another 1566 Setthathirat creation, this *wat* houses the foundation pillar of the city. According to legend, a pregnant woman named Nang Si, inspired by the gods to sacrifice herself, jumped into the pit right before the stone was lowered. She has now become a sort of patron saint for the city. The temple is very popular as a result and is the site of a colorful procession 2 days before the That Luang festival every November.

East on Samsenthai, near where it joins Setthathirat. Daily 8am–5pm.

Wat Si Saket ★★   Completed in 1818, Wat Si Saket was the only temple in Vientiane to survive the pillaging of the city by the Siamese in 1828, perhaps because the temple was built in traditional Thai style. It is renowned for the more than 10,000 Buddha images, of all shapes and sizes, in every possible nook and cranny. Look for Buddha characteristics that are unique to Laos: the standing or "praying for rain" Buddha; or the pose with arms up and palms facing forward, the "stop fighting" or "calling for peace" Buddha. The pose in which Buddha points the right hand downward signifies a rejection of evil and a calling to mother earth for wisdom and assistance. Lao Buddhas also have exaggerated nipples and square noses, to emphasize that Buddha is no longer human. The *sim* (chapel or ordination hall) features a Khmer-style Buddha seated on a coiled cobra for protection.

> **Health & Spa**
>
> The **Lao Plaza Hotel** (📞 **021/218-800**) has a basic gym and good outdoor pool open to day visitors. There are a number of small massage storefronts along Fa Ngum Road, but for good spa treatments, try **Papaya Spa** (📞 **021/216-550**; www.papayaspa. com), a Vientiane trendsetter.

At the corner of Setthathirat Rd. and Lane Xang Ave. Admission 5,000 kip (US50¢/£0.30). Daily 8am–noon and 1–4pm.

SHOPPING

Laos is famous for its hand-woven silk textiles. You can buy them as fabric or in ready-made wall hangings, accessories, and clothing. Finely crafted silver and ornamental objects are also popular souvenirs. The main shopping streets are **Samsenthai** and **Setthathirat**, around the Nam Phu Fountain area and the **Morning Market** (p. 254), where you can find the best deals on Lao silks.

Perhaps best known (not just in town but worldwide) is **Carol Cassidy: Lao Textiles,** off Setthathirat on Nokeo Koummane Road (✆ **021/212-123;** www.laotextiles.com). Since 1990, Carol has employed local weavers who create fine contemporary pieces, using traditional Lao motifs as a base. The cool colonial house alone is worth a visit, and be sure to stroll through the busy workshop area where up to 10 weavers work the looms and are happy to chat.

Satri Lao Silk, at 79/4 Setthathirat Rd., has fabrics, clothing, and housewares. **Couleur d'Asie,** Namphu Square (✆ **021/223-008**), has a fine ready-to-wear line. The unusual furniture and artworks displayed at **T'shop Lai Gallery,** Vat Inpeng Road (✆ **021/223-178**), are also worth a visit. And the **Mixay Boutic,** Ban Mixay (✆ **021/216-592**), sells a host of silks, clothing, and souvenirs from its two shops in the town center. You can also watch the looms at work in the weaving studio.

For a unique shopping experience in Vientiane, contact Sandra Yuck at her private studio, **Caruso,** housed in a charming colonial property west of the hospital on Fa Ngum Road (✆ **021/223-644;** www.carusolao.com). Sandra carries a line of ebony wood boxes, trays, and accessories, as well as unique Lao bedspreads.

Monument Books, 124/1 Nokeokumman Rd. (✆ **021/243-708**), next door to the Vayakorn Guesthouse, has the best selection of guidebooks, novels, and newspapers. For foreign goods, check out **Phimphone Minimart,** 110/1 Samsenthai Rd. (✆ **021/216-963**), or the **AM Minimart,** on Lane Xang Avenue, just past the Morning Market.

VIENTIANE AFTER DARK

At dusk, wander down to the riverside quay on Fa Ngum Road. The **Lane Xang Sunset Cruise** (✆ **020/771-1003** or 020/551-7133) boards at 7pm and includes meals from US$8 (£4.40) and affordable drinks. Passage is free and the cruise lasts about an hour and a half.

Back on land, there are a few places to meet and greet. The **Khop Chai Deu** (p. 251), on the southwest corner of the Nam Phu Fountain, is the hot spot for expats and travelers, and a good place to find out what's going on in town. For a more laid-back atmosphere, try **Jazzy Brick,** across from Khop Chai Deu, or the **Chicago Bar,** on Rue Nokeokoumane across from Wat Mixay. If dancing is your thing, check out **Dtec Disco** at the Novotel hotel. For live music, try **Chess Café,** on Sakkaline Road, just off Fa Ngum Road east of town, or **On the Rock,** an intimate affair on the corner of Fa Ngum and Manthatulat Road.

5 Vang Vieng ✫

When you arrive in Vang Vieng, a visually unappealing town, you'll be faced with a choice: fight or flight. Resist the urge to flee. Fight through the central backpacker ghetto, with its guesthouse restaurants blasting *Friends* DVDs on a constant, mind-numbing loop, and make your way to the Nam Song River and the breathtaking karst peaks beyond. The surrounding natural beauty more than makes up for the appearance of the town itself, and a few days spent exploring caves, kayaking, trekking, or just sitting at a riverside bar and enjoying a cocktail while admiring the scenery (a personal favorite) is highly recommended. If you're traveling by car, Ngam Ngum dam and lake, some 85km (53 miles) north of Vientiane, is a good stop along the way.

GETTING THERE

Vang Vieng is a smooth 3-hour bus ride north on Highway 13 from Vientiane. There are numerous daily departures from the **Morning Market** (✆ **021/216-507**), and tickets are just 25,000 kip (US$2.50/£1.40) on a regular bus and 45,000 kip (US$4.50/£2.50) on a minibus. Bus connection to Luang Prabang is a popular option, a rugged but scenic all-day ride for just 90,000 kip (US$9/£4.95). However, attacks just north of town mean that road travel must be undertaken with caution. Ask around about the current situation and do not be surprised if there is a bus-company employee toting a machine gun on board.

VISITOR INFORMATION & TOURS

Diethelm Travel (see "Planning Your Trip to Laos," p. 233) includes Vang Vieng in many of its tours and can make any custom arrangements. The town itself is brimming with small operators. For good eco-tours, contact the local branch of **Green Discovery** (see "Outdoor Activities," below).

WHERE TO STAY

Ban Sabai Bungalow ✦   This quiet collection of riverside bungalows, owned by the same folks who run the Xayoh Café and Green Discovery tours, provides a real lesson in the Lao language. *Ban* means "house"; *sabai* means "calm and relaxed"; and you'll pick up words like *ngiep* ("quiet") and *baw mi banha* ("no problem") if you stay long enough. Rooms are simple, rustic, but clean bungalows. One bungalow abuts the river, while the others form a quiet courtyard area. The riverside restaurant is tops.

Along the river just south and west of the town center. ✆ **023/511-088.** 13 units. US$25 (£14) standard; US$28 (£15) double; US$30 (£17) deluxe. MC, V. **Amenities:** Restaurant; bar; tour desk; laundry service. *In room:* A/C.

Bungalow Thavansouk ✦   In this prime riverside spot, you'll find a range of neatly fitted, affordable bungalows. Accommodations start at basic guesthouse standards and go all the way up to a unique riverside suite with—get this—a picture window next to the bathtub with views of the river. Rooms vary in age, quality, and mildew smell at this casual work in progress, so ask to have a peek before checking in. Lounge chairs on the lawn face the breathtaking wall of karst peaks across the river. The attached Sunset restaurant and bar serves good local fare and is a happening spot at dusk.

Along the Nam Song just south and west of the town center. ✆ **023/511-096.** Fax 023/511-096. www.thavonsouk. com. 29 units. US$18–US$35 (£9.90–£19) bungalow; US$40 (£22) suite. No credit cards. **Amenities:** Restaurant; concierge can arrange tours and all rentals; business center w/Internet access; laundry service. *In room:* A/C.

Vansana Vangvieng Hotel ✦✦   On the bank of the Nam Song, the Vansana is your best option in Vang Vieng. From the open-air lobby and restaurant to the bedroom balconies, everything is oriented towards the river and karst peaks. Rooms still have that new-car smell, with shiny wood floors, teak furniture, and a few Lao fabrics to add some flair. Stick with the doubles, as the suites are just standards with a couch. The inviting pool and restaurant are both right on the river and great places to have a drink and watch the sunset. Nonguests can use the pool for a US$2 (£1.10) fee.

Along the Nam Song just south and west of the town center. ☏ 023/511-598. Fax 023/511-602. www.vansana hotel-group.com. 44 units. US$40 (£22) double; US$50 (£28) suite. MC, V. **Amenities:** Restaurant; nice pool; business center; massage; laundry service. *In room:* A/C, TV.

WHERE TO DINE

There are lots of small eateries of the storefront variety all over town, and you can get decent, basic travelers' fare (fried noodles, rice, and faux-Western food) for next to nothing. **Nazim Restaurant,** on the main drag (☏ 023/511-214), serves the same good, affordable Indian cuisine as in its other locations in Laos. **Xayoh Café,** at the main intersection in town (☏ 023/511-403), serves reliable burgers and basics. For Lao fare, try **Nokeo,** across from the old market (☏ 020/2411203), or **Phay Kam,** on the west side of the old airstrip (☏ 023/511-095), a locals' favorite.

OUTDOOR ACTIVITIES

Eco-tour operators offering kayak tours now line the main road, but the folks at **Green Discovery,** at the main intersection in town (☏ 023/511-440; www.green discoverylaos.com), are your best bet for a fun day in inflatable two-man kayaks on the small rapids of the Nam Song. The trip will take you to some of the local caves, including one where you'll actually swim, wearing a headlamp. A more relaxing option is to spend a half-day tubing down the river. This is by far the most popular activity in Vang Vieng. Transportation is provided upriver—all you have to do is let the current bring you back to town. Another good half-day excursion is a visit to **Phu Kham Cave,** located about 7km (4⅓ miles) from town. Best reached by bicycle, the cave contains a bronze reclining Buddha as well as a swimming hole out front where you can cool down after the journey. The scenery along the way is spectacular.

6 Luang Prabang ⟨★⟨★⟨★

Many a traveler's tale in Luang Prabang begins like this: "Well, I was only supposed to stay here for a couple days, but . . . ." The quiet street-side cafes, ancient temples, and laid-back, friendly locals give this town a tranquillity that has sucked many unsuspecting visitors in for weeks (or years) at a time. A visit here feels like a vacation from your vacation.

Start your day at dawn, when the temple drums break the early morning silence and saffron-clad monks walk the misty streets to receive rice from the townspeople for their daily meal. Buddhists believe that by giving rice in this life ("making merit"), they are ensuring that they will not go hungry in their next life. Tourists can also participate in this ancient tradition, but should understand that although it has become an attraction of sorts, it is still a sacred ritual.

The rest of the day can be spent seeing the sights or relaxing and soaking in the atmosphere. The town itself is the main attraction, though, and the time-worn streets will undoubtedly reveal hidden gems and memorable encounters, whether it's a store selling the perfect antique or a temple housing monks anxious to practice their English.

Although UNESCO's designation of Luang Prabang as a World Heritage Site in 1995 raised the town's international profile and contributed to a mass influx of tourists, the designation also means that the town's growth will be managed and will hopefully retain its charm for years to come.

GETTING THERE

BY PLANE   Lao Airlines (☏ 021/212-057, or 021/214-427 for reservations; www. laoairlines.com) has daily flights from Vientiane to Luang Prabang for US$52 (£29)

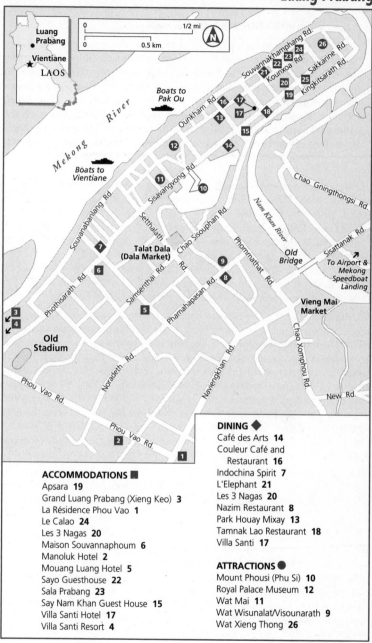

Luang Prabang

LAOS
Luang Prabang
Vientiane

Boats to Pak Ou

Boats to Vientiane

Mekong River

Nam Khan River

Talat Dala (Dala Market)

Old Bridge

To Airport & Mekong Speedboat Landing

Vieng Mai Market

Old Stadium

Souvannabanlang Rd.
Sisavangvong Rd.
Ounkham Rd.
Souvannakhamphang Rd.
Kounxoa Rd.
Sakkarine Rd.
Kingkitsarath Rd.
Chao Gningthongsi Rd.
Sisattanak Rd.
Setthalath Rd.
Phothisarath Rd.
Samsenthai Rd.
Chao Sisouphan Rd.
Phommathat Rd.
Pharnahapasan Rd.
Noradeth Rd.
Naviengkhan Rd.
Chao Xomphou Rd.
New Rd.
Phou Vao Rd.
Phou Vao Rd.

ACCOMMODATIONS ■
Apsara **19**
Grand Luang Prabang (Xieng Keo) **3**
La Résidence Phou Vao **1**
Le Calao **24**
Les 3 Nagas **20**
Maison Souvannaphoum **6**
Manoluk Hotel **2**
Mouang Luang Hotel **5**
Sayo Guesthouse **22**
Sala Prabang **23**
Say Nam Khan Guest House **15**
Villa Santi Hotel **17**
Villa Santi Resort **4**

DINING ◆
Café des Arts **14**
Couleur Café and Restaurant **16**
Indochina Spirit **7**
L'Elephant **21**
Les 3 Nagas **20**
Nazim Restaurant **8**
Park Houay Mixay **13**
Tamnak Lao Restaurant **18**
Villa Santi **17**

ATTRACTIONS ●
Mount Phousi (Phu Si) **10**
Royal Palace Museum **12**
Wat Mai **11**
Wat Wisunalat/Visounarath **9**
Wat Xieng Thong **26**

Tips Where the Streets Have No Names

In Luang Prabang, though you'll see street signs, the same road can change names as it progresses through the city, making things confusing. For example, the main street (I refer to it as "restaurant row" at the town center) is Chao Fa Ngum, Sisavongvong, or Sakkarine Road, depending on where you are. Locals use village names, not streets, to navigate, and villages are commonly named for the local *wat*. When checking into your hotel, get a business card or ask the name of the local *wat* to tell taxi and tuk-tuk drivers. Also note that the Western spelling of many street and *wat* names is very inconsistent. Just sound it out.

---

one-way. Two flights weekly connect Luang Prabang with Xieng Khouang (US$40/£22) and Pakse (US$135/£74). There are no direct flights to the far north; for that, you'll need to fly directly from Vientiane.

The **Luang Prabang International Airport** handles international flights from Chiang Mai, Bangkok, Hanoi, and Siem Reap. On Lao Airlines, the cost is US$118 (£65) to Bangkok, US$72 (£40) to Chiang Mai, US$115 (£63) to Hanoi, and US$135 (£74) to Siem Reap. On Thai Air, Chiang Mai flights are US$85 (£47). Visas are available on arrival at the airport. Airport transport is best arranged through any hotel. Otherwise, hop a shared, three-wheeled jumbo for US$1 (£0.55) or so.

BY BUS/MINIVAN   The overland route to Luang Prabang from Vientiane takes about 10 hours by public bus, assuming there are no difficulties (breakdowns are common). There are international warnings about travel on this stretch, and though it has been quiet in recent years, you should ask around before hitting the road. The trip is bumpy and winding, and local buses are often packed. However, the jaw-dropping scenery, past the mountains and limestone formations at Vang Vieng and several Hmong hill villages, is well worth it. The bus costs 90,000 kip (US$9/£4.95) and has a few morning departures from Vientiane's Northern Bus Station. Go early to get a seat. Luang Prabang's NaLuang (Southern) Bus Station is a 10,000 kip (US$1/£0.55) per person shared tuk-tuk ride from the town center. There are also daily connections to Phonsavan (90,000 kip/US$9/£4.95) and the far north.

BY CAR/JEEP   The mountain route by rented vehicle takes 7 hours and costs about 2,300,000 kip (US$230/£127), plus 600,000 kip (US$60/£33) per day, *plus* extra for the driver's meals and accommodations. If it seems steep, blame all the NGOs operating in Laos for driving up the prices—they all get reimbursed from expense accounts (in case you were wondering where your charity money ends up).

BY BOAT   Boat travel to and from Luang Prabang is quite popular. The local boat (called the **slow boat**) from Houayxay (near the Thai border) departs for Luang Prabang every morning. Arrive early at the riverside quay. The trip costs 120,000 kip (US$12/£6.6) and takes about 1½ days to complete. You'll stay overnight in Pak Beng, a village with basic accommodations, before arriving in Luang Prabang on the afternoon of the next day (assuming no engine trouble or other delays). Be prepared for all kinds of discomfort, though you'll have many tales to tell afterward. The chug upriver from Luang Prabang takes up to 3 days and is not recommended.

Speedboats also connect Luang Prabang with Houayxay if they get enough passengers to make the trip worthwhile (contact the main port at © **021/215-924**).

Speedboat travel is uncomfortable, noisy, and dangerous, but it cuts the travel time to around 7 hours. Tour operators in town offer tickets for US$30 (£17).

Luang Say Cruises (Ban Vat Sene, Sakkarine Rd., Luang Prabang, near Diethelm Travel; ✆ **071/252-553;** www.asian-oasis.com) also operates **tour boats** on the same route between Thailand and Luang Prabang. Starting at around US$268 for a single in high season, there are both 2- and 3-day trips that take you on the river in style, catered to and comfortable, with 1-night stops at the Luang Say Lodge and/or the Kamu Lodge, both charming, rustic eco-lodges on the banks of the Mekong.

On all other river routes, like the Nam Tha between Luang Namtha and Pak Beng and the Nam Ou from Nong Kiao to Luang Prabang, you essentially have to charter your own boat with other tourists. Contact any travel agent or tour provider to make arrangements and get more details (availability varies by season).

GETTING AROUND

Luang Prabang is easy to cover on foot or bicycle. If you get tired, tuk-tuks and jumbos cost about 5,000 kip (US50¢/£0.30) per trip (less with more people and some haggling). *Note:* Citing the many accidents in recent years, local officials have put the kibosh on motorbike rentals (which also ensures work for local transportation providers). Luang Prabang is a town for walking, really, but it is a shame that you can no longer go put-putting out to the waterfalls.

Vatthanaluck Vehicle Rental, around the corner from the Villa Santi (✆ **071/212-838**), covers all the bases for rentals and is the best bet of the many competitors. Bicycles go for just US$1 (£0.55) per day; a rented car with driver is US$25 (£14). For sights outside the city, jumbos and tuk-tuks usually gather along Xieng Thong Road across from the popular cafes and restaurants; prices are negotiable.

Longtail boats are for hire at Luang Prabang's main pier and can take you to adjacent villages and the Pak Ou Caves (p. 272).

VISITOR INFORMATION & TOURS

In addition to the following recommendations, small tour offices with good budget ticket services are chockablock in town, especially on "restaurant row." Try **All Lao Services** (5/7 Sisavangvong Rd.; ✆ **071/252-785;** fax 071/253-522) for ticketing, rentals, and Internet access.

- **Diethelm Travel,** Sakkarine Road, near the Villa Santi (✆ **071/212-277;** fax 071/212-032; www.diethelmtravel.com). The top agent in town, Diethelm arranges city tours and excursions to out-of-town sights.
- **Exotissimo Travel,** Ban Xieng Keo (✆ **071/253-851;** fax 071/253-027; www. exotissimo.com).
- **Inter-Lao Tourism,** in the Maison Souvannaphoum on Phothisarat and on Kingkitsarath Road near the Talat Dala (Dala Market) (✆ **071/212-034;** www. interlao.laopdr.com).

FAST FACTS: Luang Prabang

Currency Exchange U.S. dollars and Thai baht are both widely accepted here. The **Lane Xang Bank** is at Phothisarat Road near the post office. Hours are Monday through Saturday from 8:30am to 3:30pm. You can exchange cash and traveler's checks in most major currencies. You can also withdraw cash using a Visa card. There's another Lane Xang money-changing office on Xieng Thong Road next to the Luang Prabang Bakery. **Banque Pour Le Commerce Exterieur Lao** has an office on "restaurant row" (© **071/252-983**).

Emergencies For police, dial © **071/212-453**; for a medical emergency, call © **071/252-049**.

Internet Access Service was once patched through Vientiane, but now cable and satellite connections mean you can easily keep in touch from Luang Prabang. Internet cafes line the busy block of Phothisarat, "restaurant row," and are also scattered about town. Expect to pay around 100 kip per minute (US60¢/£0.30 per hr.).

Mail The post office is on the corner of Phothisarat and Kitsalat roads, across from Luang Prabang Travel and Tourism. Hours are Monday through Friday from 8am to noon and 1 to 5pm, Saturday from 8am to noon.

Telephones The city code for Luang Prabang is **71**. The telephone center in town consists of two booths around the corner from the post office on Kitsalat Road. You can buy local and international phone cards in an office across the street.

WHERE TO STAY

Luang Prabang's UNESCO World Heritage status mercifully prevents large-scale construction in the historic center. As a result, developers have renovated existing hotels and completed boutique conversions of old guesthouses. A few resorts have also sprung up on the outskirts of town to keep up with demand. Promotional and low-season rates are available at most hotels, but be aware that a surcharge is often levied in the busy months. Book ahead from November through March and during the Lao New Year festivities in mid-April.

EXPENSIVE

Grand Luang Prabang (Xieng Keo) ★   Despite new road signs and advertising, you won't get far in a taxi if you ask to go to "The Grand." The site will forever be known to locals by its former name, Xieng Keo, in reverence to its previous owner, Lao nationalist and peace broker Prince Petsarath. The site of Petsarath's former palatial home is on a high, sloping hill at the apex of a wide bend in the Mekong. Words can't describe the views of river and mountains from the open campus. The hotel's aptly named Sunset Bar overlooks such an impressive vista that you might want to make a visit here just to see the afterglow during the "magic hour." The rooms are average in size but are quite lovely, with teak floors and high ceilings. Tile bathrooms are smallish but spotless, and the one wall left in rough brick is a unique touch. All units have a balcony and a view of either the colonnaded walkways and the courtyard or the majestic Mekong. Prince Petsarath's home stands at the middle of the compound and promises to be a museum honoring his legacy. The biggest drawback of staying here is the distance from town, though the hotel runs regular shuttles and will arrange boats to Xieng Thong for a small fee. Although at press time amenities were sparse, there are plans for a riverside swimming pool by the summer of 2007, with a luxury spa to follow. A first-class resort in the making.

Baan Xiengkeo, Khet Sangkalok (about 6km/3¾ miles south of the town center), Luang Prabang. © 071/253-851. Fax 071/253-027. www.grandluangprabang.com. 78 units. US$150 (£83) deluxe; US$250–US$300 (£138–£165) suite. AE, MC, V **Amenities:** 2 restaurants; bar; concierge; airport and city shuttle; business center w/Internet access; 24-hr. room service; babysitting; laundry service; rooms for those w/limited mobility. *In room:* A/C, satellite TV, minibar, safe, IDD phone.

La Résidence Phou Vao ★★ Luang Prabang's finest hotel offers deluxe accommo-
dations, excellent service, and a lofty perch away from the fray of the busy town center. Rooms are priced accordingly, but worth it. The Phou Vao is named for the hill on which it stands. Shallow ponds trace the courtyards that connect the buildings, and bushes of bougainvillea, palm, and frangipani frame views of Phoussi hill in the distance. The views are especially lovely from the pool area and the balconies of the more choice rooms. The accommodations are like small suites, decorated with a bamboo-and-wood inlaid headboard, fine rosewood furniture, and retro fixtures like fans and mosquito netting. The large marble bathrooms feature oversize tubs, dark-teak sink stands, and wooden slat blinds that open to reveal private balconies with low, Lao-style divans. The Phou Vao combines the amenities of a city hotel with a boutique, upscale rustic charm. The recently opened spa, consisting of luxury cottages set around an infinity-edge pool and lily pond overlooking the town below, further solidifies the Phou Vao's position as the premier hotel in Luang Prabang.

Phou Vao St., P.O. Box 50, Luang Prabang. © 071/212-194. Fax 071/212-534. www.pansea.com. 34 units. US$276 (£152) deluxe double; US$400 (£220) residence suite. Ask about off-season discounts. AE, MC, V. **Amenities:** Restaurant; bar; outdoor pool; spa w/sauna and steam room; business center w/Internet access; shopping; limited room service; massage; babysitting; laundry service; library. *In room:* A/C; satellite TV; minibar; fridge; safe; IDD phone.

Les 3 Nagas ★ This hotel's original structure was built in 1898 as an unofficial
reception area for the royal family before being converted into an ice-cream factory in the 1930s. A newer wing across the street was built in 1903 by a counselor to King Sisavangvong. The inspired recent renovation has just the right mix of style, convenience, and connection with local living and history. That style can be seen in the clean-lined rosewood interiors, contemporary Asian furniture, and Lao touches like woven floor mats and ladders to upper floors. Bathrooms are done in dark wood, shower and all. Convenience points are earned because the hotel is close to the town center, but far enough from the din to afford some peace. The connection to history comes as the very professional staff welcomes you to a place that provides a glimpse into an aristocratic Indochine of a bygone era. The hotel restaurant (p. 267) is tops, too.

Just further along the peninsula from "restaurant row," P.O. Box 772, Luang Prabang. © 071/252-079. www.3nagas.com. 15 units. US$105 (£58) double; US$140 (£77) junior suite; US$180 (£99) executive suite. MC, V. **Amenities:** Restaurant; cafe/bar; outdoor pool; bicycle rental; tour desk; laundry service; Internet access. *In room:* A/C, Internet access, minibar, fridge, hair dryer.

Maison Souvannaphoum ★ Set amongst the trees and manicured gardens just
off Nam Phou fountain, the Maison is steeped in history and colonial charm. Until 1975 the private residence of Prince Souvanna Phoumma, former prime minister in the Royal Lao Government, the old L'Hotel Souvannaphoum has been given a face-lift and reopened under the Colours of Angsana banner. The beautifully restored La Residence wing offers one twin and three suites, the largest of which, the Maison Suite, was the prince's bedroom. La Residence rooms retain their original parquet floors and guests here receive nice perks like afternoon tea and discounts at the boutique. Rooms in the newer Garden Wing are small but elegant, with recessed lighting,

unique wall nooks, and oversized daybeds that convert into extra beds. Spacious marble balconies, furnished with comfortable wicker chairs, overlook the gardens and small but inviting swimming pool. Unfortunately, the spa is not up to Angsana's normally high standards. Due to UNESCO restrictions, it is housed in tents set close to the main road, rendering the treatment areas noisy and lacking in privacy. Head to the Phou Vao for your spa needs instead.

Rue Chao Fa Ngum (on Namphou Sq.), P.O. Box 741, Luang Prabang. ✆ 071/254-609. Fax 071/212-577. www. coloursofangsana.com. 24 units. US$200 (£110) garden room; US$220 (£121) veranda room; US$250 (£138) La Residence twin; US$300–US$400 (£165–£220) suite. AE, MC, V. Amenities: Restaurant; small pool; spa; bicycle rental; boutique; laundry service; wireless Internet access. *In room:* A/C, satellite TV, minibar, coffeemaker, hair dryer, safe, IDD phone.

Villa Santi Hotel 🏵   For charm and convenience, the Villa Santi is the top in-town residence. Formerly the home of Lao princess Manilay, this low-key villa reopened in 1992. Whether in the original building, in the nearby annex, or at the latest venture some 6km (3¾ miles) from town (see Villa Santi Resort, below), you'll find peaceful elegance and a connection with culture and nature. The decor is deluxe colonial, with overstuffed pillows, fine linens, mosquito netting, local weaving, parquet floors, and rosewood furniture. The tile bathrooms are small but neat. Nice touches include old-fashioned sun umbrellas available for borrowing, plus fresh flowers in every room. The newer annex just across the street has common balcony sitting areas and a charm all its own. Only four rooms have king beds, so be sure to specify when you book if that's what you want. The staff is friendly and professional. The downtown location is terrific, right in the thick of things.

Sakkarine St., P.O. Box 681, Luang Prabang. ✆ 071/212-267. Fax 071/252-158. www.villasantihotel.com. 25 units. Low season US$80 (£44) deluxe, US$200 (£110) suite; high season US$150 (£83) deluxe, US$250 (£138) suite. Special Internet rates available. AE, MC, V. Amenities: Restaurant; bar; tour desk; limited room service; laundry service; dry cleaning. *In room:* A/C, minibar, fridge, safe, IDD phone.

Villa Santi Resort 🏵🏵   This resort is a roomier rural companion to the popular downtown Villa Santi and similarly sophisticated, without being stuffy. Tucked among lush rice paddies and picturesque hills, this little Eden has a tranquil stream that tiptoes through the grounds, a placid pond, and an open garden area. The buildings seem at ease with the surroundings, and from the open-air, high-ceilinged lobby to the two-story villas scattered about, there's a certain harmony to the place. Rooms are larger versions of those at the downtown Villa Santi, with similar tile floors, dark rosewood trim, and local decoration. The hotel has laid claim to the largest swimming pool in town and plans to add tennis courts and a fitness center in the near future. The staff is kind and courteous, and will ensure efficient transport to and from town (as with the other resorts, distance is the biggest drawback here).

Santi Resort Rd., Ban Nadeuay, P.O. Box 681 (6km/3¾ miles from town, a 10-min. drive), Luang Prabang. ✆ 071/253-470. Fax 071/252-158. www.villasantihotel.com. 52 units. US$170 (£94) deluxe double; US$300–US$500 (£165–£275) suite. AE, MC, V. Amenities: Restaurant; bar; limited room service; laundry service. *In room:* A/C, satellite TV w/in-house movies, minibar, fridge, hair dryer, IDD phone.

MODERATE

Apsara 🏵🏵   Named after the celestial nymphs in Hindu mythology that grace the frescoes of Angkor Wat, the British-owned Apsara is a stylish choice. Set on the less-developed Nam Khan River side of the Luang Prabang isthmus, rooms are split between two beautiful colonials. Superior units are like loft spaces with high ceilings, old wood floors, and fashionable room dividers separating the bathroom area from the living space. Modern dark-wood furniture is highlighted by four-poster beds covered with handwoven silks and plush pillows. Smaller standard rooms are just as airy. French doors leading to either a patio by the road or a second-floor balcony let in an abundance of light, especially in the morning. The bar and restaurant are top-notch, but early-to-bedders beware: Two second-story rooms are immediately above the restaurant and can be noisy until closing time. Large families or groups should inquire about the nearby Villa Savanh, a three-bedroom traditional house that the hotel rents on a nightly basis.

Kingkitsarath Rd. (on the Nam Khan River), Ban Wat Sene, Luang Prabang. ℭ 071/254-670. Fax 071/254-252. www.theapsara.com. 13 units. US$55–US$65 (£30–£36) standard; US$65–US$85 (£36–£47) superior. MC, V. Amenities: Restaurant; bar. In room: A/C.

Le Calao ★★   This restored 1904 villa stands near the tip of Luang Prabang's peninsula on the banks of the Mekong. Unique and picturesque, it has a location and style all its own. The second-floor rooms are a nice size, with high sloping ceilings, wood furniture, neat tile floors, and firm beds. Bathrooms have wood cabinetry but are otherwise rather spartan, with no tubs. The staff is, well . . . hey, where did the staff go? What sells these rooms and commands the seemingly high price tag is that each unit has a large private balcony facing the majestic Mekong. The casual ambience at the Calao comes at a premium, but the place is quite popular (be sure to book ahead). The newly renovated downstairs suite (formerly a kitchen and staff room) has two double beds and a private balcony, perfect for a family with kids.

Khaem Khong Rd. (on the Mekong River, close to Wat Xieng Thuong), Luang Prabang. ℭ 071/212-100. Fax 071/212-085. www.calaoinn.laopdr.com. 6 units. US$70–US$75 (£39–£41) double. V. Amenities: Cafe/bar; laundry service. In room: A/C.

Manoluk Hotel   An interesting choice, the Manoluk: It's eccentric, but comfy and affordable. You're a bit away from town, though, which is a drawback. The spacious rooms have polished wood floors, high ceilings, big clunky tables and chairs, and comfortable beds. The bathrooms are similarly large and clean. The huge restaurant and second-floor lounge, complete with wooden deer heads, give the place a lodge feel. If your taste runs to quality kitsch, the Manoluk is the "Velvet Elvis" of Luang Prabang: You'll appreciate the many carved elephants, fluorescent village-scene paintings, and shiny bedspreads with fringe. The lone suite is fancy in a way that your oddball uncle might like. The staff seems to be nonexistent, save for a person or two at the front desk watching the lobby TV. Somehow, that seems to suit the laid-back, private feel of the place.

121/3 Phou Vao St., Luang Prabang. ℭ 071/212-250 or 071/212-509. Fax 071/212-508. 30 units. US$40–US$45 (£22–£25) double; US$70–US$80 (£39–£44) suite. MC, V. Amenities: Restaurant; bar; motorcycle and bicycle rental; laundry service. In room: A/C, TV, IDD phone.

Mouang Luang Hotel ★   A 10-minute walk from town on a quiet street north of the Souvanophoum, the Mouang Loung is adorned with traditional Lao temple-style roofs. Comparable to the Manoluk (above) in amenities and value, the rooms at the Mouang Luang are clean, with parquet floors and marble-tiled bathrooms (all with smallish tubs). Street-side rooms have balconies. There's an open-air Lao restaurant in the back, and just above it is an enormous balcony reserved for Baci ceremonies. Mouang Luang has the distinction of being one of the only hotels in town with a pool (there's a charge of US$4/£2.20 for nonguests). The staff is very friendly, and the place is popular with groups. If it's full, try **Le Parasol Blanc,** its sister property (© 071/252-124).

Bounkhong Rd, P.O. Box 779, Luang Prabang. © 071/212-791. Fax 071/212-790. mgluang@laotel.com. 35 units. Low season US$35 (£19) single, US$40 (£22) double; high season US$53 (£29) single, US$60 (£33) double. AE, DC, MC, V. **Amenities:** Restaurant; outdoor pool; laundry service; dry cleaning; conference room. *In room:* A/C, TV, mini-bar, IDD phone.

Sala Prabang 🌟🌟 *(Finds)*   Here's a trendsetter in developing Luang Prabang: an old riverside colonial that's been refurbished and refitted by its architect/owner, the walls reinforced with stone, and good hot-water showers and air-conditioning installed. The renovation was done with some panache, with beams and supports made of rough natural wood, sponge painting, and cool neutral tones throughout. The lobby area is a chic open-air space overlooking the Mekong, and top-end rooms on the second floor are large and have great balcony views. A recent expansion added seven naturally styled rooms in a riverfront villa down the street, as well as Nadao (under construction at press time), an offshoot of the Vientiane favorite Le Nadao, promising the same high-quality French cuisine at its riverside perch. Sala Prabang is a boutique guesthouse at its best, and a model that will likely be copied.

Mekong Riverside Rd., 102/6 Thanon Ounkham, Xieng Mouane, P.O. Box 902, Luang Prabang. © 071/252-460. Fax 071/252-472. www.salalao.com. 29 units. Low season US$50–US$60 (£28–£33) double; high season US$60–US$75 (£33–£41) double. MC, V. **Amenities:** Restaurant; cafe; airport transfer; Internet access; laundry service; Internet access. *In room:* A/C, hair dryer.

INEXPENSIVE

Another good budget choice is the **Senesouk,** Ban Vat Sene (© 071/212-074), with tidy, quiet rooms from US$25 (£14).

Say Nam Khan Guest House 🌟   Here is an unassuming little gem: In a renovated colonial on the banks of the Nam Khan River, Say Nam Khan is basic but centrally located, with its own quiet, riverside charm. Nothing here is plush. Rooms are small, with comfortable beds and wood furniture. Bathrooms are basic tile, with shower-in-room. The recent renovations mean clean parquet flooring can be found throughout. The hotel is close to "restaurant row" and has a laid-back balcony area for watching the sun go down.

Ban Wat Sene (off Kingkitsarath Rd., near the Nam Khan River), Luang Prabang. © 071/212-976. Fax 071/213-009. saynamkhane_lp@hotmail.com. 16 units. US$25 (£14) single; US$30 (£17) twin; US$50 (£28) VIP room. No credit cards. **Amenities:** Bar; laundry service. *In room:* A/C.

Sayo Guesthouse 🌟   This guesthouse isn't trying to be anything more than it is, and that's its charm. Service is nonexistent, and the lobby is just a little hallway, but the rooms on the second floor are enormous. Ceilings are practically barn height, and the rooms are done up with tasteful Lao decorations. Bathrooms are clean, large, and of the all-in-one variety (shower and toilet together). The rooms in the back are smaller, with exposed brick and unique loft spaces like little crows' nests. Sayo Guesthouse is basic, but it's an eccentric place with a lot of character. The location is convenient to the main street.

In front of Vat Xieng Mouane (between main rd. and the Mekong), P.O. Box 1060, Luang Prabang. © 071/252-614. 10 units. US$15–US$40 (£8.25–£22). No credit cards. **Amenities:** Laundry service.

Villa Sokxai   This is just a basic guesthouse in an attractive colonial that happens to be in one of my favorite spots in town. Clean rooms have wood floors, soft beds, and both A/C and a fan, a real plus for some. Try for an upstairs room overlooking the balcony and Wat Phon Heuang—this is one of the first spots where monks receive their morning alms, and the hotel staff can help you buy sticky rice if you'd like to make merit. At dusk, you can sit on the balcony and listen to the hypnotic chanting drone of the evening prayers. One drawback is the Sokxai's poorly run reservations system; you should confirm your reservation more than once before arriving. If full, look for its sister hotel, **Villa Sokxai 2,** on the other side of Mount Phousi.

Sakalin Rd. (across from Wat Phon Heuang), Ban Kilee, Luang Prabang. ℂ/fax **071/254-309.** sokxaigh@yahoo.com. 7 units. US$25–US$30 (£14–£17) double. No credit cards. **Amenities:** Laundry service. *In room:* A/C.

WHERE TO DINE

New, upmarket bistros, many run by foreign restaurateurs, have added to the culinary diversity of little Luang Prabang. Affordable open-air Lao eateries still cater to hungry backpackers returning from the back of beyond, and Luang Prabang remains a wonderful place to explore authentic Lao cuisine or savor some excellent French and Western meals. Whatever your cuisine of choice, dining in this sleepy northern burg is a delight.

EXPENSIVE

L'Elephant ☆☆ FRENCH   This stylish bistro is where it's at for fine dining in Luang Prabang. Run by French expats, it has a laid-back, retro-chic atmosphere inside a high-ceilinged colonial. There are daily and weekly specials, and just about everything is good, especially the imported steaks. Tasty cheeses and wines are also imported, though local stock is used whenever possible. Boar and venison specials are popular, for example. The wine list could hold its own in a much larger city, and it's unlikely that you'll stump the barman. Daily set menus explore the best of what's available in the kitchen. A range of tasty dishes, from coq au vin to grilled buffalo to a vegetarian savory baked eggplant, covers all the bases. L'Elephant is very expensive for Laos, but more than worth it. Be sure to make a reservation—it's quite often fully booked.

Ban Vat Nong. ℂ **071/252-482.** www.elephant-restau.com. Main courses US$8–US$18 (£4.40–£9.90). MC, V. Daily noon–2:30pm and 6–10pm.

Les 3 Nagas ☆☆ LAO   You can get real Lao cuisine done right at this new open-air spot on the quiet end of "restaurant row." Dining here is as sumptuous an affair as a stay at the connected 3 Nagas boutique hotel (p. 263). Meals are based on the culinary styles of the chef's own hometown, presented by a meticulous and capable waitstaff on fine china (you won't find the bones and gristle of traditional Lao restaurants here). Start your meal with betel-leaf soup before moving on to sautéed local mushrooms (when in season), *laap,* and grilled delicacies, from chicken satay to whole chunks of hearty river fish, lightly marinated in lemongrass and chiles. For dessert, go for the Lao-style crème brûlée, a custard of pumpkin and coconut that's divine. Great coffee, too.

In Les 3 Nagas hotel, just further along the peninsula from "restaurant row." ℂ **071/252-079.** www.3nagas.com. Main courses US$2–US$35 (£1.10–£19). AE, MC, V. Daily 7am–10pm.

MODERATE

Couleur Café and Restaurant ☆ LAO/FRENCH   This unassuming but atmospheric down-alley bistro features affordable fine dining. The decor is elegantly sparse, with colonial-size high ceilings and walls adorned with the work of local artists. Though run by a young French expat, the bistro has Lao specialties like steamed fish with coconut in banana leaf, or perhaps fried prawns in oyster sauce. Both are served with sticky rice, of course. Eggplant, mushrooms, and crispy green beans are combined in a tasty Casserole Luang Prabang. Order up some Mekong seaweed for an interesting appetizer, and ask about the fine Lao whiskey and imported wines. It's a quiet little getaway for next to nothing.

48/5 Ban Vat Nong. ℂ 020/562-1064. Main courses US$1–US$2 (£0.55–£1.10). No credit cards. Daily 8am–10pm.

Indochina Spirit ⍟ LAO/THAI/WESTERN   Housed in a restored 70-year-old wooden home, Indochina Spirit, as its name suggests, dishes up as much atmosphere as it does good grub. This gorgeous Lao home has been put to lovely use and now features traditional Lao music most evenings from 7:30 to 8pm (check the chalkboard in front to make sure). Indochina Spirit has done a great job with the simple local decor inside and charming garden dining outside. The menu is an ambitious list of Lao, Thai, and Western dishes. It's a good place to have a drink, enjoy an affordable appetizer plate, and hear some good music before strolling the city at night.

Ban Vat That 52, opposite the fountain across from L'Hotel Souvannaphoum. ℂ 071/252-372. Main courses US$5–US$10 (£2.75–£5.50). MC, V. Daily 8am–10pm.

Tamnak Lao Restaurant ⍟⍟ LAO   A renovated colonial like seemingly every other restaurant in the temple district, what caught my eye walking past the Tamnak Lao were the conspicuous DAILY COOKING CLASS signs. If a restaurant offers cooking classes, then the food should be good enough that I'd want to learn how to prepare it at home. As it turns out, yes, I would definitely like to cook this food at home. For the best variety, try one of the Tamank's three set menus. I sampled two, offering a total of 10 dishes, and the chef batted a solid .900. Notable were the pork casserole in coconut milk, *lahp pla* (spicy fish salad), and pork stuffed in crispy bamboo shoots. Daily cooking classes cost US$25 (£14). If they can teach you to cook half as well as they do, it will be money well spent.

Sakhalin Rd., Ban Wat Sene. ℂ 071/252-525. Main courses US$2–US$10 (£1.10–£5.50). Set menus US$7–US$9 (£3.85–£4.95). MC, V. Daily 8am–10:30pm.

Villa Santi ⍟⍟ LAO/CONTINENTAL   On the upper floor of the popular hotel's main building (p. 264), this atmospheric open-air perch has just the right angle on the busy street below. Set with linen and silver, a candlelight table on the balcony is hands-down the town's most romantic spot. The food is local and traditional Lao, along with some creative Asian-influenced Continental (on the whole, though, it's a bit uninspired—stick to Lao and Thai specials, and sample one of the fine curries). The daily set menus are always a good choice. The desserts are scrumptious: Try bananas flambéed in Cointreau, or fruit salad in rum. There are more casual offerings for lunch, including burgers. Most evenings feature traditional music and dancing in the courtyard below.

In Villa Santi Hotel, Sakkarine St. ℂ 071/212-267. Main courses US$4–US$8 (£2.20–£4.40). V. Daily 6:30am–10:30pm.

INEXPENSIVE

For good, cheap eats and the company of many fellow travelers, don't miss what we've called **"restaurant row"** (it's hard to miss on any trip to Luang Prabang). It is the only place in town alive past 9pm, though it quickly dies at 11pm. This fun, affordable place is great for exploring—almost like a Khao San Road.

Café des Arts ✦ FRENCH/CONTINENTAL   Pasta, hamburgers, crepes, *filet de boeuf*, and tartines round out the very appetizing menu here. Breakfast brings omelets galore. Open-air like all the others on "restaurant row," Café des Arts has a better atmosphere than most, with real tables and chairs (not plastic), linen tablecloths, and a gallery of local artwork for sale.

Sisavangvong Rd. (on "restaurant row"). ℂ/fax 071/252-162. Main courses US70¢–US$5 (£0.40–£2.75). MC, V. Daily 6:30am–11pm.

Nazim Restaurant ✦ INDIAN   Just like the other Nazim outlets in Vientiane and Vang Vieng, Nazim serves a fine complement of good curries and halal food. The dining area is kind of grubby, but the food is great and Nazim is always packed. There's another location on "restaurant row," Sisavangvong Road, at the town center (ℂ 071/253-493).

78/4 Ban Visoun, Visounnarath Rd. ℂ 071/252-263. www.nazim.laopdr.com. Main courses US80¢–US$2.50 (£0.45–£1.40). No credit cards. Daily 8:30am–11pm.

Park Houay Mixay ✦ LAO   A popular lunch option for package tours, this looks more like a traditional Lao restaurant than the places on "restaurant row." Note the tin roof, beat-up wood floors and tables, and numerous pets and kids running around—but you come here for the food, not the ambience. The large portions of delicious and deliciously cheap Lao and Thai dishes are not watered down for Western palates. If you're here for lunch, make sure the ubiquitous tour group has been served already, or else you're in for a long wait.

Ban Xieng Mouane. ℂ 071/212-260. Main courses US$2–US$4.50 (£1.10–£2.50). MC, V. Daily 10:30am–2pm and 5:30–10:30pm.

SNACKS & CAFES

For atmosphere, there is nowhere better than **L'étranger: Books and Tea** (booksin-laos@yahoo.com), in Ban Vat Aphay on the back side of Phousy Hill (the opposite side from the main street and royal palace) near the Nam Khan River. The friendly Canadian owners are full of good advice and lend books from their downstairs collection. Have a pot of tea or a cocktail (don't miss the *lao-lao* margarita) in their atmospheric upstairs teahouse and gallery; it's also a good place on a steamy afternoon to relax on the floor against a cozy Lao cushion while perusing one of the old *National Geographic* magazines. Young travelers descend for the films, played each day at 4 and 7pm.

A popular restaurant on "restaurant row," the **Luang Prabang Bakery,** 11/7 Sisavangvong Rd. (ℂ 071/212-617), serves some good pizza as well as a host of baked goods, plus has an extensive collection of books. Farther east, the **Scandinavian Bakery,** 52/6 Sisavangvong (ℂ 071/252-223), and chic, air-conditioned **Joma** (ℂ 071/252292) both serve similar fine coffee and baked goods.

The same team of expats who run L'Elephant (see above) own **Café Vat Sene** (ℂ 071/212-517), an atmospheric, open-air space with an upstairs gallery. Their desserts and coffee are excellent, as are their light lunch specials of sandwiches and salads. They also offer wireless Internet access. Find them just across from the Villa Santi.

The best place in town for authentic French crepes, savory or sweet, is **Dao Fa,** on Sisavangvong Rd. (ℂ 071/252-656), also a good spot for people-watching. It has excellent Mediterranean entrees and homemade pastas cooked to order, too.

Vegetarians should be on the lookout for the side-street buffets by the **Night Market,** along Phothisarat Road. Only 5,000 kip (US50¢/£0.30) gets you a bowl and all the non-meaty goodness you can handle.

WHAT TO SEE & DO

Mount Phousi ⚔⚔   Rising from the center of town, Phousi has temples scattered on all sides of its slopes and a panoramic view of the entire town from its top. **That Chomsi Stupa,** built in 1804, is its crowning glory. Taking the path to the northeast, you will pass **Wat Tham Phousi,** which has a large-bellied Buddha, Kaccayana. **Wat Phra Bat Nua,** farther down, has a yard-long footprint of the Buddha. Be prepared for the 355 steps to get there. Try to make the hike, which will take about 2 hours with sightseeing, in the early morning or late afternoon to escape the sun's burning rays. A great spot for sunset.

Admission 10,000 kip (US$1/£0.55). Daily dawn–dusk.

Royal Palace Museum ⚔⚔   The palace, built for King Sisavang Vong from 1904 to 1909, was the royal residence until the Pathet Lao seized control of the country in 1975. The last Lao king, Sisavang Vattana, and his family were exiled to a remote region in the northern part of the country and never heard from again. Rumor has it that they perished in a prison camp, though the government has never said so. The palace remains as a repository of treasures, rather scanty but still interesting. You can begin your tour by walking the length of the long porch; the gated open room to your right has one of the museum's top attractions, a replica of a golden standing Buddha that was a gift to King Fa Ngum from a Khmer king. Known as "The Prabang" (thus the town's name), which translates to "holy image," the original was cast in Sri Lanka in the 1st century A.D.

Don't miss the busts of the last dynasty of kings. The central throne room is done in colorful glass mosaics dating from a renovation in the 1930s. Past the throne rooms is a compound of large, spartan bedrooms with what little finery was left after the departure of the last king. The temple at the compound entrance is a gilded wedding cake, and the large Soviet-made statue of Sisavang Vong, the first king under the Lao constitution, has a stiff raised fist like a caricature of Lenin.

The palace hosts a growing troupe of dancers who perform at the Royal Theater. On Monday, Wednesday, and Friday, tourists can take part in a Baci ceremony and view the historical reenactment of the *Ramayana.* Tickets are US$5/£2.75.

Phothisarat Rd. ✆ 071/212470. Admission 20,000 kip (US$2/£1.10). Mon–Sat 8–11am and 1:30–4pm. **Warning:** At 11am the museum will kick you out, and you'll have to pay *again* to come back after lunch.

Wat Mai ⚔⚔   Wat Mai is one of the jewels of Luang Prabang. Its golden bas-relief facade tells the story of Phravet, one of the last avatars, or reincarnations, of the Buddha. This *wat* held the Pra Bang Buddha from 1894 until 1947. Stop by at 5:30pm for the evening prayers, when the monks chant in harmony.

Phothisarat Rd., near the Lane Xang Bank. Daily dawn–dusk.

Wat Wisunalat/Visounarath ⚔   Wisunalat is known for its absolutely huge golden Buddha in the *sim,* the largest in town at easily 6m (20 ft.) tall. The *wat* was constructed in 1512 and held the famous Pra Bang Buddha from 1513 to 1894. On the grounds facing the sim is the famous **That Makmo,** or watermelon stupa, a survivor since 1504. Wat Aham is a few steps away from the Wisunalat sim.

At the end of Wisunalat Rd. Daily 8am–5pm.

Taking Refuge: Making Friends at the Temple

There is little that's spectacular on the sleepy peninsula of Luang Prabang. Rather, time spent here is about soaking up the atmosphere and taking leisurely walks along dusty lanes lined with French colonial buildings. Another great local activity is to stop in at a temple—any temple, really—and meet up with the monks or young novices. The monks are great sources of information and insight into Laos culture, Buddhism, and the vagaries of human existence. Language is a big part of their training, and they study Pali and Sanskrit as well as English and French (and even Chinese and Japanese). Novices are keen to practice their English or even get help with their homework. Women should be careful not to touch or sit too close to monks and novices, but all are welcome in the temple. Don't give in to any pleas for sponsorship (unless you want to); monks live through the generosity of the sangha, or monastic community, and don't need sponsors.

Wat Xieng Thong ⭐⭐   Xieng Thong is the premier *wat* of Luang Prabang. Built in 1560 by King Say Setthathirat, it is situated at the tip of Luang Prabang's peninsula where it juts out into the Mekong. Xieng Thong survived numerous invading armies, making its facade one of the oldest originals in the city. To the left of the main temple, find the "red chapel" and its rare statue of a reclining Buddha that dates back to the temple's construction. The statue is one of the premier Buddha images in the country, with an attitude sublime; the piece actually traveled to the World's Fair in Paris in 1931. The glass mosaics adorning all external buildings date from only the 1950s, but are fun depictions of popular folk tales and Buddhist history; note the "tree of life" on the side of the main temple. Facing the courtyard from the temple steps, the building on the right contains the funeral chariot of King Sisavang Vong with its seven-headed *naga* (snake) decor. The chariot was carved by venerated Lao sculptor Thid Tun. There are also some artifacts inside, including ancient marionettes.

At the end of Xieng Thong Rd. Admission 10,000 kip (US$1/£0.55). Daily 8am–6pm.

SIGHTS OUTSIDE THE CITY

Other sights outside of town include **Wat Phon Phao (Peacefulness Temple),** a golden stupa on a hilltop about 5km (3 miles) away, best viewed from afar—though the view back to town from its height is worth the trek. From here, visit nearby **Ban Phanom Weaving Village,** a now rather commercialized weaving collective where you can find deals on Lao Ikat patterns and hand-woven bags. Just past Ban Phanom and hidden in a jungle riverside area (signs point the way down the embankment), find the **Tomb of Henri Mouhot,** the 19th-century French explorer credited with the rediscovery of Cambodia's Angkor Wat. He died in Luang Prabang of malaria while hunting the source of the Mekong. **Day trips across the Mekong** to small temples and villages are also popular and can be arranged with boat drivers at quayside.

Kuangsi Waterfall   As famous now for its recent collapse as anything, Kuangsi was a tower of champagne-glass limestone formations until the whole structure fell in on itself in 2003. Locals say that tour operators became too greedy and neglected local spirits, called Pi. The falls are still beautiful, but less so. The ride here, however, is quite spectacular. You'll have to travel by *songthaew* (covered pickup) for US$5 (£2.75) per person if shared, or by boat and tuk-tuk for the same fee.

Another option, **Tad Se Waterfall,** is 21km (13 miles) from town and good for swimming, even if it's less spectacular in height than Kuangsi. During the rainy season, the falls are stunning. Hire a driver for about US$5 (£2.75) or pay a bit extra for a ferryboat.

36km (20 miles) south of town. Admission 10,000 kip (US$1/£0.55). Daily dawn–dusk.

Pak Ou Caves &&   The longtail-boat ride on the Mekong is alone a worthy day trip. This stretch of river is lovely—and from the base of the cave entrance, you get a view of the high cliffs and swirling water of the Nam Ou River as it joins the Mekong. Inside the caves are enshrined a pantheon of Buddhist statuary. A day tour costs US$5/£2.75 per person in a boat shared by many tourists (more for a private charter). Arrangements can be made at any hotel front desk at an inflated rate, or you can just go down along the Mekong and negotiate with boat drivers directly (these guys are sure to find you). The half-day trip often includes a visit to a weaving village or the **Lao Whiskey village,** where you'll have a chance to try some really potent local brew.

25km (16 miles) from town on the Mekong. Admission 10,000 kip (US$1/£0.55).

OUTDOOR ACTIVITIES

Luang Prabang is a good base for exploring the jungly north. The folks at **Green Discovery,** in the center of town (✆ 071/212-093; www.greendiscoverylaos.com), are a top choice. They offer tours and connections to the far north in Luang Namtha, in addition to multisport adventures along the Mekong and the picturesque Nam Ou out of Nong Kiaw (east of Luang Prabang).

SHOPPING

Luang Prabang is a good place to find unique hand-woven textiles. The **Night Market** opens at dusk each evening, near Wat Mai along Phothisarat Road at the town center. Everything from good silk to jewelry to T-shirts sells for a song.

Ban Lao Natural Products, on the Mekong riverfront (✆ 030/514-555; www.ban-lao.com), offers locally produced hand-made silks, handicrafts, clothing, and naturally made soaps and beauty products, while promising fair trade with its local producers to help increase sustainable development. **Kopnoi,** in Ban Aphay on the back side of Mount Phousi by the Nam Kham River, also offers a diverse product line, including jewelry and clothing, and promotes the exportation of products made in Laos (it also has an art gallery upstairs).

Spa Treatments for All Budgets

The newly opened spa at **La Résidence Phou Vao** (p. 263) is by far the most luxurious in town. Like the hotel itself, treatments are pricey but well worth the money. The **Red Cross of Luang Prabang,** near Wat Visoun to the southeast of the city, offers traditional massage and herbal sauna to raise money for its education programs. The Red Cross is the cheapest place in town, in addition to funding a good cause. The herbal sauna is open daily from 4:30 to 8:30pm; a 1-hour massage (9am–8:30pm) costs just US$3 (£1.65).

Natural papermaking has taken the town by storm, and **Baan Khily Gallery,** on the eastern end of Sisavangvong Road (© 071/212-611), is where long-time German expat Oliver Bandmann produces and exhibits. Ask about papermaking classes.

Caruso, Sandra Yuck's inspired collection of houseware, furnishings, and silk, has an outlet in a renovated colonial along Sisavangvong, as well as a display area above Ban Vat Sene (see "Snacks & Cafes," above). And **Ban Mixay** (© 071/253-535) is a branch of the popular Vientiane boutique that sells the same quality silks, clothes, and handicrafts.

Lisa Regale (© 071/253-224) has a collection of ready-to-wear silk, including some very unique antique pieces, at her gallery behind Wat Xieng Thong.

Satri Lao Silk, on "restaurant row," has good, affordable cloth, while **Naga Creations** (© 071/212-775) presents an eclectic mix of jewelry. **Walkman Village** (© 020/567-3909) is the place to find jackets, packs, and other travel gear before heading up north.

LUANG PRABANG AFTER DARK

Luang Prabang is a morning town, really, but there are a few good spots for drinks and music. Backpackers fill the quiet lanes of **Ban Wat That,** the old silversmith quarter near the Mekong on the east end of town, and you'll sometimes find folks up late. Take a walk down any alley for budget guesthouses and adjoining bamboo bars. **Lemongrass,** near the Sala Prabang, is an attractive wine bar with a small sitting area overlooking the Mekong. On "restaurant row," **Luang Prabang Restaurant** always seems to attract a large after-dinner crowd enjoying a Beer Lao or four. The **Hive,** just next door to L'étranger (p. 269) and run by the same folks, plays drum-and-bass and hip-hop to a young crowd until late into the evening.

7 Luang Namtha & the Far North

North of Luang Prabang, things get a little rough. It's where Laos travel separates the "travelers" from the "tourists." Roads here are, on the whole, just dirt tracks, and most towns are outposts, like the dusty main streets in the American Old West. This part of the country is best visited with a tour company (try **Diethelm Travel** out of Luang Prabang, p. 261) or with a private car and driver.

Luang Namtha itself is not much to see, really—just a row of low concrete-and-wood storefronts on a dusty avenue and a few miles of bucolic road that take you to the picturesque little **Old Town** (6km/3¾ miles down the main road); nonetheless, it's connected by air with Vientiane and is a great base to explore the surrounding countryside. Trekking, kayaking, and visiting remote villages in the phenomenal **Nam Ha Biodiversity Conservation Area,** named an ASEAN Heritage Park in 2005, bring many up to this outpost. Come with the knowledge that travel here is off the beaten track, you are far from all but the most basic medical assistance, and electricity flows only a few hours each day.

GETTING THERE

BY PLANE   From Vientiane, there are a few flights each week, depending on the season, and they cost US$84 (£46). The airport is 6km (3¾ miles) from town; a *songthaew* (covered pickup) will run about US$4 (£2.20) with some friendly bargaining.

BY BUS   Luang Namtha is a major hub in the north, connected by bus with Jinhong, China, via the Laos towns of Boten (you'll need to have a prearranged visa),

Muang Sing, and Huay Xai (at the Thai border—this route is currently plagued by construction, with traffic delays expected to last well into 2007). From Luang Prabang, you'll be bounced and jounced for 5 hours (25,000 kip/US$2.50/£1.40) until the dusty bus stop in Oudomxay. If your teeth are still in your head and buses are leaving (most buses have morning departures), you can connect with Luang Namtha for 20,000 kip (US$2/£1.10); sometimes there is no same-day connection, and travelers hole up for a US$2 (£1.10) night in Oudomxay before the early-morning connection with Luang Namtha. You can also hop on the through bus from Vientiane. Arriving sometime between 4 and 6pm in the afternoon, it's 10 hours overnight. Bus travel in the far north offers beautiful views and a chance to meet locals, but it is pretty grueling in the best of circumstances.

BY CAR   Contact **Diethelm Travel** in Luang Prabang (© 071/212-277; fax 071/212-032; www.diethelmtravel.com) for jeep or minivan rental. It's expensive, but a decent option for the north.

VISITOR INFORMATION & TOURS

Green Discovery (© 086/211-484; www.greendiscoverylaos.com), in cooperation with the New Zealand– and UNESCO-backed **Nam Ha Ecotourism Project** (© 086/312-150; www.unescobkk.org) and the **Boat Landing Eco-Lodge,** puts together community-based ecotourism tours to Khmu and Hmong villages in the area, as well as great kayak and raft trips in the pristine Nam Ha NBCA. You'll visit villages where they'll ask, through a translator, "Why are you here?" because foreign wayfarers are still an anomaly. The Nam Ha River is an exciting whitewater ride through cavernous jungle overgrowth or steep-walled gullies teeming with life. The folks at Green Discovery ensure that their clients set a good example and tread lightly in the villages, while the Nam Ha Ecotourism Project is designed so that revenue generated from the program goes directly to the villages and guides, developing the local economy and thereby encouraging forest conservation by reducing reliance on natural resources. Highly recommended.

FAST FACTS: Luang Namtha

Currency Exchange There are a few foreign exchange counters on the main road (Rte. 3), and **Lane Xang Bank** has a branch on the south end of town. You can also change U.S. and Thai currency to kip in the central market.

Internet Access There is one Internet cafe on the southern end of the main street, with service at 600 kip (US6¢/£0.03) per minute.

Telephones Most guesthouses can do callback service. There are also phone booths on the main road that are IDD-capable and require a local card, which you can buy at any store or the post office.

WHERE TO STAY & DINE .

For lodging, the **Boat Landing** (© 086/312-398; www.theboatlanding.laopdr.com) is a rustic little gem on the banks of the Nam Tha River some 6km (3¾ miles) from the town center (just past the old town in Luang Namtha). It has teamed up with

Green Discovery to provide eco-friendly treks and tours to local villages and the Nam Ha Biodiversity Conservation Area. In Luang Namtha proper, an array of budget accommodations start at US$2 (£1.10). Try **Oudomsinh Hotel** (© 086/312-077).

8 Xieng Khouang Province: Phonsavan & the Plain of Jars

Xieng Khouang has the dubious distinction of being one of the most heavily bombed provinces in the most heavily bombed country on earth. For centuries, it has been at the crossroads of war, culminating in the U.S.'s "secret war" against the Pathet Lao and North Vietnamese Army. The former capital city of Muang Khouang was so thoroughly destroyed by American bombing raids that the capital was moved in 1975 to Phonsavan, itself heavily damaged. However, the people do not seem to harbor any ill will and have taken the tragedy of the war years in stride, incorporating the remnants of war into their daily lives. Halved bombshells serve as pig troughs, ammunition cases function as lunchboxes, metal tracks airlifted for makeshift runways are converted to convenient driveways, and there is even a village dedicated to and decorated by found shrapnel and bomb material. Today, Xieng Khouang is gaining recognition as home to the **Plain of Jars,** a little-understood group of archaeological sites of enormous stone jars, or drums, buried in the earth. **Phonsavan,** which has virtually no buildings remaining from the pre-war years, is merely a base from which to explore the area and not much else. The jars themselves are a fun and interesting mystery. A visit to this region is certainly educational: You'll learn about the Hmong rebels, the mysterious recent history, and the many demining projects. Spring for a good guide to take you around to the many sites. *Note:* Higher altitude and weather patterns mean that it can get chilly here, especially in the rainy season, so bring a few layers.

GETTING THERE

BY PLANE   **Lao Airlines** (© 021/214-427; www.laoairlines.com) flies to Xieng Khouang from Vientiane (US$53/£29), five times weekly, and Luang Prabang (US$40/£22), twice weekly, with return flights now offered to both cities. Schedules change with the seasons. Make sure you reconfirm your flight out *every day until you leave* to guarantee a seat back (flights overbook in the high season and get canceled in the low season).

BY BUS   Daily buses connect Phonsavan with Vientiane (6–8 hr.; 90,000 kip/ US$9/£4.95) and Luang Prabang (6–8 hr.; 85,000 kip/US$8.50/£4.70). Route 7, a spur of the main north–south artery, Route 13, begins 150km (93 miles) north of Vientiane; the road, once a contender for the world's worst, is now in great condition. The ridge-top scenery is spectacular, but buses are overcrowded and slow. The road is also prone to landslides, so ask travel agents and fellow travelers about current conditions before setting out. Private vehicle hire is costly, but the best choice.

Warning   **Beware of Unexploded Ordnance**

Xieng Khouang province is one of the most heavily bombed areas on earth. UXO, or unexploded ordnance, is numerous, particularly in the form of small cluster bombs, blue or gray metal balls about the size of a fist. Don't stray into uninhabited, unexplored areas without a good guide, and don't touch anything on the ground. The jar sites are safe.

VISITOR INFORMATION & TOURS

At **Sousath Travel,** adjoining Maly Guesthouse, a short ride south from the town center (℃ **061/312-031;** fax 061/312-395), the effusive Mr. Sousath is the definitive source on local history and a true steward of the jar sites; he has been featured in a number of local history and archaeology books and was in a documentary, *Ravens,* about the covert CIA pilots who flew from the area during the Vietnam War. A tour with Mr. Sousath himself, if you are so fortunate, is one of the town's most interesting activities. A car and driver can be arranged.

Diethelm Travel, on the main road in Phonsavan (℃ **061/211-118;** www.diethelm travel.com), meets its usual high standards and can cater guided tours to any sights, local or remote.

Local guides will come and find you upon arrival or if you're wandering central Phonsavan. Make sure they have been certified by the government, be specific about the itinerary, and barter for price. Freelance guides usually charge about US$30 (£17) for tour and transport.

For information on the ongoing unexploded ordinance (UXO) cleanup effort in Xieng Khouang, talk to the knowledgeable staff at the **Mines Advisory Group** (MAG), on the main road. MAG has been working in Laos since 1994 to clear the country of the deadly remnants of the U.S.'s "secret war" that continue to kill to this day.

FAST FACTS: Phonsavan

Currency Exchange There are a few foreign exchange counters on the main road (Rte. 7) near the central market, and **Lane Xang Bank** has a branch near the post office.

Internet Access Internet access is hard to come by, but there are a few spots where you can log on. Connections are of the dial-up variety, slow and prone to disconnecting mid-email. Patience is essential. Try **Hot Net,** near the main intersection, the cheapest in town at 300 kip per minute (US$1.80/£0.99 per hr.).

WHERE TO STAY & DINE

Budget accommodations line the main street (Rte. 7), and if you don't care to dine at your hotel, take a short stroll and you'll find a few good noodle and snack shops near the town center, **Sangha Restaurant** being the best. For Western dishes, stop by **Craters,** next door to the Mines Advisory Group and owned by an Australian expat who used to work for MAG.

Maly Hotel Owned and operated by local historian and raconteur Mr. Sousath, this is a good, low-luxe, but comfortable base for exploring the jars. Built pell-mell in a series of additions, the rooms vary and the decor runs the gamut from comfortable wooden lodge to musty cell. Ask to see your room before checking in. A few luxe setups have floor-to-ceiling windows and fine views. Bathrooms are guesthouse basic with fickle solar showers. Good Lao and Western food can be found in the popular lobby restaurant, whose walls are covered with land mines and various other objects of destruction. The staff is friendly and helpful, and the convenient offices of **Sousath Travel** are the best place in town to arrange for a guide. Don't miss any chance to chat with Mr. Sousath.

A short ride south from the town center, P.O. Box 649, Phonsavan. © 061/312-031. sousathp@laotel.com. 24 units. US$8–US$55 (£4.40–£30) double. MC, V. **Amenities:** Restaurant; tour service; car/jeep rental. *In room:* TV.

Vansana Plain of Jars Hotel ✮ Perched on a hill just off the main road, the Vansana was voted "hotel number one" in my unofficial straw poll of Phonesavanians. Luxurious by local standards, the rooms are no-frills but clean. Standard units sport tile floors and balconies facing the town below. Suites are a good upgrade, with the extra US$10 getting you a fireplace in the living area, a valuable addition during the winter months. The main drawback is the lack of an in-house travel agency for trips to the jars, but the town center is just a short stroll down the hill. A good choice.

Atop a hill northwest of the town center, Phonsavan. © 061/213-170. Fax 061/213-174. www.vansanahotel-group.com. 36 units. US$40 (£22) twin/double; US$50 (£28) suite. MC, V. **Amenities:** Restaurant; bar; shuttle service; business center; laundry service. *In room:* A/C, satellite TV, minibar.

WHAT TO SEE & DO

Thought to date back some 2,000 years, the archaeological finds at the **Plain of Jars** are stunning and mysterious. Hundreds of stone jars of varying sizes, the largest a bit over 2.7m (9 ft.) high, cover a plateau stretching across 24km (15 miles). Jars have been found in 15 different sites in the area so far. Visit these sites with a guide, if only to allay any fears over land mines (all areas within the sites are safe, though) and to get some perspective on local history. Be sure to get the obligatory "This is me in a jar!" shot before officials make restrictions on touching or climbing on them. You can cover the main sites in a day, but you might want to take a few days and explore the surrounding Hmong villages. **Na Sala,** a busy Hmong village, is a good destination. Be sure to go with a guide who can translate and make introductions.

Plain of Jars: Site 1 ✮✮ If you're short on time, this is the one to see. Set on a high hill is one of the largest of the jars, called the Doloman jar, amid a cockeyed collection of 300 jars. It's all quite surreal and a unique photo op; a visit here gives you a great perspective on the surrounding countryside. Burn scars still dot the area, and legend has it that a few enterprising members of the American military once tried to lift one of the jars with a helicopter and failed. This is the easiest site to access and the most picturesque.

11km (7 miles) from town, near Ban Hang Village. Admission 7,000 kip (US70¢/£0.40).

Plain of Jars: Sites 2 and 3 ✮ These sites are both off the beaten track and require some fancy driving and a bit of picturesque rice-paddy and pasture walking to reach, but they are certainly worth it. Site 2 is situated near a small waterfall and has some 60 jars in a grove atop a small hill. Site 3 will have you crossing a bamboo bridge and picking your way through fields to get to open pasture on a high hill with some 100 jars.

Site 2 is 22km (14 miles) from town, and Site 3 is just a short drive from there. Both have admission fees of 7,000 kip (US70¢/£0.40).

9 The Far South: Pakse & Champasak Provinces

South of Vientiane, Route 13 traces the Mekong River as it forms the border with Thailand. The river passes through Savannakhet, a French colonial outpost, and then Pakse, a midsize town, before reaching the wide Mekong floodplain, where the river spreads into hundreds of rivulets before cascading over dynamic **Phapheng Falls** to Cambodia. What brings many to this little-visited region is **Wat Phou,** a pre-Angkorian ruin

Finds Luxury on the Mekong

The **Vat Phou Cruise** operated by the folks at **Luang Say Cruises** (© 021/215-958 in Vientiane; www.asian-oasis.com) is a 3-day, 2-night excursion between Pakse and the 4,000 Islands (Si Phan Don) in the far south. In high season, trips cost a whopping US$479 (£263) for a single, or US$362 (£199) per person in a shared double, but it's worth it. The boat is large and luxurious, with a top deck replete with quiet corners in which to relax and enjoy the passing scenery. Private state rooms are small but air-conditioned and comfortable. All trips begin in Pakse. Trips include stops at small villages, the unique pre-Angkorian ruins of Oum Muong, and, of course, the south's premier attraction, Wat Phou. The food is ample, guides are informative and professional, and service is very friendly.

---

on a hilltop overlooking the river near the town of **Champassak.** The city of **Pakse** is the best base for exploring, and there are some great new luxury options, like a multiday cruise on Luang Say's Wat Phou riverboat. **Si Phan Don,** in the far south, literally means "the 4,000 Islands." Here, the Mekong spreads out like the branches of a tree and you'll find stunning waterfalls and quaint island towns like **Don Khong.** The town of **Savannakhet** is a good stop for those connecting overland with Vientiane, and there are also some good rustic resorts like those at Tad Lo, Saravan, and the Bolavan Plateau. Arranging a tour with Diethelm Travel (p. 234) or Exotissimo Travel (p. 234), even just for transport, is a good choice.

GETTING THERE

BY PLANE   Lao Airlines (© 021/214-427; www.laoairlines.com) flies regularly from Vientiane to Pakse for US$95 (£52). The airport in Pakse is on the opposite side of the river from the main town. Tuk-tuks connect to town for 8,000 kip (US80¢/£0.45) with bargaining.

BY BUS   Buses connect from Vientiane via Savannakhet. The road is good thanks to the many new Japanese-funded bridges, but it's 2 long days of travel. It is 8 hours from Vientiane to Savannakhet and then up to 10 hours from Savannakhet to Pakse. It's worth a flight, even if just one-way.

Pakse is just a short ride from the Thai border and a few hours by bus from Ubon Ratchatani.

WHERE TO STAY

Accommodations choices are limited in the far south. **Champa Residence,** on Route 13, east of town in Ban Phonosath (© 031/212-120), has tidy rooms in a former colonial from US$30 (£17). The **Champasak Palace Hotel,** half a mile east of town on Route 13 (© 031/212-263), on the banks of the Se Don River, has rooms from US$40 (£22). In the heart of town, **Hotel Pakse,** Street 5, Ban Watlouang (© 031/212-131), has basic concrete rooms with air-conditioning and cable TV from US$18 (£9.90).

WHAT TO SEE & DO

Wat Phou ★★   Predating the temples of Angkor (sometime before the 9th century), this stunning hilltop site is a highlight in Laos. Wat Phou was built in homage to the

Hindu god Shiva, on grounds once used for animist worship. Some archaeologists posit that the temple is also homage to the Mekong and a copy of a similar site along the Ganges in India. The compound is symmetrical, with a broad causeway as the central axis and expansive reflecting *barays,* or ponds, now gone dry, as flanks. The approach to the main temple site passes between two pavilions, crumbling but still grand, before ascending the steep central stair.

The upper level is the main sanctuary, which was converted to Buddhism in the 13th century and now houses nonhistoric Buddhist statues and an altar. The temple exterior is decorated in fine reliefs of Apsara, alluring mythical female dancers. The sanctuary was reportedly a site of human sacrifices from the pre–Wat Phou temple era. Today, in a ceremony conducted on the fourth day of the waxing moon in the sixth lunar month, a bull is ritually slaughtered by members of a nearby Mon-Khmer (an ethnic group closely related to the Khmer) tribe in honor of the founding father of the temple. The view of the surrounding Mekong basin is spectacular. Don't miss the spring at the base of the cliff behind the main temple. The water is thought sacred and visitors anoint themselves to receive a blessing.

There is a small museum at the entrance featuring artifacts from the original site. Wat Phou is best visited with a tour. Diethelm Travel (p. 234) and Exotissimo Travel (p. 234) can make any arrangements. The *wat* is also a stop on the **Vat Phou Cruise** (see above).

14km (8¾ miles) southwest of Champasak; 45km (28 miles) from Pakse. Admission 30,000 kip (US$3/£1.65). Daily 8am–4pm.

6

Vietnam

by Brian Calvert

For many Westerners, Vietnam was a war. Now, though, it has come into itself as a destination, with beauty, idiosyncrasies, and a people longing to put Vietnam's many conflicts and occupations behind them. Its mountains, jungles, and coastlines range from virtually untouched to well-groomed and welcoming, and the country now offers anything a traveler might hope for. Villages remain quaint and hospitable. Major cities are cosmopolitan but retain much of their old charm; a duck off a main street can lead a visitor down old stone corridors, into bustling markets, or through neighborhood enclaves with individual personalities. Ethnic hill tribes live much the way they always have, albeit with some finding themselves now melding into something not old, not new, but simply different. Where it might have once been said that Vietnam was struggling to put its past behind it, there is now plenty of evidence to say that it has finally succeeded. Even a short trip to this multifaceted country will confirm this.

Vietnam's more than 2,000 years of history was shaped by occupation: The Chinese, French, and Americans left a brutal imprint on the Vietnamese story, but also left a rich cultural footprint. Chinese and French food, language, and architecture have been assimilated smoothly into the already fascinating Vietnamese culture. An ancient Confucian university, a Zen monastery, a Buddhist temple built in the Hindu style, a Vietnamese puppet show, French country chalets, and gourmet restaurants—you'll find them all in Vietnam.

Vietnam claims 54 minority groups, mostly in rural, mountainous areas. The distinct clothing, language, and customs of each indigenous group present another side of the country entirely. The Kingdom of Cham, an Indian- and Khmer-influenced nation, also made what is present-day Vietnam its home from the 2nd through 18th centuries, leaving a stunning legacy of art and architecture.

This is a land of rich natural beauty. From plunging mountains and craggy limestone formations to dense jungles, vast river deltas, and pristine beaches, Vietnam's ecological treasures alone are worth a trip. Adventure- and outdoor-travel outfitters abound, and many visitors come to trek, bicycle, and paddle their ways to scenic serenity.

If you want to see the country's past in terms of its wars, you can easily do so. Many sights, like the tunnel city of **Vinh Moc,** near **Hue;** crumbling pill-boxes of the **DMZ** (demilitarized zone); or old Viet Cong hideouts in the **Mekong Delta** or in the areas outside Ho Chi Minh City (Saigon) serve as somber reminders of the past. American veterans and history buffs of all nationalities visit former bases and battle sites. The Vietnamese, though, have moved on; the sentiment is almost a public policy, and you'll hear it like a mantra. You might have a chance to talk about the wars on a casual basis with people, and some might even share their stories, but expect no recrimination.

Instead, the Vietnamese are going forward to establish their country as a strong nation at peace. Since the inception of *doi moi*, the Communist Party's policy of loosening stringent economic restrictions and opening trade, Vietnam has enjoyed exponential growth. From the smallest northern village to the placid capital of **Hanoi** to frantic **Ho Chi Minh City (Saigon)** in the south, all are rushing for a slice of the pie. National infrastructure is improving, foreign investment flowing, and tourism booming. The central business districts rank with any in the world for quantity of glass and steel, and they're peopled by an increasing number of Western businesspeople. Expat residents bring along their pocketbooks and appetites, and local hotels and restaurants rise to the challenge.

Travel here is a breeze; English speakers are many and, though the touts are plenty, you'll have your pick of tour guides, ticket agents, and drivers. Vietnam's relatively good roadways and efficient, inexpensive air system—indeed, its very shape—put much of this small country within easy reach of the casual traveler. Vietnam also hosts an ever-expanding collection of affordable, luxury resorts.

So, whether you want to close a chapter on the past, experience a lively ancient culture, see beautiful countryside, get your adventure fix, or just enjoy a bit of beachside or cosmopolitan comfort, Vietnam has it all. Now is the time to go: The word is out, and the number of visitors is steadily swelling. Be sure to bring your camera—the whole country is a photo op on the go.

1 Getting to Know Vietnam

THE LAY OF THE LAND

Vietnam is an S-shaped strip that borders China in the north, Laos in the west, and Cambodia in the southwest. Covering about 331,520 sq. km (129,293 sq. miles), it is roughly the size of Italy. It has a varied and lush topography, with two deltas, tropical forests, craggy mountains and rock formations, and a coastline that stretches for 3,260km (2,021 miles), much of it white-sand beaches. Vietnam also claims thousands of islands off its coast.

THE REGIONS IN BRIEF

THE NORTH The scenic northern highlands have craggy mountains hovering over sweeping green valleys. The inhabitants of the region are ethnic minorities and hill tribes, scratching out a living from subsistence farming and still somewhat isolated from civilization. Popular tourism destinations are **Sapa, Lao Cai, Son La,** and **Dien Bien Phu,** the former French military garrison. Vietnam's tallest mountain, Fansipan (3,143m/10,309 ft.), hovers over Sapa near the border with China in the northwest, part of the mountain range the French dubbed the "Tonkinese Alps." The **Red River Delta** lies to the east of the highlands. It is a triangular shape off the **Gulf of Tonkin,** an extension of the South China Sea. In the gulf is spectacular **Halong Bay,** 3,000 limestone formations jutting from still blue waters. South of the highlands but still in the northern region is **Hanoi,** Vietnam's capital city.

THE CENTRAL COAST To the east is the central coastline, location of major cities **Hue, Hoi An,** and **Danang.** Hue is Vietnam's former capital and Imperial City (1802–1945). Hoi An, a major trading port in the mid–16th century, still shows the architectural influences of the Chinese and Japanese traders who passed through and settled here, leaving buildings that are perfectly preserved. Danang, Vietnam's fourth-largest city, is a port town whose major attractions include the museum of Cham antiquities and nearby China Beach. Major flooding in the year 2000 caused immeasurable damage to the lowlands here.

THE SOUTH-CENTRAL COAST & HIGHLANDS   The central highlands area is a temperate, hilly region occupied by many of Vietnam's ethnic minorities. Travelers are most likely to visit historic **Dalat,** a resort town nestled in the Lang Bien Plateau, established by the French at the turn of the 20th century as a recreation and convalescence center. On the coast is **Nha Trang,** Vietnam's preeminent sea resort.

THE MEKONG DELTA   Farthest south, the Mekong Delta is a flat land formed by soil deposits from the Mekong River. Its climate is tropical, characterized by heat, high rainfall, and humidity. The delta's sinuous waterways drift past fertile land used for cultivating rice, fruit trees, and sugar cane. The lower delta is untamed swampland. The region shows the influences of ancient Funan and Khmer cultures, as well as the scars from war misery, particularly in battles with neighboring Cambodia. **Ho Chi Minh City (Saigon),** Vietnam's largest cosmopolitan area, lies just past its northern peripheries.

A LOOK AT THE PAST

Vietnam began in the Red River Valley, around the time of the 3rd century B.C., with a small kingdom of Viet tribes called Au Lac. The tiny kingdom was quickly absorbed into the Chinese Qin Dynasty in 221 B.C., but as that dynasty crumbled, it became part of a new land called Nam Viet, ruled by a Chinese commander. In 111 B.C., it was back to China again, this time as part of the Han empire. It remained part of greater China for the next thousand years or so. The Chinese form of writing was adopted (to be replaced by a Roman alphabet in the 17th century), Confucianism was installed as the leading ideology, and Chinese statesmen became the local rulers. Few effectively challenged Chinese rule, with the exception of a nobleman's two daughters, the Trung sisters, who led a successful but short-lived revolt in A.D. 39.

In A.D. 939, the Chinese were finally thrown out and the Vietnamese were left to determine their own destiny under a succession of dynasties. The kingdom flourished and strengthened, enough for the Vietnamese to repel the intrusion of Mongol invaders under Kublai Khan from the north, and armies from the kingdom of Champa from Danang and the east, in the mid–13th century. Gathering strength, Vietnam gradually absorbed the Cham empire and continued to move south, encroaching upon Khmer land, taking the Mekong Delta and almost extinguishing the Khmer as well. There followed a brief period of Chinese dominance in the early 1400s, but the biggest risk to the country's stability was to come from the inside.

Torn between rival factions in court, the country split along north–south lines in 1545; the north followed the Le Dynasty, while the south followed the Nguyen. The country was reunited under Emperor Gia Long in 1802, but by the 1850s, the French, already settled and on the prowl in Indochina, launched an offensive that resulted in the Vietnamese accepting protectorate status 3 decades later.

Although the French contributed greatly to Vietnamese infrastructure, the proud people of Vietnam bridled under colonial rule. In 1930, revolutionary Ho Chi Minh found fertile ground to establish a nationalist movement. As in China, World War II and occupation by the Japanese in 1940 helped fuel the movement by creating chaos and nationalist fervor. Upon the retreat of the Japanese, Ho Chi Minh declared Vietnam an independent nation in August 1945.

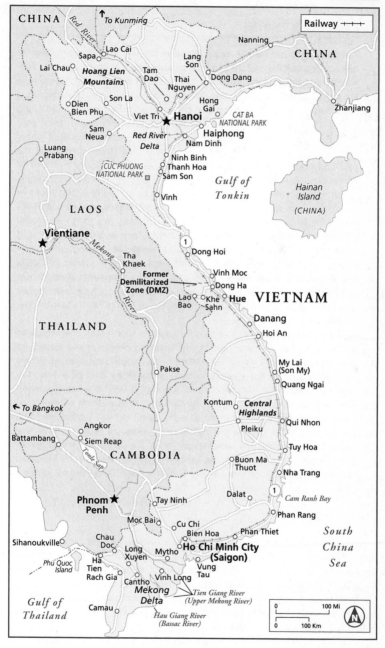

Vietnam

Responsible Tourism

Tourists in Vietnam are a relatively new species, and it's important to respect local culture and try to minimize our impact on the country. In Vietnam try to keep personal ideologies and political debate quiet. Vietnamese are proud of their triumph over outside threats, autonomy that came at a great cost in lives and suffering, and the doors are just opening after a long period of isolation (both because of external sanctions and internal policies). The common sentiment among Vietnamese, more than half of whom were born after the end of conflict with the United States, is to forget the past and push on into an ever brighter future, economically and socially. There are, however, many monuments to Vietnam's years of struggle. When visiting monuments to war—or one of the many sights that depict or revisit the years of struggle against the Chinese, French, or Americans—it's important to practice restraint. Refrain from jokes, try to go in smaller groups, and engage in debates or personal feelings in discreet tones or at a later time. In places like **Ho Chi Minh's Mausoleum** in Hanoi, the monument to the **My Lai Massacre** in central Vietnam, at the tunnels of **Cu Chi** and **Vinh Moch,** in the **Hanoi Hilton,** or in the **War Remnants Museum,** discretion is not only requested, it's often enforced (visitors have been known to receive actual hand slaps and barked orders at Ho Chi Minh's Mausoleum, for example).

Our strongest impact as visitors is through our money and how we spend it. Giving gifts in Vietnam, particularly to young people or the many who approach foreign visitors with calls of help, is a double-edged sword. Where it might gratify in the short-term to help someone and fill a few outstretched hands with sweets or school supplies, it sets up a harmful precedent, and props up the image of foreign visitors as walking ATMs—to be bilked, begged, and bamboozled at every turn. You will be followed and harried in Vietnam quite a bit, and in some areas, particularly Hanoi, the young book-and-postcard salesmen and touts are part of organized gangs and very persistent (although the hard-sell has lessened with the increased number of tourists). Saying a polite but firm "No" to persistent hawkers goes a long way to alleviating the problem.

The French did not agree, however, and the two sides fought bitterly until 1954. The French, having lost a decisive battle at Dien Bien Phu, agreed to a cease-fire at the Geneva Convention that year. The two sides determined that the country would be split along north and south at the 17th Parallel, with the Viet Minh (League for the Independence of Vietnam) having control of the north and the French supporters having control of the south. Elections were to be held in 2 years to determine who would lead a new, unified Vietnam.

Because of resistance to the American-supported regime in the south, led by Ngo Dinh Diem, the elections were never held. The communists continued to gain power, and Diem was assassinated, putting the southern regime in peril. Finally, in 1965,

Among **Vietnam's ethnic minorities** in the Central Highlands and the far north, be most careful about your impact. These are communities that are on the fringes of Vietnamese culture, distinct enclaves where ancient practices of animistic faiths still hold sway. Photographers should be sure to ask before snapping portraits or images of ceremonial sights; increasingly, asking for permission to photograph is met with pleas for money, but say "No" and move on. It's important not to assault locals with a camera, however uniquely attired and exotic they may be. Gifts of clothes or medicines might seem helpful but only diminish already-eroding ancient cultures and customs of clothing manufacture, where in fact one's clothing is an integral part of status in the community, and traditional medicines, erasing ancient traditions passed on from the time of migration from China. Learn about these people and their traditions as much as you can before traveling among them—in fact, your knowledge about any place that you travel makes you less likely to make uncomfortable blunders. Keep an open mind, and be ready to learn, not teach. Below are a few good guidelines for environmental and cultural stewardship:

Don't litter: Sounds simple, but in a country where you will rarely find a public trash receptacle (most things are discarded on the street and swept up en-masse), it is difficult. As unimportant as it might feel to drop a gum wrapper, more important is your example of *not* dropping a gum wrapper. On rural hiking trails or in national parks, tie a garbage bag to the outside of your pack and pick up wrappers along the way. Don't preach, but if locals ask what you are doing—and they certainly will—explain that you are keeping the park clean and that it is something that anyone can do.

Wherever possible, try to **support the local economy**—eat at local joints, buy essentials like bottled water and soap at small mom-and-pop shops instead of big air-conditioned department stores, even try public transport (if you are a hearty soul). Don't buy any animal products, even the likes of snake wines or lizard-skin bags, and try to find out if souvenirs are produced locally.

Your behavior as a tourist also reflects on the many tourists who will come after you. Set a good precedent, even when if doesn't feel important.

American president Lyndon Johnson dispatched the first American combat troops to Danang to prop up the south. The Soviet Union and China weighed in with assistance to the north. The rest is history. After a decade of heavy fighting that took 58,000 American and as many as four million Vietnamese lives, the communists took Saigon on April 30, 1975. In 1976, north and south were officially reunited. Rather than enjoying the newfound peace, Vietnam invaded Cambodia after border skirmishes in 1978. China, friend of Cambodia, then invaded Vietnam in 1979.

In the mid-1980s, Vietnam began moving toward *doi moi,* a free-market policy, to save itself from bankruptcy. To further ingratiate itself with the international community, it withdrew its army from Cambodia in 1989, and as the 1990s began, the country began opening to the world. It reorganized its economy toward a market-oriented model, sought diplomatic relations, and in 1991 signed a peace agreement with Cambodia. In 1994, America capitulated and lifted its long-standing trade embargo against Vietnam, and the two countries established diplomatic relations in 1995. Vietnam also joined ASEAN (Association of Southeast Asian Nations).

VIETNAM TODAY

The modern portrait of this once-troubled land is rosy. Today, Vietnam is the world's third-largest rice exporter, and the country is tentatively finding its way in the global economy. Normalization of ties between the U.S. and Vietnam in 1995 was followed by a series of ongoing resolutions and agreements contingent upon Vietnamese complicity with international human-rights and trade standards. President Clinton visited the reunified country in 2000, the first U.S. president since Richard Nixon in 1969, and Vietnam is now a member of the World Trade Organization (WTO).

American Secretary of Defense Donald Rumsfeld met with Vietnam's defense minister in Washington in 2003, and the USS *Vandergrift* pulled into port in Ho Chi Minh City at about the same time, the first U.S. navy ship to dock in a Vietnamese port since hasty withdrawal in 1975. In 2006, Vietnam hosted an Asian-Pacific Economic Cooperation (APEC) summit, welcoming world leaders such as U.S. President George W. Bush. Telling signs.

The road has not always been smooth, however: Pell-mell growth in certain industries—catfish and shrimp hatcheries, for example—circumvents international standards, disrupting markets and raising U.S. ire; and continued reports of humanitarian violations are under close international scrutiny.

Per-capita income in Vietnam is estimated at a meager US$500/£275 per person, but increases steadily each year, especially in urban centers. Rural poverty and lack of good medical services are still major problems. Vietnam hosted the Asian Games in 2003, putting its best foot forward in what was a coup for international opinion. Recent international airline agreements and new direct flights to the U.S. and Europe signify further international cooperation. As a stable, safe, rapidly developing nation, Vietnam appeals to travelers of all tastes and budgets.

VIETNAM'S PEOPLE & CULTURE

Vietnam has a cultural landscape as varied and colorful as its topography. The Viet ethnic group is well in the majority, comprising about 88% of the population, but there are 54 other minority ethnic groups, many of whom are hill tribes living in villages largely untouched by modern civilization.

Though Vietnam has rushed into modernization over the past several years, the economy has remained largely agrarian, with farmers, fishermen, and forestry workers accounting for 73% of the workforce and most of the population still residing in small villages. The Vietnamese have a strong sense of family and of community, and are accustomed to close human contact and far-reaching interrelationships. This might be one of the reasons why, despite centuries of occupation by foreigners, Vietnamese cultural traditions have survived. Moreover, outsiders are still welcomed. Americans, in fact, will get a wide smile and a thumbs up, although the reception is better in the south than in the north.

RELIGION Approximately 70% of all Vietnamese are Buddhists, mainly Mahayana practitioners of Chinese influence (see "Buddha & Buddhism in Southeast

Asia," p. 30). About 10% are Catholics, and the rest are Confucianists, animists (believing in gods of nature), or followers of the unique Vietnamese religion Cao Dai (see the listing on the Cao Dai Holy See Temple, p. 403), an interesting combination of the major world faiths. Islam and Protestantism also have small pockets of believers. While we're on the topic of -isms, it's hard for the casual observer to see any observance of communism at all, other than the prevalence of state-owned entities and the bureaucratic hoops you might have to jump through.

CUISINE   Each region has its specialties, but the hallmarks of Vietnamese food are light, fresh ingredients, heavy on the rice, pork, and fish, with garnishes such as mint, coriander, fish sauce, and chile pepper. Two of the local dishes you're most likely to encounter are *pho,* a noodle soup in a clear broth, and *bun cha,* fresh rice noodles with barbecued pork in sauce. Chinese-influenced dishes can be found, including hot pot, a cook-your-own group activity in which fresh vegetables and chunks of meat and fowl are dipped into boiling broth and then consumed. The French have left their mark as well: Along with excellent restaurants, you'll find espresso and crusty French bread on every street corner.

THE ARTS   Ancient, distinctive Vietnamese art forms remain today, like **water puppetry,** with wooden hand puppets actually dancing across water, and *cheo,* traditional **folk opera.** There is an emerging interest in fine arts, with countless galleries in almost every major Vietnamese city, and an emphasis on traditional techniques such as lacquer and silk painting and wood blocking. Vietnamese **music,** using string and woodwind instruments, bamboo xylophones, and metal gongs, is delicate, distinctive, and appealing. **Literature** has existed since the forming of the nation in folklore, proverbs, and idioms singular to each village and ethnic group, and passed down from century to century. Many of the old tales have been translated and printed in books that you can easily find in foreign-language bookstores.

ETIQUETTE

Although the Vietnamese are generally tolerant of foreign ways, they dress very modestly. Foreigners wearing hot pants or displaying navels, chests, or shoulders will attract stares. Swimsuit thongs and nude beach bathing are out of the question. Some temples flatly refuse to admit persons in shorts, and some smaller towns like Hoi An post signs asking tourists to dress "appropriately," which means you might have a run-in with the police if you don't.

Unfortunately, one byproduct of the relative newness of tourism in Vietnam is an eagerness to separate you from your money. The child hawkers, "tour guides," and cyclo drivers can be extraordinarily persistent, following you for blocks, grabbing your arm, and hounding you at temples and open-air restaurants. Saying "no" is just an invitation to turn up the sales pitch; even if you don't want to be rude, avoiding eye contact and saying nothing is the best way to extricate yourself. It can be wearying, but things have calmed down a bit in recent years. In tour centers like Hoan Kiem Lake in Hanoi or the major sights in Ho Chi Minh City, however, you'll still be besieged; remember that you're not going to hurt anyone's feelings by ignoring them (but it's hard to do).

LANGUAGE

The ancient Vietnamese language, though not complex structurally, is tonal and therefore difficult for many Westerners to master. In its earliest written form, it was based on the Chinese pictographic writing forms—you'll see remnants of that tradition on temple walls—but in the 17th century, a French scholar developed the Roman alphabet that is used today. Unlike other Asian countries, it looks like you can read this stuff, but the system of accent marks is quite involved. Today, most city dwellers seem to speak at least a little English, the older generation speaks some French, and, with growing influence from China (the Chinese comprise well over 50% of all visitors here), younger people are increasingly studying Mandarin. Students especially will be eager to practice English with you. Solo travelers, being less intimidating, are at an advantage; they'll get many opportunities (and invitations) to have a squat on a street corner, drink a "Bia Hoi" (beer Hoi), and meet people.

USEFUL VIETNAMESE PHRASES

English	Vietnamese	Pronunciation
Hello	**Xin chao**	Seen chow
Good-bye	**Tam biet**	Tam bee-et
Thank you	**Cam on**	Cahm un
You're welcome	**Khong co gi**	Kawng koe gee
Yes	**Vang**	Bahng
No	**Khong**	Kawng
Excuse me	**Xin loi**	Seen loy
I don't understand	**Toi khong hieu**	Toy kawng hew
When?	**Luc nao?**	Look now?
Where is . . . ?	**O dau . . . ?**	Er dow . . . ?
drinking water	**nuoc khoang**	nook kwang
hotel	**khach san**	kak san
restaurant	**nha hang**	nya hahng
toilet	**nha ve sinh**	nya vay shin
Turn right	**Re phai**	Ray fie
Turn left	**Re trai**	Ray chrai
How much?	**Bao nhieu?**	Baugh nyew?
I need a doctor	**Toi can bac si**	Toy cahn back see

2 The Best of Vietnam in 2 Weeks

Vietnam's serpentine curve along the South China Sea is the perfect shape for a linear trip that starts in Hanoi and ends in Ho Chi Minh City, often called by its pre-war name, Saigon. Vietnam encompasses the cultures of more than 50 ethnic groups, was ruled by both the Chinese and the French, and is the prototypical Indochinese country. That's a lot to take in.

Days ❶–❷: Hanoi ⭑

Stay in a guest room in the old wing of the **Sofitel Metropole.** The hotel is a short ride or walk from the **Old Quarter,** which you can explore by foot or by cyclo pedicab. Reserve your sleeper berth on a night train to Lao Cai and Sapa for the next night. Then stretch your legs with a walk around **Hoan Kiem Lake** and end your first evening with dinner at **Restaurant Bobby Chinn,** on the southwest corner of the lake. Spend the next day exploring Hanoi's attractions—the **Ho Chi Minh Museum and Mausoleum,** the **Vietnam National Museum of Fine Arts,** the **Hoa Lo Prison**—and grabbing lunch at **Quan An Ngon,** where many local dishes are on offer. Take an early dinner at **Vine,** known for its wine. Thus fortified, board your night train.

Days ❸–❹: Sapa ⭐⭐⭐

You'll arrive before dawn at the border town of Lao Cai; from there, take a minivan to Sapa, a hub of hill-tribe (and tourist) activity in the Tonkinese Alps. Stay at the **Topas Eco-Lodge,** 18km (11 miles) out of town. Rest in the morning, trek in the afternoon, and spend the evening relaxing at the simple, green resort, which overlooks a quiet, plunging valley of jungle and terraced rice fields. The next morning, go trekking with a guide and learn about different minority tribes along the way. Catch the return night train to Hanoi.

Day ❺: Transit to Halong Bay

If you plan it right, you can arrive in Hanoi in the early morning and be on your way to Halong Bay not long after.

Days ❻–❼: Halong Bay ⭐⭐

The spires and coves of Halong Bay can best be experienced aboard the replica French steamer **Emeraude.** Swim and relax, watch the sun set from the boat's decks, and fall asleep to the lull of the sea.

Days ❽–❾: Hue ⭐⭐

Return to Hanoi to catch an evening flight to Hue, the old imperial capital. Stay at **La Résidence,** an Art Deco gem with an excellent restaurant, **Le Parfum.** Dine here, on the edge of the Perfume River, and relax with a spa treatment or nighttime dip in the pool. The city has a dish named after it, *bun bo Hue,* so be sure to sample this during your stay. Spend your second day exploring the walled **Citadel** and **Imperial City** by foot and the **tombs of the Nguyen Dynasty emperors** by boat. Or make a trip to the **DMZ (demilitarized zone)** of the American War.

Days ❿–⓫: Hoi An

Take an early morning bus to Hoi An, which features the southern stretches of **China Beach** and the UNESCO World Heritage Site **old town.** The **Hoi An Riverside Resort** is a good bet, located at equal distances from both the beach and the town, making getting to either a pleasant bike ride. Schedule your trip to coincide with a full moon in order to see the city's **lantern festivals.** Take a quick evening flight to Saigon.

Days ⓬–⓭: Ho Chi Minh City (Saigon) ⭐⭐

Saigon is Vietnam's most chaotic city; come here for cosmopolitan buzz mixed with nostalgia for the city's past, typified in design by the new **Park Hyatt,** where you can grab dinner or drinks at any of the hotel's venues. Spend your first day on the must-sees: the **Vietnam History Museum;** the **War Remnants Museum;** and **Cholon,** the Chinese district. Have a drink or snack on the rooftop bar of the **Majestic** or the **Rex**—either will give you a feel for long-gone Saigon. On your second day, take a tour of the **Mekong Delta,** try Vietnamese *pho* from any street vendor, and cap off your travels at the **Q Bar,** in the old opera house.

Day ⓮: Return to Hanoi

A daytime flight back to Hanoi will put you on track for a flight home in the evening. Sleep on the plane—you'll have earned the rest.

3 Planning Your Trip to Vietnam

VISITOR INFORMATION

Vietnam's national tourism administration has a fairly good website at **www.vietnam tourism.com**, but it's more bureaucracy than information source. It operates mainly through state-run tourism agencies, **Saigontourist** (www.saigon-tourist.com) and **Hanoi Tourism** (hanoitourism.com.vn), which have offices all over Vietnam and provide comprehensive tours and booking services. For more online info, click on "Vietnam" at the Mekong subregion's cross-referenced site, **www.visit-mekong.com**. Also check out the **Friends of Vietnam Heritage,** in Hanoi (© **04/942-0737;** www.fv heritage.org), which supports cultural events and programs.

The website of the Vietnam Embassy in the U.S., **www.vietnamembassy-usa.org**, is very helpful. Below are Vietnam embassy and consulate locations overseas.

- **In the U.S.:** 1233 20th St. NW, Suite 400, Washington, DC 20036 (© **202/861-0737;** fax 202/861-0917; www.vietnamembassy-usa.org); 866 United Nations Plaza, Suite 435, New York, NY 10017 (© **212/644-0594;** fax 212/644-5732); or 1700 California St., Suite 430, San Francisco, CA 94109 (© **415/922-1577;** fax 415/922-1848).
- **In Canada:** 470 Wilbrod St., Ottawa, Ontario, K1N 6M8 (© **613/236-0772;** fax 613/236-2704).
- **In the U.K.:** 12–14 Victoria Rd., London W8-5RD (© **0171/937-1912;** fax 0171/937-6108).
- **In Australia:** 6 Timbarra Crescent, Malley, Canberra, ACT 2606 (© **2/6286-6059;** fax 2/6286-4534); or 489 New South Head Rd., Double Bay, Sydney, NSW 2028 (© **02/9327-2539;** fax 02/9328-1653).
- **In Thailand:** 82/1 Wireless Rd., Bangkok 10500 (© **251-7202,** 251-5835; fax 251-7201, 251-7203).

ENTRY REQUIREMENTS

Residents of the U.S., Canada, Australia, New Zealand, and the U.K. need both passport and prearranged visa to enter Vietnam. A tourist visa lasts for 30 days and costs US$65/£36. You'll pay a bit more through an agent, but will save yourself some paper

---

Tours for Vietnam Veterans

U.S. veterans are returning to Vietnam—some to see how the story ended, others to stage memorial services, find closure by crossing the 17th Parallel, or just experience Vietnamese culture this time around.

Tours of Peace (TOP), a nonprofit organization started by Jess DeVaney, a retired U.S. Marine, runs tours where veterans not only come to terms with their past by visiting important sights in the Mekong Delta and the DMZ (among others), but also participate in the future. The folks at TOP believe that through helping others, we heal ourselves, so humanitarian aid projects are part of every tour. Financial assistance is available. Check www.topvietnam veterans.org, or write to TOP Vietnam Veterans, 7400 N. Oracle Rd., Suite 100-W, Tucson, AZ 85704.

Another popular veterans' tour operator is **Nine Dragons Tours** (P.O. Box 24105, Indianapolis, IN 46224-0105; © **317/329-0350;** www.nine-dragons.com).

shuffling (it can be done for a nominal fee at any travel agent in Bangkok). Getting a visa takes 5 to 7 days for processing. Applicants must submit an application, a passport, and two passport photos. Tourist visas can be extended twice, each time for 30 days (best done through a travel agent). Multiple-entry business visas are valid for up to 3 months, but require a sponsor in Vietnam. Visas are good for any legal port of entry. *Note:* The visa begins on the date that you specify on your application.

CUSTOMS REGULATIONS

If you're entering the country as a tourist, you do not need to declare any items for personal use. You must declare cash in excess of US$3,000 (£1,650) or the equivalent. You can also import 200 cigarettes, 2 liters of alcohol, and perfume and jewelry for personal use. Antiques are forbidden from export.

MONEY

The official currency of Vietnam is the **dong (VND),** which comes in notes of 500,000, 200,000, 100,000, 50,000, 10,000, 5,000, 1,000, 500, and 200VND. At press time, the exchange rate was **16,000 Vietnamese dong = US$1.** The U.S. dollar is used as an informal second currency, and most items that cost more than a few dollars are priced in the greenback. Prices in this guide are listed as they are quoted, in either U.S. dollars or Vietnam dong.

ATMs Tourist areas have ATMs that dispense cash in Vietnam dong.

CURRENCY EXCHANGE You can exchange currency at banks in any city. Every hotel, no matter how small, will also change money at a slightly lower rate (or charge a small commission). Don't accept torn or very grubby bills. A service charge of anywhere between US$1 and US$4 (£0.55–£2.20) will be levied.

TRAVELER'S CHECKS Banks everywhere can cash traveler's checks in U.S., Canadian, and Australian dollars or pounds sterling. Vendors and retailers usually don't accept traveler's checks, however.

CREDIT CARDS Credit cards are accepted at major hotels, in upmarket restaurants, by tour operators, in most big Hanoi and Ho Chi Minh City outlets, and increasingly outside these two major cities as well. Any Vietcombank branch, as well as big foreign banks, will handle credit card cash advances.

To report lost or stolen credit cards, call the nearest branch of **Vietcombank.** Otherwise, you can go to a post office to place a collect call to the card's international toll-free collect number for cash and a card replacement. The following international numbers are operational 24 hours: **Visa** Global Customer Assistance Service, *✆* **410/581-3836;** and **MasterCard** Global Services, *✆* **314/542-7111.** Note that foreigners aren't permitted to make collect calls, so you'll have to get a local to assist you. Or you can use AT&T, whose access number in Vietnam is *✆* **1/201-0288.** For **American Express,** visit or call the nearest representative, listed below in "Fast Facts: Vietnam."

WHEN TO GO

September through April are the peak months, but with a range of climatic variation in the different regions of the country, there are always areas of Vietnam where you can find favorable weather.

CLIMATE Vietnam's climate varies greatly from north to south. The north has four distinct seasons, with a chilly but not freezing winter from November to April. Summers are warm and wet. The south (which means Nha Trang on down) has hot, humid weather throughout the year, with temperatures peaking March through May into the 90s Fahrenheit (30s Celsius). The south has a monsoon season from April to mid-November. Vietnam is also affected by weather to the east, bearing the brunt of Pacific typhoons, especially August through September.

If you follow a south–north or north–south sweep, you might want to avoid both the monsoons and heat in the south by going sometime between November and February. If you're planning a beach vacation, however, keep in mind that the surf on the south-central coast (China Beach, Nha Trang) is too rough for watersports from October through March (but brings out the windsurfers in droves). Dalat, a hill station in central Vietnam, stays cool all year; and Sapa, in the far north, is at some altitude and gets quite chilly. Otherwise, prepare for heat.

PUBLIC HOLIDAYS & EVENTS   Public holidays are **New Year's Day,** on January 1; **Tet/Lunar New Year,** the 4-day state holiday that falls between late January and mid-February; **Saigon Liberation Day,** on April 30; **International Labour Day,** on May 1; and **National Day of the Socialist Republic of Vietnam,** on September 2. Government offices and tourist attractions are closed at these times.

While **Tet,** the Lunar New Year, is Vietnam's biggest holiday, it's very much a family-oriented time, something like American Thanksgiving. Folks travel far to get home for some of Mom's cooking. Beginning on the evening exactly 3 days from the Lunar New Year and lasting for 4 days, much of the country closes down, including stores, restaurants, and museums, and accommodations may be difficult to find.

HEALTH & SAFETY
HEALTH CONCERNS   See chapter 3's "Health & Safety" section (p. 43) for information on the major health issues that affect travelers to Southeast Asia. It's always good to check the most recent information at the **Centers for Disease Control** (click "Travelers' Health" at **www.cdc.gov**). Health considerations are an important part of trip planning in Vietnam. You will need to get special vaccinations if rural areas are on your itinerary, and that means consulting a doctor at least a few weeks before your trip. If you follow the guidelines here and those of your doctor, there's no reason you can't have a safe and healthy trip.

Your biggest safety precaution is to take care with food. Drink only bottled or boiled water, without ice. Wash your hands often. And follow the old adage: Boil it, cook it, peel it, or forget it.

The following vaccinations are important for Vietnam: **hepatitis A** or **immune globulin (IG)** and **typhoid.** Injections for **Japanese encephalitis** are recommended if you plan to visit rural areas during the rainy season, as well as **rabies** in rural areas where you might be exposed to wild animals. You should also consider booster doses for **tetanus-diphtheria, measles,** and **polio.**

According to the CDC, travelers in Vietnam should take an oral prophylaxis for **malaria** if traveling extensively in rural parts; malaria is not a problem anywhere in the Red River Delta, in coastal areas north of Nha Trang, nor in any of the major cities: Ho Chi Minh City (Saigon), Hanoi, Haiphong, Nha Trang, or Danang. Consult a physician, but the common recommendations for malarial preventative are as follows: atovaquone/proguanil (Malarone), doxycycline, mefloquine (Larium), or primaquine in special circumstances. Side effects abound, so be sure to discuss with a medical professional and follow any treatment regimen to the letter. The best prevention is to cover exposed skin and to use an insect repellent that contains DEET (diethylmethyltoluamide).

SAFETY CONCERNS Vietnam is a safe destination, but take heed of the following: First, the traffic is deadly, so be cautious when crossing the street anywhere; in big cities, pedestrians cross in groups and, if alone, wade out into the street and maintain a steady pace. Second, women should play it safe and avoid going out alone late at night. Third, and most important, beware of unexploded mines when hiking or exploring, especially through old war zones such as the DMZ or My Son. Don't stray off an established path, and don't touch anything you might find lying on the ground. Before you depart, you may want to check with your home country's overseas travel bureau or with the **U.S. State Department** (click "Travel Warnings" at **www.travel. state.gov**) to keep abreast of travel advisories and current affairs that could affect your trip.

Violent crime isn't common in Vietnam, but petty thievery, especially against tourists, is a risk. Pick-pocketing is rampant, and Ho Chi Minh City (Saigon), in particular, has a special brand of drive-by purse snatching via motorbike. Don't wear flashy jewelry or leave valuables in your hotel room, especially in smaller hotels. There are small-time rackets perpetrated against tourists by taxi and cyclo drivers, usually in the form of a dispute on the agreed-upon price after you arrive at your destination. Or else the driver doesn't seem to have change. Simply agree on a price by writing it down first, and always smile and demand change.

GETTING THERE

BY PLANE A cooperative treaty between the U.S. and Vietnam means that there are now direct flights between the two ex-enemies. **United Airlines** flies from the U.S. West Coast, and promotional rates are now available.

Most travelers connect to Vietnam via Bangkok, Hong Kong, Taipei, or Tokyo. See the "Getting There" section (p. 53) in chapter 3 for more international flight tips. **Malaysia Airlines, Singapore Airlines, Thai Airways, Bangkok Airways,** and **EVA Air** fly regular routes from the big hubs. **Vietnam Airlines** connects Vietnam (Ho Chi Minh City) with Vientiane, Phnom Penh, Siem Reap, Bangkok, Kuala Lumpur, Singapore, and Manila.

Reconfirmation for flights 72 hours before departure from Vietnam is a must. Be prepared for a 200,000VND (US$13/£6.90) departure tax for your international flight out. The 20,000VND (US$1.35/£0.70) airport domestic departure tax is usually included in the ticket price.

BY BUS From Laos, it is possible to enter Vietnam overland via a bus ride from Savannakhet in the south. It's 520km (324 miles) to Danang (US$27/£15) or 405km (251 miles) to Hue (US$22/£12). Buses leave at midnight. In Laos, contact **Savanbanhao Tourist Co. (© 041/212-202).** The overnight is long and bumpy, and the road often washes out in rainy season, so be sure to ask around first.

BY BOAT Convenient boat service now connects Vietnam with neighboring Cambodia by way of one of the larger tributaries of the Mekong between Phnom Penh, Cambodia's capital, and the Mekong Delta border town Chau Doc. The trip takes all day and costs US$15 (£8.25). Contact the **Capitol Guesthouse (© 023/217-627),** Cambodia's budget travel cafe, or make more luxury arrangements on a private outboard speedboat with the **Victoria Chau Doc Hotel (© 076/865-010;** www.victoria hotels-asia.com). Be sure to have a prearranged Vietnam visa. The trip takes from morning until late afternoon, depending on water level and weather, and is an interesting adventure with great perspective on Indochine river life.

Tips **Have You Hugged Your Taxi Driver Today?**

"Motorbike? Motorbike? Where you go?" You'll hear it on every street corner in most cities, the relentless pleas of the motorbike-taxi drivers. These guys drive like maniacs, but, especially for the individual traveler, there is no better way to get around any town in Vietnam. They're called Honda Om in Vietnamese, with Om meaning "hug"—thus, it's really a "hugging taxi." These huggers will, after bargaining, take you on a short ride at rates starting from 10,000VND (US65¢/£0.35), or US$2 (£1.10) per hour. Ask for a helmet, and don't be afraid to tap the guy's shoulder and give a "slow-down" hand signal.

GETTING AROUND

The large number of tour operators—from big, inefficient government operations to slick, high-end tour companies and on down to the many budget tourist cafes—means that getting around Vietnam is quite easy. Stay with well-established agencies or the recommendations listed under "Visitor Information" in each section of this chapter. Before booking any kind of transport, be sure to confirm details: meal inclusions, air-conditioning, and so on.

BY PLANE   **Vietnam Airlines** is the country's only domestic air carrier, but prices are reasonable and the service is good. Seats are usually easy to come by if you book a few days in advance. Purchasing tickets is also very easy; all travel agents book for a nominal fee, and many major hotels have V.A. agents in the lobby.

BY TRAIN   Vietnam's major rail network runs from Hanoi to Ho Chi Minh City (Saigon) and back, with stops in Hue, Danang, and Nha Trang. To give you an idea of timing, from Hanoi all the way to Saigon takes 34 hours on the express train; from Hanoi to Hue is about 14 hours on an overnight express. The train is an interesting way to get around, although not much cheaper than flying. Soft-sleeper berths and special tourist cars are available on most routes and are worth the upgrade. Hard-sleeper berths are a good value, but you're stacked three high and cannot sit when the bunks are down. Air-conditioning will cost more per ticket, but is definitely worth it.

It's not difficult to buy tickets at any station, but most hotels and tour agencies will gladly simplify the process and arrange tickets for you for only a nominal fee (check each section of this chapter for contacts). Try **Ratraco**, Vietnam's rail tour provider (just across from the station: 95–97 Le Duan St., 2nd floor, Hanoi; ✆ **04/942-2889;** ratraco@hn.vnn.vn), or book through any travel agent. If you're going from Hanoi to Lao Cai (Sapa) near the China border, be sure to check out the new luxury cars on the *Victoria Express,* run by the **Victoria Sapa Resort** (✆ **20/871-522;** www.victoria hotels-asia.com). See "Getting There" in specific destination sections for more info.

BY BUS/MINIVAN   Public buses are recommended to only the most intrepid travelers. Local transport is slow, crowded, and prone to break down.

Begun as small storefronts making arrangements for early backpackers in the 1990s, Vietnamese **tourist cafes** are the best option for seat-in-coach tours. Now franchised, with offices dotting the country, these convenient outfits run **open-tour bus tickets** that connect all the major points: Ho Chi Minh City (Saigon), Dalat, Phan Thiet, Nha Trang, Hoi An, Danang (optional), Hue, and Hanoi. You can travel in either direction, north to south or vice versa, for under US$30 (£17). The buses leave at set times (most in the morning, though a few overnights are possible); you just decide the day before if you want to be on one. This gives you tremendous freedom to plan your own itinerary. In recent years, **Sinh Café,** which now has computerized reservations services, has really beat out the pack, but all of the cafes match prices and often consolidate services. **A–Z Queen Café, Kim Café,** and **TM Brothers** (in the south) all have comparable service. Check "Visitor Information & Tours" in the destination sections that follow.

BY CAR   For safety (and sanity) in Vietnam, it is best to rent a car only with a hired driver. Rates are reasonable, making this a good way to see things outside urban centers or to take a 1-day city tour of major sights. All major hotels and travel agents can arrange rental.

TIPS ON ACCOMMODATIONS
Vietnam is gaining in popularity among travelers and tourists, so book early, especially during the high season of November and December; accommodations ranging from the glitziest five-stars to the grungiest guesthouses are often booked up and are able to demand high rates. Always ask about seasonal reductions or promotional rates; low-season discounts can be as high as 50%. *Note:* A 20% VAT was instituted for hotels and restaurants in 1999, but expect variation in how it's followed. Some establishments might add the full 20%, while others might charge as little as 10%, and still others will ignore it entirely. Be sure to inquire.

TIPS ON DINING
Many of the world's finest culinary traditions are represented in Vietnam, including French, Chinese, Japanese, and, of course, Vietnamese. Local French cuisine is affordable and authentic. There are some interesting new upscale Vietnamese food venues,

---

⌐Tips   Telephone Dialing at a Glance

- **To place a call from your home country to Vietnam:** Dial the international access code (011 in the U.S. and Canada, 0011 in Australia, 0170 in New Zealand, 00 in the U.K.), plus Vietnam's country code (**84**), the city or local area code (**4** for Hanoi, **8** for Ho Chi Minh City, **54** for Hue, **511** for Danang, **510** for Hoi An, **63** for Dalat, **58** for Nha Trang), and the phone number (for example, 011 84 4 000-0000).

- **To place a call within Vietnam:** Dial the city or area code preceded by a **0** (the way numbers are listed in this book), and then the local number (for example, 04 000-0000). Note that not all phone numbers have seven digits after the city code.

- **To place a direct international call from Vietnam:** Dial the international access code (**00**), plus the country code, the area or city code, and the number (for example, to call the U.S., you'd dial 00 1 000/000-0000).

- **International country codes are as follows:** Australia, 61; Cambodia, 855; Canada, 1; Hong Kong, 852; Indonesia, 62; Laos, 856; Malaysia, 60; Myanmar, 95; New Zealand, 64; the Philippines, 63; Singapore, 65; Thailand, 66; U.K., 44; U.S., 1.

Tips **Smoker's Paradise**

There is no such thing as "nonsmoking" in Vietnam. Only top-end restaurants serving Western cuisine are likely to have a nonsmoking section, and even then it's unlikely that there will be any partition or distance to contain the fumes. Some hotels offer nonsmoking guest rooms or floors. Inquire when booking, especially at hotels popular with business travelers, as the rooms can get pretty musty.

---

but ask locals where to eat, and you'll get a blanket recommendation for the local market or street stalls. Regardless of whether you are with locals or at high-end eateries, try local delicacies like *bun bo* (cold rice noodles with fried beef), *banh khoi* (crispy thin rice-based crepes filled with chopped meat and shrimp), and *chao* (rice porridge with garnishes of meat, egg, or chiles). Note that many upscale places levy a 10% government tax plus a 5% service charge; some places might absorb the tax in their prices, while others add the full 20% VAT, which was instituted in 1999.

TIPS ON SHOPPING

Bring an empty suitcase—or buy one in-country for peanuts. Vietnam offers fabulous bargains on silk, as both fabric and made-to-order clothing, as well as lacquerware, silver, and fine art. Hanoi is probably best for most buys, particularly paintings; save the lacquerware and home furnishings for Ho Chi Minh City (Saigon). Furthermore, all prices are negotiable except for those in the most upscale shops; the more relentless bargainers can walk away with incredible deals on some unique finds.

In 2004, Vietnam committed to the Berne Convention for the Protection of Literary and Artistic Works, a consortium of over 150 nations working together to protect international copyright. Any stroll through a local market will tell you that this pledge is a tall order. Vietnamese have long followed the socialist ideal that all intellectual property—literary, artistic, or scientific—benefits the collective and should be shared; in fact, copying, under the communist regime, was encouraged. Today, this means rampant pirating of CDs and DVDs for resale. The tide is slowly turning, however, and Customs checks (upon return to Western countries) are increasingly sensitive to pirated material.

FAST FACTS: Vietnam

American Express AmEx is represented by **Exotissimo Travel** (in Hanoi at 24–26 Tran Nhat Duat St.; ⓒ 04/828-2150; in Ho Chi Minh City at Saigon Trade Center, 37 Ton Duc Thang St.; ⓒ 08/825-1723). *Be warned:* It does not provide complete travel services, but can direct you if you lose your card. Hours are Monday through Friday from 8am to 5pm.

Business Hours Vendors and restaurants tend to be all-day operations, opening at about 8am and closing at 9 or 10pm. Government offices, banks, travel agencies, and museums are usually open from 8 to 11:30am and 2 to 4pm.

Drug Laws Possessing drugs can mean a jail sentence, and selling them or possessing quantities in excess of 300g means a death sentence. Don't take any chances.

Electricity Vietnam's electricity carries 220 volts, so if you're coming from the U.S., bring a converter and adapter. Plugs have either two round prongs or two flat prongs. If you're toting a laptop, bring a surge protector as well. Big hotels will have all these implements.

Embassies **U.S.:** 7 Lang Ha St., Ba Dinh District, Hanoi (℡ **04/843-1500;** http://hanoi.usembassy.gov). **Canada:** 31 Hung Vuong St., Ba Dinh District, Hanoi (℡ **04/823-5500;** www.hanoi.gc.ca). **Australia:** 8 Dao Tan, Van Phuc Compound, Ba Dinh District, Hanoi (℡ **04/831-7755;** www.vietnam.embassy.gov.au). **New Zealand:** 32 Hang Bai St., Hoan Kiem District, Hanoi (℡ **04/824-1481**). **U.K.:** 31 Hai Ba Trung St., 4th Floor, Hoan Kiem District, Hanoi (℡ **04/825-2510;** www.britishembassy.gov.uk/vietnam).

Emergencies Nationwide emergency numbers are as follows: For police, dial ℡ **113;** for fire, dial ℡ **114;** and for ambulance, dial ℡ **115.** Operators speak only Vietnamese.

Hospitals Vietnamese health care is not yet up to Western standards. However, there are competent clinics in Hanoi and Ho Chi Minh City (Saigon), with international, English-speaking doctors and dentists. If your problem is serious, it is best to get to either one of these cities as quickly as possible. The clinics can arrange emergency evacuation. If the problem is minor, ask your hotel to help you contact a Vietnamese doctor. He or she will probably speak some English, and pharmacies throughout the country are surprisingly well stocked and require no prescriptions (check expiration, though).

International SOS has a 24-hour service center and both Vietnamese and foreign doctors. In Hanoi, go to 31 Hai Ba Trung St. (24-hr. hot line ℡ **04/934-0056.** In Ho Chi Minh City (Saigon), go to 65 Nguyen Du St., District 1 (24-hr. hot line ℡ **8/829-8424**). Also in Hanoi, the **French Hospital,** 1 Phuong Mai St. (℡ **574-0740**), provides fine medical attention at a fraction of the cost of SOS.

Internet Access There are heaps of Internet cafes in cities throughout Vietnam, the best in popular guesthouse and hotel areas. Cafe rates are dirt cheap—usually around 4,000VND per hour (a little less than US25¢/£0.15). In rural areas, it can be as much as 500VND per minute (US$2/£1.10 per hr.), and hotel business centers usually charge at least triple that. Take a short walk in most towns, and you can find affordable service.

Language Vietnamese is the official language of Vietnam. Older residents speak and understand French, while young folks are busily learning Chinese these days. Although English is widely spoken among folks in the service industry in Hanoi and Saigon, it is harder to find in other tourist destinations. Off the beaten track, arm yourself with a dictionary and as many Vietnamese words as you can muster. See "Language," p. 287, for more information.

Liquor Laws There are virtually no age-restriction laws limiting when or where you can buy or consume drink. It's not uncommon to find that your motorbike or taxi driver has had a few, so be cautious, especially at night.

Mail A regular airmail letter will take about 10 days to reach North America, 7 to reach Europe, and 4 to reach Australia or New Zealand. Mailing things from Vietnam is expensive. A letter up to 10g costs 13,000VND (US85¢/£0.45) to North

America, 11,000VND (US75¢/£0.40) to Europe, and 9,000VND (US60¢/£0.30) to Australia or New Zealand; postcards, respectively, cost 8,000VND (US55¢/£0.25), 7,000VND (US45¢/£0.25), and 6,000VND (US40¢/£0.20). Express services such as **FedEx** and **DHL** are easily available and are usually located in or around every city's main post office.

Police You won't find a helpful cop on every street corner—just the opposite. Count on them only in cases of dire emergency. Police can even be part of the problem. Especially in the south, you and your car/motorbike driver might, for instance, be stopped for a minor traffic infraction and "fined." If the amount isn't too large, cooperate. Corruption is the rule, and palm greasing and graft pose as police process. Be aware.

Safety Vietnam is a generally safe destination, but watch out for crazy traffic, especially in big cities, and for unexploded mines in rural areas. Women should avoid going out alone at night. Beware of pickpockets, especially in Ho Chi Minh City (Saigon), where drive-by purse snatching is rampant. Don't wear flashy jewelry or leave valuables in your hotel room, especially in smaller lodgings. See "Health & Safety," p. 292, for more tips on keeping yourself safe.

Telephones The international country code for Vietnam is **84.** Most hotels offer international direct dialing, but with exorbitant surcharges of 10% to 25%. It is far cheaper to place a call from a post office. There are plenty of phone booths that accept phone cards (local and international), which can be purchased at any post office or phone-company branch. A local call costs 1,000VND (US5¢/£0.03) per minute. See "Telephone Dialing at a Glance," p. 295, for details.

Time Zone Vietnam is 7 hours ahead of Greenwich Mean Time, in the same zone as Bangkok. It is 12 hours ahead of the U.S. Eastern Standard Time during the winter months, and 3 hours behind Sydney.

Tipping Tipping is common in Hanoi and in Saigon. In a top-end hotel, feel free to tip bellhops anywhere from 10,000VND to 15,000VND (US60¢–US95¢/£0.35–£0.50). Most upscale restaurants throughout the country now add a service surcharge of 5% to 10%. If they don't, or if the service is good, you might want to leave another 5%. Taxi drivers will be pleased if you round up the bill (again, mainly in the big cities). Use your discretion for tour guides and others who have been particularly helpful.

Toilets Public toilets *(cau tieu)* are nonexistent in Vietnam outside of tourist attractions, but you'll be welcome in hotels and restaurants. Except for newer hotels and restaurants, squat-style toilets prevail. You'll often see a tub of water with a bowl next to the toilet. Throw two or three scoops of water in the bowl to flush. Finally, bring your own paper and antiseptic hand wipes—just in case.

Water Water is not potable in Vietnam. Outside of top-end hotels and restaurants, drink only beverages without ice, unless the establishment promises that it manufactures its own ice from clean water. Bottled mineral water, particularly the reputable La Vie and A&B brands, is everywhere. Counterfeits are a problem, so make sure you're buying the real thing, with an unbroken seal. A sure sign is typos. "La Vile" water speaks for itself.

4 Hanoi ✶

Vietnam's capital, Hanoi, ranks among the world's most attractive and interesting cities. Originally named Thang Long, it was first the capital of Vietnam in 1010, and even when the nation's capital moved to Hue under the Nguyen Dynasty in 1802, the city continued to flourish, especially after the French took control in 1888. In 1954, after the French departed, Hanoi was declared Vietnam's capital once again. The city boasts 1,000 years of history, and that of the past few hundred years is marvelously preserved.

Hanoi has a reputation, doubtless accrued from the American war years, as a dour northern political outpost. While the city is certainly smaller, slower, and far less developed than chaotic Ho Chi Minh City (Saigon), and there are some vestiges of Soviet-influenced concrete monolith architecture, there are also beautiful streets and neighborhoods in Hanoi, and such placid air gives it a gracious, almost regal flavor. The city is dotted with dozens of lakes small and large, around which you can usually find a cafe, a pagoda or two, and absorbing vignettes of street life. Hanoi's 3.5 million residents all seem to be in constant motion, as part of the endless stream of motorbike and bicycle traffic, but there are plenty of quiet corners and tranquil neighborhoods to explore.

Among Hanoi's sightseeing highlights are the **Ho Chi Minh Museum and Mausoleum,** the **Vietnam National Museum of Fine Arts,** the grisly **Hoa Lo Prison** (also known as the infamous Hanoi Hilton), and the **Old Quarter,** whose ancient winding streets are named after the individual trades practiced there. Hanoi is also Vietnam's cultural center: The galleries, puppetry, music, and dance performances are worth a stay of at least a few days. You might also want to use the city as a base for excursions to Halong Bay, to Cuc Phuong nature reserve, or north to Sapa.

GETTING THERE

BY PLANE Hanoi, along with Ho Chi Minh City (Saigon), is a major international gateway. For details, see Vietnam's "Getting There" section (p. 293). The **Noi Bai International Airport** is located about a 45-minute drive outside Hanoi. If you haven't booked a transfer through your hotel, you can take an airport taxi for US$10 (£5.50). To save a few dollars, hop on the Vietnam Airlines minivan into town. It costs US$2 (£1.10) for a drop-off at the Vietnam Airlines office, but sometimes for an extra buck you can get the driver to take you to your hotel.

BY TRAIN Located on the western edge of Hoan Kiem District, **Hanoi Railway Station** (120 Le Duan; ✆ 04/942-3949) is a terminal stop on the Reunification Railroad. For US$35 (£19), you'll get a comfortable, air-conditioned soft-berth to Hue, or pay US$87 (£48) for the same to Ho Chi Minh City (Saigon). Buying tickets at the stations is easy (but takes time); any travel agent can handle it for a small fee.

BY BUS Tourist cafe open-tour options are numerous in the Old Quarter on Hang Bac or Hang Be streets. Services and prices are similar: About US$27 (£15) earns you an open-tour ticket from Hanoi to Ho Chi Minh City (Saigon), with all stops in between. See "Tourist Cafes" under "Visitor Information & Tours," below.

GETTING AROUND

Hanoi is divided into districts. Most sights and accommodations are in **Hoan Kiem District** (downtown), centered around picturesque Hoan Kiem Lake, or in **Ba Dinh District** (west of town) or **Hai Ba Trung District** (south of town). Most addresses

Hanoi

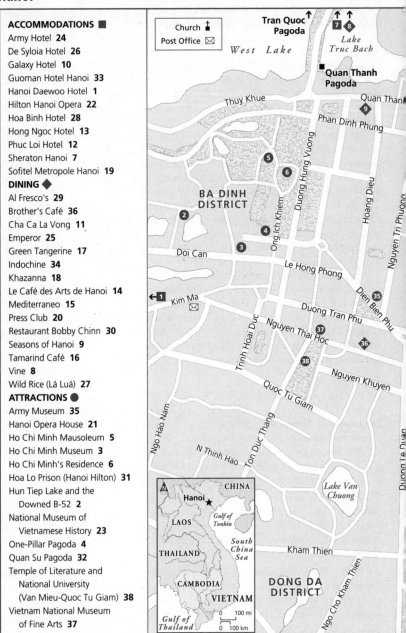

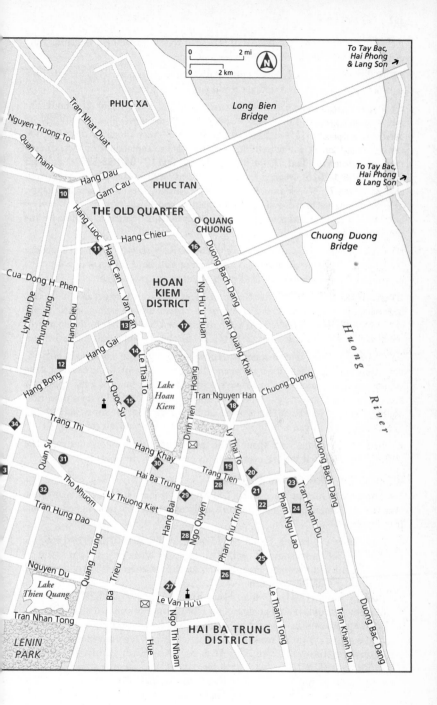

include a district name. You'll want to plan your travels accordingly, as getting from district to district can be time-consuming and expensive.

BY BUS Hanoi has only buses in the way of public transport. They are extremely crowded, and using them is difficult if you don't speak Vietnamese.

BY TAXI Taxis can be hailed off the street, at hotels, and at major attractions. The meter should read 14,000VND (US90¢/£0.50) to start, plus 4,000VND to 5,000VND (about US25¢–US30¢/£0.15–£0.20) for every kilometer thereafter. You can call ahead (or ask at any front desk or concierge) to contact one of a few companies, including **Vina Taxi** (© 04/811-1111), **52 Taxi** (© 04/852-5252), and **Taxi CP** (© 04/826-2626). Make sure the cabbie turns on the meter. Be sure to get your change; drivers often seek a surreptitious tip by claiming they don't have the change. Tell the driver that you'll wait until it's obtained, and it will materialize. *Warning:* Stick with accredited taxi companies; some independents rig meters. If you have any problems, take your case to the concierge of your hotel.

BY CAR Renting a car with driver is convenient. Rates start at US$33 (£18) per day (or US$5/£2.75 per hr., minimum 3 hr.). If an upscale hotel quotes you more, call a tourist cafe (combination eatery and travel agent) or any travel agent.

BY MOTORBIKE Motorcycle taxis are a cheap and easy way to get around the city, but they go like madmen, so this is only for the brave. With haggling, expect to pay about 10,000VND (US65¢/£0.35) for short trips, or US$1 (£0.55) by the hour. Self-rental at the tourist cafes starts at US$6 (£3.30) for the day and is only for the fearless.

BY CYCLO Cyclos are two-seated carts powered by a man on a foot-pedal bike riding behind you. Flag them down anywhere (these guys find you). Being trundled along among whizzing motorcycles isn't always very comfortable, but it is a fun option for touring the Old Quarter. Pay as low as 10,000VND (US65¢/£0.35) for a short ride, 15,000VND (US95¢/£0.50) for a longer haul, or by the hour for about 30,000VND (US$1.90/£1.05). If you're inclined, they'll let you try and ride just for fun.

BY BICYCLE Rental costs about US$1 (£0.55) from a hotel or tourist cafe. The traffic is daunting, but the brave learn quickly how to join the flow.

VISITOR INFORMATION & TOURS

Most tour companies are based in Ho Chi Minh City (Saigon); however, many have branches in Hanoi as well. Operators can usually assist with local tours as well as countrywide services.

- **Ann Tours** (18 Duong Thanh St., Hoan Kiem District; © 04/923-1366; fax 08/832-3866; www.anntours.com). This company offers private deluxe tours to Halong Bay and elsewhere. Frommer's readers have written to tell us of their good experiences with this operation.
- **Buffalo Tours** (13 Hang Muoi, Hoan Kiem District; © 04/828-0702; www.buffalotours.com). This reputable outfit offers a range of standard tours and some good eco-adventures, like cycling, trekking, and kayaking. Its boat, *Jewel of the Bay,* is a great choice for trips in Halong. Friendly and professional staff.
- **Exotissimo Travel** (26 Tran Nhat Duat St., Hoan Kiem District; © 04/828-2150; fax 04/828-2146; www.exotissimo.com). Comprehensive services.
- **Handspan** (80 Ma May St., Hoan Kiem District; © 04/962-0446; fax 04/926-0445; www.handspan.com). A good option for organized trips around Hanoi or adventures to the northern hills and Halong Bay.

BUDGET TOURS

Another good option for tours and transport or for 1- or 2-day excursions is to book with one of the tourist cafes, which are small eateries, Internet cafes, and travel agents all rolled into one. For good, affordable seat-in-tour coach, try:

- **Sinh Café** (25 Hang Be St., Hoan Kiem District; © **04/926-1288;** fax 04/756-7862; www.sinhcafevn.com).
- **A–Z Queen Café** (65 Hang Bac, Hoan Kiem District; © **04/826-0860;** fax 04/826-0300; www.azqueentravel.com).
- **Kim Tours** (82 Ma May St., Hoan Kiem District; © **04/926-0804**).
- **An Phu Tours** (50 Yen Phu, Tay Ho District; © **04/927-3585**).

FAST FACTS: Hanoi

American Express The local AmEx representative, **Exotissimo Travel,** 24–26 Tran Nhat Duat St. (© **04/828-2150**), does not provide complete travel services, but can direct you if you lose your card. Hours are Monday through Friday from 8am to 5pm.

Currency Exchange Major banks in Hanoi include **Australia New Zealand Bank (ANZ),** 14 Le Thai To St. (© **04/825-8190**); **Citibank,** 17 Ngo Quyen St. (© **04/825-1950**); and **Vietcombank,** 198 Tran Quan Khai (© **04/826-8045**). ATMs are located at ANZ Bank, at Citibank, and in various locations throughout the city. Money-changing offices abound in places like Hang Bac, in the heart of the backpacker area of the Old Quarter—**Hanoi Sacombank,** 87 Hang Bac (© **04/261-392**), is typical of many. Black-market money changers will approach you outside the major banks. Best to just avoid the temptation, as you'll often be left with a few counterfeit or out-of-circulation notes in the mix.

Emergencies For police, dial © **113;** for fire, dial © **114;** and for ambulance, dial … **115.**

Internet Access The **Emotion CyberNet Café,** at 60 Tho Nhuom and 52 Ly Thuong Kiet (© **04/934-1066**), across from the Hilton, sells snacks and Internet access. Small Internet storefronts are numerous in the Old Quarter on Hang Bac or Hang Be; all tourist cafes have Internet access as well. **A–Z Queen Café,** 65 Hang Bac (© **04/826-0860**), is a good bet with affordable service and a pay-as-you-use honor system.

Mail The general post office is at 6 Dinh Le St., Hoan Kiem District (© **04/825-7036**). It's open daily from 6:30am to 10pm. You can also send faxes or telexes and make international phone calls. **FedEx** (© **04/826-4925**) is located in the same building as the post office but has its own storefront.

Telephones The city code for Hanoi is **4.** Most hotels provide international direct dialing, although none allows you to access an international operator or AT&T (whose Vietnam access code is 12010288). To do that, you will have to go to the general post office (above). There are public phone booths throughout the city for local calls; these accept phone cards purchased from the post office.

WHERE TO STAY

Hanoi has everything from historic charm to slick efficiency to budget hole-in-the-wall. Amenities and cleanliness levels are high and prices low, making Hanoi a good place for an upgrade. Most hotels over US$15 (£8.25) per night will have a phone, air-conditioning, in-room safe, and hair dryer. Children under 12 usually stay free. Prices shown here are rack rates, and discounts abound—just ask. Note that hotels charge a VAT of up to 20%.

VERY EXPENSIVE

In addition to the top-rated hotels listed below, options on the pricier end include the mammoth **Melia Hanoi** (© 04/934-3343; www.meliahanoi.com), the plush **Hotel Nikko** (© 04/822-3535; www.hotelnikkohanoi.com), and the **Horizon Hotel** (© 04/733-0808).

Hanoi Daewoo Hotel 🏵🏵   Now 10 years in business, the Daewoo has been the most popular choice for heads of state and dignitaries (with a long list including Bill Clinton and Jiang Zemin). Fittingly, everything is done large—the lobby, the bars, the rooms with king beds, and the 80m (262-ft.) curving pool. All interior space is tessellated in marble, deep-toned wood, or sumptuous fabrics. It's almost a bit *too* much. The plush guest rooms are decorated with local accents; interesting modern works of Vietnamese artists grace the walls. Bathrooms are surprisingly small in the lower-end rooms, but are still quite well appointed. The hotel is far from the town center, but its many amenities make it sufficiently self-contained. Overlooking the large park surrounding Thu Le Lake, the Daewoo is like a city unto itself.

360 Kim Ma St., Ba Dinh District, Hanoi. © 04/831-5000. Fax 04/831-5010. www.hanoi-daewoohotel.com. 411 units. US$220 (£121) double; US$310 (£171) executive-floor double; US$420–US$4,500 (£231–£2,475) suite. AE, DC, MC, V. **Amenities:** 4 restaurants (international, Italian, Chinese, Japanese); 2 bars; 80m (262 ft.) pool; outdoor tennis court; elegant health club; spa; Jacuzzi; sauna; children's program; concierge; tour desk; car rental; limo service; very efficient business center w/Internet access; shopping arcade; salon; 24-hr. room service; massage; babysitting; laundry service; dry cleaning; 3 nonsmoking floors. *In room:* A/C, satellite TV, dataport, minibar, fridge, coffeemaker, hair dryer, safe, IDD phone.

Hilton Hanoi Opera 🏵🏵   The Hilton is a reproduction colonial that makes an elegant arc around the perimeter of the splendid Hanoi Opera building. The inside matches the fine facade, with a lobby done on a grand scale. Rooms are outfitted with richly colored carpet, unique cushioned wallpaper, subdued lighting, and faux Chinese lacquer cabinets. Those on the fifth floor have balconies. Suites are much larger and nicely appointed. Daily newspaper delivery, voice mail, and in-room broadband Internet access keep business travelers up to speed. Leisure travelers can enjoy the inviting courtyard pool, get tips from the helpful concierge, and take advantage of in-house tour services with Exotissimo. There is fine dining at Turtle's Poem (try the dim sum for lunch); Café Opera has gourmet sandwiches and baked goods; and JJ's Sports Bar is a good place to shoot some pool.

1 Le Thanh Tong St., Hoan Kiem District, Hanoi. © 800/774-1500 or 04/933-0500. Fax 04/933-0530. www.hilton.com. 269 units. US$290–US$325 (£160–£179) double; US$325 (£179) executive room; US$440 (£242) suite. AE, MC, V. **Amenities:** 3 restaurants; bar; pool; fitness center; concierge; tour desk; car rental; business center; salon; 24-hr. room service; babysitting; rooms for those w/limited mobility; executive-level rooms. *In room:* A/C, satellite TV, dataport, hair dryer, safe.

Sheraton Hanoi 🏵🏵   Just a 10-minute ride north of town, this smart, upscale hotel sits on a peninsula jutting into Hanoi's picturesque West Lake in a neighborhood popular with the local expat community (which means good restaurants and services in the area). The hotel makes up for any inconvenience to town by being completely self-contained, with fine dining options, a top fitness center, and services that cover all bases, from local touring to business support. Rooms are done in an ultra-tidy, contemporary style typical of Sheraton hotels—certainly nothing to write home about, but cozy and familiar nonetheless. All units have fine views of the lake. Bathrooms are large, with big tubs, separate showers, and wood and granite detail. In-house dining is tops; transport to town is available 24 hours. The hotel is a popular meeting destination and has room for many.

K5 Nghi Tam, 11 Xuan Dieu Rd., Tay Ho District, Hanoi. ℂ **04/719-9000.** Fax 04/719-9001. www.sheraton.com. 156 units. US$200–US$270 (£110–£149) double; from US$320 (£176) suite. AE, MC, V. **Amenities:** 2 restaurants; bar; outdoor pool; tennis court; health club; Jacuzzi; sauna; concierge; tour desk; car rental; business center w/Internet access; shopping; 24-hr. room service; massage; babysitting; laundry service; dry cleaning; nonsmoking rooms; executive-level rooms. *In room:* A/C, satellite TV, Internet access, minibar, fridge, hair dryer, safe, IDD phone.

Sofitel Metropole Hanoi ⚑⚑⚑ Hanoi's top choice. Built in 1901, the Metropole is a historic treasure. It's where invading, liberating, or civil armies have found billet and raised their flags, where the first film was shown in Indochina, where Charlie Chaplin spent his honeymoon, where Jane Fonda and Joan Baez took cover in a bomb shelter, and where heads of state and embassy officials resided for many years. In fact, the history of the Metropole is the history of the last hundred years in Hanoi, and the folks here have even published a short volume telling the tale.

The hotel has been through numerous renovations, and a new building was added in 1994. Rooms in the new wing are more spacious, but go for the old wing and walk into a bit of history: Your medium-size room will have wood floors, cane furniture, classic fixtures, and high ceilings. The large, modern bathrooms come with little touches like wood-frame mirrors, fresh flowers, and a fine line of in-house products. The staff couldn't be nicer or more efficient. The pool is small, but the adjoining Bamboo Lounge is an oasis of calm in the city center. The health club is superb and has a good street view. Le Beaulieu is popular for classic French fare, while the Spices Garden is a great place to sample local delights (the lunch buffet is a safe and tasty place to try Hanoi street fare like *pho* and *bun cha*). The Metropole even offers cooking classes. The Met Pub is a casual spot to have a beer and listen to live music. The downtown location can't be beat, and there's a nice mix of tourists and businesspeople here.

15 Ngo Quyen St., Hoan Kem District, Hanoi. ℂ **800/221-4542** or 04/826-6919. Fax 04/826-6920. www.sofitel.com. 266 units. US$350–US$700 (£193–£385) double; from US$660 (£363) suite. AE, DC, MC, V. **Amenities:** 2 restaurants; 3 bars; nice courtyard pool; top-notch health club; spa; Jacuzzi; sauna; concierge; tour desk; car rental; limo service; business center; shopping; salon; 24-hr. room service; massage; babysitting; laundry service; dry cleaning; wireless Internet access. *In room:* A/C, satellite TV, dataport, minibar, fridge, hair dryer, safe, IDD phone.

EXPENSIVE

De Syloia Hotel ⚑ The De Syloia is a cozy little treasure just south of the city center. Rooms are large and clean—not especially luxurious, but comfortable with tidy carpet, dark-wood appointments, and large bathrooms with tubs (deluxe rooms have Jacuzzis). The lobby is compact and clean but not particularly atmospheric, and the whole setup is a Hanoi mini hotel gone upscale, with a good standard throughout. The staff is friendly on a good day, and the amenities are limited, but this is a popular choice away from the downtown traffic.

17a Tran Hung Dao St., Hoan Kem District, Hanoi. ℂ **04/824-5346.** Fax 04/824-1083. www.desyloia.com. 33 units. US$90–US$110 (£50–£61) double; US$115 (£63) deluxe; US$145 (£80) suite. Internet rates available. AE, MC, V. **Amenities:** Restaurant; bar; mini gym; tour desk; car rental; business center; room service; laundry service; dry cleaning; wireless Internet access. *In room:* A/C, satellite TV, dataport, minibar, fridge, hair dryer, safe, IDD phone.

Guoman Hotel Hanoi ★★ For a high standard of service and comfort in Hanoi, the Guoman is a real find. This uppity downtown four-star caters to the business crowd and is popular with semipermanent residents; however, with such a good location and amenities, it's a great choice for all. From the chandelier and filigree of the stylish lobby to the subdued Helmsman lounge's live music, there is a laid-back boutique feel here that's much finer than the low price tag. Rooms are big, carpeted, and nicely furnished if a bit bland. Other highlights include comfy firm beds, fat pillows, and spic-and-span marble-and-tile bathrooms. The restaurant serves a great breakfast and good Western and Asian cuisine (lots of promotional specials). There are two nonsmoking floors, a rarity in Vietnam. Service is excellent—the staff can help you with any business or travel need.

83A Ly Thuong Kiet St., Hoan Kem District, Hanoi. ℂ 04/822-2800. Fax 04/822-2822. www.guomanhotels.com. 149 units. US$70–US$75 (£39–£41) double; US$120–US$180 (£66–£99) suite. AE, MC, V. **Amenities:** 2 restaurants; 2 bars (w/live music); good gym; dry sauna; concierge; tour desk; car rental; limo service; business center; 24-hr. room service; massage; babysitting; nonsmoking floors. *In room:* A/C, satellite TV, dataport, Wi-Fi, minibar, fridge, coffeemaker, hair dryer, safe.

MODERATE

Army Hotel ★★ (Value) For comfort and value close to downtown (plus a nice pool), the Army Hotel is a find. In a sprawling complex owned by the Vietnamese military—thus the name—there's no need to salute here, and the friendly staff won't ask you to drop for 20 push-ups. Located on a quiet street just a short walk east of downtown (behind the opera house), the Army is popular with long-term visitors, especially couples who come to adopt in Vietnam. Rooms vary, so ask to see one before you check in; most are large and clean, with tile floors and nice-size bathrooms with combination tub/showers. Each room has a balcony, some with direct pool access. The staff is friendly, the lobby business center is convenient, and the pool is inviting and unique in this price range. Ask about the eclectic suites, some with Japanese-style rooms and private balcony.

33 C Pham Ngu Lao St. (just behind the opera house), Hoan Kem District, Hanoi. ℂ 04/825-2896. Fax 04/825-9276. armyhotel@fpt.vn. 69 units. US$50–US$60 (£28–£33) standard double; US$70 (£39) deluxe double; US$72–US$198 (£40–£109) suite. AE, MC, V. **Amenities:** Restaurant; outdoor pool in large central courtyard; basic fitness equipment; sauna; small business center w/Internet access (US$3/£1.65 per hr.); room service (6am–10pm); babysitting. *In room:* A/C, satellite TV, fridge, hot water for coffee, hair dryer, IDD phone.

Galaxy Hotel ★★ Popular with tour groups, the Galaxy is on a busy corner just north of the Old Quarter—a comfortable spot to begin exploring this colorful part of the city. Converted from a 1929 factory, the recently renovated building is colorless but comfortable. Good-size rooms are spotless, with familiar amenities and nondescript decor. The tile bathrooms are small but neat. Corner suites are a great option, with windows facing two directions over the Old Quarter. On the premises are a good Asian restaurant and a nice little lobby bar. Staff members will remember your name and are helpful with advice and suggestions.

1 Phan Dinh Phung St., Ba Dinh District, Hanoi. ℂ 04/828-2888. Fax 04/828-2466. galaxyhtl@netnam.org.vn. 60 units. US$60 (£33) double; US$80 (£44) suite. Rates include breakfast. AE, DC, MC, V. **Amenities:** 2 restaurants; bar; tour desk; car rental; 24-hr. room service; babysitting; laundry service; dry cleaning. *In room:* A/C, satellite TV, minibar, fridge, coffeemaker, hair dryer, safe, IDD phone.

Hoa Binh Hotel ★ Built in 1926 and recently renovated, the Hoa Binh is an atmospheric choice. Comfort and history meet at a good level, and whether you're walking up the creaky grand staircase or opening French doors onto a balcony overlooking the busy street, you know that you're in Hanoi here. Sizable rooms have original light fixtures, molded ceilings, and glossy wood furniture. Everything is done a bit low-luxe, however: The shiny polyester bedspreads, velveteen drapes, and spongy mattresses detract from the overall effect. Bathrooms are plain and small but spotless. The hotel is in a prime downtown location, and the bar has a view of the city. Ask to see a room before checking in, as they vary in size, shape, and degree of smoke or mustiness; in general, though, this is a good bet. It's popular with tour groups.

27 Ly Thuong Kiet St., Hoan Kiem District, Hanoi. ℂ 04/825-3315 or 04/825-3692. Fax 04/826-9818. www.hoabinh hotel.com. 103 units. US$75 (£41) double; US$90–US$130 (£50–£72) suite. Rates include breakfast. AE, MC, V. **Amenities:** 2 restaurants; 2 bars; sauna; concierge; tour desk; car rental; small business center; shopping; limited room service; massage; laundry service; dry cleaning; nonsmoking rooms. *In room:* A/C, TV, minibar, fridge, hair dryer, safe.

INEXPENSIVE

Hong Ngoc Hotel ☆☆ With three locations all in the heart of the Old Quarter, this is a good no-frills option close to Hoan Kiem Lake. Friendly to a fault, the staff has a can-do attitude and can help you with any detail, such as renting a car, motorcycle, or bicycle. Rooms are compact, but all have dark-wood trim and the quality amenities of a proper hotel. Larger suites are a good choice. Bathrooms are small and clean. This is top-notch downtown affordability, a mini hotel with attitude—like a terrier who thinks himself a Great Dane.

14 Luong Van Can St., Hoan Kiem District, Hanoi. ℂ 04/826-7566. Fax 04/8245362. 34 Hang Manh St., Hoan Kiem District. ℂ 04/828-5053. Fax 04/828-5054. 14 Hang Van Can St., Hoan Kiem District. ℂ 04/826-7566. Fax 04/824-5362. www.hongngochotel.com.vn. Total of 40 units. US$30–US$50 (£17–£28). MC, V. **Amenities:** Restaurant; tour desk; limited room service; Internet access. *In room:* A/C, satellite TV, minibar, fridge, safe.

Phuc Loi Hotel ☆ This is the standard Old Quarter mini hotel, but everything at the Phuc Loi is super-tidy and ornate. Rooms are small but spotless, with faux-wood floors and high ceilings. This place is relatively new and everything is in good shape. The bathrooms are a nice size, with tub/shower combo and granite counters. Try for one of the three split-level VIP rooms; they're very comfortable and a steal at US$35 (£19). Rooms on higher floors have great views of the Old Quarter. The staff is friendly and helpful.

128 Hang Bong St., Old Quarter, Hoan Kiem District, Hanoi. ℂ 04/928-5235. Fax 04/828-9897. www.phucloihotel.com. 20 units. US$30–US$50 (£17–£28). **Amenities:** Restaurant; bar; small gym; bike rental; tour desk. *In room:* A/C, satellite TV, Wi-Fi, minibar, fridge, hair dryer, IDD phone.

WHERE TO DINE

It's hard to have a bad meal in Hanoi. The French influence is everywhere, with both classical French and Vietnamese fusion fare, all priced for any budget. Almost every ethnic food variation is well represented in the city as well.

Hanoi has savory specialties that must be sampled. For that, hit the streets and dine in small local eateries. *Pho*, by far the most popular local dish, is noodles with slices of beef *(bo)* or chicken *(ga)*, fresh bean sprouts, and condiments. *Bun cha*, a snack of rice noodles and spring rolls, has made the **Dac Kim** restaurant (at 1 Hang Manh, in the Old Quarter) city-renowned. And don't miss **Cha Ca**, Hanoi's famed spicy fish fry-up (p. 310).

EXPENSIVE

Emperor ☆☆☆ VIETNAMESE For atmosphere and decor alone, the Emperor is Hanoi's address of note. A beautiful restored colonial building stands sentinel at the busy street-side entrance; this is the fine-dining area, posh and elegant. But this muted elegance, a bit stiff really, gives way to an interior courtyard and a laid-back, classy, open-air dining space. With torches and candlelight, hushed conversation, and the gliding forms of staff in traditional *ao-dai* dresses, you might think you've entered a time warp. The price of admission is none too dear by Western standards; basic dishes fit any budget, though specialty items like the ubiquitous bird's-nest or shark's-fin soup will run up the bill. This is Vietnamese fine dining at its best, a tourist and expat favorite. Try the soft-shell crab, spicy grilled squid, or any seafood specials of the day. Whether you're sampling light fare in the bar area or putting on a spread in the main dining room, you'll appreciate the affordable elegance here.

18B Le Thanh Tong St., Hoan Kiem District. ⓒ 04/826-8801. Fax 04/824-0027. Reservations highly recommended. Main courses US$4.75–US$29 (£2.60–£16). MC, V. Daily 11am–2pm and 5:30–10:30pm (pub until midnight).

Green Tangerine 🕿🕿 FRENCH   The Green Tangerine is set in a lovingly restored 1928 colonial right in the center of the Old Quarter. Its small courtyard, just a few steps off busy Hang Be, is great for an afternoon drink, while the air-conditioned dining room is a real sanctuary for a luxurious meal. It's very popular with expats, and that makes for a constantly evolving menu to keep up with repeat customers. I had a delicious *mille-feuille* of scallops cooked in white wine and garnished with Parmesan and eggplant. For a main, savory lasagna was made of wide noodles stuffed with a pâté of crab and broccoli cooked in cognac and layered with spicy mashed carrot—very original. The rack of lamb served in coffee is unique; the set menus are popular as well. Everything here is rich and delicious.

48 Hang Be, Hoan Kiem District. ⓒ 04/825-1286. Reservations not necessary. Main courses US$7.70–US$15 (£4.25–£8.25). AE, MC, V. Daily 9am–11pm.

Press Club 🕿🕿 CONTINENTAL   Subdued and elegant, this place says "power lunch"—and offers cuisine and prices to match. The indoor restaurant is sizable yet private, done in dark tones of maroon and forest green with solid wood furniture and detailing. There is outdoor seating on the terrace, facing a stage that features regular live acts. The menu is full of sumptuous Continental standards: antipasto starters, goat-cheese salad, tuna steak, smoked trout and baked grouper, and various wood-grilled imported steaks and meat dishes. Unique is the "deconstructed" Vietnamese *pho* noodle soup with lobster, foie gras, and truffle. For dessert, try the white-chocolate sticky rice or rich rice pudding. The service here is impeccable.

The Deli, on the ground floor, is a good, cozy place to grab a local or international paper (and browse the book corner), accompanied by a relaxed lunch of sandwiches or gourmet pizzas, not to mention the Aussie pie with chips or "Mom's Meatloaf." A good choice for a casual dose of home. There's also a casual coffee corner here. The second and third floors house event facilities and meeting rooms.

59A Ly Thai To St., Hoan Kiem District. ⓒ 04/934-0888. www.hanoi-pressclub.com. Reservations recommended. Main courses US$13–US$48 (£6.90–£26). AE, MC, V. Daily 7am–10:30pm (Sat–Sun brunch 11am–3pm).

Vine 🕿🕿🕿 FUSION   Away from all the hubbub of the Old Quarter, but still within a short taxi ride, is this elegant venture from a former chef and wine connoisseur. A spiral staircase connects four floors, a bar, and a cigar humidor, all softly lit in reds and mauves, with bottle after bottle of wine lining the walls. Choose your wine from the menu or from the wall, or have one of the capable staff select a bottle for you. The temperature at Vine is kept pretty chilly, in order to protect the restaurant's wines and Cubans, but heavy silk jackets are always within arm's reach. The food, meanwhile, is

some of the finest in Hanoi: no small feat. There are no bad choices, and it's all according to taste, but you can't go wrong with any of the fish or pasta dishes. Make sure to
try at least one or two—or three—of Vine's innovative appetizers. Pay attention to
your palate, and order wine by the glass accordingly. For a special evening, reserve the
table in the private wine cellar.

1A Xuan Dieu St., Ho Tay District. ℂ 04/719-8001. Reservations recommended. Main courses $5–$30 (£2.75–£17).
AE, MC, V. Daily 9am to last order.

Wild Rice (Lá Luá) ✦ ASIAN FUSION   Nothing about Lá Luá portends to be
authentic Vietnamese, and everything from the decor to the dining is in fact an amalgam of traditions and customs. The place looks like an upmarket L.A. bistro borrowing Japanese themes, with tall stands of bamboo encased in glass, slate floors, and
white walls that shine with the mellow glow of indirect lighting. The food is good,
Vietnamese-influenced fare. Try the barbecued squid or beef with coconut; I had
grilled chicken in chile with lemongrass—deliciously spicy and savory. Presentation is
Zen simple: white linen with black chopsticks, a plate, a bowl, and a candle. It's all a
bit studied, really, but the food is very good.

6 Ngo Thi Nham St., Hai Ba Trung District. ℂ 04/943-8896. Fax 04/943-6299. Main courses 60,000VND–160,000VND
(US$3.75–US$10/£2.05–£5.50). AE, MC, V. Daily 11am–2pm and 5:30–10pm.

MODERATE

Al Fresco's ✦✦ TEX-MEX   Run by Australian expats, Al Fresco's is two floors of
friendly, casual dining. With checkered tablecloths, oldies music, and a great view from
the second floor to the street below, this is the place to bring the kids (or yourself) when
they're in need of a slice of home. The place serves very good Tex-Mex fare, excellent
imported and local Aussie steaks, and pizza, chicken wings, and the like. Ribs are the
house specialty. The burgers are the real deal, with all the fixin's. Desserts are good old
standbys like brownies a la mode. The wine list is heavy on Australian and inexpensive South American reds. If you've had enough of fried rice or noodle soup, come here
for something that sticks to your ribs, accompanied by a chat with the friendly owner.

23L Hai Ba Trung St., Hoan Kiem District. ℂ 04/826-7782. Main courses US$5–US$12 (£2.75–£6.60). MC, V. Daily
9:30am–midnight.

Brother's Café ✦ VIETNAMESE   The buffet-only Brother's is an inexpensive
starting point to explore gourmet Vietnamese cuisine. Lunch includes dishes such as
salted chicken, sweet-and-sour bean sprouts, shrimp, noodles, and spring rolls; a full
dessert table of sweet tofu, sweet baby rice, dragon fruit, and other exotic offerings;
and fresh lemon or melon juice. Dinner features grilled items—shrimp, fish, lamb,
and pork—and a glass of wine. The faux street stalls encircling the garden serve Vietnamese favorites like *pho* (noodle soup) and *bun cha* (cold rice noodles, spring rolls,
and lettuce eaten by dipping into a slightly sweet sauce with meat). Don't expect anyone to explain anything, though; the staff here does little more than schlep drinks and
smilingly point to the buffet—but it's about the food, really, and a meal here is not
without nice details such as pressed napkins and tiny fresh flowers. There is seating in
both the courtyard (under canvas umbrellas) and the casual corners of this lushly
restored colonial. The word is out, though, so it's not uncommon to see tour buses
pulled up in front (especially at lunch). Get here early or be ready for an old-time
smorgasbord push and shove.

26 Nguyen Thai Hoc St., Ba Dinh District. ℂ 04/733-3866. www.brothercafe.com. Buffets US$6.50 (£3.60) lunch;
178,000VND (US$11/£6.15) dinner. AE, DC, MC, V. Daily 11:30am–2pm and 6:30–10pm.

The Best Authentic Local Fare

Hanoi's local cuisine is some of the best in Vietnam, and the finest local dishes are served at small one-dish restaurants, usually just open-air joints at street-side, where you might wonder why there's a line out the door. To Vietnamese, it's about the food, not the atmosphere. Some of the best meals in the capital, or anywhere in Vietnam for that matter, are eaten on squat stools with disposable chopsticks. Standards of hygiene might appear poor, but do as locals do and wipe down bowls and chopsticks with a napkin before tucking in. Yes, eating on the street does mean you might have some tummy trouble, but if you stick to the few places recommended below, you should be okay.

The ubiquitous *pho*—noodle soup served with slices of beef *(bo)* or chicken *(ga)*, fresh bean sprouts, and condiments—can be found anywhere. And don't miss *cha ca*, Hanoi's famed spicy fish fry-up (see below).

Bun Bo Nam Bo (✮✮, 67 Hang Dieu St. (© **04/923-0701**), only serves one main course:*bun bo,* a dish of fresh rice noodles with herbs and spices, topped with beef that only costs 12,000VND (US75¢/£0.40). Sound simple? It is. It is the subtlety of the flavors of this dish and the stock that brings 'em here in droves. Just order by holding up as many fingers as you want bowls of *bun bo,* take a seat at the low tables in the brightly lit interior, and wait. A spartan atmosphere, but a rich and delicious dish worth hunting down. No credit cards. Daily 7am to 10:30pm.

Cha Ca La Vong (✮✮, 14 Cha Ca St. (© **04/825-3929**), is on a street called Cha Ca, and it serves one dish . . . you guessed it . . . *cha ca.* So what's the story with *cha ca?* Very simple: It's a delicate white fish, fried at high heat in peanut oil with dill, turmeric, rice noodles, and peanuts—and it's delicious. The place is pretty grungy, and to call the service "indifferent" would be to sing its praises, but that's the beauty here: It's all about the food. You order by saying how many you are, and how many bottles of beer or soda you'd like. Then it's do-it-yourself, with some gruff guidance, as you stir in the ingredients on a frying pan over a charcoal hibachi right at the table. It's a rich dish and great with some hot sauce (go easy on it at first), and it makes for a fun and interesting evening. Just say "Cha Ca" and any cab driver can take you there. Avoid copycats: The original Cha Ca La Vong is the only game in town. No credit cards. Daily 10am to 2pm and 4 to 10pm.

Gia Thuyen Pho (Noodle Soup): 49 Bat Danh St. (✮✮, (on the west side of the Old Quarter near the old citadel wall), is a very popular storefront *pho* noodle soup stant in Hanoi's Old Quarter. If you've seen the Japanese film *Tampopo* about the making of the perfect noodle soup, or saw the *Seinfeld* episode about New York City's "Soup Nazi" who, because of his quality broth, chose his customers instead of vice versa, you'll have an idea what it's like. The line is around the block day and night, as Hanoians of all stripes humbly cue up for a taste of the best. The formula is simple: delicious cured beef, fresh noodles, and spices—done the same way, over and over, for years. Just order "One please" (it is *pho* with beef or nothing) and pay the surly lady, who might even let a few customers go ahead of you if she doesn't like the cut of your jib. Unlike in most *pho* joints, no one serves you, so you have to carry your own bowl to an open slot at a crowded table (if you come with a friend, you might have to separate), and the place is as grotty as any little noodle stand, but when you pull those first noodles off the chopsticks and follow with a spoonful of broth, you'll know why you came. No phone. One bowl of *pho* is 12,000VND (US75¢/£0.40). Daily 6am to 11pm.

Nguyen Sinh Restaurant Francais, 17 Ly Quoc St. directly north on the street that runs in front of the Nha Tho Cathedral (tel] **04/826-5234).** What is so Vietnamese about this French restaurant? Everything. Founded in 1950, these folks were the ones (among many) who kept alive the art of baking bread and cooking French foods. Vietnamese French has its own bend, say French expats, and in Hanoi it's a cuisine of its own. This little storefront offers good imported cheese and wine; it's sort of like Hanoi's de facto New York deli (it'll do in a pinch, anyway, for that late-night snack). Here you can get a delicious baguette with cheese and pâté for just 10,000VND (US60¢/£0.35) or a savory steak fry-up French-style. You'll find locals in berets trying out their newest licks on the saxophone, and French expats getting a little taste of home, chatting with the Francophone clientele. Très chic. Daily 8am to 10pm.

Restaurant Lau Tu Xuyen,163 Yen Phu, with another location at 199 Duong Nghi Tam, (© **04/714-0289),** is a fun adventure. Way out on the eastern shore of West Lake (about 30,000VND/US$2/£1 by taxi from the city center), this big warehouse of a restaurant is the best place in town to enjoy the real *lau,* or Vietnamese hot pot. Go with a Vietnamese friend or be open to some creative charades with your waitress; there's no English menu and foreign visitors are rare. The official directions for cooking hot pot? As my friend says, "You just put." Add whatever you like—fresh seafood, beef, poultry, and vegetables—to a shared pot of boiling broth on a hot plate in the center of the table. They also can bring out a barbecue set-up for small kabobs. You order like you would order dim sum, choosing plates of raw ingredients off a tray. The place is packed in the evenings, especially in the winter (this is Vietnam's version of stew) and on weekends. The entry is just adjacent to the Thang Loi Lakeside hotel. The local draft beer flows freely and costs little. Make a night of it and end with a walk in this busy expat neighborhood. Expect to pay about US$5 (£2.75) per person in a group. No credit cards. Daily 11am to 10pm.

Indochine ★ VIETNAMESE   Set in a beautifully restored colonial, this place is a longtime tourist favorite. The food, like that at many restaurants in Hanoi, is Vietnamese cuisine toned down for foreign palates, but Indochine does it well. The spring rolls are great, as are both the banana-flower salad and the crispy fried prawn-cakes with ginger. Ask about daily specials. With indoor and patio seating and traditional Vietnamese performances in the evening (call ahead for times), Indochine is well worth a visit for the beautiful colonial setting alone. Take a cab; it's hard to find. *Warning:* The restaurant fills with tour groups at lunchtime, which brings a rise in noise level and a drop in service quality.

16 Nam Ngu St., Hoan Kiem District. © **04/942-4097.** Main courses US$2–US$6.50 (£1.10–£3.60). MC, V. Daily 11:30am–10pm.

Khazanna ★★ INDIAN   The current incarnation of this restaurant serves a fine menu of northern and southern Indian dishes, complemented by the tidy Indian-themed Western decor and the excellent service and presentation: The curries are served in small metal crocks with brass ladles. The affordable lunch menu brings in crowds of businesspeople. In the evening, choose from an extensive selection of curries, grilled dishes, and naan breads. Everything's good here.

1C Tong Dan St., Hoan Kiem District. © **04/934-5657.** Main courses 39,000VND–79,000VND (US$2.45–US$4.95/£1.35–£2.70). MC, V. Daily 11am–2:30pm and 6–10:30pm.

Restaurant Bobby Chinn ★★ CALIFORNIA/VIETNAMESE/FRENCH   With a decor and panache that would hold its own on a side street of SoHo or a lofty perch in the Bay Area, Restaurant Bobby Chinn makes for an interesting evening. It's on the southwest corner of Hoan Kiem Lake, where longtime expat and raconteur Mr. Chinn holds court and runs the show from behind the large, open bar at the entrance. It's the place to see and be seen these days in Hanoi, and it's a popular late-night spot where local jazz artists like to drop by. A revolving collection of local artists' works adorn the walls, and good music is always playing (a sign on the door reads: KENNY G–FREE ZONE). Out front, guests dine at simple tables and in a few booths with picture-window views of the lake and the street. In the back, diners lounge on overstuffed couches at low tables in a maze of discreet nooks—it's all quite cinematic. However you feel about the atmosphere, Mr. Chinn serves up a delightfully eclectic menu of fine French and Vietnamese-inspired dishes, all with a playful, cross-cultural flair. To start, try the rib sampler or "symphony of flavors" from the tapas menu. Main courses like pan-roasted salmon with wasabi mashed potatoes, or perhaps green-tea–smoked duck, have a certain Franco-Japanese appeal all their own.

1 Ba Trieu St., Hoan Kiem District. © **04/934-8577.** www.bobbychinn.com. Reservations recommended. AE, MC, V. Main courses US$12–US$22 (£6.60–£12); tapas menu from US$2 (£1.10). Daily 11:30am to last customer.

Seasons of Hanoi ★ VIETNAMESE   The atmosphere is picture-perfect at Seasons: intimate, candlelit, earth-toned surroundings in a casual yet beautifully restored colonial with authentic native furniture. The spring rolls are heaven, as are the tempura soft-shell crabs. The kitchen serves great fish the way you like it—fried, boiled, on kabobs, or in hot pots. Try the sautéed eel with chile and lemongrass or the fried chicken in panda leaves. Presentation is elegant and the wine list long. *Tip:* Sit on the first floor to avoid the group tours that take over the second floor.

95B Quan Thanh St., Ba Dinh District. © **04/843-5444.** Reservations recommended, especially for groups. Main courses 40,000VND–80,000VND (US$2.50–US$5/£1.40–£2.75). MC, V. Daily 11:30am–2pm and 6–11pm.

INEXPENSIVE

Le Café des Arts de Hanoi ✹ BISTRO/CONTINENTAL   After strolling around Hoan Kiem Lake, stop off its northwest end for a drink or a bite at this friendly bistro-style eatery, run by French expats and open all day. Spacious, with tiled floors and shuttered windows looking into the narrow Old Quarter street below, the cafe has casual rattan furniture and a long, inviting bar. It doubles as an art gallery, which explains the interesting paintings hanging throughout. The Vietnamese art crowd also adds some attractive local color. Most inviting, however, is the excellent food. Ask for the special of the day, and stick to bistro standbys like the omelets or a *croque madame*—toasted bread and cheese sautéed in egg—and house specialty *salade bressare* (very fresh chicken and vegetables in a light mayonnaise sauce). You'll also find good house wine by the glass and excellent lunch specials.

11B Ngo Bao Khanh, Old Quarter, Hoan Kiem District. ☎ **04/828-7207**. Main courses US$6–US$12 (£3.30–£6.60). No credit cards. Daily 9am–11pm (bar open until midnight).

Mediterraneo ✹ ITALIAN   You'll find a tasty but typical range of northern Italian fare at this mellow, street-side cafe on Nha Tho, Hanoi's stylish cafe area (called Church Street). Prosciutto with melon, tomato, and homemade mozzarella is a good starter. Follow with good homemade pasta, a choice of grilled dishes, or pizza. It's affordable, cozy, and casual. There are daily specials and a good wine list, too.

23 Nha Tho St. (near the Old Church), Hoan Kiem District. ☎ **04/826-6288**. Main courses US$6–US$15 (£3.30–£8.25). MC, V. Daily 10am–11pm.

Quan An Ngon ✹✹ VIETNAMESE   For a lively local lunch or dinner, the energy and extensive menu of Quan An Ngon are hard to top. Sit at the elbow-to-elbow tables in the open air or else inside, where it's cooler and quieter. The bustling courtyard, filled with Vietnamese professionals and students, is surrounded by well-stocked, clean food stalls, reminiscent of what you might find, at random, on the street, but without some of the, uh, hygiene concerns. Try the pancakes; try the noodles; try as much as you can. Everything on the menu is good, the staff is on the ball, and the prices are reasonable, so visitors can get a wide-ranging sample of Vietnamese fare.

18 Phan Boi Chau St., Hoan Kiem District. ☎ **04/942-8162-0580**. www.anan-vietnam.com. Main courses US$1–US$5 (£0.55–£2.75). MC, V. Daily 7am–10pm.

Tamarind Café ✹✹ VEGETARIAN   Even if you're not a vegetarian, this welcoming cafe's inventive menu will tickle your fancy. Vegetarian wonton soup and two-color soup (spinach and sweet potato) take the chill off Hanoi winter nights and go great with the selection of sandwiches. Other inventive options include "ratatofu" (ratatouille over tofu) and an all-day breakfast served with delicious homemade fruit condiments. Fruit shakes and excellent teas round out the meal. With a bottomless cup of coffee for just US$1 (£0.55), this is a great place to take a break from the hectic Old Quarter. There are street-side tables out front and funky seating in back. A good place to meet other travelers and pick up advice.

80 Ma May St., Hoan Kiem District. ☎ **04/926-0580**. Main courses US$2–US$5 (£1.10–£2.75). MC, V. Daily 5:30am–11pm.

SNACKS & CAFES

For great coffee and desserts, try **Moca Café** (14–16 Nha Tho St., Hoan Kiem District; ☎ **04/825-6334**). This area has become the popular spot for a growing little bohemian community in Hanoi, and businesses are sprouting up all along Nha Tho, the street that extends from St. Christopher's Church. **Paris Deli** (13 Nha Tho St., Hoan Kiem District; © **04/928-6697**) is a popular spot with great breads and deli sandwiches.

One of the main attractions around Hoan Kiem Lake (for me) is **Fanny's Ice Cream** (48 Ly Thai To St., Hoan Kiem District), on the west side of the lake. Fanny's serves exquisite gelato-style ice cream. You can also find local ice-cream shops along Trang Tien between the lake and the Press Club. For 5,000VND (US30¢/£0.15), enjoy a cone and be part of the local scene.

(Finds) Have You Tried the Snake?

Six kilometers (3¾ miles) to the east of Hanoi, across the Red River, lies the town of **Le Mat,** also known as the "snake village." Among shanty houses and winding alleys, you'll find Chinese-style roofs sheltering the elegant dining areas of flashy little restaurants, all strangely tucked away. What's the big secret? The town is the hub of the very taboo snake industry. The Vietnamese taboo is not much different from that in the West (something like "Eat snake? Ooooh, yuck!"). Snake is also considered a male aphrodisiac, a kind of fried Viagra, so at night it's not uncommon to see groups of businessmen drunk as skunks piling into these places for a bit of medicine.

So, here's the drill. Finding it is half the battle (or adventure). Any taxi driver will be happy to take you to his friend's place in anticipation of a commission. Feel free to ask to see another restaurant (some of them are pretty grotty), but expect to pay about US$5 (£2.75) to get here. There are lots of restaurants in Le Mat, but try **O Sin** (© **04/827-2984**).

You'll be greeted by a friendly owner who'll usher you back to the cages and put on quite a show of stirring up the snakes before selecting one he thinks will feed your party. He'll then quote you a ridiculous price, but expect to pay somewhere between US$5 and US$10 (£2.75–£5.50) per person, after bargaining.

Then the show begins. Before your eyes, the owner kills the snake, drains the blood into a jar of rice whiskey, and systematically disembowels the animal, extracting the liver and showing you the still-beating heart before adding it to the whiskey/blood concoction. The guest of honor eats the heart and takes the first sip of whiskey. Thus begins a lengthy seven-course meal, starting with fried snake skin, grilled snake filet, snake spring rolls, snake soup with rice cake, minced snake dumpling, and copious amounts of rice whiskey. It's a decent meal, really, and certainly something to write home about.

Be warned that many of these places are part of the underground market in endangered species, but the snakes are common cobras found everywhere in Vietnam. Be clear with the driver about where you want to go (in other words, not to a brothel afterward), and don't pay until you arrive at your destination.

Pepperonis (29 Ly Quoc Su St., Hoan Kiem District; ☏ **04/928-5246**) serves up the pizza that backpackers have been longing for along the tough travel trails throughout Asia. The pizza is cheap and best on the popular bar street, across from Café des Arts.

Little Hanoi (21 Hang Gai St., Hoan Kiem District; ☏ **04/828-8333**), just north of the lake, is a little local-styled fast-food joint, with basic but tidy bamboo and wood decor. With a limited menu of favorites like banana-flower salad and noodle soup (without the resulting bellyache), it's a good place for a light meal (and a good central meeting point). Little Hanoi delivers, too.

Highland's Coffee is the local version of Starbucks and a popular place to beat the heat. Find it at lakeside (38–40 Ly Thai To St., Hoan Kiem District; ☏ **04/828/7043**) or on a perch overlooking the north end of the lake (Hoan Kiem Terrace, 6th floor; ☏ **04/928-7369**).

WHAT TO SEE & DO

Remember that state-owned attractions usually close for lunch from 11:30am to 1:30pm. Be sure not to accept any extraneous pamphlets or unwanted guides at sights; all come with a nominal but frustrating fee.

BA DINH DISTRICT

Army Museum ☘☘   This museum, opened in 1959, presents the Vietnamese side of the country's struggle against colonial powers. There are three buildings of odds and ends from both the French and American wars here, including evocative photos. Most interesting, though, is the actual war equipment on display, including aircraft, tanks, bombs, and big guns, some with signs indicating just how many of which enemy the piece took out. There is a tank belonging to the troops that crashed through the Presidential Palace gates on April 30, 1975, Vietnamese Liberation Day. Outside, you'll see a spectacular display of downed French and U.S. aircraft wreckage. Also on the grounds is Hanoi's ancient flag tower (Cot Co), constructed from 1805 to 1812. The exhibits have English translations, which makes this an easy and worthwhile visit.

28A Dien Bien Phu St., Ba Dinh District. ☏ 04/823-4264. Admission 10,000VND (US65¢/£0.35). Tues–Thurs and Sat–Sun 8–11:30am and 1:30–4:30pm.

Ho Chi Minh Mausoleum ☘☘   In an imposing, somber, granite-and-concrete structure modeled on Lenin's tomb, Ho lies in state, embalmed and dressed in his favored khaki suit. He asked to be cremated, but his wish was not heeded. A respectful demeanor is required, and the dress code mandates no shorts or sleeveless shirts. *Note:* The mausoleum is usually closed in October and November, when Ho goes to Russia for body maintenance of an undisclosed nature. The museum might be closed during this period as well.

On Ba Dinh Sq., Ba Dinh District. Tues–Thurs and Sat 8–11am.

Ho Chi Minh Museum ☘☘   English-language explanations help to piece together the fragments of Ho's life and cause at this museum tribute; you'll see personal items, photos, and documents detailing the rise of the nation's communist revolution. The rhetoric is laid on a bit thick, but all in all it's an interesting and informative display. Completely unique to Vietnam are the conceptual displays symbolizing freedom, reunification, and social progress through flowers, fruit, and mirrors. Have a look.

3 Ngo Ha (left of 1 Pillar Pagoda, near Ba Dinh Sq.), Ba Dinh District. ☏ 04/845-5455. Admission 10,000VND (US65¢/£0.35). Tues–Sun 8–11:30am and 1:30–4pm.

Ho Chi Minh's Residence ★★ Ho's residence, the well-known house on stilts, is behind the Presidential Palace, a gorgeous French colonial building built in 1901 for the resident French governor. Shunning the glorious structure nearby, Ho instead chose to live here from 1958 to 1969. Facing an exquisite landscaped lake, the structure does have its charm, and the spartan room is an interesting glimpse into the life of this enigmatic national hero. The basement was a meeting place for the politburo; upstairs are the bedroom and a study. Little details like his phone and walking cane are kept behind glass. Behind the house is a garden of fruit trees, many of them exotics imported from other lands, including miniature rose bushes and areca trees from the Caribbean.

Behind the Presidential Palace at Ba Dinh Sq., Ba Dinh District. Admission 10,000VND (US65¢/£0.35). Tues–Sun 8–11am and 1:30–4:30pm.

Hun Tiep Lake and the Downed B-52 This place won't blow you away for its size or beauty; in fact, what brings many here is that it's an ordinary neighborhood, a maze of quiet lanes broken only by a small pond and, in the brackish water, the wreckage of an American B-52 shot down during the Christmas air raids of 1972. Many folks, veterans among them, find that a visit here puts a perspective on the war and that the rusting wreckage brings our abstract historical impressions back to the concrete present; others see landing gear, struts, and metal sheathing in a grungy pond. There's a partly submerged memorial plaque, and the area is cordoned off; entrance fees are soon to follow, no doubt. Most taxi drivers know it, or else some creative charades will get the point across. Drivers will drop you off at the head of the alley (Lane 55) leading to the site (a handwritten sign reads "B-52" with an arrow).

Located just south of West Lake along Hoang Hoa Tham Rd., and a short walk down Lane 55 heading south, Ba Dinh District.

One-Pillar Pagoda ★ To the right of the Ho Chi Minh Museum is the unique One-Pillar Pagoda, a 1049 wooden structure that sits on stilts over a lake. A king of the Ly Dynasty, Ly Thai Thong King, had it built after having a dream in which Bodhisattva Avalokitesvara, the goddess of mercy, presented him with a lotus flower. The existing pagoda is a miniature reproduction of the original, which was said to represent a lotus emerging from the water. It is certainly interesting, and a prayer here is said to bring fertility and good health. It's best to wear something full length (skirt or trousers), not shorts.

Right of Ho Chi Minh Museum, near Ba Dinh Sq., Ba Dinh District.

Vietnam National Museum of Fine Arts ★★ This very worthwhile museum features Vietnamese art of the 20th century, up to the 1970s or so. While the presentations are a bit crowded and rustic, there are explanations in English. Much of the art is outstanding, although you won't really see any works of an innovative or controversial nature. Entire rooms are devoted to the Vietnamese style of lacquer and silk painting, woodblock, and folk art. Techniques are explained—a nice touch. Interesting also are the modern works of wood statuary interspersed among the exhibits. Some are patriotic in nature, depicting daily life or events during the war or done in Soviet-influenced caricature, with heavy-limbed peasants striking triumphant poses. The top floors are devoted to prehistoric artifacts and Buddhist sculptures, some of which are huge and impressive. Don't miss the famous 11th-century goddess of mercy (Kouan Yin), with her thousand arms and eyes in the far-left room on the second floor. Best

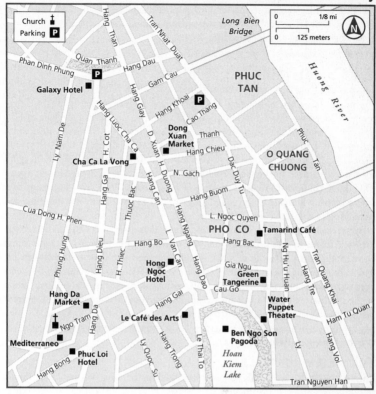

of all, the museum itself is in an old colonial, and, unless there's a tour group milling around, you can stroll around in relative serenity and rest on one of the many benches provided (no napping). The gift shop has some modern works by well-known artists for sale.

66 Nguyen Thai Hoc St., Ba Dinh District. © **04/846-5801.** Admission 15,000VND (US95¢/£0.50). Tues, Fri, Sun 8:30am–5pm; Wed and Sat 8:30am–9pm.

West Lake ⊛⊛   In Hanoi, West Lake is second only to Hoan Kiem as a nerve center for the city, steeped in legend and sporting several significant pagodas. Vietnam's oldest pagoda, **Tran Quoc,** was built in the 6th century and is located on Cayang Island in the middle of the lake, a beautiful setting. An actual fragment of the Bodhi tree under which Buddha achieved enlightenment was given as a gift from the Prime Minister of India in 1959 and now grows proudly in the main courtyard. Constructed by an early Zen sect and a famous center for Dharma study, and later an imperial feasting grounds, the temple has a visitors' hall, two corridors, and a bell tower; it still houses a group of diligent monks. (They recommend not wearing shorts here, but this is not enforced.) Farther along the lake, **Quan Thanh Temple,** by the northern gate, was built during the reign of Le Thai To King (1010–28). It is dedicated to Huyen Thien Tran Vo, the god who reigned over Vietnam's northern regions. Renovated in the 19th century, the impressive temple has a triple gate, courtyard, and 3.6m (12-ft.) bronze statue of the god. West Lake is also a hub of local activity, particularly on weekends when families go paddle-boating here.

Bordered by Thuy Khue and Thanh Nien sts., Ba Dinh District.

DONG DA DISTRICT

Temple of Literature and National University (Van Mieu–Quoc Tu Giam) ★★

If Vietnam has a seat of learning, this is it. There are two entities here: Van Mieu, a temple built to worship Chinese philosopher Confucius in 1070; and Quoc tu Giam, literally "Temple of the King Who Distinguished Literature," an elite institute established in 1076 to teach the doctrines of Confucius and his disciples. It existed for more than 700 years as a center for Confucian learning. Moreover, it is a powerful symbol for the Vietnamese, having been established after the country emerged from a period of Chinese colonialism that lasted from 179 B.C. to A.D. 938. It's a testament to the strong cultural heritage of the Mandarins; as such, it stands for independence and a solidifying of national culture and values.

What exists today is a series of four courtyards that served as an entrance to the university. Architecturally, it is a fine example of classic Chinese with Vietnamese influences. Still present are 82 stone stelae—stone diplomas, really—erected between 1484 and 1780, bearing the names and birthplaces of 1,306 doctoral laureates who managed to pass the university's rigorous examinations. Beyond the final building, known as the sanctuary, the real university began. Damaged in the French war, it is currently being restored.

Quoc Tu Giam St., Dong Da District. ℂ **04/845-2917**. Admission 5,000VND (US30¢/£0.15); 3,000VND (US20¢/£0.10) for English-language brochure. Daily 8am–5pm.

HOAN KIEM DISTRICT

Hanoi Opera House   This gorgeous Art Nouveau building was built near the turn of the 20th century. Unfortunately, to get inside, you'll have to attend a performance, but that should be enjoyable as well (see "Hanoi After Dark," p. 322).

1 Trang Tien St. (at Le Thanh Tong St.), Hoan Kiem District. ℂ **04/933-0113**.

Hoa Lo Prison (Hanoi Hilton) ★★   For sheer gruesome atmosphere alone, this ranks near the top of the must-see list. It was constructed by the French in 1896 mainly to house political prisoners; the Vietnamese took it over in 1954. It was subsequently used to house prisoners of war. From 1964 to 1973, it was a major P.O.W. detention facility. U.S. Sen. John McCain was a particularly famous inmate, as was Pete Peterson, the ambassador to Vietnam, and Lt. Everett Alvarez, officially the first American pilot to be shot down over Vietnam. Their stories are told from the Vietnamese perspective in photographs and writings grouped in one small room. To the west is the guillotine room, still with its original equipment, and the female and Vietnamese political prisoners' quarters. The courtyard linking the two has parts of original tunnels once used by a hundred intrepid Vietnamese revolutionaries to escape in 1945. Only part of the original complex is left; the rest of the original site was razed and is ironically occupied by a tall, gleaming office complex popular with foreign investors. There are basic English explanations, but this is a good spot to have a guide, who is certain to be armed with a tale or two.

1 Hoa Lo St., off Quan Su St., Hoan Kiem District. ℂ **04/824-6358**. Admission 10,000VND (US65¢/£0.35). Tues–Sun 8am–4:30pm.

Flying Dragons & Thieving Turtles: Hanoi's Founding

Originally, at its prehistorical founding as Thang Long, Hanoi was called **"the Ascending Dragon."** The dragon that ascended, so the story goes, created civilization as we know it along the Red River Valley, and then plunged to his sleep in Halong Bay, thereby creating the grand karst slopes—today a UNESCO World Heritage Site. The dragon is the symbol of the city, and you'll find references to it wherever you go.

Hanoi's other important creation myth is one oddly echoed by the legendary tale of King Arthur and his rise to the throne after receiving the sword Excalibur from the Lady of the Lake. "Strange women lying in ponds distributing swords is no basis for a system of government," says Eric Idle's character in Monty Python's spoof of the Arthur legend, and Hanoi's mandate granted by a giant turtle in Hoan Kiem is equally ridiculous, but a great one for putting the kids to bed to at night.

Le Loi, the first king of a united Viet people, asked the powers in heaven to help him vanquish the Chinese in the 2nd century A.D. His answer came from a giant turtle that rose from the depths of Hoan Kiem Lake and offered him the sword that he would use to drive the Chinese out. (Vietnamese history is full of valiant tales about driving the Chinese out.) When Le Loi returned to the lake to give thanks, the turtle rose again out of the water and took a firm jaw hold of the sword and dragged it to the watery depths, a sign that the citizens could lay down their arms and the city would prosper in peace. The turtle fooled old Le Loi, because the Vietnamese would suffer under Chinese oppression for centuries to come. The myth is best depicted at the Thang Long Water Puppet Theater (p. 322). And keep an eye out for a unique breed of lake turtles—you'll see them basking on the central island. See the section on Hoan Kiem (p. 318) for details on the lake's temples and sights, and note that most addresses in this chapter are given in relation to the lake, so you should get to know it during your stay in the Vietnamese capital.

National Museum of Vietnamese History   This is an exhaustive repository of Vietnamese historic relics nicely displayed with some bare-bones explanations in English. Housed in a building that was the French consulate until 1910 and a museum in various incarnations since, the collection walks you from prehistoric artifacts and carvings to funerary jars and some very fine examples of Dong Son drums from the north, excavations of Han tombs, Buddhist statuary, and everyday items of early history. It's the kind of place where schoolchildren are forced to go (be careful if you see buses out front), and for anyone but history buffs, you might feel just as bored as the kids. For those on any kind of historic mission in Vietnam, it's best to contact a tour agency and book a knowledgeable guide for an excellent overview and a good beginning to any trip.

1 Trang Tien St. (just east of the opera house), Hoan Kiem District. ✆ 04/825-3518. Admission 15,000VND (US95¢/£0.50). Daily 8–11:30am and 1:30–4:30pm.

Old Quarter and Hoan Kiem Lake ★★★   The Old Quarter evolved from workshop villages clustered by trades, or guilds, in the early 13th century. It's now an area of narrow, ancient, winding streets, each named for the trade it formerly featured. Even today, streets tend to be for silk, silver, or antiques. It's a fascinating slice of centuries-old life in Hanoi, including markets that are so pleasantly crowded that the street itself narrows to just a few feet.

Hoan Kiem is considered the center of the city. It is also known as the Lake of the Recovered Sword. In the mid–15th century, the gods gave emperor Le Thai To a magical sword to defeat Chinese invaders. While the emperor was boating on the lake one day, a giant tortoise reared up and snatched the sword, returning it to its rightful owners and ushering peace into the kingdom. Stroll around the lake in the early morning or evening to savor local life among the willow trees and see elders playing chess or practicing tai chi. In the center of the lake is the Tortoise Pagoda; on the northern part is Ngoc Son Pagoda, reachable only by the Bridge of the Rising Sun.

Bordered by Tran Nhat Duat and Phung Hung sts., Hoan Kiem District. Daily 8am–5pm.

Quan Su Pagoda ★   Quan Su is one of the most important temples in the country. Constructed in the 15th century along with a small house for visiting Buddhist ambassadors, in 1934 it became the headquarters of the Tonkin Buddhist Association and today it is headquarters for the Vietnam Central Buddhist Congregation. The active pagoda is usually thronged with worshippers; the interior is dim and smoky with incense. To the rear is a school of Buddhist doctrine. For good luck (or for fun), visitors of any stripe are welcome to buy sticks of incense and make offerings at the various altars and sand urns. It's easy to just follow suit, and folks will be glad to show you what to do.

73 Quan Su St. (at intersection with Tran Hung Da), Hoan Kiem District. Daily 8–11am and 1–4pm.

OUTSIDE THE CITY CENTER
Vietnam Ethnology Museum ★★   To learn more about the 53 ethnic minorities populating Vietnam's hinterlands, make the jaunt out to this sprawling compound (go by cab). The different ethnic groups' history and customs are explained in photos, videos, and displays of clothing and daily implements. Out back are a number of re-creations of the village homes, from a low Cham house to the towering peak of a thatched Banhar communal home. You'll come away with a good historic perspective on the many groups in the far north and in parts of neighboring Laos and Thailand.

Nguyen Van Huyen, 6km (3¾ miles) west of town. © 04/756-2193. Admission 10,000VND (US65¢/£0.35). Tues–Sun 8:30–11:30am and 1:30–4:30pm.

OUTDOOR ACTIVITIES
Wake up early and join the hordes of people doing tai chi, stretching, walking, and running in the parks of Hanoi. This town is a great place for people-watching and a little morning wake-up; the best spots are near the Botanical Gardens, Lenin Park, and Hoan Kiem Lake. Get your run in before about 6:30am, though, before traffic starts to snarl. Or rent a bicycle from almost any hotel for about US$1 (£0.55) a day. The **Clark Hatch Fitness Center,** at the Sofitel Metropole Hotel (© **04/826-6919**), has top-end equipment, a sauna, and a Jacuzzi, with day rates for nonguests.

SHOPPING
Hanoi is a fine place to shop for silk, silver, lacquerware, embroidered goods, and ethnic minority crafts. Silk is of good quality and an easy buy. Shops will tailor a suit in

as little as 24 hours, but allow yourself extra time for alterations. Many of the shops are clustered along **Hang Gai Street,** also called "Silk Street," on the northeast side of the Old Quarter. A silk suit will run from about US$35 to US$75 (£19–£41), depending on the silk, and a blouse or shirt will cost US$15 to US$20 (£8.25–£11). Virtually every shop accepts MasterCard and Visa. Bargain hard for all but the silk; offer 50% of the asking price and end up paying 70% or so.

Khai Silk, with branches in various hotel lobbies and at 96 Hang Gai St. (© 04/825-4237) and 121 Nguyen Thai Hoc St. (© 04/823-3508), is justly famous for its selection, silk quality, and relatively pleasant store layout. Also try **Thanh Ha Silk** (114 Hang Gai St.; © 04/928-5348) and **Oriental House** (28 Nha Chung; © 04/828-5542). **Tan My** (109 Hang Gai St.; © 04/826-7081) has exquisite embroidery work, especially for children's clothing and bedding. **F Silk** (82 Hang Gai St.; © 04/928-6786) features a fine line of silk ready-to-wear. Near the Sheraton, check out the high-end boutiques along Xuan Dieu Street, like **So 9** (© 04/716-0400), where you can also make an appointment for massage therapy from a certified therapist.

For decorative items and souvenirs, shopping is chockablock on the streets surrounding Hoan Kiem Lake. One good place to start is **Nha Tho Street,** also called "Church Street" since it terminates at the town's largest cathedral. Here you'll discover silk and houseware designers among the quiet cafes. Unique lacquerware and furnishings can be found at **Delta Deco** or **La Casa** (12 Nha Tho St.; © 04/828-9616; www.lacasavietnam.com). Nearby, **Indochine House** (13 Nha Tho St.; © 04/824-8071) has a good selection of handicrafts and souvenirs. These are just a few of the many options here.

For silver, antique oddities, and traditional crafts, try **Hong Hoa** (18 Ngo Quyen St.; © 04/826-8341), located near the Sofitel Metropole Hotel. **Giai Dieu** (82 Hang Gai St.; © 04/826-0222; also at 93 Ba Trieu St.) has interesting lacquer paintings and decorative items.

For fine ceramics, look to **Quang's Ceramics** (22 Hang Luoc St.; © 04/828-3440), in the Old Quarter. Wood, stone, and brass lacquer reproduction sculptures of religious icons are sold at **KAF Traditional Sculptures and Art Accessories** (31B Ba Trieu St.; © 04/822-0022).

ART GALLERIES Vietnam has a flourishing art scene, and Hanoi has many galleries featuring oil, silk, watercolor, and lacquer paintings. Don't forget to bargain here. Keep in mind that any paintings you buy are not originals, but copies of works by well-known Vietnamese artists.

Galleries are chockablock in the Old Quarter and on the perimeters of Hoan Kiem. Try **Linh Gallery** (13 Hang Gai; © 04/928-7013; www.vangallery.com) or **Van Gallery,** its sister shop on Trang Tien near the Dan Chu Hotel. Next door is **Nam Son** (41 Trang Tien; © 04/826-2993).

Others include **Thanh Mai** (64 Hang Gai St.; © 04/825-1618), **Apricot Gallery** (40B Hang Bong St.; © 04/828-8965), and **Thang Long** (15 Hang Gai St.; © 04/825-0740), in the Old Quarter.

BOOKSTORES For foreign books in Hanoi, check out one of the many shops lining Trang Tien or Ma May streets, where you'll find backpacker book repositories and some good deals on photocopied bootlegs. Also try the few similar shops on Bao Khan Street, a popular nightlife area.

CONVENIENCE STORES   To pick up good snacks for a long train or bus ride, check out **Intimex** (22–23 Le Thai To St.; ℂ **04/825-6148**), a spiffy grocery down a small alley on the west side of Hoan Kiem Lake. For Western wines and canned products from home, try the aptly named **Western Canned Foods** (66 Ba Trieu; ℂ **04/822-9217**), just south of Hoan Keim.

HANOI AFTER DARK

When it comes to nightlife, Hanoi is no Saigon, but there are a variety of pleasant watering holes about town as well as a few rowdy dance spots.

Hanoi is also the best city in which to see **traditional Vietnamese arts** such as opera, theater, and water-puppet shows. Invented during the Ly Dynasty (1009–1225), the art of water puppetry is unique to Vietnam. The puppets are made of wood and really do dance on water. The shows feature traditional Vietnamese music and depict folklore and myth. Book tickets for the popular puppets at least 5 hours ahead.

Real cinema (and absinthe) can be found at **Hanoi Cinematheque** (22A Hai Ba Trung St.; ℂ **04/824-4433**), near Hoan Kiem Lake.

THE PERFORMING ARTS

The **Hanoi Opera House,** or Hanoi Municipal Theatre (1 Trang Tien St., Hoan Kiem District; ℂ **04/933-0113**), hosts performances by local and international artists. The **Hanoi Traditional Opera** (15 Nguyen Dinh Chieu, Ba Dinh District; ℂ **04/826-7361**) has shows on Monday, Wednesday, and Friday at 8pm.

Central Circus (in Lenin Park, Hai Ba Trung District; ℂ **04/822-0277**) has shows at 7:45pm every day except Monday. It's a real circus done on a small scale, so see it only if you're desperate to entertain the kids.

Thang Long Water Puppet Theater ✦✦✦ (finds)   This might sound like one for the kids, but there is something enchanting about the lighthearted comedy and intricately skilled puppetry of this troupe. They perform numerous vignettes of daily life in the countryside as well as ancient tales, including the legend of Hoan Kiem Lake and the peaceful founding of the city of Hanoi. Puppeteers use bamboo poles to extend their puppets from behind the proscenium and up through the surface of a small pond that forms the stage. You will be amazed at their ingenuity, and it doesn't take much to suspend disbelief and get caught up in a magical hour of escape. The kids will like it, too. In high season, buy tickets early. The theater is poorly raked, which means that although seats in the front cost a bit more, you'll have a better view—and not look at the back of someone's head—from the middle or the back (pick from a seating chart at the ticket office). You'll also get a better effect of verisimilitude from the back, where it looks more real.

57B Dinh Tien Hoang St., Hoan Kiem District. ℂ **04/825-5450**. Fax 04/824-9494. www.thanglongwaterpuppet.org. Admission 20,000VND–40,000VND (US$1.25–US$2.50/£0.70–£1.40). Shows daily at 5:15, 6:30, and 8pm.

BARS, PUBS & DISCOS

Bao Khanh Street, just down a short lane in the northwest corner of Hoan Kiem Lake (near Café des Arts), is home to lots of popular bars. Some are a bit seedy, but there are a few comfortable places. Most popular is the **Funky Monkey** (15B Hang Hanh; ℂ **04/928-6113**), which has music, pool tables, and pizzas. Also check out **Polite Pub** (5 Bao Khanh; ℂ **04/825-0959**), open from 5pm until 2 or 3am, and **Amazon Bar** (across from Café des Arts; ℂ **04/928-7338**).

For a night out with the boys, the **Spotted Cow** (23C Hai Ba Trung, next to Al Fresco's; © 04/824-1028) is a good choice—there's just drinking and darts here.

For a more upscale experience, sip a cocktail at the famous **Press Club** (59A Ly Thai To; © 04/934-0888) or head up the street to the **Diva Café** (57 Ly Thai To; © 04/934-4088), where bartenders put on a flamboyant fire show when preparing their special Irish coffee.

In the heart of the Old Quarter, **Cau Lac Bo Nhac Jazz Club** (31 Luong Van Can St; © 04/828-7890) has no cover and offers some of the best local acts. Call ahead to see what's going on that evening.

The **New Century** (10 Trang Thi; © 04/928-5285) is a popular club for locals—a bit seedy, really, but that's its very charm, according to many.

Finally, the folks at **Restaurant Bobby Chinn** (p. 312), on the south end of Hoan Kiem Lake, can serve up just about any cocktail. It can be a hip, late-night hangout, depending on the crowd.

SIDE TRIPS FROM HANOI
HALONG BAY ⭑⭑

A Vietnamese fable tells that the towering limestone rock formations, called karst, at Halong were formed with the crash landing of a dragon sent by the gods of early Vietnamese animism to protect the country from an invading navy. The picturesque area did in fact play host to some important Vietnamese naval victories against Chinese forces, but the bay is most famous today for its UNESCO World Heritage status, its emerald-green water, and 3,000 islands of towering limestone in the Gulf of Tonkin.

The bay itself is a 4-hour drive from Hanoi; a visit usually includes an overnight stay of at least 1 night (though it can be done in a long day trip). Given the logistics, the trip is best done through an agent or with a group. If you book a tour with an overnight stay, you'll probably cruise on a junk for 4 to 6 hours along the bay, stopping to explore two grottos. You might pause for swimming or kayaking as well. Overnight trips can cost anywhere from US$16 (£8.80) to upward of US$150 (£83); it depends on whether you hire a bus or a private driver, where you stay, and what you eat.

Sinh Café (© 04/926-1288; www.sinhcafevn.com) does a fine job on the low end, but don't expect much. Our recommendation is to contact the helpful folks at **Buffalo Tours** (© 04/828-0702; www.buffalotours.com/jewel). Its luxury boat, *Jewel of the Bay,* runs overnight trips that include kayaking, touring, and fine dining. Buffalo is just one of the best of a handful of operators; **Handspan** (© 04/962-0446; www.handspan.com) runs similar tours from Hanoi, and **HuangHai** (www.halongtravels.com) manages a fleet of junks.

For a unique high-end experience, book passage aboard the ***Emeraude,*** a copy of a French steamer that once plied these waters in the early 20th century. Certainly the largest boat at 55m (180 ft.), the *Emeraude* offers real luxury in each of its 38 cabins, and it comes with prices to match. The 2-day, 1-night cruise is well worth it, though. Go to www.emeraude-cruises.com or contact the offices at the Press Club in Hanoi (© 04/934-0888; fax 04/934-0899).

Eco-tourism is taking off here, and the steep karst outcrops of the bay are not only beautiful, but also ideal for exploration. You might want to consider one of the 2- or 3-day **sea-kayaking** adventures becoming popular here. Contact Buffalo Tours or Handspan for memorable packages starting from US$180 (£99) for multiday trips.

CUC PHUONG NATIONAL PARK

Cuc Phuong, established in 1962 as Vietnam's first national park, is a lush mountain rainforest with more than 250 bird and 60 mammal species, including tigers, leopards, and the unique red-bellied squirrel. The park's many visitors—and poachers—might keep you from the kind of wildlife experience you might hope for in the brush, however. It's still the perfect setting for a good hike, and the park features goodies like a 1,000-year-old tree, a waterfall, and Con Moong Cave, where prehistoric human remains have been discovered. Cuc Phuong is a good day trip from Hanoi, and some tourist cafes offer programs for as little as US$20 (£11) if you have four people in your group. It is also possible to overnight here in the park headquarters.

HOA LU

From A.D. 968 to 1010, Hoa Lu was the capital of Vietnam under the Dinh Dynasty and the first part of the Le Dynasty. Located in a valley surrounded by awesome limestone formations, it's known as the inland Halong Bay—it's a similarly picturesque sight, but much easier to reach. Most of what remains of the kingdom are ruins, but there are still temples in the valley that were renovated in the 17th century. The first honors Dinh Tien Hoang and has statues of the king. The second is dedicated to Le Dai Hanh, one of Dinh's generals and the first king of the Le Dynasty, who grabbed power in 980 after Dinh was mysteriously assassinated. Hoa Lu can easily be seen on a day trip from Hanoi. Seat-in-coach tours from a tourist cafe run about US$12 (£6.60) per person.

5 Sapa ⭐⭐⭐ & the Far North

The north and northwest highland regions are popular destinations for hardy travelers. In addition to the breathtaking **Tonkinese Alps** and off-the-map destinations like **Dien Bien Phu,** one of the main attractions are the **villages of the ethnic minority hill tribes.**

Sapa is a small market town that has been a gathering spot for many local hill tribes for nearly 200 years. Hmong and Yao people, among others, still come here to conduct trade, socialize, and attend an ephemeral **"love market"** where young men and women choose one another for marriage (these days, it's not likely you'll see anything but a staged re-creation of it). Seeing this, French missionaries as early as 1860 said "Mon Dieu!" and set up camp to save souls; their stone church still stands sentinel and is well attended at the center of town. Sapa, with its mercifully cool climate, later became a holiday escape for French colonists, complete with rail connection, upscale hotels, and a tourist bureau as early as 1917. The outpost was retaken by the Vietnamese in 1950 and attacked and destroyed later by the French, followed by a brief occupation by Chinese troops. The town reopened for tourism in the 1990s.

Now connected by luxury train with Hanoi, Sapa boasts good accommodations and is a great jumping-off point for trekking and eco-tours. Even a 1- or 2-day trip, bracketed by overnight train journeys from Hanoi, will give you a unique glimpse of local hill-tribe culture. Trek out to nearby villages with or without a guide, or meet with the many hill-tribe people who come to town to sell their wares. Hill-tribe costumes are colorful embroidered tunics embellished with heavy silver ornaments that signify marital status or place in the group's hierarchy.

Finally, the Tonkinese Alps are a feast for the eyes: The hills striated by terraced rice farms in vast, green valleys are like a stairway up to **Mount Fansipan,** Southeast Asia's tallest mountain, which, at 3,143m (10,309 ft.), smiles down on all the proceedings. **Note:** Bring a few layers here, as it can get quite chilly, especially in the winter months.

GETTING THERE

BY TRAIN   The *Victoria Express* train from Hanoi to Sapa—with wood-paneled luxury sleeping cars and a restaurant billed as the finest dining between the two towns—is an exciting new option. Trains depart four times per week with a similar return schedule, making possible convenient 2- or 3-day trips with overnight transport. Prices range from US$85 (£47) for a midweek round-trip in superior class to US$220 (£121) in a deluxe compartment on the weekend. Contact the Victoria Sapa Resort (© 20/871-522; www.victoriahotels-asia.com) for details and reservations.

A number of standard and tourist trains also make the overnight run from Hanoi. You can make arrangements with any travel agent for a small fee, or do it yourself at the **Hanoi Railway Station** (120 Le Duan; © 04/942-3949), located where the western edge of Hoan Kiem District meets Dong Da District. Prices range from US$16 (£8.80) for a hard berth to US$30 (£17) for a soft berth with air-conditioning. Trains passing through Lao Cai also continue north and make connections in China. (*Note:* This requires a Chinese visa.)

To get to Sapa from the train station in Lao Cai, you'll need to transfer by bus for the 2-hour ride. This can mean anything from a 25,000VND (US$1.60/£0.85) fare in a rattle-trap Russian cast-off, or a price of US$40 (£22) for a ride in a Japanese Pajero Mini (S.U.V.). The road is cut into the hillside and is bumpy and windy, but the views of the terraced rice farms of the valley are beautiful as you ascend.

Note: All trains to Sapa leave from the **Hanoi Railway Station** at 120 Le Duan St., often confused with Hanoi's other station. Be sure to show your taxi driver the correct address.

BY BUS   Hanoi's tourist cafes all run frequent buses to Sapa for US$12 (£6.60) one-way. Some include Sapa in larger tours of the north. You get what you pay for, though—the train is still the best option.

BY CAR   Any tourist cafe or travel agent in Hanoi can arrange trips by private jeep or a combo jeep-and-train tour. Apart from Sapa, the vast tracts of the north are untouristed and best visited with a tour company. Look under "Visitor Information & Tours" in the Hanoi section (p. 302). **Ann Tours, Buffalo Tours,** and **Handspan** all offer comprehensive itineraries. Avoid the temptation to book budget tours with the tourist cafes, especially for areas off the beaten track.

VISITOR INFORMATION & TOURS

There are a few storefront Internet cafes on Cau May Street in Sapa. All hotels provide exchange service for traveler's checks and even credit card cash advances.

For tours and trekking in the region, the Danish outfit **Topas Travel** (26 Cau May, Sapa; © 020/871-331; fax 020/871-596; www.topas.dk/vietnam), with offices worldwide and experienced guides, is a great option. Whether it's a day trek to nearby villages, an extended tour with home stays in villages, or the 5-day push to the top of Fansipan, these guys can cover it.

WHERE TO STAY
EXPENSIVE

Topas Eco-Lodge 🌟🌟   Set atop a hill overlooking terraced rice fields 18km (11 miles) from now-bustling Sapa, the Eco-Lodge's biggest assets are peace and quiet—in nearly no other place in all of Vietnam can you experience silence like this. Each villa is made of locally quarried stone and blond wood. Decks overlook the deep valleys and plunging mountains of Sapa, and the few other residences you'll see are those of the hill tribes, far in the distance. When night falls, darkness is complete, and the only light comes from the stars overhead and a few wood fires down in the valley. At the Eco-Lodge, simplicity is the rule: Each villa is powered by solar panels. All guests eat the same dish at mealtime, with vegetables that come from the lodge's own garden. Make reservations by e-mail or fax only.

16 Pham Xuan Huan, Sapa District, Lao Cai Province. ✆ 020/872-404. Fax 020/872-405. www.topas-eco-lodge. com. info@topas-eco-lodge.com. 25 units. US$158–US$169 (£87–£93) double. AE, MC, V. **Amenities:** Restaurant; bar; tour desk (trek arrangements); guides. *In room:* No phone.

Victoria Sapa Resort ★★★   This is Sapa's crème de la crème and one of the nicest rural resorts in Indochina, set on a small hill with panoramic views of the town. The standards here, from the comfortable rooms and fine dining to the incredible hilltop health club and pool, are without rival. Situated around a cozy courtyard, all bedrooms have balconies and wood floors offset by saturated wall colors, cane and fine wooden finishes, and local weavings and artwork that remind guests of the local hill-tribe culture. The bathrooms are large, with granite counters, wood fixtures, and even a small heater to warm up the tiles. If you're here with the kids, you'll appreciate the huge family rooms, with up to six beds and bunks (they can rearrange them). Suites feature elegant canopy beds and sitting areas. With amenities like a billiards table, comfortable reading nooks, and scenic viewing points here and there, this hotel is so inviting that many prolong their stay. Don't miss having at least one meal in the Tavanh restaurant (p. 327).

At the top of the hill overlooking town, Sapa District, Lao Cai Province. ✆ 020/871-522. Fax 020/871-539. www. victoriahotels-asia.com. 77 units. US$165–US$270 (£91–£149) double; US$270 (£149) suite. Promotional rates available. AE, MC, V. **Amenities:** Restaurant; bar; indoor/outdoor heated pool; tennis court; health club; sauna; kids' playroom; tour desk (trek arrangements w/Topas); car rental; salon; massage; babysitting; laundry service; nonsmoking rooms; Internet access. *In room:* Satellite TV w/in-house movies, minibar, fridge, coffeemaker, hair dryer, safe, IDD phone.

MODERATE

Bamboo Sapa Hotel   This good budget standby is a large concrete block near the town center. Just over 4 years old, its rooms are clean and spacious, done in shiny tile. Most have balconies, and all are oriented to the valley view. Shower-in-room–style bathrooms are large and clean; mattresses are sturdy, firm foam; and the staff is quite friendly. A good in-house tour operator, **Sapa Trekking Tour,** can plan any trip. An open-air restaurant under the lobby holds fun cultural dance shows.

Cau May St., Sapa, Lao Cai Province. ✆ 020/871-076. Fax 020/871-945. www.sapatravel.com. 60 units. US$40–US$50 (£22–£28). MC, V. **Amenities:** Restaurant; bar; bicycle rental; tour desk; car rental; laundry service. *In room:* TV, minibar, hair dryer, safe, IDD phone.

Chau Long Sapa Hotel ★   A tour-group favorite, the Chau Long has the look of an old hilltop castle in Europe, but that's just the facade. Rooms are none too special, but they are cleanly crafted in dark wood and come with small, tidy bathrooms. Most units have balconies with good views—but despite the hotel's location down a quaint off-the-main-drag street, those views are now blocked in part by new hotels, so ask to see the room before checking in. The friendly staff will bend over backward to make your stay fun. The roof-top restaurant is a unique place to have a spot of grog and take in the valley below.

24 Dong Loi, Sapa, Lao Cai Province. ✆ 020/871-245. Fax 020/871-844. www.chaulonghotel.com. 95 units. US$80–US$100 (£44–£55) double; US$160 (£88) suite. MC, V. **Amenities:** Restaurant; bar; pool; spa; Jacuzzi; steam room; car rental; limited room service; laundry service; Internet access. *In room:* TV, hair dryer, IDD phone.

INEXPENSIVE

Cat Cat Guesthouse   The view: That's what it's all about here. At this basic guest-house, buildings are stacked like an unlikely pile of children's blocks against a steeply sloping hill. At the top of the hill is a large guesthouse block and popular restaurant. Rooms are concrete and plain—a backpacker's standard—but most have big windows, balconies, and fireplaces. Stop for a coffee even if you don't stay the night; the bar here has the best view in town.

Cat Cat Rd. (at the base of the town on the way down to the Cat Cat Village), Lao Cai Province. Ⓒ **020/871-946** or 020/871-387. Fax 020/871-133. catcathotelst@yahoo.com. 60 units. US$5–US$30 (£2.75–£17) double. No credit cards. **Amenities:** Restaurant; bar. *In room:* Satellite TV.

Royal Hotel   It's backpacker central at this little five-story tower in the heart of town, the very terminus of central Cau May Street. The sparse tile-and-concrete decor, busy hallways, and hit-or-miss service are a bit of a turnoff. The hotel's Friendly Café is aptly named, though; the waitstaff here seem to have been hired based on their desire (read: not ability) to speak English, and the food is good, basic traveler fare (fried rice, fried noodles, and beer). Every room has a balcony; some even come with a fireplace. Ask about Royal trains and travel services.

Cau May St., Sapa, Lao Cai Province. Ⓒ/fax **020/871-313.** 30 units. US$12–US$15 (£6.60–£8.25) double. AE, MC, V. **Amenities:** Restaurant; laundry service. *In room:* TV, IDD phone.

WHERE TO DINE

Tavanh   FRENCH/VIETNAMESE   This is the most elegant dining in the Tonki-nese Alps. The menu is rich with imports; everything from lamb to salmon steaks is shipped in. Tavanh serves all the right dishes to keep you warm on a chilly eve; be sure to try the cheese fondue. There are good Vietnamese specials on an evolving menu, and the pastas are homemade and delicious. The romantic, candlelit dining room is done up with burgundy walls, rich wood floors, a central fireplace, and local hangings.

At the Victoria Sapa Resort, at the top of the hill overlooking town. Ⓒ **020/871-522.** Main courses US$6–US$19 (£3.30–£10). AE, MC, V. Daily 7am–10pm.

WHAT TO SEE & DO

The town itself is the attraction here. Sapa's small alleys are eminently strollable, and a short walk in any direction offers great views. On any given day, **Cau May Street** (the main drag) and the **central market area** are teeming with hill-tribe folks in their spangled finery, putting on the hard sell for some great weaving, fine silver work, and interesting trinkets like mouth harps and flutes. Especially on the weekend, it can be quite a scene. On the high end of Cau May is the **Mission Church** , an aging stone edifice. This was the church of the early French missionaries and is still a popular meeting point for locals. Masses are held on Saturday night and throughout the day on Sunday.

At the base of the hill below the town of Sapa is **Cat Cat Village** ⊛, with a small waterfall that makes a good spot to kick back. This Hmong village is accessible by road most of the way, and cement path for the rest. The whole trip can be made in just a few hours and offers a unique glimpse of rural life. Admission (paid at the top of the hill) is 20,000VND (US$1.35/£0.70). You can either walk all the way down or hire a motorbike or car taxi for pick-up and drop-off.

The premier day trip in this area is from **Lao Cai to Tavanh** ⊛⊛, a good opportu-nity to traipse around the rice terraces and experience a bit of rural village life. Hire a car or motorbike for the 9km (5½-mile) ride down the valley from Sapa to the Hmong village of Lao Cai (some folks even walk it); it's a nice ride in itself, with great views of the lush terraces. From there, follow the valley for a few miles to the next town of Tavanh. The short trek leads through the picturesque hill-tribe villages of Hmong, Zay, and Dao people. It's good to have a guide along to explain any customs and perhaps translate for you. You're sure to see other tourists on the trail (which puts many people off), but this is a good example of the many great treks in the area. Ask at your hotel or contact **Topas Travel** (© 020/871-331; www.topas.dk/vietnam) for longer, less touristy options. You'll still be greeted with *"Bonjour, madame! Bonjour, monsieur!"* wherever you go. Drop-off at Lao Cai and later pickup at Tavanh will cost about US$4 (£2.20) by motorbike taxi or US$25 (£14) by jeep; contact any hotel for a guide.

If you're heading even further north from Sapa, some 100km (62 miles) from town is the very popular **Bac Ha Market,** a more authentic version of Sapa's love market, held early on Sunday mornings. **Mai Chau,** a gorgeous valley, is home to ethnic Tai people; it's about 4 hours from Hanoi. **Dien Bien Phu,** to the far northwest, is a former French commercial and military outpost, as well as the site of one of Vietnam's biggest military victories over the French. You can fly directly to Dien Bien Phu from Hanoi.

6 An Introduction to the Central Coast

Many of Vietnam's most significant historic sights and some of its best beaches are clustered along its central coast. Popular destinations are **Hue,** the former Vietnamese

Who Are the Cham?

With little written history, what we do know of the Cham is from Chinese written texts and from the splendid religious art attributed to the Cham Empire (note the many Khmer-style Prang towers scattered along Vietnam's central coastline). Migrating from Indonesia, the Cham people settled in central Vietnam in the 2nd century A.D. and fought Chinese incursions from their stronghold in and around Danang.

The Cham belong to the Malayo-Polynesian language family and have their own Sanskrit-based script. Cham communities lived by rice farming, fishing, and trading pepper, cinnamon bark, ivory, and wood with neighboring nations via Hoi An. Hinduism was their dominant religion, with Buddhist influences and an infusion of Islam starting in the 14th century. In the middle of the 10th century, internal warfare, as well as battles against both Khmer to the south and Dai Viet to the north, began to erode the Cham kingdom. By the mid–15th century, it had been almost entirely absorbed into Vietnam.

The Cham today are an ethnic minority; many are still Hindu, but many have converted to Islam. Cham enclaves subsist by fishing, farming, and sales of handicrafts. The premiere Cham site is at **My Son** (see "Side Trips from Hoi An," p. 355), but other Cham sites can be found near Nha Trang and as far south as Phan Thiet. The best Cham artifacts are on view at the Cham Museum (p. 341).

capital, with its Imperial City and emperors' tombs, and **Hoi An,** a historic trading town with many original 17th-century buildings. Formerly the seat of the Cham kingdom from the 2nd through 14th centuries, the central coast also has the greatest concentration of Cham relics and art. Transport between each of these nearby towns is quite good.

GETTING THERE

BY PLANE   You can fly into both Hue and Danang from Saigon or Hanoi.

BY TRAIN   Both Hue and Danang are stops on the north–south rail line.

BY CAR/BUS/MINIVAN   Tourist-cafe buses connect all major towns in this region. Traveling with a rented vehicle and driver is possible, but will probably cost several hundred dollars and leave your teeth chattering from the bumpy roads.

GETTING AROUND

The three main coastal towns in the central part of the country are linked by roads that are prone to flooding, and traffic can be heavy, but the roads are in better shape now than before. You can easily rent a car or get a seat on a bus or minivan in any of the towns or through a hotel or booking agency. The trip from Hue to Danang is about 3½ hours; from Danang to Hoi An, about 90 minutes. See individual city listings, later in this chapter, for suggested prices.

7 Hue ★★

Hue (pronounced "hway") was once Vietnam's Imperial City, the capital of the country from 1802 to 1945 under the Nguyen Dynasty, and is culturally and historically significant. While much of Hue—tragically including most of Vietnam's walled Citadel and Imperial City—was decimated during the French and American wars, there is still much to see. Perhaps most captivating is simply observing daily life on the **Perfume River,** its many dragonboats, houseboats, and longtail vessels dredging for sand. You can visit many of the attractions, including the **tombs of Nguyen Dynasty emperors,** by boat. The enjoyable town has a seaside-resort sort of air, with a laid-back attitude; low-slung, colorful, colonial-style buildings; and strings of lights at outdoor cafes. There are many local cuisine specialties to sample as well.

You might want to plan for a full-day **American war memorial excursion** to the nearby demilitarized zone **(DMZ),** the beginning of the **Ho Chi Minh trail,** and underground tunnels at **Vinh Moc.**

GETTING THERE

BY PLANE   **Vietnam Airlines** connects to Hue from both Hanoi and Ho Chi Minh City (Saigon). A taxi from the airport costs 100,000VND (US$6.25/£3.45). There's also an airport bus that will pick you up at your hotel; it covers the half-hour trip for 25,000VND (US$1.55/£0.85). Book through your hotel or any tour operator.

BY TRAIN   Trains to Hue depart daily from both Hanoi and Ho Chi Minh City (Saigon). The trip from Hanoi to Hue takes 14 hours on the express trains, which depart nightly at 7 and 11pm; these trains have soft-berth compartments with air-conditioning for about US$35 (£19). From Saigon, in a soft-berth, it's about US$50 (£28), which is a good way to go.

BY CAR   If you're coming from the south, Vietnamtourism Danang can arrange a car for the 3½-hour ride from Danang to Hue for US$40 (£22). Contact travel agents in any section to rent a car with driver.

BY BUS   Many travelers choose to take a nerve-rattling overnight bus or minivan from Hanoi to Hue. Tickets are US$9 (£4.95) through one of Hanoi's tourist cafes; the trip takes an excruciating 17 hours. Hue is a major stop on any open-tour ticket, and open-tour cafe buses connect with Danang and Hoi An for just US$2 (£1.10), or Nha Trang for US$6 (£ 3.30); these are long, bumpy trails but are cheap and convenient.

GETTING AROUND

Taxis are much cheaper here than in Hanoi: 5,000VND (US30¢/£0.15) starting out and 5,000VND for each kilometer thereafter. Flag 'em down or call **Gili** (① **054/ 828-282**) or **ThanhDo** (① **054/835-835**). Because Hue is relatively small, renting a cyclo by the hour for 15,000VND to 20,000VND (US95¢–US$1.25/£0.50–£0.70) also works well. Even the tiniest hotel provides motorbike rentals at US$3 to US$5 (£1.65–£2.75) per day and bicycles for US$1 (£0.55).

VISITOR INFORMATION & TOURS

A number of tour companies in Hue can book boat trips and visits to the DMZ for you. Every hotel will also be able to assist you, although the tour companies will be cheaper, especially for car services. Hue's most efficient group, as well as the most expensive, is the **Huong Giang Tourist Company** (17 Le Loi St.; ① **054/832-220;** www.huonggiangtourist.com), which organizes good, personalized tours to the tombs and the DMZ at a premium (or you can join one of its group tours). A half-day tour by car and boat, with guide, to the Citadel and Thient Mu Pagoda is US$25 (£14) for one, US$30 (£17) for two. A private boat up the Perfume River will cost US$29 (£16). On the budget end, **Sinh Café** (7 Nguyen Tri Phuong or 12 Hung Vuong St.; ① **054/845-022;** www.sinhcafevn.com) takes big groups upriver for US$2 (£1.10) and has very reasonable junkets to the DMZ.

FAST FACTS: **Hue**

Currency Exchange Most hotels in Hue will change currency. **Vietcombank** is at 46 Hung Vuong St. (① **054/846-058**). The foreign exchange bank, **Vietinde,** has an office at 41 Hung Vuong St. (on the roundabout at the terminus of the main tourist drag); it can do cash advances and is also a Western Union representative.

Internet Access **Sinh Café** (7 Nguyen Tri Phuong; ① **054/845-022;** www.sinh cafevn.com) has good service for 10,000VND (US65¢/£0.35) per hour. There are also many good spots on Hung Vuong (the main tourist street south of the river), Pham Ngu Lao Street (just across from the Century Riverside), and Doi Cung Street.

Mail There are mini–post offices in both the Century and Huong Giang hotels. The main post office, at 8 Hoang Hoa Tham St., is open from 7am to 9pm.

Telephones The city code for Hue is **54.** You can place IDD calls at the post office (above) and from most hotels.

Hue

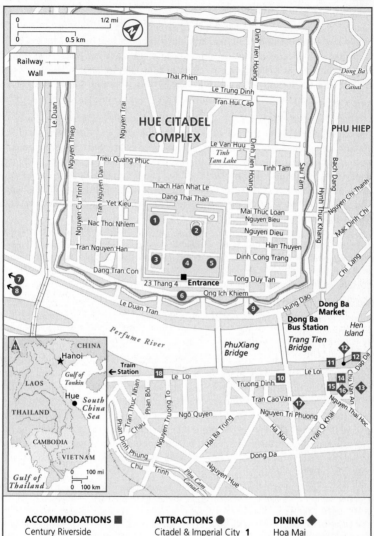

WHERE TO STAY

Considering the volume of travelers coming through this town, there isn't much in the way of quality accommodations, and even the best options are bland, with lots of "It's nice, but . . . ." Budget choices abound, but there are some real duds. Always ask to see the room first, before checking in. Hotel amenities are limited, but most have basic tour services and include breakfast. Prices are flexible, so press for a discount.

EXPENSIVE

Century Riverside Hotel ⟨⟨ Rooms at the Riverside are in bland chain-hotel style and show their age, but they're clean and comfortable enough, with new tile-and-marble bathrooms (be sure to ask for a recently renovated room). Standard units are rather small, with older carved-wood furniture. The river-view rooms are more than worth the extra outlay (usually about US$10/£5.50); there are great views from the upper floors of the longtail boats puttering by and the fisherman paddling small dugouts. The pool is in a prime lounging spot by the river, while the Riverside Restaurant has nice views and serves familiar fare.

49 Le Loi St., Hue. ⟨ 054/823-390. Fax 054/823-394. www.centuryriversidehue.com. 135 units. US$155 (£85) double; US$165–US$500 (£91–£275) suite. AE, MC, V. **Amenities:** 3 restaurants; bar; outdoor pool overlooking river; 2 tennis courts; small gym; bicycle/motorbike rental; concierge; tour desk (arranges popular boat trip to tombs); car rental; small business center; salon; 24-hr. room service; massage; laundry service; Internet access. In room: A/C, satellite TV, minibar, fridge, hair dryer, IDD phone.

Hotel Saigon Morin ⟨⟨⟨⟨ The Saigon Morin is a government-run, refurbished colonial block near the main bridge in town. The hotel forms a large courtyard around a central garden and pool area. A recent renovation of the third floor puts the Morin in a class of its own, with fine linens, wood floors, and stylish bathrooms that connect to the room via a fun "peek-a-boo" shuttered opening. The lower standard rooms, however, are still the same Chinese business-hotel basic, with old laminated furniture and threadbare carpeting dotted with cigarette burns. Over 100 years old, the Morin was originally the colonist's address of note; photos line the halls of that bygone era. The street in front of the Morin was where a young Ho Chi Minh carried his first placard in protest of foreign occupation. If he could only see the place now! The exterior maintains some of that old charm, but common areas are brash and busy, neon-lit and cluttered with souvenir stalls—all kind of fun, though. Service is a bit hit or miss, but usually friendly.

30 Le Loi St., Hue. ⟨ 054/823-526. Fax 054/825-155. www.morinhotel.com.vn. 127 units. US$120–US$140 (£66–£77) double; US$160 (£88) deluxe double; US$250–US$500 (£138–£275) suite. Rates include breakfast. AE, MC, V. **Amenities:** Outdoor buffet area; lobby restaurant; 2 bars/cafes (1 on roof w/good views); small outdoor pool; small gym; sauna; bicycle/motorbike rental; concierge; helpful in-house tour desk; car rental; salon; 24-hr. room service; massage; laundry service; Internet access. In room: A/C, satellite TV, Internet access, minibar, fridge, coffeemaker, hair dryer, safe, IDD phone.

Huong Giang Hotel ⟨⟨⟨⟨ This hotel is a veritable Asian wonderland, so enamored is it of heavy carved wood and bamboo furnishings in its faux "imperial" theme. Tacky? Yes, but also kind of fun. Standard rooms are clean and comfortable, but the bathrooms are a disappointing dormitory style, with plastic shower curtains and no counter space. Try to get a good deal on one of the Royal Suites, with carved-wood walls, grandiose furniture with inlaid mother-of-pearl, and a massive wood room divider—sort of a mini pagoda right in your room. (The words *emperor* and *bordello* both leap to mind.) The Royal Restaurant, worth a photo just for its gaudy gold-and-red-everything design alone, is for prearranged group dinners; its costumed staff serves a fancy traditional dinner at a hefty price (popular in town). The Terrace Bar is the best place in Hue to have a drink and watch life on the river. Be sure to splurge for a river-view room and enjoy a fine meal at the Hoa Mai Restaurant (reviewed below). To lay some money on a horse race, seek out the e-casino.

51 Le Loi St., Hue. (℃) 054/822-122 or 054/823-958. Fax 054/823-102. www.huonggiangtourist.com. 165 units. US$55–US$75 (£30–£41) garden-view double; US$65–US$85 (£36–£47) river-view double; US$160–US$230 (£88–£127) suite. AE, MC, V. **Amenities:** 3 restaurants; 2 bars; pool; basic health club; sauna; concierge; tour desk; car rental; small business center w/Internet access; cool, kitschy shopping area; salon; massage; laundry service. *In room:* A/C, cable TV, dataport, minibar, fridge, hair dryer, safe, IDD phone.

La Résidence Hôtel & Spa ⭑⭑⭑   Once home to France's envoy to central Vietnam, or Annam, La Résidence has been re-thought and added onto and is now one of the best-designed boutique hotels in the country. Warm colors and dark wood combine with unobtrusive, elegant Art Deco patterns befitting a colonial villa, while black-and-white pictures on the wall are reminiscent of Indochina. Nooks and crannies of private space abound, so a guest can easily find a quiet corner to himself. Rooms are spacious, with clean lines, parquet floors, and views of the Perfume River and the Citadel. The cuisine at Le Parfum is carefully prepared and excellent; the staff is exceptional.

5 Le Loi St., Hue. (℃) 054/837-475. Fax 054/837-476. www.la-residence-hue.com. 122 units. US$216–US$306 (£119–£168) double; US$342–US$531 (£188–£292) suite. AE, MC, V. **Amenities:** Restaurant; bar; outdoor pool; nice gym; spa; bicycle/motorbike rental; concierge; tour desk; car rental; business center; fine shopping; salon; 24-hr. room service; laundry service; wireless Internet access. *In room:* A/C, satellite TV, minibar, fridge, hair dryer, safe, IDD phone.

MODERATE

Hoa Hong Hotel ⭑   Though showing its age, the Hoa Hong has bargain rates and is a good midrange choice. Rooms are nondescript—think navy and beige, with ugly polyester spreads—but all are comfortable, with good, firm beds. The tidy bathrooms are a nice size, with tubs. Ask for a room with a city view rather than a noisy street view. The suites have authentic Asian furniture and are worth the extra cost. There are two restaurants, one of which specializes in the popular "royal dinner" theme evening, when both staff and guests dress like emperors and empresses. The lobby has a fun little bar that serves flowery umbrella drinks. Book early, as this place often fills up with tour groups.

1 Pham Ngu Lao St., Hue. (℃) 054/824-377 or 054/826-943. Fax 054/826-949. hoahonghotel@dng.vnn.vn. 50 units. US$30–US$60 (£17–£33) double; US$80 (£44) suite. Rates include breakfast. AE, MC, V. **Amenities:** Large restaurant; tour desk; car rental; 24-hr. room service; laundry service; Internet access. *In room:* A/C, satellite TV, minibar, fridge, IDD phone.

Ngoc Huong Hotel ⭑   Comparable to Hoa Hong (above), Ngoc Huong is newer, clean, and already quite popular. Rooms have the unfortunate fluorescent polyester blankets and gaudy drapery of most hotels this size, only here it's all new and clean. Larger suites overlook the river (peeking over the fronts of the Riverside and Huong Giang hotels). The seventh-floor restaurant serves good Vietnamese fare and offers 180-degree views.

8–10 Chu Van An St., Hue. (℃) 054/830-111. Fax 054/829-316. www.ngochuonghotels.com. 45 units. US$30–US$40 (£17–£22) double; US$80 (£44) suite. AE, MC, V. **Amenities:** 2 restaurants; bar; tour desk; car rental; laundry service; Internet access. *In room:* A/C, satellite TV, minibar, fridge, IDD phone.

WHERE TO DINE

Hue cuisine is unique, with a focus on light ingredients in choices like the popular fresh spring rolls; *bun bo Hue,* a noodle soup with pork, beef, and shredded green onions; and *banh khoi,* a thin, crispy pancake filled with ground meat and crispy vegetables. Local dishes are best at street side—there are a few good spots with English menus along the river and in the backpacker area, along Hung Vong.

MODERATE

Hoa Mai Restaurant ★★ VIETNAMESE   Hoa Mai is decked out in kitschy bamboo furnishings and set in an open area on the top floor of the Huong Giang Hotel. Great views of the Perfume River accompany the good Vietnamese fare. Try *banh rom hue,* triangular fried rolls stuffed with ground meat, shrimp, and vegetables. Daily special set menus are a good idea; mine featured a unique fried cuttlefish with grapefruit, crab soup, and shrimp with fig and rice cake. Be sure to choose a table near the riverside window and away from any banquet-size setups that say RESERVED.

At the Huong Giang Hotel, 51 Le Loi St., 3rd floor. © 054/822-122. Main courses US$2–US$6 (£1.10–£3.30); set menus US$7–US$15 (£3.85–£8.25). AE, MC, V. Daily 6am–10pm.

Tropical Garden ★★ VIETNAMESE   Though a popular tour-bus stop, Tropical Garden has a nice laid-back feel. The restaurant, with a sister location called **Club Garden** just down the road (08 Vo Thi Sau St.; © **054/826-327**), serves fine Vietnamese fare from an English-language menu, plus stages a live music show nightly. Even when it's packed, there are enough intimate corners that you'll feel comfortable. The place specializes in "embarrassing entrees," the kind of flaming dishes that would impress that eccentric uncle of yours. I got spring rolls served on toothpick skewers around the rind of a hollowed pineapple with a candle in the middle, a la a Halloween jack-o'-lantern. It's all good fun, so just go with it. The food is good, but a bit overpriced for a la carte items. Set menus are quite reasonable and walk you through some house specialties, like the banana-flower soup, the grilled chicken with lemon leaf, and the steamed crab with beer. As an appetizer, don't miss the grilled minced shrimp with sugarcane wrapped in rice paper and served with peanut sauce—unique and delicious. Service is a bit hit-or-miss, either fawning or forgetful.

27 Chu Van An St. © **054/847-143.** Fax 054/828-074. adongcoltd@dng.vnn.vn. Main courses US$2–US$4 (£1.10–£2.20); set menus US$7–US$25 (£3.85–£14). MC, V. Daily 8:30am–11pm.

INEXPENSIVE

La Carambole ★★ VIETNAMESE/CONTINENTAL   Good music is the first thing you might notice at La Carambole; I heard an unlikely mix from CCR to Beck on one relaxing evening. The decor is cheerful: cool indirect lighting, red tablecloths, and playful mobiles hanging from the ceiling, all as welcoming as the kind waitstaff. The French proprietor, Christian, and his wife, Ha, will certainly make you feel at home, and the comfort items on the menu—spaghetti, burgers, pizzas, and various French-style meat-and-potatoes specials—will stick to your ribs. The set menus are a good deal (salad and pizza at US$5/£2.75, for example), and portions are ample. There's a game table, and you're sure to meet lots of other travelers here.

19 Pham Ngu Lao St. © 054/810-491. Fax 054/826-234. Main courses US$2–US$5 (£1.10–£2.75); set menus US$5–US$9 (£2.75–£4.95). No credit cards. Daily 7am–midnight.

Lac Thanh Restaurant ★ VIETNAMESE   Everybody knows Lac Thanh, so there's a good chance you'll run into some fellow wayfarers at this popular crossroads. The place is a bit grimy, but the food is great: Try the grilled pork wrapped in rice paper, sautéed bean sprouts, grilled crab, and the popular spareribs, among others. For dessert, get the local specialty, *ché nong,* a warm congee with coconut, bananas, and nuts. Sit on the second-floor balcony and don't miss any opportunity to interface with Mr. Lac, the gregarious owner who speaks the international language of food and laughter despite his hearing impairment. Don't be fooled by the copycats next door (Lac Thanh has a RECOMMENDED BY FROMMER'S sign).

6A Dien Tien Hoang St. ℂ 054/824-674. Main courses 7,000VND–50,000VND (US45¢–US$3.15/£0.45–£1.75). No credit cards. Daily 7am–midnight.

Mandarin Café ⍟ VIETNAMESE/CONTINENTAL   In a busy storefront just a short walk from the riverside (near the Hotel Saigon Morin), Mandarin is always full of young backpackers, and for a reason: Good, affordable Vietnamese fare, predominantly one-dish items like fried rice or noodles, top a roster of comfort foods. Have a banana pancake and be one with the universe. Owner Mr. Cu (pronounced *Coo*) is a practiced photographer; his works, classic images of rural Vietnam, line the walls and are for sale as postcards or prints. For the amateur shutterbug, the images are inspiring, and the best part is that Mr. Cu is more than happy to share secrets and talk shop. Come here for both a casual meal and conversation with fellow travelers.

3 Hung Vuong St. ℂ 054/821-281. mandarin@dng.vnn.vn. Main courses 7,000VND–25,000VND (US45¢–US$1.65/£0.25–£0.85). No credit cards. Daily 6am–10pm.

WHAT TO SEE & DO IN THE CITADEL & IMPERIAL CITY ⍟⍟⍟

The Citadel is often used as a catchall term for Hue's Imperial City, built by Emperor Gia Long beginning in 1804 for the exclusive use of the emperor and his household, much like Beijing's Forbidden City. The city actually encompasses three walled enclosures: the Exterior Exclosure, or **Citadel;** the Yellow Enclosure, or **Imperial City,** within that; and, in the very center, the **Forbidden Purple City,** where the emperor actually lived. The Citadel itself is a square 2km (1¼-mile) wall, 7m (14 ft.) high and 20m (66 ft.) thick, with 10 gates. Ironically, it was constructed by a French military architect, though it failed to prevent the French from destroying the complex many years later. The main entrance to the Imperial City is the Noon Gate (Cua Ngo Mon, the southwest gate); this is where you can get a ticket and enter the site. Admission is 55,000VND (US$3.65/£3.45). Hours are daily from 7am to 5:30pm.

Flag Tower ⍟⍟   The focal point of the Imperial City, a large rampart to the south of the Noon Gate, this tower was built in 1807 during Gia Long's reign. The yellow flag of royalty was the first to fly here and was exchanged for and replaced by many others in Vietnam's turbulent history. It's a national symbol.

Forbidden Purple City ⍟   Once the actual home of the emperor and his concubines, this second sanctum within the Citadel is a large open area dotted with what's left of the king's court. Almost completely razed in a fire in 1947, the sanctum is now a few buildings among the rubble. The new **Royal Theater** behind the square, a lookalike of the razed original, is under construction. To the left as you head north is the partially restored **Thai Binh Reading Pavilion,** notable mostly for its beautifully landscaped surroundings, including a small lake with a Zen-like stone sculpture, and the ceramic and glass mosaic detailing on the roof and pillars, favored by flamboyant emperor Khai Dinh.

Catch a performance of the **Royal Traditional Theater** at the Hue Monuments Conservation Center. Eight performances daily, from 9am to 4pm, highlight the ancient art of *nha nhac* (courtly dance), at a cost of 20,000VND (US$1.25/£0.70).

Imperial Tombs As befits its history as an Imperial City, Hue's environs are studded with tombs of past emperors. They are spread out over a distance, so the best way to see them is to hire a car for a half day or take one of the many organized boat tours up the Perfume River. Altogether, there were 13 kings of the Nguyen Dynasty, although only 7 reigned until their death. As befits an emperor, all had tombs of stature, some as large as a small town. Most tomb complexes usually consist of a courtyard, a stele (a large stone tablet with a biography of the emperor), a temple for worship, and a pond.

Mieu Temple 🐦🐦 Constructed in 1921 to 1922 by Emperor Minh Mang, this temple has funeral altars paying tribute to 10 of the last Nguyen Dynasty emperors, omitting two who reigned for only days, with photos of each emperor and his empress(es) and various small offerings. The two empty glass containers to the side of each photo should contain bars of gold, probably an impractical idea today.

Across from the Mieu is Hien Lam, or the Glorious Pavilion, to the far right, with the **Nine Dynastic Urns** in front. Cast from 1835 to 1837, each urn represents a Nguyen emperor and is richly embellished with all the flora, fauna, and material goods that Vietnam has to offer, mythical or otherwise.

Noon Gate (Cua Ngo Mon) 🐦🐦 One of 10 entrances to the city, this southern entrance is the most dynamic. It was the royal entrance, in fact, and was built by Emperor Gia Long in 1823. It was used for important proclamations, such as announcements of the names of successful doctoral candidates (a list still hangs on the wall on the upper floor) and, most memorably, the announcement of the abdication of the last emperor, Bao Dai, on August 13, 1945, to Ho Chi Minh. The structure, like most here, was damaged by war but is now nicely restored, with classic Chinese roofs covering the ritual space, complete with large drums and an altar. Be sure to climb to the top and have a look at the view.

Thai Hoa Palace Otherwise known as the Palace of Supreme Harmony, this structure was built in 1833 and is the first one you'll approach at the entrance. It was used as the throne room, a ceremonial hall where the emperor celebrated festivals and received courtiers; the original throne still stands. The Mandarins sat outside. In front are two mythical *ky lin* animals, which walk without their claws ever touching ground and which have piercing eyesight for watching the emperor, tracking all good and evil he does. Note the statues of the heron and turtle inside the palace's ornate lacquered interior: The heron represents nobility and the turtle represents the working person. Folklore has it that the two took turns saving each other's lives during a fire, symbolizing that the power of the emperor rests with his people, and vice versa.

Thien Mu Pagoda 🐦🐦 Often called the symbol of Hue, Thien Mu is one of the oldest and loveliest religious structures in Vietnam. Set on the bank of the Perfume River, it was constructed beginning in 1601. The Phuoc Dien Tower in front was added in 1864 by Emperor Thieu Tri. Each of its seven tiers is dedicated to either one of the human forms taken by Buddha or the seven steps to enlightenment, depending upon whom you ask. There are also two buildings housing a bell that reportedly weighs 2 tons, plus a stele inscribed with a biography of Lord Nguyen Hoang, founder of the temple.

Once past the front gate, observe the 12 huge wooden sculptures of fearsome temple "guardians"—note the real facial hair. A complex of monastic buildings lies in the center, offering glimpses of the monks' daily routines. Stroll all the way to the rear of the complex to look at the graveyard at the base of the Truong Son mountains and to wander through the well-kept garden of pine trees. Hours are daily from 8am to 5pm, but try not to go between 11:30am and 2pm, when the monks are at lunch, because the rear half of the complex will be closed.

Tomb of Khai Dinh ★★   Completed in 1931, the tomb is one of the world's wonders. The emperor himself wasn't particularly revered, being overly extravagant and flamboyant (reportedly he wore a belt studded with lights that he flicked on at opportune public moments). His tomb, a gaudy mix of Gothic, baroque, Hindu, and Chinese Qing Dynasty architecture at the top of 127 steep steps, is a reflection of the man. Inside, the two main rooms are completely covered with fabulous, intricate glass and ceramic mosaics in designs reminiscent of Tiffany and Art Deco. The workmanship is astounding. The outer room's ceiling was done by a fellow who used both his feet and his hands to paint, in what some say was a sly mark of disrespect for the emperor. While in most tombs the location of the emperor's actual remains are a secret, Khai Dinh boldly placed his under his de facto tomb itself.

Admission 55,000VND (US$3.45/£1.90). Summer daily 6:30am–5:30pm; winter daily 7am–5pm.

Tomb of Minh Mang ★   One of the most popular Nguyen emperors and the father of the last emperor, Bao Dai built a restrained, serene, classical temple, much like Hue's Imperial City, located at the confluence of two Perfume River tributaries. Stone sculptures surround a long walkway, lined with flowers, leading up to the main buildings.

Admission 55,000VND (US$3.65/£2). Summer daily 6:30am–5:30pm; winter daily 7am–5pm.

Tomb of Tu Duc ★★   With the longest reign of any Nguyen Dynasty emperor, from 1848 to 1883, Tun Duc was a philosopher and scholar of history and literature. His reign was unfortunate: His kingdom unsuccessfully struggled against French colonialism, he fought a coup d'état by members of his own family, and although he had 104 wives, he left no heir. The "tomb" was constructed from 1864 to 1867 and also served as recreation grounds for the king, having been completed 16 years before his death. In fact, he actually engraved his own stele. The largest in Vietnam, at 20 tons, it has its own pavilion in the tomb. The highlight of the grounds is the lotus-filled lake ringed by frangipani trees, with a large pavilion in the center. The main cluster of buildings includes Hoa Khiem (Harmony Modesty) Pavilion, where the king worked; it still contains items of furniture and ornaments. Minh Khiem Duong, constructed in 1866, is said to be the country's oldest surviving theater. It's great fun to poke around in the wings. There are also pieces of original furniture lying here and there, as well as a cabinet with household objects: the queen's slippers, ornate chests, and bronze and silver books. The raised box on the wall is for the actors who played emperors; the real emperor was at the platform to the left.

Admission 55,000VND (US$3.45/£1.90). Summer daily 6:30am–5:30pm; winter daily 7am–5pm.

SHOPPING

All along Le Loi Street, you'll see souvenir stalls that vary from the cute to the kitschy. You can find good deals on commemorative spoons and velvet Ho Chi Minhs here, but nothing too traditional or authentic. There are a few good silversmiths, however. A few tailors are based in and among the souvenir shops, or you can stop by **Seductive** (40 Le Loi St.; ✆ **054/829-794**), a small, ready-to-wear silk boutique. **Bambou Company** (21 Pham Ngu Lao St., next to La Carambole) produces unique T-shirts of local theme and design.

Tips **Taking a Boat to the Tombs**

Expect to pay between US$2 and US$4 (£1.10–£2.20) for a shared boat ride to the temples (depending on which agent you use), *plus* 55,000VND (US$3.45/£1.90) for *each* tomb. Be prepared for when the boat pulls to shore at the first two tombs; you'll have to hire one of the motorcycle taxis at the bank to shuttle you to and from the site. You will not have enough time to walk there and back, so you're basically at their mercy. Haggle as best you can—about 10,000VND (US65¢/£0.35) is a good starting point.

HUE AFTER DARK

Across from the major riverside hotels is the **DMZ Café,** which stays up late a la a beer-swilling frat party. Along Hung Vuong, you'll find a few backpacker bars open till midnight, but overall this is a pretty sleepy town. **Bar Why Not?** (21 Vo Thi Sau St.; ✆ 054/824-793) is a cool open-air joint at the intersection of Pham Ngu Lao and Vo Thi Sau (near La Carambole); it has a good pool table and hot dogs cooked to order. **Newspace Bar** (22 Pham Ngu Lao; ✆ 054/810-310) has a pool table fronting a chic bistro/bar setup, with a gallery space next door. **Brown Eyes** (55 Nguyen Sinh Cung; ✆ 054/827-494) is a late-night bar and cafe that's a short taxi ride from the town center.

SIDE TRIPS FROM HUE

Except for the remains of its fabulous Imperial City, Hue in itself has sadly seen the worst of the French and American wars. Most of the star attractions other than the Citadel, therefore, involve half- or full-day trips outside the city.

THE DMZ & VINH MOC TUNNELS 𝕽𝕽

If you're old enough to remember the Vietnam War, you'll know Hue from the large-scale battles waged there. A day trip to the nearby DMZ and Vinh Moc Tunnels is a sobering revisit to that tumultuous time.

Under the Geneva Accords of 1954, an agreement struck to bring peace to Indochina after its struggle with French colonists, Vietnam was divided into North and South along the **17th Parallel.** What was meant to be a short-term political fix became a battle line, and the 17th Parallel, aka the **DMZ** or demilitarized zone, became a tangle of barbed wire and land mines, bombed and defoliated into a waste-land. Today, the area is green with growth again and completely unremarkable except for its history. Nearby are strategic sites with names you may recognize: the Rockpile, Hamburger Hill, Camp Carroll, and Khe Sanh, a former U.S. marine base that was the site of some of the war's most vicious and deadly fighting. If you take a tour of the area, you will also visit Dakrong Bridge, an official entryway into the Ho Chi Minh trail. *Warning:* The route over Highway 9 to the sites is narrow and bumpy. Rethink this trip if it's a rainy day, or if you are faint of either heart or stomach.

Most tours to the DMZ area include a visit to the **Vinh Moc Tunnels,** a site that is a testament to human tenacity. Like the tunnels in the south at Cu Chi (p. 403), soldiers and civilians took to the underground, literally, digging over a mile of tunnels from 1965 to 1966 to support Viet Cong troops and confound U.S. battalions at this strategic position near the line of north–south demarcation. Up to 20m (about 66 ft.) below the surface, multilevel tunnels formed a real community haven, with "living rooms" for families, a conference and performance room, a field hospital, and exit points inland and along the coast. Visitors walk through about 300m (984 ft.) of the tunnels in a main artery that is 1.6m high by 1.2m wide (5¹/₄×4 ft.), going down three stages. It's dirty, clammy, and a bit claustrophobic—dress accordingly. A museum at the entrance has photos and testimony of survivors. Admission is 25,000VND (US$1.55/£0.85).

These sites are some 60km (37 miles) north of Hue. Contact Hue tourist cafes such as **Sinh Café** for group excursions, or for a good private tour try **Huong Giang Tourist Company** (see "Visitor Information & Tours," earlier in this section).

LANG CO BEACH

A good day stop along Route 1A between Hue and Danang/Hoi An, Lang Co Beach is a sweeping expanse of sand where you can dip your toes and take a rest en route. The absence of group tours and touts is the main draw. For a spartan but cozy overnight getaway, try the **Lang Co Beach Resort** (✆ **054/873-555;** www.huong giangtourist.com), where stylish poolside rooms start at US$60 (£33).

8 Danang & China Beach

Danang, the fourth-largest city in Vietnam, is one of the most important seaports in the central region. It played a prominent role in the American war, serving as the landing site for the first American troops officially sent to Vietnam. Danang has nothing in the way of charm and has no major attractions except for the **Cham Museum,** which has become just a quick stop on the tourist-cafe buses between Hoi An and Hue. **Furama Resort,** a short ride from the city center, is one of the finest high-end resorts in Indochina, and there are also some excellent-value hotels in town (some use this as a base to explore nearby Hoi An).

China Beach, or **My Khe** as it's known locally, is worth a stop. This former U.S. recreation base has a light-sand coast with excellent views of the nearby Marble Mountains, and is just beginning to draw international visitors.

GETTING THERE

BY PLANE   You can fly to Danang from both Hanoi and HCMC. A taxi from the airport costs about US$3 (£1.65).

BY BUS   If you're traveling on the open-tour ticket, Danang is not a specified stop, but you can be dropped off at the Cham Museum. You'll have to call the office in either Hue or Hoi An for pickup when you're ready to leave. Travelers to Laos should contact **Vietnamtourism** for buses to Savannakhet (US$25/£14).

BY CAR   Danang is about 3½ hours by car from Hue. You'll pay US$40 (£22) for the trip. From Hoi An, it's about an hour and costs US$25 (£14). This ride makes a good day trip along with the Marble Mountains (see "What to See & Do," below). Contact **Vietnamtourism** for good rentals.

VISITOR INFORMATION & TOURS

Vietnamtourism Danang (83 Nguyen Thi Minh Khai; ✆ **0511/823-660** or 0511/822-142; fax 0511/821-560) can arrange trips to the Marble Mountains and My Son. **Exotissimo Travel Danang** (73 Ham Nghi, Thanh Khe District; ✆ **0511/ 690-364;** fax 0511/891-553; www.exotissimo.com) can make any arrangements. **An Phu Tourist** (147 Le Loi St; ✆ **0511/818-366;** anphutourist@hotmail.com) is the local tourist-cafe contact and can arrange any low-budget connections (it also has offices in Hoi An).

FAST FACTS: Danang

Currency Exchange The **Vietcombank** branch is at 104 Le Loi St. (℡ **0511/821-955**).

Internet Access Like many Vietnamese cities, Danang is experiencing a boom in Internet cafes. Look for one near the Torino Jazz Club on Nguyen Chi Thanh Street.

Telephones The city code for Danang is **511**.

WHERE TO STAY
EXPENSIVE

Furama Resort Danang ⭐⭐   Just a short ride southwest of Danang and situated in elegant relation to a beautiful sandy beach, the Furama greets you in style with a grand lobby that is more or less the gilded frame to the beautiful scenery: sand, sun, and sky. Whether you're a sailor, a beach bum, or a comfort junkie, you'll find what you want. There are two gorgeous swimming pools: one a multitiered minimalist still life overlooking the open beach, and the other a faux lagoon, complete with small waterfall and bridge. It's a good place to just relax, but there is always something to do, too: The hotel offers local tours, yoga, tai chi, a spa, and a full salon. Rooms are large and comfortable with wood floors, Vietnamese-style furniture, and sliding doors to balconies that overlook the ocean or pool. Large marble bathrooms have all the amenities. Prices are determined by view; oceanfront units are only steps from the beach and well worth it. Note that watersports are available only February through September—the surf is far too rough the rest of the year. Resort amenities are extensive, but they have to be, as the site is quite isolated. There are shuttles to the city, but there isn't much to entice in bustling Danang.

68 Ho Xuan Huong St. (oceanside 11km/7 miles southwest of town), Danang. ℡ 0511/847-333. Fax 0511/847-220. www.furamavietnam.com. 200 units. US$200–US$220 (£110–£121) garden view; US$260–US$280 (£143–£154) ocean view; US$500–US$600 (£275–£330) suite. AE, MC, V. **Amenities:** 3 restaurants; 3 bars; 2 outdoor pools; 4 lighted tennis courts; luxe health club; spa; sauna; diving; sailboat (Laser) and kayak rental; concierge; tour desk; business center w/Internet access; shopping; salon; 24-hr. room service; massage; laundry service; dry cleaning. *In room:* A/C, satellite TV, dataport, minibar, fridge, coffeemaker, hair dryer, safe, IDD phone.

MODERATE

Bamboo Green Hotel ⭐⭐   The best choice in Danang proper, Bamboo Green is operated by Vietnamtourism and is the best of its three properties in town (Bamboo Green II and III are comparable but less luxe). Rooms are large, with beige carpets and light-wood furnishings (try to overlook the hideous poly bedspreads). The nice-size marble bathrooms look brand-new. Ask for a room on the top floor for a city view. Hotel features include a big restaurant with decent Asian/Vietnamese fare, good tour services, and a friendly staff. Overall, this is as cozy as any midrange U.S. chain.

158 Phan Chau Trinh St., Danang. ℡ 0511/822-996 or 0511/822-997. Fax 0511/822-998. 46 units. US$99–US$119 (£54–£65) superior; US$119–US$139 (£65–£76) deluxe; US$149–US$169 (£82–£93) suite. AE, MC, V. **Amenities:** 2 restaurants; bar; sauna; tour desk; motorbike/car rental; limited room service; massage; laundry service; dry cleaning. *In room:* A/C, satellite TV, dataport, minibar, fridge, coffeemaker, hair dryer, IDD phone.

Saigon Tourane Hotel ⭐   Popular with European tour groups, this nondescript, friendly, three-star standard hotel offers comfort at low cost. The rooms are carpeted, clean, and come with tidy, good-size bathrooms; some upper-floor units have city views. Nonetheless, it's all a bit low-luxe, with a general atmosphere marked by failing neon signs and worn carpets that speak of the volumes that pass through. The hotel is owned by Saigontourist; thus guests are well connected and can make any necessary arrangements with little hassle. The staff couldn't be more kind. Be sure to ask for a room away from the karaoke—far away.

5 Dong Da St. (on the north end of town), Danang. ℭ 0511/821-021. Fax 0511/895-285. 82 units. US$50–US$70 (£28–£39) double; US$80–US$90 (£44–£50) suite. **Amenities:** 2 restaurants; bar; basic gym; sauna; Saigontourist tour desk; car rental; business center; massage; laundry service; dry cleaning; nonsmoking rooms; karaoke. *In room:* A/C, satellite TV, minibar, fridge, hair dryer, IDD phone.

WHERE TO DINE

If you're at the **Furama Resort,** that's where you'll find the best fine dining, but beach-side seafood shacks adjacent to the property also serve good barbecue for a fraction of resort prices. In Danang proper, choices are few, but they do exist. **Kim Do Restaurant** (180 Tran Phu St.; ℭ 0511/821-846), a popular Chinese restaurant of long standing, serves good stir-fries and steamed Cantonese specials. A notable find are the small storefronts adjacent to the Cham Museum that serve good duck and rice dishes. A block up the river from the Cham Museum and 2 blocks in, the **Torino Jazz Club** (283 Nguyen Chi Thanh St.; ℭ 0511/565-124) is a welcome oasis in central Vietnam, serving perfect pasta, homemade tiramisu, and Chilean wine, all priced very reasonably. Near the Jazz Club, the **Apsara** offers superb Vietnamese dining and a show.

WHAT TO SEE & DO

Cham Museum 🐨🐨 The Cham Museum was established in 1936 (originally the Ecole Française d'Extreme Orient) to house the relics of the powerful Hindu culture that once ruled vast tracts of central Vietnam. The museum has the largest collection of Cham sculpture in the world, in works ranging from the 4th to 14th centuries, presented in a rough outdoor setting that suits the evocative, sensual sculptures well. The more than 300 pieces of sandstone artwork and temple decorations were largely influenced by Hinduism and, later, Mahayana Buddhism. Among the cast of characters, you'll see symbols of Uroja, or "goddess mother," usually breasts or nipples; the linga, the phallic structure representing the god Shiva; the holy bird Garuda; the dancing girl Kinnari; the snake god Naga; and Ganesha, child of the god Shiva, with the head of an elephant. Note the masterpiece Tra Kieu altar of the late 7th century, with carved scenes telling the story of the Asian epic *Ramayana.* The story is of the wedding of Princess Sita. Side one tells of Prince Rama, who broke a holy vow to obtain Sita's hand. Side two tells of ambassadors sent to King Dasaratha, Prince Rama's father, to bring him the glad tidings. Side three is the actual ceremony, and side four depicts the celebrations after the ceremony. There is also a permanent photo exhibit of the many Cham relics in situ at various locations throughout Vietnam.

At Tran Phu and Le Dinh Duong sts. Admission 20,000VND (US$1.35/£0.70). Daily 7am–6pm.

Marble Mountains 🐨 The "mountains" are actually a series of five marble and limestone formations, which the locals liken to the shape of a dragon at rest. The hills are interlaced with caves, some of which are important Buddhist sanctuaries. These caves, like so many in the country, served as shelter for the Viet Cong during the American war. The highest mountain, Thuy Son, is climbable via a series of metal ladders beginning inside the cave and extending to the surface at the top. Ling Ong Pagoda, a shrine within a cave, is a highlight. The quarries in Non Nuoc village, at the bottom of the mountains, are as interesting as the caves. Fantastic animals and fanciful statues of folk tales and Buddhist figures are carved from the rock. Try to get a good look before you're set upon by flocks of hawkers. What's more, even if you're interested in the items they hawk—incredibly cheap mortar-and-pestle sets, some very nice chess sets, turtles, and small animals—any amount of marble adds considerable weight to luggage. You can easily see the mountains as part of your trip en route to or from Hoi An; most cafe tour buses stop here.

11km (7 miles) south of Danang and 9.5km (6 miles) north of Hoi An along Hwy. 1. All tours stop here. Admission 30,000VND (US$1.90/£1.05).

9 Hoi An

A visit to this old-world gem, which was designated a UNESCO World Heritage Site in 1999, is a sure cultural highlight of any Vietnam tour. From the 16th to the 18th centuries, Hoi An was Vietnam's most important port and trading post, particularly of ceramics with nearby China. Today, it is a quaint, picturesque town of some 844 structures protected as historic landmarks, and the unique influence of Chinese and Japanese traders who passed through (or settled) can still be felt.

Hoi An is small enough to cover easily on foot, with many nooks and crannies, shops, and gastronomic delights to discover. Wander among historic homes and temples, lounge in an open-air cafe, gaze at the exotic foods in the market, or take a sampan ride down the lazy river. You can still see local craftspeople at work in some parts of the city. In the afternoons when school is out, the streets are thronged with skipping children, the girls in their *ao dai* uniforms.

On the full moon of every month, local shop owners turn off the electricity and hang lanterns bearing their shop's name; a candlelight lantern procession, complete with a few small floats, makes its way through the old town and along the riverfront. It's worth timing a visit to enjoy the spectacle and the postprocessional festivities.

GETTING THERE

BY PLANE/TRAIN   Major transport connections go through Danang. From there, you can take a car to Hoi An for between US$8 and US$25 (£4.40–£14).

BY BUS   Hoi An is a major stop on all open-tour cafe buses. Connection with Danang is just US$3 (£1.65).

GETTING AROUND

Hoi An is so small that you'll be able to memorize the map in an hour or two. Most hotels and guesthouses rent **bicycles** for 5,000VND to 7,000VND (US30¢–US45¢/£0.15–£0.25) a day, a great way to explore the outer regions of the city or Cua Dai Beach. **Motorbikes** are US$3 to US$5 (£1.65–£2.75) per day and are not difficult to drive in this tiny, calm city. **Cyclos** are here and there; 10,000VND (US65¢/£0.35) or so should get you anywhere within the city. Car hire is also available anywhere; try **Faifoo Travel** (✆ 0510/914-580) for rentals by the hour or for a full day.

VISITOR INFORMATION & TOURS

- **Hoi An Tourist Guiding Office** (1 Nguyen Truong To, ✆ 0510/861-327; or 12 Phan Chu Trinh St., ✆ 0510/862-715) sells the Hoi An World Cultural Heritage tickets. A one-ticket purchase offers limited admission to the town's museums, old houses, and Chinese assembly halls. For more information about the tickets, see "What to See & Do," later in this chapter.

Hoi An

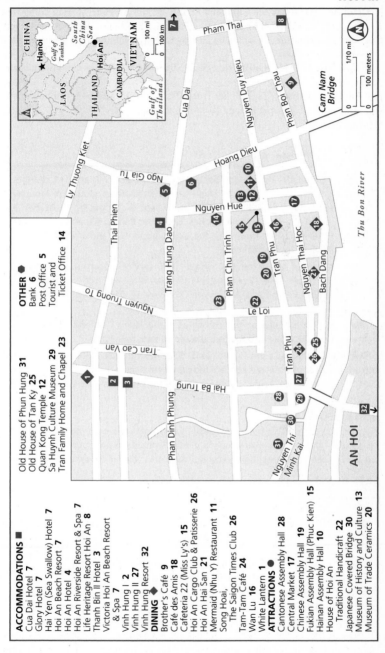

ACCOMMODATIONS ■
Cua Dai Hotel **7**
Glory Hotel **7**
Hai Yen (Sea Swallow) Hotel **7**
Hoi An Beach Resort **7**
Hoi An Hotel **4**
Hoi An Riverside Resort & Spa **7**
Life Heritage Resort Hoi An **8**
Thanh Bin II Hotel **3**
Victoria Hoi An Beach Resort
& Spa **7**
Vinh Hung I **2**
Vinh Hung II **27**
Vinh Hung Resort **32**

DINING ◆
Brother's Café **9**
Café des Amis **18**
Cafeteria 22 (Miss Ly's) **15**
Hoi An Cargo Club & Patisserie **26**
Hoi An Hai San **21**
Mermaid (Nhu Y) Restaurant **11**
Song Hoai,
The Saigon Times Club **26**
Tam-Tam Café **24**
Wan Lu **16**
White Lantern **1**

ATTRACTIONS ●
Cantonese Assembly Hall **28**
Central Market **17**
Chinese Assembly Hall **19**
Fukian Assembly Hall (Phuc Kien) **15**
Hainan Assembly Hall **10**
House of Hoi An
Traditional Handicraft **22**
Japanese Covered Bridge **30**
Museum of History and Culture **13**
Museum of Trade Ceramics **20**

Old House of Phun Hung **31**
Old House of Tan Ky **25**
Quan Kong Temple **12**
Sa Huynh Culture Museum **29**
Tran Family Home and Chapel **23**

OTHER ◆
Bank **6**
Post Office **5**
Tourist and
Ticket Office **14**

- **Hoi An Tourist Service Company,** inside the Hoi An Hotel (6 Tran Hung Dao St.; ✆ **0510/861-373;** fax 0510/861-636), is a reliable operation that books every type of tour of the city and surrounding areas, including China Beach and the Marble Mountains.
- **Sinh Café IV** (18B Hai Ba Trung St.; ✆ **0510/863-948**) provides bus tours and tickets onward.
- **An Phu Tourist** (722 Hai Ba Trung St.; ✆ **0510/862-643;** anphutourist@ hotmail.com) does everything that Sinh Café does.

FAST FACTS: Hoi An

Currency Exchange The **Vietcombank** (4 Huong Dieu St.) has an ATM, changes most major currencies, and does credit card cash advances. Hours are Monday through Saturday from 7:30am to 7pm. **Incombank** exchanges money at its 9 Le Loio St. and 4 Hoang Diet St. branches. **Exchange Bureau #1,** across from the Hoi An Hotel at 37 Tran Hung Dao, has exchange services and an ATM. There is also an ATM at the post office.

Internet Access Along Le Loi, you'll find service at around 4,000VND (US40¢/£0.20) per hour. Access is generally slow dial-up. On the northern end of town, **Min's Computer** (131 Nguyen Duy Hieu; ✆ **0510/914-323**) is as good as it gets.

Mail The post office is at the corner of Trang Hong Dao and Huong Dieu streets; open Monday through Saturday from 6am to 9:30pm.

Telephones The city code for Hoi An is **510.** You can place international calls from the post office listed above and from most hotels.

WHERE TO STAY

Hoi An has seen a recent boom in upscale resorts, with more on the way along Cua Dai Beach. Large-scale new construction in Hoi An proper is prohibited by UNESCO, but smaller hotels are going upmarket, and there are a few new options closer to town.

EXPENSIVE

Hoi An Beach Resort ✿ Opened in 2000, this is the flagship of Hoi An Tourist, a government-owned company, and it's their answer to recent upscale development in town. The resort is across the road from Cua Dai Beach and close to the small "restaurant row" and popular tourist sunbathing area. Everything here—from the casual open-air restaurant to the more expensive rooms and suites—faces the De Vong River as it approaches the sea, offering a unique glimpse of everyday riverside life. At the bar and upscale access point to the beach, you can sit in private chairs without harassment from beachside sellers. All rooms here are nice, but the villas are certainly worth the extra few bucks: They're quite large, with high ceilings and private balconies. Villas and suites have vaulted ceilings, and some have separate entrances with a shower area for cleanup after the beach. Service and general standards are comparable to the high-end competition in town. It's a popular choice for large European tours and can get a bit wild in the busy season, but it's all good fun. There are frequent shuttles to town.

1 Cua Dai, Cua Dai Beach, Hoi An. ℂ **0510/927-011** or 0510/927-015. Fax 0510/927-019. www.hoiantourist.com. 110 units. US$100 (£55) garden deluxe double; US$150 (£83) ocean- or river-view villa; US$200 (£110) suite. AE, MC, V. **Amenities:** Restaurant; 2 bars; 2 large outdoor pools; small health club; spa; Jacuzzi; sauna; steam bath; bike rental; concierge; tour desk; car rental; business center; shops; salon; limited room service; foot massage; babysitting; laundry service; Internet. *In room:* A/C, satellite TV, minibar, fridge, coffeemaker, hair dryer, safe, IDD phone.

Hoi An Riverside Resort & Spa ★★

For tranquil and intimate surroundings, you'll find no better place than this lush little resort between road and river outside of Hoi An. The place has a cozy feel, as if guest rooms kind of grew around the winding path of the garden and courtyard pool. Rooms are neat and clean, not especially big, but with nice views of the meandering bend in the river or the quiet garden. Vietnamese- or Japanese-themed accommodations have smallish, spotless bathrooms and nice wood appointments throughout. The staff is invisible, meaning that this place carries on like an immaculately trimmed golf course that gets a once-over each night. The Song Do restaurant serves fine Vietnamese and Continental fare; a visit to the Faifo bar harks back to another era. The central pool is a relaxing spot—great after wandering the town labyrinths. The staff is very professional and informative. The resort offers Vietnamese cooking lessons and lazy canoe trips on the picturesque river.

175 Cua Dai Rd. (3km/1¾ miles from town), Hoi An. ℂ **0510/864-800.** Fax 0510/864-900. www.hoianriverresort. com. 60 units. US$129 (£71) Vietnamese standard; US$139 (£76) Japanese standard; US$149 (£82) superior (river view); US$189 (£104) deluxe (river view). Off-season promotional rates available. AE, DC, MC, V. **Amenities:** Restaurant; bar; outdoor pool; health club; business center w/Internet access; nice souvenir shop; salon; 24-hr. room service; foot massage; babysitting; laundry service; dry cleaning; small library; snooker/billiards room. *In room:* A/C, satellite TV, dataport, minibar, fridge, coffeemaker, safe, IDD phone.

Life Heritage Resort Hoi An ★

New in 2004, the Life Resort is the only resort within walking distance of Hoi An—a good start. The chic, minimalist accommodations have a certain spartan charm, but already feel a bit musty. Rooms are split-level, with the slightly raised sleeping area done in cool slate tiles. Bathrooms are large, open-plan affairs. Views of the river are good, and deluxe units have quiet sitting areas out front that are perfect for meditation or a respite from the noonday sun. The dining outlets, housed in a faux-colonial block at riverside, are atmospheric; the quiet, air-conditioned cafe has good coffee and desserts. The whole place has an overly studied feel, but for location alone, it's a good choice.

1 Pham Hong Thai St., Hoi An. ℂ **510/914-555.** Fax 510/914-515. www.life-resorts.com. 94 units. US$145–US$198 (£80–£109) double, depending on view; US$250–US$280 (£138–£154) family villa. AE, MC, V. **Amenities:** 2 restaurants; 2 bars; outdoor pool; tour desk; limited room service; massage; babysitting; laundry service; Internet access. *In room:* A/C, satellite TV, minibar, fridge, safe, IDD phone.

Victoria Hoi An Beach Resort & Spa ★★

It's peace and palm trees just a short ride from ancient Hoi An. The comfortable Victoria, with top-notch amenities and lots of activities, begs at least a few nights' stay. Guest rooms have it right in every detail, from fine rustic decor to in-room sandals and beach robes. Rooms are either the bungalow variety in low-slung buildings at beachside or set in parallel two-story rows to mimic Hoi An's ancient streets—not displeasing, but a bit like a theme park. Prices reflect beachside proximity, but even the least expensive units are laid-back and classy. Some bungalows are decorated in French country style, with canopy beds and wicker; others are unique Japanese rooms, with open-timber construction, bamboo floors, and large tubs. There is a certain flow to this property, from beach to garden, rooms to common spaces, that invites guests to wander; everything's connected by catwalk. Convenient shuttles connect to town frequently; or you can rent a motorcycle with sidecar. Other perks include a private boat for transfer to town, kitesurfing equipment, and cooking courses. Victoria Hoi An is the only hotel in the area with full body massages.

Cua Dai Beach (5km/3 miles from town), Hoi An. ⓒ 0510/927-040. Fax 0510/927-041. www.victoriahotels-asia. com. 105 units. US$160 (£88) superior w/river/sea view; US$210–US$250 (£116–£138) deluxe w/river/sea view; US$310 (£171) suite. **Amenities:** 2 restaurants; 3 bars; large outdoor beachside pool; 2 tennis courts; nice health club; spa; Jacuzzi; kayak/windsurfer/Hobie Cat rental; children's play area; tour desk; car rental; shopping; extensive salon; 24-hr. room service; massage; babysitting; laundry service; dry cleaning; small library; Internet access; snooker/billiards room. *In room:* A/C, satellite TV, minibar, fridge, coffeemaker, safe, IDD phone.

MODERATE

Cua Dai Hotel ⭐⭐   A budget gem on the beach road just out of town (like nearby Hai Yen, below), the Cua Dai is a good marriage of affordability and comfort. It's easy to settle in here, with the open sitting areas furnished in wicker and the basic but comfy rooms. The very kind staff will make you feel right at home, too, and can help with any travel need. The only drawback is the busy road out front, but all units have double-paned windows and are relatively quiet. Rooms in the new wing in back have fine wooden appointments and creative, local decor; older rooms in the main building are quite large, basic, and comfortable. Cua Dai makes a good base to explore or meet the many expats and long-stay travelers here on cultural or humanitarian missions.

18A Cua Dai St., Hoi An. ⓒ 0510/862-231 or 0510/864-604. Fax 0510/862-232. 25 units. US$20–US$35 (£11–£19) double. MC, V. **Amenities:** Restaurant; bicycle/motorbike available; laundry service. *In room:* A/C, TV, minibar, fridge, IDD phone.

Glory Hotel   On Cua Dau Street just east of town (heading toward the beach), this newer hotel has a fine standard of rooms, all very large if rather spartan, set in a four-story block around a central pool area. The price is right, everything is clean, and the hotel covers all the bases. The pool is but a postage stamp, but the courtyard is tranquil.

538 Cua Dai St., Hoi An. ⓒ 0510/914-444. Fax 0510/914-445. www.gloryhotelhoian.com. 65 units. US$60–US$80 (£33–£44) double; US$95 (£52) suite. AE, MC, V. **Amenities:** Restaurant; bar; small outdoor pool; tour desk; business center w/Internet access; limited room service; laundry service. *In room:* A/C, satellite TV, minibar, fridge, IDD phone.

Hai Yen (Sea Swallow) Hotel ⭐   This is a good, basic hotel on the edge of the old town (a short walk or ride to the beach); it's a popular choice for large budget tour groups. Slick tile throughout gives everything a tidy edge. Spacious rooms have funky Chinese relief carvings, overly fancy curtains, and shiny polyester spreads—an A for effort, but the general effect is kind of unsettling. The nice (if small) pool is a surprise luxury in this price range. It's all a bit rough around the edges here, with a kind of faded pallor over the whole place. The staff is friendly, though, and can help with any detail.

22A Cua Dai St., Hoi An. ⓒ 0501/862-445 or 0501/862-446. 41 units. US$20–US$35 (£11–£19) double (seasonal). AE, MC, V. **Amenities:** Restaurant; bar; small outdoor pool; all rentals available; tour desk; laundry service. *In room:* A/C, satellite TV, minibar, fridge, IDD phone.

Hoi An Hotel ⭐⭐   Still the best and most convenient in-town address, the Hoi An Hotel was the first high-end hotel and works hard to keep that reputation. As a result, it's pretty busy here, with lots of tour groups. The friendly staff does a great job, though, and handles large numbers with a modicum of grace. Don't expect anything fancy, but rooms are unusually large and impeccably clean, with tile floors and comfortable beds. The newest building has upscale rooms with dark-wood floors and a fun, contemporary Chinese theme (but the older rooms are just as good). The central pool is large, though often overcrowded. The folks at the tour desk are very helpful.

10 Tran Hung Dao St., Hoi An. (© **0510/861-373**. Fax 0510/861-636. www.hoiantourist.com. 160 units. US$50–US$90 (£28–£50) double; US$100 (£55) suite. AE, MC, V. **Amenities:** Restaurant; garden bar; nice courtyard pool; tennis court; Jacuzzi; concierge; tour desk; car rental; business center; 24-hr. room service; babysitting; laundry service; dry cleaning; wireless Internet access. *In room:* A/C, satellite TV, minibar, fridge, hair dryer, IDD phone.

Vinh Hung Resort ✠ Chinese-style entrepreneurs follow the "start small; go big" model, and that's what the folks at Vinh Hung have done. Their small in-town properties (Vinh Hung I and II, below) are popular, so they've turned that income back into this latest project: a self-contained, midlevel resort on Hoi An Island. The area, slated for further development in coming years, is just a 10- to 15-minute walk from the canal bridge at Hoi An's center. Deluxe rooms are the best bet—large and tidy, with wood floors, Chinese tapestries, and carpeted sitting areas. High-end rooms are enormous, some with Jacuzzis. Ask for one overlooking the wide river. Although services are limited, and everything is a bit compact, Vinh Hung Resort is an affordable and convenient getaway. Rental kayaks make for a unique commute to the town center, or you can catch a ferry to town if you prefer.

111 Ngo Quyen, on Hoi An Island (across the small bridge connecting to town near Bach Dang St. and a short ride to the opposite end of the island), Hoi An. (© **0510/910-577**. Fax 0510/864-094. www.vinhhunghotel.com. 82 units. US$70–US$90 (£39–£50) double (depending on view); US$100–US$110 (£55–£61) suite. AE, MC, V. **Amenities:** Restaurant; 2 bars; 2 outdoor pools; tennis court; small fitness center; Jacuzzi; sauna; kayak rental (guests can paddle to town); tour desk; car rental; business center w/Internet access; salon; limited room service; babysitting; laundry service. *In room:* A/C, satellite TV, minibar, fridge, safe, IDD phone.

INEXPENSIVE

Thanh Bin II Hotel ✠ The Thanh Bin II is newer and nicer than its sister property, the **Thanh Bin I** (© **0510/861-740**), which has a good location on Le Loi Street but just basic rooms. This three-story building has a Chinese-inspired lobby, with carved dark-wood furnishings and cafe tables. Upstairs are the very clean, spacious guest rooms. The decor is a color-coordinated mishmash, but there's not a musty smell to be found, the bathrooms are tidy, and the staff is really friendly. For fun, ask about a suite: a huge room that sports wood paneling, carved Chinese-style furnishings, a mosquito net over the bed, a nice balcony with beaded curtains, and, in the center of everything, a large wooden carving of a fat, happy Buddha. Another location, **Thanh Bin III,** is also on Hai Ba Trung Street (© **0510/916-777**).

712 Hai Ba Trung St., Hoi An. (© **0510/863-715**. vothihong@dng.vnn.vn. 31 units. US$12–US$30 (£6.60–£17) double. AE, MC, V. **Amenities:** Restaurant; rentals; laundry service. *In room:* A/C, TV, minibar, fridge, IDD phone.

Vinh Hung I and II ✠ Standard rooms in both Vinh Hung I and II are large, with wooden appointments and cool retro features like mosquito nets and Chinese latticework balconies. Vinh Hung I, a downtown property set in an old wooden Chinese house, is a Hoi An institution; its two signature rooms are almost museum pieces and are alone worth a visit, but they're not especially luxe or comfortable. Vinh Hung II is a tour-group favorite and often full—and for good reason (the central pool is unique in this category). Popularity means heavy use, though, and the place is getting a bit rough around the edges. The new Vinh Hung Resort (see above) is an improvement on an old theme.

Vinh Hung 1: 143 Tran Phu St., Hoi An. (© **0510/861-621**. Fax 0510/861-893. **Vinh Hung II:** Hai Ba Trung St., Hoi An. (© **0510/863-717**. Fax 0510/864-094. www.vinhhunghotels.com. 64 units. US$15–US$45 (£8.25–£25) double. AE, MC, V. **Amenities:** Restaurant; small outdoor pool; rentals; tour desk; laundry service. *In room:* A/C, TV, IDD phone.

WHERE TO DINE

Hoi An is a feast for the stomach as well as the eyes. Local specialties include *cao lau* (rice noodles with fresh greens, rice crackers, and croutons), white rose dumplings of shrimp in clear rice dough, and savory fried wontons. Good, fresh seafood is available everywhere (don't miss the morning market). There are some new high-end options in town alongside the popular standbys, and each of the resorts has its own fine dining (see "Where to Stay," above).

The riverfront road, **Bach Dang,** has become the de facto "restaurant row," where you're sure to be besieged by friendly but persistent touts who will try to drag you bodily into their restaurants. Since many places here are comparable in price and cuisine (fried rice and noodles), it's sometimes fun to let the restaurant choose you. *Note:* If you do eat on Bach Dang but you'd like a quieter meal, choose a table a bit off the street and say a calm "No, thank you" to the many young Tiger Balm and chewing-gum salesmen.

EXPENSIVE

Brother's Café ✿✿✿ VIETNAMESE   Serving fine Vietnamese fare like its sister restaurant in Hanoi (but here it's a la carte, not buffet), Brother's Café is the town's top choice for both cuisine and atmosphere. A bland street-side facade gives way to the lush garden sanctuary formed by this grand U-shaped colonial by the river. Indoor seating is upscale Indochina of a bygone era, while the courtyard is dotted with canvas umbrellas to shade you on a balmy afternoon. The food is gourmet Vietnamese at its finest, with changing daily set menus and great specials; be sure to ask for a recommendation. It's a good place to try local items like the white rose (a light Vietnamese ravioli) or *cao lao* noodles. Groups can order family style and sample it all. Ask the friendly staff about the cooking school here.

27 Pham Boi Chau St. © **0510/914-150.** Main courses US$1.50–US$12 (£0.85–£6.60). AE, MC, V. Daily 10am–11pm.

Hoi An Cargo Club & Patisserie ✿ INTERNATIONAL   Ms. Vy has expanded her Hoi An empire—which includes the Mermaid and White Lantern restaurants (p. 350) and the Cua Dai Hotel (p. 346)—with this unique, open-air patisserie and French cafe. The stylish storefront serves light meals in a casual lounge on the first floor; upstairs is a refined restaurant specializing in contemporary Vietnamese cuisine. Sandwiches are made from fresh bread baked on-site. Seafood dishes abound, like the crab in five spices or jumbo shrimp with tamarind sauce. Curries and good veggie dishes round out a good, affordable menu. If you dine upstairs, you can sit on the cool balcony overlooking the river.

107–109 Nguyen Thai Hoc St. © **0510/910-489.** www.hoianhospitality.com. Main courses 25,000VND–65,000VND (US$1.55–US$4.05/£0.85–£2.25). MC, V. Daily 7am–midnight.

Song Hoai, The Saigon Times Club ✿✿ VIETNAMESE   Set in the most picturesque period building in town, on a corner overlooking riverside Bach Dang, this Saigon-managed restaurant is as much about atmosphere as it is about food. Rivaled only by Brother's (above), the two open floors here exemplify true old Hoi An elegance. The second floor has views of the river and dramatic touches, like a high ceiling and languid ceiling fans. Song Hoai serves regional dishes like Hanoi *cha ca* and *mi quang* wide noodles; try the Vietnamese-style ravioli, the local white rose specialty, and the fresh pan-fried shrimp. Presentation is arguably the classiest in town, with fine china, stemware, and lacquered dishes on linen, and the service is professional if a bit hovering. A good choice for a romantic evening, Hoi An style.

119–121 Nguyen Thai Hoc St. © 0510/910-369. Fax 0510/910-436. Main courses US$1–US$11 (£0.55–£6.05). AE, MC, V. Daily 10am–11pm.

Tam-Tam Café ✦✦ ITALIAN/CONTINENTAL/VIETNAMESE   Tam-Tam is the place to be in Hoi An. The brainchild of three French expats, it is historic and laid-back, serving good, familiar food. The decor is authentic local style, with hanging bamboo lamps, a high ceiling, and fantastic wooden figurines. The dinner menu, served in a separate room with checkered tablecloths, is simple—generous portions of homemade pastas, steaks, and salads—but the food is delicious. Desserts include flam-béed crepes, sorbet, and hot chocolate. There are two bar rooms: The bigger one to the left of the entry has a pool table, a book-swap shelf, and comfortable lounge chairs and sofas—it's the place to hang out in Hoi An. The extensive drinks menu features all kinds of bang-for-the-buck rum specials. There's even a small counter on the bal-cony where you can sip a cocktail and watch life go by on the street below. Even if it's just for a coffee, don't miss this place.

110 Nguyen Thai Hoc St., 2nd floor. © 0510/862-212. Main courses US$2–US$10 (£1.10–£5.50). AE, MC, V. Daily 24 hr.

MODERATE
Café des Amis ✦✦ VIETNAMESE   What's on the menu? There isn't one. It's your choice of set menu, either seafood or vegetarian, and the details are, well, a surprise. And the surprise is always good—one of the best meals in Vietnam, if you ask me. But don't ask me. Just read the straight dope from the many people who sign the lengthy guest book. I enjoyed a leisurely dinner of savory clear soup, fried wontons with shrimp, broiled fish, stuffed calamari, and scallops on the half shell. Sit back and sur-render yourself to the surprises of the effusive Mr. Kim and his attentive staff. Mr. Kim is a practiced raconteur with rich material from his years as a taster for the army and a chef for heads of state. He is careful to explain the intricacies of each dish and even demonstrates how to eat some of the more unique entrees. A meal here makes for a memorable evening.

52 Bach Dang St. © 0510/861-616. Set menu 90,000VND (US$5.60/£3.10). No credit cards. Daily 6–10pm.

Cafeteria 22 (Miss Ly's)   You're greeted by the kind proprietor herself, always dressed to the nines and welcoming. The menu is limited, but that means everything is always fresh in this hole-in-the-wall cafe in the heart of the old town. It's the best place in Hoi An to try the town's famous fried wontons, a rice pastry stuffed with meat, shrimp, and onion and topped with Miss Ly's special sauce, onion, and tomato—messy and delicious. Since Ly has been at it for over 10 years now, she has just the right formula. There's nothing fancy here, and that's just the appeal for folks who tire easily of trumped-up atmosphere and overpriced versions of local fare. Come meet Ly and try the real deal.

22 Nguyen Hue St. © 0510/861-603. Main courses 8,000VND–40,000VND (US50¢–US$2.50/£0.25–£1.35). No credit cards. Daily 8am–11pm.

Hoi An Hai San VIETNAMESE/CONTINENTAL   *Hai-san* means "seafood" in Vietnamese and "hello" in Swedish. The owners, Swedish expat Calle and his Viet-namese wife, Hoa, offer just that: "Hello, seafood!" This is one of the few spots on Bach Dang that won't try to drag you in—instead, it's the food that brings folks here.

Everything's good: grilled tuna with ginger, garlic, and lemongrass, served in a light coconut milk; sea scallops in cream sauce, a favorite; and Swedish lingonberry ice cream. It's a good place to linger and watch the goings-on on busy Bach Dang.

64 Bach Dang St. ⓒ 0510/861-652. Main courses 20,000VND–75,000VND (US$1.25–US$4.70/£0.70–£2.60). Daily 9am–10pm.

Mermaid (Nhu Y) Restaurant   VIETNAMESE   This quiet spot in the heart of downtown is an unassuming, ivy-draped storefront that serves some of the best authentic Vietnamese food in town (for next to nothing). The tuna filet, cooked in a banana leaf with turmeric, is scrumptious; the spring rolls are light and fresh, with a whole jumbo shrimp in each; and the Mermaid serves a most unique dish called white eggplant: It's eggplant covered in spring onion, garlic, and chile, and then pressed, sliced, and served in a light oil. If you like what you eat, stick around and take a **cooking class**—a unique chance to bring some of Vietnam home to your kitchen.

02 Tran Phu St. ⓒ 0510/861-527. www.hoianhospitality.com. Main courses 20,000VND–70,000VND (US$1.25–US$4.40/£0.70–£2.40). No credit cards. Daily 10am–10pm.

White Lantern   VIETNAMESE   This is a very popular tour-group stop, so get here early (or late); if you see buses parked out front, head for the hills. Everyone's here for good reason, though: delicious, affordable Vietnamese cuisine and a mellow atmosphere. Strumming guitarists roam the tables playing Beatles tunes and local numbers; both the large open area on the first floor and the balcony space upstairs are dimly lit and romantic. Set menus are a great bet: I had a fine meal of delicate wonton soup, spring rolls, and chicken in a light curry. Owned by the same folks that run Nhu Y, above, this is a slightly upscale version.

710 Hai Ba Trung St., just north of the town center. ⓒ 0510/863-023. www.hoianhospitality.com. Main courses 30,000VND–45,000VND (US$1.90–US$2.80/£1.05–£1.55); set menus 60,000VND–120,000VND (US$3.75–US$7.50/£2.05–£4.10). MC, V. Daily 9am–10pm.

INEXPENSIVE

Wan Lu 🍴   It's an open-air place, and the atmosphere is a little rough, but it serves a nice selection of local favorites, all for next to nothing. Try the special, *cao lao,* a thick but tender white noodle in light soy with fresh vegetables, garnishes, and croutons. This is where the locals eat it—but if it's not your cup of tea, then you're out only 6,000VND (about US40¢/£0.20). The portions are big and everything's authentic, right down to the kindness in this little mom-and-pop. There are no touts here; it's the food that brings 'em in.

27 Tran Phu St. ⓒ 0510/861-212. Main courses 5,000VND–30,000VND (US30¢–US$1.90/£0.15–£1.05). No credit cards. Daily 7am–11pm.

WHAT TO SEE & DO

The whole town is an attraction, its narrow streets buzzing with open-air crafts shops, woodworkers, and carvers based in lovely historic buildings. Most Hoi An buildings have been lovingly restored and transformed into cafes, art galleries, and silk and souvenir shops, while retaining their dignity. If you're an artist, bring your sketch pad and watercolors; photographers, bring plenty of film. Tran Phu and Nguyen Thai Hoc streets are crowded with the shops of the original Chinese merchants and clan associations.

WORLD CULTURAL HERITAGE SIGHTS

The **Hoi An World Cultural Heritage Organization** (www.hoianworldheritage.org) has the dilemma of financing restorations and maintaining the old portions of the town. It sells a 50,000VND (US$3.15/£1.70) ticket that allows limited admission to the sights within the old town, each of which is listed below. "Limited" means a "one from column A, one from column B" formula. That is, one ticket gets you one of the three museums, one of the two assembly halls, one of the four old houses, plus a choice of the Japanese Covered Bridge, the Quan Cong Temple, or the local handicrafts workshop; finally, a "wild card" lets you see one additional place in any category. So, in order to see everything, you'd have to purchase three tickets. See "Visitor Information & Tours," earlier, for where to buy tickets.

Museums
Museum of History and Culture (★)   This tottering building, erected in 1653, houses works that cover 2,000 years of Hoi An history, from Cham relics to ancient ceramics and photos of local architecture. The English-language explanations are scanty. If you're seeing only one museum, make it the Museum of Trade Ceramics (below). One interesting tidbit: The name Hoi An literally means "water convergence" and "peace."

7 Nguyen Hue St. Daily 8am–5pm.

Museum of Trade Ceramics (★★★)   Located in a traditional house, this museum describes the origins of Hoi An as a trade port and displays its most prominent trade items. Objects are from the 13th through 17th centuries and include Chinese and Thai works as well. While many of the exhibits are in fragments, the museum does have very thorough descriptions in English, giving you a real sense of the town's origins and history. Furthermore, the architecture and renovations of the house are thoroughly explained, and you're free to wander through its two floors, courtyard, and anteroom. After all the scattered explanations at the other historic houses, you'll finally get a sense of what Hoi An architecture is all about.

80 Tran Phu St. Daily 8am–5pm.

Sa Huynh Culture Museum (★)   After local farmers around Hoi An dug up some strange-looking pottery, archaeologists identified 53 sites where a pre-Cham people, called the Sa Huynh, buried their dead in ceramic jars. The two-room display here includes some of the burial jars, beaded ornaments, pottery vessels, and iron tools and weapons that have been uncovered. English descriptions are sketchy. Upstairs, the little-visited Museum of the Revolution includes such intriguing items as the umbrella "which Mr. Truong Munh Luong used for acting a fortune-teller to act revolution from 1965 to 1967." Huh? This is for connoisseurs only.

149 Tran Phu St. Daily 8am–6pm.

Old Houses
Old House of Phun Hung (★)   This private house, constructed in 1780, comprises two floors of various architectural influences. The first floor's central roof is four-sided, showing Japanese influence, while the upstairs balcony has a Chinese rounded "turtle shell" roof with carved beam supports. The house has weathered many floods; in 1964, during a particularly bad bout, its third floor served as a refuge for other town families. The upstairs is outfitted with a trap door for moving furniture rapidly to safety. You might be shown around by Ms. Anh, who claims to be an eighth-generation member of the family. Although tour guides at every house make such claims, the family really does seem to live here.

4 Nguyen Thi Minh Khai St. Daily 8am–5pm.

Old House of Tan Ky ⭐   There have been either five or seven generations of Tans living here, depending on whom you speak with. Built over 200 years ago, the four small rooms are crammed with dark-wood antiques. The room closest to the street was for greeting visiting merchants. Farther in are the living room, then the courtyard, and, to the back, the bedroom. The first three are open to the public. A guide, who will greet you at the door, will hasten to explain how the house is a perfect melding of three architectural styles: ornate Chinese detailing on some curved roof beams, a Japanese peaked roof, and a simple Vietnamese cross-hatch roof support. The mosaic decorations on the wall and furniture are aged, intricate, and amazing. Take your time and look around.

101 Nguyen Thai Hoc St. Daily 8am–5pm.

Tran Family Home and Chapel ⭐⭐⭐   In 1802, a civil service mandarin named Tran Tu Nhuc built a family home and chapel to worship his ancestors. A favorite of Viet Emperor Gia Long, he was sent to China as an ambassador, and his home reflects his high status. Elegantly designed with original Chinese antiques and royal gifts such as swords, two parts of the home are open to the public: a drawing room and the ancestral chapel. The house does a splendid job of conveying all that is interesting about these people and their period; it has even been featured in a fashion magazine. The drawing room has three sections of sliding doors: the left for men, the right for women, and the center, open only at Tet and other festivals, for dead ancestors to return home. The ancestral altar in the inner room has small boxes behind it containing relics and a biography of the deceased; their pictures hang, a little spookily, to the right of the altar. A 250-year-old book with the family history resides on a table to the right of the altar. In back of the house are a row of plants, each buried with the placenta and umbilical cord of a family child, so that the child will never forget its home. As if it could.

21 Le Loi St. (at corner of Phan Chu Trinh St.). Daily 8am–5pm.

Assembly Halls

Cantonese Assembly Hall (Quang Trieu/Guangzhou Assembly Hall)   Built in 1885, this hall is quite ornate and colorful. All of the building materials were brought here from China and then reassembled. The center garden sports a fountain with a dragon made of chipped pottery. Inside, look for the statues depicting scenes from famous Cantonese operas and, in the rooms to each side, the ancestral tablets of generations past.

176 Tran Phu St. Daily 8am–6pm.

Fukian Assembly Hall (Phuc Kien)   This is the grandest of the assembly halls, built in 1697 by Chinese merchants from Fukian Province. It is a showpiece of classical Chinese architecture, at least after you pass the first gate, which was added in 1975. It's loaded with animal themes: The fish in the mosaic fountain symbolizes scholarly achievement, the unicorn flanking the ascending stairs symbolizes wisdom, the dragon symbolizes power, the turtle symbolizes longevity, and the phoenix symbolizes nobility. The main temple is dedicated to Thien Hau, goddess of the sea, on the main altar. To the left of her is Thuan Phong Nhi, a goddess who can hear ships within a range of thousands of miles; on the right is Thien Ly Nhan, who can see them. Go around the altar for a view of a fantastic detailed miniature boat. There are two altars to the rear of the temple, the one on the left honoring a god of prosperity and the one on the right honoring a goddess of fertility. The goddess of fertility is often visited by local couples hoping for children. She is flanked by 12 fairies or mid-wives, each responsible for one of a baby's functions: smiling, sleeping, eating, and so forth.

46 Tran Phu St. Daily 7am–6pm.

More World Cultural Heritage Sights

Japanese Covered Bridge ✮✮✮   The name of this bridge in Vietnamese, Lai Vien Kieu, means "Pagoda in Japan." No one is quite sure who first built it in the early 1600s (it has since been renovated several times), but it is usually attributed to Hoi An's Japanese community. The dog flanking one end and the monkey at the other were considered sacred animals by the ancient Japanese. My guide claimed this was because most Japanese emperors were born in the Asian zodiac year of either the mon-key or the dog. Later I read that perhaps the animals' presence means construction began in the year of the dog and was completed in the year of the monkey. I'm sure there are many other interesting dog-and-monkey stories going around—pick your favorite. The small temple inside is dedicated to Tran Vo Bac De, god of the north, beloved (or cursed) by sailors because he controls the weather.

At the west end of Tran Phu St.

Quan Kong Temple ✮   This temple was built in the early 1600s to honor a famous Chin Dynasty general. Highlights inside are two gargantuan 3m (10-ft.) wooden stat-ues flanking the main altar, one of Quan Kong's protector and one of his adopted son. They are both fearsome and impressive. The temple was reportedly a stop for mer-chants who came in from the nearby river to pay their respects and pray for the gen-eral's attributes of loyalty, bravery, and virtue.

168 Tran Phu St. (at corner of Nguyen Hue). Daily 8am–5pm.

OTHER ATTRACTIONS

Central Market ✮✮   If you see only one Vietnamese market, make it this one. There are endless stalls of exotic foodstuffs and services, plus a special shed for silk tai-loring at the east end (these tailors charge much less than the ones along Le Loi). Check out the ladies selling spices—curries, chile powders, cinnamon, peppercorns, and especially saffron. But don't buy from the first woman you see; the stuff gets cheaper and cheaper the deeper you go into the market. Walk out to the docks to see activity there (best early in the morning), but be careful of fish flying through the air, and stand back from the furious bargaining (best before 7am).

At Nguyen Hue and Tran Phu sts. along the Thu Bon River, on the southeast side of town.

Chinese Assembly Hall ✮   This hall was built in 1740 as a meeting place for all of the resident Chinese, regardless of their native province.

64 Tran Phu St. Daily 8am–5pm.

Hainan Assembly Hall   The Chinese merchants from Hainan Island, in the South China Sea east of Danang, built this hall. Although it is newer than most and is mainly made of concrete, it is still nice.

178 Nguyen Duy Hieu St. Daily 8am–5pm.

House of Hoi An Traditional Handicraft ✮✮   This is basically a silk shop with an interesting gimmick: On the first floor, you can see a 17th-century silk loom and a working, machine-powered cotton one. On the second floor, you can see where silk comes from: There are trays of silkworms feeding, then a rack of worms incubating, and then a tub of hot water where the pupae's downy covering is rinsed off and then pulled, strand by strand, onto a large skein. It's cool. The shop has the best selection of silks, both fine and raw, in many colors and weights good for clothing and for home interiors.

41 Le Loi St. Daily 8am–5pm.

SHOPPING

Southeast Asia is packed with would-be Buddhists, travelers on a real spiritual mission espousing lives of detachment from material desires. These folks usually walk away with just the "one suit, two shirts, trousers, and a tie package" when they leave Hoi An. Shopaholics wander the streets in a daze.

Hoi An is a silk mecca. The quality and selection are the best in the country, and you'll have more peace and quiet at fittings here than in Hanoi. **Silk suits** are made to order within 24 hours for about US$35 (£19); **cashmere wool suits** are US$45 (£25). There are countless shops, and the tailoring is all about the same quality and speed. A good way to choose a shop is by what you see out front—if you spot a style you like, it will help with the ordering. Make sure you take the time to specify your style, down to the stitch (it can come back looking pretty cheap without specifics). Try any of the shops along Le Loi; to recommend one in particular would be like choosing one snowflake over another. The tailoring is very fast, but not always great, so plan to have two or three fittings. Be choosy about your cloth, or go to the market and haggle over it yourself (try **Hoi An Cloth Market** at 1 Tran Phu St.). It's not a bad idea to bring an actual suit or piece of clothing that you'd like to have copied. *Tip:* Get measurements from friends and relatives for good gifts.

If you have a hard time choosing from among the many budget tailors, consider **Yaly Couture** (47 Nguyen Thai Hoc St.; ✆ 0510/910-474). It has higher prices, but its quality comes with more of a guarantee.

After shopping for your new suit, seek out one of the town's skilled cobblers, who make **custom shoes** at affordable rates. You'll find them near the market on Tran Phu Street.

Tran Phu Street is also lined with **art galleries** and vendors of good **pottery** and **carved wood.** Along the river, lots of places sell blue-and-white **ceramics.** Among the fine high-end galleries springing up in town, try **Lyly 2 Gallery** (83 Nguyen Thai Hoc St.; ✆ 0510/863-184). The nearby **Bambou Company** (96 Nguyen Thai Hoc St.) produces unique (Western-size) T-shirts of local theme and design. Regardless of how cumbersome your finds are—like those lovely **Chinese lanterns**—shopkeepers are masters at packing goods for travel and to fit in your luggage, and will do so before you've even agreed on a price or decided to buy. Haggle hard.

Finally, **hand-painted Chinese scrolls** make a great souvenir, and **Mr. Ly Si Binh** (21 Nguyen Thai Hoc St.; ✆ 0510/910-721) can script you anything from *Peace* or *Determination* to your best buddy's name. It's fun to watch cheery Mr. Binh at work, too.

HOI AN AFTER DARK

For the most part, Hoi An is a town that sleeps early, but there are a few good nightspots. **Tam-Tam Café** (p. 349) is a popular spot for travelers, expats, and locals. Another late-night tourist hangout, **Hai's Scout Café** (98 Nguyen Thai Hoc St.;

© **0510/863-210**), features your standard bar drinks, cappuccino, and great baked treats. **Treat's Same Same Café** (158 Tran Phu St., at Le Loi; *©* **0501/861-125**) is usually hopping; it even has a pool table and a guillotine (for show, of course). Also try **Same Same Not Different Café,** on Phan Dinh Phung next to An Phu Tourist (both locations are, in short, similar).

The **Yellow Star Café** (73 Nguyen Thai Hoc St.; *©* **090/512-4422;** www.yellow starcafe.com) serves up drinks, while the next-door **ChamPa** (75 Nguyen Thai Hoc St.; *©* **0510/862-974**) has a cozy atmosphere, good wine, and frequent cultural dance performances. **Lounge Bar** (102 Nguyen Thai Hoc St.; *©* **0510/910-480**) is a chic, laid-back stop, while nearby **Mango Rooms** (111 Nguyen Thai Hoc St.; *©* **0510/910-839**) is similarly hip and mellow.

SIDE TRIPS FROM HOI AN
CUA DAI BEACH ★★
Cua Dai Beach is a 25-minute bike ride from Hoi An on a busy road with views of lagoons, rice paddies, and stilt houses. Take Tran Hung Dao Street to Cua Dai Street to the east of town and follow it for 3km (2 miles). The beach is thin and crowded with hawkers, but there are cozy deck chairs (for a small fee). The sand, surf, and setting, with views of the nearby Cham Islands, are worth the trip. In season (Mar–Sept), tour companies will tout boat excursions to the **Cham Islands,** a group of seven islands about 13km (8 miles) east of Hoi An; prices vary, but expect to pay about 30,000VND (US$1.90/£1.05). Contact the tourist cafes in town for details. Boat trips on the Thu Bon River are another option.

MY SON ★★
My Son, some 40km (25 miles) from Hoi An and 71km (44 miles) from Danang, is an important temple ruin of the Cham people, a once-powerful Hindu empire. The temples were constructed as a religious center for citizens of the Cham capital, Danang, from the 7th through 12th centuries during the height of Cham supremacy. My Son (pronounced *mee sun*) might also have been used as a burial site for Cham kings after cremation. Originally, there were over 70 towers and monuments at the site, but bombing during the war with the U.S. (the Viet Cong used My Son as a munitions warehouse) has sadly reduced many to rubble. Additionally, many of the smaller structures have been removed to the Cham Museum in Danang. The complex is a very serene and spiritual setting, however, and what does remain is powerful and evocative. It's not hard to imagine what a wonder My Son must once have been.

Much of what remains today are structures built or renovated during the 10th century, when the cult of Shiva, founder and protector of the kingdom, was predominant in the Cham court. Each group had at least the following structures: a **kalan,** or main tower; a **gate tower** in front of that, with two entrances; a **mandapa,** or meditation hall; and a **repository building** for offerings. Some have towers sheltering stelae with kingly epitaphs. A brick wall encircles the compound.

Architecturally, the temple complex shows Indian influences. Each temple grouping is a microcosm of the world. The foundations are earth, the square bases are the temple itself, and the pointed roofs symbolize the heavens. The entrance of the main tower faces east, and surrounding smaller towers represent each continent. A trench, representing the oceans, surrounds each group. Vietnamese architecture is represented in decorative patterns and boat-shape roofs.

Group A originally had 13 towers. A-1, the main tower, was a 21m-high (69-ft.) masterpiece before it was destroyed in 1969. Group B bears the marks of Indian and Indonesian influence. Note that B-6 holds a water repository for statue-washing ceremonies. Its roof is carved with an image of the god Vishnu sitting beneath a 13-headed snake god, or naga. Group C generally followed an earlier architectural style called Hoa Lai, which predominated from the 8th to the beginning of the 9th century. Groups G and H were the last to be built, around the end of the 13th century.

Arrange a half-day trip to My Son with any tourist agent in Hoi An (see "Visitor Information & Tours," earlier in this section). Entrance to the site is 50,000VND (US$3.15/£1.75); a private half-day tour with a guide is US$35 (£19) for a car and US$43 (£24) for a van. The half-day seat-in-coach tour by **Sinh Café** costs US$2 (£1.10) per person and is nothing more than a ride here, with no explanations. Less frequent tours also depart from Danang.

10 An Introduction to South-Central Vietnam

South-central Vietnam comprises the highlands, a land of rugged mountainous terrain, as well as a stunning coastal area popular with Vietnamese vacationers. The area saw its share of fighting during the American war; names like Buon Me Thot and Pleiku will undoubtedly ring a bell. **Dalat,** a former French colonial outpost nestled among the hills, retains a serene, formal air of another time. Cooler weather makes it a popular escape for expats and travelers, as well as a favorite honeymoon destination for Vietnamese. **Nha Trang,** not far from Dalat on the coast, is an easygoing seaside town that is growing into a top international resort destination.

GETTING THERE

BY PLANE   Both Nha Trang and Dalat are easily accessible by plane from Hanoi and Ho Chi Minh City (Saigon).

BY TRAIN   Nha Trang is a stop on the north–south railway line.

BY BUS/MINIVAN   Both towns are included on most tourist-cafe open tours.

GETTING AROUND

Travel between the two major cities involves a 6-hour ride by bus or minivan, easily organized through any local travel agency.

11 Nha Trang ⍟

Welcome to Vietnam's Ocean City! The capital of Khanh Hoa Province, Nha Trang has a full-time population of about 200,000, but it far exceeds that with the heavy local and international tourist influx, especially in summer. While it's not a particularly charming town, the surf isn't bad and the beach is breathtaking, with views of more than 20 surrounding islands. There is a growing collection of high-end hotels and resorts here, as well as good budget options. Dining is all about fresh seafood.

Nha Trang is also a very popular vacation spot for Vietnamese; especially in the summer months, the town is chockablock with tourists and young kids out cruising the strip on motorbikes—a bit much for folks looking to relax. It's a fine place to spend 2 or 3 days frolicking in the surf, snorkeling and diving, or taking a cruise to the nearby islands.

Nha Trang

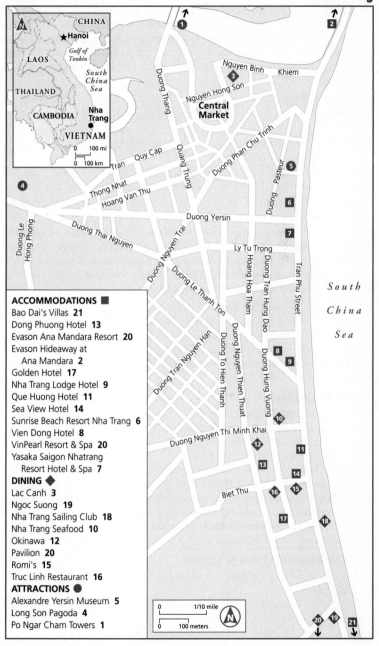

ACCOMMODATIONS ■
Bao Dai's Villas **21**
Dong Phuong Hotel **13**
Evason Ana Mandara Resort **20**
Evason Hideaway at
  Ana Mandara **2**
Golden Hotel **17**
Nha Trang Lodge Hotel **9**
Que Huong Hotel **11**
Sea View Hotel **14**
Sunrise Beach Resort Nha Trang **6**
Vien Dong Hotel **8**
VinPearl Resort & Spa **20**
Yasaka Saigon Nhatrang
  Resort Hotel & Spa **7**

DINING ◆
Lac Canh **3**
Ngoc Suong **19**
Nha Trang Sailing Club **18**
Nha Trang Seafood **10**
Okinawa **12**
Pavilion **20**
Romi's **15**
Truc Linh Restaurant **16**

ATTRACTIONS ●
Alexandre Yersin Museum **5**
Long Son Pagoda **4**
Po Ngar Cham Towers **1**

Culturally, there are a few things to keep you occupied. The **Pasteur Institute** offers a glimpse into the life and work of one of Vietnam's most famous expats; also interesting are the **Long Son Pagoda** and the well-preserved **Po Nagar Cham Temple.**

If you're traveling in the off season, from October to March, note that the surf is far too rough for swimming and sports—you might want to rethink stopping at Nha Trang at all.

GETTING THERE
BY PLANE   Nha Trang is 1,350km (837 miles) from Hanoi and 450km (279 miles) from Ho Chi Minh City (Saigon). There are daily connections on **Vietnam Airlines** (in Nha Trang at 91 Nguyen Thien Thuat St.; © **058/826-768**) between the country's urban centers and nearby Dalat. The Nha Trang airport, once in the center of town, has traded places with a larger military facility and is now called **Cam Ranh Airport,** some 35km (22 miles) north of town. The 30-minute taxi ride costs 150,000VND (US$9.40/£5.15). The larger resorts offer more affordable group connections or limousine service.

BY TRAIN   Nha Trang, a stop on the *Reunification Express,* is 12 hours from Ho Chi Minh City (Saigon) on a soft sleeper for US$18 (£9.90), and 20 hours from Hanoi for US$67 (£37). Buy your ticket at least a day in advance at the Nha Trang train station, at 17 Thai Nguyen St. (© **058/822-113**), or from any travel agent. There is convenient overnight connection with Ho Chi Minh.

BY CAR/BUS   If you drive from Hoi An to Nha Trang, the 10-hour trip will cost about US$120 (£66). An arduous 12-hour bus or minibus ride with a cafe tour bus will cost only US$8 (£4.40). There are overnight schedules to Ho Chi Minh City and Hoi An; the trip is long and tiring, but it's a good option if you're short on time and don't want to waste your precious daylight hours looking out the window of a tour bus.

GETTING AROUND
The main street in Nha Trang, **Tran Phu,** runs along a 4km (2½-mile) beach lined with the myriad minihotels and beach attractions that make the town center. **Biet Thu Street,** perpendicular to Tran Phu, is where you'll find lots of smaller restaurants and budget tour operators and tourist cafes.

Taxis are scarce, but a few tend to congregate around the major hotels. Renting a **bicycle** from your hotel for 15,000VND to 30,000VND (US95¢–US$1.90/£0.50–£1.05) a day is a good option, as are cyclos, which you can rent for US$3 (£1.65) per hour from your hotel. A **cyclo** ride across town will cost about 10,000VND (US65¢/£0.35). In addition, **motorcycle taxis** can be had for 20,000VND (US$1.25/£0.70) per hour and on short trips starting at 5,000VND (US30¢/£0.20).

VISITOR INFORMATION & TOURS
All hotels in Nha Trang can book city tours, day boat trips, or onward travel to your next destination.

One-day city tours visit Long Son Pagoda, Bao Dai's Villas, the Oceanographic Institute, and Cham Tower. Country tours take you to Ba Ho Waterfall and secluded Doc Let Beach, as well as Monkey Island. *Important:* No matter what anyone tells you, Monkey Island is not worth the trip, especially if you like animals and don't like wasting your time (you can just buy a "monkeys on bikes" postcard and be done with it).

For bus tickets and connection to Dalat, contact **TM Brothers Café** (22B Tran Hung Dao St.; ℂ **058/814-556**), **Sinh Café III** (10 Biet Thu St.; ℂ **058/811-981**), or **An Phu** (1/24 Tran Quang Khai St.; ℂ **058/524-471**).

FAST FACTS: Nha Trang

Currency Exchange The local **Vietcombank** branch is at 17 Quang Trung St. (℗ℂ **058/821-483**). Hours are 7:30 to 11am and 1:30 to 4pm. It offers the usual currency and traveler's-check exchange as well as credit card cash advances. Along Biet Thu, some of the tour operators will cash traveler's checks and change money—rates are the same as at the bank (except for a small service fee), and they're open longer hours.

Internet Access Biet Thu has a cluster of Internet cafes that charge between 200VND and 300VND (a couple cents) per minute.

Mail The main post office is at 4 Le Loi St. (℃ **058/823-866**). Hours are Monday through Saturday from 6:30am to 10pm. **DHL** express services and Internet access are available. There is another branch at 50 Le Thanh Ton St.

Telephones The city code for Nha Trang is **58**.

WHERE TO STAY

There are 270 minihotels in Nha Trang, most quite basic and geared to the summer influx of Vietnamese vacationers. Evason Ana Mandara Resort (below) still stands in a class all its own, but recent construction means there are a few mid- and high-range choices, and development on outlying islands (see VinPearl and the new Evason Hideaway, below) adds even more options.

VERY EXPENSIVE

Evason Ana Mandara Resort ★★★ *(Kids)*   One of the finest resorts in the region, the Ana Mandara is a real seaside dreamscape. The name means "beautiful home" in the Cham language, and, though it comes with a high price tag, the hospitality extended here is quite sincere. The staff is very kind, even making a point of learning guests' names. Such personalized service in a beautiful beachside setting, with a spa, pool, fine dining, and a host of activities, means you won't want to leave. Recent renovations added a large, luxurious pool and a spa with outdoor massage areas. But it's the little things that make this resort special: native art and handiwork all about, in-room touches like slippers and umbrellas, bowls with floating flowers in the bathrooms, the basin of rainwater on your private veranda for rinsing sandy feet, the burning incense in the open-air lobby. Each room is double-height and airy with wood beams, rattan ceiling, and stylish furniture. Bathrooms have a large window facing a private outdoor enclosure, like your own Zen garden. Thirty-six units face the beach, while others look onto a courtyard with exotic plants. The Pavilion (p. 363) has the best food and atmosphere in town; the new beachside eatery is tops, too. The resort offers lots of great excursions, like informative market tours where guests can learn about Vietnam cuisine and find out where it all comes from. Tai chi and yoga classes are also available.

Beachside, off Tran Phu Blvd., Nha Trang. © **058/522-222.** Fax 058/525-828. www.sixsenses.com. 74 units. Low season US$236–US$390 (£130–£215) double/villa, US$450-US$468 (£248–£257) suite villa; high season US$269–US$438 (£148–£241) double/villa, US$486-US$513 (£267–£282) suite villa. AE, DC, MC, V. **Amenities:** 2 restaurants; 2 bars; 2 large outdoor pools w/hot tub; tennis court; health club; fine spa; Jacuzzi; sauna; watersports rentals; cyclo rental (US$3/£1.65 per hr.); concierge; tour desk and in-house tour programs (diving can be arranged); business center; shopping; 24-hr. room service; massage; laundry service; dry cleaning; nonsmoking rooms; library w/games and Internet access. *In room:* A/C, satellite TV, dataport, minibar, fridge, coffeemaker, hair dryer, safe, IDD phone.

Evason Hideaway at Ana Mandara ★★★ This cluster of private villas hidden in a secluded cove in Ninh Van Bay, north of the city, can only be reached by boat and is as good as it gets in Nha Trang. Each three-room villa has its own private pool, outdoor shower, and butler, and the Hideaway premise to keep natural surroundings intact means you almost feel marooned. All units at this resort, a sister to Evason Ana Mandara (above), share a pristine beach, but it's the surrounding forest and mountains that make the place special. Choose a villa on the beach, on the hillside, or perched on huge boulders on the water. The spa menu is extensive, and the service is top-notch. It's a great place for a honeymoon—or to get hitched, as there's a wedding chapel on site. *A word of warning:* Once you're here, it's hard to leave. No boats run after dark, and there's only one restaurant and bar. Not the place for partyers, but a nice place to disappear for a day or two.

Ninh Van Bay, Ninh Hoa, north of Nha Trang. Get information at Evason Ana Mandara Resort, beachside, off Tran Phu Blvd., Nha Trang. © **058/522-222.** Fax 058/524-704. www.sixsenses.com. 58 units. Low season US$550–US$880 (£303–£484) villa, US$1,800 (£990) presidential villa; high season US$700–US$1,030 (£385–£567) villa, US$2,000 (£1,100) presidential villa. AE, DC, MC, V. **Amenities:** Restaurant; bar; outdoor pool; tennis court; health club; fine spa; Jacuzzi; sauna; watersports rentals; tour desk and in-house tour programs; business center w/Internet access; 24-hr. room service; massage; laundry service; nonsmoking rooms; library; dive masters; butler. *In villa:* A/C, satellite TV, dataport, minibar, fridge, coffeemaker, hair dryer, safe, IDD phone.

EXPENSIVE

Sunrise Beach Resort Nha Trang ★ The grand edifice of the Sunrise Beach Resort is all polished marble and white columns. The massive hotel is 10 floors of pomp, a bit like an oversize mafia don's palace, but everything about the place is shiny and new. Large rooms are clean-lined and tastefully decorated in a soothing off-white, all with great views of oceanside Tran Phu Street and the beach. The second-floor circular pool is surrounded by ostentatious columns, but makes for a luxurious getaway. Dining options are many, and the rooftop rotunda houses a classy lounge with views of the big blue beyond.

12 Tran Phu St., Nha Trang. © **058/820-999.** Fax 058/822-866. www.sunrisenhatrang.com.vn. 120 units. US$138–US$148 (£76–£81) double; US$168 (£92) deluxe; US$178 (£98) studio; US$198 (£109) club room; US$298 (£164) junior suite; US$398–US$498 (£219–£274) suite. AE, MC, V. **Amenities:** 3 restaurants (Japanese, Vietnamese, international); 2 bars; outdoor pool; small health club and spa; tour desk; car rental; business center w/Internet access; shopping; 24-hr. room service; massage; babysitting; laundry service; dry cleaning. *In room:* A/C, satellite TV, minibar, fridge, coffeemaker, safe, IDD phone.

VinPearl Resort & Spa ★ "If you build it, they will come," or so the voices have said to some visionaries and entrepreneurs. The verdict is still out on the VinPearl (that is, whether or not they'll come), but this enormous resort on Bamboo Island, a 10-minute boat ride from coastal Nha Trang, gets an A for effort. Everything on the island, from construction materials to the very water that comes out of the taps, is transported by large tankers—an incredible undertaking. Guests connect via a fleet of sturdy, high-speed crafts that keep a regular schedule (usually every 30 min.). Public

spaces, like the marble lobby rotunda, are grand in scale but rather uninteresting, though everything is new and tidy. Rooms are similarly large and comfortable, though plain. The resort is designed in an arc around the vast central pool—reputedly the largest in the region, with fun slides, meandering river areas, and bridges, all overlooking a secluded bay. The VinPearl offers lots of activities, group trips, a top-notch watersports facility, a scuba school, and a variety of classes, from yoga and aerobics to "crazy cricket" (you have to ask what it is). Dining is familiar but uninspired. The resort is just getting up and running, which means good incentive packages are on offer. VinPearl is so far a favorite with wealthy Vietnamese weekenders and Korean group tours, but time will tell. They're talking about a casino in the future.

7 Tran Phu, Vinh Nguyen, Nha Trang. Connect by boat from the pier on beachside Tran Phu, just south of Evason Ana Mandara. (C) 058/598-188. Fax 058/598-199. www.vinpearlresort.com/contact.asp. 500 units. US$150–US$190 (£83–£105) double (depending on view); US$220 (£121) junior suite; US$250–US$1,750 (£138–£963) presidential suite. AE, MC, V. **Amenities:** 2 restaurants; 3 bars; enormous outdoor pool; tennis courts; health club; luxe Shiseido Spa; Jacuzzi; sauna; extensive watersports rental; children's center; concierge; tour desk; car rental (on mainland); business center w/Internet access; shopping; salon; 24-hr. room service; massage; babysitting; laundry service; non-smoking rooms. In room: A/C, satellite TV, minibar, fridge, coffeemaker, hair dryer, safe, IDD phone.

Yasaka Saigon Nhatrang Resort Hotel & Spa 🐟🐟 On the main strip overlooking Tran Phu and the ocean blue, this Japan/Vietnam joint venture bridges the gap between the ultraluxe resorts and low-end minihotels—a good compromise. Rooms have all the basic amenities and are about as cozy as your favorite highway hotel chain back home. Upper-level units have good views of the sea, some with balconies; the vista from corner suites is quite spectacular and worth the upgrade. The standard superior rooms are comfortable, if bland; the deluxe rooms, on higher floors, are the best bet for atmosphere. Service is friendly, there are lots of good on-site dining options (the Red Onion is a local favorite), the pool is small but inviting, and it's just a short hop across busy Tran Phu Street to the beach.

18 Tran Phu St., Nha Trang. (C) 058/820-090 or 058/825-227. Fax 058/820-000. www.yasanhatrang.com. 201 units. US$98 (£54) superior; US$118 (£65) deluxe; US$158 (£87) senior deluxe; US$178 (£98) executive; US$198–US$350 (£109–£193) suite. Rates include breakfast. AE, MC, V. **Amenities:** 4 restaurants; bar; nightclub; karaoke; pool w/ocean view; tennis court; small health club; Jacuzzi; sauna; all rentals available; Saigontourist tour desk; car rental; business center; 24-hr. room service; massage; laundry service. In room: A/C, satellite TV w/in-house movies, minibar, fridge, safe, IDD phone.

MODERATE
Bao Dai's Villas Built in 1923 as a seaside resort for then-emperor Bao Dai, the hotel is a cluster of plain colonial-style buildings set high on an oceanside hill south of Nha Trang—so far south that you're in the next town, really. There's an interesting Gothic quality to the place, and one could certainly imagine a king wandering the promontory at night, watching the hotel's lighthouse scan the sea and sky, and worrying about the loss of his kingdom (which was the case). Bao Dai's very room is the master suite, which makes for a memorable stay. The less-expensive units are musty monks' cells, but the villa-style rooms have high ceilings and large, shuttered windows overlooking the coast—a good bet. The higher-end rooms vary, but all are palatial in size even if lacking in amenities. The bathrooms are nothing special, but are sizable and clean, with tubs. Some of the buildings have creaky old wooden staircases and rooftop access. The restaurant serves buffet breakfasts and delicious evening meals for little money. The staff can arrange private boat trips.

Cau Da, Vinh Nguyen, Nha Trang. (C) 058/590-147 or 058/590-148. Fax 058/590-146. www.vngold.com/nt/baodai. 45 units. US$25–US$50 (£14–£28) standard; US$70 (£39) superior; US$80 (£44) suite. Rates include breakfast. MC,

V. **Amenities:** Restaurant; bicycle/motorbike rental; in-house tour desk for island/snorkeling trips; car rental; souvenir shop; limited room service; laundry service; Internet access (500VND/US3¢/£.02 per min.). *In room:* A/C, satellite TV, minibar, fridge, hair dryer, IDD phone.

Nha Trang Lodge Hotel   This well-run, 12-story high-rise has average-size rooms in chain-hotel style, with clean carpets, floral bedspreads, and marble finishes in the bathroom. Spring for an oceanview room with balcony (on an upper floor away from street noise, if possible). It's a nice, uninspired, affordable standard here—a bit like the younger, less-accomplished brother of the Yasaka (above).

42 Tran Phu St., Nha Trang. ℂ 058/521-500 or 058/521-900. Fax 058/521-800. www.nhatranglodge.com. 121 units. US$60 (£33) standard; US$90 (£50) superior; US$130 (£72) suite. AE, MC, V. **Amenities:** Restaurant; bar; pool; tennis court; small fitness center; sauna; tour desk; car rental; business center; salon; 24-hr. room service; massage; laundry service; dry cleaning. *In room:* A/C, satellite TV, minibar, fridge, IDD phone.

Que Huong Hotel   A Khanh Hoa Tourism property, like the Vien Dong Hotel (below), this is a bright, bland, four-story block just across the street from the beach—quiet and convenient. Rooms surround a large central courtyard and pool. All are average size, with clean but worn carpets, pastel tones, nice padded wooden furniture, and balconies. There are signs of wear here and there, like crumbly tile bathrooms, but the suites are huge and a nice option for families (some even have two bathrooms). This is the land of the tour group, though, and the staff is not versed in individual graces; in high season, the front desk is run like a busy Manhattan deli: "Next!" That said, it's affordable, clean, and close to the beach, and the pool is quite lovely. Nice amenities include an Asian/Continental restaurant, small pool hall, fun little disco, and capable travel agents in the lobby.

60 Tran Phu St., Nha Trang. ℂ 058/525-047 or 058/522-365. Fax 058/523-344. www.nhatrangtourist.com.vn. 56 units. US$50–US$60 (£28–£33) single/double deluxe; US$100 (£55) suite. MC, V. **Amenities:** Restaurant; bar/club/karaoke lounge; nice outdoor pool; tennis; sauna; billiards; tour desk; car rental; small business center w/Internet access; salon; massage; laundry service. *In room:* A/C, satellite TV, minibar, fridge, hair dryer, IDD phone.

Vien Dong Hotel   Connected with Hai Yen Hotel, another large government tour-agency hotel, the Vien Dong is showing its age after years of heavy tour-group use, but it's still a relatively comfortable three-star with all the amenities. The large pool is a highlight. Smallish rooms have tatty carpet, simple wood furnishings, and sturdy foam mattresses. Bathrooms are clean but bare. A college dorm room comes to mind. Suites are not worth the extra cost. An inviting outdoor restaurant features cultural music and dance shows. You're sure to meet other travelers here, and the general atmosphere is friendly, which helps. The staff, though taxed by the many groups coming and going, is kind and helpful. The **Hai Yen,** next door at 42 Tran Phu St. (ℂ **058/522-422**), is a similar standard but *really* showing its age.

1 Tran Hung Dao St., Nha Trang. ℂ 058/523-606 or 058/521-608. Fax 058/521-912. www.nhatrangtourist.com.vn. 102 units. US$20–US$30 (£11–£17) double; US$90 (£50) suite. AE, MC, V. **Amenities** (shared w/Hai Yen Hotel): Large restaurant; open-air poolside bar; big outdoor pool; tennis courts; bicycle rental; tour desk; limited room service; laundry service; dry cleaning; Internet access (1,000VND/10 min., or US6¢/£0.03 per min.). *In room:* A/C, satellite TV, minibar, fridge, hair dryer, IDD phone.

INEXPENSIVE
Dong Phuong Hotel ⭐   It's function, not form, in this motel-style block that's typical of the budget accommodations in town (this is one of three properties of the same name and standard in Nha Trang). Rooms are bright but spartan, with not much more than a bed and a shower-in-room style of bathroom. Some units have a good city view. If you're lucky, you'll be blessed with a classy nude done in painted tile mosaic in the

bathroom (the only decoration I could find throughout). Family rooms are a good value, and the penthouse room adjoins a huge rooftop area with 365-degree views of town. It's your standard minihotel service, though: just rooms.

103 Nguyen Thien Thuat St., Nha Trang. © 058/526-986 or 058/526-247. Fax 058/526-986. dongphuongnt@dng. vnn.vn. 60 units. US$5–US$20 (£2.75–£11) double; US$30 (£17) deluxe (family). MC, V. **Amenities:** Restaurant; tours can be arranged; laundry service. *In room:* A/C, satellite TV, fridge, hair dryer, IDD phone.

Golden Hotel   You'll get little more than a surly welcome and a room, but with no other expectations than these, you can't go too wrong. Private spaces in this hotel are actually quite nice, done with dark-wood trim, crown molding, and filigree—cozier than other basic minihotels in the area. Amenities are bare bones: just good tour services and a lobby safe deposit box.

1K–2K Hung Vuong, Nha Trang. © 058/524-496. Fax 058/524-498. 31 units. US$12–US$30 (£6.60–£17) double. MC, V. **Amenities:** Tour desk; laundry service. *In room:* A/C, satellite TV, fridge, IDD phone.

Sea View Hotel   Here's another good, relatively new, and clean option comparable to those above. The Sea View is right in the heart of the busy backpacker area, and you'll have to be on a higher floor to get any actual sea view, but rooms are large, simple, and clean, with tile floors and shower-in-room-style bathrooms. Some units have balconies. Amenities are few, but the hotel is convenient to the busy downtown.

4 Biet Thu St., Nha Trang. © 058/524-333. Fax 058/524-335. seaviewhotel@dng.vnn.vn. 60 units. US$12–US$20 (£6.60–£11) double. MC, V. **Amenities:** Tour desk; laundry service. *In room:* A/C, satellite TV, fridge, IDD phone.

WHERE TO DINE
EXPENSIVE

Pavilion ★★★ ASIAN/CONTINENTAL   Without question the finest dining on this beautiful stretch of coast, the Pavilion is the jewel in the crown of the Evason Ana Mandara Resort, serving exquisite cuisine in elegant, natural surroundings. Whether you're perched on the oceanfront veranda, shaded by a canvas umbrella in the courtyard, or dining by candlelight over the open ocean on the seaside jetty, the location alone is breathtaking. The food is creatively prepared and beautifully presented. The ever-evolving roster of local and seasonal specials means anything from sandwiches (made with bread baked on-site) and imported cheese to local favorites like banana-flower salads and even sushi done to a T for the many Japanese guests. Don't miss the seafood hot pot, served in a coal-fired crock and brimming with the catch of the day delicately stewed with vegetables. There is an excellent daily lunch buffet, and evening set menus are a great value. This is the best choice for romantic ambience and fine dining.

At the Evason Ana Mandara Resort, Tran Phu Blvd. © 058/829-829. Main courses US$7–US$19 (£3.85–£10); prix-fixe menus US$15–US$22 (£8.25–£12). AE, MC, V. Daily 6am–11pm.

MODERATE

Ngoc Suong ★★ SEAFOOD   Nha Trang has dozens of good seafood restaurants, but this one leads the pack. Whether in the very pleasant thatched outdoor pavilion or the vaguely nautical, softly lit interior, it's "seafood as you like it" served by a helpful, friendly staff. Whole fish and crustaceans can be chosen by pointing at the large tank and smiling greedily; the day's catch, including shrimp and crab, is ordered by the pound, grilled, fried, or boiled with basic spices like tamarind or pepper and lemon. The oysters, if available, are small but succulent. The name of the restaurant refers to a delicate marinated whitefish salad, one of the specialties and a great appetizer. This is a popular local and expat favorite.

96A Tran Phu (south of the town center at beachside). © **058/525-656**. Main courses 20,000VND–240,000VND (US$1.25–US$15/£0.70–£8.25). No credit cards. Daily 10am–midnight.

Nha Trang Sailing Club ★ VIETNAMESE/CONTINENTAL   Stop by this open-air bar/restaurant for a real Western breakfast, if nothing else. A good bet is the pancakes, not greasy (as usual) and served with real butter. Other menu items include tasty (though not authentic) burgers and macaroni and cheese, plus the usual Nha Trang seafood selections. There are now different "stations" for dining here, including good Japanese eats, an Italian menu, and even an Indian menu. The setting, in a large hut just off the beach, can't be beat. You can lounge on the beach, buy or swap a book from the well-stocked rack, and book a boat tour or a day of scuba with Rainbow Divers. The bar swings at night.

72–74 Tran Phu St. © **058/826-528**. Main courses 30,000VND–125,000VND (US$1.90–US$7.80/£1.05–£4.30). No credit cards. Daily 7am–11pm (bar until 2am).

Nha Trang Seafood ★★ SEAFOOD/VIETNAMESE   Popular with Japanese groups (or local fat cats out to impress their mistresses), Nha Trang Seafood serves it up fresh, just as you like it: grilled, steamed, or fried. Viet-style preparation is sweet, sour, and/or spicy; grilled items are a good way to go. The shrimp in coconut, clay-pot dishes, and hot pots are affordable and delicious. The atmosphere is plain and dull by the light of day; it's best by candlelight on the second floor when the place is crowded. The staff is fun-loving and friendly.

46 Nguyen Thi Minh Khai St. © **058/822-664**. Main courses 25,000VND–200,000VND (US$1.55–US$13/ £0.85–£6.90). No credit cards. Daily 9:30am–10pm.

Okinawa JAPANESE   Pop into Okinawa for a miso-soup break, a couple slabs of sashimi, or a full meal. Prices are affordable, the food is fresh, and the owner plays piano nightly. Got a tune you want to pound out? You're invited to as well. A nice break from the standard seafood or backpacker fare usually found on this little side street.

55/2 Nguyen Thien Thuat St. © **058/524-890**. Main dishes US$4–US$8 (£2.20–£4.40). No credit cards. Daily from 4pm.

INEXPENSIVE

Lac Canh CHINESE/VIETNAMESE   Two words: grilled shrimp. The Chinese-influenced Vietnamese cuisine here is all about the ingredients, so go for the basics: fresh seafood in a light marinade that you grill yourself on a rustic, cast-iron brazier. The new location is a little more airy, but try to sit outdoors because the atmosphere is smoky. This is definitely the town's "greasy spoon," packed with both locals and tourists, and it makes for a fun evening.

11 Hang Ca St. © **058/821-391**. Main courses US$1.25–US$7.95 (£0.70–£4.40). No credit cards. Daily 9am–9:30pm.

Romi's VIETNAMESE/WESTERN   This ice-cream parlor, in the middle of the backpacker area, is a good place to meet fellow wanderers over a snack or break-fast. The owners and staff are friendly, the list of fruit shakes is as long as a sunny beachside day, and the ice cream is tops. Opt for the strawberry shake for a quick pick-me-up.

1C Biet Thu. © **058/527-677**. Main courses US66¢–US$4 (£0.35–£2.20). No credit cards. Daily 7am–11pm.

Truc Linh Restaurant VIETNAMESE   The eclectic menu here has everything from the backpacker standbys of fried rice and noodles to sirloin steak and T-bone. It's got fondue and clay-pot specials, barbecued beef on clay tile, and delicious rice-paper spring rolls with shrimp. Or you can choose your own jumbo shrimp, crab, squid, or fresh fish of the day and then have it weighed and cooked to your taste.

21 Biet Thu St. ℂ **058/521-089**. Main courses US80¢–US$10 (£0.45–£5.50). Daily 6am–11pm.

WHAT TO SEE & DO

Alexandre Yersin Museum   Here you can get an inkling of the work of one of Vietnam's greatest heroes. Swiss doctor Yersin founded Dalat, isolated a plague-causing bacteria, and researched agricultural methods and meteorological forecasting, all to the great benefit of the Vietnamese. He founded the institute in 1895. On display are his desk, overflowing library, and scientific instruments.

In the Pasteur Institute, 10 Tran Phu St. ℂ **058/822-355**. Admission 26,000VND (US$1.65/£0.90). Mon–Sat 8–11am and 2–4:30pm.

Long Son Pagoda   The main attraction at this 1930s pagoda is the huge white Buddha on the hillside behind, the symbol of Nha Trang. Around the base of the Buddha are portraits of monks who immolated themselves to protest the corrupt Diem regime. After climbing the numerous flights of stairs, you'll be rewarded with a bird's-eye view of Nha Trang.

Thai Nguyen St. Free admission. Daily 8am–5pm.

Po Ngar Cham Towers 🏵   Starting in the 8th century, the Cham people, an early Hindu empire in central Vietnam (see "Who Are the Cham?" p. 328), built the Po Ngar Cham temple complex to honor Yang Ino Po Ngar, mother of the kingdom. Set on the site of an earlier wooden temple burned by the Javanese in A.D. 774, there were originally 10 structures here; today, just four remain. The main tower, or Po Ngar Kalan, is one of the tallest Cham structures ever built. Its square tower and three-story cone roof are exemplary of Cham style. It has more remaining structural integrity than many sites, giving you a good idea of how it might have looked in all its glory. In the vestibule, you can see two pillars of carved epitaphs of Cham kings; in the sanctuary, there are two original carved doors. The statue inside is of the goddess Bharagati (also called Po Ngar), on her lotus throne. It was carved in 1050. The Po Ngar temples are still in use by local Buddhists, and the altars and smoking incense add to the intrigue of the architecture. Detracting from the whole experience are the kitsch stands and lots of hawkers.

2 Thang 4, at the end of Xom Bong Bridge (2km/1¼ miles out of the city center). Admission 10,000VND (US65¢/£0.35). Daily 7:30am–5pm.

OUTDOOR ACTIVITIES

Diving is big in Nha Trang, in season (Mar–Sept). There are a number of professionally run operations here; whether you're a beginner or an expert, make your choice based on safety more than anything. **Rainbow Divers** (ℂ **058/524-351;** www. divevietnam.com) has taken advertising to the level of pollution in Nha Trang, with seemingly every storefront claiming a connection, but these guys really are among the best in town. You can book with them anywhere—try the **Nha Trang Sailing Club** (ℂ **058/826-528;** see "Where to Dine," above). For a guaranteed safe and fun time, try the folks at **Octopus Diving** (62 Tran Phu St.; ℂ **058/810-629;** octopusdiving club@yahoo.com; or through the Evason Ana Mandara Resort), where the expert, mostly expat staff can devise dives for any and all. **Vietnam Explorer** (2 Tran Quang Khai; ℂ **058/524-490**) is another good outfit.

Also popular are the 1-day boat cruises to some of Nha Trang's 20 surrounding islands. For years, Nha Trang was famed for rowdy trips that were more like daytime raves. **Hahn's Green Hat Boat Tour** (2C Biet Thu St.; *©* **058/824-494**) is the long-time favorite, a remnant of the old "Mama Hahn" days (Mama Hahn was famous for saying, "Smoke and drink! Don't be lazy!"), but the trips have toned down significantly. **Mama Linh** (*©* **058/826-693**) offers similar tours, as do **Sinh Café** and **TM Brothers** (see "Visitor Information & Tours," at the beginning of this section). The going rate is US$7 (£3.85) per day and includes 9am hotel pick-up and afternoon drop-off. The mellow day of motoring through lovely bays to three different islands guarantees you some snorkeling, a big feast for lunch, and a great spread of fruit in the afternoon. Beer and drinks are available all day (at one point, you can swim out to a floating bar for complimentary wine). The tour terminates at a fish farm and a small harbor, where you can rent a traditional bamboo-basket boat to paddle about. Just about everyone in town will want to book you on one of these tours, so ask at any hotel front desk and be sure to nail down all specifics (meals, transport included, and so forth).

For sailing, contact the **Nha Trang Sailing Club** (*©* **058/826-528**) or the **Evason Ana Mandara Resort** (*©* **058/829-829**). Go for a Hobie Cat if it's available and hire a captain if you are not experienced; the strong ocean breezes and choppy waters will make for a memorable sail. Runabouts and jet skis are also available.

If you want to get to the popular **Thapba Mud Bath & Hotspring Resort** (*©* **058/834-939**), just outside town, hire a car or ask any hotel front desk to call the resort directly for you.

NHA TRANG AFTER DARK

Nha Trang has a few lively beachfront bars where tourists congregate to swap stories. The **Nha Trang Sailing Club** (72–74 Tran Phu St., across from the Hai Yen Hotel) has open-air bamboo huts and a dance scene on some nights until late (it gets pretty seedy past midnight). **Crazy Kim Bar** (19 Biet Thu St.; *©* **058/816-072**), in the backpacker area, is open late and asks customers to "Be hot. Be cool. Be crazy. Just be." There are many versions of that mantra around town, and it's popular with the diving crowd and the few expats here. **Guava,** next door to Kim's at 17 Biet Thu, has a similar scene.

12 Dalat

Known as "Le Petit Paris" by the early builders and residents of this hillside resort town, Dalat is still considered a kind of luxury retreat for city dwellers and travelers tired out from trudging along sultry coastal Vietnam. In Dalat, you can play golf on one of the finest courses in Indochina, visit beautiful temples, and enjoy the town's honeymoon atmosphere and delightfully hokey tourist sights.

At 1,500m (4,920 ft.) elevation, Dalat is mercifully cool year-round—there's no need for air-conditioning here—and is a unique blend of pastoral hillside Vietnam and European alpine resort. Alexander Yersin, the Swiss geologist who first traipsed across this pass, established the town in 1897 as a resort for French commanders weary of the Vietnamese tropics. In and around town are still scattered the relics of colonial mansions, as well as some serene pagodas in a lovely natural setting—you've escaped from big-city Vietnam for real here. You can also visit the small villages of a few ethnic minorities, including the Lat and the Koho, who live in and around the picturesque hills surrounding Dalat.

Dalat is a top resort destination for Vietnamese couples getting married or honeymooning. If the lunar astrological signs are particularly good, it's not unusual to see 10 or so wedding parties in a single day. Many of the local scenic spots, like the Valley of Love and Lake of Sighs, pander to the giddy couples. The waterfalls swarm with vendors, costumed bears, and "cowboys" complete with sad-looking horses and fake pistols. A carnival air prevails. It's tacky, but it's one of those "so bad that it's good" feelings that's kind of fun.

GETTING THERE

BY PLANE   The only direct flights to Dalat are from Ho Chi Minh City (flight time: 50 min). Once you're in Dalat, you should call to confirm your ticket. You can reach **Vietnam Airlines** at ✆ 063/822-895. A taxi from the airport to the city is US$3 (£1.65) and takes about 30 minutes.

BY BUS/CAR   Dalat is the first stop on the open-tour bus from Ho Chi Minh City. Buses from both north and south first stop at Phan Rang, an old Cham temple site, where the road turns inland for the hills of Dalat. The ride up is winding and spectacular, at one point following hairpin after hairpin beneath a large hydroelectric project. The trip from Nha Trang (to the north) or Ho Chi Minh City (to the south) takes 7 hours and costs US$5 (£2.75) at any tourist cafe. Alternatively, you can hire a private car for the trip and save about an hour.

GETTING AROUND

There are no cyclos in Dalat, but walking is very pleasant in the cool air. You can reach most of the city sights, like the market and the lake, on foot. On weekends, the busy streets of the central city are closed to motorbike and auto traffic. Try **Dalat Taxi** (✆ 063/830-830) if you need a cab in town.

Dalat is a good place to rent a **motorbike,** which will cost about US$3 (£1.65) per day at the street-side places on Nguyen Thi Minh Khai (between the market and the lake), or US$4 to US$5 (£2.20–£2.75) from hotels and cafes. This is a good, adventurous way to get to all the funky sights outside the city. The winding roads will have you feeling like you're born to be wild, if you can forget that you're riding the motorcycle equivalent of a hair dryer. Be sure to check the brakes and the horn: You should beep-beep all the way, especially when passing or on curves.

Another option is to get a **motorbike with driver** (look for jackets with an Easyrider logo). You'll pay about US$1 to US$2 (£0.55–£1.10) per hour, or you can fix a rate for the day and the destinations. A **car with driver** runs about US$25 (£14) per day. Because most sights are outside city limits, it makes sense to take a half- or full-day tour through your hotel or a tourist cafe.

VISITOR INFORMATION & TOURS
ECO-TOURS

Young U.S. expats Brian and Kim, of **Phat Tire Ventures** (73 Truong Cong Dinh; ✆ 063/823-104; fax 063/829-422; www.phattireventures.com), can arrange anything from day treks to jungle expeditions, mountain biking (they have a stable of top-quality bikes and hold daily clinics), rock climbing, rappelling, or canyoning. Daily rates for most activities start at US$19 (£10) and include lunch, transport, and a knowledgeable guide. Safety and environmental stewardship are their trademark. They also book classic tours through their affiliate, **Dalat Tours.**

BUDGET TOURS

- **Sinh Café** (4A Bui Thi Xuan St.; ✆ 063/822-663) has an information and tour office adjacent to Trung Cang Hotel, the company's budget accommodations (p. 370).
- **TM Brothers** (2 Nguyen Chi Thanh St.; ✆ 063/828-282) can book standard budget tours for you from its office on "cafe street."
- **An Phu Tourist Co.** (7 Hai Thuong St.; ✆ 063/823-631) is located here, too.

FAST FACTS: Dalat

Currency Exchange **Industrial & Commercial Bank** (46 Hoa Binh St.; ✆ 063/822-495) offers the best rate, but most hotels have comparable exchange services for a small fee. There are no ATMs in Dalat.

Internet Access The most accessible Internet cafe in town is on the hill that overlooks the main market street: **Viet Hung Internet Café** (7 Nguyen Chi Thanh; ✆ 063/835-737), which charges 5,000VND (US35¢/£0.15) per hour. There are many others scattered about as well.

Mail The main post office is at 14 Tran Phu St., across from the Novotel. Open Monday through Saturday from 6:30am to 9:30pm.

Telephones The area code for Dalat is **63**.

WHERE TO STAY

With its long history as a resort area for both foreigners and Vietnamese, Dalat offers some choice lodgings. There are plenty of minihotels, but they're not of the quality you might find in Hanoi, for example. Keep an eye on new developments in the hills outside the city center. Efforts are underway to restore and preserve the many 1950s-era French colonial homes, and many are converting to guesthouses. **Villa 28** (28 Tran Hung Dao; ✆ 063/822-764) is a very basic guesthouse, but a harbinger of things to come. *Note:* No Dalat hotels have air-conditioning; with the year-round temperate weather, none is needed.

VERY EXPENSIVE

Evason Ana Mandara Villas & Spa at Dalat   For a real taste of colonial living, the Villas provide an experience unrivaled in Dalat. It's as though the designers made a trip back to the 1930s, bought up an entire neighborhood, and brought the whole place into the present. Twenty renovated villas are spread over 14 hectares (35 acres) a short ride from central Dalat, and all are as distinct as their first owners. Each is a thematic homage to French colonialist professions, from winemakers to archaeologists to the Citroën family, which used to sponsor a race from Paris to Vietnam. All the original structures have been retained, so floors are polished with age and creak in a nostalgic way that can't be replicated by new construction. Most villas are designed with guest rooms sharing a common area, but a private butler in each building means that even the most reclusive visitor will be satisfied. (For complete privacy, opt for the single-occupancy villa.) The grounds are sealed off from traffic and still heavily timbered with trees planted by the original French planners of Dalat; a crumbling church on a gardened hillside constitutes part of the view. The only sounds you hear might be the rumble of classic Citroën or Peugot cars, which carry guests to their villas.

Le Lai St., Ward 5, Dalat. ℂ **063/560-719**. Fax 063/560-718. www.sixsenses.com. 70 units. Low season US$155–US$195 (£85–£107) double, US$280-US$380 (£154–£209) suite; high season US$190–US$230 (£105–£127) double, US$315–US$415 (£173–£228) suite; year-round US$400–US$435 (£220–£239) spa villa suite. AE, DC, MC, V. **Amenities:** Restaurant; bar; pool; gym; spa; all rentals available; children's center; butler; tour desk; business center; 24-hr. room service; laundry service; dry cleaning. *In room:* Satellite TV, DVD, safe, IDD phone.

Sofitel Dalat Palace   Opened in 1922 as the address of choice for French colonists on holiday and once headquarters of the occupying Japanese, this recently renovated beauty, with its understated old-world opulence, is one of the finest five-star choices in all of Indochina. From the huge fireplace and mosaic floor in the lobby to the hanging tapestries and 500 oil reproductions of classic European art, it's a French country chateau with a Southeast Asian colonial flair. The large rooms, with glossy original wood floors, are finished with fine fabrics and throw rugs, and all beds are crowned with an ornate wooden housing for an ornamental mosquito net. The bathrooms feature hand-painted tiles and claw-foot tubs with antique-style fixtures. Foyers and fireplaces in every room complete the picture. Lakeview units open to a huge shared veranda with deck chairs. The high, high ceilings and huge corridors with hanging lamps contribute to the palatial feeling. Service is superb. All in all, this is an exquisite place that should not be missed.

The whole place is the brainchild of the late Larry Hillblom, the enigmatic American entrepreneur and co-owner of DHL who invested heavily in the property out of love and generosity as much as anything. He is still remembered and revered by the many who knew him; Larry's Bar, a great little grotto with a pool table, darts, and good pub grub, does his memory proud. The in-house dining at Le Rabelais (p. 371) is unrivaled. The hotel offers a tour of the city in a vintage Citroën that should not be missed if you want to learn a lot in a hurry about Dalat's colonial architecture.

12 Tran Phu St., Dalat. ℂ **063/825-444**. Fax 063/825-666. www.sofitel.com. 43 units. US$160–US$270 (£88–£149) double; US$400 (£220) suite. Extra bed US$40 (£22). Ask about discounts and specials. AE, DC, MC, V. **Amenities:** 2 restaurants; 3 bars; golf arrangements; tennis; all rentals available; kids' playroom and outdoor playground; concierge; tour desk; business center w/Internet access; shopping; 24-hr. room service; laundry service; dry cleaning; horseback riding/carriage rental; hotel history corner. *In room:* Satellite TV, Wi-Fi, minibar, fridge, hair dryer, safe, IDD phone.

EXPENSIVE

Novotel Dalat   This is the scaled-down companion hotel to the Sofitel Palace. Lovely renovations in 1997 converted the 1932 building, which was originally the Du Parc hotel. The lobby has a unique wrought-iron elevator. The smallish rooms have attractive historic touches: glossy wood floors, tastefully understated wood furniture, and high molded ceilings. A superior room (the lowest standard) is a bit cramped and not the greatest value, but deluxe rooms are clean, classy, and worth the upgrade. The bathrooms are efficient and spotless, with sleek granite and dark-wood trim. Everything is tidy and convenient, with local artwork throughout and a warm, homey atmosphere. The staff is businesslike and friendly, and the Novotel shares fine amenities with neighboring Sofitel Dalat Palace (above).

7 Tran Phu St., Dalat. ℂ **800/221-4542** or 063/825-777. Fax 063/825-888. www.novotel.com. 140 units. US$116–US$139 (£64–£76) double; US$162 (£89) suite. Ask about discounts and specials. AE, MC, V. **Amenities:** 2 restaurants; 3 bars; golf arrangements; tennis; all rentals available; concierge; tour desk; business center w/Internet access; shopping; 24-hr. room service; laundry service; dry cleaning. *In room:* Satellite TV, minibar, fridge, coffeemaker, hair dryer, safe, IDD phone.

MODERATE

Empress Hotel ★★ This Hong Kong/Vietnamese joint venture is an upscale but affordable oasis just a stone's throw from the lake and close to all the action. Tucked into the side of a hill, the hotel has rooms that form a courtyard, with the steep gable of a European lodge-style reception and restaurant on one side and two floors of rooms (all facing the courtyard) on the other. The comfortable accommodations have dark-wood walls, terra-cotta tile floors, rattan furniture, nice local artwork, and elegant bedspreads. Bathrooms are large, with granite counters and nice fixtures, some with tubs and others an open arrangement with a combined shower/toilet area (like a guesthouse, but spotless). The suites are large and luxe, with a sunken tub and sitting area, but the deluxe rooms are a better deal, with views of the stone courtyard and lake below. Go for a room on the second floor, as those on the first are getting a bit musty. The restaurant serves good local and Continental fare; if the staff is slightly cool, it's almost refreshingly real of them. The hotel also has a great old Mercedes for rental or airport transfers.

5 Nguyen Thai Hoc St., Dalat. ✆ 063/833-888. Fax 063/829-399. empresdl@hcm.vnn.vn. US$60–US$80 (£33–£44) double (superior/deluxe); US$110–US$198 (£61–£109) suite. AE, MC, V. **Amenities:** Restaurant; tour desk; car rental (classic Mercedes to airport for US$16/£8.80); laundry service; dry cleaning. *In room:* Satellite TV w/in-house movies, minibar, fridge, hair dryer, safe, IDD phone.

Golf III Hotel ★ The Golf is a three-star chain hotel and a good choice in Dalat (Golf I and II are low-end versions). Large rooms are upholstered in purple with gaudy carved-wood details. Some units are a bit frayed around the edges, but they're perfectly clean and comfortable. It's worth springing for a deluxe room (US$50/£28), a Vietnamese honeymooner favorite, with parquet floors rather than carpet, and larger bathrooms with big sunken tubs. The constant stream of Vietnamese wedding parties in and out lends a welcome festive air to the place. Golf III is right in the center of the busy market area, but set back far enough from the road that rooms are relatively quiet. Amenities are basic, like a rooftop steam, sauna, and massage area (a little seedy); the lobby restaurant serves a fine breakfast. As the name implies, the Golf properties all have an arrangement with the local course at a good rate.

4 Nguyen Thi Minh Khai St. (near the market), Dalat. ✆ **063/826-042** or 063/826-049. Fax 063/830-579. 78 units. US$45–US$60 (£25–£33) double; US$70–US$100 (£39–£55) suite. AE, MC, V. **Amenities:** Restaurant; bar; golf arrangements; sauna; steam room; tour desk; small business center; limited room service; massage; laundry service. *In room:* Satellite TV, minibar, fridge, safe, IDD phone.

INEXPENSIVE

Hotel Dai Loi (Fortune Hotel) ★★ If you want value for money, look no further. The US$25 (£14) rooms here have two double beds and large tubs; most have balconies as well. Even the lowest-priced rooms are terrific, with high ceilings, fresh paint, firm mattresses, marble floors, and nicely tiled bathrooms. Most other places in this category have musty smells and dingy decor, but not the Fortune. The place is spotless, the location is far enough from the town center for quiet yet close enough for access, and the price is right. The second-floor restaurant is open and inviting. The staff members speak little English but are quite helpful.

3A Bui Thi Xuan, Dalat. ✆ 063/837-333. 39 units. US$14–US$25 (£7.70–£14) double. AE, MC, V. **Amenities:** Restaurant; bar; all rentals available; laundry service. *In room:* TV, minibar, fridge, IDD phone.

Trung Cang Hotel ★★ The Sinh Café expands its monopoly on budget-traveler services with this centrally located little gem. Rooms have clean tile floors and basic amenities. Time will tell with this place, but get here while it's new, ask to see a room, and do a bit of haggling. The folks at Sinh Café are always accommodating when arranging tours or getting you around town.

4A Bui Thi Xuan St., Dalat. © 063/822-663. 27 units. US$10–US$20 (£5.50–£11) double. Rates include breakfast. MC, V. **Amenities:** Restaurant; all rentals available; tour desk; laundry service. *In room:* Satellite TV, minibar, fridge, IDD phone.

WHERE TO DINE

Dalat dining is pretty basic. Meals are simply prepared and heavily influenced by Chinese cuisine. The huge variety of local ingredients, particularly fruit and vegetables, makes for fresh-tasting food. Many small restaurants are located on **Phan Dinh Phung Street,** and some of the best dining, according to locals, is at the stalls in the **central market.** Do try the artichoke tea and strawberry jam, two local specialties (and good souvenirs to take home from the market).

Café de la Poste ★★ CONTINENTAL   This cozy, colonial gem, part of the Sofitel Dalat Palace hotel, is located in an open, airy corner building across from the post office (go figure). It's more restaurant than cafe, really, and has a great selection of light choices, sandwiches, and desserts (don't miss the cheesecake), along with hearty entrees like T-bone steak and fresh pasta. The salads are big and fresh, and the French onion soup is great. It's pricey for Dalat, but worth it.

12 Tran Phu St. © 063/825-444. Main courses US$4–US$11 (£2.20–£6.05). MC, V. Daily 6am–10pm.

Dalat House ★ ASIAN/WESTERN   It's out of the town center, so you'll have to take a cab, but that somehow adds to the experience of dining at this dolled-up new restaurant, a place where local businessmen go to impress clients. (Did someone hear the theme to *The Godfather?*) You'll find a mix of Asian and Western cuisine served on fine white china at candlelit, linen-covered tables. The best local choices are the good stews that take the chill out of a cool Dalat evening: hot-pot dishes great for sharing, or baked clay-pot specials. Western meals are all country-club standbys: meat and potatoes, fish, and pasta. If you crave steak, a house specialty, you have a choice of imported beef or locally grown at half the price (pay the extra for imported). Dessert is crème caramel, apple tart, or soufflé.

34 Nguyen Du (about 4 km/2½ miles east of town, past the railway station). © 063/811-577. Main courses 50,000VND–350,000VND (US$3.15–US$22/£1.70–£12). No credit cards. Daily 6am–2pm and 5–10pm.

Le Rabelais ★★ FRENCH   A meal at Le Rabelais is a genuine French colonial fine-dining experience. Prices are high, but so is the standard of preparation and service. The Sofitel people work closely with local organic farms, thus all dishes are prepared with the finest fresh produce. In the tradition of the original 1922 Langbian Palace Hotel, Le Rabelais serves from a limited menu, which ensures that everything is done just right. Beginning with a tantalizing *amuse bouche,* dinner is a slow progression of delicious courses. I had rich lobster bisque and a beef sirloin, succulent and satisfying in a savory pepper sauce. The wine list is long and, unusual in this region, the staff knows the right suggestions for any given meal; in fact, the service here is uniquely efficient and professional, attentive without fawning or hovering, and meticulous with every detail. It's a great place to take that special someone for an evening of candlelit opulence. Follow up with coffee or after-dinner drinks and cigars down in the very atmospheric Larry's Bar.

At the Sofitel Dalat Palace, 12 Tran Phu St. © 063/825-444. Evening set menus US$18–US$35 (£9.90–£19). MC, V. Daily 6am–10pm.

Long Hoa ★★ VIETNAMESE/CONTINENTAL   On a busy street just opposite the hilltop cinema, this small bistro has checkered tablecloths and a cozy atmosphere. The owner, a vivacious, self-taught linguist, is very welcoming and will talk you through the menu, travel recommendations, or local lore in the language of your choice. You'll feel like a regular, or you will become one, even if you're in town for only a few days. The menu is grouped by ingredients (chicken, beef, fish) and lists any kind of sauté or steamed dish you can imagine, as well as a variety of hot pots and soups for those cold Dalat nights. It's inexpensive, excellent local fare with a French flair; I had a delicious meal of barbecued deer with fries. Don't miss the homemade yogurt, a real treat.

6 Duong 3 Thang 2 (Duy Tan). ⓒ **063/822-934**. Main courses US$1–US$4 (£0.55–£2.20). No credit cards. Daily 10:30am–9:30pm.

Lyla Hotel and Restaurant de Famille ★ VIETNAMESE/CONTINENTAL   It's real family dining, heavy on good French, in a closed, quiet dining room along Dalat's busy cafe street. This is a longtime expat favorite where everything is good. I had a "real" Continental meal of French onion soup (absolutely delicious), fries with mayonnaise, and a niçoise salad. The menu features great steaks, pasta, and seafood, too. Very family-friendly.

18A Nguyen Chi Thanh. ⓒ **063/834-540**. Main courses 19,000VND–59,000VND (US$1.20–US$3.70/£0.65–£2). V, MC. Daily 7am–10pm.

Ngoc Hai Restaurant ★ VIETNAMESE/CHINESE   Just down the street from the market, this local spot is two floors of bright, clean, indoor/outdoor dining. It's nothing spectacular, but the staff is friendly and the menu is ambitious; ask for anything, and you'll hear hearty replies of "Have, have." Selections from the Western end of the spectrum include roasted chicken with potatoes and a mock-up of British fish and chips, but go for the Chinese-influenced Vietnamese stir-fries, one-dish meals, and soups. Reasonable set menus are a safe bet. Good veggie selections, too.

6 Nguyen Thi Minh Khai St. ⓒ **063/825-252**. Main courses US$2–US$5.35 (£1.10–£2.95); set menus US$3.35–US$8 (£1.85–£4.40). Daily 9am–10pm.

V Café ★★ *Finds* CONTINENTAL   It's good for the budget and good for the tummy here at homey V Café. Tell me where you can sit at a table with linen and candles and enjoy a great burger for a buck? You'll also find the only burritos in town here. The owner, V, and her husband, Michael, a long-time expat, serve up hospitality smothered in gravy and will welcome you as their own. The place is full of travelers and expats, but there's room for one more. Pull up a chair!

1/1 Bui Thi Xuan St. (across from Sinh Café). ⓒ **063/837-576**. Main courses 10,000VND–40,000VND (US65¢–US$2.50/£0.35–£1.40). No credit cards. Daily 8:30am–10pm.

SNACKS & CAFES

Nguyen Chi Thanh Street is lined with cafes, one indistinguishable from the next in many ways. Each building hangs over the main market street and all serve ice cream, tea, and beer to ogling couples. Try **Coffee Artista** (9 Nguyen Chi Thanh St.; ⓒ **063/821-749**) for good ice cream, classic rock, and friendly folks. Just next door, the **Viethung Internet Café** (ⓒ **063/835-737**) has laid-back porch seating.

For a peek into the local arts scene, see if you can find Mr. **MPK** (you have to ask him what it means). He makes his home at the back of a little villa guesthouse overlooking a beautiful valley (Khach San Van Khanh; 11/8 Khoi Nghia Bac Son, up in the hills near the Bao Dai Palace II). MPK is an inspired photographer, best when he is up close to his subject. He uses a rusty old camera and turns the lens backwards, shooting through a rough-hewn tube to get incredible macro close-ups. Have a coffee, peruse his photos, and buy something (if he's selling). A unique visit. Also see his works at **V Café** (above).

WHAT TO SEE & DO

Much of what there is to see in Dalat is natural: Lakes, waterfalls, and dams dominate the tourist trail. Sights are spread over quite some distance, so consider booking a tour or renting your own car or motorbike with driver. *Note:* Avoid visiting pagodas between 11:30am and 2pm, when nuns and monks have their lunch. You might disturb them and also miss a valuable opportunity for a chat. You should also leave one or two thousand dong in the donation box near the altar.

Bao Dai's Palace ⟨★⟩   Completed in 1938, this monument to bad taste provided Bao Dai, Vietnam's last emperor, with a place of rest and respite with his family. It has never been restored and, indeed, looks veritably untouched since the emperor's ousting and hasty exile; on a busy weekend in high season, you might get a rush by pretending you're here to liberate the place and are part of the looting masses—it's not hard to imagine, with the crowds ignoring any velvet ropes and posing for pictures in the aging velvet furniture. You'll be asked to go in stocking feet or wear loose shoe covers, which make it fun for sliding around the home's 26 rooms, including Bao Dai's office and the bedrooms of the royal family. You can still see the grease stains on Bao Dai's hammock pillow and the ancient steam bath in which he soaked. The explanations are in English; most concern Bao Dai's family members. There is pathos in reading them and piecing together the mundane fate of the former royals: This prince has a "technical" job, while that one is a manager for an insurance company. There are three other Bao Dai palaces in town, the Sofitel Dalat Palace hotel among them, but this is the best choice.
South of Xuan Huong Lake and up the hill behind "Crazy House." Admission 5,000VND (US30¢/ £0.20). Daily 7am–8pm.

Dalat Market (Cho Da Lat) ⟨★★★⟩   Huge, crowded, and stuffed with produce of all varieties, this is the top stroll-through destination in Dalat. Come see all the local specialties—and even have a try! Some of the vendors will be happy to give you a sample of local wine or a few candied strawberries. Dalat in general is low on the annoying touts who plague the big towns and tourist sights in Vietnam, and entreaties from the merchants here are friendly; you can walk around without too much hassle since the locals are doing all the shopping.
Central Dalat. Daily from early morning until night.

Dalat Railway Station (Cremaillaire Railway)   Built in 1943, the Dalat station offers an atmospheric slice of the area's colonial history. You can see an authentic old wood-burning steamer train on the tracks to the rear, and stroll around inside looking at the iron-grilled ticket windows, empty now. Although the steamer train no longer makes tourist runs, a newer Japanese train makes a trip to Trai Mat Street and the Linh Phuoc Pagoda (below). The ride costs US$5 (£2.75) and leaves when full.
Near Xuan Huong Lake, off Nguyen Trai St. Daily 8am–5pm.

French Quarter ⟨★★⟩   The whole town has the look and feel of a French replica, but on the ridge-running road, Tran Hung Dao, don't miss the derelict shells of the many

French colonial summer homes; it's where the connected and successful came to escape the Saigon summer heat. Most are owned by the folks at Sofitel, and who's to say what will become of them in years to come, but they are a beautiful and eerie reminder of the recent colonial past. The road itself, one you'll take to many of the sights outside of town, offers panoramic views.

Follow Tran Hung Dao Rd. a few kilometers southeast from town. Some of the houses are on private roads at the ends of promontories. Best visited by motorbike or car w/driver.

Hang Nga Guest House and Art Gallery ("Crazy House") ★★ *Kids* This Gaudí-meets-*Sesame Street* theme park is one not to miss. It's a wild mass of wood and wire fashioned into the shape of a giant treehouse and smoothed over in concrete. It sounds simple, but there's a vision to this chaos; just ask the eccentric owner/proprietor and chief architect, Ms. Dang Viet Nga. Daughter of aristocracy, Ms. Nga is well heeled after early schooling in China and a degree in architecture from a university in Moscow. In Dalat, she has been inspired to undertake this shrine to the curved line, what she calls an essential mingling of nature and people. The locals deem her eccentric, but she's just misunderstood; don't pass up any opportunity to have a chat with her. On a visit here, you'll follow a helpful guide and are sure to have fun clambering around the concrete ladders, tunnels, hollowed-out nooks, and unique "theme" rooms of this huge fantasy tree trunk. It's an actual guesthouse, too. It says a lot about Vietnam's refreshingly lax zoning laws, but to many it's an interesting, evolving piece of pop art—a fun place to visit.

3 Huynh Thuc Khang St. ✆ **063/822-070**. Admission 6,000VND (US40¢/£0.20). Daily 7am–7pm.

Lake of Sighs (Ho Than Tho) ★ This lake has such romantic connotations for the Vietnamese that you would think it was created by a fairy godmother rather than French dam work. Legend has it that a 15-year-old girl named Thuy drowned herself after her boyfriend of the same age, Tam, fell in love with another. Her gravestone supposedly still stands on the side of the lake, marked with the incense and flowers left by other similarly heartbroken souls (even though the name on the headstone reads "Thao," not "Thuy"). The place is crammed with honeymooners in paddle boats and motorboats.

Northeast of town, along Ho Xuan Huong Rd. Admission 5,000VND (US30¢/£0.20). Daily 7am–5pm.

Lam Ty Ni Pagoda (Home of Thay Vien Thuc, "The Crazy Monk") A visit with the man is a highlight for some and just plain creepy for others. The temple itself is nothing special, though the immaculate garden in the back is nice; the real attraction is the studio of Mr. Thuc, a Vietnamese Zen practitioner who seems to be painting, drawing, and scribbling his way to nirvana. It's a unique glimpse into the inner sanctum of a true eccentric, and though locals say that he's not a real monk, just a painter and salesman, it's an interesting visit. A polyglot afflicted with graphophilia perhaps (a language genius who can't stop drawing), Mr. Thuc has a message of peace and connectedness characteristic of the Zen sect, and he conveys that message in Vietnamese, Chinese, French, English, Japanese, German, and Swedish as he continually cranks out poems with small stylized drawings while you talk with him. For US$1 (bargain if you will), he'll scribble an original before your eyes and pose for a photo. You're free to ask questions, browse his stacks of finished works in the studio, and sign the guest book. This is a standard stop on city/country tours.

2 Thien My. ✆ **063/822-775**. Free admission, but most feel obliged (or compelled) to buy one of his paintings.

Linh Phuoc Pagoda ⚡ Here is another example of one of Vietnam's fantasyland glass-and-ceramic mosaic structures. Refurbished in 1996, this modern temple features a huge golden Buddha in the main hall, plus three floors of walls and ceilings painted with fanciful murals. Go to the top floor for the eye-boggling Bodhisattva room and views of the surrounding countryside. In the garden to the right, there is a 3m-high (10-ft.) dragon climbing in and out of a small lake. You'll find very cool little nooks and crannies to explore.

At the end of Trai Mat St. (20 min. by car or bike). Daily 8am–5pm.

Prenn Falls ⚡ The falls are quite impressive, especially after a good rain. You can ride a rattle-trap cable car over them if you're brave, or else follow a stone path behind the falling water (prepare to get your feet wet). That's a minor thrill, of course, but the true Prenn experience is all about staged photos for Vietnamese tourists: couples preening, boys acting macho, and girls looking wan and forlorn. Professional photographers run the show and pose their willing actors on a small wooden bridge, on the back of a costumed horse, with an arm around a guy in a bear suit, on a small inflatable raft in front of the falls, or perched in one of the cool treehouses high above (be careful of the loose rungs when climbing up). Come here to have a laugh and observe until you find out that, as a foreign tourist, it's you that's being observed; in that case, say "Xin Chao" or return a few "hellos" and go from there (you'll be getting your photo snapped for sure). You might walk away with some new chums, not to mention some tourist tchotchkes, if that's your wont (plastic samurai sword, anyone?).

At the foot of Prenn Mountain pass, 10km (6¼ miles) from Dalat. Admission 6,000VND (US40¢/£0.20). Daily 7am–5pm.

Thien Vuong Pagoda ⚡ Otherwise known as the Chinese Pagoda, built as it was by the local Chinese population, this 1958 structure is unremarkable except for its serene setting among the hills of Dalat and the very friendly nuns who inhabit it. It does have three awe-inspiring sandalwood Buddhist statues that have been dated to the 16th century: Dai The Chi Bo Tat, god of power; Amitabha or Sakyamuni, Buddha; and Am Bo Tat, god of mercy. Each is 4m (13 ft.) high and weighs 1½ tons.

3km (2 miles) southeast of town at the end of Khe Sanh St. Daily 9am–5pm.

Truc Lam (Bamboo Forest) Zen Monastery ⚡⚡ What's refreshing is that you can walk around Truc Lam with no harassment, unlike many other temples and most pagodas in Vietnam. This is a working temple, and though it's packed with tourists at certain times of the day, you'll be wandering amid meditation halls and classrooms that are utilitarian, not museum pieces. You'll get to see monks at work and have an informative glimpse into the daily rhythms of temple life. The complex was completed in 1994 with the aim of giving new life to the Truc Lam Yen Tu Zen sect, a uniquely Vietnamese form of Zen founded during the Tran Dynasty (1225–1400). Adherents practice self-reliance and realization through meditation. The shrine, the main building, is notable mainly for its simple structure and peaceful air. There is a large relief sculpture of Boddhidarma, Zen's wild-eyed Indian heir, at the rear of the main temple. The scenery around the monastery, with views of the nearby man-made lake, Tuyen Lam Lake, and surrounding mountains is breathtaking. Truc Lam can now be reached by a scenic **tram ride** from a hilltop overlooking Dalat; a motorbike or taxi to the tram station costs little, and the round-trip is 50,000VND (US$3.15/£1.70).

Near Tuyen Lam Lake, 6km (3¾ miles) from Dalat. A popular spot on any countryside tour. Daily 7am–5pm.

Valley of Love 🐝🐝   The Valley of Love is scenic headquarters in Dalat and a popular stopover for honeymooners. It's a good place to find some real bizarre kitsch, the kind whose precedent can only be roadside America. We're talking guys in bear suits and huge-headed cowboys with guns that spout "bang" flags. There are a few nice paths among the rolling hills and quaint little lakes, and everyone enjoys the antics of Vietnamese honeymooners zipping around on motorboats and posing for pictures with guys in fuzzy jumpsuits. Don't miss it.

Phu Dong Thien Vuong St., about 3.2km (2 miles) north of town center. Admission 5,000VND (US30¢/£0.20). Daily 6am–5pm.

Xuan Huong Lake 🐝🐝   Once a trickle originating in the Lat village, Dalat's centerpiece, Xuan Huong, was created from a dam project that was finished in 1923, demolished by a storm in 1932, and reconstructed and rebuilt (with heavier stone) in 1935. You can rent windsurfers and swan-shaped paddle boats, although in two visits here I have yet to see anyone actually using them—I cannot vouch for the cleanliness of the water.

Central Dalat.

OUTDOOR ACTIVITIES

Dalat is the perfect setting for hiking and mountain biking. Check with the folks at **Phat Tire Ventures** (73 Truong Cong Dinh; ✆ **063/823-104;** see "Visitor Information & Tours," earlier in this section) for remote jungle treks to hill-tribe towns, good mountain biking, or any kind of day trip. This company is extremely amenable and can customize to your needs.

Golfers can try the impressive 18-hole course at the **Dalat Palace Golf Club** (✆ **063/821-201**). One round costs Sofitel Palace or Novotel guests US$65 (£36); all others pay US$85 (£47), plus a mandatory caddie fee of US$6 (£3.30) for 9 holes, US$12 (£6.60) for 18 holes. Call for reservations. Rental clubs and shoes are available, as are private lessons (by appointment), which begin at US$30 (£17) for a half-hour. There is a nice driving range, too.

13 Phan Thiet Town & Mui Ne Beach

This is one of the best laid-back getaways in Vietnam. **Phan Thiet** itself is a bustling little fishing port, quite picturesque and good for a day's visit. It's famous for a brand of fish sauce *(nuoc mam)* made here. The town, and especially the market, is worth exploring, but you'll definitely want to get out to the long stretch of beach to the east: the sprawling sandy shore at **Mui Ne.** This is a popular weekend escape from nearby Ho Chi Minh City (Saigon), and development in recent years has been rapid. Still, there are some very nice upscale resorts and comfy little boutique bungalow properties here.

The Nick Faldo–designed golf course at the Novotel in Phan Thiet is a big draw, and the consistent winds of Mui Ne bay bring wind- and kitesurfers from all over the world. Farther east and north along the coast are vast sand dunes, like a beachside Sahara, and inland is the famous and strangely verdant **Lotus Lake** amid the towering, shifting sands—a good day trip. These spots, as well as other small fishing villages and some local Cham ruins, make for great day trips.

GETTING THERE

Phan Thiet is just 3 to 4 hours by bus or car from Ho Chi Minh City (Saigon). The tourist-cafe buses connect here from Nha Trang and Dalat as well as Saigon, and

Sinh Café covers all the bases from its new **Mui Ne Resort** (144 Nguyen Dinh Chieu St., Ham Tien, Mui Ne; © 062/847-542; www.sinhcafevn.com). Another option is **TM Brothers,** with an office at Km 10, Nguyen Dinh Chieu St. (© 062/741-166). Any hotel front desk can make the necessary arrangements for car rental or bus tickets.

WHERE TO STAY

The Novotel is the only international standard hotel in Phan Thiet proper. Along the beach at Mui Ne, about 9km (5½ miles) to the east, you'll find a growing clutch of luxury resorts in every price range. Ask to see the hotel's beach before you commit to a place; not all are created equal. *Note:* Addresses are listed by their distance from Phan Thiet.

EXPENSIVE

Novotel Ocean Dunes & Golf Resort ☆ "Fore!" Sandwiched between Nick Faldo's golf course and an open lawn and sandy beach, the Novotel is a popular choice for both golfers and Saigon expats on holiday. It's got all the amenities of a resort, but rooms and facilities are in a "traditional" hotel style, with clean carpets and floral prints. The original hotel is an old Soviet-era resort, thus the concrete-block rooms—comfy, but small and not particularly luxe. Every unit has a balcony, though, and prices vary according to the view of the beach or the golf course. The property is right in the town of Phan Thiet, but it's insulated by the surrounding golf course and far from any road (so no honking). It's about 9km (5½ miles) to the popular beaches of Mui Ne. The beach here is narrow and rocky, but the pool area is expansive and great for kids (there's even a jungle gym). The hotel has lots of activities and rents jet skis and sailboats as well.

> **Tips** **Internet Access**
>
> You can find Internet access at most resorts at inflated prices, or check out **Coco Café** (Km 13.5; © 062/847-729), the only reasonably priced and efficient place going.

1 Ton Duc Than St., Phan Thiet. © 062/822-393. Fax 062/828-045. www.novotel.com. 123 units. US$115–US$150 (£63–£83) golf/sea view; US$210 (£116) suite; US$115–US$165 (£63–£91) villa. AE, MC, V. **Amenities:** Restaurant (indoor/outdoor seating); bar; 2 pools; golf course; 2 tennis courts; health club; watersports equipment rental; children's club and playground; concierge; tour desk; car rental; business center; wireless Internet access; shopping; salon; 24-hr. room service; massage; babysitting; laundry service; dry cleaning; nonsmoking rooms. *In room:* A/C, TV, minibar, fridge, coffeemaker, hair dryer, safe, IDD phone.

Victoria Phan Thiet Beach Resort & Spa ☆☆ Just as the road descends from Phan Thiet to meet the sandy beaches of Mui Ne, the Victoria stands on a quiet knoll overlooking the sea. The grass-and-garden property is traced by small brick paths leading to upscale bungalows. The layout is unique, with catwalks connecting the main buildings, most made of rough stone. The overall atmosphere is laid-back, private, and very family-friendly. Two different pool areas are great places to while away the day, or you can pamper yourself at the massage facility in a seaside grove. Guest rooms are large, private bungalows, some with two tiers and all done in terra cotta and dark wood; the decor is refined comfort with nice touches, like stylish indirect lighting disguised as pottery, private outdoor showers, and local artwork. Family bungalows have multiple sleeping areas and pullout couches. The newer rooms, further from the beach, are double-height and quite spacious. The beach is rocky, but the resort overlooks its own quiet cove and has beachside thatch awnings. Come for the weekend and you'll want to stay for the week.

Km 9, Phu Hai, Phan Thiet. © **062/813-000.** Fax 062/813-007. www.victoriahotels-asia.com. 50 units. US$150–US$240 (£83–£132) bungalow; US$600 (£330) villa. AE, MC, V. **Amenities:** Restaurant (indoor/outdoor dining); large thatch-roofed poolside bar areas; outdoor pool w/Jacuzzi; tennis court; small health club; all rentals available; children's club; shopping; massage; babysitting; laundry service; Wi-Fi; billiards room; private tours available. *In room:* A/C, satellite TV, minibar, fridge, coffeemaker, safe, IDD phone.

MODERATE
Coco Beach Resort
Here's that little slice of heaven you've been looking for in your hard travels along the coast. On the main strip in Mui Ne, Coco Beach doesn't look like much from the road—just a wall to keep out the noise—but it is a real seaside oasis. It was the first to build along the strip here, and it's still the best. Rooms are wooden bungalows on stilts, each with a comfy balcony, vaulted ceiling, thatch roof, and mosquito net. They're intimate and tidy, offering an authentic rustic luxury (plus maintenance here is tops—no musty smells!). Bathrooms are small but tidy, with glass shower stalls. Prices vary depending on proximity to the beautiful beach, where you'll find private lounge chairs and umbrellas. Service is attentive and genuine, the best along the main strip of Mui Ne. The resort's two restaurants, the seaside Paradise Beach Club and the more upscale Champa, are the best in town (see "Where to Dine," below). The quiet garden is a good place to just relax after a day of swimming or boating. There's even an open-air massage facility at the center.

Km 12.5 Ham Tien, Phan Thiet. © **062/847-111.** Fax 062/847-115. 31 units. US$85–US$105 (£47–£58) bungalow; US$170–US$210 (£94–£116) 2-room villa (long-stay rates available). **Amenities:** 2 restaurants; pool/beach bar; pool; Jacuzzi; motorboat/sailboat rental; children's programs; in-house tour programs; car rental; business center; limited room service; massage; babysitting; laundry service; library; Internet access. *In room:* A/C, minibar, fridge, IDD phone.

Mui Ne Sailing Club Resort
This seaside spot is owned by the same Aussie folks who run the popular Sailing Club in Nha Trang. Accommodations run the gamut from budget units with fans, like American motel rooms, to top-notch bungalows at seaside. Ask to see your room before checking in, as some are a bit musty. All units have terra-cotta tile with bamboo matting, cloth hangings, and bamboo floor lamps. There is an American Southwest feel in the artful beveled edges of the plaster walls and in the similarly rounded built-in nightstands. Large bathrooms are nicely appointed in tile and stripped-wood trim; they're separated from the bedroom by hanging cloths, a nice touch. The high-end bungalows are the best choice and worth the upgrade. The pool is small but set in a picturesque courtyard adjoining the open-air colonial-style restaurant. The owners have also added a spa, though no sauna. This is a popular stop for windsurfers and kitesurfers—both rentals and lessons are available.

24 Nguyen Dinh Chieu St., Phan Thiet. © **062/847-440.** Fax 062/847-441. www.sailingclubvietnam.com. 30 units. US$60 (£33) double; US$75–US$115 (£41–£63) bungalow. AE, MC, V. **Amenities:** Restaurant; bar; outdoor pool; spa; all rentals available; tour desk; business center w/Internet access; room service (7am–10pm); babysitting; laundry service. *In room:* A/C, satellite TV, minibar, IDD phone.

Pandanus Resort
The best of a new clutch of resorts under construction at the foot of the famous Red Sand Dunes north of Phan Thiet, this large property is as self-contained as any in Mui Ne proper, but a bit more remote. The resort is spread out, with ponds and manicured greens; the central pool area is cozy; and the beach is

expansive, though dirty and unused. Rooms vary greatly, but all are comfortable, with cool terra-cotta tile offset by dark-wood trim.

Quarter 5, Mui Ne, Phan Thiet. ✆ 062/849-849. Fax 062/849-850. www.pandanusresort.com. 134 units. US$65–US$75 (£36–£41) double; US$125 (£69) family; US$95 (£52) bungalow. MC, V. **Amenities:** Restaurant; 2 bars; outdoor pool; tennis court; small fitness center; spa; sauna, steam room; tour desk; car rental; free use of bicycles; free shuttle service; business center w/Internet access; limited room service; massage; laundry service. *In room:* A/C, satellite TV, minibar, fridge, coffeemaker, hair dryer, IDD phone.

Saigon Mui Ne Resort ✿   The Saigon Mui Ne is the most popular spot in town for larger group tours. Run by Saigontourist, the resort has all the amenities, but not a lot of charm. Rooms are comparable to any in this category in town, but there's that hazy indifference of a government-run, tour-group hotel. The good news: the affordable rates and the many amenities. The sprawling property has manicured lawns and tidy bungalows with terra-cotta tile floors, wrought-iron furniture, and bathrooms with granite counters and bamboo latticework. The hotel-block rooms are spacious, but go for a bungalow with balcony, ideally facing the sea or the pool area. There is talk of a casino soon, heaven help us.

Km 12.3 Ham Tien, Phan Thiet. ✆ 062/847-302. Fax 062/847-307. www.saigonmuineresort.com. 87 units. US$50–US$95 (£28–£52) double (bungalow or hotel block); US$125 (£69) family room. AE, MC, V. **Amenities:** Restaurant; beachside bar; nice courtyard pool; tennis court; Jacuzzi; sauna; all rentals available; Saigontourist tour desk; car rental; salon; 24-hr. room service; massage; laundry service; Internet access. *In room:* A/C, TV, minibar, fridge, IDD phone.

INEXPENSIVE

Budget options line the main drag in Mui Ne. The scene is constantly changing, but expect to pay US$8 to US$15 (£4.40–£8.25) for basic guesthouse accommodations. If you come by cafe bus, you'll be taken around to shop for a spot you like. It gets cheaper and more rustic the farther east you go on the main road.

Sinh Café, ever expanding its monopoly of the budget-traveler market in Vietnam (it runs all the buses), has just opened the **Mui Ne Resort** (144 Nguyen Dinh Chieu St., Ham Tien; ✆ 062/847-542; www.sinhcafevn.com), a 48-room hotel on the furthest end of Mui Ne. If you come by one of its buses, it'll strand you here as long as it can in the hopes that you'll stay. Rooms start at US$20 (£11) and aren't a bad bet. There's a pool and all the basics. A festive atmosphere prevails (lots of young partyers).

Another good choice is **Full Moon Beach** (14km/8¾ miles from Phan Thiet, Thon 3–Xa Ham Tien; contact Phuong or Pascal at ✆ 062/847-008; www.windsurf-vietnam.com). A popular spot for kitesurfers and windsurfers, it offers everything from wood perches overlooking the beach to midrange comfort in the newest building.

WHERE TO DINE

The **Mui Ne Sailing Club** (24 Nguyen Dinh Chieu St., Ham Tien; ✆ 062/847-440) serves good, basic Western in a nice open-air building at poolside overlooking the ocean. Farther east, **Full Moon Beach** (14km/8¾ miles from Phan Thiet, Thon 3–Xa Ham Tien; ✆ 062/847-008) is a good stop for coffee or breakfast on your way to Lotus Lake or the big dunes north of town.

Thatched-roof eateries line the main beachside road in Mui Ne. **Luna d' Autuno** (Km 12 Ham Tien; ✆ 062/847-591), a popular Saigon pizzeria, has a cool new restaurant under a high thatched roof. **Good Morning Vietnam Restaurant** (Km 11.8 Ham Tien; ✆ 091/802-2760), a branch of Vietnam's pizza and pasta franchise, serves affordable, familiar meals. The **Hot Rock** (Km 12.5, across from Bien Xanh

Resort; © **062/847-608**) is a good late-night hangout where you can get basic Western fare like fresh, grilled seafood.

Paradise Beach Club ✹ SEAFOOD   Set in a soothing seaside pavilion at the popular Coco Beach Resort (see "Where to Stay," above), the Paradise Beach Club is the place for fine fresh seafood and barbecue. Choose from a raw bar and have it cooked to order. The menu covers everything from light snacks and sandwiches to hearty Western meals. For dessert, check out the unique sundaes. The resort's more upscale restaurant, **Champa,** is also a great choice, but only for dinner.

At the Coco Beach Resort, Km 12.5, Ham Tien. © **062/847-111**. Main courses 30,000VND–200,000VND (US$1.90–US$13/£1.05–£6.90). MC, V. Daily 6:30am–11pm.

WHAT TO SEE & DO

At **Cape Mui Ne** ✹✹, some 20km (13 miles) northeast of town, you'll find Mui Ne's sprawling sand dunes. A trip out this way brings you through lots of quaint seaside villages that are worth a look. Coming from Mui Ne Beach, you'll first reach a small fishing town with a fine little rural market—great in the early morning. Heading inland away from the beach, you'll come to the towering **Red Dunes** ✹✹. A walk to the top offers views of the town and surrounding countryside; you're sure to be followed by a gaggle of friendly kids trying to sell you on the idea of renting one of their plastic sleds for the ride down the steep dune slopes—kind of fun. From the Red Dunes, if you have time, take a long and bumpy ride to unique **Lotus Lake** ✹✹. The views of the coast are dynamic, and this unique verdant lake in the parched silver dune makes the trip worth it. It's a long day, though. Ask at any hotel for tour arrangements. Expect to pay US$14 (£7.70) per person for two or more to go to the tip of the cape and the Red Dunes, more to go inland.

At the highest point on the road between Phan Thiet Town and Mui Ne Beach, you won't miss **Cham Tower,** an impressive spire of crumbling brick. The tower dates from the end of the 13th century and is worth a stop if you weren't able to catch any of the Cham sites near Hoi An and Danang. Any taxi will be happy to make a brief stop on the way. There are also Cham sites some 2 hours' drive inland near Phan Rang; all hotels can arrange tours.

Phan Thiet Market ✹ is a large but pretty standard central market in town. This is where you can pick up a bottle of locally made *nuoc mam* (fish sauce). Go early for the bringing in of the day's catch, and don't forget your camera.

OUTDOOR ACTIVITIES

The wind conditions in Mui Ne are steady and strong in the dry season (Oct–May), and the beach is becoming a real kitesurfing and windsurfing mecca (it's over 12 knot winds for two-thirds of the year). **Jibe's** (Km 14, Ham Tien, Muin Ne; © **062/847-405**; www.windsurf-vietnam.com), a popular rental shop, windsurfer club, and bar, is a good place to check in or rent a board. It's also a great opportunity for first-time kitesurfers: A 2-hour private lesson with an IKO-certified instructor, including gear, starts at just US$100 (£55). The focus is on safety, of course, and the savings are significant here (similar lessons elsewhere cost a mint).

Sailors will want to contact the folks at the **Mui Ne Sailing Club** (24 Nguyen Dinh Chieu St., Ham Tien, Phan Thiet; © **062/847-440**), or at any hotel or resort, about renting Hobie Cat and Laser sailboats, windsurfers, jet skis, and runabouts.

Finally, the outstanding Nick Faldo–designed **Ocean Dunes Golf Course** (1 Ton Duc Than St., Phan Thiet; © **062/821-511**) is a big draw here in town.

14 Ho Chi Minh City (Saigon) ★★

Ho Chi Minh City—or Saigon, as it is once again commonly known—is a relatively young Asian city, founded in the 18th century. Settled mainly by civil-war refugees from northern Vietnam as well as Chinese merchants, it quickly became a major commercial center. When the French took over the country they called Cochin China, Saigon became the capital. After the French left in 1954, Saigon remained the capital of South Vietnam until national reunification in 1975.

Saigon is still Vietnam's commercial headquarters, brash and busy, with a keen sense of its own importance. Located on the Saigon River, it's Vietnam's major port and largest city, with a population of almost seven million people. True to its reputation, the city is noisy, crowded, and dirty, but the central business district is rapidly developing in steel-and-glass precision to rival any metropolis on the globe. Still, the old Saigon survives in wide downtown avenues flanked by pristine colonials. Hectic and eclectic, this place has an attitude all its own.

Some of Saigon's tourism highlights include the **Vietnam History Museum;** the grisly **War Remnants Museum;** and **Cholon,** the Chinese district, with its pagodas and exotic stores. **Dong Khoi Street**—formerly fashionable Rue Catinat during the French era and Tu Do, or Freedom Street, during the American war—is still lined with grand colonial hotels, chic shops, and cafes. The food in Saigon is some of the best Vietnam has to offer, the nightlife sparkles, and the shopping is good. The city is also a logical jumping-off point for excursions to other southern destinations: the Mekong Delta (p. 404), the Cu Chi Tunnels (p. 403), and Phan Thiet Town and Mui Ne Beach (see previous section).

GETTING THERE

BY PLANE   Most regional airlines connect with Ho Chi Minh, including Malaysian Airlines, Thai Airways, Bangkok Airways, Silk Air/Singapore Airlines, Lao Airlines, Garuda Indonesia, Philippine Airlines, United Airlines, and Cathay Pacific. **Vietnam Airlines** usually has the best fares, thanks to government controls; to confirm or book flights, you can call its local office at 116 Nguyen Hue, District 1 (✆ **08/829-2118;** fax 08/823-8454). If you're flying to Vietnam directly from North America, check with **United Airlines** and **Cathay Pacific** for good fares and itineraries. Domestically, Ho Chi Minh City (Saigon) is linked by Vietnam Airlines flights from Hanoi, Hue, Danang, Hoi An, Nha Trang, and Dalat.

At the **Tan Son Nhat International Airport,** you can change foreign currency for VND, but taxi drivers to town won't mind payment in U.S. dollars, either. Arranging a hotel limousine to greet you will certainly make life a bit easier, but taxis are plentiful outside the arrivals hall. The trip to town is US$5 (£2.75). To get to the airport, if you can't find a cab on the street, call **Airport Taxi** (✆ **08/844-6666**).

BY BUS/MINIVAN   By bus, Saigon is about 5½ hours from Dalat, the nearest major city. All of the cafe buses connect here, of course, and line the streets around the Pham Ngu Lao area. See "Visitor Information & Tours," below.

BY CAR   For safety reasons alone, if you're taking wheels, it is better to book a minivan with a tour or group.

GETTING AROUND

Saigon is divided into districts, as is Hanoi, and is very easy to navigate. Be sure to know the district along with the address of your destinations, and try to group your

Ho Chi Minh City (Saigon)

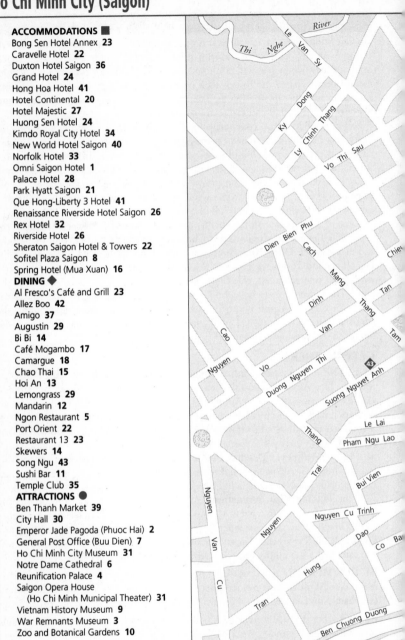

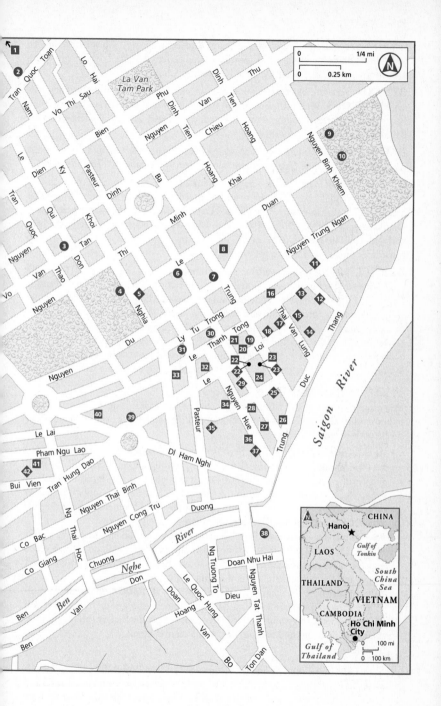

La Van Tam Park

Saigon River

sightseeing accordingly (avoid criss-crossing districts in a day). Most of the hotels, bars, shops, and restaurants are in District 1, easily covered on foot, while sightseeing attractions are spread among Districts 1, 3, and 5 (Cholon).

BY TAXI   Taxis are clustered around the bigger hotels and restaurants. They cost 12,000VND (US75¢/£0.40) to start and 6,000VND or so (US40¢/£0.20) for every kilometer thereafter. If you need to call ahead, try **Airport Taxi** (© **08/844-6666**) or **Saigon Taxi** (© **08/822-6688**).

BY CAR   You can simplify your sightseeing efforts if you hire a car and driver for the day from **Ann Tours** or **Saigontourist** (see "Visitor Information & Tours," below).

BY MOTORBIKE/BICYCLE   Saigon is cursed with the country's most chaotic traffic, so you might want to think twice before renting a motorbike or bicycle, which aren't as easily available as in other towns. You can, however, hop a **motorcycle taxi—** a quick trip is 5,000VND (US30¢/£0.20), while hourly booking can be in the ball-park of 15,000VND (US95¢/£0.50) with some haggling. It's a bit hair-raising sometimes, but a good way to get around.

BY CYCLO   Cyclos are available for an hourly rental of about 20,000VND (US$1.25/£0.70), but they simply are not a good option in Saigon, especially outside District 1. First, drivers have an odd habit of not speaking English (or indeed, any other language) halfway through your trip and taking you to places you never asked to see, or driving around in circles pretending to be confused. Second, riding in a slow, open conveyance amid thousands of motorbikes and cars is unpleasant and dangerous—plus cyclo passengers are low to the ground and in the front, functioning something like a bumper. Third, drive-by thefts from riders are common even during daylight hours!

VISITOR INFORMATION & TOURS

Every major tourist agency has its headquarters or a branch in Saigon. All will be able to book tours and travel throughout the city and the southern region, and usually the countryside as well.

- **Ann Tours** (58 Ton That Tung St., District 1; © **08/833-2564** or 08/833-4356; fax 08/832-3866; www.anntours.com) has a great reputation that is well deserved. It specializes in custom tours for individuals and small groups. It can be relatively expensive, but that's compared to the seat-in-coach cattle-drive tours. These guys will help you with virtually anything you want to do in Vietnam. Ask for director Tony Nong, and tell him Frommer's sent you.

- **Exotissimo Travel** (Saigon Trade Center, 37 Ton Duc Than, District 1; © **08/825-1723;** fax 08/829-5800; www.exotissimo.com) has a chic downtown office and can arrange just about any tour or international itinerary. It's popular with expats and has convenient offices throughout the region.

- **Saigontourist** (49 Le Thanh Ton St., District 1; © **08/824-4554;** fax 08/822-4987; www.saigontourist.net) is a large government-run group, but it'll get you where you want to go and is a far better choice than the budget cafes (below). It maintains desks in the Majestic, Rex, and Sheraton hotels.

BUDGET TOURS

- **Sinh Café** (246–248 De Tham St., District 1; © **08/369-420** or 08/836-9322; sinhcafevietnam@hcm.vnn.vn) is a backpacker's choice for inexpensive travel and tours. On paper, the tours seem exactly the same as others offered through private tour agents, but the price tags are cheaper.

- **TM Brothers** (269 De Tham St. or 139 Bui Vien St., District 1; ✆ **08/836-1791**) is pure "same-same but different here" compared to the various tourist cafes. It's a good place to compare with Sinh.
- **TNK** (230 De Tham St.; ✆ **08/837-8276;** www.tnktravelvietnam.com) is just another of the many options.

FAST FACTS: Ho Chi Minh City (Saigon)

American Express AmEx is represented in Saigon by **Exotissimo Travel** (Saigon Trade Center, 37 Ton Duc Thang St.; ✆ **08/825-1723**). *Be warned:* It does not provide complete travel services, but can direct you if you lose your card. Hours are Monday through Friday from 8am to 5pm.

Currency Exchange You can change money in banks, hotels, and jewelry stores. The exchange rate in Saigon is better than in many smaller cities. There's a convenient currency-exchange storefront at 4C Le Loi St., right in the town center—a good spot for the right rates on traveler's checks.

Major banks include: **ANZ Bank**, 11 Me Linh Sq., District 1 (✆ **08/829-9319**); **Citibank**, 115 Nguyen Hue St., District 1 (✆ **824-2118**); **HSBC**, 75 Pham Hong Thai St., District 1 (✆ **08/829-2288**); and **Vietcombank**, 29 Ben Chuong Duong, District 1 (✆ **08/829-7245**). ANZ Bank, Citibank, and HSBC all have **ATMs** dispensing dollars and VND around the clock.

Embassies & Consulates For embassies, see "Fast Facts: Vietnam," p. 296. Consulates are all in District 1, as follows: **U.S.,** 4 Le Duan St. (✆ **08/822-9433**); **Canada,** 235 Dong Khoi St. (✆ **08/824-5025**); **Australia,** 5B Ton Duc Thang St. (✆ **08/829-6035**); **New Zealand,** 41 Nguyen Thi Minh Khai St. (✆ **08/822-6908**); and **U.K.,** 25 Le Duan St. (✆ **08/829-8433**).

Emergencies For police, dial ✆ **113;** for fire, dial ✆ **114;** and for an ambulance, dial ✆ **115.** Have a translator on hand, if necessary; operators don't speak English.

Internet Access Almost every upscale hotel provides Internet services, but you can bet they charge a pretty penny. You won't find any service on Dong Khoi, but a short walk in any direction brings you to storefronts that charge an average of 200VND (US1¢/£0.006) per minute. Thumbs up to **Café Cyber Business Center** (48 Dong Du St., just off Dong Khoi in District 1; ✆ **08/823-3668**; info@cgcybercfe.com; 300VND/US2¢/£0.01 per min.) for serving drinks as well as providing full business services in a laid-back, plush atmosphere with very private terminals. Another option is **Welcome Internet** (15B Le Thanh Ton St.; ✆ **08/822-0981**). Service in the Pham Ngu Lao backpacker area is fast and cheap; Internet cafes line De Tham and charge 5,000VND per hour (US30¢/£0.20 per min.).

Mail The main post office is at 2 Coq Xu Paris, District 1 (✆ **08/823-2541** or 08/823-2542), just across from Notre Dame Cathedral. It's open daily from 6:30am to 10pm. All services are available here, including long-distance calling and callback. The building itself is a historic landmark (see "What to See & Do," later in this chapter). Postal service is also available in most hotels and at various locations throughout the city.

Safety The biggest threat to your health in Saigon is likely to be the traffic. Cross the wildly busy streets at a slow, steady pace. If you're having a really hard time getting across, find a local who is crossing and stick to his heels!

Pick-pocketing is a big problem, especially the motorbike drive-bys in which someone slashes the shoulder strap of your bag and drives off. Keep your bag close and away from traffic. Hang on to your wallet, don't wear flashy jewelry, and be especially wary in crowded places like markets. Women should avoid wandering around alone past 11pm or so. Contact your consulate or hotel if you have a serious problem. If you insist on going to the local police, bring a translator. Know that the Saigon police tend to throw up their hands at "minor" infractions such as purse snatching or thievery.

Telephones The city code for Saigon is **8.**

WHERE TO STAY

Saigon has the best variety of accommodations in Vietnam, from deluxe business and family hotels to spotless smaller options. Most hotels are clustered around Nguyen Hue Street in District 1, as are the restaurants, shops, and bars.

Remember that prices listed here are the "rack rates" and should be considered only a guideline. Internet, group, and standard promotional rates are the rule. Especially in the off season (Mar–Sept), expect discounts of up to 50%. Note that many hotels levy a VAT of up to 20%.

VERY EXPENSIVE

Caravelle Hotel Named for a type of light, fast ship, this sleek downtown hotel gives you that very impression. A French company built the original in 1956 and, after honeymoon years as the town's address of note, the place became a shabby hangout for wartime journalists and then fell into obscurity as the Doc Lap (Independence) Hotel in postwar years. In 1998, the Caravelle was renovated beyond recognition and is now an extremely attractive, efficient, and well-appointed hotel. Business travelers and well-heeled tourists enjoy the plush rooms, with neutral furnishings, firm beds, and marble bathrooms; higher floors have great views. The executive signature rooms have fax machines, computer hookups, VCRs, and CD players. The suites are luxe beyond belief. And the classic character of the old hotel lives on in the rooftop Saigon Saigon bar, an open-air colonial throwback with rattan shades, low-slung chairs, and twirling ceiling fans. If you let your imagination go, you might just see Graham Greene sidling up to the bar. The popular restaurant, Port Orient, serves fine international and Vietnamese fare. There is new competition from the nearby Sheraton and the Hyatt around the corner, but that just ups the ante on service, and the Caravelle, with its long tradition of excellence, is sure to top any list.

19 Lam Son Sq., District 1, Ho Chi Minh City. © **08/823-4999.** Fax 08/824-3999. www.caravellehotel.com. 335 units. US$230–US$280 (£127–£154) double; US$330–US$345 (£182–£190) executive double; US$380–US$1,200 (£209–£660) suite. AE, DC, MC, V. **Amenities:** 2 restaurants; 3 bars; lovely rooftop pool; top-notch health club; spa; Jacuzzi; sauna; all rentals available; tour desk; expensive but extensive business center; salon w/facials and manicures; 24-hr. room service; massage; laundry service; dry cleaning; executive-level rooms; rooms for those w/limited mobility; small casino. *In room:* A/C, satellite TV, dataport, minibar, fridge, coffeemaker, hair dryer, safe, IDD phone.

Hotel Majestic This 1925 landmark, on the riverside corner of Dong Khoi Street (formerly Rue Catinat), still has some historic charm despite many renovations—and it's a real picture-postcard colonial from the outside. Owned by Saigontourist, the Majestic is always full, as it is a good, affordable, atmospheric choice. Botched details abound on the inside, however, like tacky decor, but the rooms and facilities are still classy and comfortable for the price. High ceilings, original wood floors, and retro fixtures are a nice touch. Bathrooms are large, with tubs and old-style taps. The small courtyard pool area is lined with picturesque shuttered windows and walkways; in fact, the best choices are the deluxe rooms facing this quiet spot. Suites are just larger versions of deluxe rooms, while standards are small and quite basic. Buffet meals at the fine restaurant, Cyclo, are accompanied by either piano or traditional music and sometimes dance. The staff has a genuine desire to make your stay memorable, whether that means explaining the eccentricities of Vietnamese cuisine or hailing you a taxi. Don't miss the great views from the rooftop bar, a good spot to have a chat and popular for weddings and parties.

1 Dong Khoi St., District 1, Ho Chi Minh City. © 08/829-5514. Fax 08/829-5510. www.majesticsaigon.com.vn. 175 units. US$170 (£94) single; US$185 (£102) standard double; US$223–US$255 (£123–£140) deluxe; US$321–US$590 (£177–£325) suite. AE, DC, MC, V. **Amenities:** 2 restaurants; 3 bars; small courtyard pool; basic health club; spa; sauna; Saigontourist tour desk; car rental; business center w/Internet access; shopping; massage; babysitting; laundry service; dry cleaning. *In room:* A/C, satellite TV w/HBO, Wi-Fi, minibar, fridge, hair dryer, safe, IDD phone.

New World Hotel Saigon 🐙🐙

President Clinton called this first-rate hotel home during his brief stay in Saigon; it's a fine choice, indeed, whether you're a business traveler, tourist, or world leader. The location is in the very center of town, a short walk from Ben Thanh Market (p. 398). A popular park is right out front, and there's a nice bustle and feeling of connectedness to the place that's rarely found at the self-contained luxury hotels. The impeccable rooms are done in a soothing array of neutrals, while the bathrooms are a sharp contrast in black-and-gray marble. The fat pillows are a little mushy and the beds are a bit too firm, but you can't have everything. The executive floors have a lounge and an impressive list of perks: all-day refreshments, free pressing, computer hookups, and free access to financial newswire information. The staff snaps to; service is ultraefficient. It's also one of the few hotels that asks straightaway if you'd like a nonsmoking room.

76 Le Lai St., District 1, Ho Chi Minh City. © 08/822-8888. Fax 08/823-0710. www.newworldvietnam.com. 536 units. US$160 (£88) double; US$230–US$320 (£127–£176) executive double; from US$300 (£176) suite. AE, DC, MC, V. **Amenities:** 2 restaurants; bar; outdoor pool; lighted tennis court; health club; spa; sauna; all rentals available; concierge; tour desk; business center; shopping; 24-hr. room service; massage; babysitting; laundry service; dry cleaning; executive-level rooms. *In room:* A/C, satellite TV, Internet access, minibar, fridge, coffeemaker, safe, IDD phone.

Omni Saigon Hotel 🐙🐙

Once quarters for the C.I.A. and later the U.S. army, the hotel's edifice recalls a Soviet-era post office. Inside is another story. The lobby, with a colonial flavor and Art Deco details, is gorgeous. The rooms are quite comfortable, and the amenities—like the many fine-dining outlets, popular Irish pub Mulligan's, and extensive fitness center—rival those of any hotel in town. Here's the drawback: Though it's just 10 minutes from the airport, you're in District 3 and some 15 minutes from town. Shuttles and taxis are consistent, but traffic can be hellish and you might feel distanced from the action. There are many perks, though: Rooms are luxurious and well equipped, done in a somewhat formal but immaculate decor. The executive floor has a small business center, in-room faxes and broadband Internet access, and a particularly elegant lounge. The Omni is most popular with Asian visitors and business travelers.

253 Nguyen Van Troi St., Phu Nhuan District (District 3), Ho Chi Minh City. (C) **08/844-9222.** Fax 08/844-9198. www.omnisaigonhotel.com. 240 units. US$90–US$120 (£50–£66) double; US$150 (£83) executive double; US$250–US$500 (£138–£275) suite. Long-stay rates available. AE, DC, MC, V. **Amenities:** 4 restaurants; bar; outdoor patio pool; health club; nice spa; Jacuzzi; sauna; steam room; tour desk; car rental; business center w/Internet access; shopping; salon; 24-hr. room service; massage; babysitting; laundry service; book-borrowing corner; executive-level rooms. *In room:* A/C, TV, dataport, minibar, fridge, hair dryer, safe, IDD phone.

Park Hyatt Saigon (★★★ The brand-new kid on the block, the Park Hyatt manages to capture the old feel of Vietnam while integrating all the modern amenities worthy of a world-class hotel. Lines are clean and elegant, and teak floors and antique glass combine with traditional lacquer to create instant nostalgia. The rooms, which feel like a Vietnamese residence, are spacious and well appointed; some have verandas that open directly onto the pool. Modern features include soundproofed windows and 25-inch flatscreen TVs. That outdoor pool—with midstream jets to massage you while you swim—and the accompanying landscaped green space give the place a resort feel. On-site restaurants include Square One, which serves seafood and Vietnamese along with grilled steaks, and Opera, which is strictly Italian down to its exclusively Italian wine list. The Park Hyatt lacks a wartime or French colonial history, so any nostalgia you may feel here is carefully designed. That said, the hotel is becoming the hot spot for international jet-setters (the private driveway and back entrance help), and Brad Pitt and Angelina Jolie were rumored to have stayed here in 2006. Still, you don't have to be the biggest superstar in the world to find the Park Hyatt a good choice for a luxury stay in the center of Saigon.

2 Lam Son Sq., District 1, Ho Chi Minh City. (C) **08/824-1234.** Fax 08/823-7569. www.saigon.park.hyatt.com. 252 units. US$180–US$350 (£99–£193) double; US$560–US$2,260 (£308–£1243) suite. AE, MC, V. **Amenities:** 2 restaurants; bar/lounge; outdoor pool; health club; spa; Jacuzzi; concierge; tour desk; car rental; business center w/Internet access; shopping; salon; 24-hr. room service; massage; babysitting; laundry service; dry cleaning; executive-level rooms; rooms for those w/limited mobility; cooking classes. *In room:* A/C, flatscreen satellite TV, high-speed Internet access, minibar, coffeemaker, hair dryer, safe, IDD phone.

Renaissance Riverside Hotel Saigon (★ Managed by Marriott, the Renaissance Riverside is a convenient downtown address. The lobby is done in a colonial theme with a grand spiral staircase connecting to the mezzanine. Rooms have black-and-white tile entries, tidy carpeting, and light furnishings done in cool pastels. Electronic control panels near the headboard might remind you of a 1970s bachelor pad. Bathrooms have black-marble counters. You could be anywhere, really—everything's nice in the same way an upscale hotel might look in Bangkok, Paris, or Pittsburgh; nevertheless, the amenities, like the small rooftop pool and health club, are good. The Riverside is a popular business hotel, which means smoking everywhere: All public spaces are a bit musty, even on designated nonsmoking floors. If you want a nonsmoking room, ask to see it before checking in. Don't miss the dim sum lunch at the fine Cantonese restaurant, Kabin.

8–15 Ton Duc Thang St., District 1, Ho Chi Minh City. **08/822-0033.** Fax 08/823-5666. www.renaissancehotels.com/ sgnbr. 349 units. US$135 (£74) single/double; US$250–US$700 (£138–£385) suite. AE, MC, V. **Amenities:** 2 restaurants; bar; rooftop pool w/great city view; health club; nice massage/spa facility; all rentals available; concierge; business center; shopping; 24-hr. room service; babysitting; nonsmoking rooms; executive-level rooms. *In room:* A/C, satellite TV, dataport, minibar, fridge, coffeemaker, iron, safe, IDD phone.

Sheraton Saigon Hotel & Towers (★★ The tallest, most expensive, and one of the newest hotels in Ho Chi Minh, the Sheraton is the talk of the town. Everything is done on a grand scale, from colossal meeting rooms and top business facilities to plush guest rooms. It's high-end comfort from a brand that you can bank on. Rooms have it all: flatscreen TVs, broadband Internet, large desks, and great views of town. Bathrooms are huge, with separate shower and tub. The Sheraton seemingly covers every amenity, from a host of fine-dining options to the spa area (with squash courts and an outdoor pool) to the popular **Level 23** nightspot, which plays host to live bands on the 23rd floor. From the moment your car pulls up out front, you'll know you've arrived: Every guest here is given the red-carpet treatment.

88 Dong Khoi St., District 1, Ho Chi Minh City. (C) 08/827-2828. Fax 08/827-2929. www.sheraton.com/saigon. 382 units. US$180–US$240 (£99–£132) double; US$260–US$440 (£143–£242) suite. AE, MC, V. **Amenities:** 4 restaurants; 2 bars; outdoor pool; tennis courts; health club; spa; Jacuzzi; steam room; concierge; tour desk; car rental; airport limousine; business center; shopping; 24-hr room service; massage; babysitting; laundry service; dry cleaning; nonsmoking rooms; executive-level rooms (w/separate check-in). *In room:* A/C, satellite TV, Internet access, minibar, fridge, coffeemaker, hair dryer, safe, IDD phone.

Sofitel Plaza Saigon ☆☆
The Sofitel chain is famous in Southeast Asia for finding grand old colonial dames and converting them into the most charming hotels. This is not one of them. Opened in 1999, the Sofitel Plaza is one of the shiny new towers on the Saigon skyline; what it lacks in colonial charm, however, it more than makes up for in luxury, convenience, and comfort. Accommodations are handsome, with fine Art Deco touches like the curving, clean-lined desks in most rooms. You'll never lack for any amenity here, and the staff is helpful and professional. In a convenient spot just across from the former U.S. and French embassies, this is a popular choice for the international business crowd and long-stay executives, who enjoy the sleek executive floor with private lounge, buffet, drinks, and business services.

17 Le Duan Blvd., District 1, Ho Chi Minh City. (C) **800/221-4542** in the U.S., or 08/824-1555. Fax 08/824-1666. www. sofitel.com. 290 units. US$140 (£77) superior; US$250–US$1,500 (£138–£825) suite. AE, MC, V. **Amenities:** 2 restaurants; bar; luxury rooftop pool; health club; spa; sauna; steam room; concierge; car rental; business center w/Internet access; 24-hr. room service; massage; babysitting; laundry service; dry cleaning; nonsmoking rooms; executive-level rooms. *In room:* A/C, satellite TV, dataport, minibar, fridge, coffeemaker, safe, IDD phone.

EXPENSIVE
Duxton Hotel Saigon ☆☆
Formerly the Prince before becoming part of the popular Australian chain, the Duxton Saigon is efficient, affordable, and stylish (if a bit studied). The beige rooms are tasteful, with plush beds and carpeting. The bathrooms are done in smart black-and-white marble. The lobby, entered by swooping stairs from a circular drive, is classy but not overly grand; it makes a good downtown meeting point. This place is popular with business travelers, especially those on an extended stay, who come here for all the comforts of home. The staff is efficient and personable. The spa offers excellent Hong Kong massages (ask about special midweek spa rates). Be sure to try the authentic Japanese restaurant on the mezzanine floor.

63 Nguyen Hue Blvd., District 1, Ho Chi Minh City. (C) **08/822-2999.** Fax 08/824-1888. www.duxton.com. 203 units. US$200–US$250 (£110–£138) deluxe double; US$300–US$350 (£165–£193) suite. Promotional and long-stay rates available. AE, DC, MC, V. **Amenities:** Restaurant; bar; nightclub; small health club; Jacuzzi; sauna; steam room; concierge; tour desk; car rental; business center w/Internet access; 24-hr. room service; massage; laundry service; dry cleaning; nonsmoking rooms. *In room:* A/C, satellite TV, minibar, fridge, coffeemaker, safe, IDD phone.

Grand Hotel ☆☆
This 1930s colonial, another owned by Saigontourist, is done just right (well, close, at least). The renovated Grand has a serene atmosphere, with some choice features like the lovingly restored iron elevator at center. The Grand is at its best when taking advantage of its long history, thus rooms in the older block are much more charming than the bland, chain-hotel units in the new wing. Deluxe rooms clustered in the old building near the elevator have classic high ceilings, wood

floors, and a comfortable colonial charm. All units are big, with simple dark-wood furniture—and without the musty smell that plagues many Saigon hotels. The bathrooms are small, but have plenty of counter space. The lobby is bright, the staff is friendly, and the location on Dong Khoi couldn't be better. The quiet atmosphere suggests leisure rather than business travelers, though, and the hotel boasts all the right amenities, including the central courtyard's small but peaceful pool area, a unique escape from busy Ho Chi Minh City.

8–24 Dong Khoi St., District 1, Ho Chi Minh City. © 08/823-0163. Fax 063/823-5781. www.grandsaigon.com. 107 units. US$110–US$125 (£61–£69) double; US$160 (£88) deluxe; US$260 (£143) suite. AE, MC, V. **Amenities:** 2 restaurants; bar; nice outdoor courtyard pool; small health club; Jacuzzi; sauna; tour desk; car rental; business center; shopping; salon; 24-hr. room service; massage; laundry service; dry cleaning. *In room:* A/C, satellite TV, Wi-Fi, minibar, fridge, hair dryer, safe, IDD phone.

Hotel Continental ⓡ

This hotel is a big shame. It's not that it's so bad really, but it could have been a world-class heritage hotel—instead, it's a shambles, thanks to the shortsightedness of the folks at Saigontourist. Built in 1890, it is the preeminent historic hotel in the city, of Graham Greene's *The Quiet American* fame. Located at the very heart of Saigon's downtown, the colonial facade attracts shutter-clicking tourists and admirers, but that's where the love affair ends. Its last renovation was in 1980, which left the lobby gaudy with oversize chandeliers, Chinese vases, and that fake, semigloss shine of a low-end business hotel. Rooms are enormous, with high ceilings, but the red velveteen curtains, tatty red carpets, and general run-down feel spoil the fantasy. It looks more like an aging cathouse, unfortunately, and the furniture can't seem to fill the big, empty spaces. "First-class rooms" have roll-top desks, ornate columns, and a wood archway separating a small sitting area—a good bet. The restaurant is a lovely period piece. The hotel staff is friendly, but more or less dazed and confused. With a renovation, this historic gem could be a contender.

132–134 Dong Khoi St., District 1, Ho Chi Minh City. © 08/829-9201. Fax 08/824-1772. www.continentalvietnam.com. 83 units. US$75–US$85 (£41–£47) double; US$150 (£83) suite. AE, MC, V. **Amenities:** 2 restaurants; 2 bars; small fitness center; tour desk; car rental; small business center w/Internet access; limited room service; massage; laundry service; dry cleaning. *In room:* A/C, satellite TV w/video rental, minibar, fridge, IDD phone.

Norfolk Hotel ⓡⓡ

This snappy little business hotel has one of the highest occupancy rates in town, and for good reason: It's affordable, it's convenient, and it covers all the bases. Rooms are large and bright, furnished in slightly mismatched chain-hotel style, but everything is like new. The beds are soft and deluxe, the TVs are large, and the bathrooms are small but finished in marble. The staff is efficient and helpful. The restaurant has extensive breakfast and lunch buffets, as well as monthly themes and special menus. It's perfect for the business traveler or tourist seeking lots of amenities—all at reasonable prices. Book early.

117 Le Thanh Ton St., District 1, Ho Chi Minh City. © 08/829-5368. Fax 08/829-3415. www.norfolkgroup.com. 104 units. US$110–US$170 (£61–£94) double; from US$220 (£121) suite. Promotional and Internet rates available. AE, MC, V. **Amenities:** Restaurant; bar/club; small health club; sauna; steam room; concierge; tour desk; airport limousine; business center w/Internet access; 24-hr. room service; massage; laundry service; dry cleaning; nonsmoking rooms. *In room:* A/C, satellite TV, Internet access, minibar, fridge, coffeemaker, safe, IDD phone.

MODERATE

Huong Sen Hotel

Huong Sen is a good hotel for the price and the downtown location, but it's just another of the many government-owned places whose service is marked by varying levels of indifference. The decor is kind of a downer, too. It's a popular choice for big tours, and group and Internet rates are usually available. Rooms are big and newly renovated, with simple, colorfully painted wood furniture, ultracomfortable beds, and floral drapes. Nice touches include molded ceilings and marble-topped counters in the spotless bathrooms. Some units have balconies. The hotel is comparable to any other in this category, but quite bland.

66–70 Dong Khoi St., District 1, Ho Chi Minh City. ✆ **08/829-9400.** Fax 08/829-0916. www.vietnamtourism.com/huongsen. 76 units. US$50–US$70 (£28–£39) double. AE, DC, MC, V. **Amenities:** Restaurant; bar; sauna; steam room; car rental; business center w/Internet access; limited room service; massage; laundry service; dry cleaning. *In room:* A/C, TV, minibar, fridge, IDD phone.

Kimdo Royal City Hotel 🎔🎔

This is a good, basic bargain right downtown. The Kimdo is the kind of place with a wooden tree-trunk clock in the lobby, pink plastic hangers, and shiny polyester bedspreads. The rooftop massage area has electric blinking stars on the ceiling and a hot tub surrounded by plaster reliefs of sea nymphs. The original hotel was built nearly 100 years ago and underwent a renovation in 1994, so everything is still in good shape. All rooms are quite large and have interesting Asian carved furniture, tidy carpets, and rock-hard beds (you can request a softer one). Bathrooms are clean but basic, with no counter space.

133 Nguyen Hue Ave., District 1, Ho Chi Minh City. ✆ **08/822-5914** or 08/822-5915. Fax 08/822-5913. www.kimdohotel.com. 135 units. US$77–US$142 (£42–£78) double; US$162 (£89) suite. Great Internet discounts available. AE, DC, MC, V. **Amenities:** Rooftop restaurant; steam bath; all rentals available; concierge; tour desk; car rental; business center w/Internet access; 24-hr. room service; massage; laundry service; dry cleaning; nonsmoking rooms. *In room:* A/C, TV, Internet access, minibar, fridge, coffeemaker, hair dryer, safe, IDD phone.

Palace Hotel

This downtown tower has been around for a while. In fact, it was popular with U.S. soldiers on R & R during the war years. There have been some recent updates, but the history shows. Standard rooms are nondescript and a bit run-down, with older carpet and lots of chipped paint. The high-end suites have large beds, desks, and raised sitting areas with decent views—a better bet. The group and Internet rates attract lots of big groups, but the friendly staff isn't yet jaded. The small rooftop pool is unique: "Small" is the operative word (like a bathtub, really).

56–66 Nguyen Hue Blvd., District 1, Ho Chi Minh City. ✆ **08/824-4231.** Fax 08/824-4229. www.palacesaigon.com. US$54–US$64 (£30–£35) double; US$74–US$84 (£41–£46) suite. AE, MC, V. **Amenities:** 2 restaurants; 2 bars; nightclub; rooftop pool; car rental; business center w/Internet access; 24-hr. room service; laundry service; dry cleaning. *In room:* A/C, TV, minibar, fridge, safe, IDD phone.

Rex Hotel 🎔🎔

The Rex has an unorthodox history; it used to be a French garage, was expanded by the Vietnamese, and then was used by the United States Information Agency (and some say the C.I.A.) from 1962 to 1970. The hotel was transformed in a massive renovation and opened in 1990 as the hugely atmospheric government-run place it is today. There are a variety of rooms, but all are large and clean, with fluffy carpets and bamboo detailing on the ceilings, the mirrors—everywhere, in fact. The lampshades are big royal crowns, which are a hoot. Some suites have beaded curtains and Christmas lights over the bathroom mirrors. The beds and pillows are incredible—firm but fat—and there are good views from some balconies. The Rex has a fabulous location downtown, across from a square that has a lively carnival atmosphere at night. It is also known for its rooftop bar, with its panoramic Saigon view. The pool is small, just a toe-dipper, but is set in a quiet courtyard. Amenities here cover all the bases, if you can find them in this labyrinth. Much-needed renovations are planned.

141 Nguyen Hue Blvd., District 1, Ho Chi Minh City. ✆ **08/829-2185** or 08/829-3115. Fax 08/829-6536. www.rexhotelvietnam.com. 207 units. US$105–US$115 (£58–£63) double; US$130–US$290 (£72–£160) suite. AE, MC, V. **Amenities:** 2 restaurants; 2 bars; outdoor pool; tennis court; small health club; Jacuzzi; sauna; tour desk; car rental;

business center w/Internet access; salon; 24-hr. room service; massage; babysitting; laundry service; dry cleaning; non-smoking rooms. *In room:* A/C, satellite TV, hair dryer, safe, IDD phone, fax machine.

INEXPENSIVE

If you're on a tight budget, head for **De Tham,** a backpacker haven loaded with guest-houses and minihotels; a fan-cooled room with a cold-water shower goes for as little as US$5 (£2.75) per night, or an air-conditioned room with hot water for around US$15 (£8.25). Most of these places are very basic (and a bit noisy from street traffic) but tidy, well run, and friendly.

Bong Sen Hotel Annex   This small annex to the large Saigontourist-owned Bong Sen provides many of the same amenities at a lower price. Rooms are very basic but tidy, with light-wood furniture, thin carpet, and blue-tile bathrooms. Everything is on the small side, though, and the economy rooms have only one small window (even a junior suite isn't much bigger). Make sure you're getting the Annex and not the main Bong Sen, which, though recently renovated, isn't much of a value. Service is indifferent, but this is a good place to just lay your head for cheap. You can arrange any travel necessities elsewhere.

61–63 Hai Ba Trung St., District 1, Ho Chi Minh City. ⓒ 08/823-5818. Fax 08/823-5816. www.hotelbongsen.com. 57 units. US$40–US$50 (£22–£28) double; US$65 (£36) junior suite. AE, MC, V. **Amenities:** Restaurant; rentals available; tour desk; laundry service. *In room:* A/C, TV, minibar, fridge, hair dryer, IDD phone.

Hong Hoa Hotel 🏵🏵   This minihotel is the top dog of the lower-end category in the Pham Ngu Lao backpacker area. Rooms are small but tidy, with real wood furniture and tile floors. It's backpacker basics here—low foam beds and little charm—but the satellite TV and IDD phones are a real luxury in this price range. It's a funny spot: If it looks like two addresses, it is, with one entrance through a small grocery storefront on busy De Tham and the other off Pham Ngu Lao. The hotel is cozy, safe, and friendly, and if you stay long enough, you'll be adopted (and certainly learn some Vietnamese). If the place is full, which is more often than not the case, ask for a recommendation and they'll point you to a good neighbor.

185/28 Pham Ngu Lao St., 250 De Tham St., District 1, Ho Chi Minh City. ⓒ 08/836-1915. www.honghoavn.com. 7 units. US$12–US$18 (£6.60–£9.90) double. Rates include tax and service charge. MC, V. **Amenities:** Rentals available; tour information; laundry service; popular Internet center (free access for guests); small grocery. *In room:* A/C, satellite TV, IDD phone.

Que Huong–Liberty 3 Hotel   As the name suggests, the Liberty 3 is part of a chain. No. 3 is right in the heart of the Pham Ngu Lao backpacker area and arguably the best choice down that way. Rooms have all the amenities of a proper hotel, but are priced just above the average minihotel. It's thin office carpets and bland decor throughout, but everything is clean. Standard rooms are a bit too small; a superior is your best bet. Be sure to ask for a window and take a peek at the room before checking in, as some are worse than others (and many are musty from smokers). The adjoining **Allez Boo Bar & Restaurant** is an old backpacker standby and now managed by the hotel. The chain's flagship hotel, the **Metropole** (148 Tran Hung Dao; ⓒ **08/920-1937**), is a popular business address.

187 Pham Ngu Lao, District 1, Ho Chi Minh City. ⓒ 08/836-9522. Fax 08/836-4557. www.libertyhotels.com.vn. 60 units. US$58–US$88 (£32–£48) double. AE, V, MC. **Amenities:** Restaurant; tour desk; laundry service; dry cleaning. *In room:* A/C, satellite TV, Wi-Fi, minibar, fridge, hair dryer, IDD phone.

Riverside Hotel 🏵   Wedged into an old colonial storefront area between the hulking Renaissance Riverside and the wedding-cake Majestic, the Riverside is a good little budget stop. It's popular with young Japanese visitors, thus most services cater to them (tours and shopping). Public spaces are a bit banged and battered (worn carpets all around), but private spaces are clean and expansive for the price. It's an old building, so some rooms conform to the angled footprint in unique ways. Bathrooms are huge, plain affairs with no counter space, but again, they're tidy. Deluxe units are worth the upgrade; they're much larger and have better amenities like in-room safes. The leopard-pattern synthetic blankets are kind of fun. The staff is quite helpful.

18–20 Ton Duc Thang St., District 1, Ho Chi Minh City. © 08/822-4038. Fax 08/825-1417. www.riversidesaigon hotel.com. 73 units. US$50–US$60 (£28–£33) standard double; US$70 (£39) deluxe double; US$90–US$120 (£50–£66) suite. MC, V. **Amenities:** Restaurant; tour desk; business center; laundry service. *In room:* A/C, satellite TV, minibar, fridge, hair dryer, IDD phone.

Spring Hotel (Mua Xuan) ✿✿   If you don't care about fancy amenities and want to be downtown, look no further than the Spring, with nicer rooms than those at many hotels twice the price. Accommodations are neat and clean, with comfy beds, big TVs, and solid dark-wood or rattan furniture. The floral motif isn't bad, and the carpeted floors are impeccably clean. The lowest-priced "economy" rooms have no windows. Suites are large, with couches in separate sitting rooms. Go as high up as you can to escape street noise, which is the hotel's one failing (the elevator's kind of slow, too). The Spring has an unsettling Greco-Roman motif, with statues and filigree here and there; if the lobby's hanging ivy, colonnades, and grand staircase are a bit over the top, the rooms are a bit more toned down and utilitarian. A short walk from Dong Khoi and the central business district, this is a popular choice for long-term business travelers. The staff couldn't be nicer or more helpful.

44–46 Le Thanh Ton St., District 1, Ho Chi Minh City. © 08/829-7362. Fax 08/822-1383. 45 units. US$36–US$53 (£20–£29) double; US$67 (£37) suite. Rates include breakfast. AE, MC, V. **Amenities:** Restaurant; bar; rentals and tours can be arranged; room service (7am–10pm); laundry service; Wi-Fi. *In room:* A/C, TV w/HBO, minibar, fridge, wooden safe, IDD phone.

WHERE TO DINE

Saigon has the largest array of restaurants in Vietnam, with virtually every world cuisine represented. The area around **Dong Khoi** has lots of fine-dining choices. Ask locals where to eat, though, and they'll point you to the **Ben Thanh Market** or a local vendor on wheels. Ho Chi Minh's famous street stalls serve up local specials like *mien ga,* vermicelli, chicken, and mushrooms in a delicate soup; *lau hai san,* a tangy seafood soup with mustard greens; and, of course, *pho,* Vietnam's staple noodle soup.

EXPENSIVE

Amigo ✿✿ ARGENTINE/STEAKHOUSE   This is one of those expat gems you'll want to seek out. It served one of the best steaks I've ever had—and I don't mean just in Saigon. The roomy two-floor downtown setting has an Argentine steakhouse theme, laid-back but classy. The friendly staff and chummy atmosphere around the imposing bar will make you feel at home. But it's the food that sells this place: imported steak done just how you like it, chargrilled to perfection (not pan-fried, as is common in this part of the world). The filet mignon with red shallots would hold its own in the heart of Chicago. There's also a full raw bar and a roster of seafood specials and salads. Entrees come with baked potatoes and corn; for a real slice of home, follow up with apple strudel or ice-cream roulade. The great wine list features Argentine and Chilean reds, among others; there's also a full-service bar.

55 Nguyen Hue St., District 1. © 08/836-9890. Main courses 59,000VND–350,000VND (US$3.70–US$22/£2–£12). AE, MC, V. Daily 11am–2pm and 5–11pm.

Bi Bi FRENCH/MEDITERRANEAN   The food is the star at this small restaurant and art cafe, though the atmosphere has its charms as well. Bi Bi's cozy interior is adorned with bright Mediterranean-style furnishings and Impressionist paintings. Chairs are embossed with names of notorious or beloved expat patrons, past and present. A table near the front is devoted to drinking and card playing, while upstairs there are a few sofas for lounging. The menu is an interesting mix: cannelloni, ratatouille, pastas, and veal escalope, plus fine hot and cold starters like goat-cheese salad and grilled items. The beef tenderloin is *trés bien*. For dessert, try a perfect crème brûlée, mousse, or homemade ice cream. This is one of Saigon's more expensive choices; the food is well worth it, though, and service is seamless.

8A/8D Thai Van Lung, District 1. ⓒ 08/829-5783. Main courses 90,000VND–190,000VND (US$5.65–US$12/ £3.10–£6.65). MC, V. Daily 11:30am–2pm and 5:30–10:30pm.

Camargue ⓕ FRENCH/CONTINENTAL   Camargue, two floors of an enchanting renovated colonial, offers both softly lit interior seating and outdoor terrace tables surrounded by palm fronds. The menu changes regularly, but might list warm goat-cheese salad, roast pork, and venison, as well as the ubiquitous lower-priced pasta dishes (a nod to tourists, perhaps). The food, alas, isn't as perfect as the surroundings, and the service is substandard, but it's a quaint, laid-back spot downtown. The first-floor bar, **Vasco's,** is very popular and open late on Fridays.

16 Cao Ba Quat St., District 1. ⓒ 08/824-3148. Reservations recommended Fri–Sat. Main courses US$8–US$20 (£4.40–£11). AE, DC, MC, V. Daily 6pm–midnight (later Fri–Sat).

Hoi An ⓕⓕ VIETNAMESE   Run by the same folks who bring you Mandarin just around the corner (see below), Hoi An serves a similar complement of fine, authentic Vietnamese; here the focus is on central Vietnam's lighter fare and cuisine from Hoi An, Hue, and Saigon. On busy Le Thanh Ton just north of the town center, the building is a nice re-creation of a traditional Vietnamese home, and the upstairs dining room is an interesting faux-rustic blend of wood and bamboo. Presentation here is original; witness the hollowed coconut used to serve fine crab and asparagus. Try the drunken shrimp, large prawns soaked in rice whiskey and pan-fried at tableside. Order a cover-the-table meal for a group, and you're sure to go away smiling. Call ahead to ask about the authentic Vietnamese classical music (most nights).

11 Le Thanh Ton St., District 1. ⓒ 08/823-7694. Main courses US$5.70–US$34 (£3.15–£19). AE, MC, V. Daily 5:30–11pm.

Mandarin ⓕⓕ VIETNAMESE/CHINESE   On a quiet side street between busy Le Than Thon and the river, cross the threshold at Mandarin and enter a quaint, elegant oasis that will have you forgetting the city outside. The decor is an upscale Chinese motif with timber beams, fine screen paintings, and artwork. It's plush but not stuffy; you'll feel comfortable in casual clothes or a suit. The staff is attentive but doesn't hover, and is helpful with suggestions and explanations. Ask about daily specials and set menus. Don't miss the excellent spicy sautéed beef, served in bamboo with rice, or the famed duck done in sweet "Mandarin style." The steamed garlic in lobster is as good as it sounds; the seafood steamboat for four is a real coup. The restaurant features a live classical trio (call ahead for the schedule).

11A Ngo Van Nam, District 1. ⓒ 08/822-9783. Fax 08/825-6185. Main courses US$5.70–US$18 (£3.15–£9.90); set menus from US$17 (£9.35) per person (min. 2 people). AE, MC, V. Daily 11:30am–2pm and 5:30–10:pm.

Skewers ⓕ MEDITERRANEAN   The best food at this chic bistro does in fact come on skewers; barbecue entrees, particularly the lamb kabobs, are delicious. Also try the moussaka, grilled Moroccan sea bass, good pastas, vodka-flamed beef, or ribs dipped in honey. All the flame-bursting barbecuing is done in an open-air kitchen at the front of the restaurant—fun to watch. The salads are delicious, and the light meals and apps include great dips like hummus and baba ganoush. The atmosphere is candlelit and cozy, a great spot for a romantic evening.

9A Thai Van Lung St., District 1. © **08/829-2216.** Main courses 50,000VND–150,000VND (US$3.15–US$9.40/£1.70–£5.15). MC, V. Mon–Fri 11:30am–2pm; daily 6–10:30pm.

Song Ngu ✿ VIETNAMESE/SEAFOOD   Ask any Saigonese, and they'll help you find Song Ngu. Offset from a relatively quiet street, the restaurant is a popular place for locals and tour groups (who sit in a separate room). It's an old standby for good reason: Though the interior is nothing special, the food is anything but bland. The chefs are imaginative, the ingredients are fresh, and the portions are plentiful. And if it comes out of the water, Song Ngu does it right. Crab spring rolls, scallops, and steamed clams with lemongrass are a good start, but for the indecisive, there's an extensive list of the chef's recommendations.

70 Suong Nguyen Anh St., District 1. © **08/832-55017.** A la carte dishes 70,000VND–380,000VND (US$4.40–US$24/£2.40–£13). MC, V. Daily 11am–2pm and 5–10pm.

Sushi Bar ✿✿ JAPANESE   The food speaks for itself (in Japanese, no less) at this friendly corner sushi bar. At the end of Le Thanh Ton's "Little Tokyo," this is one of many Japanese eateries popping up and is popular among longtime residents. It's a typical busy, big-city sushi bar, complete with a wise-cracking chef from Japan. There are tatami rooms upstairs, and the place always seems full, which is a good sign. Everything's fresh—the sushi and sashimi are worth the price. Lunch specials are a good bargain.

2 Le Thanh Ton, District 1. © **08/823-8042.** A la carte dishes US$1–US$5.35 (£0.55–£2.95); set menus US$2.35–US$12 (£1.30–£6.60). MC, V. Daily 11:30am–2pm and 5:30–11:30pm. Delivery until 10pm.

MODERATE

Al Fresco's Café and Grill ✿ *Kids* WESTERN   Just like the popular Al Fresco's in Hanoi, this new location in the heart of Saigon (just a stone's throw from the Sheraton) is Vietnam's answer to TGI Friday's. Burgers, steaks, popular ribs, good pizzas, pastas, and hearty salads all stick to your ribs. Worthwhile starters include chicken wings, satay, and fried calamari. Al Fresco's is the best choice for Western comfort foods or for something familiar—kids love it. Expat management and ultrafriendly waitstaff make a visit here a welcome slice of home.

27 Dong Du, District 1. © **08/822-7317.** Main courses 40,000VND–300,000VND (US$2.50–US$19/£1.40–£10). MC, V. Daily 9am–11pm.

Augustin ✿ FRENCH   On the quaint, up-and-coming "restaurant row" of Ngueyen Thiep (just off Don Khoi), this bright, lively restaurant is a favorite with French expats and tourists. The food is simple yet innovative French fare, including beef *pot-au-feu* and sea-bass tartare with olives. Try the seafood stew, lightly seasoned with saffron and packed with fish, clams, and shrimp. The seating is quite cozy, especially since the place is always full, and the Vietnamese staff is exceptionally friendly, speaking both French and English. The menu is bilingual, too. A large French wine list and classic dessert menu finish off a delightful meal.

10 Nguyen Thiep. District 1. © **08/829-2941.** Main courses 100,000VND–170,000VND (US$6.25–US$11/£3.45–£5.85). No credit cards. Daily 11:30am–2pm and 6–10:30pm.

Café Mogambo AMERICAN   Run by American expat Mike and his Vietnamese wife, Lani, laid-back Mogambo is a longtime Yank hangout in Saigon. It's a small, dimly lit place with cane ceilings and walls, animal-head trophies, and memorabilia. A row of regulars bellies up to the long bar and television. Before long, you'll be joining in the conversation and staying longer than you'd planned. The burgers and steaks are the real thing, as are the sausages and meat pies. Entrees are all quite affordable; it's just the steaks that jack up the high end of the price range. Dessert is apple pie, of course, washed down with a hearty cup of coffee.

20 Bis Thi Sach St., District 1. ℂ **08/825-1311.** Main courses US$4–US$13 (£2.20–£7.15). MC, V. Daily 7am–11pm.

Chao Thai THAI   Chao Thai is two floors of an elegant, roomy Thai longhouse, with wide plank floors, black-and-white photos of Thai temples, and some small statuary. The restaurant is famous for its fiery papaya salad, fried catfish with basil leaves, and prawn cakes with plum sauce. The flavors are subtle and not overdone; you won't leave feeling drugged on spices or too much chile. It's a popular lunch spot, but the atmosphere is most welcoming in the candlelit evening. The service is gracious and efficient.

16 Thai Van Lung, District 1. ℂ **08/824-1457.** Reservations recommended only for groups of 5 or more. Main courses 55,000VND–75,000VND (US$3.45–US$4.70/£1.90–£2.60); set lunch menus from 80,000VND (US$5/£2.75). AE, MC, V. Daily 11am–2pm and 6–10:30pm.

Lemongrass VIETNAMESE   On a romantic side street that's becoming its own "restaurant row" in the downtown area, this place has three floors of subdued fine dining—a great place to duck out of the midday sun. The atmosphere is candlelit and intimate, very Vietnamese, with cane furniture and tile floors, yet it's not overly formal. Set lunches are an affordable and light option: soup, spring rolls, and a light curry for US$2 (£1.10). The extensive menu emphasizes seafood and seasonal specials. Particularly outstanding are the deep-fried prawns in coconut batter and the crab sautéed in salt-and-pepper sauce. Go with a group, if possible, and sample as many delicacies as possible.

4 Nguyen Thiep St., District 1. ℂ **08/822-0496.** Main courses 50,000VND–390,000VND (US$3.10–US$24/£1.70–£13); lunch set menus from 50,000VND (US$3.10/£1.70). AE, MC, V. Daily 11am–2pm and 5–10pm.

Temple Club ★★ VIETNAMESE   For atmosphere alone, the Temple Club is a must-see in Ho Chi Minh. As the name suggests, this is a turn-of-the-20th-century Chinese temple with original wood and masonry. The ceiling is high, the walls are exposed brick, the floor is terra cotta draped in antique throw rugs, and there are some great Buddhist tapestries and statuary on display. Patrons gather at a classic wooden bar and in a formal but comfortable dining room, as well as in the lounge area in the back for coffee and dessert. The cuisine is standard Vietnamese from all parts of the country. This place does a good Hanoi-style *cha ca,* fried monkfish; the *tom me,* prawns in tamarind sauce, is a smart choice as well. A "Western Corner" serves sandwiches and salads. The banana-coconut-cream pudding with sesame seeds is a decadent dessert, and the coffee is the real thing.

29 Ton That Thiep St., District 1. ℂ **08/829-9244.** Main courses US$3–US$8 (£1.65–£4.40). Daily 10am–2pm and 5–11pm.

INEXPENSIVE

Ngon Restaurant ★★★ *Finds* VIETNAMESE   *Ngon* means "delicious," and, for authentic Vietnamese, this restaurant lives up to its name and gets my vote for the best in Vietnam. This Ho Chi Minh institution is always packed with both locals and tourists; it has even built a new location nearby to handle the overflow. The atmosphere is chaotic: a cacophony of chattering guests, shouting waiters, and clanging pots and pans. Fans blow mist to quell the smoky cooking fires of the open-air kitchen. Seating is a mix of regular tables in the colonial and those on the balcony or in the courtyard out back. The main building is surrounded by cooking stations, each serving a regional specialty; it's like someone went around the country head-hunting all of the best street-side chefs. Waitstaff simply act as liaisons among the many cooks. The menu is a survey course in Vietnamese cooking, and the tuition is low. Go with a Vietnamese friend, if you can, or someone who can explain the regional specialties. If you're alone, just point and shoot; everything is good. There's Hue-style *bun bo,* cold noodles with beef; a catalog of *pho,* noodle soup; and all kinds of seafood prepared the way you like. Meals here are best done as leisurely, multicourse affairs, but stop by for a snack if you're visiting the Reunification Palace or any sights downtown. Don't miss it!

138 Nam Ky Khoi Nghia, District 1. ✆ **08/829-9449.** Main courses 16,000VND–115,000VND (US$1–US$7.20/£0.55–£3.95). AE, MC, V. Daily 7am–10:30pm.

Restaurant 13 ✦ VIETNAMESE   With all the upscale eateries popping up downtown, you might miss out on an old-school standby like this little storefront. Tucked between high-rises and just off Dong Khoi, it's one of many restaurants whose name is its street number (if this one is busy, try no. 19). The atmosphere is plain, but the kitchen serves excellent traditional Vietnamese food without any bells, whistles, or sticker shock. The place is jolly and filled with locals, tourists, and expats. Ask what's good, or try the seafood, anything done in coconut broth, or the sautéed squid with citronella and red pepper. The food is carefully prepared and the waitstaff is very professional for this price range.

13 Ngo Duc Ke, District 1. ✆ **08/239-314.** Main courses 18,000VND–60,000VND (US$1.10–US$3.75/£0.60–£2.05). No credit cards. Daily 7am–10:30pm.

SNACKS & CAFES

While shopping on Dong Khoi, stop to savor a few moments at the **Paris Deli** (31 Dong Khoi St., District 1), a retro spot with fantastic pastries and sandwiches. There's another storefront at 65 Le Loi St. (✆ **08/821-6127**) that serves the same good sandwiches and treats.

Brodard Café (131 Dong Khoi St., District 1; ✆ **08/822-3966**) is a cozy international diner-style spot with lots of familiar choices, good coffee, and air-conditioning—a good spot to beat the heat and take a shopping break.

Bach Dang ✦ (26 Le Loi St., District 1), in the heart of old Saigon, is three floors of always crowded fun. It's the best place in town for ice cream and to meet local people—a Saigon institution, really.

Café Central, in the Sun Wah Tower (115 Nguyen Hue St., District 1; ✆ **08/821-9303**), is a great little international deli. Stop in for breakfast or a sandwich any time; the kind staff makes you feel like you've stepped into an old greasy spoon (with all the same standbys on the menu).

Ciao Café (2 Hang Bai St., District 1; ✆ **08/822-9796**) is a good downtown spot for snacks and ice cream. **Fanny,** just below the Temple Club (48 Ton That Thiep St., District 1; ✆ **08/821-1630**), serves the real-deal French glacées.

Café L'Opera (11–13 Cong Truong Lam Son St., District 1; ✆ **08/827-5946**) is a cozy, upmarket coffee corner right next to the Caravelle Hotel.

Zen & the Art of *Pho*

Pho, or Vietnamese noodle soup, has become a popular dish in the West, but in Vietnam it is a national obsession, a dish eaten any time of day. Its simplicity is the attraction: beef stock with rice noodles garnished as you like, with meat and herbs, all ingredients left to speak for themselves. You can eat pho on any street corner and in any market, but there are a few good places in Saigon with English menus and a high standard of cleanliness. **Pho 2000**, on Tran Hung Dao just catercorner to the Benh Thanh Market, is a Saigon institution and a beehive of activity day or night. Bill Clinton even made a visit here, and if Bubba liked it, it has to be good. **Pho 24**, on Nguyen Thiep Street, a little "restaurant row" off busy Don Khoi, serves a busy crowd all day long in its cool, clean storefront. On Don Khoi, across from the Grand Hotel, look for the large **Pho** sign and Japanese characters at 37 Don Khoi St.; inside, the place is covered in woodcarvings and serves great soups—popular with Japanese tourists.

WHAT TO SEE & DO
IN DISTRICT 1

Ben Thanh Market ⭐⭐⭐   The clock tower over the main entrance to what was formerly known as Les Halles Centrale is the symbol of Saigon, and the market might as well be, too. Opened first in 1914, it's a crowded place, a boon for pickpockets with its narrow, one-way aisles, and loaded with vendors clamoring to sell you postcards and cheap goods (T-shirts, aluminum wares, silk, bamboo, and lacquer). There will be so many people calling out to you that you'll feel like the belle of the ball—or a wallet with legs. The wet market, with its selection of meat, fish, produce, and flowers, is interesting and hassle-free; no one will foist a fish on you. In open-air stalls surrounding the market are some nice little eateries. The adventurous can try all kinds of local specialties for next to nothing.

At the intersection of Le Loi, Ham Nghi, Tran Hung Dao, and Le Lai sts., District 1. Daily from early morning until night.

City Hall   Saigon's city hall was constructed between 1902 and 1908, a fantastic and ornate example of colonial architecture. Unfortunately, it's not open to the public.

Facing Nguyen Hue Blvd., District 1.

General Post Office (Buu Dien) ⭐   In this grand old colonial building, you can check out the huge maps of Vietnam on either side of the main entrance and the huge portrait of Uncle Ho in the rear. The specialty-stamps counter has some great collector sets for sale.

2 Coq Xu Paris, District 1. Daily 6:30am–10pm.

Ho Chi Minh City Museum ⭐   Originally built in 1890 by the French as a commercial museum, then turned into a governor's palace, a committee building, and later the Revolutionary Museum, the institution today covers a broad range, from archaeology to ethnic survey and documents from the city's founding in the 1600s. The second floor is heavy on Vietnam's ongoing revolution, with displays of weaponry and memorabilia from the period of struggle against imperialism and many flags, placards, and dispatches from the rise of communism, beginning with the August Revolution of 1945 all the way to the fall of Saigon. The bias is heavy, of course, but it is interesting to note how the displays, not unlike socialist ideals, are a bit frayed around the edges in a land that is racing pell-mell toward a market economy. The grounds are picturesque, which explains the many young couples posing for wedding photos, and there is an interesting collection of captured U.S. fighter planes, tanks, and artillery in the main courtyard. Underneath the building is a series of tunnels (closed to the public) leading to the Reunification Palace, once used by former president Ngo Dinh Diem as a hideout before his execution in 1962.

65 Ly Tu Trong St., District 1. ℃ 08/829-8250. Admission 10,000VND (US65¢/£0.35). Daily 8:30am–4:30pm.

Notre Dame Cathedral *

The neo-Romanesque cathedral was constructed between 1877 and 1883 using bricks from Marseilles and stained-glass windows from Chartres. The cathedral is closed to visitors except during Sunday services, which are in Vietnamese and English. Whatever your faith is, don't miss it.

Near the intersection of Dong Khoi and Nguyen Du sts., District 1.

Reunification Palace *

Designed as the home of former president Ngo Dinh Diem, the U.S.-backed leader of Vietnam in the 1960s, this building is most notable for its symbolic role in the fall of Saigon in April 1975, when its gates were breached by North Vietnamese tanks and the victor's flag hung on the balcony. Those very tanks that crashed through the gates are enshrined in the entryway, and photos and accounts of their drivers are on display. Built on the site of the French governor general's home, called the Norodom Palace, the current modern building, designed when "modern" meant "sterile," was completed in 1966. Like the Bao Dai Palace in Dalat, the Reunification Palace is a series of rather empty rooms that are nevertheless interesting because they specialize in period kitsch and haven't been gussied up a bit. The private quarters, dining rooms, entertainment lounges, and president's office look like everybody just up and left. Most interesting is the war command room, with its huge maps and old communications equipment, as well as the basement labyrinth. There is an ongoing screening of a propagandistic video about the war years in the basement.

106 Nguyen Du St., District 1. Admission 15,000VND (US95¢/£0.50). Daily 7:30–11am and 1–4pm.

Saigon Opera House (Ho Chi Minh Municipal Theater)

This magnificent building was built at the turn of the 20th century and renovated in the 1940s. Its three stories hold 1,800 seats. Today, it hosts very little in terms of performances, but it is a stalwart atmospheric holdout amid steel-and-glass downtown.

At the intersection of Le Loi and Dong Khoi sts.

Vietnam History Museum **

Housed in a rambling new concrete pagodalike structure, the museum presents a clear picture of Vietnamese history, with a focus on the south. Highlights include an excellent selection of Cham sculpture and the best collection of ancient ceramics in Vietnam. Weaponry from the 14th century on is displayed; one yard is nothing but cannons. One wing is dedicated to ethnic minorities of the south, including photos, costumes, and household implements. Nguyen Dynasty (1700–1945) clothing and housewares are also on exhibit, as are archaeological artifacts from prehistoric Saigon. Its 19th- and early-20th-century histories are shown using photos and, curiously, a female corpse unearthed as construction teams broke ground for a recent housing project. There are even some general background explanations in English, something missing from most Vietnamese museums.

2 Nguyen Binh Khiem, District 1. ℭ **08/829-8146.** Admission 10,000VND (US65¢/£0.35). Daily 8–11:30am and 1:30–4:30pm.

IN OTHER DISTRICTS

Cholon (District 5) 𝕽𝕽 Cholon is the sizable Chinese district of the city and probably the largest Chinatown in the world. It exists in many ways quite apart from Saigon. The Chinese began to settle the area in the early 1900s and never quite assimilated with the rest of Saigon, which causes a bit of resentment among the greater Vietnamese community. You'll sense the different environment immediately, and not only because of the Chinese-language signs.

A bustling commercial center, Cholon is a fascinating maze of temples, restaurants, jade ornaments, and medicine shops. Gone, however, are the brothels and opium dens of earlier days. You can lose yourself walking the narrow streets, but it makes sense to take a cyclo by the hour to see the sights.

Start at the **Binh Tay Market** 𝕽𝕽, on Phan Van Khoe Street, which is even more crowded than Ben Thanh and has much the same goods, but with a Chinese flavor. You'll see a lot more produce, along with medicines, spices, cooking utensils, and plenty of hapless ducks and chickens tied in heaps. From Binh Tay, head up to Nguyen Trai, the district's main artery, to see some of the major temples on or around it. Be sure to see Quan Am, on Lao Tu Street off Luong Nhu Hoc, for its ornate exterior. Back on Nguyen Trai, Thien Hau Pagoda is dedicated to the goddess of the sea and was popular with seafarers making thanks for their safe trip from China to Vietnam. Finally, as you follow Nguyen Trai Street past Ly Thuong Kiet, you'll see the Cholon Mosque, the one indication of the district's small Muslim community.

Bordered by Hung Vuong to the north, Nguyen Van Cu to the east, the Ben Nghe Channel to the south, and Nguyen Thi Nho to the west, District 5.

Emperor Jade Pagoda (Phuoc Hai) 𝕽𝕽 One of the most interesting pagodas in Vietnam, the Emperor Jade is filled with smoky incense and fantastic carved figurines. It was built by the Cantonese community around the turn of the 20th century and is still buzzing with worshippers, many lounging in the front gardens. Take a moment to look at the elaborate statuary on the pagoda's roof. The dominant figure in the main hall is the Jade Emperor himself; referred to as the "god of the heavens," the emperor decides who will enter and who will be refused. He looks an awful lot like Confucius, only meaner. In an anteroom to the left, you'll see Kim Hua, a goddess of fertility, and the King of Hell in another corner with his minions—he undoubtedly gets those the Jade Emperor rejects. It's spooky.

73 Mai Thi Luu St., District 3. Daily 8am–5pm.

Giac Lam Pagoda 𝕽 Giac Lam, built in 1744, is the oldest pagoda in Saigon. The garden in front features the ornate tombs of venerated monks, as well as a rare Bodhi tree. Next to the tree is a regular feature of Vietnamese Buddhist temples, a gleaming white statue of Quan The Am Bo Tat (Avalokitesvara, the goddess of mercy) standing on a lotus blossom, a symbol of purity. Inside the temple is a spooky funerary chamber, with photos of monks gone by, and a central chamber chock-full of statues. Take a look at the outside courtyard as well.

118 Lac Long Quan St., District 5. Daily 8am–5pm.

War Remnants Museum 𝕽𝕽 This museum has a comprehensive collection of the machinery, weapons, photos, and documentation of Vietnam's wars with the both the

French and Americans (the emphasis is heavily on the latter). It was once called the War Crimes Museum, which should give you an idea of whose side of the story is being told here. Short of being outright recrimination, this museum is a call for peace and a hope that history is not repeated—visitors are even asked to sign a petition against the kind of aerial carpet-bombing that so devastated the people of Vietnam. The exhibit begins to the right of the entrance with a room listing war facts: troop numbers, bomb tonnage, and statistics on international involvement in the conflict and numbers of casualties on both sides. Next is a room dedicated to the journalists who were lost in wartime. The exhibits are constantly evolving; one room is devoted to biological warfare, another to weaponry, and another to worldwide demonstrations for peace. The explanations, which include English translations, are very thorough. There is a large collection of bombs, planes, tanks, and war machinery in the main courtyard. Kids will love it, but you might want to think twice before taking them inside to see things like wall-size photos of the My Lai massacre and the bottled deformed fetus supposedly damaged by Agent Orange. There is also a model of the French colonial prisons, called the Tiger Cages, on the grounds.

28 Vo Van Tan St., District 3. ℂ **08/829-0325.** Admission 10,000VND (US65¢/£0.35). Daily 7:30–11:30am and 1:30–5:15pm.

OUTDOOR ACTIVITIES

There are two excellent 18-hole golf courses at the **Vietnam Golf & Country Club.** The clubhouse is at Long Thanh My Ward, District 9 (ℂ **08/733-0126;** fax 08/ 733-0102; www.vietnamgolfcc.com). Fees are US$50 to US$80 (£28–£44) during the week for nonmembers, depending on which course you want to play, and US$100 (£55) on Saturday and Sunday.

Tennis enthusiasts can find courts at **Lan Anh International Tennis Court** (291 Cach Mang Than Tam, District 10; ℂ **04/862-7144**).

The pool and well-equipped gym and spa at the **Caravelle Hotel** (p. 386) are available for nonguests at a day rate of US$12 (£6.60).

SHOPPING

Saigon has a good selection of silk, fashion, lacquer, embroidery, and housewares. Prices are higher than elsewhere in Vietnam, but the offerings are more sophisticated. Stores are open daily from around 8am to 7pm. Credit cards are widely accepted, except for in the markets.

Dong Khoi is the city's premier shopping street. Formerly Rue Catinat, it was a veritable Rue de la Paix in colonial times. Notable shops include **Heritage** (53 Dong Khoi St.; ℂ **08/823-5438**) for woodcarvings and other ethnic arts. **Les Epices** (25 Dong Khoi St.; ℂ **08/823-6795**) also has a nice collection of lacquerware and other gift items, while **Authentique Interiors** (38 Dong Khoi St.; ℂ **08/822-133**) specializes in fine pottery and table settings. **Viet Silk** (21 Dong Khoi St.; ℂ **08/823-4860**) has a quality selection of ready-made clothing and can, of course, whip something up for you in a day. **Khai Silk** (107 Dong Khoi St.; ℂ **08/829-1146**) has a fine outlet right in the heart of the city and offers ready-to-wear and fitted silk clothing.

Nearby Le Thanh Ton Street is another shopping avenue. Look for **Kenly Silk** (132 Le Thanh Ton St.; ℂ **08/829-3847**), a brand-name supplier with the best ready-to-wear silk garments in the business. Unique, tasteful, hand-embroidered pillows, table linens, and hand-woven fabrics can be found at **MC Decoration** (92C5 Le Thanh Ton St., across from the Norfolk Hotel; ℂ **08/822-6003**).

ART GALLERIES The **Ho Chi Minh Fine Arts Museum** (97A Pho Duc Chinh St., District 1; © **08/829-4441;** Tues–Sun 9am–4:45pm; admission 10,000VND/ US65¢/£0.35) is the place to start if you're truly keen; the evolving collection features area artists' works in sculpture, oil, and lacquer—a good glimpse into the local scene. **Lac Hong Art Gallery,** on the ground floor of the museum (© **08/821-3771**), features the works of many famous Vietnamese artists.

Slip into **Hanoi Gallery** (43 Le Loi St; © **08/821-8211**) to see a variety of propaganda posters. Collectors will find original works (with prices to match), but the bargains are in the reproductions, whose classic communist-style images and messages range from a call to arms during the American war to a call to plant more trees during peacetime. It's worth a perusal to find a unique gift.

There are galleries throughout the city, many clustered around Dong Khoi and near the major hotels. Reproduction artists are everywhere. Here are a few popular galleries in town: **Ancient Gallery** (50 Mac Thi Buoi St., District 1, near Saigon Sakura Restaurant; © **08/822-7962**), **Hien Minh** (32 Dong Khoi St., District 1; © **08/829-5520**), **Particular Art Gallery** (123 Le Loi St., District 1; © **08/821-3019**), and **101 Catinat** (101 Dong Khoi St.; © **08/822-7643**). If these pique your curiosity, pick up a copy of *Vietnam Discovery* or *The Guide* for further listings.

BOOKSTORES Ho Chi Minh City's official foreign-language bookstore, **Xuan Thu** (85 Dong Khoi St., across from the Continental Hotel; © **08/822-4670**) has a good selection of classics, as well as some foreign-language newspapers. There are also several small bookshops on De Tham Street in the backpacker area.

HO CHI MINH CITY AFTER DARK

When Vietnam made a fresh entry onto the world scene in the mid-1990s, Ho Chi Minh City quickly became one of the hippest party towns in the East. The mood has sobered somewhat, but it's still a fun place. Everything is clustered in District 1; ask expats in places like **Saigon Saigon** (below) about any club happenings. As for cultural events, Saigon is sadly devoid of anything really terrific, except for a few cultural dinner and dance shows.

BARS & CLUBS Head to the basement of the central opera house for **Q Bar** (7 Cong Truong Lam Son; © **08/824-6325;** www.qsaigon.com), the town's hippest club. It's a funky catacomb with good music, cocktail nooks, and an eclectic mix of homo sapiens. It has also just opened up a chic new restaurant space called **Qucina.**

Atop the Caravelle Hotel, **Saigon Saigon** (19 Lam Son Sq.; © **08/823-4999**) is a very popular spot featuring live music and a terrific view. Next door at the Sheraton, **Level 23** (88 Dong Khoi St.; © **08/827-2828**) is a double-height rotunda overlooking town. Good live bands play here—it's Indochina meets the Hard Rock Cafe on any given evening.

Pacharan (97 Hai Ba Trung St.; © **08/825-6024**), a swanky Spanish tapas bar downtown, is a great place to start your evening. **Vasco's Bar,** at the Camargue restaurant (16 Cao Ba Quat St.; © **08/824-3148**), is an atmospheric choice. On Nguyen Thiep Street, an alleyway off Dong Khoi that is becoming a little restaurant row, you'll find **Alibi** (6 Nguyen Thiep St.; © **08/822-8855**), a cozy bar and club.

Don't miss the brick-walled Irish pub **O'Briens** (74A Hai Ba Trung St.; © **08/ 829-3198**) for pints and pizza. **Sheridan's** (17/13 Le Thanh Ton St.; © **08/823-0793**) is another friendly watering hole with character.

The Pham Ngu Lao area stays up late, and **Allez Boo** (187 Pham Ngu Lao; ✆ **08/ 837-2505**) is always up till the wee hours, as are the many street-side beer stalls selling Bia Hoi for pennies a glass.

THE PERFORMING ARTS   A few hotels stage traditional music and dance shows. The **"Au Co" Traditional Troupe** has performed abroad, but calls the Skyview Restaurant (at the Mondial Hotel, 109 Dong Khoi St., District 1; ✆ **08/849-6291**) home. The **Rex Hotel** (141 Nguyen Hue Blvd.; ✆ **08/829-2185**) has regular performances as well. Call each place ahead of time to check the performance schedule.

SIDE TRIPS FROM HO CHI MINH CITY

See "Visitor Information & Tours," earlier in this section, for tour providers to the following sights.

Cao Dai Holy See Temple 𝒦𝒦   The Cao Dai religion is less than 100 years old and is a broad, inclusive faith that sprang from Buddhist origins to embrace Jesus, Mohammed, and other nontraditional, latter-day saints such as Louis Pasteur, Martin Luther King, Jr., and Victor Hugo. Practitioners of Cao Daism are pacifists, pray four times daily, and follow a vegetarian diet for 10 days out of every month. Cao Daism is practiced by only a small percentage of Vietnamese people, mostly in the south, but you'll see temples scattered far and wide—easily recognizable by the all-seeing eye, which, oddly enough, looks something like the eye on the U.S. dollar. Often included with trips to the Cu Chi Tunnels (below), the temple at Tay Ninh is the spiritual center—the Cao Dai Vatican, if you will—and the country's largest. Visitors are welcome at any of the four daily ceremonies, but all are asked to wear trousers covering the knee, remove their shoes before entering, and act politely, quietly observing the ceremony from the balcony area. The temple interior is a colorful wedding cake, with bright murals and carved pillars. Cao Dai supplicants wear either white suits of clothing or colorful robes, each color denoting what root of Cao Daism they practice: Buddhist, Muslim, Christian, or Taoist. On the ride here, you'll pass through the town of Trang Bang, site of the famous photo of 9-year-old Kim Phuc, who was burned by napalm. The road also passes Nui Ba Den, the Black Virgin Mountain, which marked the end of the Ho Chi Minh trail from the north and was a Viet Cong stronghold during the war era. About 90km (56 miles) northwest of Ho Chi Minh City. Daily dawn–dusk.

Cu Chi Tunnels 𝒦𝒦   Vietnamese are proud of their resolve in their long history of struggle against invading armies, and the story of the people of Cu Chi is indicative of that spirit. The Cu Chi area lies at the end of the Ho Chi Minh trail and was the base from which Ho Chi Minh gorillas used to attack Saigon. As a result, the whole area became a "free fire zone" and was carpet-bombed in one of many American "scorched-earth" policies. But the residents of Cu Chi took their war underground, literally, developing a network of tunnels that, at its height, stretched as far as Cambodia and included meeting rooms, kitchens, and triage areas, an effective network for waging guerilla warfare on nearby U.S. troops. The U.S. Army's 25th Infantry Division was just next door, and there are detailed maps denoting land that was either U.S.-held, Vietminh-held, or in dispute.

Visitors first watch a war-era propaganda film that is so over the top, it's fun. The site supports a small museum of photos and artifacts, as well as an extensive outdoor exhibit of guerilla snares and reconstructions of the original tunnels and bunkers. Dress appropriately if you choose to get down in the tunnels; the experience is dirty and claustrophobic. There is also a shooting range where, for US$1 per bullet, you can try your hand at firing anything from a shotgun to an AK-47. At the end of the tour, visit the dining hall and try the steamed tapioca that was a Cu Chi staple. Souvenir hawkers abound. A half-day trip can be arranged with any tour company in Saigon, often including a visit to the Cao Dai Temple (above).

About 65km (40 miles) northwest of Ho Chi Minh City. Daily dawn–dusk. Admission 65,000VND (US$4.05/£2.25).

15 The Mekong Delta

Don't leave without seeing the Mekong Delta, even for just a day. The delta is a region of waterways formed by the Mekong River, covering an area of about 60,000 sq. km (37,200 sq. miles) and with a population of 17 million, most engaged in farming and fishing. Often called the breadbasket of Vietnam, the Mekong Delta accounts for more than an estimated 50% of rice production. The land is tessellated with bright-green rice paddies, fruit orchards, sugarcane fields, and vegetable gardens, and its waters are busy with boats and fish farms.

The region's urban centers, Can Tho and Chau Doc, are good bases for tours and exploration of the countryside by road and canal. As you cruise slowly along the meandering canals, you'll see locals living right beside the water on stilt houses or houseboats—a fascinating glimpse into a way of life that has survived intact for hundreds of years. In the many floating markets, trade is conducted from boat to boat in areas teeming with activity and sellers touting their wares. Delta people are friendly and unaffected, and their cuisine is delicious—lots of good seafood, of course.

Coming south from Ho Chi Minh City (Saigon), the town you'll probably reach first is **My Tho,** but you should try to make it down at least as far as **Can Tho,** the delta's largest city. It has a bustling riverfront and waterway. About 32km (20 miles) from Can Tho is **Phung Hiep,** the biggest water market in the region. **Chau Doc** is another picturesque town and a popular gateway to Cambodia. Look for unique floating markets, weaving villages, and expansive fish farms, all visited on tours.

VISITOR INFORMATION & TOURS

To cope with the necessary logistics, going with a travel agent is your best bet in the Mekong Delta. They offer everything from day trips to 3-day tours. Our pick is **Ann Tours** (58 Ton That Tung St., District 1; ℂ 08/833-2564 or 08/833-4356; fax 08/832-3866; www.anntours.com) for custom excursions that take you off the beaten path; prices start at US$45 (£25) per day with a group.

Saigontourist (49 Le Thanh Ton St., District 1; ℂ **08/829-8914;** fax 08/822-4987; www.saigon-tourist.com) is a large government operation that runs regular buses and tours for groups big and small. Tour quality—and price—is higher than at the budget tourist cafes.

The tourist cafes all run standard, affordable trips to the Mekong Delta. Contact **Sinh Café** (246–8 De Tham St., District 1; ℂ 08/369-420) or **TM Brothers** (269 De Tham St. or 139 Bui Vien St., District 1; ℂ **08/836-1791**) for 2- and 3-day tours starting at US$10 (£5.50) per day (with optional connection to Cambodia).

WHERE TO STAY

Victoria Hotels (www.victoriahotels-asia.com) has two properties on the Mekong Delta, in Can Tho (ℂ **071/810-111**) and Chau Doc (ℂ **076/865-010**). New but unique colonial-style rooms and services at riverside come priced from just US$125 (£69). Nothing compares.

7

Cambodia

by Brian Calvert

It wasn't long ago that travel guidebooks about Cambodia weren't much more than protracted warnings and lists of safety precautions, and for good reason: Following years of war, the chaos and genocide of Pol Pot's Khmer Rouge, and a long period of civil and political instability, Cambodia was until recently an armed camp closed to foreign visitors (or open only to travelers of the danger-seeking variety). But Cambodia is healing, and, though this is a process that will take years, the country is enjoying a period of relative stability under a coalition government. Cambodia offers travelers a host of experiences, from the legacy of ancient architecture to a growing urban capital and beautiful countryside. Even the shortest visit offers a look into a vibrant ancient culture and a chance to meet with a very kind and resilient people, one of the country's greatest attributes.

What brings so many to this Buddhist land of smiles is **Angkor Wat,** the ancient capital and one of the man-made wonders of the world. Visiting the monumental Hindu complex of behemoth block temples, towering spires, giant carved faces, and ornate bas-reliefs is a once-in-a-lifetime experience. Angkor Wat is a pilgrimage point for temple aficionados and a place of spiritual significance to many.

Most travelers limit their visit to a few days at the temples and the major sites in the growing capital, **Phnom Penh,** which is tatty but charming, with crumbling French colonial architecture and a splendid palace.

But these days, travel in rural Cambodia, once unheard of, is now limited only by your tolerance for bumpy roads and rustic accommodations (though this, too, is changing in places). Bouncing around the hinterlands of Cambodia still begs caution, though, and travelers should be aware of the mass amounts of UXO (unexploded ordnance, or mines), poor road conditions, and the absence of proper medical services. Dusty roads pay off, however, when they connect hamlets rarely visited by outsiders or lead to unexplored rural ruins.

Cambodia is resplendent with natural gifts, and any of the larger tour operators are a good bet for arranging trips to the likes of mountainous **Rattanakiri,** in the northeast; the Thai border area; or rural towns along the **Mekong River,** the country's lifeline. The river connects with **Tonle Sap Lake,** Southeast Asia's largest lake, which is surrounded by fertile lowlands.

The country's only port, **Sihanoukville,** is a popular beach destination, and **Kep,** sometimes called the Cambodian Riviera, remains an under-discovered gem. Intrepid travelers commonly rent motorcycles or brave rattletrap buses to explore the country.

Known for warm, beguiling smiles, smiles that have weathered great hardship, Khmer people are very friendly, approachable, and helpful; but be warned that the hard sell is on in Cambodia, and you're sure to be harried, especially by the persistent young sellers at Angkor Wat and the motorcycle and tuk-tuk drivers in

Phnom Penh. Nevertheless, with a little patience and an exploratory attitude, travelers here are sure to meet with great kindness.

For years, the lawlessness of Cambodia attracted some rather dubious foreign visitors who came in droves for budget drugs and prostitution. Phnom Penh's expatriate community was notorious during years of instability. Even the U.N. troops that arrived in 1992 were as much a part of the problem in their support of local vice as they were in maintaining order and ensuring fair elections. "Sexpats" and drug tourists are on the wane in Cambodia, but, sadly, there still is a contingent of folks who come to take advantage of Cambodia's seedier stock-in-trade. There are new extradition treaties in place whereby foreign sex offenders in Cambodia can be tried for their crimes in their home country, but the prosecution process is still full of gaping loopholes and offenders easily fall through the cracks.

Tourism is growing in leaps and bounds, though, and there are many non-governmental organizations (NGOs) here to do their part to rebuild and support the growing nation. Their activities, centered in offices in Phnom Penh, are what keep social services and the infrastructure at subsistence levels. Volunteer opportunities abound. The number of foreign aid workers means increased quality of services, and the hotels and restaurants in Siem Reap and Phnom Penh are on par with any in the region (although outside of these two centers, choices are sparse).

For the Angkor temples alone, the trip to Cambodia is well worth it. A visit here is a chance to see a beguiling land shaking off the shackles of a devastating recent history to become an exciting tourist destination.

1 Getting to Know Cambodia

THE LAY OF THE LAND

About the size of Missouri, some 181,035 sq. km (70,604 sq. miles), Cambodia has 20 provinces that are bordered by Laos in the north, Vietnam in the east, Thailand to the west, and the Gulf of Thailand to the south. There is just one marine port in Cambodia: Sihanoukville, connected via a major American-built highway with the capital and largest city, Phnom Penh, and now linked by air to Siem Reap.

The mighty Mekong River enters from Laos to the north and nearly bisects the country. It divides into two main tributaries at Phnom Penh before it traces a route to the delta in Vietnam, and most areas of population density lie along the valleys and fertile plains of this great river and its tributaries. Near Siem Reap, the Tonle Sap Lake is the largest lake in Southeast Asia. In the monsoon summer months, when the Mekong is swollen from the snows of Tibet, the river becomes choked with silt and backs up on the Mekong Delta. The result is an anomaly: The Tonle Sap River relieves the pressure by changing the direction of its flow and draining the Mekong Delta hundreds of miles in the opposite direction and into the Tonle Sap Lake.

The northeast of the country, Ratanakiri Province, and areas bordering Vietnam are quite mountainous and rugged, as are the Thai border areas defined by the Dangrek Mountains in the northwest and the Cardamom Mountains in the southwest. These jungle forests are a rich source for timber in the region, and steps toward preservation come slowly.

A LOOK AT THE PAST

Cambodia is populated by people of the **Mon-Khmer** ethnic group, who probably migrated from the north as far back as 1,000 B.C. The area they settled was part of the

kingdom of Funan, an empire that extended into Laos and Vietnam, until the 6th century, when it was briefly absorbed into a rebel nation called Chenla. It then evolved into its glorious Angkor period in the 8th century, from which sprung many of Cambodia's treasures, most notably the lost city of Angkor.

The story of Khmer civilization is one of a slow decline from the zenith of the powerful Angkor civilization of the 11th century. The late 12th century was marked by internal rebellions. Angkor was lost to the Kingdom of Siam in 1431. Vietnam also had a hand in controlling the kingdom, to some degree, beginning in the 17th century. The French took over completely in 1863, followed by the Japanese, and then the French again. Cambodia finally regained independence in 1953 under the leadership of **Prince Norodom Sihanouk.** These years of alternating occupation had the country bouncing like a strategic Ping-Pong ball, and the Khmer kingdom's size was chiseled away considerably. Remaining is what we know today as Cambodia, a tiny land half the size of Germany.

Vietnamese communist outposts in the country drew Cambodia into the Vietnam conflict. The country was heavily bombed by American forces in the late 1960s. A U.S.–backed military coup followed in 1970, but in 1975 the infamous **Khmer Rouge,** led by the tyrannical **Pol Pot,** took over Cambodia, renamed it Kampuchea, and established a totalitarian regime in the name of communism. Opposition—even imaginary opposition—was brutally crushed, resulting in the death of over two million Cambodians. The civil and Vietnam wars decimated Cambodian infrastructure. Cambodia became, and still is, one of the world's poorest nations, with a mainly agrarian economy and a literacy rate of about 35%.

In response to Khmer Rouge infractions into its country, Vietnam invaded Cambodia in 1978 and occupied it with a small number of troops until 1989, installing a puppet regime led by **Hun Sen** as prime minister. When Vietnam departed, the United Nations stepped in and engineered a fragile coalition government between the Sihanouk and Hun Sen factions. There was never full agreement, however, and Hun Sen took over in a violent 1997 coup. The Khmer Rouge subsequently waned in power, and its former leader, Pol Pot, died in 1998.

In November 1998, a new coalition government was formed between the two leading parties, leading to relative political peace. Cambodia is now leaning toward a war crimes tribunal for Khmer Rouge perpetrators, but it still has not decided how to confront its vicious and bloody past and move forward.

The name Cambodia hardly evokes thoughts of ancient glory. To those of us born in the late 20th century, especially in the West, Cambodia suggests instead a history of oppression, civil war, genocide, drug running, and coups d'état. Constant political turbulence, armed citizenry, bandits, and war fallout, such as unexploded mines, have given the country a reputation as one of the world's most dangerous places to travel rather than a repository of man-made and natural wonders. It's important to have perspective on the country's troubled history in order to understand the present. Only then can we appreciate the current civil order and the fact that citizens have been or are being disarmed, and that Cambodia is making the slow push into this new century.

CAMBODIA TODAY

July 2003 elections went off without incident, but it took nearly a year for the negotiation of a government coalition. Hun Sen still reigns as prime minister, but ministries are shared with the royalists of FUNCINPEC. They face a dizzying backlog of legislation. In the fall of 2004, King Norodom Sihanouk, Cambodia's longtime standard-bearer through the many violent regime changes and trying times, abdicated, selecting his son Norodom Sihamoni, a retired ballet dancer, to take up the symbolic post of king. Meanwhile, work got underway in 2006 for a joint tribunal to bring justice to the former leaders of the Khmer Rouge.

The country's economy is experiencing a 5% annual growth rate, mostly spurred by tourism, but the scene in rural Cambodia is bleak. Basic medical services are nonexistent; education and job training are out of reach for rural peasantry. International monitors and aid organizations look to the youthful population (some 60% under the age of 20), the survivors of and the next generation after genocide, to foster peace and productivity. The forecast is not good. The proliferation of new AIDS cases in Cambodia, and the inability to treat patients, is a major concern. Rural travel entails following safety precautions to the letter (see below) and staying abreast of the current political situation—instability being the hallmark—but know that the Cambodia of today is a much safer and saner land than only a few years ago. Our tourist dollars are a big reason why.

THE KHMER PEOPLE & CULTURE

The name Cambodia is an Anglicized version of the French *Cambodge,* a bastardized name of the northern Indian tribe from which the Khmer are said to descend. Both

---

Tips "Heritage Friendly" Establishments

Much of Cambodia's ancient history has been lost, thanks to its violent past and the continued looting and trafficking of Khmer artifacts. To help prevent this, look for the "Heritage Friendly" logo. This logo was created by the Heritage Foundation (www.heritagewatch.org), an organization working to preserve Khmer antiquities and culture. The presence of the logo indicates that a business or organization has met certain standards that help protect Cambodian heritage. Travel to Cambodia is good, but responsible travel is even better.

---

citizens and language are alternately referred to as Khmer or Cambodian. Ninety percent of Cambodia's 14 million people are ethnic Khmer, the remainder a mix of ethnic Vietnamese, Chinese, hill tribes, and a small pocket of Cham Muslims.

The country's history is a road map of incursions and invasion. Cambodia is a geographic and cultural crossroads of the two powers, India and China, that shaped Southeast Asia and, more than any country in the region, reflects the French term *Indochine*. Khmer culture, like that of nearby Laos, is defined by Theravada Buddhism, but in other matters, one gets the distinct impression that Cambodia is still searching for its identity.

ETIQUETTE

Traditions and practices in Cambodia, like those in neighboring Thailand and Laos, are closely tied with Theravada Buddhism. Modest dress is expected of all visitors, and bare midriffs or short shorts are an offense to many and will cause a stir. Men and women should go easy on public displays of affection. As in all Buddhist countries, it is important to respect the space around Buddhist monks; women especially should avoid touching and even speaking to the men in orange robes anywhere outside the temple.

In personal interaction, keep it light and friendly, especially when bargaining or handling any business affairs. If Khmer people are confused, misunderstand, or are in disagreement, they do what many Westerners find inconceivable: smile, nod, and agree while whole in the knowledge that they will do something different. This is difficult to understand, but try to remember that if you're angry and lots of people around you are smiling, you're unlikely to have achieved your desired aim (in short, you're doomed). Direct discourse is certainly not standard procedure here, and many Western visitors can feel cheated by that misunderstanding. Be clear in what you expect from someone—whether a guide, a motorbike driver, or a business associate—and get firm affirmation of that fact. Listen closely to what comes after the *but* in "Yes, but . . . ."

On the list of cultural no-nos, it's important to remember that the feet are considered dirty and that the head is sacred and pure. This means that even pointing the feet in the direction of another or stepping over someone, thus exposing the soles of the feet, is impolite. Touching someone's head, even tussling a child's hair, should be avoided.

Hospitality has its own elaborate rules, and, like in any culture, it is important to accept when possible, or comfortable, and to say thank you: *Awk Koun*.

LANGUAGE

The language of Cambodia is called either Cambodian or Khmer, a term that refers to the ethnic majority of the country but is also used to describe all things Cambodian:

Khmer people (the Khmer), Khmer food, and Khmer culture. The Khmer language belongs to the Mon-Khmer family and is a derivative of Sanskrit and Pali, the language spoken by Buddha. Unlike in neighboring Thailand and Laos, the Khmer language is not tonal and is thus more merciful to the casual learner. Basic pronunciation is still frustrating and difficult, though. Khmer script is based on a south Indian model and is quite complex.

Khmer embraces many loaner words from French, Chinese, and now English, especially technical terms. Older Khmers still speak French, and young people are quite keen to learn and practice English. In the major tourist centers, speaking slowly and clearly in basic English phrases will do the trick, but a few choice phrases in Khmer will get you far.

USEFUL KHMER PHRASES

English	Khmer	Pronunciation
Hello	**Soa s'day**	Sew sadday
Good-bye	**Lia haoy**	Lee howie
Thank you	**Awk koun**	Awk coon
Thank you very much	**Awk koun chelan**	Awk coon chalan
How are you?	**Sohk sabai?**	Sook sabai?
I am fine	**Sohk sabai**	Sook sabai
Yes (man)	**Baat**	Baht
Yes (woman)	**Jaa**	Jya
No	**Ah te**	Ah tay
I'm sorry	**Sohm to**	Sum tow
Toilet?	**Bawngku uhn?**	Bangku oon?
Do you have . . . ?	**Men awt men?** (lit. do you have or don't you?)	Mien ought mien?
Water?	**Tuhk sot?**	Took sawt?
How much?	**Th'lai pohnmaan?**	Tlai bawn mahn?
Can you make it cheaper?	**Som joh th'lai?**	Sum joe tlai?

2 The Best of Cambodia in 1 Week

Cambodia's Angkor Wat temple complex could occupy you for a full week. But there is more to Cambodia than those old stones, and in just 7 days you can get a good sampling of this tragic, enigmatic country.

Day ❶: Siem Reap

Many carriers fly to Siem Reap, and you'll want to start your trip here. Check into the **Shinta Mani,** a quaint resort that helps train underprivileged Cambodians and provides excellent service along the way. Take a tuk-tuk to the temples and pick up your 3-day pass. Enter for sunset at **Ta Prohm Kel,** a small hilltop temple near Angkor Wat. Return to town for dinner at **Khmer Kitchen Restaurant,** which serves inexpensive, authentic Khmer food.

Days ❷–❸: Angkor Wat ✵✵✵

Devote your first day to the outer temples and sites. Stop by the **Blue Pumpkin** to pick up sandwiches for a picnic lunch;

then take a rented car to **Kabal Spean** for a small hike through the forest to a river whose bedrock has been carved into many Hindu reliefs. The water is blessed by these carvings before running into Angkor. On your return from this revered site, stop at **Banteay Srei,** a temple of pink stone. Return to Siem Reap and dine at the **Red Piano,** a restaurant made famous by Angelina Jolie during her filming of *Tomb Raider.* Wake early the following morning to watch the sun rise over Angkor Wat. Spend the day roaming the temples (you'll want to hire a tuk-tuk driver in town for this). Take your time at **Ta Prohm, Angkor Thom,** and the **Bayon,** but also explore some of the smaller temples. Save the best for last: **Angkor Wat.** Allow plenty of time for this one, as the details carved in stone here can be captivating. Have a hearty dinner on the outside patio of the **FCC (Foreign Correspondents Club).**

Day ❹: Phnom Penh

Take a morning flight from Siem Reap to the capital, Phnom Penh. Stay at the **Raffles Hotel Le Royal,** a colonial-era hotel that has retained much of its class. Spend some time strolling along the riverfront on **Sisowath Quay.** Then check out the **National Museum,** the **Silver Pagoda,** and **Tuol Sleng, Museum of Genocide.** Each of these will give you a clearer picture of the tragedies that have befallen this nation. Have dinner at the **FCC (Foreign Correspondents Club)** and watch as night falls over the confluence of the Sap and Mekong rivers.

Days ❺–❻: Kep 🏖🏖🏖

Kep is Cambodia's best-kept secret. A small beach town, Kep can be reached by an early morning bus out of Phnom Penh; the ride will give you a feel for Cambodian rural life. Stay at the **Veranda Natural Resort** in a hillside bungalow overlooking the Gulf of Thailand. Take a swim and try some crab at one of the little restaurants on the beachfront. Hop a morning bus to Phnom Penh and an evening flight to Siem Reap the next day.

Day ❼: Siem Reap

Save the last day for shopping at the **Old Market** and the stores that flank it. Look for silk and sculpture as well as souvenirs. Fly out in the evening with your bags laden with gifts for grateful friends.

3 Planning Your Trip to Cambodia

VISITOR INFORMATION

You'll find a wealth of information at **www.gocambodia.com,** or click on "Cambodia" at **www.visit-mekong.com.** The Cambodian Embassy to the U.S. sponsors **www. embassy.org/cambodia.** Below are Cambodian embassy and consulate locations overseas.

- **In the U.S.:** 4500 16th St. NW, Washington, DC 20011 (© **202/726-7742;** fax 202/726-8381; www.embassy.org); or 866 United Nations Plaza, Suite 420, New York, NY 10017 (© **212/421-7626;** fax 212/421-7743).
- **In Australia/New Zealand:** 5 Canterbury Crescent, Deakin, ACT 2600, Canberra (© **61-6/273-1259;** fax 61-6/273-1053; www.embassyofcambodia.org.nz).
- **In Thailand:** No. 185 Rajdammri Rd., Lumpini Patumwan, Bangkok 10330, Thailand (© **662/254-6630;** fax 662/253-9859; recanbot@loxinfo.co.tlt).

ORGANIZED TOURS & TRAVEL AGENTS

Many visitors choose to see Cambodia with the convenience of a guided tour, which is a good idea: It's not only safer and easier, but also means that you won't miss the finer details of what you're seeing and can visit rural Cambodia in as much comfort as possible. Being part of a larger group tour is a good, affordable option. Even if you travel independently, you might want to sign up with a local tour operator (like Diethelm or Exotissimo, below) once you're in Cambodia. Below are recommended tour operators that offer Cambodia excursions.

INTERNATIONAL

- **Abercrombie & Kent,** 1520 Kensington Rd., Suite 212, Oakbrook, IL 60523-2141 (② **800/323-7308;** fax 630/954-3324; www.aandktours.com).
- **Asia Transpacific Journeys,** 2995 Center Green Court, Boulder, CO 80301 (② **800/642-2742** or 303/443-6789; fax 303/443-7078; www.asiatranspacific.com).

REGIONAL

- **Diethelm Travel,** House #65, St. 240, P.O. Box 99, Phnom Penh (② **023/219-151;** fax 023/219-150; www.diethelmtravel.com), or House #4, Road #6, Krum #1, Sangkat #2, Phum Taphul, Siem Reap (② **063/963-524;** fax 063/963-694).
- **Exotissimo Travel,** #46, Norodom Blvd., Phnom Penh (② **023/218-948;** fax 023/426-586; www.exotissimo.com).

ENTRY REQUIREMENTS

All visitors are required to carry a passport and visa. A 1-month visa can be issued on arrival at the Phnom Penh or Siem Reap airports for about US$20/£11, and an overland visa-upon-arrival is available from both Thailand (overland from Poipet) and Vietnam (by boat from Chau Doc or by bus through Moc Bai) for US$22/£12. Bring two passport photos for your application or be prepared to pay a few extra dollars. For other entry points, you must obtain your visa before arrival. There is an overland crossing between Laos and Cambodia via Stung Treng, but it is a trip reserved only for the hearty.

Tourist visas can be extended three times for a total of 3 months. Any travel agent can perform the service for a small fee. Business visas, for just US$25/£14 upon entry, can be extended indefinitely.

CUSTOMS REGULATIONS

For visitors 18 and older, allowable amounts of goods when entering are as follows: 200 cigarettes or the equivalent quantity of tobacco; one opened bottle of liquor; and a reasonable amount of perfume for personal use. Currency in possession must be declared on arrival. Cambodian Customs on the whole is not stringent. Due to a long, sad history of theft from the Angkor temples, it is forbidden to carry antiques or Buddhist reliquaries out of the country, but Buddhist statues and trinkets bought from souvenir stalls are fine.

MONEY

Cambodia's official currency is the **riel,** but the Cambodian economy is tied to the fate of its de facto currency, the **U.S. dollar.** Greenbacks can be used anywhere. The exchange rate at the time of publication was **4,000 riel = US$1.** Prices for all but the smallest purchases are in U.S. dollars and are listed as thus in this chapter. The **Thai baht** is also widely accepted in the western region of the country.

It's important to have riel for smaller purchases, but there is no point in exchanging large amounts of foreign currency into the local scrap. You'll commonly receive small change in riel as well. The riel comes in denominations of 100, 200, 500, 1,000, 2,000, 5,000, 10,000, 50,000, and 100,000. You cannot change Cambodia's riel outside the country, so anything you carry home is a souvenir.

ATMs   ATMs are now available at major banks in both Siem Reap and Phnom Penh.

CURRENCY EXCHANGE   You can change traveler's checks in banks in all major towns. Because the U.S. dollar is the de facto currency, it's not a bad idea to change traveler's checks to dollars for a 1% or 2% fee and make all purchases in U.S. cash.

TRAVELER'S CHECKS   Traveler's checks are accepted in most major banks for exchange, but not commonly at individual vendors. American Express is a good bet and is represented by **Diethelm** (see "Recommended Tour Operators," above).

CREDIT CARDS   Cambodia has a cash economy, but credit cards are becoming more widely accepted. Most large hotels and high-end restaurants accept the majors, but you'll want to carry cash for the majority of transactions—and certainly in the countryside. To report a lost or stolen card, see "Lost & Found" under "Fast Facts: Southeast Asia" (p. 68).

WHEN TO GO
CLIMATE   Cambodia's climate falls under the pattern of the southern monsoons that also hit neighboring Thailand and Vietnam from May to November. There is little seasonal temperature variation, meaning that it's always hot (a yearly mean of about 82°F/28°C). The best time to go is in the dry season from December to April.

CLOTHING CONSIDERATIONS   Keep it light and loose; it's always hot. "Less is more" applies here; bulky luggage is an albatross in Cambodia. Loose, long-sleeved shirts and long pants are recommended. Cotton is the best choice, and long trousers are better than shorts. First, long pants are the best way to fend off mosquitoes. Second, culturally, shorts are worn by children, not adults (although long shorts are more accepted, especially for young men), and for women only rarely (with sporting events being the exception). A wide-brimmed hat is essential protection from the sun, and some even carry an umbrella to be used either as a parasol or as cover from sporadic rains. Sandals are acceptable in most arenas, but shoes are a better idea, given some of the tumbledown qualities of most areas in the country.

PUBLIC HOLIDAYS & EVENTS   **Khmer New Year** is in the middle of April. The **Angkor Festival** is held at the end of July. **King Sihanouk's Birthday** is October 31. **Independence Day** is November 9 (1953) and is celebrated throughout the country like the American Fourth of July. There are water festivals and boat races at the end of November, including a huge festival in Phnom Penh.

HEALTH & SAFETY
DRUGS   Cambodia is one of the world's biggest producers of cannabis—not to mention heroin, amphetamines, and other substances—and peddlers abound. You might be tempted to buy or sample substances offered, but if caught, you could face a lengthy jail sentence, which is guaranteed to be uncomfortable. Enough said.

HEALTH CONCERNS   See chapter 3's "Health & Safety" section (p. 43) for information on health concerns and general issues that affect the region. Remember that no tap water in Cambodia is considered potable, so stick with bottled water. It's also a good idea to check the most recent information at the **Centers for Disease Control** (click "Travelers' Health" at **www.cdc.gov**).

Health considerations should comprise a good part of your trip planning for Cambodia, even if you're going for only a few weeks. If rural areas are on your itinerary, you'll need to get special vaccinations far enough in advance to give them time to take effect. If you follow the guidelines here and those of your doctor, there's no reason you can't have a safe and healthy trip.

Malaria is not a concern in Phnom Penh and any of the larger towns, but upcountry and even in and around Siem Reap and Angkor Wat, it's quite common. Many travelers take preventative medication. Check with the Centers for Disease Control (CDC) at www.cdc.com for current information. An **antimalarial prophylaxis** is recommended everywhere but in Phnom Penh. Take atovaquone proguanil (brand name Malarone), doxycycline, or mefloquine (brand name Lariam). If you plan to travel extensively in the rural areas on the western border with Thailand, primaquine is the only effective preventative.

Other mosquito-borne ailments, such as **Japanese encephalitis** and **dengue fever,** are also prevalent. Your best protection is to wear light, loose-fitting clothes from wrist to neck and ankles; use a bug repellent with DEET; and be particularly careful at sunset or when out and about early in the morning.

(*Tips* **Some Important Safety Tips**

- Remember that the police and military of Cambodia are not there to protect and serve. Any interaction with the constabulary usually results in frustration and/or your coming away short a few dollars. Contact your embassy for major problems, and call for police assistance only in cases of theft or extreme danger. Demand a ticket if threatened with a fine of any sort (although often, especially for small traffic infractions, it's best to just cough up a buck or two).

- Women should take extra caution in Cambodia, as recent years have seen an increase in sexual assaults on foreign women, in both Phnom Penh and Siem Reap and even in the Angkor temple complex. Don't travel alone, and try not to isolate yourself in areas around the temples.

- Rural travel is really opening up, and you'll find a hearty welcome in even the most remote hamlet, but roads are rough and travel of any distance is best done in an off-road conveyance with a sturdy suspension: Motorbikes or four-wheel-drive trucks are best. Know, too, that you're really on your own out in the sticks, with no hospitals and limited support services available.

- Especially at night, travelers should stay aware, just as they would in any big city. Purse snatching is not uncommon in Phnom Penh, and pickpockets are as proficient here as anywhere in the region, so take care.

- Land mines and unexploded ordnance (UXO) can be found in rural areas in Cambodia, but especially in Battambang, Banteay Meanchey, Pursat, Siem Reap, and Kampong Thom provinces. Don't walk in heavily forested spots or in dry rice paddies without a local guide. Areas around small bridges on secondary roads are particularly dangerous.

> **⌐Warning**   **Medical Safety & Evacuation Insurance**
>
> The Cambodian medical system is rudimentary at best and nonexistent at worst. Make sure that you have medical coverage for overseas travel and that it includes emergency evacuation. For more information on insurance, see p. 41. There are a few clinics in Phnom Penh and Siem Reap, but for anything major, evacuation to Bangkok is the best option.

Hepatitis is a concern, as it is anywhere. Reliable statistics on **AIDS** are not out, but with rampant prostitution and drug abuse, Cambodia is certainly fertile ground for the disease. Recent efforts to educate needle users about the dangers of substance abuse and the importance of clean needles, as well as increased condom use, are positive signs, but statistics show that the tide of new AIDS cases is still rising.

SAFETY CONCERNS   It is recommended that you check with your home country's overseas travel bureau or with the **U.S. State Department** (click "Travel Warnings" at **www.travel.state.gov**) to keep abreast of travel advisories and current affairs that could affect your trip.

If you encounter problems during your visit, go to your country's embassy. Addresses for embassies in Phnom Penh are listed under "Fast Facts: Cambodia" (p. 417).

The days of the Khmer Rouge taking backpackers hostage are long gone, and the general lawlessness and banditry that marked Cambodia as inaccessible and dangerous only a short time ago has abated. Gun-toting thugs, once a common sight in any town, have been disarmed. Old habits die hard, however, and in general travelers should take caution. Poverty in rural areas breeds desperation and a volatile climate.

GETTING THERE

BY PLANE   International flights to Cambodia from neighboring countries are numerous and affordable. Cambodia's two main hubs, **Siem Reap International Airport** and **Phnom Penh International Airport,** are served by the following: **Bangkok Airways** from Thailand; **Malaysia Airlines** from Kuala Lumpur; **Lao Airways** from Vientiane; **Vietnam Airways** from Ho Chi Minh and Hanoi; **Silk Air** from Singapore; and **EVA Air** from Taipei. **Shanghai Air, President,** and **China Southern** provide connections between Phnom Penh and points in China. There is a US$25/£14 international departure tax.

BY BUS   Pickup trucks and limited bus service connect with Poi Pet, near Thailand, a journey that is like crossing the craters of the moon—you'll come away exhausted and caked with dust. This trip is recommended only for the rough and ready. Arriving from Vietnam, private minibuses and taxis can be chartered from the border near Moc Bai to Phnom Penh. The ride is bumpy but manageable, though flying in or out of Phnom Penh or Siem Reap is recommended.

BY BOAT   There are daily boats between Phnom Penh and Vietnam's border town, Chau Doc. From Vietnam, contact the **Victoria Chau Doc Hotel** (© 076/865-010) for expensive, private services, or one of the traveler cafes, such as **Sinh Café** (© 08/369-420), for a budget trip. From Phnom Penh, make arrangements through any hotel or travel agent.

Tips **Telephone Dialing at a Glance**

- **To place a call from your home country to Cambodia:** Dial the international access code (011 in the U.S. and Canada, 0011 in Australia, 0170 in New Zealand, 00 in the U.K.), plus Cambodia's country code (**855**), the city code (**23** for Phnom Pehn, **63** for Siem Reap), and the six-digit phone number (for example, 011 855 23 000-000). *Important note:* Omit the initial "0" in all Cambodian phone numbers when calling from abroad.
- **To place a call within Cambodia:** Dial the city or area code preceded by a **0** (the way numbers are listed in this book), and then the local number (for example, 023 000-000). Note that all phone numbers are six digits after the city code.
- **To place a direct international call from Cambodia:** To place a call, dial the international access code (**00**), plus the country code, the area or city code, and the number (for example, to call the U.S., you'd dial 00 1 000/000-0000).
- **International country codes are as follows:** Australia, 61; Canada, 1; Hong Kong, 852; Indonesia, 62; Laos, 856; Malaysia, 60; Myanmar, 95; New Zealand, 64; the Philippines, 63; Singapore, 65; Thailand, 66; U.K., 44; U.S., 1; Vietnam, 84.

GETTING AROUND

BY PLANE Connection between Phnom Penh and Siem Reap is frequent and regular on **President Air** and **Siem Reap Airways.** There is a US$6/£3.30 domestic departure tax in both Phnom Penh and Siem Reap. After many years' delay, Sihanoukville's airport is expected to be open in 2007.

BY BUS Most travelers find local buses rough going in the extreme. Contact the folks at an old travelers' standby, **Capitol Tour** (144, Rd. 182, Sangkat Beng Prolitt; © 023/217-627), for inexpensive seat-in-coach connections and tours throughout the country. **Ho Wah Genting Transport Company** (Rd. 67, just west of the Central Market, Phnom Penh; © 023/210-859) provides service between Siem Reap and Phnom Penh for just US$3.50/£1.90. **Mekong Express** (87 Sisowath Quay, Phnom Penh; © 023/427-518) connects Phnom Penh and Siem Reap with daily luxury (well, air-conditioned) buses for just US$6/£3.30.

BY CAR/MOTORBIKE Hiring a car with a driver, driving yourself, or going by rented motorbike is a great way to see Cambodia's rural highways and byways. Rough country roads mean that you'll need to rent the most durable of vehicles, with good suspension. Hiring a driver is smart, too. Contact a travel agent or your hotel for recommendations. A reputable driver trusted by aid workers and journalists is a man named **Bon Thim** (© 092/800-128).

BY BOAT Speedboats make the 5-hour trip between Phnom Penh and Siem Reap. The cost is US$25/£14; any hotel can arrange a ticket. Boats leave from the pier near the Japanese Bridge in the north end of town or connect with Siem Reap's Tonle Sap docks by taxi. **Mekong Express** (87 Sisowath Quay, Phnom Penh; © 023/427-518) charges US$35/£19 for a ride on its larger, more comfortable boat. Visit its offices adjacent to the ferry terminal.

TIPS ON ACCOMMODATIONS

The only quality accommodations that you'll find are in Phnom Penh and Siem Reap, but their standards are high. Some budget options are updating themselves and turning into rustic boutique properties. Be warned that accommodations often fill up in the winter high season, especially at the finer hotels near Angkor Wat. There is a 10% VAT charge at most hotels. Expect discounts in the low season.

TIPS ON DINING

In this old French colony, the cuisine is heavily French, all affordable and often quite good. There's also good Thai, and tourist centers are chockablock with storefronts that serve up reasonable facsimiles of Western favorites.

TIPS ON SHOPPING

There are lots of antiques stores and boutiques in the major tourist centers, but shopping for trinkets and memorabilia is best at the big markets: the Russian Market and Central Market in Phnom Penh, and the Old Market in Siem Reap.

FAST FACTS: Cambodia

American Express For basic American Express services (such as reporting lost checks) contact **Diethelm Travel,** House #65, St. 240, P.O. Box 99, Phnom Penh (℡ **023/219-151;** www.diethelmtravel.com).

Business Hours Vendors and restaurants tend to be all-day operations, opening at about 8am and closing at 9 or 10pm. Government offices, banks, travel agencies, and museums are usually open from 8am to 4 or 5pm, with an hour break for lunch.

Drug & Liquor Laws There is no minimum legal drinking age in Cambodia. When it comes to drugs, however, availability can look like permission, but it's often not the case. It's said that you can bribe your way out of (or into) anything in corrupt Cambodia, but it's best not to test that theory. Police are crooked and may be the ones who sell (out of uniform) in order to collect the bribe. Like anywhere, dabbling in this arena makes you friends in all the wrong places, and Cambodia is not a good place to have the wrong friends.

Electricity Cambodia runs on 220-volt European standard electricity, with rounded, two-prong plugs. If you're coming from the U.S., bring an adapter, as well as a surge protector for delicate gadgets.

Embassies **U.S.:** #1, St. 96, Sangkat Wat Phnom, Phnom Penh (℡ **023/728-000;** http://phnompenh.usembassy.gov). **U.K.:** #27–29 Botum Soriyavong, St. 75, Phnom Penh (℡ **023/427-124;** www.britishembassy.gov.uk/cambodia). **Australia:** #11, St. 254, Phnom Penh (℡ **023/213-470;** www.cambodia.embassy. gov.au). The Australian embassy also assists nationals of Canada and New Zealand.

Emergencies In Phnom Penh, dial ℡ **117** for police, ℡ **119** for an ambulance.

Hospitals You'll want to take care of any medical or dental issues before arriving in Cambodia. The **SOS Clinic** in Phnom Penh, #161 St. 51 (© **023/216-911**), is your best bet in a pinch.

Internet Access Reliable service can be found in the major centers, with prepaid wireless connections a recent innovation.

Language The Cambodian language is Khmer, an amalgam of ancient Sanskrit and Pali. English and French are spoken widely, as is Mandarin. See "Language," p. 409, for more information.

Mail Hotels usually sell stamps and send postcards for guests. See specific cities for locations of post offices.

Police Khmer police exist to harass and collect, not to protect and serve. Contact them only in the event of a major emergency, by calling © **117**. The expat hot line is © **023/724-793**.

Safety Once a place where violence and banditry were an everyday occurrence, Cambodia has become much safer in recent years. The civilian population is more or less disarmed and civil authorities have firm control, but stay on your toes. It's best not to be out on the roads too late at night. Beware of unexploded bombs and mines in rural areas. Also remember to lock valuables in hotel safes. In the event of trouble, comply and report any incidents to local officials. See "Health & Safety," p. 413, for more information.

Telephones The international country code for Cambodia is 855. Phones in the major centers are reliable, and international direct dial is common—for a price. Most hotels levy exorbitant surcharges of 10% to 25%. See "Telephone Dialing at a Glance," p. 416, for details.

Time Zone Cambodia is 7 hours ahead of Greenwich Mean Time, in the same zone as Bangkok. It is 12 hours ahead of U.S. Eastern Standard Time during the winter months, and 3 hours behind Sydney.

Tipping Tipping is not obligatory, but it is appreciated. A blanket 10% to 20% is exorbitant. It's best to just round up the check, or leave a buck or so.

Toilets Public toilets are a little rough. Many are the Asian-style "squatty-potty" variety, rather grungy with an attendant at the door charging a small fee for entrance and a few squares of gritty paper. It's not a bad idea to bring your own bog roll (toilet paper) and maybe some germ-fighting hand lotion. Facilities in Western accommodations will be more familiar.

Water No tap water is potable. Buy bottled water, which is widely available.

4 Phnom Penh

Founded in the mid–14th century by the Khmers as a monastery, Phnom Penh replaced Angkor Thom a century later as the country's capital. The city has long been a vital trading hub at the confluence of three rivers: the Mekong, Tonle Sap, and Bassac. The city's most dramatic history was when it lay vacant; following an eviction order from Pol Pot, the city was deserted in a period of hours. Almost all of Phnom Penh's residents moved to the countryside in 1975, not to return until 1979 under the authority of Vietnamese troops.

Phnom Penh

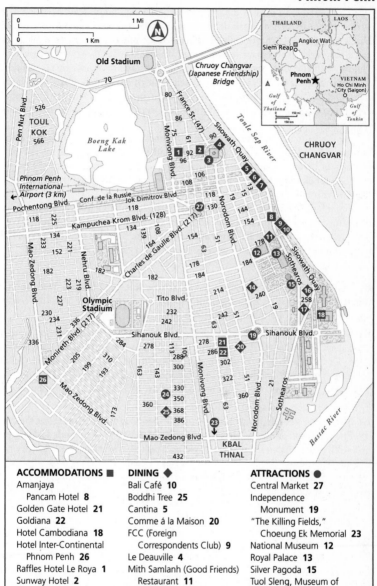

ACCOMMODATIONS ■

Amanjaya
    Pancam Hotel **8**
Golden Gate Hotel **21**
Goldiana **22**
Hotel Cambodiana **18**
Hotel Inter-Continental
    Phnom Penh **26**
Raffles Hotel Le Roya **1**
Sunway Hotel **2**

DINING ◆

Bali Café **10**
Boddhi Tree **25**
Cantina **5**
Comme á la Maison **20**
FCC (Foreign
    Correspondents Club) **9**
Le Deauville **4**
Mith Samlanh (Good Friends)
    Restaurant **11**
Rendezvous Café **6**
River House **7**
Tamarind Café **14**
Topaz **17**

ATTRACTIONS ●

Central Market **27**
Independence
    Monument **19**
"The Killing Fields,"
    Choeung Ek Memorial **23**
National Museum **12**
Royal Palace **13**
Silver Pagoda **15**
Tuol Sleng, Museum of
    Genocide **24**
Wat Phnom **3**

It has been a long road to the peaceful and growing Phnom Penh of today. There were many years of frontier-style anarchy after the city was repopulated in 1979. Drugs and prostitution are still big downtown commodities, but it's unlikely that you'll be caught in the crossfire, something you couldn't say 4 or 5 years ago. Today, Phnom Penh enjoys its own kind of harmony of opposites. Visitors are offered peaceful moments like a sunset at riverside, as well as dusty, motorbike-choked labyrinthine alleys and cacophonous markets. The city is an incongruous cluster of crumbling French colonials, and the central riverside area has a pace all its own that's great for wandering.

There's also much of historic interest in Phnom Penh. Its **Royal Palace** is a stone showpiece of classical Khmer architecture, and the **Silver Pagoda,** on the palace grounds, is a jewel-encrusted wonder. Throughout the city, you'll see the faded glory of aged **French colonial architecture.** There are also many notable *wats,* Buddhist temples with resident monks.

Of more grisly interest is the **Tuol Sleng,** or Museum of Genocide, a schoolhouse-turned-prison where up to 20,000 victims of Pol Pot's excesses were tortured before being led to the **Choeung Ek,** otherwise known as the Killing Fields, about 16km (10 miles) from Phnom Penh. It's a town certainly worth exploring for a few days.

GETTING THERE

BY PLANE   All major airlines in the region connect here. **Phnom Penh International Airport** is just a 15-minute drive from the city center. A cab costs US$7/£3.85, a ride on the back of a motorbike just US$2/£1.10.

BY BOAT   Speedboats connect with Siem Reap and leave every morning from the main dock on the north end of town. Tickets are available just about anywhere in town. The price is US$25/£14 from most hotels or the Capitol Guesthouse (below). **Mekong Express** (87 Sisowath Quay; © **023/427-518**) charges US$35/£19 for the 5-hour trip on a larger, more comfortable boat. Its office is just across from the ferry terminal.

BY BUS   Buses connect with neighboring Vietnam and points throughout the country. From Vietnam, contact **Saigontourist** (© **08/829-8914**) or **Sinh Café** (© **08/369-420**). To get from Cambodia to Vietnam, ask at any travel agent, hotel, or the Capitol Guesthouse (see below). A tourist bus to Siem Reap takes 6 to 7 hours and costs US$5/£2.75. **Ho Wah Genting Transport Company** (© **023/210-859**), with an office just west of the Central Market, sells tickets to all the major stops and minor hamlets in the country. **Mekong Express** (see "By Boat," above) has daily connections to Siem Reap on an air-conditioned bus for US$6/£3.30.

GETTING AROUND

Phnom Penh's downtown is accessible on foot, and it's easy to find your way because the streets are arranged in a numbered grid. For sites farther afield, like the Killing Fields or any temples, you'll need wheels. Metered taxis are everywhere in town, and any hotel can arrange daily car rental (with driver). Or contact the folks at **Lucky! Lucky!** (413 Monivong Blvd.; © **023/212-788**), who rent high-quality motorbikes for rural touring (available for long-term rental) as well as jeeps and even luxury cars.

Motorcycle taxis, also called **motodups,** can be hired anywhere and cost about 4,000 riel (about US$1/£0.55) for short trips in town. Bargain hard. These guys are everywhere, especially on the riverside, and the competition is in your favor. Add a tip and you'll have a friend for life.

VISITOR INFORMATION & TOURS

DELUXE

- **Diethelm Travel,** House #65, St. 240, P.O. Box 99, Phnom Penh (℡ **023/219-151;** fax 023/219-150; www.diethelmtravel.com), or House #4, Road #6, Krum #1, Sangkat #2, Phum Taphul, Siem Reap (℡ **063/963-524;** fax 063/963-694).
- **Exotissimo Travel,** #46, Norodom Blvd., Phnom Penh (℡ **023/218-948;** fax 023/426-586; www.exotissimo.com).

BUDGET

- **Capitol Guesthouse Tours,** #14 AEO, Road 182, Sangkat Beng Prolitt (℡ **023/217-627**). This is the town's budget travel cafe and a good place to arrange inexpensive rural and local tours and onward connections by bus and boat. Remember that you get what you pay for, but the services are convenient.
- Small tour operators and ticket shops abound along Sisowath. For flights and other services, try **K.U. Travel & Tours** (#38AB, St. 240; ℡ **023/723-456;** www.kucambodia.com), in the cafe and gallery area.

FAST FACTS: *Phnom Penh*

American Express For basic American Express services (such as reporting lost checks) contact **Diethelm Travel,** House #65, St. 240, P.O. Box 99, Phnom Penh (℡ **023/219-151;** www.diethelmtravel.com).

Currency Exchange **Canadia Bank,** #265, St. 110 (℡ **023/215-284**); **Mekong Bank,** #1, St. 114 (℡ **023/217-112**); and **Cambodian Commercial Bank** (CCB), #26 Monivong Rd. (℡ **023/426-208**), are just three of many in the downtown area that can cash traveler's checks and give cash advances. There is a also a **Western Union** office at Cambodia Asia Bank (℡ **023/210-900**), in the Naga, a floating casino behind the Cambodiana Hotel.

Emergencies For police, dial ℡ **117**; for fire, dial ℡ **118**; and for the expat hot line, dial ℡ **023/724-793**.

Hospitals The **International SOS Medical and Dental Clinic,** #161, St. 51 (℡ **023/216-911**), is the best place for minor emergencies. **Naga Clinic,** #11, St. 254 (℡ **011/811-175**), is another. For any major emergency or injury, however, you'll want to arrange medical evacuation.

Internet Access Internet outlets line the riverside Sisowath Street. Hourly access starts at US$1/£0.55. **Friendly Web,** near Capitol Guesthouse, has good access from its office at #199 EO, St. 107 (℡ **012/843-246**), at the corner of Rd. 182. **KIDS** is an NGO where American owner Bill Herod brings Internet technology to Khmer students. It has good, inexpensive access in its offices at #17A, St. 178 (℡ **023/218-452**; kids@camnet.com.kh).

Mail The post office is located in the north end of town on Street 13, east of Wat Phnom. It's open daily from 6:30am to 5pm, and has standard delivery service and an international phone. **DHL** has an office at #28 Monivong Rd. (℡ **023/427-726**). **FedEx** is at #701D Monivong Rd. (℡ **023/216-712**).

Telephones The local code for Phnom Penh is **23**. International direct dialing is available in most hotels and at the post office. Storefront Internet cafes along

Sisowath offer inexpensive Internet calls or direct dialing. Cellphones are very popular in the city, and you'll find street-side stalls on wheels where you can make local and international calls for next to nothing, with a good cellular connection.

WHERE TO STAY

There are some choice hotels in town, from old, upscale gems to budget minihotels and even a few small boutique properties. I recommend spending a little more for bargain luxury, as the midrange properties of Phnom Penh are run-down, at best. Always ask about seasonal rates. Some hotels charge a 10% VAT.

VERY EXPENSIVE

Hotel Inter-Continental Phnom Penh ✿✿✿   For the high-end business traveler, the Inter-Continental is definitely the place. This luxury behemoth has every amenity and in-room convenience imaginable, including wireless Internet access. It's just a short ride from the city center, but there's no reason to leave this self-contained, upscale gem. Rooms are outfitted with tidy carpeting, elegant wood furnishings, overstuffed couches, floral curtains and bedspreads, fluffy and comfortable king beds, and fine marble detailing in the entry. The large, well-appointed bathrooms come with separate shower and tub. Art Deco oak desks and floor-to-ceiling windows give guests that "power broker" feel (even if you're just a small fish). The large outdoor pool has a fun elephant fountain and elegant water-level bar, and the Clark Hatch fitness center is the best in town. Dining options include fine Chinese and Western cuisine. The lobby is pure marble elegance, and the staff is superefficient and professional. The services in the executive lounge are certainly worth the extra fee. The regency suite is fit for kings, literally. Toto, I don't think we're in Cambodia anymore.

Regency Sq., 296 Blvd. Mao Tse Toung, P.O. Box 2288, Phnom Penh. ✆ **023/424-888**. Fax 023/424-885. www.inter conti.com. 372 units. US$190 (£105) single; US$220 (£121) double; US$330–US$1,500 (£182–£825) suite. Seasonal and Internet rates available. AE, MC, V. **Amenities:** 2 restaurants; 2 snack bars; bar; outdoor pool; great fitness center; sauna; children's playroom; concierge; tour desk; car rental; business center w/Internet access; shopping; 24-hr. room service; massage; babysitting; laundry service; dry cleaning; executive-level rooms. *In room:* A/C, satellite TV, dataport, minibar, fridge, safe, IDD phone.

Raffles Hotel Le Royal ✿✿   Built in 1929, this is Phnom Penh's most atmospheric hotel, an authentic Art Deco and colonial classic. Reopened and expanded with a new wing in 1997, everything from the vaulted ceilings in the lobby to the classic original central stairs breathes history and charm. Rooms are done with fine tiled entries, high ceilings, indirect lighting, a sitting area with inlaid furniture, and ornate touches like antique wall sconces and fine drapery. The scale is large but not imposing. Landmark rooms, just one step above the standard, are a good choice in the older building and are larger, with nice appointments like claw-foot tubs. It's luxury with a price tag, but it's worth it. There are also some interesting theme suites named for famous visitors, including Stamford Raffles. Even Jacqueline Kennedy has a room dedicated to photos and memorabilia of her 1967 visit. The central pool area is a tranquil oasis divided by a unique pavilion, and the amenities throughout, such as the fine massage facility, are luxe. The staff is very professional.

92 Rukhak Vithei Daun Penh (off Monivong Blvd.), Sangkat Wat Phnom, Phnom Penh. ✆ **023/981-888**. Fax 023/ 981-168. www.phnompenh.raffles.com. 170 units. US$290–US$320 (£160–£176) double; US$350–US$2,000

(£193–£1100) suite. AE, MC, V. **Amenities:** 2 restaurants; 2 bars; 2 outdoor pools; health club; Jacuzzi; sauna; concierge; tour desk; car rental; business center w/Internet access; shopping; 24-hr. room service; massage; babysitting; laundry service; dry cleaning. *In room:* A/C, satellite TV, dataport, minibar, fridge, coffeemaker, hair dryer, safe, IDD phone.

EXPENSIVE

Hotel Cambodiana 🏵🏵   The Cambodiana nearly has it all. With a convenient location, atmosphere, and all the amenities, this is a good jumping-off point for the sights downtown. The building looks like a giant gilded wedding cake, and its vaulted Khmer-style roofs dominate the sky in the southern end of downtown. The lobby is abuzz with activity, whether it's visiting dignitaries or disembarking tour buses, but the helpful staff handles it all with grace. The large riverside pool is great, and there are some fine choices in international dining. All rooms have picture windows and good views of town or the river. They're priced according to their view of the river, and executive floors are maintained to high standards. Everything is tidy, but the decor is a chain-hotel style in plain wood and office carpeting; it's a bit dull, and some floors reek of pungent deodorizers. Deluxe riverview rooms are your best bet. The high-end suites are richly decorated and the executive privileges on the top floors are luxe. Wireless Internet access (with prepaid cards) is available in all public spaces.

313 Sisowath Quay, Phnom Penh. © **023/426-288.** Fax 023/982-380. www.hotelcambodiana.com. 267 units. US$175–US$180 (£96–£99) double; US$200 (£110) on Chactomuk floors; US$225–US$500 (£124–£275) suite. AE, MC, V. **Amenities:** 4 restaurants; bar; outdoor pool; tennis court; small health club; Jacuzzi; sauna; concierge; car rental; business center w/Internet access; shopping; limited room service; massage; laundry service; dry cleaning; executive-level rooms. *In room:* A/C, satellite TV, minibar, fridge, safe, IDD phone.

Sunway Hotel 🏵🏵   The Sunway is a very comfortable high-end choice. Just west of Wat Phnom in the north end of town, the facade and entry are grand, and the small wrought-iron chandelier suspended in the cool marble of the lobby completes the fine effect. The staff snaps to and is courteous even when busy. The Sunway covers all the bases for amenities, with a good health club and large downstairs salon and massage area. The dining room and laid-back lobby lounge are stylish and inviting. Rooms are chain-hotel bland, but large, clean, and very comfortable, with white walls, carpeting with a tight geometric design, and wooden valances. They have a good feel—though they could do without the bad "hotel art." Bathrooms are large, with combination tub/showers and granite counters.

#1, St. 92, Sangkat Wat Phnom, P.O. Box 633, Phnom Penh. © **023/430-333.** Fax 023/430-339. www.sunway.com.my. 138 units. US$140–US$160 (£77–£88) deluxe; US$280–US$850 (£154–£168) suite. AE, MC, V. **Amenities:** Restaurant; cafe; bar/lounge (w/live entertainment on Sat); health club; Jacuzzi; sauna; steam room; concierge; tour desk; car rental; business center; shopping arcade; 24-hr. room service; massage; babysitting; laundry service; dry cleaning. *In room:* A/C, satellite TV, dataport, minibar, fridge, coffeemaker, safe, IDD phone.

MODERATE

Amanjaya Pancam Hotel 🏵🏵   Riverside at Sisowath Quay, this three-story corner building is a true house of style. The porous laterite walls of the lobby, the same stone used in Angkor, and Buddhist statues throughout contribute to a cool boutique vibe. Though sparse in services and amenities, the rooms are spacious, done in rich red silk hangings and bedspreads that contrast boldly with the dark-wood trim and floors. All units have king beds. The suites are enormous and worth the extra outlay. Bathrooms are immaculate affairs done in wood and tile, with neat tub/shower units in standard rooms and separate shower and tub in suites, delineated by unique stone paths in concrete. Accommodations vary in size and shape, with the corner suites the best, offering panoramic views of the river and busy street below. Noisy traffic is the only drawback.

#1, St. 154, Sisowath Quay, Phnom Penh. ⓒ 023/214-747. Fax 023/219-545. www.amanjaya.com. 21 units. US$115–US$195 (£63–£107) double; US$185–US$265 (£102–£146) suite. MC, V. **Amenities:** Restaurant; limited room service; laundry service; dry cleaning. In room: A/C, satellite TV, minibar, fridge, safe, IDD phone.

Juliana Hotel 🍂 The Thai-owned and -managed Juliana is a good distance from the center of town and popular with both group tours and regional businessmen. Rooms are situated around a luxuriant central pool shaded by palms and with a terrace and lounge chairs: a bright spot in an otherwise dull landscape. Standard rooms aren't especially attractive, with their aging red carpeting and the nicks and scrapes of heavy use. That said, superior and deluxe rooms are large and well appointed, with tidy carpet and light-wood trim. Regal headboards top the large beds, and there are nice rattan furnishings throughout. Be sure to request a nonsmoking room—and check it out before checking in. Calling itself a "city resort" isn't quite accurate, but the Continental restaurant is inviting and the pool is a standout, even if the rooms don't quite pass muster.

16 Juliana 152 Rd., Sangkhat Vealvong, Phnom Penh. ⓒ 023/366-070-72 or 023/880-530-31. Fax 023/366-070-72. www.julianacambodia.com. 93 units. US$70 (£39) standard; US$120 (£66) superior; US$160 (£88) deluxe; US$240 (£132) suite. AE, MC, V. **Amenities:** 2 restaurants; small lobby bar; outdoor pool; small health club; sauna; car rental; business center w/Internet access; shopping; salon; room service (5am–11pm); large massage complex; babysitting; laundry service; nonsmoking rooms. In room: A/C, satellite TV, dataport, minibar, fridge, IDD phone.

INEXPENSIVE

Golden Gate Hotel 🍂 The standard US$15 (£8.25) rooms here are basic, but clean and quite livable. The Golden Gate also has deluxe rooms that are larger but just as plain. This is a popular spot for long-staying expat business visitors and NGO folks, as the suites, with kitchenette and small living room, are like one-room apartments. Accommodations are outfitted in either tile or office-style carpeting and have mismatched but tidy upholstered and rattan furniture. Bathrooms are the small shower-in-room type typical of guesthouses. The best choice is a deluxe room on a higher floor (with view). Be sure to ask to see the room first, as they really vary.

#9, Rd. 278, Sangkat (just south of the Independence Monument), Phnom Penh. ⓒ 023/7211-161. Fax 023/721-005. goldengatehtls@hotmail.com. US$15 (£8.25) standard single; US$20 (£11) standard double; US$30 (£17) deluxe; US$40 (£22) suite. MC, V. **Amenities:** Restaurant; car rental; business center w/Internet access; limited room service; laundry. In room: A/C, satellite TV, minibar, fridge, IDD phone.

Goldiana 🍂🍂 A labyrinthine complex, the result of many construction phases, the Goldiana is one of the best budget choices in the Cambodian capital. The hotel is just south of the Victory Monument and a short ride from the main sights. It's low-level luxe, but squeaky clean. Rooms are very large, with either carpeting or wood flooring. The hotel's standard of maintenance, unlike that of similar properties in town, is meticulous. Although that new-car smell is long gone, rooms are low on the mildew and musty odors commonly found at the in-town competition. Bathrooms are small-ish but comfortable, with a tub/shower combo and granite tile. The third-floor pool is a real bonus in this category. The lobby is a designer muddle of heavy curtains, large pottery with fake flowers, mirrors, and bright-colored carved wood, but it acquires a certain appeal once it becomes familiar. The staff is kind and helpful and is used to the questions and concerns of long-staying patrons, tourists, and business clients. Even guests on short stays, however, will be made to feel at home.

#10–12, St. 282, Sangkat Boeng Keng Kang I, Phnom Penh. ℭ **023/219-558.** Fax 023/219-558. www.goldiana.com. 144 units. US$28–US$38 single; US$38–US$48 double; US$58–US$90 suite. MC, V. **Amenities:** Restaurant; outdoor rooftop pool; basic gym; car rental; courtesy car; business center w/Internet access; room service (6am–10pm); laundry service; dry cleaning. *In room:* A/C, TV, minibar, fridge, IDD phone.

BUDGET

Affordable accommodations abound in the Cambodian capital, but they can be a bit rough—thin-walled cacophony, bad smells, surly proprietors, and poor security are the hallmarks. In and around Sisowath Quay, the busy riverside boulevard, you'll find minihotels and budget lodging of all kinds starting at about US$10/£5.50 per night. The eastern shore of the **Boeung Kak Lake,** just north of town, is also a popular backpacker ghetto. It's cheap sleeps and eats with no frills (or nothing even close to frills), but you're sure to meet some fellow travelers.

A good budget option is the **Last Home Guesthouse** (#47, St. 108; ℭ **023/724-917**), on the promenade south of Wat Phnom, with concrete-block basic rooms above a popular little storefront eatery. Rooms range from US$2 to US$8 (£1.10–£4.40).

Capitol Guesthouse (#14 AEO, Rd. 182; ℭ **023/217-627**) is the town's backpacker information center and offers very basic concrete rooms from US$2/£1.10.

WHERE TO DINE

Between remnants of French colonialism and the recent influx of humanitarian aid workers, international cuisine abounds in the Cambodian capital. Some restaurants themselves are actually NGO (nongovernmental organization) projects designed to raise money for local causes or provide training. Ask Khmer folks where to eat, and you'll be pointed to any of the street-side stalls or storefront Chinese noodle shops south of the Central Market. Good eats can also be had on riverside Sisowath or in and among the lazy alleys of the town center.

EXPENSIVE

FCC (Foreign Correspondents Club) ⭐ CONTINENTAL   With a long history as Phnom Penh's place to see and be seen, the FCC is as much tour stop as restaurant. Once the gathering place of the dust-caked, camera-toting, intrepid breed who came to chronicle the country's troubled times, the FCC is now a multifloor affair of restaurant, bar, and shops done in dark wood and terra cotta. There are low reclining chairs in the cafe area, a fine-dining room, and a bar that serves as the stalwart centerpiece. The whole second floor is oriented to the fine views of the river and busy Sisowath below. Ceiling fans dangle from the high, exposed roof and spin oblong patterns; geckos, as everywhere in town, chase along the walls. Come for a drink and pretend

---

Finds Prek Leap

For an interesting evening of local fun and frolic, cross the Cambodian–Japanese Friendship bridge on the Tonle Sap River in the north end of town and follow the main road a few short clicks to the town of **Prek Leap,** a grouping of large riverside eateries that's always crowded with locals on the weekend. Some of these places put on popular variety shows, combining the universal language of slapstick with a good chance to eat, talk, and laugh with locals. The restaurants serve similar good Khmer and Chinese fare. Go by taxi and pick the most crowded place—the more, the merrier.

you're here on assignment. The food is uninspired Western, but the execution is good. The FCC makes fine pizza in its wood-fired oven and has good snacks like nachos and enchiladas, as well as treats like "Death by Chocolate," a fudge cake with mousse and ice cream. The upstairs bar is very popular in the evening, and the whole place is abuzz with activity day and night, whether for power lunches or late-night laughs. There is also wireless Internet available (buy a prepaid card). The FCC is a good place to pick up information on travel, volunteering, or work in the area.

#363 Sisowath St. (C) 023/724-014. www.fcccambodia.com. Main courses US$5–US$16 (£2.75–£8.50). MC, V. Daily 7am–midnight.

River House 🐟🐟 FRENCH/CONTINENTAL   One of many along the riverside, this bar and restaurant, like the nearby FCC (above), stands out by virtue of size and style. A classic corner colonial, its downstairs is an open-air bar area with quaint patio seating under canvas umbrellas. There's also a new, elegant air-conditioned dining room. Upstairs is a bass-thumping, dimly lit club with a dance floor that's a popular late-night haunt. Elegant rattan chairs, two stately bars in wood and glass, and the fine linen and silver presentation are luxurious far beyond the price tag. The food is excellent, characterized by French specials like duck done as you like, coq au vin, and a popular chateaubriand with morel mushrooms. Come for a romantic dinner and stay for dancing.

#6, St. 110 (corner of Sisowath). (C) 023/212-302. Main courses US$4–US$17 (£2.20–£9.35). AE, MC, V. Daily 10:30am–11pm (till 1am Sat–Sun).

Topaz 🐟🐟 FRENCH/CONTINENTAL   Good familiar food and atmosphere that's sophisticated and stylish are the hallmarks of Topaz, an 8-year-old French bistro with a new location. In air-conditioned comfort, guests sit at elegant tables with fine linen, silver, and real stemware in a formal dining room unrivaled in town. The menu features great steaks, pasta, and salad. The Caesar salad is noteworthy. Daily lunch sets are popular with the business crowd, and daily specials are contingent on the day's imports of fish or steaks. Wine abounds, with some great choices. *Bon appétit!*

#182 Norodom Blvd. (near downtown sites). (C) 023/221-622. Main courses US$7–US$21 (£3.85–£12). MC, V. Daily 11am–2pm and 6–11pm.

MODERATE

Bali Café INDONESIAN/WESTERN   This smart little second-floor cafe has a vaulted ceiling and open plan that faces busy Sisowath and the picturesque riverside: a good spot to relax and beat the heat. The unique Indonesian cuisine is heavy on curry of the sweet, coconut-milk variety. The *gado gado* is a popular Indonesian dish of steamed mixed vegetables in peanut sauce. Views from the window seats are good, but go for a spot in the raised central area, where comfy chairs have the best angle on the busy street below. It's also a popular bar in the evening.

#379 Sisowath St. (C) 023/982-211. Main courses US$3–US$5 (£1.65–£2.75). No credit cards. Daily 7am–10pm.

Cantina 🐟🐟 MEXICAN   This riverfront restaurant holds the distinction of being one of the only decent Mexican joints for miles—and miles. While it might not stand its ground in Texas or California, the place does provide a bit of comfort food for the homesick. Inside, Cantina's walls are filled with the works of local photographers, notable among them a chronicler of conflicts in Vietnam and Cambodia, Al Rockoff. It is also a de facto headquarters for local journalists and aid workers. Try anything from the tostadas to the burritos, and finish up with an ice-cream sundae or banana split.

#347 Sisowath St. ⓒ 023/222-502. Main courses US$2.50–US$5 (£1.40–£2.75). No credit cards. Sun–Fri 4–10pm.

Comme á la Maison ⚜ CONTINENTAL   Expats love this place. It's quiet, with the biggest commotion on weekend mornings, when a steady stream of deliveries leaves the bakery. Light fare tops the bill, with good soups and salads perfect for sopping up with something freshly baked. Comme á la Maison also features heartier French entrees and meat and cheese platters, as well as good pizzas and pastas. Follow up with fresh yogurt, fruit, and tasty desserts. Breakfast is good, too. The quiet courtyard area is at the top of the list for escaping the chaos of busy Phnom Penh.

#13 St. 57 (around the corner from Goldiana, southwest of town center). ⓒ 023/360-801. www.commealamaison-delicatessen.com. Main courses US$3–US$9.50 (£1.65–£5.20). No credit cards. Daily 6am–10:30pm.

Le Deauville ⚜ FRENCH   This open-air French bar and brasserie, on the north end of the Wat Phnom roundabout, is a good, mellow choice for affordable French and Khmer dishes. The atmosphere is unpretentious and cozy, with a large open bar at the center and tables scattered in the street-side courtyard (and shielded from the traffic by a wall of potted greenery). Daily lunch set menus give you a choice of salad and entree, including local specialties like Mekong fish with lime or beef medallions. The restaurant serves good pizzas and spaghetti, and its wine list fits just about any taste or budget. Le Deauville is also a popular spot for a casual drink in the evening.

Kj St. 94 (just north of Wat Phnom). ⓒ 012/843-204. Main courses US$3.50–US$9.50 (£1.90–£5.20). V. Daily 7am–11pm.

Rendezvous Café ⚜ CONTINENTAL   There are so many little eateries lining the riverfront of Sisowath Road, it's hard to pick. Here's one of the best, an open-air corner bar with big, comfy rattan chairs in a prime people-watching location on the north end of Sisowath Quay, the riverside road. The Rendezvous serves solid Western pub grub: burgers, steaks, and chicken dishes, as well as good pizzas and sandwiches. This is a great place to have a cold beer and a meat-and-potatoes meal, or perhaps a groovy fruit shake and a simple salad or sandwich. The staff members here couldn't be nicer; they're amenable to suggestions (such as burgers cooked to order), and they'll make you feel like a local from the get-go. The bar hops late into the night.

#127Eo, corner of Sisowath Quay and St. 108. ⓒ 023/986-466. Main courses US$2.80–US$6.80 (£1.55–£3.75). No credit cards. Daily 6:30am–midnight.

Tamarind Café ⚜ FRENCH/MEDITERRANEAN   Good tapas, *mezze* (Middle Eastern appetizers), salads, and a host of French and Mediterranean entrees make Tamarind's cool perch, overlooking busy Street 240, an excellent choice. This spot in the popular cafe and gallery area makes a perfect break for Dad to prop his feet up (after grabbing a book or a local rag at the nearby London Book Centre) while Mom goes boutiquing. The pastas and pizzas are delicious, and fresh salads and light menu items are just right on a hot day. The bar is always busy and stays open late.

#31, St. 240. ⓒ 012/830-139. Main courses US$4.50–US$11 (£2.50–£6.05). MC, V. Daily 10am until last customer.

INEXPENSIVE

In addition to the following options, there are lots of affordable open-air cafes along riverside Sisowath.

Boddhi Tree ✿ ASIAN/KHMER   You can easily combine lunch here with a trip to nearby Tuol Sleng prison (p. 430), a site that doesn't inspire an appetite, really, but the Boddhi Tree is a peaceful oasis and not a bad spot to collect your thoughts after visiting vestiges of Cambodia's late troubles. Named for the tree under which the Buddha "saw the light," this verdant little garden courtyard and rough-hewn guesthouse has comfy balcony and courtyard seating, where it seems to serve up as much calm as the coffee, tea, and light fare that make it so popular. There are daily specials and often visiting chefs. All the curries are good, as are the great baguette sandwiches. Established in 1997 as a way to drum up funds and support for Khmer kids and families in challenging circumstances, the folks here welcome your suggestions and invite visitors to get involved in their important work.

#50, St. 113, Beong Keng Kong (across from Tuol Sleng Museum). ✆ 011/854-430. www.boddhitree.com. Main courses US$2.50–US$3.95 (£1.40–£2.15). No credit cards. Daily 7am–9pm.

Mith Samlanh (Good Friends) Restaurant ✿✿ KHMER/INTERNATIONAL
Not to be missed is this friendly little gem, an NGO project where Khmer street kids are given shelter and taught useful skills for their reintegration into society: It's a unique opportunity to meet young folks who've found a new lease on life. The food is great, mind you, an ever-changing menu of local and international favorites like spring rolls, fried rice, good salads, and a host of desserts, such as a delicious sweet sticky rice with local fruit. Stop by to cool off and have a light bite while touring the city center (it's right across from the must-see National Museum); the place is a cozy open-air colonial in a courtyard done up in murals of the kids' drawings. The name of the restaurant means "good friends"—and you might even find yourself giving English lessons, laughing, and smiling with these young survivors. The helpful staff members are happy to talk about their many efforts, including drug and AIDS programs and a 500-student vocational facility. They also run a boutique next door called **Friends and Stuff,** which sells reconditioned electronics and new crafts from their training center.

#215, St. 13 (near entrance to National Museum). ✆ 012/802-072. www.streetfriends.org. Main courses US$4–US$5 (£2.20–£2.75). No credit cards. Daily 11am–9pm.

SNACKS & CAFES

Java Café and Gallery (#56 E1 Preah Sihanouk Blvd.; ✆ 012/833-512) is a good spot in town to relax and escape the midday heat. Just south of the main sights (near the Independence Monument), this popular second-story oasis has casual seating on a large balcony and an open gallery interior. It serves real coffee and cappuccino as well as good cakes and other baked goods. Evenings can feature live music. Open 7am to 10pm.

The Shop is a nice little stop on popular Street 240 (✆ 023/986-964), now with a new location on the north end of Sisowath Quay. It serves fine baked goods and great teas and coffees in a friendly and comfortable storefront at each location. There are neat details, like butcher-block tables and fresh flowers, and the Shop can arrange picnic lunches for day trips from Phnom Penh.

Sugar Palm Café (#19, St. 240; ✆ 023/220-956) serves good Khmer dishes at street side or from its upstairs balcony. The interior also functions as a gallery, with local crafts on display. This is a great place to relax and enjoy real Khmer atmosphere.

Pizza can be found at any number of storefronts on the crowded riverside; **Happy Pizza** (#223 Sisowath Quay; ✆ 012/559-114) is among them. Beginning with the name, there are cute little codes in play here, so to be direct: Tell the staff, "Please don't put marijuana on my pizza," unless you want it. Same drill at **Ecstatic Pizza** (193 Norodom Blvd.; © **023/365-089**). Both are good and will deliver.

WHAT TO SEE & DO

All downtown attractions can be reached on foot, but you'll want to hire a car with a driver or, for the brave, a motorcycle taxi to reach sights outside the city center. **Tuol Sleng** and the **Killing Fields** can be visited together; arrangements can be made in any hotel lobby.

Central Market   This Art Deco behemoth, built in 1937, is a city landmark and, on any given day, a veritable ant hill of activity. Locals call it *Psar Thmei*, or New Market. The building has a towering rotunda with busy wings extending in four directions. The eastern entrance is the best spot to find T-shirts, hats, and all manner of trinkets and souvenirs, as well as photocopied bootlegs of popular novels and books on Cambodia. Goldsmiths, watch repair, and sales counters predominate in the main rotunda; you can find some good deals here. Spend time wandering the nooks and crannies, though, and you're sure to come across something that strikes your fancy, whether that's a chaotic hardware shop, a cobbler hard at work with an awl, or just the cacophony and carnival-barker shouts of salesmen and haggling shoppers. Be sure to bargain for any purchase.

Between sts. 126 and 136 in town center. Daily 5am–5pm.

Independence Monument   Built in the late 1950s to commemorate Cambodia's independence from the French on November 9, 1953, this towering obelisk is crowned with Khmer *nagas* and is reminiscent of Angkor architecture and Hindu influence. The area is at its most majestic when all lit up at night.

South of town center at intersection of Norodom and Sihanouk boulevards.

"The Killing Fields," Choeung Ek Memorial   Originally a Chinese cemetery before becoming the execution grounds for the Khmer Rouge during their maniacal reign under Pol Pot from 1975 to 1979, the site is a collection of mounds, mass graves, and a towering monument of catalogued human skulls. It's often visited in conjunction with a tour of Tuol Sleng (below).

15km (9¼ miles) south of Phnom Penh. Arrange a private car or motorcycle.

National Museum ★★★   What the British Museum is to the Elgin Marbles of Greece's Parthenon, the National Museum of Phnom Penh, opened in 1920 by King Sisowath, is to the statuary of Angkor Wat. This important storehouse holds artifacts and statuary from all over the country. The sad fact is that many pieces didn't make it here, but were plundered and smuggled out of the country. Nevertheless, this grand red-sandstone edifice contains a beautiful and informative collection of Khmer pieces. From the entrance, begin on your left with a room of small prehistoric artifacts. A clockwise loop around the central courtyard walks you through time, from static, stylized pieces of stiff-legged, standing Buddhas, to contra-posed and contorted forms in supplication. There are good accompanying descriptions in English, but this is not a bad place to have a knowledgeable guide (ask in the lobby). The central courtyard features a *Shiva lingum* (icon of the god Shiva) and large temple fragments. At the more significant works (the statue of Javaryman, for example), elderly ladies, looking like museum docents, hand out incense and flowers and instruct visitors to place them on makeshift altars. Don't feel obliged—it's kind of off-putting to some. If you do participate, drop a few riel and ignore entreaties for a larger donation.

Just north of Royal Palace at St. 178, and a short walk from the river. Admission US$3/£1.65. Daily 8–11am and 2–5:30pm.

Royal Palace and Silver Pagoda ★★★   Don't miss this glittery downtown campus, the ostentatious jewel in the crown of Cambodia's monarchy. Built in the late 1860s under the reign of Norodom, the site comprises many elaborate gilded halls, all with steep tile roofs, stupa-shaped cupolas, and golden temple *nagas* denoting prosperity. The grand **Throne Hall** at the center is the coronation site for Khmer kings and the largest gilded cathedral in the country. Don't miss the many royal busts and the gilded umbrella used to shade the king when in procession. The French built a small exhibition hall on the temple grounds, a building that now houses the many gifts given to the monarchy, among them cross-stitch portraits of the royal family and all manner of bric-a-brac. Just inside the door, don't miss an original by Cézanne that has suffered terrible water damage and hangs in a ratty frame like an unwanted diploma—a shame. The balcony of the exhibition hall is the best bird's-eye view of the gilded temples. The facade of the neighboring **Royal Residence** is just as resplendent and is still the home of the now abdicated King Sihanouk and his son and successor.

The **Silver Pagoda** is just south of the palace; entrance is included with the Royal Palace ticket. The floors of this grand temple are covered with 5,000 blocks of silver weighing more than 6 tons. The temple houses a 17th-century Buddha made of Baccarat crystal, and another made almost entirely of gold and decorated with nearly 10,000 diamonds. That's not exactly what the Buddha had in mind, perhaps, but it's quite beautiful. The temple courtyard is encircled by a covered walkway with a contiguous mural of Cambodia's history and mythology. On the southern end of the complex is a small hill covered in vegetation and said to be a model of the sacred Mount Meru; there's a large Buddha footprint and a small temple that provokes very devout practice in Khmer visitors.

Between sts. 240 and 184 on Sothearos (entrance on east side facing the river). Admission US$3/£1.65 (US$5/£2.75 w/still camera; US$8/£4.40 w/video camera). Daily 7:30–11am and 2:30–5pm.

Russian Market   This bustling market in the south end of town is comparable to the Central Market and equally worthy of a visit (it's a good stop on the return trip from the Killing Fields; otherwise, go by cab). The real deal on souvenirs can be had here, though it takes hard haggling to get the best prices on neat items like opium paraphernalia, carvings, and ceramics. It's all authentic-looking, even if it's made in China.

South of town center between sts. 440 and 450. Daily dawn to dusk.

Tuol Sleng, Museum of Genocide ★★   The grounds of this high-school-turned-prison-and-torture-chamber are like they were in 1979 at the end of Cambodia's bloody genocide. A stop here is a visceral revisiting of some very horrible events, and guides are often just as brutal in their portrayal of it, too much so for some visitors. From 1975 until 1979, an estimated 17,000 political prisoners, most just ordinary citizens, were tortured at Tuol Sleng and died, or were executed in the nearby Killing Fields. If you don't come with a guide, you'll certainly want to hire one at the entrance, although you're free to roam the grounds on your own. Local guides often have personal experience with the prison and are vital sources of oral history. They are open to questions, but go easy on any debate. Recrimination against the perpetrators of these horrible events is an important issue here; Cambodians hope to move on into the future, but they fear revisiting the past in the current international tribunals. The prison population of Tuol Sleng, also known as S-21, was carefully catalogued; in fact, the metal neck brace, employed for holding subjects' heads in place for the admitting photograph, is on display. There are some written accounts in English, paintings done by a survivor, and gory photos of the common torture practices in the prison, but perhaps what is most haunting is the fear in the eyes of the newly arrived; one wing of the buildings is dedicated to these very arrival photos. This sight is a bit overwhelming for some, so be prepared.

South of town at corner of sts. 350 and 113. Admission US$3/£1.65; guide fees vary, but are usually US$2–US$3 (£1.10–£1.65) per person. Daily 8am–noon and 1–5pm.

Wat Phnom ⭐⭐   This is Cambodia's "Church on the Hill." Legend has it that in the 14th century, a woman named Penh found sacred Buddhist objects in the nearby river and placed them here on the small hill that later became a temple. Well, the rest is history. *Phnom,* in fact, means "hill," so the name of the city translates to "Penh's Hill."

The temple itself is a standard Southeast Asian *wat,* with *naga* (snakes) on the cornered peaks of the roof and didactic murals of the Buddha's life done in day-glow allegories along interior walls. Don't miss the central ceiling, which, unlike the bright walls, is yet to be restored and is gritty and authentic.

The hillside park around the temple was once a no-go zone peopled by armed dealers and pimps, and in the evening you should still be careful, though now it's a laidback little park. You're sure to meet with some crafty young salesmen here who'll offer you the chance to show your Buddhist compassion by buying a caged bird for a dollar and letting it go; if you stick around long enough, you'll see the bird return to the comfort of the cage.

OUTDOOR ACTIVITIES

If your hotel lacks an outdoor pool, head to the **Clark Hatch Fitness Center** (✆ **023/424-888**), at the Hotel Inter-Continental. This place has it all in the way of equipment. Daily visitors are invited for a fee (US$8/£4.40), with pool and sauna included. It's open daily from 6am to 10pm.

SHOPPING

Shops and galleries are growing in number in the developing capital. The best shopping in town, for everything from souvenirs and trinkets to the obligatory kitchen sink, is at any of the large local markets (see the Central Market and Russian Market under "What to See & Do," above).

All along Street 178, interesting little outlets are springing up, including a few affordable silk dealers like **Lotus Pond** (#57Eo, St. 178; ✆ **012/833-149**) and **House Kravan** (#13Eo, St. 178; ✆ **012/771-936**). At **Asasax Art Gallery** (#192, St. 178; ✆ **023/217-795;** www.asasaxart.com.kh), you'll see unique local works. **Photo Click Gallery** (#65, St. 178) features the tinted black-and-white images of long-time expat and photographer Pier Poretti.

Street 240 is also developing its own cafe culture. It has a few little hole-in-the-wall antiques shops and boutiques, such as **Bliss** (#29, St. 240; ✆ **023/215-754**), which sells some unique beaded and embroidered cushions and quilts.

Near the Independence Monument, **Bazar** (28 Sihanouk Blvd.; ✆ **012/866-178**) has a small but refined collection of Asian antiques and furniture.

For CDs, DVDs, and cool T-shirts and hip-hop fashions, stop by the **Boom Boom Room,** on Street 93 in the backpacker area near Boeung Kok Lake, or at its new location just across from the Golden Gate Hotel (#1C, St. 278; ✆ **012/560-944**).

For essentials and Western groceries, stop by the **Lucky Market** (#160, Sihanouk Blvd.; ✆ **023/426-291**). For fresh organic produce and fine canned goods, try **Veggy's** (#23, St. 240; ✆ **023/211-534**).

Monument Books (#111, Norodom Blvd.; ✆ **023/217-617**) has a great selection of new titles; it's a good spot to find books on Khmer language and culture. Stop by the **London Book Centre** (#51, St. 240), among the new bistros and cafes, to exchange or buy new and used books; there's a good selection here.

PHNOM PENH AFTER DARK

Phnom Penh is notorious for some of the seedier nightlife in all of Southeast Asia. There are some good, friendly bars in town, though many are of the "hostess bar" variety. Most good romps start or end at the town's counterculture hub, the **Heart of Darkness** (#38, St. 51, Pasteur), open from 7pm until sunrise. Done in burgundy tones and cluttered with statuary and memorabilia, the Heart, as it's called, has had a face-lift in recent years and is not as seedy as its reputation of yore (though it's still a bit of a relief to see the metal detectors). It's where to go to find out what's on in town.

The downtown area along the riverside is chockablock with small storefront bars and a few upscale spots. For good atmosphere with less chaos than the Heart, try either the bar at **River House** (see "Where to Dine") or **Pontoon** (on the river bank near the Rendezvous Café), a barge bar with a hip interior. The **Rising Sun** (#20, St. 178; ✆ **023/986-270**) is one of the more comfy holes in the wall, a dark wooden stopover great for a few pints and a game of darts near the town center. Near the Golden Gate Hotel, **Tom's Irish Bar** (#170, St. 63; ✆ **023/363-161**) is a comparable and friendly choice south of town, a longtime local and tourist favorite that has a classy wooden bar as well as comfy chairs in the roadside courtyard.

SIDE TRIPS FROM PHNOM PENH
MEKONG RIVER CRUISE

To escape the clamor of Phnom Penh, look no farther than the riverfront on Sisowath Boulevard between the Amanjaya Hotel and the River House Restaurant, where you can rent a whole boat for US$10 (£5.50) per hour. You'll find these boats moored along the bank, with names like Paris Boat Tours. Bring your own food and beverages and cast off, up the Mekong, where you'll catch glimpses of river life as you navigate between fishing boats and barges and watch the muddy banks drift by. It's best done between 4 and 7pm, to catch the setting sun.

OUDONG

Following defeat at Angkor by the Thais, the Khmer capital moved to Oudong, and kings ruled from here for more than 100 years until the power center shifted to nearby Phnom Penh in 1866. The area was a monastic center, and the 13th-century temples, like most others, pale in comparison to those of the Angkor complex. Still, the hills of Oudong offer breathtaking views. It's an hour west of Phnom Penh and is best reached by rented vehicle.

PHNOM CHISOR & TONLE BATI

If you have been or are going to Angkor Wat, these temples will also pale in comparison, but the ride through the countryside and among rural villages makes for a good day trip. Tonle Bati (33km/21 miles south of Phnom Penh) is a small collection of Angkor-style temples. Admission is US$3/£1.65. Nearby Phnom Chisor is a group of 10th-century ruins atop a picturesque hill. Phnom Penh travel agents can make all the arrangements.

SIHANOUKVILLE

In Cambodia, your only bet for a dip in the ocean and beachside R & R is at Sihanoukville, some 230km (143 miles) south of Phnom Penh on the American-built highway. A popular summertime spot for Khmers, Sihanoukville is really a port town, and though the beaches don't stack up to the likes of Thailand's, they aren't bad, either. Trips to outlying islands for scuba diving and snorkeling are attracting more and more Western visitors. To get there, contact **Capitol Tour** (© 023/217-627) or **Ho Wa Genting Bus Co.** (© 023/210-859), each with daily connections for the 3- to 4-hour ride. You can also contact any hotel front desk or travel agent about renting a car for the ride from Phnom Penh.

Where once it was only low-end accommodations and seedy casinos, there is now the **Sokha Beach Resort & Spa** (© 034/935-999; www.sokhahotels.com), with 180 upmarket rooms starting at US$120/£66. Amenities include a nice central pool and frontage on a stretch of private beach. There are a number of smaller hotels and guest-houses as well: Try **Orchidee Guesthouse** (© 034/933-639; www.orchideeguesthouse. com) or **Golden Sand Hotel** (© 034/933-607; www.hotelgoldensand.com), a business hotel with bland but clean rooms.

For dining, you'll find good seafood at low prices at lots of little oceanside budget stops. Don't miss a visit to the unique **Snakehouse** (© 012/782-873), a restaurant and menagerie of local cold-blooded inhabitants (for viewing, not eating).

For tours to outlying islands, contact the folks at **EcoAdventures South East Asia LTD** (in the Samudera Market, Town Center, Sihanoukville; © 012/654-104; www. ecosea.com). It arranges great day tours with stops in remote coves where clients can snorkel or take a course in scuba.

KEP ⭐⭐⭐

Once known as the country's emerging Riveria, following the exit of the French from Indochina, Kep fell into obscurity during Cambodia's violent years. It is making a comeback, however, and visitors can now get here by comfortable bus. Still, the town remains basically undiscovered, and is certainly off the map for most tours.

There are several nice places to stay, including **Knai Bang Chatt** (Phum Thmey Sangkat Prey, Thom Khan Kep; © 012/879-486; www.knaibangchatt.com), a seaside property of three renovated and one new villas, built in what was called the New Modern Khmer style of the 1960s. Rooms are US$350/£193 per night. At the more moderately priced **Veranda Natural Resort** (Kep Hillside Rd., Krong Kep; © 012/888-619; www.veranda-resort.com), hillside bungalows go for US$20 to US$60 (£11–£33). Other guesthouses can be found near the Crab Market.

From Kep, travelers can take day excursions to lush Rabbit Island, motorcycle to the top of Bokor Mountain or explore surrounding countryside roads, and visit limestone caves and temples. Book these activities from your hotel or guesthouse.

To get here, go to the Olympic Market in Phnom Penh, near the Olympic Stadium, and find the Hua Lian transportation company's kiosk. Tickets cost US$4/£2.20, the ride takes 5 hours, and buses leave at 7:30am and 1pm.

5 Siem Reap & Angkor Wat ✦✦✦

The ruins of the ancient city of **Angkor,** capital of the Khmer kingdom from 802 until 1295, are one of the world's marvels. The largest religious monument ever constructed, it's a vast and mysterious complex of hulking laterite and sandstone blocks. Unknown to the world until French naturalist Henri Mouhot literally stumbled onto it in 1861, the area of Angkor existed for centuries only as a myth—a wondrous city (or cities, to be exact), its exact location in the Cambodian jungle unknown.

The temple complex covers some 96.6 sq. km (37 sq. miles) and includes the remains of passageways, moats, temples, and palaces that represent centuries of building in the capital. The temples are served by the nearby town of **Siem Reap,** some 6km (3¾ miles) to the south.

A 3- or 4-day visit will suffice (though many do it in fewer). More than a few visitors come away with a newfound love for ancient cultures, Asian religions, and sunsets.

GETTING THERE

BY PLANE Siem Reap Airways, Royal Phnom Penh Airways, President Airlines, and Bangkok Air all fly the 1-hour connection to Siem Reap from Phnom Penh.

If you just want to see the great temples at Angkor, the process is simplified with international arrivals: Bangkok Airways flies directly from Bangkok, and you can check flights by Silk Air, Lao Aviation, Vietnam Airlines, and Royal Camboge Airline for other routes. *Note:* The international departure tax (from both Phnom Penh and Siem Reap) is US$25/£14; the domestic tax is US$10 to US$14 (£5.50–£7.70), depending on where you're flying.

BY BOAT A ride on the 5-hour boat connection between Phnom Penh and Siem Reap costs US$25/£14. Contact any hotel or travel agent, as they all sell the same tickets at the same price. The trip connects to Siem Reap via the great Tonle Sap Lake, with some good scenery en route. Also see the new, more luxurious boat service run by **Mekong Express** (87 Sisowath Quay, Phnom Penh; ⓒ **023/427-518**), which costs US$35/£19.

BY BUS **Capitol Tour** (#14 AEO, Rd. 182, Sangkat Beng Prolitt; ⓒ **023/217-627**) runs daily minivans along the much-improved road between Phnom Penh and Siem Reap. Tickets for the all-day ride are just US$5/£2.75.

GETTING AROUND

You'll need some kind of wheeled conveyance to make your way around Siem Reap and to and from the temples. Any hotel front desk or travel agent can make arrangements for you.

A **rented car with driver** is about US$25/£14 (double that with a guide). A **motorcycle taxi** is a good, cheap option for US$8/£4.40 per day, and there are also motorbikes that pull **tuk-tuks,** small, covered trailers for two (kind of fun, really), for about US$11/£6.05 per day.

Riding your own motorbike was once the most popular choice, but local officials have put a stop to it, citing the many road accidents. **Bicycles** are still a possibility, however, and the temple roads are flat and well paved. Bikes rent for US$2 to US$3 (£1.10–£1.65) per day from guesthouses and hotels. Take care in the scorching midday heat and drink plenty of fluids.

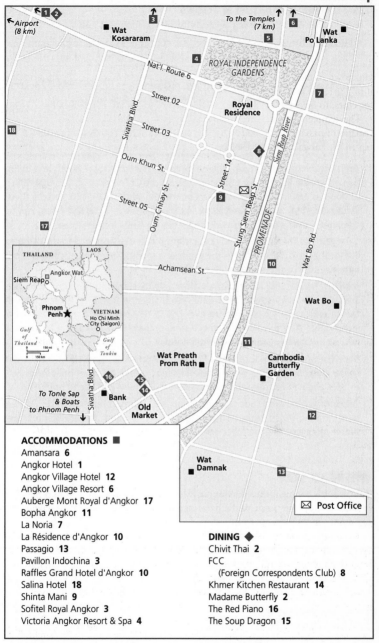

Siem Reap

ACCOMMODATIONS ■
Amansara **6**
Angkor Hotel **1**
Angkor Village Hotel **12**
Angkor Village Resort **6**
Auberge Mont Royal d'Angkor **17**
Bopha Angkor **11**
La Noria **7**
La Résidence d'Angkor **10**
Passagio **13**
Pavillon Indochina **3**
Raffles Grand Hotel d'Angkor **10**
Salina Hotel **18**
Shinta Mani **9**
Sofitel Royal Angkor **3**
Victoria Angkor Resort & Spa **4**

DINING ◆
Chivit Thai **2**
FCC
    (Foreign Correspondents Club) **8**
Khmer Kitchen Restaurant **14**
Madame Butterfly **2**
The Red Piano **16**
The Soup Dragon **15**

⊠ **Post Office**

VISITOR INFORMATION & TOURS

Contact either of the following agencies for information and tours.

- **Diethelm Travel,** House #4, Airport Rd. #6, Krum #1, Sangkat #2, Phum Taphul, Siem Reap (© **063/963-524;** fax 063/963-694; dtc@dtc.com.kh). All local and regional services.
- **Exotissimo Travel,** #300, Airport Rd. #6, Siem Reap (© **063/964-323;** fax 063/963-621; www.exotissimo.com). All local and regional services.

FAST FACTS: Siem Reap

Currency Exchange You can change traveler's checks in some hotels and in any bank; **Canadia Bank** (on the western side of the Old Market; © **063/964-808**) is as good as any in town. **Cambodia Commercial Bank (CCB)** (130 Siwatha Blvd.; © **063/380-154**) and **Mekong Bank** (43 Siwatha Blvd.; © **063/964-420**) can do credit card cash advances as well. There are no ATMs in Siem Reap.

Emergencies There is a tourist police station near the entrance to the temples. For local police, dial © **117**. In the event of a medical emergency, contact **International SOS Clinic**, in Phnom Penh (© **023/216-911**).

Internet Access Small storefront offices aplenty surround the Central Market area. On the main street, try **E-Café** (#011, Siwatha Blvd.), an air-conditioned facility with speedy ADSL, for just over US$2/£1.10 per hour. If you have a wireless-capable laptop, you can connect using prepaid PIC cards at the **FCC** restaurant or the **Raffles Grand** and **Sofitel** hotels.

Mail The post office is located on Pokambor Avenue, at riverside near the town center (next to the FCC; see "Where to Dine," later). It's open daily from 7am to 5pm and can handle foreign and domestic regular and parcel post.

Telephones The area code for Siem Reap is **63**. Most hotels have international direct dialing (IDD). Many of the Internet cafes around the Old Market have better rates and offer callback service or Internet phones.

WHERE TO STAY

Tourist levels are high, thus development has really revved up in tiny Siem Reap. Visitors can choose from some of the finest upscale accommodations in the region—more five-star properties than we can list.

For midrange hotels (below US$100/£55), there are lots of bland choices, especially on the airport road. Some smaller properties are sprucing themselves up to a more boutique-hotel standard—there are a few atmospheric gems here.

In high season, high-end accommodations often fill up, so be sure to book ahead. During the low season, ask for a discount. Most hotels levy a 10% VAT.

VERY EXPENSIVE

Amansara 🖈🖈🖈 If there's one place to splurge in Southeast Asia, Amansara is it. Transformed into an ultra-luxury resort from former King Norodom Sihanouk's private guesthouses, the space at Amansara alone is worth it. Suites—there are no "rooms" here—are elegant and minimalist, with bas-reliefs on creamy walls, dark-wood trim, and polished stone floors. Baths are drawn with warm water each afternoon; the separate shower looks out onto a courtyard or a private saltwater swimming pool. The dining is fabulous here, in a restaurant that was once King Sihanouk's private screening room (in his heyday, he was a prolific filmmaker).

But what really sets Amansara apart is the way it brings Khmer culture—both ancient and modern—inside the walls. Lectures and performances are frequent occurrences, the library is stocked with helpful books, and the staff members feel more like friendly neighbors than anything else. It's all done on a first-name basis, without being obtrusive. Ask about the traditional water blessing and other activities. Amansara has also taken great care to research the Angkor temples, in an effort to get its guests to both the main attractions and the out-of-the-way structures; guides and drivers are knowledgeable as well. Walk into Amansara for a stay and you'll walk out again feeling relaxed, replenished, and educated.

Road to Angkor, Siem Reap. ℂ 063/760-333. Fax 063/760-335. www.amanresorts.com. 24 units. US$675 (£371) suite; US$875 (£481) pool suite. AE, MC, V. **Amenities:** Restaurant; bar; outdoor pool; spa; all rentals available; shopping; 24-hr. room service; laundry service; dry cleaning; excellent library w/Internet access; tuk-tuks; guide. *In room:* A/C, Internet access, minibar, fridge, hair dryer, safe, IDD phone.

La Résidence d'Angkor 🐾🐾

Formerly the Pansea, La Résidence d'Angkor is a stylish, self-contained sanctuary managed by the people at Orient-Express. You'll cross a small moat to enter the cool interior of the steeply gabled, dark wooden lobby with its grand Angkor-inspired reliefs. The tranquil central courtyard is lined with palms and dominated by a small but stylish pool. The resort area is small, but everything from the gardens to the room decor is tidy and designed for quiet privacy. Rooms are large, well appointed, open, and elegant, with cloth divans, retro fixtures, and nice local touches. Spacious bathrooms connect with the bedrooms via a bamboo sliding door, and another glass slider opens to a small private balcony with views of the courtyard and lounges. The lobby restaurant offers fine dining. There are some great sitting areas for drinks, as well as a library with books, chess, and a conference table.

River Rd., Siem Reap. ℂ 063/963-390. Fax 063/963-391. www.pansea.com. 55 units. US$285–US$340 (£156–£187) deluxe double; US$440 (£242) suite. AE, MC, V. **Amenities:** Restaurant; bar; outdoor pool; all rentals available; business center w/Internet access; shopping; 24-hr. room service; laundry service; dry cleaning; library. *In room:* A/C, satellite TV, dataport, minibar, fridge, hair dryer, safe, IDD phone.

Raffles Grand Hotel d'Angkor 🐾🐾🐾

For luxury, atmosphere, and convenience, there is no better choice in Siem Reap. Rebuilt in 1994 from the shell of a classic 1929 structure, this is authentic old Indochina that's neither museum piece nor overly stuffy. Right in the center of town, the imposing colonial facade gives way to a marble lobby with an open metal elevator—an original period piece that's still functional. Staterooms are large, with classic French doors and windows, tiled entries, fine furnishings, and an almost out-of-place high-tech entertainment module. Landmark rooms, a step up, are similar but have four-poster beds, a balcony with rattan furniture, and nice touches like porcelain bathrooms and more antique detail. The courtyard pool is large and inviting—like a commercial set—and the nearby massage and health facilities are quite something. It's expensive, very expensive, but the price includes very fine service and a unique revisiting of old Indochina that you can't find elsewhere. The nightly *apsara* show is a traditional women's temple dance to welcome goddesses.

1 Vithei Charles de Gaulle, Khum Svay Dang Kum, Siem Reap. ℂ 063/963-888. Fax 063/963-168. www.raffles.com. 131 units. US$360–US$390 (£198–£215) double; US$410–US$1,900 (£226–£1,045) suite. AE, MC, V. **Amenities:** 4 restaurants; 2 bars; outdoor pool; 2 tennis courts; health club; spa; Jacuzzi; sauna; steam room; kids' club; concierge;

tour desk; car rental; shopping; massage; laundry service; dry cleaning; wireless Internet access. *In room:* A/C, satellite TV, dataport, minibar, fridge, coffeemaker, hair dryer, safe, IDD phone.

Sofitel Royal Angkor ✹✹   Sofitel is famed for bringing life back to the classic hotels of old Indochina, but in Siem Reap, it started fresh in 2000 with a project limited only by the designer's imagination. The lobby is an old-world Indochine replica with an antique Khmer pagoda and a menagerie of overstuffed European furniture. Design and decor throughout nicely marry Khmer and French styles, with vaulted *naga* roofs high above the sculpted central garden and tranquil pond area. The courtyard pool is large, open, and fun, including a short river meander crossed by a small bridge that's great for kids. Rooms are spacious, with dark-wood floors and rich touches like designer throw rugs and elegant built-in cabinetry. All bathrooms are large, with tubs and granite counters. Spring for a superior room with a balcony and a view of the central courtyard—it's worth it. Not surprisingly, there's an Angkor theme throughout, but the statuary is not overdone and is quite pleasing in both common areas and sleeping quarters (unique in a town of gaudy reproductions of the sites). Be sure to find a moment, preferably near the magic hour of sunset (though any time will do), to take it all in from the island pagoda in the central pond.

Vithei Charles de Gaulle (on the way to temples, just north of town center), Khum Svay Dang Kum, Siem Reap. ✆ 063/964-600. Fax 063/964-610. www.sofitel.com. 238 units. US$338 (£186) superior double; US$360 (£198) deluxe double; US$320–US$1,815 (£176–£998) suite. AE, MC, V. **Amenities:** 4 restaurants; 3 bars; large outdoor pool; health club; Jacuzzi; sauna; steam room; concierge; tour desk; business center; shopping; 24-hr. room service; fine massage facility; laundry service; dry cleaning; nonsmoking rooms; wireless Internet access; small library. *In room:* A/C, satellite TV w/in-house movies, fax, dataport, minibar, fridge, coffeemaker, hair dryer, safe, IDD phone.

Victoria Angkor Resort & Spa ✹✹   The Victoria expands its empire of fine Indochine hotels (mostly in Vietnam) with this latest offering—an oversize but tasteful replica of a French colonial hotel, but with all of the amenities of a modern five-star. Public spaces are done in earth tones, rattan and wood accents, designer tiles, and fun local bric-a-brac. The effect is at times reminiscent of the days of pith helmets and gripes about local inefficiency. A large central atrium, with a period-piece elevator and a towering courtyard staircase, greets the visitor to this downtown setting, just a stone's throw from the Raffles (above). The central pool is large and inviting; there are good spa services; and fine dining at the bistro is tops. Guest rooms are typical of Victoria hotels: large, luxurious, and decorated with location in mind (in other words, you know you're in Cambodia). All units have balconies. The wood floors are bordered with a fine tile that matches the luxurious woven bedspreads. Bathrooms are midsize, with separate tub and shower. The service is efficient and the list of amenities is extensive.

Central Park, P.O. Box 93145, Siem Reap. ✆ 063/760-428. Fax 063/760-350. www.victoriahotels-asia.com. 130 units. US$285–US$320 (£157–£176) double; US$440 (£242) colonial suite. AE, MC, V. **Amenities:** 2 restaurants; bar; large outdoor pool; spa; Jacuzzi; children's center; concierge; tour desk; car rental; business center; shopping arcade; 24-hr. room service; massage; babysitting; laundry service. *In room:* A/C, satellite TV, minibar, fridge, coffeemaker, hair dryer, safe, IDD phone.

EXPENSIVE

Angkor Hotel ✹   Of the many newer hotels along the airport road, Route 6, the Angkor Hotel is the best—and only slightly more expensive than the rest. It's large and ostentatious, with high, Khmer-style roofs and large reproductions of temple statuary in the entry. Everything is clean and comfortable, if a bit sterile. Guest rooms are bland but spacious, with crown molding, clean carpet, and familiar amenities like minibars and safes. The bathrooms are a little small, though. Ask for a room facing the pool or in the new building in the back. The Angkor Hotel is a good, comfortable step down from the glitzier properties in town, and the best choice if they're full. The lobby is always busy with tour groups, but the staff remains friendly and expedient. The hotel is sufficiently self-contained, with all of the basic amenities and services, an outdoor pool, and a good restaurant.

Rte. 6, Phum Sala Kanseng, Siem Reap. ✆ 063/964-301. Fax 063/964-302. www.angkor-hotel-cambodia.com. 193 units. US$125 (£69) standard double; US$145 (£80) deluxe; US$190 (£105) suite. V. **Amenities:** Restaurant; bar; outdoor pool; basic gym; tours; business center w/Internet access; shopping; massage; laundry service. *In room:* A/C, TV, minibar, fridge, hair dryer, safe, IDD phone.

Angkor Village Hotel ★★
For comfortable, rustic atmosphere, Angkor Village is without rival. Located in a quiet neighborhood not far from the main market, this hideaway is a unique maze of wood bungalows connected by covered boardwalks surrounding a picturesque pond. Rooms have high bamboo ceilings, wood beams, built-in cabinetry, and decorative touches like traditional Khmer shadow puppets and statuary. Top units have balconies overlooking the central pond. Bathrooms are all large, with combination tub/showers and sinks set in oversize ceramic cauldrons. The central lobby is a series of platforms and private sitting areas, a good place to rest after a day at the temples. The pool is small but picturesque, set in a verdant courtyard at the rear. L'Auberge de Temples, on a small island in the central pond, serves fine French and Khmer cuisine. The hotel's **Apsara Theatre Restaurant,** just outside the gate, has Khmer-style banquet dining and performances of Khmer Apsara dancing nightly. The whole property is infused with Khmer culture and hospitality—be sure to book ahead, as it's often full. In fact, the hotel is so popular that it's expanded; see the Angkor Village Resort, below.

Wat Bo Rd., Siem Reap. ✆ 063/963-5613. Fax 063/963-363. www.angkorvillage.com. 52 units. US$89–US$165 (£49–£91) double; off-season discounts available. AE, MC, V. **Amenities:** Restaurant; bar; outdoor pool; business center w/Internet access; shopping; limited room service; laundry service; small library. *In room:* A/C, minibar, fridge, coffeemaker, hair dryer, safe, IDD phone.

Angkor Village Resort ★★ (Kids)
This place brings all of the taste and class of the Angkor Village Hotel (above) into a resort atmosphere. A serpentine pool, hidden by lush gardens, is its premier attraction, but the Khmer architecture, attention to detail in local wood, and spacious breathing room all make it a good bet. Room rates are the same for bottom- or top-floor rooms, but the top floor is a better choice, with four-poster beds and higher ceilings reminiscent of a Khmer home. The resort is a bit off the beaten path, but not far from the town center, and is linked to its sister hotel and her offerings.

Phum Traeng. Siem Reap. ✆ 063/963-561. Fax 063/963-363. www.angkorvillage.com. 80 units. US$181 (£100) high season; US$155 (£85) low season. AE, MC, V. **Amenities:** Restaurant; bar; outdoor pool; spa; business center w/Internet access; shopping; room service; laundry service; small library. *In room:* A/C, dataport, minibar, fridge, coffeemaker, hair dryer, safe, IDD phone.

Shinta Mani ★
A member of the Sanctuary Resorts group, a Hong Kong– based hotel organization dedicated to sustainable tourism, environmental stewardship, and holistic practices, Shinta Mani is both a small boutique hotel and a school of hospitality. One of its goals is to create opportunities in health, beauty, and hospitality professions for the next generation of underprivileged kids in Siem Reap. While the public spaces are done on a small scale—the pool is quite tiny—fine guest rooms and cool minimalist decor set this place apart. Each unit is large and stylish, with cool tile

and polished wood features. Bathrooms connect to the guest rooms via large sliding doors. The overall effect is chic, clean, and luxurious.

Junction of Oum Khum and 14th St. (near FCC), Siem Reap. ℂ 063/761-998. Fax 063/761-999. www.sanctuary resorts.com/shintamani. US$144–US$160 (£79–£88) double. MC, V. **Amenities:** Restaurant; bar; small outdoor pool; limited room service; massage; laundry service; library w/Internet access. *In room:* A/C, satellite TV, fridge, safe, IDD phone.

MODERATE

Salina Hotel 🏵 This recently renovated and expanded hotel is popular with tour groups and offers clean, utilitarian comfort. Affordable rates bring 'em in in droves. The new pool at this unpretentious three-star is small but cozy. Rooms are clean, large, and well appointed, with fresh carpeting, wood furnishings, and that new-car smell. Bathrooms are small but tidy. The staff is friendly and can help arrange necessities, like guides and rentals. This is an overall good value, but there's little atmosphere to speak of.

#125, Rd. 6, Siem Reap. ℂ **063/380-221.** Fax 063/380-224. www.salinahotel.com. 133 units. US$45 (£25) single; US$55–US$65 (£30–£36) double; US$100 (£55) suite. AE, MC, V. **Amenities:** Restaurant; 2 bars; outdoor pool; small gym; tour desk; car rental; business center w/Internet access; limited room service; laundry service. *In room:* A/C, satellite TV, minibar, fridge, IDD phone.

INEXPENSIVE

The downtown area of Siem Reap, on either side of the main road, is brimming with budget accommodations.

Auberge Mont Royal d'Angkor 🏵🏵 *(Kids)* Down a lazy lane just to the west of the town center, this quiet inn is a much better choice than the larger tourist hotels in this category. The cozy, Canadian-owned and -managed hotel features a genial staff, inviting restaurant, and standard rooms that are quite chic for the low price tag. Terra-cotta tile covers the open areas, while atmospheric touches include canvas lamps, carved wood beds, and traditional hangings, curtains, and bedspreads. The traditional decor is pleasant and inviting. Bathrooms are done in clean tile, but aren't particularly large or luxe. Deluxe rooms are worth the upgrade.

497 Taphul, P.O. Box 34, west of town center, Siem Reap. ℂ 063/964-044. www.auberge-mont-royal.com. 28 units. US$30 (£17) standard; US$50 (£27) deluxe double. AE, MC, V. **Amenities:** Restaurant; bar; tour desk; car rental; laundry service. *In room:* A/C, satellite TV, minibar, fridge, no phone.

Bopha Angkor 🏵 With its popular nightly dance show and Khmer restaurant, there is a certain cultural-theme-park vibe to this place, but nevertheless, Bopha Angkor is tidy, affordable, and quite genuine about providing a culturally infused visit to Siem Reap. Rooms are arranged in a U-shaped courtyard around a lush garden. Private spaces are large but not luxe and feature fun local accents like mossy nets and souvenir-shop trinkets on the walls. Bathrooms are small. The hotel is close to the Old Market area.

#0512, Acharsvar St. (across canal from market), Siem Reap. ℂ 063/964-928. Fax 063/964-446. www.bopha-angkor. com. 39 units. US$45–US$77 (£25–£42) double; US$180 (£99) suite. MC, V. **Amenities:** Restaurant; bar; tour desk; laundry service; Internet access. *In room:* A/C, satellite TV, minibar, fridge.

La Noria 🏵🏵 With a similar sister property, Borann Auberge de Temples, La Noria is a mellow group of bungalows connected by a winding garden path. The guesthouse is near the town center, but you wouldn't know it in the hush of this little laid-back spot. Rooms are basic but tidy, with pleasing traditional decor and nice touches such as terra-cotta floors, wooden trim, small balconies, and fine hangings and details like shadow puppets and authentic Khmer furniture. Bathrooms are small but clean, with a guesthouse-style shower-in-room setup. The place is light on amenities, though it does have a small pool and makes up for any deficiency with gobs of charm. The open-air restaurant is a highlight, serving good Khmer and French food. The hotel is affiliated with Krousar Thmey "New Family," a humanitarian group doing good work, and there is a helpful information board about rural travel and humanitarian projects.

Down small lane off Rte. 6 to the northeast of town, Siem Reap. ✆ 063/964-242. Fax 063/964-243. 28 units. US$29 (£16) w/fan; US$39 (£21) w/A/C. MC, V. **Amenities:** Restaurant; outdoor pool; laundry service; Internet access. *In room:* A/C (optional).

Passagio ✦   This unpretentious little workhorse of a hotel is convenient to downtown and adjoins its own helpful travel agent, Lolei Travel. Rooms are large and tidy and not much more, but that's the beauty here: three floors that are something like an American motel, complete with tacky hotel art. The one suite has a bathtub; all others have stand-up showers in bathrooms that are nondescript. The friendly staff can arrange any detail and is eager to please.

Watdamanak Village (across river to east of town), Siem Reap. ✆ 063/760-324. Fax 063/760-163. 17 units. US$33 (£18) double; US$69 (£38) suite. AE, MC, V. **Amenities:** Restaurant (breakfast only); travel agent; car rental; business center w/Internet access; laundry service. *In room:* A/C, satellite TV, minibar, fridge, no phone.

Pavillon Indochina ✦✦   This converted traditional Khmer house and garden is the closest you'll get to the temples. It's quite peaceful, even isolated, in a quiet neighborhood. Really it's an upscale guesthouse, charming and surprisingly self-contained, with a good restaurant and a friendly, knowledgeable French proprietor whose staff can help arrange any detail in the area. Just a few years old, the rooms are large, clean, and airy, with terra-cotta tile and wood trim. The courtyard has a picturesque garden dotted by quiet sitting areas with chairs or floor mats and comfy pillows. A good information corner lists the current happenings in town and at the temples.

Wat Thmei, on back road to temples, Siem Reap. ✆ 012/804-952. www.pavillon-indochine.com. US$25–US$30 (£14-£17). V. **Amenities:** Restaurant; tour desk; car rental; outdoor massage pavilion; laundry service. *In room:* A/C, no phone.

WHERE TO DINE

Dining in Siem Reap is not a pricey affair. In addition to the choices listed below, all of the major hotels have fine upscale restaurants. The area around the Old Market is a cluster of storefront eateries, all affordable and laid-back.

MODERATE

Chivit Thai ✦✦ THAI   You found it! Authentic Thai in an atmospheric, traditional wood house. The food is great, the prices are low (try one of the set menus), and there's casual floor seating and a rustic but comfortable dining room, romantic in the candlelight. Name your favorite Thai dish and they do it here, and do it well. The *tom yum* (sweet, spicy Thai soup) is excellent.

House #129, Rd. 6, next to Angkor Hotel. ✆ 012/830-761. Main courses US$2.50–US$5 (£1.40–£2.75). No credit cards. Daily 7am–10pm.

FCC (Foreign Correspondents Club) ✦✦ CONTINENTAL   The glowing white modern cube of the FCC would be at home in a nouveau riche California suburb or a Jacques Tati film, but it is a bit jarring canal-side in the center of Siem Reap. The first floor offers boutique shopping, while the second floor is an elegant open space with high ceilings: a modern colonial. You'll find an Art Deco bar, low lounge chairs

at the center, and standard dining space on the balcony. The main room is flanked on one end by an open kitchen. The FCC is the town's runway and hosts numerous functions as well as live music. The menu is the same as that of the original FCC in Phnom Penh, with good soups, salads, and Western standards like pasta, steaks, and wood-fired pizzas. The staff still can't believe they work here, and service is hot and cold but friendly. It has wireless Internet access and is the de facto Starbucks in Siem Reap. Even if it's just for drinks, you won't want to miss this place.

Pokambor Ave. (next to the Royal Residence). © 063/760-280. www.fcccambodia.com. Main courses US$5–US$20 (£2.75–£11). MC, V. Daily 6am–midnight.

Madame Butterfly ★★ KHMER/THAI   Serving the finest authentic Khmer- and Thai-influenced cuisine in town, Madame Butterfly is very pleasant—its setting alone is worth a visit. Located in a converted traditional wooden home, the seating is in low rattan chairs and the decor is characterized by a tasteful collection of Buddhist and Khmer artifacts. The whole effect is casually romantic. The menu reads like a short course in local cuisine, heavy on the curries and hot-pot dishes. The helpful staff and French proprietor will gladly explain the daily specials. Look for the delicious poached fish in coconut sauce with sticky rice; the divine *masaman* curry; or the rich *mchou pous*, a chicken-and-shrimp bisque. For a leisurely evening, this is a great pick.

Short ride west on Airport Rd. #6. © 016/909-607. Main courses US$3–US$10 (£1.65–£5.50). V. Daily 6am–10:30pm.

The Red Piano ★★ INTERNATIONAL   Ever since Angelina Jolie and cast and crew of the film *Tomb Raider II* made this their second home while filming at the temples, this atmospheric corner bar and restaurant has been "the place" to be in town. Imported steaks, spaghetti, sandwiches, salads, and international specialties like Indian samosas or chicken cordon bleu round out a great menu of familiar fare. This place is always hoppin' late into the evening; due to popular demand (reservations aren't accepted), they've expanded onto a second floor. Renovations throughout have created a tidy, upscale charm. The best choice in town.

50m (164 ft.) northwest of the Old Market. © 063/964-750. Main courses US$2.50–US$9 (£1.40–£4.95). No credit cards. Daily 7am–midnight.

INEXPENSIVE

Khmer Kitchen Restaurant ★★ KHMER   This busy little storefront is hidden down an alley on the north end of the Old Market, but still draws a busy crowd for big portions of simple, delicious Khmer fare. Good curries and Khmer stir-fries share menu space with unique dishes like baked pumpkin. It's about the food here, not the service—but these folks are friendly enough, considering how busy they usually are.

Down alley just north of the Old Market. © 012/763-468. Main courses US$2.50–US$3 (£1.40–£1.65). No credit cards. Daily 10am–10pm.

The Soup Dragon ★ VIETNAMESE/KHMER   This long-running street-side cafe in the center of the Old Market area serves up good Khmer and Western dishes, though its fame comes from authentic Vietnamese fare like *pho,* fresh spring rolls, and all manner of wok-fried dishes. Two floors of open-air dining overlook the busy street at the center of town. It's always packed, making this a good place to meet up with other travelers.

#369 Group 6, Mondol 1 (north of the Central Market). © 063/964-933. Main courses US$2.50–US$8 (£1.40–£4.40). No credit cards. Daily 6am–10pm.

DINING AT THE TEMPLES

Across the busy parking lot closest to Angkor Wat, you're sure to spot the snazzy **Angkor Café** (② 012/826-346). This little gallery and souvenir shop serves—for a mint by Khmer standards—good coffee, tea, and sandwiches.

For a very affordable and hearty meal while touring the temples, try **Sunrise Angkor** (② 012/946-595), one of many open-air eateries and the first one you'll see behind and to the left of Angkor Café. It has good breakfasts for very low prices.

In and among all the major temples, you'll see lots of small, bamboo-roofed eateries, and all will implore you to enter. The competition means that you have more leverage when haggling: "Are you sure this Coke is US$2? Someone over there said it was . . . ." You get the picture.

SNACKS & CAFES

For a good breakfast, real coffee, baked goods, and snacks, try **Blue Pumpkin** (#365, Mondol 1; ② 063/963-574), a posh little cafe north of the market that's also a great stop for sandwiches to go—for a perfect temple picnic.

Butterfly Café ⊛, located just across the river and north of the market, is one not to miss. This netted enclosure is a butterfly farm and menagerie of local flora and fauna, including a pond filled with Japanese carp. There are detailed descriptions of all the plants and some individual butterflies, but you're sure to meet the friendly U.K.-born owner, Ian, who's a great source of local information and will gladly answer questions. The cafe serves drinks and a limited lunch menu daily from 8am to 5pm. Admission is US$2/£1.10.

WHAT TO SEE & DO

Angkor Wat is the Disneyland of Buddhist temples in Asia. The temple complex covers 97 sq. km (37 sq. miles) and requires at least a few busy days to thoroughly explore the major sites. Everyone has his or her favorite, but a few must-sees are highlighted below. Be sure to plan carefully and catch a sunrise or sunset from one of the more prime spots; it's a photographer's dream. ***Note:*** The temples are magnificent in and of themselves, and days spent clambering around are inherently interesting, but be careful not to come away from a visit to ancient Angkor with a memory of an oversize rock collection or jungle gym. There's much to learn about Buddhism, Hinduism, architecture, and Khmer history; it's useful to hire a well-informed guide or join a tour group. There are also subtleties to temple touring, and a good guide is your best chance to beat the crowds and catch the intricacies, or be in the right place for the magic moments of the day. Contact your hotel front desk or one of the tour agencies listed at the beginning of this section.

THE TEMPLES

Entrance fees for Angkor Wat are as follows: A 1-day ticket is US$20/£11, a 3-day ticket is US$40/£22, and a 1-week ticket is US$60/£33. Tickets are good for all sites within the main temple compound, as well as Banteay Srei, to the north, and the outlying temples of the Roluos Group.

Angkor Wat ⊛⊛⊛   The symbol of Cambodia, the four spires of the main temple of Angkor are known the world over. In fact, this is the most resplendent of the Angkor sites, one certainly not to miss even on the most perfunctory of tours.

Built under the reign of Suryavarman II in the 12th century, this temple, along with Bayon and Baphuon, is the pinnacle of Khmer architecture. From base to tip of the

Moments **The Magic Hours at Angkor Wat**

The skies over Angkor always put on a show. With just a bit of prior planning, you can see the dawn or the day's afterglow framed in temple spires, glowing off the main *wat*, or reflected in one of the temple reservoirs. Photographers will swoon. Here are a few hints for catching the magic hours at the temples.

The sunrise and sunset views from the upper terraces of **Angkor Wat,** the main temple, are among the best, though it's a tough climb for some. At dusk, temple staff start clearing the main temple area just as the sun dips. Smile, avoid them, and try to stay for the afterglow.

For the classic photographers' view of the main temple, Angkor Wat, at sunset—with the image of the temple reflected in a pool—enter the first wall of the temple compound, walk halfway down the front gangway, and then take a right, down a set of stairs, and out into the field. The view from the water's edge, with warm light bouncing off the temple, is stunning.

Okay, so it's a bit crowded, but the views from **Phnom Bakeng (Bakeng Hill),** just a short drive past the entrance to Angkor Wat, are amazing at both sunrise and sunset. It's a good little climb up the hill; those so inclined can go by elephant.

The open area on the eastern side of **Banteay Kdey** looks over one of Angkor's many reservoirs, this one full and a great reflective pool for the rising glow at sunrise.

For the best view of the temples, hands down, contact **Helicopters Cambodia Ltd.** at © **023/213-706.** For a hefty fee, you can see the sites from any angle you choose. Balloon rides are also available.

highest tower, it's 213m (669 ft.) of awe-inspiring stone in the definitive, elaborate Khmer style.

The famous bas-reliefs encircling the temple on the first level depict the mythical "Churning of the Ocean of Milk," a legend in which Hindu deities stir vast oceans in order to extract the elixir of immortality. This churning produced the Apsaras, Hindu celestial dancers, that can be seen on many temples.

The most measured and studied of all the sites, Angkor Wat is the subject of much speculation: It's thought to represent Mount Meru, home of Hindu gods and a land of creation and destruction. Researchers measuring the site in *hat,* ancient Khmer units of measure, deduce that the symmetry of the building corresponds with the timeline of the Hindu ages—as a map or calendar of the universe, if you will. The approach from the main road crosses the *baray* (reservoir) and is an ascending progression of three levels to the inner sanctum. The T-shirt hawkers are relentless, and the tricky steps and temple height are a challenge to those with vertigo, but the short trip is inspiring and the views from the top are breathtaking. ***Note:*** There is a guide rope on the southern face (and often a long line up).

Angkor Thom ✯✯✯ The temple name means "the great city" in Khmer and is famed for its fantastic 45m (148-ft.) central temple, Bayon. The vast area of Angkor

Thom, over a mile on one side, is dotted with many temples and features; don't miss the elaborate reliefs of the **Terrace of the Leper King** and the **Terrace of Elephants.**

The **Bayon** is a Buddhist temple built under a later king, Jayavarman VII (1190), but the temple nevertheless adheres to Hindu cosmology and can be read as a metaphor for the natural world. It has four huge stone faces, with one facing out and keeping watch at each compass point. The curious smiling image, thought by many to be a depiction of Jayavarman himself, is often considered the enigmatic Mona Lisa of Southeast Asia. Bayon is also surrounded by two long walls with bas-relief scenes of legendary and historic events, probably painted and gilded originally. There are 51 smaller towers surrounding Bayon, each with four faces of its own.

Just north of the Bayon is the stalwart form of the **Baphuon,** a temple built in 1066 that is in the process of being put back together in a protractive effort that gives visitors an idea of what original temple construction might have been like.

Ta Prohm 🐸🐸🐸 The jungle foliage still has its hold on this dynamic temple. Ta Prohm was the only one that was left in such a ruinous state when early archaeologists freed the rest of the Angkor Wat temples from the jungle. Ta Prohm is a favorite for many; in fact, the ruinous roots appeal to most. As large around as some tree trunks, the roots of fig, banyan, and kapok trees cleave massive stones in two or give way and grow over the top of temple ramparts. It's quite dramatic, and there are a few popular photo spots where the collision of temple and vine are most impressive. Sadly, Ta Prohm was looted quite heavily in recent years, and many of its stone reliquaries have been lost.

ATTRACTIONS FARTHER AFIELD

Banteay Srei 🐸🐸 True temple buffs won't want to miss this distinct complex: The 10th-century buildings of Banteay Srei are done in a style unique to the high spires of Angkor. The site is a collection of low walls surrounding low-rise peaked structures of deep-red sandstone. Translated as the "Citadel of Women," it has well-preserved relief carvings on the squat central buildings and intricate tellings of ancient Hindu tales. Go with a guide who can explain the finer details of temple inscriptions.

32km (20 miles) north of the main temples of Angkor Wat.

Kabal Spean *Finds* Known as the "River of a Thousand Linga" (a *linga* is a phallic symbol representing the Hindu god Shiva), Kabal Spean lay undiscovered by Westerners until a French researcher stumbled across it only recently. Dating from the early 11th century, the relief carvings that line the stream beds are said to purify the water before it fills the reservoirs (called *barays*) of Angkor. It's the journey here that's really interesting, along rough roads through rural villages north of Banteay Srei, and there's also a fun 30-minute forest hike to the first waterfall. Khmer folks come to picnic, and it's a good spot to swim or follow the path that trips along the brook; from there, you can view the many carvings in relief on the banks and creek bed.

5km (3 miles) north of Banteay Srei. Admission US$3/£1.65.

Land Mines Museum You won't find signs leading you to this seemingly impromptu museum; Cambodian officials prefer their own rhetoric to that of the owner and curator, Mr. Akira. The museum itself is just a corrugated-roof area stacked high with disarmed ordnance and detailed data on the country's UXO (unexploded ordnance). Most interesting is the small grove out back, an exhibit of how mines are placed in a real jungle setting. The museum is a call to action for de-mining in the country. Resist any temptation to volunteer (unless properly trained), but you can chat with Mr. Akira, peruse his recent book on the subject, and sign a petition (he's hoping to achieve NGO status). It's an interesting visit.

On the main rd. to the temples, just before the checkpoint and a few clicks east. Free admission (voluntary contributions). Daily 7am–5pm. Go by motorbike or taxi.

Roluos Group   These three temples are best viewed in the context of Angkor architecture's progression, as the forefathers of the more dynamic of Angkor's main temples. A visit to these temples is included in the main temple ticket, but will cost you a bit extra for transport.

13km (8 miles) east of the town center.

SHOPPING

The **Old Market,** in the center of Siem Reap, is the best place to find Buddhist trinkets, souvenirs like T-shirts, and even good books on the temples. Just outside the market, you'll see a whole array of small storefront boutiques.

Large, mall-style souvenir venues line the road just north of town on the way to the temples. These are a good stop for the obligatory collector's spoon or plastic replica of the temples.

The **Lazy Mango Bookshop,** a block west of the Old Market (lazymangobooks@ yahoo.com), is where you can exchange that novel you've been dragging around for a new one and talk with Don, the kind American owner.

SIEM REAP AFTER DARK

Siem Reap is a town where most visitors are up with the sun and out visiting the temple sites, but there are a few good evening options.

Apsara dance is an ancient art in Cambodia. Dancers in traditional gilded costume practice their slow art, characterized by the elegant contortions of the wrists. Combined with a fine buffet dinner in the traditional indoor banquet-house theater, this is a fun evening out. Contact the folks at the **Angkor Village** (© 063/963-5613) to make reservations for the nightly show. The **Raffles Grand Hotel d'Angkor** (© 063/963-888) has a similar show in an open pavilion on the lawn. At both, dinner begins at 7pm; the show starts at 7:30pm. Tickets cost US$20/£11.

Dr. Beat (Beatocello) Richner plays the works of Bach and some of his own comic pieces between stories and vignettes about his work as director of the **Kanth Bopha Foundation** (www.beat-richner.ch), a humanitarian hospital just north of the town center. Admission is free, but donations are accepted in support of their valiant efforts to serve a steady stream of destitute patients, mostly children, who suffer from treatable diseases such as tuberculosis. Dr. Richner is as passionate about his music as he is about his cause. You're in for an enjoyable, informative evening. Performances are every Saturday at 7:15pm, just north of the town center on the road to the temples.

There are a few popular bars near the Old Market in Siem Reap. The **Angkor What?** (1 block west of the Old Market) seems to be where it's at, and next door the **Easy Speaking Café and Pub** handles the spillover. The whole street, in fact, hops late into the evening. Nearby, the funky, black-lit **Laundry,** on a side street to the north of the Old Market, has good special events. **Dead Fish Tower** (© 012/630-6377), on the main road heading toward the temples, is set up like the rigging of a tall ship, with precarious perches, funky nooks, and unique drinks.

8

Singapore

by Jennifer Eveland

Singapore thrives on a history that has absorbed a multitude of foreign elements over almost 2 centuries, melding them into a unique modern national identity. Beginning with the landing of Sir Stamford Raffles in 1819, add to the mix the original Malay inhabitants, immigrating waves of Chinese traders and workers, Indian businessmen and laborers, Arab merchants, British colonials, European adventure seekers, and an assortment of Southeast Asian settlers—this tiny island rose from the ingenuity of those who worked and lived together here. Today, all recognize each group's importance to the heritage of the land, each adding unique contributions to a culture and identity we know as Singaporean.

With all its shopping malls, fast-food outlets, imported fashion, and steel skyscrapers, Singapore could look like any other contemporary city you've ever visited—but to peel through the layers is to understand that life here is far more complex. While the outer layers are startlingly Western, just underneath lies a curious area where East blends with West in language, cuisine, attitude, and style. At the core, you'll find a sensibility rooted in the cultural heritage of values, religion, superstition, and memory. In Singapore, nothing is ever as it appears to be.

For me, this is where the fascination begins. I detect so many things familiar in this city, only to discover how these imported ideas have been altered to fit the local identity. Like the Singaporean shophouse—a jumble of colonial architectural mandates, European tastes, Chinese superstitions, and Malay finery. Or "Singlish," the unofficial local tongue, which combines English language with Chinese grammar, common Malay phrases, and Hokkien slang to form a patois unique to this part of the world. This transformation of cultures has been going on for almost 2 centuries. So, in a sense, Singapore is no different today than it was 100 years ago. And in this I find my "authentic" travel experience.

1 Getting to Know Singapore

THE LAY OF THE LAND

On a world map, Singapore is nothing more than a speck nestled in the heart of Southeast Asia, at the tip of the Malaysian peninsula. In the north, it's linked to Malaysia by a causeway over the Strait of Johor, which is its only physical connection to any other body of land. The country is made up of one main island, Singapore, and around 60 smaller ones, some of which—like Sentosa, Pulau Ubin, Kusu, and St. John's Island—are popular retreats. The main island is shaped like a flat, horizontal diamond, measuring in at just over 42km (26 miles) from east to west and almost 23km (14 miles) north to south. With a total land area of only 584.8 sq. km (228 sq. miles), Singapore is almost shockingly tiny.

Singapore's geographical position, sitting approximately 137km (85 miles) north of the equator, means that its climate features uniform temperatures, plentiful rainfall, and high humidity.

Singapore is a city-state, which basically means the city *is* the country. The urban center starts at the Singapore River at the southern point of the island. Within the urban center are neighborhoods that are handy for visitors to become familiar with: the Historic District, Chinatown, Orchard Road, Kampong Gelam, and Little India.

THE CITY   The urban center of Singapore spans quite far from edge to edge, so walking from one end to the other, say from Kampong Gelam to Chinatown, will be too much for a relaxed walk. But within each neighborhood, the best way to explore is by foot, wandering along picturesque streets, in and out of shops and museums.

The main focal point of the city is the **Singapore River,** which on a map is located at the southern point of the island, flowing west to east into a marina. It's along the banks of this river that Sir Stamford Raffles landed and built his settlement for the East India Trading Company. As trade prospered, the banks of the river were expanded to handle commerce, behind which neighborhoods and administrative offices took root. In 1822, he developed a town plan which allocated neighborhoods to each of the races who'd come in droves to find work and begin lives. The lines drawn then remain today, shaping the major ethnic enclaves held within the city limits.

On the south bank of the river, go-downs, or warehouses, lined the waterside. Behind, offices and residences sprang up for the Chinese community of merchants and "coolie" laborers who worked the river and sea trade. Raffles named this section **Chinatown,** a name that stands today.

Neighboring Chinatown to the southwest is **Tanjong Pagar,** a small district where wealthy Chinese and Eurasians built plantations and manors. With the development of the steamship, Keppel Harbour, a deep natural harbor just off the shore of Tanjong Pagar, was built up to receive the larger vessels. Tanjong Pagar quickly developed into a commercial and residential area filled with workers who flocked there to support the industry.

In the early days, both Chinatown and Tanjong Pagar were amazing sights of city activity. Row houses lined the streets, with shops on the bottom floors and homes on the second and third. Chinese coolie laborers commonly lived 16 to a room, and the area flourished with gambling casinos, clubs, and opium dens in which they spent their spare time and money. Indians also thronged to the area to work on the docks, a small reminder that although races had their own areas, they were never exclusive communities.

As recently as the 1970s, a walk down the streets in this area was an adventure. The shops housed Chinese craftspeople and artists. On the streets, hawkers peddled food and other merchandise. Calligrapher scribes set up shop on sidewalks to write letters for a fee. Housewives bustled through their daily errands. Overhead, laundry hung from bamboo poles.

Today, both of these districts are sleepy in comparison. New Towns offering affordable housing have siphoned residents off to the suburbs, and though the government has renovated many of the old shophouses in an attempt to preserve history, they're now tenanted by law offices and architectural, public-relations, and advertising firms. About the only time you'll see this place hustle any more is during weekday lunchtime, when all the professionals dash out for a bite.

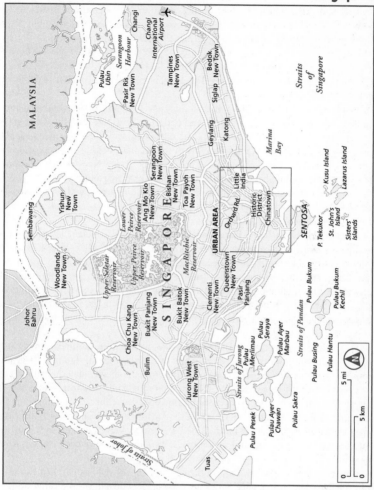

The **north bank** was originally reserved for colonial administrative buildings and is today commonly referred to as the **Historic District.** The center point was the Padang, the field on which the Europeans would play sports and hold outdoor ceremonies. Around the field, the Parliament Building, Supreme Court, City Hall, and other municipal buildings sprang up in grand style. Government Hill, the present-day **Fort Canning Hill,** was home of the governors. The Esplanade along the waterfront was a center for European social activities and music gatherings, when colonials would don their finest Western styles and walk the park under parasols or cruise in horse-drawn carriages. These days, the Historic District is still the center of most of the government's operations and home to numerous high-rise hotels and shopping malls. The area on the bank of the river is celebrated as Raffles's landing site.

To the northwest of the Historic District, in the area along **Orchard Road** and **Tanglin,** a residential area was created for Europeans and Eurasians. Homes and plantations were eventually replaced by apartment buildings and shops, and in the early 1970s, luxury hotels ushered tourism into the area in full force. In the 1980s, huge malls were erected along the sides of Orchard Road, turning the Orchard-scape into the shopping hub it continues to be. The Tanglin area is home to most of the foreign embassies in Singapore.

The landscape of **Little India** made it a natural location for an Indian settlement. Indians were the original cattle hands and traders in Singapore, and this area's grasses and springs provided their cattle with food and water, while bamboo groves supplied necessary lumber for their pens. Later, with the establishment of brick kilns, Indian construction laborers flocked to the area to find work. Today, many elements of Indian culture persist, although Indians make up a small percentage of the current population. Shops, restaurants, and temples still serve the community, and on Sundays Little India is a true mob scene, when all the workers have a day off and come to the streets here to socialize and relax.

Neighboring Little India, **Kampong Gelam** was given to Sultan Hussein and his family as part of his agreement to turn Singapore over to Raffles. Here he built his Istana (palace) and the Sultan Mosque, and the area subsequently filled with Malay and Arab Muslims who imported a distinct Islamic flavor to the neighborhood. The area is still a focal point of Muslim society in Singapore thanks to Sultan Mosque, and the Istana has recently been opened as a new exhibit celebrating Malay culture. **Arab Street** is a regular draw for both tourists and locals, who come to find deals on fabrics and local and regional crafts.

Two areas of the city center are relatively new, having been built atop huge parcels of reclaimed land. Where the eastern edges of Chinatown and Tanjong Pagar once touched the water's edge, land reclamation created the present-day downtown business district, which is named after its central thoroughfare, **Shenton Way.** This Wall Street–like district is home to the magnificent skyscrapers that grace Singapore's skyline, and to the banks and businesses that have made the place an international financial capital. During weekday business hours, Shenton Way is packed with scurrying businesspeople; after hours and on weekends, it's a quiet forest of concrete, metal, and glass.

The other area is **Marina Bay,** on the opposite side of the Marina, just east of the Historic District. **Suntec City,** Southeast Asia's largest convention and exhibition center, is located here and has become the lynchpin of a thriving hotel, shopping-mall, and amusement zone.

OUTSIDE THE URBAN AREA   The heart of Singapore centers around the Singapore River, but outside the city proper are suburban neighborhoods and rural areas. In the immediate outskirts of the main urban area are the older suburban neighborhoods, such as **Katong, Geyland,** and **Holland Village,** which feature prewar homes with charming architectural details. Beyond these are the newer suburbs, called **HDB New Towns.** The HDB, or Housing Development Board, is responsible for creating large towns, such as **Ang Mo Kio** and **Toa Payoh,** which are clusters of government-subsidized housing that have sprung up around the island, supported by their own shops, schools, and clinics, and many of them connected by the subway system.

ETIQUETTE

While in Singapore, try to use only your right hand in social interaction. Why? Because in Indian and Muslim society, the left hand is used only for bathroom chores. Not only should you eat with your right hand and give and receive all gifts with your right hand, but you should make sure all gestures, especially pointing (particularly in temples and mosques), are made with your right hand. Also try to point with your knuckle rather than your finger, to be more polite.

The other important etiquette tip is to remember to remove your shoes before entering places of worship (except for churches and synagogues) and all private residences.

In cosmopolitan Singapore, most people will shake hands in greeting, but it's good to remember that Muslim women are not allowed to touch men to whom they are not related by blood or marriage. Unless they initiate a handshake, a simple smile and nod is fine.

Also, it's common for Singaporeans to exchange business cards. Always receive cards with two hands, and always treat the card with respect—don't stash it in your pocket without paying attention to it.

If you're touring during the day, shorts and a T-shirt are fine; however, if you plan to enter a temple or mosque, you will be required to cover your legs and upper arms. If you're dining in a restaurant or attending a business function, the dress code is "dress casual," meaning slacks and pressed shirt for men, and a dress, slacks, or skirt for women. For most business meetings, a suit and tie are still necessary, but you needn't wear your jacket everywhere. For women, business suits are also expected.

If you would like to give a gift to a Singaporean, my advice is to consult your hotel concierge for appropriate recommendations. For example, avoid giving sweets or foods to Muslim friends, unless you are certain the gift is *halal* (permitted within Islamic dietary practice). For the Chinese, it's trickier. Gifts should never be knives, clocks, handkerchiefs, or white flowers. (The sharp blades of knives symbolize the severing of a friendship; in Cantonese, the word for clock sounds the same as the word for funeral; handkerchiefs bring to mind tears and sadness; and white is the color of funeral mourning—you get the drift.)

The main rules regarding table manners revolve around the use of chopsticks. Don't stick them upright in any dish, don't gesture with them, and don't suck on them. Dropped chopsticks are also considered bad luck. Southern Indian food can be eaten with your hands, but make sure you wash them first, and always use your right hand.

LANGUAGE

Singapore's four official languages are Malay, Chinese (Mandarin), Tamil, and English. Malay is the national language, while English is the language for government operations, law, and major financial transactions. Most Singaporeans are at least bilingual, with many speaking one or more dialects of Chinese, English, and some Malay.

USEFUL MALAY PHRASES

English	Malay	Pronunciation
Hello	**Selamat**	Seh-*lah*-maht
Good-bye	**Selamat tinggal**	Seh-*lah*-maht *teen*-gahl
Thank you	**Terima kasih**	*Tree*-mah *kah*-say
You're welcome	**Sama-sama**	*Sah*-mah-*sah*-mah

English	Malay	Pronunciation
How are you?	**Apa khabar?**	*Ah*-pah *kah*-bahr?
I'm fine	**Khabar baik**	*Kah*-bahr *bah*-ee
Yes	**Ya**	Yah
No	**Tidak**	*Tee*-dah
Excuse me	**Ma'afkan saya**	Mah-*ahf*-kahn *sah*-yah
I'm sorry	**Ma'af**	Mah-*ahf*
I don't understand	**Saya tidak faham**	*Sah*-yah *tee*-dah *fah*-hahm
Do you speak English?	**Bolehkah anda bercakap bahasa inggeris?**	*Boh*-lay-kah *ahn*-dah ber-*chah*-kahp bah-*hah*-sah *een*-ger-ees?
Where is the toilet?	**Di mana ada inggeris?**	Dee *mah*-nah *ah*-dah *tahn*-dahs?
I want to go to . . .	**Tolong hantar saya ke . . .**	*Toh*-long *hahn*-tahr *sah*-yah keh . . .
Do you have . . . ? drinking water a room	**Saudara ada . . . ? air minuman bilik**	Sah-oo-*dah*-rah *ah*-dah . . . ? *ah*-yer *mee*-noo-mahn *bee*-lee
I would like . . . coffee tea	**Saya mau . . . kopi the**	*Sah*-yah maow . . . *koh*-pee tay
How much?	**Berapa harganya?**	Ber-*ah*-pah hahr-*gahn*-yah?
Too expensive	**Terlalu mahal**	Ter-*lah*-loo mah-*hahl*
Can you make it cheaper?	**Boleh kurang?**	*Boh*-lay *koo*-rahng?

2 The Best of Singapore in 1 Week

If you've made it all the way to Southeast Asia, you'll likely be on a limited schedule—especially if you've arrived via a long-haul flight from Europe or North America. The good news is, Singapore is easy. It's such a small place that virtually every sight is relatively close. If your time is very limited, I recommend you bypass the museums and head straight for the streets, where you'll find a "living museum" of sorts, with local people, food, shops, and places of worship, plus a couple interesting cultural displays.

Days ❶–❷: Arrive in Singapore

After arriving in Singapore, allow yourself time to recover and just spend your time wandering through the city's streets. **Arab Street** is lined with shops that sell Malaysian and Indonesian batik cloth and home-decor items, baskets, carved wood, objets d'art, and other gifts. Just off Arab Street, you can't miss the towering onion dome of the **Sultan Mosque.**

The most historical in Singapore, its grounds are open, so feel free to explore within its walls, including the ablutions area. Take a walking tour of the **Historic District,** where you'll pass the Old Parliament House, the Padang, the Supreme Court, City Hall, and St. Andrew's Cathedral. Cool off in the afternoon at the **Asian Civilisations Museum.**

Days ❸–❹: Chinatown 🅖

Explore the sights of Chinatown and visit the **Chinatown Heritage Centre.** The streets surrounding the center are packed with souvenir shops with tons of curious finds, plus some beautiful art and antiques galleries, so be sure to wander around a bit. Spend some time at **Yue Hwa,** a Chinese emporium that is practically a museum of Chinese handicrafts, filled with floor after floor of fabulous shopping. Excellent buys here include ready-made silk clothing, embroidered handbags, carved jade, pottery, and cloisonné.

Day ❺: Little India 🅖🅖

Tour the temples and streets of Little India. **Serangoon Road** is the heart of Singapore's Indian community, a long strip where the locals come to buy spices, flowers, Bollywood DVDs, saris, and all kinds of ceremonial items, many of which make excellent gifts. This is one of the few old neighborhoods in Singapore that hasn't been "Disney-fied" by the government. Midway down Serangoon Road you'll find **Sri Veerama Kaliamman,** a brightly colored temple that hums with devotees all times of the day. Take off your shoes to explore the dioramas inside. Further along Serangoon Road, **Mustapha's**

is a crazy Indian emporium. Explore the basement sari-fabric department, one of the largest in Singapore. I love the groceries section with row after row of boxed curry mixes—great to take back home! Or check out Mustapha's three floors of the most elaborate gold jewelry you've ever seen.

Day ❻: Natural Singapore 🅖🅖

Take an early-morning stroll through the **Singapore Botanic Gardens.** You'll beat the heat and you won't feel rushed as you meander through the beautiful displays of tropical plants, shady trees, vivid blooms, and delicate bonsai. Don't forget to visit the National Orchid Garden (open at 8:30am) while you're there. Later, take in a rare chance to see nocturnal animals. **Night Safari** is the one place where all Singaporeans bring their foreign visitors, and I have yet to see anyone walk away unimpressed. Also, an easy dinner can be had from local and fast-food stalls at the park entrance.

Day ❼: Try to Leave

As hard as it might be to accept, the real world beckons. Say goodbye to Singapore, and prepare for your return flight home.

3 Planning Your Trip to Singapore

VISITOR INFORMATION

The long arm of the **Singapore Tourism Board (STB)** reaches many overseas audiences through its branch offices, which will gladly provide brochures and booklets to help you plan your trip. Check out its website at **www.visitsingapore.com**.

ENTRY REQUIREMENTS

To enter Singapore, you must have a passport valid for at least 6 months from your date of entry. Visitors from the United States, Canada, Australia, New Zealand, and the United Kingdom are not required to obtain a visa prior to arrival. A Social Visit Pass (with combined social and business status) good for up to 30 days (up to 90 days for U.S. visitors) will be awarded upon entry for travelers arriving by plane, or for 14 days if your trip is by ship or overland from Malaysia or Indonesia. Immigrations officers are not required to grant you the maximum amount of days allotted, but rather have the discretion to grant you as many days as they feel you need.

Urban Singapore Neighborhoods

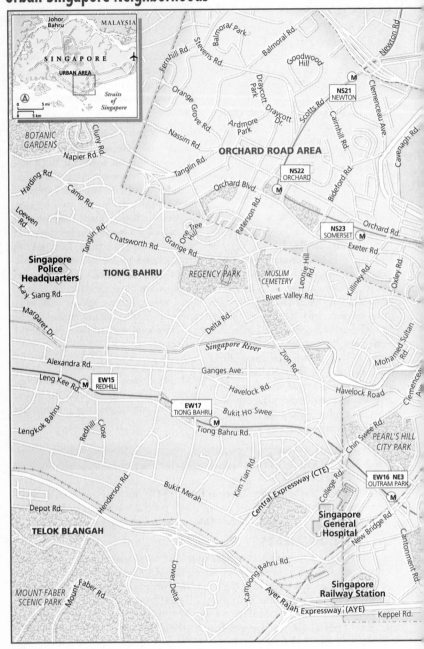

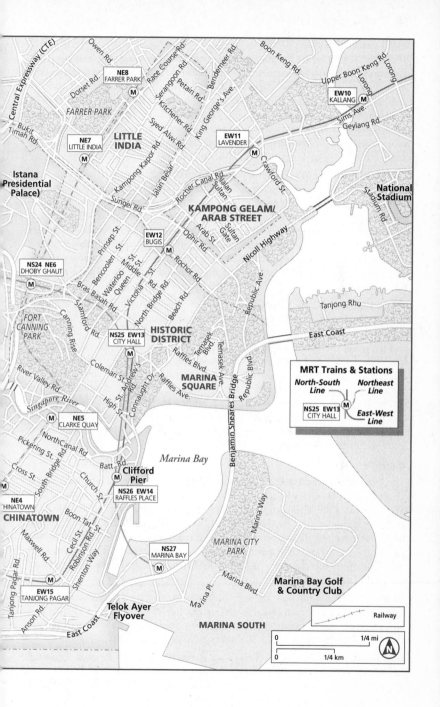

CUSTOMS REGULATIONS

There's no restriction on the amount of currency you can bring into Singapore. For those over age 18 who have arrived from countries other than Malaysia and have spent more than 48 hours outside Singapore, allowable duty-free concessions are 1 liter of spirits; 1 liter of wine; and 1 liter of either port, sherry, or beer, all of which must be intended for personal consumption only. There are no duty-free concessions on cigarettes or other tobacco items. If you exceed the duty-free limitations, you can bring your excess items in upon payment of goods and services tax (GST) and Customs duty.

PROHIBITED ITEMS It is important to note that Singapore has some very unique prohibitions on the import of certain items. While pretty much every country in the world, including Singapore, prohibits travelers from bringing items like plutonium, explosives, and firearms through Customs—same goes with agricultural products such as live plants and animals, controlled substances, and poisons—Singapore adds to the list any type of printed or recorded pornography; pirated movies, music, or software; and toy or decorative guns, knives, or swords. A detailed rundown of prohibited items can be found at the Ministry of Home Affairs website, **www.mha. gov.sg**.

SINGAPORE'S DRUG POLICY With all of the publicity surrounding the issue, Singapore's strict drug policy shouldn't need recapitulation, but here it is: Importing, selling, or using illegal narcotics is absolutely forbidden. Punishments are severe, up to and including the death penalty (automatic for morphine quantities exceeding 30g, heroin exceeding 15g, cocaine 30g, marijuana 500g, hashish 200g, opium 1.2kg, or methamphetamines 250g). If you're carrying smaller sums (anything above: morphine 3g, heroin 2g, cocaine 3g, marijuana 15g, hashish 10g, opium 100g, or methamphetamines 25g), you'll still be considered to have intent to traffic and may face the death penalty if you can't prove otherwise. If you're crazy enough to try to bring these things into the country and are caught, no measure of appeal to your home consulate will grant you any special attention.

MONEY

The local currency unit is the **Singapore dollar (S$),** commonly referred to as the "Sing dollar." Notes vary in size and color, and are issued in denominations of S$2, $5, $10, $50, $100, $500, and $1,000. S$1 bills exist but are rare. Coins are issued in denominations of S1¢, 5¢, 10¢, 20¢, 50¢, and the fat, gold-colored S$1. Singapore has an interchangeability agreement with Brunei Darussalam, so don't be alarmed if you receive Brunei currency with your change, as it's legal tender. The exchange rate used throughout this chapter is **S$1.60 = US$1,** which is about the average exchange rate during the year 2006.

ATMs The easiest and best way to get cash away from home is from an ATM, sometimes referred to as a "cash machine" or "cashpoint." It's not an absolute necessity to buy Singapore dollars before your trip, since you can find ATMs at Changi International Airport's Terminals 1 and 2 as you exit the baggage-claim area.

CURRENCY EXCHANGE There's an **American Express Foreign Exchange** (© 65/6543-0671) office at Changi International Airport's Terminal 2, open from noon to midnight daily. In town, it's best to exchange currency at a local authorized money changer, found in most shopping malls throughout the city. They'll give you the best rate. You'll lose money with the high rates at banks, hotels, and shops.

TRAVELER'S CHECKS   You can exchange traveler's checks at any local authorized money changer in town.

CREDIT CARDS   American Express, Visa, MasterCard, Diners Club, and JCB (Japan Credit Bureau) are accepted at virtually all major hotels, restaurants, nightclubs, and shopping centers. Even taxis accept payment by credit card. Smaller food and retail merchants generally don't accept plastic. Be advised, if you're trying to negotiate a discount with a vendor, you will always get a better price with good old-fashioned cash. Some retailers will insist on adding a credit card "service charge" to your bill. While it is true that the credit card companies charge the retailers a small fee each time a customer uses a card, it is a cost the retailers are supposed to bear themselves.

WHEN TO GO

A steady supply of business travelers keep occupancy rates high year-round; however, some hotels report that business travel gets sluggish during the months of July and August. This is probably your best time to negotiate a favorable rate. Peak season for travel falls between December and June, with "superpeak" beginning in mid-December and lasting through the Chinese Lunar New Year, which falls in January or February, depending on the moon's cycle. During this season, Asian travel routes are booked solid and hotels are maxed out. Good deals are rare, since most of Asia takes annual leave at this time.

CLIMATE   Singapore lies between two monsoon winds, and rainfall varies greatly. The Northeast Monsoon arrives at the beginning of November and stays until mid-March; temperatures are slightly cooler, relatively speaking, than at other times of the year. The heaviest rainfall occurs between November and January, with daily showers that sometimes last for long periods of time; at other times, it comes down in short heavy gusts and goes away quickly. Wind speeds are rarely anything more than light. The Southwest Monsoon falls between June and September. Temperatures are much higher and, interestingly, it's during this time of year that Singapore gets the *least* rain (with the very least reported in July).

By and large, year-round temperatures remain uniform, with a daily average of 81°F (27°C), afternoon temperatures reaching as high as 87°F (31°C), and an average sunrise temperature as low as 75°F (24°C). Relative humidity often exceeds 90% at night and in the early morning. Even on a "dry" afternoon, don't expect it to drop much below 60%. (The daily average is 84% relative humidity.)

PUBLIC HOLIDAYS & EVENTS   There are 11 official public holidays: **New Year's Day,** on January 1; **Chinese New Year** or **Lunar New Year,** 2 days in January or February; **Good Friday,** the Friday before Easter Sunday; **Labour Day,** on May 1; **Vesak Day,** in May or June; **National Day,** on August 9; **Hari Raya Puasa,** in October; **Deepavali,** in October or November; **Hari Raya Haji,** in December or January; and **Christmas,** on December 25. On these days, expect government offices, banks, and some shops to be closed.

HEALTH & SAFETY

HEALTH CONCERNS   Food is clean virtually everywhere, tap water is potable, restaurants and food vendors are regulated by the government, and many other airborne, bug-borne, and bite-borne what-have-yous have been eradicated.

Singapore doesn't require that you have any vaccinations to enter the country, but does recommend immunization against diphtheria, tetanus, hepatitis A and B, and typhoid for anyone traveling to Southeast Asia in general. If you're particularly worried, follow this advice; if not, don't worry about it. See chapter 3's "Health & Safety" section (p. 43) for information on the major health issues that affect travelers to Southeast Asia.

SAFETY CONCERNS   You'll be fairly safe out during the wee hours in most parts of the city, and even a single woman alone has little to worry about. Occasionally, groups of young men may catcall, but by and large those groups are not hanging out in the more cosmopolitan areas. You can always get home safely in a taxi, which fortunately isn't too hard to find even late at night, with one exception: When Boat Quay clubs close, there's usually a mob of revelers scrambling for cabs. (Note that after midnight, a 50% surcharge is added to the fare, so make sure you don't drink away your ride home!)

GETTING THERE

BY PLANE   If you're hunting for the best airfare, plan your trip for the low season, which runs from September 1 to November 30. Between January 1 and May 31, you'll pay the highest fares. In my experience, the best deals are offered through Asian carriers; remember to compare fares at Japan Airlines, Korean Air, Cathay Pacific, Malaysia Airlines, and Thai Airways in addition to the following.

Singapore's national carrier, **Singapore Airlines** (© **800/742-3333** in the U.S. and Canada, 0870/608-8886 in the U.K., or 65/6223-8888 in Singapore; www.singapore air.com), is arguably one of the finest airlines in the world, with reliable service that is second to none. It's the most luxurious way to fly to Singapore, but also the most expensive. Major cities in North America, Europe, Australia, and New Zealand are served by daily flights to Singapore.

From North America, **United Airlines** and **Northwest Airlines** link major destinations in the U.S. with Singapore. **British Airways** and **Qantas** collaborate to provide flights to Asia from major cities in the U.K. and Australia. **Air New Zealand** has daily flights from Auckland and Christchurch.

GETTING INTO TOWN FROM THE AIRPORT   Most visitors to Singapore will land at **Changi International Airport** (© **65/6542-4422** for arrival and departure information), located toward the far eastern corner of the island. Compared with other international airports, Changi is a dream come true, providing clean and very efficient facilities. Expect to find in-transit accommodations, restaurants, duty-free shops, money changers, ATMs, car-rental desks, hotel assistance, and tourist information all marked in English with clear signs. When you arrive, keep your eyes peeled for the many Singapore Tourism Board brochures that are so handily displayed throughout the terminal.

The city is easily accessible by public transportation. A **taxi** to the city center will cost around S$22 to S$25 (US$14–US$16/£7.70–£8.80), which is the metered fare plus an airport surcharge of S$3 to S$5 (US$1.90–US$3.20/£1.05–£1.75), depending on the time of pickup. It takes around 20 minutes to reach the city, double that during weekday rush hours.

If you've got a lot of luggage, **CityCab** offers a six-seater maxicab to anywhere in the city for a flat rate of S$35 (US$22/£12). Inquire at the taxi queue or call © **65/6542-8297.** There's also an **airport shuttle,** a six-seater maxicab that traverses between the airport and all major hotels, plus stops at Orchard Road, Chinatown, and Bugis Junction. The booking counter (© **65/6542-8297**) at both terminals is open daily from 6am to 2am. When you book your trip into town, you can also make a reservation for your departure. Pay S$7 (US$4.50/£2.50) for adults or S$5 (US$3.20/£1.75) for children directly to the driver.

The **MRT,** Singapore's subway system (see "MRT Transit Map," below), now operates to the airport, linking it with the city and areas beyond. STB will tell you the trip takes 30 minutes, but give yourself at least an hour, as you'll need time to wait for the train to arrive, you'll have to transfer at Tanah Merah station, and if you're arriving in Terminal 1, you'll need to hop on yet another train—a shuttle between terminals. After you get to your station in town, you'll still have to find your way, with your luggage, to your hotel. Personally, I think it's a pain in the neck, but hey, it only costs S$1.40 (US90¢/£0.50) to get to City Hall station. Trains operate roughly from 6am to midnight daily.

A couple of **buses** run from the airport into the city as well. SBS bus no. 36 is the best, saving time by hopping on East Coast Parkway before making stops through the Historic District and along Orchard Road. Pick up the bus in the basement of either terminal. The trip will take over an hour, and you'll need to get exact change before you board. A trip to town will be roughly S$1.40 (US90¢/£0.50).

GETTING AROUND

The many inexpensive mass-transit options make getting around Singapore pretty easy. Taxis are also very affordable and, by and large, drivers are helpful and honest, if not downright personable. The Mass Rapid Transit (MRT) subway has lines that cover the main areas of the city and run out to the farther parts of the island. Buses present more of a challenge because there are so many routes snaking all over the island, but they're a great way to see the country while getting where you want to go.

Of course, if you're just exploring the urban area, many sights are within walking distance—but going on foot to the different neighborhoods can be a hike, especially in the heat. The STB visitor centers carry free city maps and walking-tour maps of individual neighborhoods to help you find your way around.

BY TAXI   Taxis are by far the most convenient way to get around Singapore. Fares are cheap, cars are clean, and drivers speak English. Taxi queues can be found at every hotel, shopping mall, and public building; otherwise, you can flag one down from the side of the road. Most destinations in the main parts of the island can be reached fairly inexpensively, while trips to the outlying attractions can cost from S$10 to S$15 (US$6.25–US$9.40/£3.45–£5.15) one-way. That said, I caution you against becoming too dependent on them. During the morning and evening rush, you can wait a maddeningly long time in the queue, and sometimes if you're at a destination outside the main city area, cabs are far between. If it's raining, you might as well stay put—you'll never get a cab.

If you do find yourself stranded, call **CityCab** (© **65/6552-2222**), **Comfort** (© **65/6552-1111**), or **TIBS** (© **65/6555-8888**). There's an extra charge of S$2 (US$1.25/£0.70) or S$3 (US$1.90/£1) for booking by phone. If you're at a restaurant or attraction, ask the cashier or information desk to call a taxi company for you.

Taxis charge the metered fare, which is S$2.50 (US$1.60/£0.90) for the first kilometer (.6 mile) and S10¢ (US5¢/£0.03) for each additional 175 to 210 meters (575–690 ft.) or 25 seconds of waiting. A variety of extra charges are levied depending on where you're going and when you go—for example, during peak hours, from midnight to 6am, on holidays, for travel within the Central Business District (CBD), each time you travel through an Electronic Road Pricing (ERP) underpass, and for credit card payments (add an extra 10%).

BY MASS RAPID TRANSIT (MRT)   The MRT is Singapore's subway system. It's cool, clean, safe, and reliable, providing service around the central parts of the city and extending into the suburbs around the island. There are stops along Orchard Road into the Historic District, to Chinatown and Little India—chances are there will be a stop close to your hotel.

Fares range from S80¢ to S$1.80 (US50¢–US$1.20/£0.25–£0.60), depending on distance. System charts are prominently displayed in all MRT stations to help you find your fare, which you pay with an **EZ-Link fare card.** These cards, which are good on both the subway and buses, can be purchased at TransitLink offices in MRT stations; single-fare cards can be purchased at vending machines. The card does carry a S$5 (US$3.15/£1.75) deposit—so for a S$15 (US$9.40/£5.15) initial investment, you'll get S$10 (US$6.25/£3.40) worth of travel credit. (**One caution:** A fare card cannot be used by two people for the same trip; each must have his own.)

Tip: When you pick up your EZ-Link card at a TransitLink office, get the latest edition of the *TransitLink Guide* for about S$3.90 (US$2.50/£1.40). This tiny book details both MRT and bus routes, with connections marked between the two systems. It also tells you fares for each trip.

MRT operating hours vary among lines and stops, with the earliest train beginning service daily at 5:15am and the last train ending at 12:47am. For more information, call the **TransitLink Hot Line** (© **1800-767-4333**), which operates daily 24 hours.

BY BUS   Singapore's bus system comprises an extensive web of routes that reach virtually everywhere on the island. It can be intimidating for newcomers, but after you get your feet wet, you'll feel right at home. Start off by purchasing an **EZ-Link fare card,** so you can pay for your trips without the bother of digging up exact change, and the *TransitLink Guide,* so you can find your way around (see above for more details). All buses have a gray TransitLink machine with a sensor pad close to the driver. Tap your EZ-Link card when you get on and off the bus, and the fare will be automatically deducted. It'll be anywhere between S80¢ and S$1.80 (US50¢–US$1.20/£0.25–£0.60). If you're paying cash, be sure to have exact change; place the coins in the red box by the driver and announce your fare to him. He'll issue a ticket, which will pop out of a slot on one of the TransitLink machines behind him.

Tips   Telephone Dialing at a Glance

- **To place a call from your home country to Singapore:** Dial the international access code (011 in the U.S. and Canada, 0011 in Australia, 0170 in New Zealand, 00 in the U.K.), plus Singapore's country code **(65),** and then the eight-digit number (for example, 011 65 0000-0000).

- **To place a direct international call from Singapore:** Dial the international access code **(00),** plus the country code, the area or city code, and the number (for example, to call the U.S., you'd dial 00 1 000/000-0000).

- **International country codes are as follows:** Australia, 61; Cambodia, 855; Canada, 1; Hong Kong, 852; Indonesia, 62; Laos, 856; Malaysia, 60; Myanmar, 95; New Zealand, 64; the Philippines, 63; Singapore, 65; Thailand, 66; U.K., 44; U.S., 1; Vietnam, 84.

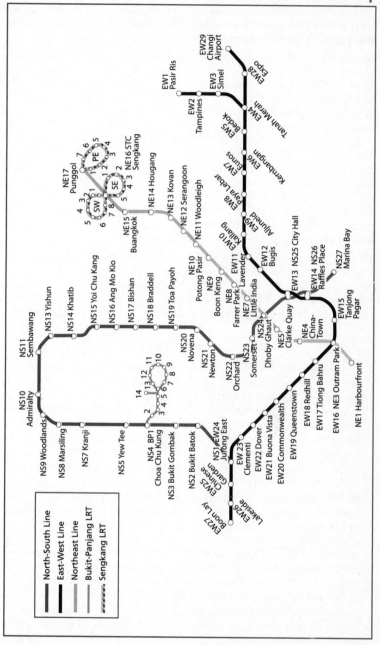

For more information, contact either of the two operating bus lines during standard business hours: **Singapore Bus Service** (SBS; ✆ 1800-287-2727) or **Trans-Island Bus Service** (TIBS; ✆ 1800-482-5433).

BY TROLLEY Both trolley services are offered for the convenience of travelers, making stops at most major tourist destinations. The **Singapore Explorer** (✆ 65/6339-6833) goes down Orchard Road, through the Historic District, over the Singapore River, and down to Marina Square. For S$9 (US$5.65/£3.10) per adult and S$7 (US$4.40/£2.40) per child, you can enjoy unlimited rides for 1 day. Buy your ticket either from your hotel front desk or directly from the driver.

Singapore Airlines operates the **SIA Hop-On Bus.** Plying between Suntec City, the Historic District, the Singapore River, Chinatown, Orchard Road and the Singapore Botanic Gardens, Little India, and Sentosa, the Hop-On comes every 30 minutes between 9am and 7.30pm. Unlimited rides for 1 day cost S$12 (US$7.50/£4.10) for adults and S$6 (US$3.80/£2.10) for children. If you flew Singapore Airlines to get here, you only have to pay S$3 (US$1.90/£1) if you flash your boarding pass. Buy your tickets from your hotel front desk, from a Singapore Airlines office, or from the bus drivers. For info, call **SH Tours** (✆ 65/6374-9923).

BY CAR Visitors to Singapore rarely rent cars for sightseeing. Why? Because they cost a bomb. At Avis, a compact car rents for S$260 (about US$153) per day. It's just not worth it, especially when the excellent, affordable local transportation means you don't have to worry about adjusting to local driving rules or finding parking. Still, if you must, contact **Avis** at Changi International Airport, Terminal 2 (✆ 65/6542-8855).

FAST FACTS : Singapore

American Express The American Express office is at 300 Beach Rd., #18-01 The Concourse (✆ 65/6880-1333). It's open Monday through Friday from 9am to 5pm and Saturday from 9am to 1pm. There's a more convenient kiosk that handles traveler's checks and simple card transactions (including emergency check guarantee) on Orchard Road just outside the Marriott Hotel at Tangs (✆ 65/6735-2069); open daily from 9am to 9pm. An additional foreign exchange office is at Changi International Airport, Terminal 2 (✆ 65/6546-5456), open from noon to midnight daily.

Business Hours Shopping centers are open Monday through Saturday from 10am to 9pm (until 10pm on some public holidays). Banks are open from 9:30am to 3pm Monday through Friday and from 9 to 11am on Saturday. Restaurants open at lunchtime from around 11am to 2:30pm; for dinner, they reopen around 6pm and take the last order sometime around 10pm. Government offices are open Monday through Friday from 9am to 5pm and Saturday from 9am to 1pm. Post offices conduct business Monday through Friday from 8:30am to 5pm and Saturday from 8:30am to 1pm.

Drugstores **Guardian Pharmacies** fills prescriptions (from a licensed physician within Singapore) with name-brand drugs. Convenient locations include #B1-05 Centrepoint Shopping Centre (✆ 65/6737-4835), Changi International Airport, Terminal 2 (✆ 65/6545-4233), #02-139 Marina Sq. (✆ 65/6333-9565), and #B1-04 Raffles Place MRT station (✆ 65/6535-2762).

Electricity Standard electrical current is 220 volts AC (50 cycles). Local outlets are made for plugs with three square prongs. Ask your concierge to see if your hotel has converters and plug adapters for guests' use. If you're using sensitive equipment, do not trust cheap voltage transformers. Nowadays, a lot of electrical equipment—including laptop computers—comes with built-in converters, so you can follow the manufacturer's directions for changing them over. FYI, videocassettes taped on different voltage currents are recorded on machines with different record and playback cycles. Prerecorded videotapes are not interchangeable between currents unless you have special equipment that can play either kind.

Embassies & Consulates U.S.: 27 Napier Rd. (© 65/6476-9100; http://singapore. usembassy.gov). **Canada:** 80 Anson Rd. (© 65/6325-3240; www.singapore. gc.ca). **Australia:** 391A Orchard Rd., Ngee Ann City Tower A, #15-06 (© 65/ 6836-4100; www.singapore.embassy.gov.au). **New Zealand:** 391A Orchard Rd., Ngee Ann City Tower A, #15-06 (© 65/6235-9966; www.nzembassy.com/ singapore). **U.K.:** Tanglin Road (© 65/6473-9333; www.britishhighcommission. gov.uk/singapore).

Emergencies For police, dial © **999.** For medical or fire emergencies, dial © **995.**

Hospitals If you require hospitalization, the centrally located **Mount Elizabeth Hospital** is near Orchard Road at 3 Mount Elizabeth (© 65/6737-2666); for accidents and emergencies, call © 65/6731-2218. You can also try **Singapore General Hospital,** Outram Road (© 65/6222-3322); for accidents and emergencies, call © 65/6321-4311.

Internet Access Internet cafes are becoming common throughout the city, with usage costs about S$5 (US$3.15/£1.75) per hour. (Hotel businesses charge a much higher rate.) Almost every shopping mall has one, especially along Orchard Road, and there are cybercafes in both terminals at Changi International Airport. In the Historic District, there are a few in Stamford House, just across from City Hall MRT station. Check out **Chills Café,** #01-07 Stamford House, 39 Stamford Rd. (© 65/6883-1016), open daily from 9am to midnight.

Language Singapore's four official languages are Malay, Chinese (Mandarin), Tamil, and English. Malay is the national language, while English is the language for government operations, law, and major financial transactions. See "Language," p. 451, for more information.

Liquor Laws The legal age for alcohol purchase and consumption is 18—but clubs rarely check foreigners. Bars and pubs usually open in the afternoon and stay open until 1am on weeknights or 2am on Friday and Saturday. Clubs and discos open around 8pm and stay open until 2am on weekdays or 3am on Friday and Saturday. Unless you come from New York, London, or Tokyo, you'll find alcohol very expensive here because of heavy "sin taxes."

Lost & Found Be sure to tell all of your credit card companies the minute you discover your wallet has been lost or stolen. File a report at the nearest police precinct; your credit card company or insurer may require a police report number or record of the loss. Most credit card companies have an emergency toll-free number to call if your card is lost or stolen; they may be able to wire you a cash advance immediately or deliver an emergency credit card in a day or two. Within Singapore, use the following toll-free hot lines: **American Express** (© 800/737-8188), **MasterCard** (© 800/110-0113), **Visa** (© 800/110-0344).

If you need emergency cash over the weekend when all banks and American Express offices are closed, you can have money wired to you via **Western Union** at most Sing Post branches.

Mail Most hotels have mail service at the front desk. Singapore Post has centrally located offices at #04-15 Ngee Ann City/Takashimaya Shopping Centre (© 65/6738-6899); Chinatown Point, 133 New Bridge Rd. #02-42/43/44 (© 65/6538-7899); Change Alley, 16 Collyer Quay #02-02 Hitachi Tower (© 65/6538-6899); and 231 Bain St. #01-03 Bras Basah Complex (© 65/6339-8899). There are also five branches at Changi International Airport.

The going rate for airmail letters to North America and Europe is S$1 (US64¢/£0.35) for 20g plus S35¢ (US22¢/£0.10) for each additional 10g. For airmail service to Australia and New Zealand, the rate is S70¢ (US45¢/£0.24) for 20g plus S30¢ (US19¢/£0.10) for each additional 10g. Postcards and aerograms to all destinations are S50¢ (US32¢/£0.15).

Newspapers & Magazines Local English newspapers available are the *International Herald Tribune,* the *Business Times,* the *Straits Times, Today,* and *USA Today International.* Following an article criticizing the Singapore government, the *Wall Street Journal Asia* was banned from wide distribution in Singapore. Most of the major hotels carry it, though, so ask around. *I-S Magazine* is a good resource for nightlife happenings. The STB visitor centers carry a few free publications for travelers, including *Where Singapore, This Week Singapore,* and *Singapore Business Visitor.* Major bookstores and news shops sell a wide variety of international magazines.

Police Given the strict reputation of law enforcement in Singapore, you can bet the officers here don't have the greatest sense of humor. If you find yourself being questioned about anything, big or small, be dead serious and most respectful. For emergencies, call © 999. If you need to call police headquarters, dial © 1800-255-0000.

If you are arrested, you have the right to legal counsel, but only when the police decide you can exercise that right. Bottom line: Don't get arrested.

Smoking It's against the law to smoke in public buses, elevators, theaters, cinemas, air-conditioned restaurants, shopping centers, government offices, and taxi queues.

Taxes Many hotels and restaurants will advertise rates followed by "+++." The first + is the goods and services tax (GST), which is levied at 5% of the purchase. The second + is 1% cess (a 1% tax levied by the STB on all tourism-related activities). The third is a 10% gratuity. See "Shopping," later in this chapter, for information on the GST Global Refund Scheme, which lets you recover the GST for purchases of goods over S$300 (US$192/£105) in value.

Telephones Public telephones can be found on the street or back near the toilets in shopping malls, public buildings, or hotel lobbies. Because most Singaporeans now carry mobile phones, public phones aren't always properly maintained. Local calls cost S10¢ (US5¢/ £0.03) for 3 minutes at coin- and card-operated phones.

International calls can be made only from public phones designated specifically for this purpose; these will accept either a phone card or credit card. Phone cards for local and international calls can be purchased at Singapore Post branches, 7-Eleven convenience stores, or money changers—make sure you specify local or international card when you make your purchase.

For **directory assistance,** dial ℂ **100** if you're looking for a number inside Singapore; dial ℂ **104** for numbers to all other countries, as well as for operator assistance in making a call. See "Telephone Dialing at a Glance," p. 460, for details on how to make calls.

Note: Numbers beginning with **1800** within Singapore are toll-free, but calling a 1-800 number in the U.S. from Singapore is not toll-free. In fact, it costs the same as an overseas call.

Time Zone Singapore is 8 hours ahead of Greenwich Mean Time (GMT). International time differences will change during daylight saving or summer time. Basic time differences are: New York -13, Los Angeles -16, London -8, Brisbane +3, Melbourne +2, Sydney +3, and Auckland +4. For the current time within Singapore, call ℂ **1711.**

Tipping Tipping is discouraged in hotels, bars, and taxis. Basically, the deal here is not to tip. A gratuity is automatically added to guest checks, and there's no need to slip anyone an extra buck for carrying bags or such—it's not expected.

Toilets Clean public toilets can be found in all shopping malls, hotels, and public buildings. Smaller restaurants may not be up on their cleanliness, and beware the Asian-style squat toilet, which you see in the more "local" places. Carry plenty of tissues with you.

Water Tap water in Singapore is potable and passes World Health Organization standards.

4 Where to Stay

Budget accommodations are not a high priority on the island. Between the business community's demand for luxury on the one hand and the inflated Singaporean real estate market on the other, rates tend to be high. Don't fret, though: I'm here to tell you that there's a range of accommodations out there—you just have to know where to find them.

Think about what you'll be doing in Singapore—that way, you can choose a hotel that's close to the particular action that suits you. (On the other hand, since Singapore is a small place and public transportation is excellent, really nothing's ever too far away.) **Orchard Road** has the largest cluster of hotels in the city, right in the heart of Singaporean shopping mania. The **Historic District** hotels are near museums and sights, while those in **Marina Bay** center more around the business professionals who come to Singapore for Suntec City, the giant convention and exhibition center. **Chinatown** and **Tanjong Pagar** have some lovely boutique hotels in quaint back streets, while **Shenton Way** has a couple of high-rise places for the convenience of people visiting the downtown business district. Many hotels have free morning and evening shuttle buses to Orchard Road, Suntec City, and Shenton Way.

Where to Stay in Urban Singapore

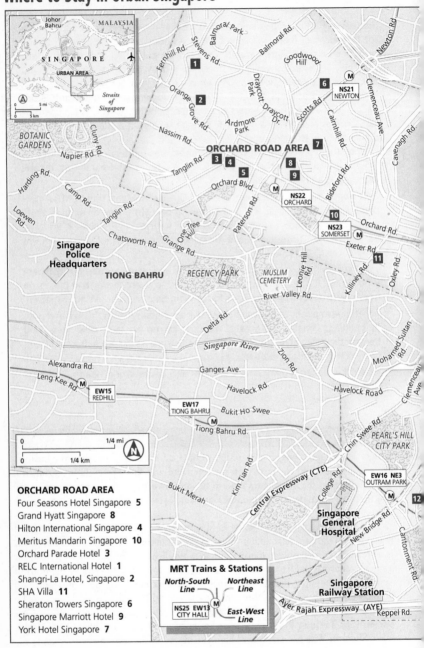

ORCHARD ROAD AREA

Four Seasons Hotel Singapore	**5**
Grand Hyatt Singapore	**8**
Hilton International Singapore	**4**
Meritus Mandarin Singapore	**10**
Orchard Parade Hotel	**3**
RELC International Hotel	**1**
Shangri-La Hotel, Singapore	**2**
SHA Villa	**11**
Sheraton Towers Singapore	**6**
Singapore Marriott Hotel	**9**
York Hotel Singapore	**7**

MRT Trains & Stations

North-South Line — *Northeast Line*

NS25 EW13
CITY HALL
East-West Line

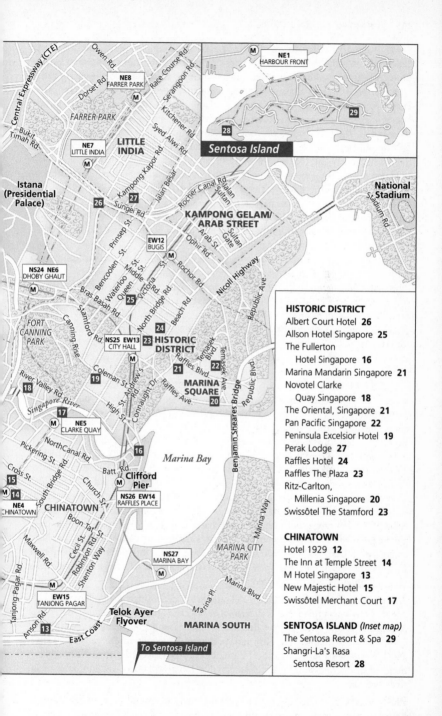

HISTORIC DISTRICT
Albert Court Hotel **26**
Allson Hotel Singapore **25**
The Fullerton
   Hotel Singapore **16**
Marina Mandarin Singapore **21**
Novotel Clarke
   Quay Singapore **18**
The Oriental, Singapore **21**
Pan Pacific Singapore **22**
Peninsula Excelsior Hotel **19**
Perak Lodge **27**
Raffles Hotel **24**
Raffles The Plaza **23**
Ritz-Carlton,
   Millenia Singapore **20**
Swissôtel The Stamford **23**

CHINATOWN
Hotel 1929 **12**
The Inn at Temple Street **14**
M Hotel Singapore **13**
New Majestic Hotel **15**
Swissôtel Merchant Court **17**

SENTOSA ISLAND *(Inset map)*
The Sentosa Resort & Spa **29**
Shangri-La's Rasa
   Sentosa Resort **28**

While budget hotels have very limited facilities and simpler decor, you can always expect a clean room. What's more, service can sometimes be more personal in smaller hotels, where the staff has fewer faces to recognize and is accustomed to helping guests with the sorts of things a business center or concierge would handle in a larger place. Par for the course, many of the guests in these places are backpackers, and mostly Western backpackers at that. However, you will see some regional visitors staying in these hotels. *Note:* The budget accommodations listed here are places decent enough for any standards. While cheaper digs are available, those rooms can be dreary and depressing, musty and old, or downright sleazy.

Unless you choose one of the extreme budget hotels, there are some standard features you can expect to find everywhere. Many hotels have courtesy shuttles to popular parts of town. Most places have adequate fitness-center facilities. Pools tend to be on the small side, and Jacuzzis are often placed in men's and women's locker rooms, making it impossible for couples to use them together. While tour desks are in some lobbies, car-rental desks are nonexistent.

A newer trend is the boutique hotel. Conceived as part of the Urban Restoration Authority's renewal plans, rows of old shophouses and historic buildings in ethnic areas like Chinatown and Tanjong Pagar have been restored and transformed into small, lovely accommodations. Places like Albert Court Hotel and the Inn at Temple Street are beautiful examples of local flavor turned into quaint lodging. While these places can put you closer to the heart of Singapore, they do have their drawbacks— for one, the hotels and their rooms are small and, due to building codes and lack of space, they're unable to provide facilities like pools, Jacuzzis, or fitness centers.

Many of the finest restaurants in Singapore are located in hotels, whether they're operated by the hotel directly or just inhabiting rented space. Some hotels can have up to five or six restaurants, each serving a different cuisine. Generally, you can expect these restaurants to be more expensive than places located outside hotels. In the hotel reviews below, distinguished restaurants have been noted.

RATES   Singapore's hotel industry experienced a record year in 2006, with September witnessing a record high average room rate of S$190 (US$120/£65), the highest it's been since before the 1997 East Asian economic crisis. In general, rack rates for double rooms range from as low as S$100 (US$64/£35) at the Strand on Bencoolen (a famous backpacker strip) to as high as S$1,000 (US$640/£350) a night at the exclusive Raffles Hotel. Rack rates for average rooms are usually in the S$350 (US$220/£120) range, but keep in mind that although all prices listed in this book are the going rates, they rarely represent what you'll actually pay. Always ask the hotel about special deals and how you can get the lowest price for your room. Many have weekend discounts, long-term stay programs, free add-ons, or complimentary breakfasts and other services with added value.

TAXES & SERVICE CHARGES   All rates listed are in Singapore dollars, with U.S. dollar equivalents provided as well (remember to check the exchange rate when you're planning, though, since it may fluctuate). Most rates do not include the so-called "+++" taxes and charges: the 10% service charge, 5% goods and services tax (GST), and 1% cess (a tax levied by the STB on all tourism-related activities). Keep these in mind when figuring your budget. Some budget hotels will quote discount rates inclusive of all taxes.

PEAK SEASON   The busy season is from January to around June. In late summer, business travel dies down and hotels try to make up for drooping occupancy rates by

---

Tips **Hotel Reservations—In Advance & On Arrival**

The website **www.asiarooms.com** offers the best rates I've seen for Internet bookings, particularly for accommodations in the "Very Expensive" and "Expensive" categories; however, it doesn't have deals for every hotel property. It's worth it to browse and compare.

If you aren't able to book a room before your trip, don't worry: The **Singapore Hotel Association** operates desks in both Terminals 1 and 2 of Changi International Airport, with reservations services based upon room availability for many hotels. The desks are open daily from 7:30am to 11:30pm.

---

going after the leisure market. In fall, tourism drops off somewhat, making the season ripe for budget-minded visitors. Probably the worst time to negotiate will be between Christmas and the Chinese New Year, when folks travel on vacation and to see their families.

HISTORIC DISTRICT
VERY EXPENSIVE

The Fullerton Hotel Singapore 𝕮𝕮   Standing guard at the mouth of the Singapore River, the Fullerton's historic edifice holds ground against a backdrop of the city's modern skyline. Originally built in 1928, this squat administrative building once housed the general post office. Today, it's flanked by the urban skyline, and its classical facade, with Doric columns and tall porticos, looks more mundane than opulent. But designers have done a superb job, restoring Italian marble floors, coffered ceilings, and cornices inside. The courtyard lobby is grand, with skylights above and guest-room windows lining the inner face of the building. Rooms have been cleverly arranged to fit the original structure, featuring vaulted ceilings and tall windows. Although the architectural style is antique, the rooms are anything but. They have large writing desks, flatscreen TVs, Sony PlayStations, and electronic safes big enough to hold your laptop. Big bathrooms have separate tub and shower stalls, mini-StairMasters, and stylish Philippe Starck fixtures. The attentive service here is second to none.

1 Fullerton Sq., Singapore 049178. (✆) **800/44-UTELL** in the U.S. and Canada, 800/221-176 in Australia, 800/933-123 in New Zealand, or 65/6733-8388. Fax 65/6735-8388. www.fullertonhotel.com. 400 units. S$670 (US$419/£230) double; from S$900 (US$563/£309) suite. AE, DC, MC, V. 5-min. walk to Raffles Place MRT. **Amenities:** 3 restaurants; bar and lobby lounge; outdoor infinity pool w/view of the Singapore River; fitness center w/Jacuzzi, sauna, and steam; spa w/massage and beauty treatments; concierge; limousine service; business center; shopping arcade; salon; 24-hr. room service; babysitting; laundry service; dry cleaning; nonsmoking rooms; executive-level rooms. *In room:* A/C, satellite TV w/in-house movies, dataport w/direct Internet access, minibar, coffeemaker, hair dryer, iron, safe.

Raffles Hotel 𝕮𝕮   Legendary since its establishment in 1887 and named after Singapore's first British colonial administrator, Sir Stamford Raffles, this posh hotel is one of the most recognizable names in Southeast Asian hospitality. Originally it was a bungalow, but by the 1920s and 1930s it had expanded to become a mecca for celebrities like Charlie Chaplin and Douglas Fairbanks, writers like Somerset Maugham and Noël Coward, and various and sundry kings, sultans, and politicians (the famous Long Bar, where the Singapore Sling was invented, is located here). Always at the center of Singapore's colonial high life, the Raffles hosted balls, tea dances, and jazz functions, and during World War II was the last rallying point for the British in the face of Japanese occupation—and the first place for refugee prisoners of war released from concentration camps. In 1987, the hotel was declared a landmark and restored to its early-20th-century splendor, with grand arches, 4.2m (14-ft.) molded ceilings with spinning fans, tiled teak and marble floors, Oriental carpets, and period furnishings. Outside, the facade of the main building was similarly restored, complete with the elegant cast-iron portico and the verandas that encircle the upper stories.

Because it is a national landmark, thousands of people pass through the open lobby each day, so the hotel maintains a private inner lobby marked off for "residents" only. Nothing feels better than walking along the teak floors of the verandas, past little rattan-furnished relaxation areas overlooking the tropical courtyards. Each suite entrance is like a private apartment door: Enter the small living and dining area dressed in Oriental carpets and reproduction furniture, then pass through louvered doors into the bedroom with its four-poster bed and period armoire, ceiling fan twirling high above. Raffles is the only hotel in Singapore where you can play out the colonial traveler fantasy, and it can be a lot of fun. Other unique features include a hotel museum, popular theater playhouse, and excellent culinary academy.

1 Beach Rd., Singapore 189673. © 800/232-1886 in the U.S. and Canada, or 65/6337-1886. Fax 65/6339-7650. www.raffleshotel.com. 103 suites. From S$1,000 (US$625/£344) suite. AE, DC, MC, V. Next to City Hall MRT. **Amenities:** 8 restaurants; 2 bars; small outdoor pool; fitness center w/Jacuzzi, sauna, steam, and spa; concierge; limousine service; business center; shopping arcade; salon; 24-hr. room service; babysitting; laundry service; dry cleaning; personal butler service; billiards room. *In room:* A/C, satellite TV w/in-room VCR, fax, dataport w/direct Internet access, minibar, coffeemaker, hair dryer, safe.

Raffles The Plaza ✦✦✦ This has to be the best location in the city. Above an MRT hub and next to one of the largest shopping centers in Singapore, you won't find any inconveniences here. The lobby is peaceful with soft lighting and music, a lovely escape from the crazy mall and hot streets. Perhaps the best reason to stay is the Amrita spa and fitness center; Singapore's largest spa, it features a huge state-of-the-art gym with exercise and relaxation classes, a swimming pool, hot and cold plunge pools, steam and sauna, and endless treatment rooms with Asian and European recipes for beauty and rejuvenation. Standard rooms are large and comfortable. Premier deluxe rooms are stunningly contemporary, with cushy bedding, Bose Wave systems, and incredible bathrooms—crisp white tiles, glistening glass counters, polished chrome fixtures, and a shower that simulates rainfall.

2 Stamford Rd., Singapore 178882. © 65/6339-7777. Fax 65/6337-1554. http://singapore-plaza.raffles.com. 769 units. S$520 (US$325/£179) double; suites from S$1,600 (US$1,000/£550). AE, DC, MC, V. City Hall MRT. **Amenities:** 10 restaurants; martini bar; lobby lounge; live-jazz venue; outdoor pool; spa w/gym, Jacuzzi, sauna, steam, and massage; concierge; limousine service; business center; shopping arcade adjacent; 24-hr. room service; babysitting; laundry service; dry cleaning; nonsmoking rooms; executive-level rooms. *In room:* A/C, satellite TV w/in-house movies, minibar, coffeemaker, hair dryer, safe.

Ritz-Carlton, Millenia Singapore ✦✦ The ultimate in luxury hotels, the Ritz-Carlton blazes trails with sophisticated ultramodern design, sumptuous comfort, and stimulating art. Grand public spaces—splashed with artworks from the likes of Frank Stella, Dale Chihuly, David Hockney, and Andy Warhol—are a welcome change from international chain-hotel design clichés. In comparison, guest rooms display a great deal of warmth and hominess. All units have spectacular views of either Kallang Bay or the more majestic Marina Bay. Even the bathrooms have views, as the huge tubs are placed under octagonal picture windows so you can gaze as you bathe. Oh, the decadence! Rooms here are about 25% larger than most five-star rooms elsewhere, providing ample space for two-poster beds and full walk-in closets.

7 Raffles Ave., Singapore 039799. ✆ **800/241-3333** in the U.S. and Canada, 800/241-33333 in Australia, 800/241-33333 in New Zealand, 800/234-000 in the U.K., or 65/6337-8888. Fax 65/6338-0001. www.ritzcarlton.com. 610 units. S$560 (US$350/£192) double; from S$820 (US$515/£285) suite. AE, DC, MC, V. 10-min. walk to City Hall MRT. **Amenities:** 3 restaurants; lobby lounge; outdoor pool and Jacuzzi; outdoor lighted tennis court; fitness center w/sauna, steam, and massage; concierge; limousine service; business center; shopping mall adjacent; 24-hr. room service; babysitting; laundry service; dry cleaning; nonsmoking rooms; executive-level rooms. *In room:* A/C, satellite TV w/in-house movies, dataport w/direct Internet access, minibar, coffeemaker, hair dryer, iron, safe.

EXPENSIVE

Marina Mandarin Singapore 🌟🌟   A few hotels in the Marina Bay area are built around the atrium concept, and of them, this one is the loveliest, having just come out of an enormous renovation to all guest rooms and public spaces. The atrium lobby opens up to ceiling skylights 21 stories above, guest-corridor balconies fringed with vines line the sides, and in the center hangs a glistening metal mobile sculpture in red and gold. One of the most surprising details is the melodic chirping of caged songbirds, which fills the open space every morning. In the evening, live classical music from the lobby bar drifts upward. The guest rooms are equally impressive: large and cool, with built-in desk spaces and entertainment consoles, plus balconies standard for each room. Try to get the Marina view for that famous Shenton Way skyline towering above the bay. All bathrooms have double sinks, separate shower and tub, and bidet. Unique Venus Rooms, for women travelers, include potpourri, bath oils, custom pillows, and hair curlers. The Marina Square Shopping Center, adjacent to the lobby, adds scores of shops, services, restaurants, and entertainment options.

6 Raffles Blvd., Marina Square, Singapore 039594. ✆ **65/6845-1000.** Fax 65/6845-1001. www.marina-mandarin. com.sg. 575 units. S$450 (US$280/£154) double; from S$700 (US$437/£240) suite. AE, DC, MC, V. 10-min. walk to City Hall MRT. **Amenities:** 3 restaurants; English pub and lobby lounge; outdoor pool; outdoor lighted tennis courts; squash courts; 24-hr. fitness center, spa w/Jacuzzi, sauna, steam, and massage; concierge; limousine service; 24-hr. business center; shopping mall adjacent; salon; 24-hr. room service; babysitting; laundry service; dry cleaning; nonsmoking rooms; executive-level rooms. *In room:* A/C, satellite TV w/in-house movies, minibar, coffeemaker, hair dryer, safe.

Novotel Clarke Quay Singapore 🌟   Novotel took over the old Hotel New Otani and reopened in 2005 after a complete renovation. The hotel towers over the Singapore River just next to Clarke Quay (a popular spot for nightlife, dining, and shopping); it's just a stroll away from the Historic District. At night, you have access to nearby Boat Quay bars and restaurants to one side and to the unique clubs of Mohamed Sultan Road on the other. All guest rooms have small balconies with good views of the river, the financial district, Fort Canning Park, or Chinatown, and the standard units have large bathrooms like those you typically see in more deluxe accommodations. Room decor is contemporary in shades of brown and tan, with small desks next to floor-to-ceiling picture windows and ergonomically designed chairs. The main lobby is an elevator ride up from the ground level. A small adjacent shopping mall has groceries in the basement and a few handy shops.

177A River Valley Rd., Singapore 179031. ✆ **800/515-5679** in the U.S. and Canada, or 65/6338-3333. Fax 65/6339-2854. www.novotel.com. 398 units. S$450 (US$280/£155) double; from S$630 (US$395/£217) suite. AE, DC, MC, V. 5-min. walk to Clarke Quay MRT. **Amenities:** 3 restaurants; lobby lounge; outdoor pool; fitness center; Jacuzzi; concierge; tour desk; limousine service; shuttle service; business center; shopping mall adjacent; 24-hr. room service; babysitting; laundry service; dry cleaning; executive-level rooms. *In room:* A/C, satellite TV, minibar, coffeemaker, safe.

The Oriental, Singapore 🌟🌟🌟   Another atrium-concept hotel similar to neighboring properties Marina Mandarin and the Pan Pacific, the Oriental is one notch above the others. Public spaces are quiet, the lobby adorned with polished black marble, leather seating, and Asian decorative accents. A recent renovation has introduced a sophisticated contemporary Asian look to guest rooms, with plush carpeting and shimmering silk throw pillows and bed runners. Pay more for a room with a view of the city's skyline through floor-to-ceiling windows—it's worth it. Also worth it: The Oriental Spa drips with a studied sense of serenity, through quiet spaces graced with Chinese antiques and a spa menu that focuses on Asian beauty and relaxation techniques. The staff is always available but never in your face. The Oriental also benefits from the adjacent Marina Square Shopping Center's multitude of shops, services, restaurants, and entertainment options.

5 Raffles Ave., Marina Sq., Singapore 039797. © 800/526-6566 in the U.S. and Canada, 800/123-693 in Australia, 800/2828-3838 in New Zealand or the U.K., or 65/6338-0066. Fax 65/6339-9537. www.mandarinoriental.com/singapore. 524 units. S$450 (US$280/£154) double; from S$780 (US$487/£268) suite. AE, DC, MC, V. 10-min. walk to City Hall MRT. **Amenities:** 4 restaurants; bar and lobby lounge; outdoor pool; fitness center; spa w/Jacuzzi, sauna, and steam; concierge; limousine service; business center; salon; 24-hr. room service; babysitting; laundry service; dry cleaning; nonsmoking rooms; executive-level rooms. *In room:* A/C, satellite TV w/in-house movies, minibar, coffeemaker, hair dryer, safe.

Pan Pacific Singapore 🌟🌟   Few know this, but Pan Pacific is Singapore's largest hotel, with over 780 rooms. But a recent face-lift has given the hotel a new look, and due to a clever atrium layout, you'd never know you were in a building that huge. Competing with Marina Mandarin and the Oriental to grab a slice of the Suntec City Convention Center and business-travel pie, Pan Pac avoids the Asian flavor for something a bit more colorful—a lobby with a checkerboard-inlay reception counter, vibrant carpeting, and a lounge with walls of lights that change colors. Guest rooms are large, with wood paneling in geometric patterns, Asian-inspired fabrics, and large oval desktops with Herman Miller chairs. Hands down, Pan Pac has Singapore's best business center—a full floor designated to private offices, with full secretarial services, every piece of office equipment you'd need, meeting rooms, and even snacks and cocktail lounges. The hotel's many restaurants are some of the top choices in Singapore. The rooftop pool has a huge open sun deck.

7 Raffles Blvd., Marina Square, Singapore 039595 (near Suntec City). © 800/327-8585 in the U.S. and Canada, 800/525-900 in Australia, 800/969-496 in the U.K., or 65/6336-8111. Fax 65/6339-1861. www.singapore.panpacific.com. 784 units. S$480 (US$300/£165) double; from S$510 (US$320/£176) suite. AE, DC, MC, V. 10-min. walk to City Hall MRT. **Amenities:** 6 restaurants; lobby lounge; outdoor pool; 2 outdoor lighted tennis courts; fitness center w/Jacuzzi, sauna, steam, massage, and spa treatments; concierge; limousine service; shuttle service; extensive business center; shopping arcade adjacent; 24-hr. room service; babysitting; laundry service; dry cleaning; nonsmoking rooms; executive-level rooms. *In room:* A/C, satellite TV w/in-house movies, dataport w/direct Internet access, minibar, coffeemaker, hair dryer, safe.

Swissôtel The Stamford 🌟 *Value*   You'd think a room in the tallest hotel in Southeast Asia would cost a bundle, but this gem is reasonably priced. Besides, with an amazing location, right on top of a subway hub and a huge shopping complex, within walking distance of many attractions, the Swissôtel is a great value for the money. On a clear day, you can see over urban Singapore's downtown financial district, so make sure you request a room with a view. However, guest rooms, while larger than the city's average, feel bland and barren, in boring neutral tones with few decorator touches. In some spots, furnishings and carpets could use a face-lift—while a good bargain, this hotel is desperate for an overhaul to keep up with its neighbors.

2 Stamford Rd., Singapore 178882. © 800/637-9477 in the U.S. and Canada, 800/121-043 in Australia, or 65/6338-8585. Fax 65/6338-2862. www.swissotel-thestamford.com. 1,200 units. S$480 (US$300/£165) double; S$1,300 (US$813/£448) suite. AE, DC, MC, V. City Hall MRT. **Amenities:** 10 restaurants; martini bar, lobby lounge, live-jazz

venue; outdoor pool; spa w/gym, Jacuzzi, sauna, steam, and massage; concierge; limousine service; business center; shopping arcade adjacent; 24-hr. room service; babysitting; laundry service; dry cleaning; nonsmoking rooms; executive-level rooms. *In room:* A/C, satellite TV w/in-house movies, minibar, coffeemaker, hair dryer, safe.

MODERATE

Albert Court Hotel *(★) (Value)*   This hotel was first conceived as part of the Urban Renewal Authority's master plan to revitalize this block, which involved the restoration of two rows of prewar shophouses. The eight-story boutique hotel that emerged has all the Western comforts but has retained the charm of its shophouse roots. Decorators placed local Peranakan touches everywhere, from the carved-teak furnishings in traditional floral design to the antique china cups used for tea service in the rooms. (Guaranteed: The sight of these cups brings misty-eyed nostalgia to the hearts of Singaporeans.) Guest-room details like teak molding, bathroom tiles in bright Peranakan colors, and old-time brass electrical switches give this place true local charm and distinction; a recent refurbishment provides an added freshness. The new courtyard rooms, in the renovated houses that front the hotel's courtyard, still contain all the local touches that make this hotel stand out from the rest. Albert Court is especially attractive if you wish to spend time shopping and eating in Little India, which is just across the street.

180 Albert St., Singapore 189971. © **65/6339-3939.** Fax 65/6339-3252. www.albertcourt.com.sg. 136 units. S$180 (US$113/£62) double; S$350 (US$218/£119) suite. AE, DC, MC, V. 5-min. walk to either Bugis or Little India MRT. **Amenities:** 3 restaurants; small lobby lounge; tour desk; limited room service; babysitting; laundry service; dry cleaning. *In room:* A/C, satellite TV, minibar, coffeemaker, hair dryer, safe.

Allson Hotel Singapore *(★) (Value)*   Allson continues to be a strong tourist-class hotel in the city's Historic District. In 2003, the facade got a complete face-lift, adding a soundproofing layer to keep out traffic noise from busy Victoria Street below. Guest rooms have fresh carpeting, paint, drapes, bed coverings, and upholstery. Carved-rosewood headboards, side tables, and armchairs in quaint Ming-style designs are an elegant touch for such a moderately priced lodging. Even the heavy doors leading into the rooms are carved rosewood. Bathrooms have been recently retiled. The small pool area and even smaller gym have received some maintenance touch-ups. With a good location and modest prices, Allson is a great choice for value-conscious leisure travelers.

101 Victoria St., Singapore 188018. © **65/6336-0811.** Fax 65/6339-7019. www.allsonhotels.com. 450 units. S$260 (US$163/£90) double; from S$450 (US$281/£155) suite. AE, DC, MC, V. 5-min. walk from Bugis Junction MRT. **Amenities:** 3 restaurants; lounge; small outdoor pool; fitness center w/Jacuzzi, sauna, steam, and massage; tour desk; business center; salon; 24-hr. room service; babysitting; laundry service; dry cleaning; nonsmoking rooms; executive-level rooms. *In room:* A/C, satellite TV w/in-house movies, minibar, coffeemaker, safe.

Peninsula Excelsior Hotel *(★★) (Value)*   Recently, two of Singapore's busiest tourist-class hotels merged, combining their lobbies and facilities into one giant value-for-money property. The location is excellent, in the Historic District within walking distance to Chinatown and Boat Quay. It's a popular pick for groups, but don't let the busloads of tourists steer you away. There are some great deals to be had here, especially if you request a room in the Peninsula tower. These are large and colorful, with big picture windows, some of which have stunning views of the city, the Singapore River, and the marina. Surprisingly, they're priced the same as rooms in the Excelsior tower, which are smaller and, frankly, look like they haven't seen a decor update since the far-out 1970s.

5 Coleman St., Singapore 179805. © **65/6337-2200**. Fax 65/6336-3847. www.ytchotels.com.sg. 600 units. S$170 (US$106/£58) double; from S$550 (US$344/£189) suite. AE, DC, MC, V. 5-min. walk to City Hall MRT. **Amenities:** Restaurant; bar and lobby lounge; 2 outdoor pools; fitness center w/Jacuzzi; concierge; tour desk; business center; shopping mall adjacent; 24-hr. room service; babysitting; laundry service; dry cleaning. *In room:* A/C, TV, minibar, coffeemaker, hair dryer, safe.

INEXPENSIVE

Perak Lodge ★ Set in a cozy corner on the edge of Little India, this place is popular with backpackers; the lobby is a nice place to read the paper or chat with other travelers from around the world. Located on a quaint alley in a row of restored pre-war shophouses, the lodge feels very homey, with a family-run ambience. The lobby cafe has only simple wooden tables and chairs, serving breakfast and snacks to house guests only. Upstairs, guest-room corridors can be a bit noisy from footsteps on the wooden floors, but otherwise the place is quite smart. Small, tidy rooms have simple furniture; spotless bathrooms with shower stalls; and some local textiles to add a bit of charm. Good management and a congenial atmosphere make this a top pick for budget-conscious travelers.

12 Perak Rd., Singapore 208133. © **65/6299-7733**. Fax 65/6392-0919. www.peraklodge.com. 34 units. S$98 (US$61/£34) double, S$138 (US$86/£48) triple, including breakfast. AE, DC, MC, V. 5-min. walk to Bugis or Little India MRT. **Amenities:** Cafe; tour desk; business center; laundry service; dry cleaning. *In room:* A/C, TV.

CHINATOWN

EXPENSIVE

M Hotel Singapore ★★ If you absolutely must stay in the Shenton Way downtown business district, then M Hotel is your best bet. Cornering the international business-travel market, everything here is designed to make life easier for those with places to go and people to see. Rooms feature large, comfortable workspaces in clutter-free tones (blond-wood furnishings, bone upholstery, tan carpeting), with some splashes of darker textiles for variety. Broadband Internet access and laptop safes make for extra convenience. The 11th floor is reserved for unwinding, with pool, spa, and fitness center all in sanitary contemporary white, with glass-and-chrome accents everywhere. Operated by local firm Haach, the spa has an excellent menu and reputation for quality. M Hotel's restaurants are packed for power lunches, so book in advance.

81 Anson Rd., Singapore 079908. © **866/866-8086** in the U.S. and Canada, 800/147-803 in Australia, 800/782-542 in New Zealand, 800/8686-8086 in the U.K., or 65/6224-1133. Fax 65/6222-0749. www.millenniumhotels.com. 413 units. S$300 (US$188/£103) double; S$700 (US$438/£241) suite. AE, DC, MC, V. 10-min walk to Tanjong Pagar MRT. **Amenities:** 3 restaurants; bar; outdoor pool w/2 Jacuzzis; fitness center w/rock-climbing wall; spa; business center; 24-hr. room service; babysitting; laundry service; dry cleaning; executive-level rooms. *In room:* A/C, satellite TV, minibar, coffeemaker, hair dryer, safe.

Swissôtel Merchant Court Merchant Court's convenient location and facilities make it very popular with leisure travelers. Situated on the Singapore River, the hotel has easy access not only to Chinatown and the Historic District, but also to Clarke Quay and Boat Quay, with their multitude of dining and nightlife options. In 2003, it became even more convenient when the new MRT stop opened just outside its doors. While this hotel's guest rooms aren't the biggest or most plush in the city, you'll never feel claustrophobic thanks to the large windows, uncluttered decor, and cooling atmosphere. Try to get a room with a view of the river or pool. The Merchant Court touts itself as a city hotel with a resort feel, with a small but nicely landscaped pool area—with a view of the river, naturally.

20 Merchant Rd., Singapore 058281. ℂ **800/637-9477** in the U.S. and Canada, 800/121-043 in Australia, 800/637-94771 in the U.K., or 65/6337-2288. Fax 65/6334-0606. www.swissotel-merchantcourt.com. 476 units. S$400 (US$250/£138) double; from S$850 (US$531/£292) suite. AE, DC, MC, V. Clarke Quay MRT. **Amenities:** Restaurant; bar; outdoor pool; fitness center and spa w/Jacuzzi, sauna, steam, massage, and beauty treatments; 24-hr. room service; babysitting; laundry service; dry cleaning; nonsmoking rooms; executive-level rooms. *In room:* A/C, satellite TV w/in-house movies, dataport w/direct Internet access, coffeemaker, hair dryer, safe.

MODERATE

The Inn at Temple Street   They've done a lovely job with this boutique hotel. In the heart of Chinatown's tourism hustle and bustle, step into the small lobby to be greeted by pretty antiques and tasteful Chinese trappings. To the side of the lobby, a charming cafe serves Western and local meals three times a day. The front desk handles everything from business services to arranging laundry, tours, and postal services, but never seems frazzled. Rooms are quite modern for this type of hotel, with keycard locks, in-room safe, minibar, and room service. Decor is atmospheric as well, with local touches of carved woods and rich fabrics, plus neat black-and-white-tiled bathrooms. This place is a welcome addition to Singapore's smattering of affordable accommodations.

36 Temple St., Singapore 058581. ℂ **65/6221-5333.** Fax 65/6225-5391. www.theinn.com.sg. 42 units. S$228 (US$143/£78) double; S$328 (US$205/£113) family. AE, DC, MC, V. 5-min. walk to Chinatown MRT. **Amenities:** Restaurant; lounge; limited room service; laundry service; dry cleaning. *In room:* A/C, TV, minibar, coffeemaker, safe.

New Majestic Hotel   A Chinatown landmark, the old 1928 Art Deco Majestic building is now a swank hotel, and Singapore's hottest spot for culture vultures. Each guest room was individually designed by an emerging Singaporean artist. With wood floors, mosaic tiled bathrooms with claw-foot cast-iron tubs, and lots of glass and contemporary fittings, these small rooms come alive with murals and artworks that say a little something about Singapore and the local arts scene. Themed units include garden rooms with wooden decks and outside tubs, hanging-bed rooms, loft rooms, a mirror room, and an aquarium room. The devil is in the details: Top-of-the-line bedding, toiletries by Kiehl's, Bose systems, and Wi-Fi throughout add real value. The lobby is special as well, in stark white, with polished terrazzo floors, a spiral staircase, and the owner's collection of vintage design-icon chairs. The rooftop lap pool is small, in contrasting black-and-white tiles, and the hotel's Chinese restaurant is as chic and quirky as the rest of the place.

31-37 Bukit Pasoh Rd., Singapore 089845. ℂ **65/6511-4700.** Fax 65/6227-3301. www.newmajestichotel.com. 30 units. S$280 (US$175/£96) double; from S$600 (US$375/£206) suite. AE, MC, V. 5-min. walk to Chinatown MRT. **Amenities:** Restaurant; outdoor pool; fitness center; concierge; laundry service; dry cleaning. *In room:* A/C, satellite TV, Wi-Fi, minibar, coffeemaker, hair dryer, safe.

INEXPENSIVE

Hotel 1929 ★ *Finds*   Run by the same people behind the New Majestic Hotel, this tiny boutique hotel shares the same love for vintage chairs as its more upmarket sister property. Located in a row of restored pre-war shophouses in a former red-light district of Chinatown (with some elements remaining . . .), this building has no space for big guest rooms. In fact, sizes and shapes can be a bit awkward at times, and the cheapest rooms have no windows, but what they lack in size they make up for in style, bright colors, and humor. The hotel doesn't have much in the way of facilities—a rooftop Jacuzzi and wooden sun deck about cover it—but if you're in town to shop and sightsee, then this is a good way to save some money but still enjoy a little style.

50 Keong Saik Rd., Singapore 089154. ℂ **65/6347-1929**. fax 65/6327-1929. S$140 (US$88/£48) double, from S$280(US$175/£96) suite. AE, DC, MC, V. 10-min. walk to Chinatown MRT. **Amenities:** Restaurant; Jacuzzi; laundry service. *In room:* A/C, TV, minibar, coffeemaker, hair dryer, safe.

ORCHARD ROAD AREA
VERY EXPENSIVE

Four Seasons Hotel Singapore ✸✸✸ Many upmarket hotels strive to convince you that staying with them is like visiting a wealthy friend. Four Seasons delivers on this promise. The guest rooms are very spacious and inviting, and even the standard rooms have creature comforts you'd expect from a suite, such as complimentary fruit, terry bathrobes and slippers, CD and video disk players, and an extensive complimentary video disk and CD library that the concierge is just waiting to deliver selections from. Each room has two-line speakerphones with voice mail and an additional dataport. The Italian marble bathrooms have double vanities, deep tubs, bidets, Neutrogena amenities, and surround-sound speakers for the TV and stereo. Did I mention remote-control drapes? Everything here is comfort and elegance done to perfection. In the waiting area off the lobby, you can sink into the sofas and appreciate the antiques and artwork selected from the owner's private collection. The fitness center has a state-of-the-art gymnasium with TV monitors, videos, CD and video disk players, a virtual-reality bike, aerobics, sauna, steam rooms, massage, facials, body wraps and aromatherapy treatments, and a staff of fitness professionals. Two indoor, air-conditioned tennis courts and two outdoor courts are staffed with a resident professional coach to provide instruction or play a game. There are two pools: a 20m (66-ft.) lap pool and a rooftop sun-deck pool, each with adjacent Jacuzzis. Consider a standard room here before a suite in a less expensive hotel—you won't regret it.

190 Orchard Blvd., Singapore 248646. ℂ **800/332-3442** in the U.S., 800/268-6282 in Canada, or 65/6734-1110. Fax 65/6733-0682. www.fourseasons.com. 254 units. S$550 (US$344/£189) double; from S$720 (US$450/£248) suite. AE, DC, MC, V. 10-min. walk to Orchard MRT. **Amenities:** 2 restaurants; bar; 2 outdoor pools w/adjacent Jacuzzis; 2 outdoor lighted tennis courts and 2 indoor air-conditioned tennis courts; Singapore's best-equipped fitness center; spa w/sauna, steam, massage, and beauty and relaxation treatments; billiards room; concierge; limousine service; business center; 24-hr. room service; babysitting; laundry service; dry cleaning; nonsmoking rooms; executive-level rooms. *In room:* A/C, satellite TV w/in-room video disk player and complimentary disks available, minibar, coffeemaker, hair dryer, safe.

Shangri-La Hotel, Singapore ✸✸✸ The Shangri-La is a lovely place, with gardens and an outdoor pool paradise that are great diversions from the hustle and bustle all around. Maybe that's why visiting VIPs like George Bush (both of them), Benazir Bhutto, and Nelson Mandela have all stayed here.

The hotel has three wings: The Tower Wing is the oldest, housing the lobby and most of the guest rooms. Instead of the standard square hotel rooms of typical city hotels, Shang's have unusual angles and curves, sophisticated contemporary furnishings, and a refreshing wall of glass blocks that welcomes natural light into the giant bathroom and dressing area. Balconies are melded into the rooms to become reading nooks. The Garden Wing surrounds an open-air atrium with cascading waterfall and exotic plants. Rooms here are more resortlike, with natural textured wall coverings, tweed carpeting, and woven bedspreads. These larger rooms also have bougainvillea-laden balconies overlooking the landscaped pool area. The exclusive Valley Wing has a private entrance and very spacious rooms (I'd say the largest rooms in Singapore), linked to the main tower by a sky bridge that looks out over the hotel's 6 hectares (15 acres) of lawns, fruit trees, and flowers. These rooms, which reopened after a massive-scale renovation, come with personalized butler service, personalized stationery, and access to complimentary airport limousine service and a champagne bar in the lobby. The new decor reflects the exclusivity of the facility, a veritable Asian sanctuary.

22 Orange Grove Rd., Singapore 258350. ℂ 800/942-5050 in the U.S., 866/344-5050 in Canada, 800/222-448 in Australia, 800/442-179 in New Zealand, or 65/6737-3644. Fax 65/6737-3257. www.shangri-la.com. 750 units. S$640 (US$400/£220) Tower double; S$740 (US$463/£255) Garden double; S$875 (US$547/£301) Valley double; from S$1,000 (US$625/£344) suite. AE, DC, MC, V. 10-min. walk to Orchard MRT. **Amenities:** 5 restaurants; lobby lounge; resort-style outdoor landscaped pool; 3-hole pitch-and-putt course; 4 outdoor lighted tennis courts; fitness center w/glass walls looking out into gardens; Jacuzzi; sauna; steam; concierge; limousine service; business center; shopping arcade; salon; 24-hr. room service; massage; babysitting; laundry service; dry cleaning; nonsmoking rooms; executive-level rooms. *In room:* A/C, satellite TV w/in-house movies, minibar, coffeemaker, hair dryer, iron, safe.

Sheraton Towers Singapore ✦✦

One of the first things you see when you walk into the lobby of the Sheraton Towers is the service awards the place has won; check in, and you'll begin to see why. With the deluxe (standard) room, you'll get a suit pressing on arrival, daily newspaper delivery, shoeshine service, and complimentary movies. These refurbished rooms are handsome, with textured walls, plush carpeting, and beds luxuriously fitted with down pillows and dreamy Egyptian-cotton bedding. Upgrade to a Tower room and you get a personal butler, complimentary nightly cocktails and morning breakfast, free laundry, free local calls, your own pants press, and free use of the personal trainer in the fitness center. The cabana units, off the pool area, have all the services of the Tower Wing in a very private resort room. The 23 one-of-a-kind suites each feature a different theme—Chinese Regency, French, Italian, jungle, you name it. Although Sheraton is a luxe choice, you can find better deals, price-wise.

39 Scotts Rd., Singapore 228230. ℂ 800/325-3535 in the U.S. and Canada, 800/073-535 in Australia, 800/325-35353 in New Zealand, 800/353535 in the U.K., or 65/6737-6888. Fax 65/6737-1072. www.sheraton.com. 413 units. S$520 (US$325/£179) double; from S$1,200 (US$750/£413) suite. AE, DC, MC, V. 5-min. walk to Newton MRT. **Amenities:** 3 restaurants; lobby lounge; outdoor landscaped pool; fitness center w/sauna and massage; concierge; limousine service; 24-hr. business center; 24-hr. room service; babysitting; laundry service; dry cleaning; nonsmoking rooms; executive-level rooms. *In room:* A/C, satellite TV w/in-house movies, dataport w/direct Internet access, minibar, coffeemaker, hair dryer, safe.

Singapore Marriott Hotel ✦✦

You can't get a better location than this—at the corner of Orchard and Scotts roads. Marriott's green-roofed pagoda tower is a well-recognized landmark on Orchard Road, but guest rooms inside tend to be smaller than average to fit in the octagonal structure. Luckily, the recent refurbishing scheme added lively colors to brighten the spaces with natural greens and floral fabrics. The palatial lobby has been overtaken by the Marriott Cafe, with weekend buffets that are so popular with the locals that there's a long queue. Outside, the Crossroads Cafe, spilling out onto the sidewalk, is a favorite of international and Singaporean celebrities who like to be seen. Service in this hotel is very personable and professional.

Marriott, which took over management of this property in 1995, caters to the business traveler, so the rooms on the club floors get most of the hotel's attention. The club lounge, for instance, has a great view, and there's not a tacky detail in the comfortable seating and dining areas.

320 Orchard Rd., Singapore 238865. ℂ 800/228-9290 in the U.S. and Canada, 800/251-259 in Australia, 800/22-12-22 in the U.K., or 65/6735-5800. Fax 65/6735-9800. www.singaporemarriott.com. 373 units. S$500 (US$313/£172) double; from S$800 (US$500/£275) suite. AE, DC, MC, V. Orchard MRT. **Amenities:** 4 restaurants; lobby lounge, bar w/live jazz, dance club w/live pop bands; outdoor pool w/Jacuzzi; outdoor basketball court; fitness center w/Jacuzzi, sauna, steam, and massage; concierge; limousine service; 24-hr. business center; shopping arcade; 24-hr. room service; babysitting; laundry service; dry cleaning; nonsmoking rooms; executive-level rooms. *In room:* A/C, satellite TV w/in-house movies, dataport w/direct Internet access, minibar, coffeemaker, hair dryer, iron, safe.

The Best of Singapore's Spas

In the mid–'90s, spas began making a splash in the Singapore hotel scene. By the millennium, every luxury hotel was planning either a full-blown spa facility or at least offering spa services to its residents. At the same time, day spas sprouted up in shopping centers; despite the economic downturn, these businesses have stayed afloat. Now, the Singapore Tourism Board is positioning Singapore as an urban spa hub in Southeast Asia, luring visitors from the region and beyond with luxurious facilities that go above and beyond the call of relaxation and hedonistic pampering. Here are the best among many:

Singapore's most celebrated spa, **Amrita** (Raffles The Plaza, Level 6, 2 Stamford Rd.; ✆ 65/6336-4477; and Swissôtel Merchant Court, Level 2, 20 Merchant Rd.; ✆ 65/6239-1780; www.amritaspas.com), is operated by Raffles International and has proven so wildly successful that the hotel chain has opened Amritas in Germany, Switzerland, and beyond. This flagship spa at Raffles The Plaza is the largest spa in Singapore, with Southeast Asian–inspired interiors and treatments—over 1,000 to choose from.

Amrita is convenient if you want to stay in the city center; however, if you want more of a retreat experience, **Spa Botanica** (2 Bukit Manis Rd., The Sentosa; ✆ 65/6371-1318; www.spabotanica.com) is a gorgeous pick. It's located at the Sentosa, a scenic resort dripping with laid-back, yet elegant, tropical Southeast Asian decor. Spa Botanica has 6,000 sq. m (64,584 sq. ft.) of designated spa space, with pools, mud baths, and treatment pavilions nestled in lush gardens. Treatments center around natural recipes for beauty and relaxation, including spices and floral essences.

EXPENSIVE

Grand Hyatt Singapore ✦✦   Despite its fantastic location, this hotel was doing pretty poorly until it had a feng shui master come in and evaluate it for redecorating. According to the Chinese monk, because the lobby entrance was a wall of flat glass doors that ran parallel to the long reception desk in front, all the hotel's wealth was flowing from the desk right out the doors and into the street. To correct the problem, the doors are now set at right angles to each other, a fountain was built in the rear, and reception was moved around a corner to the right of the lobby. Since then, the hotel has enjoyed some of the highest occupancy rates in town. Feng shui or not, the new decor is modern, sleek, and sophisticated, an elegant combination of polished black marble and deep wood. Terrace Wing guest rooms invite with plush duvets and golden colors, plus unique glass-enclosed alcoves looking over the hotel gardens. Bathrooms are large, with lots of marble counter space. If you've booked through a travel agent, these are the rooms you'll get. If you book on your own, you're more likely to be put in a Grand Wing room. These are really suites with separate living areas, small walk-in closets, and separate work area. They're very deluxe since a 2003 refurbishment that freshened up the decor. The pool and fitness center are amazing. Located in the center of this city hotel, a four-story waterfall provides the perfect soundscape to match a lush jungle garden hugging the freeform pool and state-of-the-art gym. **Note:** Grand

Hyatt no longer publishes a rack rate; rather, it selects the "best rate" for the dates of your stay; thus the prices below reflect the average best rates for January 2007.

10 Scotts Rd., Singapore 228211. ℂ **800/223-1234** in the U.S. and Canada, or 65/6738-1234. Fax 65/6732-1696. www.singapore.grand.hyatt.com. 685 units. S$380 (US$238/£131) double; from S$720 (US$450/£248) suite. AE, DC, MC, V. Near Orchard MRT. **Amenities:** 3 restaurants; lobby lounge; live-music bar; landscaped outdoor pool; 2 outdoor lighted tennis courts; squash court and badminton court; excellent fitness center w/Jacuzzi, sauna, steam, massage, and spa treatments; concierge; limousine service; business center; 24-hr. room service; babysitting; laundry service; dry cleaning; executive-level rooms. *In room:* A/C, satellite TV w/in-house movies, dataport w/direct Internet access, minibar, coffeemaker, hair dryer, iron, safe.

MODERATE

Hilton International Singapore   If you count the luxury cars that drive up to the valet at the Hilton, you'd think this is a good address to have while staying in Singapore. Well, to be honest, this Hilton doesn't measure up with some of its other properties worldwide and definitely can't compete with other hotels in this price category in Singapore. The most famous feature of the Hilton is its glamorous shopping arcade, where you can find your Donna Karan, Louis Vuitton, Gucci—all the greats. Ask the concierge for a pager, and they'll page you for important calls while you window-shop or try some of the 45 fragrant vodkas at the lobby bar. With all this, the guest rooms should be pretty sumptuous, no? Well, no. The rooms are simpler than you'd expect, with nothing flashy or overdone. Floor-to-ceiling windows are in each, and although views in the front of the hotel are of Orchard Road and the Thai Embassy property, views in the back are not so hot. In this day and age, when business-class hotels are wrestling to outdo each other, Hilton has a lot of catching up to do. *Note:* Hilton no longer publishes a rack rate; rather, it selects the "best rate" for the dates of your stay. The prices below reflect the average best rates for January 2007.

581 Orchard Rd., Singapore 238883. ℂ **800/445-8667** in the U.S., or 65/6737-2233. Fax 65/6732-2917. www. singapore.hilton.com. 423 units. S$300 (US$188/£103) double; from S$660 (US$413/£227) suite. AE, DC, MC, V. Near Orchard MRT. **Amenities:** 2 restaurants; lobby lounge; outdoor pool; fitness center w/sauna and steam; concierge; limousine service; business center; shopping arcade; salon; 24-hr. room service; babysitting; laundry service; dry cleaning; nonsmoking rooms; executive-level rooms. *In room:* A/C, satellite TV w/in-house movies, minibar, coffeemaker, hair dryer, safe.

Meritus Mandarin Singapore ⊛   Smack in the center of Orchard Road is the Mandarin Hotel, a two-tower complex with Singapore's most famous revolving restaurant topping it off like a little hat. The 39-story Main Tower opened in 1973, and with the opening of the South Wing 10 years later, the number of rooms expanded to 1,200. True to its name, the hotel reflects a Chinese aesthetic, beginning in the lobby with the huge marble mural of the "87 Taoist Immortals" and the carved-wood chairs lining the walls. The South Wing is predominantly for leisure travelers, who have access to the tower through a side entrance. These guest rooms are the same size as those in the Main Tower but feel slightly smaller, most likely because of the dark-wood modular units that fill up major wall space with imposing TV and minibar cabinets. Mandarin refurbished the carpets, drapes, and linens in this wing in 2003, which really freshened up the space. While rooms in this wing are priced for greater value, be warned that this is where all the tour groups are put. Be prepared for large groups milling around the public spaces during peak tourist seasons.

333 Orchard Rd., Singapore 238867. ℂ **65/6737-4411.** Fax 65/6732-2361. www.asiatravel.com/singapore/ mandarin. 1,200 units. S$240 (US$150/£83) double; from S$840 (US$525/£289) suite. AE, DC, MC, V. Near Orchard MRT. **Amenities:** 4 restaurants; revolving observation lounge and lobby lounge; outdoor pool; fitness center

w/Jacuzzi, sauna, steam, and massage; concierge; tour desk; limousine service; business center; shopping arcade; salon; 24-hr. room service; babysitting; laundry service; dry cleaning; nonsmoking rooms; executive-level rooms. *In room:* A/C, satellite TV w/in-house movies, minibar, coffeemaker, safe.

Orchard Parade Hotel ★★ *Value* *Kids*   This fine hotel, after a S$40-million, 2-year renovation, sports a new pool, guest rooms, lobby, driveway, front entrance, and eateries, decorated in a Mediterranean theme integrating marble mosaics, plaster walls, beamed ceilings, and wrought-iron railings. The midsize pool on the sixth-floor roof features colorful tiles and draping arbors, a motif carried over through the new fitness center. Rooms also reveal Mediterranean style in their terra-cotta wall sconces, wrought-iron table legs, and shades of teal and aqua. If it's important to you, specify a room with a view here. For good value, the family studio fits a king-size bed and two twins, with separate family room and dining area and plenty of space, for just S$100 (US$63/£34) extra. Just outside, a long terrace along Orchard Road hosts many restaurant choices; the most popular, Modestos, serves good pasta and pizzas at affordable prices.

1 Tanglin Rd., Singapore 247905. ℂ **65/6737-1133.** Fax 65/6733-0242. www.orchardparade.com.sg. 387 units. S$300 (US$192/£99) double; S$550 (US$352/£182) family studio; from S$450 (US$290/£149) suite. AE, DC, MC, V. Orchard MRT. **Amenities:** 5 restaurants; lobby lounge; outdoor pool; fitness center; concierge; tour desk; business center; salon; 24-hr. room service; babysitting; laundry service; dry cleaning; executive-level rooms. *In room:* A/C, satellite TV, minibar, coffeemaker, hair dryer.

York Hotel Singapore ★   This small tourist-class hotel has some of the most consistently professional and courteous staff I've encountered. A short walk from Orchard, York is convenient, though far enough removed to provide a relaxing atmosphere. Guest rooms reflect a sharp contemporary style in light woods, natural tones, and simple lines. Combined with an already spacious room, the result is an airy, cooling effect. Bathrooms throughout are downright huge. Cabana rooms look out to a pool and sun deck decorated with giant palms. Despite surrounding buildings, it doesn't feel claustrophobic, as do some of the more centrally situated hotels. The rates here have gone up a bit, so make sure you ask for a promotional discount.

21 Mount Elizabeth, Singapore 228516. ℂ **800/223-5652** in the U.S. and Canada, 800/553-549 in Australia, 800/447-555 in New Zealand, 800/89-88-52 in the U.K., or 65/6737-0511. Fax 65/6732-1217. www.yorkhotel.com.sg. 406 units. S$190 (US$119/£65) double; from S$340 (US$213/£117) suite. AE, DC, MC, V. 10-min. walk to Orchard MRT. **Amenities:** Restaurant; lobby lounge; outdoor pool; tiny fitness center; Jacuzzi; tour desk; tiny business center; 24-hr. room service; babysitting; laundry service; dry cleaning. *In room:* A/C, satellite TV, minibar, coffeemaker.

INEXPENSIVE

RELC International Hotel ★★ *Value*   RELC offers real value-for-money in terms of location (a 10-min. walk to Orchard Rd.) and an excellent facility. I found the service and convenience here superior to those of some hotels in the higher-priced categories. RELC has four types of rooms—superior twin, executive twin, Hollywood queen, and alcove suite—but no matter what the size, none of the rooms ever feel cluttered or cramped. Every unit has a balcony, TV, and fridge with free juice boxes and snacks. Bathrooms are large, with full-length tubs. If you're interested in the higher-priced rooms, choose the Hollywood queen over the alcove suite—its decor is better and it can sleep a family very comfortably.

30 Orange Grove Rd., Singapore 258352. ℂ **65/6885-7888.** Fax 65/6733-9976. www.relc.org.sg. 128 units. S$129 (US$81/£45) double; from S$175 (US$109/£60) suite. AE, DC, MC, V. 15-min. walk to Orchard MRT. **Amenities:** Restaurant; tour desk; laundry service; self-service laundry; nonsmoking rooms. *In room:* A/C, TV w/in-house movies, dataport w/direct Internet access, minibar, fridge, coffeemaker (in some rooms), hair dryer.

SHA Villa ★★ (Finds)   SHA Villa is an interesting pick. Formerly the Regalis Court, this charming colonial-style mansion has been restored beautifully and outfitted with Peranakan-inspired touches. Everything here will make you feel as if you're staying in a quaint guesthouse rather than a hotel, from the open-air lobby (under the porte-cochere) to the guest rooms, which have comforting touches like teak furnishings, textile wall hangings, Oriental throws over wooden floors, and bamboo blinds to keep out the sun. What makes this place truly unique is its management. SHA stands for Singapore Hotel Association—this property serves as a training ground for hospitality service staff, from bellhops to chefs. Everyone is eager to please because, well, they're being graded. Centrally located just a 10-minute walk from Orchard Road and with an excellent Western restaurant, you can't go wrong here.

64 Lloyd Rd., Singapore 239113. (C) 65/6734-7117. Fax 65/6736-1651. www.sha.org.sg. 40 units. S$180 (US$113/£62) double. AE, DC, MC, V. 10-min. walk from Somerset MRT. **Amenities:** Restaurant; car rental; babysitting; laundry service; nonsmoking rooms. *In room:* A/C, TV, dataport w/direct Internet access, coffeemaker, safe.

SENTOSA ISLAND

There are only two hotel properties on Sentosa Island, the Shangri-La Rasa Sentosa, located right on the water and designed for families and fun, and the Sentosa Resort & Spa, located on a cliff above the water, closer to golfing and ideal for secluded, romantic getaways.

The Sentosa Resort & Spa ★★   Designed with romance in mind, the Sentosa Resort & Spa's small resort-style buildings, fashioned after the famous resorts of Phuket, Thailand, are connected with covered walkways encircling lily ponds and courtyard gardens. The designers have done a great job combining clean modern lines with tropical touches to produce a sophisticated getaway with relaxing charm. Lazy terraces and cozy alcoves tucked all over the grounds invite guests to unwind in privacy—perfect for intimate candlelight dinners that can be requested anywhere you like. The centerpiece is the new spa, built into a garden setting—both opulent and relaxing.

The standard guest rooms in the five-story hotel building are small but stunning, featuring camphor burl-wood doors and accents, Thai silk screens in natural browns and greens, and deep tubs and separate showers in the bathrooms, surrounded by celadon-green tiling and sleek black-granite details. Ask for views of the golf course, which are prettier than the views of the hotel courtyards and buildings. Butlers wait around the clock to serve you—a standard feature for all rooms.

2 Bukit Manis Rd., Sentosa, Singapore 099891. (C) 65/6275-0331. Fax 65/6275-0228. www.thesentosa.com. 214 units. S$380 (US$238/£131) double; from S$550 (US$344/£189) suite; S$1,500 (US$938/£516) villa. AE, DC, MC, V. See "Sentosa Island," later in this chapter, for public transportation. **Amenities:** 2 restaurants; lounge; gorgeous midnight-blue-tiled outdoor pool w/views of the harbor; golf at nearby facilities; 2 outdoor lighted tennis courts w/pro; 2 squash courts; fitness center w/20m lap pool, Jacuzzi, and sauna; brand-new luxury spa w/private pool, mud baths, steam, Jacuzzis, exercise and relaxation classes, salon, beauty treatments, and massage; concierge; tour desk; limousine service; shuttle service; 24-hr. room service; babysitting; laundry service; dry cleaning. *In room:* A/C, satellite TV w/in-house movies, dataport w/direct Internet access, minibar, coffeemaker, hair dryer, safe.

Shangri-La's Rasa Sentosa Resort (Kids)   Set on an immaculate white-sand beach fringed with coconut palms, Shangri-La's Rasa Sentosa Resort is Singapore's only true beachfront hotel. It's frequented by Singaporeans looking to get away from it all, but as a visitor to Singapore you may find it isolated from the city's attractions. Still, you can always take advantage of the resort's complimentary shuttle service for trips to the action, only to return to the serenity of the resort at the end of a busy day. As for the rooms, the decision between whether to take the hill-view room or the slightly more expensive sea-facing room is a no-brainer: The view of the sea is exceptional, and if you don't go for it, you'll be missing out on glorious mornings, when you can throw back the curtains and take in the scenery from your balcony.

Great outdoor activities make the Rasa Sentosa particularly attractive. The resort's extensive recreational facilities, including a sea-sports center, offer windsurfing, sailing, and paddle skiing. Other pluses are a large outdoor freeform pool, jogging track, aqua-bike rentals, outdoor Jacuzzi, and fully equipped spa with gym, sauna, body and facial treatments, hydromassage, and massage therapies. The hotel organizes nature walks, cycling tours, rock-wall climbing, and beach volleyball. For children, there is a separate pool with water slides (no lifeguard, though), playground, nursery, and video arcade.

101 Siloso Rd., Sentosa, Singapore 098970. © 800/942-5050 in the U.S. and Canada, 800/222-448 in Australia, 800/442-179 in New Zealand, or 65/6275-0900. Fax 65/6275-1055. www.shangri-la.com. 459 units. S$375 (US$234/£129) double; from S$870 (US$544/£299) suite. AE, DC, MC, V. **Amenities:** 3 restaurants; poolside bar and lobby lounge; outdoor lagoon-style pool w/children's pool and Jacuzzi; golf at nearby facilities; fitness center; spa w/sauna, steam, and massage; children's center; game room; shuttle service; business center; 24-hr. room service; babysitting; laundry service; dry cleaning; executive-level rooms. *In room:* A/C, satellite TV w/in-house movies, dataport w/direct Internet access, minibar, coffeemaker, hair dryer, iron, safe.

5 Where to Dine

So what do Singaporeans do for boredom relief? They eat. Dining out in Singapore is the central focus of family quality time, the best excuse for getting together with friends, and the proper way to close that business deal. That's why you'll find such a huge selection of local, regional, and international cuisine here, served in settings that range from bustling hawker centers to grand and glamorous palaces of gastronomy. But to simply say, "If you like food, you'll love Singapore!" doesn't do justice to the modern concept of eating in this place. The various ethnic restaurants, with their traditional decor and serving styles, hold their own special sense of theater for foreigners; but Singaporeans don't stop there, dreaming up new concepts in cuisine and ambience to add fresh dimensions to the fine art of dining. For a twist, new variations on traditions pop up, like the East-meets-West fusion cuisine dished up at Doc Cheng's. Theme restaurants turn regular meals into attractions; take, for example, Imperial Herbal's intriguing predinner medical examination or True Blue Cuisine's Peranakan home feeling.

It is estimated that Singapore has over 2,000 eating establishments, so you'll never be at a loss for a place to go. I'll begin by providing an overview of the main types of traditional cuisine to help you decide, and also list those signature dishes that each style has contributed to the "local cuisine," dishes that have crossed cultures to become time-honored favorites—the Singaporean equivalent of bangers and mash or burgers and fries. These suggestions are especially helpful when navigating the endless choices at hawker centers.

SINGAPOREAN CUISINE

CHINESE   The large Chinese population in Singapore makes this obviously the most common type of food you'll find, and any good description of Singaporean food should begin with the most prevalent Chinese regional styles. Many Chinese restaurants in the West are lumped into one category—Chinese—with only mild acknowledgment of Sichuan and dim sum. But China's a big place, and its size is reflected in its many different tastes, ingredients, and preparation styles.

A lot of hawker-center fare is inspired by regional Chinese home cooking. Local favorites include **carrot cake** (white radishes that are steamed and pounded until soft, then fried in egg, garlic, and chili), *Hokkien bak ku teh* (boiled pork ribs in a seasoned soup), *Teochew kway teow* (stir-fried rice noodles with egg, prawns, and fish), and the number-one favorite for foreigners, **Hainanese chicken rice** (boiled sliced chicken breast served over rice cooked in chicken stock). On p. 497, I've provided an overview of the hawker scene so you'll know where to find local food the way the locals eat it.

MALAY   Malay cuisine combines Indonesian and Thai flavors, blending ginger, turmeric, chilis, lemongrass, and dried shrimp paste to make unique curries. Heavy on coconut milk and peanuts, Malay food can at times be on the sweet side. The most popular Malay curries are *rendang,* a dry, dark, and heavy coconut-based curry served over meat; *sambal,* a red and spicy chili sauce; and *sambal belacan,* a condiment of fresh chilis, dried shrimp paste, and lime juice. The ultimate Malay dish in Singapore is *satay,* sweet barbecued meat kabobs dipped in chili peanut sauce. *Nasi lemak*—coconut rice surrounded by an assortment of fried anchovies, peanuts, egg, and sambal—is primarily a breakfast dish, but can be eaten anytime.

PERANAKAN   This type of food came out of the Straits-born Chinese community and combines such mainland Chinese ingredients as noodles and oyster sauces with local Malay flavors of coconut milk and peanuts. *Laksa lemak* is a great example, mixing Chinese rice-flour noodles into a soup of Malay-style spicy coconut cream with chunks of seafood. Another favorite, *popiah,* is the Peranakan version of a spring roll, combining sweet turnip, chopped egg, chili sauce, and prawns in a delicate wrap. *Otak-otak* is unique: toasted mashed fish with coconut milk and chili, wrapped in a banana leaf and grilled over flames.

INDIAN   **Southern Indian** food is a superhot blend of spices in a coconut-milk base. Rice is the staple, along with thin breads such as *prata* and *dosai,* which are good for scooping up drippy curries. Vegetarian dishes are abundant, a result of Hindu-mandated vegetarianism, and use lots of chickpeas and lentils in curry and chili gravies. *Vindaloo,* meat or poultry in a tangy and spicy sauce, is also well known. **Banana-leaf restaurants,** surely the most interesting way to experience southern Indian food in Singapore, serve up meals on banana leaves cut like place mats. It's very informal. Spoons and forks are provided, but if you want to act local and use your hands, remember to use your right hand only (see "Etiquette," earlier in this chapter), and don't forget to wash up before and after at the tap.

Northern Indian food combines yogurts and creams with a milder, more delicate blend of herbs and chilis. It's served most often with breads like fluffy *nan* and flat *chapati.* Marinated meats like chicken or fish, cooked in the tandoor clay oven, are always the highlight of a northern Indian meal. Northern Indian restaurants are more upmarket and expensive than the southern ones, but while they offer more of the comforts associated with dining out, the southern banana-leaf experience is more of an adventure.

Some Singaporean variations on Indian cuisine are *mee goreng,* fried noodles with chili and curry gravy, and **fish-head curry,** a giant fish head simmered in a broth of coconut curry, chilis, and fragrant seasonings.

Muslim influences on Indian food have produced *roti prata,* a humble late-night snack of fried bread served with lentil gravy, and *murtabak,* a fried prata filled with minced meat, onion, and egg. Between the Muslims' dietary laws *(halal)* forbidding

Where to Dine in Urban Singapore

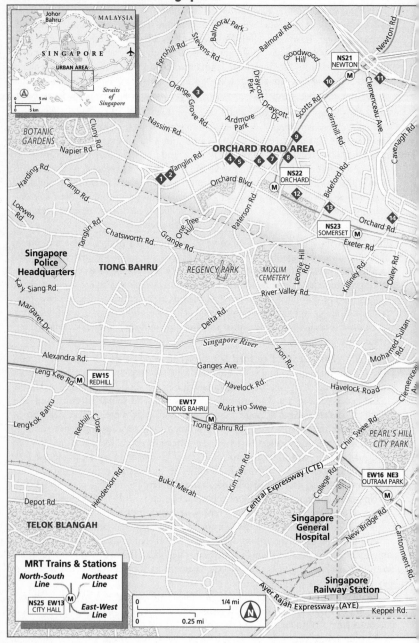

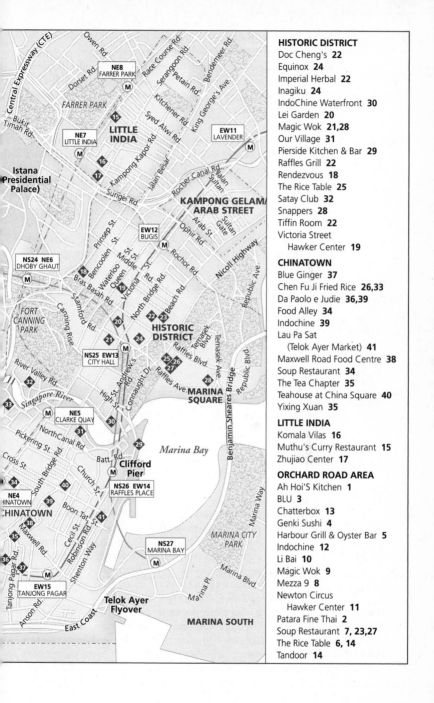

HISTORIC DISTRICT

Doc Cheng's **22**
Equinox **24**
Imperial Herbal **22**
Inagiku **24**
IndoChine Waterfront **30**
Lei Garden **20**
Magic Wok **21,28**
Our Village **31**
Pierside Kitchen & Bar **29**
Raffles Grill **22**
Rendezvous **18**
The Rice Table **25**
Satay Club **32**
Snappers **28**
Tiffin Room **22**
Victoria Street
  Hawker Center **19**

CHINATOWN

Blue Ginger **37**
Chen Fu Ji Fried Rice **26,33**
Da Paolo e Judie **36,39**
Food Alley **34**
Indochine **39**
Lau Pa Sat
  (Telok Ayer Market) **41**
Maxwell Road Food Centre **38**
Soup Restaurant **34**
The Tea Chapter **35**
Teahouse at China Square **40**
Yixing Xuan **35**

LITTLE INDIA

Komala Vilas **16**
Muthu's Curry Restaurant **15**
Zhujiao Center **17**

ORCHARD ROAD AREA

Ah Hoi'S Kitchen **1**
BLU **3**
Chatterbox **13**
Genki Sushi **4**
Harbour Grill & Oyster Bar **5**
Indochine **12**
Li Bai **10**
Magic Wok **9**
Mezza 9 **8**
Newton Circus
  Hawker Center **11**
Patara Fine Thai **2**
Soup Restaurant **7, 23,27**
The Rice Table **6, 14**
Tandoor **14**

pork and the Hindus' regard for the sacred cow, Indian food is the one cuisine that can be eaten by every kind of Singaporean.

SEAFOOD   One cannot describe Singaporean food without mentioning the abundance of fresh seafood. But most important is the uniquely Singaporean **chili crab,** chopped and smothered in a thick, tangy chili sauce. **Pepper crabs** and **black-pepper crayfish** are also a thrill. Instead of chili sauce, these shellfish are served in a thick black-pepper-and-soy sauce.

FRUITS   A walk through a wet market at any time of year will show you just what wonders the tropics can produce. Varieties of banana, coconut, papaya, mango, and pineapple are available year-round; in addition, Southeast Asia has an amazing selection of exotic and almost unimaginable fruits. From the light and juicy star fruit to the red and hairy rambutan, they are all worthy of a try, either whole or juiced. If you dare, the fruit to sample—the veritable king of fruits—is the *durian,* a large, green, spiky fruit that, when cut open, smells worse than old tennis shoes. The "best" ones are in season every June, when Singaporeans go wild over them. In case you're curious, the fruit has a creamy texture and tastes lightly sweet and deeply musky.

TIPS ON DINING

- Most restaurants are open for lunch as early as 11am, but close around 2:30 or 3pm to give them a chance to set up for dinner, which begins around 6pm. Where closing times are listed, that is the time when the last order is taken. If you need to eat at odd hours, food centers serve all day and some hawker centers are open all night—see "Hawker Centers," p. 497.

- Don't tip. Restaurants always add a gratuity to the bill. You can leave the small change, but the government discourages this practice.

- Some restaurants, especially the more fashionable or upscale ones, may require that reservations be made up to a couple days in advance. Reservations are always recommended for Saturday and Sunday lunch and dinner, as eating is a favorite national pastime and a lot of families go out for weekend quality time together.

- Because Singapore is so hot, "dress casual" (meaning a shirt and slacks for men and a dress or skirt/slacks and top for women) is always a safe bet in moderate to expensive restaurants. For the very expensive restaurants, more formal attire is required, which in Singapore means jacket and tie for men, and a dressier outfit for women. For the cheap places, come as you are, as long as you're decent.

- If you're on a budget, remember that lunch at a hawker center can be as cheap as S$3.50 (US$2.19/£1.20), truly a bargain. Many places have set-price buffet lunches, but these can be as high as S$45 (US$28/£15). Indian restaurants are great deals for inexpensive buffet lunches, which can be found as reasonably as S$10 (US$6.25/£3.44) per person for all you can eat. Fortunately, Singapore is a haven for culinary diversity where it's possible to eat exotic foods to your heart's content, all while maintaining a shoestring budget.

- In recent years, Singaporeans have become more wine savvy and have begun importing estate-bottled wines from California, Australia, New Zealand, Peru, South Africa, France, and Germany. However, these bottles are heavily taxed. A bottle of wine with dinner starts at around S$50 (US$31/£17) and a single glass runs between S$10 and S$25 (US$6.25–US$16/£3.44–£8.80), depending on the wine and the restaurant. Chinese restaurants usually don't charge corkage fees for bringing your own.

HISTORIC DISTRICT
VERY EXPENSIVE

Inagiku ✹✹ JAPANESE   Inagiku's excellent Japanese food gets top marks for ingredients, preparation, and presentation. In delicately lighted and subtle decor, you can enjoy house favorites like sashimi, tempura, and teppanyaki—with separate dining areas for tempura and the sushi bar. The *tokusen sashimi morikimi* is masterful in its presentation: An assortment of raw fish—including salmon, prawns, and clams—is laid out on an ice-filled shell, inside of which nestles the skeleton of a whole fish. It's odd and delightful at the same time. I recommend the tempura *moriawase,* a combination of seafood and vegetables that's very lightly deep-fried, and the teppanyaki prawns. In addition to sake, there is a good selection of wines.

At Raffles The Plaza, Level 3, 80 Bras Basah Rd. ℂ **65/6431-6156.** Reservations recommended. Set lunches S$40–S$100 (US$25–US$63/£14–£35); set dinners S$180–S$220 (US$113–US$138/£62–£76). AE, MC, V. Daily noon–2:30pm and 6:30–10:30pm.

Raffles Grill ✹✹✹ FRENCH   The grande dame of Singapore achieves a level of sophistication unmatched by any other five-star restaurant. The architectural charm and historic significance of the old hotel will transform dinner into a cultural event, but don't just come here for the ambience; the food is outstanding as well. Anything you order from the ever-changing menu will be divine. The *degustation* menu, seven courses at S$180 (US$115/£59), is the best way to explore the restaurant's finest dishes if you have trouble choosing from an a la carte menu that features pigeon, lamb, suckling pig, veal, and a carving trolley of amazing cuts of beef prepared to perfection. The 400-label wine list (going back to 1890 vintages) could be a history lesson, and if you'd like, you can request the cellar master to select a wine to match each course. The fabulously attentive service will make you feel like you own the place. Formal dress is required.

At the Raffles Hotel, 1 Beach Rd. ℂ **65/6331-1612.** Reservations required. Main courses S$65–S$79 (US$41–US$49/ £23–£27). AE, DC, MC, V. Mon–Fri noon–2pm and 7–10pm; Sat 7–10pm.

EXPENSIVE

Doc Cheng's ✹✹ FUSION   If you're growing tired of your travel partner, I recommend Doc Cheng's. The witty menu tells the story of Doc Cheng, a mythological colonial figure who was a sought-after physician, local celebrity, and notorious drunk. His concept of "restorative foods" is therefore rather decadent, and on the menu you'll find fabulous "fusion" dishes that are more flavorful than medicinal. Guest chefs make the menu ever changing—the latest and greatest was a trio of beef cuts prepared in three different styles (Western, Indian, and Chinese) on the same plate. The house wine is a Riesling (sweet wines are more popular with Singaporeans) from Raffles's own vineyard. Two dining areas allow you to eat alfresco under the veranda or in cool air-conditioning inside.

1 Beach Rd., Raffles Hotel Arcade #02-20, Level 2. ℂ **65/6331-1612.** Reservations required. Main courses S$32–S$41 (US$20–US$26/£11–£14). AE, DC, MC, V. Mon–Fri noon–1:30pm and 7–9:30pm; Sat–Sun 7–9:30pm.

Equinox ✹ CONTINENTAL/ASIAN   What a view! From the top of the tallest hotel in Southeast Asia, you can see out past the marina to Malaysia and Indonesia—and the restaurant's three-tier design and floor-to-ceiling windows mean every table has a view. It's decorated in contemporary style with nice Chinese accents. Lunch is an extensive display of seafood served in a host of international preparations, with chefs searing scallops to order. Dinner is a la carte, with a menu that's divided between

Eastern and Western cuisine, plus some dishes that combine Eastern and Western ingredients and cooking styles—such as *yuzu* marinated cod with braised *enoki* (mushrooms) and *tasoi* (spinach). For dessert, order the Equinox Temptation sampler plate.

At Raffles City, 2 Stamford Rd., Level 70. ✆ 65/6837-3322. Reservations required. Daily buffet lunch S$56 (US$35/£19); dinner main courses S$24–S$48 (US$15–US$30/£8.25–£17). AE, DC, MC, V. Mon–Sat noon–2:30pm and 6:30–11pm; Sun 11am–2:30pm and 7–11pm.

IndoChine Waterfront ✿✿✿ VIETNAMESE/LAO/CAMBODIAN/FRENCH IndoChine Waterfront shares the stately Empress Place Building with the Asian Civilisations Museum, enhancing the sophistication of its chic Asian decor. The views over the water make for true romance. The menu combines the best dishes from the Indochinese region, many with hints of the French cuisine that was added to regional palates during colonial days. The two most popular dishes are the house-specialty beef-stew ragout and the pepper beef with sweet-and-sour sauce. More traditional Vietnamese favorites, like spring rolls and prawns grilled on sugarcane, are fresh starters. After dinner, don't miss the Vietnamese coffee; it's mindblowingly delicious. Indo-Chine has two sister restaurants, one in a quaint Chinatown shophouse (49B Club St.; ✆ 65/6323-0503) and another in Wisma Atria on Orchard Road #01-18/23 (✆ 65/6238-3470).

At the Asian Civilisations Museum, 1 Empress Place. ✆ 65/6339-1720. Reservations required. Small dishes S$20–S$38 (US$13–US$24/£6.90–£13). AE, DC, MC, V. Sun–Thurs noon–2:30pm and 6:30–11pm; Fri–Sat noon–2:30pm and 6:30pm–midnight.

Lei Garden ✿✿ CANTONESE Lei Garden lives up to a great reputation for the highest quality Cantonese cuisine in one of the most elegant settings, nestled within the unique ambience of CHIJMES just outside its towering picture windows. Highly recommended dishes are the "Buddha jumps over the wall," a very popular Chinese soup made from abalone, fish maw (stomach), shark's fin, and Chinese ham. It's generally served only on special occasions. To make the beggar's chicken, they take a whole stuffed chicken and wrap and bake it in a lotus leaf covered in yam, which makes the chicken moist with a delicate flavor you won't forget. For either of these dishes, you must place your order at least 24 hours in advance when you make your reservation. Also try the barbecued Beijing duck, which is exquisite. Dim sum here is excellent, too. A small selection of French and Chinese wines is available.

30 Victoria St., CHIJMES #01-24. ✆ 65/6339-3822. Reservations required. Small dishes S$18–S$58 (US$11–US$36/£6.05–£20). AE, DC, MC, V. Daily 11:30am–2:30pm and 6–10:30pm.

Snappers ✿✿ SEAFOOD With a view of the Ritz-Carlton's lovely pool and gardens, this restaurant is hardly your typical poolside snack bar. Snappers invents mouthwatering recipes for new ways to enjoy fresh seafood. The grilled halibut with artichoke is served with potato confit, rocket salad, and marinated octopus. If the menu doesn't include what you're looking for, you can have your choice of live seafood prepared to your specs. This is one of the city's top choices for delicious dining, with a terrific wine list and impeccable service. You won't be disappointed.

At the Ritz-Carlton Millenia Singapore, Level 1, 7 Raffles Ave. ✆ 65/6434-5288. Reservations required. Live seafood priced by weight; average dish is S$65 (US$41/£23). Main courses S$40–S$148 (US$25–US$93/£14–£51). AE, DC, MC, V. Sun–Thurs noon–2pm and 6:30–10pm; Sat–Sun noon–2pm and 6:30–10:30pm.

Tiffin Room ✿ NORTHERN INDIAN Tiffin curry came from India and is named after the three-tiered containers that Indian workers would use to carry their lunch. The tiffin-box idea was stolen by the British colonists, who changed around the recipes a bit so they weren't as spicy. The cuisine that evolved is pretty much what you'll find served at Raffles's Tiffin Room, where a buffet spread lets you select from a variety of curries, chutneys, rice, and Indian breads. The restaurant is just inside the lobby entrance of Raffles Hotel and carries the trademark Raffles elegance throughout its decor. Very British Raj.

At the Raffles Hotel, 1 Beach Rd. ⓒ 65/6331-1612. Reservations recommended. All meals served buffet style. Breakfast S$42 (US$26/£14); lunch S$43 (US$28/£14); high tea S$37 (US$24/£12); dinner S$46 (US$29/£15). AE, DC, MC, V. Daily 7–10:30am, noon–2:30pm, 3:30–5:30pm (high tea), and 7–10:30pm.

MODERATE

Imperial Herbal ✦✦ CHINESE HERBAL   People come again and again for the healing powers of the food served here, enriched with herbs and other secret ingredients prescribed by a resident Chinese herbalist. Upon entering, you'll be ushered to the herb counter. The herbalist, who is also trained in Western medicine, will ask for the symptoms of what ails you and take your pulse. While you sit and order (from an extensive menu of meats, seafood, and vegetable dishes that are delicious in their own right), he'll prepare a packet of ingredients and ship them off to the kitchen, where they'll be added to the food in preparation. Surprisingly, dishes turn out tasty, without the anticipated medicinal aftertaste.

The herbalist is in-house every day but Sunday. It's always good to call ahead, though, as he's the main attraction. When you leave, present him with a small *ang pau*—a gift of cash in a red envelope—maybe S$5 (US$3.20/£1.65) or S$7 (US$4.50/£2.30). Red envelopes are available in any card or gift shop.

At the Metropole Hotel, 3rd Floor, 41 Seah St. (near Raffles Hotel). ⓒ 65/6337-0491. Reservations recommended for lunch, necessary for dinner. Small dishes S$12–S$25 (US$7.70–US$16/£3.95–£8.25). AE, DC, MC, V. Daily 11:30am–2:30pm and 6:30–10:30pm.

Pierside Kitchen & Bar ✦ SEAFOOD   A light and healthy menu centers on seafood prepared with fresh flavors in a wide variety of international recipes, like the house-specialty cumin-spiced crab cakes with marinated cucumber and chili, or the grilled hazelnut-crusted king prawns in lobster and lemongrass sauce. Raw oysters are served with a tangy lime-and-chili sauce that is out of this world. The place itself is airy, sparsely decorated with light wood and white walls. Nothing can compete with the view, really—the panoramic vista of the Esplanade Theatres and the marina is lovely. After sundown, the alfresco dining area cools off with breezes from the water, and the stars make for some romantic dining. Relax, enjoy the scenery, and order dessert from a gorgeous selection of chocoholic sugar-coma treats.

Unit 01-01, One Fullerton, 1 Fullerton Rd. ⓒ 65/6438-0400. Reservations recommended. Main courses S$21–S$55 (US$13–US$35/£6.95–£18). AE, DC, MC, V. Mon–Thurs 11:30am–2:30pm and 7–10:30pm; Fri–Sat 7–11pm.

INEXPENSIVE

Magic Wok ⓥ*alue* THAI   Here's an excellent value-for-money restaurant in town. The decor doesn't do much, it's usually crowded, and the staff doesn't pamper, but the food is reliably good and cheap. Thai favorites include a spicy tom yam seafood soup that doesn't skimp on the seafood, a mild green curry with chicken, and sweet pineapple rice. If you come too late, the yummy fried chicken chunks wrapped in pandan leaf will be sold out. If you're adventurous, the fried baby squid look like cute, tiny octopi and are crunchy and sweet. During busy times, you'll have to queue, but it moves fast. Other outlets are located at #04-22/24 Far East Plaza on Scotts Road (ⓒ **65/6738-3708**) and #02-05 Marina Liesureplex (ⓒ **65/6837-0826**).

#01–20 Capitol Building, Stamford Rd. ✆ **65/6338-1882.** Reservations not accepted. Small dishes S$4–S$18 (US$2.60–US$12/£1.30–£5.95). MC, V. Daily 11am–10pm.

Our Village ✦ NORTHERN INDIAN   With its antique white walls stuccoed in exotic patterns and glistening with tiny silver mirrors, you'll feel like you're in an Indian fairyland here. Even the ceiling twinkles with silver stars, and hanging lanterns provide a subtle glow for the heavenly atmosphere—it's the perfect setting for a delicate dinner. Every dish is made fresh from hand-selected imported ingredients, some of them from secret sources. In fact, the staff is so protective of its recipes, you'd almost think their secret ingredient was opium—and you'll be floating so high after tasting the food that it might as well be. There are vegetarian selections as well as meats (no beef or pork), prepared in luscious gravies or in the tandoor oven. The dishes are light and healthy, with all-natural ingredients and not too much salt.

46 Boat Quay (take elevator to 5th floor). ✆ **65/6538-3058.** Reservations recommended on weekends. Small dishes S$9–S$20 (US$5.80–US$13/£2.95–£6.60). AE, MC, V. Mon–Fri 11:30am–1:30pm and 6–10:30pm; Sat–Sun 6–10:30pm.

Rendezvous MALAY/INDONESIAN   I was sad when, after a few months away from Singapore, I couldn't find Rendezvous at its previous location in Raffles City Shopping Center, only to learn it had shifted to a nicer space at the new (coincidentally named?) Rendezvous Hotel. Line up to select from a large number of Malay dishes, cafeteria style, like sambal squid in a spicy sauce of chili-and-shrimp paste. The staff will bring your order to your table. The coffee-shop setting is as far from glamorous as the last Rendezvous, but black-and-white photos on the wall trace the restaurant's history back to its opening in the early 1950s. It's a great place to experiment with a new cuisine.

#02-02 Hotel Rendezvous, 9 Bras Basah Rd. ✆ **65/6339-7508.** Reservations not necessary. Meat dishes sold per piece S$3–S$5 (US$1.90–US$3.20/£1–£1.65). AE, DC, MC, V. Daily 11am–9pm.

CHINATOWN
MODERATE
Da Paolo e Judie ✦✦✦ ITALIAN   This shophouse restaurant, remodeled with contemporary elegance, has beautiful ambience, alfresco dining, and a wine bar. At press time, this restaurant was closed for renovations, so expect it to be reopened and ultra-swank by the time you arrive. The Italian fare features fresh seafood in classic and modern recipes, with main courses prepared to perfection. No doubt the entire city will be excited to sample the new menu in the new digs, so make your reservations early. For the quality of food and service, the prices can't be beat.

The owners have other branches that are equally satisfying: **Da Paolo il Ristorante** (80 Club St., also in Chinatown; ✆ **65/6224-7081**), **Da Paolo il Giardino** (501 Bukit Timah Rd., #01-05 Cluny Court, beside the Singapore Botanic Gardens; ✆ **65/6463-9628**), and **Da Paolo la Terrazza** (44 Jalan Merah Saga, #01-56, at Chip Bee Gardens in Holland Village; ✆ **65/6476-1332**).

81 Neil Rd. ✆ **65/6225-8306.** Reservations highly recommended for dinner. Main courses S$24–S$34 (US$15–US$22/£7.90–£11). AE, DC, MC, V. Mon–Sat 11:30am–2:30pm and 6:30–10:30pm.

INEXPENSIVE
Blue Ginger ✦ PERANAKAN   The standard belief is that Peranakan cooking is reserved for home-cooked meals, and therefore restaurants are not as plentiful—and where they do exist, are very informal. Not so at Blue Ginger, where traditional and

modern mix beautifully in a style so fitting for Singapore. Snuggled in a shophouse, the decor combines clean and neat lines of contemporary styling with paintings by local artists and touches of Peranakan flair like carved wooden screens. The cuisine is Peranakan from traditional recipes, making for some very authentic food—definitely something you can't get back home. A good appetizer is the *kueh pie tee:* bite-sized "top hats" filled with turnip, egg, and prawn with sweet chili sauce. A wonderful entree is the *ayam panggang* "Blue Ginger," tender grilled chicken with a mild coconut-milk sauce. One of the most popular dishes is the *ayam buah keluak,* a traditional chicken dish made with a hard black Indonesian nut with sweet meat inside. The favorite dessert here is *durian chendol,* red beans and *pandan* jelly in coconut milk with durian purée. Served with shaved ice on top, it smells strong.

97 Tanjong Pagar Rd. ✆ 65/6222-3928. Reservations recommended. Small dishes S$6.50–S$23 (US$4.20–US$15/£2.15–£7.60). AE, DC, MC, V. Daily 11:30am–2:30pm and 6–10pm.

Chen Fu Ji Fried Rice SINGAPOREAN   With bright fluorescent lighting, the fast-food ambience is nothing to write home about, but after you try the fried rice here, you'll never be able to eat it anywhere else again, ever. These people take loving care of each fluffy grain, frying the egg evenly throughout. The other ingredients are added abundantly, and there's no hint of oil. On the top is a crown of shredded crabmeat. If you've never been an aficionado, you'll be one now. Other dishes are served to accompany the fried rice, and the soups are also very good. There is an additional branch, the **Chen Fu Ji Noodle House,** at Suntec City Mall, 3 Temasek Blvd. #03-020 Sky Garden (✆ **65/6334-2966**).

#02-31 Riverside Point, 30 Merchant Rd. ✆ 65/6533-0166. Reservations not accepted. Small dishes S$10–S$20 (US$6.40–US$13/£3.30–£6.60). No credit cards. Daily noon–2:30pm and 6–9:45pm.

Soup Restaurant ✪ CHINESE   Tasty, traditional, exotic, and affordable. This eatery specializes in Samsui ginger chicken—moist, fragrant steamed chicken dipped in ginger sauce and wrapped in lettuce. It is both unique and delicious. The menu is limited, but simple dishes like stews of meats simmered in herbs and served in "beggars' bowls" or baked in clay pots are as authentic as they come. The quaint coffee-shop decor is also a treat. If you're game to try something new, I highly recommend this place.

More locations: 39 Seah St., across from Raffles Hotel (✆ **65/6333-9388**); #B1-44 Paragon, 290 Orchard Rd. (✆ **65/6333-6228**); DFS Scottswalk, 25 Scotts Rd. #02-01 (✆ **65/6333-8033**); and #B1-59 Suntec City Mall (✆ **65/6333-9886**).

25 Smith St. ✆ 65/6222-9923. Reservations not necessary. Small dishes S$6–S$24 (US$3.80–US$15/£2–£7.90). AE, DC, MC, V. Daily noon–2:30pm; Mon–Fri 6–10pm; Sat–Sun 5:30–10pm.

Teahouse at China Square CANTONESE   For those who dare, the Teahouse is a terrific place for dim sum served in traditional style. The coffee-shop atmosphere is as loud and chaotic as you'd imagine a Chinese eatery should be, but the dim sum is served in the authentic style, by staff who push carts around to each table. If you ask, they will tell you what is inside each dumpling and bun. Baskets of goodies are slammed on the table as soon as you can wink, so make sure you get only what you order. The dishes are mouthwatering. *Tip:* Arrive at the very beginning of mealtime so you can get the waitresses' attention and spend less time shouting over the munching hordes.

China Square Food Centre Level 3, 51 Telok Ayer St. ✆ 65/6533-0660. Reservations recommended. Small dishes S$2.20–S$6 (US$1.40–US$3.80/£0.75–£2). AE, DC, MC, V. Daily 11am–10:30pm.

LITTLE INDIA
INEXPENSIVE

Komala Vilas ⍟ SOUTHERN INDIAN/VEGETARIAN   Komala Vilas is famous with Singaporeans of every race. Don't expect the height of ambience—it's pure fast food, local style—but to sit here during a packed and noisy lunch hour is to see all walks of life come through the doors. Komala serves vegetarian dishes in southern Indian style, so there's nothing fancy about the food; it's just plain good. Order the *dosai*, a huge, thin pancake used to scoop up luscious and hearty gravies and curries. Even for carnivores, it's very satisfying. What's more, it's cheap: Two samosas, *dosai*, and an assortment of stew-style gravies *(dhal)* for two are only S$8 (US$4.70/£2.65) with tea. For a quick fast-food meal, this place is second to none.

76/78 Serangoon Rd. ✆ **65/6293-6980.** Reservations not accepted. Dosai S$2 (US$1.30/£0.65); lunch for 2 S$8 (US$5.10/£2.65). No credit cards. Daily 11:30am–3pm and 6:30–10:30pm.

Muthu's Curry Restaurant SOUTHERN INDIAN   Muthu's is a local institution that is synonymous with one local delicacy, fish-head curry, a giant fish head floating in a huge portion of delicious curry soup, its eye staring and teeth grinning. The cheek meat is the best part of the fish, but to be truly polite, let your friend eat the eye. The list of accompanying dishes is long and includes crab masala, chicken biryani, and mutton curry, with fish cutlet and fried chicken sold by the piece. We're not talking the height of dining elegance here, but Muthu's really has come a long way since its simple coffee-shop opening—its recent shift to newer, larger digs even means matching tables and chairs! I miss the old grotty ambience, but still it's a good place to try this dish. Go either at the start or toward the end of mealtime, so you don't get lost in the rush and can find staff with more time to help you. Another branch in town has opened at 3 Temasek Blvd., #B1-056, Suntec City Mall (✆ **65/6835-7707**).

138 Race Course Rd. ✆ **65/6293-2389.** Reservations not accepted. Small dishes S$3.50–S$6.50 (US$2.20–US$4.20/£1.15–£215); fish head curry from S$18 (US$12/£5.95). AE, DC, MC, V. Daily 10am–10pm.

ORCHARD ROAD AREA
EXPENSIVE

BLU ⍟⍟⍟ CONTEMPORARY   Commanding an awe-inspiring view of Orchard Road from its 24th-floor perch, BLU represents the best in stylish dining. A perfect spot for a get-together or a little quiet self-indulgence, the restaurant is appointed with modern glass sculptures by Danny Lane, Philippe Starck table lamps, fiber optics on the glass bar and floor, and Wedgwood table settings. With new Michelin-starred chef de cuisine Robin Zavou on board, expect mind-blowing signature dishes such as pan-fried foie gras with vanilla apples and black truffle, scallops with cauliflower mousse and spiced carrot sauce, fillet of beef with onion ice cream, and ginger parfait with green tea and peppermint jelly. The wine list is extensive, with over 200 sparkling, white, red, and dessert wines, including rare and vintage choices. Jazz performances are Monday through Thursday from 8:30 to 11:15pm and Friday and Saturday from 9pm to 12:30am.

At the Shangri-La Hotel, 22 Orange Grove Rd., 24th floor. ✆ **65/6213-4598.** Reservations recommended. Main courses S$40–S$60 (US$26–US$38/£13–£20). AE, DC, MC, V. Daily 7–10:30pm.

Harbour Grill & Oyster Bar ⍟⍟⍟ CONTINENTAL   Grilled seafood and U.S. prime rib are perfectly prepared and served with attentive style in this award-winning restaurant. The Continental cuisine is lighter than most, with recipes that focus on the natural freshness of their ingredients rather than on creams and fat. Caesar salad is made at your table, so you can request your preferred blend of ingredients, and the oyster bar serves juicy fresh oysters from around the world. For a main course, the prime rib is the best and most requested entree, but the rack of lamb is also worth considering—it melts in your mouth. Guest chefs from international culinary capitals are flown in for monthly specials. The place is small and cozy, with nautical-inspired murals and a finishing kitchen in the dining room.

At the Hilton Singapore, Level 3, 581 Orchard Rd. © **65/6730-3393**. Reservations recommended. Main courses S$42–S$50 (US$27–US$32/£14–£17). AE, DC, MC, V. Mon–Fri noon–2pm; Mon–Sat 7–10pm.

Li Bai ✦✦✦ CANTONESE   Chinese restaurants are typically unimaginative in the decor department—slapping up a landscape brush painting or two here and there is sometimes about as far as they go. Not at Li Bai, which is sleekly decorated in contemporary black and red lacquer, with comfortable black-leather seating. Guest chefs turn out a constantly evolving menu, refining their specialties, and jade-and-silver chopsticks and bone china add opulent touches to their flawless meals. Shark's fin soup and abalone creations are a requirement for any self-respecting Cantonese restaurant, and although Li Bai's preparation of these delicacies is tops, I recommend you bypass them—too much hype and expense. Go for the chef's special creations, which are always imaginative. Or try the duck smoked with jasmine tea leaves, a succulent dish. The crab fried rice is fabulous, with generous chunks of fresh meat, and the beef in mushroom and garlic brown sauce is some of the most tender meat you'll ever feast upon. The wine list is international, with many vintages to choose from.

At the Sheraton Towers, Lower Lobby Level, 39 Scotts Rd. © **65/6839-5623**. Reservations required. Small dishes S$16–S$48 (US$10–US$31/£5.30–£16) and up. AE, DC, MC, V. Daily 11:30am–2:30pm and 6:30–10:30pm.

Mezza9 ✦✦ FUSION   This is your best bet if your party can't agree on what to eat: Mezza9 offers an extensive menu that includes Chinese steamed treats, Japanese, Thai, Italian, fresh seafood, deli selections, and Continental grilled specialties. Start with juicy raw oysters on the half shell. If you want more raw seafood, the combination sashimi platter is also very fresh. Grilled meats include various cuts of beef, rack of lamb, and chicken dishes with a host of delicious sides to choose from. The enormous 450-seat restaurant has a warm atmosphere, with glowing wood and contemporary Zen accents, but service can be harried. Before you head in for dinner, grab a martini in the très chic martini bar.

At the Grand Hyatt, 10 Scotts Rd. © **65/6416-7189**. Reservations recommended. Main courses S$25–S$45 (US$16–US$29/£8.25–£15). AE, DC, MC, V. Daily noon–3pm and 6–11:30pm.

MODERATE
Chatterbox SINGAPOREAN   If you'd like to try the local favorites but don't want to deal with hawker food, then Chatterbox is the place for you. Its Hainanese chicken rice is highly acclaimed, though the famous chef behind the recipe left this past year. Other dishes—like *nasi lemak, laksa,* and carrot cake—are as close to the street as you can get. For a quick and tasty snack, order *tahu goreng,* deep-fried tofu in peanut chili sauce. This is also a good place to experiment with some of those really weird local drinks. *Chin chow* is the dark-brown grass-jelly drink; *chendol* is green jelly, red beans, palm sugar, and coconut milk; and *bandung* is pink rose syrup milk with jelly. For dessert, order the ever-favorite sago pudding, made from the hearts of the sago palm. This informal and lively coffee shop dishes out room service for the Mandarin Hotel and is open 24 hours a day.

At the Mandarin Hotel, 333 Orchard Rd. © **65/6737-4411**. Reservations recommended for lunch and dinner. Main courses S$15–S$39 (US$9.60–US$25/£4.95–£13). AE, DC, MC, V. Daily 24 hr.

Patara Fine Thai THAI   Patara may say fine dining in its name, but the food here is home cooking: not too haute, not too traditional. Seafood and vegetables are the stars here. Deep-fried *garoupa* (grouper) is served in a sweet sauce with chili that can be added sparingly upon request. Curries are popular, too. The roast-duck curry in red-curry paste with tomatoes, rambutans, and pineapple is juicy and hot. For something really different, Patara's own invention, the Thai taco, isn't exactly traditional, but it *is* good, filled with chicken, shrimp, and sprouts. Its green curry, one of my favorites, is perhaps the best in town. The Thai-style iced tea (which isn't on the menu, so you'll have to ask for it) is fragrant and flowery. A small selection of wines is also available. Patara has another outlet at Swissôtel The Stamford, Level 3, Stamford Road (☏ **65/6339-1488**).

#03-14 Tanglin Mall, 163 Tanglin Rd. ☏ **65/6737-0818.** Reservations recommended for lunch, required for dinner. Small dishes S$12–S$49 (US$7.70–US$31/£3.95–£16). AE, DC, MC, V. Daily noon–2:30pm and 6–10:30pm.

Tandoor ✮✮ NORTHERN INDIAN   Live music takes center stage in this small restaurant, which is adorned with carpets, artwork, and wood floors and furnishings. Entrees prepared in the tandoor oven come out flavorful and not too salty. The tandoori lobster is rich, but the chef's specialty is crab *lababdar:* crabmeat, onions, and tomato sautéed in a coconut gravy. Fresh cottage cheese is made in-house for *saag panir,* a favorite here. Chefs keep a close eye on the spices to ensure they enhance the flavor rather than drowning it out—more times than not, customers ask them to add more spices. A final course of creamy masala tea will perk you up and aid digestion.

At the Holiday Inn Parkview, 11 Cavenagh Rd. ☏ **65/6730-0153.** Reservations recommended. Small dishes S$20–S$40 (US$13–US$26/£6.60–£13). AE, DC, MC, V. Daily noon–2:30pm and 7–10:30pm.

INEXPENSIVE

Ah Hoi's Kitchen SINGAPOREAN   I like Ah Hoi's for its casual charm and its selection of authentic local cuisine. The menu is extensive, specializing in local favorites like fried black-pepper *kuay teow* (noodles), *sambal kang kong* (a spinach-like vegetable fried with chili), and fabulous grilled seafood. The alfresco poolside pavilion location gives it a real "vacation in the tropics" relaxed feel—think of a hawker center without the dingy florescent bulbs, greasy tables, and sludgy floor. Also good here is the chili crab; if you can't make it out to the seafood places on the east coast of the island, it's the best alternative for tasting this local treat. Make sure you order the fresh lime juice—it's very cooling.

At the Traders Hotel, 1A Cuscaden Rd., 4th level. ☏ **65/6831-4373.** Reservations recommended. Small dishes S$12–S$24 (US$7.70–US$15/£3.95–£7.90). AE, DC, MC, V. Daily 11:30am–2:30pm and 6:30–10:30pm.

Genki Sushi *Value* JAPANESE   I ducked into Genki Sushi for lunch. I sat at the counter, where a tiny conveyor belt snaked along in front of me carrying colored plates full of glistening sushi, rolls, sashimi, and other treats. Just pick and eat—and pay per plate. So the goofy Japanese guy next to me got chatty. We discussed the conveyor-belt sushi-bar concept and how much we both loved it, then he poked some buttons on his electronic translator and showed me the screen. "This name in Japan." The translator spelled *revolution.* Makes sense, the "revolution" sushi bar, but now I'll never shake the image of Che Guevara sitting there plucking sushi off the belt.

#01-16 Forum The Shopping Mall, Orchard Rd. ☏ **65/6734-2513.** Reservations not accepted. Revolving plates S$1.90–S$6.50 (US$1.20–US$4.20/£0.65–£2.15). AE, DC, MC, V. Sun–Thurs 11:30am–9pm; Fri–Sat 11:30am-10pm.

The Rice Table ⚜ MALAY/INDONESIAN/DUTCH   Indonesian Dutch *rijsttafel,* meaning "rice table," is a service of many small dishes (up to almost 20) with rice. Traditionally, each dish would be brought to diners by beautiful ladies in pompous style. Here, busy waiters bring all the dishes out and place them in front of you—you can feast on favorite Indo-Malay wonders like beef *rendang,* chicken satay, *otak otak,* and *sotong assam* (squid) for a very reasonable price. It's an enormous amount of food and everything is terrific. Pay extra for your drinks and desserts.

There's an additional outlet at Cuppage Terrace at 43-45 Cuppage Rd. (© **65/6735-9117**) and a new one at Suntec City Mall, #03-028 Sky Garden (© **65/6333-0248**).

At the International Bldg., 360 Orchard Rd., #02-09/10. © **65/6835-3783**. Reservations not necessary. Lunch set menus S$15 (US$9.80/£5.05); dinner set menus S$23 (US$15/£7.65). AE, DC, MC, V. Tues–Sun noon–2:45pm and 6–9:45pm.

A LITTLE FARTHER OUT

Many travelers will choose to eat in town for convenience, and although there's plenty of great dining in the more central areas, there are some other really fantastic dining finds if you're willing to hop in a cab for 10 or 15 minutes. These places are worth the trip—for a chance to dine along the water at UDMC or to get superior seafood at Long Beach Seafood Restaurant. And don't worry about finding your way back: Most places always have cabs milling about. If not, restaurant staff will always help you call a taxi.

EXPENSIVE

Halia ⚜ CONTINENTAL/FUSION   Most notable for its location within the Singapore Botanic Gardens, Halia is where you really need to come for a daytime meal—perhaps a weekend breakfast buffet, relaxing lunch, or weekday high tea—if you want to enjoy the lush greenery of the surrounds. Cuisine is contemporary fare, with ginger permeating quite a few of the recipes—*halia* meaning "ginger" in Malay. The specialty of the house is the chunks of seafood stewed in chili and lemongrass, served over a bed of pappardelle pasta. To get here, ask the taxi driver to take you along Tyersall Avenue and look for the HALIA signboard at the Tyersall Gate near the Ginger Garden.

1 Cluny Rd., in the Singapore Botanic Gardens, Tyersall Gate. © **65/6476-6711**. Reservations recommended. Main courses S$26–S$43 (US$17–US$28/£8.60–£14); breakfast buffet S$18 (US$12/£5.95). AE, DC, MC, V. Daily noon–3pm and 6:30–11pm; breakfast Sat–Sun 8–10:45am; high tea Mon–Sat 3–5:30pm.

MODERATE

Long Beach Seafood Restaurant SEAFOOD   They really pack 'em in at this place. Tables are crammed together in what resembles a big indoor pavilion, complete with festive lights and the sounds of mighty feasting. This is one of the best places for fresh seafood of all kinds: fish like *garoupa* (grouper), sea bass, marble goby, and kingfish, plus other creatures of the sea from prawns to crayfish. The chili crab here is good, but the house specialty is really the pepper crab, chopped and deliciously smothered in a thick concoction of black pepper and soy. Huge chunks of crayfish are also tasty in the black-pepper sauce and can be served in variations like barbecue, sambal, steamed with garlic, or in a bean sauce. Don't forget to order buns so you can sop up the sauce. You can also get vegetable, chicken, beef, or venison dishes to complement, or choose from the menu of local favorites.

1018 East Coast Pkwy. © **65/6445-8833**. Reservations recommended. Seafood sold by weight according to seasonal prices. Most non-seafood dishes S$9–S$16 (US$5.80–US$10/£2.95–£5.30). AE, DC, MC, V. Daily 11am–3pm; Sun–Fri 5pm–12:15am; Sat 5pm–1:15am.

Original Sin ✿ MEDITERRANEAN/VEGETARIAN   This cozy place is a perennial favorite with Singapore's expatriate population. Located in Holland Village, Singapore's expat enclave, the restaurant is close to shopping, pubs, and numerous other dining choices that cater to this international group. This particular place serves up generous portions of baba ganoush, tzatziki, and hummus accompanied by olives, feta, and pita bread. And although the menu features standard Mediterranean fare like moussaka and risotto, people always seem to go for the pizzas, which are loaded with interesting Middle Eastern toppings.

The owners also run two other properties of equal quality and popularity in Chip Bee Gardens, Italian restaurants **Michelangelo's,** Block 44, Jalan Merah Saga #01-60 (✆ **65/6475-9069**); and **Sistina,** Block 44, Jalan Merah Saga #01-58 (✆ **65/6476-7782**). All of these restaurants have a casual, congenial bistro-style atmosphere inside and sidewalk dining outside.

Block 43 Jalan Merah Saga, #01-62, Chip Bee Gardens, Holland Village. ✆ **65/6475-5605**. Reservations recommended. Main courses S$24–S$28 (US$15–US$18/£7.90–£9.25). AE, DC, V, MC. Tues–Sun 11:30am–2:30pm and 6–10:30pm; Mon 6–10:30pm.

True Blue Cuisine ✿✿ PERANAKAN   Katong, the central neighborhood of the Peranakan (Straits Chinese) community, is also famous for excellent local cuisine. True Blue, housed in a restored pre-war shophouse in this historic neighborhood, shares a block with other Peranakan heritage sights, like Rumah Bebe, a shop for Peranakan fashions. Inside, the restaurant is decorated with cultural trappings that will make Singaporeans feel nostalgic and foreigners feel as if they've been welcomed into a private home. Home-cooked from family recipes (the owner's mother runs the kitchen), luscious favorites such as *ayam buah keluak* (chicken- and mincemeat-stuffed nuts in a sourish curry) are some of the best I've tasted. The friendly staff will help you navigate other classics on the menu, like *otak-otak,* pounded fish and chili grilled in banana leaves; and beef *rendang,* beef stewed in a thick, mildly spicy coconut gravy. Tell your taxi driver to take you to East Coast Road at the junction with Joo Chiat Road. You can follow the shop numbers a short walk until you find the place. Taxis back to town are plentiful.

117 East Coast Rd., 2nd floor. ✆ **65/6440-0449**. Reservations required. Small dishes S$12–S$24 (US$7.70–US$15/£3.95–£7.90). AE, DC, MC, V. Daily noon–2:30pm and 6–9:30pm.

UDMC Seafood Centre ✿✿ SEAFOOD   Eight seafood restaurants are lined side by side in 2 blocks, their fronts open to the view of the sea outside. UDMC is a fantastic way to eat Singapore-style seafood, in the open air, in restaurants that are more like grand stalls than anything else. Try the famous local chili crab and pepper crab here, along with all sorts of squid, fish, and scallop dishes. Noodles are also available, as are vegetable dishes and other meats. But the seafood is the thing to come for. Of the eight restaurants, there's no saying which is the best, as everyone seems to have his own opinions about this one or that one (I like **Jumbo** at the far eastern end of the row; call ✆ **65/6442-3435** for reservations, which are recommended for weekends). Have a nice stroll along the walkway and gaze out at the water while you decide which one to try.

Block 1202 East Coast Pkwy. No phone. Seafood dishes charged by weight, starting from around S$12 (US$7.70/£3.95). AE, DC, MC, V. Daily 5pm–midnight.

INEXPENSIVE

Samy's Curry Restaurant ✿ SOUTHERN INDIAN   There are many places in Singapore to get good southern Indian banana leaf, but none quite so unique as

Samy's out on Dempsey Road. Because it's part of the Singapore Civil Service Clubhouse, at lunchtime nonmembers must pay S50¢ (US30¢/£0.20) to get in the door. Not that there's much of a door, as Samy's is situated in a huge, high-ceilinged, open-air hall, with shutters thrown back and fans whirring above. Wash your hands at the back and have a seat, and soon someone will slap a banana-leaf place mat in front of you. A blob of white rice will be placed in the center, and then buckets of vegetables, chicken, mutton, fish, prawn, and you name it will be brought out, swimming in the richest and spiciest curries to ever pass your lips. Take a peek in each bucket, shake your head yes when you see one you like, and a scoop will be dumped on your banana leaf. Eat with your right hand or with a fork and spoon. When you're done, wipe the sweat from your brow, fold the banana leaf away from you, and place your tableware on top. Samy's serves no alcohol, but the fresh lime juice is nice and cooling.

Block 25 Dempsey Rd., Civil Service Club. **© 65/6472-2080.** Reservations not accepted. Sold by the scoop or piece, S80¢–S$3 (US50¢–US$1.90/£0.25–£1). V. Daily 11am–3pm and 6–10pm. No alcohol served.

HAWKER CENTERS

Hawker centers—large groupings of informal open-air food stalls—were Singapore's answer to fast and cheap food in the days before McDonald's. They're still the best way to sample every kind of Singaporean cuisine. The traditional hawker center is an outdoor venue, usually under cover with fans whirring above, and individual stalls each specializing in different dishes. In between rows of cooking stalls, tables and stools offer open seating for diners.

Each center has an array of food offerings, with most dishes costing between S$3.50 to S$5 (US$2.20–US$3.20/£1.15–£1.65). You'll find traditional dishes like *char kway teow,* flat rice noodles fried with seafood; **fishball noodle soup,** with balls made from pounded fish and rice flour; **claypot chicken rice,** chicken and mushrooms baked with rice and fragrant soy sauce; *bak kut teh,* pork ribs stewed with Chinese herbs; **Hainanese chicken rice,** soft chicken over rice prepared in rich chicken stock; *laksa,* seafood and rice noodles in a spicy coconut chili soup; *popiah,* turnip, egg, pork, prawn, and sweet chili sauce wrapped in a thin skin; *rojak,* fried dough, tofu, cucumber, pineapple, and whatever the chef has handy, mixed with a sauce made from peanuts and fermented shrimp paste; plus many, many more Chinese, Malay, and Indian specialties. You'll also find hot and cold drink stalls and usually a stall selling fresh fruits and fruit juices.

If you want to become a real Singapore foodie, buy a copy of *Makansutra,* by K. F. Seetoh (Makansutra Publishing), at any bookstore. Seetoh's the local guru of hawker foods and has sniffed out the tastiest, most authentic local delicacies you can imagine.

Within the city limits, most traditional-style hawker centers have been closed down, but you can still find a few. Singapore's two most famous, or notorious, hawker centers are **Newton** and the **Satay Club.** Newton, a 24-hour center near the Newton MRT stop, is a tour-bus darling; beware of gouging, especially when ordering seafood dishes, which are sold by the kilo. The Satay Club, at Clarke Quay, is a touristy version of a Singaporean institution. The original Satay Club was a simple gathering of stalls by the water where Esplanade–Theatres on the Bay is now located. This reincarnation of the Satay Club is certainly not as authentic, in atmosphere or in food quality, but generally hawkers here tend to be an honest lot.

For local-style hawker centers, in Chinatown you can find stalls at the **Maxwell Road Food Centre,** at the corner of Maxwell and South Bridge roads, or you can try **Lau Pa Sat,** at the corner of Raffles Way and Boon Tat Street. A new food attraction, a row of stalls along Smith Street called **Food Alley,** was conceived by the STB. Rumor has it, these guys are having a hard time making a living selling local food to the very touristy crowd that passes down this street in the evenings. In the Historic District, try the **small center next to Allson Hotel,** on Victoria Street, or **Makansutra,** next to the Esplanade–Theatres on the Bay. In Little India, **Zhujiao Centre** features more Indian and Muslim hawker fare, as opposed to the mainstay Chinese cuisine at most places.

When you eat at a hawker center, the first thing to do is claim a seat at a table (local trick: if you put a tissue packet down on the table in front of your seat, people will understand it's reserved). Remember the number on your table so that when you order from each stall, you can let them know where you're seated. They will deliver your food to the table, and you must pay upon delivery. Change will be provided. When you are finished, there's no need to clear your dishes; it will be taken care of for you.

The modern version of the hawker center is the **food court.** Similar to hawker centers, food courts are air-conditioned spaces inside shopping malls and public buildings. They also have individual stalls offering a variety of foods and tables with free seating. Generally, food courts offer a more "fast-food," less authentic version of local cuisine, but you also get greater variety—many food courts have stalls that sell Western burgers and fish and chips, Japanese *udon,* or Korean barbecue. Food courts also differ in that they're self-service. When you approach the stall, you take a tray, pay when you order, and then carry the food yourself to your own table. When you finish, you are not expected to clear your tray.

Food courts are everywhere within the city, most of them operated by popular chains like **Food Junction, Kopitiam,** and **Banquet.** You'll find them in shopping malls and public buildings, most likely on the top floor or in the basement. Your hotel's concierge will be able to point you to the nearest food court, no problem.

6 What to See & Do

The city's many old buildings and well-presented museum displays bring history to life. Chinese and Hindu temples and Muslim mosques welcome curious observers to discover their culture as they play out their daily activities, and the country's natural parks make the great outdoors easily accessible from even the most urban neighborhood. Singapore also has a multitude of planned attractions for visitors and locals alike. Theme parks devoted to cultural heritage, sporting fun, and even kitsch amusement pop up all over the island.

The places of worship listed in this section are open to the public and free of entrance charges. Expect temples to be open from sunup to sundown. Visiting hours are not specific to the hour, but, unless it's a holiday (when hours may be extended), you can expect these places to be open during daylight hours.

HISTORIC DISTRICT

Armenian Church ✪ The first permanent Christian church in Singapore, it was funded primarily by the Armenian community, which was at one time quite powerful. Today, few Singaporeans can trace their heritage back to this influential group of immigrants. The church was consecrated in 1836, and the last appointed priest serving the parish retired in 1936. Although regular Armenian services are no longer held, other religious organizations make use of the church from time to time. The cemetery

in the back is the burial site of many prominent Armenians, including Ashgen Agn.
Joachim, discoverer of the Vanda Miss Joachim, Singapore's national flower.

60 Hill St., across from the Grand Plaza Hotel. (℃ **65/6334-0141**. Free admission. 15-min. walk from City Hall MRT.

Asian Civilisations Museum ★★★ If you only have time for one museum, make
it this one. The fantastic and well-executed exhibit of Southeast Asian culture highlights
the history of the region and explores the Chinese, South Indian, and Islamic heritages
that helped to shape regional cultures here. Well-planned galleries showcase fine arts,
furniture, porcelain, jade, and other relics, with excellent descriptions. The Empress
Place Building that houses the museum stood as a symbol of British colonial authority as sea travelers entered the Singapore River. The stately building housed almost the
entire government bureaucracy around the year 1905 and was a government office until
the 1980s, housing the Registry of Births and Deaths and the Citizenship Registry.

Don't forget to stop at the **Museum Shop** (℃ **65/6336-9050**) to browse exquisite
ethnic crafts of the region. Also check out the museum's website to find out more
about its free lecture series.

1 Empress Place. (℃ **65/6332-7798**. www.acm.org.sg. Admission S$5 (US$3.20/£1.65) adults, S$2.50
(US$1.60/£0.85) children and seniors; free on Fri 7–9pm. Mon 1–7pm; Tues–Sun 9am–7pm (extended hours Fri until
9pm). Free guided tours in English Tues–Fri 11am and 2pm, w/an extra tour Sat–Sun at 3:30pm. 15-min. walk from
City Hall MRT.

Asian Civilisations Museum at Armenian Street This small branch of the
Asian Civilizations Museum (see above) is currently closed for a major renovation. At
press time, no official information had been released about the focus of future
exhibits, which are slated for launch in 2008. The quaint building was the former Tao
Nan School, which dates from 1910.

39 Armenian St. (℃ **65/6332-3015**. www.acm.org.sg. Closed until 2008. 15-min walk from City Hall MRT.

Cathedral of the Good Shepherd This cathedral was Singapore's first permanent
Catholic church. Built in the 1840s, it brought together many elements of a fractured
parish—Portuguese, French, and Spanish—to worship under one roof. Designed in a
Latin cross pattern, much of its architecture is reminiscent of St. Martin-in-the-Fields
and St. Paul's in Covent Garden.

4 Queen St. (at corner of Queen St. and Bras Basah Rd.). (℃ **65/6337-2036**. Free admission. Open to the public during the day. 5-min. walk from City Hall MRT.

CHIJMES (Convent of the Holy Infant Jesus) As you enter this bustling enclave
of retail shops, restaurants, and nightspots, it's difficult to imagine this was once a convent which, at its founding in 1854, consisted of a lone, simply constructed bungalow. After decades of building and add-ons, this collection of unique yet perfectly
blended structures—a school, a private residence, an orphanage, a stunning Gothic
chapel, and many others—were enclosed within walls, forming peaceful courtyards
and open spaces encompassing an entire city block. Legend has it the small door on
the corner of Bras Basah and Victoria streets welcomed hundreds of orphan babies,
girl children who just appeared on the stoop each morning, born either during inaus-
picious years or to poor families. In late 1983, the convent relocated to the suburbs,
and some of the block was leveled to make way for the MRT Headquarters. Thankfully, most of the block survived and the Singapore government, in planning the
renovation of this desirable piece of real estate, wisely kept the integrity of the architecture. For an evening out, the atmosphere at CHIJMES is exquisitely romantic.

Urban Singapore Attractions

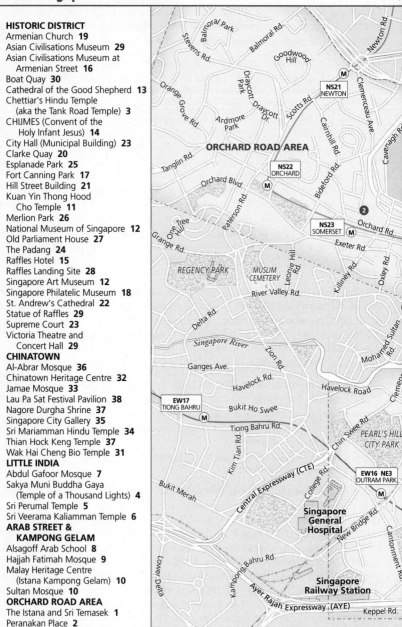

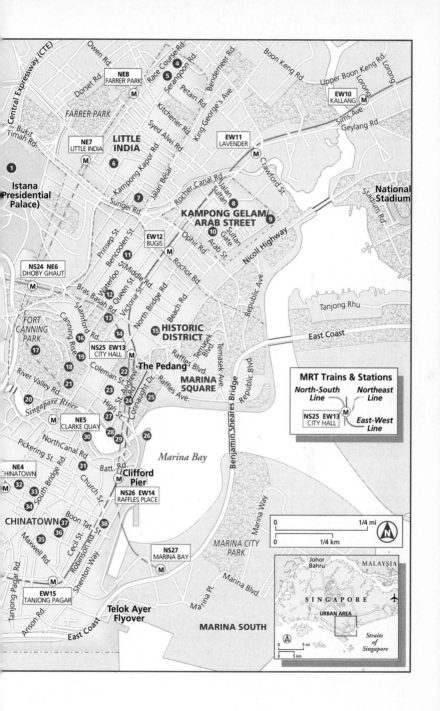

A note on the name: CHIJMES is pronounced "Chimes"; the "Chij," as noted, stands for Convent of the Holy Infant Jesus, and the "mes" was just added on so it could be pronounced "Chimes."

30 Victoria St. © 65/6336-1818. Free admission. 5-min. walk from City Hall MRT.

City Hall (Municipal Building)   During the Japanese occupation, City Hall was a major headquarters, and it was here in 1945 that Adm. Lord Louis Mountbatten accepted the Japanese surrender. In 1951, the Royal Proclamation from King George VI was read here, declaring that Singapore would henceforth be known as a city. Fourteen years later, Prime Minister Lee Kuan Yew announced to its citizens that Singapore would henceforth be called an independent republic.

City Hall, along with the Supreme Court, was judiciously sited to take full advantage of the prime location. Magnificent Corinthian columns march across the front of the symmetrically designed building, while inside, two courtyards lend an ambience of informality to otherwise officious surroundings. For all its magnificence and historical fame, however, its architect, F. D. Meadows, relied too heavily on European influence. The many windows afford no protection from the sun, and the entrance leaves pedestrians unsheltered from the elements. In defining the very nobility of the Singapore government, it appears the Singaporean climate wasn't taken into consideration.

3 St. Andrew's Rd., across from the Padang. Entrance is not permitted. 5-min. walk from City Hall MRT.

Fort Canning Park   When Stamford Raffles first navigated the Singapore River, he was already envisioning a port settlement and had designs to build his own home atop the hill that is today this park. His home, a simple wooden structure (at the site of the present-day lookout point), later became a residence for Singapore's Residents and Governors. In 1860, the house was torn down to make way for **Fort Canning,** which was built to quell British fears of invasion but instead quickly became the laughing-stock of the island. In 1907, the fort was demolished to make way for a reservoir. Today, the only reminders of the old fort are some of the walls and the Fort Gate, a deep stone structure. Behind its huge wooden door, you'll find a narrow staircase that leads to the roof of the structure.

Fort Canning was also the site of a **European cemetery.** To make improvements in the park, the graves were exhumed and the stones were placed within the walls surrounding the outdoor performance field that slopes from the Music and Drama Society building. A large Gothic monument was erected in memory of James Napier Brooke, infant son of William Napier, Singapore's first law agent, and his wife, Maria Frances, the widow of prolific architect George Coleman. Although no records exist, Coleman probably designed the cupolas as well as two small monuments over unknown graves. The Music and Drama Society building itself was constructed in 1938. Close by, in the wall, are the tombstones of Coleman and of Jose D'Almeida, a wealthy Portuguese merchant.

Inside the park, the **Battle Box** (© 65/6333-0510) is an old WWII bunker displaying wax dioramas and a multimedia show on the surrender of Singapore. It's open Tuesday through Sunday from 10am to 6pm; admission is S$8 (US$5/£2.75) for adults, S$5 (US$3.10/£1.70) for children.

51 Canning Rise. © 65/6332-1302. www.nparks.gov.sg. Free admission. Major entrances are from behind the Hill Street Building, Percival Rd. (Drama Centre), National Library Carpark, and Canning Walk (behind Park Mall). Dhoby Ghaut or City Hall MRT.

Kuan Yin Thong Hood Cho Temple   It's said that whatever you wish for within the walls of Kuan Yin Temple comes true, so get in line and have your wishes ready. It must work—there's a steady stream of people on auspicious days of the Chinese calendar. The procedure is simple: Wear shoes easily slipped off before entering the temple. Light several joss sticks. Pray to the local god, pray to the sky god, and then turn to the side and pray some more. Now pick up the container filled with inscriptions and shake it until one stick falls out. After that, head for the interpretation box office to get a piece of paper with verses in Mandarin and English to look up what your particular inscription means. (For a small fee, there are interpreters outside.) Now for the payback: If your wish comes true, be prepared to return to the temple and offer fruits and flowers to say thanks (oranges, pears, and apples are a thoughtful choice; jasmine petals are especially nice). Be careful what you wish for. Once you're back home and that job promotion comes through, your new manager might nix another vacation so soon. To be on the safe side, bring the goods with you when you make your wish.

Waterloo St., about 1½ blocks from Bras Basah Rd. Free admission. Open to the public during the day. 15-min. walk from Bugis MRT.

National Museum of Singapore ★★★   The once-little history museum, the former Singapore History Museum, closed its dusty halls in 2003 and has now reopened after a massive renovation. Today, this beautiful 120-year-old building has not only been restored, but has also been expanded to more than twice its original size. It features state-of-the-art multimedia exhibits designed to bring history to life and to make it accessible to all visitors. The History Gallery tells the story of Singapore from two points of view: from a historian's perspective and from the "man on the street." You decide which story you'd like to hear, then choose the corresponding audio headset that will guide you through the exhibit. The four Living Galleries show objects and elements of everyday Singaporean life: Food, Fashion, Film, and Photography. The museum conducts free guided tours in English Monday through Friday at 11am and 2pm, Saturday and Sunday at 11:30am and 3:30pm; the tour takes 1 to 1½ hours. The building itself is a gorgeous mix of colonial and contemporary architecture; a free tour that focuses just on the architecture is offered Friday through Sunday at 3:30pm.

93 Stamford Rd. (✆ 65/6332-3659. www.nationalmuseum.sg. Admission S$10 (US$6.40/£3.20) adults, S$5 (US$3.20/£1.60) children and seniors; free admission to the Living Galleries daily 6–9pm. History Gallery daily 10am–6pm; Living Galleries daily 10am–9pm. 5-min. walk from Dhoby Ghaut or City Hall MRT.

Old Parliament House   The Old Parliament House is probably Singapore's oldest surviving structure, even though it has been renovated so many times it no longer looks the way it was originally constructed. It was designed as a home for John Argyle Maxwell, a Scottish merchant, but he never moved in. In 1822, Raffles returned to Singapore and was furious to find a residence being built on ground he'd allocated for government use. The government took over the house for its court and other offices. In 1939, when the new Supreme Court was completed, the judiciary moved into Maxwell's House; then, in 1953, following a major renovation, the small structure was renamed Parliament House and was turned over to the legislature.

Today, the building has been transformed once again—reopened in 2004 as the Arts House at the Old Parliament, with lovingly restored spaces for visual and performance arts plus special cultural events. A couple highbrow eateries offer Thai and Western cuisine. Singapore's parliament now operates out of the new Parliament Building just next door.

1 Old Parliament Lane, at the south end of the Padang, next to the Supreme Court. ℂ **65/6332-6900.** www.thearts house.com.sg. Free admission; extra charge for tickets to events. 15-min. walk from City Hall MRT.

The Padang This large field—officially called Padang Besar but known as the Padang—has witnessed its share of historic events. It is bordered on one end by the Singapore Recreation Club and on the other end by the Singapore Cricket Club, and flanked by City Hall. The Padang is mainly used for public and sporting events— pleasant activities—but in the 1940s, it felt more forlorn footsteps when the invading Japanese forced the entire European community onto the field. There they waited while the occupation officers dickered over a suitable location for the "conquered." Presently, they ordered all British, Australian, and Allied troops as well as European prisoners on the 22km (14-mile) march to Changi.

An interesting side note: Frank Ward, designer of the Supreme Court, had big plans for the Padang and surrounding buildings. He would have demolished the Cricket Club, Parliament House, and the Victoria Theatre and Concert Hall to erect an enormous government block if World War II hadn't arrived, ruining his chances.

St. Andrew's Rd. and Connaught Dr. Free admission. 5-min walk from City Hall MRT.

Raffles Hotel 🦀🦀 Built in 1887 to accommodate the increasing upper-class trade, the Raffles Hotel was originally only a couple of bungalows with 10 rooms, but, oh, the view of the sea was perfection. The owners, Armenian brothers named Sarkies, already had a couple of prosperous hotels in Southeast Asia (the Eastern & Oriental in Penang and the Strand in Rangoon) and were well versed in the business. It wasn't long before they added a pair of wings and completed the main building—and reading rooms, verandas, dining rooms, a grand lobby, the bar and billiards room, a ballroom, and a string of shops. By 1899, electricity was turning the cooling fans and providing the pleasing glow of comfort.

As it made its madcap dash through the 1920s, the hotel was the place to see and be seen. Vacancies were unheard of. Hungry Singaporeans and guests from other hotels, eager for a glimpse of the fabulous dining room, were turned away for lack of reservations. The crowded ballroom was jumping every night of the week. During this time, Raffles's guest book included famous authors like Somerset Maugham, Rudyard Kipling, Joseph Conrad, and Noël Coward. These were indeed the glory years, but the lovely glimmer from the chandeliers soon faded with the stark arrival of the Great Depression. Raffles managed to limp through that dark time—and, darker still, through the Japanese occupation—and later pull back from the brink of bankruptcy to undergo modernization in the '50s. But fresher, brighter, more opulent hotels were taking root on Orchard Road, pushing the "grand old lady" to the back seat.

In the 1980s, Raffles was brought back to its former glory. History-minded renovators selected 1915 as a benchmark and, with a few changes here and there, faithfully restored the hotel to that era's magnificence and splendor. Today, the hotel draws thousands of visitors daily to its open lobby, its theater playhouse, the Raffles Hotel Museum, and 65 exclusive boutiques. Its 15 restaurants and bars—especially the Tiffin Room, Raffles Grill, and Doc Cheng's, all reviewed earlier in this chapter—are a wonder, as is its famous Bar and Billiards Room and Long Bar.

1 Beach Rd. ℂ **65/6337-1886.** Free admission. City Hall MRT.

Raffles Landing Site The polymarble statue at this site was unveiled in 1972. It was made from plaster casts of the original 1887 figure located in front of the Victoria

Theatre and Concert Hall (see below), and it stands on what is believed to be the site where Sir Stamford Raffles landed on January 29, 1819.

North Boat Quay. Free admission. 15-min. walk from City Hall MRT.

St. Andrew's Cathedral

Designed by George Coleman and erected on a site selected by Sir Stamford Raffles himself, St. Andrew's was the colonial's Anglican Church. Completed toward the end of the 1830s, its tower and spire were added several years later to accord the edifice more stature. By 1852, because of massive damage sustained from lightning strikes, the cathedral was deemed unsafe and was torn down. The cathedral that now stands on the site was completed in 1860. Of English Gothic Revival design, the cathedral is one of the few standing churches of this style in the region.

11 St. Andrew's Rd., across from the Padang. ℂ 65/6337-6104. Free admission. Open during daylight hours. City Hall MRT.

Singapore Art Museum ⭐

The Singapore Art Museum (SAM) officially opened in 1996 to house an impressive collection of over 6,500 pieces of art and sculpture, most of it by Singaporean and Malay artists. Limited space requires the curators to display only a small number at a time, but these are incorporated in interesting exhibits to illustrate particular artistic styles, social themes, or historical concepts. A large collection of Southeast Asian pieces rotates regularly, as do visiting international exhibits. Besides the main halls, the museum offers a gift shop with fine souvenir ideas, a cafe, a conservation laboratory, an auditorium, and the E-mage Gallery, where multimedia presentations include not only the museum's own acquisitions but also works from public and private collections in the region. Once a Catholic boys' school established in 1852, SAM has retained some visible reminders of its former occupants: Above the front door of the main building, you can still see inscribed "St. Joseph's Institution," and a bronze-toned, cast-iron statue of St. John Baptist de la Salle with two children stands in its original place.

71 Bras Basah Rd. ℂ 65/6332-3222. www.singart.com. Admission S$5 (US$3.10/£1.70) adults, S$2.50 (US$1.60/£0.85) children and seniors; free Fri 6–9pm. Sat–Thurs 10am–7pm; Fri 10am–9pm. Free guided tours in English Mon–Fri 11am and 2pm, Sat–Sun 3:30pm. 5-min. walk from City Hall MRT.

Singapore Philatelic Museum

This building, constructed in 1895 to house the Methodist Book Room, recently underwent a nearly US$4-million restoration and reopened as the Philatelic Museum in 1995. Exhibits include a fine collection of old stamps issued to commemorate historically important events, first-day covers, antique printing plates, postal-service memorabilia, and private collections. Visitors can trace the development of a stamp from idea to the finished sheet, and can even design their own. Free guided tours are available upon request.

23B Coleman St. ℂ 65/6337-3888. www.spm.org.sg. Admission S$5 (US$3.20/£1.65) adults, S$4 (US$2.50/£1.30) children and seniors. Mon 1–7pm; Tues–Sun 9am–7pm. 10-min walk from Clarke Quay MRT.

Statue of Raffles

This sculpture of Sir Stamford Raffles was erected on the Padang in 1887 and moved to its present position after getting in the way of one too many cricket matches. During the Japanese occupation, the statue was placed in the Singapore History Museum (then the Raffles Museum) and was replaced here in 1945. The local joke is that Raffles's arm is outstretched to the Bank of China building, and his pockets are empty. (*Translation:* In terms of wealth in Singapore, it's Chinese one, Brits nil.)

Behind the Victoria Theatre and Concert Hall, 9 Empress Place. Free admission. 15-min. walk from City Hall MRT.

Supreme Court   The Supreme Court stands on the site of the old Hotel de L'Europe, a rival of Raffles Hotel until it went bankrupt in the 1930s. The court's structure, a classical style favored for official buildings the world over, was completed in 1939. With its spare adornment and architectural simplicity, the edifice has a no-nonsense, utilitarian attitude, and the sculptures across the front, executed by the Italian sculptor Cavaliere Rodolpho Nolli, echo what transpires within. Justice is the most breathtaking, standing 2.7m (9 ft.) high and weighing almost 4 tons. Kneeling on either side of her are representations of Supplication and Thankfulness. To the far left are Deceit and Violence. To the far right, a bull represents Prosperity; two children hold wheat, to depict Abundance.

Two and a half million bricks were used in building this structure, but take a moment to note the stonework: It's fake! Really a gypsum type of plaster, it was applied by Chinese plasterers who molded it to give the appearance of granite. A dome, a copy of the one at St. Paul's Cathedral in London, covers an interior courtyard, which is surrounded by the four major portions of the Supreme Court building.

Visitors can go inside and take a peek at the Supreme Court Gallery, a historical exhibit of the courts system. You're also welcome to attend court hearings, provided appropriate dress and etiquette codes are observed.

1 St. Andrew's Rd., across from the Padang. (C) **65/6336-0644**. Free admission. Mon–Fri 8:30am–5pm, Sat 8:30am–1pm. 10-min. walk from City Hall MRT.

Victoria Theatre and Concert Hall   Designed by colonial engineer John Bennett in a Victorian Revival style that was fashionable in Britain at the time, the theater portion was built in 1862 as the Town Hall. Victoria Memorial Hall was erected in 1905 as a memorial to Queen Victoria, retaining the same style of the old building. The clock tower was added a year later. In 1909, with its name changed to Victoria Theatre, the hall opened with an amateur production of the *Pirates of Penzance*. Another notable performance occurred when Noël Coward passed through Singapore and stepped in at the last moment to help out a traveling English theatrical company that had lost a leading man. The building looks much the same as it did then, though the interiors have been modernized. It was completely renovated in 1979, conserving all the original details, and was renamed Victoria Concert Hall. It housed the Singapore Symphony Orchestra until the opening of Esplanade–Theatres on the Bay, when it shifted to the larger digs.

1 St. Andrew's Rd., across from the Padang. (C) **65/6336-0644**. Free admission. Mon–Fri 8:30am–5pm, Sat 8:30am–1pm. 10-min. walk from City Hall MRT.

ALONG THE RIVER

The Singapore River had always been the heart of life in Singapore even before Raffles landed, but for many years during the 20th century, life here was dead—quite literally. Rapid urban development that began in the 1950s turned the river into a giant sewer, killing all plant and animal life in it. In the mid-1980s, though, the government began a large and very successful cleanup project, and shortly thereafter, the buildings at Boat Quay and Clarke Quay were restored. Now the areas on both banks of the river offer entertainment, food, and pubs day and night.

Boat Quay ⊛   Known as "the belly of the carp" by the local Chinese because of its shape, this area was once notorious for its opium dens and coolie shops. Nowadays, thriving restaurants boast every cuisine imaginable, and the rocking nightlife offers a variety of sounds—jazz, rock, blues, Indian, and Caribe—that are lively enough to get any couch potato tapping his feet. Remember to pronounce *quay* as "key" if you don't want people to look at you funny.

On the south bank of the Singapore River, between Cavenagh Bridge and Elgin Bridge. Free admission. 5-min. walk from Clarke Quay MRT.

Chettiar's Hindu Temple (Tank Road Temple)   One of the richest and grandest
of its kind in Southeast Asia, the Tank Road Temple is most famous for a *thoonganai maadam,* a statue of an elephant's backside in a seated position. It's said that there are only four others of the kind, located in four temples in India. The original temple was completed in 1860, restored in 1962, and practically rebuilt in 1984. Used daily for worship, the temple is also the culmination point of Thaipusam, a celebration of thanks, and the Festival of Navarathiri.

15 Tank Rd., near intersection of Clemenceau Ave. and River Valley Rd. © 65/6737-9393. Free admission. 20-min. walk from Clarke Quay MRT.

Clarke Quay   The largest of the waterfront developments, Clarke Quay was named
for the second governor of Singapore, Sir Andrew Clarke. In the 1880s, a pineapple cannery, iron foundry, and numerous warehouses made this area bustle. Today, with 60 restored warehouses hosting restaurants and a shopping section known as Clarke Quay Factory Stores, the Quay still hops. **River House,** formerly the home of a *towkay* (company president), occupies the oldest building. In the evenings, you can find the **Satay Club** here, a spot where satay sellers gather to sell the juicy little Malay meat kabobs dipped in yummy peanut chili sauce. On Sunday, get up early, forgo the comics section, and take in the **flea market,** which opens at 9am and lasts all day. You'll find lots of bargains on unusual finds.

Also here, **G-Max Reverse Bungy** (3E River Valley Rd., © 65/6338-1146; www. gmax.co.nz) will strap you and two buddies into a cage and fling you around at the end of giant bungee cords for only S$35 (US$22/£12) each. You'll go up to 60m (197 ft.) high at 200kmph (124 mph). Woo! Stop by Monday through Friday from 3pm to 1am, Saturday and Sunday from noon till late.

River Valley Rd., west of Coleman Bridge. © 65/6337-3292. www.clarkequay.com.sg. Free admission. Clarke Quay MRT.

Esplanade Park   Esplanade Park and Queen Elizabeth Walk, two of the most
famous parks in Singapore, were established in 1943 on land reclaimed from the sea. Several memorials are located here. The first is a fountain built in 1857 to honor **Tan Kim Seng,** who gave a great sum of money toward the building of a waterworks. Another monument, the **Cenotaph,** commemorates the 124 Singaporeans who died in World War I; it was dedicated by the Prince of Wales. On the reverse side, the names of those who died in World War II have been inscribed. The third prominent memorial is dedicated to **Major General Lim Bo Seng,** a member of the Singaporean underground resistance in World War II who was captured and killed by the Japanese. His memorial was unveiled in 1954 on the 10th anniversary of his death. At the far end of the park, the Esplanade–Theatres on the Bay opened in 2002. Fashioned after the Sydney Opera House, the unique double-domed structure is known locally as the Durians, because their spiky domes resemble halves of durian shells (the building itself is actually smooth—the "spikes" are sun shields).

Connaught Dr., on the marina, running from the mouth of the Singapore River along the Padang to the Esplanade–Theatres on the Bay. Daily until midnight. Free admission. 10-min. walk from City Hall MRT.

Merlion Park   The Merlion is Singapore's half-lion, half-fish national symbol, the lion representing Singapore's roots as the "Lion City" and the fish representing the nation's close ties to the sea. Bet you think a magical and awe-inspiring beast like this has been around in tales for hundreds of years, right? No such luck. Rather, he was the creation of some scheming marketers at the Singapore Tourism Board in the early 1970s. Talk about the collision of ancient culture and the modern world. Despite the Merlion's commercial beginnings, he's been adopted as the national symbol and spouts continuously every day at the mouth of the Singapore River.

South bank, at the mouth of the Singapore River, adjacent to One Fullerton. Free admission. Daily 7am–10pm. 15-min walk from either City Hall or Raffles Place MRT.

CHINATOWN & TANJONG PAGAR

Al-Abrar Mosque   This mosque was originally erected as a thatched building in 1827 and was also called Masjid Chulia and Kuchu Palli, which in Tamil means "hut mosque." The building that stands today was constructed in the 1850s, and even though it faces Mecca, the complex conforms with the grid of the neighborhood's city streets. In the late 1980s, the mosque underwent major renovations that enlarged the mihrab and stripped away some of the ornamental qualities of the columns in the building. The one-story prayer hall was extended upward into a two-story gallery. Little touches like the timber window panels and fanlight windows have been carried over into the new renovations.

192 Telok Ayer St., near the corner of Amoy St., near Thian Hock Keng Temple. Free admission. 15-min. walk from either Raffles Place or Tanjong Pagar MRT.

Chinatown Heritage Centre 🎢🎢   This block of old shophouses in the center of the Chinatown heritage district has been converted into a display that tells the story of the Chinese immigrants who came to Singapore to find work in the early days of the colony. Walk through rooms filled with period antiques replicating coolie living quarters, shops, clan associations, and other places that were prominent in daily life. The display has detailed descriptions to explain each element of the immigrant experience.

48 Pagoda St. 🄲 **65/6325-2878**. www.chinatownheritage.com.sg. Admission S$8.80 (US$5.64/£2.65) adults, S$5.30 (US$3.40/£1.75) children. Daily 9am–8pm. English-language tour every hr. 5-min. walk from Chinatown MRT.

Jamae Mosque   Jamae Mosque was built by the Chulias, Tamil Muslims who were some of the earlier immigrants to Singapore, and who had a very influential hold over Indian Muslim life centered in the Chinatown area. It was the Chulias who built not only this mosque, but also Masjid Al-Abrar and the Nagore Durgha Shrine. Jamae Mosque dates from 1827 but wasn't completed until the early 1830s. The mosque stands today almost exactly as it did then.

18 South Bridge Rd., at corner of Mosque St. Free admission. 10-min. walk from Chinatown MRT.

Lau Pa Sat Festival Pavilion   Though it used to be well beloved, the locals think this place has become an atrocity. Once the happy little hawker center known as Telok Ayer Market, it began life as a wet market, selling fruits, vegetables, and other foodstuffs. Now it's part hawker center, part Western fast-food outlets, and all tourists. Lau Pa Sat is one of the few hawker centers that's open 24 hours, in case you need a coffee or snack before retiring.

18 Raffles Quay, the entire block flanked by Robinson Rd., Cross St., Shenton Way, and Boon Tat St. Free admission. Daily 24 hr. 10-min. walk from Raffles Place MRT.

Nagore Durgha Shrine   Although this is a Muslim place of worship, it is not a mosque but a shrine, built to commemorate a visit to the island by a Muslim holy man of the Chulia people (Muslim merchants and money lenders from India's Coromandel Coast), who was traveling around Southeast Asia spreading the word of Indian Islam. The most interesting visual feature is its facade: Two arched windows flank an arched doorway, with columns in between. Above these is a "miniature palace"—a massive replica of the facade of a palace, with tiny cutout windows and a small arched doorway in the middle. The cutouts in white plaster make it look like lace. From the corners of the facade, two 14-level minarets rise, with three little domed cutouts on each level and onion domes on top. Inside, the prayer halls and two shrines are painted and decorated in shockingly tacky colors.

140 Telok Ayer St., at corner of Boon Tat St. © 65/6324-0021. Free admission. 15-min. walk from either Raffles Place or Tanjong Pagar MRT.

Singapore City Gallery   This enormous exhibit is perhaps of real interest only to Singaporeans and civic planners, but if you're in the neighborhood, it's worth a pop inside to see the giant plan of the city in miniature. Very cool. If you have time, sift through the 48 permanent exhibits and 25 interactive displays that paint a historical picture of the development of urban Singapore.

URA Centre, 45 Maxwell Rd. © 65/6321-8321. www.ura.gov.sg. Free admission. Mon–Fri 9am–5pm; Sat 9am–1pm. 10-min. walk from Tanjong Pagar MRT.

Sri Mariamman Hindu Temple   As the oldest Hindu temple in Singapore, Sri Mariamman has been the central point of Hindu tradition and culture. In its early years, the temple housed new immigrants while they established themselves and also served as social center for the community. Today, the main celebration here is the Thimithi Festival in October or November. The shrine is dedicated to the goddess Sri Mariamman, who is known for curing disease, but as is the case at all other Hindu temples, the entire pantheon of Hindu gods is present to be worshipped as well.

244 South Bridge Rd., at corner of Pagoda St. © 65/6223-4064. Free admission. 10-min. walk from Chinatown MRT.

Thian Hock Keng Temple ★★★   Thian Hock Keng, the "Temple of Heavenly Bliss," is one of the oldest Chinese temples in Singapore. Before land reclamation, when the shoreline came right up to Telok Ayer Road, the first Chinese sailors landed here and immediately built a shrine, a small wood-and-thatch structure, to pray to the goddess Ma Po Cho for allowing their voyage to be safely completed. For each subsequent boatload of Chinese sailors, the shrine was always the first stop upon landing. Ma Po Cho, the Mother of the Heavenly Sages, was the patron goddess of sailors, and every Chinese junk of the day had an altar dedicated to her. The temple that stands today was built in 1841 over the shrine, with funds from the Hokkien community. All of the building materials were imported from China, except for the gates, which came from Glasgow, Scotland, and the tiles on the facade, which are from Holland.

158 Telok Ayer St., ½ block beyond Nagore Durgha Shrine. © 65/6423-4616. Free admission. 15-min. walk from Tanjong Pagar MRT.

Wak Hai Cheng Bio Temple ★★   Like most of Singapore's Chinese temples, Wak Hai Cheng Bio had its start as a simple wood-and-thatch shrine where sailors, when they got off their ships, would go to express their gratitude for sailing safely to their destination. Before the major land-reclamation projects shifted the shoreline outward, the temple was close to the water's edge, so it was named "Temple of the Calm Sea

Built by the Guangzhou People." It's a Teochew temple, located in a part of China-town populated mostly by the Teochews. The temple itself is quite a visual treat, with ceramic figurines and pagodas adorning the roof, and every nook and cranny of the structure adorned with tiny three-dimensional reliefs that depict scenes from Chinese operas. The spiral joss hanging in the courtyard adds an additional picturesque effect.

30-B Phillip St., at corner of Church St. Free admission. 5-min. walk from Raffles Place MRT.

LITTLE INDIA

Little India did not develop as a community planned by the colonial authorities like Kampong Gelam or Chinatown, but came into being because immigrants to India were drawn to business developments here. In the late 1920s, the government estab-lished a brick kiln and lime pits that attracted Indian workers, and the abundance of grass and water made the area attractive to Indian cattle traders. **Desire Paths** (65 Kerbau Rd.; ℭ **65/6392-1772**) leases headsets with an audio tour of Little India, guiding you through the streets and giving you all kinds of insight into this part of town. Headsets are available Tuesday through Saturday from 10am to 4pm for S$18 (US$12/£5.95) each.

A word of advice: If you visit Little India on a Sunday, be prepared for a mob scene the likes of Calcutta. Sunday is the only day off for Singapore's many immigrant Indian and Bangladeshi laborers, so Serangoon Road gets a little difficult to navigate.

Abdul Gafoor Mosque   This charming little mosque is resplendent, thanks to a loving restoration completed in 2003. Nestled behind a row of shophouses, it can't really be seen until you arrive at the gate. Inside the compound, the bright yellow-and-green facade and minarets reflect an Indian Muslim architectural preference, most likely imported with the mosque's builder, Sheik Abdul Gafoor. The original mosque on this site, called Al-Abrar Mosque, was constructed of wood in 1859, and is com-memorated on a granite plaque within the compound above what could have been either an entrance gate or part of the mosque itself. The newer mosque on the site was built in 1907 and includes some unusual features, including ornate European-style columns and the sunburst above the main entrance. This "sundial" has 25 rays in Ara-bic calligraphy relief, said to represent the 25 prophets in the Koran.

Note: Inside the courtyard, an information office provides robes for those in shorts and sleeveless tops. As in every mosque, the main prayer hall is off-limits to non-Muslims.

41 Dunlop St., between Perak Rd. and Jalan Besar. ℭ **65/6295-4209**. Free admission. 15-min. walk from Little India MRT.

Sakya Muni Buddha Gaya (Temple of a Thousand Lights)   Thai elements influence this temple, from the *chedi* (stupa) roofline to the huge Thai-style Buddha image inside. Often this temple is brushed off as strange and tacky, but there are all sorts of surprises inside, making the place a veritable Buddha theme park. On the right side of the altar, statues of baby bodhisattvas receive toys and sweets from worshippers. Around the base of the altar, murals depict scenes from the life of Prince Siddhartha (Buddha) as he searches for enlightenment. Follow them around to the back of the hall, and you'll find a small doorway to a chamber under the altar. Another Buddha image reclines inside, this one shown at the end of his life, beneath the Yellow Seraka tree. On the left side of the main part of the hall is a replica of a footprint left by the Buddha in Ceylon. Next to that is a wheel of fortune. For US50¢ (£0.30), you get one spin.

336 Race Course Rd., 1 block past Perumal Rd. ℭ **65/6294-0714**. Free admission. 5-min. walk from Farrer Park MRT.

Sri Perumal Temple   Sri Perumal Temple is devoted to the worship of Vishnu. As part of the Hindu trinity, Vishnu is the sustainer, balancing out Brahma the creator and Shiva the destroyer. When the world is out of whack, he rushes to its aid, reincarnating himself to show mankind that there are always new directions for development. The temple was built in 1855 and was most recently renovated in 1992. During Thaipusam, the main festival celebrated here, male devotees who have made vows over the year carry *kavadi*—huge steel racks decorated with flowers and fruits and held onto their bodies by skewers and hooks—to show their thanks and devotion, while women carry milk pots in a parade from Sri Perumal Temple to Chettiar's Temple on Tank Road.

397 Serangoon Rd., ½ block past Perumal Rd. Free admission. Best times to visit are daily 7–11am or 5–7:30pm. 5-min. walk from Farrer Park MRT.

Sri Veerama Kaliamman Temple 👁👁   This Hindu temple is used primarily for the worship of Shiva's wife Kali, who destroys ignorance, maintains world order, and blesses those who strive for knowledge of God. The box on the walkway to the front entrance is for smashing coconuts, a symbolic smashing of the ego, asking God to show "the humble way." The coconuts have two small "eyes" at one end so they can "see" the personal obstacles to humility they are being asked to smash. Inside the temple in the main hall are three altars, the center one for Kali (depicted with 16 arms and wearing a necklace of human skulls) and the altars on either side for her two sons—Ganesh, the elephant god, and Murugan, the four-headed child god. To the right is an altar with nine statues representing the nine planets. Circle the altar and pray to your planet for help with a specific trouble.

On Serangoon Rd. at Veerasamy Rd. Free admission. Daily 8am–noon and 5:30–8:30pm. 10-min. walk from Little India MRT.

ARAB STREET & KAMPONG GELAM

Hajjah Fatimah Mosque 👁👁   Hajjah Fatimah was a wealthy businesswoman from Malacca and something of a local socialite. She originally built a home on this site, but after it was robbed a couple of times and later set fire to, she decided to build a mosque here and moved to another home. Inside the high walls of the compound are the prayer hall, an ablution area, gardens and mausoleums, and a few other buildings. You can walk around the main prayer halls to the garden cemeteries, where flat square headstones mark the graves of women and round ones mark the graves of men. Hajjah Fatimah is buried in a private room to the side of the main prayer hall, along with her daughter and son-in-law.

4001 Beach Rd., past Jalan Sultan. ✆ 65/6297-2774. Free admission. 20-min. walk from Bugis MRT.

Malay Heritage Centre (Istana Kampong Gelam) 👁👁   When the Malay Heritage Centre opened its doors in 2004, it became the first museum dedicated to the history, culture, and arts of this oftentimes marginalized ethnic group. The center has lovingly displayed exhibits that offer a glimpse into Singapore's early Malay settlements, the sultan's royal family, Malay arts, and 20th-century Malay life.

There's a bit of irony here. The museum is housed in the Istana Kampong Gelam, the former royal palace that housed the descendents of the original sultan that oversaw Singapore. In 1819, Sultan Hussein signed away his rights over the island in exchange for the land at Kampong Gelam, plus an annual stipend for his family. After the sultan's death, the family fortunes began to dwindle and disputes broke out among his descendants. In the late 1890s, they went to court, where it was decided that because no one in the family had the rights as the successor to the sultanate, the land should be reverted to the state. The family was allowed to remain in the house, but because they didn't own the property, they lost the authority to improve the buildings. Over the years, the compound fell into a very sad state of dilapidation. Eventually, Sultan Hussein's family was given the boot by the government to make way for this museum heralding the value of the Malay, and the sultan's, cultural contribution to Singapore. Hmm.

The house to the left before the main gate of the Istana compound is called **Gedong Kuning,** or Yellow Mansion. It was the home of Tenkgu Mahmoud, the heir to Kampong Gelam. When he died, it was purchased by local Javanese businessman Haji Yusof, the belt merchant. Today it houses a Malay restaurant, **Tepak Sireh** (© **65/ 6393-4373**), open daily from 11:30am to 2:30pm and 6:30 to 9:30pm.

Every Wednesday at 3:30pm and Sunday at 11:30am, there's a cultural show with live music, costumes, and dancing.

85 Sultan Gate. © **65/6391-0450.** Admission S$3 (US$1.90/£1) adults, S$2 (US$1.30/£0.65) children. Culture show S$10 (US$6.40/£3.30) adults, S$5 (US$3.20/£1.65) children. Mon 1–6pm, Tues–Sun 10am–6pm. 15-min. walk from Bugis MRT.

Sultan Mosque ⟨⟩   Though there are more than 80 mosques on the island of Singapore, Sultan Mosque is the real center of the Muslim community. The mosque that stands today is the second Sultan Mosque to be built on this site. The first was built in 1826, partially funded by the East India Company as part of its agreement to leave Kampong Gelam to Sultan Hussein and his family in return for sovereign rights to Singapore. The present mosque was built in 1928 and was funded by donations from the Muslim community. The Saracenic flavor of the onion domes, topped with crescent moons and stars, are complemented by Mogul cupolas. Funny thing, though: The mosque was designed by an Irish guy named Denis Santry, who was working for the architectural firm Swan and McLaren.

Sultan Mosque, like all the others, does not permit shorts, miniskirts, low necklines, or other revealing clothing to be worn inside. However, it does realize that non-Muslim travelers like to be comfortable as they tour around, and so provides cloaks free of charge. They hang just to the right as you walk up the stairs.

3 Muscat St. © **65/6293-4405.** Free admission. Daily 9am–1pm and 2–4pm. No visits allowed during mass congregation Fri 11:30am–2:30pm. 15-min. walk from Bugis MRT.

ORCHARD ROAD AREA

The Istana and Sri Temasek   This building serves as the official residence of the president of the Republic of Singapore. Used mainly for state and ceremonial occasions, the grounds are open to every citizen on selected public holidays, though they're not generally open for visits. The house's domain includes several other homes of senior colonial civil servants.

Orchard Rd., between Claymore and Scotts roads. Free admission. 5-min. walk from Dhoby Ghaut MRT.

Peranakan Place ⟨⟩   The houses along Emerald Hill have all been renovated, and the street has been closed to vehicular traffic. As you pass Emerald Hill, though, don't just blow it off as a tourist trap. Walk through the cafe area and out the back. All of the terrace houses have been redone magnificently. The facades have been freshly painted and the tiles have been polished, and the dark-wood details add a contrast that is truly elegant. When these places were renovated, they could be purchased for a song, but as Singaporeans began grasping at their heritage in recent years, their value shot up, and now these homes fetch huge sums.

Intersection of Emerald Hill and Orchard Rd. Free admission. 5-min. walk from Somerset MRT.

WESTERN SINGAPORE

The attractions grouped in this section are on the west side of Singapore, beginning from the Singapore Botanic Gardens at the edge of the urban area all the way out to the Singapore Discovery Centre past Jurong. If you're traveling around this area, remember that transportation can be problematic; the MRT system rarely goes directly to any of these places, taxis can be hard to find, and bus routes get more complex. Keep the telephone number for taxi booking handy. Sometimes ticket salespeople at the attractions can help make the call for you.

Bukit Timah Nature Reserve ★★ Bukit Timah Nature Reserve is pure primary rainforest. Believed to be as old as 1 million years, it's the only place on the island with vegetation that exists exactly as it was before the British settled here. The park is more than 81 hectares (202 acres) of soaring canopy teeming with mammals and birds and a lush undergrowth with more bugs, butterflies, and reptiles than you can shake a vine at. You can see more than 700 plant species, many of which are exotic ferns, plus mammals like long-tailed macaques, squirrels, and lemurs. There's a visitor center and four well-marked paths, one of which leads to Singapore's highest point. At 163m (535 ft.) above sea level, don't expect a nosebleed, but some of the scenic views of the island are really nice. Also at Bukit Timah is Hindhede Quarry, which filled up with water at some point, so you can take a dip and cool off during your hike. The National Parks Board gives free guided tours on the first Sunday of the month at 9:30 and 10:30am; call ⓒ **65/6554-5127** to register.

177 Hindhede Dr. [tel] **65/6488-5736**. www.nparks.gov.sg. Free admission. Daily 8:30am–6:30pm. Newton MRT, then bus no. 171 to park entrance.

Chinese and Japanese Gardens Situated on two islands in Jurong lake, the gardens are reached by an overpass and joined by the Bridge of Double Beauty. The **Chinese Garden** dedicates most of its area to "northern-style" landscape architecture. The style of Imperial gardens, the northern style integrates brightly colored buildings with the surroundings to compensate for northern China's absence of rich plant growth and natural scenery. The Stoneboat is a replica of the stone boat at the Summer Palace in Beijing. Inside the Pure Air of the Universe building are courtyards and a pond; there's also a seven-story pagoda, with the odd number of floors symbolizing continuity. Around the gardens, special attention has been paid to the placement of rock formations to resemble true nature, and also to the qualities of the rocks themselves, which can represent the forces of yin and yang, female and male, passivity and activity, and so on.

I like the Garden of Beauty, in Suzhou style, representing the southern style of landscape architecture. Southern gardens were built predominantly by scholars, poets, and men of wealth. Sometimes called Black-and-White gardens, these smaller gardens had more fine detail, featuring subdued colors, as the plants and elements of the rich natural landscape gave plenty to work with. Inside the Suzhou garden are 2,000 pots of *penjiang* (bonsai) and displays of small rocks.

While the Chinese garden is more visually stimulating, the **Japanese Garden** is intended to evoke feeling. Marble-chip paths lead the way so that as you walk, you can hear your own footsteps and meditate on the sound. They also serve to slow the journey for better gazing upon the scenery. The Keisein, or Dry Garden, uses white pebbles to create images of streams. Ten stone lanterns, a small traditional house, and a rest house are nestled between two ponds with smaller islands joined by bridges.

Toilets are situated at stops along the way, as are benches where you can have a rest or take in the sights. Paddleboats can be rented for S$5 (US$2.85/£1.40) per hour just outside the main entrance.

1 Chinese Garden Rd. (C) **65/6261-3632**. Free admission to grounds. Admission to bonsai garden S$2 (US$1.25/£0.70) adults, S$1 (US60¢/ £0.35) children. Daily 6am–11pm. Chinese Garden MRT.

Haw Par Villa (Tiger Balm Gardens) ⚓

In 1935, brothers Haw Boon Haw and Haw Boon Par—creators of Tiger Balm, the camphor-and-menthol rub that comes in those cool little pots—took their fortune and opened Tiger Balm Gardens as a venue for teaching traditional Chinese values. They made more than 1,000 statues and life-size dioramas depicting Chinese legends and historic tales and illustrating morality and Confucian beliefs. Many of these were gruesome and bloody; some of them were really entertaining.

But Tiger Balm Gardens suffered a horrible fate. In 1985, it was converted into an amusement park and reopened as Haw Par Villa. Most of the statues and scenes were taken away and replaced with rides. Well, business didn't exactly boom. In fact, the park lost money fast. But recently, in an attempt to regain some of the original Tiger Balm Garden edge, management has replaced many of the old statues, some of which are a great backdrop for really kitschy vacation photos, and ditched the rides. They also decided to open the gates free of charge.

262 Pasir Panjang Rd. (C) **65/6774-0300**. Free admission. Daily 9am–7pm. Buona Vista MRT, then bus no. 200.

Jurong BirdPark ⚓ (Kids)

Jurong BirdPark, with a collection of 8,000 birds of more than 600 species, showcases Southeast Asian breeds plus other colorful tropical beauties, some of which are endangered. The more than 20 hectares (50 acres) can be easily walked or, for a couple dollars extra, you can ride the panorail for a bird's-eye view (so to speak) of the grounds. The Waterfall Aviary, the world's largest walk-in aviary, affords an up-close-and-personal experience with African and South American birds, plus a pretty stroll through landscaped tropical forest. This is where you'll also see the world's tallest man-made waterfall, but the true feat of engineering here is the panorail station, built inside the aviary. Another smaller walk-in aviary is for Southeast Asian endangered bird species; at noon every day, this aviary experiences a man-made thunderstorm. The daily guided tours and regularly scheduled feeding times are enlightening. Other exhibits include the flamingo pools, the World of Darkness (featuring nocturnal birds), and the penguin parade, a favorite for Singaporeans, who adore all things Arctic. The **World of Hawks** show, at 10am and 4pm, features birds of prey either acting out their natural instincts or performing falconry tricks. The **All-Star Birdshow** takes place at 11am and 3pm, with trained parrots that race bikes and birds that perform all sorts of silliness, including staged birdie misbehaviors.

2 Jurong Hill. (C) **65/6265-0022**. www.birdpark.com.sg. Admission S$16 (US$10/£5.30) adults, S$8 (US$5.10/£2.65) children under 12. Daily 9am–6pm. Boon Lay MRT, then bus no. 194 or 251.

Singapore Botanic Gardens ⚓⚓

In 1822, Singapore's first botanic garden was started at Fort Canning by Sir Stamford Raffles. After it lost funding, the present botanic garden came into being in 1859, thanks to the efforts of a horticulture society; it was later turned over to the government for upkeep. More than just a garden, this space occupied an important place in the region's economic development when "Mad" Henry Ridley, one of the garden's directors, imported Brazilian rubber tree seedlings from Great Britain. He devised improved latex-trapping methods and led the campaign to convince reluctant coffee growers to switch plantation crops. The garden also pioneered orchid hybridization, breeding a number of internationally acclaimed varieties.

Carved out within the tropical setting are a rose garden, sundial garden with pruned hedges, banana plantation, and spice garden, dotted with sculptures by international artists. As you wander, look for the Cannonball tree (named for its cannonball-shaped fruit), Para rubber trees, teak trees, bamboos, and a huge array of palms, including the sealing wax palm—distinguished by its bright scarlet stalks—and the rumbia palm, which bears the pearl sago. The fruit of the silk-cotton tree is a pod filled with silky stuffing that was once used for stuffing pillows. Flowers like bougainvilleas and heliconias add beautiful color.

The **National Orchid Garden** is 3 hectares (7½ acres) of gorgeous orchids growing along landscaped walks. The **English Garden** features hybrids developed here and named after famous visitors to the garden—there's the Margaret Thatcher, the Benazir Bhutto, the Vaclav Havel, and more. The gift shops sell live hydroponic orchids in test tubes for unique souvenirs.

The gardens have three lakes. **Symphony Lake** surrounds an island band shell for "Concert in the Park" performances by the local symphony and international entertainers. Call visitor services at the number below for performance schedules.

The National Parks Board gives free guided tours on the second Saturday of the month at 9am, 10am, 11am, and 4pm; free guided tours of the Orchid Garden are given on the third Saturday of the month at 9am, 10am, 11am and 4pm. Register 15 minutes before the walk at the visitor center near Nassim Gate.

Main entrance at corner of Cluny and Holland roads. (*C*) 65/6471-7361. www.nparks.gov.sg. Free admission. Daily 5am–midnight. National Orchid Garden S$5 (US$3.20/£1.65) adults, S$1 (US60¢/ £0.35) children under 12 and seniors. Daily 8:30am–7pm. Orchard MRT, then bus no. 7, 105, 106, or 174 from Orchard Blvd.

Singapore Discovery Centre *(Kids)*   This cool display of the latest military technology has hands-on exhibits that cannot be resisted—one of 19 interactive information kiosks, for instance, lets you design tanks and ships. Airborne Rangers, a virtual-reality experience, allows you to parachute from a plane and manipulate your landing to safety. In the motion simulator, feel your seat move in tandem with the fighter pilot on the screen. The Shooting Gallery is a computer-simulated combat firing range using real but decommissioned M16 rifles. IMAX features roll at the five-story iWERKS Theatre regularly. If you get hungry, there's a fast-food court. You can also take a 30-minute bus tour of the neighboring Singapore Air Force Training Institute, free with SDC admission. Inquire about tour times at the front counter.

510 Upper Jurong Rd. (*C*) 65/6792-6188. www.sdc.com.sg. Admission S$10 (US$6.40/£3.30) adults, S$6 (US$3.80/£2) children under 12. Tues–Fri and Sun 9am–6pm, Sat 9am–8pm. MRT to Boon Lay, then SBS no. 192 or 193.

Singapore Science Centre *(Kids)*   The center features hands-on exhibits in true science-center spirit. Interestingly, the 7,500 sq. m (80,729 sq. ft.) of exhibits directly relate to the science syllabuses of the local school system, from primary-school level all the way through junior college. The galleries are all clearly marked to explain their interactive use, and study sheets are also available. The Technology Gallery is one of the more interesting exhibits if you can wrestle the kids away from the machines.

There's a Virtual Voyages simulation theater plus the Omni Theatre planetarium, which has a projection booth encased in glass so you can check out how it works. Best to avoid visits during weekends and school holiday time in June and December.

15 Science Centre Rd., off Jurong Town Hall Rd. ⓒ 65/6425-2500. www.science.edu.sg. Admission S$6 (US$3.80/£2) adults, S$3 (US$1.90/£1) children under 16. Tues–Sun and public holidays 10am–6pm. Jurong East MRT, then bus no. 66 or 335.

CENTRAL & NORTHERN SINGAPORE

The northern part of Singapore contains most of the island's nature reserves and parks. Here's where you'll find the Singapore Zoological Gardens, in addition to some sights with historic and religious significance. Despite the presence of the MRT in the area, there is not any simple way to get from attraction to attraction with ease. Bus transfers to and from MRT stops are the way to go—or you could stick to taxis.

Kong Meng San Phor Kark See Temple   The largest and most modern religious complex on the island, this place, called Phor Kark See for short, comprises prayer and meditation halls, a hospice, gardens, and a vegetarian restaurant. The largest building is the Chinese-style Hall of Great Compassion. There is also the octagonal Hall of Great Virtue and a towering pagoda. For S50¢ (US30¢/£0.20), you can buy flower petals to place in a dish at the Buddha's feet. Compared to other temples on the island, Phor Kark See seems shiny—having only been built in 1981. As a result, the religious images inside carry a strange, almost artificial, cartoon air about them.

88 Bright Hill Dr., in the center of the island to the east of Bukit Panjang Nature Preserve (Bright Hill Dr. is off Ang Mo Kio Ave.). ⓒ 65/6453-4046. Bishan MRT, then bus no. 410.

Kranji War Memorial   Kranji commemorates the men and women who fought and died in World War II. Prisoners of war in a camp nearby began a burial ground here, and after the war it was enlarged to provide space for all the casualties. The Kranji War Cemetery is the site of 4,000 graves of servicemen, while the Singapore State Cemetery memorializes the names of more than 20,000 who died and have no known graves. Stones are laid geometrically on a slope with a view of the Strait of Johor. The memorial itself is designed to represent the three arms of the services.

Woodlands Rd., in the very northern part of the island. Daily 7am–6pm. Kranji MRT.

MacRitchie Nature Trail   Of all the nature reserves in Singapore, the Central Catchment Nature Reserve is the largest, at 2,000 hectares (5,000 acres). Located in the center of the island, it's home to four of Singapore's reservoirs: MacRitchie, Seletar, Pierce, and Upper Pierce. The rainforest here is secondary forest, but the animals don't care; they're just as happy with the place. There's one path for walking and jogging (no bicycles allowed) that stretches 3km (1.75 miles) from its start in the southeast corner of the reserve, turning to the edge of MacRitchie Reservoir, then letting you out at the Singapore Island Country Club. The National Parks Board gives free guided tours on the second Sunday of the month at 9:30 and 10:30am; to register, call ⓒ 65/6554-5127.

Central Catchment Nature Reserve. ⓒ 65/6468-5736. www.nparks.gov.sg. Free admission. From Orchard Rd., take bus no. 132 from the Orchard Parade Hotel. From Raffles City, take bus no. 130. Get off at the bus stop near Little Sisters of the Poor. Next to Little Sisters of the Poor, follow the paved walkway, which turns into the trail.

Mandai Orchid Gardens   Owned and operated by Singapore Orchids Pte Ltd. to breed and cultivate hybrids for international export, the gardens double as an STB tourist attraction. Arranged in English-garden style, orchid varieties are separated in beds that are surrounded by grassy lawn. Tree-growing varieties prefer the shade of the covered canopy. On display is Singapore's national flower, the Vanda Miss Joaquim, a natural hybrid in shades of light purple. Behind the gift shop is the Water Garden, where a stroll will reveal many houseplants common to the West, but as you would find them in the wild.

Mandai Lake Rd., on the route to the Singapore Zoo. (C) 65/6269-1036. Admission S$3 (US$1.90/£1) adults, S$1 (US60¢/£0.35) children under 12. Mon 8am–6pm; Tues–Sun 8am–7pm. Ang Mo Kio MRT, then bus no. 138.

Night Safari   Singapore takes advantage of its unchanging tropical climate and static ratio of daylight to night to bring you the world's first open-concept zoo for nocturnal animals. Here, as in the zoological gardens, animals live in landscaped areas, their barriers virtually unseen by visitors. These areas are dimly lit to create a moonlit effect, and a guided tram leads you through "regions" designed to resemble the Himalayan foothills, the jungles of Africa, and, naturally, Southeast Asia. Some of the free-range prairie animals come very close to the tram. The 45-minute ride covers almost 3.5km (2 miles) and has regular stops to get off and have a rest or stroll along trails for closer views of smaller creatures.

Staff, placed at regular intervals along the trails, help you find your way, though it's almost impossible to get lost along the trails; however, it *is* nighttime, you are in the forest, and it can be spooky. The guides are there more or less to add peace of mind (and all speak English). Flash photography is strictly prohibited. Be sure to bring plenty of insect repellent. *A weirder tip:* Check out the open-air, Bali-style bathrooms.

Singapore Zoo, 80 Mandai Lake Rd., at the western edge of the Bukit Panjang Nature Reserve, on the Seletar Reservoir. (C) 65/6269-3411. www.zoo.com.sg. Admission S$20 (US$13/£6.60) adults, S$10 (US$6.40/£3.30) children under 12. Combination Zoo & Night Safari tickets S$28 (US$18/£9.25) adults, S$14 (US$9/£4.60) children. Daily 7:30pm–midnight. Ticket sales end at 11pm. Entrance Plaza, restaurant, and fast-food outlet open 6:30–11:30pm. Ang Mo Kio MRT, then bus no. 138.

Sasanaransi Buddhist Temple   Known simply as the Burmese Buddhist Temple, it was founded by a Burmese expat to serve the overseas Burmese Buddhist community. His partner, an herbal doctor also from Burma, traveled home to buy a 10-ton block of marble from which was carved the 3.3m (11 ft.) Buddha image that sits in the main hall, surrounded by an aura of brightly colored lights. The original temple was off Serangoon Road in Little India and was moved here in 1991 at the request of the Housing Development Board. On the third story is a standing Buddha image in gold, along with murals of events in the Buddha's life.

14 Tai Gin Rd., next to the Sun Yat-sen Villa near Toa Payoh New Town. Daily 6:30am–9pm. Chanting Sun 9:30am, Wed 8pm, and Sat 7:30pm. Toa Payoh MRT, then take a taxi.

Singapore Zoo (Kids)   It calls itself the Open Zoo because, rather than coop the animals in jailed enclosures, it lets them roam freely in landscaped areas. Beasts of the world are kept where they are supposed to be by using psychological restraints and physical barriers that are disguised behind waterfalls, vegetation, and moats. Some animals are grouped with other species to show them coexisting as they would in nature. For instance, the white rhinoceros is neighborly with the wildebeest and ostrich—not that wildebeests and ostriches make the best company, but certainly contempt is better than boredom. Guinea and pea fowl, Emperor tamarinds, and other creatures are free-roaming and not shy; however, if you spot a water monitor or long-tailed macaque, know that they're not zoo residents—just locals looking for a free meal.

Major features are the Primate Kingdom, Wild Africa, Reptile Garden, children's petting zoo, and underwater views of polar bears, sea lions, and penguins. Daily shows include primates and reptiles at 10:30am and 2:30pm, and elephants and sea lions at 11:30am and 3:30pm. You can have your photograph taken with an orangutan, chimpanzee, or snake, and there are elephant and camel rides, too.

Zoo literature includes half- and full-day agendas to help make the most of your visit. The best time to arrive, however, is at 9am, to have breakfast with an orangutan, which feasts on fruits and puts on a hilarious and very memorable show. If you miss that, you can also have tea with it at 4pm. Another good time to go is just after a rain, when the animals cool off and get frisky. See also the "Night Safari" listing, above.

80 Mandai Lake Rd., at the western edge of the Bukit Panjang Nature Reserve, on the Seletar Reservoir. ⓒ 65/ 6269-3411. www.zoo.com.sg. Admission S$15 (US$9.60/£4.95) adults, S$7.50 (US$4.80/£2.50) children under 12. Combination Zoo & Night Safari tickets S$28 (US$18/£9.25) adults, S$14 (US$9/£4.65) children. Daily 8:30am–6pm. Ang Mo Kio MRT, then bus no. 138.

Sungei Buloh Wetland Reserve

Located to the very north of the island and devoted to the wetland habitat and mangrove forests that are so common to the region, 87-hectare (215-acre) Sungei Buloh is out of the way, and not the easiest place to get to; but it's a beautiful park, with constructed paths and boardwalks taking you through tangles of mangroves, soupy marshes, grassy spots, and coconut groves. Of the flora and fauna, the most spectacular sights here are the birds, of which there are somewhere between 140 and 170 species in residence or just passing through for the winter. Of the migratory birds, some have traveled from as far as Siberia to escape the cold months from September to March. Bird observatories are set up at different spots along the paths. Also, even though you're in the middle of nowhere, Sungei Buloh has a visitor center, a cafeteria, and souvenirs. Go early to beat the heat.

301 Neo Tiew Crescent. ⓒ 65/6794-1401. Admission S$1 (US60¢/£0.35) adults, S50¢ (US30¢/£0.15) children and seniors. Mon–Sat 7:30am–7pm; Sun and public holidays 7am–7pm. Audiovisual show Mon–Sat 9am, 11am, 1pm, 3pm, and 5pm; hourly Sun and public holidays. Kranji MRT, then bus no. 925. Stop at Kranji Reservoir Dam and cross the causeway to the park entrance.

Sun Yat-sen Nanyang Memorial Hall

Dr. Sun Yat-sen visited Singapore eight times to raise funds for his revolution in China, and he made Singapore his headquarters for gaining the support of overseas Chinese in Southeast Asia. A wealthy Chinese merchant built the villa around 1880 for his mistress, and a later owner permitted Dr. Sun Yat-sen to use it. The house reflects the classic bungalow style, which is becoming endangered in modern Singapore. Its typical bungalow features include a projecting carport with a sitting room overhead, verandas with striped blinds, second-story cast-iron railings, and first-story masonry balustrades. A covered walkway leads to the kitchen and servants' quarters in the back. Inside, the life of Dr. Sun is traced in photos and watercolors, from his birth in southern China through his creation of a revolutionary organization.

12 Tai Gin Rd., near Toa Payoh New Town. ⓒ 65/6256-7377. Admission S$3 (US$1.90/£1) adults, S$2 (US$1.30/ £0.65) children and seniors. Tues–Sun 9am–5pm. Toa Payoh MRT, then bus no. 45.

EASTERN SINGAPORE

The east coast leads from the edge of Singapore's urban area to the tip of the eastern part, at Changi Point. Eastern Singapore is home to Changi International Airport, nearby Changi Prison, and the long stretch of East Coast Park along the shoreline. The MRT heads east in this region, but swerves northward at the end of the line. Not all attractions are served by MRT, and bus travel is time consuming. You're better off taking a taxi to these sights.

Changi Museum ⚐ Upon successful occupation of Singapore, the Japanese marched all British, Australian, and allied European prisoners to Changi by foot, where they lived in a prison camp for 3 years, suffering overcrowding, disease, and malnutrition. Prisoners were cut off from the outside world except to leave the camp for labor duties. The hospital conditions were terrible; some prisoners suffered public beatings, and many died. In an effort to keep hope alive, they built a small chapel from wood and attap. Years later, at the request of former POWs and their families and friends, the government built this replica.

The museum displays sketches by W. R. M. Haxworth and secret photos taken by George Aspinall—both POWs who were imprisoned here. Displayed with descriptions, the pictures, along with writings and other objects from the camp, bring this period to life, depicting the day-to-day horror with a touch of high morale.

1000 Upper Changi Rd., in the same general area as the airport. ✆ 65/6214-2451. www.changimuseum.com. Free admission. Guided tour or audio-tour headset rental S$8 (US$5.10/£2.65) adults, S$4 (US$2.60/£1.30) children. Daily 9:30am–4:30pm. Tanah Merah MRT, then bus no. 2.

East Coast Park East Coast Park is a narrow strip of reclaimed land, only 8.5km (5¼ miles) long, tucked in between the shoreline and East Coast Parkway. It serves as a hangout for Singaporean families on the weekends. Moms and dads barbecue under the trees while the kids swim at the beach, which is nothing more than a narrow lump of grainy sand sloping into yellow-green water that has more seaweed than a sushi bar. Paths for bicycling, in-line skating, walking, and jogging run the length of the park and are crowded on weekends and holidays. On Sunday, you'll find kite-flyers in the open grassy parts. The lagoon is the best place to go for bicycle and in-line skate rentals, canoeing, and windsurfing.

Because East Coast Park is so long, getting to the place you'd like to hang out can be a bit confusing. Many of the locators I've included sound funny (for example, McDonald's Carpark C), but are recognizable landmarks for taxi drivers. Sailing, windsurfing, and other watersports happen at the far end of the park, at the lagoon, which is closer to Changi Airport than it is to the city. Taxi drivers are all familiar with the lagoon as a landmark. Unfortunately, public transportation to the park is tough—you should bring a good map and expect to do a little walking from any major thoroughfare.

East Coast Park is also home to **UDMC Seafood Centre** (p. 496), located not far from the lagoon.

East Coast Pkwy. Free admission. Bus no. 36 to Marine Parade; use the underpass to cross the hwy.

Escape Theme Park (Kids If you think your kids will pass out at the sight of another museum, Singapore's newest and best amusement park will keep them occupied. There are rides for small kiddies and families, plus exciting ones for big kids as well. The go-kart circuit is happening. There are also carnival games with prizes, plus snacks and beverages. If it gets too hot, visit Wild Wild Wet (see below). A beach and good seafood hawker fare are nearby.

Downtown East 1, Pasir Ris Close. ✆ 65/6581-9112. www.escapethemepark.com.sg. Admission S$17 (US$11/£5.45) adults, S$8.30 (US$5.30/£2.75) children. Sat–Sun and public and school holidays 10am–8pm. Pasir Ris MRT.

Malay Village In 1985, Malay Village opened in Geylang as a theme village to showcase Malay culture. It's always been a sort of tatty display, but since the opening of the Malay Heritage Centre in Kampong Gelam 2 years ago, it's grown even more obscure and has almost completely dropped off the Singapore Tourism Board's radar. There's a small cultural display and lots of shops that cater to the local Malay community in Geylang, a neighborhood with a strong Malay heritage. While not nearly as shiny as the new center, there's something more authentic about Malay Village, probably because it's in the heart of a residential district.

Malay Village still hosts the **Kuda Kepang,** a fascinating traditional Malay dance, on Saturday nights at 8pm, free of charge. It's a long performance, but worth the wait: At the end, the dancers are put in a trance and walk on glass, eat glass, and rip coconuts to shreds with their teeth. Arrive early—the place gets packed with locals.

39 Geylang Serai, in the suburb of Geylang. ✆ 65/6748-4700. Free admission. Daily 10am–10pm. 10-min. walk from Paya Lebar MRT.

Wild Wild Wet 𝘒𝘪𝘥𝘴   Beat the heat at this waterpark, with flumes, raft slides, a wave pool, and lots of water activities for children. A locker room and food and beverage facilities are all convenient, plus water safety is provided by trained lifeguards. Wild Wild Wet and neighboring Escape Theme Park both opened in 2003, so the facilities haven't gotten the worn and tatty look that older theme parks take on after a while.

Downtown East 1, Pasir Ris Close. ✆ 65/6581-9128. www.wildwildwet.com. Admission S$13 (US$8.30/£4.25) adults, S$8.80 (US$5.60/£2.90) children. Mon and Wed–Fri 1–7pm, Sat–Sun and public and school holidays 10am–7pm. Pasir Ris MRT.

SENTOSA ISLAND

In the 1880s, Sentosa was a hub of British military activity, with hilltop forts built to protect the harbor from sea invasion from all sides. Today, it has become a weekend getaway spot and Singapore's answer to Disneyland. Tomorrow it will be the site of one of Singapore's new "integrated resorts"—hotels, resorts, amusement and entertainment parks, plus gambling casinos—slated for opening in 2010. In the meantime, Sentosa is spending gobs of money to upgrade all existing facilities to meet the bar raised by the coming attractions.

If you're spending the day, there are numerous restaurants and a couple of food courts. For a unique dining option, consider **Sky Dining,** aboard a glass-bottomed cable car, where you can spend a couple hours eating a three-course Western meal (set menus S$88/US$56/£29 or S$158/US$101/£52 for two; children's set menu S$20/US$6.40/£3.60). It's especially popular on Valentine's Day or for birthdays and wedding proposals. Meals are pretty tasty (provided by the Jewel Box restaurant). For information, call ✆ 65/6377-9688 or visit www.mountfaber.com.sg.

For overnights, the **Shangri-La's Rasa Sentosa Resort and Spa** (p. 481) and the **Sentosa Resort & Spa** (p. 481) are popular hotel options. For general Sentosa inquiries, call ✆ 1800/736-8672 or visit www.sentosa.com.sg.

GETTING THERE   Island admission is S$2 (US$1.30/£0.65) for adults and children, payable at the visitor center upon entry, with tickets to additional attractions and activities purchased separately once inside.

The most entertaining way to get here is via cable car. From the Cable Car Towers (✆ 65/6270-8855), the cable cars make the trip daily from 8:30am to 11pm at a cost of S$9.90 (US$6.30/£3.25) per adult and S$4.50 (US$2.90/£1.50) per child one-way, or S$11 (US$7/£3.60) per adult and S$5.50 (US$3.50/£1.80) per child round-trip. The view is okay (but too far from the city to see the skyline); the ride is especially fun for kids. The cable cars also extend up Mount Faber on the Singapore side. If you

Sentosa Island

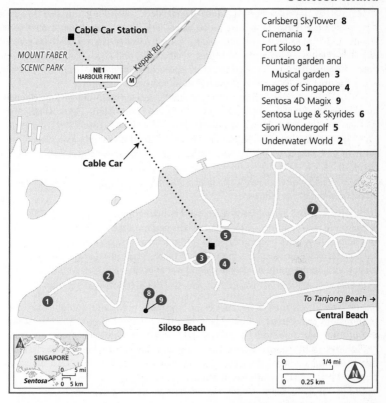

Cable Car Station

MOUNT FABER SCENIC PARK

NE1 HARBOUR FRONT Ⓜ

Keppel Rd.

Cable Car

Carlsberg SkyTower **8**
Cinemania **7**
Fort Siloso **1**
Fountain garden and
    Musical garden **3**
Images of Singapore **4**
Sentosa 4D Magix **9**
Sentosa Luge & Skyrides **6**
Sijori Wondergolf **5**
Underwater World **2**

To Tanjong Beach →

Central Beach

Siloso Beach

SINGAPORE
0   5 mi
Sentosa   0   5 km

0   1/4 mi
0   0.25 km

choose to take a cable car up to the top, you can take it back down again. Otherwise, if you opt to alight at this stop, you can take a taxi back to civilization.

The new **Sentosa Express** opened in January 2007. This light-rail train operates between Vivo City at the HarbourFront MRT station and Sentosa, with stops at the beach, major attractions, and the future site of the integrated resort. Pick up the train to Sentosa at Vivo City, third level, where you can purchase tickets for S$3 (US$1.90/ £0.90), which includes all-day rides, plus Sentosa admission.

A **bus** operates from the HarbourFront Bus Terminal (near Harbourfront MRT), daily from 7am to 11pm, with extended hours until 12:30am on Friday, Saturday, and the eve of public holidays. It costs S$1 (US60¢/£0.35) per person, paid upon arrival at Sentosa. Or any city **taxi** can take you here; just pay the entrance fee after you cross the causeway, and the driver can drop you anywhere you'd like to go within the island.

GETTING AROUND   Once on Sentosa, you can take advantage of a free bus system, with four color-coded routes that snake around the island.

ATTRACTIONS   The most notable attractions that you get free with your Sentosa admission are the **Fountain Gardens and Musical Fountain,** a nightly show of fountain, lights, and lasers (aimed at junior audiences); the **Dragon Trail Nature Walk,** a 1.5km (1-mile) stroll through secondary rainforest to see dragon sculptures and local flora and fauna; and the **beaches.**

Sentosa has three beaches. At **Siloso Beach,** deck chairs, beach umbrellas, and a variety of watersports equipment (pedal boats, aqua bikes, fun bugs, canoes, surfboards, and banana boats) are available for hire at nominal charges. Bicycles are also available. Shower and changing facilities, food kiosks, and snack bars are at rest stations. **Palawan Beach** has a greater assortment of beachside bars and restaurants, while **Tanjong Beach** is the quietest and most laid-back of the three.

Several attractions on Sentosa charge separate entrance fees; they include the **Sentosa Luge & Skyride** (S$8/US$5.10/£2.65) per ride; Mon–Thurs 10am–6pm, Sat–Sun 10am–7pm), **Sijori WonderGolf** (adults S$8–S$10/US$5.10–US$6.40/£2.65–£3.30, children S$4–S$7/US$2.60–US$4.50/£1.30–£2.30; daily 9am–7pm), **Sentosa 4D Magix** motion cinema (adults S$16/US$10/£5.30, children S$9.50/US$6.10/£3.15; daily 10am–9pm), and the **Carlsberg Sky Tower** (adults S$10/US$6.25/£3.45, children S$6/US$3.80/£3.30; daily 9am–9pm.) The best attractions, in my opinion, are as follows:

Fort Siloso   Fort Siloso guarded Keppel Harbour from invasion in the 1880s. It's one of three forts built on Sentosa, and it later became a military camp in World War II. The buildings have been outfitted to resemble barracks, kitchen, laundry, and military offices as they looked back in the day. In places, you can explore the underground tunnels and ammunition holds, but they're not as extensive as you would hope.

© 65/6275-0388. Admission S$8 (US$5.10/£2.65) adults, S$5 (US$3.20/£1.65) children. Daily 10am–6pm.

Images of Singapore 🔆🔆   Images of Singapore is without a doubt one of the main reasons to come to Sentosa. There are three parts to this museum: the Pioneers of Singapore, the Surrender Chambers, and Festivals of Singapore, a recent addition.

Pioneers of Singapore is an exhibit of beautifully constructed life-size dioramas that place figures like Sultan Hussein, Sir Stamford Raffles, Tan Tock Seng, and Naraina Pillai, to name just a few, in the context of Singapore's timeline and note their contributions to its development. Also interesting are the dioramas depicting scenes from the daily routines of the different cultures as they lived during colonial times. It's a great stroll that brings history to life.

The powers that be have tried to change the name of the **Surrender Chambers** to the Sentosa Wax Museum, but it still hasn't caught on because the Surrender Chambers are oh-so-much-more than just a wax museum. The gallery leads you through authentic footage, photos, maps, and recordings of survivors to chronologically tell the story of the Pacific theater activity of World War II and how the Japanese conquered Singapore. The grand finale is a wax museum depicting a scene of the British surrender and another of the Japanese surrender.

The newest addition, **Festivals of Singapore,** is another life-size diorama exhibit depicting a few of the major festivals and traditions of the Chinese, Malay, Indian, and Peranakan cultures in Singapore.

© 65/6275-0388. Admission S$10 (US$6.40/£3.30) adults, S$7 (US$4.50/£2.30) children. Daily 9am–7pm.

Underwater World 🔆 *Kids*   Underwater World is without a doubt one of the most visited attractions on Sentosa. Everybody comes for the tunnel: 83m (272 ft.) of transparent acrylic tube through which you glide on a conveyor belt, gaping at sharks, stingrays, eels, and other creatures of the sea drifting by, above and on both sides. At 11:30am, 2:30pm, and 4:30pm daily, a scuba diver hops in and feeds them by hand. In smaller tanks, you can view other unusual sea life, like the puffer fish and the mysteriously weedy and leafy sea dragons. The price also includes admission to the

Dolphin Lagoon, with pink dolphin shows daily at 11am, 1pm, 3:30pm, and 5pm. Then there's the latest display of bamboo-shark embryos, developing within egg cases—what's keeping you?

(C) 65/6275-0388. www.underwaterworld.com.sg. Admission S$20 (US$13/£6.45) adults, S$13 (US$8/£4.15) children. Daily 9am–9pm.

ORGANIZED TOURS

Although touring Singapore is simple enough for do-it-yourself travelers, visitors with little time or who want to delve deeper into local sights can take advantage of convenient organized activities.

COACH TOURS   Tour East (C) 65/6738-2622) organizes typical half-day bus tours of the city (adults S$30/US$19/£9.90, children S$15/US$9.60/£4.95), along with full-day excursions to some of the main attractions around the island (adults S$70/US$45/£23, children S$35/US$22/£12), some with meals included. The Peranakan Trail takes visitors out to Katong, a suburban neighborhood that is the focal point of Peranakan heritage (adults S$40/US$26/£13, children S$20/US$13/£6.60).

For something different, consider **DUCKTours** (C) 65/6338-6877; www.duck tours.com.sg), a combined coach-and-boat tour in an amphibious vehicle, a decommissioned military craft, that circles the Historic District for a tour of the harbor. The 1-hour tour starts every hour, departing from the Suntec City Mall Galleria, with additional transfers from the DUCKTours office on Orchard Road (at Cairnhill Rd.) Reservations are highly recommended; tours cost S$33 (US$21/£11) for adults, S$17 (US$11/£5.60) for children 4 to 12, and S$2 (US$1.30/£0.65) for kids under 3. DUCKTours also operates the **HiPPO Tours** aboard an open-top double-decker bus, cruising Orchard Road, Little India, Kampong Gelam, Chinatown, and the Historic District. Pick it up at the DUCKTours office on Orchard Road or at Suntec City, then get on and off at sights that interest you along the way. The day ticket costs S$33 (US$21/£11) for adults, S$13 (US$8.30/£4.30) for children 4 to 12, and S$2 (US$1.30/£0.65) for kids under 3. Call DUCKTours for information.

WALKING TOURS   The **National Museum of Singapore** (C) 65/6332-4075; www.nhb.gov.sg) usually offers a selection of tours that I highly recommend. The Overview of Singapore History & Culture is a half-day historical look at the city's ethnic enclaves. The Cemetery Tour takes you outside the city to see a side of local culture that is rarely explored. At press time, tours were temporarily on hold until after the festivals surrounding the reopening of the museum cool down. Tours were expected to resume in early 2007; call for details.

Singapore Walks (C) 65/6325-1631; www.singaporewalks.com) is another reputable outfit that organizes guided walking tours of the Historic District, Chinatown, Little India, Kampong Gelam, and other neighborhoods Monday through Saturday. Call to find out the meeting time and place for the tour you want; adults pay S$18 (US$12/£5.95), children S$12 (US$7.70/£3.95).

RIVER TOURS & CRUISES   Singapore Explorer (C) 65/6339-6833; www. singaporeexplorer.com.sg) operates boats up and down the Singapore River and into the harbor from 9am to 11pm daily. A bumboat ride with recorded info about the riverside sights costs adults S$12 (US$7.70/£3.95) and children S$6 (US$3.80/£2). If you want to ride in an air-conditioned glass-top boat, tickets for adults are S$15 (US$9.60/£4.95), children S$6 (US$3.80/£2). The boats can be met at Clarke Quay or the Raffles Place MRT Jetty.

The *Imperial Cheng Ho,* operated by **Watertours** (© **65/6533-9811;** www.water tours.com.sg), is a huge boat modeled after the sort of Chinese junk that Admiral Cheng Ho might have sailed when he explored this region in the 15th century. A 2½-hour cruise takes you past the Singapore skyline, the mouth of the Singapore River, then out past Sentosa with a stop on Kusu Island. I recommend the Morning Glory Cruise at 10am (adults S$25/US$16/£8.25, children S$12/US$7.70£3.95). There's also a High Tea Cruise at 2:30pm and a dinner cruise at 5:30pm. Watertours can arrange hotel transfer with your booking.

TRISHAW TOURS   These cycle rickshaws were once a staple form of public trans-portation. Now they're only permitted on busy streets with special permits, and only for guided tours. **Singapore Explorer** (© **65/6339-6833;** www.singaporeexplorer.com.sg) coordinates regular outings through Chinatown from 10am to 7pm daily. You can either call ahead to book a ride, or just show up at the corner of Sago and Terrenganu streets; you'll see the collection of trishaws under cover. The half-hour trip takes you through Chinatown's quaint streets for a charge of S$36 (US$23/£12) per person. You can also combine the trishaw tour with a half-hour bumboat trip for only S$2 (US$1.30/£0.65) extra. Singapore Explorer can arrange pick-up from anywhere if you book in advance.

7 Outdoor Activities

BICYCLING

Bicycles are not for rent within the city limits, and traffic does not really allow for cycling on city streets, so sightseeing by bicycle is not recommended for city touring. One favorite place where the locals go for mountain-biking adventures (and to cycle amidst the old kampung villages) is **Pulau Ubin,** off the northeast coast of Singapore.

If you plan a trip out to **Sentosa,** cycling provides a great alternative to that island's tram system and gets you closer to the parks and nature there. Try a couple of rental places on Siloso Beach off Siloso Road, a short walk from Underwater World (see "Sentosa Island," earlier in this chapter). There's a kiosk at **Sakae Sushi** (© **65/6271-6385**) and another at **Costa Sands** (© **65/6275-2471**). Both are open daily from around 10am to 6:30 or 7pm. Rental for a standard bicycle is S$4 (US$2.60/£1.30) per hour. A mountain bike goes for S$8 (US$5.10/£2.65) per hour. Identification is required.

For a little light cycling, most people head out to **East Coast Park,** where rentals are inexpensive, the scenery is nice on cooler days, and there are plenty of great stops for eating along the way. Bicycles can be rented at East Coast Park from **SDK Recre-ation** (© **65/6445-2969**), near McDonald's at Carpark C; open daily from about 11am to 8 or 9pm. Rentals are S$4 to S$6 (US$2.60–US$3.80/£1.30–£2) per hour. Identification may be requested, or leave a S$50 (US$32/£17) deposit.

GOLF

Golf is big in Singapore, and although there are quite a few clubs, many are exclusively for members only. However, many other places are open for limited play by nonmem-bers. All will require that you bring an international par certificate. Most hotel concierges will be glad to make arrangements for you, which may be the best way to go. It's also very popular for Singaporeans to go on day trips to Malaysia for the best courses.

Changi Golf Club   This 9-hole walking course is par 34; nonmembers may play at this private club only on weekdays (walk-ins are okay, but advance booking is recommended). They may even be able to set you up with other players. The course opens at 7:30am. Last tee time is 4:30pm.

20 Netheravon Rd. (*C*) **65/6545-5133**. Greens fees S$40 (US$26/£13); caddy fees S$10 (US$6.40/£3.30). Mon–Fri 7:30am–4:30pm.

Seletar Base Golf Course   A public course, Seletar's 9-hole, par 36 is open 7 days a week. Very low-cost cart and equipment rentals are available with deposit. First tee is at 7am except for Monday and Thursday, when first tee is at 11am. Last tee is 5:30pm.

244 Oxford St., 3 Park Lane. (*C*) **65/6481-4745**. Greens fees Mon–Fri S$30 (US$19/£9.90); Sat–Sun S$40 (US$27/£13). Tues–Wed, Fri–Sun 7am–5:30pm; Mon and Thurs 11am–5:30pm.

Sentosa Golf Club   The best option if you're traveling with your family and want to get in a game, Sentosa's many activities will keep the kids happy while you practice your swing guilt-free at one of the club's two 18-hole 72-par courses. This private course charges much more for nonmembers than other courses—and weekend play for nonmembers is restricted to Sunday afternoon—but it's a beautiful championship course and a relaxing time away from the city. Advance phone bookings are required.

27 Bukit Manis Rd., Sentosa Island. (*C*) **65/6275-0022**. Greens fees Mon–Fri S$231 (US$148/£76); Sun S$315 (US$202/£104). Daily 7am–7pm.

DIVING

The locals are crazy about scuba diving, but are more likely to travel to Malaysia and other Southeast Asian destinations for good underwater adventures. The most common complaint is that the water surrounding Singapore is really silty—sometimes to the point where you can barely see your hand before your face. See chapter 9 for scuba activities in Malaysia.

SEA CANOEING

Rubber sea canoes and one- or two-person kayaks can be rented at Siloso Beach on Sentosa, the beach at East Coast Park (near McDonald's Carpark C), and the beach at Changi Point. Prices range from S$6 to S$12 (US$3.80–US$7.70/£2–£3.95) per hour, depending on the type of craft. Life jackets are provided. These places don't have phones, so just go to the beach and scout out the rental places on the sand.

TENNIS

Quite a few hotels in the city provide tennis courts for guests, many floodlit for night play (which allows you to avoid the daytime heat), and even a few that can arrange lessons, so be sure to check out the hotel listings earlier in this chapter. If your hotel doesn't have tennis facilities, ask your concierge to arrange a game at a facility elsewhere. Many hotels have signing agreements with sister hotel properties or special rates with independent fitness centers within the city.

WATER-SKIING & WAKEBOARDING

The Kallang River, located to the east of the city, has hosted quite a few international water-skiing tournaments. If this is your sport, contact the Cowabunga Ski Centre, the authority in Singapore. Located at **Kallang Riverside Park,** 10 Stadium Lane ((*C*) **65/6344-8813;** www.extreme.com.sg), it will arrange lessons for adults and children as well as water-skiing and wakeboarding trips. Beginner courses will set you back S$130 (US$83/£43), while more experienced skiers and boarders can hire a boat plus equipment for 4 hours for S$300 (US$192/£99) on weekdays and S$360 (US$230/£119) on weekends. It's open Tuesday through Friday from noon to 7pm; Saturday, Sunday, and public holidays from 9am to 7pm. Call in advance for a reservation.

WINDSURFING & SAILING

You'll find both windsurf boards and sailboats for rent at the lagoon in East Coast Park, which is where these activities primarily take place. The largest and most reputable firm has to be the **Pasta Fresca Seasport Centre,** at 1212 East Coast Pkwy. (© **65/6449-5118**). For S$24 (US$15/£7.90) an hour you can rent a Laser, or for S$22 (US$14/£7.25) an hour you can rent windsurf gear. Expect to leave a deposit of around S$20 (US$13/£6.60).

8 Shopping

In Singapore, shopping is a sport—from the practiced glide through haute couture boutiques to skillful back-alley bargaining to win the best prices on Asian treasures. The shopping here is always exciting, with something to satiate every pro shopper's appetite.

HOURS Shopping malls are generally open from 10am to 8pm Monday through Saturday, with some stores keeping shorter Sunday hours. The malls sometimes remain open until 10pm on holidays. Smaller shops are open from around 10am to 5pm Monday through Saturday, but are almost always closed on Sunday. Hours vary from shop to shop. Arab Street is closed on Sunday.

PRICES Almost all of the stores in malls have fixed prices. Sometimes these stores have seasonal sales, especially in July, when the month-long **Great Singapore Sale** means prices are marked down up to 50% or 75%. In the smaller shops and at street vendors, prices are never marked, and vendors will quote you higher prices than the going rate, in anticipation of the bargaining ritual. These are the places to find good prices, if you negotiate well.

DUTY-FREE ITEMS Changi International Airport has a large duty-free shop that carries cigarettes, liquor, wine, perfumes, cosmetics, watches, jewelry, and other designer accessories. There's also a chain of duty-free stores in Singapore called **DFS.** The main branch is at #01-58 Millenia Walk, 9 Raffles Blvd., next to the Pan Pacific Hotel (© **65/6332-2188**). The store is huge and impressive, but unfortunately, the only truly duty-free items are liquor, which you can arrange to pick up at the airport before you depart—everything else carries the standard 5% GST. Feel free to apply for the Global Refund Scheme here, though.

GLOBAL REFUND SCHEME When you shop in stores that display the blue TAX-FREE SHOPPING logo, the government will refund the goods and services tax (GST) you pay on purchases totaling S$100 (US$64/£33) or more. Upon request, the sales clerk will fill out a Tax Free Shopping Cheque, which you retain with your receipt. If you've purchased that S$100 (US$64/£33) worth at the same store but on different dates, you can still claim the refund for all of the items. When you leave Singapore, present your checks at Customs along with your passport and let them see the goods you've purchased to show that you're taking them out of the country with you.

Customs will stamp the forms, which you then present at any of the Global Refund Counters in the airport for an on-the-spot cash refund (in Singapore dollars), a check, a direct transfer of the amount to your credit card account, or an airport shopping voucher. To qualify, you must spend at least S$300 (US$192/£99) overall, and you can't receive a refund of more than S$500 (US$320/£165) per person. You can also claim cash or credit refunds anytime during your stay at one of four downtown counters: Centrepoint Shopping Centre Customer Service Counter, Level 1, 176 Orchard Rd.; Funan Digitalife Mall, Information Counter Level 2, 109 North Bridge Rd.; Sim Lim Square, Information Counter, Level 1, 1 Rochor Canal Rd.; and Wisma Atria, Customer Service Centre, Level 1, 435 Orchard Rd. If you chose to claim your refund downtown, you only need to show receipts; however, goods and all paperwork still must be shown upon departure at the airport. For complete details, call the Global Refund Scheme hot line at ✆ **65/6225-6238,** or go to www.globalrefund.com. Another company, Premier Tax Free (www.premiertaxfree.com), also offers GST refunds at kiosks at the airport.

THE SHOPPING SCENE, PART 1: WESTERN-STYLE MALLS

Orchard Road is the biggie, but other good mall spots are at Marina Bay, Bugis Junction, Raffles City, and Raffles Hotel. The hottest thing on the shopping mall scene is **Vivo City** (1 Harbourfront Walk; ✆ **65/6377-6860**). Opened in November 2006, it's Singapore's biggest shopping mall, with 300 retailers, dining, entertainment, and even a rooftop sun deck with a bandshell and kiddie wading pool. Within walking distance from the Harbourfront MRT station, the mall is positioned in an area that will boom with the new Sentosa Integrated Resort opening up in 2010.

ORCHARD ROAD AREA

The malls on Orchard Road are a tourist attraction in their own right, with smaller boutiques and specialty shops intermingled with huge department stores. **Takashimaya** and **Isetan** have been imported from Japan. **Tangs** is historic, having grown from a cart full of merchandise nurtured by the business savvy of local entrepreneur C. K. Tang. **John Little** is the oldest department store in Singapore, followed by **Robinson's.** Boutiques range from the younger styles of Stussy and Guess? to the sophisticated fashions of Chanel and Salvatore Ferragamo. You'll also find antiques, Oriental carpets, art galleries, Kinokuniya and Borders bookstores, video arcades, and scores of restaurants, local food courts, fast-food joints, and coffeehouses—even a few discos. It's hard to say when Orchard Road is not crowded, but it's definitely a mob scene on weekends.

Centrepoint   Centrepoint is home to Robinson's department store, which first opened in Singapore in 1858. Here you'll find about 150 other shops, plus fast-food outlets and a Times bookstore. 176 Orchard Rd. ✆ 65/6235-6629.

Far East Plaza   At this crowded mall, the bustling little shops sell everything from CDs to punk fashions, luggage to camera equipment, eyewear to souvenirs. Mind yourself here: Most of these shops do not display prices, but rather gauge their quoted price depending on how wealthy the customer appears. If you must shop here, use your shrewdest bargaining powers. It may pay off to wear an outfit that's seen better days. 14 Scotts Rd. ✆ 65/6374-2325.

The Heeren   Thanks to the opening of a Singapore branch of Britain's HMV music stores, the Heeren is the big hangout for teens. The front entrance of the mall hums with towers of video monitors flashing and blaring the latest in American and British chart toppers. There is also a nice cafe to the side, with a garden for enjoying a coffee, tea, or snack. 260 Orchard Rd. ℂ **65/6733-4725.**

Hilton Shopping Gallery The arcade at the Hilton International Hotel is the most exclusive shopping in Singapore. Gucci, Donna Karan, Missoni, and Louis Vuitton are just a few of the international design houses that have made this their Singapore home. 581 Orchard Rd. ℂ **65/6737-2233.**

Lucky Plaza The map of this place will take hours to decipher, as more than 400 stores are here (no kidding). It's known for sportswear, camera equipment, watches, and luggage. If you buy electronics, make sure you get an international warranty with your purchase. Also, like Far East Plaza, Lucky Plaza is a notorious rip-off problem for travelers. Make sure you come here prepared to fend off slick sales techniques. It may also help to take the government's advice and avoid touts and offers that sound too good to be true. 304 Orchard Rd. ℂ **65/6235-3294.**

Ngee Ann City/Takashimaya Shopping Centre Takashimaya, a major Japanese department-store import, anchors Ngee Ann City's many smaller boutiques. Alfred Dunhill, Chanel, Coach, Royal Copenhagen, Tiffany & Co., Waterford, and Wedgwood are found here, along with many local and international fashion shops. 391 Orchard Rd. ℂ **65/6739-9323.**

Palais Renaissance Shops here include upmarket boutiques like Prada, Versus, and DKNY. 390 Orchard Rd. ℂ **65/6737-1520.**

Paragon Another upmarket shopping mall, with tenants including Diesel, Emanuel Ungaro, Escada, and Ferragamo. 290 Orchard Rd. ℂ **65/6738-5535.**

Shaw House The main floors of Shaw House are taken up by Isetan, a large Japanese department store with designer boutiques for men's and women's fashions, accessories, and cosmetics. On the fifth level, the Lido Theatre screens new releases from Hollywood and around the world. 350 Orchard Rd. ℂ **65/6235-1150.**

Specialists' Shopping Centre The anchor store in this smaller mall is John Little, Singapore's oldest department store, which opened in 1845. The prices, however, are very up-to-date. 277 Orchard Rd. ℂ **65/6737-8222.**

Tanglin Mall 🅚 This mall has a few charming boutiques filled with regional handicrafts for home and neat ethnic fashions from Singapore's neighboring countries. 163 Tanglin Rd. ℂ **65/6736-4922.**

Tanglin Shopping Centre 🅚🅚 Tanglin Shopping Centre is unique and fun. You won't find many clothing stores here, but you will find shop after shop selling antiques, art, and collectibles—from curios to carpets. 19 Tanglin Rd. ℂ **65/6373-0849.**

Tangs Once upon a time, C. K. Tang peddled goods from an old cart in the streets of Singapore. An industrious fellow, he parlayed his business into a small department store. A hit from the start, Tangs has grown exponentially over the decades and now competes with the other international megastores that have moved in. But Tangs is truly Singaporean, and its history is a local legend. 320 Orchard Rd. ℂ **65/6737-5500.**

Wisma Atria Wisma Atria caters to the younger set, with everything from Nine West to a Levi's store mixed in with numerous eyewear, cosmetics, and high- and low-fashion boutiques, all under one roof. 435 Orchard Rd. ℂ **65/6235-2103.**

MARINA BAY

The Marina Bay area arose from a plot of reclaimed land and now boasts the giant Suntec City convention center and all the hotels, restaurants, and shopping malls that have grown up around it. Shopping in the Marina Bay area is popular because of its convenience, with the major malls and hotels all interconnected by covered walkways and pedestrian bridges, making it easy to get around with minimal exposure to the elements.

Marina Square   Marina Square is a huge complex that, in addition to a wide variety of shops, has a cinema, fast-food outlets, cafes, pharmacies, and convenience stores. 6 Raffles Blvd. ℂ 65/6335-2613.

Millenia Walk   Smaller than Marina Square, Millenia Walk has more upmarket boutiques like Fendi, Guess?, and Liz Claiborne, to name a few. 9 Raffles Blvd. ℂ 65/6883-1122.

Suntec City Mall   Here are tons of shops selling fashion, sports equipment, books, and CDs, plus restaurants and food courts, along with a cinema adjacent to the Suntec Convention Centre. 3 Temasek Blvd. ℂ 65/6821-3668.

AROUND THE CITY CENTER

Although the Historic District doesn't have as many malls as the Orchard Road area, it still has some good shopping. Raffles City can be overwhelming in its size, but it can be convenient because it sits right atop the City Hall MRT stop. One of my favorite places to go, however, is the very upmarket Raffles Hotel Shopping Arcade, where I like to window-shop and dream about actually being able to afford some of the stuff on display.

Parco Bugis Junction   Here you'll find restaurants—both fast food and fine dining—mixed in with clothing retailers, most of which sell fun fashions for younger tastes. 230 Victoria St. ℂ 65/6334-8831.

Raffles City Shopping Centre   Raffles City sits right on top of the City Hall MRT station, which makes it a very well-visited mall. Men's and women's fashions, books, cosmetics, accessories, and gifts are sold in shops here. 252 North Bridge Rd. ℂ 65/6338-7766.

Raffles Hotel Shopping Arcade   These shops are mostly haute couture; however, there is the Raffles Hotel gift shop for interesting souvenirs. For golfers, there's a Jack Nicklaus signature store. 328 North Bridge Rd. ℂ 65/6337-1886.

THE SHOPPING SCENE, PART 2: MULTICULTURAL SHOPPING

The most exciting shopping has got to be in all the ethnic enclaves throughout the city. Down narrow streets, bargains are to be had on all sorts of unusual items. If you're stuck for a gift idea, read on.

CHINATOWN

For Chinese goods, nothing beats **Yue Hwa** ★★, 70 Eu Tong Sen St. (ℂ 65/6538-4222), a five-story Chinese emporium that's an attraction in its own right. The superb inventory includes all manner of silk wear (robes, underwear, blouses), embroidery and house linens, bolt silks, tailoring services (for perfect mandarin dresses!), cloisonné (enamel work) jewelry and gifts, pottery, musical instruments, traditional Chinese clothing for men and women (from scholars' robes to coolie duds), jade and gold, cashmere, art supplies, herbs—I could go on and on. Prices are terrific. Plan to spend some time here.

For one-stop souvenir shopping, you can tick off half your list at **Chinatown Point,** aka the **Singapore Handicraft Center,** 133 New Bridge Rd. (© **6534-0112**), with dozens of small shops that sell mainly Chinese handicrafts, from carved jade to imported Chinese classical instruments and lacquerware. The best gifts include hand-carved chops (Chinese seals); a few shops offer good selections of stone, wood, bone, glass, and ivory chops ready to be carved to your specifications. Simple designs are affordable, although some of the more elaborate chops and carvings fetch a handsome sum. You can also commission a personalized Chinese scroll painting or calligraphy piece.

My all-time favorite gift idea? Spend an afternoon learning the traditional Chinese tea ceremony at the **Tea Chapter,** 9–11 Neil Rd. (© **65/6226-1175**), and pick up a tea set—there's a lovely selection of tea pots, cups and accessories, as well as quality teas for sale. When you return home, you'll be ready to give a fabulous gift—not just a tea set, but your own cultural performance as well. Another neat place is **Kwong Chen Beverage Trading,** 16 Smith St. (© **65/6223-6927**), for Chinese teas in handsome tins. Although the teas are really inexpensive, they're packed in lovely tins—buy lots to bring back as smaller gifts. For serious tea aficionados or those curious about Traditional Chinese Medicine (TCM), stop by **Eu Yan Sang,** 269 South Bridge Rd. (© **65/6223-6333;** www.euyansang.com.sg), which stocks very fine (and expensive) teas, plus herbal remedies for health.

For something a little more unusual, check out **Siong Moh Paper Products,** 39 Mosque St. (© **65/6224-3125**), which also carries a full line of ceremonial items. Pick up some joss sticks (temple incense) or joss paper (books of thin sheets of paper, stamped in reds and yellows with bits of gold and silver leaf). Definitely a conversation piece, as is the Hell Money, stacks of "money" that believers burn at the temple for their ancestors to use in the afterlife. Perfect for that friend who has everything?

Also, if you duck over to **Sago Lane** while you're in the neighborhood, there are a few souvenir shops that sell Chinese kites and Cantonese opera masks—cool for kids.

ARAB STREET

Over on Arab Street, shop for handicrafts from Malaysia and Indonesia. **Hadjee Textiles,** 75 Arab St. (© **65/6298-1943**), has stacks of folded sarongs in beautiful colors and traditional patterns. They're perfect for traveling, as they're lightweight but can serve as a dressy skirt, bedsheet, beach blanket, window shade, bath towel, or whatever you need—when I'm on the road I can't live without mine. Buy a few here and the prices really drop. If you're in the market for a more masculine sarong, **Goodwill Trading,** 56 Arab St. (© **65/6298-3205**), specializes in *pulicat,* or the plaid sarongs worn by Malay men.

For modern styles of batik, check out **Basharahil Brothers,** 101 Arab St. (© **65/ 6296-0432**), for very interesting designs, but don't forget to see the collection of fine silk batiks in the back. For batik household linens, you can't beat **Maruti Textiles,** 93 Arab St. (© **65/6392-0253**), where you'll find high-quality place mats and napkins, tablecloths, pillow covers, and quilts from India. The buyer for this shop has a good eye for style.

A few shops on Arab Street carry handicrafts from Southeast Asia. For antiques and curios, try **Gim Joo Trading,** 16 Baghdad St. (© **65/6293-5638**), a jumble of the unusual, some of it old. A departure from the more packed and dusty places here,

Suraya Betawj, 67 Arab St. (© **65/6398-1607**), carries gorgeous Indonesian and Malaysian crafted housewares in contemporary design—the type you normally find for huge prices in catalogs back home.

Other unique treasures include the large assortment of fragrance oils at **Aljunied Brothers,** 91 Arab St. (© **65/6293-2751**). Muslims are forbidden from consuming alcohol in any form (a proscription that includes the wearing of alcohol-based perfumes as well), so these oil-based perfumes re-create designer scents. Check out the delicate cut-glass bottles and atomizers as well.

Finally, for the crafter in your life, **Kin Lee & Co.,** 109 Arab St. (© **65/6291-1411**), carries a complete line of patterns and accessories with which to make local Peranakan beaded slippers. In vivid colors and floral designs, these traditional slippers have always been made by hand, to be attached later to a wooden sole. The finished versions are exquisite, plus they're fun to make.

LITTLE INDIA

Serangoon Road is where Singapore's Indian community shops for Indian imports and cultural items. The best place to start is **Mustapha's** ✹✹, 320 Serangoon Rd./145 Syed Alwi Rd., at the corner of Serangoon and Syed Alwi roads (© **65/6299-2603**), but be warned, you can spend the whole day here—and night, too, because Mustapha's is open 24 hours every day. This maze of a department store fills two city blocks full of imported items from India. Granted, much of it is everyday stuff, but the real finds are rows of saris and silk fabrics; two floors of jaw-dropping gold jewelry; an entire supermarket packed with spices and packets of instant curries; readymade Indian-style tie-dye and embroidered casual wear; incense and perfume oils; cotton tapestries and textiles for the home; and the list goes on. Prices can't be beat, seriously.

Little India offers all sorts of small finds, especially throughout **Little India Arcade,** 48 Serangoon Rd., and just across the street at **Kuna's,** 3 Campbell Lane (© **65/6294-2700**). Here you can buy inexpensive Indian costume jewelry like bangles, earrings, and necklaces in exotic designs, plus a wide assortment of decorative dots (called *pottu* in Tamil) to grace your forehead. Indian handicrafts include brasswork, woodcarvings, dyed tapestries, woven cotton household linens, small curios, inexpensive incense, colorful pictures of Hindu gods, and other ceremonial items.

Across the street from Little India Arcade, the second floor of **Zhujiao Centre** is packed with stall after stall of inexpensive *salwar kameez,* or Punjabi suits, the three-piece outfits—long tunic over pants, with matching shawl—worn by northern Indian ladies. Don't be afraid to bargain. **Punjab Bazaar,** 01–07 Little India Arcade, 48 Serangoon Rd. (© **65/6296-0067**), carries a more upmarket selection, in many styles and fabrics. If nothing strikes your fancy at Punjab Bazaar, try **Roopalee Fashions,** a little farther down at 84 Serangoon Rd. (© **65/6298-0558**). Both these shops carry sandals, bags, and other accessories to complement your new outfit.

9 Singapore After Dark

Major cultural festivals are highly publicized by the **Singapore Tourism Board (STB),** which will give you complete details at its visitor centers or on its website. A great source is the "Life!" section of *Straits Times,* which lists events for each day, plus theater and cinema listings. *I-S Magazine,* a free publication, promotes Singapore's clubbing lifestyle.

TICKETS   Two ticket agents, **TicketCharge** (② **65/6296-2929;** www.ticketcharge. com.sg) and **Sistic** (② **65/6348-5555;** www.sistic.com.sg), handle bookings for almost all theater performances, concerts, and special events. Before your trip, you can browse schedules at their websites. When in Singapore, call for more information or stop by one of their centrally located outlets: TicketCharge is at Centrepoint, Forum–The Shopping Mall, Funan–The IT Mall, Marina Square Shopping Centre, and Tanglin Mall. Sistic is at the Victoria Concert Hall Box Office, Parco Bugis Junction, Raffles Shopping Centre, Scotts, Specialists' Shopping Center, Suntec Mall, and Wisma Atria.

HOURS   Theater and dance performances can begin anywhere between 7:30 and 9pm. Be sure to call for the exact time, and don't be late—at Esplanade, latecomers are not allowed in. Many bars open in the late afternoon, a few as early as lunchtime. Disco and entertainment clubs usually open around 6pm, but generally don't get lively until 10 or 11pm. Closing time for bars and clubs is 3am on Friday and Saturday, 1 or 2am the rest of the week. A rare few have extended hours until 6am.

DRESS CODE   Many clubs require smart casual attire. Feel free to be trendy, but stay away from shorts, T-shirts, sneakers, and torn jeans. Be forewarned that you may be turned away if not properly dressed. Many locals dress up for a night on the town, usually in elegant garb or fashionista threads.

DRINK PRICES   Because of the government's added tariff, alcoholic beverage prices are high everywhere, whether in a hotel bar or a neighborhood pub. "House-pour" drinks (generics) are between S$8 and S$14 (US$4.70–US$8.25/£2.60–£4.55). A glass of house wine will cost S$10 to S$15 (US$5.90–US$8.80/£3.25–£4.85). Local draft beer (Tiger), brewed in Singapore, is around S$10 (US$5.90/£3.25). Hotel establishments are, on average, the most expensive venues, while stand-alone pubs and cafes are better value. Almost every bar and club has an early-evening happy hour, with discounts of up to 50% for house pours and drafts. Most of the disco and entertainment clubs charge covers, but they will usually include one drink. Hooray for ladies' nights—at least 1 night during the week—when those of the feminine persuasion get in for free.

THE BAR & CLUB SCENE

Singaporeans love to go out at night, whether it's to lounge around in a cozy wine bar or to jump around a dance floor until 3am. This city has become pretty eclectic in its entertainment choices, so you'll find everything from live jazz to acid jazz, from polished cover bands to internationally acclaimed guest DJs. The nightlife is happening. Local celebrities and the young, wealthy, and beautiful are the heroes of the scene, and their quest for the "coolest" spot keeps the club scene on its toes.

BARS

The **Hard Rock Cafe,** #02-01 HPL House, 50 Cusacaden Rd. (② **65/6235-5232**), is just like the one in your hometown, so why bother? The resident band is pretty good and, of course, so are the burgers, but beyond that it's not much more than a tourist pickup joint.

Bar Cocoon   The IndoChine group of restaurants operates several chic bars throughout the city. They're loungey, with the feel of a luxe opium den; you'll feel enveloped in stylish Southeast Asian decor and groovy textural music. A sensual place to meet for a cocktail before dinner, to relax for a nightcap, or to just loll away the hours. Also check out sister bars: **Bar Opiume,** 1 Empress Place, Asian Civilisations Museum (✆ **65/6339-2876**), and **Bar SaVanh,** 49A Club St. (✆ **65/6323-0145**). Open Sunday through Thursday from 5pm to 3am, Friday and Saturday from 5pm to 6am. 3A Merchant's Court, Clarke Quay, River Valley Road #01-02. ✆ **65/6557-6268.**

Brix   Brix hosts a good house band and international visiting groups. A pickup joint of sorts, it's a bit more sophisticated than others. The Music Bar features live jazz and R & B, while the Wine & Whiskey Bar serves up wine, Scotch, and cognac. Open Sunday through Thursday from 7pm to 2am, Friday and Saturday from 7pm to 3am. Happy hour is nightly from 7 to 9pm. At the Grand Hyatt, 10 Scotts Rd., basement. ✆ **65/ 6416-7292.** Cover after 9pm S$35 (US$22/£12).

Coastes   In urban Singapore, you can almost forget that technically you're on a tropical island. When that happens, trek out to Coastes, an open-air bar where you can step off the deck and into the sand. Cold beer and exotic cocktails are served at shady tables or at lounge chairs under the sun while you chill out to cool Ibiza party music. Coastes also serves pizza, burgers, and pasta for lunch and dinner daily. Open Monday through Thursday from 10am to midnight, Friday from 10am to 1am, Saturday from 9am to 1am, and Sunday from 9am to midnight. 50 Siloso Beach Walk, #01-05-06, Sentosa Island. ✆ **65/6274-9668.**

Crazy Elephant   The Crazy Elephant is the city's address for blues rock. Breezes blow off the river while you listen to classic rock and blues by resident bands. This place has hosted, in addition to some excellent local and regional guitarists, international greats such as Rick Derringer, Eric Burdon, and Walter Trout. It's an unpretentious place to chill out and have a cold one. Open Sunday through Thursday from 5pm to 1am, Friday and Saturday from 5pm to 2am, with happy hour daily from 5 to 9pm. 3E River Valley Rd., #01-06/07 Traders Market, Clarke Quay. ✆ **65/6337-1990.**

Dubliner Singapore   Located in a restored colonial building, the Dubliner's got great atmosphere, with vaulted ceilings, tiled floors, pretty plasterwork, and outdoor seating on the veranda. It's also a decent Irish pub, with a friendly staff and a cast of regulars from the local expat crowd. Sports matches are broadcast regularly (mainly soccer), and there's a variety of cold beer on tap. Open Sunday through Thursday from 11am to 1am, Friday and Saturday from 11am to 2am; daily happy hour runs from 5 to 8pm. Winsland Conservation House, 165 Penang Rd. ✆ **65/6735-2220.**

Long Bar   Here's a gem of a bar, even if it is touristy and expensive. With tiled mosaic floors, shuttered windows, and fans moving in waves above, Raffles Hotel has tried to retain much of the charm of yesteryear, so you can enjoy a Singapore Sling in its birthplace and take yourself back to when history was made. And truly, the thrill at the Long Bar is tossing back one of these sweet juicy drinks while pondering the adventures of all the famous actors, writers, and artists who came through here in the early 20th century. If you're not inspired by the poetry of the moment, stick around till 9pm for the pop/reggae band, which is quite good. Open Sunday through Thursday from 11am to 1am, Friday and Saturday from 11am to 2am. Happy hour is nightly from 6 to 9pm, with special deals on pitchers of beer and some mixed drinks. A Singapore Sling is S$21 (US$13/£6.95); a Sling with souvenir glass costs S$32 (US$20/£11). At the Raffles Hotel Arcade, Raffles Hotel, 1 Beach Rd. ✆ **65/6337-1886.**

Muddy Murphy's   This is another popular Irish bar, with big-screen viewing of international soccer and rugby matches, plus live bands on weekends (otherwise it's canned Irish music). The ambience is created by the mostly Irish imported trappings around the place. A limited menu for lunch, dinner, and snacks is available. Open Sunday through Thursday from 11am to 1am, Friday and Saturday from 11am to 3am. Happy hour is daily from 11am to 7:30pm (its happy hour begins earlier, but the discount is not as great as at other places). #B1-01/01-06 Orchard Hotel Shopping Arcade, 442 Orchard Rd. ℂ 65/6735-0400.

Next Page   Few bars stand out like the Next Page, a freaky Chinese dream in an old Singaporean shophouse. Creep through the *pintu pagar* front door into the main room, its old walls of crumbling stucco washed in sexy Chinese red, the lanterns glowing crimson in the air shaft rising above the island bar. The crowd is mainly young professionals who have been known to dance on the bar. The back has a bit more space for seating, darts, and a pool table. A small snack menu is available. Open daily from 3pm to 3am. Happy hour is daily from 3 to 9pm. 17 Mohamed Sultan Rd. ℂ 65/6235-6967.

No. 5   Down Peranakan Place is no. 5, a cool, dark spot just dripping with Southeast Asian ambience, from its old shophouse exterior to its partially crumbling interior walls hung with rich woodcarvings. The hardwood floors and beamed ceilings are complemented by seating areas cozied up with Oriental carpets and kilim throw pillows. Upstairs is more conventional table-and-chair seating. This is an ideal place to stop for a cool drink on a hot afternoon. In the evenings, be prepared for a lively mix of people. Open Monday through Thursday from noon to 2am, Friday and Saturday from noon to 3am, Sunday from 5pm to 2am. Happy hour is daily from noon to 9pm. 5 Emerald Hill. ℂ 65/6732-0818.

MICROBREWERIES

Brewerkz   Brewerkz, with outside seating along the river and an airy contemporary style inside—like a giant IKEA warehouse built around brewing kettles and copper pipes—brews the best house beer in Singapore. The bar menu features five tasty selections from recipes created by the English brewmaster: Nut Brown Ale, Red Ale, Wiesen, Bitter, and Indian Pale Ale (which, by the way, has the highest alcohol content). The American cuisine for lunch, dinner, and snacks is also very good—I recommend planning a meal here as well. Open Sunday through Thursday from 5pm to 1am, Friday and Saturday from 5pm to 3am. Happy hour is daily from 3 to 9pm. #01-05 Riverside Point, 30 Merchant Rd. ℂ 65/6438-7438.

JAZZ BARS

Harry's Bar   The official after-work stop for finance professionals from nearby Shenton Way, Harry's biggest claim to fame is that it was bank-buster Nick Leeson's favorite bar. But don't let the power ties put you off. Harry's is a cool place, from its airy riverside seating to cozy tables next to the stage. It's known for its live jazz and R & B music. Of all the choices along Boat Quay, Harry's remains the classiest; and even though it's also the most popular, you can usually get a seat. Upstairs, the wine bar is very laid-back, with plush sofas and dimly lit seating areas.

Recently, Harry's outposts have been opening all over the city: **Harry's @ Esplanade,** Esplanade Mall #01-05/07, 8 Raffles Ave. (ℂ 65/6334-0132); **Harry's @ HarbourFront,** HarbourFront Centre, #01-64 Maritime Sq. (ℂ 65/6271-8234); **Harry's @ Orchard,** Orchard Towers, #01-05 and #02-08/09, 1 Claymore Dr. (ℂ 65/6736-7330); **Harry's @ Holland V,** Holland Village, 27 Lorong Mambong (ℂ 65/6467-4222); and two branches at **Changi Airport.** Open Sunday through Thursday from 11am to 1am, Friday and Saturday from 11am to 2am. Happy hour is daily from 11am to 9pm. 28 Boat Quay. ℂ 65/6538-3029.

Jazz@Southbridge   This is the only true jazz bar in Singapore. Most other "jazz" joints mix in a bit of blues and rock to attract a wider audience—but owner Eddie Chan wouldn't allow such a thing! The resident band is fun and very good. The place gets crowded and smoky, but people are friendly, especially if you want to talk about music. When visiting performers play, a cover is charged. Open Tuesday through Sunday from 5:30pm to 1am (sometimes later). 82B Boat Quay. ✆ 65/6327-4671.

Raffles Bar & Billiards   Talk about a place rich with the kind of elegance only history can provide. Raffles Bar & Billiards began as a bar in 1896 and over the decades has been transformed to perform various functions as the hotel's needs dictated. In its early days, legend has it that a patron shot the last tiger in Singapore under a pool table here. Whether or not the tiger part is true, one of its two billiards tables is an original piece, still in use after 100 years. In fact, many of the fixtures and furniture here are original Raffles antiques, including the scoreboards. In the evenings, a jazzy little trio shakes the ghosts out of the rafters, while the well-heeled lounge around enjoying single malts, cognacs, coffee, port, chocolates, and imported cigars. Expect to drop a small fortune. Open daily from 11:30am to 12:30am. Raffles Hotel, 1 Beach Rd. ✆ 65/6331-1746.

CLUBS

Bar None   In Singapore's trendy club scene, nightclubs come and go. Bar None is one place that has enjoyed steady success, probably because it does a great job keeping up with its patrons' needs, with regularly scheduled theme parties and comedy nights. Resident band Jive Talking plays a high-voltage mix of R & B, Top 40, and rock. Be prepared to queue up on weekends. On some Mondays, Bar None opens its stage to local indie bands. Open Tuesday through Sunday from 7pm to 3am, Monday from 7pm to 2am. Happy hour is 7 to 9pm. Marriott Hotel, 320 Orchard Rd., basement. ✆ 65/6831-4656. Cover Fri S$25 (US$16/£8.25) for men, S$20 (US$13/£6.60) for women; includes 1 drink.

DBL O   Singapore's cheapest club has S$12 (US$7.50/£4.10) jugs of bottom-shelf mixed drinks and draft beer all night, every night (a jug is about four drinks). A cavernous place with a Top 40 dance music, it's popular with those who want to hang out without the pretenses of some of the newer fashion-victim clubs. Two bars within the club have a garden terrace and pool tables. Open Wednesday through Friday from 8pm to 3am and Saturday from 8pm to 4am. 11 Unity St. #01-24 Robertson Walk. ✆ 65/6735-2008. Cover varies for men and women, from S$15 to S$25 (US$9.60–US$16/£4.95–£8.25).

Thumper   Amid all the new hot spots that come and go, Thumper's held ground, with a steady stream of high-profile celebs keeping it hip. It does have one timeless feature: a really nice terrace for happy-hour cocktails as the sun sets over Scotts Road. In the early evenings, you'll hear live soul; later on, a live funk band gets the dance floor moving. Open Monday and Tuesday from 6pm to 2am, Wednesday and Thursday from 6pm to 3am, and Friday and Saturday from 6pm to 4am. Happy hour is daily from 11am to 9pm. At the Goodwood Park Hotel, 22 Scotts Rd. ✆ 65/6735-0827. Cover varies; includes 1 drink.

Top Ten   The most notoriously sleazy joint in Singapore throws a wild party every night of the week. The huge space is like an auditorium, with multilevel loungey areas looking down onto one of Singapore's best soundstages and dance floors. A cover band plays three sets of pop and rock 7 days a week, but people don't come here for the decor or the music: Top Ten is a pickup joint for Thai working girls. Other clubs in the building, called Orchard Towers, host ladies from other parts of the region, which is how the building got its unofficial name . . . Four Floors of Whores. No joke. Open daily from 5pm to 3am, with happy hour from 9 to 11pm. #04-35/36 Orchard Towers, 400 Orchard Rd. ☏ 65/6732-3077. Cover Fri–Sat S$18 (US$12/£5.95); includes 1 drink.

Zouk/Phuture/Velvet Underground   Singapore's first innovative danceteria, Zouk introduced the city to house music, which throbs nightly in its cavernous disco, comprising three warehouses joined together. It plays the best in modern music, so even if you're not much of a groover, you can still have fun watching the party from the many levels that tower above the dance floor. If you need a bit more intimacy, Velvet Underground, within the Zouk complex, drips in red velvet and soft lighting—a good complement to the more soulful sounds spinning here. The newer addition to Zouk, Phuture, draws a younger, more hip-hop–loving crowd than VU. Including the outdoor wine bar, Zouk is your one-stop shop for a party; in Singapore, this place is legendary. All clubs are open daily from 6pm to 3am. 17 Jiak Kim St. ☏ 65/6738-2988. Cover varies. Pay the highest cover of the 3 clubs (S$12–S$28/US$7.70–US$18/£3.95–£9.25) and freely hop between them; otherwise, pay extra as you go from one to the next.

GAY NIGHTSPOTS

Singapore's gay clubbing scene is alive and well, but still very underground. Bars come and go, so to get the very latest happenings, you'll have to go beyond mainstream media. The Web has listings at **www.utopia-asia.com**, where you'll find the best information on the most recent parties and hangouts. For the latest info, I'd recommend one of the chat rooms suggested at the address above. **Velvet Underground,** part of the Zouk complex (see above), also welcomes a mixed clientele of gays, lesbians, and straight folks.

WINE BARS

Beaujolais   This little gem, in a shophouse built on a hill, is tiny, but its charm makes it a favorite for regulars. Two tables outside (on the Five-Foot-Way, which serves more as a patio than a sidewalk) and two tables inside don't seem like much room, but there's more seating upstairs. The owners believe that wine should be affordable, so their many labels tend to be more moderately priced per glass and bottle. Open Monday through Friday from 11am to 1am and Saturday and Sunday from 6pm to midnight; happy hour runs from opening until 9pm. 1 Ann Siang Hill. ☏ 65/6224-2227.

Que Pasa   One of the more mellow stops along Peranakan Place, this little wine bar serves up a collection of some 70 to 100 labels with plenty of atmosphere and a nice central location. It's another bar in a shophouse, but this one has as its centerpiece an unusual winding stairway up the air shaft to the level above. Wine bottles and artwork line the walls. In the front, you can order tapas and cigars. The upstairs VIP club looks and feels like a formal living room, complete with wing chairs and board games. Open Sunday through Thursday from 6pm to 2am, Friday and Saturday from 6pm to 3am. 7 Emerald Hill. ☏ 65/6235-6626.

THE PERFORMING ARTS

The **Singapore Symphony Orchestra** (www.sso.org.sg) performs regularly in its new home at Esplanade–Theatres on the Bay (www.esplanade.com), with regular guest appearances by international musicians. The **Singapore Lyric Opera** (Stamford Arts Centre, 155 Waterloo St. #03-06; ☏ 65/6336-1929) also performs regularly. The **Singapore Chinese Orchestra,** the only professional Chinese orchestra in Singapore, has won several awards for its classic Chinese interpretations. It performs every 2 weeks at a variety of venues (including outdoor concerts at the Botanic Gardens). Information is available through People's Association, Block B, Room 5, no. 9 Stadium Link (© **65/6440-3839**). Ticket sales are handled by Sistic (© **65/6348-5555; www.sistic.com.sg**).

Most international theater companies perform at the new **Esplanade–Theatres on the Bay** (1 Esplanade Dr., 10-min. walk from City Hall MRT; © **65/6828-8222; www.esplanade.com**). For local theater, the best are **ACTION Theatre** (42 Waterloo St.; © **65/6837-0842**), **Necessary Stage** (126 Cairnhill Arts Centre, Cairnhill Rd.; © **65/6738-6355**), and **Singapore Repertory Theatre** (DBS Arts Centre, 20 Merbau Rd., Robertson Quay; © **65/6733-0005**).

Once upon a time, Cantonese opera could be seen under tents on street corners throughout the city. These days, local and visiting companies still perform, but very sporadically. For a performance you can count on, the **Chinese Theatre Circle,** 5 Smith St. (© **65/6323-4862**), has a 2-hour show on Friday and Saturday with excerpts from the most famous and beloved tales, accompanied by explanations of the craft. Come at 7pm for the show with "dinner" (chicken nuggets, really; tickets are S$35/US$22/£12) or at 8pm to catch the last half, with tea only (S$20/US$13/£6.60).

For something relevant to Malay culture, **Malay Village,** 39 Geylang Serai (© **65/6748-4700**), has a program on weekends that is highly commendable. Every Saturday, the troupe performs the Kuda Kepang, a traditional dance from Johor in southern Malaysia. Featuring male dancers on wooden horses, this long performance is well worth the wait. During the grand finale, the dancers walk on glass, eat glass, and tear coconuts with their teeth.

9

Malaysia

by Jennifer Eveland

Compared with spicy Thailand to the north and cosmopolitan Singapore to the south, Malaysia is a relative secret to many from the West, and most travelers to Southeast Asia skip over it, opting for more heavily traversed routes.

Boy, are they missing out. Those who venture here wander through streets awash with international influences from colonial times and trek through mysterious rainforests and caves, sometimes without another tourist in sight. They relax peacefully under palms on lazy white beaches that fade into blue, blue waters. They spy the bright colors of batik sarongs hanging to dry in the breeze. They hear the melodic drone of the Muslim call to prayer seeping from exotic mosques. They taste culinary masterpieces served in modest local shops—from Malay dishes with their deep mellow spices to succulent seafood punctuated by brilliant chile sauces. In Malaysia, I'm always thrilled to witness life without the distracting glare of the tourism industry, and I leave impressed by how accessible the country is to outsiders while remaining true to its heritage.

Malaysia just doesn't get the tourism press it deserves, but it's not because foreign travelers aren't welcome. True, the Malaysian Tourism Board has almost no international advertising campaign—and you'll be hard-pressed to get any useful information out of them—but everyone from government officials in Kuala Lumpur to boat hands in Penang seem delighted to see the smiling face of a traveler who has discovered just how beautiful their country is.

This chapter covers the major destinations of peninsular Malaysia. We begin with the country's capital, **Kuala Lumpur,** then tour the peninsula's west coast—the cities of **Malacca (Melaka),** plus islands like the popular **Penang** and luxurious **Langkawi.** Coverage also includes **Taman Negara National Park,** peninsular Malaysia's largest national forest. Finally, we cross the South China Sea to the island of **Borneo,** where the Malaysian states of **Sarawak** and **Sabah** feature Malaysia's most impressive forests as well as unique and diverse cultures.

Malaysia is accessible to the rest of the world through its international airport in Kuala Lumpur. Or if you want to hop from another country in the region, daily flights to Malaysia's many smaller airports give you access to all parts of the country, and you can also travel by car, bus, or train from Singapore or Thailand.

1 Getting to Know Malaysia

THE LAY OF THE LAND

Malaysia's territory covers peninsular Malaysia—bordering Thailand in the north just across from Singapore in the south—and two states on the island of Borneo, Sabah and Sarawak, approximately 240km (150 miles) east across the South China Sea. All

Peninsular Malaysia

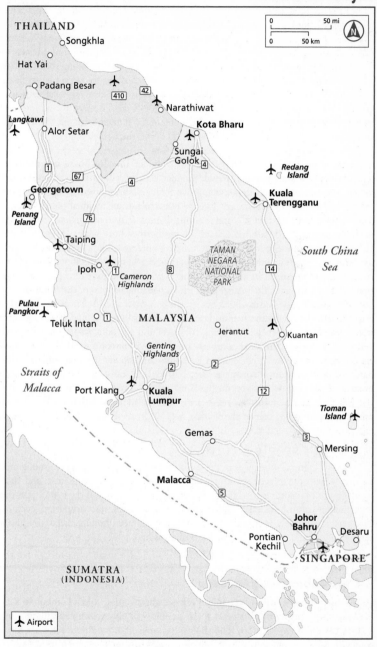

THAILAND

0 — 50 mi
0 — 50 km

Songkhla

Hat Yai

Padang Besar

Langkawi

410 42

Narathiwat

Kota Bharu

Alor Setar

Sungai
Golok 4

Georgetown

1 67

4

Redang
Island

76

**Kuala
Terengganu**

**Penang
Island**

Taiping

*South China
Sea*

Ipoh 1

*Cameron
Highlands*

8

TAMAN
NEGARA
NATIONAL
PARK

14

*Pulau
Pangkor*

MALAYSIA

Teluk Intan 1

Jerantut

Kuantan

*Genting
Highlands*

2

2

*Straits of
Malacca*

Port Klang **Kuala
Lumpur**

12

*Tioman
Island*

Gemas

3

Mersing

Malacca

5

**Johor
Bahru** Desaru

Pontian
Kechil

SINGAPORE

SUMATRA
(INDONESIA)

✈ Airport

539

13 of its states total 329,749 sq. km. (127,316 sq. miles) of land. Of this area, peninsular Malaysia makes up about 132,149 sq. km. (51,023 sq. miles) and contains 11 of Malaysia's 13 states: Kedah, Perlis, Penang, and Perak are in the northwest; Kelantan and Terengganu are in the northeast; Selangor, Negeri Sembilan, and Melaka are about midway down the peninsula on the western side; Pahang, along the east coast, sprawls inward to cover most of the central area (which is mostly forest preserve); and Johor covers the entire southern tip from east to west, with two vehicular causeways linking it to Singapore, just over the Strait of Johor. Kuala Lumpur, the nation's capital, appears on a map to be located in the center of the state of Selangor, but it is actually a federal district similar to Washington, D.C., in the United States.

Tropical evergreen forests, estimated to be some of the oldest in the world, cover more than 70% of Malaysia. The country's diverse terrain allows for a range of forest types, such as montane forests, sparsely wooded tangles at higher elevations; lowland forests, the dense tropical jungle; mangrove forests along the waters' edge; and peat swamp forest along the waterways. On the peninsula, three national forests—Taman Negara (or "National Forest") and Kenong Rimba Park, both inland, and Endau Rompin National Park, located toward the southern end of the peninsula—welcome visitors regularly, for either quiet nature walks to observe wildlife or hearty adventures like whitewater rafting, mountain climbing, caving, and jungle trekking. Similarly, the many national forests of Sabah and Sarawak provide a multitude of memorable experiences, which can include brushes with the indigenous peoples of the forests.

Surrounded by the South China Sea on the east coast and the Strait of Malacca on the west, the waters off the peninsula vary in terms of sea life (and beach life). The waters off the east coast house a living coral reef and gorgeous tropical beaches, with beach-resort areas in the more southerly parts. By way of contrast, the surf in southern portions of the Strait of Malacca is choppy and cloudy from shipping traffic—hardly ideal for diving or for the perfect Bali Hai vacation. But once you get as far north as Penang, the waters become beautiful again. Meanwhile, the sea coast of Sabah and Sarawak counts numerous resort areas that are ideal for beach vacationing and scuba diving. In fact, one of the world's top 10 dive sites is located at Sipadan, in Sabah.

MALAYSIA'S PEOPLE & CULTURE

The mix of cultural influences in Malaysia is the result of centuries of immigration and trade with the outside world, particularly with Arab nations, China, and India. Early groups of incoming foreigners brought wealth from around the world, plus their own unique cultural heritages and religions. Furthermore, once imported, each culture remained largely intact; that is, none has truly been homogenized. Traditional temples and churches exist side by side with mosques.

Tips Abbreviating Malaysia

The first tip here is that people are always abbreviating Kuala Lumpur to KL. Okay, that's pretty obvious. But these people will abbreviate everything else they can get away with. So, Johor Bahru becomes JB; Kota Bharu, KB; Kota Kinabalu, KK—you get the picture. Malaysia itself is often shortened to M'sia. To make it easier for you, the only shortened term used in this chapter is KL.

Likewise, **traditional art forms** of various cultures are still practiced in Malaysia, most notably in the areas of dance and performance art. Chinese opera, Indian dance, and Malay martial arts are all very popular cultural activities. Silat, originating from a martial arts form (and still practiced as such by many), is a dance performed by men and women. Religious and cultural festivals are open for everyone to appreciate and enjoy. Unique arts and traditions of indigenous people distinguish Sabah and Sarawak from the rest of the country.

Traditional **Malaysian music** is very similar to Indonesian music. Heavy on rhythms, its constant drum beats underneath the light repetitive melodies of the stringed gamelan (no relation at all to the Indonesian metallophone gamelan, with its gongs and xylophones) will entrance you with its simple beauty.

ETIQUETTE

Questions of etiquette in Malaysia are very similar to those in Singapore, so please see "Etiquette" in chapter 8 for more information.

LANGUAGE

The national language is Malay, or Bahasa Malaysia, although English is widely spoken. Chinese dialects and Tamil are also heard here. For a list of useful Malay phrases, please see "Language" in chapter 8.

2 The Best of Malaysia in 2 Weeks

Most visitors to Malaysia will arrive at Kuala Lumpur's (KL's) international airport, spend a day in the capital, then run around the country trying to see as much as they can in a short span of time. While it's natural to want to maximize your vacation time, I am of the philosophy that to try to pack too much into your holiday will actually detract from your overall travel experience. I recommend that you see no more than three destinations in 1 week, preferably only two. That way you have time not just to see the sights, but to stop and feel the rhythm of local life—to eat the food, smell the smells, speak with the people.

This route gives you some choices, depending on your particular interests. It brings you to Peninsular Malaysia's most historically significant destinations: Kuala Lumpur, Penang, and Malacca. You'll learn about the earliest trading ports and colonial history, and have time to shop and savor local treats. If you want to mix history and nature, the Taman Negara preserve is within hopping distance from KL; it's very easy to combine an overnight trip to Malacca with a 3-night package to the park. If you want to delve deeper into rainforest habitats, fly to Kota Kinabalu and sign up for a tour of the area's national parks; if it's indigenous cultures you'd like to visit, fly out to Sarawak, spend a day exploring Kuching, then join a boat trip into the interior to visit longhouse communities. Remember, if you go the outdoor-adventure route, be sure to check monsoon seasons with your tour coordinator. Also, for dive tours you'll have to allow extra time between flights and dives for your body to acclimate to the change in altitudes.

Days ❶–❸: Arrive in Kuala Lumpur
After arriving in Malaysia's capital city, allow yourself a full day to recover and just spend your time wandering through the city's streets. Start at **Merdeka Square,** the focal point of Colonial KL. Just behind the Moorish Sultan Abdul Samad Building, in the streets surrounding the Jame Mosque, you'll find KL's Little India of sorts. Continue your walk to the **Central Market,** where nearby coffee shops can provide a place to rest. After exploring stall after stall of Malaysian handicrafts at the Central Market, if you still have time and energy, cross the street to **Chinatown,** where you'll find more shopping, a street bazaar, and the **Sri Mahamariaman Hindu Temple.**

Day ❹: Malacca 🎔🎔
Take an early-morning bus to Malacca and spend the day exploring the town's historic heart. The most important things to see here are the **Stadthuys,** the history

museum, located in the hard-to-miss red colonial building; the **Cultural Museum,** in a replica of a Malay-style palace; and the **Baba Nyonya Heritage Museum,** located inside an old millionaire's mansion. From the Baba Nyonya Museum, head to **Jonker Walk** to wander through temples and antiques shops.

Days ❺–❻: Penang 🎔🎔🎔
Take an early-morning bus back to KL, then board a flight to Penang. Allow 1 day for the journey. Check into your resort at **Batu Feringgi** so that when you arrive, you can unwind with a cocktail as you watch the setting sun from the beach.

Day ❼: Georgetown 🎔🎔🎔
Here's what I have to say about Georgetown: Don't plan your time too closely. Start off at the **Penang Museum and Art Gallery,** where you'll get a brilliant overview of the island's history and cultures, and then just spend your time walking through the streets. Attractions

are all situated within walking distance, but don't rush: Take time to peek in the shop doors and snack on the local treats you'll find along the way. Just make sure you're at the **Cheong Fatt Tze Mansion** in time for the 11am or 3pm tour—consider it a must! Afterwards, mosey over to the **E&O Hotel** for either lunch or high tea in the old colonial grande dame.

Day ❽: Penang Hill

The funicular train up the side of Penang Hill was built in 1923 to take British colonials up to the cooler climate of the hill, where they built lovely country homes and gardens. Today the train still operates as a commuter service to the communities in this part of the island. Get there before 9am to beat the long queue. At the top of the hill you'll find restaurants, temples, and trails, one of which will lead you down to the botanical gardens.

Days ❾–❶❷: Taman Negara National Park ✿✿✿

Take an early-morning bus back from Malacca to KL; then board an afternoon bus to Malaysia's premier, and most accessible, national park. Hop a boat upstream to the resort and check in for a good night's rest. Taman Negara can be done very nicely in a full-board package. You'll have the chance to jungle trek, traverse a canopy walk, view wildlife from observation stations, go on a night hike, river raft and fish, and meet *orang asli* communities.

Days ❶❸–❶❹: Back to KL

Hop a flight back to KL to prepare for your return home. If you have time, you can stock up on gifts at **KL Craft Complex**—you'll find something for everyone on your list, in all price ranges, at this handicrafts showroom.

3 Planning Your Trip to Malaysia

VISITOR INFORMATION

The **Malaysia Tourism Board** (**MTB;** www.tourismmalaysia.gov.my) can provide some information by way of pamphlets and advice before your trip, but keep in mind that it's not as sophisticated as, say, the Singapore Tourism Board. Much of the information it provides is vague, broad-stroke descriptions with few concrete details that are useful for the traveler—a lot of it quite outdated.

Within Malaysia, each state or tourist destination has its own tourism board that operates a website and local offices for visitor information. These are your best bets, as they have on-the-ground knowledge that's more current. For each destination below, the relevant tourist offices' websites and contact information are listed.

ENTRY REQUIREMENTS

To enter the country, you must have a valid passport. Citizens of the U.S. do not need visas for tourism and business visits, and upon entry are granted a Social/Business Visit Pass good for up to 3 months. Citizens of Canada, Australia, New Zealand, and the U.K. can also enter the country without a visa; they will be granted a pass for up to 30 days' stay upon entry. For other countries, please consult the nearest Malaysian consulate before your trip for visa regulations. Also, note that travelers holding Israeli passports are not permitted to travel within Malaysia (likewise, Malaysians are forbidden from traveling to Israel).

If you are arriving from an area in which yellow fever has been reported, you will be required to show proof of yellow-fever vaccination. Contact your nearest MTB office to research the specific areas that fall into this category.

CUSTOMS REGULATIONS

You can bring into the country as many foreign currency notes or traveler's checks as you please, but you are not allowed to leave the country with more foreign currency or traveler's checks than you had when you arrived.

Social visitors can enter Malaysia with 1 liter of hard alcohol and one carton of cigarettes without paying duty—anything over that amount is subject to local taxes. Prohibited items include firearms and ammunition, daggers and knives, and pornographic materials. Be advised that, similar to Singapore, Malaysia enforces a very strict drug policy that includes the death sentence for convicted drug traffickers.

MONEY

Malaysia's currency is the **ringgit (RM).** Notes are issued in denominations of RM1, 2, 5, 10, 20, 50, 100, 500, and 1,000. One ringgit is equal to 100 sen. Coins come in denominations of 1, 5, 10, 20, and 50 sen, and there's also a 1-ringgit coin. In 2005, Malaysia ended a 7-year peg of the ringgit at RM3.80 to US$1. Now, the country uses a managed float system that measures the currency against a basket of several major currencies. At the time of writing, the exchange rate was approximately **RM3.57 = US$1.**

ATMs Kuala Lumpur, Penang, and Johor Bahru have quite a few ATMs scattered around, but they are few and far between in smaller towns and nonexistent on smaller islands and in remote beach areas. In addition, some ATMs will not accept credit or debit cards from your home bank. Debit cards on the MasterCard/Cirrus or Visa/PLUS networks are almost always accepted at **Maybank,** which has at least one location in every major town. Cash is dispensed in ringgit, deducted from your account at the day's rate.

CURRENCY EXCHANGE Currency can be changed at banks and hotels, but you'll get a more favorable rate if you go to one of the money changers that seem to be everywhere: in shopping centers, in little lanes, and in small stores (just look for signs). They are often men in tiny booths with a lit display on the wall behind them showing the exchange rate. All major currencies are generally accepted, and there is never a problem with the U.S. dollar.

TRAVELER'S CHECKS Generally, travelers to Malaysia will never go wrong with American Express and Thomas Cook traveler's checks, which can be cashed at banks, hotels, and licensed money changers. Unfortunately, they are often not accepted at smaller shops. Even in some big restaurants and department stores, many cashiers don't know how to process these checks, which might lead to a long and frustrating wait.

CREDIT CARDS Credit cards are widely accepted at hotels and restaurants, and at many shops as well. Most popular are American Express, MasterCard, and Visa. Some banks may also be willing to advance cash against your credit card, but this service is not available everywhere. To report a lost or stolen card, call **American Express** at its head office in Kuala Lumpur (© **03/2050-8888**). For **MasterCard,** call © **800/804-594,** and for **Visa,** call © **800/800-159;** both of these numbers are toll-free from anywhere in Malaysia.

WHEN TO GO

There are two peak seasons in Malaysia, one in winter and another in summer. Both seasons experience approximately equal tourist traffic, but in summer months, that traffic may ebb and flow.

The peak winter season falls roughly from early December through January, covering the major winter holidays—Christmas, New Year's Day, and Chinese New Year. Hari Raya Puasa, celebrating the end of Ramadan, shifts dates from year to year. If you plan to travel to Malaysia between November and January, call the MTB to find out exactly when this holiday will fall.

Malaysia's school holidays last about 1 or 2 weeks each during March, June, and August, then again from November through December. Singapore's school holidays occur from mid-May through June, and again during November and December, when families are likely to flock to Malaysia's seaside resorts, particularly the budget and midpriced properties. I hate to say it, but I've heard numerous complaints about resort holidays that have become nightmares when guests have to wrestle to get to the breakfast buffet and suffer screaming children around the pool.

The peak summer season falls in June, July, and August, and can last into mid-September. During this period, hotels are booked solid with families from the Middle East, as this is school-holiday season for many of the region's countries. After September, it's quiet again until December.

CLIMATE   Climate considerations will play a role in your plans. If you want to visit any of the east coast's resort areas, the low season is between November and March, when the monsoon tides make the water too choppy for watersports and beach activities. During this time, many island resorts will close. On the west coast, the rainy season is from April through May, and again from October through November.

The temperature is basically static year-round. Daily averages are between 67° and 90°F (19° and 32°C). Temperatures in the hill resorts get a little cooler, averaging 67°F (19°C) during the day and 50°F (10°C) at night.

PUBLIC HOLIDAYS & EVENTS   During Malaysia's official public holidays, expect government offices to be closed, as well as some shops and restaurants, depending on the ethnicity of the owner. During **Hari Raya Puasa** and **Chinese New Year,** you can expect many shop and restaurant closings. However, also look out for special sales and celebrations. Count on parks, shopping malls, and beaches to be more crowded during public holidays, as locals will be taking advantage of their time off.

Official public holidays fall as follows: **New Year's Day** (Jan 1), **Chinese New Year** (Feb 18–19, 2007; Feb 7–8, 2008), **Prophet Muhammad's Birthday** (Mar 31, 2007), **Labor Day** (May 1), **Wesak Day** (May 1, 2007; May 19, 2008), **King's Birthday** (June 2), **National Day** (Aug 31), **Hari Raya Aidil Fitri** (also called **Hari Raya Puasa,** Oct 13–14, 2007; Oct 2–3, 2008), **Deepavali** (Nov 8, 2007; Oct 27, 2008), **Hari Raya Haji** (Dec 20–21, 2007; Dec 9–10, 2008), and **Christmas** (Dec 25). *Note:* Please confirm all 2008 dates listed above before you plan your trip; at the time of writing, dates beyond 2007 could not be confirmed by any authority. In addition, each state has a public holiday to celebrate the birthday of the state sultan.

HEALTH & SAFETY

HEALTH CONCERNS   See chapter 3's "Health & Safety" section (p. 43) for information on the major health issues that affect travelers to Southeast Asia. It's always good to check the most recent information at the **Centers for Disease Control** (click "Travelers' Health" at **www.cdc.gov**).

The tap water in Kuala Lumpur is supposedly potable, but I don't recommend drinking it—in fact, I don't recommend drinking tap water anywhere in Malaysia. Bottled water is inexpensive enough and readily available at convenience stores and food stalls. Food prepared in hawker centers is generally safe. If you buy fresh fruit, wash it well with bottled water and carefully peel the skin off before eating it.

Malaria has not been a major threat in most parts of Malaysia, even Malaysian Borneo. **Dengue fever,** on the other hand, which is also carried by mosquitoes, remains a constant threat in most areas, especially rural parts. Dengue, if left untreated, can cause fatal internal hemorrhaging, so if you come down with a sudden fever or skin rash, consult a physician immediately. There are no prophylactic treatments for dengue; the best protection is to wear plenty of insect repellent. Choose a product that contains DEET or is specifically formulated to be effective in the tropics.

In 2003, SARS seemed to skip right over Malaysia, but **avian influenza,** or bird flu, did find its way here, particularly in the northern state of Kelantan. The CDC advises travelers to avoid contact with live or raw poultry.

SAFETY CONCERNS Malaysia has a terrible problem with thievery. "Snatch thieves" are becoming bolder and bolder, riding on motorcycles through heavily populated areas in KL, Johor Bahru, and other cities, snatching handbags from women's shoulders. Some victims have been dragged and seriously injured. When you're out, don't wear your handbag on the side of you that's facing the street; better yet, don't carry a handbag at all. Also be careful when traveling on overnight trains and buses, where there are great opportunities for theft (many times by fellow tourists, believe it or not). Keep your valuables close to you as you sleep.

When you check into a hotel, it's a good idea to put your passport, international tickets, extra cash, and traveler's checks (plus any credit or ATM cards you don't need to use right away) straight into the safe, either in your room or behind the hotel's front desk.

GETTING THERE

BY PLANE Malaysia has six international airports—at Kuala Lumpur, Penang, Langkawi, Kota Kinabalu, Kuching, and Johor Bahru—and 14 domestic airports at locations that include Kota Bharu, Kuantan, and Kuala Terengganu. Specific airport information is listed with coverage of each city.

A passenger service charge, or airport departure tax, is levied on all flights. A tax of RM5 (US$1.40/£0.80) for domestic flights and RM40 (US$11/£6.15) for international flights is usually included in your ticket price.

Few Western carriers fly directly to Malaysia. If **Malaysian Airlines** (✆ 800/552-9264 in the U.S., or 0870/607-9090 in the U.K.; www.malaysiaairlines.com) does not have suitable routes from your home country, you'll have to contact another airline to work out a route that connects. Malaysia Airlines has a very good standard of service, not to mention possibly the lowest rates to Southeast Asia from North American destinations. It has flights to Kuala Lumpur from Los Angeles and Newark in the U.S.; London's Heathrow Airport in the U.K.; Perth, Adelaide, Brisbane, Sydney, and Melbourne in Australia; and Auckland in New Zealand.

BY TRAIN The **Keretapi Tanah Melayu Berhad (KTM),** Malaysia's rail system, runs express and local trains that connect the cities along the west coast of Malaysia with Singapore to the south and Thailand to the north. Kuala Lumpur's **KL Sentral** train station (✆ 03/2267-1200) is a 10-minute taxi ride from the center of town and is connected to the Putra LRT, the KL Monorail city public transportation trains, and the Express Rail Link (ERL) to Kuala Lumpur International Airport (KLIA).

Trains to Kuala Lumpur depart daily from the **Singapore Railway Station,** on Keppel Road in Tanjong Pagar (© **65/6222-5165**), not far from the city center. Fares run S$34 to S$68 (US$21–US$43/£12–£23). The trip takes around 6 hours on an *ekspres* train—avoid the 10am mail train if you want to get here before your next birthday.

In Bangkok, trains depart from the **Hua Lamphong Railway Station** (© **662/223-7010** or 662/223-7020), with service to Hua Hin, Surat Thani, Nakhon Si Thammarat, and Hat Yai in Thailand's southern peninsula. The final stop in Malaysia is at Butterworth (Penang), so passage to KL will require you to catch a connecting train onward. The daily service departs at 3:15pm and takes approximately 22 hours from Bangkok to Butterworth. There is no first- or third-class service on this train, only air-conditioned second-class; an upper berth goes for about US$20 (£11), lower for US$23 (£13).

For a fascinating journey from Thailand, you can catch the *Eastern & Orient Express (E&O)* (www.orient-express.com), which operates a route between Chiang Mai and Bangkok, Kuala Lumpur, and Singapore. Traveling in the luxurious style for which the Orient Express is renowned, you'll finish the entire journey in about 42 hours. Your entry-level cabin is Pullman, priced at approximately US$1,375 (£756) per person double occupancy, with State and Presidential Suites also available. All fares include meals on the train. Overseas reservations can be made through a travel agent or by calling © **800/524-2420** in the U.S. and Canada. From Singapore, Malaysia, and Thailand, contact the E&O office in Singapore at © **65/6392-3500.**

BY BUS   There are many bus routes from Singapore to Malaysia. If you want to travel on land, I personally prefer the bus over the train for the Singapore–Kuala Lumpur route. Executive coaches operated by **Grassland Express** (© **65/6292-1166** in Singapore) have huge seats that recline, serve a box lunch on board, and show movies. There's also express service to Malacca, Genting Highlands, Penang, and more. Buses depart from Golden Mile Complex, 5001 Beach Rd., for the 5-hour trip (S$30–S$42/US$19–US$26/£10–£14 one-way).

Buses to Johor Bahru and Malacca can be picked up at the Ban Sen terminal, at the corner of Queen and Arab streets. Call © **65/6292-8149** for buses to Johor Bahrum, or © **65/6293-5915** for buses to Malacca.

From Thailand, you can grab a bus in either Bangkok or Hat Yai (in the southern part of the country) heading for Malaysia. However, the ride from Bangkok is just too long a journey to be confined to a bus; you're better off taking the train. From Hat Yai, many buses leave regularly for northern Malaysian destinations, particularly Butterworth (Penang). Be forewarned that the U.S. Department of State does not recommend traveling in southern Thailand, due to terrorist violence.

BY TAXI FROM SINGAPORE   From the Johor-Singapore bus terminal at Queen and Arab streets, the **Singapore Johor Taxi Operators Association** (© **65/6296-7054**) can drive you to Johor Bahru for S$40 (US$25/£14).

BY CAR   Major international car-rental agencies operating in Singapore will rent cars that you can take over the causeway to Malaysia, but be prepared to pay a small fortune. They're much cheaper if you rent within the country. At Kuala Lumpur International Airport, find **Avis** at Counter B-16 in the main terminal (© **03/8776-4540**). There's another branch at the international airport in Penang (**04/643-9633**), or make a reservation through www.avis.com.

GETTING AROUND

The modernization of Malaysia has made travel here—whether by plane, train, bus, taxi, or self-driven car—easier and more convenient than ever. Malaysia Airlines has service to every major destination within the peninsula and East Malaysia, and now budget carrier AirAsia connects all major towns for cheap. Buses have a massive web of routes between every city and town. Train service up the western coast and out to the east provides even more options. And a unique travel offering—the outstation taxi—is available to and from every city on the peninsula. All these options make it convenient enough for you to hop from city to city and not waste too much precious vacation time.

By and large, all the modes of transportation between cities are reasonably comfortable. Air travel can be the most costly of the alternatives, followed by outstation taxis, and then buses and trains.

BY PLANE   Malaysia Airlines (© 1300/883-000; www.malaysiaairlines.com) links from its hub in Kuala Lumpur to the cities of Johor Bahru, Kota Bharu, Kota Kinabalu, Kuala Terengganu, Kuantan, Kuching, Langkawi, Penang, and other smaller towns not covered in this chapter. The phone number listed here can be dialed from anywhere in the country. Individual airport information is provided in sections for each city that follows. One-way domestic fares average RM100 to RM400 (US$28–US$112/£15–£62).

AirAsia (© 03/8775-4000 in Kuala Lumpur; www.airasia.com), a new budget airline, has incredibly affordable rates. It links all the country's major cities with fares that on average run from RM40 and up (US$11/£6.15)—seriously. **Berjaya Air** (© 03/2145-2828;** www.berjaya-air.com) operates a small fleet of aircraft that services the peninsula's island resorts, with flights that link KL to Pankor, Langkawi, Tioman, and Redang islands, with another flight between Singapore and Tioman.

BY TRAIN   The **Keretapi Tanah Melayu Berhad (KTM)** provides train service throughout peninsular Malaysia. Trains run from north to south between the Thai border and Singapore, with stops between including Butterworth (Penang), Kuala Lumpur, and Johor Bahru. A second line branches off at Gemas, midway between Johor Bahru and KL, and heads northeast to Tempas near Kota Bharu. Fares range from RM64 (US$18/£9.85) for first-class between Johor Bahru and KL, to RM85 (US$24/£13) for first-class passage between Johor Bahru and Butterworth. Train-station information is provided for each city under individual headings in the following sections.

BY BUS   Malaysia's intercity coach system is extensive and inexpensive, but not really recommended. With the exception of executive coach services between KL and Singapore, which are excellent, standard coaches get dirtier and dirtier each year, maintenance issues are a question mark, and road safety is a roll of the dice. Still, if you must, bus-terminal locations are listed for each city covered in this chapter, but scheduling information must be obtained from the bus company itself.

BY TAXI   You can take special hired cars, called **outstation taxis,** between every city and state on the peninsula. Rates depend on the distance you plan to travel. They are fixed and stated at the beginning of the trip, but many times can be bargained down. In Kuala Lumpur, go to the second level of the Puduraya Bus Terminal to find cabs that will take you outside the city, or call the **Kuala Lumpur Outstation Taxi Service Station** (© 03/2078-0213). A taxi from KL to Malacca will cost approximately RM140 (US$39/£22); KL to Cameron Highlands, RM220 (US$62/£34); KL to Butterworth or Johor Bahru, RM300 (US$84/£46). Outstation taxi-stand locations are included under each individual city heading in the following sections. These cars are usually basic older-model sedans.

Also, within each of the smaller cities, feel free to negotiate with unmetered taxis for hourly, half-day, or daily rates. It's an excellent way to get around for sightseeing and shopping without transportation hassles. Hourly rates are anywhere from RM15 to RM25 (US$4.20–US$7/£2.30–£3.85).

BY CAR The cities along the west coast of the peninsula are linked by the North–South Highway. There are rest areas with toilets, food outlets, and emergency telephones at intervals along the way. There is also a toll that varies depending on the distance you're traveling.

Driving along the east coast of Malaysia is much more pleasant than driving along the west coast. The highway is narrower and older, but it takes you through oil-palm and rubber plantations, and the essence of kampung Malaysia permeates throughout. As you near villages, you'll often have to slow down and swerve past cows and goats, which are quite oblivious to oncoming traffic.

The speed limit on highways is 110kmph (68 mph). On the minor highways, the limit ranges from 70 to 90kmph (43–56 mph). Do not speed, as there are traffic police strategically situated around certain bends.

To rent a car in Malaysia, you must produce a driver's license from your home country that shows you have been driving at least 2 years. There are desks for major car-rental services at the international airports in Kuala Lumpur and Penang, plus additional outlets throughout the country (see individual city sections for this information).

Tips **Telephone Dialing at a Glance**

- **To place a call from your home country to Malaysia:** Dial the international access code (011 in the U.S. and Canada, 0011 in Australia, 0170 in New Zealand, 00 in the U.K.), plus the country code **(60)**, the city or local area code (Cameron Highlands 5, Desaru 7, Genting Highlands 9, Johor Bahru 7, Kuala Lumpur 3, Kuala Terengganu 9, Kota Bharu 9, Kota Kinabalu 88, Kuantan 9, Kuching 82, Langkawi 4, Malacca 6, Mersing 7, Penang 4, Tioman 9), and the six-, seven-, or eight-digit phone number (for example, 011 60 3 0000-0000). *Important note:* Omit the initial "0" in all Malaysia phone numbers when calling from abroad.

- **To place a call within Malaysia:** Dial the city or area code preceded by a **0** (the way numbers are listed in this book), and then the local number (for example, 03 0000-0000). You must use area codes if calling between states.

- **To place a direct international call from Malaysia:** Dial the international access code **(00)**, plus the country code, the area or city code, and the number (for example, to call the U.S., you'd dial 00 1 000/000-0000).

- **International country codes are as follows:** Australia, 61; Cambodia, 855; Canada, 1; Hong Kong, 852; Indonesia, 62; Laos, 856; Myanmar, 95; New Zealand, 64; the Philippines, 63; Singapore, 65; Thailand, 66; U.K., 44; U.S., 1; Vietnam, 84.

TIPS ON ACCOMMODATIONS

Peak months of the year for hotels in western peninsular Malaysia are December through February and July through September. For the east coast, the busy times are July through September. You will need to make reservations well in advance to secure a room during these months.

Except for the budget accommodations, all hotels charge a 10% service charge and 5% government tax. As such, there is no need to tip. But bellhops still tend to be tipped at least RM2 (US55¢/£0.30) per bag, and car jockeys or valets should be tipped at least RM4 (US$1.10/£0.60) or more.

TIPS ON DINING

Malaysian food seems to get its origins from India's rich curries, influenced by Thailand's herbs and spices. You'll find delicious blends of coconut milk and curry, shrimp paste, and chiles, accented by exotic flavors of galangal (similar to turmeric), lime, and lemongrass. Sometimes pungent, a few of the dishes have a deep flavor from fermented shrimp paste that is an acquired taste for Western palates. By and large, Malaysian food is delicious, but in multicultural Malaysia, so is the Chinese food, the Peranakan food, the Indian food—the list goes on. The Chinese brought their own flavors from their points of origin in the regions of southern China. Teochew, Cantonese, and Szechuan are all styles of Chinese cuisine that you'll find throughout the country. Peranakan food is unique to Malacca, Penang, and Singapore. The Peranakans, or "Straits Chinese," combined local ingredients with some traditional Chinese dishes to create an entirely new culinary form. And Indian food, both northern and southern, can be found in almost every city, particularly in the western part of the peninsula. Of course, you'll find gorgeous, fresh seafood almost everywhere.

Try to eat in a hawker stall when you can, especially in Penang, which is famous for its local cuisine. You'll notice many Malaysians eat with their hands off banana leaves when they're having *nasi padang* or *nasi kandar* (rice with mixed dishes). This is absolutely acceptable. If you choose to follow suit, wash your hands first and try to use your right hand, as the left is considered unclean (traditionally, it's the hand used to wash after a visit to the toilet). While almost all of the food you encounter in a hawker center will be safe for eating, it is advisable to go for freshly cooked hot or soupy dishes. Don't risk the precooked items.

Avoid having ice in your drink in the smaller towns, as it might come from a dubious water supply. If you ask for water, make sure it's boiled—or buy bottled water.

A 10% service charge and 5% government tax are levied in proper restaurants, but hawkers charge a flat price.

TIPS ON SHOPPING

Shopping is a huge attraction for tourists in Malaysia. In addition to modern fashions and electronics, there are great local handicrafts. Prices can vary considerably: There are many handicrafts centers such as Karyaneka, with outlets all over the country, where goods can be a bit more expensive, but where you are assured of good quality. Alternatively, you can hunt out bargains in markets and at roadside stores in little towns, which can be much more fun.

Batik is one of the most popular arts in Malaysia, and the fabric can be purchased just about anywhere in the country. It can be fashioned into outfits and scarves or purchased as sarongs. Another beautiful textile craft is *songket* weaving. These beautiful cloths are woven with metallic threads and are usually sold as sarongs.

Traditional woodcarvings have become popular collectors' items. Carvings by *orang asli* groups in peninsular Malaysia and by the indigenous tribes of Sabah and Sarawak have traditional uses in households or are employed for ceremonial purposes. Malaysia's pewter products are also famous; Selangor Pewter is the brand that seems to have the most outlets, with anything from picture frames to dinner sets. Silver designs are very refined, and jewelry and fine home items are still made by local artisans, especially in the northern parts of the peninsula. In addition, crafts such as *wayang kulit* (shadow puppets) and *wau* (colorful Malay kites) make great gifts.

FAST FACTS: Malaysia

American Express The main office for American Express is located in KL at Menara Maybank, Ground Level banking hall, Jalan Perak (℃ **1300/886-688**).

Business Hours Banks are open Monday through Friday from 10am to 3pm and Saturday from 9:30 to 11:30am. Government offices are open Monday through Friday from 8am to 12:45pm and 2 to 4:15pm, Saturday from 8am to 12:45pm. Smaller shops like provision stores may open as early as 6 or 6:30am and close as late as 9pm, especially those near the wet markets. Many such stores are closed on Saturday evenings and Sunday afternoons and are busiest before lunch. Other shops are open 9:30am to 7pm. Department stores and shops in malls tend to open later, about 10:30 or 11am till 8:30 or 9pm throughout the week. Note that in Kuala Terengganu and Kota Bharu, the weekday runs from Saturday to Wednesday.

Doctors & Dentists All hotels and resorts have qualified physicians on call who speak English. These doctors will come directly to your room for treatment. If your condition is serious, he or she can help you check in to a local hospital. Call ℃ **999** for emergencies.

Drug Laws As in Singapore, the death sentence is mandatory for drug trafficking (defined as being in possession of more than 15g of heroin or morphine, 200g of marijuana or hashish, or 40g of cocaine). For lesser quantities, you'll be thrown in jail for a very long time and flogged with a cane.

Electricity Malaysia's electricity carries 220–240 volts AC (50 cycles). Three-point square plugs are used, so buy an adapter if you plan to bring any gadgets. Many larger hotels can provide adapters upon request.

Embassies & Consulates **U.S.:** 376 Jalan Tun Razak, Kuala Lumpur (℃ **03/2168-5000;** http://malaysia.usembassy.gov). **Canada:** 207 Jalan Tun Razak, 17th floor, Menara Tan & Tan, Kuala Lumpur (℃ **03/2718-3333;** www.kualalumpur.gc.ca). **Australia:** 6 Jalan Yap Kwan Seng, Kuala Lumpur (℃ **03/2146-5555;** www.malaysia.embassy.gov.au). **New Zealand:** 8 Jalan Sultan Ismail, Level 21, Menara IMC, Kuala Lumpur (℃ **03/2078-2533;** www.nzembassy.com/malaysia). **U.K.:** 85 Jalan Ampang, Kuala Lumpur (℃ **03/2148-2122;** www.britishhighcommission.gov.uk/malaysia).

Emergencies Call ℃ **999** for emergencies.

Internet Access Although the major international hotels will have access for guests in their business centers, charges can be very steep. Internet cafes can be found in the most surprisingly remote places; but because these small places come and go overnight, it's impossible to list accurate information here. Wherever you are, your best bet is to ask your concierge or the local tourism information office for nearby Internet cafes. Usage only costs about RM5 to RM10 (US$1.40–US$2.80/£0.80–£1.55).

Language The national language is Malay, or Bahasa Malaysia, although English is widely spoken. Chinese dialects and Tamil are also heard here. See "Language," p. 541, for more information.

Liquor Laws Liquor is sold in pubs and supermarkets in all big cities, as well as in provision stores. If you're going to an island, your resort will have limited alcohol selections; otherwise you can bring your own. In Terengganu and Kelantan, liquor is strictly limited to a handful of Chinese restaurants. Pubs and other nightspots should officially close by 1am nationwide, but there are places in KL that stay open later. The legal drinking age in Malaysia is 18.

Mail Post office locations are listed in each city's coverage later in this chapter. Overseas airmail rates are RM0.50 (US10¢/£0.05) for a postcard and RM1.50 (US40¢/ £0.20) for a 100g letter.

Newspapers & Magazines English-language papers such as the *New Straits Times*, the *Star*, the *Sun*, and the *Edge* can be bought in hotel lobbies and at magazine stands. Of the local KL magazines, *Day & Night* has great listings and information on local happenings for travelers.

Taxes Hotels add a 5% government tax to all rates, plus an additional 10% service charge. Larger restaurants also figure the same 5% tax into your bill, plus a 10% service charge, whereas small coffee shops and hawker stalls don't charge anything above the cost of the meal. Although most tourist goods (such as crafts, cameras, sports equipment, cosmetics, and select small electronic items) are tax-free, a small, scaled tax is issued on various other goods such as clothing, shoes, and accessories that you'd buy in the larger malls and department stores.

Telephones The international country code for Malaysia is **60**. To reach the international operator, dial ⓒ **108**. See "Telephone Dialing at a Glance," p. 549, for details on how to make calls to, from, and within the country.

Time Zone Malaysia is 8 hours ahead of Greenwich Mean Time, 16 hours ahead of U.S. Pacific Standard Time, 13 ahead of U.S. Eastern Standard Time, and 2 hours behind Sydney. It is in the same time zone as Singapore. There is no daylight saving time here.

Tipping People here don't really tip, though you might want to give your bellhop something. In a nicer hotel, at least RM5 (US$1.40/£0.80) per bag should be fine. In a budget hotel, they'll probably be shocked.

Toilets To find a public toilet, ask for the *tandas*. In Malay, *lelaki* is male and *perempuan* is female. Be prepared for pay toilets. Coin collectors sit outside almost every public facility, taking RM0.20 (US5¢/£0.03) per person, RM0.30 (US8¢/£0.05) if you want paper. Once inside, you'll find that your money doesn't go for cleaning crews. Public toilets are pure filth. They smell horrible and the floors are always an inch deep in stagnant water. While most toilets are of the "squatty-potty" variety (a porcelain bowl set into the floor), even if you find a seat-style toilet bowl, the locals always place their feet on the seat to squat. The best toilets can be found in hotels, upmarket shopping malls, and restaurants.

Water Water in Kuala Lumpur is supposed to be potable, but most locals boil the water before drinking it—and if that's not a tip-off, I don't know what is. I advise against drinking the tap water anywhere in Malaysia. Hotels will supply bottled water in your room. If they charge you for it, expect inflated prices. A 1.5-liter bottle goes for RM7 (US$2/£1) in a hotel minibar, but RM2 (US55¢/£0.30) at a 7-Eleven.

4 Kuala Lumpur ★★

Kuala Lumpur (or KL, as it is commonly known) is more often than not a traveler's point of entry to Malaysia. As the capital it is the most modern and developed city in the country, with contemporary high-rises and world-class hotels, glitzy shopping malls, and international cuisine.

Today, the original city center at **Merdeka Square** is the core of KL's history. Buildings like the Sultan Abdul Samad Building, the Royal Selangor Club, and the Old Kuala Lumpur Railway Station are gorgeous examples of British style peppered with Moorish flavor. South of this area is KL's **Chinatown.** Along Jalan Petaling and surrounding areas are markets, shops, food stalls, and the bustling life of the Chinese community. There's also a **Little India,** around the area occupied by Masjid Jame, with flower stalls, Indian Muslim and Malay costumes, and traditional items. Across the river, you'll find **Lake Gardens,** a large sanctuary that houses KL's bird park, butterfly park, and other attractions and gardens. Modern Kuala Lumpur is rooted in the city's **Golden Triangle,** bounded by Jalan Ampang, Jalan Tun Razak, and Jalan Imbi. This section is home to most of KL's hotels, office complexes, shopping malls, and sights like the KL Tower and the Petronas Twin Towers, which were temporarily the tallest buildings in the world.

GETTING THERE

BY PLANE The **Kuala Lumpur International Airport (KLIA)** (© 03/8776-2000) is located in Sepang, 53km (33 miles) outside the city. KLIA is a huge complex with business centers, dining facilities, a fitness center, medical services, shopping, post offices, and an airport hotel operated by **Pan Pacific** (© 03/8787-3333). While there are money changers, they are few and far between, so hop in the first line you see and don't assume there's another one just around the corner.

City taxis are not permitted to pick up fares from the airport (avoid the illegal gypsy cabs!), but special **airport taxis** (© 03/8787-3678) operate round the clock, charging RM92 (US$26/£14) for a premier car (Mercedes) and RM67 (US$19/£10) for a standard vehicle (the locally built Proton). Vans that seat up to eight can also be hired for RM180 (US$50/£28). Coupons must be purchased at the arrivals concourse.

The **Express Rail Link** (© 03/2267-8000) runs between KLIA and KL Sentral train station from 5am to 1am daily. Trains depart every 15 minutes and take 28 minutes to complete the trip. Tickets cost RM35 (US$9.80/£5.40) for adults and RM15

(US$4.20/£2.30) for children. From KL Sentral, taxis are always on hand, or you can catch one of the city's commuter trains to a station near your hotel.

An **express coach** (© 03/2730-2000) connects KLIA to KL Sentral train station and most of the city's major hotels. It costs RM35 (US$9.80/£5.40), so you may as well take the Express Rail Link, which is faster.

BY TRAIN KL's shiny new station, **KL Sentral** (© 03/2267-1200) is a clean, safe, and orderly base from which to take the train, as well as a hub for local commuter services around the city; it's got tons of facilities, money changers, ATMs, fast food, and shops. It also has an easy taxi coupon system (about RM7/US$2/£1 or RM8/US$2.25/£1.25 to central parts of the city)—cabs are really easy to find here.

BY BUS If you're arriving in KL by bus, be warned that different bus companies drop off at different locations around the city. **Grasslands Express** (© 65/6292-1166), which runs buses from Singapore, will drop you off either at the Puduraya Bus Terminal in the center of town or on Jalan Imbi just opposite the Times Square shopping mall—a much preferred location. KL has three official bus terminals that handle inter-city bus departures and arrivals to all parts of the country: the aforementioned Puduraya Terminal on Jalan Pudu, Putra Terminal on Jalan Tun Ismail, and Pekililing Terminal on Jalan Ipoh. If you arrive at Puduraya, the biggest of the three, good luck! It's congested—both with toxic fumes and traffic jams (one of the reasons I avoid standard bus travel in Malaysia). Taxis are not hard to find at any of these terminals.

GETTING AROUND

Kuala Lumpur is a prime example of a city that was not built according to a master plan. Rather, because of its beginnings as an outpost, it grew as it needed to, expanding outward and swallowing up rural surrounds. The result is a tangled web of streets too narrow to support the traffic of a capital city. Cars and buses weave through one-way lanes, with countless motorbikes sneaking in and out, sometimes in the opposite direction of traffic or up on the sidewalks. Expect traffic jams from 6 to 9am and again from 4 to 7pm. At other times, taxis are a convenient way of getting around, but the commuter-train system is perhaps the best value and easiest route. City buses are hot and crowded, with some very confusing routes. Walking can also be frustrating; many sidewalks are in poor condition, with buckled tiles and gaping gutters. The heat can be prohibitive as well. However, areas within the colonial heart of the city, Chinatown, Little India, and some areas in the Golden Triangle are within walking distance of one another.

BY TRAIN KL has a network of mass-transit trains that snake through the city and out to the suburbs, and it'll be worth your time to become familiar with them, as taxis are sometimes unreliable and traffic jams can be unbearable. Trouble is, there are five train routes and each one is operated by a different company. How confusing! The lines don't seem to connect in any logical way.

The four lines that are most useful to visitors are the **Kelana Jaya Line,** the **Ampang & Sri Petaling Line,** the **KL Monorail,** and the **ERL Express Rail Link** to the airport. The latter route is explained under "Getting There," above.

The **Kelana Jaya Line,** formerly called Putra LRT, has stops at Bangsar (see "Kuala Lumpur After Dark," later), KL Sentral (train station), Pasar Seni (Chinatown), Masjid Jamek, Dang Wangi, and KLCC shopping center. The **Ampang & Sri Petaling Line,** formerly called the Star LRT, is only convenient if you need to get to the

Kuala Lumpur

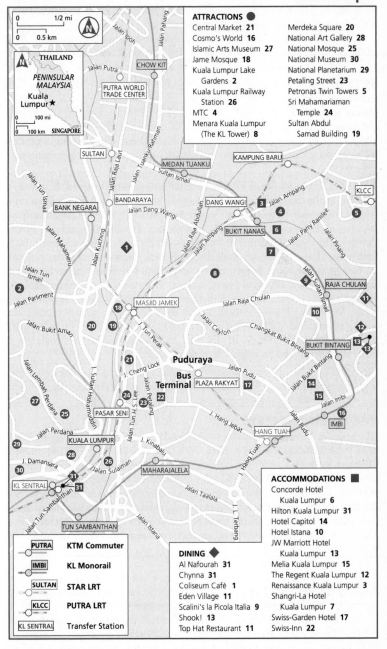

ATTRACTIONS ●

Central Market **21**
Cosmo's World **16**
Islamic Arts Museum **27**
Jame Mosque **18**
Kuala Lumpur Lake
   Gardens **2**
Kuala Lumpur Railway
   Station **26**
MTC **4**
Menara Kuala Lumpur
   (The KL Tower) **8**

Merdeka Square **20**
National Art Gallery **28**
National Mosque **25**
National Museum **30**
National Planetarium **29**
Petronas Twin Towers **5**
Petaling Street **23**
Sri Mahamariaman
   Temple **24**
Sultan Abdul
   Samad Building **19**

ACCOMMODATIONS ■

Concorde Hotel
   Kuala Lumpur **6**
Hilton Kuala Lumpur **31**
Hotel Capitol **14**
Hotel Istana **10**
JW Marriott Hotel
   Kuala Lumpur **13**
Melia Kuala Lumpur **15**
The Regent Kuala Lumpur **12**
Renaissance Kuala Lumpur **3**
Shangri-La Hotel
   Kuala Lumpur **7**
Swiss-Garden Hotel **17**
Swiss-Inn **22**

DINING ◆

Al Nafourah **31**
Chynna **31**
Coliseum Café **1**
Eden Village **11**
Scalini's la Picola Italia **9**
Shook! **13**
Top Hat Restaurant **11**

Legend:
PUTRA — KTM Commuter
IMBI — KL Monorail
SULTAN — STAR LRT
KLCC — PUTRA LRT
KL SENTRAL — Transfer Station

Map labels: THAILAND, PENINSULAR MALAYSIA, Kuala Lumpur ★, SINGAPORE

CHOW KIT, PUTRA WORLD TRADE CENTER, SULTAN, MEDAN TUANKU, KAMPUNG BARU, BANK NEGARA, BANDARAYA, DANG WANGI, BUKIT NANAS, KLCC, MASJID JAMEK, RAJA CHULAN, BUKIT BINTANG, Puduraya Bus Terminal, PLAZA RAKYAT, IMBI, HANG TUAH, PASAR SENI, KUALA LUMPUR, MAHARAJALELA, KL SENTRAL, TUN SAMBANTHAN

Putra World Trade Centre. It also stops at Masjid Jamek and Plaza Rayat. Average trips on both lines will cost around RM2 (US60¢/£0.30).

The **KL Monorail** provides good access through the main hotel and shopping areas of the city, including stops at KL Sentral, Imbi, Bukit Bintang (the main shopping strip), and Raja Chulan (along Jalan Sultan Ismail, where many hotels are located). Fares range between RM1.20 (US30¢/£0.15) and RM 2.50 (US70¢/£0.35).

As a rough guide, all lines operate from 5 or 6am to around midnight, with trains coming every 10 minutes or so. Tickets can be purchased at any station, either from the stationmaster or from single-fare electronic ticket booths.

BY BUS   I don't recommend travel on city buses. They're cheap but not dependable, with city routes that will get newcomers lost for sure. It's not the most relaxing way to get around.

BY TAXI   If you ask me, KL cabbies should have their tires slashed. If you can get one to stop, the driver will almost always refuse to use the meter (which is against the law), quoting what seems to be the standard—RM10 (US$2.80/£1.55), usually for a trip that normally costs RM4 (US$1.10/£0.60). If it's raining, expect that quote to double. I usually don't dicker over the price because it's only a buck and a half. It's just frustrating when cab after cab passes you by. In some places within the city, taxi stands try to solve this problem. Be prepared for taxis to pull over, roll down the window, and hear the pleas from the queue before deciding which passenger to take, regardless of the order of the queue. Somewhere there are numbers to call for taxi booking—what a joke! Maybe they'll show, and maybe they won't. Don't even waste your time. Technically, the metered fare is RM2 (US55¢/£0.30) for the first 2km (1¼ miles) and an additional RM0.10 (US3¢/£0.02) for each 200m after that. Between midnight and 6am, you'll be charged an extra 50% of the total fare.

ON FOOT   The heat and humidity can make walking between attractions pretty uncomfortable. However, sometimes the traffic is so unbearable that you'll get where you're going much faster by strapping on your shoes and hoofing it.

VISITOR INFORMATION

The Malaysia Tourism Board has several offices in Kuala Lumpur. The largest is at the **MTC,** the **Malaysia Tourist Centre,** 109 Jalan Ampang (© **03/2164-3929;** see "What to See & Do," later in this chapter), open daily from 8am to 10:30pm. In addition to a tourist information desk, MTC has a money changer; ATM; tourist police post; travel-agent booking for Taman Negara trips, city tours, and limited hotel reservations; souvenir shops; an amphitheater; and Transnasional bus-ticket bookings.

Vision KL Magazine is offered for free in many hotels and has listings for events in KL and around the country, plus ads for restaurants and shops. At newsstands, it costs RM6.80 (US$1.90/£1.05).

FAST FACTS: **Kuala Lumpur**

American Express The main office for American Express is in KL at Menara Maybank, Ground Level banking hall, Jalan Perak (© **1300/886-688**).

Currency Exchange You'll find headquarters for all Malaysian and many international banks, most of which have outlets along Jalan Sultan Ismail, plus ATMs at countless locations throughout the city. Look for money changers in just about every shopping mall; they're a better bargain than banks or hotel cashiers.

Emergencies If you have a medical, police, or fire emergency, the number to dial is © **999.**

Internet Access Internet service in KL will run about RM3 to RM6 (US85¢– US$1.70/£0.45–£0.90) per hour. Internet cafes come and go, popping up in backpacker areas like Chinatown and the streets around BB Plaza off Jalan Bukit Bintang.

Mail KL's general post office, on Jalan Sultan Hishamuddin in the enormous Pos Malaysia Komplex Dayabumi (© **03/2274-1122**), can be pretty overwhelming. Try to use your hotel's mail service for a much easier time.

Telephones The area code for Kuala Lumpur is 03. The city's phone numbers have an eight-digit format. Numbers in the rest of the country have seven digits.

WHERE TO STAY

The hotels listed below represent only those properties I think are best for leisure travelers. Even the very expensive hotels I've chosen have qualities that extend beyond the business center. If you plan to travel to KL in July or August and want to stay in an upmarket hotel, you'll need to book your room well in advance. KL's superpeak season falls during these months, when travelers from the Middle East take a break from scorching temperatures back home.

VERY EXPENSIVE

The Regent Kuala Lumpur 🍊   Of the best five-star properties in Kuala Lumpur, nobody delivers first-class accommodations with the finesse of the Regent. A landmark along KL's fashionable Jalan Bukit Bintang shopping strip, the Regent has an ever-bustling lobby to match the excitement along the sidewalks outside—the lobby lounge is filled night and day. Surprisingly, the staff always seems polite and professional despite the barrage. The Regent's guest rooms are spacious, quiet, and cool, with huge plush beds covered in soft cotton sheets and down comforters. Bathrooms are large, marble affairs with plenty of counter space. The outdoor pool is a palm-lined freeform escape, and the fitness center is state-of-the-art, with sauna, steam, spa, and Jacuzzi. In the plot directly next to the hotel, construction has begun on a new, mammoth shopping-and-apartment complex. Ask about it when you make your booking: Nobody wants to hear driving piles when they're trying to nap.

160 Jalan Bukit Bintang, 55100 Kuala Lumpur. © **800/545-4000** in the U.S. and Canada, 800/022-800 in Australia, 800/440-800 in New Zealand, 800/917-8795 in the U.K., or 03/2141-8000. Fax 03/2142-1441. www.regenthotels. com. 468 units. RM700 (US$196/£108) double; from RM950 (US$266/£146) suite. AE, DC, MC, V. 5-min. walk to Bukit Bintang Monorail station. **Amenities:** 3 restaurants; bar and lobby lounge; outdoor pool; 2 squash courts; 24-hr. fitness center with Jacuzzi, sauna, steam, and massage; concierge; limousine service; business center; 24-hr. room service; babysitting; laundry service; dry cleaning; nonsmoking rooms; executive-level rooms. *In room:* A/C, satellite TV w/in-house movies, minibar, coffeemaker, hair dryer, safe.

Shangri-La Hotel Kuala Lumpur 🍊🍊🍊   In 2003, Shangri-La emerged from a massive face-lift that enhanced its "tropical oasis in the city" ambience. I'm a big fan of Shangri-La, an Asian hotel chain that seeks to create luxury accommodations within lush gardens—something different from the typically faceless city tower of most urban hotels. Complete renovations to the guest rooms included new carpets, upholstered furniture, drapes, and bed linens in bright, natural colors and textures. Flatscreen TVs and broadband access come standard (although Internet usage is extra). Of all the upmarket hotels in the city, the Shang has the most attractive facilities for leisure travelers, with a pretty landscaped outdoor pool and fitness center stocked with the latest equipment.

11 Jalan Sultan Ismail, 50250 Kuala Lumpur. © 800/942-5050 in the U.S. and Canada, 800/222-448 in Australia, 0800/442-179 in New Zealand, or 03/2032-2388. Fax 03/2070-1514. www.shangri-la.com. 701 units. RM810 (US$227/£125) double; from RM1,420 (US$398/£219) suite. AE, DC, MC, V. 10-min. walk to Bukit Nanas Monorail station. **Amenities:** 5 restaurants; outdoor pool; outdoor lighted tennis courts; fitness center with Jacuzzi, steam, sauna, and massage; concierge; limousine service; salon; 24-hour room service; babysitting; laundry service; dry cleaning; nonsmoking rooms; executive-level rooms. *In room:* A/C; satellite TV w/in-house movies; Internet access; minibar; coffeemaker; hair dryer, safe.

EXPENSIVE

Hilton Kuala Lumpur ✪✪✪   The absolute hottest hotel in KL, and probably one of the most innovative hotels in the world—forget anything you've ever experienced in a Hilton. From the airy, art-filled public spaces to the rooftop lagoon pool, everything is done with edgy style and sophistication. Large rooms have sleek, contemporary decor, with a desk area wired for work, mood lighting, stocked minibar with a coffee plunger and heavy mugs, and a 42-inch plasma TV. A "magic button" handles all service requests, and three "lifestyle boxes" provide little extras like desk accessories, bath treats, and games. Bathrooms are great: deep tubs, "rainshower" showerheads, and a mini LCD TV built into the shaving mirror! The hotel's fitness center is operated by the very competent Clarke Hatch company; the rooftop pool and Bali spa are great escapes. Hilton hotels use the best-rate-of-the-day system, so I've listed a general rate during peak season below, as opposed to rack rates listed for other properties.

3 Jalan Stesen Sentral, 50470 Kuala Lumpur. © 800/HILTONS in the U.S. and Canada, 800/293-229 in Australia, 800/448-002 in New Zealand, 0875/909090 in the U.K., or 03/2264-2264. Fax 03/2264-2266. www.hilton.com. 542 units. RM425 (US$119/£65) double; from RM690 (US$193/£106) suite. AE, DC, MC, V. Opposite KL Sentral station. **Amenities:** 5 restaurants; 2 bars; outdoor pool; fitness center; spa; concierge; limousine service; business center; 24-hr. room service; babysitting; laundry service; dry cleaning; nonsmoking rooms; executive-level rooms. *In room:* A/C; satellite TV w/in-house movies, minibar, coffeemaker, hair dryer, safe.

Hotel Istana ✪   Fashioned after a Malay palace, Hotel Istana is rich with Moorish architectural elements, and *songket* weaving patterns are featured in decor elements throughout. The guest rooms were recently refurbished with Malaysian touches like handwoven carpets and upholstery in local fabric designs, capturing the exotic flavor of the culture without sacrificing modern comfort and convenience. Located on Jalan Raja Chulan, Istana is in a favorable Golden Triangle location, within walking distance of shopping and some of the sights in that area.

73 Jalan Raja Chulan, 50200 Kuala Lumpur. © 03/2141-9988. Fax 03/2144-0111. www.hotelistana.com.my. 516 units. RM550 (US$154/£85) double; from RM740 (US$207/£114) suite. AE, DC, MC, V. 5-min. walk to Raja Chulan Monorail station. **Amenities:** 4 restaurants; lobby lounge; outdoor pool; 2 outdoor lighted tennis courts; 2 squash courts; fitness center with Jacuzzi, sauna, steam, and massage; concierge; limousine service; business center; 24-hr. room service; babysitting; laundry service; dry cleaning; executive-level rooms. *In room:* A/C, satellite TV w/in-house movies, minibar, coffeemaker, hair dryer, safe.

JW Marriott Hotel Kuala Lumpur ✪   Opened in 1997, the JW Marriott is finding itself overshadowed by some of the city's newer properties. But the small lobby area still allows for a very dramatic entrance, complete with wrought-iron filigree and marble. The modern guest rooms have a European flavor, decorated in deep greens and reds with plush carpeting, large desks, and leather executive chairs that are all beginning to show wear. If you've stayed at a Marriott in other locations, this one might disappoint you. It's not the chain's hottest property, yet the staff is very motivated and enthusiastic. Another great plus: The hotel is next door to some of the most upmarket and trendy shopping complexes in the city. Similar to the Regent, this hotel is adjacent to what appears to be a new construction site, so ask about noise pollution when booking.

183 Jalan Bukit Bintang, 55100 Kuala Lumpur. © **800/228-9290** in the U.S. and Canada, 800/251-259 in Australia, 800/221-222 in the U.K., or 03/2715-9000. Fax 03/2715-7000. www.marriott.com. 518 units. RM700 (US$196/£108) double; RM6,000 (US$1,681/£924) suite. AE, DC, MC, V. 10-min. walk to Bukit Bintang Monorail station. **Amenities:** 4 restaurants; lounge and cigar bar; outdoor pool; outdoor lighted tennis court; fitness center with Jacuzzi, sauna, and steam; new spa with massage and beauty treatments; concierge; limousine service; business center; shopping mall with designer boutiques adjacent; salon; 24-hr. room service; babysitting; laundry service; dry cleaning; executive-level rooms. *In room:* A/C, satellite TV, dataport, minibar, coffeemaker, hair dryer, safe.

Renaissance Kuala Lumpur Hotel ★★ *Value*

The Renaissance offers a terrific value for the money. It's basically two hotels in one: the posh Renaissance Wing and the New World Wing, its budget neighbor, with both properties sharing all hotel facilities. Each wing has its own entrance, connected in the middle where the ballroom and banquet rooms are housed. Guest rooms in the Renaissance Wing have an "official" feel to them—very bold and impressive, and completely European in style. In fact, you'll never know you're in Malaysia. The New World Wing is contemporary, with simpler decor, but is no less comfortable. The enormous outdoor pool, which sits between the two hotel towers, is second only to Shangri-La's (reviewed above).

Corner of Jalan Sultan Ismail and Jalan Ampang, 50450 Kuala Lumpur. © **800/HOTELS-1** in the U.S. and Canada, 800/251-259 in Australia, 800/441-035 in New Zealand, or 03/2162-2233. Fax 03/2163-1122. 910 units. Renaissance Wing: RM695 (US$195/£107); from RM1,400 (US$392/£216) suite. New World Wing: RM625 (US$175/£96) double, from RM950 (US$266/£146) suite. AE, DC, MC, V. 5-min. walk to Bukit Nanas Monorail and Dang Wangi LRT stations. **Amenities:** 3 restaurants; lounge; landscaped outdoor pool; outdoor lighted tennis court; fitness center w/sauna and massage; concierge; limousine service; business center; shopping arcade; salon; 24-hr. room service; babysitting; laundry service; dry cleaning; nonsmoking rooms; executive-level rooms. *In room:* A/C, satellite TV w/in-house movies, minibar, coffeemaker, hair dryer, safe.

MODERATE

Concorde Hotel Kuala Lumpur ★★ *Value*

Concorde is one of my favorites in this price category for its central location and quality accommodations at an incredible price. Although rooms are not as large as those in more expensive hotels, they're well outfitted with desks, side chairs, comfortable beds, and tidy bathrooms in an up-to-date style that can compete with the best of them. Concorde has a small outdoor pool with a charming cafe and small fitness center. The lobby lounge is noisy at night because it's popular. The Hard Rock Cafe is also on the premises, one of the more fun clubs in town.

2 Jalan Sultan Ismail, 50250 Kuala Lumpur. © **03/2144-2200**. Fax 03/2144-1628. www.concorde.net/kl. 570 units. RM250 (US$70/£39) double; from RM1,000 (US$280/£154) suite. AE, DC, MC, V. 5-min. walk to Bukit Nanas Monoroal station and 10-min. walk to Dang Wangi LRT station. **Amenities:** 3 restaurants; lobby lounge and Hard Rock Cafe; small outdoor pool; fitness center w/sauna, steam, and massage; concierge; limousine service; business center; shopping arcade; salon; 24-hr. room service; babysitting; laundry service; dry cleaning; executive-level rooms. *In room:* A/C, satellite TV w/in-house movies, minibar, coffeemaker, safe.

Meliá Kuala Lumpur ★ *Value*

This tourist-class hotel had nothing special to boast until recently. The opening of a KL Monorail station just outside, combined with the mind-bogglingly enormous Times Square shopping-and-entertainment complex across the street, has certainly added great value. The small lobby is functional, with space for tour groups and a very active and efficient tour desk. Newly renovated guest rooms have light-wood furnishings, contemporary fixtures, wall desks with a swivel arm for extra space, and big-screen TVs. Bathrooms, although small, are well maintained with good counter space. Mealtimes in the hotel's coffee shop can be a little crowded.

16 Jalan Imbi, 55100 Kuala Lumpur. © 03/2142-8333. Fax 03/2142-6623. www.solmelia.com. 301 units. RM500 (US$140/£77) double; from RM1,200 (US$336/£185) suite. AE, DC, MC, V. Imbi Monorail station. **Amenities:** 2 restaurants; bar and karaoke lounge; small outdoor pool; health center w/massage; tour desk; small business center; shopping arcade; salon; 24-hr. room service; babysitting; laundry service; dry cleaning; nonsmoking rooms. *In room:* A/C, satellite TV w/in-house movies, minibar, coffeemaker, iron.

Swiss-Garden Hotel For midrange prices, Swiss-Garden offers reliable comfort, an okay location, and affordability that attracts many leisure travelers to its doors. It also knows how to make you feel right at home, with a friendly staff (the concierge is on the ball) and a lobby bar that actually gets patronized (by travelers having cool cocktails at the end of a busy day of sightseeing). The guest rooms are simply furnished, but are neat and comfortable. Swiss-Garden is just walking distance from KL's lively Chinatown district, and close to the Puduraya bus station (which unfortunately makes traffic ugly at rush hour).

117 Jalan Pudu, 55100 Kuala Lumpur. © 03/2141-3333. Fax 03/2141-5555. www.swissgarden.com. 310 units. RM200 (US$56/£31) double; from RM350 (US$98/£54) suite. AE, DC, MC, V. **Amenities:** 2 restaurants; lobby lounge; small outdoor pool; small fitness center; small spa w/massage; concierge; limousine service; business center; 24-hr. room service; babysitting; laundry service; dry cleaning; nonsmoking rooms. *In room:* A/C, satellite TV w/in-house movies, minibar, coffeemaker, hair dryer, safe.

INEXPENSIVE

Hotel Capitol ★ *Value* A top pick for a budget hotel, Capitol is located in an up-and-coming part of the city's popular Golden Triangle district, close to the junction of Jalan Sultan Ismail and Jalan Bukit Bintang. In the surrounding lanes, you'll find small eateries and shops for necessities; the Times Square megamall is a short hop away. The place has been nicely refurbished, with a minimalist lobby that's function over frills. Inside the redone guest rooms, the wooden furniture seems like it's been around a while, but the upholstery, bedding, carpeting, and drapes are all fresh. There are no leisure facilities to speak of, but if you've come to KL to sightsee, you won't miss them.

Jalan Bulan, off Jalan Bukit Bintang, 55100 Kuala Lumpur. © 800/448-8355 in the U.S. and Canada, 800/221-176 in Australia, or 03/2143-7000. Fax 03/2143-0000. 225 units. RM250 (US$70/£39) double. AE, DC, MC, V. 10-min. walk to Imbi Monorail station. **Amenities:** Restaurant; limited room service; laundry service; nonsmoking rooms. *In room:* A/C, satellite TV w/in-house movies, minibar, coffeemaker, hair dryer, safe.

Swiss-Inn This mini-size hotel is one of KL's most popular budget places. Tucked away in the heart of Chinatown, Swiss-Inn's best asset is its location, amid the jumble of vibrant night-market hawkers. The place is small and offers almost no facilities. Higher-priced rooms have a small window and a bit more space (but are still compact), and are somewhat better maintained. Budget rooms, on lower floors, are very small, the cheapest having no windows at all. The beige carpeting can use a deep cleaning, the walls a fresh coat of paint, and the bathrooms some new grout work. On my last visit, housekeeping wasn't up to snuff, which added to the problem. Still, the hotel often has good promotional rates. Make sure you reserve your room early—this place runs at high occupancy year-round. The cafe, hidden behind market stalls, is an interesting place to have a beer and people-watch.

62 Jalan Sultan, 50000 Kuala Lumpur. © 03/2072-3333. Fax 03/2031-6699. www.swissgarden.com/hotel/sikl. 110 units. RM180 (US$50/£28) double. AE, DC, MC, V. **Amenities:** Restaurant; bar; tour desk; limited room service;

babysitting; laundry service; dry cleaning; nonsmoking rooms; Internet access. *In room:* A/C, TV w/in-house movies, coffeemaker.

WHERE TO DINE

Kuala Lumpur, like Singapore, is very cosmopolitan. Here you'll find not only delicious and exotic cuisine, but also some pretty trendy settings.

Al Nafourah ✦✦✦ LEBANESE   Dripping with the magical allure of a desert oasis, Al Nafourah is pure *Arabian Nights*. Moorish arches, twinkling lanterns, carved screens, silken hangings, mosaic tiles, and woven carpets abound; the restaurant also has booths in private nooks for extra romance. The Lebanese cuisine is some of the best around, with lamb, chicken, and fish dishes in tangy herbs and warm flatbreads straight from a wood-fired oven. Outside on the terrace, sit back and drink a heady coffee and smoke from a hookah while taking in belly-dance performances. A truly memorable evening.

At Le Meridien Kuala Lumpur, 2 Jalan Stesen Sentral. (℃ **03/2263-7888.** Reservations recommended. Main courses RM25–RM80 (US$7–US$22/£3.85–£12). AE, DC, MC, V. Daily noon–2:30pm and 6:30–10:30pm.

Chynna ✦✦ CANTONESE   Chynna is pure dinner theater: From the Madame Wong–style red lanterns to the Old China antique-replica furnishings, you'll think you're in a highly stylized Shanghai of yesteryear. For fun, there's a show kitchen where you can watch delectable dim sum being prepared, or you can just sit at your table and watch the tea master refill your cup with acrobatic moves. Pure genius! The delicious lunch dim sum menu is extensive, with most dishes between RM8 and RM12 (US$2.25–US$3.35/£1.25–£1.85). Dinner is standard Cantonese fare, with a lengthy menu of soups and rice and noodle dishes.

At the Hilton Kuala Lumpur, 3 Jalan Stesen Sentral. (℃ **03/2264-2264.** Reservations recommended. Small dishes RM28–RM56 (US$7.85–US$16/£4.30–£8.60). AE, DC, MC, V. Daily noon–2:30pm and 6:30–10:30pm.

Coliseum Cafe *(Finds* WESTERN/LOCAL   What can I say about Coliseum? Okay, the place is 86 years old, and so is the staff (seriously, some have worked here their whole lives). Located in the grottiest hotel I've ever seen, with stained white walls, worn tile floors, and threadbare linens, this is KL's authentic "greasy spoon." It sounds dreadful, but the place is legendary, and someday it will be gone and there will never be anything else like it. It used to be The Place for the starched-shirt colonial types to get real Western food back in the day. Now it's a favorite with the locals, who come for enormous sizzling steaks (which fill the place with greasy smoke), baked crabmeat served in the shell, and the house favorite: caramel custard pudding. Actually, the food is quite nice, and the prices are terrific for the steaks, which I highly recommend. You either get this place or you don't.

98-100 Jalan Tuanku Abdul Rahman. (℃ **03/2692-6270.** Reservations not accepted. Main courses RM10–RM34 (US$2.80–US$9.50/£1.55–£5.25). MC. Daily 8am–10pm.

Eden Village SEAFOOD   Uniquely designed inside and out to resemble a Malay house, Eden Village has great local atmosphere. It was once KL's most famous "fancy place" for a night out. Now it's visited by as many tourists as locals, but still retains some authenticity. Waitresses are clad in traditional *sarong kebaya* and serve up popular dishes like braised shark's fin in a clay pot with crabmeat and roe. The Kingdom of the Sea is a half lobster baked with prawns, crab, and cuttlefish. Terrace seating is the best in the house.

260 Jalan Raja Chulan. (℃ **03/2141-4027.** Reservations recommended. Main courses RM18–RM100 and up (US$5–US$28/£2.80–£15). AE, MC, V. Mon–Sat noon–3pm; daily 7pm–midnight.

Feast Village 🌟🌟 INTERNATIONAL   I'm one of those people who can never decide what I want to eat. This is the place for me! Located in the basement of Starhill Gallery, the city's most exclusive shopping mall, Feast Village isn't a single restaurant, but a cluster of 13 restaurants arranged like a small Malay village. As you stroll along stone-and-timber pathways, you'll pass cafes that serve seafood, steaks, Malay, Chinese, Thai, Korean, Indian and more. Within each cafe, the menu is unique and so is the decor. Wander, smell the smells, read the menus, check out the sights, and find the perfect food for your mood.

At the Starhill Gallery, 181 Jalan Bukit Bintang, basement. ✆ **03/2782-3800**. Reservations not required. Main courses vary from outlet to outlet. AE, DC, MC, V. Most outlets daily noon–2:30pm and 6:30–10:30pm.

Scalini's la Piccola Italia 🌟🌟 ITALIAN   Four chefs from Italy create the dishes that make Scalini's a favorite among KL locals and expats. From a very extensive menu, you can select pasta, fish, or meat, as well as a large selection of pizzas. The specials are superb and change all the time. Some of the best dishes are salmon with creamed asparagus sauce and ravioli with goat cheese and zucchini. Scalini's has a large wine selection (that is actually part of the romantic decor), with labels from California, Australia, New Zealand, France, and, of course, Italy.

19 Jalan Sultan Ismail. ✆ **03/2145-3211**. Reservations recommended. Main courses RM28–RM56 (US$7.85–US$16/£4.30–£8.60). AE, DC, MC, V. Sun–Thurs noon–2:30pm and 6–10:30pm; Fri noon–2:30pm and 6–11pm; Sat 6–11pm.

Shook! JAPANESE/CHINESE/ITALIAN/WESTERN GRILL   This place is unique for a number of reasons. First, Shook! is located on the ground floor of a shopping center, in a cavernous space decorated in a sort of Zen minimalism with splashes of color. Above, escalators glide shoppers to floors over the glass stage, where the pop and jazz band plays nightly. Second, the menu features four different types of cuisine that are prepared in four separate show kitchens. It will take a few minutes to read the menu, which offers a mind-boggling selection of Japanese, Chinese, Italian, and Western grill specialties. Very inventive. A good spot if your party can't agree on where to eat—there's something for everyone. One caveat: The staff sometimes seem lost in Shook's enormity.

Starhill Centre, 181 Jalan Bukit Bintang, Lower Ground Floor. ✆ **03/2716-8535**. Main courses RM20–RM200 (US$5.60–US$56/£3.10–£31). AE, DC, MC, V. Daily noon–2:30pm and 6:30–10:30pm.

Top Hat Restaurant 🌟🌟🌟 *Finds* PAN-ASIAN   Let me tell you about my favorite restaurant in Kuala Lumpur. First, Top Hat has a unique atmosphere. In a 1930s bungalow that was once a school, the place winds through room after room, its walls painted in bright hues and furnished with an assortment of mix-and-match teak tables, chairs, and antiques. Second, the menu is fabulous. While a la carte is available, Top Hat puts together set meals featuring Nonya, Malacca Portuguese, traditional Malay, Thai, Western, and even vegetarian recipes. They're all brilliant. Desserts are huge and full of sin.

7 Jalan Kia Peng. ✆ **03/2142-8611**. Reservations recommended. Main courses RM28–RM60 (US$7.85–US$17/£4.30–£9.25). Set meals RM30–RM100 (US$8.40–US$28/£4.60–£15). AE, DC, MC, V. Mon–Fri noon–2:30pm; daily 6–10:30pm.

WHAT TO SEE & DO

Most of Kuala Lumpur's historic sights are located in and around the Merdeka Square/Jalan Hishamuddin area, while many of the gardens, parks, and museums are out at Lake Gardens. Taxi fare between the two locations should run you about RM5 (US$1.40/£0.80).

City tours can be booked through **Tour Fifty-one,** located at the MTC (Malaysia Tourism Centre) on Jalan Ampang (℃ **03/2161-8830**). It coordinates a half-day coach tour for RM50 (US$14/£7.70) for adults and RM30 (US$8.40/£4.60) for children. The tour swings by most of the places listed here, but is a rushed experience.

Central Market ⚔ The original Central Market, built in 1936, used to be a wet market, but the place is now a cultural center (air-conditioned!) for local artists and craftspeople selling antiques, crafts, and curios. It's fantastic for buying Malaysian and Asian crafts and souvenirs, with two floors of shops to choose from. The Central Market also stages evening performances (7:45pm on weekends) of Malay martial arts, Indian classical dance, or Chinese orchestra. Call for performance information.

Jalan Benteng. ℃ **03/2274-6542.** Daily 10am–10pm. Shops open until 8:30 or 9pm.

Cosmo's World Theme Park ⚔⚔⚔ *Kids* I don't care if you have kids or not, Cosmo's rocks. The world's largest indoor amusement park is literally built into the walls of this 900-outlet shopping mall. You don't even need to ride the looping roller coaster to feel that thrill in the pit of your stomach. Just stand and watch it overhead as it flashes by—it really takes your breath away. There are saner rides, too, plus a host of kiddie rides. Highly recommended for families with bored kids.

Berjaya Times Square Shopping Mall, 1 Jalan Imbi. ℃ **03/2117-3118.** Admission RM25 (US$7/£3.85) adults, RM15 (US$4.20/£2.30) children. Daily 10am–10pm.

Islamic Arts Museum ⚔⚔ The seat of Islamic learning in Kuala Lumpur, the center has displays of Islamic texts, artifacts, porcelain, and weaponry in local and visiting exhibits.

Jalan Lembah Perdana. ℃ **03/2274-2020.** Admission RM12 (US$3.35/£1.85) adults, RM6 (US$1.70/£0.90) children. Daily 10am–6pm.

Jame Mosque (Masjid Jame) The first settlers landed in Kuala Lumpur at the spot where the Gombak and Klang rivers meet, and in 1909 a mosque was built here. Styled after an Indian Muslim design, it is one of the oldest mosques in the city. It is supposed to be opened to the public, but many foreigners, even those properly attired, have been shooed away at the gate.

Jalan Tun Terak. Free admission.

Kuala Lumpur Lake Gardens (Taman Tasik Perdana) Built around an artificial lake, the 91.6-hectare (229-acre) park has plenty of space for jogging and rowing, plus a playground for the kids. It's the most popular park in Kuala Lumpur. Inside the Lake Gardens, you'll find the **Kuala Lumpur Bird Park** ⚔ (Jalan Perdana; ℃ **03/2273-5423;** www.birdpark.com.my; adults RM30/US$8.40/£4.60, children RM22/US$6.15/£3.40; daily 9am–6pm) nestled in beautifully landscaped gardens, with over 3,000 birds in a huge walk-in aviary. Quite impressive. **Kuala Lumpur Orchid Garden** (Jalan Perdana; ℃ **03/2693-5399;** weekend and public holiday admission adults RM1/US30¢/£0.15, children free; free weekday admission for all; daily 9am–6pm) has a collection of over 800 orchid species from Malaysia, plus thousands of international varieties. The **Kuala Lumpur Butterfly Park** (Jalan Cenderasari; ℃ **03/2693-4799;** adults RM15/US$4.20/£2.30, children RM8/US$2.25/£1.25; daily 9am–6pm) has over 6,000 butterflies belonging to 120 species making their home in this park, which has been landscaped with more than 15,000 plants to simulate the butterflies' natural rainforest environment. There are also other small animals and an insect museum.

Enter through Jalan Parliament. Free admission. Daily 9am–6pm.

Kuala Lumpur Railway Station Built in 1910, the KL Railway Station is a beautiful example of Moorish architecture.

Jalan Sultan Hishamuddin. Free admission. Daily 7:30am–10:30pm.

Malaysia Tourist Centre (MTC) At MTC, you'll find an exhibit hall, tourist information services for Kuala Lumpur and Malaysia, and other travel-planning services. On Tuesday, Thursday, Saturday, and Sunday, there are cultural shows at 2pm, featuring Malaysian dance and music. Shows are RM5 (US$1.40/£0.80) for adults and free for children.

Jalan Ampang. ✆ **03/2164-3929**. Free admission. Daily 9am–6pm.

Menara Kuala Lumpur Standing 421m (1,389 ft.) tall, this concrete structure is the third-tallest tower in the world, and the views from the top reach to the far corners of the city and beyond. At the top, the glass windows are fashioned after the Shah Mosque in Isfahan, Iran.

Bukit Nanas. ✆ **03/2020-5448**. Admission RM10 (US$2.80/£1.55) adults, RM5 (US$1.40/£0.80) children. Daily 9am–10pm.

Merdeka Square Surrounded by colonial architecture with an exotic local flair, the square was once the site of British social and sporting events. These days, Malaysia holds its spectacular Independence Day celebrations on the field, which is home to the world's tallest flagpole, standing at 100m (330 ft.).

Jalan Raja. Free admission.

National Art Gallery The building that now houses the National Art Gallery was built as the Majestic Hotel in 1932 and has been restored to display contemporary works by Malaysian artists. There are also international exhibits.

Jalan Temerloh off Jalan Tun Razak. ✆ **03/4025-4990**. Free admission. Daily 10am–6pm.

National Mosque (Masjid Negara) Built in a modern design, the most distinguishing features of the mosque are its 73m (243-ft.) minaret and the umbrella-shaped roof, which is said to symbolize a newly independent Malaysia's aspirations for the future. Could be true, as the place was built in 1965, the year Singapore split from Malaysia.

Jalan Sultan Hishamuddin (near the KL Railway Station). Free admission. Daily 9am–6pm.

National Museum (Muzim Negara) 🌟🌟 Located at Lake Gardens, the museum has more than 1,000 items of historic, cultural, and traditional significance, including art, weapons, musical instruments, and costumes.

Jalan Damansara. ✆ **03/2282-6255**. Admission RM2 (US60¢/£0.30) adults, free for children under 12. Daily 9am–6pm.

National Planetarium (Kids) The National Planetarium has a Space Hall with touch-screen interactive computers and hands-on experiments, a Viewing Gallery with binoculars for a panoramic view of the city, and an Ancient Observatory Park with models of Chinese and Indian astronomy systems. The Space Theatre has two different outer-space shows at 11am, 2pm, and 4pm for an extra charge of RM3 (US80¢/£0.40) for adults and RM2 (US60¢/£0.30) for children.

Lake Gardens. ✆ **03/2273-5484**. Admission to exhibition hall RM1 (US30¢/£0.15) adults, free for children. Tues–Sun 10am–4pm.

Petaling Street ☞ This is the center of KL's Chinatown district. By day, stroll past hawker stalls, dim sum shops, wet markets, and all sorts of stores, from pawn shops to coffin makers. At night, a crazy bazaar (which is terribly crowded) pops up—look for designer knockoffs, fake watches, and pirated VCDs (Video CDs).

Petronas Twin Towers ☞ Standing at an awesome 451.9m (1,482 ft.) above street level, with 88 stories, the towers were the tallest buildings in the world from 1998 to 2004 (when Taipei 101 snatched the title). From the outside, the structures are designed with the kind of geometric patterns common to Islamic architecture, and on levels 41 and 42 the two towers are linked by a bridge. Visitors are permitted on the viewing deck on the bridge from 10am to 8pm every day except Mondays and public holidays; otherwise, the building is accessible only if you are conducting business inside.

Kuala Lumpur City Centre. ℗ **03/2051-7770.** Free admission.

Sri Mahamariaman Temple With a recent face-lift (Hindu temples must renovate every 12 years), this bright temple livens the gray street scene around it. It's a beautiful temple tucked away on a narrow street in KL's Chinatown area. It was built by Thambusamy Pillai, a pillar of old KL's Indian community.

Jalan Bandar. Free admission.

Sultan Abdul Samad Building In 1897, this exotic building was designed by Regent Alfred John Bidwell, a colonial architect responsible for many of the buildings in Singapore. He chose a style called "Muhammadan" or "neo-Saracenic," which combines Indian Muslim architecture with Gothic and other Western elements. Built to house government administrative offices, today it is the home of Malaysia's Supreme Court and High Court.

Jalan Raja. Free admission.

GOLF

People from all over Asia flock to Malaysia for its golf courses, many of which are excellent standard courses designed by pros. The **Kuala Lumpur Golf & Country Club,** 10 Jalan 1/70D, off Jalan Bukit Kiara (℗ **03/2093-1111**), has two courses, 18 holes each, par 71 and 72, designed by R. Nelson and R. Wright, with greens fees of RM189 (US$53/£29) weekdays. The club is closed to nonmembers on weekends and holidays. **Suajana Golf & Country Club,** Km 3, Jalan Lapangan Terbang Sultan Abdul Aziz Shah, Subang Selangor (℗ **03/7846-1466;** fax 03/7846-7818), has two 18-hole courses, each par 72, designed by Ronald Fream. Greens fees are RM223 (US$62/£34) on weekdays, RM353 (US$99/£54) on weekends and holidays.

SHOPPING

Kuala Lumpur is a truly great place to shop. In recent years, mall after mall has risen from city lots, filled with hundreds of retail outlets selling everything from haute couture to cheap chic clothing, electronic goods, jewelry, and arts and crafts. The **major shopping malls** are located in the area around Jalan Bukit Bintang and Jalan Sultan Ismail. There are also a few malls along Jalan Ampang. **Suria KLCC,** just beneath the Petronas Twin Towers, is KL's most upmarket mall, while **Berjaya Times Square** wins the prize for excess, with 900 shops, food and entertainment outlets, and the world's largest indoor amusement park.

Still the best place for Malaysian handicrafts, the huge **Central Market,** on Jalan Benteng (℗ **03/2274-6542**), keeps any shopper satiated for hours. Here you'll find a jumble of local artists and craftspeople selling their wares in the heart of town. It's also a good place to find Malaysian handicrafts from other regions of the country. One specific shop for Malaysian handicrafts is **KL Craft Complex,** Section 3 Jalan Conlay (✆ **03/2162-7533**), with its warehouse selection of assorted goods from around the country, all of it fine quality. Don't forget to walk through the gardens to see the artists' village. In the bungalows towards the side of the building, you'll find some of Malaysia's finest contemporary artists displaying their works. Wear comfy shoes, as you may need to walk back to the main road to get a cab.

Another favorite haunt is **Chinatown,** along Petaling Street. Day and night, it's a great place to wander and bargain for knockoff designer clothing and accessories, sunglasses, T-shirts, souvenirs, fake watches, and pirated videos.

Pasar malam (**night markets**) are very popular evening activities in KL. Whole blocks are taken up with these brightly lit and bustling markets, packed with stalls selling everything you can dream of. They are likely to pop up anywhere in the city. Two good bets for catching one: Go to Jalan Haji Taib after dark until 10pm; on Saturday nights, head for Jalan Tuanku Abdul Rahman.

KUALA LUMPUR AFTER DARK

There's nightlife to spare in KL, from fashionable lounges to sprawling discos to pubs perfect for hanging out. Basically, you can expect to pay about RM11 to RM20 (US$3.10–US$5.60/£1.70–£3.10) for a pint of beer, depending on what and where you order. Although quite a few pubs are open for lunch, most clubs won't open until about 6 or 7pm. These places must all close by 1 or 2am, so don't plan on staying out too late. Nearly all have a happy hour, usually between 5 and 7pm, when drink discounts apply on draft beers and "house-pour" (lower-shelf) mixed drinks. Generally, "dress casual" attire is expected for these places, but avoid old jeans, tennis shoes, and very revealing outfits.

The center of nightlife is at the corner of Jalan Sultan Ismail and Jalan P. Ramlee. Walk along P. Ramlee and you'll find bars of all kinds, plus cafes and coffee shops.

For a little live music with your drinks, the **Hard Rock Cafe,** Jalan Sultan Ismail next to the Concorde Hotel (✆ **03/2715-5555**), hosts the best of the regional bands, which play nightly for a crowd of locals, tourists, and expats who take their parties very seriously.

The biggest dance club in town is **Zouk,** 113 Jalan Ampang, down the street from MTC (✆ **03/2171-1997**), fashioned after the ultra-successful Zouk in Singapore. There's a cover of anywhere from RM25 to RM40 (US$7–US$11/£3.85–£6.15), depending on what's going on inside.

Bangsar, just outside the city limits, is 2 or 3 blocks of bars, cafes, and restaurants that cater to a variety of tastes. In fact, so many expats hang out here, they call it *Kweiloh Lumpur,* "Foreigner Lumpur" in Mandarin. Every taxi driver knows where it is; just ask to go to Jalan Telawi Tiga in Bangsar. The fare should be no more than RM5 to RM6 (US$1.40–US$1.70/£0.80–£0.90). Once there, it's very easy to catch a cab back to town. During the week, it's kind of quiet.

SIDE TRIPS FROM KUALA LUMPUR
TAMAN NEGARA NATIONAL PARK ✸✸✸

Malaysia's most famous national park, Taman Negara, covers 434,300 hectares (1,072,721 acres) of primary rainforest estimated to be as old as 130 million years, and encompasses within its borders **Gunung Tahan,** peninsular Malaysia's highest peak at 2,187m (7,173 ft.) above sea level.

Prepare to see lush vegetation and rare orchids, some 250 bird species, and maybe, if you're lucky, some barking deer, tapir, elephants, tigers, leopards, and rhinos. As for primates, there are longtailed macaques, leaf monkeys, gibbons, and more. Malaysia has taken the preservation of this forest seriously since the early part of the last century, so Taman Negara showcases those efforts to keep this land in as pristine a state as possible while still allowing humans to appreciate the splendor.

There are outdoor activities for any level of adventurer. Short jungle walks to observe nature are lovely, but then so are the hard-core 9-day treks or climbs up Gunung Tahan. There are also overnight trips where you can observe animals up close. The jungle canopy walk is the longest in the world, and at 25m (82 ft.) above ground, the view is spectacular. There are also rivers for rafting and swimming, fishing spots, and a couple of caves.

If you plan your trip through one of the main resort operators, it can arrange accommodations, all meals, treks, and a coach transfer to and from Kuala Lumpur. Prices vary wildly, depending on the time of year, the level of comfort desired, and the extent to which you wish to explore the forests. The best time to visit the park is between the months of April and September; other times it will be a tad wet, and that's why it's called a rainforest.

Mutiara Taman Negara Resort ⍟ (Kuala Tahan, Jerantut, Pahang; ✆ **09/266-3500,** or 03/2145-5585 for sales office in KL), well established in the business of hosting visitors to the park, is the best lodging in terms of comfort. It organizes trips for 3 or 4 days, as well as an a la carte deal in which you pay for lodging and activities separately. Accommodations come in many styles: a bungalow suite for families; a chalet and chalet suite, both good for couples; standard guesthouse rooms in a motel-style longhouse; and dormitory hostels for budget travelers. To get an idea of pricing, a 3-day, 2-night package runs about RM765 (US$214/£118) per person, double occupancy in a chalet, with air-conditioning and attached bathroom, plus full board and activities. What it doesn't include is bus transfer from KL (RM80/$22/£12 per person round-trip) and the boat upriver from the park entrance (RM56/$16/£8.60 per person round-trip). A la carte activities include a 3-hour jungle trek, a 1½-hour night jungle walk, the half-day Lata Berkoh river trip with swimming, a 2-hour cave exploration, and a trip down the rapids in a rubber raft.

GENTING HIGHLANDS

Malaysia's answer to Las Vegas, Genting comes complete with bright lights (which can be seen from Kuala Lumpur) and gambling. And while most people come here for the casino, there's a wide range of other activities, although most of them seem to serve the purpose of entertaining the kids while you bet their college funds at the roulette wheel.

The 24-hour **casino** charges a refundable deposit of RM200 (US$56/£31) entry for people over 21 years of age. Outside of the casino, there's also a pond, a bowling alley, and an indoor heated pool. The **Awana Golf & Country Club** (✆ **03/6101-3025**) is the premier golf course in these hills. For children, the **Genting Theme Park** covers 100,000 square feet of mostly rides, plus many Western fast-food outlets, games, and other attractions.

Genting Highlands Transport (✆ **03/6251-8398**) operates buses from KL every half-hour from 6:30am to 9pm daily, departing from the Pekeliling Bus Terminal on Jalan Ipoh for RM7.40 (US$2.10/£1.15). The hour-long trip lets you off at the foot of the hill, where you take the cable car to the top for RM3 (US85¢/£0.45). You can also get here by hiring an **outstation taxi,** which should cost RM40 ($11/£6.15).

Genting has four hotels of varying prices within the resort. The **Genting Highlands Resort** is owned and operated by Resorts World Berhad, which will be glad to provide you with hotel reservations if you call ℂ **03/2718-1118.**

CAMERON HIGHLANDS

Located up in the hills, this colonial-era resort town has a cool climate, which makes it the perfect place for agriculture, as well as for weekend getaways by Malaysians and Singaporeans who are sick of the heat. Temperatures in the highlands average 70°F (21°C) during the day and 50°F (10°C) at night.

There are no visitor information services here, but you'll find banks with ATMs and money changers along the main road in Tanah Rata, the main town.

Most of the sights can be seen in a day. Contact **C. S. Travel & Tours** (47 Main Rd., Tanah Rata; ℂ **05/491-1200**), a highly reputable agency that will plan half-day tours for RM20 (US$5.60/£3.10) or full-day tours starting from RM80 (US$22/£12). On your average tour, you'll see the Boh tea plantation and factory, flower nurseries, rose gardens, strawberry farms, butterfly farms, and the Sam Poh Buddhist Temple. You're required to pay admission to each attraction yourself. C. S. Travel also provides trekking and overnight camping trips in the surrounding hills with local guides.

If you want to hit some balls, **Padang Golf** (Main Rd., between Tanah Rata and Brinchang; ℂ **05/491-1126**) has 18 holes at par 71, with greens fees around RM53 (US$15/£8.15) on weekdays and RM84 (US$24/£13) on weekends. It provides club rentals, caddies, shoes, and carts.

The best choice for accommodations here is the **Smokehouse Hotel** (Tanah Rata, Cameron Highlands, Pahang Darul Makmur; ℂ **05/491-1215;** fax 05/491-1214), a picturesque Tudor mansion with pretty gardens outside and a charming old-world ambience inside. Rates are RM460 to RM730 (US$129–US$204/£71–£112).

Kurnia Bistari Express Bus (ℂ **05/491-2978**) has service between Kuala Lumpur and Tanah Rata daily for around RM17 (US$4.75/£2.60) one-way. **Outstation taxis** from KL will cost RM220 (US$62/£34) for the trip; call ℂ **03/2078-0213** for booking.

5 Malacca ⭑

Malacca became the birthplace of Islam in Malaysia when Arab traders imported the faith in the early 1400s. Around that time, the port city rose to international attention as a major center for Southeast Asian trade with China and the Middle East. European powers conquered, first the Portuguese, then the Dutch, and finally the British; however, over the centuries Malacca lost its status to neighboring Singapore. Today, the sleepy backwater town reveals remnants of past conquerors, settlers, and traders in its architecture.

GETTING THERE

BY TRAIN   Malacca doesn't have a proper train station, but the **KTM** stops at Tampin (ℂ **06/441-1034**), 38km (24 miles) north of the city. It's not the most convenient way in and out of Malacca, but if you decide to stop en route between Kuala Lumpur and Johor Bahru, you can easily catch a waiting taxi to your hotel in town for RM40 (US$11/£6.15).

BY BUS   From Singapore, contact **Grassland Express** (ℂ **65/6293-1166**). A bus departs at 8am daily for the 4½-hour trip (S$27/US$17/£9.30). From KL's **Puduraya Bus Terminal** on Jalan Pudu, **Transnasional** (ℂ **03/6201-3463**) has hourly buses

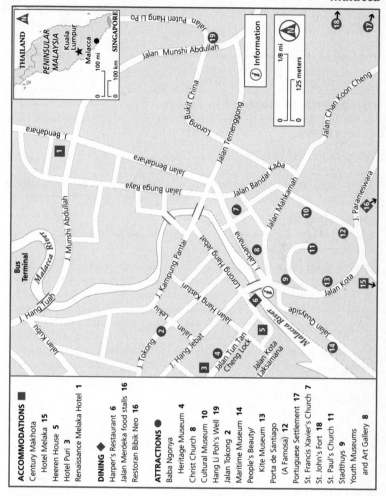

between 8am and 10pm for about RM9.50 (US$2.65/£1.45). The trip takes about 2½ hours. The bus station in Malacca is at Jalan Kilang, within the city. Taxis are easy to find from here.

BY TAXI   Outstation taxis can bring you here from Kuala Lumpur for RM140 (US$39/£22). The outstation taxi stand in Malacca is at the bus terminal on Jalan Kilang.

GETTING AROUND

Most of the historic sights around the town square are within walking distance. For other trips, **taxis** are the most convenient way around, but are at times difficult to find. They're also not as clearly marked as in KL or Johor Bahru. They are not metered, so be prepared to bargain. Basically, no matter what you do, you'll always be charged a higher rate than a local. Tourists are almost always quoted RM10 (US$2.80/£1.55) for local trips; Malaysians pay RM5 (US$1.40/£0.80). If you're feeling sporty, you can bargain for a price somewhere in between. **Trishaws** (bicycle rickshaws) are all over the historic areas of town, and in Malacca they're renowned for being very, very garishly decorated (which adds to the fun). Negotiate for hourly rates of about RM20 (US$5.60/£3.10) for two people.

VISITOR INFORMATION
The **Malacca Tourism Centre** is on Jalan Kota, at the town square next to the bridge (© **06/281-4803**).

FAST FACTS: MALACCA
Malacca's **area code** is 06. Major **banks** are located in the historic center of town, with a couple along Jalan Putra. **Internet** places come and go; your best bet is to ask your hotel's concierge or the Malacca Tourism Centre (see above) for the nearest cybercafes.

WHERE TO STAY
Malacca is not very large, and most of the places to stay are well within walking distance of attractions, shopping, and restaurants.

Century Mahkota Hotel Melaka *(Kids)*   Set along the waterfront, the hotel is within walking distance of sightseeing, historic areas, shopping, and commercial centers. Rooms are more like holiday apartments, with mini-kitchens and up to three bedrooms—a big hit with Malaysian and Singaporean families. Each apartment has a tiled main room with cooking space at one end and simple rattan furnishings at the other—only the bedrooms are air-conditioned. The views are of the pools, the shopping mall across the street, or the muddy reclaimed seafront. The sprawling complex includes two outdoor pools and facilities for children, and it's across from the largest shopping mall in Malacca. This place gets especially crowded during the school holidays in June and December.

Jalan Merdeka, 75000 Malacca. © 06/281-2828. Fax 06/281-2323. 617 units. RM178–RM408 (US$50–US$114/£27–£63) 1- to 3-bedroom apt. AE, DC, MC, V. **Amenities:** 3 restaurants; lounge and piano bar; 2 outdoor pools; outdoor lighted tennis courts; squash courts; fitness center w/sauna and massage; children's playground; game room; tour desk; car rental; shuttle; business center; 24-hr. room service; babysitting; laundry service; dry cleaning. *In room:* Satellite TV, coffeemaker, hair dryer.

Heeren House *(★★)*   This is the place to stay for a taste of the local culture. Started by a local family, the small guesthouse is a renovated 100-year-old building furnished in traditional Peranakan and colonial style and located right in the heart of historic European Malacca. All bedrooms have views of the Malacca River, and outside the front door of the hotel is a winding stretch of old buildings housing antiques shops—just walk out and wander. The small rooms have very basic amenities. The rooms on the second floor are somewhat larger. There's a cafe and gift shop on the premises. Everybody is nice as pie. Reserve well in advance.

1 Jalan Tun Tan Cheng Lock, 75200 Malacca. © 06/281-4241. Fax 06/281-4239. 7 units. RM139 (US$39/£21) double; RM239 (US$67/£37) family suite. No credit cards. **Amenities:** Restaurant; laundry service. *In room:* A/C, TV.

Hotel Puri *(Value)*   In the olden days, Jalan Tun Tan Cheng Lock was known as "Millionaires' Row" for all the wealthy families that lived here. This old "mansion" has been converted into a guesthouse, its tiled parlor has become a lobby, and the courtyard is where breakfast is served each morning. Although Hotel Puri isn't big on space, it is big on value (discount rates can be pretty low). Rooms are very clean, and while not overly stylish, they're comfortable enough for any weary traveler. A friendly and responsive staff adds to the appeal.

118 Jalan Tun Tan Cheng Lock, 75200 Malacca. ✆ 06/282-5588. Fax 06/281-5588. 50 units. RM127 (US$36/£20) double; RM265 (US$74/£41) triple; suites from RM322 (US$90/£50). AE, MC, V. **Amenities:** Restaurant; tour desk; limited room service; babysitting; laundry service. *In room:* A/C, satellite TV, fridge, coffeemaker, hair dryer.

Renaissance Melaka Hotel ✿   Renaissance is one of the posher hotels in Malacca, and, according to business travelers, is the most reliable place for quality accommodations—but aside from the pieces of Peranakan porcelain and art in the public areas, you could almost believe you weren't in Malacca at all. The hotel is, however, in a good location, though you'll still need a taxi to reach most of the sights. Renovations in 2002 upgraded the guest rooms, which are fairly large and filled with Western comforts. Don't expect much from the views, as the hotel is in a more business-minded part of the city (no historic landmarks to gaze upon here).

Jalan Bendahara, 75100 Malacca. ✆ 800/228-9898 in the U.S. and Canada, 800/251-259 in Australia, 800/441-035 in New Zealand, 800/181-737 in the U.K., or 06/284-8888. Fax 06/284-9269. 294 units. RM480 (US$134/£74) double; from RM620 (US$174/£96) suite. AE, MC, V. **Amenities:** 3 restaurants; bar and lobby lounge; outdoor pool; golf nearby; 2 indoor squash courts; fitness center w/sauna, steam, and massage; concierge; tour desk; limousine service; business center; salon; 24-hr. room service; babysitting; laundry service; dry cleaning; executive-level rooms. *In room:* A/C, satellite TV w/in-house movies, minibar, coffeemaker, safe.

WHERE TO DINE

In Malacca, you'll find the typical mix of authentic Malay and Chinese food, and because the city was the major settling place for the Peranakans in Malaysia, their unique style of food is featured in many of the local restaurants.

If you're strolling in the historic area, a good recommendation for a quick lunch or dinner is the long string of open-air food stalls along Jalan Merdeka, just between Mahkota Plaza Shopping and Warrior Square. **Mama Fatso's** is especially good for Chinese-style seafood and Malay sambal curry. A good meal will run you about RM35 to RM40 (US$9.80–US$11/£5.40–£6.15).

Try local Peranakan cuisine at **Restoran Bibik Neo** (no. 6, ground floor, Jalan Merdeka, Taman Melaka Raya; ✆ 06/281-7054), a small coffee shop that's about as authentic as you can get. *Ikan assam* with eggplant is a tasty mild fish curry that's very rich and tart; I always go for the *otak-otak* (pounded fish and spices baked in a banana leaf).

For a taste of Portuguese Malacca, the **Portuguese Settlement** (Jalan d'Albuquerque, off Jalan Ujon Pasir) has some open-air food stalls by the water, where in the evenings hawkers sell an assortment of dishes inspired by these former colonial rulers, including many fresh seafood offerings. Saturday nights are best—at 8pm, there's a cultural show with music and dancing. Other times it may be slow business. Dinner will be around RM15 (US$4.20/£2.30).

My favorite place in town is **Harper's Restaurant** (Harper's Building, Jalan Hang Jebat; ✆ 06/282-8800), which serves Nyonya, Chinese, and Western food in a terrific riverside setting. This combination watering hole and bistro has a relaxed Asian feel, with open-air verandas and cane furnishings—simple but atmospheric. The menu serves local dishes and a selection of steaks prepared Western style. Prices range from RM20 (US$5.60/£3.10) for simple Asian small dishes to RM45 (US$13/£6.95) for the surf and turf. It's open daily from 10am to 1:30am, but the Asian kitchen is only open from noon to 2:30pm and 6 to 10:30pm. Western food is served anytime between noon and 11:30pm. Visa and MasterCard are accepted.

WHAT TO SEE & DO

To get the most out of Malacca, it's best to have a bit of knowledge about the history of the place. Most of the preserved historic sights are on both sides of the Malacca River. Start at **Stadthuys** (the old town hall, pronounced *Stat*-highs) and you'll see most of Malacca pretty quickly.

MUSEUMS

Baba Nyonya Heritage Museum ⟨★⟩   Called "Millionaires' Row," Jalan Tun Tan Cheng Lock is lined with row houses that were built by the Dutch and later bought by wealthy Peranakans; the architectural style reflects their East-meets-West lifestyle. The Baba Nyonya Heritage Museum sits at nos. 48 and 50 as a repository of Peranakan heritage. The entrance fee includes a guided tour.

48–50 Jalan Tun Tan Cheng Lock. ⓒ **06/283-1273**. Admission RM8 (US$2.25/£1.25) adults, RM4 (US$1.10/£0.60) children. Daily 10am–12:30pm and 2–4:30pm.

Cultural Museum (Muzium Budaya) ⟨★⟩   A replica of the former palace of Sultan Mansur Syah (1456–77), this museum was rebuilt according to historical descriptions to house a fine collection of cultural artifacts such as clothing, weaponry, and royal items. The gardens are quite nice.

Kota Rd., next to Porta de Santiago. ⓒ **06/282-6526**. Admission RM2 (US60¢/£0.30) adults, RM0.50 (US10¢/£0.05) children. Daily 9am–5:30pm.

Maritime Museum and the Royal Malaysian Navy Museum   These two museums are located across the street from each other but share admission fees. The Maritime Museum is in a restored 16th-century Portuguese ship, with exhibits dedicated to Malacca's history with the sea. The Navy Museum is a modern display of Malaysia's less-pleasant relationship with the sea.

Quayside Rd. ⓒ **06/282-6526**. Admission RM3 (US80¢/£0.40) adults, RM1 (US30¢/£0.15) children. Daily 9am–5:30pm.

The People's Museum, the Museum of Beauty, the Kite Museum, and the Governor of Melaka's Gallery   This strange collection of displays is housed under one roof. The People's Museum is the story of development in Malacca. The Museum of Beauty is a look at cultural differences of beauty throughout time and around the world. The Kite Museum features the traditions of making and flying *wau* (kites) in Malaysia, while the governor's personal collection is on exhibit at the Governor's Gallery.

Kota Rd. ⓒ **06/282-6526**. Admission RM2 (US60¢/£0.30) adults, RM0.50 (US10¢/£0.05) children. Daily 9am–5:30pm.

Stadthuys—The Museums of History & Ethnography and the Museum of Literature ⟨★⟩   The Stadthuys Town Hall was built by the Dutch in 1650, and it's now home to the Malacca Ethnographical and Historical Museum, which displays customs and traditions of all the peoples of Malacca; it also takes you through the rich history of this city. Behind Stadthuys, the Museum of Literature includes old historical accounts and local legends. The admission price covers both exhibits.

At the circle intersection of Jalan Quayside, Jalan Laksamana, and Jalan Chan Koon Cheng. ⓒ **06/282-6526**. Admission RM5 (US$1.40/£0.80) adults, RM2 (US55¢/£0.30) children. Daily 9am–5:30pm.

Youth Museums and Art Gallery   In the old general post office are these displays dedicated to Malaysia's youth organizations and to the nation's finest artists. An unusual combination.

Laksamana Rd. © **06/282-6526**. Admission RM2 (US55¢/£0.30) adults, RM0.50 (US15¢/£0.10) children. Tues–Sun 9am–5:30pm.

HISTORIC SIGHTS

Christ Church   The Dutch built this place in 1753 as a Dutch Reform Church, and its architectural details include such wonders as ceiling beams cut from a single tree and a *Last Supper* glazed-tile motif above the altar. It was later consecrated as an Anglican church, and mass is still performed today in English, Chinese, and Tamil.

Jalan Laksamana. Free admission.

Hang Li Poh's Well   Also called "Sultan's Well," Hang Li Poh's Well was built in 1495 to commemorate the marriage of Chinese Princess Hang Li Poh to Sultan Mansor Shah. It is now a wishing well, and folks say that if you toss in a coin, you'll someday return to Malacca.

Off Jalan Laksamana Cheng Ho (Jalan Panjang). Free admission.

Jalan Tokong 🔾   Not far from Jalan Tun Tan Cheng Lock is Jalan Tokong, called the "Street of Harmony" by the locals because it has three coexisting places of worship: the Kampong Kling Mosque, the Cheng Hoon Teng Temple, and the Sri Poyyatha Vinayar Moorthi Temple.

Porta de Santiago (A Famosa) 🔾   Once the site of a Portuguese fortress called A Famosa, all that remains today is the entrance gate, which was saved from demolition by Sir Stamford Raffles. When the British East India Company demolished the place, Raffles realized the arch's historical value and saved it. The fort was built in 1512, but the inscription above the arch, "Anno 1607," marks the date when the Dutch overthrew the Portuguese.

Jalan Kota, at the intersection of Jalan Parameswara. Free admission.

Portuguese Settlement and Portuguese Square   The Portuguese Settlement was an enclave once designated for Portuguese settlers after they conquered Malacca in 1511. Some elements of their presence remain in the Lisbon-style architecture. Later, in 1920, the area was a Eurasian neighborhood. In the center of the settlement, Portuguese Square is a modern attraction with Portuguese restaurants, handicrafts, souvenirs, and cultural shows. It was built in 1985 in an architectural style to reflect the surrounding flavor of Portugal.

Down Jalan d'Albuquerque off Jalan Ujon Pasir in the southern part of the city. Free admission.

St. Francis Xavier's Church   This church was built in 1849 and dedicated to St. Francis Xavier, a Jesuit who brought Catholicism to Malacca and other parts of Southeast Asia.

Jalan Laksamana. Free admission.

St. John's Fort   The fort, built by the Dutch in the late 18th century, sits on top of St. John's Hill. Funny how the cannons point inland, huh? At the time, threats to the city came from land. It was named after a Portuguese church to St. John the Baptist, which originally occupied the site.

Off Lorong Bukit Senjuang. Free admission.

St. Paul's Church The church was built by the Portuguese in 1521, but when the Dutch came in, they made it part of A Famosa, converting the altar into a cannon mount. The open tomb inside was once the resting place of St. Francis Xavier, a missionary who spread Catholicism throughout Southeast Asia, and whose remains were later moved to Goa.

Behind Porta de Santiago. Free admission.

SHOPPING

Antiques hunting has been a major draw for decades. Distinct Peranakan and teak furniture, porcelain, and household items fetch quite a price these days, due to a steady increase in demand for these rare treasures. The area down and around Jalan Hang Jebat and Jalan Tun Tan Cheng Lok called **Jonker Walk** sports many little antiques shops that are filled with as many gorgeous items as any local museum. You'll also find handmade crafts, ready-made batik clothing, and other souvenirs. Whether you're buying or just looking, it's a fun way to spend an afternoon. For crafts and souvenirs, you'll also find a row of shops along the lane beside Stadthuys. Most prices seem fair, but you may need to do a little bargaining.

6 Penang ★★★

Penang is unique in Malaysia because, for all intents and purposes, Penang has it all. Malacca has historic sights and museums, but it doesn't have a good beach for miles. Similarly, while KL has shopping, nightlife, and attractions, it also has no beach resorts. Penang has all of it: beaches, history, diverse culture, shopping, food—you name it, it has it. If you have only a short time to visit Malaysia but want to take in a variety of experiences, Penang is your place.

Since Malaysia's independence in 1957, Penang has had relatively good financial success. Today, the state of Penang is made up of the island and a small strip of land on the Malaysian mainland. Georgetown is the seat of government for the state. Penang Island covers an area of 285 sq. km (111 sq. miles) and has a population of a little more than one million. Surprisingly, the population is mostly Chinese (59%), followed by Malays (32%) and Indians (7%).

GETTING THERE

BY PLANE **Penang International Airport** (© 04/643-4411) has flights that connect from all over the world. **Malaysia Airlines** has about 20 flights each day from KL, plus connecting flights from all over the country and region. **Singapore Airlines, Thai Airways, Cathay Pacific,** and the popular budget carrier **AirAsia** also serve Penang.

The airport is 20km (12 miles) from the city. To get into town, you must purchase fixed-rate coupons for taxis (RM38/US$11/£5.85 to Georgetown; RM60/US$17/£9.25 to Batu Feringgi). There are also car rentals at the airport; go with **Avis** (© 04/643-9633).

BY TRAIN By rail, the overnight trip from KL to Butterworth takes 10 hours and costs RM85 (US$24/£13) in first-class passage, or as low as RM17 (US$4.75/£2.60) for economy class. The prices vary depending on whether you choose upper or lower berth, as well as what class you take. Call **KL Sentral** (© 03/2267-1200) for schedule information.

Penang Island

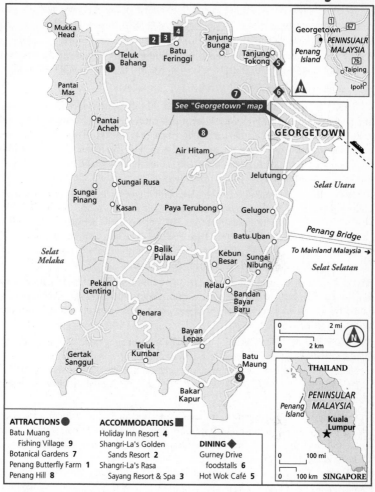

ATTRACTIONS ●
Batu Muang
    Fishing Village **9**
Botanical Gardens **7**
Penang Butterfly Farm **1**
Penang Hill **8**

ACCOMMODATIONS ■
Holiday Inn Resort **4**
Shangri-La's Golden
    Sands Resort **2**
Shangri-La's Rasa
    Sayang Resort & Spa **3**

DINING ◆
Gurney Drive
    foodstalls **6**
Hot Wok Café **5**

The train will let you off at the **Butterworth Railway Station** (© **04/323-7962**), on Jalan Bagan Dalam (near the ferry terminal) in Butterworth, on the Malaysian mainland. From there, you can take a taxi to the island or head for the ferry close by.

BY FERRY   The ferry to Penang is nestled between the Butterworth Railway Station and the Butterworth bus terminal. It operates 24 hours a day and takes 20 minutes from pier to pier. From 6am to midnight, ferries leave every 10 minutes. From midnight to 1:20am, boats run every half-hour, and from 1:20 to 6am, they run hourly. Purchase your passage by dropping RM1.20 (US35¢/£0.20) exact change in the turnstile (there's a change booth if you don't have it). Fare is paid only on the trip to Penang; the return is free. The ferry lets you off at Weld Quay.

BY BUS Many buses will bring you to Butterworth or Georgetown, but only gluttons for punishment should attempt this. Transnasional stopped its executive coach service, and if you take a standard coach, the trip will be horrible.

BY TAXI The **outstation taxi** stand is in Butterworth next to the bus terminal (© **04/323-2045**). Fares to Butterworth from KL will be about RM300 ($84/£46).

GETTING AROUND

BY TAXI Taxis are abundant, but be warned they do not use meters, so you must agree on the price before you ride. Most trips within the city are between RM3 and RM6 (US85¢–US$1.70/£0.45–£0.90). If you're staying out at the Batu Feringgi beach-resort area, expect taxis to town to run RM20 (US$5.60/£3.10), or RM30 (US$8.40/£4.60) at night. The ride is about 15 or 20 minutes, but can take 30 minutes during rush hour.

BY BUS Buses also run all over the island and are well used by tourists who don't want to spring RM20 (US$5.60/£3.10) every time they go to the beach. The dark-blue no. 93 and the white-with-blue no. 202 both operate between KOMTAR in Georgetown and the beach resorts at Batu Feringgi. The fare is anywhere under RM3 (US85¢/£0.45). Get exact change from your hotel's cashier before you set off and ask the bus driver about the exact fare to your destination.

BY CAR If you want to drive, call **Avis** (© **04/643-9633**) at the Penang International Airport. It can also provide a car with driver for RM80 (US$22/£12) per hour, with a minimum booking of 4 hours. If you plan to visit areas off Penang Island, the rate will increase.

BY BICYCLE/MOTORCYCLE Along Batu Feringgi, there are bicycles and motorcycles (little 100cc scooters, really) available for rent. Avoid the scooters—you can never be certain of their maintenance record, and Penang's drivers are careless about watching your back. A sad number of visitors are injured or worse because of scooter accidents.

BY TRISHAW In Georgetown, it's possible to find some trishaw action for about RM20 (US$5.60/£3.10) an hour. It's kitschy and touristy and I completely recommend it for traveling between in-town sights, at least for an hour or two. Bargain hard: These guys are skilled negotiators.

ON FOOT Everyone should walk at least part of the time to see the sights of Georgetown—in between each landmark and exhibit, there's so much more to see. A taxi, even a trishaw, will whisk you right by back alleys where elderly haircutters set up alfresco shops, bicycle repairmen sit fixing tubes in front of their stores, and Chinese grannies fan themselves in the shade. Georgetown is stimulating, with the sights of old trades still being plied on these living streets, the noise of everyday life, and the exotic smells of an old Southeast Asian port. Give yourself at least a day here. Start wandering early in the morning, by the waterfront, down the back alleys, before the heat of the sun takes hold—the lighting is perfect for photography and you will find fantastic subjects here.

VISITOR INFORMATION

The main **Malaysia Tourism Board (MTB)** office is at 10 Jalan Tun Syed Sheh Barakbah (© **04/261-9067**), just across from the clock tower by Fort Cornwallis. There's another information center at **Penang International Airport** (© **04/643-0501**) and a

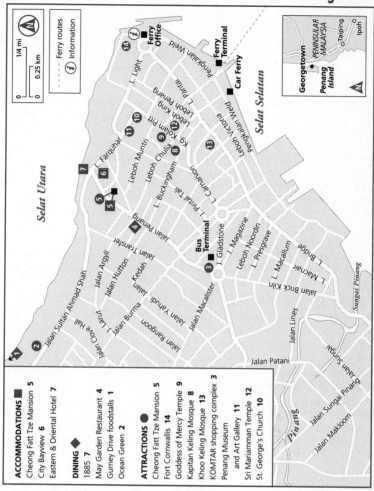

Georgetown

N
1/4 mi
0.25 km
Ferry routes
i Information

Selat Utara

Selat Selatan

Ferry Office

Ferry Terminal

Car Ferry

PENINSULAR MALAYSIA
Georgetown
Penang Island
Taiping
Ipoh

Pengkalan Weld

L. Light
Leboh King
Leboh Penang
Kg. Kolam Pitt
L. Pantai
Leboh Victoria
Pengkalan Weld
L. Farquhar
Leboh Muntri
Leboh Chulia
L. Carnarvon
L. Buckingham
J. Pitali Tali
Jalan Penang
Jalan Transfer
Jalan Argyll
Jalan Sultan Ahmad Shah
Jarut Clove Hall
J. Larut
Jalan Hutton
Jalan Burma
Jalan Yahudi
Kedah
Jalan Rangoon
Jalan Macalister
Bus Terminal
J. Gladstone
J. Magazine
Leboh Noordin
L. Presgrave
L. Macallum
L. Macnair
L. Bridge
Jalan Brick Kiln
Jalan Lines
Jalan Patani
Sungai Pinang
Pinang
Jalan Sungai Pinang
Jalan Sungai
Jalan Makloom

ACCOMMODATIONS ■
Cheong Fatt Tze Mansion 5
City Bayview 6
Eastern & Oriental Hotel 7

DINING ◆
1885 7
May Garden Restaurant 4
Gurney Drive foodstalls 1
Ocean Green 2

ATTRACTIONS ●
Cheong Fatt Tze Mansion 5
Fort Cornwallis 14
Goddess of Mercy Temple 9
Kapitan Keling Mosque 8
Khoo Keling Mosque 13
KOMTAR shopping complex 3
Penang Museum and Art Gallery 11
Sri Mariamman Temple 12
St. George's Church 10

branch on the third level at **KOMTAR (Kompleks Tun Abdul Razak),** on Jalan Penang (☎ **04/261-4461**).

FAST FACTS: PENANG

Penang's **area code** is 04. The **banking center** of Georgetown is in the downtown area (close to Fort Cornwallis) on Leboh Pantai, Leboh Union, and Leboh Downing, but you'll find **ATMs** in KOMTAR and other smaller shopping plazas as well. **Internet** cafes come and go, so it's best to ask your hotel's concierge for the closest place. If you're in town, Chulia Street, the main drag for backpacker tourists, has Internet access in a few places.

WHERE TO STAY

Although Georgetown has many hotels right in the city for convenient sightseeing, most visitors stay at one of the beach resorts 30 minutes away at Batu Feringgi. Trips back and forth can be a bother (regardless of the resorts' free shuttle services), but if you're not staying in a resort, most of the finer beaches are off-limits.

Cheong Fatt Tze Mansion ⭐⭐ *(Finds)*   This is hands-down the most unique and memorable hotel experience in all of Malaysia—to sleep inside the walls of one of Asia's most carefully restored heritage homes, the huge and opulent mansion of 19th-century millionaire Cheong Fatt Tze. The lobby is a simple desk in the courtyard, and inside the only facilities to speak of are a courtyard breakfast area, a library, and a TV room (guest rooms do not have TVs). Guest rooms are each distinctive in shape and decor, all with plank floors, charming architectural detail, and antiques and replicas of the period. Double rooms have either twin beds or one king; suites are also available. All have private bathrooms, though they are pretty small and bare. The experience is described by the management as an "owner-hosted home-stay," which is quite accurate. Don't expect the professional polish of the Shangri-La, but then, with so much beauty around you, who cares?

13 Leith St., 10200 Penang. ✆ **04/262-0006.** www.cheongfatttzemansion.com. 16 units. RM350 (US$98/£54) double; from RM420 (US$118/£65) suite. AE, DC, MC, V. **Amenities:** Breakfast area; laundry service; nonsmoking rooms; library; TV room; valet service. *In room:* A/C, coffeemaker.

The City Bayview Hotel, Penang   This city hotel is perfect for those who visit Penang for its cultural treasures rather than its beaches. A good budget choice, it has a number of fair dining venues, including a rooftop revolving restaurant with excellent views of the island. Choose from guest rooms in the newer wing, completed in 1999, or those in the old wing, which have been recently refurbished. Either wing offers cool rooms in neutral tones, not as elegant as many, but they're comfortable and definitely offer value for the money.

25-A Farquhar St., Georgetown, 10200 Penang. ✆ **04/263-3161.** Fax 04/263-4124. www.bayviewintl.com. 320 units. RM425 (US$119/£65) double; from RM828 (US$232/£128) suite. AE, DC, MC, V. **Amenities:** 3 restaurants; club with live entertainment, lobby lounge; outdoor pool; concierge; limousine service; business center; 24-hr. room service; babysitting; laundry service; dry cleaning; nonsmoking rooms. *In room:* A/C, TV w/in-house movies, minibar, coffeemaker, hair dryer, safe.

Eastern & Oriental (E&O) Hotel ⭐⭐   E&O first opened in 1884, established by the same Sarkies brothers who were behind Raffles Hotel in Singapore. Closed for many, many years (it was desperately in need of an overhaul), it reopened in 2001. It is without a doubt the most atmospheric hotel in Penang, its manicured lawns and tropical gardens flanking a white colonial-style mansion with a lacelike facade and Moorish minarets. Accommodations are all suites, with cozy sitting nooks and sleeping quarters separated by pocket sliding doors. You can expect molding details around every door and paned window, Oriental carpets over polished plank floorboards, and Egyptian-cotton linens dressing each poster bed. Dining along the hotel's many verandas is gorgeous. One caveat—no beach, but the pool in the seafront garden is very pretty.

10 Farquhar St., 10200 Penang. ✆ **04/222-2000.** Fax 04/261-6333. www.e-o-hotel.com. 101 units. RM900–RM2,050 (US$252–US$574/£139–£316) suite. AE, DC, MC, V. **Amenities:** 2 restaurants; English-style pub; outdoor pool; small fitness center w/sauna; concierge; limousine service; 24-hr. room service; laundry service; dry cleaning. *In room:* A/C, satellite TV, minibar, coffeemaker.

Golden Sands Resort by Shangri-La ⭑ 🄺🄸🄳🅂 Shangri-La has been operating resorts on Penang longer than anyone else, and because it got here first, you can bet it laid claim to the best beach. Shangri-La has two neighboring properties on this site, Golden Sands and its more exclusive sister, Rasa Sayang. A newer resort, Golden Sands is priced lower than the Rasa Sayang, so it attracts more families. The beach, pool area, and public spaces fill up fast in the morning, and folks are occupied all day with parasailing, jet-skiing, and pool games. For the younger set, a kids' club keeps small ones busy while Mom and Dad do "boring stuff." Rooms are large with full amenities, and the higher-priced categories have views of the pool and sea.

Batu Feringgi Beach, 11100 Penang. 🕻 **800/942-5050** in the U.S. and Canada, 800/222-448 in Australia, 800/442-179 in New Zealand, or 04/881-1911. Fax 04/881-1880. www.shangri-la.com. 395 units. RM700 (US$196/£108) double; RM1,750 (US$490/£270) suite. AE, DC, MC, V. **Amenities:** 3 restaurants; lobby lounge; 2 outdoor lagoon-style pools; outdoor lighted tennis courts; watersports equipment and activities; children's center; game room; concierge; tour desk; car rental; limousine service; shuttle service to Shangri-La Hotel in Georgetown; business center; salon; 24-hr. room service; babysitting; laundry service; self-service laundry; dry cleaning. *In room:* A/C, satellite TV w/in-house movies, fridge, coffeemaker, hair dryer, safe.

Holiday Inn Resort Penang 🄺🄸🄳🅂 This is a recommended choice for families, but be warned this resort has little appeal for vacationing couples or singles sans children. For families, it has everything—special Kidsuites have a separate room for the wee ones with TV, video, and PlayStation, some with bunk beds (choose from jungle, treasure-island, or outer-space themes). Holiday Inn also has a children's club, fully supervised daycare with activities and games and a lifeguard. Older kids can join in beach volleyball, water polo, bike tours, and an assortment of watersports arranged by the staff. Guest rooms are in two blocks: a low-rise structure near the beach and a high-rise tower along the hillside, connected by a second-story walkway. Naturally, the beachside rooms command the greater rate. Beachside rooms also have better ambience and slightly larger space with wood floors and details, while tower rooms have less charm. The lack of dining options gets tiring.

72 Batu Feringghi, 11100 Penang. 🕻 **04/881-1601.** Fax 04/881-1389. www.penang.holiday-inn.com. 362 units. RM450–RM550 (US$126–US$154/£69–£85) hill-view double; RM530–RM650 (US$148–US$182/£82–£100) seaview double; RM800 (US$224/£123) Kidsuite; from RM800 (US$224/£123) suite. AE, DC, MC, V. **Amenities:** Restaurant; lobby lounge; outdoor pool and children's pool; outdoor lighted tennis courts; fitness center; watersports equipment rental; children's club; game room; concierge; tour desk; limousine service; 24-hr. room service; massage; babysitting; laundry service; dry cleaning. *In room:* A/C, satellite TV w/in-house movies, minibar, coffeemaker, hair dryer, iron, safe.

Shangri-La's Rasa Sayang Resort & Spa ⭑⭑⭑ Rasa Sayang reopened in 2006 after an RM10.5 million (US$3 million/£1.6 million) renovation that saw the original buildings gutted and reformed into a state-of-the-art facility to compete with the deluxe resorts of Langkawi to the north. This was the original resort to be built along Batu Feringgi, so it commands the best beach of all the properties, with 12 hectares (30 acres) of grounds—enough for a par-3 executive golf course, three pools, and plenty of gardens. Standard rooms are gorgeous, most with sea views, in contemporary style and natural tones, wood built-ins, and big fluffy beds. In the Rasa Wing, guest rooms have private verandas and gardens, or balconies with tubs outside. Rasa Sayang also launched the Shangri-La's new spa brand, CHI, with decor and treatments based on Chinese principles of yin and yang and the five elements: metal, wood, water, fire, and earth. Guests here also share facilities with sister property Golden Sands.

Batu Feringgi Beach, 11100 Penang. 🕻 **800/942-5050** in the U.S. and Canada, 🕻 800/222-448 in Australia, 🕻 800/442-179 in New Zealand, or 🕻 04/888-8888. Fax 04/881-1880. www.shangri-la.com. 304 units. RM1,491 (US$418/£230) double; RM2,266 (US$635/£349) Rasa Wing double. AE, DC, MC, V. **Amenities:** 4 restaurants; 2 bars;

3 outdoor lagoon-style pools; outdoor lighted tennis courts; fitness center; spa; watersports equipment and activities; concierge; tour desk; car rental; limousine service; shuttle service to Shangri-La Hotel in Georgetown; business center; salon; 24-hr. room service; babysitting; laundry service; self-service laundry; dry cleaning. *In room:* A/C, satellite TV w/in-house movies, fridge, coffeemaker, hair dryer, safe.

WHERE TO DINE

The 1885 ✸✸ CONTINENTAL   If you're celebrating a special occasion while in Penang, the 1885 will make the experience beyond memorable. The nostalgic romance of the E&O Hotel—its colonial architecture, interiors, and manicured lawns evoking times when tigers probably roamed the grounds after dark—provides the most incredible backdrop for a perfect meal. From an ever-changing menu, poultry, special cuts of meats, and fresh seafood are prepared in delicate contemporary Western style. Candlelight, starched linens, silver service, and extremely attentive staff create a magical experience. The wine list is extensive. By Malaysian standards, this is very expensive, but if you consider the quality of the service and cuisine, plus the stellar surrounds, really, you will never find such elegance for this price in Europe or the States. Note that men are asked to kindly wear a shirt with a collar.

At the Eastern & Oriental (E&O) Hotel, 10 Lebuh Farquhar. © **04/222-0000.** Reservations recommended. Main courses RM50–RM100 (US$14–US$28/£7.70–£15). AE, DC, MC, V. Daily 7–10:30pm.

Hot Wok Café ✸ PERANAKAN   This place is the number-one recommended Peranakan restaurant in the city, and small wonder: The food is great and the atmosphere is fabulous. Filled with local treasures such as wooden latticework, wooden lanterns, carved Peranakan cabinets, tapestries, and carved-wood panels, the decor will make you want to just sit back, relax, and take in sights you'd only ever see in a Peranakan home. The curry capitan, a famous local dish, is curry chicken stuffed with potatoes, served with a thick, delicious coconut-based gravy. The house specialty is a mean *perut ikan* (fish intestine with roe and vegetable).

125-D Desa Tanjung, Jalan Tanjung. © **04/899-0858.** Reservations recommended for weekends. Main courses RM9–RM15 (US$2.50–US$4.20/£1.40–£2.30). AE, DC, MC, V. Daily 11am–3pm and 6–11pm.

May Garden Restaurant CANTONESE   This is a top Cantonese restaurant in Georgetown, and while it's noisy and not too big on ambience, it has excellent food. But how many Chinese do you know who go to places for ambience? It's the food that counts! Outstanding dishes include the tofu and broccoli topped with sea-snail slices or the fresh steamed live prawns. There's also suckling pig and Peking duck. Don't agree to all the daily specials or you'll be paying a fortune.

70 Jalan Penang. © **04/261-6806.** Reservations recommended. Main courses from RM8 (US$2.25/£1.25). Seafood is priced by weight in kg. AE, DC, MC, V. Daily noon–3pm and 6–10:30pm.

Ocean Green ✸✸ SEAFOOD   I can't rave enough about Ocean Green. If the beautiful sea view and ocean breezes don't make you weep with joy, the food certainly will. A long list of fresh seafood is prepared steamed or fried, with your choice of chile, black-bean, sweet-and-sour, or curry sauces. On the advice of a local food expert, I tried the lobster thermidor, expensive but divine, and the chicken wings stuffed with minced chicken, prawns, and gravy.

48F Jalan Sultan Ahmad Shah. © **04/226-2681.** Reservations recommended. Main courses from RM12 (US$3.35/£1.85); seafood priced according to market value. AE, MC, V. Daily 9am–11pm.

FOOD STALLS

No discussion of Penang dining would be complete without coverage of the local food-stall scene, which is famous. Penang hawkers can make any dish you've had in Malaysia, Singapore, or even southern Thailand—only better. Penang may be attractive for many things—history, culture, nature—but it is loved for its food.

Gurney Drive Food Stalls, toward the water just down from the intersection with Jalan Kelawai, is the biggest and most popular hawker center. It has all kinds of food, including local dishes with every influence: Chinese, Malay, Indian. Find *char kway teow* (fried flat noodles with seafood), *char bee hoon* (a fried thin rice noodle), *laksa* (noodles and seafood in a tangy and spicy broth), *murtabak* (mutton, egg, and onion fried inside Indian bread and dipped in dhal), *oh chien* (oyster omelet with chile dip), and *rojak* (a spicy fruit and seafood salad). After you've eaten your way through Gurney Drive, you can try the stalls on Jalan Burmah near the Lai Lai Supermarket.

WHAT TO SEE & DO
IN GEORGETOWN

Cheong Fatt Tze Mansion ✹✹✹ Cheong Fatt Tze (1840–1917), once dubbed "China's Rockefeller" by the *New York Times,* built a vast commercial empire in Southeast Asia, first in Indonesia, then in Singapore. He came to Penang in 1890 and continued his success, giving some of his spoils to build schools throughout the region. His mansion, where he lived with his eight wives, was built between 1896 and 1904. It is truly a sight to behold: Mr. Cheong spent lavishly for Chinese detail that reflects the spirit of his heritage and the fashion of the day as well as the rules of traditional feng shui. Every corner is dripping with stained glass, carved moldings, gilded wood-carved doors, and ceramic ornaments; don't miss the lovely courtyard and gardens, plus the seven staircases.

In 2000, the mansion won UNESCO's Asia-Pacific Heritage Award for Conservation, so lovingly has this historic treasure been preserved. Guided tours explain the history, personalities, and culture behind the home, plus the details of the conservation efforts. If you're really hooked, the owners host a home-stay program.

Lebuhraya Leith. © 04/262-0006. Admission RM12 (US$3.35/£1.85) adults, RM6 (US$1.70/£0.90) children 6–12. Daily guided tours at 11am and 3 pm.

Fort Cornwallis Fort Cornwallis is built on the site where Capt. Francis Light, founder of Penang, first landed in 1786. The fort was first built in 1793, but this site was an unlikely spot to defend the city from invasion. In 1810, it was rebuilt in an attempt to make up for initial strategic planning errors. In the shape of a star, the only actual buildings still standing are the outer walls, a gunpowder magazine, and a small Christian chapel. The magazine houses an exhibit of old photos and historical accounts of the old fort.

Lebuhraya Leith. No phone. Admission RM3 (US80¢/£.40) adults, RM2 (US60¢/£.30) children. Daily 8am–7pm.

Goddess of Mercy Temple Dedicated jointly to Kuan Yin, the goddess of mercy, and Ma Po Cho, the patron saint of sea travelers, this is the oldest Chinese temple in Penang. On the 19th of each second, sixth, and ninth month of the lunar calendar (the months that fall between February/March, June/July, and September/October, respectively), Kuan Yin is celebrated with Chinese operas and puppet shows.

Leboh Pitt. Free admission.

Kapitan Keling Mosque   Captain Light donated a large parcel of land on this spot for the settlement's sizable Indian Muslim community to build a mosque and grave-yard. The leader of the community, known as Kapitan Keling (or Kling, which ironi-cally was once a racial slur against Indians in the region), built a brick mosque here. Later, in 1801, he imported builders and materials from India for a new, brilliant mosque. Expansions in the 1900s topped the mosque with stunning domes and tur-rets, adding extensions and new roofs.

Jalan Masjid Kapitan Keling (Leboh Pitt). Free admission.

Khoo Khongsi ⓐ   The Chinese who migrated to Southeast Asia created clan asso-ciations in their new homes. Based on common heritage, these social groups formed the core of Chinese life in the new homelands. The Khoo clan, who immigrated from Hokkien province in China, acquired this spot in 1851 and set to work building row houses, administrative buildings, and a clan temple around a large square. The tem-ple here today was actually built in 1906 after a fire destroyed its predecessor. It was believed the original was too ornate, provoking the wrath of the gods. One look at the current temple, a Chinese baroque masterpiece, and you'll wonder how that could possibly be. Come here in August for Chinese opera.

Leburaya Cannon. ⓒ **04/261-4609.** Free admission. Daily 9am–5pm.

Penang Museum and Art Gallery ⓐ★★   The historical society has put together this marvelous collection of ethnological and historical findings from Penang, tracing the port's history and diverse cultures through time. It's filled with paintings, photos, costumes, and antiques, all presented with fascinating facts and trivia. Upstairs is an art gallery. Originally the Penang Free School, the building was built in two phases, the first half in 1896 and the second in 1906. Only half of the building remains; the other was bombed to the ground in World War II. It's a favorite stop on a sightseeing itinerary because it's air-conditioned!

Leburaya Farquhar. ⓒ **04/261-3144.** Admission RM1 (US30¢/£0.14) adults, children RM.50 (US10¢/£.07) children. Sat–Thurs 9am–5pm.

St. George's Church   Built by Rev. R. S. Hutchins (who was also responsible for the Free School next door, home of the Penang Museum) and Capt. Robert N. Smith, whose paintings hang in the museum, this church was completed in 1818. Although the outside is almost as it was then, the contents were completely looted during World War II. All that remains are the font and the bishop's chair.

Farquhar St. Free admission.

Sri Mariamman Temple   This Hindu temple was built in 1833 by a Chettiar, a group of southern Indian Muslims, and received a major face-lift in 1978 with the help of Madras sculptors. The Hindu Navarithri festival is held here, whereby devo-tees parade Sri Mariamman, a Hindu goddess worshipped for her powers to cure dis-ease, through the streets in a night procession. It is also the starting point of the Thaipusam Festival, which leads to a temple on Jalan Waterfall.

Leburaya Queen. Free admission.

OUTSIDE GEORGETOWN

Batu Muang Fishing Village   If you'd like to see a local fishing village, here's a good one. This village is special for its shrine to Admiral Cheng Ho, the early Chinese sea adventurer.

Southeast tip of Penang. Free admission. From Georgetown take the Jelutong Expwy.; then take Teluk Tempoyak into the village.

Botanical Gardens   Covering 30 hectares (70 acres) of landscaped grounds, this botanical garden was established by the British in 1884. It's perfect for a shady walk—and a ton of fun if you love monkeys. They're crawling all over the place and will think nothing of stepping forward for a peanut (which you can buy beneath the DO NOT FEED THE MONKEYS sign). Also in the gardens are a jogging track and kiddie park.

About a 5- to 10-min. drive west of Georgetown. ℂ 04/227-0428. Free admission. Daily 7am–7pm.

Penang Butterfly Farm   This butterfly farm is the largest in the world. On its 0.8-hectare (2-acre) landscaped grounds, there are more than 4,000 flying butterflies representing 120 species. At 10am and 3pm, there are informative butterfly shows. Don't forget the insect exhibit—there are about 2,000 or so bugs.

Jalan Teluk Bahang, toward northwest corner of the island. ℂ **04/885-1253**. Admission RM15 (US$4.20/£2.30) adults, RM7.50 (US$2.10/£1.15) children, free for children 4 and under. Daily 9am–5pm.

Penang Hill   Covered with jungle growth and 20 nature trails, the hill is great for trekking. Or you can go to Ayer Hitam, a town in the central part of Penang, and take the Keretapi Bukit Bendera funicular railway to the top. It sends trains up and down the hill every half-hour from 6am to 9pm, weekends from 6am to 11pm, and costs adults RM4 (US$1.10/£0.60) and children RM2 (US55¢/£0.30), round-trip. If you prefer to make the trek on foot, go to the "Moon Gate" at the entrance to the Botanical Garden for a 5.5km (3.4-mile), 3-hour hike to the summit.

A 20- to 30-min. drive southwest from Georgetown. The funicular station is on Jalan Stesen Keretapi Bukit.

SHOPPING

The first place anyone here will recommend for shopping is **KOMTAR.** Short for "Kompleks Tun Abdul Razak," it is the largest shopping complex in Penang, a full 65 stories of clothing shops, restaurants, and a couple of large department stores. There's a **duty-free shop** on the 57th floor; a **tourist information center** is on the 3rd floor.

Good shopping finds in Penang are batik, pewter products, locally produced curios, paintings, antiques, pottery, and jewelry. If you care to walk around in search of finds, there are a few streets in Georgetown that are the hub of shopping activity. In the city center, the area around Jalan Penang, Lebuhraya Campbell, Lebuhraya Kapitan Keling, Lebuhraya Chulia, and Lebuhraya Pantai is near the Sri Mariamman Temple, the Penang Museum, the Kapitan Keling Mosque, and other sites of historic interest. Here you'll find everything from local crafts to souvenirs and fashion, and maybe even a bargain or two. Most of these shops are open from 10am to 10pm daily.

Out at Batu Feringgi, the main road turns into a fun **night bazaar** every evening just at dark. During the day, there are also some good shops for batik and souvenirs here.

PENANG AFTER DARK

If you're looking for a bar that's a little out of the ordinary, visit **20 Leith Street,** 11-A Lebuh Leith (℃ **04/261-8873**). Located in an old 1930s house, the place has seating areas fitted with traditional antique furniture in each room of the house. Possibly the most notorious bar in Penang is the **Hong Kong Bar,** 371 Lebuh Chulia (℃ **04/261-9796**), which opened in 1920 and was a regular hangout for military personnel based in Butterworth. It has an extraordinary archive of photos of the servicemen who have patronized the place throughout the years, plus a collection of medals, plaques, and buoys from ships.

7 Langkawi ✦✦

Where the beautiful Andaman Sea meets the Strait of Malacca, Langkawi Island positions itself as one of the best emerging island paradise destinations in the region. Since 1990, the Malaysian Tourism Board has dedicated itself to promoting the island and developing it as an ideal travel spot. Now, after a decade and a half of work, the island has proven itself as one of this country's holiday gems.

Note: Malaysia has declared Langkawi a duty-free zone, so take a peek at some of the shopping in town, and enjoy RM4 (US$1.10/£0.60) beers!

GETTING THERE

BY PLANE **Malaysia Airlines** and **AirAsia** make Langkawi very convenient from either mainland Malaysia or Singapore. **Singapore Airlines** also flies to Langkawi.

The best thing to do is prearrange a shuttle pickup from your resort; otherwise, you can grab a taxi out in front of the airport. To Pantai Cenang or Pantai Tengah, the fare should be about RM20 (US$5.60/£3.10), while to the farther resorts at Tanjung Rhu and Datai Bay, the fare will be as high as RM40 and RM50 (US$11/£6.15 and US$14/£7.70), respectively.

BY FERRY From the jetty at Kuala Kedah, about five companies provide ferry service to the island (trip time: about 1 hr. and 45 min.; cost: RM18/US$5.05/£2.80). Ferries let you off at the main ferry terminal in Kuah, where you can hop a taxi to your resort for RM20 to RM50 (US$5.60–US$14/£3.10–£7.70).

If you're coming from Penang, the ferry is the way to go. **Bahagia Express** has two early-morning speedboats from Weld Quay in Georgetown for RM45 one-way (US$13/£6.95) and RM85 round-trip (US$24/£13). Call them in Penang at © **04/263-1943** or visit the office across from the clock tower, just next to the main tourism board office. If you're heading from Langkawi to Penang, you can call Bahagia in Langkawi at © **04/966-0521.**

BY TRAIN Taking the train can be a bit of a hassle because the nearest stop (in Alor Setar) is quite far from the jetty to the island, requiring a cab transfer. Still, if you prefer rail, hop on the overnight train from KL (the only train), which will put you in to Alor Setar around 7am. Just outside the train station is the taxi stand, with cabs to take you to the Kuala Kedah jetty.

BY BUS This route isn't really recommended. If you're coming from KL, the bus ride is long and uncomfortable, catching the taxi transfer to the jetty can be problematic, and by the time you reach the island you'll need a vacation from your vacation. Fly or use the train instead. If you're coming from Penang, the direct ferry is wonderfully convenient.

GETTING AROUND

BY TAXI Taxis generally hang around at the airport, the main jetty, the taxi stand in Kuah, and some major hotels. From anywhere in between, your best bet is to ask your hotel's concierge to call a taxi for you. Keep in mind, if you're going as far as one side of the island to the other, your fare can go as high as RM50 (US$14/£7.70).

BY CAR/MOTORCYCLE At the airport and from agents in the complex behind the main jetty, car rentals can be arranged starting at RM80 (US$22/£12) per day. This is for the standard, no-frills model. Insurance policies are lax, as are rental regulations. If you're out on the beach at Cenang or Tengah, a few places rent jeeps and

Langkawi

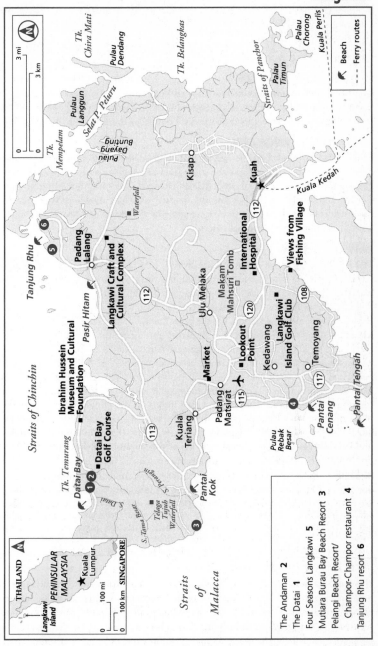

Map labels:

Straits of Chinchin

Tk. Chira Mati
Pulau Dendang
Tk. Belangkas
Pulau Langgun
Pulau Langgun
Tk. Mempelam
Selat P. Peluru
Pulau Dayang Bunting
Tanjung Rhu
Kisap
Kuah
Kuala Kedah
Straits of Panchor
Palau Timun
Palau Chorong
Kuala Perlis

Waterfall
6
5
Padang Lalang
Langkawi Craft and Cultural Complex
Pasir Hitam
Ibrahim Hussein Museum and Cultural Foundation
Datai Bay Golf Course
Datai Bay
Tk. Temurang

Ulu Melaka
Makam Mahsuri Tomb
International Hospital
Views from Fishing Village
120
108
Market
Lookout Point
Kedawang
Langkawi Island Golf Club
Temoyang
115
Padang Matsirat
117
Pantai Tengah
Pantai Cenang
Pulau Rebak Besar
4
Kuala Teriang
113
112
Kuala Kok
Pantai Kok
Telaga Tujuh Waterfall
S. Datai
S. Tama Besar
S. Petangin
3

Straits of Malacca

THAILAND
PENINSULAR MALAYSIA
Kuala Lumpur
SINGAPORE
Langkawi Island
100 mi
100 km
0

Beach
Ferry routes

3 mi
3 km

The Andaman **2**
The Datai **1**
Four Seasons Langkawi **5**
Mutiara Burau Bay Beach Resort **3**
Pelangi Beach Resort/
Champor-Champor restaurant **4**
Tanjung Rhu resort **6**

motorcycles from RM80 (US$22/£12) and RM30 (US$8.40/£4.60) per day, respectively. Pick a good helmet.

ON FOOT The main beaches at Cenang and Tengah can be walked quite easily; however, don't expect to be able to walk around to other parts of the island.

VISITOR INFORMATION

The **MTB** office is unfortunately situated in Kuah town on Jalan Persiaran Putra, far from the beach areas. For specific queries, you can call the office at ✆ **04/966-7789.** If you're arriving by plane, there's another MTB office at the airport (✆ **04/955-7155**).

FAST FACTS: LANGKAWI

The only major **bank** branches are located far from the beach areas, in Kuah town, mostly around the blocks across the street from the Night Hawker Center (off Jalan Persiaran Putra), or at the airport. Money changers keep long hours out at Pantai Cenang and Pantai Tengah, but for other resorts you'll have to change your money at the hotel itself. Along the Pantai Cenang and Pantai Tengah main road, you'll find at least a half dozen small **Internet** places.

WHERE TO STAY

The Andaman ★★ *Kids* You will be surprised how large this resort is—its buildings blend so perfectly with the jungle surrounding them. Andaman has far better landscaped garden areas than neighboring Datai (see below), with a sprawl of lush grounds hugging a beautiful white beach, as opposed to Datai, which is quite constricted architecturally by its hillside situation. On the other hand, I prefer Datai's mesmerizing tropical Asian simplicity. Sometimes the Andaman uses decorator ideas straight from the West, such as European-style furnishings and fabrics, which to me detract from the whole spirit of escapism. But there are other advantages: The Andaman has a better beach and welcomes families, with special facilities like a kids' club. The entrance and main lobby are visually quite stunning, in open-air local-style architecture with vaulted roofs built from polished hardwoods. Guest rooms, in two wings that span either side of the main building, are spacious, with wall-to-wall carpeting and Western style decor, save for a few local textiles. Ground-floor lanai rooms have private sun decks with umbrella stands. The pool is huge with lots of shady spots, and the spa features traditional Malay herbal beauty and health treatments. Gulai House serves delicious Malay and Indian cuisine in a charming open-air Malay-style house by the beach.

Jalan Teluk Datai, P.O. Box 94, 07000 Langkawi, Kedah. ✆ **04/959-1088.** Fax 04/959-1168. www.theandaman.com. RM1,000–RM1,600 US($280–US$448/£154–£246) double; RM1,600 (US$448/£246) lanai double; from RM2,170 (US$608/£334) suite. Prices jump from Dec–Jan. AE, DC, MC, V. **Amenities:** 4 restaurants; 3 lounges; outdoor pools surrounded by gardens; golf course; 2 outdoor lighted tennis courts; fitness center; spa w/Jacuzzi, sauna, steam, and massage; watersports equipment rental; mountain-bike rental; children's club; games; concierge; limousine service; 24-hr. room service; babysitting; laundry service; dry cleaning; jungle trekking. *In room:* A/C, satellite TV w/in-house movies, minibar, coffeemaker, hair dryer, safe.

The Datai ★★★ Aesthetically speaking, this is one of the most innovative resorts in Southeast Asia. Datai is the epitome of sublime, its tropical resort design incorporating nature at every turn. Beyond the graceful open-air lobby, pass the lily pond courtyard to the Datai's brilliant lounge—a hillside veranda surrounded by lush jungle and suspended above a breathtaking bay. Rooms and villas, also built into the hillside, are expert in their studied Southeast Asian elegance. Minimalist in design, the color schemes stick close to nature, with rosewood tones, rich local tapestries, and regal celadon-colored upholstery. Even lower-priced deluxe rooms have a quaint seating area with a view, plus an oversize bathroom with designer products, separate shower stall, and long bathtub. Facilities, which include two pools, a spa, and a golf course, show the same meticulous attention to luxury. A top pick.

Jalan Teluk Datai, Langkawi, Kedah. ✆ **800/223-6800** in the U.S. and Canada, ✆ 800/181-123 in the U.K., or ✆ 04/959-2500. Fax 04/959-2600. www.ghmhotels.com/thedatai. RM1,730 (US$485/£267) double; RM2,185 (US$612/£337) villa; from RM2,780 (US$779/£428) suite. Prices jump Dec–Jan. AE, DC, MC, V. **Amenities:** 3 restaurants; lounge; 2 outdoor pools surrounded by jungle; golf course; 2 outdoor lighted tennis courts; fitness center w/Jacuzzi, sauna, steam, and massage; spa; watersports equipment rental; mountain-bike rental; concierge; limousine service; limited room service; babysitting; laundry service; dry cleaning; library; jungle trekking. *In room:* A/C, satellite TV w/in-house movies, minibar, coffeemaker, hair dryer, safe.

Four Seasons Resort Langkawi ★★★   With this new property, Four Seasons raises the bar for resorts in Malaysia, and possibly in the region. Every detail is perfectly exotic, influenced by contemporary Moorish style; every view is a picture postcard. Pavilion rooms are surrounded by floor-to-ceiling windows and wraparound verandas. Under soaring ceilings, the huge bedrooms have wood floors, ceiling fans, carved-wood detailing, and plush furnishings. Through double doors, the bathrooms are majestic, with oversized terrazzo tubs built into arched nooks, separate closets for rainshower and WC, and center islands with double sinks. Throughout the rooms, you'll find touches such as lanterns, hammered bronze work, lovely toiletries on clay pedestals, and cozy throw pillows that add an intimate Middle Eastern flavor. The resort has two infinity pools that look like they're spilling onto the beach, which is a long, wide stretch of perfect sand. Every dining venue also fronts the beach. At Rhu Bar, Moorish carved latticework arches frame the seaview gorgeously—if you can't stay at the Four Seasons, at least get a cocktail here amid the Turkish water pipes, Indian Moghul hanging swings, glowing lanterns, and snug seating. The spa here is also to die for. The private pavilions are bigger than my whole house (seriously), with tubs for two, space for floor and table massages, and private showers and changing rooms all encased in glass with lovely garden views. This is the most luxurious property in this whole chapter. Period.

Jalan Tanjung Rhu, 07000 Langkawi, Kedah ✆ **800/332-3442** in the U.S., ✆ 800/268-6282 in Canada, or ✆ 04/950-8888. Fax 04/950-8899. www.fourseasons.com. US$495–US$540 (£272–£297) pavilion; from US$1,500 (£825) villa. Prices jump Dec–Jan. AE, DC, MC, V. **Amenities:** 3 restaurants; 2 bars; 2 outdoor pools; tennis; fitness center; spa w/yoga and juice bar; complimentary nonmotorized watersports; children's center; concierge; limousine service; 24-hour room service; babysitting; laundry service; dry cleaning; library; tour services; jungle trekking. *In room:* A/C, satellite TV w/in-house movies, minibar, coffeemaker, hair dryer, safe.

Mutiara Burau Bay Beach Resort   Burau offers beachside resort accommodations for less money than its upscale neighbors. Not nearly as ritzy, this place feels more like summer camp than a resort. All guest rooms are contained in cabanas, with simple decor that's a bit on the older side. For the price, though, they offer value for money. Burau also organizes golf, massage, jeep treks, jungle treks, mountain biking, tennis, canoeing, catamaran sailing, jet skiing, scuba diving, snorkeling, fishing, water-skiing, windsurfing, and yachting.

Teluk Burau, 07000 Langkawi, Kedah. ✆ **04/959-1061.** Fax 04/959-1172. www.mutiarahotels.com/mutiara_buraubay. 150 units. RM280 (us$78/£43) garden-view chalet; RM310 (US$87/£48) sea-view chalet; RM380 (US$106/£59) family chalet; RM750 (US$210/£116) suite. AE, DC, MC, V. **Amenities:** 3 restaurants; beach bar; outdoor pool; outdoor lighted tennis courts; children's center; game room; concierge; activities desk; car rental; shuttle service; business center; 24-hr. room service; massage; babysitting; laundry service; nonsmoking rooms. *In room:* A/C, satellite TV w/in-house movies, minibar, coffeemaker.

Pelangi Beach Resort ⍟   For those who prefer a more active vacation or a more family-oriented resort, book at Pelangi. A top-quality resort, this place stands out from neighboring five-star resorts for its sheer fun. A long list of organized sports and leisure pastimes makes it especially attractive for families, but surprisingly I never found children to be a distraction here. Pelangi's 51 ethnic wooden chalets are huge inside and are divided into either one, two, or four guest rooms. You'll be welcomed by vaulted ceilings, modern bathrooms, and large living spaces. But it's the little things you'll love—like the squishy down pillows and snuggly bedding. In addition, Pelangi's location, near the central beach strip for island life, means you're not cloistered away from the rest of civilization.

Pantai Cenang, 07000 Langkawi, Kedah. ℭ **04/952-8888.** Fax 04/952-8899. www.pelangibeachresort.com. 350 units. RM756 US($212/£116) double; from RM1,650 (US$462/£254) suite. AE, DC, MC, V. **Amenities:** 3 restaurants; 3 bars; 2 large outdoor pools with swim-up bar; golf nearby; miniature golf; outdoor lighted tennis courts; squash courts; fitness center w/sauna, steam, and massage; Jacuzzi; concierge; tour desk and watersports center with equipment rental, boating excursions, and jungle trekking; car rental; limousine service; shuttle service; business center; 24-hr. room service; babysitting; laundry service; dry cleaning. *In room:* A/C, satellite TV w/in-house movies, minibar, coffeemaker, hair dryer, safe.

Tanjung Rhu Resort ⍟⍟   The beach at Tanjung Rhu is a wide crescent of dazzlingly pure sand wrapped around a perfect azure bay. Tree-lined karst islets jut from the sea, dotting the horizon. Just gorgeous. This resort claims 440 hectares (1,100 acres) of jungle in this part of the island, monopolizing the scene for extra privacy, but it has its pros and cons. The pros? Guest rooms are enormous and decorated with sensitivity to the environment, from natural materials to organic recycled-paper-wrapped toiletries. A newly completed second pool and spa facility add value. The cons? Make sure you don't book your vacation during the months of June or December, when Malaysia and Singapore celebrate school holidays, because the place draws families like flies. Still, during between-holiday downtimes, I love this resort's friendly and casual atmosphere—and, of course, the beach.

Tanjung Rhu, Mukim Ayer Hangat, 07000 Langkawi, Kedah. ℭ **04/959-1033.** Fax 04/959-1899. www.tanjungrhu. com.my. 138 units. RM1,300 (US$364/£200) double; RM2,700 (US$756/£416) suite. AE, DC, MC, V. **Amenities:** 3 restaurants; bar and library; 2 outdoor pools (1 saltwater and 1 freshwater); golf nearby; outdoor lighted tennis courts; fitness center and spa w/Jacuzzi, sauna, steam, and massage; concierge; activity desk with watersports (non-motorized), trekking, and boat tours; limousine service; shuttle service; 24-hr. room service; babysitting; laundry service; dry cleaning. *In room:* A/C, satellite TV w/in-room movie library, CD player, minibar, coffeemaker, hair dryer, safe.

WHERE TO DINE

If you're out at one of the more secluded resorts, chances are you'll stay there for most of your meals. However, if you're at Pantai Cenang or Pantai Tengah, I recommend taking a stroll down to **Champor-Champor** ⍟, just across the road in the Pelangi Resort (ℭ **04/955-1449**), which has creative dinners—a local *roti canai* served like a pizza, and local fish doused in sweet sauces. Everything is incredibly fresh, wildly delicious, and amazingly inexpensive. As for decor, the imaginative catchall beach-shack atmosphere really relaxes. After dinner, hang around the bar for the best fun on the island. Because Langkawi is an official duty-free port, one beer costs a wee RM4 (US$1.10/£0.60)!

If you're in Kuah town, the best local dining experience can be found at the evening **hawker stalls,** just along the waterfront near the taxi stand. A long row of hawkers cooks up every kind of local favorite, including seafood dishes. You can't get any cheaper or more laid-back. After dinner, it's easy to flag down a taxi back to your resort.

WHAT TO SEE & DO

Fifteen years ago, Langkawi was just a backwater island supporting small fishing communities. When the government officials came in with big money to develop the place for tourism, they thought they needed a catch, so they dug up some old moldy "legends" about the island and have tried to market them as bonafide cultural attractions. Basically, these sorts of attractions are more hype than anything else. If you want to experience culture, take a ferry to Penang for an overnight in historic Georgetown. Now *that's* something to see.

In terms of beaches and watersports, most resorts are self-contained units, offering their own equipment rentals and planning their own outings.

Outside of your resort, there's some fairly decent diving to be had. **Asian Overland** (© 04/955-2002; www.asianoverland.com.my) can arrange day trips with two dives to Payar Marine Park within Langkawi's extensive island network. It charges RM280 (US$78/£43). You can also snorkel for the day for RM160 (US$45/£25) per person. There's an interesting snorkel attraction off Langkawi—a platform in the middle of the sea that floats above a coral reef. Day trips to the platform include rides in a glass-bottomed boat, snorkeling, and lunch on the platform. It's an all-day affair for RM230 (US$64/£35) per person, starting at 8am and getting you back to your resort just before dinnertime.

Asian Overland also plans round-island boat trips to "island-hop" at beaches and into mangrove swamps (interesting), with a stop at the Pregnant Maiden Lake (one of the aforementioned over-hyped places). See if you can skip the lake and go to the Batik Art Village instead. The company will cater your tour so you can see anything you want.

Perhaps one of the loveliest additions to Langkawi's attractions is the **Ibrahim Hussein Museum and Cultural Foundation,** Pasir Tengkorak, Jalan Datai (© **04/959-4669**). The artistic devotion of the foundation's namesake fueled the creation of this enchanting modern space, designed to showcase Malaysia's contribution to the international fine-arts scene. If you can pull yourself from the beach for any single activity in Langkawi, don't miss this one. Mr. Hussein has created a museum worthy of international attention—truly a gem. It's open Saturday through Thursday from 10am to 6pm; adults pay RM12 (US$3.35/£1.85), while children visit for free.

SHOPPING

Langkawi's designated Duty Free Port status makes shopping here quite fun and very popular. Two shopping malls, **Langkawi Parade** (Jalan Kelibang; © **04/966-6372**) and **Langkawi Fair** (Persiaran Putra; © **04/969-8100**), both in Kuah town, are filled with duty-free shopping. For local handicrafts, the **Langkawi Craft and Cultural Complex** (Jalan Teluk Yu; © **04/959-1913;** daily 10am–6pm) sells an assortment of batik, baskets, ceramic, silver jewelry, brassware, and more; it also has daily crafts demonstrations and cultural shows.

8 East Malaysia: Borneo

Borneo for the past 2 centuries has been the epitome of adventure travel. While bustling ports like Penang, Malacca, and Singapore attracted early travelers with dollars in their eyes, Borneo attracted those with adventure in their hearts. Today, the island still draws visitors who seek new and unusual experiences, and few leave disappointed. Rivers meander through dense tropical rainforests, beaches stretch for miles, and caves snake out longer than any in the world. All sorts of creatures live in the rain-forest: deer the size of house cats, owls only 6 inches tall, the odd proboscis monkey, and the endangered orangutan, whose only other natural home is Sumatra. It's also home to the largest flower in the world, the rafflesia, spanning up to a meter wide. Small wonder this place has special interest for scientists and researchers the world around.

The people of Borneo can be credited for most of the alluring tales of early travels. The exotically adorned tribes of warring headhunters and pirates of yesteryear, some of whom still live lifestyles little changed (though both headhunting and piracy are now illegal), today share their mysterious cultures and colorful traditions openly with outsiders.

Add to all of this the fabulous tale of the White Raja of Sarawak, Sir James Brooke, whose family ruled the state for just over 100 years, and you have a land filled with allure, mystery, and romance unlike any other.

Malaysia, Brunei Darussalam, and Indonesia have divided the island of Borneo. Indonesia claims Kalimantan to the south and east, while the Malaysian states of **Sarawak** and **Sabah** lie to the north and northwest. The small sultanate of Brunei is nestled between the two Malaysian states on the western coastline.

SARAWAK ✿✿✿ & KUCHING

Tropical rainforest accounts for more than 70% of the total land mass of **Sarawak,** providing homes for not only exotic species of plants and animals, but also the myriad ethnic groups who are indigenous to the area. With more than 10 national parks and four wildlife preserves, Malaysia shows its commitment to conserving the delicate balance of life here, while still allowing small gateways for travelers to appreciate natural wonders. The national parks located around the state's capital, **Kuching,** provide quick access to forest life, while longer, more detailed trips to northern Sarawak lead you deeper into the jungle to explore remote forests and extensive ancient cave networks. A web of rivers connects the inland areas to the main towns, and a boat trip from Kuching to visit tribal communities and trek into the surrounding forests is the most memorable attraction going.

The perfect introduction to Sarawak begins in its capital. Kuching's museums, cultural exhibits, and historic attractions will help you form an overview of the history, people, and natural wonders of the state. In Kuching, your introduction to Sarawak will be comfortable and fun—culture by day, good food and fun by night. Kuching, meaning "cat" in Malay, also has a wonderful sense of humor, featuring monuments and exhibits to its feline mascot on almost every corner.

GETTING THERE   Almost all travelers to Sarawak enter through **Kuching International Airport,** just outside the city. **Malaysia Airlines** has international flights from Singapore and Perth, with domestic service from KL, Johor Bahru, and Kota Kinabalu. **AirAsia** flies between Kuching and KL.

The brand-new airport is a terrific facility with ATMs, money changers, restaurants, and tourist information. Taxis from the airport use coupons that you purchase outside the arrivals hall. Priced according to zones, most trips to the central parts of town will be about RM18 (US$5.05/£2.80).

GETTING AROUND   Centered around a *padang*, or large ceremonial field, Kuching resembles many other Malaysian cities. Buildings of beautiful colonial style rise on the edges of the field; many of these today house Sarawak's museums. The main sights,

East Malaysia's National Parks

as well as the Chinatown area and the riverfront, are easily accessible on foot. Taxis are also available and do not use meters; most rides around town are quoted between RM6 and RM10 (US$1.70–US$2.80/£0.90–£1.55). Taxis can be waved down from the side of the road. If you're in the Chinatown area, the main taxi stand is on Gambier Road near the end of the India Street Pedestrian Mall.

VISITOR INFORMATION The **Sarawak Tourism Board's Visitor Information Centre** has literature and staff that can answer any question about activities in the state and city. This is the best place to start planning any trips to Sarawak's wonderful national parks, as the main office for the National Parks & Wildlife Centre operates a visitor center here as well. Both offices are incredibly informed and welcoming, so feel free to take advantage. You'll find them at the Sarawak Tourism Complex in the Old Courthouse opposite the Kuching Waterfront (Sarawak Tourism Board, ☎ **082/410-944;** National Parks Centre, ☎ **082/248-088;** www.sarawaktourism.com).

FAST FACTS Sarawak's **area code** is 082. Major **banks** have branches on Tunku Abdul Rahman Road near Holiday Inn Kuching or in the downtown area around Khoo Hun Yeang Road. There are a few **Internet** cafes around town; it's best to ask your hotel's concierge for the nearest one before you start wandering—they're constantly going out of business, then popping up elsewhere.

WHERE TO STAY

Holiday Inn Kuching   Holiday Inn offers Western-style accommodations at a moderate price, and you'll appreciate its location in an excellent part of town. It sits along the bank of the Kuching River, so to get to the main riverside area you need only stroll 10 minutes past some of the city's unique historic and cultural sights, shopping, and eateries. Catering to a diverse group of leisure and business travelers, the hotel has spacious, modern, and comfortable rooms. Although there are few bells and whistles, you won't want for convenience. The outdoor pool and excellent fitness center will help you unwind, and the small shopping arcade has one of the best collections of books on Sarawak in the city.

Jalan Tunku Abdul Rahman, P.O. Box 2362, 93100 Kuching, Sarawak. ✆ 082/423-111. Fax 082/426-169. www.holiday inn-sarawak.com. 305 units. RM230 (US$64/£35) double. AE, DC, MC, V. **Amenities:** 3 restaurants; bar; outdoor pool; fitness center w/sauna; concierge; tour desk; limousine service; business center; 24-hr. room service; babysitting; laundry service; dry cleaning; nonsmoking rooms; executive-level rooms. *In room:* A/C, satellite TV w/in-house movies, minibar, coffeemaker, hair dryer.

Merdeka Palace Hotel ✸   Towering over the Padang Merdeka in the center of town is the Merdeka Palace, practically a landmark in its own right (as soon as you see the easily distinguishable tower, you'll always know where you are). This is one of the most fashionable addresses in the city, for guests as well as for banquets and functions. From the marble lobby to the mezzanine shopping arcade stuffed with designer tenants, its reputation for elegance is justified. Large rooms come dressed in European-inspired furnishings and fabrics. Try to get a view of the padang, as the less expensive rooms face the parking lot. The rooftop outdoor pool is small, but the fully equipped fitness center has sauna and steam rooms, plus massage. The pub here is perhaps the most happening one in town.

Jalan Tun Abang Haji Openg, 93000 Kuching, Sarawak. ✆ 082/258-000. Fax 082/425-400. www.merdekapalace. com. 214 units. RM414 (US$116/£64) double. AE, DC, MC, V. **Amenities:** 2 restaurants; bar; outdoor pool; fitness center w/Jacuzzi, sauna, steam, and massage; concierge; limousine service; business center; shopping arcade; salon; 24-hr. room service; babysitting; laundry service; dry cleaning; nonsmoking rooms; executive-level rooms. *In room:* A/C, satellite TV, minibar, coffeemaker, safe.

Telang Usan Hotel ✸✸ *Value*   While in Kuching, I like to stay at the Telang Usan Hotel. It's not as flashy as the higher-priced places, but it's a fantastic bargain for a good room. Most guests are leisure travelers—in fact, many are repeat visitors. The small public areas sport murals in local Iban style, revealing the origin of the hotel's owner and operator. While rooms are small and decor is not completely up-to-date, everything's spotless. Some rooms have only standing showers, so be sure to specify when making your reservation if a tub is important to you. The coffee shop is a fine place to try local food, but it has Western selections as well. There is an excellent tour agency under the same ownership at the hotel.

Ban Hock Rd., P.O. Box 1579, 93732 Kuching, Sarawak. ✆ 082/415-588. Fax 082/245-316. www.telangusan.com. 66 units. RM120 (US$34/£18) double. AE, DC, MC, V. **Amenities:** Restaurant; limited room service; laundry service; Internet access. *In room:* A/C, TV, minibar (some rooms).

WHERE TO DINE

Everyone ends up at the **Top Spot Food Court,** a cheap hawker center on Jalan Bukit Mata, off Jalan Tunku Abdul Rahman just near the Holiday Inn. Various stalls cook Chinese, Malay, and Western cuisine—you'll find all sorts of exotic dishes, as well as local and seafood options. Located on the roof of a multi-story parking garage, don't

Kuching

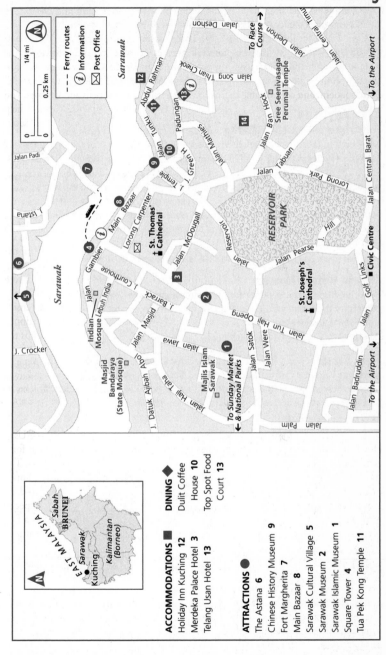

ACCOMMODATIONS ■
Holiday Inn Kuching **12**
Merdeka Palace Hotel **3**
Telang Usan Hotel **13**

ATTRACTIONS ●
The Astana **6**
Chinese History Museum **9**
Fort Margherita **7**
Main Bazaar **8**
Sarawak Cultural Village **5**
Sarawak Museum **2**
Sarawak Islamic Museum **1**
Square Tower **4**
Tua Pek Kong Temple **11**

DINING ◆
Dulit Coffee
House **10**
Top Spot Food
Court **13**

expect anything but "local charm" for decor. But the food is good and cheap, and you'll bump into plenty of other travelers and locals here to chat with.

A good pick for local specialties is the **Dulit Coffee House,** at Telang Usan Hotel (© **082/415-588**). Try its local Sarawak version of *laksa,* vermicelli noodles and seafood in a rich and spicy coconut gravy, or the Sarawak black-pepper steak, a house specialty. Entrees are reasonably priced between RM8 and RM24 (US$2.25–US$6.70/ £1.25–£3.70).

ATTRACTIONS

The Astana and Fort Margherita   At the waterfront by the Square Tower, you'll find water taxis to take you across the river to see these two reminders of the White Rajas of Sarawak. The Astana, built in 1870 by Raja Charles Brooke, the second raja of Sarawak, is now the official residence of the governor. It is not open to the public, but visitors may still walk in the gardens. The best view of the Astana, however is from the water.

Raja Charles Brooke's wife, Ranee Margaret, gave her name to Fort Margherita, which was erected in 1870 to protect the city of Kuching. Inside the great castlelike building is a police museum, the most interesting sights of which are the depictions of criminal punishment.

Across the Sarawak River from town. Fort © 082/244-232. Free admission. Daily 9am–5pm.

Chinese History Museum   Built in 1912, this old Chinese Chamber of Commerce building is the perfect venue for a museum that traces the history of Chinese communities in Sarawak. Though small, it's centrally located and a convenient stop while you're in the area.

Corner of Main Bazaar and Jalan Tunku Abdul Rahman. Free admission. Daily 9am–5pm.

Main Bazaar   Main Bazaar, the major thoroughfare along the river, is home to Kuching's antiques and handicrafts shops. If you're walking along the river, a little time in these shops is like a walk through a traditional handicrafts gallery. You'll also find souvenir shops and some nice T-shirt silk-screeners.

Along the river. Free admission.

Sarawak Cultural Village ⊛   What appears to be a contrived theme park turns out to be a really fun place to learn about Sarawak's indigenous people. Built around a lagoon, the park re-creates the various styles of longhouse dwellings of each of the major tribes. Inside each house are representative members of each tribe displaying cultural artifacts and performing music, teaching dart blowing, and showing off carving talents. Give yourself plenty of time to stick around and talk with the people, who are recruited from villages inland and love to tell stories about their homes and traditions. Performers dance and display costumes at 11:30am and 4:30pm daily. A shuttle bus leaves at regular intervals from the Holiday Inn Kuching on Jalan Tunku Abdul Rahman.

Kampung Budaya Sarawak, Pantai Damai, Santubong. © 082/846-411. Admission RM45 (US$13/£6.95) adults, RM23 (US$6.45/£3.55) children. Daily 9am–5pm.

Sarawak Islamic Museum   A splendid array of Muslim artifacts at this quiet and serene museum depicts the history of Islam and its spread to Southeast Asia. Local customs and history are also highlighted. Although women are not required to cover their heads, respectable attire that covers the legs and arms is requested.

Jalan P. Ramlee. © 082/244-232. Free admission. Sat–Thurs 9am–5pm; Fri 9am–12:45pm and 3–5pm.

Sarawak Museum 🏛 Two branches, one old and one new, display exhibits of the natural history, indigenous peoples, and culture of Sarawak, plus the state's colonial and modern history. The two branches are connected by an overhead walkway above Jalan Tun Haji Openg. The wildlife exhibit is a bit musty, but the arts and artifacts in the other sections are well tended. A tiny aquarium sits neglected behind the old branch, but the gardens here are lovely.

Jalan Tun Haji Openg. 🕾 082/244-232. Free admission. Sat–Thurs 9am–5pm; Fri 9am–12:45pm and 3–5pm.

Square Tower The tower, built in 1879, served as a prison camp, but today the waterfront real estate is better served by an information center for travel agents. The Square Tower is a prime starting place for a stroll along the river and is also where you'll find out about cultural performances and exhibitions held at the waterfront. You can also call the number below for performance schedules.

Jalan Gambier, near the riverfront. 🕾 082/426-093. Free admission.

Tua Pek Kong Temple At a main crossroads near the river stands the oldest Chinese temple in Sarawak. Although officially it dates from 1876, most locals acknowledge the true date of its beginnings as 1843. It's still lively in form and spirit, with colorful dragons tumbling along the walls and incense filling the air.

Junction of Jalan Tunku Abdul Rahman and Jalan Padungan. Free admission.

TOURING LOCAL CULTURE 🏛🏛🏛

One of the highlights of a trip to Sarawak is a visit to a longhouse community. Trips can range from simple overnight stays to 2-week intensive discovery tours. It goes without saying that shorter trips only venture as far as those longhouse villages closest to Kuching. The benefit is that these communities are at ease with foreigners and so are better able to demonstrate their culture. The drawback is that these villages are the ones most trampled by busloads of tourists looking to gawk at "primitive tribes." Basically, the more time you have, the deeper you will venture into the interior and the more time you will have to spend with different ethnic groups, allowing greater insight into these fascinating cultures.

A typical longhouse trip starts with a van ride from Kuching followed by a longtail boat ride upriver, through gorgeous scenery. If you are only stopping in for the night, you'll be welcomed, fed, and entertained—the food is generally edible and always prepared under sanitary conditions. Fruits are delicious. Your guide, through translation, will help you chat with villagers and ask questions about their lifestyle and customs. At night, you will sleep in a longhouse provided especially for guests. It's basic but cool, with mosquito nets (very necessary) provided. The following day includes a very brief jungle trek, plus hunting and fishing demonstrations before your departure back from whence you came. If your trip is for longer, you will probably avoid the closer villages and head straight for more remote communities, depending on how much time (and money) you have.

Your average overnight longhouse tour will set you back up to US$150 (£83) per person. Good tour operators are **Borneo Adventure,** 55 Main Bazaar (🕾 082/245-175; fax 082/422-626), and **Telang Usan Travel & Tours,** Ban Hock Road (🕾 082/236-945; fax 082/236-589). These agencies can also arrange trips into Sarawak's national parks.

TOURING SARAWAK'S NATIONAL PARKS

The Sarawak National Parks & Wildlife Centre has opened access to all of Sarawak's national parks to do-it-yourself travelers. From its booking center in Kuching, you can apply for parks permits and book reservations in state-run lodging within each park. It can also advise how to travel to and from each park: Those closer to Kuching will involve only local road and river transportation, while more remote parks will require commercial flights to either Sibu or Miri, plus transfers to ground and river transportation and even chartered flights. If you have the time to plan your travel this way, you will be rewarded with the thrill of "getting there," experiencing local life a little closer to the ground.

Most people do not have the luxury of time, which is why I recommend booking a trip through a tour operator, which will arrange all transportation, parks permits, lodging, meals, and guides, freeing your time to experience the attractions themselves. **Borneo Adventure** (55 Main Bazaar; ⓒ **082/245-175;** www.borneoadventure.com) costs a few dollars more than other local operations, but you'll get experienced guides and reliable services, and you do not need to join a huge touristy coach group—most of its trips are for small groups. The half-day trips from Kuching can even be combined for longer itineraries so you can maximize your time. The company can also prepare customized itineraries and special theme tours based upon your interests—for example, crafts, flora, or tribal cultures. If you want to venture further afield, Borneo Adventure books trips to national parks in other parts of the state as well. You'll have to fly to Miri or Sibu, as these two towns are the hop-off points for such excursions. Malaysia Airlines and AirAsia both serve these two towns from KL and Kuching.

NEAR KUCHING **Bako National Park** 🟊🟊🟊, established in 1957, is Sarawak's oldest national park. An area of 2,728 hectares (6,820 acres), it combines mangrove forest, lowland jungle, and high plains covered in scrub. Throughout the park, you'll see the pitcher plant and other strange carnivorous plants, plus long-tailed macaques, monitor lizards, bearded pigs, and the unique proboscis monkey. Because the park is only 37km (22 miles) from Kuching, half-day trips here are extremely convenient. A day trip for two costs RM278 (US$78/£43) per person.

Gunung Gading National Park, about a 2-hour drive west of Kuching, sprawls 4,106 hectares (10,265 acres) over rugged mountains to beautiful beach spots along the coast. Day-trippers and overnighters come to get a glimpse of the rafflesia, the largest flower in the world. The flowers are short-lived and temperamental, but the national parks office will let you know if any are in bloom. A day tour for two people costs RM278 (US$78/£43) per person.

Semenggoh Orang Utan Sanctuary is a rehabilitation center for orangutans and other endangered wildlife species who are either orphaned or recovering from illness and are being trained for eventual release into the forest. A half-day tour for two people costs RM121 (US$34/£19) per person.

A LITTLE FARTHER OUT **Gunung Mulu National Park** provides an amazing adventure with its astounding underground network of caves. The park claims the world's largest cave passage (Deer Cave), the world's largest natural chamber (Sarawak Chamber), and Southeast Asia's longest cave (Clearwater Cave). No fewer than 18 caves offer explorers trips of varying degrees of difficulty, from simple treks with minimal gear to technically difficult caves that require specialized equipment and skills. Aboveground are 544 sq. km (326 sq. miles) of primary rainforest, peat swamps, and mountainous forests teeming with mammals, birds, and unusual insects. Located in the north of Sarawak, Mulu is very close to the Brunei border. Borneo Adventure has a 2-day package for RM371 (US$104/£57) per person (min. 2 people). The trip includes accommodations; ground transportation; longboat rides; nature guides to see

Deer Cave, Sarawak Chamber, and Clearwater Cave; plus some rainforest trekking (wear a hat in the caves to protect yourself from bat droppings). It can book your flights from Kuching, but you'll have to pay extra.

SABAH 𝒜𝒜𝒜 & KOTA KINABALU

Sabah presents a wonderland of awe-inspiring natural scenery and mysterious indigenous cultures. It is, in my opinion, Southeast Asia's hidden treasure. A playground for adventure seekers, extreme sportsters, and bums in search of the ultimate beach, Sabah rewards those who venture here with a holiday in an unspoiled paradise.

Covering 73,711 sq. km (28,747 sq. miles) of the northern part of Borneo, the world's third-largest island, Sabah stretches from the South China Sea in the west to the Sulu Sea in the east, both seas containing an abundance of uninhabited islands, postcard-perfect beaches, and pristine coral reefs bubbling with marine life. In between, more than half of the state is covered in ancient primary rainforest that's protected in national parks and forest reserves. In these forests, some rare species of mammals like the Sumatran rhino and Asian elephant (herds of them) take effort to witness, but other animals, such as the orangutan, proboscis monkey, gibbon, lemur, civet, and Malaysian sun bear, can be seen on jungle treks. Of the hundreds of bird species here, the hornbills and herons steal the show.

Sabah's tallest peak also happens to be the highest mountain between the Himalayas and Irian Jaya. At 4,095m (13,432 ft.), **Mount Kinabalu** is the tallest in Southeast Asia, and a challenge to trek or climb. The state's interior has endless opportunities for jungle trekking, river rafting, mountain biking, and 4×4 exploration for every level of excitement, from soft adventure to extreme sports.

This state holds not only mysterious wildlife and geography, but also people as well. Sabahans count among their many ethnic groups some 32 different tribes whose cultures and traditions are vastly different from the Malay majority that makes up the rest of the country. In fact, ethnic Malays are a minority in Sabah.

The best place to begin exploring Sabah's marine wonders, wildlife and forests, adventure opportunities, and indigenous peoples is from its capital, **Kota Kinabalu.** A speck of a city on the west coast, it's where you'll find the headquarters for all of Sabah's adventure-tour operators and package-excursion planners. Spend at least a day here to explore your options; then set out to the wilds for the adventure of a lifetime.

GETTING THERE   Because of Sabah's remote location, just about everybody arrives by plane at the **Kota Kinabalu International Airport** (© **088/238-555**). A surprising number of direct international flights connect Sabah to the region.

⌐Warning Exercise Caution

In April 2000, 22 people, including 11 foreign tourists, were kidnapped from a dive resort on Sipadan Island off the east coast of Sabah. This would be the first of four incidents of kidnapping, mostly of Malaysian workers, in this area by the Abu Sayyaf, a terrorist group in the southern Philippines with known links to Al-Qaeda. While Malaysia responded by placing security forces on 23 islands and six additional strategic locations, the U.S. Department of State still advises Americans to exercise caution when traveling in this area. Despite the warning, foreign visitor arrivals to Sipadan have doubled since the advisory was first issued.

Malaysia Airlines flies from Hong Kong, Manila, Osaka, Seoul, Shanghai, Singapore, and Tokyo, among others, while **AirAsia** flies from Bangkok. Malaysia Airlines also has direct domestic flights to Kota Kinabalu from KL, Johor Bahru, Kuching, Sibu, and Miri, with in-state service to Sandakan and other towns. AirAsia has direct domestic flights from KL and Johor Bahru.

The airport is about a 20-minute drive south of the central part of the city. The most efficient way to get into town is by taxi. The cars line up outside the arrivals hall and are supposed to use a coupon system—look for the coupon-sales and taxi-booking counter close by. You'll pay about RM12 (US$3.35/£1.85) for a trip to town. Ignore the drivers that will try to lure you away from the coupon counter.

GETTING AROUND   In the downtown area, you can get around quite easily on foot between hotels, restaurants, tour operators, markets, and the tourism office. For longer trips, a taxi will be necessary; in-town trips cost about RM10 (US$2.80/£1.55). Taxis are flagged down on the street or by your hotel's bellhop.

VISITOR INFORMATION   The **Sabah Tourism Board** (51 Jalan Gaya; ① **088/212-121;** www.sabahtourism.com) provides the most comprehensive information about the state. It's open daily from 9am to 4pm. Although the national **MTB** has a small office on Jalan Gaya, a block down from the Sabah Tourism office, almost all of its information promotes travel in other parts of the country. Still, if you're interested, stop by Ground Floor Uni. Asia Building, no. 1 Jalan Sagunting (① **088/248-698**).

FAST FACTS   The **area code** for Sabah is **088.** Sabah time is 1 hour ahead of peninsular Malaysia. You'll find **banks** with ATMs conveniently located in the downtown area around Jalan Limabelas and along Jalan Gaya and Jalan Pantai. While there are no large **Internet** cafes, per se, you'll find access in small shopfronts around the main parts of town, especially near the shopping malls.

WHERE TO STAY

Hyatt Regency Kinabalu 🅐   The only international business-class hotel in town, in some ways the Hyatt seems a little out of place in cozy Kota Kinabalu. Still, it's located close to the waterfront, near all major shopping and travel operators, and has a fantastic assortment of restaurants to choose from. Even if you're staying elsewhere in town, you may appreciate one of its dining options. As modern as you would expect the Hyatt chain to be, rooms here are large and presented in up-to-date furnishing styles that are not so Western that they take all the charm away. Local tour and car-rental booking in the lobby make the place convenient for leisure travelers. One of the high points is Shenanigan's, the best bar in Kota Kinabalu, with live entertainment. It gets packed, mostly with locals and expats out for a sip.

Jalan Datuk Salleh Sulong, 88994 Kota Kinabalu, Sabah. ① **800/233-1234** in the U.S. and Canada, ① 800/131-234 in Australia, ① 800/441-234 in New Zealand, or ① 088/221-234. Fax 088/225-972. http://kinabalu.hyatt.com. 288 units. RM270 (US$76/£42) double; from RM470 (US$132/£72) suite. AE, DC, MC, V. **Amenities:** 3 restaurants; bar; outdoor pool; fitness center; concierge; tour desk; car rental; limousine service; business center; 24-hr. room service; babysitting; laundry service; dry cleaning; nonsmoking rooms; executive-level rooms. *In room:* A/C, satellite TV w/in-house movies, minibar, coffeemaker, hair dryer, safe.

Jesselton Hotel 🅐🅐   Listen to me rave about the Jesselton. It's such a nice surprise to find this quaint boutique hotel in the center of Kota Kinabalu, just about the last real reminder in this city of a colonial presence. Even more lovely: the level of personalized service and the comfort of the rooms, which, though completely modern, retain

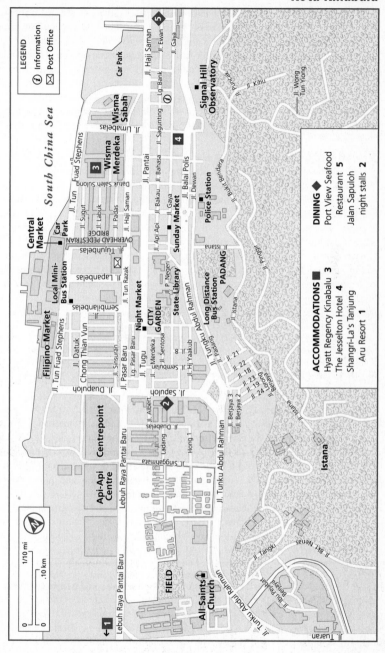

Kota Kinabalu

LEGEND
- ⓘ Information
- ⊠ Post Office

South China Sea

Car Park

Wisma Sabah

Wisma Merdeka **3**

Central Market

Car Park

Local Mini-Bus Station

Filipino Market

Signal Hill Observatory

5

Jl. Haji Saman Jl. Ewan Jl. Gaya

Lg. Bank

Jl. Limabelas

Jl. Pantai

Jl. Bahasa Jl. Sagunting

4

Jl. Tun Fuad Stephens

Datuk Saleh Sulong

Jl. Tun Sugut Jl. Labuk Jl. Padas Jl. Haji Saman

OVERHEAD PEDESTRIAN BRIDGE

Jl. Tujuhbelas

Jl. Lapanbelas

Jl. Sembilanbelas

Night Market

CITY GARDEN

Jl. Datuk Chong Thian Vun

Jl. Sinsuran

Jl. Pasar Baru

Lg. Pasar Baru

Jl. Tugu Jl. Merdeka Jl. Sentosa

Jl. P. Negeri

State Library

Jl. 8

Jl. Hj Yaakub

Centrepoint

Api-Api Centre

Lebuh Raya Pantai Baru

Jl. Albert

Jl. Duabelas

Jl. Ladang

Hong 1

Jl. Singgahmata

Lebuh Raya Pantai Baru

FIELD

All-Saints Church

Jl. Tunku Abdul Rahman

Jl. Api Api Jl. Bakau Jl. Gaya

Sunday Market

Police Station

Jl. Dewan

Jl. Balai Polis

Jl. Istana

PADANG

Long Distance Bus Station

Jl. Padang

Jl. Tungku Abdul Rahman

Jl. 21
Jl. 18
Jl. 22
Jl. 23
Jl. 19
Jl. 24

Jl. Berjaya 3
Jl. Berjaya 2

Jl. Istana

Jl. Bukit Bendera

Jl. Pinggir

Jl. Istana

Istana

Jl. Tangki

Jl. Bkt. Nenas

Jl. Ibu Pejabat Jl. Berjaya

Jl. Tunku Abdul Rahman

Jl. Tuaran

Jl. Kihu

Jl. Punai

Jl. Wong Tun Yiong

ACCOMMODATIONS ■
Hyatt Regency Kinabalu **3**
The Jesselton Hotel **4**
Shangri-La's Tanjung
Aru Resort **1**

DINING ◆
Port View Seafood
Restaurant **5**
Jalan Sapuloh
night stalls **2**

0   1/10 mi
0   .10 km

N

←**1** Lebuh Raya Pantai Baru

their charm with lovely Audubon-style inks and attractive wallpapers and fabrics—sort of a cross between a cozy guesthouse and a top-class hotel. Due to lack of space in the building, there's no pool, fitness center, or business center, but the staff at the front desk can help you with tour information and transportation. The coffee shop serves local and Western food, which is quite good. The Gardenia Restaurant looks more upmarket than it really is.

69 Jalan Gaya, 88000 Kota Kinabalu, Sabah. ℂ **088/223-333.** Fax 088/240-401. www.jesseltonhotel.com. 32 units. RM280 (US$78/£43) double; RM1,000 (US$280/£154) suite. AE, DC, MC, V. **Amenities:** Restaurant; bar and lounge; coffee shop; tour desk; limousine service; 24-hr. room service; babysitting; laundry service; nonsmoking rooms. *In room:* A/C, TV (movies available), minibar, coffeemaker, hair dryer, safe.

Shangri-La's Tanjung Aru Resort ★★★ *Kids*   A short ride southwest of Kota Kinabalu and you're at Tanjung Aru, an amazingly gorgeous beach-resort area—Sabah's Riviera. The Shangri-La here is located in a most impressive setting, surrounded on three sides by water. It serves the finest local Sabahan cuisine and freshest seafood you can get in the region. Book a room in the Tanjung Wing, which is nestled amid Shangri-La's signature lush garden setting, since the Kinabalu Wing, while newer, is more like a hotel block. Every room has a stunning view of either the sea or Mount Kinabalu, with a balcony for full appreciation. Tropical touches include rattan furnishings, local fabrics, and wood details. The tour desk can arrange everything from scuba to trekking and rafting, and the free shuttle gives you convenient access to town. Special activities for kids make this place a good choice for families, too.

Locked Bag 174, 88744 Kota Kinabalu, Sabah. ℂ **800/942-5050** in the U.S. and Canada, ℂ 800/222-448 in Australia, ℂ 800/442-179 in New Zealand, or ℂ 088/225-800. Fax 088/217-155. www.shangri-la.com. 499 units. RM700 (US$196/£108) double; from RM1,250 (US$350/£193) suite. **Amenities:** 3 restaurants; beach bar and lounge; 2 outdoor lagoon-style pools; 4 outdoor lighted tennis courts; fitness center w/Jacuzzi, sauna, steam, and massage; concierge; tour desk; shuttle service; salon; 24-hr. room service; babysitting; laundry service; dry cleaning; nonsmoking rooms. *In room:* A/C, satellite TV w/in-house movies, dataport w/direct Internet access, minibar, coffeemaker, hair dryer, safe.

WHERE TO DINE

One of the best local specialties, *hinava,* is a mouthwatering delicacy of raw fish marinated in lime juice, ginger, shallots, herbs, and chiles—I highly recommend trying it! Kota Kinabalu is known for its fresh seafood, and there are a lot of places to choose from, but the locals and expats all agree that **Port View Seafood Restaurant,** Jalan Haji Saman, across from the old Customs Wharf, near the downtown area (ℂ **088/ 252-813**), is the best. Dishes are prepared primarily in Chinese and Malay styles, moderately priced (sold by weight), and always succulent.

If you're into the dinner-and-cultural-show thing, head for **Kampung Nelayan** (Taman Tun Fuad, Bukit Padang, Luyang; ℂ **088/231-005**). This seafood-market-style restaurant is housed in a traditional Malay building floating on a lake in a botanic garden. The nightly show starts at 7:45pm.

WHAT TO SEE & DO

Sabah attracts **scuba** enthusiasts from around the world, who come to dive at Sipadan, an island resort off the east coast of the state. **Sipadan,** ranked as one of the top 10 dive sites in the world, is actually a tall limestone "tower" rising from the bed of the Celebes Sea, supporting vast numbers of marine species, some of which may still be unidentified. In December 2004, the Malaysian government revoked the licenses of the five dive operators that managed resorts on the tiny island in an effort to prevent environmental degradation—Malaysia is also applying for World Heritage Site recognition for the area. The dive operators moved their base camps to surrounding islands, offering day trips to the area or running live-aboard trips.

Borneo Divers (9th floor, Menara Jubili, 53 Jalan Gaya; ✆ **088/222-226;** www. borneodivers.info) was the first full-service dive operator in Borneo and the pioneering operator to Sipadan. It houses divers at its resort on Mabul, along a gorgeous sandy beach with easy access to dive sites around the Mabul island and Sipadan. For RM664 (US$186/£102) per night per person, you'll get accommodations, meals, airport transfers, and two dives a day. You'll have to pay extra for a round-trip flight into Tawau, which costs about RM390 (US$109/£60). Sipadan has good diving year-round, but the best weather is March through October.

A newer spot, **Layang Layang,** located off the coast of northwest Borneo in the South China Sea, is also making a splash as an underwater bounty of marine life. **Layang Layang Island Resort** (head office in KL at Block A, Ground Floor, A-0-3, Megan Ave. II, 12 Jalan Yap Kwan Seng; ✆ **03/2162-2877;** www.layanglayang.com) pioneered this area for divers. Its standard 6-day package runs RM3,500 (US$980/ £539) per person, which includes accommodations, meals, and three dives a day. Equipment is extra, as is the chartered helicopter flight to the island, which is expensive at RM714 (US$200/£110) round-trip (booked through the dive operator). Layang Layang closes during the monsoon season (early Sept–Feb).

If you want to stay close to Kota Kinabalu, Borneo Divers (see above) makes day trips to **Tunku Abdul Rahman Marine Park.** This group of five islands about 8km (13 miles) off the coast of Kota Kinabalu has been protected since the mid-1970s. Throughout the park, waters are clear and visibility is good. Although not as lauded as Sipadan and Layang Layang, it's highly recommended if you're looking for some quick diving excitement but have time and money constraints. A day trip that includes two boat dives and a shore dive costs RM265 (US$74/£41), not including equipment rentals. Borneo Divers has a base camp on the smallest island, from which it also conducts complete PADI scuba courses.

Sabah has many other dive sites, including Pulau Tiga of *Survivor* TV fame. A couple of sites also offer wreck diving, so if you're interested, inquire when you make your booking.

For other types of watersports, your best bet is to either book these activities through your resort or plan a do-it-yourself trip to Tunku Abdul Rahman Marine Park. To get to the park, catch a ferry at the Jesselton Point Jetty at the Customs House on Jalan Haji Saman, opposite Port View Seafood Restaurant (RM24/US$6.70/£3.70 round-trip). It's only 8km (13 miles) from Kota Kinabalu, so you can easily take a day trip to one or more of the park's five islands and sun on the beach. **Snorkel** rentals go for around RM10 (US$2.80/£1.55), while **parasailing** charges run RM90 (US$25/£14). The latest thrill is **seawalking**—donning an enormous helmet connected to the surface with a tube, which allows you to breathe underwater without tanks. This costs RM200 (US$56/£31) a pop. There are cafes and toilets near the jetties, plus rustic accommodations on two of the islands.

Sabah's rugged terrain makes for terrific hiking, camping, biking, and rafting for any level, be it soft adventure or extreme sports. **TYK Adventure** (Borneo Travel; Lot 48-2F, 2nd floor, Beverly Hill Plaza; ✆ **088/727-825;** www.mega-ecom.come/tham yaukong) was founded by local Chinese award-winning tour guide Tham Yau Kong, who also happens to hold records for the longest cultural walk (1998) and for leading the first group to circum-cycle Mount Kinabalu (1999). Mountain-biking day trips around Papar or Penampang run RM310 (US$87/£48) per person, including hotel transfer, mountain bike, and helmet.

Many come to Sabah to climb **Mount Kinabalu.** It's a terrific trip if you're prepared and if you hit it just right, in terms of weather and timing. It can only be done on an overnight trip, which includes a 4- or 5-hour hike from the park headquarters uphill to a ranger station, where you stay the night. Groups get up at 3am to begin the 3-hour hike to the summit. This is not light trekking, as some parts are steep, altitude sickness can cause headaches and nausea, and remember—you're tooling along in the pitch darkness, the whole point being to arrive at the summit in time for the spectacular sunrise. Come prepared with cold-weather snugglies, or at the very least a wool sweater or fleece, long pants, windbreaker, rain poncho, and hiking boots. Bring a good, strong flashlight and pack plenty of trail mix and sports drinks for rejuvenation. And finally, there's no guarantee that the weather will cooperate with your itinerary. You might hit rain or find the summit covered in clouds. There's pretty much nothing any tour operator can do to guarantee you'll get a clear view. But I've heard when you hit it right, it's really quite an experience. **TYK Adventure** can also book this tour for you—a 2-day trip will set you back RM881 (US$247/£136). Make sure you book early—the outfitter needs to make sure there's space available at park accommodations. The price includes transfer, lodging, and your guide to the summit.

TYK also plans regular trips out to Sandakan, on the eastern coast of Sabah, for trips to see the **Sepilok Orang Utan Rehabilitation Center,** the largest orangutan sanctuary in the world, with facilities to house and train hundreds of orphaned orangutans for eventual release back into the wilds. There's also a boat trip to see the **Marine Turtle Conservation Park and Hatchery.**

For a peep at a bit of local culture, explore the **Monsopiad Cultural Village,** a Kadazandusun heritage center with its creepy House of Skulls, located in Penampang, not far from Kota Kinabalu. During the 3-hour visit to the village, you'll tour the place and be treated to a cultural performance. It's about the height of "touristy" Sabah, but can be a fun half-day trip. Call ⓒ **088/774-337** to make a booking; the RM95 (US$27/£15) price includes transportation to and from your hotel, the tour, and the show, plus a welcome drink. The tour leaves daily from 9 to 9:30am and again at 2 to 2:30pm.

In 2000, the **North Borneo Railway** (Tanjung Aru Railway; ⓒ **088/263-933**) revived the old tradition of steam-train travel with the launch of a 1954 fully renovated British Vulcan steam locomotive pulling six restored carriages. Traversing a 58km (36-mile) route from Tanjung Aru, just outside Kota Kinabalu, to the rural town of Papar, the train passes lovely sea and mangrove views, past fishermen and local watercraft, through a deep mountain tunnel, and out the other side into a vast scenery of paddy fields. Carriages are open-air but comfortable, with soft seats and charming wood-and-brass accents. A swanky bar car and observation deck round out the facilities, which also include toilets. The train departs every Wednesday and Saturday at 10am, returning at 2pm; tickets are RM195 (US$55/£30).

For another unique view of the countryside, **Sabah Air** (Sabah Air Building, Old Airport Rd.; ⓒ **088/256-733;** www.sabahair.com.my) offers thrilling **helicopter tours,** flying over Kota Kinabalu, tropical wilds, and the jewel-colored sea for 20 minutes. You can also book a 1-hour aerial tour of Mount Kinabalu. You need a minimum of four people for each trip. The Kota Kinabalu trip is RM257 (US$72/£40) per person; the Mount Kinabalu trip is RM685 (US$192/£106) per person.

10

Bali (Indonesia)

by Jen Lin-Liu

A scenic land of active volcanoes, dense jungle, stunning beaches, and a rich, ancient culture, Bali is an island of tranquillity in the often-tumultuous Indonesian archipelago. Bali's peaceful way of life—one marked by colorful ritual and genuine hospitality—has drawn tourists, artists, and escapists for generations. Sadly, recent events like the terrorist attacks of October 2002 and October 2005 have shattered that image. Warnings from the U.S. government, among others, are still in place, and, though the Indonesian government has taken important steps to update security on its tourist cash cow, many balk at returning to Bali.

There has been a marked shift among Balinese, a realignment of priorities in the wake of tragedy and changing world opinion. Whereas in the past tourists were taken for granted, bilked for that extra rupiah at every turn, and hurried along, many Balinese have reassessed what life is all about. Among both tourists and expats, the impression is that the Balinese mastery of "living in the moment" and coexisting with nature has intensified. Visitors are sure to find Balinese eager to sit for a chat and share a laugh (though the transport lads are still pretty relentless). The Balinese have always welcomed visitors warmly, with a sense of hospitality that has even increased of late.

And people *are* coming back. After the most recent terrorist attack, tourism began rebounding in 2006, and hoteliers expect that 2007 will see the industry return to pre-terrorism levels. Some hotels, like the Ritz-Carlton in Jimbaran, are operating near full capacity. The market has shifted slightly, however, reflecting a greater number of visitors from other parts of Indonesia and neighboring countries like Japan. After the second attack, the number of Australian visitors dropped dramatically, while Europeans, who have had to deal with terrorism for years at home, continue to come in large numbers. Americans are still slow to return.

Though in some places tourism has spawned overdevelopment a la Thailand's Phuket, a brief ride out of Kuta or away from any resort area brings you to the pristine Bali of volcanic peaks, bubbling springs, tropical jungle, and stunning beaches.

Balinese people practice a unique amalgam of Indian Hindu traditions, Buddhism, ancient Javanese practices, and indigenous animistic beliefs. The beauty of this faith colors every aspect of life, from fresh flowers strewn everywhere in obeisance to the calm of morning prayer at temple. During your visit, you're sure to catch the soothing music of the gamelan, the music of the island, and see the enchanting Balinese dance. Despite recent events, Bali is still the beautiful island paradise that has attracted so many for so long.

1 Getting to Know Bali

THE LAY OF THE LAND

Tiny Bali has great topographical variety. Located in the center of Indonesia's vast archipelago, the island has an area of 5,620 sq. km (roughly 2,192 sq. miles), only the size of a large metropolis. The land is divided in half east to west by a volcanic mountain chain and is scored lengthwise by deep river gorges. White-sand beaches line the coast to the east, as well as near Kuta in the most populated area of wider lowlands to the south. Dotting the island are active volcanoes, including Gunung Agung, a dynamic peak and a power point of Balinese culture and belief. Central Ubud is one of the more beautiful spots, with mountainous scenery, lush vegetation, and Bali's famed terraced rice farms. The far west is the least developed area of the island, with mountainous terrain mostly given over to national park land.

A LOOK AT THE PAST

As distinct as Balinese life is, its people and culture originated elsewhere. Evidence of settlement goes back to the Neolithic period of around 3000 B.C., but the culture flourished under Chinese and Indian influences, including the introduction of Buddhism and Hinduism beginning in 800 B.C. Bali was ruled periodically by the Javanese. With the rise of Islam on the mainland, the last Javanese Majapahit king fled Jakarta for Bali in 1515, cementing the island's Javanese influence and affecting a renaissance in art and culture that would survive years of Muslim incursion.

The first real Western presence was established in 1601, when a Dutch contingent came to set up formal relations and establish trade. Attempts to expand relations were largely rebuffed—even as the **Dutch East India Company** expanded throughout the area—but Balinese slaves were shipped to Dutch and French merchants nonetheless. In the era of Napoleon, Holland's East Indian holdings passed first to the French and then to the British, who returned them to the Dutch in the peace agreement following Napoleon's Waterloo defeat in 1815. After protracted struggle, the Dutch fully secured control in 1909.

A steady stream of European settlers and visitors followed—doctors and teachers at first, then the first tourists, artists, and cultural explorers. By the 1930s, Bali's reputation as a magical paradise was spreading rapidly, and such figures as anthropologist Margaret Mead and artist Walter Spies frequented the island.

World War II saw an exodus of foreigners with the arrival of Japanese troops. For Indonesians, it was a time of both strain, under the brief Japanese occupation, and revelation, in light of the withdrawal of Dutch control. Shortly after the end of the war in 1945, Nationalist Party founder **Sukarno,** a thorn in the side of the Dutch since the 1920s, announced a declaration of Indonesian independence and was named president. The Dutch withdrew under international pressure in 1949, allowing the creation of the Republic of Indonesia, a tentative federation.

Hindu Bali was suspect under the rule of Muslim Jakarta, and the island was hit very hard by economic collapse. In 1965, **Suharto** seized control in response to a staged communist coup, and bloody conflicts continued for several years. As many as 100,000 Balinese were killed as suspected communists or as ethnic Chinese.

Under Suharto, the military gained a far-reaching influence over national affairs. For the next 3 decades, until the major economic crisis of 1997, Indonesia enjoyed a period of prosperity in spite of Suharto's embezzling autocracy. During this time, and with government attention, Bali rose to prominence as a top tourist destination in the region.

In just the last half century, Bali has undergone remarkable change and weathered turmoil on the Indonesian mainland. The riots and protests that erupted in Indonesia in 1998 were the result of 3 decades of military rule and struggles to bring the world's fourth most populous country into the modern global economy. Chafing under the yoke of President Suharto, the Indonesians finally revolted, with demonstrations turned into riots that made headlines around the world. In June 1999, Indonesians witnessed their first free parliamentary election since 1955, ousting Suharto. But riots, bombings, and separatist protests continued to plague the country, specifically in Aceh and Irian Jaya. On May 20, 2002, East Timor was internationally recognized as an independent state after a protracted struggle. Indonesia achieved a tentative peace under a provisional government headed by **President Megawati,** the daughter of Sukarno (predecessor to Suharto). Megawati inherited political instability and an economic crisis, but addressed corruption and the military's human rights record.

The elections in July 2004 brought ascendancy to **Susilo Bambang Yudhoyono,** and a certain peace prevails in the wake of a surge toward democracy. Despite the recent bombings in Jakarta and alleged terror cells throughout the archipelago, many countries have lifted travel restrictions as visitors rediscover Indonesia.

BALI TODAY

Tourism had been rebounding significantly from the October 2002 bombings (which killed 202 people) when terrorists once again struck in October 2005. The second attack was smaller, killing 20, but the use of suicide bombers in two highly touristed areas (Kuta and Jimbaran Bay) made it just as frightening. Even so, tourists, recognizing that terrorism is a modern-day problem on most of the planet, have once again begun returning to Bali. Huge foreign investments in new luxury hotels—like the Bulgari, where rooms start at US$1,000 (£550) per night—indicate that many see a hopeful future for Balinese tourism. An increase in guards, bomb-sniffing dogs, and regular vehicle checks nearly everywhere in Bali also shows that the tourism industry and the government are taking security seriously. Ironically, the areas hardest hit by the drop in tourists are the more far-flung, remote parts of Bali where terrorists are least likely to strike. Rather than skipping out on one of the world's best beach holidays, travelers can alleviate their terrorism concerns by visiting Bali's more remote destinations, asking their hotels what security measures are in place, and staying alert when visiting crowded areas.

As with any undiscovered paradise that isn't so undiscovered anymore, Bali buffs mourn the loss of the island's innocence. You're sure to meet one or two scruffy old expats who'll be more than happy to tell you about "how it once was" on the island. Where there were no hotels or even electricity only a few decades ago, the island is now spotted with cybercafes, upscale lodging, and pesky touts. Don't be dissuaded. The "real Bali" is wherever you look for it.

BALI'S PEOPLE & CULTURE

RELIGION   Over 90% of the population is Hindu, with the minority made up of Muslims, Buddhists, and Christians. Religious ritual plays into every facet of life. Balinese Hindus believe in the ascending (and confusing) pantheon of Hindu gods, as well as dharma and adharma, order and disorder, and the need for balance between the two and rituals to that end. The importance of karma, or the consequence of individual

Bali

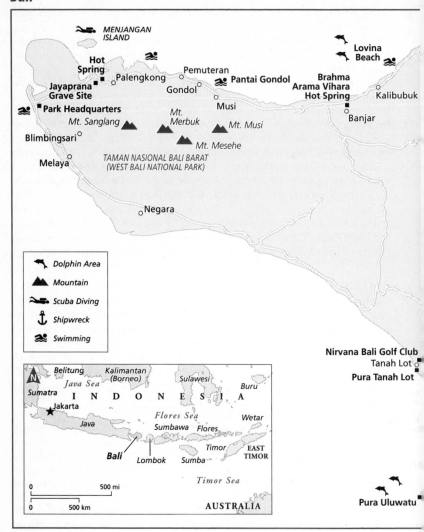

actions, plays into the peaceful daily rhythms, and forms of "making merit" are as many as the people who practice them. Whether placing daily offerings of flowers on someone's car or undertaking rigorous mountain pilgrimages, Balinese believe that, to achieve harmony, the forces of good must be saluted with offerings, while the forces of evil must be appeased. With an estimated 20,000 temples and shrines, Bali is known as the "Island of the Gods," and every village has at least one temple with buildings dedicated to Vishnu, Brahma, and Shiva (the Creator, the Preserver, and the Destroyer).

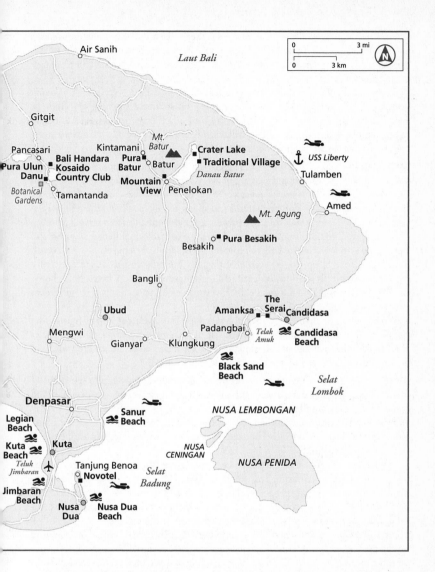

CELEBRATIONS **Tooth filing** is a rite of maturation, wherein the sharp front teeth, especially the canines, are filed down smooth (the idea being to differentiate humans from the animals). This can happen at any age, even after death, but is most often done to adolescents.

Weddings in Bali are unique, colorful affairs not to be missed, and **cremations** are surprisingly festive as well. Burning the body is the only way a soul can be freed of its earthly self and travel to its next incarnation (or to enlightenment), and death is a joyous occasion in Bali, full of floats and fanfare. Complicated towers (the higher the caste, the higher the tower) hold the body, carried aloft by cheering men who turn the tower in circles to send the spirit to heaven as they carry it to the burning ground. It's an extraordinary and wonderful event; there are even tours that will take you, or you can ask at any *losmen* (hostel) or at your hotel front desk. Cremations in Ubud are particularly noteworthy.

Compared to Western churchgoing, celebrations in Bali are very casual: Women gossip, children play, and dogs wander temple grounds freely, snacking on offerings. A priest chants, people pray and then get up, and others take their places. Ask before taking photos, and stay on your best behavior. Balinese are generally most welcoming and might even invite you for food or drinks.

MUSIC & DANCE The tones of the **gamelan**—the bright-sounding metal percussion ensembles that accompany just about every celebration and ceremony here—will first turn your head. Music is everywhere in Bali, from the raucous *dangdut,* or Indonesian pop pouring from restaurants and shops, to folk music and the refined classical music that accompanies the many staged dance performances and temple worship.

If you have a chance, don't miss a performance of traditional dance. **Legong** and **Barong dances** are intricate ballets depicting scenes from the epic *Ramayana.* **Kecak dance** is a circle of up to 100 men chanting rhythmically and telling the saga of a monkey king and his warriors. It's a colorful, fun experience. Many hotels hold shows; the Royal Palace in Ubud is a good choice. If you're lucky, you'll find a real, nontourist performance in an outlying village.

Wayang Kulit, or **shadow-puppet plays,** feature intricately cut leather figures that puppeteers use to project images against a screen. *Wayang Kulit* shows also depict tales from the Hindu epics and are accompanied by a gamelan ensemble and the voices of puppeteers (often injecting news, gossip, and bawdy jokes).

ARTS & CRAFTS Decoration and craft are as seamlessly woven into the fabric of life in Bali as are dance, music, and ritual. Fine carving and craftwork can be found adorning the most humble dwelling. Craftsmen are highly revered, and skilled wood and stone carvers turn out authentic works in street-side studios all over the island (concentrated in Ubud). Visitors are sure to walk away with some beautiful, original finds in wood and stone.

Masks used in traditional performance, many of the bug-eyed demoness Rangda, make fine souvenirs. (*Beware:* Tradition has it that even tourist copies can be inhabited!) There's a lot of mass-produced clutter, and lots of these works have been "aged" by an artful banging around on the sidewalk; authentic antiques are rare, so be cynical of claims of authenticity—though the copies can be quite good.

Ancient stylized **paintings of deities** and the delicately carved "lontar" **palm-frond books** are both still produced on the island. Expatriates have had as much influence on modern Balinese art as the ancients. As guiding patrons, men such as **Rudolf Bonnet,** a Dutchman, and **Walter Spies,** whose home on the site of the Tjampuhan Hotel in Ubud became central to the arts in Ubud, influenced local painters, opened societies, and brought the glory of Bali to the world at large. With a little searching, you can find some real masterpieces.

ETIQUETTE

Since the Balinese have been hosting foreign tourists for decades, they are fairly laid-back and accepting of Western habits—but even the Balinese have their traditions that should be respected. The most important rule is to cover up your legs and shoulders when entering a temple; most hotels supply sarongs for temple visits. The Balinese also ban menstruating women from temples. When speaking with locals, avoid pointing with your index finger. If you must point, stick out your thumb and make a fist with the rest of your fingers.

LANGUAGE

The Balinese speak both Indonesian and Balinese—the former when out in public, the latter at home. Aside from the tendency toward seemingly jaw-breaking polysyllabic phrases, Indonesian is not that hard to learn; pronunciation is pretty straightforward, and spelling is phonetic. Balinese is much more complicated, not least because there are three levels—high, middle, and low—depending on the class and authority of the person to whom you are speaking.

English is spoken widely, and if you've learned a few words of Malay, you can give them a try here as the languages are quite similar. For a list of useful Malay phrases, please see "Language" in chapter 8.

2 The Best of Bali in 2 Weeks

A visit to Bali is, as always, replete with kingly comforts, beautiful resorts, fine dining, and immersion in an ancient culture amid an island dreamscape. The following 2-week plan starts you off in Seminyak and then takes you to Ubud, Gunung Bakur, Menjangan, Jimbaran Bay, and Tanjung Banoa. The last stop is Nusa Dua, where you can treat yourself to a luxury spa.

Days ❶–❷: Seminyak ⚐

This hip, yuppie beachside enclave is a great alternative to the overrun Kuta just south of here. Lounge at the oceanfront pool at the luxurious **Legian.** The next day, take a surf lesson at the **Rip Curl School of Surf,** followed by a sunset cocktail and dinner at **Ku De Ta.** Dance late into the night at **Hu'u Bar.**

Days ❸–❹: Ubud ⚐⚐

The 1-hour drive to Ubud takes you from the shore to the lush rice paddies and jungles of Bali. The stellar **Chedi Club,** a collection of boutique private villas with personal butlers, is worth every rupiah. Take a morning trek through the rice paddies and get a back scrub and rub at **Ubud Body Works Center,** a great value spa. The next day, peruse the numerous housewares shops on Monkey Forest Road and take a break at **Monkey Forest,** where you can feed the monkeys a few bananas. Late in the afternoon, take the 1-hour drive to Penelokan, a town that sits on the outer crater's edge of **Gunung**

Batur. The digs aren't fancy here, but the best of the lot is the **Lakeview Hotel.**

Day ❺: Gunung Batur

Make the 2-hour ascent of Gunung Batur, an active volcano. At the top, you can boil eggs in pockets of erupting steam and walk along one of the volcano's ridges. In the afternoon, hire a car for the 3-hour trip to **Pemuteran,** on Bali's north shore. The **Matahari Beach Resort** provides beachside bungalows and Michelin-star-worthy dinners.

Days ❻–❼: Diving & Snorkeling in the North ⚐⚐

Enjoy a snooze on the north shore's less touristed beaches or canoe in the calm waters. The next day, take a dive boat to **Menjangan,** Bali's premier dive spot. Dive or snorkel in crystal-blue waters with ample coral, turtles, and fish of every color.

Days ❽–❾: Jimbaran Bay ⚐⚐

Hire a car to the romantic yet local area of Jimbaran Bay, home to a number of the world's top resorts. The cream of the crop are the **Ritz-Carlton Bali** and the **Four Seasons Resort at Jimbaran Bay.** Even if you don't stay at the Ritz, be sure to make an appointment at its world-class spa—it features a unique therapy pool called the Aquatonic, which delivers a massage and light workout via jet streams. Visit the cliffside temple **Uluwatu** at sunset, followed by a grilled lobster and shrimp dinner at **Menega Cafe,** the best seafood hut on Jimbaran beach.

Days ⑩–⑪: Tanjung Benoa
A half-hour taxi ride away, this fishing village offers great watersports and world-class Balinese cooking schools. For cooking fanatics like myself, I recommend the

Rumah Bali guesthouse, which offers lessons right on its premises. The next day, windsurf, water-ski, or take a catamaran out onto the sea. Relax with a poolside cocktail at **Tao** before enjoying a scrumptious Thai meal at this much-talked-about restaurant.

Days ⑫–⑭: Nusa Dua ✦
End your holiday by winding down beachside or poolside at any number of the resorts in this five-star enclave. If you're seeking a peaceful and quiet alternative to the brand-name resorts, head to the pristine **Balé,** a series of minimalist villas with ocean views. The **Westin Resort Nusa Dua** offers fantastic restaurants and a top-notch spa.

3 Planning Your Trip to Bali

VISITOR INFORMATION
The Bali Department of Tourism operates visitor information centers at a number of locations: at **Ngurah Rai International Airport** (© 361/751011); in **Ubud** at the crossroad of Monkey Forest Road and Jalan Raya Ubud; in **Kuta** at Jalan Benasari 36B, Legian (© 361/754090); in **Denpasar** at Jalan Parman Niti Mandala (© 362/222387); and in **Singaraja** at Jalan Veteran 23 (© 361/225141). Better still is the efficient **Badung Government Tourist Office** in Kuta, Jalan Raya Kuta 2 (© 361/756176). Or try the **Bali Tourism Board** (© 361/235600; www.bali-tourism-board.com).

Some good online sources include **Bali Paradise Online** (www.bali-paradise.com), **Bali Online** (www.indo.com), and **Bali Guide** (www.baliguide.com). **Bali Echo** (www.baliecho.com) is an informative arts and culture magazine.

There are lots of free pamphlets with listings, information, and maps: *Bali Plus* has general info; *The Beat* (www.beatmag.com), *What's Up Bali?*, and *Groove* are free guides to nightlife, dining, and activities. *The Yak* is a local glossy focused on nightlife in Seminyak. For information about surfing, check www.indosurf.com.au or pick up a copy of *Indo Surf Guide,* published by the same folks.

ENTRY REQUIREMENTS
Visitors from the U.S., Canada, Australia, New Zealand, and most of Europe can get visas on arrival through Ngurah Rai International Airport or the seaports of Padang Bai and Benoa. For stays of 7 days or less, the charge is US$10 (£5.50); for stays of up to 30 days, the charge is US$25 (£14). For stays of longer than 30 days, a tourist or business visa must be arranged *before* coming to Indonesia.

CUSTOMS REGULATIONS
Customs allows you to bring in, duty free, 200 cigarettes or 50 cigars or 100 grams of tobacco; cameras and film; 2 liters of alcohol; and perfume clearly intended for personal use. Forbidden are guns, weapons, narcotics, pornography (leave it at home if

you're unsure how it's defined), and printed matter with Chinese characters. Plants and fresh fruit might also be confiscated. The export of tortoise shell, crocodile skin, and ivory is prohibited.

MONEY

The currency of Indonesia is the **rupiah,** from the Sanskrit word for wrought silver, *rupya.* Coins come in denominations of Rp25, 50, 100, and 500. Notes are Rp100, 500, 1,000, 5,000, 10,000, 20,000, 50,000, and 100,000; the largest denomination is worth only about US$11 (£6.05). The rate of exchange is relatively stable. At press time, it was about **9,000 Indonesian rupiahs = US$1.**

ATMs In Bali, ATMs are common in all major tourist areas and trade at good rates.

CURRENCY EXCHANGE Most major hotels will change currency, but offer less than favorable rates. Storefront exchange services line most streets and offer the best rates, but it's important to be careful of scams such as counterfeit bills and damaged currency that won't be accepted anywhere. Ask first about commission, and be sure to count your bills before walking away. State-sponsored **Wartel Telecommunications Service** offices are the best bet.

CREDIT CARDS Credit cards are accepted at Bali's higher-end restaurants and hotels. For transactions elsewhere, be prepared to use cash. To report a lost or stolen credit card, you can call **American Express** (counter at the Grand Bali Beach Hotel) at © **361/283970,** or **MasterCard** and **Visa** at © **361/759010.**

WHEN TO GO

The high seasons are July and August and the weeks surrounding Christmas and New Year's, when prices are higher and tourist traffic is considerably increased. Try to avoid these times as well as February and March (given the heat and humidity).

CLIMATE Bali is just below the equator—so days are a consistent 12 hours long—and the temperatures always hover in the 80s Fahrenheit (upper 20s to low 30s Celsius). The rainy season lasts from October to April; rain usually comes in short, violent bursts that last an hour or so, and the humidity is at its crushing worst during this period. The hottest months are February, March, and April. Remember that it gets a bit nippy at night up in the mountains, but a light sweater will certainly be enough.

PUBLIC HOLIDAYS & EVENTS Public holidays and events include **New Year's Day** (Jan 1), **Idul Fitri** (celebration of the end of Ramadan, in late Feb), **Nyepi** (a major purification ritual and a time when Balinese are supposed to sit at home, silent, in late Mar), **Good Friday and Easter Sunday** (late Mar/early Apr), **Muslim New Year** (mid-May), **Indonesia Independence Day** (Aug 17), **Ascension Day of Mohammed** (early Dec), and **Christmas** (Dec 25).

HEALTH & SAFETY

HEALTH CONCERNS See chapter 3's "Health & Safety" section (p. 43) for information on health concerns, vaccinations, and general issues that affect the region. No inoculations are required for Bali, but it's always a good idea to get shots for hepatitis A, tetanus, polio, and typhoid (likely you've already had some of these). It's also a good idea to check the most recent information at the **Centers for Disease Control** (click "Travelers' Health" at **www.cdc.gov**).

The CDC has declared Bali malaria-free, though it is not uncommon on other islands in the Indonesian archipelago. Of concern, though, are the many stray dogs on Bali and therefore rabies, so beware of strays.

You can't drink the water on Bali, but bottled water is cheap and readily available. Just about every hotel will supply you with a couple bottles or a jug of boiled water—to be extra cautious, use it to brush your teeth as well. Restaurants in tourist areas supply safe water and ice, but to be sure, ask for *air minum* (bottled drinking water) and no ice. Avoid "Bali belly" (the Indonesian version of Montezuma's Revenge) by sticking to foods that have been peeled or cooked.

SAFETY CONCERNS   To alleviate any terrorism concerns you may have, consider visiting Bali's more remote destinations, asking hotels what security measures are in place, and staying alert when visiting crowded areas. It is recommended that you check with your home country's overseas travel bureau or with the **U.S. State Department** (click "Travel Warnings" at **www.travel.state.gov**) to keep abreast of travel advisories and current affairs that could affect your trip.

GETTING THERE

BY PLANE   **Ngurah Rai International Airport** (✆ **361/751011**) is 13km (8 miles) southwest of Denpasar. For airport information and connection to airline reservations counters, call ✆ **361/751011**, ext. 1454. When you leave Bali, there will be an airport departure tax of Rp100,000 (US$5.50/£6.10).

Most visitors from the U.S. and Canada fly here via connection in Taipei on **China Airlines** or **EVA Air,** Bangkok on **Thai Airways,** Jakarta on **Garuda Indonesia,** Singapore on **Singapore Airlines,** Tokyo on **Japan Airlines,** or Seoul on **Korean Air.** Check with travel agents for deals and package rates, some with affordable overnight connections via Bangkok. Bali is served from Europe by **Cathay Pacific** via Hong Kong; tickets can be purchased from **British Airways, Singapore Airlines,** or **Air France.** Flights from Australia and New Zealand can be booked through **Qantas** and **Australian Airlines.**

Few travelers stop in the city, but connect directly with their resort area of choice. To get to your destination from the airport, it is a good idea to prearrange pickup through your hotel (the rate is comparable to the official rates at the airport); otherwise, you can buy a ticket at the official taxi counter just outside Customs and arrange a fixed-rate ride to your hotel. Avoid the temptation to go with unofficial cabs; you might get caught in a taxi scam that will leave you frustrated, overcharged, or in the wrong place.

GETTING AROUND

BY PRIVATE CAR   Given how cheap and easy it is to hire someone to drive, many folks just avoid the headache of driving themselves. **Private taxis** are the most common choice of transport and can get you to any destination for a reasonable price. A driver and car should be around US$30 (£17), plus gas charges, for an 8-hour day. A reputable agency is **Amertha Dana** (✆ **361/735406**), which can arrange transport in most of southern Bali. Otherwise, guys offering "transport" and pantomime-steering a car will be at your heels wherever you go and, depending on your luck, can be pretty helpful. Be specific about destination and price (and check for seat belts) before setting out.

Note that, if you do drive yourself, you will need an international driver's license or a locally issued tourist driving license; 1-month licenses are issued on the spot for Rp150,000 (US$17/£9.15) at the **Foreign License Service** (Jalan Agung Tresna 14,

---

Tips A Note on Addresses

Street addresses in Bali can be as vague as "on the main street." In some areas, that's all that passes for an address. Don't worry—most are easy to find.

Renon, Denpassar; ☎ **361/243939**). Traffic is on the left side, and "third-world rules" apply: The more aggressively honking, larger vehicle goes first. Traffic police are just bribe collectors.

BY PUBLIC TRANSPORTATION   Blue and brown vans called *bemos* operate as buses in Bali. They have regular routes, but these aren't really written down. Most tourists save the headaches and go for private transport. *Bemos* are better for short hops (around town, for example) than long distances. **Metered taxis,** if you can find them, are your best bet. Be sure that the driver turns on his meter (you might have to insist more than once). One other option is to ask at your hotel or a travel agent about the **tourist shuttles** that connect the main destinations on the island.

BY MOTORBIKE   Riding a motorbike on Bali is a dangerous proposition; on even the briefest visit to the island, you will see your share of crashes. Renting a scooter or motorbike, however, is a cheap (from US$3/£1.65 per day) and fun way to see the island. Keep in mind that riding is safer and more beautiful in remote areas. The same driver's license requirements for cars apply to motorbikes and scooters.

BY BOAT   Several companies offer diving and snorkeling day trips, sunset or dinner cruises, and connection to the nearby islands of Nusa Penida and Nusa Lembongan. Both **Bounty Cruises** (☎ **361/726666;** www.balibountycruises.com) and **Bali Hai Cruises** (☎ **361/720331;** www.balihaicruises.com) run regular high-end tours from Bali's Benoa Harbor. **Sail Sensations** (☎ **361/725864;** www.bali-sailsensations.com) offers day and overnight sails. The *Wakalouka* (☎ **361/484085**), a luxury catamaran, transports you in style to its exclusive property on Nusa Lembongan.

TIPS ON ACCOMMODATIONS

Bali accommodations range from bungalows that cost Rp40,000 (US$4.40/£2.45) to luxury villas serviced by a retinue of servants and priced at over US$1,000 (£550). In between are an ever-increasing number of lodging options. Atmosphere is the rule here, and those who forgo Western chain-hotel comfort to stay in a *losmen* (traditional homestay, a bastardization of the Dutch word *logement*) or find their own rustic bungalow (more or less "roughing it") often come away from Bali with fond memories of local hospitality and the tranquillity of the island. That said, Bali's resorts and fine Western hotels cost a fraction of what luxury accommodations would elsewhere, and many come to enjoy the upgrade.

Promotional and Internet rates are available at all hotels in Bali. Paying the rack rates, or published rates (which are listed in this guide), even in high season, is almost unheard of. Especially in the off season, it pays to shop around; you can show up at the front desk of even the largest hotels and ask for the best rate.

Almost all hotels charge a 21% government tax and service charge on top of the quoted rates. Some hotels tack on a charge in high season—the 2 or 3 weeks around Christmas and New Year's, plus the months of July and August.

TIPS ON DINING

The choices in Bali are many, but it's rare to find authentic Balinese or Indonesian food on a menu for foreigners; for that, you'll have to go to a *warung,* a local cafe, and many visitors are dissuaded by the typical *warung's* appearance (some are pretty grungy). If you're not put off by a bit of grime, a la an old greasy spoon in the U.S., the food at *warungs* is authentic, delicious, and cheap. Most visitors, however, surrender to the call of high-quality international dining options, which are affordable and varied, with great options for vegetarians.

Indonesian dishes that you are most likely to encounter include *nasi goreng* (fried rice, usually topped with an egg), *mie goreng* (fried noodles), *nasi campur* (a plate of boiled rice with sides of meat and veggies and a house specialty), *ayam goreng* (fried chicken), *gado gado* (salad with peanut sauce, served hot or cold), and satay (small chunks of meat on skewers served with peanut sauce). *Padang* food (sold in little cafes called *rumah makan*) is spicy tidbits of fried fish, chicken, or veggies on a buffet; you pick what you want. A truly authentic Balinese dish found in roadside cafes is *babi guling,* delicious roast suckling pork prepared with spices over a spit. Just look for the ubiquitous signs with a picture of a pig. A good website with details on Bali dining can be found at www.balieats.com.

TIPS ON SHOPPING

The quantity of Balinese arts and crafts available on the island is overwhelming. Woodcarvers, jewelers, and craftspeople of all types line the streets around all tourist areas, particularly in and around Ubud and on the streets of Kuta. There's something

---

Tips Telephone Dialing at a Glance

- **To place a call from your home country to Bali:** Dial the international access code (011 in the U.S. and Canada, 0011 in Australia, 0170 in New Zealand, 00 in the U.K.), plus Indonesia's country code (**62**), the city or local area code (**361** for Kuta, Jimbaran, Nusa Dua, Sanur, and Ubud; **362** for Lovina; **363** for Candi Dasa; **370** for Lombok), and the six-digit phone number (for example, 011 62 362 000000).
- **To place a call within Indonesia:** You must use the area code if calling between states. For calls within the country, area codes are all preceded by a **0** (e.g., 0361 for Ubud, 0362 for Lovina, 0363 for Candi Dasa, 0370 for Lombok, and so on). Dial the city or area code preceded by a **0**, and then the local number (for example, 0362 000000).
- **To place a direct international call from Indonesia:** Dial the international access code (**00**), plus the country code, the area or city code, and the number (for example, to call the U.S., you'd dial 00 1 000/000-0000).
- **To reach the international operator:** Dial 102.
- **International country codes are as follows:** Australia, 61; Cambodia, 855; Canada, 1; Hong Kong, 852; Laos, 856; Malaysia, 60; Myanmar, 95; New Zealand, 64; the Philippines, 63; Singapore, 65; Thailand, 66; U.K., 44; U.S., 1; Vietnam, 84.

for all budgets, from tourist trinkets to fine art and antiques. It's a shopper's paradise of fabrics, clothing, wood and stone carvings, paintings, and doodads of varying quality. Generally, you get what you pay for—but with a bit of haggling, you can get a lot more for what you pay. Shop around; the same item gets cheaper the more you look at it, and it's really the same stuff everywhere. Ask the price, offer half, smile, and go from there. Even at inflated prices, you'll still come out ahead of the game.

FAST FACTS: Bali

American Express There is an American Express branch in the Grand Bali Beach Hotel, in Sanur (© 361/283970).

Business Hours Most places keep "daylight hours," which on the equator pretty much means 6am to 6pm (or a little later).

Drug Laws Though you might be offered hash and marijuana at every turn, Indonesia officially takes drug offenses very seriously. Busts are regular and jail terms stiff.

Electricity Currents can be either 110 volts (50 AC) or 220 to 240 volts (50 AC).

Embassies & Consulates **U.S.:** Jalan Hayam Wuruk 188, Denpasar (© 361/233605). **Great Britain:** Jalan Mertisari 2, Sanur (© 361/270601). **Australia:** Jalan Prof. Moch, Yamin 51, Denpasar (© 361/241118). The Australian consulate also assists nationals of Canada and New Zealand.

Emergencies Bali has a new emergency response center that coordinates all governmental bureaus and services: Just dial © **112**. Otherwise, you can call © **110** for the police, © **118** for an ambulance, © **113** in case of fire, and © **111/ 115/151** for search and rescue.

Hospitals If you need a doctor or dentist, ask your hotel for a referral—many have one on call. In Kuta, try the **Bali International Medical Centre,** Jalan Bypass Ngurah Rai 100X (© 361/761263); it's open daily from 8am to midnight and sometimes will send someone to your hotel. Another option in Kuta is the **International SOS Bali,** Jalan Bypass Ngurah Rai (© 361/710505). There is a city hospital in Denpasar, but for any serious ailment, you should evacuate to Hong Kong, Singapore, Kuala Lumpur, or Bangkok.

Internet Access Internet cafes, some with wireless laptop access, are springing up all over Bali. Expect to pay about US$1.50 (£0.80) per hr.

Language The Balinese speak both Indonesian and Balinese—the former when out in public, the latter at home. English is widely spoken throughout Bali, particularly in the major tourist areas. While not everyone is fluent, most of the people you will be dealing with will speak enough English that you can communicate with them. See "Language," p. 609, for more information.

Liquor Laws You won't find liquor in *halal* restaurants catering to Muslims, but there are no restrictions elsewhere. The legal drinking age is 17, but the police rarely enforce this law.

Mail Your hotel can send mail for you, or you can go to the post office in Denpasar, at Jalan Raya Puputan Renon (© 361/223566). Other branches are in Kuta (Jalan Raya Kuta; © 361/754012), Ubud, and Sanur. For big items, there are packing and shipping services in all major tourist areas, but the cost can be exorbitant.

Police Dial ✆ **110** for the police.

Safety Bali is by and large a safe place, even after dark. Violent crime is rare. However, pickpockets are not, so you should exercise considerable caution by using a money belt, particularly in crowded tourist areas, and being careful not to flash large wads of cash. If you need assistance, contact the **Guardian Angels Tourist Police** (✆ **361/763753**), available 24 hours a day.

Many hotels offer safety deposit boxes, the best place to keep your extra cash and other valuables. If nothing else, make sure your suitcase has a good lock on it. Even the best hotel can't always guarantee security for valuables left lying in plain sight.

Telephones The international country code for Indonesia is **62**. Because many hotels charge a great deal even for using your calling card, you're better off using the Wartel network of privately owned pay phones. There's one in every tourist center, though some work better than others. Some also have Internet access. See "Telephone Dialing at a Glance," p. 614, for details.

Time Zone Bali is 8 hours ahead of Greenwich Mean Time, except during daylight saving time, which it does not observe. That's 13 hours ahead of Eastern Standard Time in the U.S.

Tipping Tipping is not required and not even encouraged. Most restaurants include a service charge. Leave a small tip if you feel the need; more often than not, the recipient will be surprised.

Toilets Western-style toilets with seats are becoming more common than the Asian squat variety, though cheap *losmen* (homestays) and some less touristy public places still have the latter. Always carry toilet paper with you, or you might have to use your hand (the left one only, please) and the dip bucket.

Water Avoid tap water in Bali unless properly boiled. Bottled water is available everywhere, and restaurants in tourist areas seem to use it as a matter of course, but you should always ask to be sure.

4 Kuta

A quick 10 minutes from the airport and you'll be in Kuta, Bali's most developed area, a popular spot for budget travelers and a longtime favorite for weekend vacationers from nearby Australia. It's also where Abu Sayef chose to attack the island on the night of October 12, 2002, and, though it is again brimming with tourists, memories of that day are still fresh. At press time, a temple and small monument to commemorate the day were under construction.

Kuta is made up of narrow streets and alleys, and pedestrians share space with honking, mufflerless cars and motorbikes. You'll be harried by some of the most aggressive touts on the island, and the beaches are crowded with imploring sellers and masseurs; the tourist rush, however, means some of the best nightlife and dining on the island. Unfortunately, the current makes swimming difficult and dangerous.

The best compromise of all, short of staying elsewhere on the island, is to hit the quiet beaches just north of Kuta at **Legian** and **Semniyak** ⭐.

GETTING THERE

Kuta is near the airport, and most hotels offer free airport pickup. If you're hiring a cab, it's best to go to the airport's official taxi counter, where you'll pay a set fare.

GETTING AROUND

Kuta is a big rectangle. The two main north–south streets are oceanside Jalan Pantai Kuta and Jalan Legian. They're connected east–west by Jalan Benesari, Poppies Gang I, and many quaint alleys. You can easily walk all of this area or take the reasonably priced blue-and-yellow metered taxis.

FAST FACTS: Kuta

Currency Exchange There are a number of ATMs in Kuta. **Wartel** outlets are found all around the main streets.

Internet Access Internet cafes almost outnumber transport guides in Kuta. They charge between Rp10,000 and Rp37,000 (US$1.10–US$4.05/£0.60–£2.25) per hour for reliable connection. For those with a laptop and a wireless card, **ESC Urban Food Station** (JL Legian; ② 361/756362) offers free wireless Internet access 24 hours a day. Many hotel lobbies, like the Legian, also have wireless access for a fee.

Mail There is a main post office on Jalan Raya Tuban, but it's far from the town center. There are also some postal agents around town, or your hotel can send mail for you.

Telephones The area code in Kuta is **361**.

WHERE TO STAY

Kuta Beach, while still a booming resort, is quite noisy and busy. We've listed the better choices in town and at nearby Legian and Seminyak to the north.

KUTA & LEGIAN BEACH
Expensive
Hard Rock Hotel ⭐⭐ You'll be disarmed by this hotel's fun, fanciful design. The lobby is typical Hard Rock Cafe, lined with once-used guitars and gold records, and the decor throughout is bright, with corridors done in varying rock themes. Rooms are light and airy, with photos of artists, and bathrooms are done in playful geometric patterns. The pool is the largest in Bali, with slides and its own beach. You'll also enjoy the outdoor living room, the in-house radio station, and a recording studio where you can live out your own musician fantasies. Sure, rock blares around the clock in the lobby, which has a popular bar, and in other public areas, but the fabulous kids' playroom—"Little Rock"—and that pool make it a great option for boomer families. It's not really Bali, but it is good fun.

Jalan Pantai, Banjar Pande Mas, Kuta, Bali. ② 361/761869. Fax 361/761868. www.hardrockhotels.net. 418 units. US$190–US$220 (£105–£121) double; US$370–US$760 (£204–£418) suite. AE, DC, MC, V. **Amenities:** 3 restaurants; 3 bars; outdoor pool (w/swim-up bar); health club; spa; kids' club; concierge; business center; shopping; salon; 24-hr.

room service; massage; laundry service; dry cleaning; meeting rooms; wireless Internet access; rock library. *In room:* A/C, satellite TV w/on-demand movies, minibar, fridge, safe, IDD phone.

Padma Hotel 🏵

You've got all that you need at the Padma, a self-contained, comfortable compound that's just the right distance from the fray at Kuta for peace and quiet, but close enough to go play and shop. There's something for the whole family here, including a good kids' club, daily activities, a roster of day trips, the fine Mandara Spa, and cultural classes such as egg painting and musical demonstrations. Garden rooms have parquet floors and Balinese furnishings. Standard rooms, in a four-story high-rise, all have balconies and great views. Family rooms open onto a patio and central garden. There is a quiet, tout-free grassy spot between the pool and the beach where the kids can frolic. The beach is not good for swimming, however.

Jalan Padma no. 1, Legian, Bali. ⓒ 361/752111. Fax 361/752140. www.hotelpadma.com. 405 units. US$160 (£88) double; US$180 (£99) chalet; US$220–US$1,500 (£121–£825) suite. AE, DC, MC, V. **Amenities:** 3 restaurants; 3 bars; outdoor pool; tennis court; game area w/Internet and PlayStation; tour desk; car rental; business center; 24-hr. room service; babysitting; laundry service; club-level rooms; meeting rooms. *In room:* A/C, satellite TV, minibar, fridge, safe, IDD phone.

Moderate

Bounty Hotel 🏵🏵

The Bounty is popular with Australian revelers, especially at school-break times. The rooms are decidedly Western, but have traditional wood floors and are decorated with Balinese fabric. The standard rooms are slightly smaller than the deluxe, with the sink in the room. The complex, arranged around an attractive pool, features stone carvings and red-tile ornamentation. The hotel is within easy walking distance of the beach, the best shopping on Legian, and Kuta's many nightspots; the same people own the happening late-night **Bounty Bar & Restaurant.** This is a good choice if you want to be right in the middle of the fray.

Poppies Gang II, Jalan Segara Batu Bolong no. 18, Kuta, Bali. ⓒ 361/753030. Fax 361/752121. www.bounty hotel.com. 166 units. US$93–US$190 (£51–£105) double. AE, DC, MC V. **Amenities:** 2 restaurants; bar; 2 outdoor pools; car rental; 24-hr. room service; laundry service; dry cleaning. *In room:* A/C, cable TV, minibar, fridge, IDD phone.

Poppies Cottages 🏵🏵

This is by far the best midrange hotel in Kuta, with atmospheric thatched cottages set among gorgeous gardens abloom with a riot of bougainvillea. Located at the town center, the property has a small central pool designed to look like a natural pond, surrounded by lush garden nooks perfect for lounging. The rooms are a bit compact for the price, but the open-air bathrooms are done in marble, complete with sunken tubs, and everything is very clean and cozy.

Poppies Lane I, Kuta, Bali. ⓒ 361/751059. Fax 361/752364. www.poppiesbali.com. 20 units. US$85 (£47) double (seasonal rates available). AE, DC, MC, V. **Amenities:** Restaurant; bar; outdoor pool; business center w/Internet access; shopping; room service; laundry service. *In room:* A/C, TV, IDD phone.

Inexpensive

There are lots of budget options in busy Kuta. Small guesthouses crowd the back streets near the beach. You can try **Komala Indah I,** Jalan Benesari (ⓒ **361/735185**); or **Mimpi Bungalows,** Gang Sorga (ⓒ **361/751848**).

SEMINYAK
Very Expensive

Legian 🏵🏵🏵

A thousand square feet in size and impeccably decorated by well-known interior designer Jaya Ibrahim, the rooms here are some of the best in Bali. The layout is open and airy, and features like fantastic lighting, two iPods loaded with music (which you're free to take to the beach or pool), a Bose stereo system, and a cordless phone give it the feel of a luxe home rather than a hotel room. Balconies, some directly facing the ocean, offer a great place to chill out, as does the simple rectangular pool that abuts the beach. Across the street at the **Club,** you sacrifice the ocean views but get the privacy of your own contemporary villa. The latest venture is the **Beach House,** a two-story home with panoramic ocean views. It's big enough to host 60-person events. Service is very professional and the location is rivaled only by the Oberoi (below).

Jalan Laksmana, Seminyak, Kuta, Bali. © **361/730622.** Fax 361/730623. www.ghmhotels.com. 79 units. US$380–US$1,200 (£209–£660) suite; US$800–US$1,800 (£440–£990) villa; US$2,000 (£1,100) beach house. AE, DC, MC, V. **Amenities:** Restaurant; 2 bars; 2-tiered pool; watersports facilities; spa; tour desk; shuttle service; shopping; massage; babysitting; laundry service; dry cleaning; meeting rooms. *In room:* A/C, satellite TV w/in-house movies, iPods and speakers, Bose stereo system, Wi-Fi, minibar, fridge, coffeemaker, hair dryer, safe.

Oberoi ★★ The first hotel in Seminyak and one of the leading hotels of the world, the Oberoi has long attracted celebrities, from Henry Kissinger to Julia Roberts. The property is composed of individual *lanais*—native bungalows of coral stone with wood beams and thatch roofs. Rooms are cozy and strike a great balance between high-end comforts and local style. Amenities are first class all the way: raised futon beds, marble bathrooms with sunken tubs facing private gardens, and goodies like slippers, robes, and flip-flops for the beach. Private pool villas are luxurious beyond belief. The beach here is great, with a nice expanse of sand and few touts to harass you. An outdoor amphitheater hosts traditional dance performances. Service is genuinely warm and helpful without fawning, and you can feel at ease here without forgetting that you're in Bali. The fine spa is managed by Banyan Tree.

Jalan Laksmana, Seminyak, Kuta, Bali. © **361/730361.** Fax 361/730791. www.oberoihotels.com. 74 units. US$255–US$700 (£140–£385) garden-view cottage or villa; US$300–US$850 (£165–£468) ocean-view cottage or villa. AE, DC, MC, V. **Amenities:** Restaurant; bar; outdoor pool; tennis court; fitness center; spa; sauna; tour desk; car rental; 24-hr. room service; massage; babysitting; laundry service; dry cleaning. *In room:* A/C, satellite TV w/in-house movies, DVD, minibar, fridge, hair dryer, IDD phone.

Expensive

Sofitel Seminyak Bali ★ Location, location, location. You're right on the beach here and the staff is friendly and helpful, though the place is not particularly luxe. Formerly the Royal Seminyak, the hotel has undergone significant renovations since the Sofitel took over 2 years ago. Beach access, a beachside pool, and a more secluded pool in the garden give guests a range of lounging options. The airy, thatched-roof two-story villas are the main attraction: Done up in a traditional Balinese style, they're both elegant and cozy. Rooms are somewhat dark but modern, with Balinese touches. Unfortunately, the age of the place still shows (for example, the loud central air-conditioning units).

Jalan Abimanyu (Dhyana Pura), Seminyak, Bali. © **361/730730.** Fax 361/730545. www.sofitelbali.com. 145 units. US$220–US$420 (£121–£231) double; US$500–US$700 (£275–£385) villa. AE, MC, V. **Amenities:** 2 restaurants; spa; Jacuzzi; tour desk; limo service; shopping; limited room service. *In room:* A/C, cable TV, minibar, fridge, IDD phone.

Moderate

Puri Cendana Right near the ocean at the end of busy Dhyana Pura Street (Bali's newest nightlife spot), the Puri Cendana offers a good balance of affordability, comfort, and location. The oversize rooms in two-story motel blocks try to fill the space with big canopy beds and sparse furnishings. The bathrooms are stylish, with tubs looking onto private gardens, but the hallways could use some dusting. The pool is small and right near the road, as is the restaurant, but you're just a short walk from the beach at Seminyak in one direction and all of the services and nightlife of Dhyana Pura in the other.

Jalan Abimanyu (Dhyana Pura), Seminyak, Bali. ☎ **361/730869.** Fax 361/730868. http://geocities.com/puricendana. 24 units. US$80–US$100 (£44–£55) double (big discounts available). AE, MC, V. **Amenities:** Restaurant; bar; outdoor pool; tour desk; airport transfer; 24-hr. room service; laundry service; Internet access. *In room:* A/C, TV, fridge, IDD phone.

WHERE TO DINE

The international variety in Kuta is a result of homesick tourists; unfortunately, this translates into mediocre copies of Western fare. There are a couple of standouts, listed below.

KUTA

Kori Restaurant and Bar ☆☆ INTERNATIONAL/STEAKHOUSE   Valet parking in the narrow and chaotic Poppies Gang II? Finery uncharacteristic of Bali abounds at this chic venue. Sit in the dining room, replete with linen and silver, or on one of the more romantic cushioned bamboo platforms that bridge the narrow garden oasis. The lunch menu is light, featuring dishes like *malai köfte,* spicy vegetarian fritters in a curry sauce, or the mouth-burning Bali chile burger (if you dare). The dinner menu has all the bells and whistles of a Western steakhouse. Try the mixed grill of U.S. beef loin, spare ribs, pork cutlet, and Nuerberger sausages; or order the Singapore chile crab, savory and spicy fresh black Bali crabs served with a big ol' bib. At the high end of the menu is the giant seafood grill, cooked and served on a hot lava stone. To finish off your meal, there's a respectable stock of brandy and cognac.

Poppies Gang II, Kuta. ☎ **361/758605.** Main courses Rp30,000–Rp140,000 (US$3.30–US$15/£1.85–£8.55). AE, DC, MC, V. Daily noon–11pm.

Poppies Restaurant ☆☆ INDONESIAN/EUROPEAN   Poppies has a 30-year tradition of serving Indonesian and international specials on the busy beach. It's the place for your Western fix and is certainly the prettiest restaurant in the Kuta area: a garden setting with crawling vines overhead that keep the hot sun at bay, accompanied by babbling pools and waterfalls. Indonesian dishes include an outstanding *ikan pepes*—mashed fish cooked in a banana leaf with fine spices and very spicy local "pickles" (beware). The *mie goreng,* loaded with shrimp and vegetables, is also good. Service is slow, but this is a good place to dawdle.

Poppies Cottages, Poppies Lane I, Kuta. ☎ **361/751059.** www.poppiesbali.com. Reservations recommended. Men must wear shirts. Main courses Rp20,000–Rp50,000 (US$2.20–US$5.50/£1.20–£3.05). AE, MC, V. Daily 8am–11pm.

TJ's Restaurant ☆☆ MEXICAN   Set up more like a typical Asian bistro, TJ's is a real Bali original. Stop in, if only for one of the famous frozen margaritas and to listen to some good tunes in this laid-back, open-air spot. Meals start with homemade corn chips, delicious dips, and an extensive menu of specials. TJ's advertises the "best burgers in town," and though the jury is still out on that one, most everything from the quesadillas to the fish Veracruz is delicious. Order up, kick back, and enjoy the vibe in this popular spot.

Poppies Lane, Kuta. ☎ **361/751093.** Main courses Rp35,000–Rp55,000 (US$3.85–US$6.05/£2.15–£3.35). MC, V. Daily 11am–11pm.

SEMINYAK

This northern stretch of the Kuta Beach area is *the* place for fine dining and hip nightlife. The restaurants listed below are only a few of the many bistros popping up. Check out Jalan Laksmana, called "Eat Street," crammed with a growing number of international cafes and restaurants.

Kafe Warisan 🌶 FRENCH   It's fine international dining in a Balinese setting here in this open courtyard of frangipani trees overlooking green rice paddies. The standards, service, and menu are equally sophisticated, and with so many choices, you might have to come back to try everything. Be sure to order the raw oysters if you're game. Kafe Warisan serves the finest cuts of meat imported from Australia, along with local venison. On the lighter side, try the grilled Tasmanian salmon or rosemary chicken breast. You'll be treated to an extensive wine list and a range of California wines by the glass. Stop by the boutique to peruse the collection of beaded dresses, silk sarongs, jewelry, antique batik, and other collectibles.

Jalan Kerobokan, Seminyak. ℂ 361/731175. Reservations required. Main courses Rp65,000–Rp145,000 (US$7.15–US$16/£3.95–£8.85). AE, MC, V. Mon–Sat 11am–4pm and 7–11pm.

Ku De Ta 🌶🌶 BISTRO   This is Kuta's "Europe meets Asia" international bistro, aimed at an upscale clientele. It's also one of the town's hippest catwalks. The best time to go is at sunset, for the ocean views and lounge-worthy patio. Though the daytime ambience is dominated by the nearby beach, at night it's all about romantic lighting in the restaurant's open-air, minimalist rotunda. Add an elegant bar and a cigar lounge—complete with putting green—and you've got an all-purpose evening out. Happily, what comes out of the kitchen makes you want to stay: Try the signature dish of slow-roasted, yellow-curry duck or the chile-and-sea-salted squid with a mango/papaya marmalade. The cigar lounge is open from 6pm until late. The place roars with the carefree laughter of the ridiculously rich.

Jalan Oberoi 9, Seminyak. ℂ 361/736969. www.kudeta.net. Reservations recommended. Main courses Rp140,000–Rp330,000 (US$15–US$33/£8.55–£20). AE, MC, V. Daily 7am–midnight (bar open later).

La Lucciola 🌶 ITALIAN   If there's a see-and-be-seen spot among the Kuta crowd, it's La Lucciola. Even breakfast draws the beautiful people, and why not, with its prime beachfront location on this deserted stretch of Legian? Morning eye-poppers include tasty ricotta hotcakes and smoked-salmon scrambled eggs on toasted focaccia. The dinner menu is equally enticing, with choice offerings such as lemongrass bokchoy risotto with sesame ginger, or oven-baked snapper with braised shallots and oregano. The seafood specials, calamari, and a unique prawn-and-snapper pie are tops, in addition to a complement of good pasta and traditional Italian fare. End with a bracing espresso and tiramisu.

Oberoi Rd., Kayu Aya Beach, Legian. ℂ 361/730838. Main courses Rp40,000–Rp150,000 (US$4.40–US$16/£2.45–£9.15). AE, MC, V. Daily 8am–midnight.

Made's Warung 🌶🌶 *Finds* INDONESIAN   This is a longtime Bali favorite, and for good reason. The original location is an open-air place at street side in Kuta, but the new space in Seminyak is a big improvement—it's protected from the road and bustling with people, not beeping motorbikes. If it's busy, and it often is, don't be surprised if you end up sharing a table. *Gado gado,* satay, and curries are all recommended, and the price is right. Fun surprises on the menu include a bagel with smoked marlin, tofu burgers, and Caesar salad. Don't pass up the daily specials, particularly the fresh fish. Beverage choices range from iced coffee and juices to some very potent booze concoctions (be warned).

Br. Pando Mas, Kuta (℃ 361/755297), and Jalan Raya Seminyak, Seminyak (℃ 316/732130). Main courses Rp12,000–Rp30,000 (US$1.30–US$3.30/£0.75–£1.85). AE, MC, V. Daily 8am–midnight.

Ryoshi ⭑ JAPANESE   At Ryoshi, every day is special, the prices are reasonable for sushi, and there's all kinds of other Japanese fare that's done just right (just ask the many Japanese guests). Be sure to try the butterfish, a deepwater whitefish with a rich texture and savory flavor—not to be missed. There are locations all over the island, but the Seminyak outlet is by far the best (with the busy shop in Kuta a close second).

Jalan Raya Seminyak 17, Seminyak (℃ 361/731152); Jalan Melasti 42A, Kuta (℃ 361/750504); plus additional locations in Sanur, Ubud, and even on tiny Gili Trawangan island near Lombok. Main courses from Rp35,000 (US$3.85/£2.15); a la carte sushi dishes from Rp10,000 (US$1.10/£0.60). MC, V. Daily 11:30am–11:30pm.

OUTDOOR ACTIVITIES

Surfers from all over are drawn to Kuta's stupendous breakers, which are at their best between March and July. Surf shops line the main drags and can help with rentals or tide information. Any hotel can arrange a private or group lesson, or you can contact **Rip Curl School of Surf** (℃ 361/735858; www.ripcurlschoolofsurf.com). Beginners start off at Kuta or Legian (with soft-sand beaches), but the legendary surf is at the low reef breaks and "barrels" of **Kuta Reef** at the southern end.

Unfortunately, the same surf makes recreational swimming virtually impossible. Even past the breakers, the current can be too strong. Pay close attention to swimming warnings and restrictions, and be very careful if you do swim. Tanning and splashing to cool off are about all that are left to do.

You can book adventure tours to destinations across the island using Kuta as a hub. For day trips to Ubud, the volcanoes, or the temples of central Bali, contact **Sobek Tours** (℃ 361/287059) or **Bali Adventure Tours** (℃ 361/721480; www.baliadventure tours.com). One smaller operator, **Matangi Tours** (℃ 361/739820; www.traditional balitours.com), has unique cultural and adventure trips all across the island starting at US$76 (£42) per day.

If money is no obstacle, take a ride on a helicopter to remote stretches of the island and pass over volcanoes and jungle scenery. Contact **Air Bali** (℃ 361/767466; www. airbali.com) for details.

And if the kids aren't getting enough of a kick out of the busy beach at Kuta, take 'em to the **Waterbom Park,** in the south end of Kuta on Jalan Kartika Plaza (℃ 361/755676; www.waterbom.com).

SHOPPING

Shopping in Kuta is inevitable. Even if you aren't interested in buying anything, the touts are quick to steer you none-too-subtly to their merchandise (usually by waving it in your face). The streets (particularly **Poppies Gang II**) are lined with stalls offering tie-dyed sarongs, shorts, swimsuits, knock-off brand-name cologne, hats, and wristwatches. Given the hard sell, this might be the best place to hone your bargaining skills.

Kuta Square is the place to go for Western-style shopping—it might be called "Brand-Name Row," with Nike, Polo, and Armani all represented, plus fast-food outlets such as McDonald's and KFC. The **Galleria Bali** (℃ 361/761945; www.dfsgalleria. com)—a new luxury shopping mall with duty-free goods by Chanel, Coach, and other big brands—offers shuttles from many hotels.

Spa Treatments

There are some fine spas in the area, and most large hotels and resorts offer at least basic spa services—try the **Spa at the Legian** (p. 618). For a bikini wax (which is hard to come by in Bali, strangely enough), head to **Glo** (Jalan Kunti; ✆ 361/766762) or the **Westin Spa** at the Westin Resort Nusa Dua (p. 627).

Surfer Girl, on Jalan Legian (✆ 361/752693), has a good collection of women's swimwear and active clothing, while a co-ed selection can be found at **Jungle Surf,** also on Jalan Legian (✆ 361/756644; www.junglesurfworld.com).

For books, stop by **Periplus,** with locations in Kuta Square (✆ 361/763988), in Seminyak near Made's Warung (✆ 361/734843), and even at the airport.

KUTA & SEMINYAK AFTER DARK

Kuta is party central, going full-on from 11pm until dawn every night. Clubs and bars abound, each with its own flavor, though they're mostly "same-same but different." Thankfully, it is all pretty family-friendly and not the go-go bar scene you'd find in parts of Thailand and other Southeast Asian destinations.

For the club crowd, the hottest spot at the moment is **Hu'u Bar** ⚔, Jalan Dhyana Pura, Seminyak (✆ 361/736443; www.huubali.com), a beachside bar and nightclub that hosts international DJs. Other contenders, all located nearby, include the **Living Room** (✆ 361/735735), **Bacio,** and Bacio's next-door neighbor, **Double Six** (✆ 361/ 731266). A good late-night spot is **Paparazzi** (✆ 361/731155), which only gets going around 2am. The much-hyped bistro and bar **Ku De Ta** ⚔ (p. 621) still remains popular, particularly for cocktails at sunset.

For clubbing in Kuta, try **Bounty,** on Jalan Legian (✆ 361/752529), which is built to look like a galleon and has a lively dance floor and bar often playing R&B and hip-hop. Watch out for drunk Australians. **Kama Sutra** (✆ 361/761999), chock-full of local teenagers, is a busy club on the north end of Kuta; it has nightly shows and features local bands. The **Hard Rock Hotel's Centerstage** (✆ 361/755661) sometimes has good live acts, though it's known to be crowded with tourists.

SIDE TRIPS FROM KUTA

Uluwatu ⚔⚔ is a spectacular pinnacle of land at the far south of Bali. A visit at dusk reveals a sunset panorama framed by frolicking monkeys. At the right times of year, it has some of the best surfing in the world. Arrange trips to Uluwatu, Tanah Lot (below), or sights listed later in this chapter under "Side Trips from Ubud" (p. 640) by contacting any hotel concierge or tour desk. Daily car rental (with driver) starts as low as US$20 (£11).

Tanah Lot   Founded by a Brahmin priest in the 16th century, the temple at Tanah Lot is notable less for its construction than for its spectacular setting, high on craggy bluffs overlooking the Java Sea. This is a truly magnificent example of how well temples in Bali are wedded to their locations, be they lakeside, mountainside, or seaside. Legend has it that a Brahmin priest had a rivalry with the local, established priest which nearly led to his expulsion from the order; instead, he meditated so hard he pushed Tanah Lot "out to sea," where it rests on an inlet that actually becomes an island at high tide. The walk from the parking lot is not as long or as steep as at many other sites, and there are no stairs. Non-Hindus cannot enter the temple, but may access the other parts of the complex strung out across the rocks. Many of these afford stunning views. Try to come at sunset, when Tanah Lot is truly glorious. *Tip:* Skip the touristy snake cave.

15km (9¼ miles) west of Denpasar. Admission Rp3,000 (US30¢/£0.20). Open during daylight hours.

5 Jimbaran Bay ★★

Jimbaran has some of the best sandy beaches in South Bali, and the clear, calm water is great for swimming. Developers were quick to realize this; thus Jimbaran now hosts some of the finest high-end resorts on the island. Despite development, the town still looks like a fishing village, with small mom-and-pop seafood shacks serving up some of the best fish dishes on the island. It's a worthy day trip from Kuta for good eats alone, and the many resorts make it a comfy place to stay.

GETTING THERE
Jimbaran is on the road to Nusa Dua, south of Kuta. Cabs are plentiful.

WHERE TO STAY
Four Seasons Resort at Jimbaran Bay ★★★ The very picture of luxury, the exquisitely landscaped grounds of the Four Seasons are on a stunning hillside overlooking the bay. The layout is meant to suggest a series of Balinese villages, each thatched villa consisting of a large bedroom, generous dressing area, and marble bathroom with oversize tub. The little things stand out: thick towels and fancy bath amenities, two sinks, cool garden showers, a library with books for borrowing and Internet access, and snap-to service everywhere you look. There are even top spa services and a cooking school. The resort's horizon pool blends seamlessly with the ocean blue, and there are other small pools and lots of private corners where you can relax and escape from it all. Walk or be driven in a golf cart down to the beach, passing *bales* (open-air pavilions) and viewing spots along the way. The luxe beach club has all the same amenities as the pool, plus plenty of watersports activities like surfing, kayaking, and sailing on catamarans. Though the other Four Seasons Bali property, at Sayan, is equally luxurious, I prefer Jimbaran for its romantic vibe, convenient location, and superb service.

Jimbaran, Bali. © **361/701010.** Fax 361/701020. www.fourseasons.com. 147 units. US$585–US$695 (£322–£382) 1-bedroom villa; US$1,500–US$3,500 (£825–£1925) 2-bedroom villa and Royal Villa. AE, DC, MC, V. **Amenities:** 3 restaurants; 2 bars; 2 outdoor pools; tennis courts; health club; spa; Jacuzzi; sauna; watersports equipment rental; concierge; tour desk; car rental; business center w/Internet access; shopping; 24-hr. room service; massage; babysitting; laundry service. *In room:* A/C, satellite TV, DVD, stereo with CD player, Wi-Fi, minibar, fridge, safe, IDD phone.

Jimbaran Puri Bali ★★ The pioneer resort on Jimbaran beach, the Puri Bali, originally the Pansea, has stylish, self-contained garden cottages scattered among lily ponds, coconut trees, and Balinese statuary, set back from the beach. All cottages have terraces, shaded by umbrellas, with privacy-providing screens and outdoor deck showers. Rooms are done in carved teak under thatched roofing, with mosquito netting and natural linen touches. Bathrooms have sunken tubs and all the goodies. The resort is a haven of privacy and calm, a good choice for getting away from it all.

Jalan Uluwatu, Jimbaran, Bali. © **361/701605.** Fax 361/701320. www.pansea.com. 41 cottages. US$190–US$290 (£105–£160) cottage. AE, MC, V. **Amenities:** 2 restaurants; bar; outdoor pool; tour desk; business center w/Internet access; shopping; 24-hr room service; massage; babysitting; laundry service. *In room:* A/C, satellite TV, DVD player, minibar, fridge, hair dryer, safe, IDD phone.

Ritz-Carlton Bali ★★ *Value* *Kids*   Built on a sloping hill on a cliff's edge, the Ritz boasts absolutely breathtaking ocean views that immediately greet you upon arrival in the open-air lobby. The newly built ocean pool, located at the bottom of the resort down a winding flight of stairs, is one of the best in Bali—it sits right above the crashing waves at Jimbaran. The hotel is certainly not cheap, but its unique ocean views, spectacular service, and public amenities make it a good value. Rooms are comfy, with four-poster beds, marble floors, and elegant neoclassical touches. The private villas, with their own plunge pool, outdoor and indoor day beds, and ocean views, are simply stunning. The spa, designed with pavilions and running streams of water, is also one of the best in Bali. It's worth a stop even if you aren't staying here—visit the Aquatonic therapy pool (with currents and jets to give you a workout and massage) at sunset for a particularly romantic experience.

Jalan Karang Mas Sejahtera, Jimbaran, Bali. (C) **361/702222.** Fax 361/701555. www.ritzcarlton.com. 274 units. US$305–US$465 (£168–£256) double; US$440–US$550 (£242–£303) suite; US$685–US$2,640 (£377–£1452) villa. AE, DC, MC, V. **Amenities:** 5 restaurants; 2 bars; 5 pools (including separate children's pool and water slide); golf putting course; 3 tennis courts; billiards (outdoors); table tennis (outdoors); fitness center; spa; seawater therapy pool; business center w/Internet access; shopping; 24-hr room service; massage; wedding chapel; library; executive-level rooms. *In room:* A/C, satellite TV, dataport, minibar, fridge, safe.

WHERE TO DINE

Dining at Jimbaran's fine resorts is a good, safe option: Try **PJ's** at the Four Seasons for a beachside Sunday brunch or the Ritz-Carlton's **Dava** for a sexy dinner with a fantastic ocean view. But remember, folks come from far and wide for the good, fresh seafood barbecue, priced by the pound, served at beachside. Look for **Menega Cafe** ((C) **361/705888;** www.menega.com/cafe.html), which stands out for its more unique grilling approach among the row of restaurants that basically offer the same thing. Lobster and snapper are served with dipping sauces, rice, cucumber salad, and spinach cooked in sweet chile. Follow it up with some fresh fruit. It's romantic at sunset and afterwards by candlelight—and it's inexpensive, too.

6 Nusa Dua ★

In the 1970s, a French firm, commissioned by the Indonesian government, came up with the idea for a self-contained resort complex to "minimize the impact of tourism on the Balinese culture." It chose this 300-hectare (741-acre) tract of undeveloped land, devoid of any infrastructure, and basically transformed it into a theme park. Nusa Dua is now a roster of five-star, all-inclusive properties, all secluded and finely manicured. The beaches are clean and blissfully tout-free, but it can all seem a bit sterile. Still, it's suitable for families and business conventions.

GETTING THERE

Most hotels in Nusa Dua offer airport pickup, but you can find shuttles and cheap taxis at the airport and in Kuta. (Be sure to take only the official blue-and-yellow metered taxis in Kuta.) *Bemos* from Denpasar go to Nusa Dua by way of Kuta and Jimbaran.

GETTING AROUND

These big resorts make it so comfortable, you won't have to leave the grounds—but even the most starry-eyed honeymooners might want a break from expensive hotel meals. Most hotel taxis are rentable at an exorbitant US$11 (£6.05) per hour; it's smarter to hire a car and driver for a day from a private company such as **Amertha Dana** (*©* **361/735406**). A new swanky mall in Nusa Dua, the **Bali Collection** (*©* **361/ 771662;** www.bali-collection.com), has an hourly shuttle that makes the rounds to most of the hotels.

WHERE TO STAY
NUSA DUA

Nusa Dua is like a Disneyland of high-end hotels and resorts. Most of the properties have their own private beaches and many offer babysitting (some include it in the price of the room), making it a good option for families (unless otherwise noted). A good share of honeymooners come here as well. The atmosphere is a bit sterile, but you'll at least avoid the touts and tacky tourists in places like Kuta.

Very Expensive

Amanusa ★★★ It doesn't get any better than this. Typical of the refined Aman resorts in Ubud and Candi (among others), the Amanusa boasts a magnificent setting, on a high hilltop overlooking a golf course and the beaches of Nusa Dua beyond. It comes with quite a price tag, but a visit to Amanusa is an invitation to service that is gracious and intuitive, and to accommodations that are over-the-top luxurious while remaining in harmony with the surroundings. Rooms are crafted in rich redwood with four-poster beds, sunken tubs, and outdoor and indoor showers. Each suite has a small *bale,* or covered sitting area, with a stylish daybed for lounging. Cozy nooks, like the library, abound; the central 24m (79-ft.) pool is stunning; and in-house dining at the Terrace is an experience in itself, with great views and delicious local cuisine. The beach club is just a short drive down the hill; it's a collection of private *bales* that front the Bali Golf and Country Club property. The staff can arrange just about anything for you, from local cycling excursions to island cruises to cooking classes, shopping, and adventure tours.

Nusa Dua, Bali. *©* **361/772333.** Fax 361/772335. www.amanresorts.com. 35 units. US$650–US$800 (£358–£440) suite; US$1,000–US$1,300 (£550–£715) pool suite. AE, MC, V. **Amenities:** 2 restaurants; bar; outdoor pool; beach club; golf course; 2 tennis courts; watersports equipment rental; bike rental; concierge; tour desk; courtesy car; business center; boutiques; 24-hr. room service; in-room massage; babysitting; laundry service; dry cleaning; nonsmoking rooms; library w/Internet access. *In room:* A/C, TV w/DVD and stereo, minibar, fridge, safe, IDD phone.

Expensive

Ayodya Resort Bali *Kids* One of your initial thoughts might be, "Where's the ride?" This massive hotel looks like a Disneyfied fortress, complete with ornate Balinese gates and a central stage area for daily cultural performances. There is no ride, but there is free babysitting at the kids' camp, where your children will be occupied with Balinese dress-up costumes, a huge playground, and video games. Meanwhile, you can relax on the resort's private beach. When the management changed from the Hilton to a local company in 2006, a conscious effort was made to provide guests with a Balinese cultural experience, from the folk art in the rooms to music and dance performances. More effort has been directed to the common rooms than the guest rooms, which are decent but nothing special.

P.O. Box 46, Nusa Dua, Bali. *©* **361/771102.** Fax 361/771616. www.ayodyaresortbali.com. 535 units. US$220– US$365 (£121–£201) double; US$435–US$1,480 (£239–£814) suite. AE, DC, MC, V. **Amenities:** 5 restaurants; 3 bars; 3 outdoor pools; nearby golf; miniature golf; 2 tennis courts; fitness center; spa; watersports equipment rental; tour desk; business center; shopping; salon; 24-hr. room service; massage; laundry service; clinic. *In room:* A/C, satellite TV, minibar, fridge, safe, IDD phone.

Balé 🐦🐦 Balé means "bungalow" in Balinese, but the moniker is rather modest—this is an absolutely beautiful collection of villas set on a hill overlooking the ocean. After being ushered into a high-ceilinged, open-air lobby, you'll climb a set of steps that lead to the villas, all of which are walled off for privacy. Each has its own plunge pool and a daybed in the courtyard for lounging. The interiors are elegantly simple, with large bathrooms and outdoor showers. Rivers of water flow around the property; the scent of the tropical flower alang-alang wafts throughout. While not set right on the beach, the Balé has a shuttle that whisks you to the water in 2 minutes. The resort is popular with yuppies and a fair number of gay couples as well. For adults seeking peace, an added bonus is that no children under 15 are allowed.

If the private-villa-no-children-allowed concept appeals to you but the Balé seems too expensive, try the slightly cheaper **Kayumanis** (✆ 361/770777), a new property nearby that features 20 private villas, though it doesn't have the view and the beach access that Balé provides.

Jalan Raya Nusa Dua Selatan, P.O. Box 76, Nusa Dua, Bali. ✆ 361/775111. Fax 361/775222. www.thebale.com. 20 units. US$480 (£264) double; US$800 (£440) suite. AE, DC, MC, V. No children under 15 accepted. **Amenities:** Restaurant; bar; outdoor pool; nearby golf; fitness center; spa; 24-hr. room service; laundry service; library w/free Wi-Fi. *In room:* A/C, satellite TV, DVD, minibar, fridge; IDD phone.

Laguna Resort & Spa Nusa Dua 🐦 The hotel formerly known as the Sheraton underwent a US$7.5-million renovation and name change in 2006, though it's still managed by Starwood, Sheraton's parent company. The feel of the Sheraton still lurks, but the rooms, once flower-fussy, have turned modern. The main draws remain the beachfront and the meandering lagoonlike pool, which can be accessed directly by ladders from some of the ground-floor rooms. Bathrooms are large and done in marble. The amenities, like the classy restaurants and spa, have also undergone dramatic face-lifts.

P.O. Box 77, Nusa Dua, Bali. ✆ 361/771327. Fax 361/771326. www.luxurycollection.com/bali. 270 units. US$258–US$420 (£142–£231) double; US$515–US$2,800 (£283–£1540) suite. AE, DC, MC, V. **Amenities:** 3 restaurants; 3 bars; 7 outdoor pools; nearby golf; tennis court; fitness center; spa; Jacuzzi; watersports equipment rental; tour desk, car and motorbike rental; business center w/Wi-Fi; shopping; salon; 24-hr. room service; massage; laundry service. *In room:* A/C, satellite TV w/in-house movies, minibar, fridge, hair dryer, IDD phone.

Westin Resort Nusa Dua 🐦 *Kids* This resort is for those who like to combine a few hours of telecommuting with their holiday. Business travelers will appreciate the wireless Internet access, a great club lounge, and nicely appointed rooms with a safe that's big enough for a laptop. Beachside daybeds, where you can get spa treatments, are the perfect place to unwind. I like the Westin because it's a high-quality version of the McDonald's experience—that is, you know what you're going to get: great service, fantastic dining options, and beds so comfortable they're branded the "Heavenly Beds."

P.O. Box 77, Nusa Dua, Bali. ✆ 361/771327. Fax 361/771326. www.starwood.com. 270 units. US$258–US$420 (£142–£231) double; US$515–US$1,260 (£283–£693) suite. AE, DC, MC, V. **Amenities:** 3 restaurants; 4 bars; 3 outdoor pools (and kids' pool); nearby golf; tennis court; fitness center; spa; Jacuzzi; watersports equipment rental; tour desk, car and motorbike rental; shopping; salon; 24-hr. room service; massage; laundry service; meeting room. *In room:* A/C, satellite TV w/in-house movies, Internet access, minibar, fridge; hair dryer, IDD phone.

TANJUNG BENOA

Just north of Nusa Dua along the coast is the fishing village of Benoa. The labyrinth of streets in this town makes for a good stroll, certainly more interesting than sterile Nusa Dua. The coast here is lined with upscale hotels and resorts, like the **Conrad** (✆ 361/778788; www.conradhotels.com), which features a fantastic two-level spa with a private pool and bar, both of which you can visit even if you aren't a guest (stay elsewhere, as the rooms aren't particularly special here). This is a popular spot for jet-ski and motorboat rentals, as well as parasailing, so the beach is always busy.

Expensive
Novotel Coralia Benoa Bali ⍟   This hotel is slightly more upscale than your typical Novotel. Public spaces are grand, and the design throughout reflects Bali. The resort straddles the main street: The ocean side is more expensive and has better beach access, while the "garden" side is quiet and secluded. Better still, for the price, are the "beach cabanas," even bigger suites in semiprivate bungalows (two per pavilion), complete with outdoor stone tubs—most of them honeymoon-worthy. Rooms throughout are big, bright, and airy, decorated in a minimalist Asian style with coconut wood. Each of the three pools has its own flair, though none is very big. Lots of activities, including aerobics, soccer, a kids' club, and dance and cooking lessons, will keep you on the run, if you like. The free shuttle to Nusa Dua is convenient for touring, but given that this is the best of both worlds—a terrific resort and authentic Bali—it's hard to see that you would need it. The ocean up this way is much deeper and better for swimming, too.

Jalan Pratama Tanjung Benoa, P.O. Box 39, Nusa Dua, Bali. ℂ 361/772239. Fax 361/772237. www.novotelbali.com. 192 units. US$150–US$170 (£83–£94) double; US$270 (£149) beach cabana. AE, DC, MC, V. **Amenities:** 3 restaurants; 2 bars; 3 outdoor pools; tennis court; fitness center; spa; kids' club; tour desk; shuttle service; shopping; 24-hr. room service; massage; babysitting; laundry service; dry cleaning; library; Internet access; meeting room. *In room:* A/C, satellite TV, minibar, fridge, safe, IDD phone.

Moderate
Rumah Bali ⍟⍟ (Value)   This bed-and-breakfast is one of the best values in Bali. The bungalows feature outdoor kitchens and generous bathrooms (with outdoor shower!); deluxe bungalows get their own plunge pool. The people who run this hotel also own Bumbu Bali, the restaurant and cooking school, and they'll send a chef over to cook all your meals if you wish. The peaceful pool area is set in a garden, while the beach is just a 5-minute walk away. If you're on a budget, you can stay here and use the beachside pool at the restaurant Tao for something close to a five-star experience.

Jalan Pratama Tanjung Benoa, P.O. Box 132, Nusa Dua, Bali. ℂ 361/771256. Fax 361/771258. www.balifoods.com. 13 units. US$65–US$150 (£36–£83) bungalow. AE, DC, MC, V. **Amenities:** 2 restaurants; outdoor pool; tennis court; cooking school. *In room:* A/C, satellite TV, kitchen, minibar, fridge, safe, IDD phone.

WHERE TO DINE
Nusa Dua has some fine dining, mostly at the hotels, all with high prices for this part of the world. There are few other options short of the small *warungs* in town. **Bumbu Bali** (Jalan Pratama; ℂ **361/774502;** www.balifoods.com), run by former Grand Hyatt chef Heinz von Holzen, serves authentic Balinese food in a well-appointed environment. The restaurant also offers entertaining **cooking classes** ⍟⍟ on Mondays, Wednesdays, and Fridays. Across from the Ramada Resort is the new fusion restaurant **Tao** (Jalan Pratama; ℂ **361/772902;** www.taobali.com), decorated with Buddhist statues and featuring a lagoon pool, lounge chairs, and beachside tables where diners are free to laze about all day. Another good choice is **Raja's,** at the Nusa Dua Beach Hotel (ℂ **361/771219**), which serves tasty traditional Balinese fare.

OUTDOOR ACTIVITIES
Unlike Kuta, the surf here is a considerable distance offshore, making swimming in the clear blue-green water most pleasant at high tide (at low tide, it's only ankle-high).

It's a popular surf, windsurf, and jet-ski spot. Dive excursions, all arranged by the hotels, will probably take you to areas closer to Sanur or to Amed and Tambulen in the northeast.

The **Bali Golf and Country Club** (© **361/771791;** www.baligolfandcountryclub. com) sits at the southern tip of the island and has sweeping views of the beaches and clear waters off Nusa Dua. It has a fine course, worth the whopping US$142 (£78) outlay to the serious enthusiast.

SHOPPING

A new mall called the **Bali Collection** (© **361/771662;** www.bali-collection.com) offers some of the same shopping you'll find in Kuta (without the crowded streets and the touts), as well as a Starbucks and the Japanese department store Sogo, which has great cosmetic counters and name-brand clothing labels.

7 Ubud ⟨★⟨★

For a thorough exploration of Balinese culture and tradition—and a good dose of comfort and quiet—Ubud is the place. Though unabashedly touristic, the town is the cultural pulse of the island, the richest region in Bali for art production, and the very reason why so many expat artists and collectors have made Bali their home. Ubud has a royal legacy and hosts the **Royal Palace,** a center for cultural performances and dance. In and among the smaller streets of town, you'll find refined boutiques, chic galleries, and cool trinket shops, alongside open-air cafes that swallow passersby on lazy days. Outside the busy town labyrinth, the phosphorescent rice paddies, virgin jungle, gorges, and river valleys of this hilly Shangri-la are ripe for exploration. Ubud's central location makes the whole island accessible as a day trip. About the only thing it doesn't have is a beach, but they're all a short drive away.

GETTING THERE

Many hotels in the area offer pickup service, and taxis connect from the airport, about an hour away. *Bemos* drop you in the center of town, while the tourist shuttles have their own stops, usually on one of the two main drags.

GETTING AROUND

Central Ubud is small enough to see on foot, and hotels away from the main action generally provide regular shuttles into town. The main street is Jalan Raya, which runs east–west; Monkey Forest Road runs perpendicular. Transport touts in town are quite aggressive; **minivans** are for hire on every corner for either day trips or the short jaunt across town. A superb private driver is **Gusti Ngurah Nariasa** (© **081/23928171**), who often works for the Chedi Club.

Ubud is a good a place to rent a motorbike (about Rp50,000/US$5.50/£3.05 per day) if you're an experienced rider. Bicycles are available for hire at two or three street-side locations along Monkey Forest Road for about Rp10,000 (about US$1.10/£0.60).

VISITOR INFORMATION & TOURS

The **information kiosk,** on Jalan Raya (© **361/973285**), on the south side of the main street near the intersection with Monkey Forest Road, is a good place to start. There are also travel agencies all over town, each offering competitive prices for day trips and shuttles to other tourist areas.

FAST FACTS: **Ubud**

Currency Exchange There are a number of small ATMs on the main road and along Monkey Forest Road. Storefront money changers are at every turn.

Internet Access There are Internet cafes every few steps in Ubud, but for the best service, head to the center of town and find **Ubud Music,** next to Ary's Warung on Jalan Raya (© 361/972515), one of only a few with broadband.

Mail The post office is on the main road, but very far to the east. Major hotels offer postal service.

Telephones The area code in Ubud is **361.**

WHERE TO STAY

No matter what your budget is, Ubud has it all, from sublime honeymoon compounds to the humblest cottage. Below is an assortment of options, both in central Ubud and outside of town. Staying at the more rural properties might mean a long walk or ride, but the scenery is breathtaking. Many visitors come and spend a few nights before shopping around for someplace new.

VERY EXPENSIVE

Amandari ✸✸✸   If you have serious disposable income, a stay at the Amandari ensures the kind of luxurious seclusion and unrivaled service afforded celebrities (it's where Mick Jagger and Jerry Hall got married). Laid out like a fanciful Balinese village, the plush rooms are housed within huge stone cottages roofed in thatch. Each suite is enclosed in its own walled compound and appointed with every kingly comfort (some even have a private pool). Amandari is over-the-top without sacrificing local charm: There are outdoor tubs and indoor showers, Balinese decor, and a unique connection to the surrounding villages. Architects, anticipating local ceremonial processions, have designed pathways and openings in the covered walks for the passage of tall, ritual palanquins. Village suites have a first-floor common room and a cozy upstairs loft bedroom done in wood, like a rustic tree house with a quiet writing nook. The resort looks out over a beautiful jungle gorge; the Amandari's emerald-green infinity-edge pool mimics the color, to blend seamlessly with the green beyond. There is a free shuttle to Ubud, but it's hard to imagine wanting to leave very often. The terrific restaurant has a bar and serves local and European favorites.

Kedewatan, Ubud, Bali. © 361/975333. Fax 361/975335. www.amandari.com. 31 units. US$675–US$2,800 (£371–£1,540) double; US$3,600 (£1,980) villa. AE, MC, V. **Amenities:** Restaurant; bar; outdoor pool; golf course; tennis courts; health club; spa; Jacuzzi; free bicycles; concierge; tour desk; shopping; 24-hr. room service; massage; babysitting; laundry service; dry cleaning. *In room:* A/C, Wi-Fi, minibar, fridge, hair dryer, safe, IDD phone.

Chedi Club at Tanah Gajah ✸✸✸   Possibly the best resort in all of Bali, the Chedi Club (not to be confused with the Chedi) offers a small number of luxurious yet cozy villas set in rice fields and accompanied by highly tailored personal service. The freebies offered here—including breakfast brought to your villa, afternoon tea, evening drinks, yoga lessons, escorted treks, and airport transfers—make other hotels seem stingy. Did I mention there's also a personalized butler to take care of any other needs you might have? Your private courtyard offers shaded daybeds, plunge pools with rice-paddy views, a huge outdoor tub, and Bose speakers that link with an indoor stereo system that you can hook up to your iPod. The bedrooms, decorated in wood tones and Balinese art, are just as luxe. After a stay at the Chedi Club, it's likely that you'll compare every other resort to the experience and discover that they simply don't match up.

Jalan Goa Gajah, Tengkulak Kaja, Ubud, Bali. © **361/975685.** Fax 361/975686. www.ghmhotels.com. 20 units. US$300 (£165) suite; US$480–US$850 (£264–£468) villa. Rates include breakfast, afternoon tea, and evening drinks. AE, DC, MC, V. **Amenities:** Restaurant; bar; outdoor pool; tennis court; health club; spa; shuttle service to Ubud; yoga; trekking; 24-hr. personal butler service; free laundry service, complimentary afternoon tea and evening drinks. *In room:* A/C, TV, DVD player, Bose stereo w/CD player, free high-speed Internet access, free minibar, fridge, safe, IDD phone.

Four Seasons Resort at Sayan 🏵🏵

The Four Seasons here is a masterpiece of planning that takes full advantage of its extraordinary setting right on the River Ayung. It's incredibly posh, though not intimidatingly so. You enter across a long bridge leading to a lily pond that, almost unbelievably, rests atop the lobby, all in an immense crater of rice terraces. The design throughout is ultramodern, but with references to Balinese tradition. Guests stay in two-story suites (bedroom below the sitting area), deluxe suites, or high-end villas with private plunge pools. Interiors are done in gleaming woods and natural fabrics, highlighted by precious local art and artifacts. Every room has views of the deep-green gorge and/or the river. Expect luxurious bathrooms with huge tubs, showers, and dressing areas, and more plush towels than a linen shop. The two-level horizon pool follows the serpentine shape of the river below. Pampering, of course, is at a maximum and includes "seamless" transfer between here and the Four Seasons at Jimbaran Bay; the staff takes care of everything—including, if you wish, your packing. There is also regular shuttle service to Ubud.

Sayan, Ubud, Bali. © **361/977577.** Fax 361/977588. www.fourseasons.com. 46 units. US$460 (£253) suite; US$585–US$3,000 (£322–£1,650) villa. AE, DC, MC, V. **Amenities:** 2 restaurants; bar; outdoor pool; health club; spa; all rentals available; tour desk; shopping; 24-hr. room service; laundry service; dry cleaning; library w/games. *In room:* A/C, TV, stereo w/CD player, free high-speed Internet access, minibar, fridge, safe, IDD phone.

Ubud Hanging Garden 🏵

Located at the end of a long, winding road, this recent addition to the local resort scene offers peace and isolation in a jungle environment 30 minutes away from Ubud by car. The property is set in a gorge that is so steep, it's served by a tram so that guests don't have to climb too many stairs. The two infinity pools are a great place to unwind, though you may never leave the comfort of your private plunge pool and courtyard. The well-appointed guest rooms feature four-poster beds, gigantic bathrooms with huge tubs, and floor-to-ceiling windows with jungle views.

Desa Buahan, P.O. Box 80571, Ubud, Bali. © **361/982700.** Fax 361/982800. www.pansea.com. 38 units. US$350–US$800 (£193–£440) villa. AE, DC, MC, V. **Amenities:** Restaurant; bar; 2 outdoor pools; spa; tour desk; airport transfer; shuttle service; laundry service; dry cleaning; library w/Internet access; rice-paddy trek. *In room:* A/C, satellite TV, minibar, fridge, coffeemaker, hair dryer, safe, IDD phone.

EXPENSIVE

Alila Ubud 🏵 Just one step down from the ultraluxe Amandari, the Alila has a beautiful campus with fine rooms, suites, and villas overlooking the stunning northern stretch of the Ayung gorge, one of the most scenic stretches of the popular rafting trips that go through here. The infinity-edge swimming pool was voted one of the "50 Most Spectacular Pools in the World"; it's like a cube of water in otherworldly (or at least unlikely) suspension over the spectacular gorge. Accommodations are large and luxe, with top amenities (though no bathtubs), and the Mandara Spa complex is as posh as they come. The deluxe rooms even have iPods. The resort is far from town, but it's perfectly self-contained and offers regular shuttle service.

Desa Melinggih Kelod, Payangan, Gianyar, Bali. © **361/975963**. Fax 361/975968. www.alilahotels.com. 64 units. US$260–US$275 (£143–£151) double; US$450 (£248) villa. AE, MC, V. **Amenities:** Restaurant; bar; outdoor pool; spa; Jacuzzi; sauna; bike rental; concierge; tour desk; airport transfer; boutique; 24-hr. room service; massage; babysitting; laundry service; dry cleaning; library and TV room w/Internet access. *In room:* A/C, TV, minibar, fridge, coffeemaker, hair dryer, safe, IDD phone.

Bali Spirit Hotel and Spa *

Located a fair jaunt from central Ubud in the village of Nyuh Kuning, this is a reasonable alternative to the really high-end luxury hotels in the north of Ubud. At Bali Spirit, you get a great setting and comfortable rooms at a good price, without all the bells, whistles, and fees. The stunning hillside setting overlooks a river gorge. Large, well-appointed rooms come with small kitchen nooks and decks, with local fabrics and materials employed throughout. The pool is just right, a cozy perch with lounges overlooking the gorge, and there are traditional Balinese bathing pools in the holy river below. A fine spa offers a full range of services. There are regular shuttles to town, in addition to a car available to take you wherever you want to go "at a moment's notice." The lack of in-room TVs keeps your eyes on the beautiful hills.

P.O. Box 189, Nyuh Kuning Village, Ubud, Bali. © **361/974013**. Fax 361/974012. www.balispirithotel.com. 25 units. US$95–US$135 (£52–£74) double; US$145 (£80) villa. Rates include breakfast. AE, MC, V. **Amenities:** Restaurant; bar; outdoor pool; full spa; mountain-bike rental; tour desk; car rental; airport transfer; 24-hr. room service; massage; laundry service; dry cleaning; Internet access; cooking school. *In room:* A/C, TV, minibar, fridge, IDD phone.

Komaneka Resort *

Located on Monkey Forest Road right in the center of town, the Komaneka is clean, modern, and chic. Tracing a long, narrow corridor ending in a small pool with an elegant vanishing edge, guest buildings are well away from street noise and have views of gardens and rice paddies. Accommodations are done in a cool, contemporary style with shiny marble tiles and spartan wooden furnishings. The decor employs lots of natural woods and fabrics, and the beds are hung with netting suspended from the thatched ceiling. Deluxe units have unique bathrooms: Some feature outdoor-type showers and tubs, while others have sunken marble tubs. The owners have just opened a new high-end resort north of town called **Komaneka Tanggayuda,** a more deluxe compound of suites and pool villas from US$220 (£121).

Monkey Forest Rd., Ubud, Bali. © **361/976090**. Fax 361/977140. www.komaneka.com. 20 units. US$200–US$250 (£110–£138) double; US$300 (£165) garden or pool villa. AE, DC, MC, V. **Amenities:** Restaurant; outdoor pool; full spa; tour desk; car rental; shopping; 24-hr. room service; massage; laundry service; library. *In room:* A/C, TV, DVD player, CD player, minibar, fridge, IDD phone.

Maya Ubud Resort & Spa **

Just 5 years old, this fine resort is a short hop outside of Ubud proper (just to the east) and is set in a quiet, mountainous area surrounded by rice fields. The hotel's design makes elegant use of local materials, blended in an immaculate, contemporary style. Rooms reflect that refined simplicity, with cool white and yellow tones set against the dark wood of Art Deco furnishings. Floors are made of river stone and ceilings of thatch. The double-height lobby rotunda echoes the shape of a Dongsan Drum, a relic of an ancient culture and an important regional motif. The property stretches in a line of low-profile buildings all the way down to the river. An elevator transports you down the steep valley to the riverside, where the fine spa rooms literally hang over the rushing water; there's also a small restaurant and a riverside pool with a vanishing edge. Fine dining, spa facilities, and plenty of activities make the Maya quite self-sufficient, but regular shuttle service to town keeps you connected.

Jalan Gunung Sari, Peliatan, Ubud, Bali. ⓒ 361/977888. Fax 361/977555. www.mayaubud.com. 108 units. US$220–US$240 (£121–£132) double; US$330–US$1,200 (£182–£660) villa. AE, DC, MC, V. **Amenities:** 2 restaurants; bar; 2 outdoor pools; tennis courts; comprehensive spa; Jacuzzi; bike rental; tour desk; airport transfer; shopping; laundry service; dry cleaning; library w/Internet access. *In room:* A/C, satellite TV, minibar, fridge, coffeemaker, hair dryer, safe, IDD phone.

MODERATE

Agung Raka Bungalows 🍴   Just south of central Ubud, these two-story thatched bungalows are arranged around a series of working rice paddies and surrounded by a thriving village art community. Lower-end bungalows are basic two-story wood-and-bamboo constructions with rudimentary outdoor bathrooms and a staircase leading up to a cozy bedroom. Superior bungalows are single-occupancy A-frames with teak and catay accents. The bathrooms here are large, modern courtyard facilities that each include both a tile tub and a stone-floor shower. The suites are tip-top: a dizzying spectacle of stone and marble, each big enough for four and great for two.

Pengosekan Village (2km/1¼ miles south of Ubud center), Ubud, Bali. ⓒ 361/975757. Fax 361/975546. www.agungraka.com. 21 units. US$60–US$100 (£33–£55) double; US$70–US$150 (£39–£83) villa. MC, V. **Amenities:** Restaurant; bar; outdoor pool; motorbike rental; tour desk; car rental; shuttle service; laundry service. *In room:* A/C, TV, minibar, IDD phone.

Alam Sari 🍴🍴   This model hotel offers an excellent combination of comfort, social responsibility, setting, and low price. Everything the Alam Sari does is with a thought toward the local economy, ecology, and culture. Decorative touches, such as the brightly dyed fabric and wood furniture, are made locally. The hotel almost exclusively employs villagers from neighboring Keliki, to bolster the local economy. Environmentally friendly touches are everywhere, from solar water heaters to the use of recycled paper. Rooms are lovely, with views of the gorge and looming volcano. The hotel is sufficiently self-contained, making the 20-minute ride to town only an occasional necessity. Traditional music is featured at night.

Keliki, Tromoi Pos 03, Kantor Pos Tegallalang (9km/5½ miles north of Ubud), Ubud, Bali. ⓒ 361/981420. Fax 361/981421. www.alamsari.com. 12 units. US$106 (£58) double; US$119 (£65) suite; US$198 (£109) family unit. AE, MC, V. **Amenities:** Restaurant; bar; bicycle rental; tour desk; car rental; laundry service; library; Internet access. *In room:* A/C, minibar, fridge, safe, IDD phone.

Ananda Cottages 🍴   Just north of Ubud proper, Ananda Cottages is atmospheric enough for the Balinese experience you're hoping for, yet situated far enough from the town center to discourage the tourist hordes. The rice fields and thatched cottages of this bungalow campus are almost more "Balinese" than real villages you might visit (where you'll find TVs instead of shrines, and roaring machines instead of hand tools). Cozy rooms are connected by paths along terraced retaining walls, which are lit at night with miniature coal-fed, torchlike flames. The cottages are bi-level brick huts with bamboo pavilion roofs. Downstairs rooms are the better choice, with outdoor tubs and patio living rooms. Upstairs rooms have modern bathrooms and small verandas. The pool is small, but set on an interesting raised rice terrace. The three new deluxe bungalows are very cozy and well worth the outlay.

Campuhan, Ubud, Bali. ⓒ 361/975376. Fax 361/975375. www.anandaubud.com. 54 units. US$50–US$60 (£28–£33) double without A/C; US$70–US$80 (£39–£44) double w/A/C; US$175 (£96) suite villa. AE, MC, V. **Amenities:** Restaurant; bar; outdoor pool; shopping; 24-hr. room service; laundry service. *In room:* A/C (in some units), minibar, fridge, IDD phone.

Hotel Tjampuhan ⭐⭐   This hotel is a tropical sanctuary with terraces that lead to a beautiful gorge, the Tjampuhan River, and the 900-year-old Gunung Lebah Temple. The hotel was built in 1928 for guests of the prince of Ubud and was chosen by Western artists Walter Spies and Rudolf Bonnet as headquarters for their art association, Pita Maha. All units have Balinese thatched roofs. Air-conditioned rooms are larger and have better views than fan rooms. Splurge for a Raja Room (or even Spies's own villa), with verandas overlooking the gorge. The grounds are done in beautiful stonework, and immaculate gardens line the path down to the river. There are two very pretty pondlike pools and another with cold spring water, perfect for hot days.

Jalan Raya Campuhan, Ubud, Bali. © **361/975368.** Fax 316/975137. 67 units. US$70 (£39) double w/fan; US$115 (£63) double w/AC; US$175 (£96) Walter Spies villa. Rates include breakfast. AE, MC, V. **Amenities:** 2 restaurants; 4 bars; 2 outdoor pools; full spa; tour desk; car rental; shopping; massage; babysitting; laundry service; dry cleaning; library. *In room:* A/C (in some units), minibar, fridge, IDD phone.

Ubud Bungalow ⭐   These bungalows are a popular budget option in the middle of town (call ahead as it's often full). Basic rooms, all with balconies out front, are stacked two high in a long column down the length of this quiet property. There's a small pool and restaurant. Otherwise, you can just fend for yourself, which, given the central location right in the middle of busy Monkey Forest Road, won't require the use of survival skills. This is a very good budget choice.

Monkey Forest Rd., Ubud, Bali. © **361/975537.** Fax 361/971298. 18 units. US$22 (£12) double w/fan; US$33 (£18) double w/A/C. MC, V. **Amenities:** Restaurant; pool; laundry service. *In room:* A/C (in some units); no phone.

Ubud Sari Health Resort ⭐⭐   This place gets my top recommendation in this category. Nowhere else in Ubud will you find such lovely cottages, small but immaculate, with real rustic charm. Rooms are situated above a river, so many guests open the windows, hang the mossy net, and let the jungle sounds and rushing water sing them to sleep. Breakfast is served on your private balcony, and the staff is attentive without fawning. There's nothing like it at these prices. A meandering garden path leads to the rustic spa area (open to day visitors), which offers a cold plunge pool, herbal steam, sauna, and a roster of fine massage treatments at discount prices. Once you've checked in, you may not want to leave.

35 Jalan Kajeng, Ubud, Bali. © **361/974393.** Fax 361/976305. www.ubudsari.com. 10 units. US$35–US$75 (£19–£41) double. MC, V. **Amenities:** Restaurant; outdoor pool; extensive spa; whirlpool; Jacuzzi; steam room; sauna; tour desk; limited room service; massage; babysitting; laundry service. *In room:* A/C, no phone.

INEXPENSIVE

Puri Garden Bungalows (Monkey Forest Rd.; ©/fax **361/974923**) is exemplary of the good budget choices in town. Large, cozy guesthouse rooms with air-conditioning start from US$19 (£10). Also try **Ubud Bungalow** ⭐ (Monkey Forest Rd.; © **361/ 971298;** fax 361/975537), with rooms starting at US$20 (£11). Other budget choices line Monkey Forest Road and the Jalan Hanoman; better still, turn down any little alley or side street that cuts across them.

WHERE TO DINE

Ubud has many eateries, mostly international restaurants in the busy town center, though you'll also find small *warungs* or stands selling *babi guling* (suckling pig). Much of Ubud's fine dining comes with a Western price tag.

Ary's Warung ⭐ MODERN INDONESIAN   Ary's gourmet European and Indonesian specialties have fans from around the world. Stop in for at least one of the honey-ginger-lime drinks (with or without the booze) and kick back on a couch at street side for a bit of people-watching. The metallic, angular construction of this open-air bistro would look great in a big-city gallery district, but is a bit at odds with ancient Hindu temples and the adjacent Royal Palace. It is the place to see and be seen, however, and Ary's is quite pleasant at night, when tranquil trance music plays and candles light every corner. Second-floor dining gives you a good view of the busy street below or the bats swooping to catch bugs at dusk. The food is good—overpriced, but good. Try the gazpacho, perfect on a hot day, or the grilled goat-cheese salad. The grilled tuna and lamb cutlets are done to perfection, and the ponzu-grilled snapper is delicious. The tasting menu (Rp220,000/US$24/£13) includes two glasses of house wine. Ary's also makes for a good meeting place or for reconnoitering when the kids are trekking and mom is off shopping.

Main rd. C **361/975053**. www.dekco.com. Main courses Rp25,500–Rp75,000 (US$2.80–US$8.25/£1.55–£4.55); duck, lamb, and salmon dishes up to Rp150,000 (US$17/£9.15). MC, V. Daily 7:30am–10pm (last order).

Batan's Waru 🐟🐟 INDONESIAN/EUROPEAN   Tucked away on a pleasant side street, Batan's Waru is particularly atmospheric at night, when the entrance is lit with candles. The ambitious menu has traditional dishes beyond the usual suspects, and plenty of vegetarian options. For an appetizer, try *urap pakis,* wild fern tips with roasted coconut and spices; or *lemper ayam,* chicken dumplings simmered in a banana leaf. Uncle Karaman's Hummus is spicy and comes with grilled-pepper flatbread and tomato-mint relish. Everything is served with a dish of spicy condiments. Finish off with a perfect cup of decaf Illy-brand espresso. The restaurant also does smoked duck and a *babi guleng* feast, with a day's advance order, and there is a full menu of pasta, sandwiches, and light fare as well.

Jalan Dewi Sita. C **361/977528**. www.baligoodfood.com. Main courses Rp15,500–Rp43,000 (US$1.70–US$4.75/£0.95–£2.60). MC, V. Daily 8am–midnight.

Bebek Bengil (Dirty Duck) 🐟🐟 INDONESIAN/EUROPEAN   The Dirty Duck is the best place to try Ubud's famous dish. First stewed in local spices, then deep fried, the duck here is finger-lickin' good, but not quite as oily as in other restaurants. Another way to go is the stuffed chicken with shiitake, sprouts, and spinach. The menu also features salads, overstuffed crunchy sandwiches, and good veggie options. The atmosphere is romantic; book a table towards the back of the open-air restaurant, which looks out onto the paddy fields.

Padang Tegel (at end of st. as it hooks into Monkey Forest Rd.). C **361/975489**. Main courses Rp12,500–Rp35,000 (US$1.35–US$3.85/£0.75–£2.15). MC, V. Daily 10:30am–11pm.

Cafe Lotus 🐟 MODERN INDONESIAN/INTERNATIONAL   The food here isn't half bad, but the real reason to come to Cafe Lotus is for the chance to dine in the shadow of the Pura Saraswati temple (p. 637). It's cozy in the shaded dining area or on bamboo platforms overlooking the temple. The menu features good Western options, pastas and such, some modified into fiery dishes with hot chiles, black olives, and hearts of palm. Try the Balinese Satay Lilit, a mixed-fish kabob with a hint of coconut, served on skewers and presented on a plate the size of a boat. The fresh health drinks are a delight. This is a good place to just kick back when touring the town. Note that no beef is served due to the restaurant's proximity to the temple.

Main rd. C **361/975660**. Main courses Rp25,000–Rp54,000 (US$2.75–US$5.95/£1.50–£3.30). No credit cards. Daily 9am–9:30pm (last order).

Indus ∮ ECLECTIC   Indus provides two floors of open-air dining overlooking the stunning Tjampuhan Ridge. It's a bit like a mafia don's house, with marble tile and columns. The dining area is under a high thatch roof with cozy, low-slung couches and chairs to one side. This is a great spot for coffee and an escape from the heat, or for a long, languid lunch. The setting alone makes it worth the trip, and the food is tops to boot. Sample the likes of beetroot and feta empanadas, grilled calamari tostada, or fine wraps and sandwiches. Be sure to try the Balinese *tenggiri* curry, a Spanish whitefish done in ginger and coconut (or, for a lighter choice, get the *tenggiri* salad). Indus also has an extensive tapas menu and good fruit smoothies. Save room for the homemade ginger ice cream or coconut crème caramel.

Jalan Raya Sargingan, Campuhan. ℂ 361/977684. www.casalunabali.com. Dress is "neat casual." Main courses Rp27,000–Rp50,000 (US$3–US$5.50/£1.65–£3.05). MC, V. Daily 8:30am–11pm.

Mozaic ∮∮ INTERNATIONAL   The word is out: Hip Mozaic is now the only place in town where you really need a reservation. Chris Salons, the French-trained American chef and owner, brings his own distinctive French-American cooking techniques and presentation to the restaurant, which was just listed in Le Grande Tables du Monde, a prestigious French culinary fraternity. He uses fresh local ingredients, all rich and delicious but healthy, with unique local dairy substitutes. A meal at Mozaic is a languid affair, best enjoyed in multiple courses, sopped up with good bread, chased with fine wine, and shared with friends. Give yourself at least 2 hours to really enjoy it. Daytime dining features light French fare served in a quiet patio area. The evening meal is an extravaganza of Continental specialties done with local flair and served in a lush garden dining area. Try the king prawns in chilled gazpacho, followed by a pan-seared Long-Nose Emperor filet done in a Laksa Indonesian yellow emulsion with rice noodles and baby turnips. Other specials include Australian beef tenderloin and local favorites like *babi guling* and Ubud crispy duck. Finish with a fine sorbet combining melon, cherry, and pomelo. Service is ultraprofessional, attentive without being intimidating, and the atmosphere is the right mix of elegant and casual—the perfect romantic evening.

Jalan Raya Sanggingan. ℂ 361/975768. www.mozaic-bali.com. Reservations required. Tasting menu US$50–US$60 (£28–£33). AE, MC, V. Daily noon–4pm and 6–10pm.

Naughty Nuri's Warung and Grill ∮∮ BARBECUE/BALINESE   This old expat hangout has the best barbecue in town, with ribs so tender the meat falls right off the bone. On Thursday, a regular shipment of fresh tuna arrives and the place fills right up. The burgers, dogs, and local curries and satay are also good. Free-flowing drinks (try the honkin' martinis) add to the laid-back, picnic-table atmosphere at street side. Bring your appetite, a high booze tolerance, and a good sense of humor.

Tromol Pos 219 (just across from the Neka Art Museum on the road leading north of town). ℂ 361/977547. Main courses Rp15,000–Rp60,000 (US$1.65–US$6.60/£0.90–£3.65). No credit cards. Daily 9am–10pm.

TeraZo ∮∮ MEDITERRANEAN   The spacious interior of this hip bistro is simple yet welcoming, with terraces set behind a nice garden with decorative fountains. The menu is extensive. Cool tomato gazpacho is a welcome starter in the tropical heat, while the spring rolls are light and delicious. The eight-layer pie is a delicious pastry crust filled with smoked blue marlin, spinach, ricotta, and mushrooms. There's also a host of grilled items, fine pasta, and gourmet Asian-influenced dishes, like the *nasi kuning,* yellow coconut rice with raisins, cashews, and strips of egg; or the *kue tiaun,* stir-fried rice noodles, chicken, and local greens. A tempting breakfast menu features surprises like ricotta blintzes topped with honey and fresh yogurt.

Jalan Suweta. (© **361/978941.** www.baligoodfood.com. Main courses Rp60,000–Rp134,000 (US$6.60–US$15/ £3.65–£8.15). AE, MC, V. Daily 10am–11pm.

SNACKS & CAFES
Casa Luna, on the main road (© **361/977409**), is a longtime favorite with expats for its local and international cuisine, coffee, and desserts. (It also has cooking classes.) For desserts and ice cream, **Mumbul's Cafe,** also on the main road (© **361/975364**), is a tasty choice with a serene garden terrace. The town's best coffee shop is **Tutmak Warung Kopi,** on Jalan Dewi Sita, near Batan's Waru (© **361/975754**), with great desserts and a whole range of healthy treats, from salads to light lunches. There's also a good menu for kids.

    Kafe, on Jalan Hanoman (© **361/970992**; www.balispirit.com), offers fantastic vegetarian mains, California-style burritos, coffee, and desserts. It also contains a yoga and massage center and a gift shop featuring crafts from nonprofit organizations.

    Bali Buddha Cafe, Jalan Jembawan 1, in front of the post office to the east of town (© **361/976324**), is a happening little expat spot with a small grocery store that sells good fresh bread, organic vegetables, healthy snacks, and supplements. Upstairs is a popular juice bar—a good place to meet long-staying folks or get info off the bulletin board. It's New Age central here, more or less.

WHAT TO SEE & DO
Pura Saraswati 𝕬𝕬   The royal family commissioned this temple and water garden, dedicated to the Hindu goddess of art and learning, at the end of the 19th century. The main shrine is covered in fine carvings, and the *bale* houses (small pavilions) and giant *barong* masks are interesting. The restaurant **Cafe Lotus** (above) is situated at the front, on the main street, so that diners can look out over the lovely grounds.

Jalan Raya Ubud. Free admission. Daily during daylight hours.

Puri Saren Agung (Royal Palace) 𝕬   From the late 19th century to the mid-1940s, this was the seat for the local ruler. It's a series of elegant and well-preserved pavilions, many of them decorated incongruously with colonial-era European furniture. Visitors are welcome to stroll around, though there are no signs indicating what you are looking at. Evening dance performances are held in the courtyard, by far the best and most dramatic setting for these in Ubud.

Jalan Raya Ubud. Free admission. Daily during daylight hours.

MUSEUMS
Ubud has enjoyed a long relationship with foreign artists. As a result, the town has a few good museums and many galleries. All give you a crash course in authentic Balinese art, not to mention welcome respite from souvenir stalls. Of the many small museums in town, those listed below are the best choices, but don't pass up the free galleries around town, especially on Jalan Raya Sanggingan going north toward the more high-end resorts. In addition to the following, stop by the free **Seniwati Gallery of Art by Women** (Jalan Sriwedari 2B, Banjar Taman; © **361/975485;** www.seniwatigallery.com) and the **Agung Rai Museum and Gallery** (Jalan Pengosekan; © **361/975742;** www.armamuseum.com), another popular local collection.

Antonio Blanco Museum   The museum is an homage to Bali's famous Catalan expat. Born in the Philippines, Blanco arrived here penniless, but eventually befriended the king, married, had children, and lived the life of Riley all his days. He was a favorite at court and the confidant of many powerful people on Bali and in Indonesia. This grand gallery houses a collection of his work that is as much a romp through Blanco's sexual dalliances as anything, a collection of homespun, baroque pornography. Some paintings feature Blanco's raunchy prose poetry. Don't miss touring his studio space. The consummate egomaniacal artist, Blanco envisioned this monument to himself and participated fully in its creation before shuffling off this mortal coil in 1999. The museum grounds are a trip, with Blanco's menagerie of dachshunds, monkeys, and exotic birds still ruling the roost.

Jalan Campuhan, just past the bridge heading north of Ubud. ⓒ 361/975502. www.blancobali.com. Admission Rp20,000 (US$2.20/£1.20). Daily 9am–5pm.

Neka Art Museum 🏵🏵   Founded in 1982 by Suteja Neka, a former schoolteacher and patron of the arts, this museum is a good introduction to the Balinese school. Housed in several pavilions, works are labeled in English and provide informed access to rural traditions and modern movements on the island and locally in Ubud. The collection features the work of the Dutch-born Indonesian artist Arie Smit, as well as contemporary works both local and from abroad. Don't miss the view of the Campuhan Gorge from the Smit Pavilion—you can see what inspires local artists (or get inspired yourself).

Jalan Raya Campuhan (about 10 min. north of central Ubud, near Ananda Cottages). ⓒ 361/976206. www.museum neka.com. Admission Rp20,000 (US$2.20/£1.20). Mon–Sat 9am–5pm; Sun noon–5pm.

Puri Lukisan 🏵   A major renovation has turned this formerly dilapidated display into something nearly on par with the Neka Art Museum. The gorgeous gardens of lily ponds and rice paddies are worth a visit on their own. Founded in 1956 by a prince of Ubud and a Dutch artist, the collection of painting and sculpture here traces the evolution of Balinese art. One space is dedicated to a revolving exhibit of up-and-coming local artists.

Jalan Raya Ubud. ⓒ 361/975136. www.mpl-ubud.com. Admission Rp20,000 (US$2.20/£1.20). Daily 9am–5pm.

OUTDOOR ACTIVITIES

Just west of Ubud, the Ayung River has some good whitewater rafting and kayaking. The rapids aren't too impressive for experienced rafters, but the scenery along the way is, with rice paddies, deep gorges, and photo-op waterfalls. Two-hour trips include all equipment, hotel pickup, and lunch; most hotels can make the reservations. You can also contact **Bali Adventure Tours** (ⓒ 361/721480; www.baliadventuretours.com) or **Sobek** (ⓒ 361/287059).

Ubud is surrounded by fascinating villages, scenic rice paddies, gorges, and rivers, and roads and paths lead to all of them. You can just wander, but I strongly urge you to buy a copy of the *Ubud Surroundings* map, available in all shops. Then head for the picturesque village of **Penestanan** or go on the rigorous **Campuhan Ridge** walk. Hiring a local guide is also a good option.

Ever seen a Scarlet-headed Flowerpecker? For an interesting day, meet up with famed author and naturalist **Victor Mason** (ⓒ 361/975009 in the daytime, or ⓒ 812/29313801 in the evening; su_birdwalk@yahoo.com) for his popular **birdwatching tour** 🏵 of Ubud. Tours cost US$33 (£18) and leave Tuesday, Friday, Saturday, and Sunday from the bridge at Tjampuhan in the northeastern end of town. You're bound to see a good many of Bali's 100 species of birds. The scenic walk includes lunch, water, and binocular use.

Spa Treatments for All Budgets

Repeat visitors to Ubud are escapists, spiritual seekers, and relaxation junkies. The **Ubud Body Works Center** ✸ (25 Hanuman Rd.; © 361/975720; www.ubud bodyworkscentre.com) focuses on Balinese healing techniques; while the atmosphere isn't luxe, the massages and body scrubs are fantastic and inexpensive. All of the high-end resorts have good spa services as well; **Ibah** (© 361/974466;** www.ibahbali.com) and the **Four Seasons Resort at Sayan** (© 361/977577; www.fourseasons.com) are the best among them.

Elephant Safari Park ✸✸ *(Kids)* The Elephant Safari Park, run by **Bali Adventure Tours,** is less safari and more elephant ride, and it's a real hoot. These native Sumatra elephants are well cared for and live in large, lush enclosures. The owners have worked carefully with locals from Taro Village, previously one of Bali's most remote and untouched villages, to make sure they leave little more than elephant tracks. A safari starts with Pachyderm 101, as knowledgeable guides tell about the animals' care and feeding, local ecology, threats to the native population, and preservation efforts. Then, along with a *mahout* (guide), you'll have a galumphing trip through the jungle. Don't miss the antics of the youngest pachyderm; he's just taken up the game of soccer and can usually be found pouncing on an oversize ball in the central pond. A fun elephant show is staged twice daily at 12:30 and 3:30pm. The price is a bit dear, but they take good care of you here, with a tasty lunch buffet and attentive service.

Jalan Bypass Ngurah Rai, Pesanggaran. © 361/721480. Fax 361/721481. www.baliadventuretours.com. Reservations recommended. Admission (including transport, buffet lunch, and show) US$48 (£26) adults, or US$68 (£37) w/elephant ride; US$33 (£18) children, or US$47 (£26) w/elephant ride; family rates and Internet rates available.

Monkey Forest ✸ *(Kids)* Yes, there is a monkey forest at the southern end of Monkey Forest Road, and this is a popular day trip. The towering tree clusters here are home to a troop of bad-tempered but photogenic primates who swing from branches, cannonball into pools of water, and do everything short of putting on suits and paying taxes, all to the general delight of photo-snapping visitors. Signs warn you not to feed the monkeys, but locals stand under those very signs selling you bananas and nuts for precisely that purpose. Do so if you must, but do not tease the critters, who are grumpy enough as it is—just hand them the food. Make sure you have no other food on you: They will smell it. They're also known to snatch at dangling or glittering objects and to gnaw on sandals. There's a small temple in the forest, and the track also leads to Nyuhkuning, a woodcarving village.

Monkey Forest Rd. © 361/971304. Admission Rp10,000 (US$1.10/£0.60) adults, Rp5,000 (US55¢/£0.30) children. Daily during daylight hours.

SHOPPING

Ubud is the shopper's paradise of Bali, with everything from tacky plastic doohickeys to priceless works that will have you thinking of selling the S.U.V.

Start at **Ubud Market,** at the southeast corner of Monkey Forest Road and Jalan Raya Ubud. Open during daylight hours only, it's a real market—great noisy fun, with dozens of stalls selling produce and livestock along with tourist kitsch.

All along **Monkey Forest Road, Jalan Raya Ubud,** and **Jalan Hanoman,** shop after shop is filled with gorgeous sarongs, woodcarvings, mobiles, jewelry, incense, pottery, and gaily colored shirts. It's all geared to tourists, but the quality isn't bad. Elsewhere in town, you can find jewelry, housewares, and textiles.

Treasures, Toko, and **Toko East** are fine boutiques owned by the folks at Ary's Warung; find them on the main road in the center of Ubud or online at www.dekco. com. Other boutiques and galleries line the road running north of central Ubud toward the high-end resort area. The lace shop **Toko Uluwatu** has outlets all over Bali. You can find its popular storefront on Monkey Forest Road in the center of Ubud. **Okrakartini,** east of the palace on the main road (② **361/975624**), is an upmarket boutique with fine cloth, jewelry, and antiques. **Threads of Life,** Jalan Kajeng 24 (② **361/972187;** www.threadsoflife.com), a foundation that supports groups of weavers on the eastern islands of Indonesia, sells unique local patterns.

For books, stop by **Periplus,** on Monkey Forest Road (② **361/975178**); or **Ganesh Bookshop,** Jalan Raya (② **361/970320;** www.ganeshabooksbali.com), adjacent to the popular Buddha Cafe.

UBUD AFTER DARK

Ubud's nightlife scene is growing, but still rather sedate. **Jazz Café** (Jalan Sukma 2, east of Monkey Forest Rd.; ② **361/976594**), has good live jazz. There are lots of little laid-back places along Monkey Forest Road that are more than happy to stay open late. Upscale **Lamak** (② **361/974668;** www.lamakbali.com) stays up, but its scene is mostly calm. For a night of drinking and fun, hit **Naughty Nuri's** (p. 636; ② **361/ 977547**), where most dinners turn into a romp. **Exiles Café** (Jalan Pengosekan; ② **361/ 974812**) is where the disenfranchised come to fraternize and get anesthetized, particularly on Saturday nights; it's located just to the southeast of central Ubud.

For an evening of culture, there are usually several dance, music, and shadow-puppet performances to choose from every night in Ubud, both at the **Royal Palace** (p. 637) and on other nearby stages. A *barong* performance at the Royal Palace is the best and most stimulating choice; even the kids will like it. Touts selling tickets are ubiquitous; ask at any front desk for a recommendation.

SIDE TRIPS FROM UBUD

Day hiking in and around Bali is the real attraction, with rice fields set among low hills and small towns as far as the eye can see. Ask at any tour desk about day trips to the **Sayan Rice Terraces** ℛ, just north of Ubud. This deep-green valley, striated in stunning tiers and hanging with palms, is a photographer's dream.

Basakih Temple ℛ   Called the "Mother Temple," Basakih is Bali's premier Hindu site. Even if you come with your own guide, you'll have to hire a local to take you around the temple site; meet one out in front (he'll find you). The compound is a collection of 22 multi-tiered temples that look like Chinese pagodas. They're more interesting for their significance to Balinese culture than for their architectural qualities. The temples were destroyed in eruptions in 1917, and damaged in another incident in 1963. This is a working temple complex, with each compound attended by families. There are no signs for tourists, and ceremonies are often in progress—but the compulsory guides help prevent visitors from treading where they're not welcome. Be respectful and certainly ask before taking pictures, though usually foreign visitors are made welcome. This is a possible day trip from Ubud or Kuta; most visitors include a detour to the nearby volcanoes (see "Scaling the Heights: Bali's Volcanoes," below).

40km (25 miles) north of Klungkung. Admission Rp8,000 (US90¢/£0.50), plus about US$2/£1.10 for a guide.

Scaling the Heights: Bali's Volcanoes

Gunung Agung, the tallest peak on the island at 3,014m (9,886 ft.), is quite a spectacle, visible from as far away as the island of Lombok and from high buildings in busy Kuta. It is a grueling 5-hour climb to the top. Easier is nearby **Gunung Batur,** Agung's little brother, just a few hours' hike. Both Batur and Agung are still active volcanoes, with eruptions as recent as 1997. Start before first light to catch the dawn. From the top, you can see the geothermally active surrounding crater, the volcanoes of nearby Lombok, and the looming peak of Agung.

Lots of small storefront outfitters arrange group bus tours and private transport. The area makes for a good overnight, too, though it can also be done as a day trip from Ubud. Rooms in the very basic lodging at the base of Mount Batur start at Rp30,000 (US$3.30/£1.85). The town of Penelokan, a name that means "moved people" (a result of volcanic activity), stands at the rim of the crater. **Lakeview Hotel and Restaurant** (© 366/51394; www.indo.com/hotels/lakeview) is a good bet, with deluxe rooms from US$30 (£17). All rooms face the lake (thus the moniker), and helpful staff can arrange transport and trekking at a cost just slightly higher than if you go down and make your own arrangements at the trail head.

You do need a guide, however. It's not just the rules; it's a good idea. The sad part is that the local mafia masks itself as a government agency and controls the mountain guides. The cost of a tour, which includes transportation, a guide, and a breakfast of eggs, bananas, and bread, is a rather expensive US$45 (£25) per person; try to bargain down to US$35 (£19). It's best to arrange any hiking plans at your guesthouse or hotel. Be sure to be fastidious and specific about details: Is it a private tour? Is breakfast included? What route will you follow?

There are a few different routes up both peaks. Most follow the trail to the main viewing point near the top of Batur (there's a little lean-to where folks have breakfast and wait for the sunrise). From there, you can follow a short loop to the various craters. You can arrange for a basic tour and then offer the guide a little extra for an upgrade.

It makes for a fun morning, which you can follow with a visit to the small hot springs near the lake. This is a stunning part of the island and certainly worth the trip.

8 Candi Dasa

The best reason to camp out in Candi Dasa is to take advantage of the peace, relaxation, and historic riches of the eastern corner of the island. The beaches are eroded and it's overdeveloped, but you can find some of the island's finest accommodations here. Many choose to stay in nearby **Padangbai,** an atmospheric little fishing village with some basic accommodations.

GETTING THERE

There are shuttles from all major tourist areas to Candi Dasa. Most of the hotels offer airport pickup for a fee.

GETTING AROUND

There isn't much to the town of Candi Dasa itself—just one road, parallel to the beach—so your feet will do you just fine. Hotels just outside the center generally offer regular shuttles into town. Motorbike rental and *bemos* are available, too.

FAST FACTS: Candi Dasa

Car/Motorbike Rental **Safari,** on the main road (© **363/41707**), is a reliable and friendly tourist agency with a selection of cars, jeeps, and motorbikes.

Currency Exchange Money changers can be found up and down the main road, offering competitive prices.

Internet Access Internet storefronts line the main street. Service is unreliable, but costs only Rp2,400 per hour (US30¢/£0.15).

Mail **Asri Shop,** on the main street, offers postal services.

Telephones Candi Dasa's area code is **363**.

WHERE TO STAY

VERY EXPENSIVE

Amankila 🏵🏵   The name of this ultraluxe resort means "beautiful hill," and it is just that. Private villas, luxurious beyond compare, open to the most stunning views of surrounding hills and ocean below. There is nothing typical about an Aman resort, and this breathtaking perch is no exception. Accommodations have it right in every detail. A solid-wood four-poster canopy bed dominates each spacious unit, which also comes with an enormous dressing area, lavish bathroom with sunken tub, and cushioned window seats. The high-end suites have better views and private pools. The Amankila has the only beach in Candi Dasa with sand. Its most striking feature is the giant tiered pool at the center, with water that matches the color of the ocean it seems to spill into. Amankila has every amenity, of course, and rooms and restaurants beyond compare, but what really sets this place apart is its meticulous service. Everyone is a rock star here.

Manggis, Bali. © **363/41333**. Fax 363/41555. www.amankila.com. 34 units. US$675–US$1,050 (£371–£578) suite; US$1,050–US$2,700 (£578–£1485) pool suite. AE, MC, V. **Amenities:** 2 restaurants; bar; outdoor pool; tennis court; spa; watersports equipment rental; motorbike rental; tour desk; car rental; 24-hr. room service; massage; laundry service; library w/Internet access. *In room:* A/C, satellite TV, Wi-Fi; minibar, fridge, coffeemaker, safe, IDD phone.

EXPENSIVE

Alila Manggis 🏵🏵   From the outside, this comfortable, contemporary place looks more like a boxy, concrete apartment complex, but inside it's all stark luxury. Chic rooms have clean lines, and everything is new and tidy. The staff is very friendly, and there are nice little touches like afternoon tea and treats on your patio. The lush central lawn and pool area is surrounded by teak lounges and leads to a large pebble beach. Getting to town is a bit of a haul, but regular shuttles make it convenient. The hotel features its own line of special soaps which have spawned a local cottage industry. When you check in, you'll be asked your preference: coconut, loofah sponge, or seaweed (you'll also have your choice of aromatherapeutic oils). Be sure to carry some of the Sensatia products away with you. The hotel's new restaurant, Sea Salt, takes its name from nearby salt-producing villages. Days at their popular cooking school include a visit to these areas.

Buitan, Manggis, Bali. © 363/41011. Fax 363/41015. www.alilahotels.com. 58 units. US$200–US$220 (£110–£121) double; US$350 (£193) suite. AE, MC, V. **Amenities:** Restaurant; bar; watersports equipment rental; bicycle rental; tour services; shuttle bus; room service; babysitting; laundry service; Internet access; cooking lessons; trekking. *In room:* A/C, satellite TV, minibar, fridge, IDD phone.

Puri Bagus 🏵🏵   The Puri Bagus is a short ride from the town center and a good compromise between Candi Dasa's ultraluxe options and the more run-down budget stops. Pretty and romantic, this hotel is the best of its class. It's set on land jutting into the ocean, with steps leading right down to the beach. Good-size bungalows are airy and light, thanks to many large windows, and each has a small sitting area. Cool outdoor bathrooms have hand-held showers. The U-shaped pool has a deep section for scuba practice and a shallow area for kids. Dance programs and movies are offered at night, plus there's a full range of free daily activities and good dining at seaside. You'll also find a beautiful new spa area.

P.O. Box 129, Manggis, Bali. © 363/41304. Fax 363/41290. www.manggis.puribagus.net. 26 units. US$115–US$160 (£63–£88) double; US$665 (£366) 7-room pool villa. AE, DC, MC, V. **Amenities:** 2 restaurants; 2 bars; outdoor pool; nearby tennis court; watersports equipment rental; bike and scooter rental; concierge; tour desk; car rental; shopping; room service (7am–midnight); massage; laundry service. *In room:* A/C, minibar, fridge, IDD phone.

MODERATE

Kubu Bali 🏵   A great value for the price, the Kubu Bali is comfortable and atmospheric. Just off the main street, this quiet little hillside sanctuary is situated in a ravine of rice terraces, cobblestone gardens, statues, benches, aviaries, and pavilions. Handsomely decorated individual bungalows are simple, bright, and airy, with comfortable amenities. The bathrooms have tile-and-stone showers open to the sky. Each cottage has a porch with lazy lounge chairs in the shade. At the highest point on the grounds is a cozy pool area with views of the ocean.

Main rd., Candi Dasa. © 363/41532 or 363/41256. Fax 363/41531. www.kububali.com. 20 units. US$55 (£30) double; US$65 (£36) suite. MC, V. **Amenities:** Restaurant; outdoor pool; tour desk; car rental; shopping; room service (7am–10pm); massage; babysitting; laundry service. *In room:* A/C, minibar, fridge, hair dryer, safe, IDD phone.

Watergarden 🏵🏵   The simple thatched bungalows of the Watergarden may not be spectacular, but they're plenty comfortable. Each has a wide veranda overlooking the many lily ponds that give the hotel its name. The best and most private rooms are at the back. In-house dining at the Watergarden Café (see "Where to Dine," below) is some of the best in town. The place has a good laid-back feel that draws lots of return guests. The hotel is under new management, but it plans to carry on the tradition of quiet atmosphere and friendly service at a reasonable price.

Main rd., Candi Dasa. © 363/41540. Fax 363/41164. www.watergardenhotel.com. 14 units. US$95–US$110 (£52–£61) double; US$180 (£99) 2-bedroom suite. AE, MC, V. **Amenities:** Restaurant; popular bar (TJ's); small outdoor pool; tour desk; airport transfer; shopping; laundry service; library. *In room:* A/C (in some units), TV, minibar, IDD phone.

INEXPENSIVE

Dewa Bharata, on the north end of the main road in Candi Dasa (© 363/41090), is typical of the good, basic beachside accommodations available here. Rooms start at US$21 (£12).

WHERE TO DINE

Hotels offer some of the best dining choices among the myriad possibilities on the Candi Dasa strip. The **Watergarden Café** (© 363/41540) and **Kubu Bali** (© 363/41532) lead the pack with great local and Western fare (see "Where to Stay," above). Also recommended is **Kedai** (© 363/42020; www.dekco.com), a chic little bistro from the owners of Ubud's Ary's Warung.

OUTDOOR ACTIVITIES

Big, healthy reefs teeming with marine life are just a short trip from the shores of Candi Dasa. There are lots of storefront outfitters in town able to arrange snorkeling and diving trips. Some spots are fit only for advanced divers; the wreck of the World War II USS *Liberty* is offshore at Tulamben. Hotels can arrange trips with operators along the main road, or you can try **Geko Divers,** out of Padangbai to the south (© 363/41516; www.gekodive.com).

SIDE TRIPS FROM CANDI DASA

Tracing the coast north from Candi Dasa, travelers have the chance to see volcanoes to the left and stunning coast to the right. The fishing village of **Amed,** about 2 hours north of Candi Dasa, is popular for snorkeling and diving. You can come on a day trip from Candi Dasa or even Ubud (it's easy to arrange land transport), though you might want to spend the night. Lodging options are limited to either *losmen* or the very posh **Hotel Indra Udhyana** (© 361/241107; www.indo.com/hotels/indra-udhyana). A good beachside budget choice is **Amed Café** (© 363/23473; www.amedcafe.com), with rooms as low as US$10 (£5.50).

Some 4 hours of driving north and west along the coast brings you to **Lovina.** Famous for the schools of dolphins swimming just offshore, Lovina is a collection of bungalows and hotels on a quiet stretch of beach far from the madding crowd. **Damai Lovina Hotel,** Jalan Damai, Kayuputih (© 362/41008; www.damai.com) has over-the-top luxury rooms overlooking town (from US$250/£138). **Puri Bagus Lovina** (© 362/21430; www.puri-bagus.com) offers less pricey luxury, with beachside rooms starting at US$100 (£55). Budget accommodations are wall-to-wall along the beaches in Lovina. All accept cash only and cost between Rp80,000 and Rp150,000 (US$8.80–US$16/£4.90–£9.15). Check out **Angsoka,** Jalan Bina Ria, Lovina Beach (© 362/41841; www.angoka.com), a clean, comfortable choice with a pool; some rooms have air-conditioning.

Further west of Lovina is the small village of **Pemuteran,** a quiet spot with a small cluster of beachside resorts. Pemuteran is a great base for diving and snorkeling trips to **Menjangan,** a small island bordering northwestern Bali. Try **Reef Seen Aquatics** (© 362/92339; www.reefseen.com) for snorkeling and diving. The dive center has a turtle hatchery and reef gardening project, plus basic but nicely appointed rooms around US$40 (£22). The best of Pemuteran's resorts is the **Matahari Beach Resort & Spa** *⋆* (© 362/92312; www.matahari-beach-resort.com), with rooms ranging between US$186 and US$466 (£102–£256). Owned by a German butcher, the property features fantastic service, a world-class beachside restaurant, and a beautiful full-service spa. Just west of Matahari is the **Taman Selini Resort** (© **362/94746;** www.taman selini.com), with a good Greek restaurant.

Lombok, a smaller island off the east coast of Bali, is a flight into the rugged landscape of unspoiled Indonesia. With a dry climate that's dominated by central volcanic peaks, Lombok is a predominantly Muslim island that attracts travelers hoping to get off the beaten track. Tourism infrastructure is limited, but beaches are unspoiled; this is also a popular base for diving and trips to the outlying Gili Islands. With the recent drop in tourism, high-speed boats no longer connect, but there is a daily ferry from Padang Bai, just south of Candi Dasa (trip time: 5 hr.). **Merpati** (© **361/235358** in Bali, or 370/636745 in Lombok) flies several times daily from Bali to Lombok's **Selaparang Airport** (20 min.; approximately US$30/£17). From there, connect to your destination by cab. The top choice for accommodations is the self-contained, luxurious **Oberoi Lombok,** cousin of the popular Kuta resort (Medana Beach, Tanjung, West Lombok; © **370/638444;** www.oberoihotels.com), located on the far north of the island. Lombok's **Sengigi Beach** is dotted with budget accommodations as well.

Index

FROMMER'S® COMPLETE TRAVEL GUIDES

Alaska
Amalfi Coast
American Southwest
Amsterdam
Argentina & Chile
Arizona
Atlanta
Australia
Austria
Bahamas
Barcelona
Beijing
Belgium, Holland & Luxembourg
Belize
Bermuda
Boston
Brazil
British Columbia & the Canadian
  Rockies
Brussels & Bruges
Budapest & the Best of Hungary
Buenos Aires
Calgary
California
Canada
Cancún, Cozumel & the Yucatán
Cape Cod, Nantucket & Martha's
  Vineyard
Caribbean
Caribbean Ports of Call
Carolinas & Georgia
Chicago
China
Colorado
Costa Rica
Croatia
Cuba
Denmark
Denver, Boulder & Colorado Springs
Edinburgh & Glasgow
England
Europe
Europe by Rail
Florence, Tuscany & Umbria

Florida
France
Germany
Greece
Greek Islands
Hawaii
Hong Kong
Honolulu, Waikiki & Oahu
India
Ireland
Israel
Italy
Jamaica
Japan
Kauai
Las Vegas
London
Los Angeles
Los Cabos & Baja
Madrid
Maine Coast
Maryland & Delaware
Maui
Mexico
Montana & Wyoming
Montréal & Québec City
Moscow & St. Petersburg
Munich & the Bavarian Alps
Nashville & Memphis
New England
Newfoundland & Labrador
New Mexico
New Orleans
New York City
New York State
New Zealand
Northern Italy
Norway
Nova Scotia, New Brunswick &
  Prince Edward Island
Oregon
Paris
Peru
Philadelphia & the Amish Country

Portugal
Prague & the Best of the Czech
  Republic
Provence & the Riviera
Puerto Rico
Rome
San Antonio & Austin
San Diego
San Francisco
Santa Fe, Taos & Albuquerque
Scandinavia
Scotland
Seattle
Seville, Granada & the Best of
  Andalusia
Shanghai
Sicily
Singapore & Malaysia
South Africa
South America
South Florida
South Pacific
Southeast Asia
Spain
Sweden
Switzerland
Tahiti & French Polynesia
Texas
Thailand
Tokyo
Toronto
Turkey
USA
Utah
Vancouver & Victoria
Vermont, New Hampshire & Maine
Vienna & the Danube Valley
Vietnam
Virgin Islands
Virginia
Walt Disney World® & Orlando
Washington, D.C.
Washington State

FROMMER'S® DAY BY DAY GUIDES

Amsterdam
Chicago
Florence & Tuscany

London
New York City
Paris

Rome
San Francisco
Venice

PAULINE FROMMER'S GUIDES! SEE MORE. SPEND LESS.

Hawaii

Italy

New York City

FROMMER'S® PORTABLE GUIDES

Acapulco, Ixtapa & Zihuatanejo
Amsterdam
Aruba
Australia's Great Barrier Reef
Bahamas
Big Island of Hawaii
Boston
California Wine Country
Cancún
Cayman Islands
Charleston
Chicago
Dominican Republic

Dublin
Florence
Las Vegas
Las Vegas for Non-Gamblers
London
Maui
Nantucket & Martha's Vineyard
New Orleans
New York City
Paris
Portland
Puerto Rico
Puerto Vallarta, Manzanillo &
  Guadalajara

Rio de Janeiro
San Diego
San Francisco
Savannah
St. Martin, Sint Maarten, Anguila &
  St. Bart's
Turks & Caicos
Vancouver
Venice
Virgin Islands
Washington, D.C.
Whistler

FROMMER'S® CRUISE GUIDES

Alaska Cruises & Ports of Call
Cruises & Ports of Call
European Cruises & Ports of Call

FROMMER'S® NATIONAL PARK GUIDES

Algonquin Provincial Park
Banff & Jasper
Grand Canyon

National Parks of the American West
Rocky Mountain
Yellowstone & Grand Teton

Yosemite and Sequoia & Kings
Canyon
Zion & Bryce Canyon

FROMMER'S® MEMORABLE WALKS

London
New York

Paris
Rome

San Francisco

FROMMER'S® WITH KIDS GUIDES

Chicago
Hawaii
Las Vegas
London

National Parks
New York City
San Francisco

Toronto
Walt Disney World® & Orlando
Washington, D.C.

SUZY GERSHMAN'S BORN TO SHOP GUIDES

France
Hong Kong, Shanghai & Beijing
Italy

London
New York

Paris
San Francisco

FROMMER'S® IRREVERENT GUIDES

Amsterdam
Boston
Chicago
Las Vegas

London
Los Angeles
Manhattan
Paris

Rome
San Francisco
Walt Disney World®
Washington, D.C.

FROMMER'S® BEST-LOVED DRIVING TOURS

Austria
Britain
California
France

Germany
Ireland
Italy
New England

Northern Italy
Scotland
Spain
Tuscany & Umbria

THE UNOFFICIAL GUIDES®

Adventure Travel in Alaska
Beyond Disney
California with Kids
Central Italy
Chicago
Cruises
Disneyland®
England
Florida
Florida with Kids

Hawaii
Ireland
Las Vegas
London
Maui
Mexico's Best Beach Resorts
Mini Mickey
New Orleans
New York City

Paris
San Francisco
South Florida including Miami &
the Keys
Walt Disney World®
Walt Disney World® for
Grown-ups
Walt Disney World® with Kids
Washington, D.C.

SPECIAL-INTEREST TITLES

Athens Past & Present
Best Places to Raise Your Family
Cities Ranked & Rated
500 Places to Take Your Kids Before They Grow Up
Frommer's Best Day Trips from London
Frommer's Best RV & Tent Campgrounds
  in the U.S.A.

Frommer's Exploring America by RV
Frommer's NYC Free & Dirt Cheap
Frommer's Road Atlas Europe
Frommer's Road Atlas Ireland
Great Escapes From NYC Without Wheels
Retirement Places Rated

FROMMER'S® PHRASEFINDER DICTIONARY GUIDES

French
Italian
Spanish

THE NEW TRAVELOCITY GUARANTEE

EVERYTHING YOU BOOK WILL BE RIGHT, OR WE'LL WORK WITH OUR TRAVEL PARTNERS TO MAKE IT RIGHT, RIGHT AWAY.

*To drive home the point,
we're going to use the word "right" in every single sentence.*

Let's get right to it. Right to the meat! Only Travelocity guarantees everything about your booking will be right, or we'll work with our travel partners to make it right, right away. Right on!

Here's a picture taken smack dab right in the middle of Antigua, where the guarantee also covers you.

The guarantee covers all but one of the items pictured to the right.

For example, what if the ocean view you booked actually looks out at a downright ugly parking lot? You'd be right to call – we're there for you. And no one in their right mind would be pleased to learn the rental car place has closed and left them stranded. Call Travelocity and we'll help get you back on the right track.

Now, you may be thinking, "Yeah, right, I'm so sure." That's OK; you have the right to remain skeptical. That is until we mention help is always right around the corner. Call us right off the bat, knowing that our customer service reps are there for you 24/7. Righting wrongs. Left and right.

Now if you're guessing there are some things we can't control, like the weather, well you're right. But we can help you with most things – to get all the details in righting,* visit **travelocity.com/guarantee**.

*Sorry, spelling things right is one of the few things not covered under the guarantee.

I'd give my right arm for a guarantee like this, although I'm glad I don't have to.

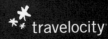
travelocity
You'll never roam alone.

IF YOU BOOK IT, IT SHOULD BE THERE.

Only Travelocity guarantees it will be, or we'll work
with our travel partners to make it right, right away.
So if you're missing a balcony or anything else you
booked, just call us 24/7 1-888-TRAVELOCITY

travelocity

You'll never roam alone